Writing About Diversity

An Argument Reader and Guide

Writing About Diversity

■ An Argument Reader and Guide

Irene L. Clark
University of Southern California

Harcourt Brace College Publishers

Fort Worth   Philadelphia   San Diego   New York   Orlando   Austin
San Antonio   Toronto   Montreal   London   Sydney   Tokyo

Editor-in-Chief: Ted Buchholz
Acquisitions Editor: Stephen T. Jordan
Developmental Editor: Fritz Schanz
Production Manager: J. Montgomery Shaw
Permissions Editor: Aimé Merizon
Editorial, Design, and Production Services: Editorial Services of New England, Inc.
Cover Design: David Day
Compositor: Dayton Typographic
Cover Artist: Zita Asbaghi, *Working Woman's Day*

Acknowledgments appear on page ACK-1, after the appendix.

Library of Congress Cataloging-in-Publication Data
Clark, Irene L.
   Writing about diversity: and argument-reader and guide/Irene L. Clark
      p.   cm.
   Includes bibliographical references and index.
   ISBN 0-15-500949-4
   1. Readers—Social sciences. 2. Pluralism (Social sciences)—Problems, exercises, etc. 3. Ethnic groups—Problems, exercises, etc. 4. English laguage—Rhetoric. 5. Persuasion (Rhetoric) 6. College readers.   I. Title.
PE1127.S6C57   1994
808'.0427—dc20   93-11785
                                                                                    CIP

Requests for permission to make copies of any part of the work should be mailed to: Permissions Department, Harcourt Brace & Company, 8th Floor, Orlando, Florida 32887

Address Editorial Correspondence To:
Harcourt Brace College Publishers
301 Commerce Street, Suite 3700
Fort Worth, TX 76102

Address Orders To:
Harcourt Brace & Company
6277 Sea Harbor Drive
Orlando, FL 32887
1-800-782-4479, or 1-800-433-0001 (in Florida)

Printed in the United States of America

3   4   5   6   090   9   8   7   6   5   4   3   2   1

To my husband, Bill,
and my children,
Elisa, Louisa, Clifton, and Justin

■ Preface

Over the past several years, during which I have taught and developed curricular materials on argumentation for the Freshman Writing Program at the University of Southern California, I have become increasingly aware of the need to connect formal argument with less formal, more personal forms of writing. Personal experience in the form of narrative and descriptive examples lend immediacy and liveliness, but students are seldom able to integrate these features in argumentation. Moreover, if there is one thing that has been learned from composition research over the past twenty-five years, it is that students will become more involved with a writing assignment and will usually produce better writing when the topic is linked to their own experience.

Most textbooks, however, present argumentation as a completely different genre, a sophisticated "second semester" concept unrelated to the less formal, more personal writing that students often engage in during their first semester. The premise of *Writing About Diversity: An Argument Reader and Guide* is that writing about any issue originates with the self and it is difficult for students to formulate an opinion, develop a thesis, and provide a convincing argument about a topic unless they first explore their own perspective on it. Therefore, one distinguishing feature of this book is that it views argumentative writing as inextricably linked to personal experience. Thus, before students begin to write on any topic in this textbook, they are encouraged to reflect on their own preconceptions, opinions, and values, some of which they may never have examined critically. Through exploration questions, students begin by looking into themselves, which sets the stage for broadening their point of view through reading and writing.

However, although *Writing About Diversity* conceives argumentative writing as beginning with personal examination, it also acknowledges the importance of expanding student understanding by reading material from newspapers, magazines, journals, and books. Thus, another distinguishing feature of this textbook is that it forges a strong link between writing a thoughtful and convincing argument and reading outside sources actively and analytically. To establish this connection, the acts of reading and writing are presented in terms of joining an on going public conversation or debate, a metaphor that is usually associated with Kenneth Burke and that is sustained throughout the initial chapters addressing the writing process.

Because *Writing About Diversity* recognizes the importance of critical reading to the writing process, a full chapter is devoted to helping students develop effective strategies for reading and evaluating outside sources. This chapter presents a "three-pass approach" for engaging in a critical dialogue with an outside text, a method that stresses the importance of developing an attitude of informed skepticism when reading published works. This three-pass approach has now become an integral component of the Freshman Writing Curriculum at the University of Southern California.

In addition to helping students read critically, *Writing About Diversity* addresses a fundamental characteristic of academic argument often omitted from argument readers—the importance of acknowledging the complexity of most debatable topics and of recognizing that argumentative writing frequently involves a negotiation between writer and reader and a navigation between extreme positions. This recognition implies that an effective thesis for academic argument uses a qualified approach to the topic and acknowledges that there is no absolutely "right" answer to social problems. Accordingly, this textbook cautions student writers against expecting to change their readers' minds completely or proclaiming that a particular position or viewpoint is absolutely right or wrong. Rather, the book emphasizes that an effective academic argument has the more modest goal of moving its readers to at least consider the thesis, think about the reasons and evidence, acknowledge that the argument has merit, and then to reevaluate and modify their point of view.

The topic of cultural diversity was selected because it is not only complex and controversial, but timely and relevant. Indeed, diversity has been referred to as the most significant issue of the 1990s and, as such, has been accorded widespread media attention and generated considerable controversy on college campuses. Aside from the "trendiness" of the topic, though, I believe that students should become aware of the conflicts associated with diversity in order to function effectively in an increasingly complex, multiethnic world.

Chapters 1 through 4 address the writing process. These include, respectively, Writing an Essay: Finding and Expanding a Thesis, Negotiating Controversy in an Argumentative Essay, Credibility and Support, and A Three-Pass Approach to Critical Reading. The final seven chapters consist of readings concerned with various facets of the topic of cultural diversity. The readings chapters begin by introducing the reader to the various controversies, providing background and some political and social context relevant to the topic. At the end of each chapter are writing assignments and exploration questions. Because research in composition suggests that students develop best as writers when they can write about something they care about, something they find personally relevant, the exploration questions are designed to generate thinking about students' own culture and the ideas associated with that culture. Students are asked to reflect on their own values and customs; to consider how these values had been communicated at home, in school, and in the social and political context; and to assess the extent to which these values reflect those of the dominant "American" culture. These questions may be assigned before the student begins the readings.

Chapter 5, Melting Pot Versus Tossed Salad, examines several perspectives on what constitutes "American" culture, in particular the controversy concerning assimilation (the "melting pot" metaphor) versus the retention of ethnic identity within each individual group (the "tossed salad" metaphor). Chapter 6, Diversity in Language, examines the complex relationship between language and culture, focusing on the debate over whether English ought to be declared the official language of the country, arguments over how non-English-speaking children should be educated, and issues concerning the legitimacy of Black dialect in school and society. Chapter 7, Controversies About Political Correctness, focuses on the debate about whether policies that mandate politically correct behavior constitute an infringement on free speech rights, on the question of whether it is desirable or possible to "teach" political correctness on college campuses, and on the related question of deciding which literature ought to be included in the literary canon. Chapter 8, Diversity in Men and Women, examines different roles assigned to men and women in various cultures, queries whether these roles are determined by nature or nurture, and includes a discussion of the women's and men's movements. Chapter 9, Diverse Concepts of the Family, raises questions about the changing nature of the family within presumably "mainstream" American culture, examines varying concepts of family life, and presents opposing views on the conflict over family values. Chapter 10, Diversity and the Workplace, discusses controversies concerned with affirmative action policies, differing views of workplace values as society becomes increasingly diverse, and the question of whether bias in the workplace contributes to or reflects social divisiveness. Finally, chapter 11, Diversity in the Media, examines the extent to which the media both reflect and create attitudes toward diverse groups and includes several readings on whether censorship of the media would be desirable. The appendix presents two systems of documentation, that of the Modern Language Association and that of the American Psychological Association. The appendix also discusses strategies to help students avoid inadvertent plagiarism and to effectively incorporate quoted material into their own texts.

My hope is that as students work with the material in *Writing About Diversity*, they will improve their writing skills and broaden and deepen their perspective on issues concerned with cultural diversity, with practice in writing serving as both an end in itself and as means of fostering understanding. As Richard Marius points out, we often think of writing simply in terms of communication, and consequently, "we may forget how much writing helps us know things—to arrange facts, to see how they are related to one another, and to decide what they mean. Nothing helps the mind and memory more than writing things down" (*A Writer's Companion*, 2nd ed., New York: McGraw Hill, 1991).

There are many people whose energy has driven this book to completion and who I would like to thank—Stephen T. Jordan, Acquisitions Editor at Harcourt Brace, whose enthusiasm for the proposal propelled him across the country within a few days of reading it and accordingly propelled me into action; Fritz Schanz, whose keen insights as developmental editor helped me to focus my thinking; my colleagues at the Freshman Writing Program at the University of Southern California, Betty Bamberg, Jack Blum, and John Holland, whose concept of composition teaching has so strongly influenced my own; my research assistant, Kathleen Forni, who always came through when I needed her, both efficiently and cheerfully; Paul Cohen and Kevin Parker, who provided additional research assistance; and my assistant in the Writing Center a U.S.C., Dana Loewy, who maintained my connection to the United States while I was working in Holland in the spring of 1993. Then, of course, there are the members of my family, my husband, Bill, and my children, Elisa, Louisa, Clifton, and Justin, whose vitality and support invigorate whatever I choose to do.

In addition, I would like to thank the following reviewers who commented on the manuscript: Marvin Diogenes, University of Arizona; David Estes, Loyola University; Lester Faigley, University of Texas; Richard Fulkerson, East Texas State University; Judith Funston, State University of New York–Postsdam; Joyce Jolly, Shelton State Community College; Carolyn Miller, North Carolina State University; Nancy Moore, University of Wisconsin–Stevens Point; Madeleine Picciotto, Oglethorpe University; Cheryl Ruggiero, Virginia Polytechnic Institute and State University; Randy Woodland, University of California–Los Angeles.

Irene L. Clark
University of Southern California

■ Contents

Part I   Argumentation

4

A THREE-PASS APPROACH TO CRITICAL READING **115**

Part II   Readings

5

MELTING POT VERSUS TOSSED SALAD **145**

6
DIVERSITY IN LANGUAGE

7
CONTROVERSIES ABOUT POLITICAL CORRECTNESS

10
DIVERSITY AND THE WORKPLACE   685

11
DIVERSITY AND THE MEDIA   769

Part III   Appendix

ACKNOWLEDGING YOUR SOURCES   A-1

Introduction

■ Why Write About Diversity?

"Can't We All Just Get Along?"

In May 1992, the verdict in the Rodney King beating case triggered a major riot in the city of Los Angeles. Stores and businesses were set ablaze, windows were smashed, millions of dollars in property was destroyed, and looters, apparently undaunted by the presence of television cameras, brazenly helped themselves to whatever they could get their hands on—televisions, VCRs, liquor, food, clothing. The concept of law and order was swiftly rendered meaningless. As a result, the public was forced to pay attention to the racial tensions and ethnic hostilities that had been escalating steadily as the city had become increasingly diverse. The media coverage of the events of that day and the days that followed raised public awareness that unless something were done to change the precipitating conditions, it could happen again, not only in Los Angeles but anywhere in the country.

The Los Angeles riots focused attention on one of the most serious issues of our time—that is, how people can live together harmoniously and productively in an increasingly multicultural society, or as Rodney King phrased it—how we can "just get along." The riots also brought the recognition that the goal of just getting along is unlikely to be realized unless people make a serious effort to make it happen. Before we can even decide what we should or can do, we will have to become aware of issues that can generate controversy. If we wish to "just get along," we can no longer afford to ignore areas of potential conflict.

This book was written to familiarize you with some of the issues concerned with the topic of cultural diversity by providing you with opportunities to think and write about them. The readings were selected because they present differing viewpoints, enabling you to examine multiple perspectives, weigh evidence, and ultimately arrive at an informed position. The book, therefore, has a dual purpose: to familiarize you with some of the issues associated with the timely and complex subject of cultural diversity and, by providing you with opportunities to read and write about it, to help you improve your writing skills.

1

Why Study Diversity?

The Los Angeles riots demonstrated that if we are not sensitive to one another's needs and if we continue to ignore the possibility of conflict, then the very fabric of our society might soon be torn apart. One justification for reading and writing about diversity is that it can ultimately pave the way for communication and mutual respect among the different groups that live in our world. In fact, the United States has become so diverse that, as a speaker at a recent conference on diversity pointed out, if any two people in the United States were randomly selected, there is a forty percent chance that they would be from two different cultures. More than ever before, the children in our classrooms come from a variety of cultural backgrounds, speak other languages, and espouse quite different values. It is, therefore, of crucial importance that we who live in this country learn to exist peacefully with one another.

Throughout the world, ethnic and racial conflicts pose a threat to peace and stability. Every day, national newspapers recount horrifying tales of one ethnic, religious, or racial group attempting to destroy another in the Middle East, Africa, Eastern Europe, South America and elsewhere in the world. People seem to have become less tolerant of one another's differences and are apparently regressing to behavior usually associated with the Dark Ages—blatant discrimination, "ethnic cleansing," warfare in the streets, torture, and mass destruction. For the sake of world, as well as national peace, it is of particular importance that diversity should become a topic addressed on college campuses.

The Approach of This Book: Looking Within, Looking Beyond

Writing about any issue originates with the self and it is difficult to formulate an opinion and develop a convincing thesis about a topic unless you first explore your own perspective on it. Therefore, before you begin to write on any of the topics in this book, you will be encouraged to reflect on your own preconceptions and opinions and gain an awareness of your own values, some of which you may not have examined critically. Such reflection will be encouraged through exploratory questions and then through writing assignments. You will begin by looking into yourself and then broadening your point of view through reading and writing.

Let us begin with a brief overview of the topic I am broadly labeling *diversity*. What does this term mean? Why are people so concerned about it? And what implications do controversies concerned with this topic have for American society?

Melting Pot or Tossed Salad?

Until fairly recently, it was common to refer to American society as a "melting pot," a metaphor that suggested that the United States was a country composed of many different ethnic groups, who had all somehow become blended or assimilated into "Americans." The concept of the melting pot was associated with the idea of the United States as a land of freedom and opportunity; it was assumed that anyone would welcome the chance of becoming an American and that anyone who wished to be an American would easily and happily relinquish other ethnic and cultural bonds. Blending was considered a realizable ideal. Today, however, the metaphor of the melting pot is being challenged by another metaphor: that of the "tossed salad. " This idea implies that although many different groups live in the United States and may, indeed, consider themselves American, each also retains its own ethnic and cultural character and that this retention is both possible and desirable. Proponents of the tossed salad view believe that assimilation can be balanced with the preservation of identity; for them, the ideal is not for the elimination of differences but for an increased awareness of and respect for cultural and ethnic diversity.

A point of disagreement about which numerous books and articles have recently been published is whether immigrants to the United States should be encouraged to retain their own ethnic identity or whether they should adopt a new blended American identity. The underlying issue of the controversy concerns the effect each choice will have on a society, assuming that people are even capable of making such a choice. Those who advocate retaining ethnic identification believe that the melting pot notion of freedom and justice for all was never a reality because only one group, consisting of white English-speaking Europeans, was ever regarded as being essentially American; those of other races and cultures were excluded and made to feel inferior. Those who favor the idea of the melting pot claim that every new immigrant group was marginalized at first but that all eventually blended into American culture within a generation. Furthermore, they maintain that lack of national identity will fan ethnic and racial conflict, ultimately contributing to the fragmentation and disintegration of the society.

Exploring Your Own Views on Diversity

You may not have spent time evaluating whether you adhere to the melting pot or tossed salad view of the United States or some combination of the two, but at some time in your own life, you have probably believed that you belonged to one group rather than to another. On holidays, for example, people often identify closely with particular religious or cultural groups, and most of us are more comfortable with others who look, speak, or act in a manner that is familiar or understandable to us. Correspondingly, many people are uneasy with those who are unfamiliar in some way; some may react with suspicion or even hostility.

To explore the topic of diversity, it is useful to begin by reflecting on your own preconception of the topic—that is, to think about your own concept of identity and how you have been brought up to view diverse groups. An effective way to begin to explore any topic is to think about how your own background may have influenced what you may already know and believe about it. Sometimes, even if we are unaware that we have a position about a given topic, our home environment or community may have unconsciously predisposed us to view it from a particular perspective. Later on, that perspective may have been modified by what we have read or experienced in school, at work, through friends, on television, and elsewhere. By thinking and writing about a topic, we can get in touch with what we already think, enabling us to evaluate what we read and write with greater objectivity.

As a first step in working with the material in this book, I suggest that you write responses to the "exploration questions," which, as the name suggests, are intended to stimulate reflection and enable you to explore your own acquaintance with the topic. Exploration questions are used throughout this book as a means of introducing new subjects or writing assignments, and in chapter 1, I suggest some general questions that you can apply to any topic in this book. In this introductory chapter, though, you will use exploration questions to help you get in touch with your own point of view on the subject of diversity.

Exploration Questions

WHAT IS THE ORIGIN OF "IDENTITY?" HOW DOES INDIVIDUAL IDENTITY RELATE TO NATIONAL IDENTITY?

The debate over whether the melting pot or the tossed salad metaphor most aptly characterizes American society raises questions about how identity is formed, how individual identity relates to national identity, and the link between identity and physical and cultural characteristics. For example, do black Americans view themselves primarily as members of the black community or as Americans? When people from Mexico move to the United States, how long do they continue to regard themselves as Mexican as opposed to American? What do these national labels mean? Do they imply a set of cultural or physical characteristics? To consider yourself an American, do you have to look, speak, or believe in a certain way? These are difficult questions to answer, but certainly worth thinking about in the context of understanding multiculturalism. To begin examining your own perspective on the relationship between individual and national identity, respond in writing to the following questions:

1. What labels do you use to identify yourself (gender, culture, race, ethnicity, religion, nationality, profession, interests, and hobbies)?
2. To what extent is your identity linked to how you look? Think about your own physical appearance, and write down as many physical characteristics of yourself that you can.
3. What racial and ethnic group do you belong to? Is this group associated with a particular skin or hair color or physical size? Do you resemble members of your family?
4. When did you become aware of your physical identity? Was it emphasized at home or at school? Was there a particular occasion on which your physical identity was mentioned?
5. What stereotypes are associated with your racial, cultural, and ethnic group?
6. Think about other racial and ethnic groups you are familiar with, either in your daily life or through the media (choose one or two). List the physical characteristics of each group. Then list the stereotypes associated with each of these groups. Your responses to these questions can be kept for your own use, but you might find it interesting to exchange responses with a member of your class.

IS DIVERSITY DESIRABLE?

As a resident of the United States, you live in a diverse society which consists of many different races and cultures, and history tells us that this country has always been this way. Suppose, however, you had a choice of two countries to live in, both of them comfortable and pleasant, but one was multicultural and the other was populated with people exactly like yourself. Which country would you choose? Would you prefer to live in a society in which your particular ethnic identity was in the majority? Would you rather live among many different races and cultures? Or could you imagine a society where racial and ethnic characteristics were not considered important?

One writer who has explored the societal impact of ethnicity and race is Marge Piercy, who, in her futuristic novel, *Woman on the Edge of Time,* imagines a society in which racial and ethnic distinctions have been deliberately blurred. The people in Piercy's society have no native, ethnic, or racial identity, except what they, themselves, might choose. They are "a mixed up bag of genes." In this society, appearance is not equated with any ethnic or national identity, nor are ethnic or national groups associated with a particular level or power in society. In fact, to ensure that ethnic identity is not inherited or passed on to one's children, people of all different colors are created in a "brooder."

One of the leaders of this future society explains that this blurring of ethnic identity had been the result of a deliberate decision to eliminate racism; he explains that

> decisions were made forty years back to breed a high proportion of darker-skinned people and to mix the genes well through the population. At the same time, we decided to hold on to separate cultural identities. But we broke the bond between genes and culture, broke it forever. We want there to be no chance of racism again. But we don't want the melting pot where everybody ends up with thin gruel. We want diversity, for strangeness breeds richness.

Think about the possibility of a society in which race and culture could not be passed on from generation to generation. Then respond to the following questions:

1. The society depicted in *Woman on the Edge of Time* presents an idealized solution to problems of racial and ethnic hostilities and to power inequities based on gender; however, many of you may have differing reactions to this type of society. To explore your own reaction, think about how you would feel if our society went in this direction. Would you be comfortable with the idea of relinquishing your family connections and with the notion of having children who were not related to you genetically? To what extent do you view people in terms of their racial or ethnic background?

2. How attached are you to your own culture? Discuss the extent to which you were brought up to believe that your own culture was the "best" in the world. To what extent were you brought up to respect the culture of others?

3. Do you feel a part of American culture? Discuss the extent to which you have felt like an outsider when you were growing up (remember that most students feel marginalized, to some extent, when they encounter unfamiliar ideas and cultures).

4. Characterize your own school experience in terms of ethnic, racial, and cultural diversity. Did you attend a school in which there were people of other cultures and races? Did the school do anything to promote ethnic pride for any of these groups?

Your responses to these questions will enable you to assess your own concept of identity and the extent to which you feel attached to a particular racial or ethnic group. It will also help you begin to reflect on the complex subject of diversity.

Questionnaire: "Are You a Racist?"

J. G. Conti and Brad Stetson, Ph.D candidates in social ethics at the University of Southern California, have written a questionnaire to enable people to assess whether or not they are racists. Respond in writing to the questions in this questionnaire. Then discuss Conti and Stetson's questions in small groups.

Are You a Racist?

J. G. CONTI AND BRAD STETSON

In an effort to understand student attitudes about race, the administration of your school has asked your writing class to respond to this questionnaire. Please answer each of the following questions with "true" or "false," and be honest. Your answers will be confidential.

T/F 1. *Only whites can be racist.*

T/F 2. *"Institutional racism" so permeates American society that it hardly matters if African-Americans go to college or not because the effects of discrimination exclude them from the job market.*

T/F 3. *Public interest in "straightening out the welfare system" is really a secret expression of racist attitudes toward the black poor.*

T/F 4. *To disagree with the views of prominent black leaders on social issues such as school busing is actually to show racist opposition to African-Americans as a group.*

T/F 5. *Talk show panels that pit white racists against black civil rights leaders accurately reflect the state of American race relations.*

T/F 6. *Given that black Ph.D.s are salaried less, on the average, than white Ph.D.s, the only credible explanation is racism.*

T/F 7. *Only persons of a certain race or ethnicity ought to speak about issues directly related to that race or ethnicity.*

1. Would your answers to the questionnaire be any different if you knew you would have to present your answers to your class? If so, speculate on the reasons for this dissonance between your private and public answers.

2. Many Americans have expressed a sense of pride in what their ancestors accomplished and endured. Others feel no particular pride in their ancestors' accomplishments or failures, believing only *individual* accomplishment can be a legitimate basis for pride. What is your view?

3. Which term do you think is more accurate description of how we form our attitudes about society and ourselves: *determinism,* which is the notion that race or ethnicity causes us to think in certain ways, or *individualism,* which is the idea that each person is free to choose his or her own attitudes.

4. How would you respond to those who criticize "group-identification"—the understanding of oneself in primarily racial or ethnic terms—as dehumanizing and as a denial of a one's true individuality?

5. Many legislative proposals and laws are justified by the claim that "most people" think they are appropriate or necessary. Is this idea a logically and morally sound warrant for public policy? Can you think of any historical examples in which "the majority" supported unfair legislation?

6. What does it mean, politically and personally, to treat all persons equally, irrespective of their color and ethnicity?

I

■ Argumentation

1 ■ Writing an Essay: Finding and Expanding a Thesis

In the introduction, you began to explore the topic broadly referred to as "diversity" by writing responses to exploration questions; throughout this textbook, exploration questions are presented to help you develop ideas for your essays. However, after you have responded to questions and generated some thoughts about the topic, you will then want to formulate a central or unifying idea for your essay. In this chapter, I discuss strategies for finding and expanding that central idea or thesis statement. I also explain essay form, examine how your intended audience can influence the sort of thesis you develop, and suggest strategies for making your writing lively and for revising your work.

Approaching a Writing Task

Many writers wait until almost the last minute to begin working on a writing assignment. Students, in particular, subject themselves to panic-filled "night before" writing marathons during which they work furiously to meet the next day's deadline. Sometimes, these last minute jobs, as weak and ineffective as they might be, seem to be inevitable—time pressures or uncontrollable writing-avoidance behaviors can make it impossible to begin sooner.

To break down the process of writing an essay into more manageable tasks, I am going to presume that you will not wait until the last minute to write your essay and that you will allow enough time to complete the following activities:

1. Explore what you already believe about the topic through reflection and respond in writing to the exploration questions.

2. Clarify the writing task.
3. Write multiple drafts and allow ample time for revision.

These three activities will maximize your chances of writing an effective essay—that is, an essay that makes a worthwhile point, develops that point in a lively and interesting manner, and influences its audience to view that point as worth considering, maybe even as significant.

Responding to Exploration Questions

In the introduction several exploration questions prompted you to begin thinking about the view of diversity you were exposed to in your own background, and for many of the assignments in this book, I will provide additional exploration questions directed at specific issues. However, you may also find it useful to have a set of generic exploration questions that you could apply to other writing tasks. The questions below, then, are intended to generate material from your own background.

1. What childhood associations do you have with this topic? What images or details come to your mind when you think of it?
2. How did your family view this topic? Can you think of specific conversations or instances in your childhood that influenced your conception of it? What incidents, scenes, or conversations come immediately to your mind?
3. How did your school experiences influence your conception of the topic? Did your teachers and classmates feel the same way about the topic as did your family? Were there any points of conflict?
4. Can you think of at least two people who held differing views about this topic? If so, describe these people and summarize what you believe were their points of view.
5. Has your opinion changed about this topic in any way? Why or why not?
6. Do you think that this topic is important for people to think about? Why or why not?

To illustrate how these questions can be used to generate material, I will discuss how Marlene used them to begin writing her essay, which is reproduced later in this chapter. Marlene used these questions to develop ideas for the following writing assignment: *"Write an essay in which you discuss a family custom involving eating (dinner, for example) that occurred regularly in your own home or community."* Here is the way Marlene responded to the exploration questions:

1. What childhood associations do you have with this topic? What images or details come to your mind when you think of it?

Dinner time at our house—towels at the table, lots of pots, messy, nothing elegant, arguing about the lighting, father hated all pretension, crude but funny. Wedding gifts, father sneering at all of them.

2. How did your family view this topic? Can you think of specific conversations or instances in your childhood that influenced your conception of it? What incidents, scenes, or conversations come immediately to your mind?

My father hated all pretension at the dinner table and insisted that we use bath towels instead of napkins because they were more practical.

He also hated anything else that wasn't practical like candles, or serving spoons, anything nice. He would go on and on about it—it was one of his pet topics.

3. How did your school experiences influence your conception of the topic? Did your teachers and classmates feel the same way about the topic as did your family? Were there any points of conflict?

Dinner at my friends' houses seemed to be more formal, nicer things at the tables, no pots, napkins instead of towels. I wanted to have some of this, but really had no power over what sort of dinner table customs we had at home. It was sort of funny, though—all of those pots, especially at breakfast when my father insisted on eating scrambled eggs directly from the pot so that they wouldn't cool off.

4. Can you think of at least two people who held differing views about this topic? If so, describe these people and summarize what you believe were their points of view.

I think my mother probably would have liked a bit more formality at our table but she usually did whatever my father said and he had such a strong opinion that it was hard to diagree with him without getting into a big argument. She didn't usually question why something was done, she just did it. My father questioned things too much, so that he had no use for anything that wasn't completely practical. Practicality became almost an obsession.

5. Has your opinion changed about this topic in any way? Why or why not?

I think I have come around more to my father's point of view than I used to think when I was growing up. I wouldn't go as far as he did, but sometimes I think people are a little extreme in the stuff they do to make their dinner tables fancy or elegant. And with my own children, I sometimes think that bath towels make a lot of sense.

6. Do you think that this topic is important for people to think about? Why or why not?

I think there is a place for ritual and elegance in the home, although in a funny sense, my father's concern with being practical was a ritual of its own although certainly not the usual kind. I think though that it is important to think about what kind of atmosphere you want to create at the dinner table, not only for yourself, but for your children. Rituals also help people feel a part of family life and I'm not sure whether my father's dislike of anything impractical at the dinner table created a bond or made us feel removed from the family scene.

Marlene used these questions to begin thinking about her topic and, as you will see in her essay, the responses she wrote to the exploration questions helped her locate her thesis and provided her with several useful examples. Of course, for some writers, exploration questions may not be as useful because they may prefer to do their exploring mentally without writing anything down. Before deciding that writing responses to exploration questions will not work for you, I suggest that you try the method at least once. You may be surprised at the amount of material you can summon from your background.

Clarifying the Writing Task

Even when you have generated a lot of preliminary material by responding to exploration questions, you may still be unsure about what type of essay to write. As a means of clarifying the writing task I suggest that you ask yourself the following questions.

What sort of essay am I supposed to write? This includes awareness of the components of the essay, understanding what sort of information is needed to provide content for the essay, and knowing where to look for this information.

Do I understand the meaning of all of the terms in the assignment? This includes defining terms that might be open to interpretation or may be used in a particular way in relation to the topic. In the context of issues concerned with diversity, for example, words such as *beneficial* or *equality, feasible, advantageous,* or *fair* can be viewed from a number of perspectives.

What Sort of Essay Am I Supposed to Write?

THE IMPORTANCE OF THE THESIS

Writing an essay for a college course usually requires you to construct a thesis—that is, an idea worth considering or a main point. This idea, or main point, does not have to be earth shaking or new, but it should present a fresh perspective on the topic from which the reader will learn something, feel something, understand something, or view something from a different angle. For some issues, the thesis may cause the reader to modify his or her position or maybe even to change his or her mind.

The thesis serves as a unifying thread throughout the essay, tying together details and examples. It helps the writer decide which ideas should be included and becomes the reference point for each component of the essay, relating information so the reader understands the essay as a whole. The thesis statement thus shapes the form and content of the essay.

ESSAY FORM

There are infinite possibilities for thesis statements and although the thesis statement helps shape your essay (implying that there are also infinite shapes that an essay can have), most teachers who assign writing at the college level expect their students' essays to adhere to a fairly predictable form. It is, therefore, useful for you to understand what sort of essay you are expected to write and how an essay is usually structured. Before I discuss form and structure, I would like to point out that many writers of college composition textbooks are hesitant to advocate a particular essay form or structure for fear of stifling student creativity or of giving students the impression that one particular form is always appropriate, no matter what the writing task may be. I worry about these misconceptions, too, because I am aware that some students come to the university thinking that every essay has a definite structure and has to adhere to a particular set of rules. In other words, many students are under the impression that writing a good essay means "getting it right."

Let me stress that I do not believe in the fixity of form and structure in an essay, that I do not believe that every essay has to have five paragraphs (or any other number, for that matter), and that I am always delighted when students experiment with new ways of making their point. But I know that if I were assigned to write an essay, I would want to know what sort of essay my instructor had in mind, and if possible, I would like to see an example of that sort of essay. It is likely that in the beginning, I might imitate the model too closely. But then, after becoming comfortable with writing it, I would be able to break away from that pattern and begin developing my own variations within that form.

Having made that qualification, I can now explain the components of an essay.

The Introduction

An essay usually begins with an introductory paragraph (sometimes two) that presents the essay's main point or thesis. Depending on the complexity, purpose, and audience of your essay, an introduction can take many forms, such as presenting a problem or issue, providing historical context, indicating the importance of the subject, or introducing the subject with a lively anecdote or description. Above all, the main purpose of the introduction is to lead the reader into the essay, give the reader a clear sense of what the essay will be about, and present the thesis statement.

Because the introduction is found at the beginning of the essay, students usually try to write the introduction first. However, I suggest that you write the introduction *after* you have written the body of your paper unless you are very familiar with your subject matter and know exactly what you want to say. When you attempt to write the introduction first, you will have much greater difficulty with it because you haven't yet clarified for yourself exactly what you want to say. After you have developed your main points and perhaps revised your thesis statement, you will be able to write the introduction more easily.

The Body

The body of an essay consists of paragraphs which support the thesis; support may take the form of subpoints or reasons which establish the validity of the essay's main point. The body of the essay develops the thesis using various strategies such as analysis, comparison-contrast, or illustration, and the information included in the body may come from various sources—from outside reading as well as from personal experience.

The Conclusion

The essay ends with a concluding paragraph that directs the reader's attention back to the overall purpose or thesis of the essay. Depending on the subject of the essay, the conclusion may reaffirm the main point of the essay, summarize what has already been stated, raise a question of policy, or indicate the significance of the topic that was discussed. Fanciful conclusions might surprise the reader with an illustrative anecdote.

For an example of this type of essay, read Marlene's essay "Of Towels, Pots, and Snuffboxes," reproduced below.

Of Towels, Pots, and Snuffboxes

Marlene

The table is set for dinner—seemingly an unremarkable, quite ordinary table—flowered vinyl tablecloth, white plates, conventional knives, forks, spoons, and glasses. But wait—something is missing! Something expected, something usual, something important. Glance again at the table and it becomes clear that the place where a snowy linen or perhaps a crisply folded paper napkin ought to appear remains conspicuously empty. Instead, tossed flaccidly across the backs of chairs with casual inappropriateness hang an unappetizing assortment of terry cloth bath towels—faded, nondescript, grayish mauve or yellowed beige, worn thin from many washings, more like rags than towels. Draped over our laps, flapping clumsily below our knees, these shabby, unattractive linen closet rejects were what our family used each night instead of dinner napkins, epitomizing the obsessive and frequently embarrassing concern with practicality that characterized all of our family meals.

Why, one might ask, would an average, solidly middle-class New York family adhere to so aberrant, unappealing, and, to a certain extent, disgusting a custom? It was not, as one might assume initially, that our family was too impoverished to buy more ordinary napkins (I know from several furtive explorations in dining room drawers that we did indeed own several lovely linen sets, gathering dust with labels still intact). Nor was it that our family was presciently concerned with saving paper. Rather, the presence of the old bath towels at the dinner table was a serious matter of principle, representing for my father a glorious victory for the forces of common sense over those of pretense and frivolity. Eminently practical and terrifyingly outspoken, my father maintained, until his dying day, that linen or even paper napkins were utterly worthless in terms of absorption and launderability. In fact, on the rare occasion that he was subjected to the more usual variety of napkin at another person's home, he was more than likely to whisper loudly that his hands had actually become stickier as a result of using it. Perched nervously around the table, my mother, sister, and

I would glance at one another in dread; we all became remarkably adept at changing the subject.

But my father's crusade for practicality extended beyond the substitution of bath towels for napkins—other equally strange customs graced our family meals under the banner of utilitarianism. One in particular was our family's practice of serving any food intended to be eaten hot directly from the pots they had been cooked in, which were brought directly from the stove to the table and remained in a circle of trivets around my mother, who served from the pot at the table. Uncompromising in his standards for food temperature, my father hotly maintained that food cooled off far too quickly when placed in traditional serving dishes, that there was nothing more irritating than eating lukewarm food when one yearned for something that was piping hot, and that serving dishes were simply an unnecessary luxury that created more washing up later on. Eggs, my father insisted, were especially susceptible to ruination from instant cooling, which meant that eggs in any form other than boiled were always to be eaten directly from the pot, without having even been transferred to a plate. This custom might have caused some difficulty if more than one person had decided to eat scrambled or fried eggs at breakfast, but since none of us were as fanatic about food temperature as my father was, we usually deferred to him, serving ourselves first, and letting him eat from the pot.

Breakfast was actually no problem. But this insistence on pots instead of serving dishes created considerable difficulty during dinner, particularly if there were several courses, since the table then became extremely crowded with multiple pots, trivets, and pot holders. In fact, it was sometimes difficult even to see my mother at the table, surrounded as she was with various cooking pots (she didn't seem to mind). It also meant that if any of us, for some reason, wished to serve ourselves, we could not simply say, "pass the carrots, please" without first requesting a pot holder, since the pots were usually too hot to touch with unprotected fingers. Sometimes the bath towels could double as pot holders, if they were not too worn out or so large that they caused something to be knocked over or spilled (which sometimes happened anyway, but then, I must admit, the towels were particularly useful).

Of course, like most adolescents, I secretly yearned for whatever appeared to be lacking in my own home, and I therefore harbored a clandestine predilection for luxurious dinner items—flower arrangements, candles ablaze in a softly lit dining room, elegantly decorative platters and bowls, all of which were anathema to my father. "It is ridiculous not to be able to see what you eat," he would remark loudly as he peered at his food in fashionably dim restaurants; similarly, he insisted that in the age of electricity, candles were necessary only during blackouts. Flower arrangements, particularly those that were large enough to obscure eye contact across the table, he similarly regarded as frivolous, unnecessary, a barrier to worthwhile conversation—the especially large ones my father would remove immediately and unceremoniously from the table, even in restaurants and sometimes in other people's homes. From time to time, I would stage a small rebellion in the form of actually setting the table with a linen napkin (I can't ever remember using it, though, since I suppose that my fingers would inevitably gravitate to the omnipresent and admittedly more absorbent towel) or of insisting on proper serving plates and bowls when guests were invited to dine with us. Most of the time, though, I paid little attention to the peculiarities of our dinner table, simply accepting them as the norm.

When I became engaged, however, the assortment of festively beribboned wedding gifts which began arriving at the house generated a new barrage of derision about frivolous dining habits and infusing new energy into the ongoing controversy. Like many prospective brides, I received a number of gifts intended for elegant dining—decorative plates, vases, bowls, napkins, candleholders, ornate serving spoons, all of which my father disdainfully termed "snuff boxes," meaning that they were outdated luxuries, and essentially useless. With feigned indifference, my father would watch me open the beautiful gift boxes, and then, as each treasure emerged from its carefully folded wrapping, he would snicker to himself and mutter, "Looks like another snuff box." In fact, so much merriment was created as a result of the "snuff box" label, that from time to time I contemplated having a set of thank-you cards printed, the front of which would say simply, "Thank you for the snuff box."

Of course, this all happened many years ago, and, I am happy to report, I now have my own home in which I use real napkins, sometimes linen, sometimes paper, along with flowers, candles, serving bowls, and other appurtenances of ordinary and sometimes elegant dining. I must confess, though, that every once in a while, when no one is at home and I find myself dining alone, I derive a curious pleasure from tossing a bath towel across my lap like a comfortable old friend and enjoying a supper of piping hot scrambled eggs, eaten, of course, directly from the pot.

MARLENE'S THESIS

In this essay, Marlene's thesis is that dining in her family was characterized by an obsessive concern with practicality. She illustrates her thesis with several descriptive anecdotes, for example, the use of towels instead of napkins at the dinner table, the serving of hot foods from pots instead of serving dishes, and the idea that almost everything should be functional rather than decorative.

Notice that in Marlene's essay the thesis appears at the end of the first paragraph. Although I would never insist that there is only one place in an essay that a thesis statement *must* appear, the first or second paragraph is a common and appropriate location for it. Theoretically, a thesis statement can appear anywhere in an essay and can even be implied rather than directly stated. However, because many of the writing assignments you will be completing in your university courses will require a thesis statement located near the beginning of the text, it is useful for you to practice writing this kind of essay.

The Role of Audience in Thesis Development

The extent to which you consider the needs of your audience is closely related to the purpose of your essay. When you are writing about a controversial issue and when your goal is to encourage your audience to modify or change its point of view, you have to be particularly sensitive to your audience's ideas and attitudes. It is best to indicate that you are aware of how your audience thinks and that you understand that position, even if you don't agree with it. The more concerned you are with persuading your audience of something, the greater your concern must be with strategies that are likely to have an effect on an audience. (See chapter 3 for a greater exploration of the role of audience.)

It is also important to consider your audience even when you are not writing about a controversial topic; you should be aware of how much your audience knows and what its attitudes are toward the topic, for such awareness will influence the content of your essay. When Marlene decided to write about the dinner rituals in her family, she assumed that her audience knew what dinner rituals were, and she did not need to define that term. In fact, it was because she assumed that her audience would have a preconceived idea of what a dinner table should look like, that she was able to develop her thesis that her own family's dining customs were not the norm. Marlene assumed that most of her readers would have a particular point of view about what is considered "usual" at a dinner table and would find it odd that her family used towels rather than napkins. It is as if she were asking, "Look, you want to hear about something strange?" But what she is pointing out is strange only in the context of what her audience may view as usual. If she were writing for an audience that had no knowledge of dining customs and no expectations of what a dinner table setting should look like, she would have had to explain what was usual, and she might have decided to write about an entirely different topic. The humor of this essay is based on the assumption that the audience will know what is customary. If she thought that everyone reading the essay also used towels at the dinner table, then her essay would have much less of an impact.

Finding a Thesis: Writing Down Details, Noting a Tension, Perceiving a Problem

How helpful a nice simple formula or maybe a foolproof machine for finding a good thesis would be. The student could fill in variables, calculate, or pour material into a funnel and press a button. Then, magically, a good thesis would emerge ready for development. Unfortunately, there is no such formula or device, but there are several strategies you can use to generate ideas. As I noted above, responding to exploration questions can be very helpful because answering questions often has the effect of generating further questions that lead to the development of ideas. Doing outside reading is especially helpful for a topic about which there may be multiple perspectives.

The other method, which in some ways is similar to writing responses to exploration questions, is to record as many details as you can about the subject, perceive a tension between some of these details, and use that tension to develop a main point. For example, after writing her responses to the exploration questions, Marlene began formulating ideas for her essay by writing down every detail she could remember about her family's dining habits. These are some of the details Marlene noted:

> dinner, towels, pots, scrambled eggs, flowers, arguing about napkins, candle-holders, electric light, candlelight

She then noted that some of these details did not seem to fit with the others, creating a tension between them. The word "dinner," for example, did not seem to fit with "towels," nor did "pots" and "scrambled eggs" fit with "flowers." Perceiving a tension between ideas sometimes means looking at the world with a critical attitude and thinking, for instance, "Something here is not as it should be" or "Something here could be different" or "Something here is out of place." Thus, in writing down details, Marlene was able to perceive a problem that led to the creation of her thesis—that her family's dining habits were focused too much on practical matters at the expense of more aesthetic concerns.

Writing down ideas, perceiving a tension between them, and actively seeking a problem make up an effective method of initiating the thinking process that will lead to a thesis. Looking at the topic with a critical eye, saying to yourself, "Something here is not as it should be," or "Something here could be different," or "Something here is out of place" problematizes the topic so that you can develop a perspective on it.

Keep in mind that deciding on a main point or thesis for an essay can take a lot of time because writers tend to modify a thesis as they develop their ideas. What we know about the writing process is that it is *recursive,* implying that writers may have an idea, start to write, then change their ideas, discover they need some additional material, start to write again, and so on. Even after writing several drafts, you may continue to refocus your thinking, and because ideas change when you think and write about them, writing is usually a messy process. So allow for the necessary time and don't be discouraged.

Broadly, though, finding a thesis usually occurs in three stages which may be repeated:

1. You select a topic (in Marlene's essay, dining customs) and assemble as much material about it as you think you will need to get started. This may include brainstorming, thinking, or writing responses to exploration questions. For some topics, it may include outside reading.

2. You narrow your topic (in Marlene's essay, the attitude her family had about non-functional dining utensils).

3. You make an assertion or express an opinion about this topic (Marlene asserts that dining customs in her family were characterized by an obsessive concern with practicality).

Narrowing the Topic

A common tendency for many students is to try to cover too many aspects of the topic in one paper. Instead of developing one or two ideas, they move frantically from one to the other, resulting in a paper made up of a list of generalizations without a great deal of development or exploration. An overly generalized topic is not as informative, interesting, or convincing as a topic that is developed with specific details, so be sure to limit your thesis to one that you can cover adequately in the designated length of your paper. Note that in the essay "Of Towels, Pots, and Snuffboxes" Marlene did not attempt to write about every custom her family might have observed, nor did she try to describe many different occasions that might have been relevant to her main point. Instead, she selected representative examples that could be illustrated briefly within the scope of the essay.

College writing assignments frequently require you to narrow the topic yourself, although sometimes a particular assignment narrows the topic for you. Marlene's assignment, to write an essay concerning a family custom involving eating (dinner, for example), focused her attention on the relatively narrow topic of a dinner ritual. Suppose, though, that her assignment had been simply to write an essay about a family custom. In that case, she might have begun with many different kinds of rituals and would have had to do a lot more narrowing before she could come up with a thesis. After you have generated some preliminary material for your writing assignments, look carefully at the assignment to determine how much narrowing you are expected to do. One way to narrow your topic is to ask yourself the questions that journalists are encouraged to use, that is, What? How? When ? Where? Why? and Who?

Marlene focused her thinking by asking, "*What* dinner rituals did my family have?" Other focusing questions that she could have asked are as follows: "*How* were these rituals performed?" "*When* were these rituals performed?" "*Where* were these rituals performed?" "*Why* were these rituals performed?" and "*Who* performed these rituals?" Because these questions focus attention on specific times, people, and places, Marlene might have used them to become aware of some of the details she eventually included in her essay, enabling her to narrow her topic.

One way to understand the concept of narrowing a thesis is to think of it in terms of a camera lens. When your topic is too broad, it is as if you are using a wide angle lens that captures a panoramic broad view of the topic. But when you narrow your vision and look at the topic more closely, you can examine a smaller area of the picture more closely, as if you are using a macroscopic lens. Most writers tend to begin with too wide a vision at first, but as they revise their work, they realize that in attempting to cover too wide a field, their coverage of the topic is superficial and they may have overlooked important and interesting details.

Expanding the Thesis: Several Strategies

Once you have formulated a thesis statement, you will need to develop and expand it so that it will be convincing and interesting. By expanding your thesis, you will be able to influence your reader to think, "I never thought of that" or "I never noticed that before," or even "I need to rethink my position on that." Strategies of expansion make your thesis lively—they enable you to flesh out generalizations, explore your topic with greater depth and complexity, and write in a springy and energetic style.

ILLUSTRATING AND EXPLAINING GENERALIZATIONS

The most obvious and useful strategy of expansion is that of illustration and explanation—the writer develops a general statement by giving specific examples and then explaining how those examples illustrate the overall statement. For example, in the following paragraph, the writer, Alison Lurie, asserts that primitive clothing is often associated with magic, and she illustrates that statement with the examples of a necklace of shark's teeth and a girdle of cowrie shells or feathers:

> However skimpy it may be, primitive dress almost everywhere, like primitive speech, is full of magic. A necklace of shark's teeth or a girdle of cowrie shells or feathers serves the same purpose as a prayer or spell, and may magically re-

place—or more often supplement—a spoken charm. In the first instance, a form of contagious magic is at work: the shark's teeth are believed to endow their wearer with the qualities of a fierce and successful fisherman. The cowrie shells, on the other hand, work through sympathetic magic: since they resemble the female sexual parts, they are thought to increase or preserve fertility.

The Language of Clothes

Note that the thesis statement appears in the first sentence of the paragraph and that Lurie illustrates her main point with the examples of the shark's teeth necklace and a girdle of cowrie shells or feathers. Then she explains why those particular examples illustrate the main point of the paragraph.

USING STRONG DETAILS

In expanding your main points, you should aim for strong, vivid details that appeal to the senses of the reader so that he or she can envision them and imagine how they look, sound, smell, or feel. Choose powerful words that capture the essence of what you want to say, details that suggest more than what appears initially on the surface. Some writers refer to this characteristic of powerful writing as the "iceberg principle," in that just as only the tip of an iceberg appears above water, the rest being hidden beneath, so do effective details suggest more than is obvious upon first reading. In *Great Expectations*, Dickens uses powerful, well-selected details to convey the terror that the boy, Pip, feels when he meets the convict, Magwitch, in the graveyard:

> A fearful man, all in coarse grey, with a great iron on his leg. A man with no hat, and with broken shoes, and with an old rag tied round his head.

This description is much more effective than a tepid generalization such as "Magwitch was a frightening sight" or "Pip was frightened." Similarly, in the essay, "Of Towels, Pots, and Snuffboxes," Marlene illustrates her initial reference to "an unappetizing assortment of terry cloth bath towels" by describing them as "faded, nondescript, grayish mauve, or yellowed beige." In another example, Alison Lurie uses an illustration to explain her statement that the original purpose of clothing was magical:

> When Charles Darwin visited Tierra del Fuego, a cold, wet, disagreeable land plagued by constant winds, he found the natives naked except for feathers in their hair and symbolic designs painted on their bodies.

COMPARISON, CONTRAST, ANALOGY

An important technique for expanding a general statement so that your reader will understand what you are trying to communicate is to use comparisons, contrasts, and analogies. Sometimes the easiest way to develop a state-ment is to describe what it is or is not like. Comparisons link similar charac-teristics from things or ideas that may not have seemed similar at first. Contrasting emphasizes differences that may not have been apparent ini-tially. Here are some examples of how comparison and contrast may be used.

Marlene emphasizes the unappetizing nature of the bath towels her fam-ily used at the dinner table by comparing them to "rags."

Evan, another student, in an essay discussing the magical effect of his lucky jeans, contrasts them with other pairs. He says, "I wore my faded denim jeans to the senior picnic, although they were not as durable or warm as my navy slacks."

The essayist, Murray Ross, in his essay, "Football Red and Baseball Green," contrasts America's two principal outdoor sports by stating that "the funda-mental difference is that football is not a pastoral game; it is a heroic one."

The writer, E. E. Evans-Pritchard, uses comparison to point out that the position of women in primitive societies was about the same as the position of women today:

> Certainly, and obviously, English women enjoy comforts and leisure and lux-uries and the advantage of Christianity, education, medicine, mechaniza-tion—everything, in fact which we speak of as civilization; and all this primitive women lack; but then the men lack them too. Indeed it might rea-sonably be held that where our womenfolk are most conspicuously better off than primitive women, this is due not so much to alteration of women's sta-tus . . . as to innovations that have affected everybody.
>
> *"The Position of Women in Primitive Societies and in Our Own"*

Related to comparison and contrast is analogy, which is an extended comparison between two things (processes, ideas, actions, etc.). Analogies are especially useful for helping readers understand something unfamiliar by pre-senting it in terms of something that is familiar. Alison Lurie uses an ex-tended analogy to compare eccentric dress with eccentric speech:

> In dress as in language there is a possible range of expression from the most eccentric statement to the most conventional. At one end of the spectrum is the outfit of which the individual parts or "words" are highly incongruent, marking its wearer (if not on stage or involved in some natural disaster) as very peculiar or possibly deranged.
>
> The Language of Clothes

A Caution. Expanding ideas with specific, powerful details, or using com-parisons, contrasts, and analogies, usually involves much thinking and addi-tional writing. Too often, students are under the impression that they have expanded an idea when they simply produce another general idea; often, that idea ineeds additional development. For example, in her first draft of an essay concerned with dining rituals, Jasmine wrote the following paragraph:

> I grew up in a very formal home in which good manners were considered very important. Particularly at the dinner table, we were all brought up to observe strict rules of etiquette.

In this paragraph, Jasmine used another generalization to support her initial generalization so that we really do not know what she meant by "strict rules of etiquette," nor did she use vivid details to make the reader "see" what she meant. Did family members sit stiffly in their chairs? Was it a silent table? Was the table set elegantly? Were people dressed up?

LEARNING TO THINK IN DETAIL

Many successful writers who use vivid details in their writing also think in vivid detail. Likewise, learning to think vividly may impart freshness to your own writing, not to mention make your own perceptions more rewarding. With this in mind, practice the habit of observation—of people, their conversations, mannerisms, and of objects and scenes around you—your room, telephone, and car. Think about how you would describe them to someone who was unfamiliar with your world—what specific details you would include, what sorts of comparisons and contrasts would bring your prose to life. Keep a pad and pencil nearby so that you can write down ideas as they come to you. If you exercise your mind in this way, you will be surprised at how fresh and energetic your writing will become.

Revising Your Essay

There is a myth in our culture that good writers can write a paper quickly, without having to revise it very much. The myth is perhaps a remnant of the romantic concept of the author who, inspired by a divine muse, receives ideas intact and, therefore, does not have to revise his or her work, obtain other people's opinions on it, or engage in any of the hard work that "less inspired" writers have to do. If you are lucky enough to be inspired by a muse, then your first draft will be perfectly fine. More likely, you should be prepared to revise your work; remember that all writers revise, even gifted writers who have published a great deal. When you realize this, you will not be discouraged when your first draft is less than perfect. Just be sure that you have allowed adequate time for revision.

WHAT IS REVISION?

Another misconception about writing is that revising a paper means simply correcting the punctuation and spelling. However, as important as it is to submit a polished paper, correcting the surface before reexamining the thesis and the structure is like polishing fifty pieces of wood before you have decided which pieces you are actually going to use to build a table. In undertaking a revision, be sure you have a solid table before you polish it.

An important step in revision is to allow at least some time between completing a draft and revising it. If you begin to revise your essay as soon as you have written it, you will be too immersed in the writing process to view your work objectively, and consequently, you will miss many areas that need improvement. However, if you put the essay aside for a while, you will return to it with fresh eyes, viewing it almost as if you were the audience rather than the writer, and you will be in a better position to notice where revision is needed.

Based on my own experience as a teacher and a writer, I suggest that you print your paper (if you are using a computer) and leave it for a little while. Then revise it by asking yourself the following questions:

1. Is there a thesis? Often in a first draft, there is a tendency to write down a lot of information about the topic, without using that information in support of a thesis or a main idea. For example, in her essay, Marlene developed the thesis that dining in her family was characterized by an obsessive concern with practicality. She did not simply describe the dinner table or narrate events of her childhood, although she may have done so in an earlier draft.

2. Is the thesis sufficiently narrow? As I noted above in the discussion of narrowing the topic, first drafts often attempt to cover too broad a field and, therefore, result in a superficial, sometimes disjointed paper. Had Marlene attempted to discuss too many rituals, her coverage of the topic would have been excessively broad and generalized, giving the reader only a vague sense of her thesis. Scrutinize your topic as if you were examining it through a close-angled lens. Have you examined the topic in sufficient depth?

3. Are supporting points and details linked to the thesis? Lack of connection between supporting points and the main task thesis is another problem in early drafts, and it is, therefore, helpful to ask yourself after reading each paragraph, "How does this paragraph relate to my thesis?" Then ask yourself the same question about each supporting point and detail within the paragraph. In looking over your examples, be sure that you have indicated to your reader why you have used them and use transition words such as "in addition to," "for example," or "in contrast to," to cue your reader about how each detail supports your main idea. Do not presume that your reader will automatically know what you have in mind and will make the necessary connection.

4. Is further elaboration needed? In writing a first or second draft, writers often omit important information or give certain points only cursory attention, which means that the essay may require additional explanations, details, or examples. In revising your paper, you should expect to do at least some additional writing because you probably left something out in your first draft. Also, remember that details make your writing interesting, so in checking for adequate details, note whether you have included any that evoke sen-

sory images—pictures, sounds, or feelings. Look also for any representative anecdotes that can help your reader's understanding of your ideas and hold your reader's attention as well.

5. Does anything need to be deleted? Adding material requires additional work, but deleting material can be painful because you may have worked hard on it and, thus, are a little reluctant to give it up. Nevertheless, as you narrow your thesis and add additional material, your conception of the topic may change so that some material will no longer be relevant to your main point. In that case, you should be prepared to delete any material that no longer has a function in the paper. Of course, all writers find it hard to delete material; nevertheless, for your paper to be coherent, it is important that you do so. To return to the wooden table metaphor, if you had originally constructed a table with straight legs and then had decided to add curved ones, you would be unlikely to leave the straight ones on as well, no matter how difficult it had been to attach them, because they would be extraneous and no longer suit the design of the table.

For example, suppose that Marlene had originally written a paper in which she had discussed some other rituals that her family had observed, but then she had decided to focus on dining rituals. As interesting and well written as those sections of her paper might have been, she would have had to delete them from her essay because they would no longer be relevant to her main point. If you delete sections of a paper, it is a good idea to save them for another use. You never know when they might come in handy for another writing assignment.

6. Does anything need to be rearranged? As you revise your paper and modify your thesis, the order of ideas may change, requiring some rearrangement. Also, as you add material, a section that might have followed naturally from another in your original draft may seem out of sequence in your revision. Check that each section follows smoothly from the previous one and leads smoothly into the next.

7. Is the surface of the paper smooth and error free? When you have checked your paper for overall coherence, focus, arrangement, and elaboration, then, finally, you can examine it for surface flaws, such as awkward sentences, misspellings, and grammatical errors. If you are using a word processor with a spell checker, be sure to leave sufficient time to use it, even though it is tempting to eliminate this step. I also suggest that you read the essay aloud because you increase your chances of noticing sentences that are awkwardly constructed if you hear them as well as read them. Some students find it useful to read their essays into a tape recorder and listen back with the text in front of them, noting places where rewriting or correction may be needed.

Finally, in thinking about revision you should use every human resource available to you. If there is a writing lab or center at your school, ask a tutor to give you feedback on your essay. Or let a friend read it, indicating areas that may not be clear. You do not always have to act on the recommendation of a tutor or a friend, but they might notice something that you, as the writer, overlooked.

Assignments

LOOKING WITHIN

Exploration Questions: Personal Level

Before responding to any of the writing assignments suggested here, assess your own background in relation to one of the topics by responding to the exploration questions below. Write down as much information as you can about the topic, and identify a problem or a tension in those details.

1. What childhood associations do you have with this topic? What images or details come to mind?
2. How did your family view this topic? Can you think of specific conversations or instances in your childhood that influenced your conception of it? What incidents, scenes, or conversations come immediately to mind?
3. How did your school experiences influence your conception of the topic? Did your teachers and classmates feel the same way about the topic as did your family? Were there any points of conflict?
4. Can you think of at least two people who held differing views about this topic? If so, describe these people and summarize what you believe were their points of view.
5. Has your opinion changed about this topic in any way? Why or why not?
6. Do you think that this topic is important for people to think about? Why or why not?

Writing Assignments: Personal Level

After working through the six exploration questions and after identifying a thesis for one of the following topics, complete the writing assignment for that topic.

1. Write an essay in which you discuss a ritual or custom involving eating (dinner, for example) that occurred regularly in your own home or community. (Use Marlene's essay as a model for this assignment.)
2. If you have eaten in the home of someone from a different culture, write an essay about that meal, indicating how it differs from what is usually done in your own home or community.
3. Write an essay about how a typical meal in which you dine with your friends is similar to or different from meals you eat with your family.

4. Think about dining customs associated with your own culture and write an essay in which you discuss what would be considered rude or impolite behavior. After you have written a draft, find a classmate whose background is different from your own. Interview that person about what was considered rude behavior at the dinner table when he or she was growing up. Compare what your classmate's family considered rude with what was considered rude in your own family.

Exploration Questions: Community Level

The writing assignments above enabled you to reflect on your own individual and national identity and on some of the habits and customs associated with your immediate family, friends, peers, and influential adults. The next writing assignment asks you to move beyond your own identity to consider the diversity to which you were exposed in the community in which you grew up and to evaluate the level of tolerance you believe might still be needed. To begin thinking about this assignment, answer the following exploration questions.

1. Where was the place that you consider the community in which you grew up?
2. How diverse was this community?
3. Describe this community's diversity:
    a. racially
    b. economically
    c. sexually
    d. religiously
    e. politically
    f. morally
4. Describe the community's tolerance level in each of the categories below:
    a. racially
    b. economically
    c. sexually
    d. religiously
    e. politically
    f. morally
5. Explain your level of tolerance in each of the categories as compared to the community (more, less, same)? If you are less tolerant, explain why. What event(s) led to your position? If you are more tolerant, explain why. What event(s) led to your position?
6. What areas could have been improved in the diversity tolerance level in the community in which you grew up?

Writing Assignment: Community Level

After you respond to the above exploration questions, write an essay which addresses the following question: What improvement would you suggest that your home community could make in its level of diversity tolerance and what impact would this change have on that community? (You might also get ideas by reading how Carol Fukui and Alexa Isbell responded to this assignment.) [Both the exploration questions and the question were written by Adrien Lowery at the University of Southern California.]

Racial Diversity

Carol Fukui

The cool tropical breeze, egg-yolk sun rising above the green mountain tops, and trickle of the valley stream continue on their course since the formation of this island paradise called Hawaii—our home. Like the serenity that accompanies the natural scenery in the valley of Pauoa, so are we the inhabitants of this small community—peaceful, without any street riots, gang warfare, or muggers. Yet, although there is no physical attack made on individuals, there is harm done on the pride, identity, and culture of whole groups of people made by another dominant group—the natives who have been here longer and who feel that the preservation of their culture is as honored as the age-old tradition of keeping the land. The Hawaiians in Pauoa Valley must be more open and accept other races without discrimination in order to eliminate the fear and intimidation that they invoke within others. This would create a higher tolerance of racial diversity through in-school exposure and social integration.

Hawaii is the "Aloha State," a well-earned title meaning "kind-heartedness," except when those of Polynesian descent feel that their ties to their ancestral roots is justification enough for self-elevation and ignorance that Hawaii is now home to others as well. For instance, this summer, while I was riding the bus to work, three preteen girls of dark brown skin tone boisterously asked me "What-u time-u is it-u? with uncouth snickering and pointing to their bare wrists in exaggerated sweeping motions, as though I was deaf and dumb. It did not matter to them that I was also dark, except that my shade was due to excessive tanning, nor that I was older than they were by at least four years. All that mattered was that I had small slanted eyes and did not look like them. When I was smaller, I used to like to get dark tans, not because it was a sign that I went to the beach frequently, but more so that I would look Hawaiian and be accepted by the "in" crowd. I grew up thinking that the Hawaiians in Pauoa were the coolest people with their "pidgin English," which is the local slang, and their strong sense of being "family," people who were connected to one another. Disconnected and alien, though, is what I felt during that short bus ride, and the immaturity of these "locals" was no reason to excuse their behavior.

Discrimination must be prevented at an early age, so as to clear the way for unbiased learning. Racial diversity should be taught in schools by emphasizing the importance of each group's individuality— culture, language, ideas, customs, traditions, and personalities. Then children could grow up in an environment where they were surrounded by the different cultures and learning about different cultures through frequent cultural activities such as simple "show and tell" about their ethnic traditions to bigger "culture-day" festivals.

Students of all grade levels in Hawaii need more diversity in the subjects taught so that we can navigate in a society that is becoming more multicultural every day. In Pauoa, only Hawaiian history was required until the tenth grade, a form of monoculturalism.

Pauoa has to expose both children and adults within the community to more diverse cultures by simply allowing people to get to know their neighbors. My family is Japanese, our neighbors are Chinese, around the corner are Caucasians, and down the street there are

Hawaiians. If we band together through community projects such as crime watch, neighbors will be forced to rely on each other for the safety of all. This social integration would make our duties to cooperate with each other more enforced because we can appreciate others by recognizing where we fall short and then learning how we can work together to fill those needs.

The Asian groups were intimidated the most by the locals simply because their differences were the most obvious. But cultural values should not have to succumb to the dominant race, but rather everyone should be proud to share themselves with others in the hopes of understanding each other more.

Some locals would protest such radical changes in the community, arguing that in order to incorporate cultural diversity teaching, Hawaiian classes would have to be cut to allot time and space for other cultural classes. This "limitation" may pose a threat to the preservation of Hawaiiana, but the goal of racial diversity is to ensure that every culture is respected.

In conclusion, the sedate Pauoa Valley should become actively involved in their surroundings for a more united community. It should ensure tolerance of racial diversity by balancing the compatibility of everyone through cultural exposure in schools and the formation of integrated social programs that would require people to cooperate more with each other.

What Difference Does a Difference Make?

Alexa Isbell

I cried when my mother made me come in early that night. "It's not safe out here," she said. I didn't understand until I heard the sirens and saw the paddy wagons. I stared out my window as navy-clad policemen bolted by, clubs in hand, chasing random men costumed in white robes as they scurried from the forest surrounding my neighborhood. My mother cried and my father shook his head in angry disbelief. Before it had always been teenagers partying in the dark woods near my house, but this time it was different; it was serious. My father tried to explain to me that these people dressed in white were members of a bad group called the Ku Klux Klan and that they were wrong about black people and other minorities. I was told never to associate with them. I was seven years old then.

This incident with the Ku Klux Klan was my first true encounter with racism. This experience was the first to make me realize that my community had a long way to go on the road to racial diversity. Recently, however, I have realized that not only is my community racially intolerant, but that it has never even been exposed to many different ethnic backgrounds. Anderson, Indiana, has basically only Afro-Americans and Caucasians; this means that there are few Asians, Hispanics, and Native Americans. Because of this incredible lack of diversity, it is a monocultural society, and many people are missing out on enlightening experiences. But the saddest part of the problem is that few people realize the lack of diversity in the area and therefore see no need to change. The community of Anderson, Indiana, must acknowledge the lack of racial diversity in the area and promote multicultural education in order to encourage racial harmony and diversity tolerance among its citizens.

The first step toward racial diversity would be to admit as a community to the lack of tolerance toward racial and ethnic minorities. An excellent example of the district's unwillingness to foster racial diversity occurred in the schoolyear of 1983 when the schoolboard attempted to make the elementary schools more integrated through busing. The chaos caused by reluctant parents was more than enough to affect the attitudes of the students. Previously racially unbiased kids became miniature reflections of their genocidal parents. Although after almost ten years the problem has been alleviated, it makes me wonder how long it will be before there is a similar encounter with the migration of additional minorities.

Another source of racial intolerance in Anderson are the minorities that actually do exist there. It is difficult enough to encourage the majority to accept the ideas and traditions of another group, but it is even more impractical if the minorities refuse to allow members of the majority to join their culture. While Caucasians are no longer allowed to form clubs advocating white supremacy, such as the aforementioned Ku Klux Klan, there are still special clubs for Afro-Americans, Hispanics, Latinos, and Native Americans. Although this example is rather drastic and such clubs exist primarily to help minorities adjust to a racially lopsided culture, they still advocate segregation according to race. How can a white teenager be expected to try to learn about a different race when he or she is told on T-shirts and posters, "It's a black thing. You wouldn't understand"? The community could be bettered in this respect by educating the minorities and majority about many different cultural backgrounds, as opposed to one general concept.

Communication, perhaps, is the key to a racially tolerant society. The minorities of today are angry because they want to learn about their true heritage and no one will teach them. The majority of today is angry because it can't understand why the minorities are so upset. Perhaps, if the two groups could communicate their frustrations, there would be fewer problems resulting from racial issues. By implanting multiculturalism into the educational system, both groups could be appeased. Everyone could learn about every group and become multiculturally enlightened. Since the basis of racism is ignorance, it is up to the educators of society to see that all ethnicities are presented equally. Because everyone is so frustrated with each other, no one listens anymore. It is the duty of the leaders of the younger generation to make the WASPs realize that minorities have had it hard throughout the years and do deserve an equal opportunity at the American Dream. However, it is also the task of the teachers to help the minorities realize that the past cannot be blamed on the youth of today because they are also the victims of misconceptions. Both of these tasks can be accomplished only if the two groups agree to at least open their minds and communicate.

The impact that a more multicultural education could have on society could produce profound effects. The deletion of monoculturalism would encourage more racial tolerance, boosting diversity. Not only would minorities benefit from this, but the majority of the people would become more culturally enlightened and generally well-rounded. The economy would also benefit because with more tolerance of diversity there would come more integration and therefore a better education for everyone. Because education boosts salary, there would be fewer ghettos and welfare recipients. By breaking a chain of racial segregation, everyone would benefit. In order to promote the tolerance of racial diversity in Anderson, Indiana, the community must first acknowledge the lack of diversity and encourage communication and multicultural education.

LOOKING BEYOND

Exploration Questions: National Level

Thus far, you have used your own background as a resource for thinking about diversity and for generating material for essay assignments. In the next assignment, you will be asked to move beyond your family and community into a wider arena that focuses on a conflict involving gender, ethnicity, or race. To generate ideas for this essay, write responses to the following exploration questions:

1. Who is involved in the conflict?
2. What issues are involved in the conflict?
3. Who is primarily affected by the conflict?
4. What do newspapers and magazines indicate are the causes? Are there points of disagreement?
5. Do you believe that one group is right or wrong? If so, why?

Writing Assignment: National Level

To prepare for this assignment, collect material from national newspapers and magazines about a specific conflict involving gender, ethnicity, or race, noting, in particular, any background material that is provided. Write an essay addressing the following question: What do newspapers or magazines suggest are the major causes of this conflict? In your essay, be sure to summarize the nature of the conflict so that the reader can understand it.

Returning to the Questionnaire: "Are You *Really* a Racist?"

In the introductory chapter, you responded to a questionnaire entitled,"Are You a Racist," created by J. G. Conti and Brad Stetson and you may also have discussed the questions that followed it. Now read their essay "Are You *Really* a Racist?" that analyzes what they believe are typical responses. Locate the thesis of their essay and compare their analysis to your own responses. Then write an essay in which you discuss the extent to which you agree with their perspective.

Are You *Really* a Racist?

J. G. CONTI AND BRAD STETSON

*The following commentary was written by two graduate students in South
Central Los Angeles, who during the riots came to see a fundamental error in
approaches to minority advocacy. In this piece, which is based on their book,*
Challenging the Civil Rights Establishment, *they argue for a "racial humanism" in place of the usual "color-coordinated thinking."*

Some time ago, a popular host of a morning television show began a discussion of racism with a quiz. It would indicate, he said, "if you're a racist or a
liberal."

Are all conservatives, then, racist? The host's assumption was that they
are. In the same way, a recent book of surveys that claimed to discover what
Americans "really" thought about controversial topics—including racial issues—asked citizens, "Do you favor affirmative action policies?" Those who
answered "no" were automatically deemed racists.

Today on newscasts, talk shows, and in polite company, it would seem
that only one set of opinions on racial issues is acceptable. But a growing number of Americans, including some black intellectuals, believe that this isn't fair.
They are troubled by what appears to be a substitution of name-calling for rational discussion. They point out that a pluralistic nation like ours is predisposed to lively and sharp debate and to the free expression of a full range of
viewpoints and ideas. Indeed, this ongoing intellectual conversation is commonly understood to be the great strength of a culturally diverse nation. But
when the issue on the table involves race, it seems that this tradition of democratic reflection is regularly overrun by a politically correct "groupthink." The
effect of this politically correct bullying is that many are pressured into silence
and made to feel guilty for questioning the "official story."

What follows is a commentary on the quiz, "Are You a Racist?" It illustrates, point by point, what we see as gaps between popular, media-sanc-
tioned opinions on race and those of the cognitive minority—the dissenters
from conventional thinking.

T/F   1. *Only whites can be racist.*

You are probably familiar with this view. It is regularly taught as rock-solid
fact in many forums, including elementary school classrooms, university lecture halls, church discussion groups, and on MTV videos. "Only people in

power can be racist," goes the reasoning, "and so only whites, the power-brokers, can be racists." Garbage! says Professor Glenn Loury, a black political economist at Boston University. Loury argues that any one who hates on the basis of race, is a racist. He suggests that we tell Reginald Denny (the truckdriver beaten to the point of death during the Los Angeles riots) that only whites can be racist—that blacks, because of their social status, are not even capable of racism on their own!

Loury, and others, see such rhetoric as insulting to the dignity of African-Americans, because it patronizingly suggests that they are limited in the kinds of judgments they can make. Ultimately, such reasoning is harmful to black progress. This is especially so in the case of black youth, because it undermines the idea of personal responsibility, which is so vital to achievement. To say that African-Americans may be prejudiced but not racist (as raptivist Sister Souljah maintains) amounts to a verbal smokescreen, one that prevents discussion within the African-American community of a serious problem: some black youth have become as racially intolerant as the white bigots whom Dr. Martin Luther King, Jr. and his followers opposed in the 1950s and 1960s.

Indeed, misleading notions like "Only whites can be racist" may have immunized a generation of youth from moral commonsense. In *Shut Up and Let the Lady Teach!*, Emily Sachar, a journalist and teacher, illustrates this with a story from her classroom in a New York City school. Annoyed at the nomination of two Asians to be class leaders, a black youngster stood up in Sachar's classroom and announced, "No way I'm staying here if two slanty-eyed kids is running things." Sachar told him that he was free to run for the position too but that he would have to refrain from racist remarks. The boy seemed truly shocked, and replied softly, "That was a racist remark?"

Jesse Peterson, a South Central Los Angeles community activist who helps troubled black youth grow into mature men, believes that racism among black teens is one of the most tragic, underreported stories in America today. "A black gang member told us during a meeting that he refuses to learn from a teacher at school—just because the man is white. He told us, 'I hate all white people.' Millions of black kids think this way, and they don't even understand how they are hurting themselves."

Those who deny that the evil of racism comes in all colors are blind to an important truth, a truth that was best expressed by Dr. Martin Luther King, Jr.: "It is not a sign of weakness, but a sign of high maturity to rise to a level of self-criticism."

T/F   2. *"Institutional racism" so permeates American society that it hardly matters if African-Americans go to college or not because the effects of discrimination exclude them from the job market.*

In a 1992 issue of *Spin* magazine, one of the most influential voices in black youth culture today, rapper Chuck D. (from Public Enemy), opined on the empty promise of a college education for blacks:

> I can go to college and high school and get top grades, and when I go out into the job market, I don't know anything about business, which means business is a family thing, you understand what I am saying? If you ain't got family, you're not going to get that f-----g job.[1]

Chuck D. is not the only one to beat the drum of futility in this way—speeches by mainstream black leaders commonly sound the same theme. But are they right? To find out, we turn to recent statistics from the U.S. Department of Labor that reveal the relationship between black educational attainment and black employment. For every significant level of increase in education realized by 25- to 34-year-old blacks, the percent of the black unemployment rate drops by one half. This means, in more concrete terms, that blacks with a four-year college degree are roughly six times as likely to be employed than those who only have a high school diploma.

Chuck D. is simply wrong when he denigrates the value of a college degree for blacks. But his futilitarianism is of a piece with that of fellow *philosophe* and millionaire rapper "Ice Cube," who insists: "The American dream is not for blacks. Blacks who [still believe in that dream] are kidding themselves. There's only room in that dream for a few blacks." Once again, the facts contradict the rap. "Ice Cube" appears unaware that black college-educated women currently earn 125 percent of what white college-educated women earn. Would he be interested in putting that fact to a beat?

T/F   3. *When people and politicians talk about "straightening out the welfare system," they are secretly expressing racist attitudes toward the black poor.*

This is a favorite of media pundits, who commonly dismiss public calls for welfare reform as "playing the race card." For instance, one famous television commentator blamed the Los Angeles riots not on the looters and arsonists who sacked the city, but on "those who fanned these flames with codewords about 'welfare queens,' 'equal opportunity,' and 'quotas.'" His unstated message was all too clear: 'If you criticize welfare programs, or expect certain behavior from those on welfare, you are a racist.'

This "decoding" breeds a palpable social silence on the issue of welfare. This silence—the refusal to voice unpopular, but heartfelt opinions—ends up being most damaging to the black poor, according to neighborhood activist Robert Woodson. Sharply criticizing the welfare system, Woodson says: "Above all, the black community must disentangle itself from the welfare professionals whose primary objective has become the maintenance of clients." He argues that this "poverty pentagon" literally rides on the backs of the black poor, with 75 percent of monies intended for the poor going instead to the bureaucratic apparatus—that is, to the "helpers" of the poor.

The black family has been especially hard hit by the welfare system, says Woodson. With few exceptions, for a mother to qualify for the largest welfare program (Aid to Families with Dependent Children), she *must* be unmarried. This policy has set into motion a tragic set of social dynamics. In Detroit's nearly all-black school district of 170,000 students, 70 percent of them are being raised by single mothers—and nearly two out of three boys entering high school in Detroit do not graduate.[2] Today, it is projected that eight out of ten black children born in 1980 will wind up on welfare. Now, there is nothing intrinsically "racial" about these dynamics, notes black economist Thomas Sowell; he points out that more than half the children born in Sweden—with its hefty welfare packages—are the result of unwed pregnancies.[3] "The issue," says Sowell, "is not that the government gives too much help to the poor. The problem is that the government creates too much harm to the poor."

T/F   **4.** *To disagree with the views of prominent black leaders is to show racist opposition to African-Americans as a group.*

It is a myth that "black leadership" somehow speaks for all African-Americans and that "community spokespersons" are voicing opinions forged through consensus, insists Ezola Foster, founder of Black Americans for Family Values. (This is true of other minority groups as well: in a nationwide survey, 90 percent of Hispanics said that they did not belong to any of the ethnic organizations that so stridently speak in their name).[4] Surveys bolster Foster's point. When *Washington Post* pollsters asked whether minorities should receive preferential treatment to make up for past discrimination, 77 percent of black leaders said *yes,* whereas an equal percentage of the black public said *no.* Asked about the death penalty, 33 percent of black leaders favored it, whereas 55 percent of the black public favored it. On forced school busing, 68 percent of black leaders supported it, whereas 53 percent of the black public strongly disapproved.[5]

These disparities stem from pressure on blacks to keep private their dissent from the so-called Black Viewpoint, which is so loudly promulgated by "community spokespersons." To dissent publically is to risk the tag, "Uncle Tom"; even to discuss certain issues, some black journalists have found, is to court the charge of racial betrayal. A clear example of this was cited in the book *Outrage: The Story Behind the Tawana Brawley Hoax,* co-authored by six reporters from the *New York Times.* In 1987, Tawana Brawley, a black teenager, made national headlines when she charged that she had been raped by a group of white policemen. When a number of black journalists covering the story reported facts that called into question the authenticity of Brawley's "nightmare," they were confronted by angry Brawley supporters, who called them "Uncle Toms" and "Traitors!" for not rubber stamping her story.[6] To Brawley's supporters, the reporters were guilty of a heinous race-betrayal for questioning the words of a young black woman. (As it turned out, the black reporters were all but proven correct as multiple inconsistencies eventually appeared in Brawley's story, rendering it incredible.)

These black journalists refused the color-coordinated thinking that was expected of them. They rejected the simplistic idea that there is just one legitimate Black Viewpoint—the point of view expressed by "community spokespersons," who somehow speak for 30 million African-Americans.

T/F   5. *Talk show panels that pit white racists against black civil rights leaders accurately reflect the state of American race relations.*

You have, undoubtedly, seen more than a few of these because they have become a staple of national talk shows. The host introduces today's guests: on the right of your screen, members of white racist groups such as the Ku Klux Klan and "Aryan Nation" and on the left, black community leaders, frequently clergy. Predictably, a shouting match ensues. As the show sizzles on and decibel levels rise, the definite impression is given that no progress in race relations has been made over the last quarter century. The audience, of course, is forced to choose sides. We can either cast our lot with the community activists and show ourselves to be champions of "civil rights" or side with the rednecks and be exposed as Archie Bunker–style "Low Rent Bigots."

But does cutting race issues along these fantastic lines really give the audience a true picture of race relations in America today? The answer is *no,* according to careful, scholarly studies that have explored changes in American racial attitudes, including Edith Efron's *The News Twisters.* Efron contends that media images of race relations have not kept pace with the progress that has been made. Television news, she points out, routinely depicts American race relations as a "crude racist cartoon—with noble blacks pitted against evil conservative white America." Efron wrote that line in the late 1970s. It has only grown truer in the years that have followed.

But as the ancient Greek philosophers demonstrated, such imagery commits the "fallacy of the false dicotomy." That is, there is no reason to believe that only two points of view on racial issues are valid. In the case of "racist cartoon" talk shows, a *third position* would seem more plausible. This perspective, at once, avoids the color consciousness of black leaders and the neofascist idiocies of snarling white bigots.

Notwithstanding the imagery of "racist cartoon" talk shows, an overwhelming majority of white Americans have come to recognize racism as an evil. Studies such as *Racial Attitudes in America* have shown significant changes in personal attitudes in recent years—so much so, that Shelby Steele, a black professor of English, affirms in *The Content of Our Character:* "For every white I have met who is a racist, I have met twenty more who have seen me as an equal." Steele hardly could have affirmed that three decades ago. Although some concede such progress in personal attitudes, they often hasten to add that the problem today is "institutional racism." The University of Michigan has been charged with such racism—even though, as of 1988, it has had more than 100 programs in effect to combat bigotry.[7] "Institutional racism" in corporate America appears on the run, too. America's fastest growing income group are black families with incomes of more than $50,000.[8]

None of this is to say that racism is dead and gone; rather, it is to say that thoughtful, sensitive dialogue—a sort of "racial humanism"—requires civil discourse to be based on facts.

T/F   6. *Given that black Ph.D.s are salaried less, on the average, than white Ph.D.s, the only credible explanation is racism.*

Statistical disparities *do* exist between black and whites in many areas—but do they *necessarily* indicate racial prejudice? Clearly not, says Thomas Sowell in the *Economics and Politics of Race*. Sowell has coined a term—the "civil rights vision"—to describe an outlook that automatically accounts for various differences of status and income by charging "racism." It is a social outlook, says Jim Sleeper in *The Closest of Strangers,* which spies "intimations of racism in every leaf that falls."

When the "civil rights vision" automatically identifies racial discrimination as the root cause of income differences, it ignores other critical factors, says Sowell. Although it is a fact that black Ph.D.s are salaried less, on the average, than white Ph.D.s, it is important to know that the economic value of a degree is related to its field of expertise because some fields pay more than others. As it happens, a great percentage of African-Americans have taken Ph.D.s in education—not a very lucrative field, relatively speaking. Had they taken Ph.D.s in fields common to non-blacks (e.g., engineering, computer science, mathematics), this "conclusive" evidence for racism would evaporate.[9] Often social and cultural factors—apart from racism—can explain statistical differences.

Again, the "civil rights vision" invariably links black poverty to racism. But this perspective ignores the crucial relationship of social mobility to individual differences, says Sowell. For instance, according to a 1986 study, young black women who graduate from high school (and avoid unwed pregnancy) have better than a 90-percent chance of living above the poverty line.[10] The poverty rate for those who either don't graduate high school or have an unwed pregnancy in their teen years is dramatically higher. "Racism" doesn't account for this disparity, but individual differences in behavior do. Indeed, for married couples outside the South, black family income was 78 percent of white family income in 1959, 91 percent in 1969, and 96 percent in 1970. Black female-headed families have had declining real incomes during a period when black husband-wife families have had rising real incomes, both absolutely and relative to white families. Again, personal behavioral choices most plausibly account for such trends.

T/F   7. *Only persons of a certain race or ethnicity ought to speak about issues related to that race or ethnicity.*

"IT'S A BLACK THING, YOU WOULDN'T UNDERSTAND." Maybe you have seen this T-shirt motto. If we take its message at face value, it calls into question the possibility of participatory democracy itself because it implies that only blacks can deliberate and comment on issues affecting blacks. But the fact is, that in our pluralistic society, there is no such thing as a social issue that only affects one sector of the population. No group exists in a social vacuum, completely isolated from all others. Our destinies, as individuals and as members of a common society, are tightly intertwined.

Put concretely, it is impossible for a white American to cast a ballot that does not somehow affect a black American and *vice versa.* And so it goes for all racial and ethnic groups. We are obligated, then, to mutually reflect on the full range of social issues, including those that uniquely affect other races. Such reflection naturally results in the expression of a variety of perspectives on racial issues, and this drives us to a clear understanding of the radical uniqueness of persons, not as racial beings, but human beings. In turn, this understanding has a humanizing effect on culture, reminding us that we must extend respect and goodwill to cognitive minorities as well as ethnic ones period. This is the meaning of racial humanism, and it is the precondition of a social discourse that aims at genuine liberty for all.

NOTES

1. Chuck D., interviewed by Vivien Goldman, *Spin,* October 1992, p. 46.
2. *New York Times,* August 14, 1991, p. A11.
3. Thomas Sowell, "Throwing Money and Intercepting It," *Washington Times,* February 19, 1991.
4. Sowell, "Are Minority 'Spokesmen' Doing the Job?," *Daily News,* L.A., Dec. 18, 1992. p. NEWS-27.
5. Walter Williams, *All It Takes Is Guts,* Washington D.C., Regnery Gateway, 1987, p. 31.
6. Robert D. McFadden, et al., *Outrage: The Story Behind the Tawana Brawley Hoax,* New York, Bantam Books, 1990, p. 325.
7. Illiberal Education, p. 140.
8. Robert Woodson, "The New Politics in Action: Beyond the Welfare State," in *Left and Right: The Emergence of a New Politics in the 1990s?,* p. 47.
9. Thomas Sowell, *The Economics and Politics of Race,* p. 140
10. William Bennett, *The De-Valuing of America,* New York, Summit Books, 1992, p. 197.

2 ■ Negotiating Controversy in an Argumentative Essay

Rodney's King's plea "Can't we all just get along?" implies that getting along is simply a matter of will—that if people really want to get along, they will find ways to make it happen. Yet, although it is true that people are unlikely to get along with one another unless they really want to, it is also true that there are certain issues about which people disagree profoundly, particularly those concerned with moral questions or decisions about how diminishing space, resources, and opportunities should be distributed among people of differing backgrounds, races, languages, and cultures. These are the issues that must be understood, considered, and negotiated before people can begin to try to get along.

An effective way of understanding and negotiating controversial issues is to write about them. As I discussed in chapter 1, the process of writing an essay requires considerable exploration of the topic, part of which involves understanding your own views and then considering what your audience might think. This chapter discusses strategies for formulating and developing a thesis when the topic is likely to generate disagreement in your audience. I will emphasize that in working with a controversial topic, it is particularly important to consider the views of your intended audience and to find points of mutual agreement to negotiate a compromise position. I will also discuss how your concept of human nature will influence the positions you are likely to advocate.

Controversy and the Argumentative Essay

An issue is considered controversial if it has the potential for dividing its audience and eliciting at least two divergent viewpoints. Sometimes when these viewpoints differ widely, it can be difficult to find any common ground, and some students find it tempting to write an essay that simply explores these positions without necessarily advocating a particular one or formulating a thesis at all. For example, if you were writing about the controversy concerned with the fairness of affirmative action programs, you might discover that there are effective arguments on both sides, and decide, then, not to formulate a thesis, but simply write an essay exploring both positions as if you were writing an overview of the topic in a textbook. Although writing an essay that acknowledges the existence of multiple viewpoints is the first step toward the goal of "just getting along," it is also important that you ultimately choose a position and engage in the negotiation that occurs when people with diverse viewpoints have to reach a decision. It may be difficult for you to decide where you stand on some of these issues, but you should ultimately find a thesis and support it with convincing reasons and evidence.

Argumentative writing has been discussed in many composition textbooks, and has been explained in a number of ways. However, for the purpose of this book, I am defining the argumentative essay in terms of the following characteristics:

1. An argumentative essay advocates a position on a complex, controversial issue.

    Argumentative essays are concerned with topics about which there are at least two points of view. A thesis statement for an argumentative essay is one with which some people are likely to disagree.

2. An argumentative essay aims to convince a reader that its thesis has merit.

    Writers of argumentative essays on complex, controversial topics do not expect to change their readers' minds completely, although that sometimes happens. Rather, in most instances, the purpose of an argumentative essay is to move readers to at least consider the thesis, think about the reasons and evidence, acknowledge that the argument has merit, and then perhaps to reevaluate and modify their point of view.

3. An argumentative essay explores its subject in sufficient depth so as to acknowledge an opposing viewpoint.

    When a topic is complex and controversial, the "truth" or a clear concept of right and wrong is difficult to "know." Therefore, the topic invites a qualified response that indicates awareness of other perspectives.

Joining a Public Conversation

When you write an argumentative essay on a controversial topic, it is like joining an ongoing conversation or debate in which many people have been participating for some time. Issues concerned with diversity in particular have always generated controversy, and when you formulate your thesis you take on the role of speaker with your goal being to earn the respect of other debaters who may have been involved in the discussion for some time. This is true to some extent whenever you write an essay that others will read; however, it is also true that some topics have a greater potential for generating discussion and controversy than others.

The Importance of a Qualified Response

The topic of diversity is well suited for argumentative writing because it is inherently controversial—a topic about which concerned, intelligent, well-meaning people have long had difficulty making decisions. One might say that the subject of diversity invites controversy simply because it is concerned with the human condition, which is always characterized by contradiction and inconsistency. Disagreement about what is best for the human race transcends time and place; a position that one group passionately and definitively views as absolutely "right," may be viewed by another as absolutely "wrong" with equal passion and certitude. A further complication in writing about diversity is that the main controversy, at its most basic level, is concerned with a very difficult issue—figuring out how diverse groups can live together in harmony and equality when, historically, humanity has not been characterized by its ready acceptance of diversity. One might make the case that whether it originates with biology or culture, human beings tend to be downright suspicious of anyone who is even slightly different; presumably, the survival impulse draws human beings toward similarity, rather than toward toleration of "otherness." For most issues, developing a position about how diverse groups can get along while sharing increasingly scant resources does not involve simply pointing out what is right or wrong because for most issues the "truth" or a clear concept of right and wrong is difficult to know.

As in writing about many areas involving human interaction, a thoughtful essay about diversity often involves navigating between extreme positions, acknowledging the difficulty of making definitive predictions or absolute value judgments, and developing a compromise position because the writer is aware of other perspectives. An intelligent statement about human beings suggests implicitly the possibility that events (or policies or results) may take an unusual turn or that people may behave unpredictably. Because human nature is so complex a great deal of academic writing in the humanities and social sciences is characterized by qualification—writers may predict consequences or present analyses of particular conditions or events, but they may also indicate the tentativeness of their observations by using terms such as "seems," suggests," "indicates," "to some degree," or "to a certain extent." For an example of how qualifying words indicate the writer's awareness of the complexity of human behavior, read the following paragraph, by journalist Michael Clough, concerned with predicting a potential outcome of the decision to send American troops to Somalia:

> Less than two years after Africa's last colony—Namibia— gained its independence, the United Nations may have taken the first step on a slippery slope leading to de facto re colonization of collapsing African states. And the

United States, which seemed to be on the verge of abandoning Africa, may soon find itself more deeply engaged in the continent's affairs than ever before.

"The Heart of the Matter"
Los Angeles Times *(Dec. 6, 1992)*

In the above paragraph, note the use of the word "may" in two instances as well as the word "seemed." These words show that the author knows he cannot predict with certainty what is going to happen, but nevertheless his article is an educated appraisal based on his expertise in African policy.

Another reason for qualifying your thesis is that for a problematic topic such as diversity, other people's opinions are difficult to change completely, and thus an accommodating approach is more effective than one which attacks the subject head-on. Even informed, concerned, and open-minded people are often set in their opinions particularly when the opinion is based on strong feeling or has been ingrained since childhood. Think about opinions you feel strongly about. Have you held these opinions for a long time? Have your opinions changed a great deal over the past few years? How about the opinions of people you have known for a long time, such as those of your parents or neighbors? Because you are enrolled in a college or university and exposed to many new ideas, you may be at a stage in your life where your opinions will change rapidly. But, for many people, opinions and ideas are often firmly ingrained, and obvious attempts to change them can engender resistance.

Exercise: Assessing Ingrained Opinions

Write a response to each the following statements, indicating the extent to which you agree or disagree. Then assess which opinions you derived from your family or community versus those you may have acquired later in your life. Has your opinion remained consistent about these topics? Or have you changed your mind at some point in your life?

1. To solve the drug problem in the United States, even minor offenses should be punished severely, a jail sentence of at least five years for smoking marijuana, for example.
2. Because affirmative action programs are unfair, they should not be required by law.
3. If a particular culture allows a man to have more than one wife, he should be allowed to do so.
4. People should not have to speak English if they move to the United States.
5. Because television has a significant impact on children, daytime programming should be closely monitored by the government.
6. People should not assume particular roles or behaviors based on gender. Boys should be brought up to think of themselves as responsible for car-

ing for children at least half the time, and girls should be brought up to have a career.

7. Standards of sexual behavior should be the same for women as for men.

8. People react too strongly to marital infidelity.

9. High school students should live in boarding schools because they don't particularly want to live with their families anyway.

After writing your responses, compare them with your classmates' in small discussion groups.

Changing Your Readers' Minds

Generally speaking, people tend to hold on to their opinions unless they are confronted with compelling reasons to change their minds, and when you realize how infrequently people actually do this, you might then wonder what is the purpose of an argumentative essay at all, if it is unlikely to result in dramatic change in a reader. Why bother, if it is not going to make any difference?

My first response to this question is that causing dramatic change in a reader is not the only reason to write an argumentative essay about diversity. In fact, one of the purposes of this book is to provide opportunities for you to think seriously about the issues; by writing argumentative essays, you will be learning a great deal whether or not you significantly affect your reader. My second response is that even if your reader feels strongly about a particular issue, new information or a different perspective on a topic can result in at least partial change. Finally, it is important to understand that for a controversial topic like diversity the goal of an argumentative essay is not to change readers' minds completely but, rather, to move your readers to consider what you are saying, think about your reasons and evidence, acknowledge that your argument makes a great deal of sense, and then perhaps to reevaluate and modify their point of view.

APPROACHING YOUR TOPIC JUDICIOUSLY

These purposes of consideration, thought, acknowledgment, and modification are unlikely to be achieved if you simply proclaim "you are absolutely wrong and I am absolutely right." As the psychologist Carl Rogers has pointed out, that approach rarely works under any circumstances. Rogers maintains that many writers do not have their intended effect on readers because the arguments they write engender hostility rather than agreement, or to use the above terms, consideration, thought, acknowledgment, and modification. Generally, you will be more successful in writing for an academic audience if you approach your subject politely and judiciously, indicate that

MOMMA by Mell Lazarus

OH, **REALLY**? EXACTLY WHICH OF MY FAULTLESS, PERFECTLY LOGICAL, CLEARLY INDISPUTABLE AND WELL-THOUGHT-OUT ARGUMENTS DON'T YOU AGREE WITH?

you understand your reader's ideas on the subject, and qualify your discussion to allow for the possibility of compromise.

QUALIFICATION ENABLES NEGOTIATION

A qualified thesis on the topic of diversity enables you to negotiate a compromise position with your reader, so that the reader moves a bit further toward your position than he or she was situated before. Because the topic is multifaceted and because even experts on the topic are reluctant to predict consequences definitively or attribute causes absolutely, some acknowledgment of uncertainty and some speculation about alternatives is suitable. Your message to your reader should be "I understand how you feel and here are the points on which we agree. But here is where I differ from you, based on the following reasons." Note how James Fallows accomplishes this in his essay "The New Immigrants. " After Fallows discusses the reasons that many people are opposed to bilingual education, he states, "this is the way many people think, and this is the way I myself thought as I began this project." On the other side of this issue, Richard Rodriguez similarly acknowledges what his opponents have to say. Usually, whether we are listening to a speech or reading an essay, we are more likely to pay attention to what someone has to say if we feel that he or she understands our own point of view.

Exercise: From the Readings

In the following readings, the writer has indicated an awareness of an opposing viewpoint. Examine the first few paragraphs of each of these readings and, in small groups, discuss how the writer has negotiated a position with the reader.

1. Charles R. Lawrence III. "The Debate Over Placing Limits on Racist Speech Must Not Ignore the Damage It Does to Its Victims," chapter 7

2. Stephen Carter. "The Special Perspective," chapter 5
3. Jane Caputi and Gordene O. MacKenzie, "Pumping Iron John," chapter 8

QUALIFICATION AND CREDIBILITY

Qualifying your thesis enhances the effectiveness of your argument in that it indicates you are a thoughtful person who is aware of the complexity of the topic—thus, it helps to establish your credibility as a writer. In writing an argumentative essay, your tone should be reasonable and your overall approach to the topic should be thoughtful and concerned. You also establish credibility by indicating to your reader that you share the same overall goals—to make fair decisions and to advocate ideas that will result in societal benefit. You are saying to your reader, "You and I want the same things. Let's work together to find ways to make these things happen."

If you can find ways to show your reader that you share common ground, you will go a long way toward gaining your reader's trust. For example, Stephen L. Carter begins his book, *Reflections of an Affirmative Action Baby,* by acknowledging what he feels is the truth about why he and other blacks were admitted to prestigious schools. He states that in the interest of bringing "honesty as well as rigor to the debate," that "I got into a top law school because I am black. Not only am I unashamed of this fact, but I can prove its truth." With this statement, Carter anticipates his reader's potential objections to affirmative action programs and in effect says to them, "Okay, you're right and I agree with you." But then he goes on to show that whether or not he was admitted to law school because of his skin color is irrelevant because the main point is that he graduated with distinction and went on to maximize his opportunity. Carter establishes common ground to make his point that if one supports racial preferences in professional school admissions, it is not racist to point out that some people have benefited from these preferences. He then goes on to argue that whether or not they are deemed fair, it is the consequences of affirmative action programs that should be used to evaluate them. In effect, then, Carter has said, "Here are the points on which I agree with you. But here is another point that you may not have considered."

A DELICATE BALANCE BETWEEN QUALIFICATION AND COMMITMENT

Thus far, I have been discussing the importance of a qualified response and of negotiating a compromise position with your reader. Suppose, though, you feel very strongly about a particular issue and wish to indicate this feeling in your writing. Does a qualified approach mean that you cannot communicate emotion? And if you aim for a measured approach that considers the needs of the reader, will your emphasis suffer so that your writing becomes lackluster and boring?

An effective piece of writing is both committed and qualified. If you combine a thoughtful presentation with intensity of feeling, you maximize the chance that your essay will accomplish its purpose. Being reasonable, measured, and clear does not mean being undecided, nor does it mean that you cannot write in a vigorous emphatic style that communicates intensity. Although it is important to indicate your awareness of multiple perspectives on a controversy and to qualify your thesis as a means of negotiating with your reader, you do not want to create the impression that you are unable to make up your mind and remain paralyzed between opposing viewpoints. Usually, there is merit on both sides of a controversy (after all, that is what makes it controversial) but ultimately, you want to formulate a thesis and support it with commitment and enthusiasm even if you also speculate about alternatives. Writers who move back and forth between several perspectives without advocating a particular one of them have little credibility, and few readers will be influenced by a vacillating essay in which the writer has not decided on a main point. Being a credible writer on the topic of diversity means finding out as much as you can about your subject, confronting contrasting viewpoints, and then exercising intellectual judgment to finally choose a position and support it, even if that position is qualified. This is not easy to do, but those who care about how society functions eventually must do it. Otherwise, no policy would ever be instituted and no action would ever be taken except by extremists who feel there is only one side and no place for compromise.

Exercise: Qualify an Approach

Rephrase the following thesis statements to reflect a qualified view of the topic. Then discuss the impact that qualification would have on the credibility and effectiveness of the statement.

1. The present call to declare English the only language that governments can use in the United States is a naked attempt to arrest growing political influence by linguistic minorities in the country.
2. The educational emphasis on ethnic distinctions and the suspicion of democratic institutions are going to wear down the bonds that hold this country together.
3. The distribution of birth control devices in the schools will undermine the efforts of parents to institute moral values in their children.
4. Television news presents a distorted picture of violence in the inner city.

A qualification about qualification: Sometimes the qualification does not have to be stated directly in the thesis statement, but instead could appear within the body of the essay. In small groups, examine the above thesis statements and discuss how each could be qualified in the body of the paper.

Formulating a Thesis for an Argumentative Essay

UNDERSTANDING THE CONTROVERSY

In chapter 1, I suggested that you find a thesis by exploring a topic, narrowing the topic, and then constructing a statement to support that topic, and these suggestions pertain to almost any subject. However, because argumentative essays are concerned with controversies, you cannot formulate an informed position unless you become aware of the various perspectives that different people or groups may have on the controversy. At first, it may seem fairly simple to define a controversy because it seems as if there are only two sides. For example, you may feel that there should or should not be bilingual education programs in the schools or that mandatory busing should or should not be used as a means of providing educational opportunities for minorities. However, if you examine these seemingly straightforward positions more carefully, you will discover that they require an explanation of the context and perhaps some definition and clarification before you formulate a decisive position.

Clarifying the context is particularly important for understanding a controversy—that is, examining the history, time, and place in which it occurs and reflecting on the implications of various viewpoints. A superficial position (i.e., "The United States has always welcomed immigrants. Therefore, all laws restricting immigration are anti-American.") overlooks the problems arising from unrestricted immigration in some of our major cities. To cite another example, although some people may be in favor of using mandatory busing as a means of improving educational opportunities for minorities, advocating mandatory busing for every minority group under all circumstances would not be feasible and might, indeed, lead to disruption in the schools or withdrawal of certain ethnic or racial groups from public education. By considering the conflict in terms of a specific context, you can avoid formulating an overly general thesis that never goes beyond surface issues.

STRATEGIES FOR UNDERSTANDING THE CONTROVERSY

A thesis on a controversial topic requires that you understand what the controversy is about. I suggest that you begin developing ideas by utilizing the following strategies:

- Write responses to exploration questions.
- Become familiar with materials written by others to discover at least two perspectives on the topic.
- Create a list of opposing viewpoints and consider the potential consequences of each.
- Examine the underlying assumptions behind each viewpoint.

At the end of this chapter, you will see how Kathleen worked with these strategies in response to an argumentative essay assignment.

WHAT IS YOUR OPINION OF THE HUMAN RACE?

Another way of exploring the topic is to think about how your view of it has been influenced by your view of human nature in general, admittedly a broad and complex subject. If you walked up to a stranger on the street and asked them, "Tell me in a few sentences, what do you think of the human race?" he or she would probably think that you were not serious, because the question is so broad and complicated. And yet, it is important that you think about how you perceive most people and the extent to which you think they are likely to behave admirably toward one another without being forced to do so and the extent to which you think it is possible to force people to behave well. For example, most of us would probably not steal our neighbors' possessions, even if it were not illegal to do so. For most of us, respecting the property of others is a question of principle and, therefore, even if we knew that our neighbors were out of town and had left their doors unlocked, we would not go into their homes and steal their things. And yet, it is also true, unfortunately, that there are some people who do not concern themselves with the morality of stealing. For these people, the desire for the goods far outweighs the immorality of the act. If we did not anticipate that some people would steal our goods, we would have need for locks, alarms, guards, and all of the other sad paraphernalia of modern living. Unfortunately, as the psychiatrist Walter Reich has pointed out in a recent article,

> the greatest religious texts wouldn't always be exhorting us to do good if they didn't recognize that we're inclined, so often, to do evil. At the simplest level, doing evil means doing harm, intentionally and unjustifiably, to others. The capacity to do evil seems to be part of being human."
>
> Los Angeles Times, *Feb. 28, 1993.*

Some of you may disagree strongly with this view of human nature. You may feel that human beings intrinsically want to "do the right thing" and get along with one another, but that the ills of society have made doing the right thing impossible for them. You may feel that if we could rectify some of the injustices in our world, people would cooperate with one another and there would be decreased need for law enforcement in all of its manifestations.

Understanding how you think human beings are likely to behave is important in the context of deciding law or policy. If you feel that most people want to help minorities advance in society, then you will probably feel that affirmative action policies to help minorities are unnecessary. Or you may not be in favor of them because you believe that some people will take unfair advantage of them. Another position you may hold is that unless people are forbidden to discriminate against minorities they are likely to do so, in which case you favor keeping such laws in operation.

Exercise: Thinking About Human Nature

Consider how you were brought up to regard human nature by responding to the following questions:

1. How did your family view humanity? Were you brought up to trust people? Or were you brought up to be suspicious?
2. Do you believe that people will "do the right thing" if they are satisfied with their lives?
3. Do you believe that laws are necessary to prevent people from hurting one another? Which laws, in particular?
4. Do you think that laws can prevent people from hurting one another? Can you cite examples on either side of the question?

READING ABOUT THE CONTROVERSY

Some composition textbooks give the impression that all of the ideas you will need for writing an essay lie hidden within your brain and that preparing to write means simply to find some mechanism for eliciting them. My feeling is that for many topics most of us don't have enough information to be able to formulate a grounded opinion. Therefore, it is useful to increase your understanding by reading what others have to say. Chapter 4 focuses on strategies for becoming an active reader who questions the material and is sensitive to authorial bias, ideological interest, fallacies, and contradictions—a reader who does not accept everything at face value. Use outside reading to understand the nature of the controversy, but reflect on whether or not the ideas you encounter are credibly presented and consistent with what you believe is possible or desirable and whether they are consistent with what you believe about the nature of humanity.

LIST OPPOSING VIEWPOINTS AND CONSIDER THE CONSEQUENCES OF EACH ONE

After you have explored your preliminary reaction to the topic and have read some material concerned with it, you can begin to focus on areas of conflict. Find these areas and list as many opposing viewpoints as you can. As I mentioned earlier in the chapter, controversies about diversity are concerned essentially with finding ways for diverse groups to share increasingly limited space peacefully and fairly. Deciding what form that effort should take, determining how, when, and where that effort should be exerted, and assessing whether or not these goals are even possible are what most of the controversies are really about. In general, controversies associated with the topic of diversity are concerned with the following:

1. Examining what is or is not "just" or "fair" or "right" about a condition or problem;
2. Discussing the causes of a condition or problem;
3. Evaluating what has already been done to create fairness, opportunity, or justice;
4. Postulating potential effects of a policy, law, or social outlook, either one that currently exists or one that has been proposed.

A thesis for an argumentative essay makes a statement about **value**, that is the rightness or wrongness of a condition or problem, **causation**, that is, the causes or effects of the problem or condition, or **policy**, either one that already exists or one that has been proposed.

Exercise: From the Readings

Find three readings in chapter 5 or chapter 7. Skim over the beginnings of these readings to understand the main ideas. Then answer the following questions:

1. Do the articles examine what is or is not "just" or "fair" or "right" about a condition or problem?
2. Do the articles discuss the causes of a condition or problem?
3. Do the articles evaluate what has already been done to create fairness, opportunity, or justice?
4. Do the articles postulate potential effects of a policy, law, or social outlook, either one that currently exists or one that has been proposed?

WHICH GROUP WILL BENEFIT?

Because different points of view suggest potentially different courses of action, controversies frequently focus on predicted consequences for different groups since most positions, even those based on compromise, are likely to favor one group over another. Understanding the conflict involves considering these potential consequences and predicting how various groups are likely to be affected. Thinking about what overall effect each perspective is likely to have and deciding who is most likely to be affected are important considerations for formulating a thesis.

To illustrate this point, let us examine the idea that bilingual education should be available in all schools in which a significant number of children do not speak English. When first considering this topic you might feel that there are actually very few perspectives on the topic because it seems straightforward—either you have bilingual programs or you don't, and, at first glance, it seems as if you would certainly want to have them. If you were to attend a school in a foreign country, naturally you would feel more comfortable if some effort were made to help you learn the language. Those on the opposing side of the issue might say that since immigrants to the United States speak so many different languages, it would be difficult to decide which language to emphasize in schools and that whatever decision were made, certain groups would be privileged at the expense of others. For instance, if it were decided that some instruction would be given in Spanish, that policy might be considered unfair to the significant number of children who speak Korean. Another opposing view might be that since bilingual instruction is likely to cost a great deal of money, it might deflect resources from programs that would benefit children who already speak English. Another view might be that the only way to learn a foreign language is by total immersion in it and that bilingual education actually inhibits language acquisition.

In thinking about an issue such as this one might ultimately decide on a compromise position—that bilingual instruction should be attempted only in certain areas of the country, on perhaps a limited basis. Yet even when you argue for a thesis that seems to be a compromise, you will often discover that the position inevitably benefits one side more than another.

UNDERLYING ASSUMPTIONS

Your understanding of a controversy will also deepen if you become aware of the underlying assumptions on which various perspectives are based, of the ideas or beliefs that we all feel are true and important and which are used as the foundational support for a thesis. Underlying assumptions are based on our views of what is possible and desirable in the world and reflect our overall perspective on humanity that, in turn, influences how we predict human beings are likely to behave. For example, a woman I know uses the following argument to oppose bilingual education and bases her argument cn assumptions that many people would perceive as true:

> My father came to this country as a young man not speaking a word of English. The first thing he did when he arrived was to study English, read English language newspapers, and take night classes so that he learned English on his own. If people come from a foreign country, it is their responsibility to learn English, and it is not the business of the schools to provide language classes.

In this example, the woman has assumed the following:

- The controversy about bilingual education is mainly concerned with immigrants, rather than with American children who come from homes and cultures where English is not the main language.
- Most people want to learn English, as her father did, and will personally take on the responsibility for doing so.

- Public funding should not be used for immigrant students.

Those in opposition to her point of view may base their arguments on completely different assumptions, such as:

- Bilingual education is not mainly concerned with immigrants. Rather, it represents an attempt to help American children who come from homes and cultures where English is not the main language.
- Unless language education is easily accessible, most people will not seek it out.
- It is in the public interest to maximize opportunities for immigrants to learn English.

Exercise: Examining Underlying Assumptions

Examine the following thesis statements. In small groups, discuss the underlying assumptions behind each.

1. The recent emphasis on multiculturalism has left America culturally centerless, posing a threat to its national identity. The only way to preserve Western culture is to enact strict immigration policies.
2. The function of public schools is to inculcate an "Americentric" education—one that creates an inclusive national identity based on our common culture.
3. The male success trip is driven by a fear of failure and the inability to feel. The male's only desire in life is to keep his head above water.
4. For men to get in touch with their basic male spirit, they need mentors, older men who can sever their feminizing attachment to their mothers.
5. The imposition of speech codes at many universities has set a dangerous precedent that will result in tighter restrictions on freedom of speech.

Justifying an Argumentative Thesis

MORALITY VERSUS POSSIBILITY

In an ideal world, all things deemed good would also be possible—everyone would have equal opportunity to be educated and wealthy, all strangers would be welcomed into new communities, people would give freely to help the poor, everyone would work and study hard for self-improvement, and everyone would be honest. Unfortunately, we live in a world that is far from ideal. Consequently, a thesis concerned with a controversial issue about diversity must grapple not only with the question of what is good or bad but also with the issue of what is or is not possible in a world where resources are limited and human behavior is not always admirable. In fact, controversies concerned with diversity often occur because a tension exists between what is regarded as moral in an abstract sense and what is deemed possible in terms of likely consequences. For example, one might argue that abortion is immoral because it involves terminating a life (or a potential life) and because our society regards the termination of life as immoral. Therefore, all abortions are immoral and should be forbidden by law. Someone else might argue that the question of morality is far less important than the question of possibility, or, in this instance, likely consequences, because even if abortion were considered immoral in an absolute sense, the morality or immorality of legalized abortion is irrelevant compared to the societal problems that would result from making it illegal, such as the birth of unwanted children or the deaths of pregnant women from unqualified, unscrupulous abortionists. In terms of an isolated act, abortion might indeed be considered immoral. But in the context of possibility, making abortion illegal might be considered equally if not more immoral, and one might vote in favor of legalized abortion simply on the basis of practicality.

One cannot, however, always equate morality with practicality. Most of us would not support a proposal to put all people over the age of eighty to death based on the fact that they often drain resources from society, even though such a proposal might be of economic benefit to society. In this instance, our moral objections to the proposal would outweigh potential practical benefits.

In formulating your own thesis, you should think about whether you personally advocate it on moral or on practical grounds. Moreover, if you are aware of the tension between morality and possibility, you will be able to anticipate potential objections from readers. Will the reader object to a thesis on moral grounds? Will the reader object that, irrespective of intrinsic merit, an idea or proposal is not possible because people are unlikely to support it, because people are not likely to behave according to prediction, or because it would cost too much money?

INDIVIDUAL VERSUS PUBLIC BENEFIT

Another area of tension inherent in developing a thesis involves assessing whether something that is good for an individual or a particular group is as good for society as a whole. For example, one might feel that a policy of instituting quotas for university admissions or places of employment is not right because it privileges certain groups over others and is therefore immoral in a society which values equal opportunity for everyone. However, another viewpoint might be that quotas are actually advantageous to society as a whole because they rectify past injustices perpetrated upon certain groups (thereby making society more just) and because they provide opportunities for those who might not otherwise have them, ultimately benefiting society by reducing economic and social inequities.

SALLY FORTH By Greg Howard and Craig MacIntosh

Copyright © 1992. Reprinted with special permission of King Features Syndicate.

Exercise: From the Readings

Choose one of the following readings and note how it justifies its main points. Does it use morality or practicality as its basis? Does it assess individual versus pubic benefit?

1. Arthur Schlesinger, Jr., "The Decomposition of America," chapter 5.
2. Shirley N. Weber, "The Need to Be: The Socio-Cultural Significance of Black Language," chapter 6.
3. Richard Perry and Patricia Williams, "Freedom of Hate Speech," chapter 7.
4. Betty Friedan, "The Second Stage," chapter 8.
5. Stephen L. Carter, "Racial Preferences? So What?" chapter 10.

The Importance of Defining Terms

Negotiating meaning with readers so that they will be influenced by your ideas also involves negotiating agreement on the meaning of the terms used in the essay. Such agreement requires you to minimize ambiguity and vagueness by carefully defining the words you use. The concept of affirmative action, for instance, is one that many people have violent reactions to because for them, the concept means simply, "hiring members of underprivileged groups, regardless of their qualifications." For others, the concept may have a more moderate meaning such as, "only when a candidate from an underprivileged group is well qualified should he or she be given precedence over another candidate." Therefore, in arguing for or against affirmative action policies, you should define and clarify which version of the concept you have in mind.

In another example, an argument against the practice of using quotas in affirmative action programs has been that quotas do not promote equal opportunity because they privilege one group over another. However, those in favor of using quotas might argue that quotas actually facilitate equal opportunity, because they provide opportunities for those who had been denied them previously, thus equalizing prior inequalities. For them, the concept of equal opportunity means *equalizing* opportunities that were rendered unequal because of unfair past policies. Finally, those who object to the concept of requiring politically correct speech sometimes argue that the PC movement violates the right to freedom of speech guaranteed in the First Amendment. For them, freedom of speech means that anyone can say anything, as long as it does not cause a threat to safety, such as calling "fire" in a crowded theater. Others might argue that freedom of speech does not mean that anyone has the right to say anything and was never intended to encompass sexist or racist speech. For them, the PC movement has nothing to do with the First Amendment. In these instances, then, it is important to define what is meant by freedom of speech.

Defining terms becomes particularly important when one uses value-laden terms such as *beneficial, good,* or *fair* because these terms are often used to justify a particular position. For example, in the context of deciding whether or not to require a diversity course at the local high school, proponents might argue that it would be beneficial to society since it would foster mutual tolerance and respect among diverse groups, presumably enhancing possibilities for peace and harmony. In this instance, a beneficial program might be defined as "one which fosters tolerance and respect among diverse groups." Those opposed to such a course might argue that it would displace other needed courses, placing students at a disadvantage. For them, the concept of beneficial might mean something entirely different.

Exercise: From the Readings

Read the following articles, and answer the questions on defining terms. Then, in small discussion groups, compare Schlesinger's and Ravitch's approaches to the concept of multiculturalism. What role does each definition play in developing the main point of the essay?

1. Arthur M. Schlesinger, Jr., "The Decomposition of America," chapter 5. How does Schlesinger define "separatism?"
2. Diane Ravitch, "Multiculturalism: E Pluribus Plures," chapter 5. How does Ravitch define "particularism?"

The Structure of an Argumentative Essay

The form of an argumentative essay depends on the goal you are trying to accomplish, and argumentative writing concerned with diversity issues can take many forms. Form must follow content, not the other way around. However, in an academic argument frequently, but not always, contains the following sections in this order:

1. INTRODUCTION

In this section, consisting only of one or two paragraphs, you indicate your topic, establish briefly why it is controversial and significant, and present your thesis.

2. EXPLAIN THE CONTROVERSY

In this section, you explain the nature of the conflict and summarize various viewpoints as a way of indicating that you understand the ideas of others and have researched the topic thoroughly. This section might define important key terms and include relevant personal experience.

3. EXPLANATION AND SUPPORT OF YOUR THESIS

In this section, you present your thesis and main points and support them with reasons and evidence that might include facts, statistics, data, and ill-ustrative examples. You may include a paragraph that establishes common ground between you and your intended readers. This is usually the longest and most substantive section of the essay.

4. ANTICIPATION AND REFUTATION OF OPPOSING VIEWPOINTS

In this section, you indicate areas where your opponent will probably agree with your thesis, and then demonstrate that you are aware of areas where you are likely to disagree. Once you have indicated that you understand your op-ponent's point of view, you can show how your own point of view is superior.

5. CONCLUSION

This section summarizes your main argument and perhaps suggests what ac-tion, if any, the readers ought to take. It also gives the reader a sense of clo-sure by restating the main thesis or postulating potential implications or consequences.

Some Suggestions for Introductions and Conclusions

THE INTRODUCTION

Some students have difficulty writing introductions because they have not clarified for themselves what they want to say. If you are having trouble (you find yourself rephrasing the same sentence over and over again without making any progress), I suggest setting the introduction aside and working on the middle of your paper where you develop your supporting points and cite your evidence. Usually, once you have involved yourself sufficiently in the topic by developing several main points, the introduction will probably be easier to write.

Below are several suggestions for writing an introduction:

1. Establish that a problem exists that needs solving. The problem may take the form of an ongoing situation, a failed plan, an inadequate proposal, etc. Your thesis, then, will be concerned with a way to solve the problem.
2. Establish that a controversy exists. Your thesis will then indicate your position in the controversy.
3. Present the background of the topic, defining relevant terms.
4. Indicate why a topic is significant—why a particular situation, plan, proposal, or policy is, or would be, good or beneficial.
5. Attract your reader with a thought-provoking or attention-getting anecdote or example.

THE INTRODUCTION AND THE "ALTHOUGH" STATEMENT

Introductions frequently introduce main ideas through the use of the "although statement," a transitional sentence that serves to distinguish the writer's main idea from ideas that have already been proposed. The although statement is used when the writer states an existing point of view or proposal and then raises an objection to it, using the word "although," which naturally leads to the thesis statement. In its essence, the although statement says that although something (another idea or proposal) may appear to be true (or good or beneficial, or inevitable), the truth is actually the writer's point. "Although" indicates to the reader that what the writer has to say is superior to what has been said before.

Here is an example of a statement using an although clause:

> Although American men often focus on their macho image and on success in their jobs, many of them experience feelings of great loneliness and isolation.

Exercise: Using Strategies

In small groups, discuss the strategies used in the following introductions:

> For 70 years, it has been public school organizing principle No. 1: Each grade has high-track students, middle-level students, and some version of the Sweathogs on "Welcome Back Kotter." While some discuss Voltaire in class, others are in metal shop. Some make the algebra-readiness cut, some do not. It's the American way.

Now a growing number of educators—most of whom, it is safe to say, never took metal shop—are convinced that it's the wrong way. Their cause is "detracking," the dismantling of the sorting mechanisms that American schools rely upon. Pressing arguments of efficacy or equity or both, they are trying to convince Americans that stratification in school hurts some and helps none.

"Should Tracking Be Derailed?"
Laura Masnerus
New York Times, *Nov. 1, 1992*

Multiculturalism—the notion that ethnic and cultural groups in the United States should preserve their identities instead of fusing them in a melting pot—has become a byword in education in Los Angeles and other cities. But now, educators at the elementary, secondary, and university levels are re-thinking that idea—and worrying that past efforts to teach multiculturalism may have widened the ethnic divisions they were meant to close.

"Multiculturalism: Building Bridges or Burning Them?"
Los Angeles Times, *Nov. 30, 1992*
Sharon Bernstein

The problem lay buried, unspoken, for many years in the minds of American women. It was a strange stirring, a sense of dissatisfaction, a yearning that women suffer in the middle of the twentieth century in the United States. Each suburban housewife struggled with it alone. As she made the beds, shopped for groceries, matched slip-cover material, ate peanut butter sand-wiches with her children, chauffeured Cub Scouts and Brownies, lay beside her husband at night—she was afraid to ask even of herself the silent ques-tion—"Is this all?"

The Feminine Mystique
Betty Friedan

THE CONCLUSION

Like introductions, conclusions can also be problematic, particularly because writers sometimes lose patience by the time they get to the conclusion and are tempted to say, "Okay, I'm finished. This is all I have to say." You must not give in to that temptation because conclusions are very important. In fact, aside from the introduction, the conclusion is often what readers re-member best. The conclusion is the place where you can direct the reader's at-tention back to the central problem discussed at the beginning of the paper, sum up your main thesis, and tie things together. Strong conclusions are usu-ally concise and sometimes can be memorable, particularly if you can think of a thought-provoking or dramatic last sentence. Drama, though, is not the main requirement of the conclusion, and a solid conclusion can be strong without punchy concluding lines. Below are some uselful suggestions for writing a conclusion.

1. Return to the Problem You Discussed Earlier

Because your thesis is likely to be concerned with a particular issue or prob-lem, it is sometimes useful to return to that problem in the conclusion to refocus your reader's attention. Perhaps you began with a specific example or a personal reference—if so, mention it again in the conclusion as a way of tying the essay together. Returning to something mentioned in your introduction can provide unity to your essay.

2. Summarize Your Main Points

Conclusions frequently contain a summary of your main points, connecting them to your thesis. This is the place where you can restate your ideas without having to provide additional explanation. Readers often find it helpful to conclude with a summary of main points because it helps them remember the focus of the essay.

3. Direct Your Reader's Attention to the Implications and Potential Consequences of Your Ideas

You might conclude your essay by showing how the issue you have discussed will impact society as a whole. A paper arguing in favor of bilingual education, for example, might conclude with a statement showing that the United States cannot afford to reduce an entire segment of society to a life of poverty because they are unable to speak English. If you use this strategy, however, be careful that you do not conclude your essay with an unsupported point.

4. Use an Illustrative Anecdote

The significance of your thesis might be reinforced for your reader if you conclude with an illustrative anecdote or description. James Fallows's essay in chapter 6 concludes with a reference to a young man originally named "Ramon," who, after having participated in a bilingual education program, wished his name to be spelled "Raymond," showing that Americanization occurs in spite of bilingual education.

Assignments

EXPLORATION QUESTIONS

Background Information

Until fairly recently, it was common to refer to American society as a melting pot, a metaphor that suggests that the United States is a country made up of many different ethnic groups that have all become blended or assimilated into Americans. Today, however, the metaphor of the melting pot is being challenged by another metaphor: that of the tossed salad. This idea implies that although many different groups live in the United States and may, indeed, consider themselves American, each also retains its own ethnic and cultural character and that this retention is both possible and desirable.

One arena where interest in multiculturalism has been most intense is in the schools, where educators at all levels have attempted to promote ethnic and cultural pride through ethnic studies courses and the celebration of special holidays and heroes. Critics of these efforts, however, claim this new emphasis on ethnic and racial differences in the schools may actually increase divisions between groups, resulting in increasing fragmentation, segregation, and hostility.

As a way of understanding the controversy, write brief responses to the following questions:

1. Why is this topic considered controversial?
2. Were you brought up to have an opinion on this controversy? What opinion did your family and community have on this topic?
3. How did your school experiences influence your conception of the controversy? Did your teachers and classmates feel the same way about it as did your family? Were there any points of disagreement?
4. Can you think of at least two people who held differing views about this controversy? If so, describe these people and summarize what you believe were their points of view.
5. Has your opinion changed about this controversy in any way? Why or why not?
6. Do you think that this controversy is important for people to think about? Why or why not?

After reading the assigned articles, try to fill in the missing components of the following sentences:

The conflict in this issue is between ⎯⎯⎯⎯⎯⎯⎯⎯⎯⎯⎯⎯ and

⎯⎯⎯⎯⎯⎯⎯⎯⎯⎯⎯⎯⎯⎯⎯⎯⎯⎯⎯⎯⎯⎯⎯⎯⎯⎯⎯⎯⎯⎯⎯⎯⎯⎯.

I am more inclined to agree with ⎯⎯⎯⎯⎯⎯⎯⎯⎯⎯⎯⎯⎯⎯⎯⎯⎯

because ⎯⎯⎯⎯⎯⎯⎯⎯⎯⎯⎯⎯⎯⎯⎯⎯⎯⎯⎯⎯⎯⎯⎯⎯⎯⎯⎯⎯.

However, it is possible that some of my readers may believe that

⎯⎯⎯⎯⎯⎯⎯⎯⎯⎯⎯⎯⎯⎯⎯⎯⎯⎯⎯⎯⎯⎯⎯⎯⎯⎯⎯⎯⎯⎯⎯⎯⎯⎯.

Kathleen's Responses to the Exploration Questions

1. Why is the topic of multiculturalism considered controversial?

I think the issue of multiculturalism is controversial because some people believe that ethnic diversity threatens national unity and that the emphasis on our differences leads to further racism and fragmentation. On the other hand, some believe that learning about other cultures will lead to greater harmony and understanding. This issue is a hot topic right now because multiculturalist educators are trying to change school curriculums so that they cater more to the needs of minority children. And I think that the problem of racism and integration has gained national attention since the Rodney King beatings and the Los Angeles riots.

2. Were you brought up to have an opinion on this topic? What was the opinion of your family or community?

Although I have always been aware that American society is diverse, I have never really considered whether or not it is important to consciously learn about other cultures because it almost seems to happen naturally. For example, I've grown up in California, which has a large Mexican-American population. We went to school together, we worked together. They were always considered Americans first, and there was no problem with just "getting along." However, some people would emphasize the cultural difference by calling them names, but most of us believed that these name-callers were just insecure and ignorant.

3. How did your schooling influence your perception of multiculturalism?

Apart from Mexican-Americans, my high school was not very culturally diverse. I remember we used to celebrate Cinco de Mayo, but I am still not entirely sure of what event that day commemorates. I vaguely remember social studies in grammar school—our book had pictures of kids in traditional costumes who would describe (in personal narratives that were idealized) what it was like to live in their countries. This gave us some idea that different cultures existed, but these portraits were obviously not very realistic.

4. Find two people with different points of view on this topic and describe their ideas.

One of my friends is angry that she has to fulfill the Non-Western Cultures requirement because she says that she knows so little about *Western* culture and history. She doesn't understand how a course in Third World Literatures and Cultures is relevant to her own life. She believes it would be better to learn about Western literature and thought first.

Another friend of mine has a class on East Asian Societies. She says it is fascinating to learn about cultures so different from her own. She says that it has given her increased respect for Asian culture and at the same time has helped her to see some of the problems with Western culture. She says that she no longer just blindly accepts the Western way of doing things as the only, or the best, way.

5. In the course of this assignment has your opinion on multiculturalism changed?

Yes, my opinion has changed. When I first started reading the articles, I believed that emphasizing cultural diversity was a good thing—it would help us to learn about each other's cultural heritage and would lead to greater respect and understanding. But now I tend to agree with the authors who believe that the emphasis on "particularism" may lead to further ethnic combat. What is happening in the former Soviet Union and Yugoslavia shows us the ultimate dangers of particularism. These political situations seem to prove that in a pluralistic society, national unity or some type of common bonds are essential for peace.

6.   Is this controversy important to think about?

This controversy is important because it is affecting the curriculum in schools. Those who advocate a multicultural curriculum believe that it is essential for students' self-esteem because it makes the material relevant to them. But it seems to me that most students know very little about American history or government, which because they are Americans and going to American schools should be relevant enough. Schools have enough problems teaching the basic kinds of knowledge needed to be a culturally literate, functioning member of American society. The curriculum may be Eurocentric but that it is because Europe has played a large part in our history.

WRITING ASSIGNMENT

Read the articles at the end of this chapter. Supplement these readings with at least three readings included in chapter 5 (the articles by Ravitch, Dasenbrock, and Rose will be particularly helpful). Write an argumentative essay addressing the following question: Is the recent emphasis on multiculturalism in education likely to help us all "just get along?" See the student sample paper that follows.

Kathleen's Paper

In a recent episode of the popular television series "Star Trek," the character Worf, a Klingon, visits a society in which his fellow Klingons, who have assimilated with another group known as the Romulons, have learned nothing of their own Klingon heritage. Worf is appalled at the ignorance of these Klingons and proclaims loudly that it is tremendously important that they learn who they are and where they come from. For Worf, the issue of ethnic pride is of crucial importance.

Worf's concern with Klingon national pride raises the question of whether learning about one's own particular culture is necessary for fostering feelings of self-worth or whether it is perhaps better to try to create one assimilated culture. It also raises the question of whether these issues ought to be addressed by educators. As American society becomes more pluralistic and ethnically diverse, the issue of a multi-cultural curriculum has gained national attention. Some educators believe that the traditional Eurocentric curriculum is not relevant to minority students and that they therefore lack the motivation and self-esteem to excel in school. The solution, they say, is to teach these students subjects that will give them pride in their heritage. I disagree with this proposal. I think the emphasis on a multicultural curriculum not only deprives students of the basic "cultural literacy" needed to succeed in American society, but also leads to institutionalized separatism and social fragmentation.

Proponents of a what Ravitch calls "particularism" believe that "an ethnocentric curriculum will raise the self-esteem and academic achievement of children from racial and ethnic minority backgrounds" (Ravitch 154). It is only by being immersed in their ancestral heritage that minority children can be inspired and feel empowered, and escape the intellectual oppression of Eurocentric thought. For instance, Professor Joseph argues that mathematics is tainted by "intellectual racism" because it has been traced to the Greeks, when in reality mathematics originated in Egypt, Babylonia, and Mesopotamia (Ravitch 158). He suggests that children study "traditional African designs, Indian Rangoli patterns and Islamic art" as well as "the language and counting systems found across the world" (158). Similarly, a black rapper, KRS-One, argues that blacks should be taught about their cultural heritage rather than about Thomas Jefferson and the Civil War, which he believes has "nothing to do . . . with black history" (157).

The assumption behind these approaches to teaching is that minority children are somehow alienated by traditional subjects (like modern mathematics) and Western history. The assumption is that despite the fact that they live in America and attend American schools, "Eurocentric" thought, which is taught in those schools, alienates them and creates low self-esteem. Even if this may be true to some extent, it seems crucial to me that American children be given the skills to succeed in American society. Ancient mathematics or counting systems used in other cultures may be interesting, but they hardly provide real-life applications, nor will they raise test scores, which is the ultimate goal of proponents of a multicultural curriculum.

Furthermore, the assertion of the rapper assumes that somehow American history, and especially the Civil War, has nothing to do with blacks. It assumes, as Ravitch says, that the culture in which these children live "is not their own culture, even though they were born here" (154). Dasenbrock points out that seeking to preserve the cultural heritage of minority students is simply "empty posturing" since Western culture is by nature "assimilative and syncretic": "Most African-Americans are no more culturally African than I am culturally German" (188). It is difficult to see how learning about African-American history is not culturally relevant. Although black American history may be a story of oppression and victimization, it is a story that needs to be told, lest we forget, or fail to learn from our past. Furthermore, a knowledge of history does not necessarily lead to a lack of self-esteem because it can be inspiring to learn about individuals who were able to overcome discrimination and bigotry and achieve success.

The type of multicultural curriculum that is constructive is that discussed by Coughlin, in which American history has been rewritten not as a "story of progress towards freedom" (192) but as "a long struggle to realize the American ideals of equality and democracy" (194). Traditionally marginalized voices—blacks, women, American Indians and other minority groups—have become incorporated into a more pluralistic and representative view of American history. This brand of multiculturalism stresses both our diversity, but also our common cultural heritage, and shows how despite our differences, we have learned to live together because we share common values and ideals. It shows how our many racial and cultural groups have contributed to, and transformed, the national culture. As Rodriguez asserts, it is only by feeling that we are part of society that we gain self-esteem: "Only when I was able to think of myself as an American, no longer an alien in gringo society, could I seek the rights and opportunities necessary for full public individuality" (quoted by Schlesinger, 177).

Because, as Dasenbrock asserts, American culture is already multicultural, "constructed out of a fusion of disparate and often conflicting cultural traditions" (184), the alternative is "not lively diversity as much as unending conflict" (189). College campuses that encourage racial and ethnic "enclaves" seem to experience the most racial tension: "The cult of ethnicity exaggerates differences, intensifies resentments and antagonisms, drives ever deeper the awful wedges between races and nationalities" (Schlesinger, 174).

The society that Worf discovered in the program "Star Trek" may have been ignorant of its ethnic heritage, but it was a peaceful society, and maybe when the advantages and disadvantages of multicultural education are considered, peace is more important than ethnic pride. With racial and ethnic tensions occurring not only in the United States but also all over the world, the new emphasis on multiculturalism is likely to make things even worse. "The division of society into fixed ethnicities nourishes a culture of victimization and contagion of inflammable sensitivities . . . it presents a threat to the brittle bonds of national identity that hold this diverse and fractious society together" (179).

Multiculturalism: Building Bridges or Burning Them?

SHARON BERNSTEIN

Sharon Bernstein is a staff writer for the Los Angeles Times. *This article is from the* Los Angeles Times *(Nov. 30, 1992).*

Multiculturalism—the notion that ethnic and cultural groups in the United   1
States should preserve their identities instead of fusing them in a melting
pot—has become a byword in education in Los Angeles and other cities.

But now, educators at the elementary, secondary and university levels are   2
rethinking that idea—and worrying that past efforts to teach multiculturalism may have widened the ethnic divisions they were meant to close.

Fearing that the current approach—which relies largely on ethnic studies   3
courses and the recognition of special holidays and heroes—may have unin-

tentionally isolated students from each other, teachers and academics are gingerly beginning to question the way multiculturalism has been taught.

"I think many people, especially in the post-Rodney King era, are beginning to realize that we can't just study ourselves as separate groups," said Ronald Takaki, ethnic studies professor at UC Berkeley. "We've gone beyond the need to recover identity and roots, and now we're realizing that our paths as members of different groups are crisscrossing each other." 4

Not that these educators have abandoned multiculturalism as a concept. Nor do they suggest themes. 5

For example, a typical class in a multicultural program would be "a course that an African-American student can take which gives him a sense of identity," said Deborah Dash Moore, director of the American Culture program at Vassar College in Poughkeepsie, N.Y., and an organizer of a recent conference on ways to teach American studies. "It gives him a cultural connection with others, respect for his past, and a sense of knowing where he fits within a larger society of which he can be proud." 6

The new movement finds particularists and pluralists moving toward a middle ground, where instead of treating each ethnic group separately, elements from all their histories are woven into discussions of particular topics. 7

"I'm in the movement toward bringing them together," said Los Angeles Board of Education member Warren Furutani, an advocate of ethnic studies who was formerly the program coordinator at UCLA's Asian American Studies Center. "Because it means people can understand their own experience, but bring it together with other people's experiences." 8

Raising questions about multiculturalism has been difficult for educators, in part because the movement has come under intense criticism from conservatives such as Dinesh D'Souza, of the American Enterprise Institute, whose book, "Illiberal Education: the Politics of Race and Sex on Campus," reached the New York Times bestseller list. 9

"Many people are very defensive, and have been put on the defensive by attacks by conservatives," Vassar's Moore said. "They feel that there is no room for them to be self-reflective, self-critical, that if they do some critical thinking they are playing into the hands of people who really want to destroy the entire enterprise." 10

In the Los Angeles public schools, teachers at all levels are encouraged to talk about the different cultures represented by their students. Most schools conduct festivals or hold special assemblies or parties to celebrate such holidays as the birthday of Martin Luther King Jr. or Cinco de Mayo, which marks the day Mexico defeated French forces in the Battle of Puebla. 11

In addition, the district has developed for high schools elective ethnic studies classes—including African-American studies, Mexican-American studies and courses about Asian and Jewish concerns. From kindergarten on up, the reading and history curricula include stories and information about diverse cultures. 12

Cultural Awareness, the class developed by Taira, explores similarities between ethnic groups and discusses the contributions of a number of cultures. 13

But Taira said if she were designing that course today, she would take   14
pains to interweave the lives and experiences of members of different ethnic
groups. Sharing her concerns, Takaki, the UC Berkeley professor, said he
wished he had made his 1989 book "Strangers from a Different Shore"—
which chronicles Asian immigration to the United States—more inclusive.

In schools and at universities, they and others said, even courses that spot-   15
light several ethnic groups tend to treat each group separately. A course might
highlight African-Americans one week, Korean-Americans the next, and so on.

And, experts said, most students tend to take only the classes that relate   16
to the group to which they belong. In Los Angeles, administrators said, many
schools offer only those courses that relate to the majority of their student
populations.

In such a climate, even the celebration of ethnic holidays has caused   17
problems, with one group believing that another got more attention or boy-
cotting another group's festivities, said Casey Browne, who heads the peer
counseling program at North Hollywood High.

"To some extent I think we bring on racial tensions when we celebrate one   18
holiday over another," Browne said. "Some schools do a better job on certain
holidays than they do on others, and then the other kids feel left out."

Such problems have developed, said Bernadine Lyles, the school district's   19
multicultural education unit adviser, because "the climate was not prepared"
for students to want to celebrate the cultures of others.

She noted that a framework for multicultural education adopted by the   20
school board last spring emphasizes "activities that would bring groups together, rather than those activities that might look like separation."

In the new course that Taira is developing, lessons are organized around   21
historical themes instead of ethnicity.

If the subject is American agriculture, Taira said, the teacher might discuss   22
how farming and ranching affected the lives of black African slaves, Chinese
and Mexican immigrants and poor whites who worked as sharecroppers—all
within broader contexts such as family farms or the plantation economy of
the South.

"There has been a drawing back from the notion that we just have to add   23
more African-Americans, or add more Latinos, as well as the notion that we
have to focus on victims," Moore said. "People are in a complex relationship
with each other. They may be victims in one set of relationships and served
in others."

Students sum up the situation most poignantly—and appear to offer the   24
most hope.

After last month's racial brawl at North Hollywood High, senior Pele   25
Keith called out to a group of African-American and Latino students who
were arguing about the events of that troubled day.

"They say brown pride, but look, I'm just as brown as she is," Pele, an   26
African-American, said, placing her arm alongside the arm of a Latino friend,
Patti Martinez.

"Look at that," Patti sang out in reply, "the same color."   27

Multicultural Education: The Context and the Case

JAMES LYNCH

This selection is from James Lynch's book, The Multicultural Curriculum *(1983).*

'Multicultural education' is simply a convenient shorthand term used in dis-   1
cussing the concept of 'education for a multicultural society'. It can only arise
in such a society and be embedded within that particular ethical context. It is
necessary, therefore, first to identify the underlying ethic of a multicultural
society before decisions and policies for its educational system can be proposed. Only then can discussion commence as to what kind of curriculum
might be appropriate for schools.

Hence, this first chapter begins with a description of how and why the   2
United Kingdom of the 1980s may be described as a multicultural society,
and what I mean by that statement. The underlying principles of that society
are then identified and I argue that a commitment to the concept of a multicultural society necessarily commits advocates of an education appropriate to
it, to those principles underlying it. My major purpose in this chapter is to
suggest that these principles are the basic means whereby rational, 'person-
respecting' decisions can be taken about the selection of valued knowledge
that we call curriculum.

In what ways is the United Kingdom a multicultural society?

But firstly, in what ways is the United Kingdom a multicultural society? Is it   3
unique in this respect? And, has it only more recently become one? In any
case, how does the concept 'multicultural' relate to similar ones in use at the
moment, such as 'multiracial', 'polyethnic', 'multicredal', 'bilingual', 'bicultural', etc.?.

The term 'multicultural' may be considered to embrace and go beyond all   4
the above terms. They are more restricted in meaning—perhaps even more
precise, but they are also exclusive of important cultural groups in our society. Take 'multiracial', for example. This refers to the existence within one social system (it may be the nation state) of several different races: caucasoid,
negroid, etc. (Examples of such societies would include Australia, Fiji, Singapore, the United States and, of course, the United Kingdom). We are certainly
a multiracial society and we must make sure that our educational system edu-

cates for racial harmony and against racial bigotry and discrimination. But we are more than that, for we are also a multicredal society and a multiethnic society, that is, we have peoples of many different faiths and religious beliefs, and none, who should all command our respect. Moreover, we have peoples who are descended from different ethnic groups, from the Celts, the Romans and the Normans to the Jews, Poles, Irish and Vietnamese of more recent settlement. We also have people who are bilingual by birth or later acquisition of a second language and many who are functional in more than one culture. All of these different cultural groups merit respect and it is therefore important that the description which we use for our society makes it clear that this is so for all legitimate cultural groups and not just for some. It is for this reason that I use the term multicultural as a comprehensive descriptor of our society which embraces the multiracial, multicredal, multiethnic and multicultural composition of that society.

Given that the United Kingdom is a multicultural society, then all else   5 should flow from that: its laws, its institutions, its schooling and its curriculum. So the question of whether our society has always been multicultural and whether other societies are such is academic, for the contemporary fact is that we are one now. That said, it will be clear from what has been written above that we have been a multicultural society for a long time and that other countries have as well. The fact that our perception (and theirs) has only more recently become sharpened towards a greater recognition of that fact merely indicates the dislocation which has been taking place between education and society, for which a reconceived multicultural education and curriculum must now seek to correct.

So, in a sense, contemporary British society is not unique in time or space   6 in being multicultural. It has always been multicultural—and at no period more markedly so than since the Industrial Revolution—and many other societies around the globe are multicultural too. So we can learn from each other in building multicultural education.

Within our society, there have always been different groups which have   7 felt a social or economic affinity that has resulted in their establishing a patterned network of human relations, and which has meant that they have thereby begun to generate and transmit cultural values and meanings. These values and meanings may have overlapped with those of other groups, but they were also clearly distinguishable from them and from those of the dominant groups of the time. At the same time, it is indisputable that English education has tended to give preferential treatment to the needs of predominant groups in society to secure the economic and political systems. This has often resulted in flight by other legitimate groups from the mainstream education which was offered, as in the case of the non-conformist Academies of the eighteenth century, the proprietary schools of the nineteenth and the alternative schools of the twentieth.

But the substantial demographic changes of the post-Second World War   8 period coincided with a period of renewed emphasis on individualism and the pursuit of equality of opportunity, which caused a fundamental reappraisal. Influences from countries abroad too, such as the United States, have meant that assimilationist 'melting pot' approaches to social organization, cultural transmission and educational opportunity could no longer be justified amongst the population at large as far as the average teacher is concerned. Rather the reverse, for the pendulum in the United States has swung from the attempt to impose a false unity (false because for some it had to be a segregated unity), through the intergroup and intercultural movements of the 1940s to the rampant cultural pluralism of the 1960s and back again to a concept somewhere between the two. That concept has been variously described, amongst other things, as multicultural and multiethnic.

In this book the term 'multicultural education' is used as going beyond 9 multiracial or multiethnic education. It embraces them both, and other concepts such as multicredal and bilingual education, but it is less exclusive. Thus, while the change to a manifestly multicultural society is more recent in the United Kingdom, the movement to recognize British society as multicultural is part of an older continuity.

Regardless of when they occur, however, such changes in the racial or cul- 10 tural composition of a society (or more precisely the increased recognition of them) make heavy demands on all members of that society, and these demands are more acutely felt in the very fulcrum of cultural transmission, the schools and other education establishments. As one infant school's policy statement succinctly puts it:

1. The school is multicultural and all that goes on within it must strive to reflect and build upon this basis;
2. Culture is central to a child's identity, and the learning environment must reflect the cultures of those learning within it and *within society at large* [my italics];
3. Teachers must become aware of the cultures from which children come and the customs and attitudes within them. . . .

It is in the schools that the newly changed perceptions of the cultural mosaic 11 of society have to be translated against the background of the rhetoric of politicians and educationists alike into the arena of decision and action. This is not to suggest either a linear process or autonomy on the part of the school, for it is clear that schools interact with, influence and are influenced by the broader society. The quotation above seems to me to allow for this. The point is that changed perceptions in the wider society pose imperatives for schools, to which they must respond, but that these imperatives are usually indistinct, oblique and hazy, sometimes illogical and contradictory.

For example, the newer commitment to multicultural education has to be 12 measured against the over-riding commitment of education in any society to secure social cohesion. Clearly, society would fall apart if this were not the case. Thus, education has to prepare us to recognize that we are alike, as for example, members of one species, but different as well, in sex, social class, religion, culture, competence and expertise: infinite in diversity but united in our humanity.

The resultant dilemma has been called by Bullivant 'the pluralist dilemma'. Essentially, Bullivant is drawing attention to the conflict between celebrating pluralism and maintaining social cohesion, to the basic contradiction of an education aimed at both diversity and unity. He might have added that, in a country such as the United Kingdom, the apparent unity in education is, in any case, a mirage, for there are many systems: for example, the Public School System and the state system, and within both there is and has been a hierarchy and differentiation according to social class, academic achievement, religion, sex, age, etc. 13

Each of the social groups which provides the clientele for such schools strives to perpetuate its concept of the most important values, meanings and knowledge, not only as the content of contemporary education, but as the determinant of future decisions about education and learning. Thus, at the same time the content of education is both substance and criteria: criteria for future substance but also for determining what is valued culture in society at large, and even more importantly what cultural capital will lead to economic wellbeing and advancement. It will thus be used as a means to influence access to power and resources in society. 14

What is the culture in multiculturalism?

Crudely stated, it is precisely because culture influences life chances as well as life styles, and is the central concept of 'multiculturalism' in education, that we need to define more closely what we mean by culture—before we can then proceed to define multicultural education. Be warned! There are many competing definitions of culture and no final agreement, and many advocates of multicultural education in the United States have argued that established definitions of culture must not be allowed to dictate the meaning of multiculturalism and that it would be premature to be too firm about definitions. But, it seems to me, we have to know, at least roughly, what it is we are debating. So, as a tentative working definition only, what I mean by culture in this book is a network of values, conceptions, methods of thinking and communicating, customs and sentiments (for it is not wholly rational) used as a socio-ecological coping mechanism by individuals, groups and nations. It is an active capital of non-material, socio-historical character which attracts 'compound interest' in interaction with the social and natural environment so as to secure the survival of the individual and the group. All accretions to the culture are achieved through the 'good offices' of the existing capital. 15

Societies, which are in practice territorially defined political units, consider their cultural 'capital' so valuable that they establish special agencies to preserve, supervise and transmit 'valued' selections to all new members of society: a process which is called enculturation. In nation states much of this process of cultural transmission is entrusted to formal institutions called schools. But how do they do this? What channels do they use? For Hirst and Peters, the transmission of valued knowledge is achieved through clearly dis- 16 tinguishable forms of knowledge, which coincide more or less with established academic disciplines, and which are fundamental to the development of rationability and thus to being educated. For others, including myself, such a view has led to an unbalanced selection of valued knowledge. Rationality, according to this view, is subject to social negotiation and would be enhanced through the pursuit of a new 'common culture' which was more socially and regionally representative, pluralist and open, and intellectually reflexive. Note, I am not denying the contemporary importance of forms of knowledge, merely arguing that they are not 'the whole story'. I am concerned, however, that there should be greater awareness of the significance of the development of shared meanings through greater social co-operation, balance and therefore equality within a multicultural society.

Jeffcoate argues that a broader, less elitist and less ethnocentric definition of a common culture (and a common curriculum no doubt) requires just such a reflexive, critical 'revaluation' as an established feature of British society and of British education. For this purpose, he envisages the school as filling the function of social critic and cultural synthesizer. Such a function would certainly be compatible with the overall functions of education in a democratic society but would place a heavier burden on them (and on teachers) than at present. It would, for instance, presuppose the existence of a set of publicly negotiated rational criteria against which contending cultural capital could be sifted and sorted for inclusion in 'school knowledge'. Likewise, it would presuppose a greater dialogue between school and community than has currently been achieved, and perhaps a realignment of our thinking on schooling towards an acceptance of Peters's view that the summit of moral development is the ability to reflect upon the principles which guide our actions. And herein, to my view, lies the nearest we shall attain to identifying, defining, utilizing and refining categorical 'imperatives' to guide opinion, value and action in a multicultural society. 17

But let us get back for a moment to the question of the selection of knowledge. The alternative to selection, namely a totally random, *en bloc* absorption of all cultural capital projected in the direction of the school, would clearly be both illogical and unacceptable, for it would inevitably imply the inclusion of anti-social capital and very rapidly lead to breakdown through overload. As Zec points out, respect for the richness and strengths of culture (and their inclusion in that valued selection which we call curriculum) presupposes evaluative criteria which he calls generalizable maxims. Only thus, he argues, can cultural diversity be reconciled with objectivity and universality as a basis for a worthwhile multicultural education for which we need to know, to use Leach's words, 'how things are related, not just how they can be taken apart'. 18

How can knowledge be selected for multicultural education?

It will be clear from what has been said above that a 'soft, folksy tokenism' approach to multicultural education, where all cultural values and meanings of all cultural groups are supposed to be equally acceptable merely because 19 they are different, is not tenable. Such a concept of multicultural education can become so diffuse that it actually blurs rather than clarifying elements, dissipating resource utilization and mushrooming to the point where it means everything to everyone. Such an intellectual position would be neither rational nor likely to be educational in its outcomes. Not only would the resulting educational policy be unlikely to succeed (for in the educational progression that is life, those who had restricted their educational intake to the functional, the rational and the educational would once again come off best, thus defeating the whole purpose of multicultural education, namely the pursuit of greater cultural respect and equality of educational opportunity, pursued through one's own legitimate culture), but it would also be a practical impossibility.

It must be apparent, moreover, that not all cultural values are of equal   20
worth. To give but one example, the practice of mutilating young girl children, prevalent and practised in some cultural groups, would never be generally acceptable as a norm for (or to) the whole of British society. The practice of some minority political groups of deliberately inciting racial hatred (of groups for instance such as the Ku Klux Klan in the United States) could not be acceptable. Nor would these two examples of cultural deviance even be acceptable as rationally founded and thus explicitly sanctioned norms for a constituent group of a society such as ours which propagates equality of the sexes, the integrity of the individual, an abhorrence of violence towards children, and racial tolerance. In the inevitable and irreconcilable clash in these cases between the rational 'universals' and the sometimes irrational particulars of a cultural group, the 'universals' must surely hold sway.

The reader will no doubt have noticed that a key, if implicit, factor in this   21
argument is that the particular requires the rational universal for its legitimation. Let me explain what I mean by that. The exploration and evaluation of local knowledge, both geographical and cultural, can only take place judged against something which has a wider validity, what I am going to call for the moment 'the universals'. It is only in terms of these latter that exploration and evaluation can take place, and moreover, a society without shared universals would disintegrate. In short, multicultural education does not mean, indeed cannot mean, that everything and anything goes, but it does offer a more objective, open and deliberate means of deciding what goes within a multicultural society.

Such considerations need not, however, be inimical to the kind of more   22
critical and evaluative role and the greater autonomy for the multicultural school, which Jeffcoate is advancing. Indeed they can enhance such a role. For, ideally, multicultural education can be considered as the initiation of children into critical-rational acceptance of cultural diversity and the creative affirmation of individual and group difference within a common humanity. That means that it is a process conducted according to explicit, rational evaluative criteria: an ethical process, celebrating both diversity and unity, social differentiation and cohesion, stability and deliberate, systematic and evaluated change according to explicit yardsticks, themselves the subject of critical discourse.

What kind of criteria could be used?

But what would these evaluative criteria be and who would decide which cri-   23
teria should be included and which not, and when they might become redundant? This is a sensitive, controversial and difficult question which has
remained largely unaddressed by advocates of multicultural education. Yet it
is central to the development of a realistic and functional multicultural education within a modern, industrial market economy and society that is tolerant, humane and politically relatively stable. Education, in brief, and
therefore the school curriculum, has to look to the good of the community,
to the provision of economic health and to the freedom and creativity of the
individual. It has to prepare children to take their places in society as citizens,
as workers and consumers, and as creative persons, working for its progression and change. Since fulfilling a range of different functions, social, political and economic, presupposes institutionalized preparation for such
roles—in schools or other educational institutions—the school needs to be
functionally related to but not dominated by such functions.

Cultural capital unrelated to that functionality by open, objective and ra-   24
tional criteria would be redundant or superfluous and, whilst such culture
would be available for preservation at the individual or small group level, according to criteria of the 'gradation of functionality', it would have a low
claim to inclusion in the valued cultural capital that we call curriculum. This
may sound hard, but once it is conceded that not all cultural capital can be
included in curriculum, the fact of selection has to be faced as has also the
continuing social viability of knowledge and therefore its redundancy. As the
allegory of the 'sabre-tooth curriculum' implies, it is possible for previously
highly functional knowledge to become degraded and even redundant, a
phenomenon which has occurred in our own time in the movement from
imperial weights, measures and currency to decimal systems.

A multicultural society is particularly demanding in regard to the selec-   25
tion of valued cultural capital, both because of the richness of capital 'on offer' and because it requires respect and tolerance for the culture of others,
which in turn demands cultural overlap to an extent which is necessary for
effective knowledge, understanding and inter-communication. To make way
for that common ground, and because there is a limit to the capital which
can comprise a curriculum, a hierarchy of functionality, rationality and universality has to be identified. These we might call the meta-values or criteria
for knowledge sorting and sifting. We shall return to this point shortly, but
for the moment let us review where we have got to so far.

To summarize, British society of the twentieth century is a multicultural   26
society, not just a multicredal or multiethnic one. Such a society necessitates
a multicultural education and a corresponding curriculum. A curriculum
based on total absorption of all available cultural capital is non-viable, however, because:

   a. It would result in overload;

   b. not all culture is equally worthy and therefore acceptable;

   c. culture needs to be adaptive and functional (if only in the interests of
      the survival of the species);

d. it would not allow for sufficient overlap or common ground to secure social cohesion.

It follows that selection is necessary from the available cultural (actually   27
multicultural) capital, and that process of selection in turn points to the need
for criteria against which such a selection can take place, and mechanisms for
the generation and consideration of criteria and their practical application.
As I suggested earlier, such criteria might be typified, in a kind of shorthand,
as concerning the functions of an individual in society as a person, as a
worker and as a citizen and they could be 'tempered' by some means of assessing their rationality, objectivity and universality. These considerations
would then yield a grid of reflexive and adaptive criteria.

The opposites of these criteria would be subjectivity, particularism and pri-   28
mordiality or assumed givenness, yielding a continuum where the locus of the
criteria would be different according to the level involved—for example, person, worker or citizen, at local, regional or national levels—and, of course, the
age range of children or learners concerned. Potentially at least, the criteria
must allow for interplay and mutual influence between the major social imperatives that constitute our contemporary society—democracy, industrialization and individualism (citizen, worker, private person)—whilst at the same
time offering some measure of both continuity and pluralism, both culturally
and geographically. Thus, whilst there are certain overarching economic activities of our society as a whole, there are also regional and local variations, such
as textile manufacture in the West Riding, coal mining in Durham, shipbuild-
ing on the Tyne. Similarly, although there are certain universals that are functionally necessary for all members of our society, for example, command of
English, commitment to democracy and the rule of law, this does not rule out
the presence of regional or local languages, local by-laws and the like. Indeed
commitment to pluralist democracy cannot so rule them out. But why not,
you may ask, seen theoretically and philosophically at least?

In embryo, this question touches on the question of the ethic of the mul-   29
ticultural society. Let us for a moment pause to look behind the social criteria
which have been suggested and ask whether there are, in fact, certain fundamental principles—perhaps universal, or even eternal ones—which are so integral a part of the multicultural society that without them it could not exist.
For I am conscious that the social criteria suggested could as well be used to
perpetuate the *status quo,* with little concern for a tolerant pluralism, unless
the core ethic of society contained such a commitment.

This brings me to the most difficult part of my own personal position on   30
the relationship between our multicultural society and its educational provision and curriculum, and one on which I have little doubt that there will be
contrary opinions.

Are there fundamental and overriding principles intrinsic to society?

A recent government publication on the school curriculum, probably with-   31
out realizing it, comes close to the core of the answer to this question, when
it states,

What is taught in schools, and the way it is taught, must appropriately reflect
fundamental values in our society.

Admittedly, the document then goes on to identify the fact that British   32
society has become multicultural as an 'issue', rather than a principle or a
value or an imperative or an ethic out of which certain kinds of decision
about education and curriculum automatically flow. But even given that the
document also made a mess of the statement of aims which it contains, the
above question does provide an important touchstone for our theme, because
behind it (implicitly and amongst other issues), as also behind the functionally identified criteria proposed above, hovers, I suggest, the question as to
the availability of fundamental principles which could be used as reference
points to decisions concerning what kind of multicultural education is appropriate to our society. Put another way, is there a yardstick for the application
of the social criteria? Further, are there, for instance, certain basic ethical
principles which could serve this purpose for all cultures?

The answer to the last question is probably a qualified 'no', in the sense   33
that, it could be argued, there do exist principles which are basic to the 'Western European Ethic'. Multicultural societies are an extension of that ethic and
its fundamental principle of respect for persons, out of which our democratic
institutions and major political concepts such as equality, freedom and justice
are derived. Multicultural education is the education appropriate for a multicultural society, and as the London Borough of Brent states in its approach to
the issue, 'Multicultural education and education cannot be seen as separate
entities in a fair and just society'. Commitment to a multicultural society thus
necessarily commits one to the ethical principles underlying that society, and
coincidentally it also rules out practices which run counter to those principles
on the grounds that commitment to the 'ethic' is logically prior.

Additionally, if the 'multicultural educator' is committed to an ethical   34
state at all, then it is to the principles underlying a multicultural society in
Britain, to the principles mentioned above, and for both of these reasons to
'respect for persons'. An understanding of how this principle works out in our
democratic institutions and political concepts is crucial to the stability and
continuing viability of a multicultural society. Moreover, although understanding is necessary, it is not sufficient as a basis for decision and action appropriate to a multicultural society, because the important momentum to the
construction and perpetuation of such a society is given by the behaviour
which flows from these principles. But in what sense is it possible to decide
on behaviour which is congruent with these principles and therefore with the
aims and ethic of a multicultural society?

Although it is not uncontroversial, it seems to me that the work of Wil-   35
son *et al.* offers some way forward in response to that question. He has suggested several principles which must govern opinions before they can be
classified as moral opinions, namely they must be autonomous, that is, subject to free will; rational; impartial, as between persons; prescriptive for all,
including the individual; and overriding, in the sense of taking precedence
over the person's other opinions. The absence of any of the principles would

render the opinion non-moral, and the same applies to action. On the other hand, the presence of all might not guarantee morality but render it subject to what I have called discourse.

It will perhaps be clear that the third principle, impartiality, implies a concern for other people's interests which may be seen as extensions of one's own. All of these principles, but particularly the third and fourth, imply, as Wilson points out, accepting others on an equal footing to ourselves: a respect for persons that is fundamental to western society and institutional concepts, as it must be to any multicultural society. Moreover, the very fact that the principles include mutual prescriptiveness means that there must be an equality of application: that any action we take must contain our acceptance of its equal applicability to ourselves.   36

Without going into the minutiae of the argument, it is from such principles that criteria for 'moral' opinions and actions, that is, behaviour congruent with the ethic of a multicultural society, may be derived, and it is from them that fundamental concepts and institutions of western democratic society are drawn in turn. Against them also can be measured the social criteria for decisions about the aims of education and the content of valued knowledge that we call a curriculum, all of which may be appropriate to a multicultural society. This complex process is neither linear nor does it exclude the central role of discourse. Rather it seeks to emphasize the importance of communicative competence amongst all cultural groups and individuals in society as an essential pre-requisite to that discourse, which will secure a functional and 'culturally fair' inclusion of content in the curriculum of a multicultural school. In that sense and with minor amendments, Jeffcoate's enunciation of respect for others as one of the major objectives dominant in multicultural education, is correct. But this is a topic which will be dealt with in greater detail later.   37

What kind of overall curriculum structure does the above argument imply?

For the moment, it is necessary to ask what kind of overall curriculum structure may fulfil the need to select in a balanced way from the available multi-culture of modern British society, whilst at the same time securing the economic and political mainstays of that society and offering respect for persons and their cultures. In other words, what kind of curriculum in outline, and what kinds of strategies put into operation the principles, criteria and processes that I have suggested in the first part of this chapter? Put differently, having briefly considered the Why?, what are the implications for the What? of education, that is, the curriculum?   38

All the above three areas, personal, economic and political, must be addressed for all children, irrespective of their regional or cultural background, or they will not be able to take a full place in society. The consequence of neglect of any one would probably be the collapse of the kind of multicultural, industrial and democratic society for which we are seeking to educate. But, in addition, the principle of respect for persons would appear to require the rep-   39 resentation, in some way or other, of all legitimate (in terms of that society's ethic) cultures for all of the population, for knowledge and awareness are pre-requisites to respect and it is illogical to expect respect without any grounding of knowledge. Thus a kind of 'knowledge chart' of our multicultural society is an essential for all members of that society. There are other essentials too, which I shall deal with in later chapters, but for the present this one example suffices to illustrate my argument. Now such a chart might not be universally considered to be directly functional in terms of the `worker' criterion suggested above. Its inclusion might not be capable of justification by reference to the vocational aims of education, necessary in our industrial and technological society. It might even (for some) be debatable whether it would be functional in terms of the 'citizen' criterion: it might not relate necessarily to the need in a democracy for articulate and participating, politically aware voter-members of society. (I believe that it does). But it could certainly be functional in terms of the 'person' criterion and the underlying principle of respect for persons discussed above, potentially expressing both individualism (and to some extent intrinsic aims for education) and creative momentum for change in society (that is, extrinsic aims for the individual addressed to the good of others).

The logic of this argument leads to the tailoring of such common elements into a curriculum related functionally to the 'person', 'worker', 'citizen' paradigm for all children, with extras, alternates, options or choices which might be more closely but not exclusively related to the 'person' dimension. And what is valid for the 'person' criterion is also valid for the 'worker' dimension, bearing in mind differential human abilities and regional distinctions and differences in the industrial and economic bases: vocational and cultural options in other words, attached to a common core curriculum, according to cultural and geographical location, and influenced of course by age-range, need and cognitive style.

But before deploying that argument more fully in later chapters, I would here return to my point about the role of discourse in the whole process of deciding the why, what, how and where of education, and the need for greater dialogue between school and society and school and community. For in a democratic and open society, such decisions cannot be subject to *Diktat*. This process is neither linear nor mechanistic but subject to the 'bonfire night bombardment' of oral, visual, aural and other stimuli, although, perhaps, slightly less predictable!

How can the necessary discourse be achieved?

The process of building an education and a curriculum appropriate to a multicultural society like ours is not to be thought of solely in terms of content and structures. Rather, respect for others implies respect for their opinions and beliefs and willingness to engage in dialogue about them and the appropriate aim of education in that society. All of this adds up to the need to cherish dialogue between individuals and groups across the whole

range of our social 'credos' and institutions. If we are indeed to have a humane multicultural society then individuals and institutions must know how
to engage in such dialogue and be willing to do so.

I am aware that the extent to which the school has done this so far is very   43
limited. But there are very welcome signs of change with the whole thrust of
the teacher self-evaluation movement, the new Schools Council Programme
orientation (and the publication of *The Practical Curriculum*) and, perhaps also
implicitly, with the imperatives of recent publications and Circulars from the
Department of Education and Science. There is certainly a healthy current
concern with accountability and monitoring although I shall argue the need
later for this to be broadened and deepened, if multicultural education is to
be achieved. More, the process of discussion will necessarily need to include a
more balanced distribution of influence between school and community and
between lay, professional, political and administrative members of society
than it currently does. It will also incidentally need to include the recognition that grown-ups do not have a monopoly of rationality nor children of
emotionality, and that this recognition will need to embrace an acknowledge-
ment of the way children can, and apparently do, take responsibility for their
own and their peers' learning.

For the moment, having briefly mapped out the field, let us consider   44
what multicultural education implies for the teacher and what efforts have
already been made in different and diverse places to design and implement
a multicultural curriculum, before returning in Chapter Four to the need
for greater discourse and its role in the construction of a multicultural curriculum.

SUMMARY

This chapter has: 45
1. suggested that recognizing the United Kingdom as a multicultural society
    presents social and ethical imperatives for education and the curriculum;
2. offered a working definition of culture as a basis for understanding multi-
    cultural education;
3. outlined a typology for social criteria to select knowledge in a multicul-
    tural society;
4. argued the presence of overriding principles to facilitate educational deci-
    sions and policy;
5. suggested that the implementation of a curriculum according to the
    above criteria and principles implies greater discourse in society at large
    and particularly between school and community;
6. promised, in the next chapter, some ideas on what multicultural edu-
    cation may mean for teachers and some examples of multicultural cur-
    ricula.

Study Details How Race Affects Neighborhood Choices

STUART WOLPERT

Stuart Wolpert is the public relations officer for UCLA Today.

People of the largest ethnic groups in Los Angeles prefer to live in neighbor- 1
hoods consisting primarily of members of their own race, a new UCLA study
shows.

Despite what people say about their willingness to live in integrated neigh- 2
borhoods, members of all races avoid neighborhoods with certain ethnic
groups, although this practice is strongest among whites, according to the
study.

"Anglos, Hispanics, Asians and, to a lesser extent, blacks, practice avoid- 3
ance," said Professor of Geography William A. V. Clark, whose article, "Residential Preferences and Residential Choices in a Multi-Ethnic Context," is
published in the current issue of the journal "Demography."

"All groups want to live in neighborhoods where their racial group is a 4
plurality," Clark said, "Own-race preferences, while strongest for Anglos, are
strong across all ethnic groups."

Clark, who teaches a course on metropolitan Los Angeles and has studied 5
demographic issues for 10 years, analyzed not only people's stated neighborhood preferences, but also their actual decisions when they moved to new
neighborhoods. When he compared the kinds of neighborhoods people said
they preferred with those in which they chose to live, he found a large discrepancy between the two.

"I was particularly interested in looking at the people who say it makes 6
no difference where they live—about one-third of the sample," Clark said.
"Those who say they will live in any neighborhood tend to move to neighborhoods much like those they already live in, whether Asians, Hispanics,
blacks or Anglos.

"Many people say they will live in a mixed neighborhood, but in fact 7
they want more of their own racial group than any other; they don't want to
be a minority in their neighborhood," he said.

Among Clark's findings: 8

■ Whites have strong preferences for neighborhoods that are at least 70%
white. When asked about living with Hispanics, more than 30% of whites
said they prefer a neighborhood that is 100% white, and another 12% prefer
a neighborhood that is 90% white.

Almost three-quarters of the white families in Clark's study chose to live   9
in neighborhoods that are at least 80% white, and almost 90% of the white
families moved into neighborhoods that are less than 10% black.

When averages are computed, whites said they prefer neighborhoods   10
with a white-black mix of 76% white and 24% black; and a white-Hispanic
mix of 79% white and 21% Hispanic.

■ Hispanics, when asked about living with blacks, stated a preference   11
for neighborhoods that are 88% Hispanic and 12% black. When asked about
living with whites, Hispanics preferred a mix of 62% Hispanic and 38%
white.

■ When asked about living with Hispanics, blacks preferred a mix of 62%   12
black and 38% Hispanic. When asked about living with whites, the majority
of black households, about 60%, said they prefer neighborhoods that are 50%
black and 50% white.

Clark said it is difficult to know from the data whether blacks really want   13
to live with large numbers of whites, or whether they simply want a "nice
neighborhood with low crime and good schools," many of which happen to
be populated primarily by whites.

"Blacks choose neighborhoods with low proportions of Hispanics, and   14
Hispanics choose neighborhoods with low proportions of blacks," Clark said.

■ When Asian families move, their new neighborhoods typically are ei-   15
ther predominantly Asian or largely white and affluent. Almost none of the
Asian families in Clark's study moved into neighborhoods that are more than
10% black.

Clark's findings are based on surveys of more than 2,600 households in   16
Los Angeles: 813 white, 805 black, 821 Hispanic and 204 Asian.

In addition to the preference responses, data on actual and previous   17
places of residence were collected for families that had moved between 1981
and 1987. The surveys were conducted in 1987.

Clark concludes that while housing affordability partly explains segrega-   18
tion, deep-seated preferences play a large role in housing decisions.

Noting that in a post-riot study by Lawrence Boho, UCLA associate pro-   19
fessor of sociology, whites expressed a greater willingness to live in integrated
neighborhoods, Clark remarked that he would like to know how many of
those people act on that expressed willingness.

"My evidence says that's nice, but there is a discrepancy between what   20
people say and what they do," Clark said.

"Anglos are leaving the city and are not moving to mixed neighborhoods,   21
but to Ventura, Santa Barbara, Orange County, Riverside and out of state.
Many blacks are moving out of state, too. Change is going to come slowly, if
at all," he said.

"My findings suggest there will not be many multi-ethnic neighborhoods   22
any time soon."

3

■ Credibility and Support

Imagine you arrive at a party at which a heated discussion is underway. Everyone involved seems excited; some guests are gesturing emphatically; a few are actually thumping chairs and tables to make a point. Intrigued by the liveliness, you approach the group and listen for a while, trying to figure out what you think about the topic. You evaluate several points of view, examine the issues, weigh alternatives, formulate a thoughtful position, and eventually feel that you would also like to speak. However, as soon as you join the debate, all eyes turn to you and people begin asking questions such as "Who says so?" "What reasons can you give for that statement?" or "How do you know that?" Everyone wants to know if you are a credible speaker and can support your position convincingly.

This chapter is concerned with various types of support you can use for an argumentative essay. No matter how well you may have thought out your position and how thoroughly you may have researched the topic, your ideas will not have an impact on your reader without adequate support. In particular, I will discuss strategies for establishing authority, types of evidence you can use for support, and ideas for arranging your thoughts and making your essay more coherent.

Authority as Support

In chapter 1, Marlene's essay about her family's obsessive concern with practicality in regard to dining customs was supported with specific examples from Marlene's background, such as the use of towels instead of napkins, and pots at the table instead of serving dishes. Because the essay was concerned with a personal topic, Marlene was able to support her thesis using only personal examples. She was the primary authority on the subject, and only readers who were family members or had been dinner guests at her home would be qualified to contradict her. Readers, of course, could question the credibility of her essay on the basis of what they felt was likely or possible.

In writing about diversity in an argumentative essay, you enter a realm where initially you are not likely to be an authority, although you may have had some personal experiences which are relevant to your thesis and you may care a great deal about the topic. For the most part, though, you are in the position of having entered a conversation in which a wide variety of people are involved who will question the truth of your statements. To establish your credibility, it is helpful to incorporate the ideas of more qualified authorities who can provide additional information you can use to support your thesis.

Looking Within: The Authority of Personal Experience

For a topic such as diversity, you may have had experiences that might provide authoritative support for your main points; however, students often wonder whether their own experience can be used in this way, and, indeed, there is no hard and fast rule that can help you decide on this definitively. My recommendation about using personal experience is based on how typical it might be and how relevant it is to the controversy. On the topic of bilingual education, for example, some of you may have grown up in a home in which two languages were spoken or perhaps your own first language is not English. In chapter 6, Richard Rodriguez, S.I. Hayakawa, and Rosalie Pedalino Porter have written compelling essays on the basis of their own experience and supplemented their personal accounts with additional information and research. I would recommend using personal experience because it can provide a liveliness and sense of immediacy that is often missing from student writing. But, if possible, reinforce the representativeness of your experience by referring to additional sources.

In the essay, "Living Under 'a Veil of Denial,'" included in this chapter, Alfee Enciso cites personal experience as a means of preparing his readers for the thesis he develops later in the essay—that all Americans are racist, whether or not they are aware of it. In the following excerpt from that essay, note how Enciso uses his own background to establish his credibility, to support his thesis, and to indicate his awareness of a possible opposing viewpoint:

> To belittle my own racism would be quite easy. I worked in Watts for 8½ years; I even asked the school district to place me there. I also hail from an oppressed minority—Mexican-American—and suffered discrimination. In fact, I even remember being called a n------ during my formative years in Glendale. My chess-playing buddies Gene, Eddie, Vince, and Charlie are all, like my wife, African-American. So how could I possibly be prejudiced or racist? Shall I bend my back some more?

In the above paragraph, Enciso is saying essentially, "Hey, I could never be considered a racist because I am a member of a minority group, have worked with African-Americans voluntarily, have African-American friends, and am married to an African-American woman." Later in the essay, though, he uses his own background to suggest that *everyone* is racist, even if they are not aware of it. He uses personal experience to set the stage for his main points, which include a definition of what he means by racism, and he indicates that his own experience is both representative and typical.

Using Information from Published Works

Even if you are quite familiar with your topic on a personal level, the inclusion of information from published works can enhance your credibility because those who publish books and articles about the topic have usually been involved in the controversy a long time, have familiarity with the issues, and bring the weight of publication to their assertions. However, as I will discuss in chapter 4, simply because someone has published an article or book on an issue does not make that person an authority. In chapter 4, I will also suggest strategies you can use to find out as much information as possible about the author and publication so that you can assess whether a particular author is worth including in your essay.

Information from published works or the opinions of authorities can be included in a number of ways such as:

- to support a statement, thus enhancing your authority
- to contradict an opposing opinion
- to indicate that an example cited is typical
- to provide another example
- to interpret facts
- to analyze the causes of a problem
- to offer a solution
- to predict a consequence.

Note the use of information from an authority in the following paragraph:

Over the past several years, many American parents are being forced to make room for their adult children, who are returning to the nest in increasing numbers. "There is a naive notion that children grow up and leave home when they're 18, and the truth is far from that," says sociologist Larry Bumpass of the University of Wisconsin in Madison. "Today, according to the U.S. Census Bureau, 59% of men and 47% of women between 18 and 24 depend on their parents for housing, some living in college dorms, but most at home.

"Show Me the Way to Go Home"
Anastasia Toufexis

In this paragraph, the use of the sociologist and the citation of statistics from the U.S. Census Bureau indicate that the tendency of adult children to return home is typical. It helps establish the credibility of the writer examining this trend.

ASSIGNMENT

Read Susan Faludi's article, "The Media and the Backlash" (in chapter 11), and note how she uses information from published works and the opinions of experts to enhance her credibility. Discuss your findings in small groups.

What Are Your Reasons?

Having credibility as a speaker or writer also means being reasonable—generally, we do not trust irrational people who simply state an idea without establishing proof; we are more likely to be convinced by those who provide us with sound reasons. For your argumentative essay to be convincing, you should understand how reasoning works so that you will be able to use it more effectively. Most discussions of argumentation identify two types of reasoning: inductive and deductive.

INDUCTIVE REASONING

Inductive reasoning is based on the principle that a conclusion may legitimately be drawn from incomplete evidence—in fact, because it is impossible for anyone to have experienced everything, this is a very common form of reasoning that we use all of the time. The following interchange is an example of inductive reasoning:

PAULA: I am going to buy a piñata for my son's birthday party.
JUAN: I can recommend a good place to buy one, because our family gets piñatas very often. But be sure that you also buy candy to put into it, because piñatas do not come with the candy already inside. You have to fill it yourself.

In this interchange, Juan indicated that he has had a lot of experience with piñatas and was able to say with relative certainty that piñatas do not come with the candy already inside. His conclusion was reached inductively in that it was based on specific instances in which his family bought piñatas. Most of what we know about the world and most of what we have been told about the world has, in fact, been obtained through induction. Having grown up in New York City where there are no tigers roaming the streets (usually), I have never encountered a live tiger except in a zoo, although I have seen tigers in pictures or films. Yet the few I have seen have stripes and look like large cats.

Therefore, I regard the few I have seen in zoos as typical tigers and, consequently, believe that most tigers have stripes and look like large cats. Although none of us have heard every dog bark or seen every fish swim, we would feel safe predicting that, in general, dogs bark and fish swim.

When you use inductive reasoning in an argument you base your conclusion on samples that are sufficient and typical (this, of course, also pertains to statistics or examples). If you say, "All people from a certain country are untrustworthy. I once knew this guy from that country and he would steal you blind," you are basing a conclusion on only one person which constitutes an insufficient sample. If you use inductive reasoning to support a position or idea, you must check that your sample has really been sufficient and typical. Otherwise, you will be drawing a hasty conclusion from an unrepresentative example, resulting in unfair stereotyping.

An inductive argument usually moves from a series of specific instances to a generalization which represents a degree of probability. Before Dr. Jonas Salk could claim that his vaccine prevented polio, he had to have tested it on a group that was both typical and of adequate size. He then concluded that it was probable that his vaccine could prevent polio in anyone. For issues concerned with human behavior it is not as easy to generalize from specific instances, as there are bound to be many exceptions. If you survey a number of businesses and discover that female employees cite problems of adequate child care as their most pressing concern, that does not mean that every female employee will necessarily feel the same way. However, it does indicate that for *many* employees, child care represents a significant problem in the workplace.

DEDUCTIVE REASONING

Deductive reasoning draws conclusions from an already established generalization such as "All human beings are mortal." The most important tool in deduction is the *syllogism,* which consists of a major premise (or fundamental truth), a minor premise, which consists of a specific instance of the major premise, and the conclusion, which states that because the major premise is true, then the minor premise is also true. A famous syllogism is the following:

All men (meaning people) are mortal. (major premise)
Socrates is a man (a person). (minor premise)
Therefore, Socrates is mortal. (conclusion)

In the above instance, both the major and the minor premises are obviously true, so the conclusion is also true. However, in writing about diversity you will be developing arguments on which the major premises might not be so obviously true, and it is important that you assess the truth of both the major and the minor premises in order to determine the truth of a given statement. For example, in the following syllogism, the major premise is not true; therefore, the conclusion drawn is also not true:

All French men eat snails.
Pierre is a French man.
Therefore, Pierre eats snails.

The major premise, "All French men eat snails," is not true (although *many* French men may eat snails, surely not all of them do). Therefore, the conclusion drawn from this premise is also not true.

In a deductive argument, specific instances are drawn from a generalization, as in the following example:

Physical strength is required for moving the piano.
Albert moved the piano.
Albert must have physical strength.

Although mortality is a fact of human nature, other generalizations are sometimes more difficult to find because there are always exceptions. In fact, one generalization about the human condition is that it is difficult to generalize about it. Here is a syllogism based on that concept:

Children develop emotionally at their own rate.
Jesse is a child.
Jesse is developing emotionally at his own rate.

INDUCTION AND DEDUCTION IN EVERYDAY ARGUMENT

Most of the arguments that we use and encounter in reading use both inductive and deductive reasoning, and frequently, it is unnecessary to distinguish between the two. For instance, although Dr. Jonas Salk had to test his vaccine on many people before he could reach the conclusion that it prevented polio, he may have initially had an idea or hypothesis that motivated him to test the vaccine in the first place. On the other hand, because most generalizations on which deductions are based were established by repeated observations, many first premises were reached originally by the process of induction.

Exercise: Thinking About Induction and Deduction

Examine the following statements and decide which are based on inductive reasoning and which on deductive reasoning. Then decide whether or not these statements are well reasoned. Discuss your observations in small groups.

1. John is one of our most punctual employees. In fact, he has never been late to work in the past five years since he joined the firm. Because he didn't arrive on time today, I assume that something serious must have happened to him.

2. People who collect snakes usually like other reptiles as well. Lisa has a large snake collection, so I think she will also like this iguana.

3. Mexican women are very warm and loving with babies, so I suggest that you hire Maria as a nanny because she comes from Mexico.

4. Students in the United States have not been given adequate preparation in geography. Seth was educated in the United States, so it is unlikely that he knows anything about geography.

5. Louisa is very athletic and works out at the gym every day, so she will probably be able to learn mountain climbing techniques easily.

6. Justin is especially interested in electronics, so if you wish to interest him in your product you should demonstrate its technical applications.

7. Clifton successfully negotiated a number of mergers in his previous job, so I suggest that you consult him about the upcoming acquisition.

THE ENTHYMEME

Although people use deductive reasoning all of the time, in casual speech as well as in formal writing, they frequently assume that the major premise is understood and leave it out, mentioning only the minor premise and the conclusion. An abbreviated form of the syllogism in which one part is left out is the enthymeme. This is the form that you are likely to use in your argumentative essay and encounter in your reading. In the following example, the enthymeme assumes agreement about the major premise:

> You cannot possibly expect peace and cooperation in the United States because it has many different ethnic groups living in it.

This statement takes for granted the major premise that "any country with many ethnic groups in it is unlikely to have peace and cooperation." If stated as a syllogism, it would be structured as follows:

> Any country with many different ethnic groups in it is unlikely to have peace and cooperation.
> The United States is a country with many different ethnic groups in it.
> Therefore, the United States is unlikely to have peace and cooperation.

In this instance, one must question whether the major premise or unstated assumption is, in fact, always true, usually true, or never true. Another way of seeing how the enthymeme works in argumentative writing is to note the presence of a "because clause" that links the main statement to unstated assumptions, as in the following sentence: "The United States is unlikely to have peace and cooperation because it is a country with many different ethnic groups in it."

Note the use of enthymeme in the following paragraph:

> Psychotherapists Louise Eichenbaum and Susie Orbach, co-authors of the recently published book, *Between Women: Love, Envy, and Competition,* point out

that as women become more successful professionally, they are also becoming more competitive and less cooperative with one another. Female bonds are broken, they say, as women discover that "the feelings of competition and envy, the scurry for approval, the wish to be acknowledged and noticed by other women are now a part of their daily work lives. Young professional women, in fact, do not seem to be interested in the feminist ideals of bonding and cooperation, and are, in fact, acting more like men.

"When Women Vie with Women"
David Brand

In this paragraph, the implied syllogism is as follows:

> People who enter the professional world become more competitive and less cooperative.
> Young women have entered the professional world.
> Therefore, young women are becoming more competitive and less cooperative.

As an enthymeme, this argument may be stated as follows:

> Young women are behaving more competitively because they have entered the professional world.

The major premise here is that entrance into the professional world causes people to value competitiveness over cooperativeness and friendship. (It should also be noted that this is an idea that some people would question.)

QUESTIONING ASSUMPTIONS

As demonstrated above, the enthymeme is based on unstated premises or assumptions. Yet for a controversial topic, the "truth" of those assumptions is frequently open to question. For example, look at the following statement about inequities in the pay scale for women:

> Women don't earn high salaries or achieve professional advancement because they are unwilling to work late.

One assumption or major premise behind this statement is that all women are unwilling to work late, which is certainly not true. The other is that low salaries and lack of professional advancement occur when people are unwilling to work late. If you share both of these assumptions, the statement above might seem valid to you, since you believe that pay increases and achievement should be linked to hard work. You might then decide that women's low salaries and lack of professional advancement are unfortunate but fair because women are not willing to work as hard as men.

If you think about this idea, though, you may question whether it is true that women are unwilling to work late, and decide that even if this is true, the statement also assumes that hard or valuable work is based on late hours. Perhaps some women are working just as hard as men, but working at different times, such as early in the day or on weekends. Or maybe it is not necessary to work late in order to do valuable work. Perhaps some people work more efficiently than others. If you feel that women are working just as hard as men, doing just as valuable work but receiving lower salaries, you may then postulate that perhaps women's lower salaries are due to other factors such as lack of opportunity for advancement, inequities in the pay scale, or sex discrimination.

Even if you decide that an assumption is true, you should examine it more carefully to consider its implications. The above statement about women's working hours, for example, does not consider possible causes—that some employees are unwilling or unable to work late due to responsibilities they have to their children. Does the statement then imply that if women (or men, for that matter) are unwilling to work late because they have to take care of their children, that those who wish to be home with their children in the evening must resign themselves to low salaries and lack of professional advancement? And if this is so, does it mean that our society does not value those who care for children, and, by implication, that it does not value children? Does such a statement imply that only those without domestic responsibilities are entitled to high salaries and professional advancement? For a complex and controversial topic such as diversity, it is important to examine assumptions carefully to evaluate whether they are always, usually, or never true, and to speculate about their implications.

Exercise: Identifying Underlying Assumptions

Try to identify the underlying assumptions in the following statements. Are these statements always, usually, or never true? What implications can be derived from them?

1. Manuel has lived in this country for five years and still cannot speak English properly. He must be stupid.
2. Segregated schools caused black children to suffer mental and emotional damage.
3. It is important to maintain ethnic identity.
4. The political correctness movement is dangerous to society because it threatens freedom of speech.
5. The women's movement has threatened the stability of the family because it took women out of the home.
6. Affirmative action policies should be made illegal because they unfairly privilege one group over another.

7. Immigration should be restricted because immigrants take jobs away from American workers.

8. The media should be censored because it presents biased pictures of minorities.

Fallacious Reasoning

If the purpose of an argumentative essay is to move readers to at least consider the thesis, think about the reasons and evidence, and acknowledge that the thesis has merit, the reasoning in the argument should be based on sound logic and clear thinking. Statements based on poor logic and mistaken belief are called fallacies, and although numerous attempts have been made to categorize them, many overlap with one another. In writing an argumentative essay, it is not necessary that you study an exhaustive list of fallacies, but it is useful to become familiar with some of them so that you can avoid using them in your writing. The following, then, is a list of the more common fallacies.

SLIPPERY SLOPE REASONING

This is an argument that assumes that one action will lead to another similar action which in turn will lead to another and to another, ultimately resulting in something quite undesirable. An example of a slippery slope argument is the following:

> Doctor-assisted euthanasia will ultimately lead to mass suicide. In the beginning, only people with incurable, painful illnesses will request to die. Then others with less drastic conditions will request it. Before you know it, people with even minor illnesses will begin thinking of assisted death as a viable option.

Slippery slope arguments are used quite frequently in the context of a variety of social situations. "Smoking marijuana will ultimately lead to heroin addiction" is a popular version. Another is "Making an exception for one minority in a school or work situation will ultimately lead to the necessity of doing so for every minority."

The essence of a slippery slope argument is that once a first step is taken, a descent all the way down is inevitable.

BLACK AND WHITE THINKING

This is a form of reasoning that presumes an "either-or" situation, such as the following:

Either we institute bilingual instruction in the schools, or recent immigrants will never learn to speak English.

This statement does not consider that immigrants might learn to speak English through some other means, or that many groups in the past have learned to speak English without formal instruction.

HASTY GENERALIZATIONS

Hasty generalizations are caused by drawing conclusions from insufficient evidence. Hasty generalizations are often used to condemn a whole group of people on the basis of an inadequate sample, such as in the following statement:

Let's invite Howard to be a club member. He's Jewish and all Jews are rich.

FALSE CAUSE

Hasty generalizations assume causal connections where none may exist, as in the following statement:

As soon as mandatory busing was instituted in the town of Glenport, many families began moving out of town.

This statement presumes that it was mandatory busing that caused people to move, when, in actuality, the move coincided with the closing of one of the town's major industries.

FALSE AUTHORITY

Authorities from one field are sometimes cited as authorities in another, a fallacy that is used regularly on television when movie stars are used to endorse particular products that they may know little about. If a famous person endorses a particular position on an issue, you should not immediately assume that the position is then worth endorsing.

RED HERRING

The name "red herring" is derived from the idea that a pack of dogs would be distracted from a scent if a herring with a strong odor was dragged across the trail. In argumentation, a red herring means that the writer has brought in a point that has little or nothing to do with the issue being discussed. An example of a red herring would be the introduction of women's child care difficulties in a discussion of sexual harassment in the workplace.

ATTACK ON THE PERSON RATHER THAN THE ISSUE (AD HOMINEM ARGUMENTS)

Arguments that attack the person rather than the issue are extremely common in controversies involving diversity. An example of a statement using this form of fallacious reasoning is as follows:

> Don't listen to what Angela has to say. She's just a typical dumb blonde.

A Caution About Fallacies: Some textbooks provide a long and detailed list of fallacies, thereby implying that all fallacies can be easily classified and that by identifying them, you will be able to write a convincing argument. My intention here, however, is simply to alert you to the possibility that reasoning can be false in a number of ways and that you must scrutinize your own arguments more carefully and approach those of others with a critical perspective.

Types of Evidence

Even if your argument is well reasoned, it will not convince your audience unless you provide adequate support. Two of the most common and effective forms of support are the use of examples and the citation of statistics.

EXAMPLES

Examples provide an important form of support. If you wish to argue that some children's toys reinforce sexual stereotypes, you might cite the example of the "Talking Barbie" who says, "Math class is hard." If you wish to argue that a particular town is guilty of racial discrimination, you can cite numerous examples to indicate that this is so. If you are examining the trend of many motorists to equip their cars as if they were homes and offices, you can cite examples of people who not only have phones and fax machines in their cars, but also video cameras, television sets, changes of clothes, and coffee-makers.

Be sure to use concrete examples and to include enough of them to be convincing. The following paragraph has little impact because it cites only a few general examples:

> Working parents are concerned about a number of problems associated with child care. Often child-care facilities are dirty and poorly supervised.

More specific examples and additional information, however, can improve this paragraph:

> Working parents are concerned about a number of problems associated with child care. Daycare is hard to find, difficult to afford, and often of distress-

ingly poor quality. Having toured over a dozen facilities, one working mother tells appalling stories of what she found. In one place the children were all lined up in front of the television like zombies. In another, the place was so filthy that she was unable to find a clean spot in which to seat her child during the interview. Because of the scarcity of good facilities, waiting lists for established day-care centers are so long that parents apply for a spot months before their children are born, and, in some cases, before the child is even conceived.

EXTENDED EXAMPLES

Sometimes it is useful to develop one example fully, rather than use several, as in the following paragraph:

> Child care has always been an issue for the working poor. Traditionally, they have relied on neighbors or extended family and, in the worst of times, have left their children to wander in the streets or tied to the bedpost. In the mid-19th century, the number of wastrels in the streets was so alarming that charity-minded society ladies established day nurseries in cities around the country. A few were sponsored by employers. Gradually, local regulatory boards began to discourage infant care, restrict nursery hours and place emphasis on a kindergarten or Montessori-style instructional approach. The nurseries became nursery schools, no longer suited to the needs of working mothers.
>
> "The Child-care Dilemma"
> *Claudia Wallis*

In this example, the main idea that "child care has always been an issue for the working poor" is supported with a historical narrative of various problems existing in the past. Although the narrative contains a series of events, it really functions as an extended example of the first idea. Extended examples can be especially effective when you are recounting a personal experience.

HYPOTHETICAL EXAMPLES

Real or personal examples can be effective, but you can also cite hypothetical examples if they seem sufficiently illustrative of the point you are attempting to develop. For example, an illustration I have heard used in favor of bilingual examination is as follows:

> Suppose you were planning to visit another country for a long period of time. Certainly, you would find it easier to maneuver in that country if you had access to someone in the country who spoke your own language, could answer your questions, and provide an overview of what you would need to know. Now imagine what it would be like if you did not have access to such a person. Without that form of assistance, your adjustment to the new country would take much longer.

Hypothetical examples can be especially useful if the concept you are explaining is difficult to understand or abstract. An essay titled, "The Case for Torture," points out that in some instances, torture would be considered a moral act, and it uses the example of a terrorist who has refused to reveal the whereabouts of a deadly virus that will destroy civilization unless found immediately. The essay points out that in this instance, the use of torture might be considered morally justifiable.

Analogy as Evidence

In chapter 1, I defined analogy as an extended comparison between two things (processes, ideas, actions, etc.) and pointed out that analogies are especially useful for helping readers understand something unfamiliar by presenting it in terms of a parallel or more familiar case. When used appropriately, analogy can be an effective strategy for convincing an audience that if two things are similar in one way, they are also similar in other ways and what is true for one is therefore true for the other.

In the following paragraph, Alfee Enciso uses an analogy to make his point that America tends to deny that it is racist.

> America's denial of its racism is tantamount to an alcoholic refuting his illness. And like an addict, if my students, city, or country continues to insist on being "colorblind" or judging all people by the content of their character, then the specter of racism will continue to rear its terrifying head.
>
> "Living Under 'a Veil of Denial'"

The analogy here attempts to establish that if America continues to deny that it is a racist country, it will never be able to improve, as is the case when an alcoholic denies his alcoholism.

Sometimes, however, an analogy may seem to strengthen a position, but when scrutinized more carefully, it breaks down. For example, look at the following paragraph which uses analogy to argue in favor of mandatory drug testing:

> Any of us who has ever gone for a medical examination has had to submit to a blood test. Blood tests are required for many jobs, entrance into schools, and even marriage licenses, and even if we think that they represent an invasion of privacy, we recognize their necessity, because we feel that they are good for society. Drug testing, which involves the testing of urine, is similarly used for the good of society. However, many people object to mandatory drug testing because they consider it an invasion of privacy. But if we allow blood testing, surely we can allow urine testing for drugs, since drug abuse is such a tremendous societal problem.

In this paragraph, the writer is arguing by analogy that blood testing is similar to urine testing, in that both may be considered invasions of privacy, but both are necessary for the good of society. However, if you examine this analogy carefully, you will see that in certain ways it doesn't completely support the case for mandatory drug testing because blood tests and mandatory drug tests are not used for the same purposes. Blood tests are used to diagnose diseases that usually can be cured, and benefit the person being tested. Urine tests for drug abuse are usually used to identify a drug user to his or her employer, and the information is often used against the person being tested. Moreover, people usually choose to have blood tests voluntarily as part of routine physical examinations whereas urine tests for drugs are usually mandatory. The effectiveness of the analogy, then, is undercut by some of these differences.

STATISTICS

Presenting statistics is another forceful way of supporting a position. However, statistics can also be misleading if they are not current, if they are atypical of the population they are intended to describe, or if they do not reflect what the author claims they reflect. Moreover, statistics are not only confusing for the average person—sometimes, even those familiar with statistical methods have difficulty interpreting them. In deciding whether or not to cite statistics in your essay you can use the following guidelines.

The Source of the Information

As a recent article in the *New York Times* points out, "the source of the report matters. Whether the study was done at Harvard or Podunk University, the most reliable reports are those that are published in peer-reviewed journals" (February 24, 1993). Another reliable source of statistics is a government organization since the government is unlikely to award money for research without seriously evaluating its importance.

In deciding whether or not to include statistical information, examine the source of the information and try to figure out how the numbers were obtained. Did the information come from a study which used a questionnaire? If so, do you have access to the questions asked and do you feel that these questions elicited the information that they claim they did? Would people be likely to misrepresent, either deliberately or unintentionally?

The Size and Representativeness of the Sample

For a statistic to be valid, it should mean what the author says it means and should be representative of the population of which it is a sample. Yet often a sample drawn from only a small segment of the population may not be representative at all. For instance, if you asked students at one table in a school cafeteria with over one hundred tables, to comment on the quality of the food and they all happened to think the food was excellent, it would not be valid to claim that all the students in the entire university (or even in the cafeteria) were happy with the food.

Another common error in sampling results from using a self-selecting population. For example, if you stood outside the cafeteria with a sign saying, "Please use this form to express your feelings about the food," it is likely that only students who disliked the food would bother to respond. You might then conclude that most of the students disliked the food, when that might not be the case at all. Some studies are actually conducted in this way, but in examining their results you should think carefully about how the information was obtained.

Percentages Versus Actual Figures

Another point to consider is whether the statistic cites percentages or actual numbers and to reflect on the significance of what is being claimed. Both percentages and actual figures may not be significant if the number is fairly small, as in the following examples:

> Twice as many college women are looking to marriage as their major goals in life, a study conducted at the University of Crockerville suggests. When questioned about their plans after college, forty percent of respondents indicated that their primary goal after graduation was to find a husband, as opposed to only twenty percent of respondents questioned two years ago.

Of course, this paragraph does not state that only twenty women participated in the study. A critical reader might also ask who conducted the study and how the question was phrased.

Here is another example of how statistics can misrepresent information:

> More college men in 1992 expected their wives to stay at home and take care of the house than they did in 1985, a study conducted at the University of Crockerville suggests. Whereas in 1985, only five hundred college men responded to a survey that they expected their wives to stay at home, in 1992, 750 college men answered the same survey in the affirmative.

What this paragraph does not state is how many people were questioned, nor does it mention that the enrollment at the University of Crockerville increased extremely rapidly during these years, from two thousand students in 1985 to twenty thousand students in 1992. Therefore, the figure cited may actually indicate a decline in the proportion of college men who said that they expect their wives to stay at home.

Caution: Association Isn't Cause. An important point to keep in mind in deciding whether or not to include statistics is that a link between two events or situations does not necessarily imply cause and effect. For example, an article in a newspaper may point out that there is a well-known association between the number of television serials in a region and death rates from heart attacks. But it may not mean that the serials, themselves, caused the heart attacks. Instead, the association might indicate that people who watch television a great deal get little exercise or perhaps eat fattier foods, both of which might be responsible for the increase in coronaries.

In writing about issues associated with the topic of diversity, it is particularly difficult to use statistics to make definitive statements because human behavior tends to be imprecise and difficult to measure. One of the difficulties of assessing the effect of bilingual education is that it is·not always easy to decide what to measure because there are many possibilities, among them, pronunciation, fluency, reading or writing ability, or simply the ability to use language conversationally. Improvement in a skill like speaking or writing sometimes is not readily reflected on tests and often does not manifest itself immediately after instruction. How then can the worth of a particular program be measured objectively?

What is also problematic about statistics is that either intentionally or unintentionally, people do not always respond to questions accurately. If you read the article entitled, "Study Details How Race Affects Neighborhood Choices" in chapter 2, you will see that although many people claimed that it made no difference to them where they might live in terms of the ethnic composition of a neighborhood, they actually chose to live in neighborhoods consisting of their own ethnic group. Thus, their real behavior contradicted the responses they gave to the questionnaire. In such a case where there is a discrepancy between what people say they would do and what they actually did, which response is most valid—the statement or the behavior?

Statistics can be useful, however, in documenting trends and reporting specific information such as salaries, types of jobs held, figures indicating the composition of households, or television-watching habits. If you examine them carefully and weigh several possibilities for interpreting them, you will find them a useful means of support.

The Arrangement of Ideas

In chapter 2, I discussed a common structure for an argumentative essay in which a position or thesis is presented in an introductory paragraph or paragraphs and then developed in the body of the essay using reason and evidence. This pattern has often been used for argumentation, because it imposes an overall deductive structure on the writer's thinking and guides the writer to proceed logically. Within that overall structure, you have a great deal of flexibility according to what you are trying to accomplish and what you wish to emphasize. There is no set number of paragraphs or requisite word or page length for an argumentative essay, nor is there any particular arrangement required.

CREATING A PRELIMINARY OUTLINE

Some writers advocate creating a formal outline before beginning to write, complete with multilayered subheadings down to the smallest detail. Other writers object to the idea of a preplanned outline, claiming that the imposition of a formal structure is unrealistic because writers often discover ideas as they write; moreover, they feel that too much planning inhibits the creative impulse. Such writers do little advance planning on paper—once they identify their preliminary thesis, they simply begin to write and see what develops, creating a concept of structure as they go along.

Unless you have already developed a system that works for you, my recommendation is to take the middle ground—once you have a fairly clear idea of what position you wish to develop, write down your main points and jot down possible examples and supporting pieces of evidence, giving you something to refer to as you write. Creating an informal outline will give you an opportunity to think through your main ideas before beginning to write and to gain a sense of the preliminary structure of your paper, enabling you to see what may be weak, missing, or disproportionately emphasized. Once you have created an outline, it can serve as a guideline for proceeding and indicate to you where your paper might need additional research, development, or balance. However, because it only involves noting ideas it will not absorb as much time as the creation of a formal outline.

ORGANIZING YOUR MAIN POINTS

Most writers prefer to organize subsections of their essays to parallel the overall structure of the essay as a whole—they use a deductive structure for each of their major points, stating the point, supporting that point, stating the next point, supporting that point, etc. For variation or for calling attention to a point you wish to emphasize, you may wish to use an inductive structure, presenting facts or observations and leading your readers to make discoveries for themselves.

When considering possibilities for arrangement, my suggestion is to begin with the most important or compelling points. Readers usually pay most attention to points presented at the beginning of a text, and therefore, you should present your most significant point first and it will have the most profound impact on your reader. Then develop your major points in descending order of importance, ultimately reminding your reader of your most important point when you refute the opposition and again in your conclusion.

Alfee Enciso's essay about racism in America develops his position through the following main points:

1. Racism is promoted through magazines, television shows, and billboards.
2. Racism is implicit in the ideal of beauty that young men and women adopt as a standard.

3. Racism is implicit in a number of ways such as confusing two people for the same one, assuming that two black people know each other, believing that all black people share the same ideology, viewing black people as unfortunate, or suspecting black students of thievery.

His main point, though, is that racism is everywhere because it is promoted through the media; therefore he presents that point at the beginning.

SIGNPOSTING YOUR IDEAS

No matter what order of presentation you select, your essay will not hold together unless you link each point to your main thesis through signposts or, as my colleague, Jack Blum, refers to them, "cueing devices." Signposts remind your reader of how each point supports the main point of the essay; signposts review where the essay has been, indicate where it is going, and keep the reader from getting lost. Most readers can focus on only a limited amount of information at any one time; therefore, signposts or cueing devices help readers understand how the essay is structured so they will not become confused.

The simplest method of signposting is to say simply, "this is my first point; this is my second" and so on. Less obvious signposts do not announce their presence so obviously, but instead smooth the transition between ideas. Alfee Enciso uses a signpost by beginning his fourth paragraph with a reference back to the main idea of his third paragraph, as follows:

> *Despite my race-relations credentials,* none of these particulars, whether isolated or bunched together, can stand up to one undeniable fact: I am an American, born and raised. To be an American is to be racist.

Signposting can be achieved through transitional words and phrases such as "however," "nonetheless," "therefore," "moreover," "additionally," "nevertheless," and many others. Here are some transitional devices that are frequently used for signposting:

- To establish cause and effect—therefore, thus, as a result, consequently
- To show similarity—similarly, in the same way
- To show difference—however, on the contrary, but, despite that
- To elaborate—moreover, furthermore, in addition, finally
- To explain or present examples—for example, for instance, such as, in particular

Signposting can also be achieved through transitional paragraphs that act as a link between two ideas and prepare the reader for a new topic or indicate a forthcoming order of ideas. Here is an example of a transitional paragraph:

But too many of those who wave the flag for multiculturalism have let enthusiasm outrun reason. In particular, I believe four major issues deserve more
debate and consideration before we embrace the brave new world of multicultural education.

"Too Many Have Let Enthusiasm Outrun Reason"
Kenneth T. Jackson

In this paragraph, Jackson refers to four issues which he explains further in
subsequent paragraphs.

Revising an Argumentative Essay

In chapter 1, I discussed several strategies for revision that are applicable to
the argumentative essay as well. In addition, the following questions may direct your attention to specific problems in an argumentative essay:

THE THESIS

Does my overall thesis make sense? Does it address a legitimate controversy?
Have I included the word "because" in my thesis statement? Is the word "because" necessary for this particular thesis? Have I qualified my position sufficiently?

SUPPORT

Credibility

How have I established credibility? Have I cited relevant personal experience?
Have I included pertinent statements from authorities? Do they strengthen
my position or have I simply quoted from outside material to fill in space?

Reasoning

Can I cite at least two reasons or supporting points for my thesis? Are these
reasons based on sound assumptions?

Evidence

Have I supported my main points with compelling evidence? Have I included
irrelevant information? Do I need more convincing evidence? Have I presented concrete examples? Do I have enough examples?

ARRANGEMENT AND STRUCTURE

Have I structured my essay and arranged my material logically, comprehen-
sively, and convincingly? Have I addressed the opposing viewpoint? Does the

introduction establish the context and introduce the controversy? Does the conclusion wrap things up adequately? Do I understand the purpose of each paragraph? Do I understand how each paragraph contributes to the overall purpose of the essay? Have I used signposts to maximize overall coherence?

SENTENCE-LEVEL COHERENCE, FLUENCY, CORRECTNESS

Reading aloud is especially useful for detecting sentence-level problems and areas where the text does not read smoothly. In reading for coherence, fluency, and correctness, ask yourself the following questions: Does one sentence lead naturally into another? Are my sentences too short? Do I need to develop them with additional details? Are my sentences too long? Should I divide a few of the longer sentences into smaller ones? Have I checked for common mechanical errors such as subject-verb agreement or pronoun reference? Have I checked for punctuation and spelling errors?

Assignment

WRITING ASSIGNMENT

Read Alfee Enciso's essay, "Living Under a 'Veil of Denial.'" Write an argumentative essay in which you consider the extent to which you agree with Enciso's point that "to be an American is to be a racist."

EXPLORATION QUESTIONS

As a way of understanding the controversy in Enciso's article, write brief responses to the following questions:

1. Why is this topic considered controversial?
2. Were you brought up to have an opinion on this controversy? What opinion did your family and community have on this topic?
3. How did your school experiences influence your conception of the controversy? Did your teachers and classmates feel the same way about it as did your family? Were there any points of disagreement?
4. Can you think of at least two people who held differing views about this controversy? If so, describe these people and summarize what you believe were their points of view.
5. Has your opinion changed about this controversy in any way? Why or why not?

6. Do you think that this controversy is important for people to think about? Why or why not?

After reading the assigned articles, try to fill in the missing components of the following sentences:

The conflict in this issue is between _____ and

_____.

I am more inclined to agree with _____

_____

because_____.

However, it is possible that some of my readers may believe that

_____.

Living Under "a Veil of Denial"

ALFEE ENCISO

Alfee Enciso teaches English at Palms Junior High School in Los Angeles. He previously taught at Markham Intermediate School in Watts.
This selection is from the Los Angeles Times *(Dec. 1992).*

Stacy Koon, one of the officers involved in the Rodney King beating case, re- 1
ferred to King as "Mandingo" and feared him because he is black, but insists
he is "not a racist." My students, in post-unrest discussions, framed their
comments with the tired "I'm not a racist but . . ." and my colleagues bend
over backward trying to show me how liberal they are. No one, it seems,
wants to admit to our country's deeply racist roots.

America's denial of its racism is tantamount to an alcoholic refuting his 2
illness. And like an addict, if my students, city or country continues to insist
on being "colorblind" or judging all people by the content of their character,
then the specter of racism will continue to rear its terrifying head.

To belie my own racism would be quite easy. I worked in Watts for 8½ 3
years; I even asked the school district to place me there. I also hail from an
oppressed minority—Mexican-America—and suffered discrimination. In fact,

I even remember being called a n----- during my formative years in Glendale. My chess-playing buddies Gene, Eddie, Vince and Charlie are all, like my wife, African-American. So how could I possibly be prejudiced or racist? Shall I bend my back some more?

Despite my race-relations credentials, none of these particulars, whether isolated or bunched together, can stand up to one undeniable fact: I am an American, born and raised. To be an American is to be racist. Anyone can see this, with their eyes closed—or can they?   4

After a few years of teaching in Watts, I developed a keener insight into the dynamics of racism or, as Malcolm X called it, Americanism. In supermarkets, I noticed the images of wealth, beauty, happiness and success in the magazines at the checkout stands. With the exception of sports magazines, where a few African-Americans—namely Michael (Jordan) and Magic (Johnson)—dominated the covers, I realized that blacks, Latinos or Asians rarely achieved front-page status. The print media's message rings loud and clear. Success is fair skin, blue eyes and a European figure. No African butts, slanted eyes or greasy hair allowed. My awareness didn't stop there. Billboards, radio and television all spoke the same message every day, "If it's dark or foreign, you're not welcome in the glamour of America's home." Even trying to find solace in a pool hall, I discovered that the eight-ball, the darkest ball in the rack, was the last to go in the pocket, leaving only the white ball to roam the green felt.   5

I asked my students how they could watch television and not be insulted by the images that brainwashed them. Outraged by such a claim, they balked. So, to prove my point, I asked the males in my class, "What's the first thing you guys do when you're together discussing a 'freak' or a 'fox?' You ask, 'Hey, what she look like? . . . Oh, man! She's real fine, man. She's light-skinned,'" at which the class got quiet and smiled. Then a young girl said, "He's right. . . ." while the rest of the students giggled, easing the embarrassment of being "moded."   6

Awareness of my Eurocentric society made me realize how my own attitudes shaped my preferences. As a child, I proudly announced to my older sister that my choice of girlfriend, when I got old enough, would be blond and blue-eyed. And through my formative years I would constantly look in the mirror, dreaming of blond locks and a surfer face, something I couldn't readily describe but tangible enough for me to know I didn't possess.   7

Walking among my students in Watts, exposed to a people from whom I'd been sheltered, I viewed American society in a different light. I started asking questions. Who had kept this rich, beautiful, African-American culture from my consciousness? Why had I never even thought of my own Latinas as gorgeous or goddess-like? And why weren't these the faces that spill out on the pages of magazines or the myriad television commercials that ingrain our preferences and desires? But despite these questions and revelations, I realized how much of America I personally swallowed.   8

Like a fugue in a G minor, my own Americanism played itself out in a variety of ways. There were the obvious ones: confusing two people for the   9 same one, assuming two black people knew each other or believing that all of my African-American colleagues shared the same political ideology. In addition, the liberal paternalism with which my mother raised me—the "Oh, these poor black people have had such a hard life," attitude—prevailed not only in me, but in many of my white colleagues. In class I would often accuse students of stealing my things only to find out I had merely misplaced them. And in college, I manifested a superiority over my own Mexican people. Apparently, I believed the constant refrain my Anglo friends intoned: "You're Mexican, but not really." As one of my African-American teammates pointed out, "You think you're better than me."

These attitudes and beliefs, since changed, nonetheless existed, a part of   10
my upbringing that subconsciously incorporated itself into my American psyche. Upon reflection of this American culture and my own experience in the inner city, I realized how incredibly powerful this disease is that brainwashed me, and how tightly its insidious grip steers the conscious and subconscious behavior of most citizens in this country.

While my experiences may be unique, the outcome—my being made   11
aware of and sensitive to the racist world I live in—should not.

Anyone willing to question themselves and the system in which we live   12
will hopefully come to one conclusion—the truth; much better than the current veil of denial under which most Americans live.

4

■ A Three-Pass Approach to Critical Reading

Joining the Conversation

In chapter 3, I asked you to imagine arriving at a party at which a heated discussion was underway and, wanting to join the conversation, you approached the group and listened for a while, trying to figure out whose point of view you found worthwhile. Suppose, though, that the speakers were strangers to you and you knew nothing about their backgrounds or interests. How, then, would you know whose opinion to take seriously? What criteria would you use to evaluate what was being said? On what basis would you be able to decide?

Reading a published work (whether in the form of a newspaper, magazine article, or material from a book) is like entering an ongoing conversation—in fact, the rhetorician, Kenneth Burke, among others, has made exactly that point—when you are not familiar with the topic the process of research is uncomfortably similar to entering a room full of strangers. I make this comparison because for you as a student being asked to develop a thoughtful position on a complex topic such as diversity, it is important to be aware that most of the controversies you encounter in print have been going on for some time and that many writers concerned with controversy, like the guests at the party, have been involved in the discussion long before your arrival. Deciding which points of view are believable will be a real challenge for you.

Although it is difficult to assess the value of a published work unless you are quite familiar with the topic, it is possible to use clues from the text to learn as much as possible. This chapter focuses on strategies for approaching published sources using what I refer to as a three-pass approach.

YOUR FAMILIARITY WITH THE TOPIC

In terms of the conversation at the party, one way to decide which speaker was credible would be to reflect on how much you, knew about the topic being discussed and then to compare what you know with what you heard in the discussion. Without some basic knowledge about the topic, you would not be able to assess anyone's opinion and would first have to acquire some basic information. If, for example, the speakers were debating the merits of various laptop computers, you would be unable to decide whose recommendation to believe if you knew nothing about laptop computers, had no idea what computers did, and had never used a computer. The first requirement for participating in the conversation would be that you know something about the subject matter, and if you know nothing about it, I suggest that you consult sources that will provide you with at least an overview. An encyclopedia, an almanac, or an introductory book on the subject can usually provide some context and background. In this book, the introductory prefaces provide you with an introduction to the controversies addressed in the readings.

In the context of the ongoing discussion at the party, the more similar a particular position was to a viewpoint you already held, the more likely you would be to agree with it. So, if the topic under discussion was the merits of the Zoink laptop computer, and if you had used a Zoink and liked it, knew others who felt the same way, and had read about the merits of the Zoink, you would be likely to agree that the Zoink was the best laptop computer on the market. Under these circumstances, you would be disinclined to change your mind unless you became aware of a new piece of information.

In addition to understanding the topic of the discussion and being aware of your own views on it, you would also be in a better position to evaluate what was being said if you knew why the discussion was being held. Had someone requested the name of a reliable, reasonably priced laptop computer, or was the discussion concerned with deciding which computer was the most technologically advanced? Had something happened recently that had sparked the debate (the release of a new model, for example)? Had the topic been raised in the context of a presumed health hazard from laptop computers? Are there any particular groups or organizations associated with a particular perspective on this controversy?

THE CREDIBILITY OF THE SPEAKERS

Aside from understanding something about the subject and context of the debate, you would also be more qualified to decide whose opinion to trust if you knew something about the participants, in particular, their qualifications for discoursing on this subject and their motives or agendas in this discussion. For example, if you discovered that the gentleman in the red jacket happened to be the president of Zoink Computers Inc., you would be somewhat suspicious of his endorsement of this particular model because he would obviously have a specific motive or agenda to promote. On the other hand, if the man in the blue T-shirt bearing the slogan, "Computers Will Destroy Humanity," was yelling that Zoink computers were infected with all sorts of dangerous viruses, causing users to break out in unsightly rashes, yet he provided no specific evidence to support his claim (and, in fact, was a member of the Delete Computers Society), you would also distrust his position. Finally, if you realized that the gentleman with the large mustache was a notorious liar who enjoyed fueling discussions whether or not he had any real information to contribute, you would not pay too much attention to his viewpoint either. However, if the woman in the gray suit introduced herself as a research consultant whose profession it was to evaluate laptop computers for a well-known corporation, and if she indicated (in measured tones) that, based on her extensive research and personal experience, the Zoink was undoubtedly the best model on the market, you would be most likely to trust her opinion rather than those of the other participants in the debate. Even if you already had an opinion on the topic, you might reevaluate your own point of view if you were sufficiently impressed with what she had to say.

Now, of course, I must qualify that it is the quality of the ideas, not the style of presentation, that you should ultimately focus on in deciding which opinions to trust because style is something that can be easily distorted. Television commercials, in particular, tend to present people who seem calm, collected, and knowledgeable, and viewers find themselves trusting what they have to say even when they know that they are simply actors being paid to endorse a particular product. On the other hand, if someone is hysterical, it does not necessarily mean that his or her opinion is not worthwhile—perhaps the situation is sufficiently alarming so that hysteria is the appropriate response. Furthermore, an obvious self-interest is not always a reason to distrust an opinion. Perhaps the president of Zoink Computers Inc., has done a great deal of research, knows a lot about computers, and wants to produce the best computer on the market. In this case, despite the fact that he stands to profit from the sale of Zoinks, his ideas could be worth believing.

In general the extent to which you will find a particular text convincing depends on the following factors:

The Controversy and the Context

- How much do you already know about the controversy?
- Do you already have an opinion about the controversy?
- Why is the controversy being discussed? Has a plan or policy been proposed? Are there any particular groups or organizations associated with it?

The Writer

- How much do you know about the expertise and motives of the writer?
- Can you trust what the writer has to say?
- Does the writer indicate that he or she is aware of the complexity of the topic?

The Quality of the Argument

- Is the argument consistent with what you believe is true or possible in the world?
- Is the argument consistent with what you believe is true about human nature?
- Is the argument supported with compelling evidence?
- Does the argument acknowledge the complexity of the topic?

Style

- Does its style fulfill your expectations of a credible text?

The Three-Pass Approach: An Overview

The three-pass approach is a method that will enable you to evaluate the credibility of the articles and books you read so that you will be able to decide whether or not to use them in your essays. At first, the method will seem as if it involves a lot of work, and maybe you will think initially that it is not worth your time. Keep in mind, though, that with practice, the first two steps quickly become collapsed into one. Any new method may seem cumbersome at first but eventually becomes easy to use. Here is an overview of the three-pass approach:

THE FIRST PASS

During the first pass, the reader reflects on the subject and context of the controversy, evaluates the qualifications and motives of the author, and examines the text for additional clues such as the title, publication information, and easily discernible strategies of organization.

THE SECOND PASS

During the second pass, the reader reads the text for meaning to determine what it is saying. To aid understanding, the reader uses structural clues within the text and facilitates his or her understanding by summarizing main points.

THE THIRD PASS

During the third pass, the reader interacts with the text, actively engaging in a critical dialogue to determine how much is acceptable. Such interaction involves distinguishing between fact and opinion, evaluating the type of evidence cited, deciding whether the writer is aware of the complexity of the topic, and paying close attention to how language is being used to shape the reader's perspective.

Taking Charge of Your Reading Through the Three-Pass Approach

When people are inexperienced in working with published works, they often approach them passively—they note that the title seems related to their topic and then they simply begin reading, trying to understand the meaning of the text. The problem with this approach is that it adheres to a submissive rather than a "take charge" model of the reading process. Reading submissively implies that the work exists as a separate, valid, believable entity, worthy of serious consideration simply because it has been published. Moreover, the submissive approach does not include the reader-initiated activities of reflecting on the subject and context of the work, questioning the motives, agendas, and qualifications of its author, or evaluating the quality of the argument.

The submissive approach to reading puts you, as the reader, at a great disadvantage in that you will not be aware of all the factors you will need to evaluate the validity of what you are reading. Recall the party discussion scenario previously outlined: The submissive approach is as if you had entered the party, had been immediately cornered by the man in the blue T-shirt who was complaining about the rash he had contracted from his Zoink laptop, and had listened only to his point of view without reflecting on your own perspective, understanding the context of the discussion, or questioning the reliability of the speaker.

To avoid being a passive reader you should keep the following principle in mind: *Very few, if any, articles or books are written simply to present information in a completely objective way.* Even what seems to be the most coldly and objectively written scientific piece of writing has at its foundation a complex set of beliefs about how the world is or should be, and if you are aware of what those might be, you will be in a better position to evaluate the text and decide whether or not it is credible. Competent readers engage actively in the reading process. They approach a published work by trying to learn as much information about it as possible before beginning to read it. Once they decide that the text is worth reading, they interact with it energetically, almost as if they were having a conversation with the author.

THE FIRST PASS: THE SUBJECT, THE CONTEXT, THE AUTHOR, AND THE CLUES

The first pass over a published work involves assessing what you already know about the subject matter, the context, and the author, and then examining the easily detectable surface clues that the work provides. Before you begin reading a published work, ask yourself the following questions:

1. What do I know about the subject matter of this work? Have I been brought up to have an opinion on this topic? Have I heard discussions on this topic or read anything about it? Is there a controversy associated with this topic?
2. What is the context of the controversy about this topic? Is there some action or policy associated with it? Was it written in response to another piece of writing? For whom is this source being written? Do I know anything about any particular groups associated with this controversy?
3. What do I know about the author? Does the author have a title or position that would indicate his or her qualifications or a particular agenda? Can I speculate on what the motive of the author might be?

Clues About the Text

Once you have reflected on the subject and context of the controversy and on the potential agenda of the author, you should then peruse the work for surface clues that can provide you with additional information. These clues include publication information such as the title, type of publication, and copyright date, and organizational clues such as section headings and bolded subtitles (for an article), or chapter headings and the table of contents (for a book). If you know something about the topic, you can get a sense of where the author is situated in the conversation by looking at the bibliography, if there is one, and noting which sources the author has cited and whether or not you can recognize any names or publications. Then, in a brief glance, you should try to determine the type of evidence cited, such as the use of charts or graphs or the inclusion of statistics.

Begin by examining the title and thinking about what the title might suggest about the author's attitude toward the subject or purpose in writing. See if you can figure out what the article or book might be about simply on the basis of the title. If the work is an article in a magazine or journal, try to grasp the overall approach or agenda of that publication. Some journals are known to endorse a particular political approach and you will be able predict the overall thrust of an article by thumbing through to see what other articles appear in the journal. If biographical information about other authors appears, read through it and see which authors are included and the kind of backgrounds they have. Finally, check the copyright date. For some topics, the fact that a particular article was written fifteen or twenty years ago might not matter. For other topics, it might matter a great deal. Reflect on whether or not the date of publication will affect the believability or validity of the work.

Sometimes you can get a sense of an article by reading an abstract or by skimming over section headings or words that appear in bold. Think about how these subheadings relate to the title. If the work you are about to read is a book or a chapter from a book, see if there is a chapter summary at the beginning or end of each chapter or part that will provide you with additional clues. Frequently, if you skim over the first few and last few paragraphs of an article or chapter, you can quickly understand its main point.

Of course, not every article or book you come upon will be easily accessible to immediate scrutiny. Even those that were not written by readily identifiable authors with easily predicted agendas, or explicitly stated main points, will usually yield some information during the first pass and enable you to approach the work with greater insight. Even if you find out very little information about the text, looking for clues in this way will help you begin looking at the work with a critical eye.

THE SECOND PASS: READING FOR MEANING AND STRUCTURE

During the second pass, you should read the material through reasonably quickly and write a summary to easily refer back to. Use the summary to encapsulate the overall point, to record component supporting points, and to make the summary sufficiently complete so that even a reader unfamiliar with the article will be able to understand what it is about. Be sure to write down all information you would need to be able to locate the article again if you wish to use it—for an article, include the title, author, title of the journal, issue number, pages, and date; for a book, include the author, title, and publication information (publisher, place of publication, and copyright date).

In reading a text for meaning, it is a good idea to focus attention on its purpose and structure.

- Is it a response to another point of view? Can you situate it in a conversation? Is there a controversy associated with it?
- Does the article or book compare and contrast two or more ideas or recommendations?
- Does it make a point about cause and effect?
- Does it pose a question and then answer it?
- Does it trace the history of something, structuring its information chronologically?
- Is it developed through the use of many examples?

During the second pass, your need to understand what the text is saying will be enhanced when you consider its organization, noting how different facets of the topic relate to the author's main point. Also look for signals in the text that indicate a shift of some sort is about to occur, noting how new content is introduced—subheadings are good indicators of this, but authors sometimes use transitional sentences.

One point to note about the second pass is that after a quick read you may decide that the work is not worth reading after all. Remember that there has been a lot written that may not be worth your time. Understanding the meaning of a text through a relatively quick appraisal can prevent you from expending unnecessary effort.

THE THIRD PASS: INTERACTING WITH THE TEXT

Once you understand the meaning and structure of the text, it is time to take charge of your reading, which means reading critically with a questioning attitude toward your material and interacting with it as much as possible. Now is the time for you to enter the conversation, not accepting what you read unless the evidence is convincing. Keep in mind what you have learned about the author's agenda or qualifications for writing this particular article or book, and use that information to formulate critical questions as you read. Below is a detailed discussion of the third pass.

Is the Argument Consistent with Your View of the World and Human Nature?

Your View of What Is Possible in the World. In order for an argument to convince a reader, it must be consistent with what the reader believes is true and possible in the world and with his or her concept of human nature. Our view of the world and our beliefs and ideas about humanity serve as a kind of filter through which we can assess the quality of the information we receive. The more we experience and read, the more we adjust our world view to accommodate new information. We believe, for example, that it is possible to fly from California to New York in about five hours, so if a friend left my home in Los Angeles at 2:00 P.M. and called me at 8:00 P.M., claiming he was in New York, I would probably believe him. But if my friend left my home in Los Angeles at 2:00 P.M. and called me at 2:30 P.M., claiming to be in New York, I would be unlikely to believe him even if he claimed he had been whisked there in a new form of airplane.

Your View of What Is Possible in Human Nature. Similarly, our concept of human nature—what we believe human beings are likely to do or are capable of doing—is another source by which we evaluate what we read. To cite an obvious example of how one's world view and concept of human nature contribute to the credibility of an idea, imagine the difficulty you would have convincing a local school board that a night watchman is needed to prevent aliens from landing on the football field at night, since most people do not believe aliens constitute much of a problem on a nightly basis (in fact, only some people believe in the existence of aliens). On the other hand, it would probably not be difficult to convince the school board that a night watchman is necessary to prevent thieves from stealing expensive computer equipment from the science lab. Our world view tells us that there are, indeed, such things as thieves, and our concept of human nature tells us that, unfortunately, some human beings will avail themselves of the opportunity to steal unless reasonable precautions are taken.

On an issue such as whether or not to have a night watchman at the local high school, most people would probably have little difficulty reaching agreement. However, on controversial, complex topics such as those associated with diversity, people will often disagree because they have differing concepts of human nature. For example, over the past twenty years or so, there has been considerable disagreement over the question of using mandatory school busing for the purpose of integrating society. The position people have taken in this debate has been strongly related to the extent to which they believed that people would cooperate. Some people maintained that racial and ethnic integration could be achieved simply by allocating children to attend certain schools. Others argued that the imposition of such a requirement would not achieve the desired goal because people would simply withdraw their children from the school district rather than allow them to be bused out of their immediate neighborhoods. To some extent, the disagreement over mandatory busing derived from differing perspectives about human nature that suggested opposing predictions about what people would be likely to do.

If people's opinions are based on their concept of human nature, and if that concept is well fixed, you might then wonder whether analyzing those views is useful in evaluating a published work. After all, if the work is based on a world view quite different from your own, you are unlikely to think it is worthwhile so why bother to read it in the first place? My response is that once you are aware of the underlying concept behind an opinion, even an opinion with which you disagree, you are then able to understand it more thoroughly and will be better able to establish common ground and negotiate the controversy more insightfully when you write your essay.

Sometimes, however, people make statements about human behavior on the basis of what they wish were true, rather than what the evidence suggests is really the case. Because we often wish that everyone was motivated by only the most noble of impulses, and that everyone wants to "do the right thing," we often have difficulty believing stories that suggest otherwise, particularly about those we have set up as heroes or role models. When a president of a country or a film star or sports celebrity behaves poorly or illegally, many people refuse to believe what seems evidently true. Many people seem to want to be deceived, easily believing reports that to others seem completely preposterous—belief in paranormal events or a chance at winning the lottery, for example.

In the third pass, then, active readers question the extent to which a particular argument is consistent with their world view and concept of human nature. They ask themselves whether the main point makes sense to them according to their own experience and what they believe is likely to be true. If it is not, active readers then attempt to try to view the issue from the author's point of view, trying to understand why the author espouses these beliefs.

Is the Argument Supported with Appropriate and Believable Subpoints, Examples, and Facts?

Distinguishing Fact from Opinion. One facet of reading a text interactively is being alert to statements that may appear to be facts but are actually opinions presented as facts. An effective way to detect the difference is to notice whether or not the main points are supported with specific appropriate details and subpoints or consist simply of observations that the author thinks are true. Keep in mind that unless a writer is an acknowledged authority, you really have no reason to accept his or her point of view, and that even an expert is obliged to provide supporting evidence. For example, examine Jenny's paragraph below, which is concerned with the question of whether novels from the Victorian period in England should be included in a required literature course.

1. Novels from the Victorian period in England should not be included in required literature courses. 2. Since these novels tend to be extremely long, students often have difficulty finishing all of the reading. 3. Moreover, these novels are usually concerned with situations which are nothing like what is happening in American society today—in particular, they discuss romantic, political, and social themes which students frequently have trouble understanding, since they are not usually familiar with this period in history. 4. Finally, the characters in these novels do not reflect the diverse populations of today's American students, so that students are unable to identify with them easily. 5. Many of today's students want to read literature that is associated with their own cultural and ethnic heritage, so that they can develop pride in their own backgrounds. 6. This is a function that the Victorian novel cannot fulfill.

In this paragraph, Jenny has written a number of statements that are stated as facts but are actually Jenny's opinion of what she believes to be facts. To determine the extent to which you should be convinced by Jenny's paragraph, read each statement carefully with a questioning attitude, reflecting on the nature of the support Jenny has provided.

1. *Novels from the Victorian period in England should not be included in required literature courses.*

This is Jenny's topic sentence. It expresses the idea that her paragraph is going to develop and Jenny states it definitively. The implication of the statement is that Victorian novels should never be included in a required literature course and you might begin by reflecting on what you know about Victorian novels and the extent to which you agree with this idea.

2. *Since these novels tend to be extremely long, students often have difficulty finishing all of the reading.*

Although it is true that Victorian novels tend to be long, the statement that "students often have difficulty finishing all of the reading" is not a fact but is actually Jenny's opinion. You, as the reader, might ask, "Which students? How much reading? How does Jenny know this?" and "Is this a good reason for not including a Victorian novel?"

3. *Moreover, these novels are usually concerned with situations which are nothing like what is happening in American society today—in particular, they discuss romantic, political, and social themes which students frequently have trouble understanding, since they are not usually familiar with this period in history.*

Jenny does not define what she means by situations which "are nothing like what is happening in American society today," nor does she clarify the "romantic, political, and social themes" she mentions. Even if one accepts that students may not be familiar with this particular period in history, one might also question whether or not this is a valid reason for excluding the Victorian novel from a required literature course.

4. *Finally, the characters in these novels do not reflect the diverse populations of today's American students, so that students are unable to identify with them easily.*

A statement like this needs additional support. What does it mean for students to identify with a set of characters? Should this be a characteristic for including or excluding a work of literature on a reading list?

5. *Many of today's students want to read literature that is associated with their own cultural and ethnic heritage, so that they can develop pride in their own backgrounds.*

Once again, you might question how Jenny knows this. Can she cite the statements of people who work with "today's students" verifying that this is so? Does Jenny have any evidence to suggest that reading literature concerned with one's own cultural and ethnic background helps develop this sort of pride? This is the type of controversial statement that people are currently debating, so there is considerable discussion about this topic that Jenny could read that might help her develop her ideas. However, in this paragraph, Jenny has not indicated that she has "joined the conversation." She is simply voicing her own opinion.

6. *This is a function that the Victorian novel cannot fulfill.*

This is a debatable statement about which there are conflicting opinions, but Jenny has not indicated that she is aware of them.

Evaluating the Assumptions Behind the Thesis. During the third pass, it is important to try to understand the assumptions that lie behind the author's position, that is, the underlying values or statements about the world that provide the foundation for the main idea. The assumptions provide the basis for the author's point and are used to justify what the author is saying. For example, Jenny's paragraph is based on a number of assumptions that derive from her view of the function of required reading. Some of these assumptions are as follows:

■ that required reading ought to be accessible to students. For an assigned work to be of benefit to students, they should be familiar with the context of the work and be able to identify with the characters. Required reading should contain material that is familiar.

■that required reading should be used to help develop ethnic and cultural pride. If a student does not perceive an ethnic or cultural affiliation with a work of literature, that work of literature will not be valuable for that student.

Once you are aware of the assumptions behind a work, you are in a better position to evaluate the quality of the argument and the extent to which you accept it. In the example of Jenny's paragraph, you may decide that you do agree with it. But, you may also feel that an assigned work of literature does not have to be quite so accessible to students in order for it to be considered worthwhile. Or you may feel that the fostering of ethnic or cultural pride is not the main function of a literature course.

One assumption behind Jenny's paragraph is that students are unlikely to read works that are long or that they cannot easily identify with and, as an active reader, you would question whether or not you think that this is true. If you do, then perhaps you will agree that Victorian novels should not be assigned because there is little benefit in assigning works that students are not going to read.

Is the Evidence Reliable?

The Quality of the Reasoning. Some arguments appear to be well thought out, but are really based on fallacious reasoning which cannot withstand careful scrutiny. To evaluate the quality of the reasoning, question whether or not the author's reasons seem logical to you and be on the alert for arguments based on fallacies, which I discussed in chapter 3

An active reader looks closely at the kind of evidence used to support an argument before deciding to accept it. As I discussed in chapter 3, evidence in an argumentative essay can take many forms such as statements from authorities and statistics, and it is important for a careful reader to examine that evidence with a questioning attitude.

Appeals to Authority. Since no one is qualified to make judgments about every topic, writers often use the statements of experts to provide support. However, when an active reader encounters a statement by an authority in a piece of writing, he or she should check that the statement does indeed substantiate what the author is saying and that the authority can really be trusted. Find out who these experts are before accepting what they say as absolute truth, and evaluate their statements carefully. Sometimes a statement by an authority is quoted out of context, or authorities in one field are quoted as experts on topics that they know little about. (The use of athletes or movie stars to endorse certain products is an example of this.) Keep in mind that you do not have to accept everything that you read just because an alleged "expert" says that something is so. Maintain a skeptical attitude and look for other perspectives on the topic before completely accepting a particular point of view, especially if it does not seem sensible to you.

Statistics. Statistics (discussed in more detail in chapter 3) constitute another means of supporting an argument and can be a very convincing means of support. In fact, many students are under the impression that when an article includes statistics, the article is then automatically more reliable. A critical reader is aware that although statistics can often provide valid support, they can also be used to distort rather than to clarify an argument. As an active reader, then, be wary of statistics—they may not indicate what is initially suggested and can be used to suit an author's purpose.

Is the Text Stylistically Trustworthy?

Detecting Vagueness and Distortion in Language. Trying to figure out what a text is really saying is sometimes like trying to read through a rain-swept window, and particularly when writers attempt to manipulate, rather than convince, their readers, they sometimes use language to disguise meaning so that readers have difficulty knowing whether to trust what they read. An important characteristic of a stylistically trustworthy text is that it uses language to communicate, not to confuse. Therefore, as an astute reader you should be aware of the following stylistic techniques that can sometimes muffle the meaning of a text:

- interpretive words
- words used for emotional effect
- excessive use of abstract rather than concrete language
- ambiguity and distortion

Interpretive Words. Reading with a questioning, critical attitude involves becoming alert to words that interpret as opposed to those that simply state the facts. For example, examine the following two statements:

1. A beautiful woman was sitting in the cafe, her elegant hand lightly holding a coffee cup.
2. A woman in her mid-thirties with long black hair was sitting in the cafe, her slender fingers lightly holding a coffee cup.

If you read the statements carefully, you will perceive that in statement 1, the reference to the woman as beautiful is only the opinion of the author. (The author thinks the woman is beautiful and the author wants the reader to think that the woman is beautiful.) The second statement presents particular facts (the woman's age, the color and style of her hair, the slenderness of her fingers, which also suggest that the woman is probably slender because it is unlikely that the author would mention the slenderness of the woman's fingers if she was overweight). One method of distinguishing between facts and opinion is to become sensitive to the many words that interpret, words such as ugly, dangerous, elegant, bad, and best.

Of course, it is not necessarily "bad" to use interpretive language, and, indeed, one could make the argument that no text is entirely interpretation-free. However, in interacting with a text, it is a good idea to be sensitive to interpretive language and the extent to which that interpretation either enhances or clouds the argument.

Words Used for Emotional Effect. Many words have positive and negative overtones and tend to trigger emotional responses in their readers or listeners. Because they stimulate an immediate response, they are sometimes used by writers as a shortcut to providing adequate support. Saying that someone is a "bleeding heart," for example, suggests that such a person is inclined to spend money recklessly in a misguided impulse toward helping the human race. A writer may use this term without indicating what sort of spending or what type of misguided humanitarian impulse he or she means. Other examples of emotionally loaded language are *nerd, loser,* or *hippie.* Moreover, not all emotionally charged words are negative. "Democracy," "freedom," and "family" are examples of words that stimulate an immediate positive response among readers. Whether positive or negative, be alert to extreme statements and exaggerated expressions—they can generate a disproportionately emotional response that can affect your judgment.

For example, reacting against the political correctness movement on college campuses, Dinesh D'Souza writes in "The Visigoths in Tweed" that the college classroom has been transformed from

> a place of learning to a laboratory of indoctrination for social change. Not long ago most colleges required that students learn the basics of the physical sciences and mathematics, the rudiments of economics and finance, and the fundamental principles of American history and government. Studies by the National Endowment for the Humanities show that this coherence has disappeared from the curriculum. As a result, most universities are now graduating students who are scientifically and culturally impoverished, if not illiterate.

In this passage, D'Souza has used several terms that are likely to trigger a strong reaction in his reader such as "laboratory of indoctrination," suggesting a dictatorial Orwellian-like atmosphere, and the reference to students as "scientifically and culturally impoverished, if not illiterate." In essence, D'Souza is implying here that the PC movement is responsible for lack of freedom, poverty, and illiteracy on college campuses.

Excessive Use of Abstract Rather than Concrete Language. In his famous and often anthologized essay, "Politics and the English Language," George Orwell argues that politicians often use abstract language to desensitize the reader to what a writer may actually be saying.

> . . . political language has consisted largely of euphemism, question begging, and sheer cloudy vagueness. Defenseless villages are bombarded from the air,

the inhabitants driven out into the countryside, the cattle machine gunned, the huts set on fire with incendiary bullets: This is called *pacification*. Millions of peasants are robbed of their farms and sent trudging along the roads with no more than they can carry. This is called *transfer of population* or *rectification of frontiers . . .*

Orwell's point pertains to a writing style that still exists today. Bureaucratic language, in particular, is often characterized by a high degree of abstraction, the idea being that the reader becomes numb or bored and, hence, more willing to accept what may be outrageous or preposterous statements.

Another form of ambiguity is manifested in words that are not adequately defined, a technique that is particularly common in advertising. A facial soap ad claims that the product will "enhance the beauty you were born with," but does not specify what "enhance" means in this context or define what it means by "the beauty you were born with." In examining a text with a critical eye, be especially suspicious of words that are not adequately defined; words such as "family values," or "work ethic" are used frequently to put down a particular ethnic or racial group, yet the terms are left undefined.

For example, in the following paragraph, Marilyn Loden and Judy B. Rosener in *Workforce America! Managing Employee Diversity as a Vital Resource* point out the problems occurring in the workplace when diverse groups attempt to conform to the values of the dominant group.

> Recognizing that their mere presence is, at times, a challenge to the mainstream culture, diverse employees often feel compelled to adopt a style of behavior that is foreign to their self-definitions. They often attempt to modify their values and experiences in order to "fit" and conform to the behavioral and stylistic standards of the dominant group. The enormous energy that is spent learning how to assimilate could be better spent solving problems, identifying new business opportunities, or developing new programs, but this is seldom the case. Instead, we see countless examples of diverse people adapting, conforming, delimiting their potential, losing their identities and self-esteem, and, on occasion, burning out as they try to be something they aren't.

This approach does not explain what these employees do to adapt or conform, nor does it define how these activities delimit employees' potential or what these activities actually involve.

The Three-Pass Approach: Using the Method

To illustrate how the three-pass approach can help you gain insight into a source, assume you have come upon the article, entitled "Educating Tomorrow's Workers: Are We Ignoring Today's Girls?" included in this chapter. Below is a procedure you might use.

THE FIRST PASS

Title and Subtitle

On first encountering the article, you might begin by thinking about what you already know or believe about the topic that is suggested by the title. What was your own educational experience like in terms of male and female education? Do you think that the educational system ignores women or discriminates against women in some way, or do you believe that discriminatory practices no longer exist? Reflect on the meaning of the title and the subtitle. The title is "Educating Tomorrow's Workers," and the subtitle asks the question, "Are We Ignoring Today's Girls?" Although the main point of the article is not directly stated here, you might presume the article's answer is "yes," and that the article is concerned with the harm awaiting tomorrow's workers because of this problem. On the basis of the title and subtitle, you might assume that the article focuses on ways that the educational system is ignoring women. Keep an open mind, though, until you have examined other clues such as headings or subheadings that, in the case of this particular article, do indeed support this assumption.

Journal (or Source)

After examining the title and subtitle, see if you can locate the name of the journal in which the article appeared. The note at the bottom of the page indicates that it was published in *National Business Woman* in the summer of 1992 and was written by Marcia Eldredge, identified as the "assistant editor of *National Business Woman*." On the basis of the journal and the identity of the author, then, you might presume that the article has a particular agenda to promote, most likely that of calling attention to educational inequities against women that still exist.

Audience

You might also think about who is likely to read *National Business Woman*. Is the journal read mostly by women who are in business as the title suggests? Do other people also read the journal—businessmen or people who are not in business? Unless you were very familiar with this journal, you would not necessarily know the answer to these questions. However, by thinking about them, you will get a better idea of the possible intentions of the article.

Of course, the existence of an identifiable agenda or a set of motives does not mean that the article is not worth reading or that the author is unworthy of trust—an assistant editor of a business-oriented journal is probably well-qualified to discuss the impact of education on business and is probably someone who is well educated with a background in journalism as well as business, who may be especially concerned with the importance of presenting information fairly. However, awareness of a potential agenda can alert you to possible bias that might be reflected in a one-sided or unintentionally distorted presentation of information or facts.

First and Final Paragraphs

Finally, read through the first and final paragraphs of the article. The first paragraph indicates that the article is concerned with a report published recently from the American Association of University Women, entitled "How Schools Shortchange Girls," and states the thesis of the article quite explicitly—that despite the passage of civil rights acts addressing women, "the rights won on Capital Hill do not always translate into action for those they are designed to protect," thereby endangering America's competitive business edge. The last paragraph summarizes the main point of the AAUW report, and makes the additional point that "what is good for America's schoolgirls will be better for higher education and could ultimately be great for America's competitive business edge."

THE SECOND PASS

During the second pass, the reader does a quick appraisal of the article, reading it for meaning and to get a sense of how it develops its main point. A quick perusal of "Educating Tomorrow's Workers" shows how the author uses subheadings to note various times and life stages that place women at an educational disadvantage. These subheadings are as follows: Early Education, The Later Years and Self-Esteem, Teen Pregnancy, Math and Science, Special Education, and Testing. These subheadings can be used to structure the summary, which might read something like this:

> In "Educating Tomorrow's Workers: Are We Ignoring Today's Girls?" Marcia Eldredge discusses a report recently published by the American Association of University Women (AAUW) which points out that despite anti-discrimination legislation passed in the early seventies, women still suffer inequities in education. According to the report, these inequities can be traced to unconscious attitudes of teachers during the early years, social pressure and loss of self-esteem during late adolescence, to the perception that teen pregnancy is only a female problem, to gender biased curriculums and tests, and to a continued stereotyping of students. The article expresses concern that an inequitable educational system is not good for American business, causing the nation to lose its competitive edge.

THE THIRD PASS

During the third pass over "Educating Tomorrow's Workers: Are We Ignoring Today's Girls?" the reader could evaluate the text by responding to the following questions:

Is the argument consistent with what you believe is true or possible about the world and with your concept of human nature? In asking yourself this question, you might reflect on your view of the educational system and the extent to which you believe that most educators are sensitive to potential bias against women. Do you believe in the possibility that unconscious bias exists both in the treatment of women in schools and in the creation of a curriculum? If so, you will be inclined to trust the observations of the author and the report she is discussing.

Is the argument supported with appropriate and believable subpoints, examples, and facts? In evaluating the support provided in this article, you might note that the author cites specific points from the report. However, in some instances, the report itself makes assertions that may not necessarily be true, such as the statement on the second page that "school is only one place where they [girls] are reminded of their treatment as second-class citizens." This is a statement that might be open to question and that some might view as an exaggeration. Similarly, under the section concerned with "Special Education" the author attributes the presumed neglect that girls suffer to the fact that they are able to sit quietly and are less likely to misbehave, another questionable assumption. Overall, however, the author's statements tend to be well-supported.

Is the evidence reliable? Although it is sometimes impossible to evaluate the reliability of statistics unless you are very familiar with the subject and the method of sampling, this article cites figures that seem consistent and realistic; moreover, the author uses them judiciously, not making outrageous claims. For example, in the third paragraph, the author cites figures showing that few women hold leadership positions even in the field of education where women usually succeed. The discussion of the gender bias in the Scholastic Aptitude Test also seems accurate.

Does the argument acknowledge the complexity of the topic? In some instances, the author acknowledges that other causes besides inequities in the educational system may be responsible for women's lack of professional equality with men. In particular, the author admits that the "report allows that schools are not responsible for the inequality women face in society." For the most part, however, the author is discussing a report that makes a strong case in favor of one position and the author personally seems in favor of it .

Is the text stylistically credible? The author uses a measured tone, devoid of language that is inflammatory or hysterical. Overall, the article seems believable.

Conclusion

This chapter has outlined a three-pass approach to reading an outside source, a method that will enable you to "join the ongoing conversation" about issues related to the topic of diversity. Some of you may be thinking, though, that analyzing a text in this way will take more time than you are in the habit of devoting to your reading. When you are in the process of writing an essay, you may wish to complete your reading as quickly and efficiently as possible. However, critical reading to evaluate the credibility of a published work requires analytical thinking, a process that usually takes more time than a quick skim will allow. Ultimately, you will be able to use the three-pass approach quickly and efficiently. Like any new procedure, once you have practiced it, the more efficiently you will be able to do it, and the gain in insight will more than compensate for the additional time you spent initially.

Below is a form you can use to evaluate outside sources using the three-pass approach.

EVALUATING OUTSIDE SOURCES

BIBLIOGRAPHIC INFORMATION

Author _____

Title _____

Publication Information (Publisher, Place, Date of Publication)

_____

Main Point _____

_____

Short Summary _____

_____

_____

THE WRITER
Describe the expertise and motives of the writer.

_____

_____

Describe how the writer acknowledges the complexity of the topic.

_____

_____

THE QUALITY OF THE ARGUMENT
Characterize the beliefs about the world implied in this argument.

_____

_____

Characterize the view of human nature that underlies this argument.

Summarize the evidence used to support this argument.

Analyze the use of language. Does it contribute to the credibility of the text?

Assignments

1. Read Dinesh D'Souza's article in chapter 7, and use the above form to analyze it critically.

2. Read Joel Kotkin's article, "Perilous Illusions About Los Angeles," at the end of this chapter. Use the three-pass approach to evaluate this article.

Educating Tomorrow's Workers: Are We Ignoring Today's Girls?

MARCIA ELDREDGE

Marcia Eldredge is the assistant editor of National Business Woman. *This article appeared in* National Business Woman *(Summer, 1992).*

Are girls treated equally to boys in America's schools? Several recent developments in education throw into question the equity of our system for preparing today's students—tomorrow's workers—for their roles in the future. If America is to remain competitive, at home and abroad, it must begin by providing *all* of its future workers with the same foundation and the same competitive edge. One major development is the recent publication of "How Schools Shortchange Girls," by the American Association of University Women (AAUW) Educational Foundation. The report examines gender issues since passage of Title IX of the 1972 Education Amendments, which prohibits discrimination in educational institutions receiving federal funds. Like many acts passed to ensure equity for women and minorities, the rights won on Capitol Hill do not always translate into action for those they are designed to protect.

"How Schools Shortchange Girls" shows how educators have ignored   2
one-half of their students and how this affects not only young girls and women, but ultimately, America's work force. An equitable education for both girls and boys means a more equitable work force. The inequities detailed in the AAUW report range from unconscious attitudes of teachers, to gender-biased curriculums and tests, to the stereotyping of students. Reports on education are nothing new. In 1983, after the release of "A Nation at Risk," a report published by the U.S. Department of Education, an agenda was set to reform America's schools. Commissions, committees and special study groups were formed to learn why schools were failing America's children. Thirty-five reports issued from these groups were reviewed by the Wellesley College Center for Research on Women for AAUW to determine how much of the material dealt with gender and sex-equity issues. Most of the reports do not define the issues by gender, but four reports do include gender as a category in defining students at risk. Only one of the 35 reviewed addresses Title IX.

As in politics, government and corporate management, America needs   3
more women involved in the decisions that set the agendas and curriculums that are carried out in the nation's classrooms. The statistics show that, although teaching is still a women's field (72 percent of elementary and secondary school teachers are women), few women hold leadership positions. In 1990, women represented only 34 percent of the nation's school board members, 28 percent of principals and 5 percent of superintendents. In 1991, only nine of the 50 chief state school officers were women. Of the 35 commissions, committees and groups evaluating American education, only two had panels of at least 50 percent women.

Early Education

According to the AAUW report, there are few studies available of the varying   4
effects of preschool environments on girls and boys. However, there is a common educational myth that suggests preprimary programs are more beneficial to girls than to boys. "How Schools Shortchange Girls" disputes this myth by noting that young girls often arrive in preschool having mastered impulse-control training, small-muscle development and language enhancement. Since these are considered important skills needed for success in early education, teachers turn their attention to the boys who have yet to master the skills. Because girls arrive at school proficient in these skills, one study suggests girls actually benefit less from the preschool experience.

According to the AAUW report, this is one of the first biases girls face as   5
they begin their educational experience and, although girls may inherently

be more proficient in some basic skills than boys, educators must establish a balanced curricula for preschoolers so that both sexes will benefit equally from their early education experience.

The Later Years and Self-Esteem

Upon high school graduation the self-esteem of girls is measurably lower   6
than their male classmates. Although adolescence is a difficult time for both sexes, the report says it is a more difficult transition for girls. The report reminds readers that girls grow into young women in a society where they are both idealized and exploited and that school is only one place where they are reminded of their treatment as second-class citizens. In one report, research shows that being popular and well-liked is more important than being perceived as competent or independent among girls in grades six and seven. Boys, however, ranked being independent and competent as more important.

According to the AAUW report, both empirical and clinical studies, as   7
well as public-opinion polls, show significant declines in girls' self-esteem and self-confidence as they move from childhood to early adolescence. The research surveyed in the report asserts that girls' significant drop in self-esteem between elementary school and middle school is due in part to the negative messages girls perceive about women's role in society. Another factor may be that girls experience puberty before boys and that puberty is often a more difficult time for girls than boys. Girls usually experience puberty while making a transition from one school to another, and this is an added stress for students who already are lacking in self-esteem. Research shows that girls' self-esteem benefits if they experience only one transition into high school, as opposed to transitions from elementary school into a middle or junior high school and then again into high school.

As girls mature into late adolescence, their self-esteem continues to de-   8
cline. They are aware that marriage, family and employment are not equal situations for women and men. Although the report allows that schools are not responsible for the inequality women face in society, it holds educators and school administrators partially responsible by suggesting that inequality will not change until schooling changes.

Teen Pregnancy

The risk of pregnancy is an obstacle to success for adolescent girls. In the re-   9
ports reviewed for the AAUW study, the majority imply that teen pregnancy and dropping out of school are the only significant problems teenage girls face. Yet more than one-half of female drop-outs do so for reasons other than pregnancy. The reports also imply teen girls who give birth are a burden on society by increasing the number of female-headed households. There is no mention of the fathers who often offer little financial support to their children and the teen mothers. The AAUW report suggests that if teen pregnancy was seen as a systemic problem rather than an individual problem, and if pol-

icy initiatives focused on improving the educational system rather than girls' personal decisions, there might be fewer high school pregnancies.

Math and Science

In the past 15 years much research has concentrated on gender and math re- 10 lationships. According to the AAUW report, the gender gap in math is small and declining. Both boys and girls take the same classes and do equally well until the later high school years, at which time boys outnumber girls in higher-level classes such as calculus. The girls who do enroll in these higher level math classes do as well or better in classroom work and tests; however, boys continue to score higher on the Scholastic Aptitude Test, the Advanced Placement Test and other national standardized tests.

According to the report, unlike math, the gender gap in science is not de- 11 creasing but may be increasing. Since 1978, the gender gap has remained largest among 17-year-olds. Biology, traditionally the science with the most female representation, is the only field that has experienced a small decline in the gender gap. Again, girls perform the same or better in classroom work and tests, but score lower on national aptitude tests.

Although girls and boys are enrolled in the same science classes until later 12 high school years and express an equal interest in sciences, studies show they have different experiences. Girls tend to be exposed to more biology-related activities than to mechanical and electrical activities. With limited exposure to other fields, it should not be surprising that more females choose to pursue biology fields. When students make course selections in high school, boys tend to enroll in advanced physics and advanced chemistry classes; girls are found in the advanced biology classes. There are repercussions in higher education, too. With such a limited science background, high school girls, including those with exceptional academic preparation in math and science, are choosing math and science careers in disproportionately low numbers— careers that are high-paid, and will be increasingly in demand in our technological economy.

Janice Earle, of the National Science Foundation affirms that women are 13 still not choosing the science careers that boys do. "It's not enough to say anyone can sign up for the class. Something more has to happen."

She attributes the lack of female science majors in college to girls' elemen- 14 tary and middle school science experience, where, she says, more emphasis on science is needed. Earle suggests that some elementary school teachers avoid science, because they are not prepared to teach it. Often science is an elective course in the master's elementary education discipline rather than a required course.

"The gross inequities [in schools] have been addressed, but the subtleties 15 have not," Earle says. There are girls in higher level classes but there are still areas where they are not well represented, such as the advanced placement physics and calculus classes. With few role models for girls, their teachers, parents and peers must encourage them to participate at the advanced levels. It is through this encouragement that some of the subtleties of inequitable teaching will be addressed, she says.

Special Education

According to the AAUW report, more than two-thirds of students in special-   16
education classes are male. One explanation given for this difference is that
boys are born more often with disabling conditions. The report then states
that existing data does not, however, support this explanation. Medical reports on learning disabilities indicate that they occur almost equally in boys
and girls. One 1988 survey revealed that 70 percent of learning-disabled students enrolled in special education classes were boys. Despite differing study
results and contradictory statistics, one statement in the AAUW report suggests that some of the boys enrolled in special-education classes may have little more than behavorial problems. Girls who are more likely to sit quietly
and less likely to misbehave, thus less likely to get the attention they deserve,
are deprived of the specialized education they may need to develop fully.

Public Boys School Rejected

Despite the acts and amendments designed to protect discriminatory behav-   17
ior in federally funded learning institutions, some administrators insist that
girls and boys can get by on "separate but equal" educations. A recent example is the Detroit Board of Education, which, in February 1991, voted to establish three male public elementary schools to combat many of the
problems young urban men face; problems such as high drop out rates, homicide, suspension, low grades and poor test scores, many of the same problems
young urban girls also face.

On behalf of a mother who sought admission to the schools for her three   18
daughters, the National Organization for Women (NOW) Legal Defense and
Education Fund and the American Civil Liberties Union of Michigan filed a
lawsuit.

According to the NOW Legal Defense and Education Fund, the suit argues   19
that separate educational environments for males suggest that girls are less in
need of enhanced educational programs, a message to girls that their educational needs are inferior to those of boys; and that education demonstrating
positive male-female interaction, not separation, is the best way to eliminate
sexual harassment and anti-women attitudes, which hurt young women and
young men.

In August 1991 a federal district court judge ruled that the Detroit Board   20
of Education must admit girls to the schools and issued a preliminary injunction against the school board ordering the development of a plan for admitting girls in the fall of that year.

Testing

Examinations of standardized tests also show bias favoring boys. The most   21
obvious bias is when the number of references to one sex outnumber those of
the other sex or if sexes are stereotypically portrayed. In the 1970s, test devel-

opers worked to equate the number of references to women and men and to exclude offensive items. Researchers analyzing tests given in 1984, however, showed twice as many references to men as to women, as well as more pictures of and references to boys than to girls. A study of the Scholastic Aptitude Test found references to 42 men and only three women in the reading comprehension passages of the four 1984–85 exams. Classroom tests given by teachers have not been researched and, according to the report, little can be generalized from such tests.

The full AAUW report contains many more examples of an inequitable   22
U.S. educational system. Many of the inequities discussed above are explored more thoroughly in the report and are supported by statistics and research notes. If the AAUW report is taken seriously by education administrators, and if school policy-makers decide girls in America's schools deserve the same education and first-class treatment as their male classmates, not only should girls' test scores and girls' self-esteem increase, the repercussions will extend far beyond primary and secondary schools. What is good for America's school girls will be better for higher education and could ultimately be great for America's competitive business edge.

Perilous Illusions About Los Angeles

JOEL KOTKIN

Joel Kotkin, a contributing editor to Opinion, *is an international fellow at Pepperdine University's School of Business and Management in Los Angeles and a senior fellow with the Center for the New West.*

This article appeared in the Los Angeles Times *(June, 1992).*

Beyond its human and material costs, the Los Angeles riots left behind a   1
residue of dangerous myths and attitudes. Left unchallenged, these myths could pave the way for a descent into a future of ceaseless racial and class strife and widening economic impoverishment.

The politically correct myth-makers portray the riots as naturally occur-   2
ring events, even as justifiable expressions of anger and despair. In their eyes, Los Angeles is a fragmented city of distinct ethnic groups, the most aggrieved of which may violently protest its grievances without fear of punishment or moral censure. Such are the seeds of a political and social culture more akin to that of Sarajevo.

Some seem to have taken root. Korean merchants negotiating jobs and   3
investments with local gang leaders, rather than with community leaders, is
one frightening example. Unless rejected by people of all races, such forms of
"governance" will become the norm of our political future.

Among the post-riot myths are: 4

The riots were a rebellion. Although the acquittals in the Rodney G. King   5
beating trial provoked an angry political protest, within hours of the verdict
the "rebellion" looked more like mayhem, with criminal intent replacing
moral outrage. Once the LAPD officers and National Guard soldiers, or even
neighborhood residents, showed any will to resist, the "rebels" quickly retreated. Authentic rebels, as were the Viet Cong in Vietnam, routinely withdraw to fight another day. And they can usually count on support from the
local population if their cause is popular. In South Los Angeles, residents
pleaded with government and law-enforcement officials for assistance.

The riots signaled the opening of race war between people of color and the white   6
Establishment. In fact, the vast majority of communities denounced the un-
rest as completely unjustified. Among Latinos, nearly three-quarters, including nearly all business and political leaders, condemned the rioting.
Latinos—and even more so, Asians—were among the prime victims of the
disturbances, owning, between them, as many as half of all the destroyed
businesses.

Even more damaging to the myth makers, nearly three of five African-   7
Americans, in contrast to some of their leaders, also shared this position.

The riots, together with economic despair in South Los Angeles, were an in-   8
evitable reaction to Reagan-Bush economic policies. In fact, the area's rapid economic decline began in the mid-'60s and continued through the '70s, due
largely to a widespread exodus of local businesses, particularly in manufacturing. During the period from 1970 to 1977, for example, median family income in South-Central rose at one-third the rate enjoyed by the rest of the
city. This gap persisted throughout the Carter Administration.

In contrast, during the much-maligned 1980s, the percentage of African-   9
Americans in the L.A. area living in poverty declined, even as the rate of non-
black poverty increased. By the late 1980s, blacks in Los Angeles suffered, on
average, a rate of poverty almost 50% below that experienced by their counterparts in other metropolitan areas. The economic problem for South-Central lay largely in the migration of upwardly mobile blacks to the suburbs,
leaving the poorest and most alienated behind. Since the late 1970s, the
African-American population in South-Central has dropped from 80% to
roughly half.

Only huge government programs tailored for the worst riot-scarred areas can   10
help overcome the area's fundamental problems of crime, lack of training and of en-
trepreneurial skills. The record of the '60s and '70s provides little comfort for
believers in this approach. When tried in communities similarly blighted, enterprise zones have proved to be not much better.

A more reasonable approach would target companies in the broader re-   11
gion—particularly in the industrial belt surrounding South Los Angeles—that

already provide decent jobs to residents. These companies, easily reachable by public transit and largely spared the problems plaguing the heart of Rep. Maxine Waters' district, have established markets and technologies. Regrettably, as demands for financing economically tenuous developments in South-Central mount, the established employers in adjacent areas become targets of opportunity for industrial recruiters from out of state and from the suburbs, particularly the Inland Empire.

Given the racist nature of L.A. society, local politicians, particularly in minority 12
communities, have little choice but to support programs rewarding narrow communal interests. Already, many African-American leaders, Waters and Diane Watson among them, seem relentless in their advocacy of a "black agenda," often seemingly indifferent to either their increasingly Latino constituencies or the overall general economy. This brand of "me-first" economic tribalism seems headed for failure, given the increasing demographic and economic power of other groups, notably Asians and Latinos, in Southern California.

The chances of building a multiracial cosmopolis rooted in a shared civic 13 culture lies in turning away from all these dangerous and, ultimately, self-destructive myths. An ethos that condones narrow communalism and violence as a response to failed governmental policies ignores the experience of other societies in which the rule of the gun gained widespread legitimacy. Our choice, as Martin Luther King Jr. said, remains between chaos or community.

Equally important, condoning violence as a legitimate response to eco- 14 nomic hardship threatens to further isolate the poor by frightening away those whose capital and skills provide the critical perquisities for ameliorating long-term urban ills. Unlike such cities as Detroit and St. Louis, Los Angeles still boasts a large, ethnically diverse middle class that only now may be beginning its final flight from the metropolitan core.

Frequently ignored by the media elite and communalist politicians, these 15 middle-income Angelenos and their families will not remain without some guarantee of basic respect for property, security and the rule of law—the essential foundation of any civic culture. They desperately require, as do all Angelenos, a government and police department that is firm *and* fair. As the ancient Jewish book of laws, the Mishnah, suggests: "Pray for the welfare of the government, since if it were not for the fear of it, men would swallow each other alive."

II

■ Readings

5 ■ Melting Pot Versus Tossed Salad

My country 'tis of thee
Sweet land of liberty.
Of thee I sing.
Land where my fathers died . . .

I grew up singing this song in school every day, right after pledging allegiance to the flag, and in schoolrooms all across the United States, other children were singing it too. As Americans, we sang proudly of our country and its heritage of freedom, repeating the same words day after day without reflecting much on their meaning. We knew that the "fathers" who "died" referred to the founding fathers, the early settlers who had arrived from Europe long ago seeking a new world, and we sang of these fathers even if our own relatives did not arrive on the *Mayflower.* As children in American schoolrooms, we were, by definition, "Americans," and all other ethnic, racial, or cultural ties were regarded as insignificant in comparison with those of being an American.

For us, there was no question that America was a melting pot—that is, a country comprising many different ethnic groups that had somehow become blended or assimilated into Americans. The concept of the melting pot was associated with the idea of America as a land of freedom and opportunity; it was assumed that *anyone* would welcome the chance of becoming an American and that anyone who wished to become an American would easily and happily relinquish other ethnic and cultural bonds. Blending was considered a realizable ideal.

Today, however, even though schoolchildren sometimes sing the same song, the possibility and, in fact, desirability of America being a melting pot is being questioned, and the metaphor of the melting pot is being challenged by another metaphor: that of the tossed salad. This idea implies that although many different groups live in the United States and may consider themselves American, each group also retains its own ethnic and cultural character. The idea also implies that this retention is not only possible and desirable but has actually always been the case. Proponents of the tossed salad view feel that assimilation can be balanced with the preservation of identity; for them, the ideal is not the elimination of differences but an increased awareness of and respect for cultural and ethnic diversity.

145

The readings in this chapter examine several perspectives on the question of whether it is desirable or possible to retain ethnic, racial, and cultural diversity while maintaining the concept of a national identity, and they examine the impact both metaphors have on how American society functions. Advocates of the tossed salad perspective believe that the melting pot notion of freedom and justice for all was never a reality because only one group, that consisting of English-speaking white Europeans, was ever regarded as being essentially American and that all of the other races and cultures were excluded and made to feel inferior. Those who favor the concept of the melting pot maintain that the new emphasis on diversity will only fan ethnic conflict, ultimately contributing to the fragmentation and disintegration of the nation.

Background: The Waves of Immigration

Whether one adheres to the melting pot or tossed salad metaphor or a combination of the two, history tells us that the United States has always been ethnically and culturally diverse and that the earliest settlers had roots in many different countries and spoke many different languages. In 1750, Hector St. John de Crevecoeur immigrated to the American colonies, and during the American Revolution, he published *Letters From an American Farmer*, where he noted the remarkable cultural and linguistic diversity of other settlers in the new world—English, Scottish, French, Dutch, Germans, and Swedes. In that work, Crevecoeur defined an American as someone who leaves "behind him all his ancient prejudices and manners, receives new ones from the new mode of life he has embraced, the new government he obeys, and the new rank he holds. The American is a new man, who acts upon new principles. . . . Here individuals of all nations are melted into a new race of men." This statement, which I quote with apologies for its assumption that only men are citizens, suggests that each individual must forsake old loyalties and relinquish roots in order to become an American.

Despite Crevecoeur's observation of the diversity of the new world, however, three of four settlers during his time came from the British Isles. Not many immigrants arrived between 1790 and 1840. Immigration increased between 1841 and 1860, mainly from European countries. Some left Europe because of poor harvests, famine, political conflicts, or revolutions, and all viewed the United States as a place for a second chance, a land of opportunity. Steamship companies, railroad lines, factory owners, and landowners sent agents to Europe to attract prospective immigrants to the new world, with the result that by 1860, about thirteen of every hundred persons in the United States had only recently arrived from somewhere else.

By the 1880s, immigrants were arriving from countries other than those of northern Europe, in particular, Italy and Austria-Hungary. Chinese and Japanese immigrants arrived as well, many of them settling on the Pacific Coast, and as the United States became more settled, concern about competition for jobs and the problems of sharing increasingly scarce resources created a desire among already established residents to limit immigration in some way. In 1921, Congress passed a quota law that limited the number of immigrants from each country. This law allowed each country to send only three percent each year of the number of persons of that nationality who were already living in America in 1910. In 1924, another immigration act changed the quota to two percent and used 1890 as the base year. Another law that went into effect in 1929 was also designed to maintain a stable population in the United States. This law set a limit on the number of immigrants that could enter the country, and used the national origin of a prospective immigrant as a criterion for admission rather than the country of residence. This law also excluded certain nationality groups, particularly those from Asia, although China was exempted from this restriction in 1943. After World War II, immigration again rose sharply, as a number of displaced persons sought a new home, and in 1952, Japan received the right to send immigrants to the United States on the same basis as European countries.

In 1965, an amendment to the Immigration and Nationality Act made the quota system more flexible, a shift that resulted in a large number of immigrants arriving from Mexico, the West Indies, and Asia, especially from Taiwan, the Philippines, Korea, and India. Currently, a large number of immigrants to the United States come from Central America (in particular, Mexico, El Salvador, and Nicaragua) and Asia (especially Korea and Taiwan).

Thus, the history of the United States has been characterized by several waves of immigrants seeking to become blended into their new country. But history also tells us is that this ideal of blending and assimilation was rarely, if ever, realized. The many periods of immigration brought groups who fit only awkwardly into American society and who found melting extremely difficult. Non-white immigrants and those from Asian or African countries experienced considerable difficulty blending in to the so-called American culture, and many of them became victims of racism and discrimination. The recent emphasis on ethnicity and diversity then may be viewed as a long overdue recognition of the role that minorities have played in the forging of American culture and to a reinterpretation of history to recognize the achievements of women, Asians, black Americans, Native Americans, and Hispanics. Nevertheless, while acknowledging this progress, historians and social analysts are also concerned that the new emphasis on cultural pluralism will result in greater divisiveness and cultural disintegration.

Multiculturalism Versus Particularism

The readings in this chapter explore issues associated with the advantages and disadvantages of retaining ethnic and cultural identity within American society and examine the extent to which such retention is possible. Diane Ravitch's essay, "Multiculturalism: E Pluribus Plures," acknowledges the existence of a pluralistic society, but also points out that pluralism could easily become "particularism"—that is, the notion that no common ground exists between cultures, that personal self-esteem depends on cultural self-esteem, and that the only culture individuals can belong to is the culture of their ancestors. Ravitch is especially concerned that "particularism" can become a threat to national unity. The *Los Angeles Times* article, "Beyond the Melting Pot," traces the history of the melting pot and tossed salad debate, weighing the pros and cons of each view. Arthur M. Schlesinger, Jr., in an excerpt, "The Decomposition of America," from *The Disuniting of America,* deals a measured but devastating attack on the concept of multiculturalism, maintaining that it will ultimately lead to virulent nationalism, destructive of national unity. He points out that when people of different ethnic origins, speaking different languages and professing different religions, settle in the same geographical location, tribal hostilities will drive them apart unless a common purpose binds them together. Reed Way Dasenbrock's article, "The Multicultural West," maintains that Western culture has always been multicultural and questions the notion that we ought to preserve the culture of minority groups.

Several articles explore the meaning of the word "culture," and question how the nation's history contributes to our concept of it. Ellen K. Coughlin's essay, "Scholars Confront Fundamental Question: Which Vision of America Should Prevail?" discusses the debate occurring among historians about how to create a multicultural approach to teaching history. The primary change in this approach has been to substitute the old view of history as a "story of progress towards freedom" to looking at our past as a "long struggle to realize the American ideals of equality and democracy." Lynda Gorov's essay, "The Myth of the Melting Pot," contains the observations of three women who discuss what it is like to be caught between cultures. Her interviews suggest that the ideal of the melting pot is partly myth. Apparently, immigrants are often torn between the pressure to adopt American culture and the need to retain their own heritage.

Specific Minority Experiences

Several readings examine the experience of specific ethnic and minority groups within American society. The excerpt from Richard Rodriguez's book,

Days of Obligation: An Argument with My Mexican Father, traces his search for his roots in a small Mexican village. Rodriguez maintains that Native Americans from both North and South America have long been marginalized from American society because "America is an idea to which natives are inimical." Moreover, Rodriguez points out, Native Americans have been largely stereotyped by the media and have only recently been shown in a positive light when used as a gauge for the extent to which industrial America has corrupted the environment. In the excerpt entitled "The Special Perspective" from *Reflections of an Affirmative Action Baby,* Stephen L. Carter, a lawyer and law professor, discusses the black experience in America and the extent to which it is similar to that of other oppressed peoples. Carter, who is black, argues that although the black experience is different from that of whites and from that of other oppressed groups, the diversity movement should not insist that whites cannot understand the black experience or that the oppression and suffering of blacks is worse than the suffering of other ethnic groups. Carter believes that to equate the black experience with suffering and oppression does not advance the black cause because it emphasizes rather than minimizes differences that contribute to stereotyping and prejudice.

Of course, to some extent, American society has always been characterized by both tolerance for and suspicion of "otherness." In the essay entitled "Prejudice," Peter Rose argues that ethnocentricity is in one sense a protective gesture, for we tend to both fear and generalize the unknown, and that ethnocentricity serves to enhance group cohesion. Rose explains how ethnocentric thinking is almost unconsciously passed on to our children through vehicles such as literature and patriotism. Sometimes, in fact, the desire to preserve group cohesion can prevent individual members of the group from striving for success. Discussing the Mexican-American experience, Ruben Navarrette, Jr. argues that Mexican-Americans have fallen behind other ethnic groups politically and economically because of the pressure of "envidia"—that is, the jealousy and hatred that some Mexican-Americans exhibit when their peers are successful. Rather than condemning those who appear to "sell out," Navarrette urges that only ethnic solidarity and support for achievement can overcome such external forces as racism and discrimination.

Future Possibilities

Included in this chapter is the famous "I Have a Dream" speech by the Reverend Martin Luther King, Jr. In this speech, originally delivered at the Lincoln Memorial in 1963 to commemorate the one-hundred–year anniversary of the Emancipation Proclamation, King calls for "the unalienable rights of life, liberty, and the pursuit of happiness," which continue to be denied to blacks and which will eventually prove "fatal" to the nation. King outlines his dream for the society of the future, which he envisions as a time of freedom for all, when all groups can join hands in unity. Such unity, according to Bebe Moore Campbell, is already physically evident in a curious trend of "cultural borrowing"—that is, the swapping among races of particularly characteristic racial features—tan skin in white people and blond hair on African-Americans, for example. Although her tone is light, Moore Campbell concludes with the hope that perhaps Americans will be able to transcend these superficialities of skin and hair to institute a more meaningful exchange that would ultimately lead to understanding and acceptance.

Multiculturalism:
E Pluribus Plures

DIANE RAVITCH

Diane Ravitch (b. 1938) has written extensively on the history of education and is the author of numerous books including The Troubled Crusade: American Education, 1945–1980 *and* Against Mediocrity *(1984). She was an adjunct professor of history and education at Teachers College, Columbia University, until 1991 when she became Assistant Secretary in the Office of Education Research and Improvement with the U.S. Department of Education.*

In this selection, Ravitch argues that the particularist approach to public education does not foster self-esteem but leads to alienation and hostility. She proposes that the function of public schools is to inculcate an "Americentric" education—one which creates an inclusive national identity based on our common culture. This selection is from the American Scholar *(1990).*

Questions of race, ethnicity, and religion have been a perennial source of 1 conflict in American education. The schools have often attracted the zealous attention of those who wish to influence the future, as well as those who wish to change the way we view the past. In our history, the schools have been not only an institution in which to teach young people skills and knowledge, but an arena where interest groups fight to preserve their values, or to revise the judgments of history, or to bring about fundamental social change. In the nineteenth century, Protestants and Catholics battled over which version of the Bible should be used in school, or whether the Bible should be used at all. In recent decades, bitter racial disputes—provoked by policies of racial segregation and discrimination—have generated turmoil in the streets and in the schools. The secularization of the schools during the past century has prompted attacks on the curricula and textbooks and library books by fundamentalist Christians, who object to whatever challenges their faith-based views of history, literature, and science.

Given the diversity of American society, it has been impossible to insulate 2 the schools from pressures that result from differences and tensions among groups. When people differ about basic values, sooner or later those disagreements turn up in battles about how schools are organized or what the schools should teach. Sometimes these battles remove a terrible injustice, like racial segregation. Sometimes, however, interest groups politicize the curriculum and attempt to impose their views on teachers, school officials, and textbook

151

publishers. Across the country, even now, interest groups are pressuring local school boards to remove myths and fables and other imaginative literature from children's readers and to inject the teaching of creationism in biology. When groups cross the line into extremism, advancing their own agenda without regard to reason or to others, they threaten public education itself, making it difficult to teach any issues honestly and making the entire curriculum vulnerable to political campaigns.

For many years, the public schools attempted to neutralize controversies over race, religion, and ethnicity by ignoring them. Educators believed, or hoped, that the schools could remain outside politics; this was, of course, a vain hope since the schools were pursuing policies based on race, religion, and ethnicity. Nonetheless, such divisive questions were usually excluded from the curriculum. The textbooks minimized problems among groups and taught a sanitized version of history. Race, religion, and ethnicity were presented as minor elements in the American saga; slavery was treated as an episode, immigration as a sidebar, and women were largely absent. The textbooks concentrated on presidents, wars, national politics, and issues of state. An occasional "great black" or "great woman" received mention, but the main narrative paid little attention to minority groups and women. 3

With the ethnic revival of the 1960s, this approach to the teaching of history came under fire, because the history of national leaders—virtually all of whom were white, Anglo-Saxon, and male—ignored the place in American history of those who were none of the above. The traditional history of elites had been complemented by an assimilationist view of American society, which presumed that everyone in the American melting pot would eventually lose or abandon those ethnic characteristics that distinguished them from mainstream Americans. The ethnic revival demonstrated that many groups did not want to be assimilated or melted. Ethnic studies programs popped up on campuses to teach not only that "black is beautiful," but also that every other variety of ethnicity is "beautiful" as well; everyone who had "roots" began to look for them so that they too could recover that ancestral part of themselves that had not been homogenized. 4

As ethnicity became an accepted subject for study in the late 1960s, textbooks were assailed for their failure to portray blacks accurately; within a few years, the textbooks in wide use were carefully screened to eliminate bias against minority groups and women. At the same time, new scholarship about the history of women, blacks, and various ethnic minorities found its way into the textbooks. At first, the multicultural content was awkwardly incorporated as little boxes on the side of the main narrative. Then some of the new social historians (like Stephan Thernstrom, Mary Beth Norton, Gary Nash, Winthrop Jordan, and Leon Litwack) themselves wrote textbooks, and the main narrative itself began to reflect a broadened historical understanding of race, ethnicity, and class in the American past. Consequently, today's history textbooks routinely incorporate the experiences of women, blacks, American Indians, and various immigrant groups. 5

Although most high school textbooks are deeply unsatisfactory (they still   6
largely neglect religion, they are too long, too encyclopedic, too superficial,
and lacking in narrative flow), they are far more sensitive to pluralism than
their predecessors. For example, the latest edition of Tod and Curti's *Triumph
of the American Nation,* the most popular high school history text, has significantly increased its coverage of blacks in America, including profiles of Phillis
Wheatley, the poet; James Armistead, a revolutionary war spy for Lafayette;
Benjamin Banneker, a self-taught scientist and mathematician; Hiram Revels,
the first black to serve in the Congress; and Ida B. Wells-Barnett, a tireless cru-
sader against lynching and racism. Even better as a textbook treatment is Jordan and Litwack's *The United States,* which skillfully synthesizes the historical
experiences of blacks, Indians, immigrants, women, and other groups into
the mainstream of American social and political history. The latest generation
of textbooks bluntly acknowledges the racism of the past, describing the
struggle for equality by racial minorities while identifying individuals who
achieved success as political leaders, doctors, lawyers, scholars, entrepreneurs,
teachers, and scientists.

As a result of the political and social changes of recent decades, cultural   7
pluralism is now generally recognized as an organizing principle of this society. In contrast to the idea of the melting pot, which promised to erase ethnic
and group differences, children now learn that variety is the spice of life.
They learn that America has provided a haven for many different groups and
has allowed them to maintain their cultural heritage or to assimilate, or—as is
often the case—to do both; the choice is theirs, not the state's. They learn
that cultural pluralism is one of the norms of a free society; that differences
among groups are a national resource rather than a problem to be solved. Indeed, the unique feature of the United States is that its common culture has
been formed by the interaction of its subsidiary cultures. It is a culture that
has been influenced over time by immigrants, American Indians, Africans
(slave and free) and by their descendants. American music, art, literature, language, food, clothing, sports, holidays, and customs all show the effects of
the commingling of diverse cultures in one nation. Paradoxical though it
may seem, the United States has a common culture that is multicultural.

Our schools and our institutions of higher learning have in recent years   8
begun to embrace what Catherine R. Stimpson of Rutgers University has
called "cultural democracy," a recognition that we must listen to a "diversity
of voices" in order to understand our culture, past and present. This understanding of the pluralistic nature of American culture has taken a long time
to forge. It is based on sound scholarship and has led to major revisions in
what children are taught and what they read in school. The new history is—
indeed, must be—a warts-and-all history; it demands an unflinching examination of racism and discrimination in our history. Making these changes is
difficult, raises tempers, and ignites controversies, but gives a more interesting and accurate account of American history. Accomplishing these changes
is valuable, because there is also a useful lesson for the rest of the world in

America's relatively successful experience as a pluralistic society. Throughout human history, the clash of different cultures, races, ethnic groups, and religions has often been the cause of bitter hatred, civil conflict, and international war. The ethnic tensions that now are tearing apart Lebanon, Sri Lanka, Kashmir, and various republics of the Soviet Union remind us of the costs of unfettered group rivalry. Thus, it is a matter of more than domestic importance that we closely examine and try to understand that part of our national history in which different groups competed, fought, suffered, but ultimately learned to live together in relative peace and even achieved a sense of common nationhood.

Alas, these painstaking efforts to expand the understanding of American culture into a richer and more varied tapestry have taken a new turn, and not for the better. Almost any idea, carried to its extreme, can be made pernicious, and this is what is happening now to multiculturalism. Today, pluralistic multiculturalism must contend with a new, particularistic multiculturalism. The pluralists seek a richer common culture; the particularists insist that no common culture is possible or desirable. The new particularism is entering the curriculum in a number of school systems across the country. Advocates of particularism propose an ethnocentric curriculum to raise the self-esteem and academic achievement of children from racial and ethnic minority backgrounds. Without any evidence, they claim that children from minority backgrounds will do well in school *only* if they are immersed in a positive, prideful version of their ancestral culture. If children are of, for example, Fredonian ancestry, they must hear that Fredonians were important in mathematics, science, history, and literature. If they learn about great Fredonians and if their studies use Fredonian examples and Fredonian concepts, they will do well in school. If they do not, they will have low self-esteem and will do badly. 9

At first glance, this appears akin to the celebratory activities associated with Black History Month or Women's History Month, when schoolchildren learn about the achievements of blacks and women. But the point of those celebrations is to demonstrate that neither race nor gender is an obstacle to high achievement. They teach all children that everyone, regardless of their race, religion, gender, ethnicity, or family origin, can achieve self-fulfillment, honor, and dignity in society if they aim high and work hard. 10

By contrast, the particularistic version of multiculturalism is unabashedly filiopietistic and deterministic. It teaches children that their identity is determined by their "cultural genes." That something in their blood or their race memory or their cultural DNA defines who they are and what they may achieve. That the culture in which they live is not their own culture, even though they were born here. That American culture is "Eurocentric," and therefore hostile to anyone whose ancestors are not European. Perhaps the most invidious implication of particularism is that racial and ethnic minorities are not and should not try to be part of American culture; it implies that American culture belongs only to those who are white and European; it implies that those who are neither white nor European are alienated from Amer- 11

ican culture by virtue of their race or ethnicity; it implies that the only culture they do belong to or can ever belong to is the culture of their ancestors,
even if their families have lived in this country for generations.

The war on so-called Eurocentrism is intended to foster self-esteem   12
among those who are not of European descent. But how, in fact, is self-esteem
developed? How is the sense of one's own possibilities, one's potential
choices, developed? Certainly, the school curriculum plays a relatively small
role as compared to the influence of family, community, mass media, and society. But to the extent that curriculum influences what children think of
themselves, it should encourage children of all racial and ethnic groups to believe that they are part of this society and that they should develop their talents and minds to the fullest. It is enormously inspiring, for example, to learn
about men and women from diverse backgrounds who overcame poverty, discrimination, physical handicaps, and other obstacles to achieve success in a
variety of fields. Behind every such biography of accomplishment is a story of
heroism, perseverance, and self-discipline. Learning these stories will encourage a healthy spirit of pluralism, of mutual respect, and of self-respect among
children of different backgrounds. The children of American society today
will live their lives in a racially and culturally diverse nation, and their education should prepare them to do so.

The pluralist approach to multiculturalism promotes a broader interpreta-   13
tion of the common American culture and seeks due recognition for the ways
that the nation's many racial, ethnic, and cultural groups have transformed
the national culture. The pluralists say, in effect, "American culture belongs
to us, all of us; the U.S. is us, and we remake it in every generation." But particularists have no interest in extending or revising American culture; indeed,
they deny that a common culture exists. Particularists reject any accommodation among groups, any interactions that blur the distinct lines between
them. The brand of history that they espouse is one in which everyone is either a descendant of victims or oppressors. By doing so, ancient hatreds are
fanned and recreated in each new generation. Particularism has its intellectual roots in the ideology of ethnic separatism and in the black nationalist
movement. In the particularist analysis, the nation has five cultures: African
American, Asian American, European American, Latino/Hispanic, and Native
American. The huge cultural, historical, religious, and linguistic differences
within these categories are ignored, as is the considerable intermarriage
among these groups, as are the linkages (like gender, class, sexual orientation,
and religion) that cut across these five groups. No serious scholar would claim
that all Europeans and white Americans are part of the same culture, or that
all Asians are part of the same culture, or that all people of Latin-American
descent are of the same culture, or that all people of African descent are of the
same culture. Any categorization this broad is essentially meaningless and
useless.

Several districts—including Detroit, Atlanta, and Washington, D.C.—are   14
developing an Afrocentric curriculum. *Afrocentricity* has been described in a
book of the same name by Molefi Kete Asante of Temple University. The

Afrocentric curriculum puts Africa at the center of the student's universe. African Americans must "move away from an [*sic*] Eurocentric framework" because "it is difficult to create freely when you use someone else's motifs, styles, images, and perspectives." Because they are not Africans, "white teachers cannot inspire in our children the visions necessary for them to overcome limitations." Asante recommends that African Americans choose an African name (as he did), reject European dress, embrace African religion (not Islam or Christianity) and love "their own" culture. He scorns the idea of universality as a form of Eurocentric arrogance. The Eurocentrist, he says, thinks of Beethoven or Bach as classical, but the Afrocentrist thinks of Ellington or Coltrane as classical; the Eurocentrist lauds Shakespeare or Twain, while the Afrocentrist prefers Baraka, Shange, or Abiola. Asante is critical of black artists like Arthur Mitchell and Alvin Ailey who ignore Afrocentricity. Likewise, he speaks contemptuously of a group of black university students who spurned the Afrocentrism of the local Black Student Union and formed an organization called Inter-race: "Such madness is the direct consequence of self-hatred, obligatory attitudes, false assumptions about society, and stupidity."

The conflict between pluralism and particularism turns on the issue of 15 universalism. Professor Asante warns his readers against the lure of universalism: "Do not be captured by a sense of universality given to you by the Eurocentric viewpoint; such a viewpoint is contradictory to your own ultimate reality." He insists that there is no alternative to Eurocentrism, Afrocentrism, and other ethnocentrisms. In contrast, the pluralist says, with the Roman playwright Terence, "I am a man: nothing human is alien to me." A contemporary Terence would say "I am a person" or might be a woman, but the point remains the same: You don't have to be black to love Zora Neale Hurston's fiction or Langston Hughes's poetry or Duke Ellington's music. In a pluralist curriculum, we expect children to learn a broad and humane culture, to learn about the ideas and art and animating spirit of many cultures. We expect that children, whatever their color, will be inspired by the courage of people like Helen Keller, Vaclav Havel, Harriet Tubman, and Feng Lizhe. We expect that their response to literature will be determined by the ideas and images it evokes, not by the skin color of the writer. But particularists insist that children can learn only from the experiences of people from the same race.

Particularism is a bad idea whose time has come. It is also a fashion 16 spreading like wildfire through the education system, actively promoted by organizations and individuals with a political and professional interest in strengthening ethnic power bases in the university, in the education profession, and in society itself. One can scarcely pick up an educational journal without learning about a school district that is converting to an ethnocentric curriculum in an attempt to give "self-esteem" to children from racial minorities. A state-funded project in a Sacramento high school is teaching young black males to think like Africans and to develop the "African Mind Model Technique," in order to free themselves of the racism of American culture. A popular black rap singer, KRS-One, complained in an op-ed article in the *New York Times* that the schools should be teaching blacks about their cultural heritage, instead of trying to make everyone Americans. "It's like trying to teach a dog to be a cat," he wrote. KRS-One railed about having to learn about Thomas Jefferson and the Civil War, which had nothing to do (he said) with black history.

Pluralism can easily be transformed into particularism, as may be seen in the potential uses in the classroom of the Mayan contribution to mathematics. The Mayan example was popularized in a movie called *Stand and Deliver,* about a charismatic Bolivian-born mathematics teacher in Los Angeles who inspired his students (who are Hispanic) to learn calculus. He told them that their ancestors invented the concept of zero; but that wasn't all he did. He used imagination to put across mathematical concepts. He required them to do homework and to go to school on Saturdays and during the Christmas holidays, so that they might pass the Advanced Placement mathematics examination for college entry. The teacher's reference to the Mayans' mathematical genius was a valid instructional device: It was an attention-getter and would have interested even students who were not Hispanic. But the Mayan example would have had little effect without the teacher's insistence that the class study hard for a difficult examination. [17]

Ethnic educators have seized upon the Mayan contribution to mathematics as the key to simultaneously boosting the ethnic pride of Hispanic children and attacking Eurocentrism. One proposal claims that Mexican-American children will be attracted to science and mathematics if they study Mayan mathematics, the Mayan calendar, and Mayan astronomy. Children in primary grades are to be taught that the Mayans were first to discover the zero and that Europeans learned it long afterwards from the Arabs, who had learned it in India. This will help them see that Europeans were latecomers in the discovery of great ideas. Botany is to be learned by study of the agricultural techniques of the Aztecs, a subject of somewhat limited relevance to children in urban areas. Furthermore, "ethnobotanical" classifications of plants are to be substituted for the Eurocentric Linnaean system. At first glance, it may seem curious that Hispanic children are deemed to have no cultural affinity with Spain; but to acknowledge the cultural tie would confuse the ideological assault on Eurocentrism. [18]

This proposal suggests some questions: Is there any evidence that the teaching of "culturally relevant" science and mathematics will draw Mexican-American children to the study of these subjects? Will Mexican-American children lose interest or self-esteem if they discover that their ancestors were Aztecs or Spaniards, rather than Mayans? Are children who learn in this way prepared to study the science and mathematics that are taught in American colleges and universities and that are needed for advanced study in these fields? Are they even prepared to study the science and mathematics taught in *Mexican* universities? If the class is half Mexican-American and half something else, will only the Mexican-American children study in a Mayan and [19]

Aztec mode or will all the children? But shouldn't all children study what is culturally relevant for them? How will we train teachers who have command of so many different systems of mathematics and science?

The efficacy of particularist proposals seems to be less important to their   20
sponsors than their value as ideological weapons with which to criticize existing disciplines for their alleged Eurocentric bias. In a recent article titled "The Ethnocentric Basis of Social Science Knowledge Production" in the *Review of Research in Education,* John Stanfield of Yale University argues that neither social science nor science are objective studies, that both instead are "Euro-American" knowledge systems which reproduce "hegemonic racial domination." The claim that science and reason are somehow superior to magic and witchcraft, he writes, is the product of Euro-American ethnocentrism. According to Stanfield, current fears about the misuse of science (for instance, "the nuclear arms race, global pollution") and "the power-plays of Third World nations (the Arab oil boycott and the American-Iranian hostage crisis) have made Western people more aware of nonscientific cognitive styles. These last events are beginning to demonstrate politically that which has begun to be understood in intellectual circles: namely, that modes of social knowledge such as theology, science, and magic are different, not inferior or superior. They represent different ways of perceiving, defining, and organizing knowledge of life experiences." One wonders: If Professor Stanfield broke his leg, would he go to a theologian, a doctor, or a magician?

Every field of study, it seems, has been tainted by Eurocentrism, which   21
was defined by a professor at Manchester University, George Ghevarughese Joseph, in *Race and Class* in 1987, as "intellectual racism." Professor Joseph argues that the history of science and technology—and in particular, of mathematics—in non-European societies was distorted by racist Europeans who wanted to establish the dominance of European forms of knowledge. The racists, he writes, traditionally traced mathematics to the Greeks, then claimed that it reached its full development in Europe. These are simply Eurocentric myths to sustain an "imperialist/racist ideology," says Professor Joseph, since mathematics was found in Egypt, Babylonia, Mesopotamia, and India long before the Greeks were supposed to have developed it. Professor Joseph points out too that Arab scientists should be credited with major discoveries traditionally attributed to William Harvey, Isaac Newton, Charles Darwin, and Sir Francis Bacon. But he is not concerned only to argue historical issues; his purpose is to bring all of these different mathematical traditions into the school classroom so that children might study, for example, "traditional African designs, Indian *rangoli* patterns and Islamic art" and "the language and counting systems found across the world."

This interesting proposal to teach ethnomathematics comes at a time   22
when American mathematics educators are trying to overhaul present practices, because of the poor performance of American children on national and international assessments. Mathematics educators are attempting to change the teaching of their subject so that children can see its uses in everyday life. There would seem to be an incipient conflict between those who want to in-

troduce real-life applications of mathematics and those who want to teach the mathematical systems used by ancient cultures. I suspect that most mathematics teachers would enjoy doing a bit of both, if there were time or student interest. But any widespread movement to replace modern mathematics with ancient ethnic mathematics runs the risk of disaster in a field that is struggling to update existing curricula. If, as seems likely, ancient mathematics is taught mainly to minority children, the gap between them and middle-class white children is apt to grow. It is worth noting that children in Korea, who score highest in mathematics on international assessments, do not study ancient Korean mathematics.

Particularism is akin to cultural Lysenkoism, for it takes as its premise the 23 spurious notion that cultural traits are inherited. It implies a dubious, dangerous form of cultural predestination. Children are taught that if their ancestors could do it, so could they. But what happens if a child is from a cultural group that made no significant contribution to science or mathematics? Does this mean that children from that background must find a culturally appropriate field in which to strive? How does a teacher find the right cultural buttons for children of mixed heritage? And how in the world will teachers use this technique when the children in their classes are drawn from many different cultures, as is usually the case? By the time that every culture gets its due, there may be no time left to teach the subject itself. This explosion of filiopietism (which, we should remember, comes from adults, not from students) is reminiscent of the period some years ago when the Russians claimed that they had invented everything first; as we now know, this nationalistic braggadocio did little for their self-esteem and nothing for their economic development. We might reflect, too, on how little social prestige has been accorded in this country to immigrants from Greece and Italy, even though the achievements of their ancestors were at the heart of the classical curriculum.

Filiopietism and ethnic boosterism lead to all sorts of odd practices. In 24 New York State, for example, the curriculum guide for eleventh grade American history lists three "foundations" for the United States Constitution, as follows:

A. Foundations
    1. 17th and 18th century Enlightenment thought
    2. Haudenosaunee political system
        a. Influence upon colonial leadership and European intellectuals (Locke, Montesquieu, Voltaire, Rousseau)
        b. Impact on Albany Plan of Union, Articles of Confederation, and U.S. Constitution
    3. Colonial experience

Those who are unfamiliar with the Haudenosaunee political system 25 might wonder what it is, particularly since educational authorities in New York State rank it as equal in importance to the European Enlightenment and suggest that it strongly influenced not only colonial leaders but the leading intellectuals of Europe. The Haudenosaunee political system was the Iroquois confederation of five (later six) Indian tribes in upper New York State, which conducted war and civil affairs through a council of chiefs, each with one vote. In 1754, Benjamin Franklin proposed a colonial union at a conference in Albany; his plan, said to be inspired by the Iroquois Confederation, was rejected by the other colonies. Today, Indian activists believe that the Iroquois Confederation was the model for the American Constitution, and the New York State Department of Education has decided that they are right. That no other state sees fit to give the American Indians equal billing with the European Enlightenment may be owing to the fact that the Indians in New York State (numbering less than forty thousand) have been more politically effective than elsewhere or that other states have not yet learned about this method of reducing "Eurocentrism" in their American history classes.

Particularism can easily be carried to extremes. Students of Fredonian descent must hear that their ancestors were seminal in the development of all human civilization and that without the Fredonian contribution, we would all be living in caves or trees, bereft of art, technology, and culture. To explain why Fredonians today are in modest circumstances, given their historic eminence, children are taught that somewhere, long ago, another culture stole the Fredonians' achievements, palmed them off as their own, and then oppressed the Fredonians.   26

I first encountered this argument almost twenty years ago, when I was a graduate student. I shared a small office with a young professor, and I listened as she patiently explained to a student why she had given him a D on a term paper. In his paper, he argued that the Arabs had stolen mathematics from the Nubians in the desert long ago (I forget in which century this theft allegedly occurred). She tried to explain to him about the necessity of historical evidence. He was unconvinced, since he believed that he had uncovered a great truth that was beyond proof. The part I couldn't understand was how anyone could lose knowledge by sharing it. After all, cultures are constantly influencing one another, exchanging ideas and art and technology, and the exchange usually is enriching, not depleting.   27

Today, there are a number of books and articles advancing controversial theories about the origins of civilization. An important work, *The African Origin of Civilization: Myth or Reality,* by Senegalese scholar Cheikh Anta Diop, argues that ancient Egypt was a black civilization, that all races are descended from the black race, and that the achievements of "western" civilization originated in Egypt. The views of Diop and other Africanists have been condensed into an everyman's paperback titled *What They Never Told You in History Class* by Indus Khamit Kush. This latter book claims that Moses, Jesus, Buddha, Mohammed, and Vishnu were Africans; that the first Indians, Chinese, Hebrews, Greeks, Romans, Britains, and Americans were Africans; and that the first mathematicians, scientists, astronomers, and physicians were Africans. A debate currently raging among some classicists is whether the Greeks "stole" the philosophy, art, and religion of the ancient Egyptians and whether the ancient Egyptians were black Africans. George G. M. James's   28

Stolen Legacy insists that the Greeks "stole the Legacy of the African Continent and called it their own." James argues that the civilization of Greece, the vaunted foundation of European culture, owed everything it knew and did to its African predecessors. Thus, the roots of western civilization lie not in Greece and Rome, but in Egypt and, ultimately, in black Africa.

Similar speculation was fueled by the publication in 1987 of Martin   29
Bernal's *Black Athena: The Afroasiatic Roots of Classical Civilization,* Volume 1, *The Fabrication of Ancient Greece, 1785–1985,* although the controversy predates Bernal's book. In a fascinating foray into the politics of knowledge, Bernal attributes the preference of Western European scholars for Greece over Egypt as the fount of knowledge to nearly two centuries of racism and "Europocentrism," but he is uncertain about the color of the ancient Egyptians. However, a review of Bernal's book last year in the *Village Voice* began, "What color were the ancient Egyptians? Blacker than Mubarak, baby." The same article claimed that white racist archeologists chiseled the noses off ancient Egyptian statues so that future generations would not see the typically African facial characteristics. The debate reached the pages of the *Biblical Archeology Review* last year in an article titled "Were the Ancient Egyptians Black or White?" The author, classicist Frank J. Yurco, argues that some Egyptian rulers were black, others were not, and that "the ancient Egyptians did not think in these terms." The issue, wrote Yurco, "is a chimera, cultural baggage from our own society that can only be imposed artificially on ancient Egyptian society."

Most educationists are not even aware of the debate about whether the   30
ancient Egyptians were black or white, but they are very sensitive to charges that the schools' curricula are Eurocentric, and they are eager to rid the schools of the taint of Eurocentrism. It is hardly surprising that America's schools would recognize strong cultural ties with Europe since our nation's political, religious, educational, and economic institutions were created chiefly by people of European descent, our government was shaped by European ideas, and nearly 80 percent of the people who live here are of European descent. The particularists treat all of this history as a racist bias toward Europe, rather than as the matter-of-fact consequences of European immigration. Even so, American education is not centered on Europe. American education, if it is centered on anything, is centered on itself. It is "Americentric." Most American students today have never studied any world history; they know very little about Europe, and even less about the rest of the world. Their minds are rooted solidly in the here and now. When the Berlin Wall was opened in the fall of 1989, journalists discovered that most American teenagers had no idea what it was, nor why its opening was such a big deal. Nonetheless, Eurocentrism provides a better target than Americentrism.

In school districts where most children are black and Hispanic, there has   31
been a growing tendency to embrace particularism rather than pluralism. Many of the children in these districts perform poorly in academic classes and leave school without graduating. They would fare better in school if they had well-educated and well-paid teachers, small classes, good materials, en-

couragement at home and school, summer academic programs, protection from the drugs and crime that ravage their neighborhoods, and higher expectations of satisfying careers upon graduation. These are expensive and time-consuming remedies that must also engage the larger society beyond the school. The lure of particularism is that it offers a less complicated anodyne, one in which the children's academic deficiencies may be addressed—or set aside—by inflating their racial pride. The danger of this remedy is that it will detract attention from the real needs of schools and the real interests of children, while simultaneously arousing distorted race pride in children of all races, increasing racial antagonism and producing fresh recruits for white and black racist groups.

The particularist critique gained a major forum in New York in 1989, with 32 the release of a report called "A Curriculum of Inclusion," produced by a task force created by the State Commissioner of Education, Thomas Sobol. In 1987, soon after his appointment, Sobol appointed a Task Force on Minorities to review the state's curriculum for instances of bias. He did this not because there had been complaints about bias in the curriculum, but because—as a newly appointed state commissioner whose previous job had been to superintend the public schools of a wealthy suburb, Scarsdale—he wanted to demonstrate his sensitivity to minority concerns. The Sobol task force was composed of representatives of African American, Hispanic, Asian American, and American Indian groups.

The task force engaged four consultants, one from each of the aforemen- 33 tioned racial or ethnic minorities, to review nearly one hundred teachers' guides prepared by the state. These guides define the state's curriculum, usually as a list of facts and concepts to be taught, along with model activities. The primary focus of the consultants, not surprisingly, was the history and social studies curriculum. As it happened, the history curriculum had been extensively revised in 1987 to make it multicultural, in both American and world history. In the 1987 revision the time given to Western Europe was reduced to one-quarter of one year, as part of a two-year global studies sequence in which equal time was allotted to seven major world regions, including Africa and Latin America.

As a result of the 1987 revisions in American and world history, New York 34 State had one of the most advanced multicultural history-social studies curricula in the country. Dozens of social studies teachers and consultants had participated, and the final draft was reviewed by such historians as Eric Foner of Columbia University, the late Hazel Hertzberg of Teachers College, Columbia University, and Christopher Lasch of the University of Rochester. The curriculum was overloaded with facts, almost to the point of numbing students with details and trivia, but it was not insensitive to ethnicity in American history or unduly devoted to European history.

But the Sobol task force decided that this curriculum was biased and Eu- 35 rocentric. The first sentence of the task force report summarizes its major thesis: "African Americans, Asian Americans, Puerto Ricans/Latinos, and Native

Americans have all been the victims of an intellectual and educational oppression that has characterized the culture and institutions of the United States and the European American world for centuries."

The task force report was remarkable in that it vigorously denounced bias 36 without identifying a single instance of bias in the curricular guides under review. Instead, the consultants employed harsh, sometimes inflammatory, rhetoric to treat every difference of opinion or interpretation as an example of racial bias. The African-American consultant, for example, excoriates the curriculum for its "White Anglo-Saxon (WASP) value system and norms," its "deep-seated pathologies of racial hatred" and its "white nationalism"; he decries as bias the fact that children study Egypt as part of the Middle East instead of as part of Africa. Perhaps Egypt should be studied as part of the African unit (geographically, it is located on the African continent); but placing it in one region rather than the other is not what most people think of as racism or bias. The "Latino" consultant criticizes the use of the term "Spanish-American War" instead of "Spanish-Cuban-American War." The Native American consultant complains that tribal languages are classified as "foreign languages."

The report is consistently Europhobic. It repeatedly expresses negative 37 judgments on "European Americans" and on everything Western and European. All people with a white skin are referred to as "Anglo-Saxons" and "WASPs." Europe, says the report, is uniquely responsible for producing aggressive individuals who "were ready to 'discover, invade and conquer' foreign land because of greed, racism and national egoism." All white people are held collectively guilty for the historical crimes of slavery and racism. There is no mention of the "Anglo-Saxons" who opposed slavery and racism. Nor does the report acknowledge that some whites have been victims of discrimination and oppression. The African American consultant writes of the Constitution, "There is something vulgar and revolting in glorifying a process that heaped undeserved rewards on a segment of the population while oppressing the majority."

The New York task force proposal is not merely about the reconstruction 38 of what is taught. It goes a step further to suggest that the history curriculum may be used to ensure that "children from Native American, Puerto Rican/Latino, Asian American, and African American cultures will have higher self-esteem and self-respect, while children from European cultures will have a less arrogant perspective of being part of the group that has 'done it all.'"

In February 1990, Commissioner Sobol asked the New York Board of Regents to endorse a sweeping revision of the history curriculum to make it more multicultural. His recommendations were couched in measured tones, not in the angry rhetoric of his task force. The board supported his request unanimously. It remains to be seen whether New York pursues the particularist path marked out by the Commissioner's advisory group or finds its way to the concept of pluralism within a democratic tradition.

The rising tide of particularism encourages the politicization of all curric-   40
ula in the schools. If education bureaucrats bend to the political and ideological winds, as is their wont, we can anticipate a generation of struggle over
the content of the curriculum in mathematics, science, literature, and history. Demands for "culturally relevant" studies, for ethnostudies of all kinds,
will open the classroom to unending battles over whose version is taught,
who gets credit for what, and which ethno-interpretation is appropriate.
Only recently have districts begun to resist the demands of fundamentalist
groups to censor textbooks and library books (and some have not yet begun
to do so).

The spread of particularism throws into question the very idea of Ameri-   41
can public education. Public schools exist to teach children the general skills
and knowledge that they need to succeed in American society, and the specific skills and knowledge that they need in order to function as American citizens. They receive public support because they have a public function.
Historically, the public schools were known as "common schools" because
they were schools for all, even if the children of all the people did not attend
them. Over the years, the courts have found that it was unconstitutional to
teach religion in the common schools, or to separate children on the basis of
their race in the common schools. In their curriculum, their hiring practices,
and their general philosophy, the public schools must not discriminate
against or give preference to any racial or ethnic group. Yet they are permitted to accommodate cultural diversity by, for example, serving food that is
culturally appropriate or providing library collections that emphasize the interests of the local community. However, they should not be expected to
teach children to view the world through an ethnocentric perspective that rejects or ignores the common culture. For generations, those groups that
wanted to inculcate their religion or their ethnic heritage have instituted private schools—after school, on weekends, or on a full-time basis. There, children learn with others of the same group—Greeks, Poles, Germans, Japanese,
Chinese, Jews, Lutherans, Catholics, and so on—and are taught by people
from the same group. Valuable as this exclusive experience has been for those
who choose it, this has not been the role of public education. One of the primary purposes of public education has been to create a national community,
a definition of citizenship and culture that is both expansive and *inclusive*.

The curriculum in public schools must be based on whatever knowledge   42
and practices have been determined to be best by professionals—experienced
teachers and scholars—who are competent to make these judgments. Professional societies must be prepared to defend the integrity of their disciplines.
When called upon, they should establish review committees to examine disputes over curriculum and to render judgment, in order to help school officials fend off improper political pressure. Where genuine controversies exist,
they should be taught and debated in the classroom. Was Egypt a black civilization? Why not raise the question, read the arguments of the different
sides in the debate, show slides of Egyptian pharoahs and queens, read books
about life in ancient Egypt, invite guest scholars from the local university,

and visit museums with Egyptian collections? If scholars disagree, students should know it. One great advantage of this approach is that students will see that history is a lively study, that textbooks are fallible, that historians disagree, that the writing of history is influenced by the historian's politics and ideology, that history is written by people who make choices among alternative facts and interpretations, and that history changes as new facts are uncovered and new interpretations win adherents. They will also learn that cultures and civilizations constantly interact, exchange ideas, and influence one another, and that the idea of racial or ethnic purity is a myth. Another advantage is that students might once again study ancient history, which has all but disappeared from the curricula of American schools. (California recently introduced a required sixth grade course in ancient civilizations, but ancient history is otherwise *terra incognita* in American education.)

The multicultural controversy may do wonders for the study of history, which has been neglected for years in American schools. At this time, only half of our high school graduates ever study any world history. Any serious attempt to broaden students' knowledge of Africa, Europe, Asia, and Latin America will require at least two, and possibly three years of world history (a requirement thus far only in California). American history, too, will need more time than the one-year high-school survey course. Those of us who have insisted for years on the importance of history in the curriculum may not be ready to assent to its redemptive power, but hope that our new allies will ultimately join a constructive dialogue that strengthens the place of history in the schools. 43

As cultural controversies arise, educators must adhere to the principle of "E Pluribus Unum." That is, they must maintain a balance between the demands of the one—the nation of which we are common citizens—and the many—the varied histories of the American people. It is not necessary to denigrate either the one or the many. Pluralism is a positive value, but it is also important that we preserve a sense of an American community—a society and a culture to which we all belong. If there is no overall community with an agreed-upon vision of liberty and justice, if all we have is a collection of racial and ethnic cultures, lacking any common bonds, then we have no means to mobilize public opinion on behalf of people who are not members of our particular group. We have, for example, no reason to support public education. If there is no larger community, then each group will want to teach its own children in its own way, and public education ceases to exist. 44

History should not be confused with filiopietism. History gives no grounds for race pride. No race has a monopoly on virtue. If anything, a study of history should inspire humility, rather than pride. People of every racial group have committed terrible crimes, often against others of the same group. Whether one looks at the history of Europe or Africa or Latin America or Asia, every continent offers examples of inhumanity. Slavery has existed in civilizations around the world for centuries. Examples of genocide can be found around the world, throughout history, from ancient times right through to our own day. Governments and cultures, sometimes by edict, 45 sometimes simply following tradition, have practiced not only slavery, but human sacrifice, infanticide, cliterodectomy, and mass murder. If we teach children this, they might recognize how absurd both racial hatred and racial chauvinism are.

What must be preserved in the study of history is the spirit of inquiry, the readiness to open new questions and to pursue new understandings. History, at its best, is a search for truth. The best way to portray this search is through debate and controversy, rather than through imposition of fixed beliefs and immutable facts. Perhaps the most dangerous aspect of school history is its tendency to become Official History, a sanctified version of the Truth taught by the state to captive audiences and embedded in beautiful mass-market textbooks as holy writ. When Official History is written by committees responding to political pressures, rather than by scholars synthesizing the best available research, then the errors of the past are replaced by the politically fashionable errors of the present. It may be difficult to teach children that history is both important and uncertain, and that even the best historians never have all the pieces of the jigsaw puzzle, but it is necessary to do so. If state education departments permit the revision of their history courses and textbooks to become an exercise in power politics, then the entire process of state-level curriculum-making becomes suspect, as does public education itself.

The question of self-esteem is extraordinarily complex, and it goes well beyond the content of the curriculum. Most of what we call self-esteem is formed in the home and in a variety of life experiences, not only in school. Nonetheless, it has been important for blacks—and for other racial groups— to learn about the history of slavery and of the civil rights movement; it has been important for blacks to know that their ancestors actively resisted enslavement and actively pursued equality; and it has been important for blacks and others to learn about black men and women who fought courageously against racism and who provide models of courage, persistence, and intellect. These are instances where the content of the curriculum reflects sound scholarship, and at the same time probably lessens racial prejudice and provides inspiration for those who are descendants of slaves. But knowing about the travails and triumphs of one's forebears does not necessarily translate into either self-esteem or personal accomplishment. For most children, self-esteem—the self-confidence that grows out of having reached a goal—comes not from hearing about the monuments of their ancestors but as a consequence of what they are able to do and accomplish through their own efforts.

As I reflected on these issues, I recalled reading an interview a few years ago with a talented black runner. She said that her model is Mikhail Baryshnikov. She admires him because he is a magnificent athlete. He is not black; he is not female; he is not American-born; he is not even a runner. But he inspires her because of the way he trained and used his body. When I read this, I thought how narrow-minded it is to believe that people can be inspired *only* by those who are exactly like them in race and ethnicity.

Questions

1. Reflect on your high school history classes. Would you describe the curriculum as "multicultural" or "Eurocentric"? Why?

2. Why do particularists oppose teaching a "common culture"?

3. Do you agree that pride in one's culture or heritage may also lead to hostility?

4. Ravitch's underlying concern is how to get marginalized ethnic minorities to perform better in school. Do you agree with her proposed curriculum? Does it have any drawbacks or problems?

5. Compare Ravitch's and Schlesinger's essays later in this chapter. In what ways do they agree or disagree?

Beyond the Melting Pot

This article questions the various labels used to define America's increasing cultural diversity, and whether the melting pot metaphor implies hegemony or harmony. The essay also explores the social, political, and economic impact this multiculturalism will have on American society and whether this pluralism will lead to cultural fragmentation. This article is from the Los Angeles Times *(1991).*

Blending in was once considered the ideal. But as the racial and ethnic nature 1
of the nation has changed, so has that ideal.

Throughout the nation, and especially in California, *multiculturalism*— 2
the concept of looking at the world through the eyes of more than one culture—is the new end-of-the-millennium buzzword.

The notion of the melting pot has seen "an astonishing repudiation," 3
said historian Arthur Schlesinger Jr. in the Wall Street Journal last year. "The contemporary ideal is not assimilation but ethnicity. We used to say *e pluribus unum*. Now we glorify *pluribus* and belittle *unum*. The melting pot yields to the Tower of Babel."

We have heard about the demographic future—seen it in Los Angeles 4
where 90 foreign languages are spoken in the public schools—but no one is sure how to define it.

Some say we should call it multiculturalism, or cultural pluralism—the 5
politically correct term on many college campuses. Or is it a salad? A mosaic? A patchwork quilt? Or is it possible to hold onto the beloved melting pot and just admit there are new ingredients in the stew?

The questions over how we define ourselves are triggered by population 6
shifts that will lead us to what demographers say will be the new majority in 21st-Century America: people of color.

A Time magazine article last year proclaimed: "By 2056, when someone 7
born today will be 66 years old, the 'average' U.S. resident will trace his or her descent to Africa, Asia, the Hispanic world, the Pacific Islands, Arabia—almost anywhere but white Europe."

This already is a reality in Southern California, where ethnic and racial 8
"minorities" compose the majority.

As 1991 begins, interpretations of multiculturalism versus the melting 9
pot are contentious and contradictory, especially among scholars on college campuses.

"Multiculturalism? I don't use it in the sense it's used today," said a leery   10
Shelby Steele, author of a widely touted book about race in America, "The
Content of Our Character." "I think it's used today as a power term.

"Behind it, you usually have people lined up demanding things: separate   11
black studies, Asian studies, women's studies. They are usually making demands on the system and the focus is on whatever their power needs are,
rather than any exposition of the culture," said Steele, an English professor at
San Jose State University.

However, sociologist Margaret L. Andersen is among those urging the   12
new multicultural century to "come on down." Multicultural studies "have
encouraged us to look at traditionally excluded cultures and study them on
their own terms rather than seeing them through the eyes of the dominant
class," said the associate provost for instruction at the University of Delaware
in Newark.

But the "spirit of multiculturalism" is not separatist, Andersen said. "It is   13
to enable people to see in plural ways, so that they are not seeing through the
lens of any single culture, but understanding the relationships of cultures to
each other. . . . "

What must yield, said literary critic and historian Henry Louis Gates, is   14
the "antebellum aesthetic position, where men were men, and men were
white, when scholar-critics were white men, and when women and persons
of color were voiceless, faceless servants and laborers, pouring tea and filling
brandy snifters in the boardrooms of old boys' clubs."

It means having "a double consciousness," said George Spindler, profes-   15
sor emeritus of anthropology at Stanford University. It means, in everyday
terms, not having to live through this seemingly surreal but true and recent
L.A. experience:

"Well now," said the blond nurse, smiling at the tense woman on the doc-   16
tor's examining table. "Don't worry if you bleed too much. I'll give you some
of my blood," she offered, then gently stroked the black woman's arm. "But
you know what they say about getting one drop of black blood," she began,
then spun into, "One drop makes you black. I heard that all my life growing
up in New Orleans. One drop does it to you, that's what I heard. . . . "

* * *

The melting pot has its defenders.   17

"I subscribe to the notion of the melting pot," said Karen Klein, a profes-   18
sor of English literature at Brandeis University and the director of a Ford
Foundation-funded project to diversify the university's curriculum. It is one
of 19 such projects nationwide funded by the foundation.

"There is a certain homogenous culture in the U.S. that is best exempli-   19
fied by something like motels"—the notion that if you've seen one Howard
Johnson's, you've seen them all. "But the melting pot concept has never
meant that we give up our sense of pluralistic identity," she said.

But isn't that exactly what the concept represents?   20

"Yes," she said, "but I am trying to redefine it."   21

Pot salvagers seek to minimize what Harvard University professor Werner   22
Sollors acknowledged is "sinister dominance." But there is a flip side to the
smelting notion, said Sollors, an expert on Afro-American literature and ethnic images in American literature as well as the author of "Beyond Ethnicity"—which provided the Ford Motor Co. Melting Pot School anecdote.

"What I like about the melting pot better than those other terms is the   23
process that is implicit in it"—a culture constantly in change:

"Japanese technology is sold by Hasidic Jews on 47th Street to imagina-   24
tive artists who . . . living in Harlem or Brooklyn use this technology to create
rap," which becomes a national music that is exported.

* * *

So far, most of the national debate about multiculturalism has occurred   25
on college campuses, but in California, the ideology of multiculturalism res-
onates far beyond the classroom.

Among the questions being raised: 26

- How will the race or ethnicity of the new majority influence the fundamental character of American society?
- Who will hold political, social as well as cultural power in an ethnically
  transformed America?
- Do we need a new social lexicon to define the changed and changing
  social landscape?
- What does the state's growing multiracial population, and its demands
  for official recognition on the U.S. Census, suggest about the nature of
  ethnic and racial identity in America?
- What will be the nature of relations among people of color, the emerging
  majority?
- What are the hopes and fears of the Anglo population in this changing
  environment?

In asking these questions and talking about them, "Californians are 75%   27
ahead of almost anybody in the country, until you get to some of the metropolitan centers of the East Coast," said Stanford's Spindler, who with his wife,
Louise, wrote "The American Cultural Dialogue and Its Transmission."

These questions are new, but the fundamental issues have been central to   28
American life for more than 200 years. Independence, freedom, conformity,
success, community, optimism, cynicism, idealism, materialism, technology,
nature and work have been the pivotal issues in the nation's cultural dialogue, the Spindlers conclude in their book.

"The balancing of assimilation and preservation of identity is constant   29
and full of conflict," they write.

Those arguing against pluralism have to recognize the need to expand   30
America's political, economic and social base with new blood, new ideas, new
cultural styles.

However, no nation can survive if it is truly pluralistic. 31

"Large groups of people with really separate identities and languages . . . 32
wouldn't be a nation," Spindler said. "The fact that the Soviet Union is breaking up right now is a case in point."

Said Spindler: "I have real questions as to whether we are going to survive 33
as a society, because it is not just a matter of ethnic combat. It is combat between pro-lifers and pro-choicers, between environmentalists and exploiters
and developers and so on. There isn't an area of American life where there
isn't a polarized opposition."

That's why the term *multiculturalism* does not accurately describe the 34
complex dynamics of current American society, sociologist Andersen said.
Multiculturalism is really about "culture and the intersection of culture with
social power." But the term *multiculturalism* obscures the issue of power, she
said.

Power implies access to economic, political and social resources, Ander- 35
sen said. "By social resources I mean how people are perceived, how they are
valued, what significance their culture is seen as having."

Linda Wong, executive director of California Tomorrow, a research and 36
advocacy organization agreed: "We need a new social lexicon to describe the
changing dynamics of American society."

In trying to get a better understanding of what multiculturalism means 37
and how the term evolved, Wong said she looked at affirmative action, diversity and cultural pluralism by turning to the civil rights movement.

"Clearly, that was the most coherent social movement to bring issues of 38
race, ethnicity and cultural pluralism to the forefront of American life," she
said. Laws were enacted "requiring equal opportunity and equal access for disenfranchised peoples in terms of gender, race, ethnicity, age and religion."

"We [tried to] eliminate differences based on gender, race or ethnicity," 39
said Wong, a former practicing attorney. The philosophy then was "colorblindness."

But did colorblindness lead to equal opportunity, equal access? It seldom 40
did, she said. Consequently, affirmative-action policies were developed and
goals and timetables were created.

"And what we found," said Wong—even in cases where benchmarks were 41
reached—"was that we could not keep the women, we could not keep the
blacks or the Latinos hired under those affirmative-action programs."

Why? Because whether it was in the private or public sector "they had to 42
accommodate themselves to a dominant culture"—Euro-Americans in general and Anglo, middle-class males in particular—"with its own set of values
and conduct deemed to be acceptable for success."

Women, blacks, Latinos and Asians couldn't accommodate themselves to 43
this environment and found they were hitting the proverbial glass ceiling.

"Many times, they found that their values, their conduct, their behavior 44
was misinterpreted by those belonging to the dominant culture in those organizational settings. So they left [the organization]," she said.

Increasingly, "as we move into this third generation of understanding,   45
people prefer to use the term *diversity*," Wong said. It doesn't automatically
conjure associations with affirmative action, she pointed out.

And it seems less loaded than multiculturalism, which in 1990 buzzed   46
638 times through the pages of the Los Angeles Times, the New York Times,
the Washington Post and the Wall Street Journal. On the other hand, "melting pot" appeared 307 times, and "cultural pluralism" finished with 13 in the
race to define the nature of America's increasingly diverse population.

Whichever word one chooses, "people are just coming to grips" with   47
what they mean, Wong said. Many corporations are training managers to
work with different styles of communication and approaches to problem-
solving. "This kind of diversity unleashes the creative, entrepreneurial potential that lies in gender-, culture- or socially based differences," Wong said.

While corporations and schools in California have begun to embrace this   48
concept of diversity, "it has not taken hold in other public institutions," said
Wong, who says it will take more than moral persuasion to make it work.

"I hate to use this analogy, but it is an accurate one," Wong said. "Califor-   49
nia—eventually the nation, if the demographic predictions are correct—is a
lifeboat. If the boat is springing leaks because of inadequate and poor quality
education, because of deepening poverty . . . the people who are sitting in the
boat are going to figure out some way of plugging those leaks and working together if they value their lives."

But no one should be misled by the "browning of America," as some have   50
labeled the demographic shifts in progress. It doesn't signal a change in the
power structure.

Education equals participation and success, said George Spindler. "It's a   51
simple equation. And if whites continue to have the best, the longest . . . the
most professional kinds of educational experience," they are going to stay in
control.

But, Spindler added: "If you have a large mass of blacks or Latinos who   52
are educated, or even a smaller group who are superiorly educated, eventually
this inequality is going to break down. But for most groups, it takes perhaps
three generations to attain that competitive socioeconomic status."

***

Potentially the most significant phenomenon in the next decades will   53
be the emergence of the multiracial population. In the United States, interracial marriages tripled from 310,000 in 1970 to 956,000 in 1988. An
estimated 1 to 2 million children have been born to interracial couples
since about 1970, according to an expert on multiracial children. And early
reports show an increase in the number of people who called themselves
"multiracial" or "biracial" on the 1990 census, according to the U.S. Census
Bureau.

The discussion generated by this new multiethnic generation is going to   54
stimulate a decades-long debate—one that may force Americans to confront
the myths that surround race and ethnicity in the United States.

What the coming multicultural, polyethnic, pluralistic—unarguably di- 55
verse—America will be no one knows for certain. There are no models anywhere for what is happening here. America is the experiment and California
is the first on-line lab.

Questions

1. According to the article what are the dangers inherent in both the melting pot
   and the salad metaphors for cultural pluralism?
2. Has the increasing cultural pluralism had any effect on your life or your education?
3. Compare the analysis in this article with Schlesinger's perspective (see next selection). With which points in this article would Schlesinger be most likely to agree?

The Decomposition of America

ARTHUR M. SCHLESINGER, JR.

Arthur M. Schlesinger, Jr. (b. 1917) currently teaches at the graduate school at University Center of City University in New York. He has received two Pulitzer Prizes, and served as a special advisor to John F. Kennedy (1961– 1964). He has published numerous books on political history and is perhaps best known for A Thousand Days: John F. Kennedy in the White House *(1965), and recently for* The Disuniting of America *(1992).*

In this excerpt, Schlesinger warns us of the dangers of separatism: the "cult of ethnicity" and bilingualism that are supposed to affirm racial and cultural pride lead instead to fragmentation, segregation, and racial hostility. However, he argues, cohesion and harmony can result from our continued devotion to democracy and human rights. This selection is from The Disuniting of America.

I

The ethnicity rage in general and Afrocentricity in particular not only divert attention from the real needs but exacerbate the problems. The recent apotheosis of ethnicity, black, brown, red, yellow, white, has revived the dismal prospect that in happy melting-pot days Americans thought the republic was moving safely beyond—that is, a society fragmented into separate ethnic communities. The cult of ethnicity exaggerates differences, intensifies resentments and antagonisms, drives ever deeper the awful wedges between races and nationalities. The endgame is self-pity and self-ghettoization.   1

Now there is a reasonable argument in the black case for a measure of regrouping and self-reliance as part of the preparation for entry into an integrated society on an equal basis. Integration on any other basis, it is contended, would mean total capitulation to white standards. Affirmation of racial and cultural pride is thus essential to true integration. One can see this as a psychological point, but as a cultural point?   2

For generations blacks have grown up in an American culture, on which they have had significant influence and to which they have made significant contributions. Self-Africanization after 300 years in America is playacting. Afrocentricity as expounded by ethnic ideologues implies Europhobia, separatism, emotions of alienation, victimization, paranoia. Most curious and unexpected of all is a black demand for the return of black-white segregation.   3

"To separate [black children] from others of similar age and qualifications solely because of their race," Chief Justice Warren wrote in the school-integration case, "generates a feeling of inferiority as to their status in the community that may affect their hearts and minds in a way unlikely ever to be undone." In 40 years doctrine has come full circle. Now integration is held to bring feelings of inferiority, and segregation to bring the cure. 4

This revival of separatism will begin, if the black educator Felix Boateng has his way, in the earliest grades. "The use of standard English as the only language of instruction," Boateng argues, "aggravates the process of deculturalization." A "culturally relevant curriculum" for minority children would recognize "the home and community dialect they bring to school." (Not all black educators, it should be said, share this desire to handicap black children from infancy. "One fact is clear," notes Janice Hale-Benson of Cleveland State University. "Speaking standard English is a skill needed by Black children for upward mobility in American society and it should be taught in early childhood.") 5

If any educational institution should bring people together as individuals in friendly and civil association, it should be the university. But the fragmentation of campuses in recent years into a multitude of ethnic organizations is spectacular—and disconcerting. 6

One finds black dormitories, black student unions, black fraternities and sororities, black business and law societies, black homosexual and lesbian groups, black tables in dining halls. Stanford, Dinesh D'Souza reports, has "ethnic theme houses." The University of Pennsylvania gives blacks—6 percent of the enrollment—their own yearbook. Campuses today, according to one University of Pennsylvania professor, have "the cultural diversity of Beirut. There are separate armed camps. The black kids don't mix with the white kids. The Asians are off by themselves. Oppression is the great status symbol." 7

Oberlin was for a century and half the model of a racially integrated college. "Increasingly," Jacob Weisberg, an editor at *The New Republic,* reports, "Oberlin students think, act, study, and live apart." Asians live in Asia House, Jews in "J" House, Latinos in Spanish House, blacks in African-Heritage House, foreign students in Third World House. Even the Lesbian, Gay, and Bisexual Union has broken up into racial and gender factions. "The result is separate worlds." 8

Huddling is an understandable reaction for any minority group faced with new and scary challenges. But institutionalized separatism only crystallizes racial differences and magnifies racial tensions. "Certain activities are labeled white and black," says a black student at Central Michigan University. "If you don't just participate in black activities, you are shunned." A recent study by the black anthropologist Signithia Fordham of Rutgers concludes that a big reason for black underachievement is the fear that academic success will be taken as a sellout to the white world. "What appears to have emerged in some segments of the black community," Fordham says, "is a 9 kind of cultural orientation which defines academic learning in school as `acting white.'"

Militants further argue that because only blacks can comprehend the   10
black experience, only blacks should teach black history and literature, as, in the view of some feminists, only women should teach women's history and literature. "True diversity," according to the faculty's Budget Committee at the University of California at Berkeley, requires that courses match the ethnic and gender identities of the professors.

The doctrine that *only* blacks can teach and write black history leads inex-   11
orably to the doctrine that blacks can teach and write *only* black history as well as to inescapable corollaries: Chinese must be restricted to Chinese history, women to women's history, and so on. Henry Louis Gates criticizes "ghettoized programs where students and members of the faculty sit around and argue about whether a white person can think a black thought." As for the notion that there is a "mystique" about black studies that requires a person to have black skin in order to pursue them—that, John Hope Franklin observes succinctly, is "voodoo."

The voodoo principle is extended from scholarship to the arts. Thus the   12
fine black playwright August Wilson insists on a black director for the film of his play *Fences*. "We have a different way of responding to the world," Wilson explains. "We have different ideas about religion, different manners of social intercourse. We have different ideas about style, about language. We have different esthetics [*sic*]. . . . The job requires someone who shares the specifics of the culture of black Americans. . . . Let's make a rule. Blacks don't direct Italian films. Italians don't direct Jewish films. Jews don't direct black American films." What a terrible rule that would be!

In the same restrictive spirit, Actors' Equity tried to prevent the British ac-   13
tor Jonathan Pryce from playing in New York the role he created in London in *Miss Saigon,* announcing that it could not condone "the casting of a Caucasian actor in the role of a Eurasian." (Pryce responded that, if this doctrine prevails, "I'd be stuck playing Welshmen for the rest of my life.") Equity did not, however, apply the same principle to the black actors Morgan Freeman and Denzel Washington who were both acting in Shakespeare at that time in New York. *The Wall Street Journal* acidly suggested that, according to the principle invoked, not only whites but the disabled should protest the casting of Denzel Washington as Richard III because Washington lacked a hunchback.

The distinguished black social psychologist Kenneth B. Clark, whose find-   14
ings influenced the Supreme Court's decision in the school-integration case, rejects the argument that blacks and whites must be separated "because they represent different cultures and that cultures, like oil and water, cannot mix." This, Clark says, is what white segregationists have argued for generations. He adds, "There is absolutely no evidence to support the contention that the inherent damage to human beings of primitive exclusion on the basis of race is any less damaging when demanded or enforced by the previous victims than when imposed by the dominant group."

II

The separatist impulse is by no means confined to the black community. An- 15
other salient expression is the bilingualism movement, ostensibly conducted
in the interests of all non-English speakers but particularly a Hispanic-American project.

Bilingualism is hardly a new issue in American history. Seven years after 16
the adoption of the Constitution, a proposal to print 3,000 sets of federal
laws in German as well as English was narrowly defeated in the House of Representatives. (This incident gave rise to the myth, later cherished by Nazi pro-
pagandists like Colin Ross, that German had nearly displaced English as
America's official language.) In the nineteenth century, newly arrived immigrants stayed for a season with their old language, used it in their homes,
churches, newspapers, and not seldom in bilingual public schools, until acculturation reduced and the First World War discouraged the use of languages
other than English.

In recent years the combination of the ethnicity cult with a flood of immi- 17
gration from Spanish-speaking countries has given bilingualism new impetus.
The presumed purpose is transitional: to move non-English-speaking children
as quickly as possible from bilingual into all-English classes. The Bilingual Education Act of 1968 supplies guidelines and funding; the 1974 Supreme Court
decision in *Lau* v. *Nichols* (a Chinese-speaking case) requires school districts to
provide special programs for children who do not know English.

Alas, bilingualism has not worked out as planned: rather the contrary. 18
Testimony is mixed, but indications are that bilingual education retards
rather than expedites the movement of Hispanic children into the English-
speaking world and that it promotes segregation more than it does integration. Bilingualism shuts doors. It nourishes self-ghettoization, and
ghettoization nourishes racial antagonism. Bilingualism "encourages concen-
trations of Hispanics to stay together and not be integrated," says Alfredo
Matthew Jr., a Hispanic civic leader, and it may well foster "a type of
apartheid that will generate animosities with others, such as Blacks, in the
competition for scarce resources, and further alienate the Hispanic from the
larger society."

Using some language other than English dooms people to second-class citi- 19
zenship in American society. "Those who have the most to lose in a bilingual
America," says the Mexican-American writer Richard Rodriguez, "are the for-
eign-speaking poor." Rodriguez recalls his own boyhood: "It would have
pleased me to hear my teachers address me in Spanish....But I would have delayed...having to learn the language of public society....Only when I was able
to think of myself as an American, no longer an alien in *gringo* society, could I
seek the rights and opportunities necessary for full public individuality."

Monolingual education opens doors to the larger world. "I didn't speak 20
English until I was about 8 years of age," Governor Mario Cuomo recently recalled, "and there was a kind of traumatic entry into public school. It made

an immense impression on me." Traumatic or not, public school taught Cuomo the most effective English among politicos of his generation.

Yet a professor at the University of Massachusetts told Rosalie Pedalino   21
Porter, whose long experience in bilingual education led to her excellent book *Forked Tongue,* that teaching English to children reared in another language is a form of political oppression. Her rejoinder seems admirable: "When we succeed in helping our students use the majority language fluently . . . we are empowering our students rather than depriving them."

Panicky conservatives, fearful that the republic is over the hill, call for a   22
constitutional amendment to make English the official language of the United States. Seventeen states already have such statutes. This is a poor idea. The English language does not need statutory reinforcement and the drive for an amendment will only increase racial discrimination and resentment.

Nonetheless, a common language is a necessary bond of national cohe-   23
sion in so heterogeneous a nation as America. The bilingual campaign has created both an educational establishment with a vested interest in extending the bilingual empire and a political lobby with a vested interest in retaining a Hispanic constituency. Like Afrocentricity and the ethnicity cult, bilingualism is an elitist, not a popular, movement—"romantic ethnicity," as Myrdal called it; political ethnicity too. Still, institutionalized bilingualism remains another source of the fragmentation of America, another threat to the dream of "one people."

III

Most ominous about the separatist impulses is the meanness generated when   24
one group is set against another. What Harold Isaacs, that acute student of racial sensitivities and resentments, called the "built-in we-they syndrome" has caused more dominating, fearing, hating, killing than any other single cause since time began.

Blacks, having suffered most grievously (at least in America) from perse-   25
cution, have perhaps the greatest susceptibility to paranoia—remembering always that even paranoids may have real enemies. After all, considering what we now know about the plots against black Americans concocted by J. Edgar Hoover and executed by his FBI, who can blame blacks for being forever suspicious of white intentions?

Still, the *New York Times*–WCBS-TV poll of New Yorkers in 1990 is star-   26
tling. Sixty percent of black respondents thought it true or possibly true that the government was making drugs available in black neighborhoods in order to harm black people. Twenty-nine percent thought it true or possibly true that the AIDS virus was invented by racist conspirators to kill blacks.

When Mayor Edward Koch invited the irrepressible Leonard Jeffries of   27
CCNY to breakfast to discuss the "ice people-sun people" theory, Jeffries agreed to come "but said he would not eat because white people were trying to poison him. When he arrived," Koch reports, "I offered him coffee and danish, but he refused it. I then offered to be his food taster, but he still declined."

On another occasion, Jeffries observed that "AIDS coming out of a labora- 28
tory and finding itself localized in certain populations certainly has to be
looked at as part of a conspiratorial process." After a Jeffries class, 10 black
students told the *Times* reporter that AIDS and drugs were indeed part of a
white conspiracy. "During the Carter administration," one said, "there was a
document put out that said by the year 2000, one hundred billion Africans
had to be destroyed." "Because of who's being devastated the most, and growing up in the U.S. and knowing the history of slavery and racism in this country," an older black man said, "you can't be black and not feel that AIDS is
some kind of experiment, some kind of plot to hit undesirable minority populations."

Nor is such speculation confined to the feverish sidewalks of New York. 29
"Let me make a speech before a black audience," testifies William Raspberry,
"and sometime during the Q & A someone is certain to ask if I believe there is
a conspiracy against black Americans. It doesn't matter whether the subject is
drugs or joblessness, school failure or teen pregnancy, politics or immigration. I can count on hearing some version of the conspiracy question."

The black case is only a more extreme version of the persecution com- 30
plex—the feeling that someone is out to get them—to which nearly all minorities on occasion succumb. Mutual suspicion and hostility are bound to
emerge in a society bent on defining itself in terms of jostling and competing
groups.

IV

"The era that began with the dream of integration," Richard Rodriguez has 31
observed, "ended up with scorn for assimilation." Instead of casting off the
foreign skin, as John Quincy Adams had stipulated, never to resume it, the
fashion is to resume the foreign skin as conspicuously as can be. The cult of
ethnicity has reversed the movement of American history, producing a nation of minorities—or at least of minority spokesmen—less interested in joining with the majority in common endeavor than in declaring their alienation
from an oppressive, white, patriarchal, racist, sexist, classist society. The ethnic ideology inculcates the illusion that membership in one or another ethnic group is the basic American experience.

Most Americans, it is true, continue to see themselves primarily as indi- 32
viduals and only secondarily and trivially as adherents of a group. Nor is
harm done when ethnic groups display pride in their historic past or in their
contributions to the American present. But the division of society into fixed
ethnicities nourishes a culture of victimization and a contagion of inflammable sensitivities. And when a vocal and visible minority pledges primary allegiance to their groups, whether ethnic, sexual, religious, or, in rare cases
(communist, fascist), political, it presents a threat to the brittle bonds of national identity that hold this diverse and fractious society together.

A peculiarly ugly mood seems to have settled over the one arena where 33
freedom of inquiry and expression should be most unconstrained and civility

most respected—our colleges and universities. It is no fun running a university these days. Undergraduates can be wanton and cruel in their exclusion, their harassment, their heavy pranks, their wounding invective. Minority students, for the most understandable reasons, are often vulnerable and frightened. Racial cracks, slurs, insults, vilification pose difficult problems. Thus posters appear around the campus at the University of Michigan parodying the slogan of the United Negro College Fund: A MIND IS A TERRIBLE THING TO WASTE—ESPECIALLY ON A NIGGER. Decent white students join the protest against white bullies and thugs.

Presidents and deans begin to ask themselves, which is more important—   34 protecting free speech or preventing racial persecution? The Constitution, Justice Holmes said, embodies "the principle of free thought—not free thought for those who agree with us but freedom for the thought that we hate." But suppose the thought we hate undercuts the Constitution's ideal of equal justice under law? Does not the First Amendment protect equality as well as liberty? how to draw a bright line between speech and behavior?

One has a certain sympathy for besieged administrators who, trying to do   35 their best to help minority students, adopt regulations to restrict racist and sexist speech. More than a hundred institutions, according to the American Civil Liberties Union, had done so by February 1991. My own decided preference is to stand by the First Amendment and to fight speech by speech, not by censorship. But then, I am not there on the firing line.

One can even understand why administrators, not sure what best to do for   36 minorities and eager to keep things quiet, accept—even subsidize—separatist remedies urged by student militants. They might, however, ponder Kenneth Clark's comment: "The white liberal . . . who concedes black separatism so hastily and benevolently must look to his own reasons, not the least of them perhaps an exquisite relief." And it is sad, though instructive, that the administrations especially disposed to encourage racial and ethnic enclaves—like Berkeley, Michigan, Oberlin, the University of Massachusetts at Amherst—are, Dinesh D'Souza (himself an Indian from India) points out, the ones experiencing the most racial tension. Troy Duster, a Berkeley sociologist, finds a correlation between group separatism and racial hostility among students.

Moderates who would prefer fending for themselves as individuals are bullied into going along with their group. Groups get committed to platforms   37 and to we-they syndromes. Faculty members appease. A code of ideological orthodoxy emerges. The code's guiding principle is that nothing should be said that might give offense to members of minority groups (and, apparently, that anything can be said that gives offense to white males of European origin).

The Office of Student Affairs at Smith College has put out a bulletin listing types of oppression for people belatedly "realizing that they are oppressed." Some samples of the Smith litany of sins: 38

ABLEISM: Oppression of the differently abled by the temporarily able.

HETEROSEXISM: Oppression of those of sexual orientation other than heterosexual, such as gays, lesbians, and bisexuals; this can take place by not acknowledging their existence.

LOOKISM: The belief that appearance is an indicator of a person's value; the construction of a standard for beauty/attractiveness; and oppression through stereotypes and generalizations of both those who do not fit that standard and those who do.

Can they be kidding up there in Northampton?

The code imposes standards of what is called, now rather derisively, "political correctness." What began as a means of controlling student incivility threatens to become, formally or informally, a means of controlling curricula and faculty too. Clark University asks professors proposing courses to explain how "pluralistic (minority, women, etc.) views and concerns are explored and integrated in this course." A philosopher declined to sign, doubting that the university would ask professors to explain how "patriotic and pro-family values are explored and integrated." 39

Two distinguished American historians at Harvard, Bernard Bailyn and Stephan Thernstrom, offered a course in population history called "The Peopling of America." Articles appeared in the *Harvard Crimson* criticizing the professors for "racial insensitivity," and black students eventually presented them with a bill of particulars. Thernstrom, an advocate of ethnic history, the editor of the *Harvard Encyclopedia of American Ethnic Groups,* was accused of racism. He had, it developed, used the term "Indians" instead of "Native Americans." He had also referred to "Oriental" religion—the adjective was deemed "colonial and imperialistic." Bailyn had recommended diaries of Southern planters without recommending slave narratives. And so on, for six single-spaced pages. 40

The episode reminds one of the right-wing students who in Joe McCarthy days used to haunt the classrooms of liberal Harvard professors (like me) hoping to catch whiffs of Marxism emanating from the podium. Thernstrom decided to hell with it and gave up the course. A signal triumph for political correctness. 41

Those who stand up for what they believe invite smear campaigns. A favorite target these days is Diane Ravitch of Columbia's Teachers College, a first-class historian of American education, an enlightened advocate of school reform, and a steadfast champion of cultural pluralism. She is dedicated to reasoned and temperate argument and is perseveringly conciliatory rather than polemical in her approach. Perhaps the fact that she is a woman persuades ethnic chauvinists that they can bully her. Despite nasty efforts at intimidation, she continues to expose the perils of ethnocentrism with calm lucidity. 42

Ravitch's unpardonable offense seems to be her concern about *unum* as well as about *pluribus*—her belief that history should help us understand how bonds of cohesion make us a nation rather than an irascible collection of unaffiliated groups. For in the end, the cult of ethnicity defines the republic not as a polity of individuals but as a congeries of distinct and inviolable cultures. When a student sent a memorandum to the "diversity education committee" at the University of Pennsylvania mentioning her "deep regard for the individual," a college administrator returned the paper with the word *individual* underlined: "This is a *red flag* phrase today, which is considered by many to 43 be *racist*. Arguments that champion the individual over the group ultimately privileges [*sic*] the 'individuals' belonging to the largest or dominant group."

The contemporary sanctification of the group puts the old idea of a co-   44
herent society at stake. Multicultural zealots reject as hegemonic the notion of a shared commitment to common ideals. How far the discourse has come from Crèvecoeur's "new race," from Tocqueville's civic participation, from Emerson's "smelting pot," from Bryce's "amazing solvent," from Myrdal's "American Creed"!

Yet what has held the American people together in the absence of a com-   45
mon ethnic origin has been precisely a common adherence to ideals of democracy and human rights that, too often transgressed in practice, forever goad us to narrow the gap between practice and principle.

The American synthesis has an inevitable Anglo-Saxon coloration, but it   46
is no longer an exercise in Anglo-Saxon domination. The republic embodies ideals that transcend ethnic, religious, and political lines. It is an experiment, reasonably successful for a while, in creating a common identity for people of diverse races, religions, languages, cultures. But the experiment can continue to succeed only so long as Americans continue to believe in the goal. If the republic now turns away from Washington's old goal of "one people," what is its future?—disintegration of the national community, apartheid, Balkanization, tribalization?

"The one absolutely certain way of bringing this nation to ruin, of pre-   47
venting all possibility of its continuing to be a nation at all," said Theodore Roosevelt, "would be to permit it to become a tangle of squabbling nationalities, an intricate knot of German-Americans, Irish-Americans, English-Americans, French-Americans, Scandinavian-Americans, or Italian-Americans, each preserving its separate nationality." Three-quarters of a century later we must add a few more nationalities to T. R.'s brew. This only strengthens his point.

Questions

1. According to Schlesinger, what are the dangers of separatism? To bilingualism?
2. What is the "voodoo principle"? Do you agree or disagree?
3. Do you agree that forcing children reared in another language to learn English is a form of political oppression? Or is it necessary to prevent what Schlesinger calls self-ghettoization?

The Multicultural West

REED WAY DASENBROCK

Reed Way Dasenbrock is a professor of English at New Mexico State University, Las Cruces.

Here, Dasenbrock argues that what ethnocentrists label "Eurocentric" culture is actually an amalgam of cultures. American culture has historically been assimilative, and our task is not to choose between "Western" and "non-Western" but to forge a "responsible and responsive" multiculturalism. This article is from Dissent *(1991).*

When we speak of a common Western culture or, more narrowly, of a common European culture, we are speaking of something that took millennia to construct and consolidate. There was no common European identity two thousand years ago, just a collection of disparate peoples and cultures ranging from the world's most powerful and sophisticated, the Roman Empire, to the rude Germanic and Celtic peoples of the North. By now, it is those rude, uncivilized people who seem to stand at the center of European culture. Joseph Conrad's brilliant frame for *Heart of Darkness* reminds his British readers of 1900 that Britain, by then the very center of European civilization, was once also a "heart of darkness," considered by its Roman conquerors to lie at the outer edges of civilization.

***

What created the relative coherence of European culture we see today out of this multiplicity of peoples, cultures, and traditions? Contemporary thinking usually answers, *domination*—assuming that we always go on being ourselves until someone else overpowers us. However, though force undoubtedly played a role, Europe did not take shape primarily through conquest or forcible assimilation. (The Roman conquest of Britain left a few ruins but had little lasting effect.) It was created primarily by cultural imitation, the mysterious process by which one culture responds to the influence of another. Indeed, the key moment in the creation of a European culture was not the initial sudden emergence of essential Western concepts such as democracy in Athenian Greece. It was, instead, the more gradual process by which another society—Rome—underwent Hellenization and took over Greek ideals and culture as its own. Differences remained, but cultural influence and imitation created a degree of commonality such that we can speak with some accuracy of a shared Greco-Roman or classical civilization. Virgil thus is in a sense more important in the creation of "Western" culture than Homer precisely

183

because of his acceptance of Homer as a normative ideal. This process of imitation, repeated many times over, gives birth to the essential Western concept
that culture is not autochthonous, that it comes from somewhere else: from
the East, if one is a Midwesterner or Westerner; from Europe, if one is American or Russian or Australian; from the Continent, if one is British; from the
Mediterranean, if one is Nordic; from Greece, if one was Roman. Culture thus
is not what we do but usually what someone else does better than we do. This
relation is always double-edged: the provincial side both resents and admires
the sophisticated side in the relationship. But there is never any ambiguity
about which is the sophisticated side: it is, simply, the side that is the object
of imitation over the long term.

Now this sense of culture as something learned, something constructed,   3
something that we share with and take from others, is in quite sharp contrast
to the anthropological sense of culture as the ensemble of practices of a given
community. The difference is between a normative, or prescriptive, and a descriptive concept. Culture in the normative sense is what we ought to do; for
an anthropologist culture is what a given people do. The anthropological
sense seems to govern the current use of the term among multiculturalists,
particularly in their assumption that it is important to "preserve" the culture
of minority students. African Americans should study African and African
American literature to maintain their own cultural identity as African Americans, and it is partly for this reason that it is deemed important to have
African Americans—not members of other groups—teaching these subjects.
Yet the educational practice urged on the society as a whole by multiculturalists is deeply Virgilian. Multiculturalists urge members of the mainstream culture to learn about other cultures so that we can learn from them as well as
learn about them. Diversity in the curriculum is seen as important because
other cultures have traits to learn from; the project is for our students and our
society to become more multicultural, not simply to be more informed about
other cultures. And if we are to become more multicultural, then we must
consciously become a combination of what we wish to retain from our culture and what we wish to adopt from that of others. We must become like
Virgil. And it is for the same reason that this project is also resisted so
strongly: those opposed to multiculturalism are just as Virgilian, insisting
that we should model ourselves on the models we have long imitated, not on
"alien" traditions and ways of being.

However, those on both sides who present Western culture and multicul-   4
turalism as if they were opposed options miss what I would call the fundamental multiculturalism of Western culture, the fact that it has been
constructed out of a fusion of disparate and often conflicting cultural traditions. The straw man of the multicultural polemics is now the dead white
European male or the Anglo; only twenty years ago the straw man of comparable polemics was the white Anglo-Saxon Protestant. Whatever happened
to the WASP?

In just one generation, it would seem, the once crucial distinctions be-   5
tween Protestant and Catholic, between Protestant and Jew, between Anglo-
Saxons and other European ethnic groups have ceased to matter: all of these

groups are seen to be part of a homogeneous "Eurocentric" tradition. But these internal barriers inside the "Western tradition" in America did not go away magically or easily, any more than the internal barriers inside of Europe did. One might remind anyone glibly referring to "the European tradition" (as if it were a harmonious whole) of the long conflict from 1914 to 1945 (or really from about 1500 to 1945) concerning who was to dominate Europe; one might remind anyone glibly talking about a homogeneous Anglo culture in the United States of the intense resistance, as recently as 1960, to the election of the Irish Catholic John F. Kennedy to the presidency. If we can talk about European unity or about a certain unified "Anglo" culture in this country, it is only as a result of a long historical process of knocking down the walls that have separated the different European communities. And that process is not complete even today.

The wall that multiculturalist slogans create between *just one* Western culture and non-Western culture thus reflects a kind of amnesia. Moreover, the disparate elements out of which "Western culture" has been created are themselves often non-Western in origin. One of the loci of the recent debates has been the argument advanced in Martin Bernal's *Black Athena* and elsewhere that classical Greek culture is deeply indebted to Egyptian (and therefore to "black") culture. The debate here is really about the extent to which Egyptian culture can be said to be African. For there is no disputing the obvious debt of Hellenic culture to ancient Egyptian and Near Eastern cultures. However, the details of this particular controversy sort out, the imitativeness of Western culture—its ability to learn from cultures outside the West as well as from other places inside the West—has obviously been one of its constitutive features. We might broaden T. S. Eliot's dictum and say that "immature cultures borrow, mature cultures steal." 6

* * *

After all, if the heritage of classical civilization is one key strand in Western culture, the second key strand would have to be Christianity. For it was really Christianity, not the classical heritage, that cemented a sense of European identity: the fundamental affirmation of European identity has come from Europeans defining themselves as Christian in opposition to cultures that were seen as heathen or pagan. Yet this is deeply paradoxical. Is Christianity a Western or European religion? Its birthplace is undoubtedly "Eastern" and non-European, and it stands in close relation to other religions seen clearly as non-Western and "other," particularly Zoroastrianism and Islam, or whose status in this cultural geography is problematic, particularly Judaism. If one master concept could be said to crystallize a Western mind-set, it is probably not democracy—which so many European countries managed to do without for so long—so much as monotheism. Monotheism allowed us to justify conquest of the "pagan" and "idolatrous" countries of the non-Western world; it also, by removing the sacred from the natural world to a metaphysical realm, justifies thinking of the natural world as something to be used, transformed, and conquered. Yet monotheism is an indigenous notion nowhere in Europe. It was introduced to Europe by Christianity, but derived immediately from Judaism, and ultimately from Zoroastrianism. This helps to 7

explain why, if classical civilization and Christianity are the two more important strands or constitutive elements of Western culture, it took an immense
synthesizing labor across centuries to bring them into some sort of harmony.
Dante, Spenser, and Milton—in seeking to fuse classical culture with Christianity—are thus in a sense just as multicultural as Virgil was, and if we fail to
realize this immediately, we are only testifying to how successful their work
of assimilation was.

* * *

Finally, the third key element in any definition of Western culture would   8
have to be science and technology. This is crucial both for the monocultural-
ist praise of the West (Jacob Neusner's insistence that "we are what the rest of
the world wants to be") and the multiculturalist critique, which tends to find
in other cultures a saner because more respectful attitude towards nature. Yet
Western science and technology (whether we think it a good or a bad thing)
is no more exclusively Western than Western religion. Even if much of it
comes from the Greeks, they took their astronomy from the Sumerians and
Egyptians, and we only know about much of Greek science because of the
Arab role in transmitting it. It is hard to imagine "Western" science without
the Chinese invention of gunpowder, rockets, and printing, without the Indian and Arab contributions to mathematics, and without the key Arab discovery of how to sail upwind.

Consider, for a final example, the "Western calendar," now sometimes re-   9
sisted for imposing a common "Eurocentric" grid on the world. How many
elements enter into a date such as Thursday, August 15, 1991? The name of
the day comes from a Norse God, the name of the month from a Roman emperor. The year comes (approximately) from the date of Christ's birth, so is
Christian in inspiration, but the numerical system is Arabic (and ultimately
Indian) in inspiration. Nor is this hybridization and syncretism anything
uniquely Western. For many of the world's central cultures are multicultural
in the sense I am describing, made up of complex mixtures of local and borrowed elements. Even when we can find someone located univocally in what
seems to be a homogeneous culture, a historical perspective shows how that
culture was itself formed at some earlier point out of a multicultural context.
The way in which successive European cultures rewrote the Homeric epics to
trace their own history back to Greece is paralleled by the successive rewriting
of the Indian epics, the *Mahabharata* and the *Ramayana,* in Southeast Asia. Indian culture is a complex mixture of indigenous Hindu and imported Muslim
elements, and Islam has been a profound influence on the culture of much of
Africa. Our current models of culture all seem to be either/or (Eurocentric vs.
Afrocentric, Western vs. non-Western, monocultural vs. multicultural), but
culture itself is both/and, not either/or. Multiculturalism is simply the standard human condition.

* * *

Now, nothing I have said so far should be controversial. I have recalled   10
some basic historical facts. Yet the facts should lead us to see the debate about
multiculturalism in an unexpected light. The choice cannot be between a

closed Western tradition and openness to other non-Western traditions, for the Western tradition itself has always been open—if not always prone to admit that it is—to other cultural traditions. If you changed into or out of pajamas, took a bath, brushed your teeth, or had a cup of tea or coffee this morning, each of these activities is something we have taken from Asia. If, say, William Bennett's attitudes toward other cultures had always been dominant in the West, we would still be worshipping Zeus and trying to use Roman numerals. The very spirit of the West when it encounters another cultural practice is to say, "Is there something we can use here?" Is tobacco good to smoke? Is coffee good to drink? Is chocolate good to eat? Not every borrowing has been wise, but by and large Western culture has been immeasurably enriched by its ability to adapt to and borrow from others.

If this history teaches us anything, it is that crises of multiculturalism   11 have deep historical roots and cannot be wished away. Early medieval England was a country riven by a schism between the indigenous culture and language of the Anglo-Saxons and the imported culture and French language of the conquering Normans: what resulted was the hybrid language of English and a profoundly hybrid and syncretic culture. Multiculturalism has emerged in the United States today out of a comparable historical exigency. On the one hand, we are faced with a new wave of immigration into the United States: our country is becoming less European, less white, more Asian and more Latin American. Europe, having for decades felt smug and superior about racial problems and tensions in America, is faced with the same phenomenon and is—if anything—considerably less prepared to deal with it. On the other hand, we and every other trading nation are faced with an increasingly integrated world, above all an increasingly integrated international economy, in which we can no longer pretend to separate ourselves from other nations. Borders are now gates, not walls, through which pour problems—drugs and too many Toyotas—but also essential ingredients such as oil. Most important, across borders now pour people. And each of these tendencies is likely to become more pronounced, not less, for the foreseeable future. How do we respond to the complex interaction of cultures that shapes the contemporary world? My answer may seem paradoxical: we need to adopt a good deal of the multiculturalist agenda precisely because it is in keeping with the best and most important aspects of Western and American culture. The great moments of our historical tradition have been moments of contact with and borrowing from other cultures: a good deal of what was important about the Middle Ages was prompted by contact with Islamic civilization: Greek exiles in Italy helped spark the Renaissance, as did the discovery of the New World; the discovery of the spiritual traditions of Asia played an important role in British and particularly American romanticism. Our historical situation is perhaps more complex than any of these, since we are now in contact with the entire world through immigration and trade, but it is nevertheless a situation these examples will help us to understand. When faced with disparate cultures in contact (which usually means conflict), the successful response has always been assimilative and syncretic, to mix and match, taking the best of each. We now need to do this with the totality of the cultures of the world. But this doesn't represent a surrender of the Western tradition as much as a reaffirmation of it.

If this is what we need to do, how can we do it responsibly? Once we see   12
the fundamental continuity between multiculturalism today and earlier moments in our history, the polemical anti-Western thrust of much multiculturalist rhetoric seems absurdly out of place, as does that side of multiculturalism seeking to "preserve" the culture of minority students by focusing their curriculum on their own culture. It is empty posturing to pretend to choose non-Western culture over Western culture when our task is to harmonize them and choose the best of both. To see the choice as one between Eurocentrism and Afrocentrism is to deny the very possibility of multiculturalism. The Afrocentric curriculum being advocated by some black intellectuals and implemented in some school systems is both impractical and no more multicultural than the suggestions of William Bennett and George Will. Moreover, this way of framing the issues ignores the degree of acculturation already undergone by minorities in this country. Most African Americans are no more culturally African than I am culturally German.

In any case, the thought of what could happen when hundreds of thou-   13
sands of not very well-informed—even if well-intentioned—schoolteachers and college professors are turned loose on the cultures of the world is enough to make anyone cringe, and certainly what passes for multiculturalism in the nation's schools is often shallow, misinformed, and intellectually shoddy. In kindergarten, my son brought home some nationally disseminated materials about Columbus Day that made an attempt (obviously influenced by multiculturalism) to show something about precontact native American culture as well as the usual stuff about the *Niña,* the *Pinta,* and the *Santa Maria.* But the worksheet identified Columbus as landing in Bermuda, not the Bahamas; when I pointed this out to his teacher, she asked me what the difference was. In 1991, in first grade, a whole section of native American culture followed, so rife with misinformation and clichés that the children wouldn't have been much worse off just playing cowboys and Indians. I would be astonished if the new Afrocentric schools conveyed a much more accurate sense of what African culture is really like. The point here is that even the best intentions are not enough, that misinformed teaching can in fact reinforce the stereotypes and prejudices it is attempting to move beyond. Moreover, given the spirit of guardianship for these cultures dominating the attempts to represent them in the curriculum, it is unlikely that anything but a sanitized, idealized portrait of these cultures could emerge, even though it is precisely such a portrait of Western culture that multiculturalism objects to.

* * *

So a responsible and responsive multiculturalism is not going to take   14
shape overnight. We are in for a period of experimentation, and we can only hope that more complex models and pedagogies slowly emerge and replace the simplistic visions and responses of both sides in the current debate. To

anyone searching in the interim for what such a multiculturalism would look like, my advice is to read contemporary non-Western literature written in English, which seems to me to be a crucial site where we can move toward a more sophisticated sense of the world's cultures. English is an international language, playing an important role inside about one fourth of the world's 160 countries, and it has therefore become an important international literary language. Important—great—writing is being done in English all over the world, on every continent today. But this body of literature has not yet played an important role in the curriculum at any level, since it doesn't seem English or American enough to make it into the English curriculum, or "different enough" to make it into those parts of the curriculum concerned with other cultures. In this context, that is precisely its virtue. The writers themselves are often attacked from both sides, precisely because they don't fit into one camp or the other, as the case of Salman Rushdie has shown most spectacularly. In fact, the discussion about "Afrocentricity" took shape first in literary criticism when critics such as Chinweizu attacked Wole Soyinka and other African writers for their "Euro-modernism." Yet the bridges these writers are building, by importing European forms into non-European contexts and by introducing non-European cultural traditions into European languages, may in retrospect seem as crucial to the formation of a world culture as the Augustan imitation of Greek culture was for the formation of classical culture and the Renaissance imitation of those classical forms and of Italian culture was for the construction of European culture.

I believe the construction of a world culture—as Wyndham Lewis said   15
more than forty years ago and V. S. Naipaul has recently reiterated—is the task that now faces us. Despite the fashionable nostalgia for pockets of difference yet unintegrated into a world community, the alternative to such a world culture is not a lively diversity of cultures as much as unending conflict among them. Will pointing this out magically transform the current debate into a less shrill one? Of course not, for there are powerful reasons why each side in this debate wants not to understand the other. On the one hand, advocates of a separatist cultural identity for minorities reserve their harshest criticism for those of their own communities like Naipaul or Richard Rodriguez who insist that a measure of assimilation is inevitable, that accommodation must be a two-way street. Ayatollah Khomeini's condemnation of Salman Rushdie is the most conspicuous exemplification of this rage: that one of "us" could be "polluted" by contact with the other side. On the other hand, a George Will or a William Bennett finds it hard to admit that the West might have something to learn from as well as something to teach the rest of the world.

My point is not just that both sides hold to blindingly narrow ideals. It is   16
rather that neither side perceives the world in which we live. Despite all of the talk on both sides about preserving earlier cultural identities, these identities are changing quickly and inexorably. It is in this sense that—despite the apparent polarization of the debate—the two sides are really one. Together, they represent a point of view that is historically irrelevant.

Questions

1. How is Dasenbrock's concept of culture different from the anthropological defini-
    tion of culture?
2. What does the author mean by a "Virgilian" approach to culture?
3. Can you think of examples of cultural practices or beliefs that one can label as
    specifically "Western" and "non-Western"?

Scholars Confront Fundamental Question: Which Vision of America Should Prevail?

ELLEN K. COUGHLIN

Ellen K. Coughlin examines the current debate over how to create a multi-cultural approach to teaching history. She notes that the primary change in this approach has been to substitute the old view of history as a "story of progress toward freedom" to looking at our past as a "long struggle to realize the American ideals of equality and democracy." This article is from the Chronicle of Higher Education *(1992).*

As the issue of multiculturalism has gathered steam over the past few years, 1 historians have been increasingly drawn, as they have not been since the turmoil of the 1960's, into public debates over how to interpret the past, especially America's.

Most often the debates have grown out of controversies over revisions in 2 public-school curricula and textbooks—as has occurred in California, New York State, and Portland, Ore. Sometimes, as on the occasion of the Columbus Quincentenary, discussions have focused on the way certain contested subjects should be understood.

Every case, however, comes down to the same fundamental question: 3 Which version of American history—or, more appropriately, *whose* version—is the one that should be told?

The latest potential battleground is a recently announced effort, sup- 4 ported by the National Endowment for the Humanities and the U.S. Department of Education, to develop national standards in history for kindergarten through 12th grade. Although the project is still in its infancy, it promises to be a contentious one, involving scholars once again in debate over competing visions of history.

"The first question one has to ask is, Whose values will be imposed?" said 5 Harvey J. Kaye, a historian who is professor of social change and development at the University of Wisconsin at Green Bay.

Series of Key Questions

Although the public debate over multiculturalism is sometimes portrayed in 6 rather stark terms—pitting charges of "Eurocentrism" against counter-charges

191

of "ethnic separatism," for example—few, if any, professional historians are
not committed in some degree to a multicultural approach to history.

But for scholars the issue raises a series of key questions about how Amer- 7
ican history should be conceived: Is the story of America that of a common
culture or of many different, perhaps irreconcilable, ones? Given the proliferation, over the last 30 years, of research in women's history, labor history,
black history, and the history of other racial and ethnic groups, is it desirable,
or even possible, to impose a single narrative line on the story of America's
evolution? If such a grand narrative is possible, what should it be?

While there has never been a single, monolithic interpretation of Amer- 8
ica, until recently many historians have subscribed to a general view of American history as the story of progress toward freedom.

Questions about how to envision American history now that the old view 9
has been seriously challenged can be especially troublesome when they require tangible answers in the form of curriculum outlines or textbooks. The
attempt to establish national standards for the teaching of history is certain
to raise those questions anew.

In a move announced in mid-December, the humanities endowment and 10
the Education Department awarded a $1.6-million grant to the National Cen-
ter for History in the Schools, a curriculum-development center at the University of California at Los Angeles, to formulate "world-class standards in
history education." The project was prompted by President Bush's call, as part
of his "America 2000" education program, for national standards in several
core subjects.

A Common Core of Knowledge

The two-year effort, said Charlotte A. Crabtree, director of the center and a 11
professor in UCLA's Graduate School of Education, will involve a broad-based
coalition of teachers, school officials, curriculum experts, academic historians, and others.

Ms. Crabtree, who is a co-author of a framework adopted a few years ago 12
for a statewide social-studies curriculum in California, acknowledged that the
breadth and diversity of current research in history could make it difficult to
set standards that are widely agreed upon. But she maintained that defining a
common core of knowledge that all American students should possess was
not impossible.

"A synthesis can be achieved; it can be done," she said. "Our common 13
culture is constantly being renewed. The problem in the past is that the story
hasn't been well told."

The project is so new that many scholars still do not know much about it, 14
but some historians familiar with the effort expressed ambivalence.

Danger of Political Manipulation

"I start with a general philosophical feeling against it," said Kenneth T. Jack- 15
son, a professor of history at Columbia University who has been asked to

participate in drawing up the new standards. "The concept is at least value free. But the danger is that it can be politically influenced by people on any side in the whole matter, and it can be difficult to find a consensus."

Mr. Jackson, a member of a committee charged with drawing up a revised   16
social-studies curriculum for New York State, last year issued a dissenting opinion on the committee's final report, criticizing the new curriculum for its overemphasis on ethnic differences in American society.

Mr. Kaye of Wisconsin also fears the danger of political manipulation in   17
writing national standards for history, but he is more decided in his opinion about where it will come from: Bush Administration officials such as NEH chairman Lynne V. Cheney and others in the press and in academe who have been critical of efforts to deemphasize the culture and values of Western civilization in college curricula, academic research, and elsewhere.

"I'm not saying that by some natural law this will turn out to be a bad   18
thing," he said, "but we should be watchful and skeptical."

Questions about how to choose among competing views of American his-   19
tory are perennials, but lately they have sometimes proved especially divisive, particularly when the issue of multiculturalism has become entwined with the issue of political correctness, as it inevitably does. Last fall, for example, senior historians who are long-time friends and allies—including C. Vann Woodward, John Hope Franklin, and George M. Fredrickson, all of whom helped pioneer the historical study of race relations—faced off against each other in the pages of the *New York Review of Books* over such questions as whether black history had fallen into the trap of preaching cultural separatism.

Broad Intellectual Issues

Underlying such debates are broad intellectual issues about where the new   20
research of the last few decades has led the discipline of history.

"What we're doing is applying democratic principles to American history,   21
to the study of American culture," said Nell Irvin Painter, professor of history at Princeton University. "People whose voices had been muted or silenced can now be heard."

Most historians would find that description unexceptionable, but would   22
differ about what that means for the interpretation of history. Many argue, for example, that the increasing diversity of viewpoints in historical research and teaching is of inestimable benefit to the field, but that that diversity should nevertheless be incorporated into an idea of America as a common culture built on such common principles as liberty, democracy, and equality.

In his book, *The Disuniting of America: Reflections on a Multicultural Society,*   23
just published in hardcover by W. W. Norton and Company, Arthur M. Schlesinger, Jr., describes the history of America as the story of the development of "a unique national character based on common political ideals and shared experiences."

"The point of America was not to preserve old cultures," he added, "but   24
to forge a new *American* culture."

Like Mr. Jackson of Columbia, Mr. Schlesinger, a professor in the humani-   25
ties at the Graduate Center of the City University of New York, also issued a
dissenting opinion on the revised curriculum for social studies in New York.

Other historians are not quite as insistent as Mr. Schlesinger on the idea   26
of a single American culture, but they do see the importance to American history of certain unifying ideas.

"Multiculturalism provides the opportunity to teach kids an inclusive his-   27
tory that will promote mutual respect among people of different religious and
cultural backgrounds," said Gary B. Nash, professor of history at UCLA. "But
it will only succeed in bringing about greater openness and sympathy if we
can all keep returning to some common values and political ideals that we
share. No curriculum reform can stand in isolation of the social and political
world around it. If that world is so deeply fractured that you have no common ground, then multiculturalism will fail."

A Single Story Line?

Mr. Nash is one of the authors of a new series of social-studies textbooks for   28
kindergarten through eighth grade in California. The books have been widely
hailed by scholars and educators for their representation of diverse racial and
ethnic groups, but have nevertheless been attacked by some critics—Mr. Nash
maintained that the number was small—as being "deeply Eurocentric."

Where Mr. Nash sees unifying threads in the American story, others take a   29
more radical view, arguing that American society is too fragmented to admit
of a single core culture or a single story line for its history.

"A number of critics of the standard version of American history say it   30
has offered a vision of American history that excludes conflicts and the different stories that other groups have to tell," said Joan W. Scott, a historian at
the Institute for Advanced Study in Princeton, N.J., who counts herself
among such critics. "Those critics are saying that there is no possibility of a
single representation of tradition or of the meaning of the American past."

Others agree that old historical understandings have been badly shaken,   31
though not irretrievably.

"There's no question but that the old grand narrative has been disturbed   32
and we don't have a narrative to put in its place," said Joyce O. Appleby, professor of history at UCLA and president of the Organization of American Historians. But she maintained that such a narrative was possible.

Some say the theme for that narrative may already be apparent in the re-   33
search on America's minority groups: the long struggle to realize the American ideals of equality and democracy.

"I think we can attempt to tell a single story," said Mr. Kaye, "but it   34
should be complex and pluralistic. It may be a theme of struggle about liberty
and democracy."

Within the confines of academe, such debates are relatively muted. When   35
they enter the public arena, and begin to involve public officials, newspaper
columnists, and others outside the universities, differences appear more stark.

Historians and the Public

Many historians say that is because the historical research of the last three   36
decades has not fully penetrated the public consciousness, and they blame
that on the failure of most scholars to make their more specialized work accessible to a general audience.

Others point to academic historians' decades-long reluctance to become   37
involved in writing curricula or textbooks for the schools. "It's only in the
last half dozen years or so that they have begun rebuilding those bridges,"
said UCLA's Mr. Nash. If historians had been working with the schools all
along, he said, the new research in history would have filtered down to pre-
college textbooks long before this.

Whatever the problem, said Princeton's Ms. Painter, many of the people   38
outside academe who seem resistant to a more multicultural history often
have little or no appreciation of the amount of work and the kinds of questions that are involved in recent historical research.

"Those questions are fundamentally recasting American studies," she   39
said.

Questions

1. What is the connection between teaching history and teaching values? What
   kinds of values would we learn in a history class?

2. Why do you think so many people object to the old narrative of American history
   which defines our past as the story of progress toward freedom?

3. What version of American history were you taught in high school? In retrospect,
   was it an idealized and sanitized version? What is the rationale behind this approach? What are the dangers?

The Myth of the Melting Pot

LYNDA GOROV

Lynda Gorov is a freelance writer living in Chicago.

In this selection, Gorov believes that her interviews with three women from different cultural backgrounds reveal that the ideal of the melting pot is partly myth. Immigrants are often torn between the pressure to adopt American culture and the need to retain their own heritage. This selection is from Self *(1989).*

Though we like to celebrate the notion that the United States is a country where people of all nationalities can settle comfortably or make a new start, "today's conservative political and social climate is breeding an increased distrust of anyone who is 'different,'" says Samuel Roll, Ph.D., director of clinical training in psychology at the University of New Mexico and an expert on assimilation and acculturation. "This current wave of intolerance affects people at the bottom of the social totem pole, those with the least power—like immigrants, minorities and women." 1

In some ways, Dr. Roll says, fitting in is easier than it used to be—especially for women, who traditionally have had a harder time assimilating. "In the past, men had work and children had school to provide contacts with the new culture and opportunities to learn the language," Roll explains. "But women were most often confined to the home, imprisoned by the cultural as well as social barriers of the time." 2

In contrast, the three women profiled here—one immigrant, two daughters of immigrants—have had far more options. They are educated, and all work outside the home. But though their circumstances are different from women of an earlier generation, they are facing similar issues: how much of their heritage to retain, what to pass on to *their* children, how to bridge the gap between two very different cultures. For them, the American melting pot is much more than a dream; it's a complex reality based on distinctive ingredients of conflict and compromise. 3

Kimberly Chung

Kimberly Chung is a Californian through and through. She was born and raised in a suburb of San Francisco. She is laid-back. She works on her tan. She speaks one language fluently, and it is English. She considers herself an American who simply happens to be of Chinese ancestry. 4

196

But not everyone sees the twenty-eight-year-old Chung the way she sees 5
herself. It was one of the lessons she learned a few years ago at Cornell University. Other students kept asking her where she was born or if she'd need a
green card to work. To them, Chung was Chinese first, American second—the
opposite of her self-image.

"It was shocking to me. I grew up in an affluent, all-American suburb, just 6
like any other lucky American kid," she says. "To me, it was quite clear what
the difference was between a Chinese-American and someone who had recently immigrated. You can tell these things by the way people dress and talk.
And I am thoroughly Americanized."

But Chung, now working toward her doctorate in development econom- 7
ics at Stanford University, got used to being mistaken for a foreign exchange
student at Cornell. "I felt that the mistake just made the other person look
foolish. It was like, 'Boy, haven't *you* led a sheltered life,'" she adds.

In California, Chinese-Americans are more the rule than the exception. 8
Chung says she fits in there to such a degree that she feels "invisible." Chung
never did come up with a stock response to the remarks. She says she usually
laughed them off. But sometimes she got testy—particularly with people she
thought should know better.

Traveling also taught Chung that people will invariably expect her to be 9
more Chinese than she is. More than a few times, Chung has had to explain
that her heritage is Chinese, but her home has always been the United States.
Then come the inevitable questions about relatives back in China; she explains she has few close ones left there. And, no, she is not a Buddhist. Her
parents raised their two daughters as Protestants.

"I identify much more with American culture than Chinese," Chung says. 10
"My parents chose the suburb Los Altos over San Francisco to give us better
schools and more opportunity. That choice meant we lost our connection to
the rich Chinese culture of San Francisco. It also meant my parents were further away from my grandparents, who were a strong link to that culture."

Chung is first-generation American. Her mother came to the United 11
States as a baby, her father at age twelve; they assimilated swiftly into their
new culture. Now retired, Chung's father was a successful chemical engineer
who made a comfortable life for his wife and daughters. But her positive personal experience has not convinced Chung that America opens its arms to all
people. She says her first cousins, who came here as teenagers, had a much
harder go of it than she did. To illustrate her point, Chung cites her cousins'
inner-city high schools, where the Chinese students stuck together and where
there were clashes between ethnic-based gangs.

Chung's own public high school experience was different. In her class, 12
there were only two black students and forty or fifty of Asian descent. Most
were born in America. Her friends were Caucasian or, like her, of Chinese
ancestry.

"My friends were like me. They grew up doing Girl Scouts or Little League 13
or anything else all-American you can think of," she says. "My whole life, I've
always been like everyone else; I never stood out among my peers in any way.

I was treated like everyone else because I acted like everyone else. So what difference did it make that I looked different?

"It's tough to try to raise kids in a really homogeneous area and to give them a sense of two cultures," Chung says. "My sister and I fit in well in American circles. But I haven't done as well in the Chinese culture. 14

"It's sad to me that I don't have stronger roots. I wish that I could speak Chinese; it's embarrassing to me that I can't. You know, my grandmother spoke no English, and so I couldn't even talk to her." Though she chuckles at the memory of her and her sister being considered the "stupid relations," Chung is serious. Her first cousins on her father's side could speak Chinese, and it was a disgrace to her father, she says, that his daughters could not. He was, after all, the eldest son in his family. "I feel bad for him," Chung says. 15

It is her father, says Chung, who has made her life as a first-generation Chinese-American so easy, so privileged. "My father was the one who was caught in the middle. He grew up under strict Chinese rules, and yet he raised totally American kids. He has spent his life going back and forth between two cultures, and because of that, he has had to compromise all the time. 16

"My father has had the worst of both worlds," says Chung. "He absorbed the shock of the cultural differences, so I wouldn't have to." 17

But Chung admits it will be hard to pass along her Chinese heritage to the next generation. "How can you pass on a culture," she asks, "that you don't know anything about?" 18

Renatta German-Adan

The day he dumped her, not long ago, is fixed in Renatta German-Adan's mind. He is twenty-six, an all-American guy. She is twenty and less certain of who she is. German-Adan is Ecuadoran on her mother's side, Mexican on her father's. But she has never lived anywhere except Merritt Island, Florida, three hours north of Miami. 19

"My boyfriend didn't like my father, and my father didn't like him at all," German-Adan says, her voice catching. "I made a big mistake, putting an American boyfriend ahead of my family. I'm sorry about it now. Friends come and go, but your family—that is a special connection." It is not surprising that German-Adan has very close ties to her family. In a community where, as she says, there are few Latinos, her family has made strong efforts to hold on to their South American traditions. 20

And German-Adan, who uses both her father's name and her mother's maiden name, as is the custom in Latin American countries, is both proud of and pained by her heritage. She is at the age when young adults' identities are naturally in turmoil. Though she is an industrious college student, and aspires to be an international lawyer, her folks insist that she live at home indefinitely, or at least until she finds a husband who suits them. It is that parental edict that most irks German-Adan. But it's hardly the only one. 21

"My friends' parents let them breathe. With me, it's like I'm suffocating. I can't escape. I hate to say it, but it depresses me. I'm an adult, I have my own life, but my parents won't let me live it," she says. 22

German-Adan says she does respect her father, a communications engi- 23
neer. It's just that she doesn't understand him. And neither parent understands the Americanization of their children. German-Adan is South
American by blood, and has visited Ecuador often. But by birth and culture,
she is American. Half here, half there, she has a sense of herself as separate
from others no matter where she is.

German-Adan is naturally outgoing. On the surface, she seems unusually 24
sure of herself. But as she speaks, the doubts show through. She has all the in-
securities of a young American woman and then some. She feels particularly
vulnerable about her language skills.

Spanish, and only Spanish, was spoken in the Adan household when she 25
was young. Today, German-Adan is grateful to be bilingual; she realizes it will
give her an edge in the job market. But it has also left her with scars. She remembers being a kindergartner unable to mingle with her English-speaking
classmates, unprepared for the pain and loneliness of that first year of school.

"I just sat by myself. I thought I was in another world. I would come 26
home to my mom and cry," recalls German-Adan, who speaks English without an accent now. "One of my friends still talks about it: how he came over
to play with me and ran away when I started talking to my mother. He
thought we were aliens.

"Watching *Sesame Street* helped me learn English. But mostly I was moti- 27
vated by the other kids saying, 'Hey, you're in America now. Why don't you
speak English?' I hated it when they said that. And I became obsessed with
speaking English clearly.

"That's partly why I would like to study law," says German-Adan. "I want 28
to be able to speak as well as a lawyer. Powerfully. I would like to use language
to command respect."

Now German-Adan has to consult the dictionary for words that come eas- 29
ily to other Americans. Sometimes, she has to look a word up in Spanish,
other times in English. Her combined vocabulary is immense, but she has
limitations in each language. She says she finds it especially troublesome in
her work as a part-time data-entry clerk at a local hospital. "If I spoke perfect
English," says German-Adan, "the doctors would have more respect for me. I
don't like being corrected. I want to tell them, 'Do you know I speak fluent
Spanish, too?'

"Sometimes I want to say something in English and I say to myself, 30
'Please don't embarrass yourself, Renatta.'

"It's not forbidden to speak English at home anymore. But my mom defi- 31
nitely prefers Spanish. She has a very strong accent and doesn't express herself in English too well, even after twenty-two years here."

To German-Adan's surprise, her teenage friends didn't think her mother's 32
stilted English was at all odd. Instead, they thought her exotic. With her own
thick black hair, dark eyes and olive skin, German-Adan has always stood out
among her friends, which served to reinforce her own awareness of the divide
between them.

"I am," she says, "really Latina." German-Adan is reluctant to explain ex- 33
actly what being "Latina" means. It seems to have more to do with *not* being

like her American friends than strongly identifying with a particular ethnic group. Finally, awkwardly, she says it means that she was raised differently from the American kids around her. No sleepovers, early curfews. Her friends, with their more liberal-minded parents, teased her relentlessly about all the rules. But it was more than rules that set German-Adan's family apart. Her parents, intent on preserving the. family's Latin American roots, seemed to have created a household in the middle of Merritt Island that might have been plucked right out of another culture.

German-Adan's mother has instilled in her daughter an appreciation of all things Latin. Her real pleasure in these things, though, comes from sharing her enthusiasm with friends. She recalls how impressed her classmates were recently with a paella she and her mother prepared together for a presentation. And she feels important when friends ask her where she got her South American jewelry and her beautifully dyed skirts. She travels to Ecuador once every few years, where her father sends her to visit with relatives. "I feel freer in Ecuador," she says. "I can be more myself; my family's customs and everybody else's are the same. I don't even think about being accepted.   34

"My mom always said, 'Be proud of who you are.' I can't change it, anyhow. At home, I was raised in the culture my parents came from," German-Adan says. "In school, all I wanted was to be accepted. I tried to be a big shot, hanging out with the older kids, smoking cigarettes in the bathroom.   35

"Today, I think the only way to be accepted is to adopt American customs. And I say, the heck with that. Sure, I was born here, I'm an American citizen, but the culture I come from is not accepted in this country.   36

"You know, sometimes people still give me a hard time about speaking Spanish, about English being my second language. But I don't care what they say about me anymore."   37

Ngoan Le

Nowhere is the contrast between this country's prosperity and the poverty of Ngoan Le's (pronounced Wan Lay) native Vietnam more obvious than at the dinner table. Sometimes, she can't help but just stare at the abundance of food. Thinking about the leftovers sometimes makes her feel sick.   38

Le says she has discussed this with her American-born friends. Actually, it is less of a discussion than a lecture. She tells them about a people who wish for one-tenth of what Americans throw away. She talks about the painfulness of that contrast. She wonders if her friends appreciate how lucky they are.   39

Fourteen years in the United States have not tempered thirty-four-year-old Le's sense of being blessed. When she first arrived in Illinois, after a brief stay in a refugee camp, that feeling consumed her. The family she'd lived with as a young foreign exchange student had agreed to sponsor her real family. Together, they settled in a rural area three hours outside Chicago, where, Le says, the number of Vietnamese families could be counted on one hand. Le felt lucky to have made it out of Vietnam but, for her first few years in the U.S., when she thought about those she had left behind, the strongest emotion she felt was guilt.   40

She was nineteen at the time she arrived, old enough to have absorbed   41
her own culture but young enough to be open to the new world around her.
The daughter of the owner of a small bookshop, she had learned English and
French in school. She knew her place in Vietnamese society. "I was born female and therefore taught how to behave as a daughter and a future wife,
how to behave within the structure of the family," Le says. "I was very aware
of the expectation that I know and accept my inferior status as a woman.

"But here it's different," she continues. "The language betrays the way   42
people relate to one another. In Vietnam, for example, there are many ways
to say 'you' and 'I,' depending on whom you talk to; their sex, status, age. I
grew up knowing how to establish my relationship to other people immediately," Le says. "Then I came here and everyone is *you*, whether it's a sixty-
year-old male professor or my roommate.

"Relationships became confusing for me," says Le. "I found myself want-   43
ing to express respect, and being given signals that respectfulness was not appropriate. I might call someone 'sir,' and see that he felt awkward. At first I
tried to explain the custom in my country, but finally I'd do what people
asked. It seemed better for me to be the one to feel awkward."

Le, soft-spoken but forthright, has adjusted to American life. After   44
earning degrees in French and Spanish from a state university in 1979,
she had the confidence to go after a job she wanted. She was chosen over
several candidates to become executive director of the Vietnamese Association of Illinois, a Chicago-based group whose mission is to ease the transition of refugees and focus attention on the needs of the statewide
community of 18,000. Last summer, she was named Special Assistant to the
Governor for Asian-American Affairs. Her new job requires her to move comfortably among both cultures, and she has learned to feel at home in either
one.

"Being an immigrant is like being a flower. You need to have a deep root,   45
but you always need to grow where the sun is shining," Le says. "Sometimes,
I see Vietnamese families that want to hang on to Vietnamese cultural values
and prohibit their children from becoming Americanized. That is a conflict I
can appreciate, but it is against the natural grain of human experience.

"I was blessed very early in my life with the recognition that most of the   46
distinctions between me and other people were man-made. People everywhere are raised with certain cultural expectations, but once you know how
to relate to their values, you then can get to the point where your differences
will actually broaden your understanding of each other."

Coming into American adulthood has meant letting go for Le. She is not,   47
by nature, aggressive or even chatty. She has had to learn to deal with the immediate familiarity and directness of Americans. Perhaps the hardest skill Le
has had to develop is to argue. In Vietnam, the emphasis is on harmony at all
costs. To challenge a statement is to insult another person. Her American
friends have had to encourage her to stand up for herself.

"I'm more reserved than Americans in general," she says. "I've learned to   48
appreciate the fact that here I have to be more outspoken. Since I'm now in a
position of advocacy for the Asian community, I can't afford *not* to be.

"Some people are strangely intimidated by my reserve; I seem to give the   49
impression that I'm very much in control of myself. Of course," she adds,
smiling. "I am not."

It is her ability to seek out common ground—common truths—between   50
people that has made the acculturation process less difficult than it might
have been for Le. "If you act like you are very different from the people
around you," she says, "you are asking people to see you differently and treat
you differently. I have never really felt a basic difference from other people. I
have never been susceptible to the signals of discrimination, unless they're
extremely blatant."

Which is not to say that Le has had an easy time learning to live in a cul-   51
ture different from her own. Le's ability to adapt, to feel comfortable in both
cultures, has made her feel sometimes as if she belongs in neither one. She is
now clearly too outspoken to fit into her former role as Vietnamese daughter.
And yet, she will never have a completely American mentality.

"I think there is such a thing as an American spirit," Le says. "Americans   52
have a sense of their place in the world as a world power. They have a kind of
can-do spirit, an ease about life and their ability to achieve things.

"But it would take people who are either second or third generation to   53
completely become part of that American mentality. For people like me, the
first ones here, there is always so much comparing—how it used to be like
that, and now it's like this. It's very hard to go totally the American way or
the Vietnamese way."

Even if it were possible right now for Le to go home again, she knows it   54
would not be easy. She is, for better or worse, an American in a number of
ways. She married an American in 1987 and has a style that might not sit well
in her homeland. After all, she works outside the home and defends her opinions. Her own nuptials illustrate how the customs that used to be second
nature do not come as easily to her now.

In Vietnam, the family of the groom prepares the wedding. In America,   55
the responsibility traditionally belongs to the bride's family. With her big day
fast approaching, Le suddenly realized none of the wedding arrangements
were being made.

"Both of our families were just sitting there," she says grinning. "Finally   56
with a month to go, we said, 'Hey, *we* had better do something.'"

The couple decided to mix American and Vietnamese music and customs.   57
They invited two hundred guests to dinner at a Korean restaurant.

"Only in America," she says.   58

One of the motivating forces in Le's life today is the memory of the indi-   59
viduals and churches that helped Vietnamese refugees. She wants to repay
their generosity and humanitarian spirit the only way she knows how: by being a productive citizen. "I have big dreams," she says. "I have seen a lot of
destruction because of the war. I have become a very strong woman. And I
continue to gain strength from living here. You have to know exactly what
you want and be willing to work hard to get it. To me, this country is not a
melting pot but a salad bowl. A carrot is a carrot, a radish is a radish; we never
become something we're not. Instead, we complement each other."

Questions

1. If you have ever traveled to a foreign country (including the United States), have you met with intolerance when you showed ignorance of its customs? How did it make you feel?

2. Why do you think Americans are often intolerant of immigrants?

3. According to Renatta German-Adan, the only way to be accepted in America is to "adopt American customs." Do you agree? Compare this pressure to conform with Marin's assertion that "freedom in America still means essentially *being left alone*."

4. Ngoan Le defines the "American spirit" as "a kind of can-do-spirit, an ease about life and their ability to do things." How would you define the American spirit?

India

RICHARD RODRIGUEZ

Of Mexican-American heritage, Richard Rodriguez was born in San Francisco in 1944. He graduated from Stanford University in 1967, received a master's degree from Columbia University in 1969, and continued his graduate study at the University of California, Berkeley. Rodriguez is now a full-time writer and is particularly known for Hunger of Memory *(1982) and* Days of Obligation: An Argument with my Mexican Father *(1992).*

In this excerpt, Rodriguez says the Native Americans have been marginalized from American society because "America is an idea to which natives are inimical." Indians are largely stereotyped by the media and are only shown in a positive light when used as a gauge for the extent to which industrial America has corrupted the environment. This selection is from Days of Obligation.

> *At sunrise the next day, the time the Indians appointed, they came according to their promise, and brought us a large quantity of fish with certain roots. . . . They sent their women and children to look at us. . . .*
> ÁLVAR NÚÑEZ CABEZA DE VACA

I used to stare at the Indian in the mirror. The wide nostrils, the thick lips. Starring Paul Muni as Benito Juárez. Such a long face—such a long nose—sculpted by indifferent, blunt thumbs, and of such common clay. No one in my family had a face as dark or as Indian as mine. My face could not portray the ambition I brought to it. What could the United States of America say to me? I remember reading the ponderous conclusion of the Kerner Report in the sixties: two Americas, one white, one black—the prophecy of an eclipse too simple to account for the complexity of my face. 1

Mestizo in Mexican Spanish means mixed, confused. Clotted with Indian, thinned by Spanish spume. 2

What could Mexico say to me? 3

Mexican philosophers powwow in their tony journals about Indian "fatalism" and "Whither Mexico?" *El fatalismo del indio* is an important Mexican philosophical theme; the phrase is trusted to conjure the quality of Indian passivity as well as to initiate debate about Mexico's reluctant progress toward modernization. Mexicans imagine their Indian part as deadweight: the Indian 4 stunned by modernity; so overwhelmed by the loss of what is genuine to him—his language, his religion—that he sits weeping like a medieval lady at the crossroads; or else he resorts to occult powers and superstitions, choosing to consort with death because the purpose of the world has passed him by.

One night in Mexico City I ventured from my hotel to a distant *colonia* to visit my aunt, my father's only sister. But she was not there. She had moved. For the past several years she has moved, this woman of eighty-odd years, from one of her children to another. She takes with her only her papers and books—she is a poetess—and an upright piano painted blue. My aunt writes love poems to her dead husband, Juan—keeping Juan up to date, while re-watering her loss. Last year she sent me her *obras completas,* an inch-thick block of bound onionskin. And with her poems she sent me a list of names, a genealogy braiding two centuries, two continents, to a common origin: eighteenth-century Salamanca. No explanation is attached to the list. Its implication is nonetheless clear. We are—my father's family is (despite the evidence of my face)—of Europe. We are not Indian.

On the other hand, a Berkeley undergraduate approached me one day, creeping up as if I were a stone totem to say, "God, it must be cool to be related to Aztecs."

I sat down next to the journalist from Pakistan—the guest of honor. He had been making a tour of the United States under the auspices of the U.S. State Department. Nearing the end of his journey now, he was having dinner with several of us, American journalists, at a Chinese restaurant in San Francisco. He said he'd seen pretty much all he wanted to see in America. His wife, however, had asked him to bring back some American Indian handicrafts. Blankets. Beaded stuff. He'd looked everywhere.

The table was momentarily captured by the novelty of his dilemma. You can't touch the stuff nowadays, somebody said. So rare, so expensive. Somebody else knew of a shop up on Sacramento Street that sells authentic Santa Fe. Several others remembered a store in Chinatown where moccasins, belts—"the works"—were to be found. All manufactured in Taiwan.

The Pakistani journalist looked incredulous. His dream of America had been shaped by American export-Westerns. Cowboys and Indians are yin and yang of America. He had seen men dressed like cowboys on this trip. But (turning to me): Where are the Indians?

(Two Indians staring at one another. One asks where are all the Indians, the other shrugs.)

I grew up in Sacramento thinking of Indians as people who had disappeared. I was a Mexican in California; I would no more have thought of myself as an Aztec in California than you might imagine yourself a Viking or a Bantu. Mrs. Ferrucci up the block used to call my family "Spanish." We knew she intended to ennoble us by that designation. We also knew she was ignorant.

I was ignorant.

In America the Indian is relegated to the obligatory first chapter—the "Once Great Nation" chapter—after which the Indian is cleared away as easily as brush, using a very sharp rhetorical tool called an "alas." Thereafter, the Indian reappears only as a stunned remnant—Ishi, or the hundred-year-old hag blowing out her birthday candle at a rest home in Tucson; or the teenager drunk on his ass in Plaza Park.

Here they come down Broadway in the Fourth of July parades of my 14
childhood—middle-aged men wearing glasses, beating their tom-toms; Hey-ya-ya-yah; Hey-ya-ya-yah. They wore Bermuda shorts under their loincloths. High-school kids could never refrain from the answering Woo-woo-woo, stopping their mouths with the palms of their hands.

In the 1960s, Indians began to name themselves Native Americans, recall- 15
ing themselves to life. That self-designation underestimated the ruthless idea Puritans had superimposed upon the landscape. America is an idea to which natives are inimical. The Indian represented permanence and continuity to Americans who were determined to call this country new. Indians must be ghosts.

I collected conflicting evidence concerning Mexico, it's true, but I never 16
felt myself the remnant of anything. Mexican magazines arrived in our mail-box from Mexico City; showed pedestrians strolling wide ocher boulevards beneath trees with lime-green leaves. My past was at least this coherent: Mex-ico was a real place with plenty of people walking around in it. My parents had come from somewhere that went on without them.

When I was a graduate student at Berkeley, teaching remedial English, 17
there were a few American Indians in my classroom. They were unlike any other "minority students" in the classes I taught. The Indians drifted in and out. When I summoned them to my office, they came and sat while I did all the talking.

I remember one tall man particularly, a near-somnambulist, beautiful in 18
an off-putting way, but interesting, too, because I never saw him without the current issue of *The New York Review of Books* under his arm, which I took as an advertisement of ambition. He eschewed my class for weeks at a time. Then one morning I saw him in a café on Telegraph Avenue, across from Cody's. I did not fancy myself Sidney Poitier, but I was interested in this moody brave's lack of interest in me, for one, and then *The New York Review*.

Do you mind if I sit here?   19

Nothing.   20

Blah, Blah, Blah . . . *N.Y.R.B.?*—entirely on my part—until, when I got up 21
to leave:

"You're not Indian, you're Mexican," he said. "You wouldn't under- 22
stand."

He meant I was cut. Diluted.   23

Understand what?   24

He meant I was not an Indian in America. He meant he was an enemy of 25
the history that had otherwise created me. And he was right, I didn't under-stand. I took his diffidence for chauvinism. I read his chauvinism as arro-gance. He didn't see the Indian in my face? I saw his face—his refusal to consort with the living—as the face of a dead man.

As the landscape goes, so goes the Indian? In the public-service TV com- 26
mercial, the Indian sheds a tear at the sight of an America polluted beyond
his recognition. Indian memory has become the measure against which
America gauges corrupting history when it suits us. Gitchigoomeism—the
habit of placing the Indian outside history—is a white sentimentality that rel-
egates the Indian to death.

An obituary from *The New York Times* (September 1989—dateline Alaska): 27
An oil freighter has spilled its load along the Alaskan coast. There is a billion-
dollar cleanup, bringing jobs and dollars to Indian villages.

> The modern world has been closing in on English Bay . . . with glacial slow-
> ness. The oil spill and the resulting sea of money have accelerated the
> process, so that English Bay now seems caught on the cusp of history.

The omniscient reporter from *The New York Times* takes it upon himself to 28
regret history on behalf of the Indians.

> Instead of hanging salmon to dry this month, as Aleut natives have done for
> centuries . . . John Kvasnikoff was putting up a three thousand dollar televi-
> sion satellite dish on the bluff next to his home above the sea.

The reporter from *The New York Times* knows the price modernity will ex- 29
act from an Indian who wants to plug himself in. Mind you, the reporter is
confident of his own role in history, his freedom to lug a word processor to
some remote Alaskan village. About the reporter's journey, *The New York
Times* is not censorious. But let the Indian drop one bead from custom, or let
his son straddle a snowmobile—as he does in the photo accompanying the
article—and *The New York Times* cries Boo-hoo-hoo yah-yah-yah.

Thus does the Indian become the mascot of an international ecology 30
movement. The industrial countries of the world romanticize the Indian who
no longer exists, ignoring the Indian who does—the Indian who is poised to
chop down his rain forest, for example. Or the Indian who reads *The New York
Times*.

Once more in San Francisco: I flattered myself that the woman staring at 31
me all evening "knew my work." I considered myself an active agent, in other
words. But, after several passes around the buffet, the woman cornered me to
say she recognized me as an "ancient soul."

Do I lure or am I just minding my own business? 32

Is it the nature of Indians—not verifiable in nature, of course, but in the 33
European description of Indians—that we wait around to be "discovered"?

Europe discovers. India beckons. Isn't that so? India sits atop her lily pad 34
through centuries, lost in contemplation of the horizon. And, from time to
time, India is discovered.

In the fifteenth century, sailing Spaniards were acting according to scien- 35
tific conjecture as to the nature and as to the shape of the world. Most thinking men in Europe at the time of Columbus believed the world to be round.

The voyage of Columbus was the test of a theory believed to be true. Brave, yes, but pedantic therefore.

The Indian is forever implicated in the roundness of the world. America   36
was the false India, the mistaken India, and yet veritable India, for all that—India—the clasp, the coupling mystery at the end of quest.

This is as true today as of yore. Where do the Beatles go when the world is   37
too much with them? Where does Jerry Brown seek the fat farm of his soul? India, man, India!

India waits.   38

India has all the answers beneath her passive face or behind her veil or   39
between her legs. The European has only questions, questions that are assertions turned inside out, questions that can only be answered by sailing toward the abysmal horizon.

The lusty Europeans wanted the shortest answers. They knew what they   40
wanted. They wanted spices, pagodas, gold.

Had the world been flat, had the European sought the unknown, then   41
the European would have been as great a victor over history as he has portrayed himself to be. The European would have outdistanced history—even theology—if he could have arrived at the shore of some prelapsarian state. If the world had been flat, then the European could have traveled outward toward innocence.

But the world was round. The entrance into the Indies was a reunion of   42
peoples. The Indian awaited the long-separated European, the inevitable European, as the approaching horizon.

Though perhaps, too, there was some demiurge felt by the human race of   43
the fifteenth century to heal itself, to make itself whole? Certainly, in retrospect, there was some inevitability to the Catholic venture. If the world was round, continuous, then so, too, were peoples?

According to the European version—the stag version—of the pageant of   44
the New World, the Indian must play a passive role. Europe has been accustomed to play the swaggart in history—Europe striding through the Americas, overturning temples, spilling language, spilling seed, spilling blood.

And wasn't the Indian the female, the passive, the waiting aspect to the   45
theorem—lewd and promiscuous in her embrace as she is indolent betimes?

Charles Macomb Flandrau, a native of St. Paul, Minnesota, wrote a book   46
called *Viva Mexico!* in 1908, wherein he described the Mexican Indian as "incorrigibly plump. One never ceases to marvel at the superhuman strength existing beneath the pretty and effeminate modeling of their arms and legs and backs. . . . The legs of an American 'strong man' look usually like an anatomical chart, but the legs of the most powerful Totonac Indian—and the power of many of them is beyond belief—would serve admirably as one of those idealized extremities on which women's hosiery is displayed in shop windows."

In Western Civilization histories, the little honeymoon joke Europe tells   47
on itself is of mistaking America for the extremities of India. But India was perhaps not so much a misnomer as was "discoverer" or "conquistador."

Earliest snapshots of Indians brought back to Europe were of naked little 48
woodcuts, arms akimbo, resembling Erasmus, or of grandees in capes and
feathered tiaras, courtiers of an Egyptified palace of nature. In European museums, she is idle, recumbent at the base of a silver pineapple tree or the
pedestal of the Dresden urn or the Sèvres tureen—the muse of European adventure, at once wanderlust and bounty.

Many tribes of Indians were prescient enough, preserved memory 49
enough, or were lonesome enough to predict the coming of a pale stranger
from across the sea, a messianic twin of completing memory or skill.

None of this could the watery Europeans have known as they marveled at 50
the sight of approaching land. Filled with the arrogance of discovery, the Europeans were not predisposed to imagine that they were being watched,
awaited.

That friend of mine at Oxford loses patience whenever I describe my face 51
as mestizo. Look at my face. What do you see?

An Indian, he says. 52

Mestizo, I correct. 53

Mestizo, mestizo, he says. 54

Listen, he says. I went back to my mother's village in Mexico last summer 55
and there was nothing mestizo about it. Dust, dogs, and Indians. People there
don't even speak Spanish.

So I ask my friend at Oxford what it means to him to be an Indian. 56

He hesitates. My friend has recently been taken up as amusing by a bunch 57
of rich Pakistanis in London. But, facing me, he is vexed and in earnest. He
describes a lonely search among his family for evidence of Indian-ness. He
thinks he has found it in his mother; watching his mother in her garden.

Does she plant corn by the light of the moon? 58

She seems to have some relationship with the earth, he says quietly. 59

So there it is. The mystical tie to nature. How else to think of the Indian 60
except in terms of some druidical green thumb? No one says of an English
matron in her rose garden that she is behaving like a Celt. Because the Indian
has no history—that is, because history books are the province of the descendants of Europeans—the Indian seems only to belong to the party of the first
part, the first chapter. So that is where the son expects to find his mother,
Daughter of the Moon.

Let's talk about something else. Let's talk about London. The last time I 61
was in London, I was walking toward an early evening at the Queen's Theatre
when I passed that Christopher Wren church near Fortnum & Mason. The
church was lit; I decided to stop, to savor the spectacle of what I expected
would be a few Pymish men and women rolled into balls of fur at evensong.
Imagine my surprise that the congregation was young—dressed in army fa-
tigues and Laura Ashley. Within the chancel, cross-legged on a dais, was a
South American shaman.

Now, who is the truer Indian in this picture? Me . . . me on my way to the 62
Queen's Theatre? Or that guy on the altar with a Ph.D. in death?

We have hurled—like starlings, like Goths—through the castle of Euro-   63
pean memory. Our reflections have glanced upon the golden coach that carried the Emperor Maximilian through the streets of Mexico City, thence
onward through the sludge of a hundred varnished paintings.

I have come at last to Mexico, the country of my parents' birth. I do not   64
expect to find anything that pertains to me.

We have strained the rouge cordon at the thresholds of imperial apart-   65
ments; seen chairs low enough for dwarfs, commodious enough for angels.

We have imagined the Empress Carlota standing in the shadows of an af-   66
ternoon; we have followed her gaze down the Paseo de la Reforma toward the
distant city. The Paseo was a nostalgic allusion to the Champs-Elyées, we
learn, which Maximilian recreated for his tempestuous, crowlike bride.

Come this way, please. . . .   67

European memory is not to be the point of our excursion. Señor Fuentes,   68
our tour director, is already beginning to descend the hill from Chapultepec
Castle. What the American credit-card company calls our "orientation tour"
of Mexico City had started late and so Señor Fuentes has been forced, regrettably,

" . . . This way, please . . . "

to rush. Señor Fuentes is consumed with contrition for time wasted this
morning. He intends to uphold his schedule, as a way of upholding Mexico,
against our expectation.

We had gathered at the appointed time at the limousine entrance to our   69
hotel, beneath the banner welcoming contestants to the Señorita Mexico
pageant. We—Japanese, Germans, Americans—were waiting promptly at nine.
There was no bus. And as we waited, the Señorita Mexico contestants arrived.
Drivers leaned into their cabs to pull out long-legged señoritas. The drivers
then balanced the señoritas onto stiletto heels (the driveway was cobbled) before they passed the señoritas, *en pointe,* to the waiting arms of officials.

Mexican men, meanwhile—doormen, bellhops, window washers, hotel   70
guests—stopped dead in their tracks, wounded by the scent and spectacle of
so many blond señoritas. The Mexican men assumed fierce expressions, nostrils flared, brows knit. Such expressions are masks—the men intend to convey their adoration of prey—as thoroughly ritualized as the smiles of beauty
queens.

By now we can see the point of our excursion beyond the parched trees of   71
Chapultepec Park—the Museo Nacional de Antropología—which is an air-
conditioned repository for the artifacts of the Indian civilizations of Meso-
America, the finest anthropological museum in the world.

"There will not be time to see everything," Señor Fuentes warns as he   72
ushers us into the grand salon, our first experience of the suffocating debris
of The Ancients. Señor Fuentes wants us in and out of here by noon.

Whereas the United States traditionally has rejoiced at the delivery of its   73
landscape from "savagery," Mexico has taken its national identity only from
the Indian, the mother. Mexico measures all cultural bastardy against the Indian; equates civilization with India—Indian kingdoms of a golden age; cities

as fabulous as Alexandria or Benares or Constantinople; a court as hairless, as subtle as the Pekingese. Mexico equates barbarism with Europe—beardedness—with Spain.

It is curious, therefore, that both modern nations should similarly apostrophize the Indian, relegate the Indian to the past.   74

Questions

1. What point is Rodriguez making with his list of personal experiences at the beginning of the essay?

2. What point is Rodriguez making about our perception of what it means to be "Indian"? How are American, Mexican, and European attitudes different?

3. Explain the following assertions using examples from your own experience or learning: "America is an idea to which natives are inimical"; "Indian memory has become the measure against which America gauges corrupting history when it suits us."

The Special Perspective

STEPHEN L. CARTER

Stephen L. Carter (b. 1954) is a lawyer and a law professor at Yale University.
Carter, as a black man, argues that although the experience of blacks is different from that of whites and other groups, the diversity movement should not insist that whites cannot understand the black experience or that the oppression and suffering of blacks is worse than the suffering of other ethnic groups. Here, he argues that this insistence on difference and on viewing suffering as a symbol of special worth does not advance the black cause because people continue to think of others "in racial terms." This selection is from Reflections of an Affirmative Action Baby *(1991).*

Traitors/patriots, dissenters/loyalists, neoconservatives/left-radicals: it is past time, surely, for black people to put an end to these efforts to divide us. Our task is to reconcile and, having done so, to work toward building a reconciled solidarity, a coalition built not on our agreement on a program, not on our willingness to profess a particular viewpoint, but on our shared love of our people and our culture. For although the diversity movement has many faults, and although those faults can lead down unhappy paths, it nevertheless possesses an underlying theme that seems to me unexceptionable.

I have in mind the notion that people of color are marked and tied together by a shared history and, to a lesser extent, by a shared present of racial oppression. We cannot shrug off this history the way a snake sheds its skin, and we shouldn't want to. I want my children to grow up in a world in which they are confident that nothing is closed to them, and I frankly believe that virtually nothing will be; but I do not want them ever to forget that generations of our people have suffered and sacrificed to build that world, and that the forces that would hold them back, while put to rout (no, one *can't* fairly draw parallels between the Reagan era, whatever its many problems, and the years of slavery and Jim Crow), still lurk in the shadows, looking for chances and occasionally taking them, and will continue to do so for as much of the future as my children and their children are likely to see. I want them to understand their rich culture and glorious history, and I want to steel them against the many forces that will seek to deny and distort both.

So, yes, a history of oppression (but also of triumph) is our shared legacy, and a certain uneasy vigilance is our responsibility to our progeny. Black people, says Alice Walker, can be "middle class in money and position, but they cannot afford to be middle class in complacency."[1] These aspects of our situation undoubtedly combine to produce a predictable, if not always unique, perspective on any number of issues, explaining everything from why black people in such overwhelming numbers vote Democratic to why opinion surveys show black people far less supportive of the death penalty than white people are.

If one wants a further example, consider the case of William Coleman, a lion of the corporate bar, a wealthy partner in one of the nation's most exclusive law firms, tailored and elegant, a Republican to his fingertips. Coleman, who is black, was an avowed supporter of President Reagan, but nevertheless felt compelled to testify—indeed, in effect to lead the charge, for his was by far the most effective testimony—against the nomination of Robert Bork as an Associate Justice of the Supreme Court. Opening his prepared statement, Coleman (who had been courted by both sides) explained his decision to oppose the nomination:

> I have tried very hard to avoid this controversy. The Supreme Court has played such an important role in ending so many of the horribly racially discriminatory practices that existed when I first came to the bar. As one who has benefitted so greatly from this country's difficult but steady march towards a free, fair and open society, the handwriting on the wall—*"mene mene tekel upharsin"* ["thou art weighed in the balances and found wanting"]—would condemn my failure to testify against Judge Bork.[2]

I do not mean to suggest that Coleman's blackness created some compulsion to oppose the nomination; Bork certainly had his black supporters. (I took no position on the nomination, although I did find much of the campaign against Bork, excepting the reasoned and stirring testimony of Coleman and some others, a triumph of rhetorical excess.)[3] But the example of Coleman's own explanation for his decision emphasizes the main point: our shared history of oppression might affect us in different ways, but affect us it does.

So, again, I do not deny that the shared history that helps define us makes black people different from white people. My quarrel with the diversity forces is that it is far from evident to me how any of this translates into a single, genuine, preferred black perspective, a voice that is specially to be valued, to be sought out for celebration when other voices are not. We are by no means the only group in society that has suffered and drawn a perspective from its suffering, and different groups will define hierarchies of suffering in sharply different ways. Other than the fact that it makes our lives (and arguments) easier, there is no *a priori* reason to prefer our vision of suffering to any other. Perhaps we should be looking for commonalities of suffering rather than parading our uniqueness. But the unhappy truth is that too much has been allowed for too long to turn on whether or not the suffering of black people is unique.

To see why this must be so, consider the matter the other way around: if all people who have suffered have suffered in essentially similar ways, then it is difficult to explain why the law should treat some sufferers differently than others. Perhaps others who have suffered the predations of racial oppression might be admitted to share in the uniqueness—but no one else. Special treatment for everyone, after all, means special treatment for no one. Everything from minority set-aside programs to diversity to good old-fashioned political solidarity rests in some way on the claim of uniqueness. Thus it ought to be unsurprising that many black people find the notion of commonality of suffering profoundly threatening. If we lose our claim to have suffered in ways that are unique in history (so the fear must run), then how much else of our hard-won political ground will we have to surrender?

The claim that the suffering of black folk is unique grounds much of the current civil rights agenda. We were dragged here unwillingly on slave ships, our culture has been forcibly abolished, our education prohibited in one century and inferior in the next, our general unfitness for the ordinary occupations of life drummed into us relentlessly for centuries, so that we have very nearly been destroyed as a people. We are society's victims. Consequently, racial preferences and other special programs are described as payment for a debt that society owes us, and whether society pays out of guilt or out of simple justice, pay it must, because we have been wronged like no people before.*   7

To expunge the debt, the society must recognize our claim on a share of such scarce resources as jobs with real prospects of advancement and education in the most selective programs of the best professional schools. The underlying assumption is that the problems the rest of the world has caused are problems the rest of the world must solve. Life may be unfair and, in the words of the aphorism, tests may measure the results, but according to the argument from difference, those are only interim results; the world that has caused the unfairness must come back later and adjust the scores.   8

The claim of uniqueness takes the majority's historical insistence on the difference between black and white and tries to make it work the other way. Once upon a time, the nation justified its oppression of us on the ground that we were different than they. It is easier to make it a crime to teach a black person to read once you are prepared to concede that it is not possible to do so. Well, fine, the argument concludes: you treated us as different then; you will choke on those differences now. And in the era of affirmative-action-as-diversity, the idea of celebrating the things that make us different is more than a rallying cry. It is also a critique of accepted understandings, a demand for a share in the interpretation of the world. It says we matter. Our oppression makes our world different from yours and our voice different from yours. Those differences matter.   9

Again, this is in a sense unexceptionable; history *does* make black people different from white people. But it is both wrong and dangerous to insist that it makes us different in some predictable, correctly black way. And, for reasons I shall explain, it is also wrong, and potentially quite dangerous as well, to insist that our differentness is to be more valued than anybody else's.   10

---

*Sometimes this proposition takes on bizarre proportions. As an undergraduate, I was part of a group of black students who went to complain to a history professor who had made the suggestion in a lecture that slavery in Brazil was far harsher than slavery in the United States. Quite apart from the point that he was of course exactly right, it is plain that politics was driving our evaluation of the facts: he had to be wrong because it was inconvenient for him to be right. To his credit, he did not apologize for insensitivity, as faculty members today seem to do all the time; instead, he told us some things that we should read.

II

The idea of difference, and its importance, has been worked out more fully by   11
feminist scholars than by those propounding what might be called the racial
critique. Most prominent is perhaps the hugely controversial work of the psychologist Carol Gilligan, who contends that from early childhood, males and
females evidence markedly different forms of moral reasoning.[4] Gilligan has
her critics, including psychologists who have questioned her methodology or
conducted independent studies that they describe as throwing doubt on her
results.[5] Other critics are fearful of the uses to which their opponents might
put the notion that there is some fundamental distinction between the way
men and women analyze problems.[6]

A vision similar to Gilligan's was long ago seized upon by scholars assert-   12
ing the "point of view" of the putatively oppressed black community. Although much of the analysis of the significance of difference requires
considerable erudition to be understood, the underlying proposition manifests a rough-and-ready common sense that probably reflects the day-to-day
experience of vast numbers of people in our "us and them" society.

The difference approach proposes, for example, that writers who are   13
white and writers who are not are on opposite sides of an unbridgeable
chasm, that their experiences of reality diverge so sharply that beyond a certain, limited point, a shared understanding is virtually impossible. Black (and
other nonwhite) writers are said to have different voices from white ones, to
think and speak and, of course, write in a way that reflects their backgrounds.
They see some things—those related to their oppression, those related to
their culture—more sharply than others possibly can. A just society, then, according to this approach, would take account of that difference rather than
seek to silence it.

This vision of difference presupposes the existence of what is often called   14
the "black experience," a uniquely black reality that has shaped in similar
ways the lives of all people who are black. The black experience, it is said,
cannot possibly be fathomed by anyone who is white. A classic statement of
this proposition is in Stokely Carmichael and Charles Hamilton's 1967 book
Black Power:

> Our point is that no matter how "liberal" a white person might be, he cannot
> ultimately escape the overpowering influence—on himself and on black peo-
> ple—of his whiteness in a racist society.
>
> Liberal whites often say that they are tired of being told "you can't un-
> derstand what it is to be black." They claim to recognize and acknowledge
> this. Yet the same liberals will often turn around and tell black people that
> they should ally themselves with those who can't understand, who share a
> sense of superiority based on whiteness.[7]

Plainly, this idea has the advantage of silencing critics. The three magic
words, "You can't understand," free the object of criticism from the need to
seek a dialogue with those who disagree; the fact of oppression becomes its
own authority.

Like the claim of gender difference, the claim of racial difference has its   15
critics. They challenge, for example, the premise of a monolithic black experience that has shaped all black people in ways that make them more like one
another than like people who are white.[8] The idea of difference, moreover,
carries a very real risk of stigmatizing and perhaps even "ghettoizing" black
intellectuals. If they—white intellectuals—can't do what we—black intellectuals—do, then perhaps we can't do what they do, either. Harold Cruse must
have been painfully aware of this possibility over two decades ago when he
wrote in *The Crisis of the Negro Intellectual:*

> Even at this advanced stage in Negro history, the Negro intellectual is a re-
> tarded child whose thinking processes are still geared to piddling intellectual
> civil writism [*sic*] and racial integrationism. This is all he knows. In the mean-
> time, he plays second and third fiddle to white intellectuals in all the estab-
> lishments—Left, Center, and Right. The white intellectuals in these
> establishments do not recognize the Negro intellectual as a man who can
> speak both for himself and for the best interests of the nation, but only as
> someone who must be spoken for and on behalf of.[9]

Small wonder that black intellectuals might be seen this way, if our claim is
that we speak, in effect, in a language that others cannot hope to understand.

Besides, there is something vaguely derisive in the conclusion that those   16
of us who are black intellectuals are stuck with doing things in one way, forever marked by race. Edward Shils, writing at about the same time as Cruse,
surely recognized this when he observed:

> [M]embers of the various communities in the major areas of intellectual life
> evaluate intellectual performance with little or no reference to nationality, re-
> ligion, race, political party, or class. An African novelist wants to be judged as
> a novelist, not an African; a Japanese mathematician would regard it as an af-
> front if an analysis of his accomplishment referred to his pigmentation; a
> British physicist would find it ridiculous if a judgment on his research re-
> ferred to his being "white."[10]

This was obviously a hope, not a statement of fact, and as hopes go, it was a
good one. But Shils's closing prediction—that "primordial attachment to
color . . . will survive but not so strongly as to deflect the intellect and imagination from their appropriate activities"[11]—is precisely what theorists of difference deny. And in that denial, they implicitly condemn all scholars of
color to a narrow and unhappy path, writing mostly for one another rather
than for a universal audience, and never able to aspire to a higher goal than,
for example, best *black* economist.*

---

*In a story that might be apocryphal, but is too good to pass up, it is said that Thomas Sowell
hung up on a member of Ronald Reagan's staff who telephoned him shortly after the 1980 election to inform him that the new president wanted Sowell to be his first black cabinet member.[12]

Theorists who believe that difference means a common perspective face a   17
further and more fundamental difficulty. Without a good deal of sidestepping
and rhetorical excesD, they are unable to account for the work of such prominent black critics of racial preferences and other aspects of the civil rights orthodoxy as Glenn Loury, Thomas Sowell, and Shelby Steele. Has the black
experience touched them? Does it touch their work? Ah, well, perhaps they
have surrendered to the racist society, sold out. In any event, the problem
must be with them, the dissenters, and not with the theory that the black experience has shaped us all in similar ways. The notion that reasonable minds,
even reasonable black minds, might differ over some part of the dominant
civil rights agenda is treated by theorists of difference as worse than absurd—
why, it isn't even worth mentioning!

The diversity theorists will very likely have similar trouble accounting for   18
the work of Julius Lester, who is nobody's conservative, neo- or otherwise,
but nevertheless is evidently a critic of difference, and on grounds that are
quite instructive. In 1988, as I discussed earlier, Lester published *Lovesong,* a
fine book in which he chronicled his evolution from a rather chic and trendy
spokesman for the black separatist movement in the 1960s to his recent con-
version to Judaism—and, along the way, his estrangement from the remnants
of the movement he had once helped lead. His narrative is a statement of the
universality of human experience—including the suffering and oppression
that are said by scholars of difference to be crucial to creating the different
voices in which different communities speak. But for Julius Lester, different
communities speak *to* one another, and there are messages for those prepared
to listen.

Thus, although he wonders as he prepares a seder whether "a Gentile can   19
understand Judaism and Jewishness," his conclusion is a rejection of the idea
that the uniqueness of black experience makes white understanding impossible:

> The thought is as repugnant to me as when blacks tell whites they cannot
> know what it is to be black. It is a statement that negates literature, art and
> music, nullifies the realm of the imaginative and says it is impossible for hu-
> man beings to reach out from one loneliness to another and assuage both. If
> that were true, I would not see aspects of myself in haiku and the poems of
> Sappho, the music of Bach and the watercolors of Winslow Homer.[13]

The point of this passage, and a good one, is surely not that the scholars of
difference are wholly wrong, but that the experiences that make us different
do not make us unable to understand or appreciate one another. Jack Greenberg *can* successfully teach a course on law and race, and can even describe a
part of the perspective of people of color. Jonathan Pryce, a white actor whose
award-winning performance in a nonwhite role nearly led to the cancellation
of the Broadway musical *Miss Saigon, can* successfully and authentically portray a Eurasian on the stage. Daniel Lewis James *can* learn what it is like to
live in a barrio and write about it. As Felix Gutierrez, then a professor at the
University of Southern California, said of the James incident: "You don't have

to be a Latino to write on the Latino experience, and Latinos should not write only on that. There's nothing to stop an Anglo from writing authentically about it if he spends the time. That's the key, get to know us."[14]

Get to know us. Why not? For those who care to, it isn't that hard. People   20 of color are not mysterious; our world is not impenetrable. But we do have background and experiences and visions that it is important to share, not as cartoon characters who are all alike, not as representatives of our people but simply as people ourselves. Difference, in short, is a bridgeable chasm. It is bridged when we "reach out from one loneliness to another," not in anger, not in frustration, not in hatred, but in love; not lifting the world up by its ears but touching it on its human heart.

Still, in order to be useful, the bridge must finally be built not simply in   21 the mind of the observer but in the world; the decision might begin with emotion, but it must end with will. This, surely, is what the theologian David Tracy had in mind when he noted that "[e]mpathy is much too romantic a category to comprehend this necessary movement . . . from otherness, to possibility, to similarity-in-difference."[15] Bridging the chasm is a choice, and not always an easy one. But it is not enough just to look at the one who is different, the lonely, suffering other, and say, "Gee, that's too bad" or "Gee, I understand." For Lester, as for Tracy, the triumph over difference is finally a social act as well as a spiritual one.

Armed with the notion of difference as a chasm to be bridged, one can   22 readily imagine an impressive panoply of lines that might be blurred or crossed by a world willing to proclaim, "We love you because you are different; we love your differentness; we value it; we want to learn from it." The continuing struggle to mend the division between black and white in the United States is only one such border crossing. The gay and lesbian rights movement and efforts to empower the homeless are plainly others. Difference ought to have a human face, and people should talk to each other.

There are borders to be crossed, fences to be mended, bridges to be built   23 within our community as well as outside, for we who are black fairly sparkle with an internal diversity that the rest of the world, so often stuck in its obsession with stereotypes, seems to ignore. We should not make the same mistake ourselves; we should love and value *us*, black people in all of our diversity: rich, poor, gay, straight, religious, secular, left, right. For it is none of these distinctions that define our blackness; what defines us, rather, is the society's attitude toward us—all of us are black before we are anything else— and our attitude toward ourselves, toward our culture, toward one another. We are defined by the choices we make.

In my other life as a scholar of the Constitution, I am fond of quoting a   24 metaphor from the late Alexander Bickel, and it seems appropriate to repeat it here. In *The Morality of Consent,* published in 1975 just after his death, Bickel warned the courts not to ignore popular response to their decisions. The public reaction, Bickel argued, is an important part of an "endlessly renewed educational conversation" between the judges and the public that must choose whether to obey their edicts. For Bickel, a lasting and insistent chorus of protest was evidence that something was wrong, that perhaps the judges had made an error. Thus he added the stern admonition that the dialogue he envisioned "is a conversation, not a monologue."[16]

We who are black, rather than establishing a hierarchy of "correct" or "more valuable" black views, should adopt the same model. We should be having a conversation, not a monologue, and certainly not this bitter argument. We should talk to each other rather than at each other. We should make our shared love for our people the center of our belief, and use that shared center as a model for the possibility of a solidarity that does not seek to impose a vision of the right way to be black.

The task that faces us, then, long before we can insist that the rest of the world shop for our perspective(s) in the market, is to build a reconciled solidarity, a world in which an appreciation of our differences, the attitudes and visions that make black people unlike one another, is the focus of our efforts to re-create ourselves and our society. And who knows? Our ability to love one another, whatever our politics and policies, might finally serve as a model for the larger white society which, in the rhetoric of diversity but also in fundamental fairness, is called upon to do the same thing.

III

The diversity movement is correct in insisting that the rest of the world—including the academic and professional world, but the larger nation as well—share in our own celebration of the aspects of our culture that mark us as special. But the point of appreciating difference is, or ought to be, that *everybody* is special. Every individual has a unique history, and so does every group. That wonderful truth is not something that should drive us apart, as racists have for too long tried to use it; it is, rather, something that should draw us together.

This much strikes me as both valuable and incontrovertible. The trouble with the diversity movement is that it goes on to insist that our specialness in effect *adds value* to us in a way that the specialness of other people does not. (If this is not true, then there is no reason for a university to search for excellent scholars who can tell our story, as the movement insists it should.) It is by taking this additional step, I think, that the diversity movement makes its analytical error, and the error, although subtle, is ultimately of sufficient import to make the theory unworkable. For there is no logical connection between the proposition that we are special people and the proposition that our voices are uniquely to be valued. The world is full of special people and all of their voices are unique.

The diversity movement proposes, however, that there are important reasons to value and search out people who can speak of *our* story, the most important among them being the fact of our oppression at the hands of people who are white. And it is that oppression that the cherishing of the special, excluded voice is meant to overcome.

But the supposition that it is white oppression of us, and our suffering   30
under that oppression, that makes our perspective more to be valued, seems
to me a rejection of the idea that recognizing difference can be a binding
force, a form of love. There shouldn't be any hierarchy of suffering, not because no one person or group has any subjective sense of having suffered
more than anyone else, and not because there are no moral standpoints from
which to judge it, but because to make the fact of suffering the badge of authority defeats the purpose of valuing diversity. To try to impose a hierarchy—to say, in effect, "We have suffered more than you have, and you are
not allowed to disagree"—is to make a potentially bitter contest of what
ought to be a solemn and shared understanding.

This becomes a matter of practical importance when critics of affirmative   31
action cite the experiences of other ethnic groups who have also been oppressed but who have, it is said, succeeded without the use of explicit preferences.[17] The responses from advocates fall into two categories: No, you are
wrong, the other groups did benefit from preferences of some informal sort;[18]
or, Yes, but that experience is not relevant because they have not suffered as
we have. The second category seems to be the very tidy way in which the diversity movement steers away from a very slippery slope.

But the strategy of deciding who has suffered more entails considerable   32
risk. To illustrate, I will borrow another story from Julius Lester, a story with
no relation to the diversity movement, but one that many black people
should find chillingly familiar nevertheless. Lester's most controversial thesis
is his suggestion that the black community, or at least its leadership, is awash
in anti-Semitic sentiment. It is tempting to dismiss his claim as lacking empirical support, as merely anecdotal, as a product of his understandable anger
at his own treatment at the hands of the Afro-American Studies Department
at the University of Massachusetts at Amherst, which I described in chapter 5.
And yet there is a plausibility to Lester's suggestion that our community has
some problems. Louis Farrakhan, who calls himself a man of God while weav-
ing into his admirable gospel of self-reliance and self-esteem a stark and unmistakable thread of hate, does draw huge and enthusiastic audiences and
sometimes his audience seems to be outnumbered by his apologists. Still, I
believe (and also hope) that there is considerably less black anti-Semitism
than Lester supposes, and in any case—and this is not to excuse any of us—in
any case, the problem of black anti-Semitism is surely dwarfed by the problem of white anti-Semitism.[19]

But this is not the place to address that rather complex issue. I raise   33
Lester's claim only as background to a story I wish to borrow from *Lovesong*.
Lester describes a scene in which one of his colleagues, on reading an essay
Lester wrote about black anti-Semitism, becomes apoplectic, and screams:
"You think I haven't studied the Holocaust? Well, I have, goddamit! I don't
see a damned thing about it that's unique. I think black folks have been
through more hell than a Jew in Auschwitz could imagine."[20] Lester, by his
own account, becomes so angry in return that he tells his colleague never to
speak to him again.

There are many layers to the tragedy in that small story. The worst, prob-   34
ably, is the way his colleague insists on making suffering a competition. The
argument is quite commonly made, and by no means by black people alone,
that the Holocaust is not unique, that it is no worse in its way than, for example, the slaughter of the Hutu by the Tutsi or the Armenian genocide. But
that is the same trap. The horror of the Holocaust does not lie in its uniqueness; the horror does not even need an explanation. It is plain on the face of
history. The same can be said of the centuries of oppression of black folk in
the Western world: the horror does not need an explanation. It is plain on
the face of history. This does not mean that the oppressions are the same, but
neither does it mean that they are different. Humanity has proved itself capable of perpetrating any number of horrors; and to those who suffer from
them, each is unique. The error comes in assuming that it matters which one
is the most horrible.

Is it anti-Semitic to criticize Jews for refusing to let the world forget the   35
Holocaust? I would rather put the question another way: Why would anyone
criticize Jews for refusing to let the world forget the Holocaust? God knows,
we who are black ought never to let the world forget the African slave trade.
Our responsibility is what Lester says it is: to share in the suffering of others.
Thus, we who are black should also refuse to let the world forget the Holocaust; and we should insist that Jews join us in refusing to let the world forget
the slave trade. Alliances among people traditionally despised are natural and
important, and with good reason: had black people been present in Europe in
significant numbers, Hitler would have had another project besides making
the continent *judenrein,* for he despised us as well.*

This brings me back to the diversity movement, which does indeed seem   36
to propose that we ought to make a contest of suffering, that we ought to
value people of color specially because of the special nature of the oppression
in our history. For a school to refuse to hire a scholar because she chooses to
embrace a history of suffering would be a terrible wrong; but for a school to
say that its faculty will be incomplete *unless* it hires one is to repeat, albeit on
a smaller canvas, the wrong of Lester's colleague. For nothing about value or
authority ought to turn on who has suffered more.

Our suffering might have marked us and it is surely a fact of history that   37
we must never forget, but it is not a symbol of special worth. In the words of
the philosopher Judith Shklar, "Victimhood happens to us: it is not a quality."[22] Besides, even were one to concede the unique value of the perspective
that our suffering or even injury brings, there is an almost quaint sentimentality in the idea that the only shared inheritance from our past is a positive
one. After all, when a taxi driver in New York City explains in the *Times* that
he refuses to pick up black males as passengers because (according to a widely

*Early in 1942, Hitler told associates: "My feelings against Americanism are feelings of hatred and
deep repugnance. . . . Everything about the behavior of American society reveals that it's half Ju-
daized and the other half Negrified."[21]

shared bit of suspicious data) black men are responsible for 85 percent of crimes against cabbies,[23] he also is making an assumption about the characteristics we share. The label that the driver proposes for our boxes may be more damaging than the one offered by the theorists of diversity, but that is a consequentialist judgment; there is no reason *in logic* that he cannot be as right as they.

There is a point here that is often overlooked in discussions about racial   38
stereotyping. The popular image of stereotyping holds that an irrationally skewed reasoning process guides it. Gordon Allport, for example, in *The Nature of Prejudice* (1955), insisted that racial prejudice is "an antipathy based upon a faulty and inflexible generalization."[24] This argument suggests that the problem with racial stereotypes is overinclusivity, a judgment less normative than empirical. Racial stereotyping is bad, in this view, because it is irrational, and therein lies the difficulty: "Don't use them *because* they don't work" carries the same normative message as "Don't use them *if* they don't work." The implication is that there might lurk somewhere a set of better, more accurate stereotypes that should not be dismissed as involving "prejudice" because they are rational.

It is dangerous to suggest that racial categorizations, even negative ones,   39
might be acceptable as long as a case can be made for rational fit between ends and means. If the result of a categorization is oppressive, the reality of that result has little to do with the rationality of the racialist categorizations that might have been involved in bringing it about. In those areas of human endeavor the law simply cannot reach with any practical effect—most areas of life traditionally, if suspiciously, considered private—virtually anyone who makes a judgment about anyone else that rests on race will believe the judgment to be a rational one.

In this sense, the diversity movement runs into the trouble that has be-   40
deviled every effort to define the special shared characteristics that would justify preferential treatment for people of color. The peculiar language forced upon us by programs that treat people as members of groups and assign characteristics on the basis of that membership has an ugly mirror image, for it is as easy to assign negative characteristics as positive ones. Preferential treatment comes in two kinds, the kind we like and the kind we hate.[25] Both kinds have roots in the idea that race is a useful proxy for other information: in the early days of affirmative action, a proxy for disadvantage; today, a proxy for the ability to tell the story of the oppressed; and, to the taxi driver, a proxy for a high potential for criminality. That is why there has always been something unsettling about the advocacy of a continuation of racial consciousness in the name of eradicating it. The one thing that every version of racial preferences has in common, by definition, is an explicit consciousness of race; the programs *insist* that an employer or college or professional school take note of the race of an individual applicant. That might be a way to ensure minority representation or diversity or better opportunities or compensation for disadvantage, but it has little to do with getting people to stop thinking of others in racial terms.

There is a surface innocence to all of this, and certainly systems of racial 41
preferences are not intended to denigrate either those permitted to benefit
from them or those who are excluded. But although those who are excluded
are plainly not victims of a system of racial subjugation, such as the one that
long oppressed people of color, they are just as plainly victims of racial discrimination, an entirely distinct wrong, but not a trivial one. The backlash
against racial preferences is not trivial, either, and explaining it away as
racism is just another way of silencing critics without debating them—and
another sign that we are losing the moral high ground, for there was a time
when the civil rights movement had no reluctance to debate. We must learn
once more to love and cherish individuals for who they are, not for what
they represent; and, having learned it once more ourselves, we can once more
teach it to a doubting world.

NOTES

1. Alice Walker, "The Civil Rights Movement: What Good Was It?" in *In Search of
   Our Mothers' Gardens* (New York: Harcourt Brace Jovanovich, 1983), pp. 119,
   127–28.

2. Quoted in Ethan Bronner, *Battle for Justice: How the Bork Nomination Shook America*
   (New York: W. W. Norton, 1989), p. 279.

3. I have written about the Bork hearings elsewhere in considerable detail. See, for
   example, Carter, "The Confirmation Mess," *Harvard Law Review* 101 (1988): 1185;
   Carter, "Bork Redux," *Texas Law Review* 69 (February 1991): 751.

4. Carol Gilligan, *In a Different Voice* (Cambridge: Harvard University Press, 1982).
   For a similar argument, see Gibbs, Arnold, and Burkhart, "Sex Differences in the
   Expression of Moral Judgment," *Child Development* 55 (1984): 1040.

5. See Lawrence Walker, Brian de Vries and Shelley Trevethan, "Moral Stages and
   Moral Orientations in Real-Life and Hypothetical Dilemmas," *Child Development*
   58 (1987): 842; idem, "Sex Differences in the Development of Moral Reasoning: A
   Critical Review," *Child Development* 55 (1984): 677 (asserting that substantial evi-
   dence of lack of sex differences in moral development is disregarded); Catherine
   Greeno and Eleanor Maccoby, "How Different Is the 'Different Voice'?," *Signs* 11
   (1986): 310 (questioning Gilligan's methodology and citing contrary evidence);
   Zetta Luria, "A Methodological Critique," *Signs* 11 (1986): 316 (rejecting Gilligan's
   methodology). For Gilligan's response to her critics, see, for example, "Reply by
   Carol Gilligan," *Signs* 11 (1986): 324.

6. See, for example, Catherine MacKinnon, *Feminism Unmodified* (Cambridge: Harvard University Press, 1982), pp. 38–39 (arguing that Gilligan's work affirms difference "when difference means dominance" and therefore affirms "the qualities
   and characteristics of powerlessness"); and Linda Kerber, "Some Cautionary
   Words for Historians," *Signs* 11 (1986): 304 (assessing dangers in suggesting biological source of differences). Some feminists who have embraced her conclusions
   have been critical of her methodology or style. See, for example, Judy Auerbach,
   Linda Blum, Vicki Smith, and Christine Williams, "Commentary: On Gilligan's *A
   Different Voice*," *Feminist Studies* (Spring 1985): 149, 160 ("The problem with her

book is not that its politics are bad, but that it lacks a politics altogether"). Others have accepted the work, and considered principally its implications. See, for example, Jessica Benjamin, "Book Review," *Signs* 8 (Winter 1983): 297, 298 ("Gilligan's work . . . points to the radical potential of women's search for universal norms through a psychological rather than a formal logical mode of thought"); Suzzana Sherry, "Civic Virtue and the Feminine Voice in Constitutional Adjudication," *Virginia Law Review* 72 (1986): 543, 591 (Gilligan's work implies "a feminine vision" of "a mature virtue-based ideology" that "has been conspicuously absent from the shaping of [American] moral or political traditions"). Cf. Lindsy Van Gelder, "Carol Gilligan: Leader for a Different Kind of Future," *Ms.* (January 1984): 37 (uncritical acceptance of the work).

7. Stokely Carmichael and Charles V. Hamilton, *Black Power: The Politics of Liberation in America* (New York: Random House, 1967), pp. 61–62.

8. See, for example, Stanley Crouch, *Notes of a Hanging Judge* (New York: Oxford University Press, 1990); Randall Kennedy, "Racial Critiques of Legal Academia," *Harvard Law Review* 102 (1989): 1745.

9. Harold Cruse, *The Crisis of the Negro Intellectual* (New York: William Morrow, 1967), p. 475.

10. Edward Shils, "Color and the Afro-Asian Intellectual," *Daedalus* (Spring 1967): 279, 288.

11. Ibid., p. 293.

12. This story is recounted by Peter Brimelow in "A Man Alone," *Forbes,* 24 August 1987, p. 40. According to Brimelow, Sowell refused to confirm or deny it.

13. Julius Lester, *Lovesong: Becoming a Jew* (New York: H. Holt, 1988), p. 172.

14. Quoted in Edwin McDowell, "A Noted 'Hispanic' Novelist Proves to be Someone Else," *New York Times,* 22 July, 1984. p. 1.

15. David Tracy, *Plurality and Ambiguity: Hermeneutics, Religion, Hope* (San Francisco: Harper & Row, 1987), pp. 20–21.

16. Alexander M. Bickel, *The Morality of Consent* (New Haven: Yale University Press, 1975), p. 111.

17. See, for example, Thomas Sowell, *Ethnic America* (New York: Basic Books, 1981).

18. See, for example, Richard Wasserstrom, "One Way to Understand and Defend Programs of Preferential Treatment," in Robert K. Fullinwider and Claudia Mills, eds., *The Moral Foundations of Civil Rights* (Totowa, N. J.: Rowman & Littlefield, 1986); Carter A. Wilson, "Affirmative Action: Exploding the Myths of a Slandered Policy," *Black Scholar* (May/June 1986): 19.

19. I discuss the problem of black anti-Semitism in Stephen L. Carter, "Loving the Messenger," *Yale Journal of Law and the Humanities* (May 1989): 317.

20. Lester, *Lovesong,* p. 65.

21. Quoted in William L. Shirer, *The Rise and Fall of the Third Reich: A History of Nazi Germany* (New York: Simon and Schuster, 1960), p. 895n.

22. Judith N. Shklar, *Ordinary Vices* (Cambridge: Harvard/Belknap, 1984), p. 17.

23. J. R. Green, letter to the editor, *New York Times,* 22 March 1990, p. A26.

24. Gordon Allport, *The Nature of Prejudice* (Garden City, NY: Doubleday, 1955), p. 9.

25. A detailed reminder of this stark fact is Thomas Sowell's *Preferential Policies: An International Perspective* (New York: William Morrow, 1990).

Questions

1. Both King (see selection later in this chapter) and Carter refer to the "debt" that is owed to blacks. How are their perceptions of this debt similar?
2. Carter compares racial difference to gender difference. Do you think his comparison is valid?
3. What are the drawbacks of the "you can't understand" approach that the diversity movement often utilizes?
4. Why does Carter feel that the diversity movement makes an "analytical error" when it insists that "our specialness *adds value* to us in a way the specialness of other people does not"?

Prejudice

PETER ROSE

Peter Rose (b. 1933) is a professor of sociology and anthropology at Smith College. He has written extensively on racial and ethnic issues. His publications include The Subject Is Race *(1968),* Strangers in Their Midst *(1977), and* They and We *(1981).*

In this excerpt, Rose explains how ethnocentric thinking is almost unconsciously passed on to our children through vehicles such as literature and patriotism. He argues that ethnocentricity is in one sense a protective gesture for we tend to both fear and generalize the unknown and that ethnocentricity serves to enhance group cohesion. This selection is from They and We.

All good people agree,
   And all good people say,
All nice people like Us, are We
   And everyone else is They.

In a few short lines, Rudyard Kipling captured the essence of what sociol- 1
ogists and anthropologists call *ethnocentric thinking*. Members of all societies tend to believe that "All nice people like Us, are We . . ." They find comfort in the familiar and often denigrate or distrust others. Of course, with training and experience in other climes, they may learn to transcend their provincialism, placing themselves in others' shoes. Or, as Kipling put it,

   . . . if you cross over the sea,
      Instead of over the way,
You may end by (think of it!) looking on We
      As only a sort of They.

In a real sense, a main lesson of the sociology of intergroup relations is to 2
begin to "cross over the sea," to learn to understand why other people think and act as they do and to be able to empathize with their perspectives even if one still does not accept them. But this is no easy task. Many barriers—political, economic, social, and personal—stand in the way of such international (and intergroup) understanding. According to William Graham Sumner, ethnocentrism "leads a people to exaggerate and intensify everything in their own folkways which is peculiar and which differentiates them from others." Intensive socialization to particular points of view and notions of what is right and wrong and good and bad has a long-lasting effect.

226

Sometimes the teaching is very explicit regarding the superior quality of   3
one's own culture; sometimes it is more subtle. Consider the following poem
written by Robert Louis Stevenson and taught to many English and American
children.

> Little Indian, Sioux or Crow,
> Little frosty Eskimo,
> Little Turk or Japanese,
> O! don't you wish that you were me?
>
> You have seen the scarlet trees
> And the lions over seas;
> You have eaten ostrich eggs,
> And turned the turtles off their legs.
>
> Such a life is very fine,
> But it's not so nice as mine;
> You must often, as you trod,
> Have wearied, not to be abroad.
>
> You have curious things to eat,
> I am fed on proper meat;
> You must dwell beyond the foam
> But I am safe to live at home.
>
> Little Indian, Sioux or Crow,
> Little frosty Eskimo,
> Little Turk or Japanese,
> O! don't you wish that you were me?

Raised on such literary fare it should not be surprising that children de-   4
velop negative ideas about the ways of others. Undoubtedly many young
people in this society still find it hard to understand how those in other lands
can become vegetarians, worship ancestors, practice infanticide, or engage in
polygamy. They are confused by the fact that many Moslem women wear the
chador (the veil to cover their faces), that Balinese women go bare-breasted,
and that some people wear no clothes at all. They are troubled when they
learn that many nations emerging from colonial status favor one-party states
and communism over our political system.

American ethnocentricity, while manifest in general attitudes toward oth-   5
ers is, of course, tempered somewhat by the very heterogeneity of the population that we have been examining. Thus, while there are the broad
standards—expressed in the ways most Americans set goals for their children,
organize their political lives, and think about their society in contrast to others—living in our racial and ethnic mosaic makes us more inclined to think
in terms of layers or circles of familiarity. A black from Chicago feels and
thinks very "American" in Lagos or Nairobi as does an Italian from Brooklyn
when visiting relatives in Calabria or Sicily. But when they get home, they
will generally revert to feeling "black" in contrast to "white" and Italian in
comparison to other Americans in their own communities.

Ethnocentrism is found in political as well as in ethnic contexts. Much of   6
the discussion of patriotism and loyalty is couched in language that reflects
rather narrow culture-bound thinking. At various periods in our history this
phenomenon has been particularly marked—we remind ourselves of the na-
tivistic movements of the pre–Civil War period, of the anti-foreign organizations during the time of greatest immigration, and the McCarthyism of the
early 1950s. During the McCarthy era there was a widespread attempt to impose the notion that anyone who had ever joined a Marxist study group, supported the Loyalists in the Spanish Civil War, or belonged to any one of a
number of liberal organizations was "un-American."

It is clear that not only those "over the sea" are viewed (and view others)   7
ethnocentrically. These distinctions between "they" and "we" exist within societies as well. In modern industrial societies most individuals belong to a
wide array of social groups that differentiate them from others—familial, religious, occupational, recreational, and so on. Individuals are frequently
caught in a web of conflicting allegiances. This situation is often surmounted
by a hierarchical ranking of groups as referents for behavior. In most societies,
including our own, the family is the primary reference group. As we have
seen in the United States, ethnic or racial identity and religious affiliation are
also relevant referents. Members of other ethnic, racial, and religious groups
are often judged on the basis of how closely they conform to the standards of
the group passing judgment.

Thus, several studies have shown that in American society many whites   8
holding Christian beliefs, who constitute both the statistical majority and the
dominant group, rank minorities along a continuum of social acceptability.
They rate members of minority groups in descending order in terms of how
closely the latter approximate their image of "real Americans." Early studies of
"social distance" indicated that most ranked groups in the following manner:
Protestants from Europe at the top, then, Irish Catholics, Iberians, Italians,
Jews, Spanish-Americans, American-born Chinese and Japanese, blacks, and
foreign-born Asians. A 1966 study suggested the following rank order: English,
French, Swedes, Italians, Scots, Germans, Spaniards, Jews, Chinese, Russians,
and blacks. (In late 1979 Iranian-Americans became scapegoats for many other
Americans frustrated by the takeover of the United States Embassy in Teheran
by supporters of the Ayatollah Khomeini. Were a social distance scale constructed at the time Iranians—and Muslims in general— probably would have
ranked very low.) While, over the years, most Americans generally have considered those of English or Canadian ancestry to be acceptable citizens, good
neighbors, social equals, and desirable marriage partners, relatively few feel
the same way about those who rank low in scales of social distance.

There is an interesting correlate to this finding. Investigators have found   9
that minority-group members themselves tend to accept the dominant
group's ranking system—with one exception: each tends to put his or her
own group at the top of the scale.

Ranking is one characteristic of ethnocentric thinking; generalizing is an-   10
other. The more another group differs from one's own, the more one is likely

to generalize about its social characteristics and to hold oversimplified attitudes toward its members. When asked to describe our close friends, we are able to cite their idiosyncratic traits: we may distinguish among subtle differences of physiognomy, demeanor, intelligence, and interests. It becomes increasingly difficult to make the same careful evaluation of casual neighbors; it is almost impossible when we think of people we do not know at first-hand. Understandably, the general tendency is to assign strangers to available group categories that seem to be appropriate. Such labeling is evident in generalized images of "lazy" Indians, "furtive" Japanese, "passionate" Latins, and "penny-pinching" Scots.

Ranking others according to one's own standards and categorizing them into generalized stereotypes together serve to widen the gap between "they" and "we." Freud has written that "in the undisguised antipathies and aversions which people feel toward strangers with whom they have to do we may recognize the expression of self-love—of narcissim." In sociological terms, a function of ethnocentric thinking is the enhancement of group cohesion. There is a close relationship between a high degree of ethnocentrism on the part of one group and an increase of antipathy toward others. This relationship tends to hold for ethnocentrism of both dominant and minority groups. 11

Questions

1. Explain what Rose means by ethnocentric thinking. Can you think of examples from your own experience in which you have been exposed to American ethnocentricity?
2. Rose says that for most people, the family is the primary reference group. Can you think of values or attitudes that have been instilled in you that are particular to your family?
3. According to Rose, why do we stereotype cultural groups with whom we are unfamiliar? Can you think of any labels given to different cultural groups?
4. What is the function of ethnocentric thinking?
5. In what ways is your thinking ethnocentric? What types of referent groups (ethnical, racial, religious, familial) have affected your attitudes and behavior?

Ethnic Envidia

RUBEN NAVARRETTE, JR.

Ruben Navarrette, Jr., is the editor of Hispanic Student USA.

In this selection, Navarrette argues that Mexican-Americans have fallen behind other ethnic groups politically and economically because of the pressure of "envidia"—the jealousy and hatred that some Mexican-Americans exhibit when their peers are successful. Rather than condemning those who appear to "sell out," Navarrette urges that only ethnic solidarity can overcome such external forces as racism and discrimination. This selection is from the Los Angeles Times *(1992).*

The savaging of one by another over individual differences is learned behavior. Learned early. A friend recalls, with pain in her voice, a certain afternoon, almost 20 summers ago, in a small town in Arizona. Her mother had gone to great expense to buy her a pretty dress for school. When she arrived, she was teased by a group of Mexican children who insulted her attire for being too prim, too proper. "Aw, look at her pretty dress. She must think she's white or something." My friend ran home with tears dripping down her face and onto her blue dress.

Privately, I wonder where children learn to devour one another so viciously. It is, I suspect, something they learn from watching their elders.

As the nation's fastest growing minority group, Mexican-Americans continue to fall behind other ethnic groups economically and politically. Part of the reason may be how they relate to one another.

On college campuses, among shelves of Shakespeare and vaulted dining halls, we train our intra-racial assassins. There, privileged young Latinos, afraid of being found out as ethnic frauds, sharpen their skills at destroying one another, fueled by hatred and competition and intolerance of personal differences.

A friend remembers seeing an ambitious Mexican-American law student at Boalt Hall sternly scolded by Chicano classmates. She had announced her intention of pursuing a career in corporate law. Since the Latino left contingent at the law school—those who did not fulfill their thirst for Mexican blood in college—had decided that the *ethnically correct* career path led not to corporate America but to public service, they took it upon themselves to harass the young woman for her error. When my friend entered the room, he found her sitting on a couch in tears while a handful of Chicano brethren lectured her with pointed fingers in a spectacle resembling a feeding frenzy.

And, there are professionals. Grown-ups who should know better. A   6
Latino attorney in Beverly Hills tells the tale of being an ethnic outcast since
he practiced law from what the Latino left considers the wrong side. As a federal prosecutor sending *Mexican-Americans* to jail, he was unpopular with old
buddies. "Can you believe what he's doing now? Putting his own people in
jail!" *Sell-out.*

And Latinos know well the concept of selling out, reserving for it in our   7
collective hearts a special place. A dark, ugly place. The Latino left considers a
sell-out someone who succeeds at the expense of his or her own cultural integrity. In Spanish, the word for such a person is an insult of particularly vicious bite. Even the angriest of Chicano activists use it sparingly. We say it
with scorn: *vendido.*

There are more euphemisms: *Un Tio Taco,* a variation of the character of   8
Uncle Tom in Harriet Beecher Stowe's classic; *Una Mosca En Leche,* referring to
a (brown) fly in (white) milk, trying to blend in. A *coconut*—literally, brown
on the outside—where it is seen, but white on the inside—where it counts.
What it means to be "white on the inside" is sorted out by those who toss
terms like hand grenades.

When the grenades miss, there is more direct action. A Latino administra-   9
tor at UCLA relays to me with glee the reaction of a group of Chicano undergraduates to a conservative Latina in the Reagan Administration. Someone
was incensed enough by her remarks to break into her car and defecate on
the front seat.

I saw the same official address a group of Latino students at Harvard Uni-   10
versity. She opened the floor to questions. In the Ivy League, our intra-racial
destruction is more subtle. A Latino graduate student fired away. "Isn't your
reconciliatory tone influenced by the fact that your husband is white?" With
that, the discourse digressed into a David Duke rally against miscegenation.

Harsh personal attacks between Mexican-Americans are old and tired   11
remnants of an earlier, darker age. We accuse those fellow Chicanos with
whom we disagree on political issues of somehow betraying us on a personal
level.

There is yet another obstacle for Latinos to overcome before they may   12
claim that elusive entity called unity. We direct it not at those who have "sold
out," but rather at those with whom we would like to trade places. Those of
whom we are jealous. We admit its cancer among ourselves in whispered,
frustrated voices. We acknowledge it with a squinted eye and a shake of our
head—*envidia.*

In English, the term means "envy," the green-eyed desire to have what   13
another has. With Mexican-Americans, the term assumes a special significance. It is an emotion directed most often at those who are considered too
close to positions of wealth, prestige, influence or power.

It is there in the heart of the teen-age girl who resents her girlfriend for   14
being more popular. It is there in the minds of Chicano students at Stanford
who wish each other well in securing that summer internship, while hoping
theirs will be the juiciest plum of all. And it is there, among family (*entre fa-*

milia) who accuse the Harvard Man in their ranks of thinking himself "better than the rest of us" and secretly hope that he will not accomplish the goals he has set for himself.

Perhaps it is there any time that a member of a disadvantaged community strives to crawl out of the bucket and is rewarded for the effort with snide remarks from those left behind. Too intelligent. Too ambitious. Too good for the lives that others live.   15

Strangely, the one individual whom I have seen generate the greatest amount of *envidia* among some Latinos has also enjoyed the most support from others. In the 1980s, Henry G. Cisneros, the former mayor of San Antonio, became the most prominent of Latino political figures.   16

During a chat with a Chicano Studies professor from Berkeley, I cited Cisneros as my choice for a speaker for a Harvard forum. He made a snide remark about what was then the mayor's admission of marital indiscretion. Just recently, at the opening of the Republican Convention, there was another such remark following a Cisneros pledge to rally Latino support for Bill Clinton— and it was traced to U.S. Treasurer Catalina Vasquez Villalpando. To appease her party's thirst for infidelity blood, this Latina on the Bush Administration offered up one of her own.   17

In my lifetime, I may see a Latino mayor of Los Angeles or governor of California. What I have not seen, perhaps will not see, are Latino professionals holding raised hands in unity. *"You be the candidate this time, I'll go next."* Ethnic solidarity, a successful economic and political tool for American Jews and other ethnic groups, eludes Latinos.   18

I had hoped my generation could stop playing these hurtful games and, finally, respect each other's personal and ideological differences. For 50 years, the Old Guard has attributed the stagnation of the Latino population to external forces like white racism and discrimination. Yet, there are *internal* forces at work as well.   19

For Latinos, there has been little cooperation or camaraderie. And so little progress. Petty competition, personal intolerance and a refusal to let any of our own progress ahead of us make it unlikely that the *children of the sun,* however numerous, will ever inherit the earth.   20

Questions

1. According to Navarrette, what is a "sell out"? Why are successful individuals often considered "ethnic frauds"?

2. Have you ever felt the pressure to conform to some kind of culturally accepted behavior? Do you agree with Navarrette that this pressure stems from jealousy?

3. In what ways are the cultural pressures that Navarrette describes the same as or different from the pressures described by Gorov?

I Have a Dream

MARTIN LUTHER KING, JR.

Martin Luther King, Jr. (1929–1968) won the Nobel Peace Prize in 1964 for his leadership in the civil rights movement and his emphasis on racial integration through nonviolent means. This speech was delivered at the Lincoln Memorial in 1963 to commemorate the 100-year anniversary of the Emancipation Proclamation. King was assassinated in Memphis in 1968.

In this speech, King calls for "the unalienable rights of life, liberty, and the pursuit of happiness," which continue to be denied to blacks, and which will eventually prove "fatal" to the nation. Perhaps in response to the more direct and violent agenda of Malcolm X, King argues that the struggle for freedom must only be conducted on "the high plane of dignity and discipline."

Five score years ago, a great American, in whose symbolic shadow we stand, signed the Emancipation Proclamation. This momentous decree came as a great beacon light of hope to millions of Negro slaves who had been seared in the flames of withering injustice. It came as a joyous daybreak to end the long night of captivity.

But one hundred years later, we must face the tragic fact that the Negro is still not free. One hundred years later, the life of the Negro is still sadly crippled by the manacles of segregation and the chains of discrimination. One hundred years later, the Negro lives on a lonely island of poverty in the midst of a vast ocean of material prosperity. One hundred years later, the Negro is still languishing in the corners of American society and finds himself an exile in his own land. So we have come here today to dramatize an appalling condition.

In a sense we have come to our nation's Capitol to cash a check. When the architects of our republic wrote the magnificent words of the Constitution and the Declaration of Independence, they were signing a promissory note to which every American was to fall heir. This note was a promise that all men would be guaranteed the unalienable rights of life, liberty, and the pursuit of happiness.

It is obvious today that America has defaulted on this promissory note insofar as her citizens of color are concerned. Instead of honoring this sacred obligation, America has given the Negro people a bad check; a check which has come back marked "insufficient funds." But we refuse to believe that the bank of justice is bankrupt. We refuse to believe that there are insufficient

233

funds in the great vaults of opportunity of this nation. So we have come to cash this check—a check that will give us upon demand the riches of freedom and the security of justice. We have also come to this hallowed spot to remind America of the fierce urgency of *now*. This is no time to engage in the luxury of cooling off or to take the tranquilizing drug of gradualism. *Now* is the time to make real the promises of Democracy. *Now* is the time to rise from the dark and desolate valley of segregation to the sunlit path of racial justice. *Now* is the time to open the doors of opportunity to all of God's children. *Now* is the time to lift our nation from the quicksands of racial injustice to the solid rock of brotherhood.

It would be fatal for the nation to overlook the urgency of the moment   5 and to underestimate the determination of the Negro. This sweltering summer of the Negro's legitimate discontent will not pass until there is an invigorating autumn of freedom and equality. 1963 is not an end, but a beginning. Those who hope that the Negro needed to blow off steam and will now be content will have a rude awakening if the nation returns to business as usual. There will be neither rest nor tranquility in America until the Negro is granted his citizenship rights. The whirlwinds of revolt will continue to shake the foundations of our nation until the bright day of justice emerges.

But there is something I must say to my people who stand on the warm   6 threshold which leads into the palace of justice. In the process of gaining our rightful place we must not be guilty of wrongful deeds. Let us not seek to satisfy our thirst for freedom by drinking from the cup of bitterness and hatred. We must forever conduct our struggle on the high plane of dignity and discipline. We must not allow our creative protest to degenerate into physical violence. Again and again we must rise to the majestic heights of meeting physical force with soul force. The marvelous new militancy which has engulfed the Negro community must not lead us to a distrust of all white people, for many of our white brothers, as evidenced by their presence here today, have come to realize that their destiny is tied up with our destiny and their freedom is inextricably bound to our freedom. We cannot walk alone.

And as we walk, we must make the pledge that we shall march ahead. We   7 cannot turn back. There are those who are asking the devotees of civil rights, "When will you be satisfied?" We can never be satisfied as long as the Negro is the victim of the unspeakable horrors of police brutality. We can never be satisfied as long as our bodies, heavy with the fatigue of travel, cannot gain lodging in the motels of the highways and the hotels of the cities. We cannot be satisfied as long as the Negro's basic mobility is from a smaller ghetto to a larger one. We can never be satisfied as long as a Negro in Mississippi cannot vote and a Negro in New York believes he has nothing for which to vote. No, no, we are not satisfied, and we will not be satisfied until justice rolls down like waters and righteousness like a mighty stream.

I am not unmindful that some of you have come here out of great trials   8 and tribulations. Some of you have come fresh from narrow jail cells. Some of you have come from areas where your quest for freedom left you battered by the storms of persecution and staggered by the winds of police brutality. You have been the veterans of creative suffering. Continue to work with the faith that unearned suffering is redemptive.

Go back to Mississippi, go back to Alabama, go back to South Carolina, go back to Georgia, go back to Louisiana, go back to the slums and ghettoes of our northern cities, knowing that somehow this situation can and will be changed. Let us not wallow in the valley of despair. 9

I say to you today, my friends, that in spite of the difficulties and frustrations of the moment I still have a dream. It is a dream deeply rooted in the American dream. 10

I have a dream that one day this nation will rise up and live out the true meaning of its creed: "We hold these truths to be self-evident; that all men are created equal." 11

I have a dream that one day on the red hills of Georgia the sons of former slaves and the sons of former slaveowners will be able to sit down together at the table of brotherhood. 12

I have a dream that the state of Mississippi, a desert state sweltering with the heat of injustice and oppression, will be transformed into an oasis of freedom and justice. 13

I have a dream that my four little children will one day live in a nation where they will not be judged by the color of their skin but by the content of their character. 14

I have a dream today. 15

I have a dream that the state of Alabama, whose governor's lips are presently dripping with the words of interposition and nullification, will be transformed into a situation where little black boys and black girls will be able to join hands with little white boys and white girls and walk together as sisters and brothers. 16

I have a dream today. 17

I have a dream that one day every valley shall be exalted, every hill and mountain shall be made low, the rough places will be made plain, and the crooked places will be made straight, and the glory of the Lord shall be revealed, and all flesh shall see it together. 18

This is our hope. This is the faith with which I return to the South. With this faith we will be able to hew out of the mountain of despair a stone of hope. With this faith we will be able to transform the jangling discords of our nation into a beautiful symphony of brotherhood. With this faith we will be able to work together, to pray together, to struggle together, to go to jail together, to stand up for freedom together, knowing that we will be free one day. 19

This will be the day when all of God's children will be able to sing with new meaning. 20

My country, tis of thee
Sweet land of liberty,
   Of thee I sing:
Land where my fathers died,

Land of the pilgrims' pride,
From every mountainside
  Let freedom ring.

And if America is to be a great nation this must become true. So let free- 21
dom ring from the prodigious hilltops of New Hampshire. Let freedom ring
from the mighty mountains of New York. Let freedom ring from the height-
ening Alleghenies of Pennsylvania!

  Let freedom ring from the snowcapped Rockies of Colorado!   22
  Let freedom ring from the curvaceous peaks of California!   23
  But not only that; let freedom ring from Stone Mountain of Georgia! 24
  Let freedom ring from Lookout Mountain of Tennessee!   25
  Let freedom ring from every hill and molehill of Mississippi. From every 26
mountainside, let freedom ring.

  When we let freedom ring, when we let it ring from every village and 27
every hamlet, from every state and every city, we will be able to speed up that
day when all of God's children, black men and white men, Jews and Gentiles,
Protestants and Catholics, will be able to join hands and sing in the words of
the old Negro spiritual, "Free at last! free at last! thank God almighty, we are
free at last!"

Questions

1. King argues for a course of nonviolent action to achieve those "unalienable
    rights" that many Americans take for granted. What are his reasons for insisting
    on nonviolence? Why is this approach effective? Why do you think some activists
    feel only direct physical force is effective?

2. List some of the metaphors King uses to describe the black condition in the 1960s.
    Why are these metaphors fitting? Why are they effective?

3. Would Martin Luther King, Jr., be satisfied with the black condition today? Why
    or why not?

Cultural Borrowing

BEBE MOORE CAMPBELL

BeBe Moore Campbell is a journalist living in Los Angeles who writes on a wide range of social issues.

In this piece, Campbell describes how different races emulate the physical appearances of each other, and questions whether this imitation is a manifestation of "racial envy" or "self-hatred." However, she argues that although the imitation of perceived physical beauty may be the first step toward racial harmony, it is more constructive "to talk to each other more . . . to exchange life stories." This selection is from NPR's "Morning Edition" (1992).

BEBE MOORE CAMPBELL (Commentator): Summertime and the living is definitely not easy. It's hard work getting a tan. Yes, Americans are making their annual trek to the beaches or the tanning salon in search of the bronze look. The quest to be beige is a ritual participated in, for the most part but by no means exclusively, by white Americans. Some may want to tan so that they can be out in the sun without danger of burning, but a lot of others simply feel that brown skin, or coppertone, if you will, is more attractive. No matter the dire warnings about wrinkling or even death, looking good—that's the name of the beauty crossover game, and tanning is only part of the cultural borrowing that many Americans are engaging in these days in the relentless search for beauty. 1

Marriages between races were illegal in most of the 50 states until the mid-'60s. One of the grand dragons of the Ku Klux Klan used to warn that if blacks and whites intermarried, they would produce a nation of mongrels. Well, only 2 percent of Americans marry outside of their race, but look around you. Our nation is becoming racially mixed without miscegenation. Even David Duke has a tan. Welcome to Muttsville, USA. A walk down any urban street will reveal Asians and Hispanics with blue and green contact lenses and salon curled hair of all shades. Thin-lipped and fat-hipped people are plumping up their mouths and their behinds with collagen, while those folks of all ethnicities with fleshy or hump noses have them surgically narrowed. Dreadlocks, once the stylistic province of rastafarians, have been adopted by some European-Americans. 2

And go to any African-American community in America and you will find some very dark-skinned women with very unnaturally blond hair and maybe a jar of Porcelana skin lightener in their medicine cabinets. Despite the tanning craze that captivates so many white Americans, a lot of black 3

237

Americans are still convinced that having light skin gives a person a decided beauty advantage. What does all this mean? To be sure, some of this cultural borrowing is about racial envy, and some, sad to say, is about self-hatred. But a lot of it is simply a matter of, "Hey, I like the way you look. I want to look like that." If imitation is the sincerest form of flattery, we all ought to feel pretty good, or at least better.

Too bad cultural borrowing doesn't come with a set of emotional require-   4
ments. If you're going to see light through someone else's eyes, breathe the air through a borrowed nose, if you're going to get into someone else's skin, it seems you ought to be able to get into her head first. It's relatively easy to look like another person, a little more difficult, but often far more beneficial, to feel like someone else. That comes not from sharing beauty secrets, but exchanging life stories. Americans need to get to know one another better, to go beyond the superficialities of skin and hair and eye color right to the heart of our diversity. We need to talk to each other more. Maybe then America would feel as good as it looks.

Questions

1. Why, in your opinion, is a tan a sign of beauty for Americans? Campbell implies that it is a sign of racial flattery or emulation. Do you agree?
2. Campbell also describes cultural borrowing as a form of "self-hatred." What does she mean by this? Do you agree with her interpretation?
3. How would Schlesinger and Dasenbrock interpret Campbell's observations?

Writing Assignments

The following writing assignments are based on the readings in this chapter. Before developing a thesis and planning your response, complete the following activities:

- Write responses to exploration questions.
- Read outside material to discover at least two perspectives on the topic.
- Create a list of opposing viewpoints and consider the potential consequences of each one.
- Examine the underlying assumptions behind each viewpoint.

To help you understand the issues and develop ideas, you can use the following form:

The conflict in this issue is between _____ and__
_____.

I am more inclined to agree with _____

because _____ .

However, it is possible that some of my readers may believe that

_____ .

Exploration Questions

1. List the qualities you believe define the American character. Compare your list with that of a classmate.
2. Describe your high school history classes. Would you describe the curriculum as multicultural or Eurocentric? Why?
3. To what extent does your lifestyle reflect a particular ethnic or racial heritage? What aspects of your lifestyle would you define as uniquely "American"?
4. In your opinion, why are Americans often intolerant of immigrants?
5. For most people, the family is the primary reference group in shaping attitudes and values. Which attitudes and values were most important in your family? Compare answers with a classmate.

ASSIGNMENT

In his recent book, *The Disuniting of America,* Arthur M. Schlesinger, Jr., warns of the dangers of separatism, maintaining that the "cult of ethnicity" and bilingualism that are supposed to affirm racial and cultural pride will lead instead to fragmentation, segregation, and racial hostility. Using the readings in this chapter, write an argumentative essay discussing the extent to which you agree or disagree with Schlesinger's position.

Using Data

ASSIGNMENTS

1. What are some conclusions that can be drawn from the following table about immigration rates?
2. How could this table be used in the debate over cultural pluralism (i.e., the melting pot vs. tossed salad)?

Immigration 1820 to 1989

Period	Number	Rate[*]
1820–1989	55,458	3.4
1820–1830	152	1.2
1831–1840	599	3.9
1841–1850	1,713	8.4
1851–1860	2,598	9.3
1861–1870	2,315	6.4
1871–1880	2,812	6.2
1881–1890	5,247	9.2
1891–1900	3,688	5.3
1901–1910	8,795	10.4
1911–1920	5,736	5.7
1921–1930	4,107	3.5
1931–1940	528	0.4
1941–1950	1,035	0.7
1951–1960	2,515	1.5
1961–1970	3,322	1.7
1971–1980	4,493	2.1
1981–1989	5,802	2.7
1970	373	1.8
1971	370	1.8
1972	385	1.8
1973	400	1.9
1974	395	1.9
1975	386	1.8
1976	399	1.9
1977	462	2.1
1978	601	2.8
1979	460	2.1
1980	531	2.3
1981	597	2.6
1982	594	2.6
1983	560	2.4
1984	544	2.3
1985	570	2.4
1986	602	2.5
1987	602	2.5
1988	643	2.6
1989	1,091	4.4

[*] Annual rate per 1,000 U.S. population. Rate computed by dividing sum of annual immigration totals by sum of annual U.S. population totals for same number of years.

Source: Based on U.S. Bureau of the Census estimates.

6 ■ Diversity in Language

With 500,000 words, the English vocabulary is larger than that of any other language, partly because 80 percent of English words come from foreign sources.
DOUGLAS CAZORT, *UNDER THE GRAMMAR HAMMER*

Many people are under the impression that just about everyone in the United States speaks English, and some, in fact, think that people in other countries also speak English or at least ought to. The stereotype of the ugly American traveler who expects everyone to speak English and is annoyed when everyone does not has become an embarrassing cultural stereotype that reflects the ambiguity with which many Americans view foreign languages. They may profess to have great admiration and tolerance for other languages and cultures and may even institute foreign language requirements in the schools. Yet, they are sometimes uneasy with non-English speakers and suspicious of people who speak English with an accent or use a nonstandard dialect. Because language is an important facet of culture and has a significant impact on how diverse groups interact with one another, this chapter examines the complex relationship between language and culture, focusing on two controversial topics: the debate over whether English ought to be declared the official language of the United States, and the conflict over methods of educating non-English-speaking children.

To begin your exploration of the issues associated with language and diversity, imagine what it would be like to attend a meeting of the United Nations without the benefits of simultaneous translation. Or, if you have had the experience of visiting a country where people do not speak your native language, recall some of the difficulties you may have had in understanding what people said or in making yourself understood. Finally, as another way of understanding this topic, turn on your television to a station that broadcasts in a language other than your own. All of these instances illustrate some of the challenges of living and working in a multilingual society, and raise the question of whether communication and understanding, not to mention peace and harmony, can ever occur unless everyone speaks a common language.

Multilingualism in the United States: The English–Only Movement

Although the United States is generally regarded as an English-speaking country, there have always been a large number of people in the United States for whom English is not a first language and who speak a language other than English at home. Throughout United States history, English-speaking Americans have, for the most part, been able to live in relative harmony with those who speak another language. However, from time to time, differences in language have generated feelings of uneasiness, and at these times, movements have arisen to make English the official language—that is, the institutionalized public language—for education and legal proceedings. The motives behind these movements have usually been in the interest of fostering national unity, of maximizing communication, or of fostering advancements for non-English-speaking minorities; generally, proponents of the English-only legislation believe that the nation will function more smoothly if everyone speaks the same language. A subset of those in favor of making English the official language, however, are motivated by concern that unless there is a law forcing immigrants to learn English, the unity of the country will suffer and the nation itself will dissolve into squabbling noncommunicating factions, a veritable tower of Babel. This group is intent on fostering assimilation as quickly as possible.

The Debate over Bilingual Education

Related to the controversy concerning the English-only movement is the question of what type of language program will provide the most effective method of preparing non-English-speaking children to live in American society. Some minority writers such as Richard Rodriguez and Rosalie Pedalino Porter, who, as children, learned English as a second language without special assistance, maintain that when one moves to a new country, the only way to learn English is through total immersion in the language. Both writers acknowledge that the process was painful and difficult and that they experienced the loss of some of their own language and culture as a result. Nevertheless, they believe strongly that their acquisition of the English language was the direct result of their having been immersed in the new language.

Other writers and educators believe that because there are so many children who do not speak English, and because many of these children come from the poorer segments of society where the inability to speak English inhibits upward mobility, the schools have an obligation to provide assistance through some form of bilingual education. Some bilingual education programs offer instruction in all subject areas in the children's own language and combine this with a course in English. The goal is that once students reach a level of proficiency in speaking and reading English, all instruction will then shift to English. Other programs use English for instruction in every subject except reading because it is presumed that children will not be able to learn to read in a language they cannot understand but will be able to make the transition to reading in English once they can read in their own language.

One reason there is conflict over how English ought to be taught in the schools is that there is no definitive evidence as to the effectiveness or lack of effectiveness of bilingual programs. Some educators maintain that these programs ease the transition into English; others maintain that they simply delay it. Another facet of the controversy concerns the debate over whether minority-language students should be encouraged to maintain their own language as well as learn English. Most educators who believe that it is important for students to maintain their own language envision a time when the United States will be a truly pluralistic society, where people will speak many languages, in particular, Spanish. These people point out that a policy of multilingualism would be advantageous to both the minority- and majority-language child: the minority-language child would feel a sense of pride in his or her own language, whereas the majority-language child would be enriched by learning another language.

Others point out, however, that aside from certain cities in the United States, such as Los Angeles, San Antonio, and Miami, there is not strong pressure for native English speakers to master Spanish or any other language. They believe that the English language is the vehicle for transmitting values and culture and that frequent use of another language will undermine the formation of an American identity. These people view mastery of English as the key to social mobility, the only way that immigrants will be able to improve their socioeconomic status. They also note that all over the world, English is becoming the true *lingua Franca*, the language that everyone speaks. They believe that the United States should make sure that all citizens learn to speak English; for them, the toleration of other languages is viewed as counterproductive to the creation of a national character.

Black English Dialect

Related to the controversy over bilingual education is the debate concerning black dialect or Black English vernacular as it is referred to by linguists, who use the word "dialect" to refer to how one speech pattern differs from another. A dialect such as black dialect may vary from Standard English by vocabulary, grammar, and pronunciation, but it is important to realize that a dialect is not, in and of itself, either inferior or superior to the standard version of the language—it is simply different. Black dialect contains a systematic internal grammatical structure and is well suited for binding the black community together, for expressing feelings, and for making a political statement about the importance of black culture in the United States. Nevertheless, although black dialect may play an important role within black culture, people who are unable to speak Standard English are often socially and economically disadvantaged.

Immigration to the United States and the Role of Language

Any discussion of how language impacts culture must acknowledge its role during the various waves of immigration to the United States. From its earliest days, the history of the United States has been characterized by a continuous flow of immigrants, many of whom had difficulty learning the language and culture of their new country. During the colonial and revolutionary periods, numerous Native American languages, as well as French, Spanish, Dutch, and German, were spoken, and, in fact, the Articles of Confederation, the document that preceded the Constitution, was translated into German to gain the support of German colonists. Although the framers of the Constitution were native speakers of English and presumed that they were creating a document for an English-speaking country, they did not formally proclaim English as the official language—they were apparently more concerned with political freedom than with establishing cultural or linguistic homogeneity.

During the nineteenth century, a number of non-English-speaking nationalities immigrated to the United States in large groups. From 1830 to 1890, 4.5 million Germans arrived, comprising one-third of the immigrant total. These Germans, like the Swedes, the Dutch, and the French who preceded them, had a great desire to preserve their native language and even succeeded in establishing their own German-speaking public schools. Toward the middle of the century, the termination of the Mexican War (1848) enabled more than 75,000 Mexicans to become American citizens, and from 1860 until 1890, more than ten million immigrants arrived in the United States from Germany, Great Britain, Ireland, Denmark, Norway, Sweden, Austria-Hungary, Italy, and Russia. In the early part of the twentieth century, immigrants streamed into the United States from Poland, Russia, Greece, Italy, and Spain.

Like most immigrants in a new country, each group initially tried hard to retain the language it knew best and, indeed, learned English quite slowly. (Think about how you would feel if you moved to another country. Would you want to give up your language? Would you be able to?) In all of these groups, the learning of the new language began with the younger generation who acted as interpreters for their parents and who ultimately assimilated into American culture. The one exception was found in the experience of Jewish immigrants from Eastern Europe in the early twentieth century who attended the Lower East Side's Educational Alliance, which enabled them to learn English more quickly than other groups. But in all cases, whether or not they learned English quickly, new immigrants were generally regarded with suspicion by those already established; their foreign language and culture rendered them alien.

During the twentieth century, a large influx of immigrants arrived from neighboring Spanish-speaking countries such as Mexico, Cuba, and Puerto Rico, and these people retained their language more persistently than did other groups partly because they continuously revitalized contact with their native land by frequent visitation back and forth. This large number of non-English-speaking immigrants revived interest among some American lawmakers for making English the official language of the country, an act that presumably would facilitate linguistic assimilation. Others disagree, claiming that this group would learn English eventually, just as other groups did and that the learning of a language can never happen by coercion.

Diversity and Language

Certainly, one might make the case that if members of a group do not speak the same language, they are less likely to relate to one another easily or to share a common perspective—indeed, a multilingual gathering of people might not be considered a group at all. According to the twentieth-century linguists Edward Sapir and Benjamin Whorf, language is so important in determining the individual's perception of reality that people who do not speak the same language do not perceive the world in the same way and thus are unable to have a common frame of reference. This view suggests that language and culture are so inextricably intertwined that translation from one language to another is virtually impossible because meaning can only be understood in the context of language. "Human beings . . . are very much at the mercy of the particular language which has become the medium for their society. . . . The fact of the matter is that the 'real world' is to a large extent built up on the language habits of the group" (from Edward Sapir, *Selected Writings*, ed. D.G. Mandelbaum, Berkeley and Los Angeles, 1949). To accept the Sapir-Whorf hypothesis unconditionally suggests that common language is an absolute essential for meaningful communication. However, a less extreme version of this theory maintains that although language certainly influences perception, it does not completely control it and that other nonlinguistic factors are also important. Moreover, as the linguist Deborah Tannen points out in her national best-seller, *You Just Don't Understand,* human beings have always had difficulty communicating, even when they do speak the same language—men and women, for example, often have great difficulty understanding one another's meaning, even when both of them are fluent English speakers.

The articles in this chapter focus on issues concerned with language in a diverse society. Amy Tan's article, "The Language of Discretion," serves as an illustration of the confusion that occurs when two linguistic cultures conflict. Tan questions whether the Chinese language is really a language of discretion, as many Americans presume, and whether this in turn accounts for Chinese peoples' apparent inability to talk candidly. Tan's conclusion is that although from the outside Chinese appears to be an indirect language, it is actually as forceful and direct as it needs to be, once one understands the context. The readings by James Fallows, Juan Cartagena, and Dennis Baron are concerned with the question of how new immigrants are best incorporated into American society and raise issues surrounding the English-only debate. In "The New Immigrants," James Fallows traces the history of immigration to the United States, and discusses his visits to bilingual schools in Texas and California to investigate the nature and the effect of English and Spanish classroom education. Fallows discovers—to his own surprise—that most of the children were unmistakably learning to speak English. Juan Cartagena brings both a general Latino and specific Puerto Rican perspective to the English-only debate in his article "English Only in the 1980s: A Product of Myths, Phobias, and Bias." Cartagena traces the non-native English experience in the United States and the peaks and valleys of measures taken by certain English-speaking bodies to legislate against immigrant groups. He accuses Dr. John Tanton, co-founder with S.I. Hayakawa of U.S. English, a pressure group lobbying to make English the official language of the United States, of racism, and argues that Latinos are learning English faster than other immigrant groups. He points out, however, that attempts to make English mandatory to Puerto Rican students have had a detrimental effect in schools, leading to higher dropout rates. The essay, "An Official Language," by Dennis Baron, taken from the opening chapter to his book, *The English-Only Question: An Official Language for Americans?* outlines the essential pluralistic nature not only of the United States from its inception but also that of the human condition. He shows how established immigrant groups look warily upon ethnic newcomers, and provides striking examples of both support for and repression of minority languages. He concludes by arguing that the continuation of, say, Spanish, will happen only if Hispanic immigration persists. If this does not occur, then Spanish, like other languages spoken by American immigrants, will ultimately be lost in the English mainstream.

The readings by Rosalie Pedalino Porter, and Richard Rodriguez are concerned with differing perspectives on bilingual education. The article, "First-hand Experience in Educating Language Minorities," by Rosalie Pedalino Porter from her book, *Forked Tongue: The Politics of Bilingual Education,* traces Porter's first exposure to English as an immigrant first-grade student, and discusses her experiences implementing some of the first bilingual education courses in the early 1970s. Porter maintains that too much teaching in the students' native language (Spanish) in her classroom hindered their transition to a full use and understanding of English, and concludes that a swifter transition to English must be effected—if, indeed, that is the aim of bilingual education in the first few grades of schooling.

Richard Rodriguez, however, points out in "Learning the Language" that whenever a student makes the transition to English, something of the original culture is lost. Rodriguez recalls his early attempts to reconcile his native tongue, so fluently articulated at home, and the sounds and demands of English in his first classroom. His childhood idea was that Spanish was for him a "private language" to be guarded, whereas English was simply the "public language." Rodriguez feels that by learning English, he lost something of the family's private nature, but this was a necessary change in order for him to access the full possibilities of the family's new society.

Shirley N. Weber and Wayne Lionel Aponte discuss the origin and significance of black dialect to black culture, and weigh the benefits of preserving it against those insisting Standard English is the only acceptable dialect in the culture. Weber illustrates in detail the power of the word in African-American language, the true meaning in its context of "rappin" and the value placed on proverbial language in the black community. Arguing here, in her essay "The Need to Be: The Socio-Cultural Significance of Black Language," that language demonstrates a culture's view of the reality, Weber forcefully asks the reader to understand that because blacks experience the world differently from other groups in America, there is a need for a language that communicates that experience, namely, black English. Wayne Lionel Aponte, in his essay "Talkin' White," does not attribute the same significance to black dialect. At a younger and more vulnerable age, Aponte became polylingual and does not feel the need to talk what he calls "slang" to prove he is black. Research suggests that employers are more likely to hire Standard English speakers, and therefore, it is often useful for speakers of black dialect, whatever its role in affirming black identity, to be able to speak Standard English as well.

As with all problematic social issues, the topic of diversity in language is complex, unlikely to be resolved with simple solutions. The historical context in which ideas about language in the United States have occurred and theories about how language impacts cultural identity constitute a beginning, but it is unlikely that these controversies are going to be resolved in the near future.

The Language of Discretion

AMY TAN

*Born in Oakland, California, in 1952, of Chinese parentage, Amy Tan first
visited China in 1987, and it was a turning point in her life. Having worked
as a free-lance writer, Tan wrote her first novel,* The Joy Luck Club, *which
spent nine months on the* New York Times *best-seller list. Her second book,*
The Kitchen God's Wife, *has enjoyed similar success.*

*In this article, Tan asks whether the Chinese language is a language of
discretion, as many Americans presume, and whether this accounts for Chinese peoples' apparent inability to talk candidly. Tan's measured response is
that Chinese is as forceful and direct as it needs to be; however, from the outside, when the contexts are not understood, Chinese seems overtly cryptic.
This selection is from* The State of the Language *(1990).*

At a recent family dinner in San Francisco, my mother whispered to me: 1
"Sau-sau [Brother's Wife] pretends too hard to be polite! Why bother? In the
end, she always takes everything."

My mother thinks like a *waixiao,* an expatriate, temporarily away from 2
China since 1949, no longer patient with ritual courtesies. As if to prove her
point, she reached across the table to offer my elderly aunt from Beijing the
last scallop from the Happy Family seafood dish.

Sau-sau scowled. *"B'yao, zhen b'yao!"* (I don't want it, really I don't!) she 3
cried, patting her plump stomach.

"Take it! Take it!" scolded my mother in Chinese. 4

"Full, I'm already full," Sau-sau protested weakly, eyeing the beloved scal- 5
lop.

"Ai!" exclaimed my mother, completely exasperated. "Nobody else wants 6
it. If you don't take it, it will only rot!"

At this point, Sau-sau sighed, acting as if she were doing my mother a big 7
favor by taking the wretched scrap off her hands.

My mother turned to her brother, a high-ranking communist official who 8
was visiting her in California for the first time: "In America a Chinese person
could starve to death. If you say you don't want it, they won't ask you again
forever."

My uncle nodded and said he understood fully: Americans take things 9
quickly because they have no time to be polite.

***

I thought about this misunderstanding again—of social contexts failing in 10
translation—when a friend sent me an article from the *New York Times Maga-*

zine (24 April 1988). The article, on changes in New York's Chinatown, made passing reference to the inherent ambivalence of the Chinese language.

Chinese people are so "discreet and modest," the article stated, there 11 aren't even words for "yes" and "no."

That's not true, I thought, although I can see why an outsider might 12 think that. I continued reading.

If one is Chinese, the article went on to say, "One compromises, one 13 doesn't hazard a loss of face by an overemphatic response."

My throat seized. Why do people keep saying these things? As if we truly 14 were those little dolls sold in Chinatown tourist shops, heads bobbing up and down in complacent agreement to anything said!

I worry about the effect of one-dimensional statements on the unwary 15 and guileless. When they read about this so-called vocabulary deficit, do they also conclude that Chinese people evolved into a mild-mannered lot because the language only allowed them to hobble forth with minced words?

Something enormous is always lost in translation. Something insidious 16 seeps into the gaps, especially when amateur linguists continue to compare, one-for-one, language differences and then put forth notions wide open to misinterpretation: that Chinese people have no direct linguistic means to make decisions, assert or deny, affirm or negate, just say no to drug dealers, or behave properly on the witness stand when told, "Please answer yes or no."

Yet one can argue, with the help of renowned linguists, that the Chinese 17 are indeed up a creek without "yes" and "no." Take any number of variations on the old language-and-reality theory stated years ago by Edward Sapir: "Human beings . . . are very much at the mercy of the particular language which has become the medium for their society. . . . The fact of the matter is that the 'real world' is to a large extent built up on the language habits of the group."

This notion was further bolstered by the famous Sapir-Whorf hypothesis, 18 which roughly states that one's perception of the world and how one functions in it depends a great deal on the language used. As Sapir, Whorf, and new carriers of the banner would have us believe, language shapes our thinking, channels us along certain patterns embedded in words, syntactic structures, and intonation patterns. Language has become the peg and the shelf that enables us to sort out and categorize the world. In English, we see "cats" and "dogs"; what if the language had also specified *glatz*, meaning "animals that leave fur on the sofa," and *glotz*, meaning "animals that leave fur and drool on the sofa"? How would language, the enabler, have changed our perceptions with slight vocabulary variations?

And if this were the case—of language being the master of destined 19 thought—think of the opportunities lost from failure to evolve two little words, *yes* and *no*, the simplest of opposites! Ghenghis Khan could have been sent back to Mongolia. Opium wars might have been averted. The Cultural Revolution could have been sidestepped.

There are still many, from serious linguists to pop psychology cultists, 20 who view language and reality as inextricably tied, one being the consequence of the other. We have traversed the range from the Sapir-Whorf hypothesis to est and neurolinguistic programming, which tell us "you are what you say."

I too have been intrigued by the theories. I can summarize, albeit badly, ages-old empirical evidence: of Eskimos and their infinite ways to say "snow," their ability to *see* the differences in snowflake configurations, thanks to the richness of their vocabulary, while non-Eskimo speakers like myself founder in "snow," "more snow," and "lots more where that came from."   21

I too have experienced dramatic cognitive awakenings via the word. Once I added "mauve" to my vocabulary I began to see it everywhere. When I learned how to pronounce *prix fixe,* I ate French food at prices better than the easier-to-say *à la carte* choices.   22

But just how seriously are we supposed to take this?   23

Sapir said something else about language and reality. It is the part that often gets left behind in the dot-dot-dots of quotes:" . . . No two languages are ever sufficiently similar to be considered as representing the same social reality. The worlds in which different societies live are distinct worlds, not merely the same world with different labels attached."   24

When I first read this, I thought, Here at last is validity for the dilemmas I felt growing up in a bicultural, bilingual family! As any child of immigrant parents knows, there's a special kind of double bind attached to knowing two languages. My parents, for example, spoke to me in both Chinese and English; I spoke back to them in English.   25

"Amy-ah!" they'd call to me.   26

"What?" I'd mumble back.   27

"Do not question us when we call," they scolded me in Chinese. "It is not respectful."   28

"What do you mean?"   29

"Ai! Didn't we just tell you not to question?"   30

To this day, I wonder which parts of my behavior were shaped by Chinese, which by English. I am tempted to think, for example, that if I am of two minds on some matter it is due to the richness of my linguistic experiences, not to any personal tendencies toward wishy-washiness. But which mind says what?   31

Was it perhaps patience—developed through years of deciphering my mother's fractured English—that had me listening politely while a woman announced over the phone that I had won one of five valuable prizes? Was it respect—pounded in by the Chinese imperative to accept convoluted explanations—that had me agreeing that I might find it worthwhile to drive seventy-five miles to view a time-share resort? Could I have been at a loss for words when asked, "Wouldn't you like to win a Hawaiian cruise or perhaps a fabulous Star of India designed exclusively by Carter and Van Arpels?"   32

And when this same woman called back a week later, this time complaining that I had missed my appointment, obviously it was my type A language that kicked into gear and interrupted her. Certainly, my blunt denial—"Frankly I'm not interested"—was as American as apple pie. And when she   33 said, "But it's in Morgan Hill," and I shouted, "Read my lips. I don't care if it's Timbuktu," you can be sure I said it with the precise intonation expressing both cynicism and disgust.

It's dangerous business, this sorting out of language and behavior. Which one is English? Which is Chinese? The categories manifest themselves: passive and aggressive, tentative and assertive, indirect and direct. And I realize they are just variations of the same theme: that Chinese people are discreet and modest. 34

Reject them all! 35

If my reaction is overly strident, it is because I cannot come across as too emphatic. I grew up listening to the same lines over and over again, like so many rote expressions repeated in an English phrasebook. And I too almost came to believe them. 36

Yet if I consider my upbringing more carefully, I find there was nothing discreet about the Chinese language I grew up with. My parents made everything abundantly clear. Nothing wishy-washy in their demands, no compromises accepted: "Of course you will become a famous neurosurgeon," they told me. "And yes, a concert pianist on the side." 37

In fact, now that I remember, it seems that the more emphatic outbursts always spilled over into Chinese: "Not that way! You must wash rice so not a single grain spills out." 38

I do not believe that my parents—both immigrants from mainland China—are an exception to the modest-and-discreet rule. I have only to look at the number of Chinese engineering students skewing minority ratios at Berkeley, MIT, and Yale. Certainly they were not raised by passive mothers and fathers who said, "It is up to you, my daughter. Writer, welfare recipient, masseuse, or molecular engineer—you decide." 39

And my American mind says, See, those engineering students weren't able to say no to their parents' demands. But then my Chinese mind remembers: Ah, but those parents all wanted their sons and daughters to be *pre-med*. 40

Having listened to both Chinese and English, I also tend to be suspicious of any comparisons between the two languages. Typically, one language—that of the person doing the comparing—is often used as the standard, the benchmark for a logical form of expression. And so the language being compared is always in danger of being judged deficient or superfluous, simplistic or unnecessarily complex, melodious or cacophonous. English speakers point out that Chinese is extremely difficult because it relies on variations in tone barely discernible to the human ear. By the same token, Chinese speakers tell me English is extremely difficult because it is inconsistent, a language of too many broken rules, of Mickey Mice and Donald Ducks. 41

Even more dangerous to my mind is the temptation to compare both language and behavior *in translation*. To listen to my mother speak English, one might think she has no concept of past or future tense, that she doesn't see the difference between singular and plural, that she is gender blind because she calls my husband "she." If one were not careful, one might also general- 42 ize that, based on the way my mother talks, all Chinese people take a circumlocutory route to get to the point. It is, in fact, my mother's idiosyncratic behavior to ramble a bit.

Sapir was right about differences between two languages and their realities. I   43
can illustrate why word-for-word translation is not enough to translate meaning and intent. I once received a letter from China which I read to non-Chinese speaking friends. The letter, originally written in Chinese, had been translated by my brother-in-law in Beijing. One portion described the time when my uncle at age ten discovered his widowed mother (my grandmother) had remarried—as a number three concubine, the ultimate disgrace for an honorable family. The translated version of my uncle's letter read in part:

> In 1925, I met my mother in Shanghai. When she came to me, I didn't have greeting to her as if seeing nothing. She pull me to a corner secretly and asked me why didn't have greeting to her. I couldn't control myself and cried, "Ma! Why did you leave us? People told me: one day you ate a beancake yourself. Your sister in-law found it and sweared at you, called your names. So . . . is it true?" She clasped my hand and answered immediately, "It's not true, don't say what like this." After this time, there was a few chance to meet her.

"What!" cried my friends. "Was eating a beancake so terrible?"   44
Of course not. The beancake was simply a euphemism; a ten-year-old boy   45
did not dare question his mother on something as shocking as concubinage. Eating a beancake was his equivalent for committing this selfish act, something inconsiderate of all family members, hence, my grandmother's despairing response to what seemed like a ludicrous charge of gluttony. And sure enough, she was banished from the family, and my uncle saw her only a few times before her death.

While the above may fuel people's argument that Chinese is indeed a language of extreme discretion, it does not mean that Chinese people speak in   46
secrets and riddles. The contexts are fully understood. It is only to those on the *outside* that the language seems cryptic, the behavior inscrutable.

I am, evidently, one of the outsiders. My nephew in Shanghai, who recently started taking English lessons, has been writing me letters in English. I   47
had told him I was a fiction writer, and so in one letter he wrote, "Congratulate to you on your writing. Perhaps one day I should like to read it." I took it in the same vein as "Perhaps one day we can get together for lunch." I sent back a cheery note. A month went by and another letter arrived from Shanghai. "Last one perhaps I hadn't writing distinctly," he said. "In the future, you'll send a copy of your works for me."

I try to explain to my English-speaking friends that Chinese language use   48
is more *strategic* in manner, whereas English tends to be more direct; an American business executive may say, "Let's make a deal," and the Chinese manager may reply, "Is your son interested in learning about your widget business?" Each to his or her own purpose, each with his or her own linguistic path. But I hesitate to add more to the pile of generalizations, because no

matter how many examples I provide and explain, I fear that it appears defensive and only reinforces the image: that Chinese people are "discreet and modest"—and it takes an American to explain what they really mean.

Why am I complaining? The description seems harmless enough (after all, 49
the *New York Times Magazine* writer did not say "slippery and evasive"). It is
precisely the bland, easy acceptability of the phrase that worries me.

I worry that the dominant society may see Chinese people from a lim- 50
ited—and limiting—perspective. I worry that seemingly benign stereotypes
may be part of the reason there are few Chinese in top management positions, in mainstream political roles. I worry about the power of language: that
if one says anything enough times—in *any* language—it might become true.

Could this be why Chinese friends of my parents' generation are willing 51
to accept the generalization?

"Why are you complaining?" one of them said to me. "If people think we 52
are modest and polite, let them think that. Wouldn't Americans be pleased to
admit they are thought of as polite?"

And I do believe anyone would take the description as a compliment—at 53
first. But after a while, it annoys, as if the only things that people heard one
say were phatic remarks: "I'm so pleased to meet you. I've heard many wonderful things about you. For me? You shouldn't have!"

These remarks are not representative of new ideas, honest emotions, or 54
considered thought. They are what is said from the polite distance of social
contexts: of greetings, farewells, wedding thank-you notes, convenient excuses, and the like.

It makes me wonder though. How many anthropologists, how many soci- 55
ologists, how many travel journalists have documented so-called "natural interactions" in foreign lands, all observed with spiral notebook in hand? How
many other cases are there of the long-lost primitive tribe, people who turned
out to be sophisticated enough to put on the stone-age show that ethnologists had come to see?

And how many tourists fresh off the bus have wandered into Chinatown 56
expecting the self-effacing shopkeeper to admit under duress that the goods
are not worth the price asked? I have witnessed it.

"I don't know," the tourist said to the shopkeeper, a Cantonese woman in 57
her fifties. "It doesn't look genuine to me. I'll give you three dollars."

"You don't like my price, go somewhere else," said the shopkeeper. 58

"You are not a nice person," cried the shocked tourist, "not a nice person 59
at all!"

"Who say I have to be nice," snapped the shopkeeper. 60

"So how does one say 'yes' and 'no' in Chinese?" ask my friends a bit warily. 61

And here I do agree in part with the *New York Times Magazine* article. 62
There is no one word for "yes" or "no"—but not out of necessity to be discreet. If anything, I would say the Chinese equivalent of answering "yes" or
"no" is dis*crete,* that is, specific to what is asked.

Ask a Chinese person if he or she has eaten, and he or she might say *chrle*   63
(eaten already) or perhaps *meiyou* (have not).

Ask, "So you had insurance at the time of the accident?" and the response   64
would be *dwei* (correct) or *meiyou* (did not have).

Ask, "Have you stopped beating your wife?" and the answer refers directly   65
to the proposition being asserted or denied: stopped already, still have not,
never beat, have no wife.

What could be clearer?   66

As for those who are still wondering how to translate the language of discre-   67
tion, I offer this personal example.

My aunt and uncle were about to return to Beijing after a three-month   68
visit to the United States. On their last night I announced I wanted to take
them out to dinner.

"Are you hungry?" I asked in Chinese.   69

"Not hungry," said my uncle promptly, the same response he once gave   70
me ten minutes before he suffered a low-blood-sugar attack.

"Not too hungry," said my aunt. "Perhaps you're hungry?"   71

"A little," I admitted.   72

"We can eat, we can eat," they both consented.   73

"What kind of food?" I asked.   74

"Oh, doesn't matter. Anything will do. Nothing fancy, just some simple   75
food is fine."

"Do you like Japanese food? We haven't had that yet," I suggested.   76

They looked at each other.   77

"We can eat it," said my uncle bravely, this survivor of the Long March.   78

"We have eaten it before," added my aunt. "Raw fish."   79

"Oh, you don't like it?" I said. "Don't be polite. We can go somewhere else."   80

"We are not being polite. We can eat it," my aunt insisted.   81

So I drove them to Japantown and we walked past several restaurants fea-   82
turing colorful plastic displays of sushi.

"Not this one, not this one either," I continued to say, as if searching for a   83
Japanese restaurant similar to the last. "Here it is," I finally said, turning into
a restaurant famous for its Chinese fish dishes from Shandong.

"Oh, Chinese food!" cried my aunt, obviously relieved.   84

My uncle patted my arm. "You think Chinese."   85

"It's your last night here in America," I said. "So don't be polite. Act like   86
an American."

And that night we ate a banquet.   87

Questions

1. Why does Tan disagree with the Sapir-Whorf hypothesis?
2. What are some of the fundamental differences in the ways in which English and
   Chinese are used?

3. Why do English speakers often misunderstand the real meaning behind Chinese utterances?

4. Have you ever had an experience in which unfamiliarity with a culture caused you to misinterpret meaning?

The New Immigrants

JAMES FALLOWS

Since 1979, James Fallows has been the Washington Editor for Atlantic *magazine. Born in Philadelphia in 1949, he graduated from Harvard and was a Rhodes scholar at Oxford in 1972. After his return to the United States, he worked as staff editor for the* Washington Monthly *and was chief speech writer for President Carter from 1977 to 1979 before taking up his present position.*

In his provocative article, Fallows visits bilingual schools in Texas and California to investigate the nature and the effect of English and Spanish classroom education, and—to his own surprise—concludes: "Most of the children I saw were unmistakably learning to speak English." This article is from Atlantic *magazine (1983).*

Assume for the moment that legal immigrants make an economy more efficient. Does that tell us all we need to know in order to understand their impact on our society? A national culture is held together by official rules and informal signals. Through their language, dress, taste, and habits of life, immigrants initially violate the rules and confuse the signals. The United States has prided itself on building a nation out of diverse parts. *E Pluribus Unum* originally referred to the act of political union in which separate colonies became one sovereign state. It now seems more fitting as a token of the cultural adjustments through which immigrant strangers have become Americans. Can the assimilative forces still prevail? 1

The question arises because most of today's immigrants share one trait: their native language is Spanish. 2

From 1970 to 1978, the three leading sources of legal immigrants to the U.S. were Mexico, the Philippines, and Cuba. About 42 percent of legal immigration during the seventies was from Latin America. It is thought that about half of all illegal immigrants come from Mexico, and 10 to 15 percent more from elsewhere in Latin America. Including illegal immigrants makes all figures imprecise, but it seems reasonable to conclude that more than half the people who now come to the United States speak Spanish. This is a greater concentration of immigrants in one non-English language group than ever before. 3

Is it a threat? The conventional wisdom about immigrants and their languages is that the Spanish-speakers are asking for treatment different from that which has been accorded to everybody else. In the old days, it is said, im- 4 migrants were eager to assimilate as quickly as possible. They were placed, sink or swim, in English-language classrooms, and they swam. But now the Latin Americans seem to be insisting on bilingual classrooms and ballots. "The Hispanics demand that the United States become a bilingual country, with all children entitled to be taught in the language of their heritage, at public expense," Theodore White has written. Down this road lie the linguistic cleavages that have brought grief to other nations.

This is the way many people think, and this is the way I myself thought   5
as I began this project.

The historical parallel closest to today's concentration of Spanish-speaking   6
immigrants is the German immigration of the nineteenth century. From 1830 to 1890, 4.5 million Germans emigrated to the United States, making up one third of the immigrant total. The Germans recognized that command of English would finally ensure for them, and especially for their children, a place in the mainstream of American society. But like the Swedes, Dutch, and French before them, they tried hard to retain the language in which they had been raised.

The midwestern states, where Germans were concentrated, established   7
bilingual schools, in which children could receive instruction in German. In Ohio, German–English public schools were in operation by 1840; in 1837, the Pennsylvania legislature ordered that German-language public schools be established on an equal basis with English-language schools. Minnesota, Maryland, and Indiana also operated public schools in which German was used, either by itself or in addition to English. In *Life with Two Languages,* his study of bilingualism, François Grosjean says, "What is particularly striking about German Americans in the nineteenth century is their constant efforts to maintain their language, culture, and heritage."

Yet despite everything the Germans could do, their language began to die   8
out. The progression was slow and fraught with pain. For the immigrant, language was the main source of certainty and connection to the past. As the children broke from the Old World culture and tried out their snappy English slang on their parents, the pride the parents felt at such achievements was no doubt mixed with the bittersweet awareness that they were losing control.

At first the children would act as interpreters for their parents; then they   9
would demand the independence appropriate to that role; then they would yearn to escape the coarse ways of immigrant life. And in the end, they would be Americans. It was hard on the families, but it built an assimilated English-language culture.

The pattern of assimilation is familiar from countless novels, as well as   10
from the experience of many people now living. Why, then, is the currently fashionable history of assimilation so different? Why is it assumed, in so many discussions of bilingual education, that in the old days immigrants switched quickly and enthusiastically to English?

One reason is that the experience of Jewish immigrants in the early twen-   11
tieth century was different from this pattern. German Jews, successful and

thoroughly assimilated here in the nineteenth century, oversaw an effort to bring Eastern European Jews into the American mainstream as quickly as possible. In New York City, the Lower East Side's Hebrew Institute, later known as the Educational Alliance, defined its goal as teaching the newcomers "the privileges and duties of American citizenship." Although many Jewish immigrants preserved their Yiddish, Jews generally learned English faster than any other group.

Another reason that nineteenth-century linguistic history is so little re-   12
membered lies in the political experience of the early twentieth century. As an endless stream of New Immigrants arrived from Eastern Europe, the United States was awash in theories about the threats the newcomers posed to American economic, sanitary, and racial standards, and the "100 percent Americanism" movement arose. By the late 1880s, school districts in the Midwest had already begun reversing their early encouragement of bilingual education. Competence in English was made a requirement for naturalized citizens in 1906. Pro-English-language leagues sprang up to help initiate the New Immigrants. California's Commission on Immigration and Housing, for example, endorsed a campaign of "Americanization propaganda," in light of "the necessity for all to learn English—the language of America." With the coming of World War I, all German-language activities were suddenly cast in a different light. Eventually, as a result, Americans came to believe that previous immigrants had speedily switched to English, and to view the Hispanics' attachment to Spanish as a troubling aberration.

The term "Hispanic" is in many ways deceiving. It refers to those whose ori-   13
gins can be traced back to Spain (*Hispania*) or Spain's former colonies. It makes a bloc out of Spanish-speaking peoples who otherwise have little in common. The Cuban-Americans, concentrated in Florida, are flush with success. Some of them nurse dreams of political revenge against Castro. They demonstrate little solidarity with such other Hispanics as the Mexican-Americans of Texas, who are much less estranged from their homeland and who have been longtime participants in the culture of the Southwest. The Cuban-Americans tend to be Republicans; most Mexican-Americans and Puerto Ricans are Democrats. The Puerto Ricans, who are U.S. citizens from birth, and who have several generations of contact with American city life behind them, bear little resemblance to the Salvadorans and Guatemalans now pouring northward to get out of the way of war. Economically, the Puerto Ricans of New York City have more in common with American blacks than with most other Hispanic groups. Such contact as Anglo and black residents of Boston and New York have with Hispanic life comes mainly through Puerto Ricans; they may be misled about what to expect from the Mexicans and Central Americans arriving in ever increasing numbers. Along the southern border, Mexican-American children will razz youngsters just in from Mexico. A newcomer is called a "TJ," for Tijuana; it is the equivalent of "hillbilly" or "rube."

Still, "Hispanic" can be a useful word, because it focuses attention on the   14
major question about this group of immigrants: Will their assimilation into

an English-speaking culture be any less successful than that of others in the past?

To answer, we must consider what is different now from the circum- 15 stances under which the Germans, Poles, and Italians learned English.

The most important difference is that the host country is right next door. 16 The only other non-English-speaking group for which this is true is the French-Canadians. Proximity has predictable consequences. For as long as the Southwest has been part of the United States, there has been a border culture in which, for social and commercial reasons, both languages have been used. There has also been a Mexican-American population accustomed to moving freely across the border, between the cultures, directing its loyalties both ways.

Because it has always been so easy to go home, many Mexicans and Mex- 17 ican-Americans have displayed the classic sojourner outlook. The more total the break with the mother country, the more pressure immigrants feel to adapt; but for many immigrants from Mexico, whose kin and friends still live across the border and whose dreams center on returning in wealthy splendor to their native villages, the pressure is weak.

Many people have suggested that there is another difference, perhaps 18 more significant than the first. It is a change in the nation's self-confidence. The most familiar critique of bilingual education holds that the nation no longer feels a resolute will to require mastery of the national language. America's most powerful assimilative force, the English language, may therefore be in jeopardy.

It is true that starting in the early 1960s U.S. government policy began to 19 move away from the quick-assimilation approach preferred since the turn of the century. After surveys of Puerto Rican students in New York City and Mexican-Americans in Texas revealed that they were dropping out of school early and generally having a hard time, educational theorists began pushing plans for Spanish-language instruction. The turning point came with *Lau* v. *Nichols,* a case initiated in 1971 by Chinese-speaking students in San Francisco. They sued for "equal protection," on grounds that their unfamiliarity with English denied them an adequate education. In 1974, the Supreme Court ruled in their favor, saying that "those who do not understand English are certain to find their classroom experience wholly incomprehensible and in no way meaningful." The ruling did not say that school systems had to start bilingual programs of the kind that the phrase is now generally understood to mean— that is, classrooms in which both languages are used. The court said that "teaching English to the students . . . who do not speak the language" would be one acceptable solution. But the federal regulations and state laws that implemented the decision obliged many districts to set up the system of "transitional" bilingual education that has since become the focus of furor.

The rules vary from state to state, but they typically require a school dis- 20 trict to set up a bilingual program whenever a certain number of students (often twenty) at one grade level are from one language group and do not speak English well. In principle, bilingual programs will enable them to keep up with the content of, say, their math and history courses while preparing them to enter the English-language classroom.

The bilingual system is accused of supporting a cadre of educational consultants while actually retarding the students' progress into the English-speaking mainstream. In this view, bilingual education could even be laying the foundation for a separate Hispanic culture, by extending the students' Spanish-language world from their homes to their schools.

Before I traveled to some of the schools in which bilingual education was applied, I shared the skeptics' view. What good could come of a system that encouraged, to whatever degree, a language other than the national tongue? But after visiting elementary, junior high, and high schools in Miami, Houston, San Antonio, Austin, several parts of Los Angeles, and San Diego, I found little connection between the political debate over bilingual education and what was going on in these schools.

To begin with, one central fact about bilingual education goes largely unreported. It is a *temporary* program. The time a typical student stays in the program varies from place to place—often two years in Miami, three years in Los Angeles—but when that time has passed, the student will normally leave. Why, then, do bilingual programs run through high school? Those classes are usually for students who are new to the district—usually because their parents are new to the country.

There is another fact about bilingual education, more difficult to prove but impressive to me, a hostile observer. Most of the children I saw were unmistakably learning to speak English.

In the elementary schools, where the children have come straight out of all-Spanish environments, the background babble seems to be entirely in Spanish. The kindergarten and first- to third-grade classrooms I saw were festooned with the usual squares and circles cut from colored construction paper, plus posters featuring Big Bird and charts about the weather and the seasons. Most of the schools seemed to keep a rough balance between English and Spanish in the lettering around the room; the most Spanish environment I saw was in one school in East Los Angeles, where about a third of the signs were in English.

The elementary school teachers were mostly Mexican-American women. They prompted the children with a mixture of English and Spanish during the day. While books in both languages are available in the classrooms, most of the first-grade reading drills I saw were in Spanish. In theory, children will learn the phonetic principle of reading more quickly if they are not trying to learn a new language at the same time. Once comfortable as readers, they will theoretically be able to transfer their ability to English.

In a junior high school in Houston, I saw a number of Mexican and Salvadoran students in their "bilingual" biology and math classes. They were drilled entirely in Spanish on the parts of an amoeba and on the difference between a parallelogram and a rhombus. When students enter bilingual programs at this level, the goal is to keep them current with the standard curriculum while introducing them to English. I found my fears of linguistic separatism rekindled by the sight of fourteen-year-olds lectured to in Spanish. I reminded myself that many of the students I was seeing had six months earlier lived in another country.

The usual next stop for students whose time in bilingual education is up 28 is a class in intensive English, lasting one to three hours a day. These students are divided into two or three proficiency levels, from those who speak no English to those nearly ready to forgo special help. In Houston, a teacher drilled two-dozen high-school-age Cambodians, Indians, Cubans, and Mexicans on the crucial difference between the voiced *th* sound of "this" and the voiceless *th* of "thing." In Miami, a class of high school sophomores included youths from Cuba, El Salvador, and Honduras. They listened as their teacher read a Rockwellesque essay about a student with a crush on his teacher, and then set to work writing an essay of their own, working in words like "garrulous" and "sentimentalize."

One of the students in Miami, a sixteen-year-old from Honduras, said 29 that his twelve-year-old brother had already moved into mainstream classes. Linguists say this is the standard pattern for immigrant children. The oldest children hold on to their first language longest, while their younger sisters and brothers swim quickly into the new language culture.

The more I saw of the classes, the more convinced I became that 30 most of the students were learning English. Therefore, I started to wonder what it is about bilingual education that has made it the focus of such bitter disagreement.

For one thing, most immigrant groups other than Hispanics take a com- 31 paratively dim view of bilingual education. Haitians, Vietnamese, and Cambodians are eligible for bilingual education, but in general they are unenthusiastic. In Miami, Haitian boys and girls may learn to read in Creole rather than English. Still, their parents push to keep them moving into English. "A large number of [Haitian] parents come to the PTA meetings, and they don't want interpreters," said the principal of Miami's Edison Park Elementary School last spring. "They want to learn English. They don't want notices coming home in three languages. When they come here, unless there is total noncommunication, they will try to get through to us in their broken English. The students learn the language *very* quickly."

Bilingual education is inflammatory in large part because of what it symbol- 32 izes, not because of the nuts and bolts of its daily operation. In reality, bilingual programs move students into English with greater or lesser success; in reality, most Spanish-speaking parents understand that mastery of English will be their children's key to mobility. But in the political arena, bilingual education presents a different face. To the Hispanic ideologue, it is a symbol of cultural pride and political power. And once it has been presented that way, with full rhetorical flourish, it naturally strikes other Americans as a threat to the operating rules that have bound the country together.

Once during the months I spoke with and about immigrants I felt utterly 33 exasperated. It was while listening to two Chicano activist lawyers in Houston who demanded to know why their people should be required to learn

English at all. "It is unrealistic to think people can learn it that quickly," one lawyer said about the law that requires naturalized citizens to pass a test in English. *"Especially when they used to own this part of the country,* and when Spanish was the *historic language* of this region."

There is a historic claim for Spanish—but by the same logic there is a   34 stronger claim for, say, Navajo as the historic language of the Southwest. The truth is that for more than a century the territory has been American and its national language has been English.

I felt the same irritation welling up when I talked with many bilingual   35 instructors and policy-makers. Their arguments boiled down to: What's so special about English? They talked about the richness of the bilingual experience, the importance of maintaining the children's abilities in Spanish—even though when I watched the instructors in the classroom I could see that they were teaching principally English.

In my exasperation, I started to think that if such symbols of the dignity   36 of language were so provocative to me, a comfortable member of the least-aggrieved ethnic group, it might be worth reflecting on the comparable sensitivities that lie behind the sentiments of the Spanish-speaking.

Consider the cases of Gloria Ramirez and Armandina Flores, who taught   37 last year in the bilingual program at the Guerra Elementary School, in the Edgewood Independent School District, west of San Antonio.

San Antonio has evaded questions about the balance between rich and   38 poor in its school system by carving the city up into independent school districts. Alamo Heights is the winner under this approach, and Edgewood is the loser. The Edgewood School District is perennially ranked as one of the poorest in the state. The residents are almost all Mexican-Americans or Mexicans. It is a settled community, without much to attract immigrants, but many stop there briefly on their way somewhere else, enough to give Edgewood a sizable illegal-immigrant enrollment.

In the middle of a bleak, sunbaked stretch of fields abutting a commercial   39 vegetable farm, and within earshot of Kelly Air Force Base, sits Edgewood's Guerra School. It is an ordinary-looking but well-kept one-story structure that was built during the Johnson Administration. Nearly all the students are Mexican or Mexican-American.

Gloria Ramirez, who teaches first grade, is a compact, attractive woman   40 of thirty-three, a no-nonsense veteran of the activist movements of the 1960s. Armandina Flores, a twenty-seven-year-old kindergarten teacher, is a beauty with dark eyes and long hair. During classroom hours, they deliver "Now, children" explanations of what is about to happen in both Spanish and English, although when the message really must get across, it comes in Spanish.

Both are remarkable teachers. They have that spark often thought to be   41 missing in the public schools. There is no hint that for them this is just a job, perhaps because it symbolizes something very different from the worlds in which they were raised.

Gloria Ramirez was born in Austin, in 1950. Both of her parents are na-   42 tive Texans, as were two of her grandparents, but her family, like many other

Mexican-American families, "spoke only Spanish when I was growing up," she says. None of her grandparents went to school at all. Her parents did not go past the third grade. Her father works as an auto-body mechanic; her mother raised the six children, and recently went to work at Austin State Hospital as a cleaner.

Ramirez began learning English when she started school; but the school, on Austin's east side, was overwhelmingly Mexican-American, part of the same culture she'd always known. The big change came when she was eleven. Her family moved to a working-class Anglo area in South Austin. She and her brother were virtually the only Mexican-Americans at the school. There was no more Spanish on the playground, or even at home. "My parents requested that we speak more English to them from then on," she says. "Both of them could speak it, but neither was comfortable."   43

"Before then, I didn't realize I had an accent. I didn't know until a teacher at the new school pointed it out in a ridiculing manner. I began learning English out of revenge." For six years, she took speech classes. "I worked hard so I could sound—like this," she says in standard American. She went to the University of Texas, where she studied history and philosophy and became involved in the Mexican-American political movements of the 1970s. She taught bilingual-education classes in Boston briefly before coming home to Texas.   44

Armandina Flores was born in Ciudad Acuña, Mexico, across the river from Del Rio, Texas. Her mother, who was born in Houston, was an American citizen, but *her* parents had returned to Mexico a few months after her birth, and she had never learned English. Flores's father was a Mexican citizen. When she reached school age, she began commuting across the river to a small Catholic school in Del Rio, where all the other students were Chicano. When she was twelve and about to begin the sixth grade, her family moved to Del Rio and she entered an American public school.   45

At that time, the sixth grade was divided into tracks, which ran from 6-1 at the bottom to 6-12. Most of the Anglos were at the top; Armandina Flores was initially placed in 6-4. She showed an aptitude for English and was moved up to 6-8. Meanwhile, her older sister, already held back once, was in 6-2. Her parents were proud of Armandina's progress; they began to depend on her English in the family's dealings in the Anglo world. She finished high school in Del Rio, went to Our Lady of the Lake College in San Antonio, and came to Edgewood as an aide in 1978, when she was twenty-two.   46

Considered one way, these two stories might seem to confirm every charge made by the opponents of bilingual education. Through the trauma of being plucked from her parents' comfortable Spanish-language culture and plunged into the realm of public language, Gloria Ramirez was strengthened, made a cosmopolitan and accomplished person. Her passage recalls the one Richard Rodriguez describes in *Hunger of Memory,* an autobiography that has become the most eloquent text for opponents of bilingual programs.   47

"Without question, it would have pleased me to hear my teachers address me in Spanish when I entered the classroom," Rodriguez wrote. "I would have felt much less afraid. . . . But I would have delayed—for how long postponed?—having to learn the language of public society."   48

Gloria Ramirez concedes that the pain of confused ethnicity and lost loy-   49
alties among Mexican-Americans is probably very similar to what every other
immigrant group has endured. She even admits that she was drawn to bilingual education for political as well as educational reasons. As for Armandina
Flores, hers is a calmer story of successful assimilation, accomplished without
the crutch of bilingual education.

Yet both of these women insist, with an edge to their voices, that their   50
students are fortunate not to have the same passage awaiting them.

It was a very wasteful process, they say. They swam; many others sank.   51
"You hear about the people who make it, but not about all the others who
dropped out, who never really learned," Ramirez says. According to the Mexican-American Legal Defense and Education Fund, 40 percent of Hispanic students drop out before they finish high school, three times as many as among
Anglo students.

"Many people around here don't feel comfortable with themselves in ei-   52
ther language," Ramirez says. Flores's older sister never became confident in
English; "she feels like a lower person for it." She has just had a baby and is
anxious that he succeed in English. Ramirez's older brother learned most of
his English in the Marines. He is married to a Mexican immigrant and thinks
that it is very important that their children learn English. And that is more
likely to happen, the teachers say, if they have a transitional moment in
Spanish.

Otherwise, "a child must make choices that concern his survival,"   53
Ramirez says. "He can choose to learn certain words, only to survive; but it
can kill his desire to learn, period. Eventually he may be able to deal in the
language, but he won't be educated." If the natural-immersion approach
worked, why, they ask, would generation after generation of Chicanos, American citizens living throughout the Southwest, have lived and died without
ever fully moving into the English-language mainstream?

These two teachers, and a dozen others with parallel experience, might be   54
wrong in their interpretation of how bilingual education works. If so, they are
making the same error as German, Polish, and Italian immigrants. According
to the historians hired by the Select Commission, "Immigrants argued, when
given the opportunity, that the security provided them by their cultures eased
rather than hindered the transition." Still, there is room for reasonable disagreement about the most effective techniques for bringing children into
English. A former teacher named Robert Rossier, for example, argues from his
experience teaching immigrants that intensive courses in English are more effective than a bilingual transition. Others line up on the other side.

But is this not a question for factual resolution rather than for battles   55
about linguistic and ethnic pride? Perhaps one approach will succeed for certain students in certain situations and the other will be best for others. The
choice between bilingual programs and intensive-English courses, then,
should be a choice between methods, not ideologies. The wars over bilingual
education have had a bitter, symbolic quality. Each side has invested the issue
with a meaning the other can barely comprehend. To most Mexican-American parents and children, bilingual education is merely a way of learning

English; to Hispanic activists, it is a symbol that they are at last taking their place in the sun. But to many other Americans, it sounds like a threat not to assimilate.

"It is easy for Americans to take for granted, or fail to appreciate, the strength   56
of American culture," says Henry Cisneros, the mayor of San Antonio. Cisneros is the first Mexican-American mayor of the country's most heavily Hispanic major city, a tall, grave man of thirty-six who is as clear a demonstration of the possibilities of ethnic assimilation as John Kennedy was. Cisneros gives speeches in Spanish and in English. Over the door that leads to his chambers, gilt letters spell out "Office of the Mayor" and, underneath, *"Oficina del Alcalde."* "I'm talking about TV programs, McDonald's, automobiles, the Dallas Cowboys. It is very pervasive. Mexican-Americans *like* the American way of life."

"These may sound like just the accouterments," Cisneros says. "I could   57
also have mentioned due process of law; relations with the police; the way supermarkets work; the sense of participation, especially now that more and more Mexican-Americans are in positions of leadership. All of the things that shape the American way of life are indomitable."

In matters of civic culture, many Mexican-Americans, especially in Texas,   58
act as custodians of the values the nation is said to esteem. They emphasize family, church, and patriotism of the most literal sort, expressed through military service. In the shrinelike position of honor in the sitting room, the same place where black families may have portraits of John F. Kennedy or Martin Luther King, a Mexican-American household in Texas will display a picture of the son or nephew in the Marines. Every time I talked with a Mexican-American about assimilation and separatism, I heard about the Mexican-American heroes and martyrs who have served in the nation's wars.

All the evidence suggests that Hispanics are moving down the path to-   59
ward assimilation. According to a survey conducted in 1982 by Rodolfo de la Garza and Robert Brischetto for the Southwest Voter Registration Education Project, 11 percent of Chicanos (including a large number of illegal immigrants) were unable to speak English. The younger the people, the more likely they were to speak English. Ninety-four percent of those between the ages of eighteen and twenty-five could speak English, versus 78 percent of those aged sixty-six to eighty-seven. Not surprisingly, the English-speakers were better educated, had better jobs, and were less likely to have two foreign-born parents than the Spanish-speakers.

The details of daily life in Hispanic centers confirm these findings. The   60
first impression of East Los Angeles or Little Havana is of ubiquitous Spanish, on the billboards and in the air. The second glance reveals former Chicano activists, now in their late thirties, bemused that their children have not really learned Spanish, or second-generation Cubans who have lost interest in liberating the motherland or in being Cubans at all.

Ricardo Romo says that when he taught Chicano studies at UCLA, his   61
graduate students would go into the San Antonio *barrio* but could not find their way around, so much had they lost touch with the Spanish language. At

a birthday party for a Chicano intellectual in Texas, amid piñatas and plates laden with *fajitas,* a birthday cake from a bakery was unveiled. It said "Happy Birthday" in Spanish—misspelled. There was pathos in that moment, but it was pathos that countless Italians, Poles, and Jews might understand.

With Mexico next door to the United States, the Mexican-American culture will always be different from that of other ethnic groups. Spanish will be a living language in the United States longer than any other alternative to English. But the movement toward English is inescapable.   62

In only one respect does the Hispanic impulse seem to me to lead in a dangerous direction. Hispanics are more acutely aware than most Anglos that, as a practical reality, English is the national language of commerce, government, and mobility. But some have suggested that, in principle, it should not be this way.   63

They invoke the long heritage of Mexican-Americans in the Southwest. As "Californios" or "Tejanos," the ancestors of some of these families lived on and owned the territory before the Anglo settlers. Others came across at the turn of the century, at a time of Mexican upheaval; still others came during the forties and fifties, as workers. They have paid taxes, fought in wars, been an inseparable part of the region's culture. Yet they were also subject to a form of discrimination more casual than the segregation of the Old South, but having one of the same effects. Because of poverty or prejudice or gerrymandered school districts, many Mexican-Americans were, in effect, denied education. One result is that many now in their fifties and sixties do not speak English well. Still, they are citizens, with the right of citizens to vote. How are they to exercise their right if to do so requires learning English? Do they not deserve a ballot printed in a language they can understand?   64

In the early seventies, the issue came before the courts, and several decisions held that if voters otherwise eligible could not understand English, they must have voting materials prepared in a more convenient language. In 1975, the Voting Rights Act amendments said that there must be bilingual ballots if more than 5 percent of the voters in a district were members of a "language minority group." The only "language minority groups" eligible under this ruling were American Indians, Alaskan natives, Asian-Americans (most significantly, Chinese and Filipinos), and Spanish-speakers. A related case extracted from the Sixth Circuit Court of Appeals the judgment that "the national language of the United States is English."   65

So it is that ballots in parts of the country are printed in Spanish, or Chinese, or Tagalog, along with English. This is true even though anyone applying for naturalization must still pass an English-proficiency test, which consists of questions such as "What are the three branches of government?" and "How long are the terms of a U.S. Senator and member of Congress?" The apparent inconsistency reflects the linguistic reality that many native-born citizens have not learned the national language.   66

By most accounts, the bilingual ballot is purely a symbol. The native-born citizens who can't read English often can't read Spanish, either. As a symbol,   67 it points in the wrong direction, away from a single national language in which the public business will be done. Its only justification is the older generation, which was excluded from the schools. In principle, then, it should be phased out in several years.

But there are those who feel that even the present arrangement is too onerous. Rose Matsui Ochi, an assistant to the mayor of Los Angeles, who served on the Select Commission, dissented from the commission's recommendation to keep the English-language requirement for citizenship. She wrote in her minority opinion, "Abolishing the requirement recognizes the inability of certain individuals to learn English." Cruz Reynoso, the first Mexican-American appointee to the California Supreme Court, was also on the Select Commission, and he too dissented. "America is a *political* union—not a cultural, linguistic, religious or racial union," he wrote. "Of course, we as individuals would urge all to learn English, for that is the language used by most Americans, as well as the language of the marketplace. But we should no more demand English-language skills for citizenship than we should demand uniformity of religion. That a person wants to become a citizen and will make a good citizen is more than enough." 68

Some Chicano activists make the same point in less temperate terms. Twice I found myself in shouting matches with Mexican-Americans who asked me who I thought I was to tell them—after all the homeboys who had died in combat, after all the insults they'd endured on the playground for speaking Spanish—what language they "should" speak. 69

That these arguments were conducted in English suggests the theoretical nature of the debate. Still, in questions like this, symbolism can be crucial. "I have sympathy for the position that the integrating mechanism of a society is language," Henry Cisneros says. "The U.S. has been able to impose fewer such integrating mechanisms on its people than other countries, but it needs some tie to hold these diverse people, Irish, Jews, Czechs, together as a nation. Therefore, I favor people learning English and being able to conduct business in the official language of the country." 70

"The *unum* demands only certain things of the *pluribus,*" Lawrence Fuchs says. "It demands very little. It demands that we believe in the political ideals of the republic, which allows people to preserve their ethnic identity. Most immigrants come from repressive regimes; we say, we're asking you to believe that government should *not* oppress you. Then it only asks one other thing: that in the wider marketplace and in the civic culture, you use the official language. No other society asks so little. 71

"English is not just an instrument of mobility. It is a sign that you really are committed. If you've been here five years, which you must to be a citizen, and if you are reasonably young, you should be able to learn English in that time. The rest of us are entitled to that." 72

Most of the young people I met—the rank and file, not the intellectuals who espouse a bilingual society—seemed fully willing to give what in Fuchs's view the nation asks. I remember in particular one husky Puerto Rican athlete at Miami Senior High School who planned to join the Navy after he got 73 his diploma. I talked to him in a bilingual classroom, heard his story, and asked his name. He told me, and I wrote *"Ramon."* He came around behind me and looked at my pad. "No, no!" he told me. "You should have put R-A-Y-M-O-N-D."

Questions

1. What is the difference between the German and the Hispanic experience of assimilation?
2. What is the author's position on the issue of bilingual education? What did he learn in the course of his research for this article?
3. Why is bilingual education the focus of such bitter disagreement?
4. Do you agree that there should be bilingual ballots? Why or why not?

English Only in the 1980s: A Product of Myths, Phobias, and Bias

JUAN CARTAGENA

Juan Cartagena is legal director of the Commonwealth of Puerto Rico's Department of Puerto Rican Community Affairs. A civil rights attorney, he has represented Puerto Rican and Latino workers fired for speaking Spanish in the workplace and parents seeking bilingual education.

Here, Cartagena brings both a general Latino and specific Puerto Rican perspective to volatile issues. Should the United States make English the official language of the country? Cartagena traces succinctly the non-native English experience in the United States and the peaks and valleys of measures taken by certain English-speaking bodies to legislate against immigrant groups. He accuses Dr. John Tanton, co-founder with S.I. Hayakawa of U.S. English, of racism, and argues that Latinos are learning English faster than other immigrant groups. He points out, however, that attempts to make English mandatory for Puerto Ricans have had detrimental effects in schools, leading to higher dropout rates. This selection is from ESL in America *(1991).*

Introduction

A Puerto Rican woman casts a vote in Jersey City after reading a ballot initia-   1
tive printed in Spanish. A public health brochure on teen pregnancy is distributed in Brooklyn in Haitian Creole. A bilingual—English, Mandarin—ad in a subway car announces low-cost checking available at a popular bank in Manhattan. A resident of Hamtramck, Michigan, fondly recalls the words of the Pope as he addressed this city in Polish in 1987. A faded wooden sign in Monsey, New York, marks the entrance to the city hall in English and Hebrew.

These are some images of today's America. They are also, in large part, the   2
images of yesterday's America. Each of them is threatened by the present call to declare English the only language that governments can use in the United States. As the present-day nativism starts to approach the fervor of the early twentieth century, three things are certain. First, the call for new laws is aimed at a different set of immigrants and migrants in the United States, a group much darker in complexion. Second, the present call is a naked at-

tempt to arrest growing political influence by linguistic minorities in the country. And, third, the present debate stands on a foundation of myths, phobias, and bias.

What follows is an exploration of these themes and a discussion about a   3
small but influential segment of the population that has confronted language restrictionist policies for nearly a century: the Puerto Ricans. Initially, however, a discussion of the historical underpinning of language policy in the United States is in order.

Historical Points in U.S. Language Policy

"The protection of the Constitution extends to all, to those who speak other languages as well as those born with English on the tongue" (*Myer* v. *Nebraska*).

The history of U.S. language policy shows a strange quilt of trends and move-   4
ments that embrace, and at times reject, accommodation of other languages in public life. This history, however, discloses that there has always been resistance to creating an exclusively monolingual society in the United States. Instead, a cyclical or spiral pattern best describes the nation's language policy. One lesson that history teaches us, however, is clear: the English only movement of the 1980s is not new in America.

Founded upon the principle of ensuring life, liberty, and the pursuit of   5
happiness, the United States contained a multiplicity of languages during the colonial and revolutionary periods. The numerous Native American languages and the arrival of the Spanish in North America before the first English settlement may have forced a more accommodationist view of language policy in this country. That is to say, the country was new and attractive to the Germans, the French, the Dutch, and many others. Thus, for example, the Articles of Confederation, the precursor of the Constitution, was translated into German to attract the support of German residents in a number of American colonies (Kloss 1977).

More importantly, the Constitution did not establish English as the offi-   6
cial language of the country. The choice apparently was deliberate, as even a proposal to establish a governmental body to regulate the English language was rejected by the Continental Congress. Political liberty, not cultural homogeneity, was much more important to the framers to the Constitution (Crawford 1989a).

As the country progressed in the 1800s, three distinct national-origin   7
groups were woven into its fabric. Each left its mark on U.S. language policy. First, the Germans quickly became the largest language minority group in the colonies, and, subsequently, the most important language minority group to have an impact upon this country's language policies. Germans created their own public schools to preserve their language and successfully thwarted attempts to establish English schools in the same areas. These practices made them the subject of scorn and the abuse by language restrictionists. Second,

the termination of the Mexican-American War in 1848 resulted in over 75,000 Mexicans becoming U.S. citizens by operation of the Treaty of Guadalupe Hidalgo (Castellanos 1983). The Treaty preserved the right of these settlers to their land and arguably to their language and culture (Cartagena, Kaimowitz, and Perez 1983) as Mexicans throughout what is now the American Southwest became citizens without having to demonstrate English proficiency. Third, in 1898 the United States invaded Puerto Rico and, in 1917, imposed U.S. citizenship on all Puerto Ricans. Once again, English proficiency was not a precondition to citizenship. Neither the Mexicans nor the Puerto Ricans, therefore, fit the typical immigration stereotype. Bridges remain behind them. Ellis Island and the Statue of Liberty have not been their gateways.

In the mid-nineteenth century, the first wave of language restrictionist   8
policies began to take hold. With the coming of large numbers of Irish and Italian immigrants, descendants of the English settlers began to harbor suspicions and resentments against these people and their Catholicism (San Miguel 1986). The arrival of Mexicans and Asians added more peoples with different languages. At first Chinese were recruited to work on the railroads, but subsequently they were barred from the United States for decades (see Nash, this volume). All new territorial acquisitions, such as the Philippines and Puerto Rico, were forced to use English; public and private schools were ordered to use English as the language of instruction; and some states began to declare English as the required language for public affairs.

But the heyday of language restrictionist policies arrived in the early   9
twentieth century. More than ever, the tie between language restrictions and immigration restrictions dominated the political scene. In 1920, Congress enacted sweeping immigration laws that placed national origin quotas on the number of visas issued annually. The quotas favored England and other northern European countries at the expense of southern European countries. The Ku Klux Klan, whose membership exceeded four million in 1925, proclaimed its mission to save the "Nordic race" from the onslaught of Jews, Slavs, and Catholics (Wittke 1939). States began to criminalize the use of German in all areas of public life, including on city streets and the telephone. Over 18,000 people in the Midwest were charged with violations of these laws (Crawford 1989a, 23). Anti-German hysteria peaked with the enactment of such laws and the country's entry into World War I in 1917. Increasingly, the arrival of Jews, Italians, and Slavs led to continued suspicions over their loyalty to the country and their capacity for change.

> Old-stock Americans, which now included children of earlier waves of immigrants, believed that the "new immigrants" lacked the assimilative qualities which the "old immigrants" possessed. Further, new immigrants were thought to lack a democratic background and understanding of American institutions, as well as to contribute to vagrancy and crime (San Miguel 1986, 13).

In 1923, the Supreme Court effectively ended this first wave of nativism,   10
at least with respect to language-restrictionist laws. The Court ruled in *Myer* v.

Nebraska that states could not, under the Constitution, criminally punish residents for teaching foreign languages to students in the schools. The defendant in this case was a private-school teacher who taught German to a young student whose parents hoped would learn the language in order to read their German Bible. Nebraska authorities tried to persuade the Supreme Court, unsuccessfully, that the state's language restriction law was constitutional because Germans had proven that they could not be assimilated into the American mainstream and because their continued use of German indicated a disloyalty to the United States (Trasvina 1988). The Court rejected these arguments, and its ruling affected the laws of over twenty states that similarly sought to outlaw the use of foreign languages (Combs and Trasvina 1986). In addition to the Midwestern states, Vermont, Connecticut, New Hampshire, and Massachusetts had enacted laws restricting the use of French in public and private schools at this time (San Miguel 1986).

The period between the 1920s and 1980 contained other important events that shaped U.S. language policies. Immigration restrictions were lessened somewhat with the elimination of the discriminatory national origin quotas in 1965. However, the implementation of English proficiency requirements for naturalization gained steam. Additional events that shaped language policy during this period have been identified (Cartagena 1989) to include: (1) the ratification by the United States of the United Nations Charter, which includes "language" as an impermissible basis of differentiation alongside "race" and "religion"; (2) the passage of the National Defense Education Act of 1958 in response to Russia's Sputnik launch, which financed the teaching of foreign languages in public schools; (3) the Voting Rights Act of 1965 and amendments to that law in 1970. The original Act exempted Puerto Ricans from English only literacy requirements for voter registration and an amendment mandated bilingual assistance in the voting process for all major language minorities; and (4) the upsurge in bilingual education as a result of the 1974 *Lau* v. *Nichols* Supreme Court opinion and the Equal Education Opportunity Act of 1974, which prohibited states from discriminating against students by failing to remove language barriers that may impede educational progress.

These events reflect a true contradiction in the United States. At times, foreign language learning has been promoted and respected. At times, English has consciously not been used as a precondition to certain rights and programs. Yet citizenship, and loyalty in the eyes of many, is still conditioned on knowledge of English, and many youngsters are still ridiculed and punished in schools for speaking Spanish.

By the 1980s the domestic economic situation, immigration patterns and, as in the early 1900s, an upsurge in xenophobic attitudes refueled controversy over the language policies of the nation. In no uncertain terms, the proponents of the new English Language Amendment repeated the same observations about Latinos in the United States that were used against previous immigrant groups. The present English only movement can only be understood in this context.

The Present English Only Movement

> We, the people of the United States, in order to form a more perfect union
> . . . U.S. English (U.S. English, Inc., motto).

> . . . put a gun to their heads, and if they say 'don't shoot', we'll know they can
> speak English (*Wall Street Journal* 1986).

U.S. English, Inc., and English First are the organizational leaders of the cur-   14
rent English only movement. These two organizations have financed the current drive at the state level to declare English the official language of each
state. Their aim, however, is clear. Only an amendment to the U.S. Constitution will suffice.

Like so many of its predecessors, the movement is aimed at immigrants.   15
Note the following reference to our latest immigrants in this letter from English First:

> They never become productive members of American society. They remain
> stuck in a linguistic and economic ghetto, many living off welfare and cost-
> ing working Americans millions of tax dollars every year (English First a).

Founded in 1983, U.S. English was created by former Senator S. I.   16
Hayakawa and Dr. John H. Tanton as an "offshoot" of the Federation of
American Immigration Reform (Crawford 1989a). Around this time, Senator
Hayakawa introduced, for the first time in American history, an amendment
to the U.S. Constitution to declare English as the country's official language.

U.S. English, Inc., has developed numerous objectives during its short ex-   17
istence. The organization is committed to the promotion of the "use of English in political and economic life" while rejecting "all manifestations of
cultural or linguistic chauvinism" (U.S. English a). Thus it calls for:

- Adoption of a Constitutional amendment to establish English as the official language of the United States.
- Repeal of laws mandating multilingual ballots and voting materials.
- Restriction of government funding for bilingual education to short-term
  transitional programs only.
- Universal enforcement of the English language and civics requirement for
  naturalization.

Not obvious in these stated objectives are the immediate targets of U.S.   18
English, which are quite different:

> At various times, leaders of U.S. English have advocated elimination of bilin-
> gual 911 operators and health services, endorsed English only rules in the
> workplace, petitioned the Federal Communications Commission to limit for-
> eign-language broadcasting, protested Spanish-language menus at McDon-
> ald's, and opposed Pacific Bell's *Paginas Amarillas en Espanol* and customer
> assistance in Chinese (Crawford 1989a, 55).

Similarly, "English First" was founded to add the English Language   19
Amendment to the U.S. Constitution. Its aim is to stop the "dangerous spread
of 'bilingualism' in our society," by ending bilingual ballots and other bilingual programs (English First a).

Recently, however, startling revelations have surfaced concerning the   20
largest of these proponents, U.S. English, Inc. A 1986 memorandum written
by cofounder John Tanton regarding the consequences of Latino immigration
in the United States revealed clear, racist motives by this influential chairman. In his memorandum, Tanton decried the "cultural threats" posed by
continued Latino immigration to include Latinos' "low educability," high
drop-out rates, failure to use birth control, tradition of the *mordida* (bribe),
"lack of involvement in public affairs," and allegiance to Roman Catholicism
that did not respect this country's separation of church and state (Tanton
1986). In a plea for action by the "majority" not unlike the white supremacist
calls in the 1920s, Tanton states:

> *Gobernar es poblar* translates "to govern is to populate." . . . Will the present
> majority peaceably hand over its political power to a group that is simply
> more fertile? . . . As Whites see their power and control over their lives declin-
> ing, will they simply go quietly into the night? Or will there be an explosion?
> We are building a deadly disunity. All great empires disintegrate; we want sta-
> bility.

Simultaneously with the disclosure of the Tanton memo, financial data revealed that the financiers of U.S. English included heiress Cordelia Scaife May
and the Pioneer Fund. The former financed the distribution of a French novel
in which third world immigrants invade and destroy Europe. The latter is
dedicated to white racial superiority and eugenics (Crawford 1988).

Despite these gaffes, U.S. English continues to push for language restric-   21
tionist policies while trying to shy away from their reactionary image. Linda
Chavez, their Hispanic president, resigned in the wake of the disclosures, calling the Tanton view "repugnant . . . anti-Hispanic and anti-Catholic."
Chavez, who had previously denied, adamantly, that the English only movement was racist, conceded that their legal initiatives "do polarize the community, whether intentionally or not, and this is not in the interest of bringing
Hispanics into the mainstream" (Crawford 1989b). Similarly, Walter Cronkite
resigned at the same time from the notable U.S. English advisory board, becoming the second such advisory board member to quit in recent years over
the direction of the organization. Author Norman Cousins resigned in October 1986 just before the election in which the California English only referendum appeared, stating that "there is a very real danger" that Proposition 63
would cause Latinos and other racial minorities to be "disadvantaged, denigrated, and demeaned" (*Los Angeles Times* b). Other members of U.S. English
who continue to serve on the advisory board despite calls for their resigna-
tions from opponents of English only measures include Walter Annenberg,
Jacques Barzun, Saul Bellow, Alistair Cooke, Barbara Mujica, Norman Pod-
horetz, and Arnold Schwarzenegger.

Nevertheless, the English only movement is quite alive today, in part be- 22
cause of the simplicity of its seemingly innocuous message. Proponents of
English only call for laws to declare English the official language of the state,
or, alternatively, the country. It is difficult to argue with this simple proposition without explaining that such laws will establish English as the *only* language that is sanctioned by the government. Accordingly, other languages
will be outlawed, to the detriment of those who need such services. On the
other hand, some modern variations of English only legislation are not so innocent. Arizona's referendum, which passed by the slimmest of margins in
November 1988, requires all state and municipal employees to conduct their
business in English—in effect, an English only workrule for all state employees. In 1989, the county legislature in Suffolk Country, New York, just barely
defeated a similar proposal that would have even required all contractors and
subcontractors of the county to conduct their business only in English. All
this in a country where 98 percent of all its residents, according to the 1980
census, understand and speak English!

In actuality, the present call for language restrictionist legislation preys 23
upon the dominant culture's fears and misconceptions about the country's
language minorities. Three myths underlie the restrictionist agenda.

"Our grandparents got by without special treatment or materials, why can't you?" 24

Proponents of language restrictionist laws have glorified the otherwise trau- 25
matic experiences of their forefathers in the debate over language restrictionist laws. In effect, they have to, for this would create imaginary divisions
between "older" immigrants and "newer" immigrants. Such divisions can
only support their call for drastic action. Former Senator Hayakawa has made
the distinction quite clear: "At one time, most immigrants' first task was to
learn English. This is no longer an accepted fact" (Hayakawa 1983). Other
leaders of the English only movement have a remarkable way of basing public policy on their own personal experiences. For example, Texas legislator
Jim Horn can somehow divine that English was so easily accessible for his
forebears: "I don't know about your forefathers but when mine came to
America, the first thing they did was learn English" (English First a). Larry
Pratt, president of English First, similarly shares his view about the complex
issues of language acquisition through the eyes of his Panamanian spouse
(English First b).

Despite these subjective claims, historically the immigrant experience has 26
not been a bed of roses in the United States, and English acquisition did not
come about so easily. Nor were immigrants able to sacrifice getting a job or a
home to immediately learn English. Immigrant children also bore the burdens and traumas of the immigrant experience. "A large percentage of immigrant children—Armenian, Irish, Italian, Polish, German, Russian, Chinese,
and Mexican—who arrived at school not understanding or speaking English
failed in school and, in failing, suffered a serious loss of self-esteem and unrealized potential" (Jimenez 1987). These patterns were officially documented

by the Federal Immigration Commission (Dillingham Commission) report in 1911, which set the stage for national origin quotas in our immigration laws. The Dillingham Commission found that 51 percent of German students were two grades behind their peers; 60 percent of the Russian students were equally behind as were 70 percent of the Italian students. In those days, government officials disclosed their prejudices openly: the newer immigrants were considered to be "less intelligent, less willing to learn English, or did not have the intention of settling in the United States" (*ibid.*).

In this context, the attempt to paint divisions between older and newer   27
immigrants is disingenuous. As will be discussed below, Latinos and Asians are acquiring English at the same rates, if not faster, than previous immigrant communities. The division, however, does serve a function, as English speakers who support English only do so believing that there's something wrong with Latinos, Asians, Haitians, and others today.

"You people don't want to learn English."   28

Assimilation is a recurrent theme in the arguments posed by current language   29
restrictionists. U.S. English alleges that Latinos refuse to learn English. Assimilation by operation of law is their solution. Again, another wedge is placed between Latinos and all other immigrant groups. Thus U.S. English states:

> The assimilative process is not working as well as it did during previous periods of large-scale immigration. Several studies, all of them undertaken under Hispanic sponsorship, indicate growing attachment to Spanish over time, and increasing separation from the mainstream (U.S. English b).

This line of argument continues by setting up Latino leaders as a straw man that must be overcome in order to save the flock. For example, Hayakawa asserts: "Nor does Hispanic leadership seem to be alarmed that large populations of Mexican Americans, Cubans, and Puerto Ricans do not speak English and have no intention of learning" (Hayakawa 1985, 12). His counterpart, John Tanton, assumes the role of liberator when he proclaims: "The way to demean minority citizens is to keep them in language ghettos, where they can be controlled by self-serving ethnic politicians" (*Los Angeles Times* b).

Quite the opposite is true for Latinos in this country. Latinos are acquir-   30
ing English at the same rate, if not faster, than other immigrant groups. As for large numbers of those who do not want to know English, the words of T. Edward Hollander, Chancellor of Higher Education in New Jersey, ring true: "There is no such person in this country who doesn't understand the value of knowledge and understanding of English as a key to individual success and achievement" (Hollander 1987).

No "study" that U.S. English can cite can refute what has been already   31
documented thoroughly. Recent studies by Calvin Veltman in this area have been highlighted by Crawford (1989a). Veltman concluded that among Spanish speakers, the shift to English dominance is already approaching a two-

generation pattern in virtually the entire country as compared to the three-generation pattern exhibited by other immigrants. The typical three-generation pattern describes language acquisition over generations of newcomers. Thus the first generation arrives in the United States proficient in their native language and generally does not obtain full English proficiency. Their children, the second generation, typically acquire English and maintain their native language. The grandchildren, however, become proficient only in English and lose the language of their parents and grandparents. In 1988, Veltman also found that seven out of ten children of Hispanic immigrants were English speakers, and in 1983 he found that bilingual education has no measurable impact on slowing the rate of acquiring English. Far from English being in danger, Veltman found that other languages in the United States are in peril. In 1984, a National Opinion Research Center survey showed that 81 percent of Hispanics believe that speaking and understanding English is a very important obligation (American Jewish Committee 1987). And in 1985, a Rand Corporation study found that 90 percent of first-generation Mexican Americans are proficient in English and over half of the second generation can only speak English (*New York Times* 1986)!

Adult English classes attract literally thousands of Latinos for registration. 32 In 1986 in Los Angeles, 40,000 were turned away from English as a second language classes offered by the Los Angeles Unified School District (*Los Angeles Times* b). In New York, thousands more are on waiting lists. And by 1989, with the passage of the Immigration Reform and Control Act, Latinos and others were competing for scarce seats in English classes (English Plus Information Clearinghouse 1988). This was caused by the Immigration Act's requirement that English proficiency be demonstrated for all applicants for legal permanent residency under the Act's amnesty provisions. Thousands of immigrants are now in need of more English classes where there are none. Facts like these led Norman Cousins to resign from U.S. English and state:

> Not until we provide educational facilities for all who are now standing in line waiting to take lessons in English should we presume to pass judgment on the non-English-speaking people in our midst (*Los Angeles Times* b).

Latinos, therefore, do not need U.S. English to liberate them. They have 33 done it themselves.

"Laws declaring English the official language will help today's immigrants learn 34 *English."*

Perhaps the most deceiving element in the jargon of English only proponents 35 is the representation that these proposed laws will assist non-English speakers learn the language. English First has stated that:

> The ELA [English Language Amendment] ensures equal opportunity for all to progress economically, *to learn English as quickly as possible,* and to be equally

and justly served by a government that refuses to discriminate against those who do not speak one of its favored languages (English First c).

Recently, a representative of U.S. English asserted that the passage of English-as-official-language laws permitted the financing of English classes, implying that the latter could not have occurred otherwise (Acle 1989). The votes in favor of official English laws in Florida in 1988 and in California in 1986 demonstrated that many Latino voters thought such laws would result in increasing English classes for adults.

The sad truth is that laws declaring English the official language of any   36
state do not address the overwhelming problem of providing educational opportunities. "It [the English Language Amendment] will not provide for one more textbook, one more teacher, one more aide, or one more classroom to teach English," states the National Education Association (1988). U.S. English refused to support the English Proficiency Bill sponsored by the Congressional Hispanic Caucus in 1987, which eventually provided a mere $4.8 million for adult English as a second language classes. These developments led many observers to question the motives of the language restrictionists. In 1987, Teachers of English to Speakers of Other Languages noted that the money used by these English only proponents could have been better spent to teach English (Crawford 1989a).

Puerto Ricans: A Community Against English Only

The Puerto Rican community in the United States has had direct experience   37
with language restrictionist policies since 1898. It is a community that is increasingly bilingual. It is a community that has shaped language policy at all levels of government in order to guarantee equal rights to all. Puerto Ricans know all too well that the imposition of English only policies does not work.

Approximately 2.7 million Puerto Ricans live in the continental United   38
States. As with all other nationalities that have arrived in the country, Puerto Ricans know the value of learning English and see its acquisition, generally, as an asset and a necessity (Pedraza 1985). Equally important, in New York City, the largest Puerto Rican community in the United States, Puerto Ricans are neither abandoning their mother tongue nor resisting English. A higher proportion of Puerto Ricans—91 percent—still speak Spanish at home, compared to all other Latino groups. Simultaneously, a higher proportion of Puerto Ricans—70 percent—speak English "well" and "very well," as compared to all other Latino groups (Rodriguez 1989, 30). Thus, for this population, especially its youth, there is no contradiction in being bilingual, bicultural, and American (*ibid.*, 149).

It is because Puerto Ricans have experienced an attempt to impose Eng-   39
lish only policies in their native land that, today, they are at the forefront of the struggle to stop U.S. English and English First (Cartagena 1989). Spanish was Puerto Rico's national language for 390 years at the time of the U.S. takeover of the island in 1898. A year later, the handpicked American in

charge of the island's education system ridiculed Puerto Ricans by proclaiming that their Spanish was a patois that possessed no literature or value (Garcia Martinez 1981). This attitude of ridicule, contempt, and superiority permeated the actions taken by the United States against the colony of Puerto Rico. Overnight, English became the medium of instruction in all public schools. American cultural and historical heroes replaced Puerto Rican culture and values. As Puerto Ricans struggled to gain some measure of control over their educational system, they organized all teachers, administrators, and legislators to pass laws to regain Spanish as the medium of instruction. In 1946, President Truman vetoed such legislation, thus becoming the first president to veto legislation originating in Puerto Rico (San Juan Cafferty and Rivera Martinez 1981). Finally, in 1949 Spanish was used as the language of instruction in the public schools.

This attempt at "Anglicization" (Rodriguez Bou 1966) had severe conse- 40 quences: a marked erosion of Puerto Rican culture, an 80 percent dropout rate in Puerto Rico's public schools at the time, and *no full English proficiency* (Zentella 1987).

An analysis of the current debate over language policy can not be com- 41 plete without addressing the relationship of these policies to the Puerto Rican question. History is not the only reason for focusing on this population. The fact is that Puerto Ricans, American citizens since 1917, have been largely ignored in the debate. The Puerto Rican experience in the United States is one that demonstrates how political power and litigation strategy can result in securing services and programs in languages other than English. This benefits all language minorities. It also provokes action to disempower the Puerto Rican community as in the drive to make English the only official language. There is little doubt left that the current language-restrictionist debate is really an anti-Spanish debate. The items cited above concerning the major actors in U.S. English and English First support this as do the written materials produced by these proponents. Some of these briefing packets are clearly directed at Spanish speakers and denounce the presence of Spanish broadcasting, the proximity of Spanish speaking countries of origin for today's immigrants, and the motives of Latino leaders (*ibid.*). The atmosphere of intolerance that English only supporters have created affects many areas of Puerto Rican life. Adult literacy classes in Puerto Rican neighborhoods have also felt the pressure to conduct literacy classes solely in English. Fortunately, many have resisted (Torruellas 1989).

Puerto Ricans and other Latinos played a leading role in forcing Congress 42 to acknowledge that the electoral and political process, when conducted only in English, discriminates and diminishes political participation by American citizens. Bilingual voting materials have played a significant role in assisting these communities and in increasing their political participation. In 1984, a survey conducted by the Southwest Voter Participation Project, found in four states that 30 percent of the Mexicans responding would not have registered to vote had it not been for bilingual voting materials. Another survey published in 1988 by the Commonwealth of Puerto Rico found that 29 percent of all Puerto Ricans surveyed in New York City listed language barriers, such as the consistent failure to secure sufficient bilingual assistance at the polls, as an impediment to voting.

The bilingual ballot and bilingual voter-registration materials are clear tar-   43
gets for elimination by U.S. English and others. Thus the stage is set. By eliminating the ballot in a language that many, but not all, Puerto Ricans can
understand, political power is diminished. None of today's language restrictionists have addressed the fact that Puerto Ricans, as U.S. citizens from a Spanish-speaking territory, must continue to receive various services in Spanish.

Instead, the only official mention of Puerto Ricans occurs when the is-   44
land's political status is at issue. The people of Puerto Rico and the U.S. Congress are beginning to debate a proposed plebiscite on the island's political
future that will include the options of independence, statehood, or continued
commonwealth status. In attempting a preemptive strike, U.S. English, Inc.,
testified before the congressional hearings to, in effect, place conditions on
statehood, should it be chosen by the Puerto Ricans:

> . . . during these historical debates, we feel it would be badly misleading for
> the people of Puerto Rico to vote in the plebiscite thinking that any language,
> other than English, can be the official language of a State of the Union (U.S.
> English c).

Once again, an attempt is made to impose English on Puerto Rico. These
machinations by U.S. English are made with the full knowledge that they are
better equipped to influence a Senate committee than to convince the residents of Puerto Rico. By using this route, the language restrictionists expose
the fact that they seek to control by force and numbers a decision that is often left to the local electorate. For example, New Mexico has Spanish and
English as official languages, and Hawaii has Hawaiian and English as official
languages. Should statehood befall Puerto Rico, it would be spared this liberty, according to U.S. English.

Puerto Ricans know better. They will continue to ensure that outside   45
forces will not impose language and cultural norms against their will. And in
the United States they will continue to uphold the principle that differentiation on the basis of language is a violation of basic human rights.

Conclusion

The present English only movement has garnered the support of sixteen   46
states that have passed English-as-official-language laws. In recent years an
equivalent number of states have rejected such laws. The debate, as demonstrated on recent television shows, becomes emotional. Revelations about the
founders and financing of U.S. English, Inc., continue to add more fire to the
dispute over the consequences of these unnecessary laws. In a world of increasing interdependence, the United States may be taking a step backwards.
Linguistic divisions tend to lead to political conflict whenever the dominant

group seeks to impose its view on all members of a society and arrests the development and empowerment of minority groups. This is exactly what is occurring in the United States. Instead of unifying the country over issues such as liberty and prosperity, today's language restrictionists are doing the opposite: "Officialization of English is more likely to create language conflict and to politicize language differences than to avoid it [*sic*]" (Guy 1988, 5).

As it strives to legislate uniformity, the English Language Amendment   47
threatens our beliefs in diversity, tolerance, and individual liberty (Ruiz 1989). The following passage from the Puerto Rican sociolinguist, Ana Celia Zentella, raises what may be the ultimate question posed by the English only movement:

> How does what starts out as an innocent "We just want to help everyone learn English so that we may communicate and they can succeed," turn into the odious impugning of the patriotism of those who support the rights of language minorities? It is because language is not the real issue, but a smoke-screen for the fact that the U.S. has not resolved the inequality that exists, and finds it convenient to blame linguistic differences. The root of the problem lies in an inability to accept an expanded definition of what it is to be an American today (1987, 21).

REFERENCES

Acle, L. 1989. Interview with author and others on WWOR-TV "People Are Talking," Mar. 13, 1989.

American Jewish Committee. 1987. "English as the official language" policy statement (on file with author).

Cartagena, J. 1989. English Only jamas. *Centro Bulletin,* 2:5 (Spring 1989) (Centro de Estudios Puertorriquenos, Hunter College, New York, NY).

Cartagena, J., G. Kaimowitz, and I. Perez. 1983. U.S. language policy: Where do we go from here? Paper presented at conference, El Espanol en los Estados Unidos IV, Hunter College, New York, NY.

Castellanos, D. 1983. *The best of two worlds: Bilingual-bicultural education in the U.S.* Trenton, NJ: New Jersey State Dept. of Education.

Combs, M. C. and J. Trasvina, 1986. Legal implications of the English Language Amendment. In *The "English Plus" project.* Washington, DC: League of United Latin American Citizens.

Crawford, J. 1988. What's behind English Only II: Strange bedfellows. *Hispanic Link Weekly Report,* Oct. 31, 1988, p. 3.

_____. 1989a. *Bilingual education: History, politics, theory and practice.* Trenton, NJ: Crane Publishing Co.

_____. 1989b. Linda Chavez gives it to us in plain English. *Hispanic Link Weekly Report,* June 19, 1989, p. 3.

English First, Soliciting letter by Jim Horn. Undated (on file with author).

_____. Soliciting letter by Larry Pratt. Nov. 19, 1986 (on file with author).

_____. Remarks by Larry Pratt. Undated (on file with author).

English Plus Information Clearinghouse. 1988. EPIC events, Mar./Apr. 1988.

Guy G., 1988. Presentation on a panel on the International Situation and Comparative Analysis of Language Policy, at the Conference on Language Rights and Public Policy, Apr. 16–17, 1988 at Stanford University organized by Californians United, English Plus Information Clearinghouse, and the Joint National Committee on Languages (on file with author).

Hayakawa, S. I. 1983. English by law. *New York Times,* Sept. 30, 1983.

_____. 1985. *The English Language Amendment, one nation . . . indivisible?* Washington, DC: Washington Institute for Values in Public Policy.

Hollander, T. E. 1987. English only? Paper presented at a conference, "Language Policy in the United States," by the Global Studies Institute, Jersey City State College, Jersey City, NJ, Oct. 6, 1987 (on file with author).

Jimenez, M. 1987. Briefing paper on English-Only legislation. Mexican American Legal Defense & Educational Fund, Oct. 26, 1987 (on file with author).

Kloss, H. 1977. *The American bilingual tradition.* Rowley, MA: Newbury House Publishers.

Los Angeles Times. Immigrants—A rush to the classrooms, Sept. 24, 1986.

_____. Norman Cousins drops his support of Prop. 63, Oct. 16, 1986.

Myer v. *Nebraska,* 262 U.S. 563 (1923).

New York Times. 1986. Editorial, English yes, xenophobia no, Nov. 10, 1986.

National Education Association. 1988. Official English/English only, More than meets the eye. Washington, DC.

Pedraza, P. 1985. Language maintenance among New York Puerto Ricans. In *Spanish Language Use and Public Life in the USA,* L. E. Olivares, E. A. Leone, R. Cisneros, J. R. Gutierrez, eds. Berlin: Mouton Publishers.

Rodriguez, C. 1989. *Puerto Ricans born in U.S.A.* London: Unwin Hyman, Inc.

Rodriguez Bou, I. 1966. Americanization of schools in Puerto Rico. Adapted from "Significant factors in the development of education in Puerto Rico," in *The Status of Puerto Rico: Selected background studies prepared for the United States—Puerto Rico Commission on the Status of Puerto Rico.* Washington, DC: Government Printing Office.

Ruiz, E. 1989. The English only movement: Is it constitutional? In *Marintaya,* State University of New York at Old Westbury Newsletter of Bilingual Teacher Education Program, Spring 1989.

San Juan Cafferty, P., and C. Rivera Martinez. 1981. Bilingual education in Puerto Rico. In *The Politics of language: The dilemma of bilingual education for Puerto Ricans.* Boulder CO: Westview Press.

San Miguel, G. 1986. One country, one language: A historical sketch of English Language movements in the United States. In *Are English Language Amendments in the national interest?* Claremont, CA: Macias, Reynaldo, ed. Tomas Rivera Center.

Tanton, J. 1986. Memorandum of Oct. 10, 1986 (on file with author).

Torruellas, R. 1989. Alfabetizacion de adultos en " 'El Barrio' "—Distrezas basicas o educacion popular? *Centro Bulletin,* 2:6 (Summer 1989). New York: Centro de Estudios Puertorriquenos, Hunter College.

Trasvian, J. 1988. Lecture presented at the Conference on Language Rights and Public Policy. See Guy 1988.

U.S. English. Pamphlet, In defense of our common language. Undated (on file with author).

_____. Frequently used arguments against the legal protection of English. Undated (on file with author).

_____. Testimony by Luis Acle before the U.S. Senate Committee on Energy and Natural Resources on S. 712. July 14, 1989 (on file with author).

Wall Street Journal. November 1986 [quoting a Monterey County, California, Superintendent of Schools].

Wittke, C. 1939. *We who built America, The saga of the immigrant.* Western Research University Press.

Zentella, A. C. 1987. Language politics in the USA: The English only movement. Paper adapted from presentation for the Dec. 29, 1987, meeting of the Modern Language Association (on file with author).

Questions

1. According to Cartagena, why are the motives of English-only advocates racist? Why do these advocates see the spread of bilingualism as a dangerous development?

2. What are the myths that underlie the drive for language restriction legislation? Do you agree that they are myths?

3. How does Cartagena's position on bilingualism compare with that of Fallows?

An Official Language

DENNIS BARON

Dennis Baron teaches in the department of English at the University of Illinois at Urbana.

Here, Baron outlines the essential pluralistic nature not only of the United States from its inception but also of the human condition. He shows how established immigrant groups look warily on ethnic newcomers, and gives striking examples of both support for and repression of minority languages. He concludes by arguing that the continuation of, say, Spanish, will only happen if Hispanic immigration persists; if the source dries up, the original language will be lost in the English mainstream. This selection is from The English-Only Question: An Official Language for Americans? *(1990).*

Section 1. The English language shall be the official language of the United States.
Section 2. The Congress shall have the power to enforce this article by appropriate legislation.
ONE VERSION OF THE PROPOSED ENGLISH
LANGUAGE AMENDMENT TO THE
U.S. CONSTITUTION

Although many Americans assume that English is the official language of the United States, it is not. That is, nowhere in the U.S. Constitution is English privileged over other languages, and while a few subsequent federal laws require the use of English for special, limited purposes—air traffic control, product labels, warnings, official notices, service on federal juries, and naturalization of immigrants (Grant 1978, 3)—no law establishes English as the language of the land. 1

On the other hand, Americans often assume that all the world speaks English, or that it should: the image of the ugly American abroad hinges in part on this frequently thwarted linguistic expectation. They further assume that everyone in the United States speaks English, or should. Moreover, many English-speaking Americans tend to regard English not just as a language, but as an essential human trait. In consequence, nonanglophones may be regarded not simply as un-American, but as subhuman. To cite one egregious example, Daniel Shanahan (1989) reports that in 1904 a railroad president 2

284

told a congressional hearing on the mistreatment of immigrant workers, "These workers don't suffer—they don't even speak English."

Just as the American stereotype assumes monolingual competence in English, American legislatures, courts, and schools have always operated on the assumption that English is indeed the official language of public expression— that English is the normal vehicle of government, the courts, the schools, and the general business community in the United States. Although the legal record is generally silent or unclear on this matter, the assumption that English is or should be official has occasionally been voiced by American political leaders and by the federal courts. For example, in 1923 the United States Supreme Court, in a decision protecting foreign language instruction in the schools, ventured the opinion that it was desirable for English to be the American national language (*Meyer v. Nebraska,* 262 U.S. 390). As early as 1780 John Adams predicted that the United States would be the vehicle for making its national language, English, the next world language, "because the increasing population in America . . . will . . . force their language into general use, in spite of all the obstacles that may be thrown in the way" (1856, 7:250). John Quincy Adams (1875, 5:401) opposed the Louisiana Purchase because "it naturalizes foreign nations in a mass." In 1807 President Thomas Jefferson, who held similar fears that immigrants coming from absolute monarchies would be unable to adjust to American principles and would transmit their language to their children, proposed settling some thirty thousand Americans—whom he assumed to be speakers of English—in the newly acquired Louisiana Territory to prevent that area from remaining French in language and law (Jefferson 1903, 11:135–37; Franklin 1906, 99). In 1937 President Franklin Delano Roosevelt asserted in a comment on language policy in Puerto Rico that "English is the official language of our country" (Roosevelt 1941, 6:161). And in the case of *Frontera v. Sindell* (1975), the Sixth Circuit of the United States Court of Appeals flatly stated, "The common, national language of the United States is English" (cited in Leibowitz 1982, 117). Frontera was a carpenter who claimed that he failed the Cleveland Civil Service Carpenter's Examination because it was in English; he sought as relief a test in Spanish. The court's opinion continued, "Statutes have been enacted which provide exceptions to our nation's policy in favor of the English language to protect other interests and carry out the policies of the Fourteenth Amendment, but these exceptions do not detract from the policy or deny the interests the various levels of government have in dealing with the citizenry in a common language." In no instance, however, did either the executive or the federal court opinions endow English with official status, and the legal position of English at the federal level remains inexplicit, a situation which proponents of English as the official language of the United States find intolerable.

Although English may be the common, national language of the United States de facto—it is, after all, the language of the Constitution, laws, and government operations—it is not and has never been the exclusive language of the country. Besides the pre-Columbian languages of the Native Americans, now greatly reduced in numbers of speakers through deliberate policies of forced extermination and assimilation, and languages such as Spanish, French, Dutch, Hawaiian, and Russian, which coexisted with English in New World territories that eventually formed or were added to the United States, we find in the United States the many languages of those who immigrated or were brought under duress to its shores.

There are now, as there have been in the past, a considerable number of 5 people in the United States for whom English is not a first language. For example, the 1970 census reported that at least 17 percent of Americans claimed a language other than English as their mother tongue, a figure "substantially larger" than that reported in 1940 or 1960, possibly due to the effect of the rise in ethnic consciousness during the 1960s (Fishman 1985, 109). The 1980 census reported that a lower figure, 10.9 percent of the population, claimed to use a language other than English at home, and that one out of every seven Americans spoke, or lived in a household with someone who spoke, such a language. However, the census also disclosed a significant degree of bilingualism among the members of this group: close to 82 percent of respondents indicated that they also spoke English well or very well.*

Despite the large percentage of bilinguals and nonanglophones who have 6 always made up part of the American population, English has frequently lived at peace with its linguistic neighbors. At other times, like the present, the language question has become a source of friction. Since colonial days, languages other than English have been used both privately and quasi-officially. However, at certain periods in American history attempts have been made to suppress at least the public use of minority languages. In the absence of overriding federal legislation, a number of states have made or are now contemplating laws to make English the official language of such public activity as education, voting, and legal and governmental services. Supporters of official-English legislation may further hope that the public restriction of minority languages will lead to their suppression in private as well.

The effect of these state official-language laws is not always easy to trace. 7 Some of them simply give English the same honorary position as the state bird, flower, or fossil, while others seek *exclusive* status for English vis-à-vis the minority languages of the United States. For example, the Illinois statute, passed in 1923 and amended in 1969, simply declares that English is the official language of the state of Illinois, whereas California's more recent official-language law specifically protects English from the encroachments of other tongues.

In addition to general official-language laws, a good many states have 8 designated English as the language of instruction in their schools, or the language of the state courts and government, and from time to time state or-

---

*U.S. Census 1980, table 99: Nativity and Language. Census data on total numbers of non-English speakers, in the years for which it exists, tends to be inaccurate, partly because the census has not always targeted language very precisely for investigation, and partly because respondents who are suspicious of the motives of the census takers often deny using languages other than English at home. In contrast, Fishman (1985) indicates that in 1970, respondents anxious to proclaim their ethnic heritage during a period of ethnic revival in American society may have exaggerated their fluency in languages other than English.

dinances have required English literacy for suffrage or jury service. Furthermore, by requiring American citizenship, which in most but not all cases presumes a knowledge of English, some states have limited entrance of nonanglophones into such professions as barber, private detective, or undertaker, and have even prevented them from obtaining hunting and fishing licenses (Foreign Language Information Service 1940).

The motives for laws privileging English are often simply practical or patriotic: proponents of official English assume that a nation functions best if its citizens share a common language, although it is clear that there are no monolingual nation-states today and that, contrary to the myth of Babel, plurilingualism may always have been the basic human condition (Calvet 1987, 32; Guy 1989, 153). In any case, supporters of official-language laws hope that imposing English by statute will accelerate its adoption among nonanglophones, though the furor over bilingual education and the generally disappointing experience with foreign language requirements in school curricula might suggest the futility of forcing anyone to learn a language.   9

Furthermore, supporters of official-English legislation frequently assume an identity between language and nation. This is a complex idea that has permeated scientific thought about language and has all too frequently taken on a reality outside of the purely linguistic arena as well. There it may have pernicious social and political effects, particularly in struggles between majority and minority languages. In elaborations of the age-old conviction that language reflects national identity, the philosopher Johannes Fichte (1808) and the philologist Wilhelm von Humboldt (1836) asserted the natural superiority of their native German in contrast to the failings of what they regarded as more primitive forms of speech. Their nationalistic essays drew legitimate charges of racism from their critics.   10

In a more scientific attempt to state the language-nation connection, the twentieth-century American linguists Edward Sapir and Benjamin Lee Whorf maintained that language controls the individual's perception of reality so that no two languages perceive the natural world in exactly the same way. Perhaps the most commonly cited example of the relation between language and perception is the number and variety of words for different kinds of snow in the Eskimo language. Eskimo has words for falling snow, snow on the ground, encrusted snow, and some twenty others, while English has only *snow, sleet, and slush*. While linguists today reject the strong, deterministic form of the Sapir-Whorf hypothesis, which would render translation, borrowing, and linguistic innovation virtually impossible, they do acknowledge a weaker version of the theory arguing that language influences perception without completely limiting or controlling it.   11

Languages carve up the color spectrum differently—the English shades of dark and light blue are two distinct colors in Russian. They also disagree on the linguistic spectrum. The very definition of what constitutes a language or a dialect is influenced by political factors as well as by linguistic ones. Though to an external observer Danish, Swedish, and Norwegian may constitute mutually understandable Scandinavian dialects, they are classified as separate languages by their speakers, who prefer that distinct tongues separate their   12 distinct political units. In contrast, the Chinese consider the mutually incomprehensible spoken varieties of Cantonese, Mandarin, Hakka, Hunan, North and South Min, Wu, and so forth not as separate languages but as dialects of an all-embracing, culturally unifying Chinese.

The linguist Richard W. Bailey (1990, 84) has suggested that the language-nation problem has become even more complex in the late twentieth century, as nationality has frequently come to be defined in terms of structures that transcend individual political states (his examples are multinational corporations, which develop their own corporate culture, and global Islamic fundamentalism, which also transcends geographical boundaries). According to Bailey, "Like nation states themselves, these movements influence political affiliation, cultural loyalty, and language choice."   13

Language is central to national culture, as well as to the more genetically defined ethnos. When language functions as an essential token of cultural identification, changes in the linguistic status quo can produce disruption. In the early 1900s, for example, attempts to modernize the literary language of Greece resulted in violence: students and faculty at the University of Athens protested publicly in order to stop a performance of Aeschylus's *Oresteia* in modern, demotic Greek, and demonstrations at the university protesting a modernized translation of the New Testament led to several deaths.   14

So central is language to political organization that in many societies defining the language has become tantamount to defining nationality. The view that to be French is to speak French underlay official efforts to spread French from the capital outward, something that took over 150 years to accomplish. The official goal was to create the French people, and the French nation, by giving them the French language. Clearly, though, in another equally important sense, being French is a function of geography rather than language: there have been many residents of the Hexagon who were French—legally, socially, culturally, politically—without having French as their mother tongue. The complexity of the *questione della lingua,* an ancient and ongoing debate in Italy from the time of Dante to the present, similarly rests on the notion that defining the language is a necessary precursor to defining the group and ultimately the polity as well. In Europe, language played an essential part in the establishment of political units, both in the Renaissance and in the nineteenth century, and political turmoil in Europe during and after World War I, and at present as well, is frequently expressed in terms of calls for language rights and linguistic independence.   15

The situation may be slightly different for English in that nationality and political loyalty are often treated as distinct. Hence, in the United States, the conversational question What nationality are you? is frequently used to elicit information about the forebears of someone suspected of not being a Mayflower descendant. In England, too, native speakers of English are frequently classified as non-English in terms of their ethnicity: American, Scottish, Irish, Welsh, Asian, West Indian, Australian, and so forth.   16

In the United States, official-English advocates firmly subscribe to the language-nation connection, though frequently on a rather superficial and   17 occasionally pernicious level. They would require English of American citizens in the belief that a nation's ideals are symbolized by and accessed through its language. Americanism, they argue, loses something in the translation, while English offers the only key to the nation's democracy, history and culture. Language thus becomes a literal shibboleth of nationality, a badge of true Americanism, and anything less than fluency in English—a foreign accent, let alone maintenance of a minority tongue—is perceived to threaten national security and subvert the national ideal. Some zealots in the cause have gone so far as to suggest changing the name of the language from English to American. (In fact, speakers of other languages sometimes consider English and American as distinct, hence the phrase occasionally appended to French translations of works by Americans, *traduit de l'américain,* while books of British provenance are labeled *traduit de l'anglais.*) But this linguistic chauvinism has a more damaging side: taking advantage of the presumed connection between English and democracy, anti-alien nativists insisted that nonanglophones could never understand the principles of American society, and produced statements like the following, by Clifford Walker, the governor of Georgia, to a national meeting of the Ku Klux Klan in St. Louis in the 1920s: "I would build a wall as high as Heaven against the admission of a single one of those South Europeans who never thought the thoughts or spoke the language of a democracy in their lives" (quoted in Bennett 1988, 223). 17

Even without the push toward official monolingualism in the name of Americanism, nonanglophones find themselves pushed by law and the conditions of American life not simply to adopt English but to abandon their mother tongue, and indeed immigration to the United States has generally been accompanied by a high degree of voluntary linguistic assimilation rather than permanent bilingualism, particularly in the second and subsequent generations. Concomitantly, there is a tendency for older generations of Americans, those already established and assimilated, to apply the bootstrap argument to newcomers: our ancestors had no special breaks, yet they assimilated; so can you. 18

Established ethnic groups perceive each new wave of immigrants as qualitatively different in its willingness to join the melting pot. In the nineteenth century, Germans and Scandinavians were often regarded by the Anglo-Saxon population as dangerous foreigners who were both racially distinct and bent on keeping their distance from American culture. In the early part of the twentieth century, newcomers from southern and eastern Europe were judged less adaptive to the American language and way of life than the northern and western Europeans who, after several generations in the New World, were finally shedding the linguistic trappings of their ethnicity. Today the same charges of unwillingness to assimilate are leveled at Hispanic and to a lesser extent at Asian Americans, despite linguistic evidence which shows that the children of these immigrants still learn English at an impressive rate. 19

This brings us to the less rational side of the official-English question. Since language retention is often the most visible badge of national origin, some English-only laws have not been attempts to ensure smooth-running

government or statements of patriotism so much as thinly disguised attacks   20
on race, religion, and ethnicity. In times of national emergency, American
legislators have often questioned the loyalty of nonanglophones, pushing for
stricter English literacy requirements to turn immigrants into 100 percent,
unhyphenated Americans, while at the same time urging that immigration be
sharply curtailed to protect the purity of the melting pot.* But these legislators have been opposed by colleagues reasoning that most if not all Americans trace their roots to someplace else, and celebrating the loyalty of newer
Americans who spoke little or no English but managed to defend their country in all its wars.

Nevertheless, when the United States entered World War I, many locali-   21
ties banned the use of German in public while schools rushed to drop German from their curricula, and the 1920s saw an end to massive immigration.
Many supporters of English-only laws today also favor immigration reform—
by which they mean the exclusion from the United States of the "new" immigrants from the Soviet bloc, Asia, the Middle East, the Pacific, and Latin
America.

While supporters of official-language laws emphasize their positive goal,   22
the spreading of English, their opponents are wary of legislation perceived as
threatening or punitive to minority-language speakers. Such fears are not
without basis. Language legislation and immigration "reform" have served in
the past as weapons against those who spoke little or no English, and supporters of today's official-language laws, in their fund-raising, routinely play
on fears of the English-speaking population that they will soon find themselves at the mercy of foreigners.

The German, Spanish, Chinese, and Native American languages, among   23
others, have been the targets of specific legal discrimination at various times
over the past two hundred years. But while there have been both well-intentioned and glaringly discriminatory attempts to promote monolingualism in
the United States, it would be wrong to assume from the foregoing that all efforts, public and private, have been directed toward the eradication of minority languages. Legislation to privilege English is sometimes balanced by
policy supporting minority languages. French was encouraged in Louisiana,
for example, even by Jefferson. He sought to make Lafayette the first governor of Louisiana, but Lafayette declined, and Jefferson then appointed
William Claiborne, an English monolingual who insisted unsuccessfully that
all laws be in English (Leibowitz 1969, 15). Jefferson was an untiring advocate
of language study, and he promoted both Greek and Anglo-Saxon as academic subjects in the United States. He knew French as well: Jefferson concluded his letter proposing the settlement of anglophones in the Louisiana
territory with a few words of French. A year later he affirmed that the French

*The phrase *hyphenated American* was common in the late nineteenth and early twentieth century
as a derogatory reference to Americans of foreign birth, implying "a withholding of full allegiance
to the adopted country" (*Webster's New International Dictionary*, 2d ed., s.v.). In this work I follow
current, more neutral practice in omitting the hyphen in such compounds as *German American*
and *Irish American*, as well as the more recent forms *African American* and *Asian American*.

laws retained jurisdiction in Louisiana unless they had been specifically superseded by congressional action (1903, 11:58–59). Some of Louisiana's constitutions have protected French, and the 1975 constitution, without mentioning that language specifically, guarantees citizens the right to preserve their linguistic and cultural origins (Kloss 1977, 114).

Hawaiian is protected by the constitution of Hawaii (a symbolic gesture, 24 since Hawaiian is for most a second language); and Spanish has been legally protected as well as attacked in New Mexico, a state which even today is proving strongly resistant to official-English legislation. In addition, local laws have favored specific minority languages (for example, German in the Midwest, German, Yiddish, and Italian in Pennsylvania), and while state courts have generally supported English-only legislation, two landmark decisions by the United States Supreme Court have protected minority-language speakers from discrimination within the context of an English-speaking country. In *Meyer v. Nebraska* (262 U.S. 390 [1923]), the court reversed state bans on foreign language instruction. More recently, in *Lau v. Nichols* (414 U.S. 563 [1974]), the court required schools to ensure that nonanglophone children were not excluded from the benefits of education. This resulted in the controversial proliferation of bilingual education programs, which we will examine more closely in chapter 5.

Although these decisions have significance for the language situation in 25 the United States, it is important to note that, despite the popular misconception that such court decisions as *Meyer*, *Lau*, or the *King* or Ann Arbor decision (473 F. Supp. 1371 [1979]) require minority-language or minority-dialect maintenance, none of these rulings guarantee language rights of any kind. Rather, these decisions deal with the rights of the individual. In the *Meyer* case, the court upheld the right of parents to direct their children's education and that of instructors to pursue their calling. In *Lau*, the court protected the plaintiffs from discrimination based on national origin. And in *King*, the court directed the Ann Arbor school board to ensure that black students learn to read standard English. In no cases have courts ordered minority-language-maintenance programs, or even transitional programs to teach English as a second or other language, though such programs have not been forbidden. Even the Bilingual Education Act of 1968 confers no minority-language rights (Macías 1979, 94). Federally sponsored bilingual programs, while not all equally accepted or effective, have all been transitional in intent: wary of permanently segregating minority language students, they are mandated to assist nonanglophones only until those students have mastered English and can join the regular curriculum.

In the nineteenth century the education community was more willing 26 than it is today to permit non-English instruction: some states or cities provided public non-English or bilingual schooling (Ohio is the major example) in an effort to woo students from the private schools. Others at least conducted school assemblies and graduations in languages accessible to parents and grandparents (minority-language religious ceremonies were also common in the nineteenth century, and they too have declined).

In addition to historical and present-day bilingual education, there have   27
always been strong efforts on the part of various ethnic groups to maintain minority languages through the foreign language press, radio, and television. Particularly challenging to the assumption that each new wave of migrants or
immigrants retains its language and resists English is the fact that ethnic
groups themselves continue to maintain private, supplementary schools to
fight language loss among their children. These schools are deemed necessary
because the children continue to pick up English and reject the minority language of their parents or grandparents, as generations before them have done.
Such schools have sometimes been maintained in the face of efforts by the
English-speaking majority to suppress them: in *Farrington v. Tokushige* (273 U.S.
284 [1927]), the U.S. Supreme Court ruled Hawaii's attempt to close Japanese
supplementary schools an infringement of Fifth Amendment guarantees. (The
Fourteenth Amendment, which pertained in the earlier *Meyer v. Nebraska* decision, did not apply to Hawaii because it was a territory, not a state, at the time;
however, the Fifth Amendment applies to territories as well as states.)

While such supplementary minority-language schools are an important   28
symbol of ethnic and cultural identity, they have not been particularly effective. Their mother-tongue instruction is more likely to resemble the foreign
language instruction found in the public schools than the maintenance of
a non-English first language (Fishman and Nahirny 1966, 104). In general,
sociolinguists have concluded that despite maintenance efforts on the part of
ethnic communities, minority languages tend to survive in the United States
more as cultural artifacts—like ethnic restaurants—than as living languages
transmitted across generations.

There is a practical side to the treatment of minority-language speakers as   29
well as a legal one. While public support for minority languages has not always been strong, government officials and politicians, particularly those
dealing with or representing ethnic districts, whether urban or rural, always
manage to communicate with their constituencies in languages other than
English when necessary. Similarly, like politicians on the lookout for votes,
the business community, where money always talks, even now seldom hesitates to speak to customers in their native tongues. Non-English advertising
thrives, particularly in urban markets, producing such materials as *Las Pagi-
nas Amarillas de Pacific Bell* (1988–89), a book which is somewhat shorter than
the various English-language *Yellow Pages* for Los Angeles, but which contains
many advertisements aimed directly at that city's Hispanics. According to
Denis P. Doyle, Spanish-language television broadcasting has become "the
fifth network" (*English Language Amendment* [henceforth, *ELA*] 1985, 229).

However, businesses do not always treat their employees with the same   30
consideration they give their customers, and reports of workers fired for using
Spanish or another language on the job continue to surface in the press. The
courts have held that employers may require their employees to use English
when dealing with the public, or when the language is otherwise essential to
the job, while prohibitions on the use of languages other than English during
work breaks tend not to be upheld. In 1987, though, a panel of the Ninth U.S.

Circuit Court of Appeals ruled that, despite California's official-English law, a regulation requiring Los Angeles municipal court employees to use only English on the job was discriminatory, fostering an "atmosphere of inferiority, isolation and intimidation." The court further found California's language law "to be primarily a symbolic statement concerning the importance of preserving, protecting, and strengthening the English language" (*Gutierrez v. Los Angeles County Municipal Court,* cited in Gonzalez, Vasques, and Bichsel 1989, 196; the opinion was vacated on a technicality in 1988).

National Language Policy

The courts, the schools, and public opinion in general have vacillated on the   31 minority-language question. In light of the checkered historical and legal record concerning English and other tongues, experts wonder whether the United States actually has any official-language policy, and if so, what that policy may be. Like American linguistic history, their conclusions are often contradictory. Shirley Brice Heath (1977) views the failure of the nation's founders to inscribe an official-English language policy into its laws as a conscious decision on their part to support cultural pluralism. In contrast, Steven Grant (1978) finds in American law a string of incoherent language policies all of which, whatever their stance on minority languages, assume that English is and ought to be official. As for linguistic assimilation and the retention of minority languages, Heinz Kloss (1977) presents clear evidence that nonanglophone Americans assimilated to English despite laws which consistently supported minority languages, while Jack Levy (1982) sees in the various language laws and lawsuits a calculated and explicit attempt to eradicate minority languages and force everyone in the nation to speak English. Embracing these opposites, Richard Thompson (1982) concludes that while English *is* the official American language, the country's implicit language policy opposes linguistic discrimination, promotes bilingualism, and encourages—or at least should encourage—the study of foreign languages. Resolving these apparent contradictions, Joshua Fishman (1985, 59) accurately characterizes current American legal practice as favoring a kind of "parsimonious equity" with regard to language. Making the least effort necessary to assure that everyone is treated fairly, American laws are—in the long run—"neither mandatory with respect to English nor prohibitory with respect to other languages."

Ironically, since American language policy is indeed fragmented and in-   32 explicit, the record supports all of these contradictory conclusions to some extent. Throughout its history, the United States has both encouraged and suppressed minority languages. American society and American law recognize the unofficial officialness of English. The federal government actively used minority languages to recruit settlers for its sparsely populated territories in the Midwest and West, then withheld statehood from territories that lacked English-speaking majorities. In addition, both economic pressure and consciously articulated public policy encourage minority language speakers to adopt English at the expense of their native tongue. And ironically, both business and government leaders—not to mention educators—bemoan the fact that Americans by and large are monolingual, a situation which, they contend, places American goods and services at a disadvantage in the international marketplace of the twentieth century. Even this support of second-language acquisition proves controversial. The linguist Peter Strevens (1988, cited in Bailey [1990, 84–85]) maintains that monolinguals dealing with language communities in a position of economic or political superiority to their own operate at a disadvantage. However, Geoffrey Nunberg (personal communication) warns that while there is much speculation, there is as yet no *proof* that monolingualism limits markets.

The pattern of American linguistic assimilation is perceived to adversely   33
affect the position of the United States in international diplomacy as well as trade, and as a result the American tendency toward monolingualism is seen by many to affect national security directly. Since the Sputnik crisis of the 1950s and the subsequent passage of the National Defense Education Act, or NDEA, knowledge of foreign languages has been defined as a military asset. But the need to speak to the world's buyers and rulers in their languages has little overall effect on the retention of ethnic mother tongues at home. Although individuals often do become bilingual, learning English and retaining an ethnic language as well, bilingualism has not become institutionalized. For many, knowledge of a language other than English marks them as unassimilated and educationally deficient, not as scholars or national assets.

Fishman (1985, xiii) is not alone in seeing non-English languages as both   34
persistent and inevitably peripheralized in the United States. Once the switch is made to English, few individuals are willing or able to maintain or return to their first language, or to learn a supplementary or foreign language. As Fishman shows, where the ethnic community remains physically or ideologically isolated from the society in general, as was the case in several areas in the nineteenth century, and as is the case today for the Old Order Amish and Hasidic Jews, the transition to English tends to be slower. And groups like American Hispanics, whose mother tongue is revitalized by continued immigration, tend to show a high degree of bilingualism which then disappears once the source of linguistic renewal dries up.

The American linguistic situation produces an almost inescapable para-   35
dox. Minority-language speakers are encouraged to abandon their native tongues and become monolingual in English to demonstrate their patriotism, their willingness to assimilate, and their desire to enter the economic mainstream. Once they do this, they are encouraged—with the same arguments of patriotism and economic advantage—to learn a foreign language in order to strengthen their country's position in the international arena. Supporters of minority-language maintenance regard this as wasteful, while more cynical observers insist that it is not a question of waste since two distinct and independent groups of people are involved. According to this view, those who need to adopt English are members of the poor and working classes whose linguistic handicaps cause them to fail in school and afterwards in adult life. Members of such a group will never become diplomats or international trade

representatives. On the other hand, the argument goes, it is the monolingual middle class, the academically and socially successful, whose second-language skills need beefing up. However, both liberal and conservative analysts admit that a national policy which promotes second-language competence— whether it is in English or another language—as a cultural asset and not a social liability, rewarding it in the schools and in the workplace, would go a long way toward unifying these two distinct populations (Doyle, *ELA* 1985; Thompson 1982).

The English Language Amendment

Recently, recognition that the United States lacks any formal, coherent language policy has led to attempts to establish such policy. For the past thirty years the American social and legal systems have moved in the direction of increased civil rights protection for individuals and groups. This has been marked on the social plane by the civil rights movement, the women's movement, and the ethnic revival. On the legal plane this trend is reflected in a variety of laws and decisions protecting Americans from discrimination on the basis of race, religion, sex, and national origin: *Brown v. Board of Education* (1954), the Civil Rights and Voting Rights acts of the mid-1960s, the *Miranda* decision protecting the rights of the arrested, *Roe v. Wade* (1978) legalizing abortion, and *Lau v. Nichols* (1974), which has become the basis of bilingual education.

These events have all produced a significant backlash. Forced busing, the primary method of desegregating schools, continues to come under attack; the Equal Rights Amendment failed at the federal level, though it succeeded in many individual states; Miranda remains under siege; and the Supreme Court has remanded the regulation of abortions to the jurisdiction of the individual states.

In a reaction against the ethnic revival of the 1970s, the most pressing aspects of American language policy today pit official-English movements against supporters of minority-language rights. Bilingual schools, ballots, and street signs inflame those monolingual English speakers who resent or fear languages they cannot understand, while in the era of the bicentennial of the U.S. Constitution, more rational Americans wonder whether English can survive what seems to be a massive assault on its two-century hegemony. As a result, the 1980s have seen a renewed interest in official-language legislation. But reacting to the monolingual revival, a significant number of educators and community leaders have emphasized the importance of acquiring English while at the same time conserving minority languages as an important national resource.

In November 1986 the voters of California passed a referendum, known as Proposition 63, making English the official language of that state. Some three-quarters of the electorate voted to make it so, which perhaps was only to be expected, for most people in the United States either speak English or feel a need to learn it, and many view such a language law as a simple reflex issue, like voting for apple pie. For others, both those who support the English-first, or English-only, movement, and those who oppose the establishment of English, the official-language question has become a matter of deep concern.

The language question has always been an important legal issue in California. The 1849 California constitution called for the publication of the future state's laws in English and Spanish (California became a territory in 1848 and entered the Union in 1850). But in 1855 English became the official language of the California schools, and when the constitution was rewritten a generation later, Spanish was dropped and all executive, legislative, and judicial proceedings were ordered to "be conducted, preserved, and published in no other than the English language" (California 1879, 801). Debate at the 1878–79 California constitutional convention was spirited, with supporters of official bilingualism arguing that the Anglos were newcomers to the state who should observe the courtesy that was becoming of conquerors; that the Treaty of Guadalupe Hidalgo, through which California was acquired from Mexico in 1848, implicitly guaranteed language rights; that most states allowed publication of laws and other documents in minority languages; and that government and business were still conducted exclusively in Spanish in many parts of Southern California, and restrictions on the use of Spanish in these areas would represent not only an injustice but a very real hardship. But opponents of Spanish, who won the roll call vote 46 to 39, countered that the treaty of cession did not guarantee Spanish-language rights; that California's Mexicans had had some thirty years to learn English, which was more than sufficient; and that privileging Spanish would open the door for concessions to speakers of French, German, even Chinese. Although the Treaty of Guadalupe Hidalgo did confer American citizenship on Mexicans who chose to stay in the region, at least one delegate, complaining of the paperwork that goes with official bilingualism, considered them to be strangers still: "We have here in the Capitol now tons and tons of documents published in Spanish for the benefit of foreigners" (801). This sentiment clearly persists in California.

The question of an official language is now before Americans at the national level, as well, in the form of the English Language Amendment to the U.S. Constitution, first proposed in 1981 by the semanticist and then senator from California Samuel I. Hayakawa. The ELA would establish once and for all the primacy of English, defending it against the imagined onslaught of competing languages, and requiring the learning of English by immigrants.

On the surface, these seem laudable aims. After all, the ELA makes legal what happens anyway. There have always been non-English speakers in the United States, and those groups who have come to the country as permanent residents have always adopted English, a process which often takes three generations to complete. But the ELA is creating just the kind of furor we might expect from a proposed constitutional amendment. Turning on such controversial social issues as bilingual education and immigration policy, language loyalty and patriotism, it provokes heated and sometimes irrational debate among legislators, civic leaders, newspaper columnists, educators, and the public at large. To point to one blatant example, audience and panelists almost came to blows when the television talk-show host Phil Donahue broadcast a program on the official-language question from Miami in 1985.

Although Congress has taken no action on the ELA, with the exception of   43
brief hearings before the Senate Judiciary Committee's Subcommittee on the
Constitution in 1984 (*ELA* 1985) and the House Subcommittee on Civil and
Constitutional Rights in 1988 (*ELCA* 1989), official-language laws were
passed in Arkansas and defeated in Texas, Oklahoma, and Louisiana. In 1986
the issue was discussed in thirty-seven state legislatures. An official-English
statute, explicitly targeted at Mexican Americans, initially failed in Texas,
though state Republicans vowed to resurrect it. Official-language amendments to state constitutions have been defeated in Louisiana, traditionally
protective of its French heritage, and Oklahoma, where opposition was led by
a Native American state senator whose constituents strongly favor minority-
language rights. In 1988 official-English measures succeeded in Florida
(where the initiative gathered 84 percent of the vote), Colorado (where 60
percent of voters supported it), and Arizona (where the margin of support was
a much narrower 51 percent of the vote), and Massachusetts will be the target
of official English supporters in 1990. The ELA has been repeatedly introduced
in Congress between 1981 and the present.

Clearly, interest in official-language legislation is high, and the status of   44
such legislation is likely to change by the time this book is published. According to a recent issue of the newsletter of the English Plus Information Clearinghouse (EPIC), official-English laws are pending in Alabama, Connecticut,
Kansas, Missouri, New York, Pennsylvania, West Virginia, and Wisconsin.
English-only legislation was defeated in Maryland and died in New Hampshire and Utah. In addition, the concept of English-plus—that is, support for
English *and* second-language study or minority-language maintenance—has
won legislative approval in Michigan and New Mexico (*Epic Events* 1.6
[Jan./Feb. 1989], 5).

The language issue arouses fear and passion on both sides. Former senator   45
Hayakawa recently warned members of U.S. English, a lobbying group that
supports the ELA, that opponents of official English in Colorado were being
aided by a "Soviet front group" of lawyers bent on undermining national
unity (memorandum of 15 July 1988). However, included among the "enemies" of official English is the U.S. Department of Justice, which is clearly on
the side of national unity. The department joined in an unsuccessful effort to
remove the official-language amendment from the Florida ballot on the
grounds that petitions had not been circulated in Spanish, as required by the
federal Voting Rights Act. Moves are still afoot to invalidate the Colorado and
Florida votes.

In the meantime, the scope and effects of the new statutes remain far   46
from clear. The passage of state official-language laws does not create instant
change, though it is often accompanied by anti—minority language incidents. California officials have treated Proposition 63 as symbolic, leaving
minority-language services intact, though in one instance the mayor of Mon-

terey Park, a city with an Asian majority, tried to prevent the public library from accepting a gift of ten thousand Chinese books on the grounds that "English is the law of the land" (Crawford 1989, 58). The Medical Center of the University of California at San Francisco permits its departments to require that English be spoken as a legitimate "business necessity," though ten employees filed a formal complaint alleging they were forced to observe the English-only rule in personal conversations and had been reprimanded for speaking Spanish and Tagalog ("'English-only' rule" 1988; the university has since backed away from the rule).

Similarly, just after the 1988 election the Associated Press reported the   47 suspension of a Miami supermarket cashier for speaking Spanish to fellow employees (*Champaign-Urbana News Gazette*, 13 November 1988, p. B7). The supermarket chain denied that the suspension was on linguistic grounds, pointing instead to "a store policy that prohibits personal conversation between employees during work hours," a policy that would seem to be unenforceable in the average grocery store. However, the employee contended a written notice clearly stated that his suspension was "for speaking a foreign language."

Passage of the Colorado official-English amendment to the state's consti-   48 tution also prompted a brief wave of anti-Hispanic discrimination: the *Chicago Tribune* reported that a school bus driver forbade children from speaking Spanish on the bus; that Anglo schoolchildren told their Spanish American confreres they had just been made unconstitutional; and that a restaurant worker was fired for translating menu items into Spanish for a customer from South America. In response to such incidents, Colorado's governor Roy Romer and Denver's mayor Federico Pena ordered both state and city policies on bilingual assistance for legal and social services to remain in force. However, such orders were viewed by supporters of the state's English Language Amendment as contrary to the English-only spirit of the new law (*Chicago Tribune*, 15 January 1989, p. 6). In contrast, while Arizona's Proposition 106, amending article 28 of the state constitution, is the most restrictive of the current wave of official-language laws, requiring that "this state and all political subdivisions of this state shall act in English and no other language," the Arizona attorney general issued a nonbinding opinion that the law "does not prohibit the use of languages other than English that are reasonably necessary to facilitate the day-to-day operation of government" (Crawford 1989, 67–68; *U.S. English Update* 7 [March/April 1989], 2).*

U.S. English was rocked by controversy in 1988 when Dr. John Tanton,   49 one of the group's founders, advocated forced sterilization as a means of population and immigration control. In response, a number of prominent supporters, including the group's president, Linda Chavez, and the television journalist Walter Cronkite, resigned from the organization. Tanton, whose

*In 1990 a federal court found the Arizona statute to be in violation of First Amendment speech guarantees.

concern that too many of the world's non-European tired, poor, huddled masses were making it to America's shores led him to found the Federation for American Immigration Reform (known, ironically, by the acronym FAIR), announced his own resignation from U.S. English. However, the group's October 1988 newsletter contained a prominent article by him debunking what he regards as the myth of the Swiss multilingual paradise. FAIR has also been accused of attempting to interfere with the publication of a recent study of bilingual education that is critical of the tactics of U.S. English (Crawford 1989, 7).

Opponents of the English Language Amendment fear it as an attack on bilingual programs, and it is true that many supporters of the ELA are opposed to bilingual education as well as continued immigration. But such an amendment may be purely symbolic and have little or no practical effect. This has been the case with official English in Arkansas, and it is clearly the case in Illinois, whose official-language law goes back to 1923. Illinois has always permitted foreign-language instruction, and it ordains English as its official language while offering bilingual ballots, bilingual education (Chicago has programs in some seventeen languages), and driver's license tests in Polish and Spanish as well as English.   50

On the other hand, the English Language Amendment and its ilk could add to the already negative climate for minority language maintenance, further impede the already difficult transition to English, and discourage much-needed foreign language instruction in this country. Unlike most state language statutes, the California official-English law has teeth, permitting ordinary citizens to sue if they feel the position of English has been harmed, diminished, or ignored in any way. U.S. English, which led the English-only drive in California, announced plans to sue several cities, including Los Angeles and San Francisco, under the provisions of the new law. An amendment to the U.S. Constitution will certainly guarantee the filing of lawsuits to test its implications.   51

Clearly, the ELA attracts a fringe of bigots and opponents of immigration; such has been the case with all nativist movements in American history. In addition, though, it appeals to middle-of-the-road Americans and even those who think of themselves as otherwise liberal, who express resentment toward aliens perceived to be illegal, intrusive, excessively fertile, and overly dependent on social services paid for by what they regard as an already overtaxed middle class. For example, the American Civil Liberties Union opposes English-only legislation. Its position, as articulated by ACLU Legislative Counsel Antonio J. Califa (1989), is that "entitlement to the rights of democracy . . . should not be predicated solely on a citizen's proficiency in the language of the majority." In response to this position, however, members and former members wrote to the ACLU newsletter to defend English-only laws and protest continued immigration. One such correspondent blamed "parochial or religious groups" for aiding "thousands and thousands of illegal immigrants," while another objected that "millions of aliens have forced their way   52 into our country, and as they gain majorities in various areas they will change the law to force Spanish in the same way the French have done in Quebec."*

Further compounding the problem of designating an official language, the rational appeal of one nation speaking one tongue also attracts the support of well-meaning citizens—perhaps a majority of Americans, English and non-English speakers alike, and even some linguists—who find the idea of linguistic and ethnic prejudice otherwise abhorrent. It is more than likely that the massive support given California's Proposition 63, and the 1988 referenda in Arizona, Colorado, and Florida, came from these rationally motivated citizens, together with an increasingly discontented middle class—including a majority of the state's schoolteachers—and not just from the radical fringe with its campaign of fear.   53

By linking immigration with the question of a national language, the current English-first debate does not differ much from earlier attempts to deal with the fact that the United States is and has always been a multilingual country whose basic language is English. Furthermore, while many believe that the ELA is aimed primarily at Hispanics, who are stereotyped as reluctant to assimilate, recent studies show that Spanish speakers rapidly adopt English, and that Spanish can be maintained as a minority language only so long as Hispanic immigration continues (Marshall 1986; Veltman 1988). Spanish is then no different from any of the other minority languages in the United States. Nonetheless, researchers are now finding that the large numbers of Hispanics who have become monolingual English speakers are not reaping the promised benefits of assimilation. Their competence in English does not readily translate into increased salaries and greater job opportunities: apparently the discrimination against American Hispanics is deeper than language alone.   54

Seeing discrimination as the main threat of official-language legislation, some opponents of the ELA have countered with their own constitutional amendment, the Cultural Rights Amendment (CRA), which seeks to bar discrimination on the basis of minority language and culture just as discrimination on the basis of national origin is already prohibited. Supporters of the CRA favor a government policy of English-plus, not English-first or English-only (Michigan recently adopted such a plan), though even if they could garner government support for minority-language maintenance, the problems of how to prevent erosion of minority languages may prove to be insurmountable. Both Doyle (*ELA* 1985) and Fishman (1985) conclude that private-sector maintenance programs have a limited appeal and effect despite their efficiency in responding to community demands. The public sector is poorly equipped to provide language maintenance in the face of ambivalence toward such programs at the community and individual levels.   55

Civil Liberties 366 (Spring 1989), 2. Although the British ended French dominance in Québec (and both groups beat out the original Native American population), it is the French who are blamed by the writer of this letter for seeking to reclaim their lost language rights. See chapter 6 for an analysis of the situation in Canada, so often alluded to by official-English proponents.

One obstacle to the ELA's success is the uncertainty over the effect it might   56
have. On one hand, it might simply prove symbolic. In the case of Arkansas
and Illinois, English-only laws have not restricted minority-language rights or
interfered with the assimilation process. On the other hand, it is difficult to
predict the effects of an amendment to the federal Constitution on the basis
of state precedents, since, as we will see in chapter 4, the states have been inconsistent in applying official-language laws, and individual statutes have
been ruled unconstitutional by federal courts.

Although gauging the effects of an English Language Amendment is a dif-   57
ficult enterprise, it is possible also to see that the ELA might change language
use in America profoundly. The House and Senate versions of the proposed
English Language Amendment are quite different. The Senate version, which
simply establishes English in the most general fashion, need not affect the
status of other languages, though supporting legislation spawned by an ELA
could either be restrictive or permissive. In and of itself, however, the Senate
version of the ELA should not put bilingual education programs in jeopardy,
nor should it require that ballots, street signs, and emergency services in multilingual areas be limited to English.

In contrast, the House version is more focused on protecting the domain   58
of English in public life, and, by implication, in private life as well. It specifically prohibits the use of any language other than English except as a means
of establishing English proficiency. This could restrict the use of multilingual
tests, forms and ballots, as well as translators for legal and emergency services. The legal analyst Charles Dale (1985) concludes that an extreme interpretation of the ELA might not only outlaw foreign language requirements in
college curricula, it could prevent the voluntary teaching of any foreign language except for the limited purpose of helping a non-English speaker to
learn English. (In order to avoid such an interpretation, Arizona's recent official-language law specifically permits both transitional bilingual education
and school foreign-language requirements.)

But whether statutes are broadly phrased or specific, there is always a   59
danger that the adoption of official-language laws may backfire by producing
an even more negative climate for minority-language speakers than presently
exists. Ironically, an English Language Amendment may not only fail to facilitate the adoption of English, it may in fact deter the learning of English by
isolating non-English speakers further from the American mainstream. However, it is not clear that a more balanced government approach to language
learning of the kind anticipated by the Cultural Rights Amendment can succeed either. For example, writing in the *Chronicle of Higher Education,* Daniel
Shanahan (1989), head of the Program in English Studies at the Monterey Institute of International Studies, describes a plan to make all Americans multilingual. Shanahan suggests calling English not the official but the "standard"
language of the United States (he finds *standard* a more neutral term), at the
same time requiring all students, regardless of their native language, to learn
a second language. Minority-language speakers would learn English as their

second language, while anglophones would choose some other language to study. Shanahan's regulations, which he would phase in over a twenty-year period, require all students to show competence in a second language for high school graduation and native-speaker fluency in that language for college graduation. While there is much to praise in such an optimistic approach to the problem of language learning, a problem which certainly merits government support, I strongly doubt that the fluency Shanahan requires can be established through coercive legislation and academic requirements alone.

On balance, the benefits of an English-only amendment to the federal   60
Constitution are not entirely clear. Sen. Orrin G. Hatch of Utah, who chaired the 1984 hearings on the ELA, warned supporters of the measure against using the constitutional amendment process, instead of specific laws, to legislate social policy. That the framers of the Constitution, who dealt with the same problems of multilingualism that face us today, chose not to adopt an English-first stance is instructive: their attitude should lead us to question the necessity of an amendment whose purpose seems not purely linguistic but either naively idealistic or, more likely, both culturally and politically divisive and isolationist in its thrust. But in order best to understand the current status and possible effects of the official-language question, we must first trace its origins in ideas about language that have been brought to bear in American political theory and legislative history.

Questions

1. How does the Sapir-Whorf hypothesis relate to the debate over bilingualism?
2. Baron says that proponents of the English-only movement draw a parallel between English as a national language and the preservation of democracy. What is the connection? Do you agree with this line of thinking?
3. Why does Baron feel that the adoption of the English Language Amendment may be harmful?
4. Compare Baron's thesis in this article with Cartagena's.

Firsthand Experience in Educating Language Minorities

ROSALIE PEDALINO PORTER

Having entered the field of bilingual education in the early 1970s, Rosalie Pedalino Porter is currently director of ESL/Bilingual Programs for Newton, Massachusetts, public schools, and has recently been a fellow of the Bunting Institute of Radcliffe College and a former visiting scholar at the University of London. She is the author of Forked Tongue: The Politics of Bilingual Education *(1990).*

In this selection, Porter traces her first exposure to English as an immigrant first-grade student, and discusses her experiences implementing some of the first bilingual education courses in the early 1970s. She found that students who were taught mostly in their first native language (Spanish) were hindered in their transition to a full use and understanding of English. Porter concludes that a swifter transition to English must occur if, indeed, that is the aim of bilingual education in the beginning grades of schooling. This reading is from Forked Tongue.

My introduction to the American school system began when I entered a first-grade classroom not long after arriving in the United States at the age of six. Feelings of fearfulness at being separated from my family were heightened when I lost my way home on the first day of school. I wandered for what seemed miles in central Newark, New Jersey, crying, until I was brought home by a policeman who lived in our neighborhood.

During those first few months, the hours I spent in the classroom were a haze of incomprehensible sounds. I copied what the other children seemed to be doing, scribbling on paper as though I were writing; otherwise, I silently watched the behavior of teachers and students. Although I cannot recall the process of learning English and beginning to participate in the verbal life of the classroom, I know it was painful. I can remember, however, that within two years I felt completely comfortable with English and with the school community—how it happened I do not know. I suspect that a combination of factors worked in my favor: a close-knit family, personal motivation, good health, sympathetic teachers, peer acceptance, and who knows what other intangibles of time and place. When it finally began to happen, I remember the intense joy of understanding and being understood, even at a simple level, by those around me.

Reading Richard Rodriguez's moving account of his experience as an un-   3
derprivileged Mexican-American child, I am surprised that it affects me so
deeply now. He said,

> One day in school I raised my hand to volunteer an answer. I spoke out in a
> loud voice. And I did not think it remarkable when the entire class under-
> stood. That day, I moved very far from the disadvantaged child I had been
> only days earlier. The belief, the calming assurance that I belonged in public,
> had at last taken hold. . . . It would have pleased me to have my teachers
> speak to me in Spanish but I would have delayed having to learn the lan-
> guage of public society. I would have evaded learning the great lesson of
> school, that I had a public identity. . . . Only later when I was able to think of
> myself as an American, no longer an alien in gringo society, could I seek the
> rights and opportunities necessary for full public individuality. . . . Those
> middle class ethnics who scorn assimilation romanticize public separateness
> and they trivialize the dilemma of the socially disadvantaged.[1]

Changing Educational Expectations

In my generation, many immigrant children did not succeed either in learn-   4
ing English or in mastering academic subjects. It was this common immigrant
experience of failure, the widespread dropping out of school, that gave rise in
the 1960s to the demand for effective, humane language programs. The expectation among educators of those earlier times was that immigrant children
would either "sink or swim." This cruel experience forced many to leave
school early, prepared only for unskilled labor. This aborted schooling was not
as serious a drawback then, however, because of the easy access to jobs in industry and agriculture. The current growth of a service/technological economy requires a much higher level of education for even entry-level jobs.

Albert Shanker, president of the American Federation of Teachers, tells   5
the story of the enormous change he has seen in the average years of education completed by Americans. As a young boy growing up on New York's East
Side in a predominantly Jewish neighborhood in the 1930s, he often heard
his elders speak with pride of someone who "has a grammar school diploma."
Until World War II only 20 percent of Americans had completed high school.
Now 70 percent have a high school diploma, and 40 percent have pursued
higher education. Dropping out of school is an almost certain predictor of a
lifetime of below-poverty-level earnings, at best.[2]

The Push for Transitional Bilingual Education

The start of the civil rights push on behalf of language minority children co-   6
incided, happily, with the years when I, like other women with career interests, was able to return to my university studies to complete an undergraduate degree. My children were all in school, and it was an ideal time
to resume my study of Spanish literature. The college of education began
transmitting such a sense of excitement about their new program to train

Spanish bilingual teachers that I eagerly changed my direction. The new method, designated Transitional Bilingual Education (TBE) but usually referred to simply as "bilingual education" or TBE, requires the teaching of all school subjects in the native language for several years, so that the students learn subject matter while making, with gradually increased English-language lessons, the transition from native language to English.

The call was out for anyone with strong skills in Spanish to join the new wave. Chicano activists from California and the Southwest, as well as Puerto Rican professors from New York and Chicago, taught us about the history and literature of the Caribbean, the phonetics of Spanish and English, psycholinguistics, multicultural sensitivity, and many other skills to prepare us to be bilingual teachers in urban schools. I entered the field of bilingual education at its very beginning and have, therefore, a direct understanding of the way it has developed. My firsthand experience provides a vivid representation of the issues in educating language minority children, a topic too often discussed abstractly by the theoreticians and ideologues.   7

The institution I attended granted credit to university students willing to tutor bilingual children in the schools of Holyoke, Massachusetts, an impoverished mill town with a large Puerto Rican population. As luck would have it, all the classroom tutoring placements were filled, and a few of us were invited to tutor families in their homes. This proved to be a rich experience for me. I worked with the Santiago family for a whole year, giving the mother, Toñita, and her two youngest children English lessons three times a week. A few of my classmates at the university declined the opportunity because they felt unsafe in the housing project where these families lived. For me it was not frightening but familiar, not unlike the original apartment in which my family lived for our first seven years in the United States.   8

In the course of these lessons I became very well acquainted not only with the daily struggles of Manuel and Toñita to create a stable life but also with their hopes for their three children. The English lessons were not about grammar rules but about understanding and making oneself understood in daily encounters—in the grocery store, at the doctor's office, or with service workers. In the process we discussed nutrition, schools, family planning, and job training opportunities for Toñita when her youngest child reached school age. Clearly, I went beyond what was expected in a tutorial sponsored by the university. Because I was a mature woman with a family who had lived the experience of being in an alien culture, I found an easy rapport with the Santiago family, and they visited occasionally with my family before returning to Puerto Rico a few years ago.   9

New Experiences and New Lessons

In 1974, with a bachelor's degree and a view of myself, at age forty-three, as the oldest "new" teacher in the world, I began teaching in Springfield, Massachusetts. Here began, first, my excitement in being part of a new experiment in education and, later, the evolution of my thinking on the impractical as-   10 pects of bilingual education in the classroom. The Armory Street School had just been desegregated in a citywide master plan that reassigned fifth- and sixth-grade students to different schools to achieve racial balance. Among the 500 students at Armory 49 percent were blacks, 10 percent were Spanish-speakers, and the rest were white students from predominantly low-income families of Irish background in the "Hungry Hill" neighborhood. Kindergarten children living in the vicinity, more than half of whom were from Puerto Rican families, also attended the school.

My prescribed teaching duties were dauntingly varied. First, I was to teach the kindergarten children *in Spanish* for about an hour daily, developing the basic concepts of size, shape, colors, numbers, and letters—in short, those things typically taught to American kindergarteners. I also was to provide twenty to thirty minutes of English for these children, usually through stories, songs, and games. The rest of the day I was to teach fifth- and sixth-grade students their subject matter—mathematics, science, and social studies—in Spanish and give them intensive lessons in English as a Second Language (ESL), the generic label for the teaching of English speaking, reading, and writing skills to speakers of other languages.   11

After the first year of groping for teaching materials and searching for good ways of getting ideas and facts across to the students, I began to feel somewhat less shaky about what we were accomplishing together in the classroom. As the only bilingual teacher in the school, I was also called on to be the interpreter for families arriving with new students to be enrolled, to make emergency telephone calls to non-English-speaking parents, to act as interpreter for parent–teacher conferences in various classrooms, and occasionally to visit the home of one of our students with the principal when some unusual situation arose.   12

I learned invaluable lessons from Jim Moriarty, the principal at the Armory Street School. By example he disproved the notion that children can only be inspired if taught or supervised by someone from their own racial group or ethnic culture. Jim's first concern was for the students—their physical safety and their opportunity for real *learning*. How did he communicate this to the students and to everyone on his staff? Not by his words, since he is not a particularly expressive or articulate person, but by his daily actions. He got to know each child and something about each family in his district early in the school year, and he certainly knew his school staff. There was no mistaking his priorities when he said to us one day when we were complaining about some onerous duty at school, "This school is not being run for the convenience of the teachers but for the benefit of the students—let's always remember that." Although he was paternalistic and authoritarian to some degree, we respected Jim for his fairness and his consistent advocacy for *all* students. In the years since desegregation, Armory, under his leadership, has established a reputation in Springfield for high student achievement. The school often ranks in first place or close to it on citywide test scores in reading and mathematics.   13

Such contacts, coupled with the generalized euphoria of starting a new career in a new field that was being created daily, carried me through the first   14 year or two of teaching. Idealism, the sense of mission, and the satisfying knowledge that I was helping students in ways that I had never been helped kept me from analyzing too closely what was going on in my classes. But the time for reflection arrived, and the questioning of my early assumptions about the value of bilingual education became a preoccupation.

Awakening to the Realities of Bilingualism

As I began to know my students and their families, I saw that very few were new to the United States and totally non-English-speaking. The small number who were came predominantly from Italy, Greece, or Central America. The large majority were Puerto Rican children who either were born on the mainland or had arrived as very young children. The languages of their homes were Spanish and English. Older brothers and sisters spoke mostly English; parents spoke mostly Spanish. Years of shuttling between San Juan and New York or Holyoke and Springfield, and perhaps moving three times in one year within the city of Springfield, produced the expected outcome of languages in transition: Spanish became stronger when the family spent some time in Puerto Rico; English became stronger when the family returned to the mainland. And there was the mixing of the two, with the words or expressions in so-called Spanish creating a neighborhood argot for informal communication. 15

I soon realized that teaching in Spanish to the kindergarten children required much preliminary work in vocabulary enrichment in standard Spanish. These children, like other children in our society from disadvantaged homes, need more language development, no matter what the language, just to help them begin academic learning. Often I found that as I spoke Spanish, they answered in English. *"Juan, que color es este?"* I would ask, as I pointed to a green box. "Green" (pronounced "grin") would be Juan's reply. So, I would correct him, *"Verde,"* and he would again say, "Green." In the early years I followed the curriculum and taught all subjects in Spanish, but I came to feel that I was going about things the wrong way around, as if I were deliberately holding back the learning of English. 16

When I gave the required thirty minutes of English-language lessons in the kindergarten, scrupulously separate from the Spanish teaching and of much shorter duration, the students responded with equal enthusiasm. They sang the songs in English, shouted the rhymes and number games, and play-acted with me "Three Billy Goats Gruff" and "Jack and the Beanstalk." I do not know how they felt about the patchwork use of two languages in the classroom, but I know how I felt: odd at first, and then very doubtful about the efficacy of what I was doing. 17

Today, fourteen years later, I open my hometown newspaper in Amherst, Massachusetts, and read a regrettably comparable story about the new bilingual classroom established in one of our elementary schools. The reporter quotes this bit of dialogue between a nine-year-old girl from Spain and her teacher: "Pointing to a picture illustrating the text, the child asks, 'Is this a *fuego*?' and the teacher replies, *'Si, por favor hable en Español.'* The teacher ex- 18 plains to the reporter, 'It's very simple. We learn easiest in the language we know best. Most of these children can speak English but their academic skills are very weak. The goal is to build up a foundation of skills in their native language and then transfer those skills to a second language.'"[3] But that child from Spain is obviously ready and eager to continue her learning in English! She is capable of thinking and speaking in grammatical English and only needs the one word *fire* in English. Why is the teacher not following the obvious course of teaching academic subjects in English since her students can already speak the language?

Refocusing on English-Language Skills

At the Armory Street School I also was teaching fifth- and sixth-grade students, who spent three hours or more with me daily. These students came to my room from their various homerooms for special instruction because the school did not have a large enough group of limited-English students to organize an entire bilingual classroom of fifth graders or sixth graders. Those whose English was sufficient to the tasks studied their subjects in their homeroom and came to me for English-language reading and writing; those whose English was very limited spent more time in my class, receiving instruction in the fifth- and sixth-grade math, science, and social studies curriculum in Spanish, in addition to an intensive English program.   19

We bilingual teachers were told by the citywide director of the program to teach spoken English but not to teach reading in English until the students could read *at grade level* in Spanish. Supposedly, the reading skills in Spanish would easily be transferred to English. This is, indeed, the common practice in bilingual programs across the country. Working with students who were ten to fourteen years old and who were not reading above the first- or second-grade level in Spanish, I doubted that this magic transfer of reading skills from Spanish to English would happen before they finished high school—if they stayed in school that long.   20

Instead, I decided, quite on my own, and based on this firsthand experience, to devote most of the teaching time to intensive work on English-language skills—speaking, reading, and writing. I reasoned that my students needed a rapid infusion of English if they were to cope with their junior high school classes and succeed. Two hours a day we moved from one activity to another to broaden their English vocabulary and focus on specific concepts related to the curriculum of the school. We did science experiments to understand the water cycle, grew plants, and demonstrated simple machines by rolling toy cars down inclined planes. We set up a classroom "grocery store" to learn hands-on about nutrition, money, and classification of objects. We wrote our own dramatic version of a children's classic, "Clever Gretel," in the students' own English and performed it for other classrooms. We had a weekly cooking lesson, and the students produced a recipe book in English with artwork, binding, and all. Everything we did in some way advanced the use of the English language for academic, as well as social, situations. I did, of   21 course, continue to provide some native-language help to the students who needed it, relying on my judgment of their abilities. But out of this highly representative classroom experience came my determination to create the most direct means for my students to reach English proficiency and academic achievement.

We did not, however, neglect the cultural background of the students! We 22 read folktales and learned songs of their island, looked at Caribbean art, and studied the history of Puerto Rico and the mainland United States. I made the culture of my students familiar to the other students in the school through various activities. An annual event at Christmas time was the serenading of each classroom by the bilingual group. We presented typical Puerto Rican songs, accompanied by maracas and bongos—sounds and rhythms unfamiliar in English Christmas carols but joyful and appreciated by the students! We gave weekly mini-lessons in Spanish for interested classes, with the bilingual students acting as expert assistants.

The Clear-Cut Need for Change

Where did all this lead me in my anxieties over the best ways to help these students after a third and fourth year went by? My conviction was strengthened that both at the youngest school age and in the higher grades in the elementary school we were not following the most natural course of concentrating on the English language and on helping students learn their subjects in English— and these are, indeed, the two stated goals of the bilingual education law and of all bilingual programs. As I visited other schools and talked with teachers at professional meetings about their experiences, I began to believe, along with many of my colleagues, that the underlying rationale of native-language-based programs was wrong-headed. How else could I account for the fact that so many of my fifth- and sixth-grade students—who had never been out of the mainland United States, and had, indeed, grown up right in Springfield—had not yet learned enough English to be taught their subjects in English? How could I account for the ability of students from other countries who arrived in the fifth and sixth grade and responded quickly to English-language instruction without bilingual support? Looking at the structure of the program in grades one through four revealed at least part of the answer.

Impediments to English-Language Learning

In Springfield, as in hundreds of other school districts across the country, the 24 TBE program, as noted previously, is based on early and extended native-language instruction. One of its central concerns is the preservation, through language, of the child's native "culture." In first grade, limited-English students are placed in a classroom where a bilingual teacher provides all instruction in their home language (typically, Spanish)—reading, language arts, spelling, mathematics, science, and social studies. For a small portion of the day—perhaps thirty minutes daily, three times a week—an ESL teacher, that

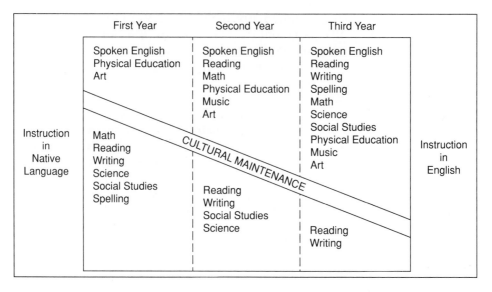

Figure 1. Transitional bilingual education model (instruction in native language and in English)

is, one skilled in intensive English-language instruction, gives oral English lessons. These language minority students may be "integrated" with English-speaking children a few times a week for art, music, or physical education. This same schedule continues in grade two, with the possibility of mathematics being taught in English. Reading in English is not introduced until third grade, and only if the bilingual teacher considers the students ready. (See figure 1.) The transition from native-language instruction to English is so gradual, and the increase in use of English and in opportunities for these students to be integrated with their English-speaking peers is so minimal, that the process is like a meandering, slow-motion dance.

Another factor contributing to the slow transition is often the composi- 25 tion of the teaching staff. As an example, during my entire time in Springfield the bilingual program director made annual trips to Puerto Rico to recruit teachers, asserting that we needed bilingual teachers with native skills in Spanish and a knowledge of the children's culture. Because the enrollment of limited-English students at Armory Street School was increasing and I could no longer teach all of them, first one and then another teacher from Puerto Rico was added to the staff, specifically to work with the kindergarten children. Competent as these teachers were, however, many of them knew little or no English and, therefore, could hardly be called "bilingual."

Clearly, the cultural identity of the teachers became a criterion for hiring, 26 and the bias became evident in other ways, as well. On three occasions I trained college students in my classroom as part of their practical experience before they received their college degree and state credentials for teaching. When Springfield had openings for bilingual teachers, I recommended two of these students for the jobs because they showed great promise. They were turned down, although they had good Spanish-speaking skills and were well prepared for elementary-level teaching. They were told that the bilingual teachers had to be from the same cultural group as the students in order to be effective. In Springfield at that time we lost some excellent candidates because of this narrowly cultural view. I believe it was a deliberate policy of the administrators in our school district to build an establishment whose primary language skills would be in Spanish, with only marginal concern for their English-language ability.

The higher education establishment supported and promoted such an approach. In order to implement the new TBE law in Massachusetts in 1971, the first to be passed in the nation, the state needed hundreds of bilingual teachers, yet very few were trained. We early candidates were subjected to examinations in Spanish and English in order to establish our oral and written competency in both. As bilingual education came under the control of a more determined element of latino activists, however, the testing procedure changed. For a number of years thereafter, testing of bilingual teacher candidates at our state university was done *only in Spanish*—prospective teachers were not even tested in English! One nonhispanic woman who had lived and taught in Mexico for several years and had completed a master's degree in languages told me of her great disappointment when she failed the examination. She was told that her Spanish-language ability was fine but that she did not have enough knowledge of Puerto Rican history and culture. She could not, for instance, name three small rivers in the interior of the island.

Another example of this exclusionary bias occurred in 1980 when, at the first meeting of a graduate course at the University of Massachusetts at Amherst, the instructor lectured for a while in Spanish and then in English. He proclaimed passionately that bilingual education meant that he could use his native language now. One of the students, a Portuguese bilingual teacher, raised her hand and asked if she could use Portuguese in class also. He replied, "No, Anna, bilingual means Spanish around here," and added, "there was a Chinese student who wanted to take this class, and I told her she could but she'd have to have a Spanish interpreter come with her." These attitudes and actions did nothing to promote the recognition that in the 1970s eight languages were used in bilingual programs in the state. Nor was there any attempt to initiate training courses for bilingual teachers of other languages to staff any of these other programs.

These stories illustrate the history of politics surrounding bilingual education in Massachusetts and at least partially explain how the programs evolved with such a heavy emphasis on native-language development and such limited concern for the stated goal of teaching English. However, these instances are not unique to Massachusetts. In my travels during the past dozen years to lecture in different states and to participate in the work of the National Advisory Council on Bilingual Education of the U.S. Department of Education, I have learned how widespread such practices are in other states with large numbers of limited-English students, principally California, Texas, and

Florida. They demonstrate the zealousness with which the search for Spanish-speaking personnel has been pursued. However, no one seems to have been asking, Who should teach English to these children, and how can this best be done?

The Travesty of Teacher Selection and Preparation

Administrators in Springfield ignored the crucial questions about teaching   30
English. I observed the haphazard assignment of ill-prepared teachers to teach ESL. In most cases, they had little idea at all of how to teach a foreign language—which is what English was to their students. My experience, once again, is representative. In the minds of school administrators, anyone who can speak English can teach English. In Springfield, they press-ganged all sorts of people into teaching limited-English students: high school English teachers and foreign language teachers, elementary classroom teachers, speech pathologists, remedial reading teachers, and teachers of the hearing impaired. Some teachers with good skills and high motivation really did a creditable job, even though it was a seat-of-the-pants effort with no curriculum, no books or materials, and some pretty odd places to work. It was not unusual for small-group English lessons to be given in hallways, broom closets, cafeterias, and boiler rooms. After two years of teaching in a coat closet at Armory School, I felt elated when a classroom was finally assigned to me.

More destructive was the practice of assigning ineffective teachers to ESL   31
classes or to some of the remedial programs serving students with serious learning problems. Teachers who could not maintain discipline, who were not competent in teaching their subjects, or who, for various reasons, were functioning at a low level were sometimes given the job of working with students whose needs were greater than those of average children, whose situations cried out for the most able teachers to work with them. While a student teacher, I was an observer for a month in the classroom of a teacher who was close to retirement and in poor health yet had been given the ESL assignment. That experience was so heartbreaking it almost dissuaded me from entering the field. The teacher had given up on these students—six- and seven-year-olds—and had no expectations for their achievement. She merely served out her time, giving them dull, repetitive exercises to copy from the board. It was a painful experience for everyone in that classroom.

Years later I added to my file a similar complaint concerning the assign-   32
ment of untrained language teachers made by linguist Christina Bratt Paulston. She writes about the situation in Sweden, where immigrant students were not receiving instruction in Swedish from trained teachers:

> I find the neglect of Swedish as a foreign language (Sfs) quite unaccountable.
> . . . Swedish is necessary for the possibility of upward social mobility, for school success, for access to good jobs, yet Sfs is neglected in funding, in teacher training, in general attention. For successful adjustment in Sweden, it is the most important subject for the immigrant students, yet they get sad-

dled with castoff teachers who lack training and inclination. I would urge National Board of Education and appropriate officials to make a major effort on behalf of improvement in teaching Sfs.[4]

Teacher-training workshops sometimes did not encourage rigorous in-   33
struction either. In the graduate courses I began to take, we were exhorted, in the jargon of the day, to teach students "where they're at" and to know "where they're coming from." I translated this to mean that we should be conscious of our students' current level of school knowledge and of their language ability so that we would not plan lessons that would be far beyond them. However, helping students feel comfortable with their own language and culture in a strange, new school setting promoted the development of some unusual, if not bizarre, strategies that the lunatic fringe in this field still promotes.

Fads and Fantasies

I once attended a workshop at Brown University in Providence, Rhode Island   34
on teaching reading skills to Cape Verdean children, whose language is a dialect of Portuguese. The speakers described a three-year federally funded project to develop a written form of the Cape Verdean dialect and then to write storybooks in that dialect. The proposal, which was very enthusiastically presented, was to teach the children to read in Cape Verdean, then to read in Portuguese so they could participate in the Portuguese bilingual program, and sometime in the future to transfer their skills to reading in English. I thought that I, like Alice in Wonderland, had fallen down the rabbit hole. Could anyone really believe that this circuitous route through a non-existent island dialect script would lead to *faster* learning of English and a better ability to learn subject matter taught in English? It seemed much more likely that the project leaders were high on the idea of Cape Verdean identity and "where the children were at" rather than on the practical outcome of such a program.

Another example of this kind of convoluted logic was described to me by   35
a teacher from Laredo, Texas, where, in the 1970s, Rodolfo Jacobson of the University of Texas, in studying the spoken language in the community, noted that people switched from English to Spanish, back and forth, sometimes within the same sentence. Professor Jacobson decided it would help students make a closer match between home and school by having teachers use the same language-switching pattern found in the community. Laredo school administrators were persuaded to train teachers to switch from one language to another in their sentences, giving equal time to each language as they taught school subjects. This method, though it has not gained many supporters, is still included in a review of teaching strategies as "the concurrent approach."[5]

Even if one ignores the obvious core of confusion in such a manner of   36
teaching, is it not one of the primary functions of education—bilingual or

not—to expand every student's repertoire of language and thought? Surely, it is counterproductive to institutionalize in the classroom the informal, non-standard language patterns of the home. The telling argument against such a teaching strategy is similar to that used by black parents against the use of Black English as a classroom language: perpetuating a language pattern that is acceptable in the home or neighborhood but inadequate for the larger world of school and work tends to exclude children from equal opportunity. I am gratified to note here that the Laredo "language switching" approach is not often mentioned in the research literature, nor have I found this method to have been adopted by other school systems.

In New York in 1970, however, an equally wrong-headed initiative was being pursued. Considering the oft-repeated, but erroneous, claim that Puerto Ricans speak neither Spanish nor English but the so-called Spanglish, an effort was made to establish Spanglish as the language of Puerto Ricans in New York. The effort was promoted by the New School for Social Research, which offered courses in Spanglish to Anglo professionals so that they could teach Puerto Rican children in their own "language." Irate Puerto Rican community groups reacted by picketing the university and, as a result of condemnatory editorials in the Spanish-language press in New York, finally forcing the cancellation of the classes.[6]

Once again, my firsthand experience highlights the difference between practical means and faddish diversions. One day in my sixth-grade social studies class I was presenting, in Spanish, a carefully constructed lesson on the natural resources of the Amazon basin. First on my list of items was the word *caucho* (meaning "latex from rubber trees"), which I asked a student to explain. William replied that he knew what it was: the thing his uncle sleeps on in the living room when he stays overnight. His brother, Nelson, shouted that William was wrong because *caucho* was that red stuff you put on hamburgers. The brothers demonstrated with wonderful clarity the limitations of Spanglish in a classroom setting.

Underlying these fanciful ideas is the decent notion of showing respect for other languages and cultures, which is certainly laudable; however, too many practitioners of this idea operate on fractured logic. In my five years of bilingual teaching in Springfield, I interviewed at least 150 families when they first registered their children for school and then later at parent-teacher conferences. Almost always the discussion was in Spanish, and always I carefully explained the bilingual program we were providing for their children. Most parents showed little interest in the details of the program, but all were earnestly concerned that their children's schooling should give them opportunities not available to their parents. They were interested in how rapidly the children would learn English. The fact that there was a teacher who could speak their language made them all feel welcome in the school and gave them the confidence to discuss their hopes for the children's futures. This was the crucial factor in establishing a basis for contact and trust between home and school. They felt respected. As with many families from other cultures, they were ready to trust the judgment of the teacher on the kind of program that would help their children the most. They did not, as advocates led us to believe, demand native-language instruction and, in some cases, were strongly opposed to it.

The Rumbles of Discontent

The growing frustrations in my bilingual teaching had nothing to do with the parents, the students, or my colleagues at the Armory Street School. Again, rather than being alone in this attitude, I was part of a nationwide group of teachers disenchanted with bilingual education. In 1987, for example, the United Teachers–Los Angeles, the union representing teachers in the nation's second largest school district, polled its membership on bilingual education. Seventy-eight percent voted against bilingual instruction and in favor of a strong emphasis on English.[7]   40

My persistent frustration had to do mainly with the imposed rules of the Springfield bilingual department. I questioned the wisdom of what we were doing. In a large school system, and rarely under the personal scrutiny of my supervisor, I took the risk of giving far more instruction in English than in Spanish to the fifth- and sixth-grade students. At the end of each year, I was called on to review with the bilingual department head all the records of students that I was recommending to leave the bilingual program and to go to regular classes. Every year we had the same disagreement. I argued that the students, according to test scores and classroom performance, had made enough progress in English to be able to work in a regular classroom, with some further attention to their reading and writing skills. The department head argued that they must remain in the bilingual program as long as they were not yet reading at grade level. It did not matter when I countered that many American students who speak only English do not read at grade level, or that after six or seven years of heavy instruction in Spanish without achieving good results it was probably time to try a different approach.   41

It is fair to say that in my last two years in Springfield I quietly followed my own inclinations, creating the richest learning environment possible in my classroom, both for English and for other subjects, and I watched many students blossom. It was not Garrison Keillor's Lake Woebegone, where everyone is above average, but there was a noticeable improvement in school attendance and an apparent growth in positive attitudes toward learning. I think the success was partly due to students' awareness that they were making progress in their daily lessons and that they were learning English rapidly and connecting socially with the other students in the school. The desire of children to be a part of their group is too strong to ignore—they truly want to "belong."   42

When strict bilingual education advocates speak of the great benefits of separating limited-English students from their classmates temporarily so that they can develop pride in their own language and culture and a sense of identity, they downplay the negative side of such an approach, namely, that this segregation reinforces the feeling of being different, of being a perpetual out-   43 sider. An integrative approach to bilingual education is difficult to achieve because the program itself is essentially segregative. All my experience bore this out.

One consummate irony came to light late in my Springfield career. I learned, through conversations with a few of the bilingual teachers, that they did not enroll their own children in the public schools but were struggling to pay the tuition required for parochial school. When I asked if they preferred to have their children receive a religious education, they said no, that they wanted their children in the parochial school *because it did not have a bilingual program and therefore the children were learning English rapidly.* It shocked me to hear from bilingual teachers that they would not have their own children in our program!

Finally, I became convinced that there was too large a gap between the establishment's forceful rhetoric and what I observed daily. I had become a serious critic of the bilingual education method. The resolution of my dilemma was presented to me when I was offered a position in Newton, Massachusetts, a suburb of Boston, as director of the bilingual and ESL programs. This opened for me the marvelous opportunity to put into practice what I believed would be a better way of educating language minority children. It was to be in Newton that my ideas would be tested, and it was here that the full force of the political pressure for TBE would come down on me.

Setting out for Newton, I had no misgivings. My five years of classroom teaching experience revealed the problems, the complexity, and the shortcomings of bilingual education as the purported solution to the education of language minority children. I was ready to make changes. I had just completed a master's degree and a year as a visiting scholar at the University of London. I was full of language-learning theory, socio- and psycholinguistics, multicultural awareness, and just enough naive confidence to think that I could successfully apply it all in some real-life situation. Like the Splendid Castle that sat waiting for the Perfect Knight, Newton and I were destined for each other.

NOTES

1. Richard Rodriguez, *Hunger of Memory: The Education of Richard Rodriguez* (Boston: David R. Godine, 1982), 22.

2. Author's notes from Albert Shanker lecture in Harvard Graduate School of Education course, 8 February 1988.

3. Daniel Gonzalez, "Classes Educating Children in Their Native Languages," *Daily Hampshire Gazette,* 25 March 1988, p. 25.

4. Christina Bratt Paulston, *Swedish Research and Debate about Bilingualism* (Stockholm: National Swedish Board of Education, 1982), 51–52.

5. Anna Uhl Chamot and Gloria Montanares, "A Summary of Current Literature on English as a Second Language" (Washington, D.C.: National Clearinghouse on Bilingual Education, March 1985), 32.

6. Ana Celia Zentella, "The Fate of Spanish in the United States: The Puerto Rican Experience," in *The Language of Inequality,* ed. Joan Manes and Nessa Wolfson (The Hague: Mouton, 1985), 47.

7. Deborah L. Gold, "Union Vote Downs Bilingual Method," *Education Week,* 9 September 1987, p. 6.

Questions

1. If you learned English as a second language in an American school, what were the methods of instruction? Given your experience, do you agree with Porter's assertion that emphasis on English is more productive?

2. If you have ever taken a second language in school, how was it taught? How well did you learn the language?

3. How does Porter's experience in learning English compare with that of Rodriguez (see next selection)?

Learning the Language

RICHARD RODRIGUEZ

Of Mexican-American heritage, Richard Rodriguez was born in San Francisco in 1944. He graduated from Stanford University in 1967, received a master's degree from Columbia University in 1969, and continued his graduate study at the University of California, Berkeley. Rodriguez is now a full-time writer and is particularly known for Hunger of Memory *(1982) and* Days of Obligation: An Argument with My Mexican Father *(1992).*

    Here, Rodriguez recalls his early attempts to reconcile his native tongue, so fluently articulated at home, and the sounds and demands of English in his first classroom. His childhood idea was that Spanish was for him "a private language" to be guarded, whereas English was simply the "public language." At about age seven, he realized he needed to develop a public identity, and after some coaxing of his parents by his teachers, English was spoken in his home whenever possible. Something of the family's private nature was lost, but Rodriguez's view is that it was a necessary change in order to access the full possibilities of the family's new society. This reading is from Hunger of Memory.

1   I remember to start with that day in Sacramento—a California now nearly thirty years past—when I first entered a classroom, able to understand some fifty stray English words.

2   The third of four children, I had been preceded to a neighborhood Roman Catholic school by an older brother and sister. But neither of them had revealed very much about their classroom experiences. Each afternoon they returned, as they left in the morning, always together, speaking in Spanish as they climbed the five steps of the porch. And their mysterious books, wrapped in shopping-bag paper, remained on the table next to the door, closed firmly behind them.

3   An accident of geography sent me to a school where all my classmates were white, many the children of doctors and lawyers and business executives. All my classmates certainly must have been uneasy on that first day of school—as most children are uneasy—to find themselves apart from their families in the first institution of their lives. But I was astonished.

4   The nun said, in a friendly but oddly impersonal voice, 'Boys and girls, this is Richard Rodriguez.' (I heard her sound out: *Rich-heard Road-ree-guess.*) It was the first time I had heard anyone name me in English. 'Richard,' the

nun repeated more slowly, writing my name down in her black leather book. Quickly I turned to see my mothers's face dissolve in a watery blur behind the pebbled glass door.

Many years later there is something called bilingual education—a scheme 5 proposed in the late 1960s by Hispanic-American social activists, later endorsed by a congressional vote. It is a program that seeks to permit non-English-speaking children, many from lower-class homes, to use their family language as the language of school. (Such is the goal its supporters announce.) I heard them and am forced to say no: It is not possible for a child—any child—ever to use his family's language in school. Not to understand this is to misunderstand the public uses of schooling and to trivialize the nature of intimate life—a family's 'language.'

Memory teaches me what I know of these matters; the boy reminds the 6 adult. I was a bilingual child, a certain kind—socially disadvantaged—the son of working-class parents, both Mexican immigrants.

In the early years of my boyhood, my parents coped very well in America. 7 My father had steady work. My mother managed at home. They were nobody's victims. Optimism and ambition led them to a house (our home) many blocks from the Mexican south side of town. We lived among *gringos* and only a block from the biggest, whitest houses. It never occurred to my parents that they couldn't live wherever they chose. Nor was the Sacramento of the fifties bent on teaching them a contrary lesson. My mother and father were more annoyed than intimidated by those two or three neighbors who tried initially to make us unwelcome. ('Keep your brats away from my sidewalk!') But despite all they achieved, perhaps because they had so much to achieve, any deep feeling of ease, the confidence of 'belonging' in public was withheld from them both. They regarded the people at work, the faces in crowds, as very distant from us. They were the others, *los gringos*. That term was interchangeable in their speech with another, even more telling, *los americanos*.

I grew up in a house where the only regular guests were my relations. For 8 one day, enormous families of relatives would visit and there would be so many people that the noise and the bodies would spill out to the backyard and front porch. Then, for weeks, no one came by. (It was usually a salesman who rang the doorbell.) Our house stood apart. A gaudy yellow in a row of white bungalows. We were the people with the noisy dog. The people who raised pigeons and chickens. We were the foreigners on the block. A few neighbors smiled and waved. We waved back. But no one in the family knew the names of the old couple who lived next door; until I was seven years old, I did not know the names of the kids who lived across the street.

In public, my father and mother spoke a hesitant, accented, not always 9 grammatical English. And they would have to strain—their bodies tense—to catch the sense of what was rapidly said by *los gringos*. At home they spoke Spanish. The language of their Mexican past sounded in counterpoint to the English of public society. The words would come quickly, with ease. Conveyed through those sounds was the pleasing, soothing, consoling reminder of being at home.

During those years when I was first conscious of hearing, my mother and father addressed me only in Spanish; in Spanish I learned to reply. By contrast, English (*inglés*), rarely heard in the house, was the language I came to associate with *gringos*. I learned my first words of English overhearing my parents speak to strangers. At five years of age, I knew just enough English for my mother to trust me on errands to stores one block away. No more.   10

I was a listening child, careful to hear the very different sounds of Spanish and English. Wide-eyed with hearing, I'd listen to sounds more than words. First, there were English (*gringo*) sounds. So many words were still unknown that when the butcher or the lady at the drugstore said something to me, exotic polysyllabic sounds would bloom in the midst of their sentences. Often, the speech of people in public seemed to me very loud, booming with confidence. The man behind the counter would literally ask, 'What can I do for you?' But by being so firm and so clear, the sound of his voice said that he was a *gringo;* he belonged in public society.   11

I would also hear then the high nasal notes of middle-class American speech. The air stirred with sound. Sometimes, even now, when I have been traveling abroad for several weeks, I will hear what I heard as a boy. In hotel lobbies or airports, in Turkey or Brazil, some Americans will pass, and suddenly I will hear it again—the high sound of American voices. For a few seconds I will hear it with pleasure, for it is now the sound of *my* society—a reminder of home. But inevitably—already on the flight headed for home—the sound fades with repetition. I will be unable to hear it anymore.   12

When I was a boy, things were different. The accent of *los gringos* was never pleasing nor was it hard to hear. Crowds at Safeway or at bus stops would be noisy with sound. And I would be forced to edge away from the chirping chatter above me.   13

I was unable to hear my own sounds, but I knew very well that I spoke English poorly. My words could not stretch far enough to form complete thoughts. And the words I did speak I didn't know well enough to make into distinct sounds. (Listeners would usually lower their heads, better to hear what I was trying to say.) But it was one thing for *me* to speak English with difficulty. It was more troubling for me to hear my parents speak in public: their high-whining vowels and guttural consonants; their sentences that got stuck with 'ch' and 'ah' sounds; the confused syntax; the hesitant rhythm of sounds so different from the way *gringos* spoke. I'd notice, moreover, that my parents' voices were softer than those of *gringos* we'd meet.   14

I am tempted now to say that none of this mattered. In adulthood I am embarrassed by childhood fears. And, in a way, it didn't matter very much that my parents could not speak English with ease. Their linguistic difficulties had no serious consequences. My mother and father made themselves understood at the county hospital clinic and at government offices. And yet, in another way, it mattered very much—it was unsettling to hear my parents   15 struggle with English. Hearing them, I'd grow nervous, my clutching trust in their protection and power weakened.

There were many times like the night at a brightly lit gasoline station (a blaring white memory) when I stood uneasily, hearing my father. He was talking to a teenaged attendant. I do not recall what they were saying, but I cannot forget the sounds my father made as he spoke. At one point his words slid together to form one word—sounds as confused as the threads of blue and green oil in the puddle next to my shoes. His voice rushed through what he had left to say. And, toward the end, reached falsetto notes, appealing to his listener's understanding. I looked away to the lights of passing automobiles. I tried not to hear anymore. But I heard only too well the calm, easy tones in the attendant's reply. Shortly afterward, walking toward home with my father, I shivered when he put his hand on my shoulder. The very first chance that I got, I evaded his grasp and ran on ahead into the dark, skipping with feigned boyish exuberance.

But then there was Spanish. *Español:* my family's language. *Español:* the language that seemed to me a private language. I'd hear strangers on the radio and in the Mexican Catholic church across town speaking in Spanish, but I couldn't really believe that Spanish was a public language, like English. Spanish speakers, rather, seemed related to me, for I sensed that we shared— through our language—the experience of feeling apart from *los gringos*. It was thus a ghetto Spanish that I heard and I spoke. Like those whose lives are bound by a barrio, I was reminded by Spanish of my separateness from *los otros, los gringos* in power. But more intensely than for most barrio children— because I did not live in a barrio—Spanish seemed to me the language of home. (Most days it was only at home that I'd hear it.) It became the language of joyful return.

A family member would say something to me and I would feel myself specially recognized. My parents would say something to me and I would feel embraced by the sounds of their words. Those sounds said: *I am speaking with ease in Spanish. I am addressing you in words I never use with* los gringos. *I recognize you as someone special, close, like no one outside. You belong with us. In the family.* (Ricardo.)

At the age of five, six, well past the time when most other children no longer easily notice the difference between sounds uttered at home and words spoken in public, I had a different experience. I lived in a world magically compounded of sounds. I remained a child longer than most; I lingered too long, poised at the edge of language—often frightened by the sounds of *los gringos,* delighted by the sounds of Spanish at home. I shared with my family a language that was startingly different from that used in the great city around us.

For me there were none of the gradations between public and private society so normal to a maturing child. Outside the house was public society; inside the house was private. Just opening or closing the screen door behind me was an important experience. I'd rarely leave home all alone or without reluctance. Walking down the sidewalk, under the canopy of tall trees, I'd warily notice the—suddenly—silent neighborhood kids who stood warily watching me. Nervously, I'd arrive at the grocery store to hear there the sounds of the *gringo*—foreign to me—reminding me that in this world so big, I was a foreigner. But then I'd return. Walking back toward our house, climbing the steps from the sidewalk, when the front door was open in summer, I'd hear voices beyond the screen door talking in Spanish. For a second or two, I'd stay, linger there, listening. Smiling, I'd hear my mother call out, saying in Spanish (words): 'Is that you, Richard?' All the while her sounds would assure me: *You are home now; come closer; inside. With us.*

'*Si,*' I'd reply.   22

Once more inside the house I would resume (assume) my place in the   23
family. The sounds would dim, grow harder to hear. Once more at home, I would grow less aware of that fact. It required, however, no more than the blurt of the doorbell to alert me to listen to sounds all over again. The house would turn instantly still while my mother went to the door. I'd hear her hard English sounds. I'd wait to hear her voice return to soft-sounding Spanish, which assured me, as surely as did the clicking tongue of the lock on the door, that the stranger was gone.

Plainly, it is not healthy to hear such sounds so often. It is not healthy to   24
distinguish public words from private sounds so easily. I remained cloistered by sounds, timid and shy in public, too dependent on voices at home. And yet it needs to be emphasized: I was an extremely happy child at home. I remember many nights when my father would come back from work, and I'd hear him call out to my mother in Spanish, sounding relieved. In Spanish, he'd sound light and free notes he never could manage in English. Some nights I'd jump up just at hearing his voice. With *mis hermanos* I would come running into the room where he was with my mother. Our laughing (so deep was the pleasure!) became screaming. Like others who know the pain of public alienation, we transformed the knowledge of our public separateness and made it consoling—the reminder of intimacy. *We are speaking now the way we never speak out in public. We are alone—together,* voices sounded, surrounded to tell me. Some nights, no one seemed willing to loosen the hold sounds had on us. At dinner, we invented new words. (Ours sounded Spanish, but made sense only to us.) We pieced together new words by taking, say, an English verb and giving it Spanish endings. My mother's instructions at bedtime would be lacquered with mock-urgent tones. Or a word like *si* would become, in several notes, able to convey added measures of feeling. Tongues explored the edges of words, especially the fat vowels. And we happily sounded that military drum roll, the twirling roar of the Spanish *r*. Family language: my family's sounds. The voices of my parents and sisters and brother. Their voices insisting: *You belong here. We are family members. Related. Special to one another. Listen!* Voices singing and sighing, rising, straining, then surging, teeming with pleasure that burst syllables into fragments of laughter. At times it seemed there was steady quiet only when, from another room, the rustling whispers of my parents faded and I moved closer to sleep.

Supporters of bilingual education today imply that students like me miss 25
a great deal by not being taught in their family's language. What they seem
not to recognize is that, as a socially disadvantaged child, I considered Spanish to be a private language. What I needed to learn in school was that I had
the right—and the obligation—to speak the public language of *los gringos*.
The odd truth is that my first-grade classmates could have become bilingual,
in the conventional sense of that word, more easily than I. Had they been
taught (as upper-middle-class children are often taught early) a second language like Spanish or French, they could have regarded it simply as that: another public language. In my case such bilingualism could not have been so
quickly achieved. What I did not believe was that I could speak a single public language.

Without question, it would have pleased me to hear my teachers address 26
me in Spanish when I entered the classroom. I would have felt much less
afraid. I would have trusted them and responded with ease. But I would have
delayed—for how long postponed?—having to learn the language of public
society. I would have evaded—and for how long could I have afforded to delay?—learning the great lesson of school, that I had a public identity.

Fortunately my teachers were unsentimental about their responsibility. 27
What they understood was that I needed to speak a public language. So their
voices would search me out, asking me questions. Each time I'd hear them,
I'd look up in surprise to see a nun's face frowning at me. I'd mumble, not really meaning to answer. The nun would persist. 'Richard, stand up. Don't
look at the floor. Speak up. Speak to the entire class, not just to me!' But I
couldn't believe that the English language was mine to use. (In part, I did not
want to believe it.) I continued to mumble. I resisted the teacher's demands.
(Did I somehow suspect that once I learned the public language my pleasing
family life would be changed?) Silent, waiting for the bell to sound, I remained dazed, diffident, afraid.

Because I wrongly imagined that English was intrinsically a public lan- 28
guage and Spanish an intrinsically private one, I easily noted the difference
between classroom language and the language of home. At school, words
were directed to a general audience of listeners. ('Boys and girls.') Words were
meaningfully ordered. And the point was not self-expression alone but to
make oneself understood by many others. The teacher quizzed: 'Boys and
girls, why do we use that word in this sentence? Could we think of a better
word to use there? Would the sentence change its meaning if the words were
differently arranged? And wasn't there a better way of saying much the same
thing?' (I couldn't say. I wouldn't try to say.)

Three months. Five. Half a year passed. Unsmiling, ever watchful, my 29
teachers noted my silence. They began to connect my behavior with the difficult progress my older sister and brother were making. Until one Saturday
morning three nuns arrived at the house to talk to our parents. Stiffly, they
sat on the blue living room sofa. From the doorway of another room, spying
the visitors, I noted the incongruity—the clash of two worlds, the faces and
the voices of school intruding upon the familiar setting of home. I overheard

one voice gently wondering, 'Do your children speak only Spanish at home, Mrs. Rodriguez?' While another voice added, 'That Richard especially seems so timid and shy.'

That Rich-heard!   30

With great tact the visitors continued, 'Is it possible for you and your hus-   31
band to encourage your children to practice their English when they are home?' Of course, my parents complied. What would they not do for their children's well-being? And how could they have questioned the Church's authority which those women represented. . . . The moment after the visitors left, the change was observed, '*Ahora,* speak to us *en inglés,'* my father and mother united to tell us.

At first, it seemed a kind of game. After dinner each night, the family   32
gathered to practice 'our' English. (It was still then *inglés,* a language foreign to us, so we felt drawn as strangers to it.) Laughing, we would try to define words we could not pronounce. We played with strange English sounds, often overanglicizing our pronunciations. And we filled the smiling gaps of our sentences with familiar Spanish sounds. But that was cheating, somebody shouted. Everyone laughed. In school, meanwhile, like my brother and sister, I was required to attend a daily tutoring session. I needed a full year of special attention. I also needed my teachers to keep my attention from straying in class by calling out, *Rich-heard*—their English voices slowly prying loose my ties to my other name, its three notes, *Ri-car-do.* Most of all I needed to hear my mother and father speak to me in a moment of seriousness in broken— suddenly heartbreaking—English. The scene was inevitable: One Saturday morning I entered the kitchen where my parents were talking in Spanish. I did not realize that they were talking in Spanish however until, at the moment they saw me, I heard their voices change to speak English. Those *gringo* sounds they uttered startled me. Pushed me away. In that moment of trivial misunderstanding and profound insight, I felt my throat twisted by unsounded grief. I turned quickly and left the room. But I had no place to escape to with Spanish. (The spell was broken.) My brother and sisters were speaking English in another part of the house.

Again and again in the days following, increasingly angry, I was obliged   33
to hear my mother and father: 'Speak to us *en inglés.' (Speak.)* Only then did I determine to learn classroom English. Weeks after, it happened: One day in school I raised my hand to volunteer an answer. I spoke out in a loud voice. And I did not think it remarkable when the entire class understood. That day, I moved very far from the disadvantaged child I had been only days earlier. The belief, the calming assurance that I belonged in public, had at last taken hold.

Shortly after, I stopped hearing the high and low sounds of *los gringos.* A   34
more and more confident speaker of English, I didn't trouble to listen to *how* strangers sounded, speaking to me. And there simply were too many English-speaking people in my day for me to hear American accents anymore. Conversations quickened. Listening to persons who sounded eccentrically

pitched voices, I usually noted their sounds for an initial few seconds before I concentrated on *what* they were saying. Conversations became content-full. Transparent. Hearing someone's *tone* of voice—angry or questioning or sarcastic or happy or sad—I didn't distinguish it from the words it expressed. Sound and word were thus tightly wedded. At the end of a day I was often bemused, always relieved to realize how 'silent,' though crowded with words, my day in public had been. (This public silence measured and quickened the change in my life.)

At last, seven years old, I came to believe what had been technically true since my birth: I was an American citizen. 35

But the special feeling of closeness at home was diminished by then. Gone was the desperate, urgent, intense feeling of being at home; rare was the experience of feeling myself individualized by family intimates. We remained a loving family, but one greatly changed. No longer so close; no longer bound tight by the pleasing and troubling knowledge of our public separateness. Neither my older brother nor sister rushed home after school anymore. Nor did I. When I arrived home there would often be neighborhood kids in the house. Or the house would be empty of sounds. 36

The silence at home, however, was finally more than a literal silence. Fewer words passed between parent and child, but more profound was the silence that resulted from my inattention to sounds. At about the time I no longer bothered to listen with care to the sounds of English in public, I grew careless about listening to the sounds family members made when they spoke. Most of the time I heard someone speaking at home and didn't distinguish his sounds from the words people uttered in public. I didn't even pay much attention to my parents' accented and ungrammatical speech. At least not at home. Only when I was with them in public would I grow alert to their accents. Though, even then, their sounds caused me less and less concern. For I was increasingly confident of my own public identity. 37

I would have been happier about my public success had I not sometimes recalled what it had been like earlier, when my family had conveyed its intimacy through a set of conveniently private sounds. Sometimes in public, hearing a stranger, I'd hark back to my past. A Mexican farmworker approached me downtown to ask directions to somewhere. *'¿Hijito . . . ?'* he said. And his voice summoned deep longing. Another time, standing beside my mother in the visiting room of a Carmelite convent, before the dense screen which rendered the nuns shadowy figures, I heard several Spanish-speaking nuns—their busy, singsong overlapping voices—assure us that yes, yes, we were remembered, all our family was remembered in their prayers. (Their voices echoed faraway family sounds.) Another day, a dark-faced old woman—her hand light on my shoulder—steadied herself against me as she boarded a bus. She murmured something I couldn't quite comprehend. Her Spanish voice came near, like the face of a never-before-seen relative in the instant before I was kissed. Her voice, like so many of the Spanish voices I'd heard in public, recalled the golden age of my youth. Hearing Spanish then, I continued to be a careful, if 38 sad, listener to sounds. Hearing a Spanish-speaking family walking behind me, I turned to look. I smiled for an instant, before my glance found the Hispanic-looking faces of strangers in the crowd going by.

Today I hear bilingual educators say that children lose a degree of 'individuality' by becoming assimilated into public society. (Bilingual schooling was popularized in the seventies, that decade when middle-class ethnics began to resist the process of assimilation—the American melting pot.) But the bilingualists simplistically scorn the value and necessity of assimilation. They do not seem to realize that there are *two* ways a person is individualized. So they do not realize that while one suffers a diminished sense of *private* individuality by becoming assimilated into public society, such assimilation makes possible the achievement of *public* individuality. 39

The bilingualists insist that a student should be reminded of his difference from others in mass society, his heritage. But they equate mere separateness with individuality. The fact is that only in private—with intimates—is separateness from the crowd a prerequisite for individuality. (An intimate draws me apart, tells me that I am unique, unlike all others.) In public, by contrast, full individuality is achieved, paradoxically, by those who are able to consider themselves members of the crowd. Thus it happened for me: Only when I was able to think of myself as an American, no longer an alien in *gringo* society, could I seek the rights and opportunities necessary for full public individuality. The social and political advantages I enjoy as a man result from the day that I came to believe that my name, indeed, is *Rich-heard Road-ree-guess*. It is true that my public society today is often impersonal. (My public society is usually mass society.) Yet despite the anonymity of the crowd and despite the fact that the individuality I achieve in public is often tenuous—because it depends on my being one in a crowd—I celebrate the day I acquired my new name. Those middle-class ethnics who scorn assimilation seem to me filled with decadent self-pity, obsessed by the burden of public life. Dangerously, they romanticize public separateness and they trivialize the dilemma of the socially disadvantaged. 40

Questions

1. Why does Rodriguez feel that it is important for bilingual children to learn the language of public society? What does a child gain by this? What does the child lose?

2. How does Rodriguez characterize those who are against assimilation? How would Porter respond to Rodriguez's position?

3. How do Rodriguez's ideas in this essay compare with those in his later work, *Days of Obligation: An Argument with My Mexican Father* excerpted in chapter 5?

4. Because of his position on bilingual education, Rodriguez has been accused of "selling out" his own people. Do you agree with this assessment?

The Need to Be:
The Socio-Cultural Significance
of Black Language

SHIRLEY N. WEBER

Shirley N. Weber is currently a professor and chairperson of African-American Studies at San Diego State University. While completing her Ph.D. at UCLA, she worked as a caseworker for the Episcopal City Mission in Los Angeles. After teaching at California State College in Los Angeles, she joined San Diego State. She has won a Woodrow Wilson Fellowship and a Carter G. Woodson Education Award from the NAACP.

Here, Weber illustrates in detail the power of the word in African-American language, the true meaning in its context of "rappin," and the value placed on proverbial language in the black community. Arguing that language demonstrates a culture's view of the reality around it, she forcefully asks the reader to understand that because blacks experience the world differently from other groups in America, there is a need for a language that communicates that experience, namely, black English. This selection is from Intercultural Communication *(1991).*

*Hey blood, what it is? Ah, Man, ain't notin to
it but I do it.
Huney, I done told ya', God, he don't lak ugly.
Look-a-there. I ain't seen nothin like these
economic indicators.*

From the street corners to the church pew to the board room, black language 1
is used in varying degrees. It is estimated that 80 to 90 percent of all black
Americans use the black dialect as least some of the time.[1] However, despite
its widespread use among blacks at all social and economic levels, there continues to be concern over its validity and continued use. Many of the concerns arise from a lack of knowledge and appreciation for the history of black
language and the philosophy behind its use.

Since the publication of J. L. Dillard's book *Black English* in 1972, much 2
has been written on the subject of black language. Generally, the research fo-

cuses on the historical and linguistic validity of black English, and very little has been devoted to the communications and cultural functions black language serves in the black community. It seems obvious that given the fact that black English is not "formally" taught in schools to black children and, yet, has widespread use among blacks, it must serve some important functions in the black community that represents the blacks' unique experience in America. If black language served no 'important function, it would become extinct like other cultural relics because all languages are functional tools that change and adapt to cultural and technological demands. If they cease to do this, they cease to exist as living languages. (The study of the English language's evolution and expansion over the last hundred years, to accommodate changing values and technological advancements, is a good example.) This article looks at the "need to be," the significance of black language to black people.

One's language is a model of his or her culture and of that culture's ad- 3 justment to the world. All cultures have some form of linguistic communications: without language, the community would cease to exist. To deny that a people has a language to express its unique perspective of the world is to deny its humanity. Furthermore, the study of language is a study of the people who speak that language and of the way they bring order to the chaos of the world. Consequently, the study of black language is really an examination of African people and of their adjustment to the conditions of American slavery. Smitherman says that black English (dialect) is

> an Africanized form of English reflecting Black America's linguistic-cultural African heritage and the conditions of servitude, oppression and life in America. . . .
>
> (It) is a language mixture, adapted to the conditions of slavery and discrimination, a combination of language and style interwoven with and inextricable from Afro-American culture.[2]

Much has been written about the origins of black language, and even 4 though the issue seems to be resolved for linguists, the rest of the world is still lingering under false assumptions about it. Basically, there are two opposing views: one that says there was African influence in the development of the language and the other that says there was not. Those who reject African influence believe that the African arrived in the United States and tried to speak English. And, because he lacked certain intellectual and physical attributes, he failed. This hypothesis makes no attempt to examine the phonological and grammatical structures of West African languages to see if there are any similarities. It places the African in a unique position unlike any other immigrant to America. Linguistic rationales and analyses are given for every other group that entered America pronouncing words differently and/or structuring their sentences in a unique way. Therefore, when the German said *zis* instead of *this,* American understood. But, when the African said *dis,* no one considered the fact that consonant combinations such as *th* may not exist in African languages.

Countering this dialectical hypothesis is the creole hypothesis that, as a   5
result of contact between Africans and Europeans, a new language formed
that was influenced by both languages. This language took a variety of forms,
depending on whether there was French, Portuguese, or English influence.
There is evidence that these languages were spoken on the west coast of
Africa as early as the sixteenth century (before the slave trade). This hypothesis is further supported by studies of African languages that demonstrate the
grammatical, phonological, and rhythmic similarities between them and
black English. Thus, the creole hypothesis says that the African responded to
the English language as do all other non-English speakers: from the phonological and grammatical constructs of the native language.

The acceptance of the creole hypothesis is the first step toward improving   6
communications with blacks. However, to fully understand and appreciate
black language and its function in the black community, it is essential to understand some general African philosophies about language and communications, and then to see how they are applied in the various styles and forms of
black communications.

In Janheinz Jahn's *Muntu,* basic African philosophies are examined to give   7
a general overview of African culture. It is important to understand that while
philosophies that govern the different groups in Africa vary, some general
concepts are found throughout African cultures. One of the primary principles is the belief that everything has a reason for being. Nothing simply exists
without purpose or consequences. This is the basis of Jahn's explanation of
the four basic elements of life, which are Muntu, mankind; Kintu, things;
Hantu, place and time; and Kuntu, modality. These four elements do not exist as static objects but as forces that have consequences and influence. For instance, in Hantu, the West is not merely a place defined by geographic
location, but a force that influences the East, North, and South. Thus, the
term "Western world" connotes a way of life that either complements or challenges other ways of life. The Western world is seen as a force and not a place.
(This is applicable to the other three elements also.)

Muntu, or man, is distinguished from the other three elements by his   8
possession of Nommo, the magical power of the word. Without Nommo,
nothing exists. Consequently, mankind, the possessor of Nommo, becomes
the master of all things.

> All magic is word magic, incantations and exorcism, blessings and curse.
> Through Nommo, the word, man establishes his mastery over things. . . .
>   If there were no word all forces would be frozen, there would be no pro-
> creation, no changes, no life. . . . For the word holds the course of things in
> train and changes and transforms them. And since the word has this power
> every word is an effective word, every word is binding. And the muntu is re-
> sponsible for his word.[3]

Nommo is so powerful and respected in the black community that only   9
those who are skillful users of the word become leaders. One of the main

qualifications of leaders of black people is that they must be able to articulate the needs of the people in a most eloquent manner. And because Muntu is a force who controls Nommo, which has power and consequences, the speaker must generate and create movement and power within his listeners. One of the ways this is done is through the use of imaginative and vivid language. Of the five canons of speech, it is said that Inventio or invention is the most utilized in black American. Molefi Asante called it the "coming to be of the novel," or the making of the new. So that while the message might be the same, the analogies, stories, images, and so forth must be fresh, new, and alive.

Because nothing exists without Nommo, it, too, is the force that creates a   10
sense of community among communicators, so much so that the speaker and audience become one as senders and receivers of the message. Thus, an audience listening and responding to a message is just as important as the speaker, because without their "amens" and "right-ons" the speaker may not be successful. This interplay between speaker and listeners is called "call and response" and is a part of the African world view, which holds that all elements and forces are interrelated and indistinguishable because they work together to accomplish a common goal and to create a sense of community between the speaker and the listeners.

This difference between blacks and whites was evident, recently, in a class   11
where I lectured on Afro-American history. During the lecture, one of my more vocal black students began to respond to the message with some encouraging remarks like "all right," "make it plain," "that all right," and "teach." She was soon joined by a few more black students who gave similar comments. I noticed that this surprised and confused some of the white students. When questioned later about this, their response was that they were not used to having more than one person talk at a time, and they really could not talk and listen at the same time. They found the comments annoying and disruptive. As the lecturer, I found the comments refreshing and inspiring. The black student who initiated the responses had no difficulty understanding what I was saying while she was reacting to it, and did not consider herself "rude."

In addition to the speaker's verbal creativity and the dynamic quality of   12
the communication environment, black speech is very rhythmic. It flows like African languages in a consonant-vowel-consonant-vowel pattern. To achieve this rhythmic effect, some syllables are held longer and are accented stronger and differently from standard English, such as DE-troit. This rhythmic pattern is learned early by young blacks and is reinforced by the various styles it complements.

With this brief background into the historical and philosophical foundation of black language, we can examine some of the styles commonly employed and their role in African-American life. Among the secular styles, the most common is *rappin'*. Although the term *rappin'* is currently used by whites to mean simply talking (as in *rap sessions*), it originally described the dialogue between a man and a woman where the main intention is to win the admiration of the woman. A man's success in rappin' depends on his ability to make creative and imaginative statements that generate interest on the part of the woman to hear more of the rap. And, although she already knows his intentions, the ritual is still played out; and, if the rap is weak, he will probably lose the woman.

To outsiders, rappin' might not appear to be an important style in the black community, but it is very important and affects the majority of black people because at some time in a black person's life, he or she will be involved in a situation where rappin' will take place. For, in the black community, it is the mating call, the introduction of the male to the female, and it is ritualistically expected by black women. So that while it is reasonable to assume that all black males will not rise to the level of "leader" in the black community because only a few will possess the unique oral skills necessary, it can be predicted that black men will have to learn how to "rap" to a woman.   14

Like other forms of black speech, the rap is rhythmic and has consequences. It is the good *rapper* who *gets over* (scores). And, as the master of Nommo, the rapper creates, motivates, and changes conditions through his language. It requires him to be imaginative and capable of responding to positive and negative stimuli immediately. For instance: 15

R: Hey Mama, how you doing?
L: Fine.
R: Yeah. I can see! (looking her up and down) Say, you married?
L: Yes.
R: Is your husband married? (bringing humor and doubt)

The rap requires participation by the listener. Thus, the speaker will ask for confirmation that the listener is following his line of progression. The rap is an old style that is taught to young men early. And, while each male will have his own style of rappin' that will adapt to the type of woman he is rappin' to, a poor, unimaginative rap is distasteful and often repulsive to black women.   16

Runnin' it down is a form of rappin' without sexual overtones. It is simply explaining something in great detail. The speaker's responsibility is to vividly recreate the event or concept for the listener so that there is complete agreement and understanding concerning the event. The speaker gives accurate descriptions of the individuals involved, describing them from head to toe. Every object and step of action is minutely described. To an outsider this might sound boring and tedious. However, it is the responsibility of the speaker to use figurative language to keep the listener's attention. In a narrative of a former slave from Tennessee, the following brief excerpt demonstrates the vivid language used in runnin' it down: 17

I remember Mammy told me about one master who almost starved his slaves. Mighty stingy I reckon he was.

Some of them slaves was so poorly thin they ribs would kinda rustle against each other like corn stalks a-drying in the hot winds. But they gets even one hog killing time, and it was funny, too, Mammy said.[4]

Runnin' it down is not confined to secular styles. In C. L. Franklin's ser-   18
mon. "The Eagle Stirreth Her Nest"—the simple story of an eagle, mistaken
for a chicken, that grows up and is eventually set free—the story becomes a
drama that vividly takes the listener through each stage of the eagle's development. And even when the eagle is set free because she can no longer live in
a cage, she does not simply fly away. Instead, she flies from one height to the
other, surveying the surroundings, and then flies away. The details are so
vivid that the listener can "see" and "feel" the events. Such is the style and
the effect of runnin' it down.

Another common style of black language is *the dozens*. The dozens is a   19
verbal battle of insults between speakers. The term dozens was used during
slavery to refer to a selling technique used by slavers. If an individual had a
disability, he was considered "damaged goods" and was sold with eleven
other "damaged" slaves at a discount rate. The term dozens refers to negative
physical characteristics. To an outsider, the dozens might appear cruel and
harsh. But to members of the black community, it is the highest form of verbal warfare and impromptu speaking. The game is often played in jest.

When the dozens is played, there is usually a group of listeners that serves   20
as judge and jury over the originality, creativity, and humor of the comments.
The listeners encourage continuation of the contest by giving comments like
"Ou, I wouldn't take that," "Cold," "Rough," "Stale," or any statement that
assesses the quality of the comments and encourages response. The battle
continues until someone wins. This is determined by the loser giving up and
walking away, or losing his cool and wanting to fight. When a physical confrontation occurs, the winner is not determined by the fight, but by the verbal confrontation. The dozens is so popular that a rock 'n' roll group made a
humorous recording of insults between friends. Some of the exchanges were:

> Say Man, your girlfriend so ugly, she had to sneak up on a glass to get a drink
> of water.
>
> Man, you so ugly, yo mamma had to put a sheet over your head so sleep
> could sneak up on you.

The dozens, like other forms of black language, calls on the speaker to use
words to create moods. More than any other form, it pits wit against wit, and
honors the skillful user of Nommo.

The final secular style to be discussed is proverbial wisdom. Sayings are   21
used in the black community as teaching tools to impart values and truths.
Their use demonstrates the African-American's respect for the oral tradition
in teaching and socializing the young. Popular phrases, such as "what goes
around comes around," "if you make you bed hard you gon lay in it," "God
don't like ugly," and "a hard head make a soft behind," are used in everyday
conversation by blacks from all social, economic, and educational strata. At
some time in a black child's life, the sayings are used to teach them what life
expects of them and what they can expect in return. It is also used to expose
the truth in an artful and less offensive manner, such as "you don't believe fat

meat is greasy." In this saying the listener is being put down for having a narrow or inaccurate view of things. And while it might appear that proverbial wisdoms are static, they are constantly changing and new ones are being created. One of the latest is said when you believe someone is lying to you or "putting you on." It is, "pee on my head and tell me it's raining." Or, if someone is talking bad about you, you might say, "don't let your mouth write a check your ass can't cash." Proverbial wisdom can be found on every socioeconomic level in the black community, and it is transmitted from generation to generation. Listening to speech that is peppered with proverbial sayings might seem strange to nonblacks. But, because proverbial sayings are generally accepted as "truths" because they are taught to children at a very early age, they effectively sum up events and predict outcome.

Like the secular, the nonsecular realm places a tremendous emphasis on the creative abilities of the speaker. The speaker (preacher) creates experiences for his listeners, who are participants in the communication event. The minister calls and his audience responds, and at some point they become one. The minister actively seeks his audience's involvement and when he does not receive it, he chides and scolds them. The audience also believes that the delivery of a good sermon is dependent upon them encouraging the minister with their "amens" and "right-ons." And if the minister preaches false doctrine, the audience also feels obliged to tell him, "Uh, oh Reb, you done gone too far now!" 22

The language used by the minister, who is probably very fluent in standard English, is generally seasoned with black English. Seldom will you hear the term *Lord* used, but you will hear *Lawd* because the *Lord* is the man in the big house who is an overseer, but the *Lawd* is a friend who walks, talks, and comforts you. The relationship between the *Lawd* and his people is more personal than the *Lord*'s. 23

Also, the speaker may overaccent a word for black emphasis. In C. L. Franklin's sermon, he said, "*extra*-ordinary sight." He then came right back and said *extraordinary*, to demonstrate that he knew how to "correctly" enunciate the word. The non-secular style of speech is generally the most dramatic of all forms and has the highest degree of audience participation. It encompasses all the elements of black language, and of all the styles it is the most African in form. 24

Black language and the numerous styles that have been developed are indications of the African-American's respect for the spoken word. The language has often been called a hieroglyphic language because of the vivid picture created by the speaker for the listener about the activities or feelings taking place. To say someone is "all jawed up," or "smacking on some barnyard pimp," or "ready to hat," is more imaginative and creative than saying they had "nothin to say," or "eating chicken," or "ready to leave." The responsibility of the speaker and the listener to participate in the communication event also emphasizes the African world view, which stresses the interrelatedness of all things to each other. And finally, the dynamics of the communication, and the responsibility of man as the user of Nommo, places 25 communication and the spoken word in the arena of forces and not static objects. The rhythm and flow of the language approximates the style and flow and unity of African life.

Despite all of the explanation of the Africanness found in black language, 26 many continue to ask, why use it? Why do blacks who have lived in America for hundreds of years continue to speak "black"? Why do those who possess degrees of higher learning and even write scholarly articles and books in standard English continue to talk "black"?

There are many reasons for the continued use of black language. A lan- 27 guage expresses an experience. If the experiences of a group are culturally unique, the group will need a different vocabulary to express them. If white folks in white churches don't *get happy* because they have been socialized to be quiet listeners in church, then they don't have the vocabulary that blacks have to describe levels of spiritual possession. And if they do not have curly hair, they probably do not *press* their hair or worry about *catching up* their *kitchins*. Thus, because blacks experience the world differently from other groups in America, there is a need for a language that communicates that experience.

Secondly, black language reaches across the superficial barriers of educa- 28 tion and social position. It is the language that binds, that creates community for blacks, so that the brother in the three-piece Brooks Brothers suit can go to the local corner where folks "hang out" and say, "hey, blood, what it is?", and be one with them. Additionally, the minister's use of black language reminds the listeners of their common experiences and struggles (for example, "I been thur the storm"). Through black language, barriers that separate blacks are lowered and they are finally "home" with each other. So, for cultural identity, the code is essential to define the common elements among them.

Finally, black language usage stands as a political statement that black 29 people are African people who have not given up a vital part of themselves in slavery: their language. They have retained the cultural link that allows them to think and to express themselves in a non-European form. As an old adage says, The namer of names is the father of things. Thus, the ability of blacks to maintain and sustain a living language shows their control over that aspect of their lives, and their determination to preserve the culture. The use of black language is the black man's defiance of white America's total indoctrination. The use of black language by choice is a reflection not of a lack of intelligence, but of a desire to retain and preserve black life styles.

The purpose of this discussion is to help others understand and appreci- 30 ate black language styles and the reasons blacks speak the way they do, in hopes of building respect for cultural difference. Now the question may be asked, what does the general society do about it? Some might ask, should whites learn black English? To that question comes a resounding *no!* Black language is, first of all, not a laboratory language and it cannot be learned in a classroom. And even if you could learn definition and grammar, you would not learn the art of creative expression that is taught when you're "knee high to a duck." Thus, you would miss the elements of rhythm and style, and you would sound like invaders or foreigners.

What one should do about the language is be open-minded and not judge the speaker by European standards of expression. If you're in a class-room and the teacher is *gettin down,* don't *wig out* because the black student says "teach." Simply realize that you must become listening participants. If some *bloods* decide to use a double negative or play *the dozens,* don't assume some social theory about how they lack a father image in the home and are therefore culturally and linguistically deprived. You just might discover that they are the authors of your college English text. 31

The use of black language does not represent any pathology in blacks. It simply says that, as African people transplanted to America, they are a differ-ent flower whose aroma is just as sweet as other flowers. The beginning of racial understanding is the acceptance that difference is just what it is: differ-ent, not inferior. And equality does not mean sameness. 32

NOTES

1. Geneva Smitherman. *Talkin' and Testifyin'.* (1972). Boston: Houghton Mifflin Company, p. 2.
2. Ibid., p. 3.
3. Janheinz Jahn. *Muntu.* (1961). New York: Grove Press, Inc., pp. 132–133.
4. Smitherman, *Talkin' and Testifyin'.* p. 156.

Questions

1. According to Weber, what is the function of language?
2. What are the two views of black language? Which view does Weber support?
3. In the essay, Weber gives different examples of how black language reflects and preserves black cultural identity. Reflect on some of your own speech habits, for instance, proverbial wisdom. How does your language communicate your experi-ence or reflect your perception of the world?

Talkin' White

WAYNE LIONEL APONTE

At the time of writing, Aponte was an English major at the University of Rochester. He has published work in the Nation *and* American Visions.

    Here, Aponte defends the fact that he talks "white." At a younger and more vulnerable age, he became polylingual, and does not feel the need to talk what he calls "slang" to prove he is black. He believes that just as "white English" has many variables, so does (or should) black English. This reading is from Essence *magazine (1989).*

Recently, during a conversation on film at a dinner party, when I was using my best college-educated English, I was asked where I was born. I received a curious look when I replied, with pride, "Harlem." The questioner, whom I had met through a mutual friend, looked at me as if I were a brother from another planet and immediately wanted to know whether I'd lived in Harlem all my life. When I responded, "Yeah, man, I been cold chillin' on Lenox Avenue ever since I was rockin' my fly diapers," he laughed, and I realized his was nervous laughter, the kind folks use to mask their thoughts. *Has he really lived in Harlem all his life? He talks white* was the thought behind his laughter, and the follow-up question asked after my departure. 1

While growing up in Harlem during my not-so-long-ago elementary and middle-school days, I often encountered the phrase "talkin' white." It was usually thrust on people who were noticed because they were speaking grammatically correct English in a community that did not. I've also heard the term applied to people who place themselves above others by verbally showboating with the elocution of a Lionel Trilling or a Sir Laurence Olivier. 2

Nevertheless, I've always loved those folks who have mastered the art of manipulating words. Eloquent oratory and masterful writing have stimulated my mind for as long as I can remember. I took great pride in my ability to mimic and to slowly transform the styles of my favorite writers and orators into my own voice. In this sense language is a form of intellectual play for me. 3

When I was a child, my reaction to the question "Why do you talk so white?" was to alter my spoken English drastically (once "Ask yo mama" became less effective and after I ran out of money for candy bribes to make the 4 kids like me). Like most children, I wanted to be liked and wanted to blend into each new social circle. But speaking as I did made blending difficult since it brought favorable attention from teachers that, outside the classroom, evoked fierce verbal attacks from my peers. I never could quite understand how talking slang proved I was Black. Nor did I understand why I couldn't be accepted as a full-fledged, card-holding member of the group by speaking my natural way.

Hearing the laughter, though, and being the butt of "proper" and "Oreo" 5
jokes hurt me. Being criticized made me feel marginal—and verbally impotent in the sense that I had little ammunition to stop the frequent lunchtime attacks. So I did what was necessary to fit in, whether that meant cursing excessively or signifying. Ultimately I somehow learned to be polylingual and to become sensitive linguistically in the way animals are able to sense the danger of bad weather.

The need to defend myself led me to use language as a weapon to deflect 6
jokes about the "whiteness" of my spoken English and to launch harsh verbal counterattacks. Simultaneously language served as a mask to hide the hurt I often felt in the process. Though over time my ability to "talk that talk"— slang—gained me a new respect from my peers, I didn't want to go through life using slang to prove I am Black. So I decided "I yam what I yam," and to take pride in myself. I am my speaking self, but this doesn't mean that I'm turning my back on Black people. There are various shades of Blackness; I don't have to talk like Paul Laurence Dunbar's dialect poems to prove I'm Black. I don't appreciate anyone's trying to take away the range of person I can be.

"Talkin' white" implies that the English language is a closed system 7
owned exclusively by whites. But my white friends from Chattanooga, Ventura, California, and New York City don't all speak the same way. Nor do the millions of poor whites working below the poverty line "talk white," as that phrase is interpreted.

But the primary reason I question this peculiar euphemism for "speaking 8
well" is that it has been used tyrannically to push to the periphery of the race people who grew up in the West Indies and attended English schools or who lived in predominantly white environments: They are perceived as not being Black enough, or as somehow being anti-Black.

It hurts to know that many people judge me and others on whether or 9
not we break verbs. If we follow this line of thought, maybe we'll also say that W.E.B. DuBois wasn't Black because he matriculated at Harvard and studied at the University of Berlin. Or perhaps that Alain Leroy Locke wasn't Black because he earned a degree from Oxford University. Or, to transfer the logic, maybe we're not all of African descent since we don't speak Swahili and some "real" Africans do.

If we can take pride in the visual diversity of the race, then surely we can 10
transfer this diversity and appreciation to spoken English. Because all of us don't be talkin' alike—ya know what I'm sayin'?

Questions

1. Would Weber agree with Aponte's assertion that he does not need to talk slang to prove he is black? Would Aponte agree with Weber's assertion that black language reflects black cultural identity? Why or why not?

2. Black language is currently considered an essential component of rap music. What reasons can you cite for this?

3. Is the current preference for Standard English on the job market simply a form of racism? Why or why not?

Writing Assignments

The following writing assignments are concerned with the topic of diversity and language. Before developing an argument on any of these assignments, be sure that you understand the controversy by completing the following exercises:

- Write responses to exploration questions.
- Read several articles in this chapter or elsewhere to discover at least two perspectives on the topic.
- Create a list of opposing viewpoints and consider the potential consequences of each.
- Examine the underlying assumptions behind each viewpoint.

To help you understand the issues and develop ideas, you can use the following form:

The conflict in this issue is between _____ and

_____.

I am more inclined to agree with _____

because _____.

However, it is possible that some of my readers may believe that

_____.

Exploration Questions

1. When you were growing up, what was your family's attitude toward people who did not speak English? Did you have contact with people whose first language was not English?
2. Perhaps you did not speak English as a first language. If so, what experiences did you have in learning the new language?
3. Do you believe that immigrants to the United States should have free access to instruction in English?
4. Do you believe that English should be declared the official language of the United States?
5. If you moved to a foreign country, would you want to keep your native language? Why or why not?
6. Do you think that people who do not speak your language are incapable of understanding you completely? Why or why not?
7. What is your reaction to regional accents? Do you tend to form an opinion of a person based on his or her accent?

8. To what extent was proper speech and pronunciation stressed in your own background?

ASSIGNMENT 1

Although the history of the United States is associated with waves of immigrants from many different countries, there is now, more than ever before, a tremendously high concentration of immigrants from Spanish-speaking countries. Given the proximity of the United States to Mexico, the historical link between the United States and Mexico, and the large influx of immigrants from Puerto Rico, Mexico, El Salvador, and Nicaragua, some have argued that all students in the United States should study Spanish in school and that ballots and directions should be printed in Spanish as well as in English.

In an argumentative essay, address the following question: Should students in the United States be required to study Spanish? In framing your response, be sure to indicate your awareness of the history of this controversy and of the opposing viewpoint.

ASSIGNMENT 2

Several of the articles in this chapter concern the question of whether bilingual education with its advantages and disadvantages is helping immigrants learn English to become a part of American culture. Read several of these articles and reflect on your own views on the relationship between language, education, and culture. Then write an argumentative essay which addresses the following question: Do you believe that bilingual education is beneficial for society? In framing your response, be sure that you define what you mean by "beneficial."

ASSIGNMENT 3

One of the issues raised in this chapter is the relationship between language and power. The ability to speak English well is usually considered a social and professional advantage. Walk around your campus, listen to how various people speak, and note what their speech seems to reveal about them. Another way of thinking about this topic is to watch several television programs and note what the speech patterns of various characters seem to indicate about them. Then write an argumentative essay addressing the following question: Is it valid to judge people by how they speak? As in all academic writing, you should narrow your topic sufficiently so that you can address it adequately. In answering this question, you should define what you mean by "judged" and specify the type of speech you are using as an example.

ASSIGNMENT 4

Read the articles concerned with the "English-only" movement, and write an essay in response to the following question: If you could construct an ideal society, would it be one in which everyone spoke the same language? Or does a society in which people speak different languages offer greater advantages?

Using Data

ASSIGNMENT

1. How do these projections of population changes lend support to the debates over bilingual education and the English-only Amendment?

Projected Components of Population Change, by Race: 1995 to 2025

YEAR AND RACE	Population at start of period (1,000)	TOTAL (Jan. 1–Dec. 31)						RATE PER 1,000 MIDYEAR POPULATION				
		Net increase[1]		Natural increase		Net civilian immigration (1,000)	Net growth rate[2]	Natural increase			Net civilian immigration rate
		Total (1,000)	Per-cent[2]	Births (1,000)	Deaths (1,000)			Total	Birth rate	Death rate	
ALL RACES											
1995	259,238	1,767	0.68	3.517	2,275	525	6.8	4.8	13.5	8.7	2.0
2000	267,498	1,522	0.57	3,389	2,367	500	5.7	3.8	12.6	8.8	1.9
2005	274,884	1,433	0.52	3,399	2,465	500	5.2	3.4	12.3	8.9	1.8
2010	281,894	1,351	0.48	3,485	2,634	500	4.8	3.0	12.3	9.3	1.8
2025	297,926	622	0.21	3,357	3,235	500	2.1	0.4	11.3	10.9	1.7
WHITE											
1995	216,267	1,074	0.50	2,744	1,966	296	5.0	3.6	12.7	9.1	1.4
2000	221,087	837	0.38	2,602	2,038	273	3.8	2.5	11.7	9.2	1.2
2005	225,048	746	0.33	2,583	2,110	273	3.3	2.1	11.5	9.4	1.2
2010	228,637	674	0.29	2,639	2,238	273	2.9	1.8	11.5	9.8	1.2
2025	235,317	79	0.03	2,490	2,684	273	0.3	0.8	10.6	11.4	1.2
BLACK											
1995	33,000	396	1.20	601	262	56	11.9	10.2	18.1	7.9	1.7
2000	34,939	379	1.08	597	272	54	10.8	9.2	17.0	7.7	1.5
2005	36,816	372	1.01	604	286	54	10.1	8.6	16.3	7.7	1.5
2010	38,653	358	0.93	616	312	54	9.2	7.8	15.9	8.0	1.4
2025	43,348	247	0.57	602	410	54	5.7	4.5	13.9	9.5	1.3
OTHER RACES											
1995	9,971	298	2.98	172	48	174	29.4	12.2	17.0	4.7	17.2
2000	11,472	305	2.66	190	58	173	26.3	11.4	16.4	5.0	14.9
2005	13,020	315	2.42	211	69	173	23.9	10.8	16.0	5.2	13.1
2010	14,604	319	2.18	230	84	173	21.6	9.9	15.6	5.7	11.7
2025	19,261	296	1.54	265	142	173	15.5	6.4	13.9	7.4	9.0

Based on U.S. Bureau of the Census estimates.

7 ■ Controversies About Political Correctness

To be PC or not to be PC—that is the question.

The term "political correctness," or "PC," refers to a particular view of the world that its proponents maintain should be actively promoted, both in school and in the workplace. This view perceives Western culture as having always been oppressive to women and racial minorities and emphasizes that in order for such oppression to end, an atmosphere of sensitivity to others should be maintained through mandating acceptable boundaries for speech and behavior. The label "politically correct" is often applied to statements, programs, or policies that foster this position and to people whose opinions are in accord with it. A particular opinion or a person holding such an opinion may be termed "politically correct." Although the term is most frequently associated with issues on university campuses, it has now moved into more general usage. Even George Bush, who was not usually involved in academic debates, used the term in a 1990 speech at the University of Michigan in which he defended the maintenance of campus freedoms from the restrictions advocated by politically correct censors.

Controversies concerned with what is or is not politically correct are closely allied with issues of diversity and multiculturalism and are, therefore, relevant to the theme of this textbook. The readings in this chapter focus on several facets of the PC debate, in particular, on the nature and origins of the controversy, on the extent to which the imposition of PC policies constitute an infringement on free speech rights, on the question of whether it is desirable or possible to institute programs fostering political correctness, or to teach political correctness on college campuses, and on the related question of deciding which literature ought to be included in the literary canon, the body of work that is generally acknowledged to be worthy of study.

SALLY FORTH By Greg Howard and Craig MacIntosh

The Origin of the PC Debate

Although one might make the case that at various historical periods, certain political and social positions have always been privileged by the intellectual elite and that dissatisfaction with political and social hierarchies has always been a part of the intellectual tradition, the current use of the term "political correctness" and the furor generated in print over the past two years began in the fall of 1990, when articles began to appear in the *New York Times,* the *Atlantic,* the *New Republic,* and the *Village Voice,* and when educators as well as television newscasters began to discuss it. According to Paul Berman in his introduction to *Debating P.C.: The Controversy over Political Correctness on College Campuses,* the overall thrust of the PC movement is associated with a political ideology that condemns the United States and Western culture in general as fundamentally oppressive to particular groups (women and minorities) and that seeks to rectify past injustice by fostering awareness of racial and gender issues. Such an atmosphere would be instituted through a prescribed set of speech and behavior codes designed to foster sensitivity to others, codes that some educators believe ought to be encouraged through special courses and policies. The concept of political correctness is also linked with proposals to revise the school curricula to acknowledge the role of minorities in American history, to incorporate minority literature into the literary canon, and to endorse cultural and ethnic pluralism.

Analysts of the PC phenomenon sometimes express concern that its most enthusiastic proponents are, at times, somewhat naive in directing their criticism toward the racism, sexism, and oppression of Western culture without acknowledging that the Third World cultures they idealize can be equally racist, sexist, and oppressive. In his essay, "The Origins of PC," John M. Ellis argues that criticism of one's own society and an overly optimistic view of other societies has often surfaced in Western thought and that concern about racism and male dominance is actually more prevalent in the West despite the condemnation of Western culture by PC critics. Dinesh D'Souza points to a similar dichotomy in "The Visigoths in Tweed." He points out that multicultural or non-Western education on campus frequently glamorizes Third World cultures while understating or overlooking the rampant sexism and racism within these societies.

Other critics of the PC movement focus on the excessive seriousness of its most ardent activists. Examining the origins of the term in her essay, "A Short History of the Term *Politically Correct,*" Ruth Perry identifies it as first appearing in the United States in the Black Power movement and the New Left and points out that the term has many meanings, including an ironic nuance—in lesbian circles at one time it was hip to be politically correct. The term also has what Perry refers to as a "double consciousness"; that is, it denotes desirable thinking, and yet at the same time, it acts as a self-mocking term to illustrate the excesses of such thinking.

Political Correctness and Free Speech

Although proponents of the PC movement view it as simply another way of requiring people to "do the right thing"; others perceive it as a potential threat to the preservation of democracy and culture. These critics are concerned that the notion of requiring PC language will endanger the right of free speech and lead ultimately to a society in which people use one language in private and another in public and where thought is mandated as well, a move in the direction of an Orwellian Big Brother society. In his article, "'Speech Codes' and Free Speech," Nat Hentoff expresses concern that so-called free speech is being curtailed by speech codes, a set of which were adopted several years ago at Stanford University. Nevertheless, Hentoff points out, at the same time, right wing campus publications that poke fun at PC speech are flourishing. Hentoff is concerned about the self-censoring some students claim to adopt in classrooms, and he also notes a worrying tinge of anti-Semitism in the choice of speakers invited by black student groups to speak on campuses. Professor Stanley Fish, however, is not concerned that the PC movement will have an adverse effect on free speech because he says that there really is no such thing as absolutely free speech. In "There's No Such Thing as Free Speech and It's a Good Thing, Too!" Fish points out that as concerned citizens, we have to be responsible for our utterances and not simply rely on the First Amendment to guarantee our right to say anything. He illustrates some of the ways in which the amendment can be circumvented, and argues that politics of the day will also influence free speech. The important thing, he says, is to be sensitive to the context in which one is making remarks and to maintain a critical perspective on speech with which one might disagree.

In his article, "The Debate over Placing Limits on Racist Speech Must Not Ignore the Damage It Does to Its Victims," Charles R. Lawrence III points out that unbridled free speech can be devastating to those injured by it. To Lawrence, real harm to both individuals and groups can arise from racial insults, and he believes that legal remedies need to be constructed to counter

Reprinted with special permission: Tribune Media Services.

the worst effects of racist and sexist speech. Finally, Richard Perry and Patricia Williams point out that whether or not we agree with speech codes, such codes, explicitly or implicitly, are not entirely new, nor do they prevent racist and sexist thought in private. They conclude their piece, "Freedom of Hate Speech," by asking for a redefinition of the standard traditional rational man to reflect our multicultural society.

IMPLICATIONS OF MANDATING POLITICAL CORRECTNESS

If political correctness denotes a new emphasis on sensitivity to others and a heightened awareness of racism, sexism, and oppression in Western culture, where should this sensitivity and awareness be learned? Some PC proponents believe these facets of the movement should be taught to students on college campuses through special PC classes, a suggestion that has generated considerable controversy. Some educators believe that to institute another required course would necessitate the elimination of some other requirement, raising questions about which requirement can be excluded. Other educators object to the notion that the university should take on this responsibility. Others, however, believe that the tensions inherent in modern society make it necessary for the university to assume such a role. The article by the National Association of Scholars, "The Wrong Way to Reduce Campus Tensions," for exam-ple, asserts that it is indeed the role of higher education to enable students to grapple with contrary or unpleas-ant ideas and that to shield them from such ideas will be detrimental in the long run.

Political Correctness and the Literary Canon

One component of the PC debate focuses on the extent to which the literary canon (the literature which is studied in school and which is generally re-garded as worthy of study) reflects and fosters ethnic and gender bias because it traditionally has consisted primarily of the work of "Eurocentric" male writers and has excluded works by women and minorities. Questions about the canon have led to a serious examination of the political and social role of literacy, of the criteria for inclusion in a traditional curriculum, and of the role of education in the forging of ethnic and national identity. As a result of these inquiries, many college campuses are now reevaluating and modifying their curriculum to include women and ethnic minority writers and to recog-nize the role of these groups in United States history. Most academics agree that the traditional literary canon should be expanded to include a greater di-versity of writers and that the narrative of history ought to be rewritten to include a more global consciousness. However, determining which writers should be included and the best way to structure an increasingly complex historical narrative has yet to be decided. Some believe that this new empha-sis on ethnicity and gender will result in a sacrifice of aesthetic and intellec-tual standards.

The question of the literary canon and its role in reinforcing societal val-ues was brought to public consciousness by E.D. Hirsch in his book, *Cultural Literacy* (1987). Hirsch maintains that to be truly successful and democratic, a society must ensure that its members are culturally literate and that such literacy extends beyond reading and writing into a proficiency with a wide base of knowledge. Its members must become knowledgeable about their own culture, other cultures, and the world at large. Such universal literacy will liberate all strata of society and enable societies to deal comfortably with one another. People who do not have cultural literacy in the present so-ciety are, according to Hirsch, disenfranchised. He argues that traditional bases of knowledge and a traditional curriculum do not mean conservative indoctrination.

The debate over the literary canon implies that it is a fixed entity; yet, as Todd Gitlin points out in "On the Virtues of the Loose Canon," the canon is always in the process of change. Gitlin attacks the excesses of both right and left wing critics in the PC debate, charging that our society is in trouble not only because it lacks cultural literacy but also because too often an individual aligns him- or herself with a particular interest group as an end in itself, squelching intellectual curiosity, openness, and tolerance for difference.

Critics of the PC movement tend to focus on its more superficial manifestations, such as the necessity of saying high school "women" instead of high school "girls" or on the application of the term to other aspects of life, such as PC sex or PC clothing, and some believe that the movement will soon fade from the national consciousness. Advocates point out, however, that political correctness is not simply a buzzword but a legitimate movement that addresses serious social issues, among them the racial and ethnic tensions characteristic of a diverse society. If this is so, it is likely that the PC movement will continue to play a significant role on the national, political, and academic scene.

The Origins of PC

JOHN M. ELLIS

Born in England, John Ellis came to the United States in 1966 after teaching in England, Wales, and Canada. He joined the faculty of the University of California, Santa Cruz, where he is now a professor of German literature. He is the author of a number of books, including studies of Kleist and Schiller, and has been a Guggeinheim Fellow.

In this article, Ellis argues that a criticism of one's own society and overly optimistic praise of others has often surfaced in Western thought. In Ellis's view, the movement away from racism and male dominance is most prevalent in Western societies despite condemnation of these same societies by "politically correct" critics. This selection is from the Chronicle of Higher Education *(1992).*

Both sides in the current debate about "political correctness" assume that modern theory—whether political, social, or literary—has produced the ideas that are the focus of the present controversies: cultural relativism, hostility toward racism and sexism in Western society, suspicion that classic books provide elitist rationales for controlling women and the lower classes, and an emphasis on power relationships. But these ideas are not new, and theory is not their source. From the earliest times, inhabitants of Western society have been prone to recurring fits of politically correct—but quintessentially Western—self-doubt. 1

In the first century A.D. the Roman historian Tacitus wrote an idyllic account of the Germanic peoples. Compared to civilized Romans they were barbarians, part of the third world of their day. Yet to Tacitus they were remarkable people—so instinctively democratic that their kings ruled only through persuasion and their generals commanded by example rather than rank. They had no greedy financiers, and they valued the opinions of women. But when Tacitus says that no one in Germany finds vice amusing and that Germans are not corrupted by the excitements of banquets and public spectacles, we become suspicious. What was really on his mind was the corruption and decadence of imperial Rome, not the virtue of Germans. 2

The situation is familiar: A sophisticated man of letters, disillusioned by the flaws, inconsistencies, and retrogressions of a great civilization, deludes himself into thinking that primitive innocence exists among people who have remained untouched by that civilization. He sees his own culture not as an improvement on brutish natural behavior but as a departure from natural 3

349

goodness. This recurring Western fantasy runs from Tacitus's idealized Germans to Margaret Mead's sentimentalized Samoans and finally to the more general form prevailing today. Notable episodes along the way include Rousseau's adulation of the Noble Savage, the German Romantics, and Marx's imagined society whose state will wither away, presumably when natural goodness can substitute for law.

History has been brutal to these illusions. Tacitus did not live to see his 4 noble Germans run amok in the centuries that followed: The victims of the reign of terror that gave us the word "vandalism" saw little "natural goodness" in the Vandals of the fourth and fifth centuries; nor did those who encountered the Goths and the Vikings find much to admire. Rousseau died too soon to witness the Terror of the French Revolution, and Marx was comfortably buried long before the world saw his proletarian leaders become too fond of the states that they ran to let them wither away.

* * *

Today's political correctness bears more than a broad-brush similarity to these 5 thinkers' recurring fantasies, however. For example, the idea that "deconstructing" the Western canon reveals how elites use their power to control the lower classes sounds as if it comes straight from Foucault, Derrida, and Gramsci. But Rousseau said as much more than 200 years ago: "Princes always view with pleasure the spread among their subjects of a taste for the arts. . . . The sciences, letters and arts . . . cover with garlands of flowers the iron chains that bind them, stifle in them the feeling of that original liberty for which they seemed to have been born, make them love their slavery, and turn them into what is called civilized people." Here are all the essential elements of the avant-garde idea of our daring modern theorists: The sciences and the arts are really all about social control.

But, unlike Rousseau, we know what happened next in history. The free 6 expression of ideas by creative writers and philosophers of the Enlightenment proved highly dangerous to princes, who correctly saw these ideas as subversive and censored them. Rousseau's idea turned out to be foolish in his time, and it surely is just as foolish in ours. Modern princes, whether they rule in Baghdad or Havana, obviously think so too, judging by their practice of censorship. Rousseau did not need modern literary theory to reach his view; nor did he "deconstruct" the canon to reveal a "repressed politics." He just invented a crude, unrealistic conspiracy theory—which is what it remains, even in its chic modern formulation.

Another old "new" idea is the fashionable theory of cultural relativism. 7 By the late 18th century, some European cultures were much more advanced than others. The cultural dominance (or should I say "hegemony"?) of France was much resented in Germany, where some began to question the right of those French cultural imperialists to judge Germany as culturally backward. The critic and philosopher Johann Gottfried Herder invented multicultural theory and cultural relativism when he proclaimed that cultures can only be judged by their own unique standards. No culture is better than another, he said; they are just different, and we should celebrate the differences. Herder proceeded, however, to disparage high culture as artificial and praised the low culture of the German *Volk* as genuine, thus breaking the cultural truce that relativism was supposed to offer. Modern multiculturalists follow Herder, first asking us to celebrate difference and then denouncing Western culture as elitist.

The advantage of locating an idea in its historical birthplace is that we   8 can see how it fared. The fate of Germany's cultural relativism was partly amusing and partly tragic. Almost immediately after Herder developed his theory, Germany began to produce a series of cultural giants: the composers Mozart, Haydn, Beethoven, and Schubert; the philosophers Kant, Hegel, and Schopenhauer; the writers Goethe, Schiller, Kleist, and Hölderlin; and many others.

***

As the Germans began to dominate European culture, cultural relativism   9 seemed less attractive to them. But the celebration of the German *Volk* sowed the seeds of a virulent and persistent German nationalism that was to become part of the Nazi ideology. Anyone who thinks that cultural relativism and the celebration of ethnicity must lead to egalitarianism is sadly mistaken: The lesson of history is that they are more likely to unleash dangerous forces of the extreme right.

The collection of fairy tales gathered by the brothers Grimm showed the   10 unreality of the second part of Herder's theory, that the German folk culture was to be preferred to any high culture. The Grimms set out to document the natural eloquence of the German *Volk* by collecting tales verbatim from untutored peasants. But the Grimms' sentimental preconceptions must have clashed with what they found in the real world. We now know that their sources were almost exclusively middle-class friends or simply books—even French books—and that they rewrote everything to create an illusion of folk narration. The familiar desire to be politically correct had led the brothers to lie.

We cannot blame Tacitus for not anticipating the Vandals and Goths, nor   11 Rousseau for not foreseeing Robespierre, nor Herder and the Grimms for not seeing where celebrating the ethnicity of the German *Volk* would lead. However, we can ask that people who want to take us through the fantasy yet one more time first confront the lessons of history that show how disastrous "politically correct" ideas have proved to be.

Moreover, modern communications give us a much greater knowledge of   12 our world than Tacitus or Rousseau had of theirs. There is no excuse now for ignoring the violent ethnic, religious, and political clashes of the non-Western third world or for sentimentalizing the often appalling treatment of women there. Nowadays, it takes an extraordinary act of self-deception to avoid seeing that it is the developed countries that are slowly leading the world *away* from racism and male dominance. In seeking an end to racism and sexism, we automatically ally ourselves with certain *Western* values.

Although proponents of ideas considered to be politically correct claim   13 that they are grounded in "theory," these ideas cannot survive theoretical, that is, analytical, scrutiny. Take the showpiece argument, which is evidently considered one of great sophistication, that language conceals hidden power relations between men and women or between different classes and ethnic groups. Thus the apparent subject of a piece of language is set aside and its underlying *real* subject is said to be power and dominance.

But any parent of a rebellious teen-ager knows this argument too well to   14
find it novel or sophisticated. Teen-agers, too, are apt to reduce any topic of discussion to one of parental control and power. A parent, trying vainly to insist that issues such as safety and responsibility are just as relevant, if not more so, easily recognizes a primitive method of argument that reduces a complex state of affairs to a single factor. The argument remains primitive, whether used by Foucault or a 15-year-old.

An additional theoretical flaw is the obvious contradiction that exists be-   15
tween ideas such as cultural relativism, on one hand, and the denunciation of sexism and racism on the other. The former stance denies that norms transcend particular cultures, while the latter asserts that certain norms should override cultural differences. Real theorists would not grab any argument that happens to suit them at the moment and then ignore the overall consistency, or inconsistency, of their position.

* * *

What troubles me most about the self-styled theorists identified with political   16
correctness is their very un-theoretical habit of evading the arguments of their critics. Sometimes, they hide: For example, as deconstruction has become more difficult to defend, many of the leading deconstructionists seem to be edging quietly toward the door, ignoring their obligation to their students and to other scholars to deal forthrightly with criticisms. That is not the way of the theorist.

Most often, those under attack dismiss counter-arguments by labeling   17
those who make them as conservative or hostile to the progress of women and members of minority groups. But this approach denigrates the critic without addressing the criticism; until now the *ad hominem* argument has not been considered serious academic analysis.

A more radical mode of avoidance has been to deny that any issues need   18
to be discussed. Stanley Fish, professor of English at Duke University, tells us that the fuss about political correctness has been stirred up by right-wingers from outside academe. Thus no legitimate scholarly debate even exists. We also are told that the press has created much of the problem or that criticism of ideas such as multiculturalism or the new literary "theory" is an anti-intellectual attack on academe in general—again, presumably from the outside.

Evidently, J. Edgar Hoover and Richard Nixon are the role models of those   19
who use such arguments to avoid responding to critics in any substantive way: Hoover routinely met criticism by claiming that it came from outside agitators and Communists, and Nixon blamed his troubles on the press. Real theorists would want to engage, rather than to evade, the arguments of their academic colleagues and to genuinely join the debate that is now under way.

The root of the problem is that the mind-set of an academic social activist 20
is not that of a theorist. Theoretical analysis follows where the argument
leads, but activism determines where the argument must go and wants only
support for that predetermined direction. Theorists are intrigued by the *structure* of arguments, while activists only want to win them. Activists see their
opponents as immoral people from whom nothing can be learned, but theorists regard intellectual opponents as useful predators who pick off weak arguments and leave the remaining ones stronger. This is why, in the hands of
academic activists, ideas atrophy into the absurdities that are pilloried in the
national press. Activists underestimate the power of ideas to move the world;
they try to impose them through political power. But the pursuit of power
corrupts ideas just as it corrupts people.

Questions

1. Ellis argues that the ideas behind PC are not new. What are some of the historical
   precedents that have led to our modern theory of political correctness?
2. In what way is Rousseau a precursor of the theory of deconstruction?
3. According to Ellis, how does the celebration of ethnicity lead to conservatism?
4. What distinction does Ellis draw between theorists and activists?

A Short History of the Term *Politically Correct*

RUTH PERRY

Ruth Perry teaches in the Program in Women's Studies at the Massachusetts Institute of Technology.

Here, Perry identifies the term "politically correct" as first appearing in the United States in the Black Power movement and the New Left. She points out that the term has many meanings, including an ironic nuance—in lesbian circles at one time it was hip to be politically correct—and how, in general, it had what Perry calls a "double consciousness": it denoted desirable thinking and yet, at the same time, acted as a self-mocking term to illustrate excesses of such thinking. This selection is from Beyond PC *(1992).*

The phrase *politically correct,* like a will-o'-the-wisp on the murky path of history, has glimmered and vanished again as successive movements for social change have stumbled across the uncertain terrain. Its erratic appearance has always brought consternation as well as relief, resistance as well as consent. Like a recurring refrain in a song, or an incantatory line in a poem, its meaning changes each time it appears. 1

The phrase seems first to have gained currency in the U.S. in the mid to late 1960s within the Black Power movement and the New Left, although the phenomenon—labeling certain acts and attitudes as right or wrong—must be as old as belief itself.[1] Indeed, anthropologists will tell you that all communities evolve group norms about behavior and ideology. But in the era in which *politically correct* emerged as a popular phrase, the various groups that made use of it were all newly organized, whistling in the dark, trying to get their bearings, reaching for common terms to name the *plastic, corporate, mechanistic, alienated, white-supremacist, sexist, militaristic* society they wanted to change. 2

Feminists of various stripes, Black Panthers, activists against the Vietnam War or against the House Un-American Activities Committee, civil rights workers, Muslims and other elements of the Black Power movement, hippies, and countercultural pacifists—all of these groups were evolving their own agendas, their own internal dynamics, their own organizing strategies, their own political tactics, their own identities. Officially suspicious of the older generation (Question authority! Don't trust anyone over thirty!), these groups saw themselves as discontinuous with past movements: fresh, new, and visionary. 3

354

In this context, the phrase *politically correct* meant as many different things as the people who used it. Usually marked with quotation marks or italics, it expressed a combination of distrust for party lines of any kind and a simultaneous commitment to whichever dimension of social change that person was working for. Used every which way—straight, ironically, satirically, interrogatively—it focused and expressed all the uncertainties about dogmatism and preachiness that these new movements were questioning, including the pieties of the Old Left, of corporate America, and of the government. 4

It probably came into the New Left vocabulary through translations of Mao Tse-tung's writings, especially in "the little red book" as it was known, *Quotations from Chairman Mao Tse-tung.* Mao used the word *correct* a lot (or rather his translators used it), as in "correct" or "incorrect" ideas. In a speech from 1957, "On the Correct Handling of Contradictions Among the People," first translated in 1966 and widely disseminated in excerpts in the little red book, he stated that "the only way to settle questions of an ideological nature or controversial issues among the people is by the democratic method, the method of discussion, of criticism, of persuasion and education, and not by the method of coercion or repression."[2] This is the same essay in which he advocated "letting a hundred flowers blossom" and "letting a hundred schools of thought contend" and "long term co-existence and mutual supervision." In other words, the Maoist position at the time was that correct thinking—thinking that would help the new socialist state survive—could be achieved by free speech, contention, and mutual criticism. These three conditions of thought and speech were assumed to entail one another rather than to inhibit one another. 5

The little red book had an enormous influence on the New Left because it was read avidly by two constituencies, by black as well as by white radicals. The Black Panthers sold it to raise money. Black revolutionaries from the cultural nationalists to the Muslim pan-Africanists quoted it. In fact the earliest memories of the term *politically correct* that I have been able to elicit from friends and acquaintances on either the New or the Old Left, are the memories of black friends guilt-tripping or being guilt-tripped about their dedication to the Black Power movement. To be politically incorrect in the late sixties as a black was to be an Uncle Tom, a nonrevolutionary, or a sloppy person—a hippie, for instance. Going with a white person was definitely incorrect. Women who stood up to their black brothers as feminists rather than staying within traditional nurturing female roles were also incorrect. 6

Indeed, the earliest textual reference to the phrase that I have found is in an essay by Toni Cade (not, as yet, Bambara), "On the Issue of Roles," in the anthology she edited in 1970, *The Black Woman.* In the essay she tells a teaching anecdote about confronting gender prejudice in a black class by reading aloud an antifeminist paper in which all the references to men and women had been changed to "us" and "them," thus disguising the sexism as racism. "And sure enough everyone reacted to phrases like 'I don't believe in the double standard, but' or 'They're trying to take over' and agreed it was the usual racist shit." When the uproar died down after she revealed her trick, the point 7 remained, as she put it: "Racism and chauvinism are anti-people. And a man cannot be politically correct and a chauvinist too."[3]

The next year, 1971, Toni Cade Bambara published a book for children, *Tales and Stories for Black Folks.* In the contributors' notes she described herself as a "young Black woman who writes, teaches, organizes, lectures, tries to learn and tries to raise her daughter to be a correct little sister." Within months, Audre Lorde responded to this with a poem with a very long title: "Dear Toni/Instead of a Letter of Congratulation/Upon your Book and Your Daughter/Whom You Say You Are Raising To Be/A Correct Little Sister."   8

Audre Lorde's poem takes issue with Bambara's boast about raising her daughter to be correct, and claims experience as the only training for "correctness":   9

> I know beyond fear and history
> that our teaching means keeping trust
> with less and less correctness
> only with ourselves—

For this poet, no less dedicated to the struggle for black women, the notion of political correctness stuck in her craw. Still she was grateful to her friend and sister Toni Cade for "going and becoming/the lessons you teach your daughter," for her warrior spirit, and for her commitment. She ends the poem hopefully, blessing both their daughters, and pointing out that she and Toni Cade together form the landscape for these girls:

> printed upon them as surely
> as water etches feather on stone.
> Our girls will grow into their own
> Black Women
> finding their own contradictions
> that they will come to love
> as I love you.

Do not lose sight of the personal in the political, she is saying. Our daughters will become who they are in relation to who we are; they will have their own battles to fight, their own contradictions to handle.

Almost from the start, then, the phrase occasioned a dispute over what defined "politically correct" and over its uncritical use. That accords with Maurice Isserman's memory about the use of the phrase in the early seventies, recently recorded in an article in *Tikkun*. "It was always used in a tone mocking the pieties of our own insular political counterculture," he wrote, "as in 'We *could* stop at McDonald's down the road if you're hungry,' or 'We *could* spend good money to get the television fixed,' etc.—'but it wouldn't be politically correct.'"[4]   10

There were some, no doubt, like the young Toni Cade, who used the phrase straight up, without irony, without self-mockery. But almost as soon as anyone did use it that way, it was picked up and parodied by the skeptics,   11 the anarchists, the individualists—whoever was worrying about the constraints of dogma.

This history was repeated with a vengeance in the so-called Sex Wars, the debates among feminists about women's sexuality, about pornography, and especially about lesbian sadomasochistic practices. Positions in the Sex Wars polarized at the famous Barnard College conference "The Scholar and the Feminist IX: Towards a Politics of Sexuality," held April 24, 1982. One of the purposes of this conference was to question whether there was such a thing as "politically correct" sexual practice, and to address issues of pleasure and fear, "acknowledging that sexuality is simultaneously a domain of restriction, repression, and danger, as well as a domain of exploration, pleasure, and agency."[5] From the earliest stages of planning for this conference, in September 1981, the question of "political correctness" had come up, in quotes, in relation to female sexuality. Muriel Dimen proposed to examine the "links between sexual 'political correctness' and other forms of 'political correctness' both on the Left and the Right."[6] What was a feminist to do if her sexual gratification was tied to "politically incorrect" fantasies? Were antipornography activists simply re-inscribing Victorian images of prudish "good girls"? Was the "prosex" faction simply enacting patriarchal paradigms of domination and submission and playing into the hands of a billion-dollar pornography industry that exploited and dehumanized women? 12

The conflict was exacerbated by a "Speakout on Politically Incorrect Sex" sponsored by the Lesbian Sex Mafia, many of whom were, according to Ann Ferguson, "self-identified 'S/M' lesbian feminists who argue that the moralism of the radical feminists stigmatizes sexual minorities such as butch/ femme couples, sadomasochists, and man/boy lovers, thereby legitimizing 'vanilla sex' lesbians and at the same time encouraging a return of a narrow, conservative, 'feminine' vision of ideal sexuality."[7] The speakout was, in turn, picketed by the Coalition for a Feminist Sexuality and against Sadomasochism, whose leaflet protested the exclusion from the conference of "feminists who have developed the feminist analysis of sexual violence, who have organized a mass movement against pornography, who have fought media images that legitimize sexual violence, who believe that sadomasochism is reactionary, patriarchal sexuality, and who have worked to end the sexual abuse of children."[8] 13

Each side felt that the other side was standing in the way of liberation; each felt that the other was working against the interests of women. The so-called radical feminists accused the Lesbian Sex Mafia of politically incorrect sexual practices, and the LSM in turn gleefully appropriated this terminology and began to flaunt it as enviable, sexy, radical. Within lesbian circles, being "politically incorrect," like being a "bad girl," was coming to mean hip, sophisticated, rebellious, impulsive. 14

Meanwhile, the organizers of the Barnard conference and their supporters circulated and published a letter deploring the censoriousness of such groups as Women Against Pornography and Women Against Violence Against Women. "Feminist discussion about sexuality cannot be carried on if one 15 segment of the feminist movement uses McCarthyite tactics to silence other voices," they wrote.[9] That was in 1982.

The point of rehearsing this history is to demonstrate that the phrase *po-*   16
litically correct has always been double-edged. No sooner was it invoked as a genuine standard for sociopolitical practice—so that we might live as if the revolution had already happened—than it was mocked as purist, ideologically rigid, and authoritarian. Although the mainstream press is obviously trying to construct the phrase on a Stalinist "party line" model, there is little evidence of its use in the Old Left, and a great deal of evidence that within the New Left it was nearly always used with a double consciousness. Indeed, the fact that the phrase has survived with these self-mocking, ironized meanings is testimony to a kind of self-critical dimension to New Left politics, a flexibility, a suspiciousness of orthodoxy of any sort.

This history makes the current media campaign to discredit the Left espe-   17
cially infuriating. *Politically correct* has long been our own term of self-criticism. For George Bush and his hired hands—Cheney, Bennett, and D'Souza—to use the term places them squarely in the camp of the leather dykes, baiting the earnest. But the motive behind the current press campaign is hardly directed toward pleasure or knowledge. The timing of the campaign to discredit "political correctness" coincides with that other media event calculated to wipe out the sixties and to "kick the Vietnam syndrome": the Gulf War.

The attack on the politically correct in the universities is an attack on the   18
theory and practice of affirmative action—a legacy of the sixties and seventies—defined as the recruitment to an institution of students and faculty who do not conform to what has always constituted the population of academic institutions: usually white, middle class, straight, male. The cultural, or as some like to say, ideological, aspect of this practice has been the reassessment of whose culture is worth studying and knowing: whose history, whose literature, whose customs, whose attitudes, whose self-definitions. This investigation has created no little excitement in departments of history, literature, psychology, sociology—and even in a number of business schools. Certainly some part of the animus against the politically correct, as newly defined by the Right, has been generated by particular battles waged on those fronts. I would feel better about the campaign to expose the politically correct if the campaigners were willing to argue about the justice of affirmative action rather than the motives of those advocating this cultural adjustment.

For that's what the stakes are, just as they were in the late '60s at the be-   19
ginning of the ferment: how to redistribute power, knowledge, and resources in this country. The appropriation of the New Left's in-joke by Bush and by the popular press, pretending to expose some narrow-minded doctrinaire position, is ludicrous in the face of the worsening economic and political position of women and African Americans in this country. Without rehearsing the depressing statistics about unemployment, salary scales, mortality, education levels, and the like, let me end by pointing out that insofar as the accusation of political correctness restrains or embarrasses anyone inclined to

point out these appalling inequalities, the phrase is now successfully fore-stalling discussion of everything it ever stood for. In this Orwellian inversion, only those who uphold the conservative status quo are exempt from ridicule; only those who believe that the existing distribution of wealth and power is "natural," or inevitable, are depicted as operating without ideological bias. Like Goliath trying to disqualify David by appealing to fair play, the government and the press are playing a disingenuous role in this contest. As our history reminds us, all we ever had were a few pebbles, and we've been polishing them for years. The point is to remember why we collected them in the first place.

NOTES

1. In a recent letter to the *Chronicle of Higher Education* (June 26, 1991), Howard M. Ziff writes that he remembers the phrase used in the early 1950s as a euphemism for "party line"; but I have found no corroboration of this usage from historians of the Old Left, card-carrying members, or longtime associates.

2. *Quotations from Chairman Mao Tse-Tung* (Peking: Foreign Languages Press, 1966), 52. Mao did not, of course, invent the concept of "correct" ideas. As far back as 1935, Joseph Wood Krutch, in an article called "On Academic Freedom" published in the *Nation* (April 17, 1935), noted that leftists were beginning to sound more like conservatives in believing that "'correct' opinions," as opposed to debate and conflicting ideas, should be taught in school.

3. This essay was excerpted from a lecture delivered to the Livingston College Black Women's Seminar in 1969.

4. Maurice Isserman, "Travels with Dinesh," *Tikkun,* vol. 6, no. 5, 1991:82.

5. This "Concept Paper" was published as an addendum to *Pleasure and Danger,* ed. Carole S. Vance (Boston and London: Routledge and Kegan Paul, 1984), 443–46.

6. Hannah Alderfer et al., eds., *Diary of a Conference on Sexuality* (New York: Faculty Press, 1982). A searching essay on the subject by Muriel Dimen was subsequently published in Carole S. Vance, ed. *Pleasure and Danger,* 138–48.

7. Ann Ferguson et al., "Forum: The Feminist Sexuality Debates," *Signs,* vol. 10, no. 1 (1984): 107. Ann Ferguson's introduction to this fascinating collection of position papers on the subject is beautifully documented. See also Carla Freccero, "Notes of a Post-Sex Wars Theorizer," in *Conflicts in Feminism,* ed. Marianne Hirsch and Evelyn Fox Keller (New York and London: Routledge, 1991): 305–25.

8. The entire leaflet is reprinted in *Feminist Studies,* vol. 9, no. 1 (Spring 1983): 180–82.

9. Ibid., 179–80.

Questions

1. How would you define the phrase "politically correct"? What does it mean to be politically correct?

2. What does Perry mean when she says that the phrase "politically correct" is double-edged?

3. Why do some conservatives say that political correctness is a "narrow-minded doctrinaire position"?

4. Would Perry agree with Ellis's position on political correctness?

The Visigoths in Tweed

DINESH D'SOUZA

*Educated at Yale and Princeton, Dinesh D'Souza is a vigorous critic of the
left wing in education.*

*In this selection, D'Souza charges that in the new curricula, an anti-
Western, anti-capitalist view of the world is foisted upon students. The problem, he writes, is not the attainment of pluralism and diversity, but how such
goals are achieved. He cites examples of the replacement of standard texts in
the liberal arts canon with newer texts that seem not to serve the best purposes of pluralism. With a flourish, he concludes that, at present, "Multicultural or non-Western education on campus frequently glamorizes Third
World cultures and omits inconvenient facts about them": namely, the levels
of sexism and racism within these societies, these being the very curses leveled continually at Western society and its literature. This reading is from*
Forbes *magazine (1991).*

"I am a male wasp who attended and succeeded at Choate (preparatory)   1
School, Yale College, Yale Law School, and Princeton Graduate School. Slowly
but surely, however, my life-long habit of looking, listening, feeling, and
thinking as honestly as possible has led me to see that white, male-dominated, western European culture is the most destructive phenomenon in the
known history of the planet.

"[This Western culture] is deeply hateful of life and committed to death;   2
therefore, it is moving rapidly toward the destruction of itself and most other
life forms on earth. And truly it deserves to die. . . . We have to face our own
individual and collective responsibility for what is happening—our greed,
brutality, indifference, militarism, racism, sexism, blindness. . . . Meanwhile,
everything we have put into motion continues to endanger us more every
day."

This bizarre outpouring, so reminiscent of the "confessions" from victims   3
of Stalin's show trials, appeared in a letter to *Mother Jones* magazine and was
written by a graduate of some of our finest schools. But the truth is that the
speaker's anguish came not from any balanced assessment but as a consequence of exposure to the propaganda of the new barbarians who have captured the humanities, law, and social science departments of so many of our
universities. It should come as no surprise that many sensitive young Americans reject the system that has nurtured them. At Duke University, according

361

to the *Wall Street Journal,* professor Frank Lentricchia in his English course shows the movie *The Godfather* to teach his students that organized crime is "a metaphor for American business as usual."

Yes, a student can still get an excellent education—among the best in the   4
world—in computer technology and the hard sciences at American universities. But liberal arts students, including those attending Ivy League schools, are very likely to be exposed to an attempted brainwashing that deprecates Western learning and exalts a neo-Marxist ideology promoted in the name of multiculturalism. Even students who choose hard sciences must often take required courses in the humanities, where they are almost certain to be inundated with an anti-Western, anticapitalist view of the world.

Each year American society invests $160 billion in higher education,   5
more per student than any nation in the world except Denmark. A full 45 percent of this money comes from the federal, state, and local governments. No one can say we are starving higher education. But what are we getting for our money, at least so far as the liberal arts are concerned?

A fair question? It might seem so, but in university circles it is considered   6
impolite because it presumes that higher education must be accountable to the society that supports it. Many academics think of universities as intellectual enclaves, insulated from the vulgar capitalism of the larger culture.

Yet, since the academics constantly ask for more money, it seems hardly   7
unreasonable to ask what they are doing with it. Honest answers are rarely forthcoming. The general public sometimes gets a whiff of what is going on— as when Stanford alters its core curriculum in the classics of Western civilization—but it knows very little of the systematic and comprehensive change sweeping higher education.

An academic and cultural revolution has overtaken most of our 3,535 col-   8
leges and universities. It's a revolution to which most Americans have paid little attention. It is a revolution imposed upon the students by a university elite, not one voted upon or even discussed by the society at large. It amounts, according to University of Wisconsin–Madison Chancellor Donna Shalala, to "a basic transformation of American higher education in the name of multiculturalism and diversity."

The central thrust of this "basic transformation" involves replacing tradi-   9
tional core curricula—consisting of the great works of Western culture—with curricula flavored by minority, female, and Third World authors.

Here's a sample of the viewpoint represented by the new curriculum.   10
Becky Thompson, a sociology and women's studies professor, in a teaching manual distributed by the American Sociological Association, writes: "I begin my course with the basic feminist principle that in a racist, classist, and sexist society we have all swallowed oppressive ways of being, whether intentionally or not. Specifically, this means that it is not open to debate whether a white student is racist or a male student is sexist. He/she simply is."

Professors at several colleges who have resisted these regnant dogmas   11
about race and gender have found themselves the object of denunciation and even university sanctions. Donald Kagan, dean of Yale College, says: "I was a

student during the days of Joseph McCarthy, and there is less freedom now than there was then."

As in the McCarthy period, a particular group of activists has cowed the authorities and bent them to its will. After activists forcibly occupied his office, President Lattie Coor of the University of Vermont explained how he came to sign a sixteen-point agreement establishing, among other things, minority faculty hiring quotas. "When it became clear that the minority students with whom I had been discussing these issues wished to pursue negotiations *in the context of occupied offices* . . . I agreed to enter negotiations." As frequently happens in such cases, Coor's "negotiations" ended in a rapid capitulation by the university authorities. 12

At Harvard, historian Stephan Thernstrom was harangued by student activists and accused of insensitivity and bigotry. What was his crime? His course included a reading from the journals of slave owners, and his textbook gave a reasonable definition of affirmative action as "preferential treatment" for minorities. At the University of Michigan, renowned demographer Reynolds Farley was assailed in the college press for criticizing the excesses of Marcus Garvey and Malcolm X; yet the administration did not publicly come to his defense. 13

University leaders argue that the revolution suggested by these examples is necessary because young Americans must be taught to live in and govern a multiracial and multicultural society. Immigration from Asia and Latin America, combined with relatively high minority birth rates, is changing the complexion of America. Consequently, in the words of University of Michigan President James Duderstadt, universities must "create a model of how a more diverse and pluralistic community can work for our society." 14

No controversy, of course, about benign goals such as pluralism or diversity, but there is plenty of controversy about how these goals are being pursued. Although there is no longer a Western core curriculum at Mount Holyoke or Dartmouth, students at those schools must take a course in non-Western or Third World culture. Berkeley and the University of Wisconsin now insist that every undergraduate enroll in ethnic studies, making this virtually the only compulsory course at those schools. 15

If American students were truly exposed to the richest elements of other cultures, this could be a broadening and useful experience. A study of Chinese philosophers such as Confucius or Mencius would enrich students' understanding of how different peoples order their lives, thus giving a greater sense of purpose to their own. Most likely, a taste of Indian poetry such as Rabindranath Tagore's *Gitanjali* would increase the interest of materially minded young people in the domain of the spirit. An introduction to Middle Eastern history would prepare the leaders of tomorrow to deal with the mounting challenge of Islamic culture. It would profit students to study the rise of capitalism in the Far East. 16

But the claims of the academic multiculturalists are largely phony. They pay little attention to the Asian or Latin American classics. Rather, the non-Western or multicultural curriculum reflects a different agenda. At Stanford, 17 for example, Homer, Plato, Dante, Machiavelli, and Locke are increasingly scarce. But often their replacements are not non-Western classics. Instead the students are offered exotic topics such as popular religion and healing in Peru, Rastafarian poetry, and Andean music.

What do students learn about the world from the books they are required   18
to read under the new multicultural rubric? At Stanford one of the non-Western works assigned is *I, Rigoberta Menchú,* subtitled "An Indian Woman in Guatemala."

The book is hardly a non-Western classic. Published in 1983, *I, Rigoberta*   19
Menchú is the story of a young woman who is said to be a representative voice of the indigenous peasantry. Representative of Guatemalan Indian culture? In fact, Rigoberta met the Venezuelan feminist to whom she narrates this story at a socialist conference in Paris, where, presumably, very few of the Third World's poor travel. Moreover, Rigoberta's political consciousness includes the adoption of such politically correct causes as feminism, homosexual rights, socialism, and Marxism. By the middle of the book she is discoursing on "bourgeois youths" and "Molotov cocktails," not the usual terminology of Indian peasants. One chapter is titled "Rigoberta Renounces Marriage and Motherhood," a norm that her tribe could not have adopted and survived.

If Rigoberta does not represent the convictions and aspirations of   20
Guatemalan peasants, what is the source of her importance and appeal? The answer is that Rigoberta seems to provide independent Third World corroboration for Western left-wing passions and prejudices. She is a mouthpiece for a sophisticated neo-Marxist critique of Western society, all the more powerful because it seems to issue not from some embittered American academic but from a Third World native. For professors nourished on the political activism of the late 1960s and early 1970s, texts such as *I, Rigoberta Menchú* offer a welcome opportunity to attack capitalism and Western society in general in the name of teaching students about the developing world.

We learn in the introduction of *I, Rigoberta Menchú* that Rigoberta is a   21
quadruple victim. As a person of color, she has suffered racism. As a woman, she has endured sexism. She lives in South America, which is—of course—a victim of North American colonialism. She is also an Indian, victimized by Latino culture within Latin America.

One of the most widely used textbooks in so-called multicultural courses   22
is *Multi-Cultural Literacy,* published by Graywolf Press in St. Paul, Minnesota. The book ignores the *The Tale of Genji,* the Upanishads and Vedas, the Koran and Islamic commentaries. It also ignores such brilliant contemporary authors as Jorge Luis Borges, V.S. Naipaul, Octavio Paz, Naguib Mahfonz, and Wole Soyinka. Instead it offers thirteen essays of protest, including Michele Wallace's autobiographical "Invisibility Blues" and Paula Gunn Allen's "Who Is Your Mother? The Red Roots of White Feminism."

One student I spoke with at Duke University said he would not study *Par-*   23
adise Lost because John Milton was a Eurocentric white male sexist. At the University of Michigan, a young black woman who had converted to Islam refused to believe that the prophet Muhammad owned slaves and practiced

polygamy. She said she had taken courses on cultural diversity and the courses hadn't taught her that.

One of the highlights of this debate on the American campus was a pas- 24
sionate statement delivered a few years ago by Stanford undergraduate William King, president of the Black Student Union, who argued the benefits of the new multicultural curriculum before the faculty senate of the university. Under the old system, he said, "I was never taught . . . the fact that Socrates, Herodotus, Pythagoras, and Solon studied in Egypt and acknowledged that much of their knowledge of astronomy, geometry, medicine, and building came from the African civilization in and around Egypt. [I was never taught] that the Hippocratic oath acknowledges the Greeks' 'father of medicine,' Imhotep, a black Egyptian pharaoh whom they called Aesculapius. . . . I was never informed when it was found that the 'very dark and wooly haired' Moors in Spain preserved, expanded, and reintroduced the classical knowledge that the Greeks had collected, which led to the 'renaissance.' . . . I read the Bible without knowing Saint Augustine looked black like me, that the Ten Commandments were almost direct copies from the 147 Negative Confessions of Egyptian initiates. . . . I didn't learn Toussaint L'Ouverture's defeat of Napoleon in Haiti directly influenced the French Revolution, or that the Iroquois Indians in America had a representative democracy which served as a model for the American system."

This statement drew wild applause and was widely quoted. The only trou- 25
ble is that much of it is untrue. There is no evidence that Socrates, Pythagoras, Herodotus, and Solon studied in Egypt, although Herodotus may have traveled there. Saint Augustine was born in North Africa, but his skin color is unknown, and in any case he could not have been mentioned in the Bible; he was born over 350 years after Christ. Viewing King's speech at my request, Bernard Lewis, an expert on Islamic and Middle Eastern culture at Princeton, described it as "a few scraps of truth amidst a great deal of nonsense."

Why does multicultural education, in practice, gravitate toward such 26
myths and half-truths? To find out why, it is necessary to explore the complex web of connections that the academic revolution generates among admissions policies, life on campus, and the curriculum.

American universities typically begin with the premise that in a democra- 27
tic and increasingly diverse society the composition of their classes should reflect the ethnic distribution of the general population. Many schools officially seek "proportional representation," in which the percentage of applicants admitted from various racial groups roughly approximates the ratio of those groups in society at large.

Thus universities routinely admit black, Hispanic, and American Indian 28
candidates over better-qualified white and Asian American applicants. As a result of zealously pursued affirmative action programs, many selective colleges admit minority students who find it extremely difficult to meet demanding academic standards and to compete with the rest of the class. This fact is reflected in the dropout rates of blacks and Hispanics, which are more than 50 percent higher than those of whites and Asians. At Berkeley a study

of students admitted on a preferential basis between 1978 and 1982 concluded that nearly 70 percent failed to graduate within five years.

For affirmative action students who stay on campus, a common strategy   29
of dealing with the pressures of university life is to enroll in a distinctive minority organization. Among such organizations at Cornell University are Lesbian, Gay & Bisexual Coalition; La Asociacion Latina; National Society of Black Engineers; Society of Minority Hoteliers; Black Students United; and Simba Washanga.

Although the university brochures at Cornell and elsewhere continue to   30
praise integration and close interaction among students from different backgrounds, the policies practiced at these schools actually encourage segregation. Stanford, for example, has "ethnic theme houses" such as the African house called Ujaama. And President Donald Kennedy has said that one of his educational objectives is to "support and strengthen ethnic theme houses." Such houses make it easier for some minority students to feel comfortable but help to create a kind of academic apartheid.

The University of Pennsylvania has funded a black yearbook, even   31
though only 6 percent of the student body is black and all other groups appeared in the general yearbook. Vassar, Dartmouth, and the University of Illinois have allowed separate graduation activities and ceremonies for minority students. California State University at Sacramento has just established an official "college within a college" for blacks.

Overt racism is relatively rare at most campuses, yet minorities are told   32
that bigotry operates in subtle forms such as baleful looks, uncorrected stereotypes, and "institutional racism"—defined as the underrepresentation of blacks and Hispanics among university trustees, administrators, and faculty.

Other groups such as feminists and homosexuals typically get into the   33
game, claiming their own varieties of victim status. As Harvard political scientist Harvey Mansfield bluntly puts it, "White students must admit their guilt so that minority students do not have to admit their incapacity."

Even though universities regularly accede to the political demands of vic-   34
tim groups, their appeasement gestures do not help black and Hispanic students get a genuine liberal arts education. They do the opposite, giving the apologists of the new academic orthodoxy a convenient excuse when students admitted on a preferential basis fail to meet academic standards. At this point student activists and administrators often blame the curriculum. They argue that it reflects a "white male perspective" that systematically depreciates the views and achievements of other cultures, minorities, women, and homosexuals.

With this argument, many minority students can now explain why they   35
had such a hard time with Milton in the English department, Publius in political science, and Heisenberg in physics. Those men reflected white male aesthetics, philosophy, and science. Obviously, nonwhite students would fare much better if the university created more black or Latino or Third World courses, the argument goes. This epiphany leads to a spate of demands: Abolish the Western classics, establish new departments such as Afro-American

Studies and Women's Studies, hire minority faculty to offer distinctive black and Hispanic "perspectives."

Multicultural or non-Western education on campus frequently glamor-   36
izes Third World cultures and omits inconvenient facts about them. In fact, several non-Western cultures are caste-based or tribal, and often disregard norms of racial equality. In many of them feminism is virtually nonexistent, as indicated by such practices as d0wries, widow-burning, and genital mutila-tion; and homosexuality is sometimes regarded as a crime or mental disorder requiring punishment. These nasty aspects of the non-Western cultures are rarely mentioned in the new courses. Indeed, Bernard Lewis of Princeton ar-gues that while slavery and the subjugation of women have been practiced by all known civilizations, the West at least has an active and effective move-ment for the abolition of such evils.

Who is behind this academic revolution, this contrived multiculturalism?   37
The new curriculum directly serves the purposes of a newly ascendant gener-ation of young professors, weaned in the protest culture of the late 1960s and early 1970s. In a frank comment, Jay Parini, who teaches English at Middle-bury College, writes, "After the Vietnam War, a lot of us didn't just crawl back into our library cubicles. We stepped into academic positions. . . . Now we have tenure, and the work of reshaping the university has begun in earnest."

The goal that Parini and others like him pursue is the transformation of   38
the college classroom from a place of learning to a laboratory of indoctrina-tion for social change. Not long ago most colleges required that students learn the basics of the physical sciences and mathematics, the rudiments of economics and finance, and the fundamental principles of American history and government. Studies by the National Endowment for the Humanities show that this coherence has disappeared from the curriculum. As a result, most universities are now graduating students who are scientifically and cul-turally impoverished, if not illiterate.

At the University of Pennsylvania, Houston Baker, one of the most promi-   39
nent black academics in the country, denounces reading and writing as op-pressive technologies and celebrates such examples of oral culture as the rap group N.W.A. (Niggers With Attitude). One of the group's songs is about the desirability of killing policemen. Alison Jaggar, who teaches women's studies at the University of Colorado, denounces the traditional nuclear family as a "cornerstone of women's oppression" and anticipates scientific advances en-abling men to carry fetuses in their bodies so that child-bearing responsibili-ties can be shared between the sexes. Duke professor Eve Sedgwick's scholarship is devoted to unmasking what she terms the heterosexual bias in Western culture, a project that she pursues through papers such as "Jane Austen and the Masturbating Girl" and "How To Bring Your Kids Up Gay."

Confronted by racial tension and Balkanization on campus, university   40
leaders usually announce that, because of a resurgence of bigotry, "more needs to be done." They press for redoubled preferential recruitment of mi-nority students and faculty, funding for a new Third World or Afro-American center, mandatory sensitivity education for whites, and so on. The more the

university leaders give in to the demands of minority activists, the more they encourage the very racism they are supposed to be fighting. Surveys indicate that most young people today hold fairly liberal attitudes toward race, evident in their strong support for the civil rights agenda and for interracial dating. However, these liberal attitudes are sorely tried by the demands of the new orthodoxy: many undergraduates are beginning to rebel against what they perceive as a culture of preferential treatment and double standards actively fostered by university policies.

Can there be a successful rolling back of this revolution, or at least of its   41
excesses? One piece of good news is that blatant forms of racial preference are having an increasingly tough time in the courts, and this has implications for university admissions policies. The Department of Education is more vigilant than it used to be in investigating charges of discrimination against whites and Asian Americans. With help from Washington director Morton Halperin, the American Civil Liberties Union has taken a strong stand against campus censorship. Popular magazines such as *Newsweek* and *New York* have poked fun at "politically correct" speech. At Tufts University, undergraduates embarrassed the administration into backing down on censorship by putting up taped boundaries designating areas of the university to be "free speech zones," "limited speech zones," and "Twilight Zones."

Even some scholars on the political left are now speaking out against   42
such dogmatism and excess. Eugene Genovese, a Marxist historian and one of the nation's most respected scholars of slavery, argues that "too often we find that education has given way to indoctrination. Good scholars are intimidated into silence, and the only diversity that obtains is a diversity of radical positions." More and more professors from across the political spectrum are resisting the politicization and lowering of standards. At Duke, for example, sixty professors, led by political scientist James David Barber, a liberal Democrat, have repudiated the extremism of the victims' revolution. To that end they have joined the National Association of Scholars, a Princeton, New Jersey–based group devoted to fairness, excellence, and rational debate in universities.

But these scholars need help. Resistance on campus to the academic revo-   43
lution is outgunned and sorely needs outside reinforcements. Parents, alumni, corporations, foundations, and state legislators are generally not aware that they can be very effective in promoting reform. The best way to encourage reform is to communicate in no uncertain terms to university leadership and, if necessary, to use financial incentives to assure your voice is heard. University leaders do their best to keep outsiders from meddling or even finding out what exactly is going on behind the tall gates, but there is little doubt that they would pay keen attention to the views of the donors on whom they depend. By threatening to suspend donations if universities continue harmful policies, friends of liberal learning can do a lot. In the case of state-funded schools, citizens and parents can pressure elected representatives to ask questions and demand more accountability from the taxpayer-supported academics.

The illiberal revolution can be reversed only if the people who foot the bills stop being passive observers. Don't just write a check to your alma mater; that's an abrogation of responsibility. Keep abreast of what is going on and don't be afraid to raise your voice and even to close your wallet in protest. Our Western, free-market culture need not provide the rope to hang itself.

Questions

1. What is D'Souza's attitude toward political correctness? How is his position similar to Ellis's?
2. Why does D'Souza say that the claims of multiculturalists are largely phony?
3. How does political correctness encourage racism and segregation? Compare D'Souza's position on this issue with Perry's.

"Speech Codes" and Free Speech

NAT HENTOFF

A columnist for the Village Voice *since 1960 and for the* Washington Post *since 1984, Nat Hentoff was educated at Northeastern University and Harvard University, and studied at the Sorbonne in Paris on a Fulbright Scholarship. In addition, he is an associate professor of music at New York University and has written on music and increasingly on education.*

In his survey of U.S. college campuses, Hentoff finds that so-called free speech is being curtailed by "speech codes," a set of which were adopted several years ago at Stanford University. At the same time, however, right wing campus publications that poke fun at politically correct speech are flourishing. Hentoff writes with concern of the self-censoring some students claim to adopt in classrooms, and he also notes a worrying tinge of anti-Semitism in the choice of speakers invited to speak on campuses by black student groups. This selection is from the Progressive *(1989).*

During three years of reporting on anti-free-speech tendencies in higher education, I've been at more than twenty colleges and universities—from Washington and Lee and Columbia to Mesa State in Colorado and Stanford. 1

On this voyage of initially reverse expectations—with liberals fiercely advocating censorship of "offensive" speech and conservatives merrily taking the moral high ground as champions of free expression—the most dismaying moment of revelation took place at Stanford. 2

In the course of a two-year debate on whether Stanford, like many other universities, should have a speech code punishing language that might wound minorities, women, and gays, a letter appeared in the *Stanford Daily*. Signed by the African-American Law Students Association, the Asian-American Law Students Association, and the Jewish Law Students Associati, the letter called for a harsh code. It reflected the letter and the spirit of an earlier declaration by Canetta Ivy, a black leader of student government at Stanford during the period of the grand debate. "We don't put as many restrictions on freedom of speech," she said, "as we should." 3

Reading the letter by this rare ecumenical body of law students (so pressing was the situation that even Jews were allowed in). I thought of twenty, thirty years from now. From so bright a cadre of graduates, from so prestigious a law school would come some of the law professors, civic leaders, col- 4

370

lege presidents, and maybe even a Supreme Court justice of the future. And many of them would have learned—like so many other university students in the land—that censorship is okay provided your motives are okay.

The debate at Stanford ended when the president, Donald Kennedy, fol-   5 lowing the prevailing winds, surrendered his previous position that once you start telling people what they can't say, you will end up telling them what they can't think. Stanford now has a speech code.

This is not to say that these gags on speech—every one of them so over-   6 board and vague that a student can violate a code without knowing he or she has done so—are invariably imposed by student demand. At most colleges, it is the administration that sets up the code. Because there have been racist or sexist or homophobic taunts, anonymous notes or graffiti, the administration feels it must *do something*. The cheapest, quickest way to demonstrate that it cares is to appear to suppress racist, sexist, homophobic speech.

Usually, the leading opposition among the faculty consists of conserva-   7 tives—when there is opposition. An exception at Stanford was law professor Gerald Gunther, arguably the nation's leading authority on constitutional law. But Gunther did not have much support among other faculty members, conservative or liberal.

At the University of Buffalo Law School, which has a code restricting   8 speech, I could find just one faculty member who was against it. A liberal, he spoke only on condition that I not use his name. He did not want to be categorized as a racist.

On another campus, a political science professor for whom I had great re-   9 spect after meeting and talking with him years ago has been silent—students told me—on what Justice William Brennan once called "the pall of orthodoxy" that has fallen on his campus.

When I talked to him, the professor said, "It doesn't happen in my class.   10 There's no 'politically correct' orthodoxy here. It may happen in other places at this university, but I don't know about that." He said no more.

One of the myths about the rise of PC is that, coming from the Left, it is   11 primarily intimidating conservatives on campus. Quite the contrary. At almost every college I've been to, conservative students have their own newspaper, usually quite lively and fired by a muckraking glee at exposing "politically correct" follies on campus.

By and large, those most intimidated—not so much by the speech codes   12 themselves but by the Madame Defarge-like spirit behind them—are liberal students and those who can be called politically moderate.

I've talked to many of them, and they no longer get involved in class dis-   13 cussions where their views would go against the grain of PC righteousness. Many, for instance, have questions about certain kinds of affirmative action. They are not partisans of Jesse Helms or David Duke, but they wonder whether progeny of middle-class black families should get scholarship preference. Others have a question about abortion. Most are not pro-life, but they believe that fathers should have a say in whether the fetus should be sent off into eternity.

Jeff Shesol, a recent graduate of Brown, and now a Rhodes scholar at Ox-   14
ford, became nationally known while at Brown because of his comic strip,
Thatch, which, not too kindly, parodied PC students. At a forum on free
speech at Brown before he left, Shesol said he wished he could tell the new
students at Brown to have no fear of speaking freely. But he couldn't tell
them that, he said, advising the new students to stay clear of talking critically
about affirmative action or abortion, among other things, in public.

At that forum, Shesol told me, he said that those members of the Left   15
who regard dissent from their views as racist and sexist should realize that
they are discrediting their goals. "They're honorable goals," said Shesol, "and
I agree with them. I'm against racism and sexism. But these people's tactics
are obscuring the goals. And they've resulted in Brown no longer being an
open-minded place." There were hisses from the audience.

Students at New York University Law School have also told me that they   16
censor themselves in class. The kind of chilling atmosphere they describe was
exemplified last year as a case assigned for a moot court competition became
subject to denunciation when a sizable number of law students said it was too
"offensive" and would hurt the feelings of gay and lesbian students. The case
concerned a divorced father's attempt to gain custody of his children on the
grounds that their mother had become a lesbian. It was against PC to represent the father.

Although some of the faculty responded by insisting that you learn to be   17
a lawyer by dealing with all kinds of cases, including those you personally
find offensive, other faculty members supported the rebellious students,
praising them for their sensitivity. There was little public opposition from the
other students to the attempt to suppress the case. A leading dissenter was a
member of the conservative Federalist Society.

What is PC to white students is not necessarily PC to black students. Most of   18
the latter did not get involved in the NYU protest, but throughout the country
many black students do support speech codes. A vigorous exception was a black
Harvard Law School student who spoke during a debate on whether the law
school should start punishing speech. A white student got up and said that the
codes are necessary because without them, black students would be driven away
from colleges and thereby deprived of the equal opportunity to get an education.

The black student rose and said that the white student had a hell of a   19
nerve to assume that he—in the face of racist speech—would pack up his
books and go home. He'd been familiar with that kind of speech all his life,
and he had never felt the need to run away from it. He'd handled it before
and he could again.

The black student then looked at his white colleague and said that it was   20
condescending to say that blacks have to be "protected" from racist speech.
"It is more racist and insulting," he emphasized, "to say that to me than to
call me a nigger."

But that would appear to be a minority view among black students. Most   21
are convinced they do need to be protected from wounding language. On the

other hand, a good many black student organizations on campus do not feel that Jews have to be protected from wounding language.

Though it's not much written about in reports of the language wars on cam-   22
puses, there is a strong strain of anti-Semitism among some—not all, by any means—black students. They invite such speakers as Louis Farrakhan, the former Stokely Carmichael (now Kwame Touré), and such lesser but still burning bushes as Steve Cokely, the Chicago commentator who has declared that Jewish doctors inject the AIDS virus into black babies. That distinguished leader was invited to speak at the University of Michigan.

The black student organization at Columbia University brought to the   23
campus Dr. Khallid Abdul Muhammad. He began his address by saying: "My leader, my teacher, my guide is the honorable Louis Farrakhan. I thought that should be said at Columbia Jewniversity."

Many Jewish students have not censored themselves in reacting to this   24
form of political correctness among some blacks. A Columbia student, Rachel Stoll, wrote a letter to the *Columbia Spectator:* "I have an idea. As a white Jewish American, I'll just stand in the middle of a circle comprising . . . Khallid Abdul Muhammad and assorted members of the Black Students Organization and let them all hurl large stones at me. From recent events and statements made on this campus, I gather this will be a good cheap method of making these people feel good."

At UCLA, a black student magazine printed an article indicating there is   25
considerable truth to the *Protocols of the Elders of Zion.* For months, the black faculty, when asked their reactions, preferred not to comment. One of them did say that the black students already considered the black faculty to be insufficiently militant, and the professors didn't want to make the gap any wider. Like white liberal faculty members on other campuses, they want to be liked—or at least not too disliked.

Along with quiet white liberal faculty members, most black professors   26
have not opposed the speech codes. But unlike the white liberals, many honestly do believe that minority students have to be insulated from barbed language. They do not believe—as I have found out in a number of conversations—that an essential part of an education is to learn to demystify language, to strip it of its ability to demonize and stigmatize you. They do not believe that the way to deal with bigoted language is to answer it with more and better language of your own. This seems very elementary to me, but not to the defenders, black and white, of the speech codes.

Consider University of California president David Gardner. He has im-   27
posed a speech code on all the campuses in his university system. Students are to be punished—and this is characteristic of the other codes around the country—if they use "fighting words"—derogatory references to "race, sex, sexual orientation, or disability."

The term *fighting words* comes from a 1942 Supreme Court decision,   28
Chaplinsky v. *New Hampshire,* which ruled that "fighting words" are not

protected by the First Amendment. That decision, however, has been in disuse at the High Court for many years. But it is thriving on college campuses.

In the California code, a word becomes "fighting" if it is directly addressed to "any ordinary person" (presumably, extraordinary people are above all this). These are the kinds of words that are "inherently likely to provoke a violent reaction, *whether or not they actually do.*" (Emphasis added.)   29

Moreover, he or she who fires a fighting word at any ordinary person can be reprimanded or dismissed from the university because the perpetrator should "reasonably know" that what he or she has said will interfere with the "victim's ability to pursue effectively his or her education or otherwise participate fully in university programs and activities."   30

Asked Gary Murikami, chairman of the Gay and Lesbian Association at the University of California, Berkeley: "What does it mean?"   31

Among those—faculty, law professors, college administrators—who insist such codes are essential to the university's purpose of making *all* students feel at home and thereby able to concentrate on their work, there has been a celebratory resort to the Fourteenth Amendment.   32

That amendment guarantees "equal protection of the laws" to all, and that means to all students on campus. Accordingly, when the First Amendment rights of those engaging in offensive speech clash with the equality rights of their targets under the Fourteenth Amendment, the First Amendment must give way.   33

This is the thesis, by the way, of John Powell, legal director of the American Civil Liberties Union (ACLU), even though that organization has now formally opposed all college speech codes—after a considerable civil war among and within its affiliates.   34

The battle of the amendments continues, and when harsher codes are called for at some campuses, you can expect the Fourteenth Amendment—which was not intended to censor *speech*—will rise again.   35

A precedent has been set at, of all places, colleges and universities, that the principle of free speech is merely situational. As college administrators change, so will the extent of free speech on campus. And invariably, permissible speech will become more and more narrowly defined. Once speech can be limited in such subjective ways, more and more expression will be included in what is forbidden.   36

One of the exceedingly few college presidents who speaks out on the consequences of the anti-free-speech movement is Yale University's Benno Schmidt: 37

> Freedom of thought must be Yale's central commitment. It is not easy to embrace. It is, indeed, the effort of a lifetime. . . . Much expression that is free may deserve our contempt. We may well be moved to exercise our own freedom to counter it or to ignore it. But universities cannot censor or suppress speech, no matter how obnoxious in content, without violating their justification for existence. . . .
>
> On some other campuses in this country, values of civility and community have been offered by some as paramount values of the university, even to the extent of superseding freedom of expression.

Such a view is wrong in principle and, if extended, is disastrous to freedom of thought. . . . The chilling effects on speech of the vagueness and open-ended nature of many universities' prohibitions . . . are compounded by the fact that these codes are typically enforced by faculty and students who commonly assert that vague notions of community are more important to the academy than freedom of thought and expression. . . .

This is a flabby and uncertain time for freedom in the United States.

On the Public Broadcasting System in June 1991, I was part of a Fred Friendly panel at Stanford University in a debate on speech codes versus freedom of expression. The three black panelists, including a Stanford student, strongly supported the codes. So did the one Asian American on the panel. But then so did Stanford law professor Thomas Grey, who wrote the Stanford code, and Stanford president Donald Kennedy, who first opposed and then embraced the code. We have a new ecumenicism of those who would control speech for the greater good. It is hardly a new idea, but the mix of advocates is rather new. 38

But there are other voices. In the national board debate at the ACLU on college speech codes, the first speaker—and I think she had a lot to do with making the final vote against codes unanimous—was Gwen Thomas. A black community college administrator from Colorado, she is a fiercely persistent exposer of racial discrimination. 39

She started by saying, "I have always felt as a minority person that we have to protect the rights of all because if we infringe on the rights of any persons, we'll be next. 40

"As for providing a nonintimidating educational environment, our young people have to learn to grow up on college campuses. We have to teach them how to deal with adversarial situations. They have to learn how to survive offensive speech they find wounding and hurtful." 41

Gwen Thomas is an educator—an endangered species in higher education. 42

Questions

1. Does your college have a speech code? What kinds of expressions are censored? Do you think that speech codes are beneficial? Why or why not?

2. Why does Hentoff feel that speech codes pose a threat to freedom of expression?

3. Should there be a distinction made between public and private speech? Is it okay to make racist or sexist remarks in private?

4. Compare Hentoff's ideas with Fish's in the following essay.

There's No Such Thing as Free Speech and It's a Good Thing, Too!

STANLEY FISH

Stanley Fish is currently a professor of law and English at Duke University. Educated at the University of Pennsylvania and Yale University, he has taught at the University of California, Berkeley and Johns Hopkins. He is the author of many books, including his seminal study of Milton in Surprised by Sin. *He has been a Guggenheim Fellow and serves on the editorial board of* Milton Studies *and the* Milton Quarterly.

Here, Fish's main point is that we have to be responsible for our utterances, and not simply rely on citing the First Amendment as our right to say anything. He illustrates some of the ways in which the Amendment can be circumvented, and argues that politics of the day will also influence "free speech." The key thing, he says, is to be sensitive to the context in which one is making remarks, and to be prepared to counter speech with which one might disagree. This selection is from the Boston Review *(Feb. 1992).*

> *Nowadays the First Amendment is the First Refuge of Scoundrels.*
> S. JOHNSON AND S. FISH

Lately many on the liberal and progressive left have been disconcerted to find that words, phrases and concepts thought to be their property and generative of their politics have been appropriated by the forces of neo-conservatism. This is particularly true of the concept of free speech, for in recent years First Amendment rhetoric has been used to justify policies and actions the left finds problematical if not abhorrent: pornography, sexist language, campus hate speech. How has this happened? The answer I shall give in this essay is that abstract concepts like free speech do not have any "natural" content but are filled with whatever content and direction one can manage to put into them. "Free speech" is just the name we give to verbal behavior that serves the substantive agendas we wish to advance; and we give our preferred verbal behaviors *that* name when we can, when we have the power to do so, because in the rhetoric of American life, the label "free speech" is the one you want your favorites to wear. Free speech, in short, is not an independent value but a political prize, and if that prize has been captured by a politics opposed to yours, it can no longer be invoked in ways that further your purposes for it is now an obstacle to those purposes. This is something that the liberal left has yet to understand and what follows is an attempt to pry its members loose from a vocabulary that may now be a disservice to them.

　　Not far from the end of his *Aereopagitica,* and after having celebrated the virtues of toleration and unregulated publication in passages that find their way into every discussion of free speech and the First Amendment, John Milton catches himself up short and says, of course I didn't mean Catholics, them we exterminate: 2

> I mean not tolerated popery, and open superstition, which as it extirpates all religious and civil supremacies, so itself should be extirpate . . . that also which is impious or evil absolutely against faith or manners no law can possibly permit that intends not to unlaw itself.

Notice that Milton is not simply stipulating a single exception to a rule generally in place; the kinds of utterance that might be regulated and even prohibited on pain of trial and punishment comprise an open set; popery is named only as a particularly perspicuous instance of the advocacy that cannot be tolerated. No doubt there are other forms of speech and action that might be categorized as "open superstitions" or as subversive of piety, faith, and manners, and presumably these too would be candidates for "extirpation." Nor would Milton think himself culpable for having failed to provide a list of unprotected utterances. The list will fill itself out as utterances are put to the test implied by his formulation: would this form of speech or advocacy, if permitted to flourish, tend to undermine the very purposes for which our society is constituted? One cannot answer this question with respect to a particular utterance in advance of its emergence on the world's stage; rather one must wait and ask the question in the full context of its production and (possible) dissemination. It might appear that the result would be ad hoc and unprincipled, but for Milton the principle inheres in the core values in whose name men of like mind came together in the first place. Those values, which include the search for truth and the promotion of virtue, are capacious enough to accommodate a diversity of views. But at some point—again impossible of advance specification—capaciousness will threaten to become shapelessness, and at that point fidelity to the original values will demand acts of extirpation.

　　I want to say that all affirmations of freedom of expression are like Milton's, dependent for their force on an exception that literally carves out the   3 space in which expression can then emerge. I do not mean that expression (saying something) is a realm whose integrity is sometimes compromised by certain restrictions, but that restriction, in the form of an underlying articulation of the world that necessarily (if silently) negates alternatively possible articulations, is constitutive of expression. Without restriction, without an in-built sense of what it would be meaningless to say or wrong to say, there could be no assertion and no reason for asserting it. The exception to unregulated expression is not a negative restriction, but a positive hollowing out of value—we are for *this,* which means we are against *that*—in relation to which meaningful assertion can then occur. It is in reference to that value—constituted as all values are by an act of exclusion—that some forms of speech will be heard as (quite literally) intolerable. Speech, in short, is never a value in and of itself, but is always produced within the precincts of some assumed conception of the good to which it must yield in the event of conflict. When the pinch comes (and sooner or later it will always come) and the institution (be it church, state or university) is confronted by behavior subversive of its core rationale, it will respond by declaring "of course we mean not tolerated _____, that we extirpate;" not because an exception to a general freedom has suddenly and contradictorily been announced, but because the freedom has never been general and has always been understood against the background of an originary exclusion that gives it meaning.

This is a large thesis, but before tackling it directly I want to buttress my   4
case with another example, taken not from the seventeenth century but from the charter and case law of Canada. Canadian thinking about freedom of expression departs from the line usually taken in the United States in ways that bring that country very close to the *Aereopagitica* as I have expounded it. The differences are fully on display in a recent landmark case, *R. v. Keegstra.* James Keegstra was a high school teacher in Alberta who, it was established by evidence, "systematically denigrated Jews and Judaism in his classes." He described Jews as treacherous, subversive, sadistic, money-loving, power hungry, and child-killers. He declared them "responsible for depressions, anarchy, chaos, wars and revolution," and required his students "to regurgitate these notions in essays and examinations." Keegstra was indicted under section 319(2) of the Criminal Code, and convicted. The Court of Appeal reversed and the Crown appealed to the Supreme Court which reinstated the lower court's verdict.

Section 319(2) reads in part, "Every one who, by communicating state-   5
ments other than in private conversation, willfully promotes hatred against any identifiable group is guilty of . . . an indictable offense and is liable to imprisonment for a term not exceeding two years." In the United States, this provision of the code would almost certainly be struck down because, under the First Amendment, restrictions on speech are apparently prohibited without qualification. To be sure, the Canadian charter has its own version of the First Amendment, in section 2(b): "Everyone has the following fundamental freedoms . . . (b) freedom of thought, belief, opinion, and expression, including freedom of the press and other media of communication." But section 2(b), like every other section of the charter, is qualified by section 1: "The Canadian Charter of Rights and Freedoms guarantees the rights and freedoms set out in it subject only to such reasonable limits prescribed by law as can be demonstrably justified in a free and democratic society." Or in other words, every right and freedom herein granted can be trumped if its exercise is found to be in conflict with the principles that underwrite the society.

This is what happens in *Keegstra* as the majority finds that section 319(2)   6
of the Criminal Code does in fact violate the right of freedom of expression
guaranteed by the charter, but is nevertheless a *permissible* restriction because
it accords with the principles proclaimed in section 1. There is, of course, a
dissent which reaches the conclusion that would have been reached by most,
if not all, U.S. courts; but even in dissent the minority is faithful to Canadian
ways of reasoning. "The question," it declares, "is always one of balance," and
thus even when a particular infringement of Charter section 2(b) has been
declared unconstitutional, as it would have been by the minority, the question remains open with respect to the next case. In the United States the
question is presumed closed and can only be pried open by special tools. In
our legal culture as it is presently constituted, if one yells "free speech" in a
crowded courtroom and makes it stick, the case is over.

Of course, it is not that simple. Despite the apparent absoluteness of the   7
First Amendment, there are any number of ways of getting around it, ways
that are known to every student of the law. In general, the preferred strategy
is to manipulate the distinction, essential to First Amendment jurisprudence,
between speech and action. The distinction is essential because no one would
think to frame a First Amendment that began "Congress shall make no law
abridging freedom of action;" for that would amount to saying "Congress
shall make no law," which would amount to saying "There shall be no law,"
only actions uninhibited and unregulated. If the First Amendment is to make
any sense, have any bite, speech must be declared not to be a species of action, or to be a special form of action lacking the aspects of action that cause
it to be the object of regulation. The latter strategy is the favored one and usually involves the separation of speech from consequences. This is what
Archibald Cox does when he assigns to the First Amendment the job of protecting "expressions separable from conduct harmful to other individuals and
the community." The difficulty of managing this segregation is well known:
speech always seems to be crossing the line into action where it becomes, at
least potentially, consequential. In the face of this categorical instability, First
Amendment theorists and jurists fashion a distinction within the speech/ac-
tion distinction: some forms of speech are not really speech because their
purpose is to incite violence or because they are, as the court declares in
Chaplinsky v. New Hampshire (1942), "fighting words," words "likely to provoke the average person to retaliation, and thereby cause a breach of the
peace."

The trouble with this definition is that it distinguishes not between fight-   8
ing words and words that remain safely and merely expressive, but between
words that are provocative to one group (the group that falls under the rubric
"average person") and words that might be provocative to other groups,
groups of persons not now considered average. And if you ask what words are
likely to be provocative to those non-average groups, what are likely to be
their fighting words, the answer is anything and everything, for as Justice
Holmes said long ago (in *Gitlow v. New York*), every idea is an incitement
to somebody, and since ideas come packaged in sentences, in words, every

sentence is potentially, in some situation that might occur tomorrow, a fighting word and therefore a candidate for regulation.

This insight cuts two ways. One could conclude from it that the fighting words exception is a bad idea because there is no way to prevent clever and unscrupulous advocates from shoveling so many forms of speech into the excepted category that the zone of constitutionally protected speech shrinks to nothing and is finally without inhabitants. Or, alternatively, one could conclude that there was never anything in the zone in the first place; and that the difficulty of limiting the fighting words exception is merely a particular instance of the general difficulty of separating speech from action. And if one opts for this second conclusion, as I do, then a further conclusion is inescapable; insofar as the point of the First Amendment is to identify speech separable from conduct and from the consequences that come in conduct's wake, there is no such speech and therefore nothing for the First Amendment to protect. Or, to make the point from the other direction, when a court invalidates legislation because it infringes on protected speech, it is not because the speech in question is without consequences, but because the consequences have been discounted in relation to a good which is judged to outweigh them. Despite what they say, courts are never in the business of protecting speech *per se*, "mere" speech (a non-existent animal); rather they are in the business of classifying speech (as protected or regulatable) in relation to a value—the health of the republic, the vigor of the economy, the maintenance of the status quo, the undoing of the status quo—that is the true, if unacknowledged, object of their protection.

But if this is the case, a First Amendment purist might reply, why not drop the charade along with the malleable distinctions that make it possible, and declare up front that total freedom of speech is our primary value and trumps anything else, no matter what? The answer is that freedom of expression would only be a primary value if it didn't matter what was said; didn't matter in the sense that no one gave a damn, but just liked to hear talk. There are contexts like that, a Hyde Park corner or a call-in talk show where people get to sound off for the sheer fun of it. These, however, are special contexts, artificially bounded spaces designed to assure that talking is not taken seriously. In ordinary contexts, talk is produced with the goal of trying to move the world in one direction rather than another. In these contexts—the contexts of everyday life—you go to the trouble of asserting that x is y only because you suspect that some people are wrongly asserting that x is z or that x doesn't exist. You assert, in short, because you give a damn, not about assertion—as if it were a value in and of itself—but about what your assertion is about. It may seem paradoxical, but free expression could only be a primary value if what you are valuing is the right to make noise; but if you are engaged in some purposive activity in the course of which speech happens to be produced, sooner or later you will come to a point when you decide that some forms of speech do not further but endanger that purpose.

Take the case of universities and colleges. Could it be the purpose of such places to encourage free expression? If the answer were "yes" it would be hard to say why there would be any need for classes, or examinations, or departments, or disciplines or libraries, since freedom of expression requires nothing but a soapbox or an open telephone line. The very fact of the university's machinery—of the events, rituals and procedures that fill its calendar—argues for some other, more substantive, purpose. In relation to that purpose (which will be realized differently in different kinds of institutions), the flourishing of free expression will in almost all circumstances be an obvious good; but in some circumstances, freedom of expression may pose a threat to that purpose, and at that point, it may be necessary to discipline or regulate speech, lest, to paraphrase Milton, the institution sacrifice itself to one of its *accidental* features.

Interestingly enough, the same conclusion is reached (inadvertently) by Congressman Henry Hyde, who is addressing these very issues in a recently offered amendment to Title VI of the Civil Rights Act. The first section of the amendment states its purpose, to protect "the free speech rights of college students" by prohibiting private as well as public educational institutions from "subjecting any student to disciplinary sanctions solely on the basis of conduct that is speech." The second section enumerates the remedies available to students whose speech rights may have been abridged; and the third, which is to my mind the nub of the matter, declares as an exception to the amendment's jurisdiction, any "educational institution that is controlled by a religious organization," on the reasoning that the application of the amendment to such institutions "would not be consistent with the religious tenets of such organizations." In effect, what Congressman Hyde is saying is that at the heart of these colleges and universities is a set of beliefs, and it would be wrong to require them to tolerate behavior, including speech behavior, inimical to those beliefs. But insofar as this logic is persuasive, it applies across the board; for all educational institutions rest on some set of beliefs—no institution is "just there" independent of any purpose—and it is hard to see why the rights of an institution to protect and preserve its basic "tenets" should be restricted only to those that are religiously controlled. Read strongly, the third section of the amendment undoes sections one and two—the exception becomes, as it always was, the rule—and points us to a balancing test very much like that employed in Canadian law: given that any college or university is informed by a core rationale, an administrator faced with complaints about offensive speech should ask whether damage to the core would be greater if the speech were tolerated or regulated.

The objection to this line of reasoning is well known and has recently been reformulated by Benno Schmidt, former President of Yale University. According to Schmidt, speech-codes on campuses constitute "well intentioned but misguided efforts to give values of community and harmony a higher place than freedom" (*Wall Street Journal,* May 6, 1991). "When the goals of harmony collide with freedom of expression," he continues, "freedom must be the paramount obligation of an academic community." The flaw in this logic is on display in the phrase "academic community"; for the phrase recognizes what Schmidt would deny, that expression only occurs in communities, if not in an academic community, then in a shopping mall community or a dinner-party community or an airplane-ride community or an office community. In these communities and in any others that could be imagined (with the possible exception of a major-league-baseball-fan community) limitations on speech in relation to a defining and deeply assumed purpose are inseparable from community membership.

Indeed "limitations" is the wrong word because it suggests that expression, as an activity and a value, has a pure form that is always in danger of being compromised by the urgings of special interest communities; but independently of a community context informed by interest (that is, purpose), expression would be at once inconceivable and unintelligible. Rather than being a value that is threatened by limitations and constraints, expression, in any form worth worrying about, is a *product* of limitations and constraints, of the already-in-place presuppositions that give assertions their very particular point. Indeed the very act of thinking of something to say (whether or not it is subsequently regulated) is already constrained—rendered impure, and because impure communicable—by the background context within which the thought takes its shape. (The analysis holds too for "freedom," which in Schmidt's vision is an entirely empty concept referring to an urge without direction. But like expression, freedom is a coherent notion only in relation to a goal or good that limits, and by limiting, shapes its exercise.)   14

Arguments like Schmidt's only get their purchase by first imagining speech as occurring in no context whatsoever, and then stripping particular speech acts of the properties conferred on them by contexts. The trick is nicely illustrated when Schmidt urges protection for speech "no matter how obnoxious in content." "Obnoxious" at once acknowledges the reality of speech-related harms and trivializes them by suggesting that they are *surface* injuries which any large minded ("liberated and humane") person should be able to bear. The possibility that speech-related injuries may be grievous and *deeply* wounding is carefully kept out of sight, and because it is kept out of sight the fiction of a world of weightlessness verbal exchange can be maintained, at least within the confines of Schmidt's carefully denatured discourse.   15

To this Schmidt would no doubt reply, as he does in his essay, that harmful speech should be answered not by regulation, but by more speech; but that would make sense only if the effects of speech could be canceled out by additional speech, only if the pain and humiliation caused by racial or religious epithets could be ameliorated by saying something like "So's your old man." What Schmidt fails to realize at every level of his argument is that expression is more than a matter of proffering and receiving propositions, that words do work in the world of a kind that cannot be confined to a purely cognitive realm of "mere" ideas.   16

It could be said, however, that I myself mistake the nature of the work done by freely tolerated speech because I am too focused on short-run outcomes and fail to understand that the good effects of speech will be realized not in the present, but in a future whose emergence regulation could only   17 inhibit. This line of reasoning would also weaken one of my key points, that speech in and of itself cannot be a value and is only worth worrying about if it is in the service of something with which it cannot be identical. My mistake, one could argue, is to equate the something in whose service speech is with some locally espoused value (e.g., the end of racism, the empowerment of disadvantaged minorities), whereas in fact we should think of that something as a now inchoate shape that will be given firm lines only by time's pencil. That is why the shape now receives such indeterminate characterizations (e.g., true self-fulfillment, a more perfect polity, a more capable citizenry, a less partial truth); we cannot now know it, and therefore we must not prematurely fix it in ways that will bind successive generations to error.

This forward-looking view of what the First Amendment protects has a great appeal, in part because it continues in a secular form the Puritan celebration of millenarian hopes, but it imposes a requirement so severe that one would except more justification for it than is usually provided. The requirement is that we endure whatever pain racist and hate speech inflicts for the sake of a future whose emergence we can only take on faith. In a specifically religious vision like Milton's this makes perfect sense (it is indeed the whole of Christianity), but in the context of a politics that puts its trust in the world and not in the Holy Spirit, it raises more questions than it answers and could be seen as the second of two strategies designed to delegitimize the complaints of victimized groups. The first strategy, as I have noted, is to define speech in such a way as to render it inconsequential (on the model of "sticks and stones will break my bones, but . . ."); the second strategy is to acknowledge the (often grievous) consequences of speech, but declare that we must suffer them in the name of something that cannot be named. The two strategies are denials from slightly different directions of the *present* effects of racist speech; one confines those effects to a closed and safe realm of pure mental activity; the other imagines the effects of speech spilling over into the world, but only in an ever receding future for whose sake we must forever defer taking action.

I find both strategies unpersuasive, but my own skepticism concerning them is less important than the fact that in general they seem to have worked; in the parlance of the marketplace (a parlance First Amendment commentators love), many in the society seemed to have bought them. Why? The answer, I think, is that people cling to First Amendment pieties because they do not wish to face what they correctly take to be the alternative. That alternative is *politics*, the realization (at which I have already hinted) that decisions about what is and is not protected in the realm of expression will rest not on principle or firm doctrine, but on the ability of some persons to interpret—recharacterize or rewrite—principle and doctrine in ways that lead to the protection of speech they want heard and the regulation of speech they want silenced. (That is how George Bush can argue *for* flag burning statutes and *against* campus hate-speech codes.) When the First Amendment is successfully invoked the result is not a victory for free speech in the face of a challenge from politics, but a *political victory* won by the party that has managed to wrap its agenda in the mantle of free speech.

It is from just such a conclusion—a conclusion that would put politics *in- side* the First Amendment—that commentators recoil, saying things like "this could render the First Amendment a dead letter," or "this would leave us with no normative guidance in determining when and what speech to protect," or "this effaces the distinction between speech and action," or "this is incom- patible with any viable notion of freedom of expression." To these statements (culled more or less at random from recent law review pieces) I would reply that the First Amendment has always been a dead letter if one understood its "liveness" to depend on the identification and protection of a realm of "mere" expression distinct from the realm of regulatable conduct; the distinc- tion between speech and action has always been effaced in principle, al- though in practice it can take whatever form the prevailing political conditions mandate; we have never had any normative guidance for marking off protected from unprotected speech; rather the guidance we have has been fashioned (and refashioned) in the very political struggles over which it then (for a time) presides. In short, the name of the game has always been politics, even when (indeed, especially when) it is played by stigmatizing politics as the area to be avoided.

In saying this, I would not be heard as not arguing either for or against regulation and speech codes as a matter of general principle. Instead my argu- ment turns away from general principle to the pragmatic (anti) principle of considering each situation as it emerges. The question of whether or not to regulate will always be a local one and we can not rely on abstractions that are either empty of content or filled with the content of some partisan agenda to generate a "principled" answer. Instead we must consider in every case what is at stake and what are the risks and gains of alternative courses of action. In the course of this consideration many things will be of help, but among them will not be phrases like "freedom of speech" or "the right of in- dividual expression," because, as they are used now, these phrases tend to ob- scure rather than clarify our dilemmas. Once they are deprived of their talismanic force, once it is no longer strategically effective simply to invoke them in the act of walking away from a problem, the conversation could con- tinue in directions that are now blocked by a first amendment absolutism that has only been honored in the breach anyway. To the student reporter who complains that in the wake of the promulgation of a speech code at the University of Wisconsin there is now something in the back of his mind as he writes, one could reply, "There was always something in the back of your mind and perhaps it might be better to have this code in the back of your mind than whatever was in there before." And when someone warns about the slippery slope and predicts mournfully that if you restrict one form of speech, you never know what will be restricted next, one could reply, "some form of speech is always being restricted; else there could be no meaningful assertion; we have always and already slid down the slippery slope; someone is always going to be restricted next, and it is your job to make sure that the someone is not you." And when someone observes, as someone surely will, that anti-harassment codes chill speech, one could reply that since speech only becomes intelligible against the background of what isn't being said, the background of what has already been silenced, the only question is the political one of which speech is going to be chilled, and, all things considered, it seems a good thing to chill speech like "nigger," "cunt," "kike," and "faggot." And if someone then says, "But what happened to free-speech principles?" one could say what I have now said a dozen times, free speech principles don't exist except as a component in a bad argument in which such principles are invoked to mask motives that would not withstand close scrutiny.

An example of a wolf wrapped in First Amendment clothing is an adver-   22
tisement that ran recently in the Duke University student newspaper, *The Chronicle.* Signed by Bradley R. Smith, well-known as a purveyor of anti-semitic neo-Nazi propaganda, the ad is packaged as a scholarly treatise: four densely packed columns complete with "learned" references, undocumented statistics, and an array of so-called authorities. The message of the ad is that the Holocaust never occurred and that the German state never "had a policy to exterminate the Jewish people (or anyone else) by putting them to death in gas chambers." In a spectacular instance of the increasingly popular "blame the victim" strategy, the Holocaust "story" or "myth" is said to have been fabricated in order "to drum up world sympathy for Jewish causes." The "evidence" supporting these assertions is a slick blend of supposedly probative facts—"not a single autopsied body has been shown to be gassed"—and sly insinuations of a kind familiar to readers of *Mein Kampf* and *The Protocols of the Elders of Zion.* The slickest thing of all, however, is the presentation of the argument as an exercise in free speech—the ad is subtitled *The Case for Open Debate*—that could be objected to only by "thought police" and censors. This strategy bore immediate fruit in the decision of the newspaper staff to accept the ad despite a long standing (and historically honored) policy of refusing materials that contain ethnic and racial slurs or are otherwise offensive. The reasoning of the staff (explained by the editor in a special column) was that under the First Amendment advertisers have the "right" to be published. "American newspapers are built on the principles of free speech and free press, so how can a newspaper deny these rights to anyone?" The answer to this question is that an advertiser is not denied his rights simply because a single media organ declines his copy so long as other avenues of publication are available and there has been no state suppression of his views. This is not to say that there could not be a case for printing the ad, only that the case cannot rest on a supposed First Amendment obligation. One might argue for example that printing the ad would foster healthy debate or that lies are more likely to be shown up for what they are if they are brought to the light of day, but these are precisely the arguments the editor *disclaims* in her eagerness to take a "principled" free-speech stand.

What I find most distressing about this incident is not that the ad was   23
printed but that it was printed by persons who believed it to be a lie and a distortion. If the editor and her staff were in agreement with Smith's views or

harbored serious doubts about the reality of the Holocaust, I would still have a quarrel with them, but it would be a different quarrel; it would be a quarrel about evidence, credibility, documentation, etc. But since on these matters the editors and I are in agreement, my quarrel is with the reasoning that led them to act in opposition to what they believed to be true. That reasoning, as I understand it, goes as follows: although we ourselves are certain that the Holocaust was a fact, facts are notoriously interpretable and disputable; therefore nothing is ever really settled, and we have no right to reject something just because we regard it as pernicuous and false. But the fact—if I can use that word—that settled truths can always be upset, at least theoretically, does not mean that we can not affirm and rely on truths that according to our present lights seem indisputable; rather it means exactly the opposite: in the absence of absolute certainty of the kind that can only be provided by revelation (something I do not rule out but have not yet experienced) we must act on the basis of the certainty we have so far achieved. Truth may, as Milton said, always be in the course of emerging, and one must always be on guard against being so beguiled by its present shape that we ignore contrary evidence, but, by the same token, when it happens that the present shape of truth is compelling beyond a reasonable doubt, it is our moral obligation to act on it and not defer action in the name of an interpretative future that may never arrive. By running the First Amendment up the nearest flagpole and rushing to salute it, the student editors defaulted on that obligation and gave over their responsibility to a so-called principle that was not even to the point.

Let me be clear. I am not saying that First Amendment principles are inherently bad (they are *inherently* nothing), only that they are not always the appropriate reference point for situations involving the production of speech, and that even when they are the appropriate reference point, they do not constitute a politics-free perspective because the shape in which they are invoked will always be political, will always, that is, be the result of having drawn the relevant line (between speech and action, or between high value speech and low value speech, or between words essential to the expression of ideas and fighting words) in a way that is favorable to some interests and indifferent or hostile to some others. This having been said, the moral is not that First Amendment talk should be abandoned. For even if the standard First Amendment formulas do not and could not perform the function expected of them (the elimination of political considerations in decisions about speech), they still serve a function that is not at all negligible: they slow down outcomes in an area in which the fear of overhasty outcomes is justified by a long record of abuses of power. It is often said that history shows (itself a formula) that even a minimal restriction on the right of expression too easily leads to ever larger restrictions; and to the extent that this is an empirical fact (and it is a question one could debate) there is some comfort and protection to be found in a procedure that requires you to jump through hoops—do a lot of argumentative work—before a speech regulation will be allowed to stand.

I would not be misunderstood as offering the notion of "jumping 25
through hoops" as a new version of the First Amendment claim to neutrality.
A hoop must have a shape—in this case the shape of whatever binary distinction is representing First Amendment "interests"—and the shape of the hoop
one is asked to jump through will in part determine what kinds of jumps can
be regularly made. Even if they are only mechanisms for slowing down outcomes, First Amendment formulas by virtue of their substantive content (and
it is impossible that they be without content) will slow down some outcomes
more easily than others, and that means that the form they happen to have
at the present moment will favor some interests more than others. Therefore,
even with a reduced sense of the effectivity of First Amendment rhetoric (it
can not assure any particular result), the counsel with which I began remains
relevant: so long as so called "free speech principles" have been fashioned by
your enemy (so long as it is *his* hoops you have to jump through), contest
their relevance to the issue at hand; but if you manage to refashion them in
line with your purposes, urge them with a vengeance.

It is a counsel that follows from the thesis that there is no such thing as 26
free speech which is not, after all, a thesis as startling or corrosive as may first
have seemed. It merely says that there is no class of utterances separable from
the world of conduct, and that therefore the identification of some utterances
as members of that non-existent class will always be evidence that a political
line has been drawn rather than a line that denies politics entry into the forum of public discourse. It is the job of the First Amendment to mark out an
area in which competing views can be considered without state interference;
but if the very marking out of that area is itself an interference (as it always
will be), First Amendment jurisprudence is inevitably self-defeating and subversive of its own aspirations. That's the bad news. The good news is that precisely *because* speech is never "free" in the two senses required—free of
consequences and free from state pressure—speech always matters, is always
doing work; because everything we say impinges on the world in ways indistinguishable from the effects of physical action, we must take responsibility
for our verbal performances—*all* of them—and not assume that they are being taken care of by a clause in the Constitution. Of course with responsibility come risks, but they have always been our risks and no doctrine of free
speech has ever insulated us from them. They are the risks, respectively, of
permitting speech that does obvious harm and of shutting off speech in ways
that might deny us the benefit of Joyce's *Ulysses* or Lawrence's *Lady Chatterly's
Lover* or Titian's paintings. Nothing, I repeat, can insulate us from those risks.
(If there is no normative guidance in determining when and what speech to
protect, there is no normative guidance in determining what is art—like free
speech a category that includes everything and nothing—and what is obscenity.) And, moreover, nothing can provide us with a principle for deciding
which risk in the long run is the best to take. I am persuaded that at the present moment, right now, the risk of not attending to hate speech is greater
than the risk that by regulating it we will deprive ourselves of valuable voices
and insights or slide down the slippery slope toward tyranny. This is a judg-

ment for which I can offer reasons but no guarantees. All I am saying is that the judgments of those who would come down on the other side carry no guarantees either. They urge us to put our faith in apolitical abstractions, but the abstractions they invoke—the marketplace of ideas, speech alone, speech itself—only come in political guises, and therefore in trusting to them we fall (unwittingly) under the sway of the very forces we wish to keep at bay. It is not that there are no choices to make or means of making them; it is just that the choices as well as the means are inextricable from the din and confusion of partisan struggle. There is no safe place.

Postscript

When a shorter version of this essay was first published it drew a number of indignant letters from readers who took me to be making a *recommendation:* let's abandon principles, or let's dispense with an open mind. But, in fact, I am not making a recommendation, but declaring what I take to be an unavoidable truth. That truth is not that freedom of speech should be abridged, but that freedom of speech is a conceptual impossibility because the condition of speech's being free in the first place is unrealizable. That condition corresponds to the hope, represented by the often-invoked "marketplace of ideas", that we can fashion a forum in which ideas can be considered independently of political and ideological constraint. My point, not engaged by the letters, is that constraint of an ideological kind is *generative* of speech and that therefore the very intelligibility of speech (as assertion rather than noise) is radically dependent on what free-speech ideologues would push away. Absent some already-in-place and (for the time being) unquestioned ideological vision, the act of speaking would make no sense, because it would not be resonating against any background understanding of the possible courses of physical or verbal actions and their possible consequences. Nor is that background accessible to the speaker it constrains; it is not an object of his or her critical self-consciousness; rather, it constitutes the field in which consciousness occurs, and therefore the productions of consciousness, and specifically speech, will always be political (that is, angled) in ways the speaker cannot know.

27

In response to this, someone might say (although the letters here discussed do not rise to this level) that even if speech is inescapably political in my somewhat rarified sense, it is still possible and desirable to provide a cleared space in which irremediably political utterances can compete for the public's approval without any one of them being favored or stigmatized in advance. But what the history of First Amendment jurisprudence shows is that the decisions as to what should or should not enjoy that space's protection and the determination of how exactly (under what rules) that space will first be demarcated and then administered are continually matters of dispute; and moreover, the positions taken in the dispute are, each of them, intelligible and compelling only from the vantage point of a deeply assumed ideology which, like the ideology of speech in general, dare not, and indeed cannot, speak its name. The structure that is supposed to permit ideological/political agendas to fight it out fairly—on a level playing field that has not

28

been rigged—is itself always ideologically and politically constructed. This is exactly the conclusion reached reluctantly by Robert Post in a piece infinitely more nuanced than the letter he now writes. At the end of a long and rigorous analysis, Post finds before him "the startling proposition that the boundaries of public discourse cannot be fixed in a neutral fashion" ("The Constitutional Concept of Public Discourse: Outrageous Opinion, Democratic Deliberation and *Hustler v. Falwell*," *Harvard Law Review*, Vol. 103, no. 3, January, 1990, 683). "The ultimate fact of ideological regulation," he adds, "cannot be blinked." Indeed not, since the ultimate fact is also the *root* fact in the sense that one cannot get behind it or around it, and that is why the next strategy—the strategy of saying "well, we can't get beyond or around ideology, but at least we can make a good faith try"—won't work either. In what cleared and ideology-free space will the "try" be made?, one must ask, and if the answer is (and it must be by Post's own conclusion) that there is no such cleared space, the notion of "trying" can have no real content. (On a more leisurely occasion I would expand this point into an argument for the emptiness of any gesture that invokes a regulative ideal.)

No such thing as free (non-ideologically constrained) speech; no such   29
thing as a public forum purged of ideological pressures or exclusions. That's my thesis, and waiting at the end (really at the beginning) of it is, as my respondents have said, politics. Not, however, politics as the dirty word it becomes in most First Amendment discussions, but politics as the attempt to implement some partisan vision. I place the word "vision" after "partisan" so as to forestall the usual reading of partisan as "unprincipled," the reading Post attributes to me when he finds me "writing on the assumption that there is some implicit and mutually exclusive dichotomy between politics and principle." In fact, my argument is exactly the reverse: since it is only from within a commitment to some particular (not abstract) agenda that one feels the deep urgency we identify as "principled," politics is the *source* of principle, not its opposite. When two agendas square off, the contest is never between politics and principle, but between two forms of politics, or, if you prefer, two forms of principle. The assumption of an antagonism between them is not mine, but Post's, and it is an assumption he doubles when he warns of the danger of "unprincipled self-assertion." This is to imagine selves as possibly motivated by "mere" preference, but (and this is the same point I have already made) preference is never "mere" in the sense of being without a moral or philosophical rationale; preference is the precipitate of some defensible (and, of course, challengeable) agenda, and selves who assert it, rather than being unprincipled, are at that moment extensions of principle. Again, it is Post, not me, who entertains a picture of human beings "as merely a collection of Hobbesian appetites." I see human beings in the grip of deep (if debatable) commitments, commitments so constitutive of their thoughts and actions that they cannot help being sincere. Franklin Haiman and Cushing Strout (two other correspondents) could not be more off the mark when they brand me cynical and opportunistic. They assume I am counseling readers to set aside principle in favor of motives that are merely political, whereas in fact I am challenging that distinction and counseling readers (the counsel

is superfluous) to act on what they believe to be true and important, and not to be stymied by a doctrine that is at once incoherent and (because incoherent) a vehicle for covert politics.

In general, the letter writers ignore my challenge to the binaries on which   30
their arguments depend, and take to chiding me for failing to respect distinctions whose lack of cogency has been a large part of my point. Thus, Professor Haiman solemnly informs me that an open mind is not the same as an empty one; but, in my analysis—which Professor Haiman is of course not obliged to accept, but is surely obliged to note—they *are* the same. An open mind is presumably a mind not unduly committed to its present contents, but a mind so structured, or, rather, *un*structured, would lack a framework or in-place-background in relation to which the world (both of action and speech) would be intelligible. A mind so open that it was anchored by no assumptions, no convictions of the kind that order and stabilize perception, would be a mind without gestalt and therefore without the capacity of keeping anything *in*. A consciousness not shored up at one end by a belief (not always the same one) whose negation it could not think would be a sieve. In short, it would be empty.

Professor Strout ventures into the same (incoherent) territory when he   31
takes me to task for "confusing toleration with endorsing" and "justifying" with "putting up with." The idea is that a policy of allowing hate-speech does not constitute approval of hate-speech, but shifts the responsibility for approving or disapproving to the free choice of free individuals. But this is to assume that the machinery of deliberation in individuals is purely formal and is unaffected by what is or is not in the cultural air. Such an assumption is absolutely necessary to the liberal epistemology shared by my respondents, but it is one that I reject because, as I have argued elsewhere, the context of deliberation is cultural (rather than formal or genetic) and because it is cultural the outcome of deliberation cannot help being influenced by whatever notions are current in the culture. (Minds are not free, as the liberal epistemology implies, for the same reason that they cannot be open). The fact that David Duke was rudely and provocatively questioned by reporters on *Sixty Minutes* or *Meet the Press* was less important than the fact that he was on *Sixty Minutes* and *Meet the Press* in the first place, for these appearances legitimized him and put his views into national circulation in a way that made them an unavoidable component of the nation's thinking. Tolerating may be different from endorsing from the point of view of the tolerator, who can then disclaim responsibility for the effects of what he has not endorsed, but, if the effects are real and consequential, as I argue they are, the difference may be cold comfort.

It is, of course, *effects* that the liberal epistemology, as represented by a   32
strong free-speech position, cannot take into account or can take into account only at the outer limits of public safety ("clear and imminent danger," "incitement to violence"). It is, therefore, perfectly apt for Professor Haiman to cite Holmes' dissent in *Abrams,* for that famous opinion at once concisely states the modern First Amendment position and illustrates what I consider to be its difficulties, if not its contradictions. Holmes begins by acknowledging the truth basic to my argument: it makes perfect sense to desire the si-

lencing of beliefs inimical to yours, because if you did not so desire, it would be an indication that you did not believe in your beliefs. But then Holmes takes note of the fact that one's beliefs are subject to change, and comes to the skeptical conclusion that since the course of change is unpredictable, it would be unwise to institutionalize beliefs we may not hold at a later date; instead, we should leave the winnowing process to the marketplace of ideas unregulated by transient political pressures.

This sounds fine (even patriotic), but it runs afoul of problems at both ends. The "entry" problem is the one I have already identified in my reply to Professor Post: the marketplace of ideas—the protected forum of public discourse—will be structured by the same political considerations it was designed to hold at bay; and therefore, the workings of the marketplace will not be free in the sense required, that is, be uninflected by governmental action (the government is given the task of managing the marketplace and therefore the opportunity to determine its contours). Things are even worse at the other end, the exit or no-exit end. If our commitment to freedom of speech is so strong that it obliges us, as Holmes declares, to tolerate "opinions . . . we . . . believe to be fraught with death" (a characterization that recognizes the awful consequentiality of speech and implicitly undercuts any speech/action distinction), then we are being asked to court our own destruction for the sake of an abstraction that may doom us rather than save us. There are really only three alternatives: either Holmes does not mean it, as is suggested by his instant qualification ("unless . . . an immediate check is required to save the country"), or he means it but doesn't think that opinions fraught with death could ever triumph in a free market (in which case he commits himself to a progressivism he neither analyzes nor declares), or he means it and thinks deadly opinions could, in fact, triumph, but is saying something like "que sera sera" as it would appear he is in a later dissent, *Gitlow v. New York*). Each of these readings of what Holmes is telling us in *Abrams* and *Gitlow* is problematic, and it is the problems in the position born out of these two dissents that have been explored in my essay. The replies to that essay, as far as I can see, do not address those problems, but continue simply to rehearse the pieties my analysis troubles. Keep those cards and letters coming.

Questions

1. Try to explain in your own words Fish's argument that freedom of expression is not protected by the First Amendment.
2. One way to get around the First Amendment is to draw a distinction between speech and action, in which "fighting words" are restricted. What kinds of phrases or words in your opinion constitute fighting words? Why does Fish say that this distinction leads him to conclude that there is nothing for the First Amendment to protect?
3. Compare Hentoff's and Fish's positions on the freedom of expression vs. speech code debate. Whose position do you favor? Why?

The Debate over Placing Limits on Racist Speech Must Not Ignore the Damage It Does to Its Victims

CHARLES R. LAWRENCE III

Charles R. Lawrence III is a professor of law at Stanford University.

In this article, Lawrence argues against unbridled free speech. To Lawrence, real harm to both individuals and groups can arise from racial insults, as well as having the effect of undermining the First Amendment. He supports the need to develop impositions on offensive speech and discourse, and writes that legal remedies need to be constructed to counter the worst effects of racist and sexist speech. This reading is from the Chronicle of Higher Education *(1989) and was adapted from a speech Lawrence gave to the American Civil Liberties Union.*

I have spent the better part of my life as a dissenter. As a high school student, I was threatened with suspension for my refusal to participate in a civil-defense drill, and I have been a conspicuous consumer of my First Amendment liberties ever since. There are very strong reasons for protecting even racist speech. Perhaps the most important of these is that such protection reinforces our society's commitment to tolerance as a value, and that by protecting bad speech from government regulation, we will be forced to combat it as a community. 1

But I also have a deeply felt apprehension about the resurgence of racial violence and the corresponding rise in the incidence of verbal and symbolic assault and harassment to which blacks and other traditionally subjugated and excluded groups are subjected. I am troubled by the way the debate has been framed in response to the recent surge of racist incidents on college and university campuses and in response to some universities' attempts to regulate harassing speech. The problem has been framed as one in which the liberty of free speech is in conflict with the elimination of racism. I believe this has placed the bigot on the moral high ground and fanned the rising flames of racism. 2

Above all, I am troubled that we have not listened to the real victims, that we have shown so little understanding of their injury, and that we have abandoned those whose race, gender, or sexual preference continues to make them second-class citizens. It seems to me a very sad irony that the first instinct of civil libertarians has been to challenge even the smallest, most narrowly framed efforts by universities to provide black and other minority students with the protection the Constitution guarantees them. 3

392

The landmark case of *Brown v. Board of Education* is not a case that we nor-   4
mally think of as a case about speech. But *Brown* can be broadly read as artic-
ulating the principle of equal citizenship. *Brown* held that segregated schools
were inherently unequal because of the *message* that segregation conveyed—
that black children were an untouchable caste, unfit to go to school with
white children. If we understand the necessity of eliminating the system of
signs and symbols that signal the inferiority of blacks, then we should hesitate before proclaiming that all racist speech that stops short of physical violence must be defended.

University officials who have formulated policies to respond to incidents   5
of racial harassment have been characterized in the press as "thought police,"
but such policies generally do nothing more than impose sanctions against
intentional face-to-face insults. When racist speech takes the form of face-to-
face insults, catcalls, or other assaultive speech aimed at an individual or
small group of persons, it falls directly within the "fighting words" exception
to First Amendment protection. The Supreme Court has held that words
which "by their very utterance inflict injury or tend to incite an immediate
breach of the peace" are not protected by the First Amendment.

If the purpose of the First Amendment is to foster the greatest amount of   6
speech, racial insults disserve that purpose. Assaultive racist speech functions
as a preemptive strike. The invective is experienced as a blow, not as a prof-
fered idea, and once the blow is struck, it is unlikely that a dialogue will follow. Racial insults are particularly undeserving of First Amendment
protection because the perpetuator's intention is not to discover truth or initiate dialogue but to injure the victim. In most situations, members of minority groups realize that they are likely to lose if they respond to epithets by
fighting and are forced to remain silent and submissive.

Courts have held that offensive speech may not be regulated in public   7
forums such as streets where the listener may avoid the speech by moving on,
but the regulation of otherwise protected speech has been permitted when
the speech invades the privacy of the unwilling listener's home or when the
unwilling listener cannot avoid the speech. Racist posters, fliers, and graffiti
in dormitories, bathrooms, and other common living spaces would seem to
clearly fall within the reasoning of these cases. Minority students should not
be required to remain in their rooms in order to avoid racial assault. Mini-
mally, they should find a safe haven in their dorms and in all other common
rooms that are a part of their daily routine.

I would also argue that the university's responsibility for ensuring that   8
these students receive an equal educational opportunity provides a compelling justification for regulations that ensure them safe passage in all common areas. A minority student should not have to risk becoming the target of
racially assaulting speech every time he or she chooses to walk across campus.
Regulating vilifying speech that cannot be anticipated or avoided would not
preclude announced speeches and rallies—situations that would give minority-group members and their allies the chance to organize counterdemonstra-
tions or avoid the speech altogether.

The most commonly advanced argument against the regulation of racist   9
speech proceeds something like this: We recognize that minority groups suffer pain and injury as the result of racist speech, but we must allow this hate
mongering for the benefit of society as a whole. Freedom of speech is the
lifeblood of our democratic system. It is especially important for minorities
because often it is their only vehicle for rallying support for the redress of
their grievances. It will be impossible to formulate a prohibition so precise
that it will prevent the racist speech you want to suppress without catching
in the same net all kinds of speech that it would be unconscionable for a
democratic society to suppress.

Whenever we make such arguments, we are striking a balance on the one   10
hand between our concern for the continued free flow of ideas and the democratic process dependent on that flow, and, on the other, our desire to further
the cause of equality. There can be no meaningful discussion of how we
should reconcile our commitment to equality and our commitment to free
speech until it is acknowledged that there is real harm inflicted by racist
speech and that this harm is far from trivial.

To engage in a debate about the First Amendment and racist speech with-   11
out a full understanding of the nature and extent of that harm is to risk making the First Amendment an instrument of domination rather than a vehicle
of liberation. We have not all known the experience of victimization by
racist, misogynist, and homophobic speech, nor do we equally share the burden of the societal harm it inflicts. We are often quick to say that we have
heard the cry of the victims when we have not.

The *Brown* case is again instructive because it speaks directly to the psy-   12
chic injury inflicted by racist speech by noting that the symbolic message of
segregation affected "the hearts and minds" of negro children "in a way unlikely ever to be undone." Racial epithets and harassment often cause deep
emotional scarring and feelings of anxiety and fear that pervade every aspect
of a victim's life.

Brown also recognized that black children did not have an equal opportu-   13
nity to learn and participate in the school community if they bore the additional burden of being subjected to the humiliation and psychic assault
contained in the message of segregation. University students bear an analogous burden when they are forced to live and work in an environment where
at any moment they may be subjected to denigrating verbal harassment and
assault. The same injury was addressed by the Supreme Court when it held
that sexual harassment that creates a hostile or abusive work environment
violates the ban on sex discrimination in employment of Title VII of the
Civil Rights Act of 1964.

Carefully drafted university regulations would bar the use of words as as-   14
sault weapons and leave unregulated even the most heinous of ideas when
those ideas are presented at times and places and in manners that provide an
opportunity for reasoned rebuttal or escape from immediate injury. The history of the development of the right to free speech has been one of carefully
evaluating the importance of free expression and its effects on other important societal interests. We have drawn the line between protected and unpro-

tected speech before without dire results. (Courts have, for example, exempted from the protection of the First Amendment obscene speech and speech that disseminates official secrets, that defames or libels another person, or that is used to form a conspiracy or monopoly.)

Blacks and other people of color are skeptical about the argument that even the most injurious speech must remain unregulated because, in an unregulated marketplace of ideas, the best ones will rise to the top and gain acceptance. Our experience tells us quite the opposite. We have seen too many demagogues elected by appealing to America's racism. We have seen too many good liberal politicians shy away from the issues that might brand them as being too closely allied with us. 15

Whenever we decide that racist speech must be tolerated because of the importance of maintaining societal tolerance for all unpopular speech, we are asking blacks and other subordinated groups to bear the burden for the good of all. We must be careful that the ease with which we strike the balance against the regulation of racist speech is in no way influenced by the fact that the cost will be borne by others. We must be certain that those who will pay that price are fairly represented in our deliberations and that they are heard. 16

At the core of the argument that we should resist all government regulation of speech is the ideal that the best cure for bad speech is good, that ideas that affirm equality and the worth of all individuals will ultimately prevail. This is an empty ideal unless those of us who would fight racism are vigilant and unequivocal in that fight. We must look for ways to offer assistance and support to students whose speech and political participation are chilled in a climate of racial harassment. 17

Civil-rights lawyers might consider suing on behalf of blacks whose right to an equal education is denied by a university's failure to ensure a nondiscriminatory educational climate or conditions of employment. We must embark upon the development of a First Amendment jurisprudence grounded in the reality of our history and our contemporary experience. We must think hard about how best to launch legal attacks against the most indefensible forms of hate speech. Good lawyers can create exceptions and narrow interpretations that limit the harm of hate speech without opening the floodgates of censorship. 18

Everyone concerned with these issues must find ways to engage actively in actions that resist and counter the racist ideas that we would have the First Amendment protect. If we fail in this, the victims of hate speech must rightly assume that we are on the oppressors' side. 19

Questions

1. On what grounds does Lawrence argue that racist speech should be regulated? Do you agree with his argument?
2. In what ways are Lawrence's and Fish's arguments similar?
3. Compare and contrast the arguments of Hentoff, Fish, and Lawrence. Do you agree that speech codes pose a threat to free speech?

Freedom of Hate Speech

RICHARD PERRY AND PATRICIA WILLIAMS

Richard Perry is a researcher in linguistics at the University of Louvain in Belgium; Patricia Williams is an associate professor of law and women's studies at the University of Wisconsin at Madison, and author, most recently, of The Alchemy of Race and Rights.

In this statement, Perry and Williams deal briefly with the changing face of students on American campuses, and argue for a realization that whether or not we agree with speech codes, such codes, explicitly or implicitly, are not entirely new, nor do they prevent racist and sexist thought in private. They conclude by asking for a redefinition of the standard "traditional rational man" to reflect our multicultural society. This selection is from Tikkun *magazine (1991).*

Until well after the Second World War, American institutions of higher educa- 1
tion were bastions of a sort of cheery and thoughtlessly jingoistic nativism (isn't this some part of what we've always meant when we spoke of "that old college spirit"?). Except for the historically black and women's colleges and a couple of schools serving immigrant populations (such as the City College of New York), the vast majority of the student bodies of America's hundreds of colleges were overwhelmingly U.S.-born, male, Christian, and of Northern European descent, and their faculties were even more so. The structure of the core liberal arts curriculum suggested that the university understood itself as an umpire of timeless values, high above the rough and tumble of mere politics, standing at the summit of Western civilization, which from this vantage point could be seen to have risen in an unbroken crescendo from Plato to NATO.

However, the assumptions that made the university an arbiter of "uni- 2
versal values" have been questioned, as multinational business and research institutions have evolved into ever more global and ethnically diverse enterprises. On the home front, meanwhile, the hard-won material gains of women and ethnic minorities have produced halting progress toward the goal of making American universities truly representative of the country's population as a whole. Responding to these historical developments, many have sought to make the core curriculum a more effective preparation for the diverse, multicultural environments of both the contemporary United States and the world. There have also been efforts to make the campus itself a more hospitable place for its newly heterogeneous population, most notably

396

amendments to the campus conduct rules intended to discourage harassment on the basis of race, religion, ethnicity, gender, and sexual orientation.

These reform efforts have been met with a virulent backlash. This backlash has recently been fueled by a series of often scurrilous stories in the most visible national magazines and by fervent denunciations from the Left, Right, and center of political debate. 3

This confusion stems largely from the dishonest manner in which the debates have been reported. Most accounts of this campus dispute have been characterized by repeated distortions of fact and a profound bad faith with history. First, it is preposterous to claim, as many opponents of multiculturalism have, that these debates are about some supposed new infringement of the First Amendment rights of American citizens. No position seriously advocated by multiculturalists would have the slightest effect upon our right as Americans to be nativist, racist, anti-Semitic, sexist, homophobic, or just as narrowly monocultural-as-we-wanna-be in our personal lives. So too it remains entirely possible to stand in the public arena and call one another any of the whole litany of terms with which we as Americans have learned throughout our history to abuse one another. One might instructively compare this situation with the new Canadian constitution, which specifically limits the protection of certain kinds of hate speech, without much evidence that this provision has started Canada down that slippery slope toward being a Stalinist police state. 4

Nor do the multiculturalist reforms pose any institutional threat to the many securely tenured professors on the most prestigious faculties who teach doctrines (such as sociobiology and kindred theories on the margins of intellectual respectability) that are patently demeaning to members of the most long-abused groups. And the debate over multiculturalism scarcely disturbs the work of eminent scholars who regularly contrive to put a revisionist happy face upon the history of slavery, the Czarist pogroms, the Nazi genocides, the colonial subjugation of indigenous peoples, or the oppression of women. 5

***

What has *never* been true is that one member of an institution has an unrestrained legal right to harass another member and remain in the good graces of the institution. 6

Yet the recent barrage of media coverage would have us believe that some *novel* restriction is being imposed in multiculturalist speech and behavior codes. This misinformation has been conveyed by those who are apparently unable to distinguish between a liberty interest on the one hand and, on the other, a quite specific interest in being able to spout racist, sexist, and homophobic epithets completely unchallenged—without, in other words, the terrible inconvenience of feeling bad about it. 7

There is a sharp paradox at the heart of all this, a contradiction whose effective message is: "I have the right to express as much hatred as I want, so you shut up about it." It may be appropriate to defend the First Amendment rights of students who, for example, openly advocate Nazi policies. However, 8

there has been a good deal of unacknowledged power-brokering that has informed the refusal even to think about the effect of relentless racist propagan-
dizing on educational institutions in particular. Now those who even criticize
this selective invocation of the First Amendment on the behalf of one social
group over another are themselves called Nazis.

This fundamental paradox has bred a host of others. Conservatives such   9
as George Will hurriedly discard their hallowed distinction between the public and private spheres when expediency beckons. Not long ago right-wingers
were asserting that the evangelical Bob Jones University should be allowed to
practice segregation and still be given a tax exemption—because it was a *private* institution. Where were these free-speech patriots in 1986 when Captain
Goldman, a U.S. Air Force officer and an Orthodox Jew, was denied by the
Reagan Supreme Court the right to wear a yarmulke at his desk job? And
where are they now, when the new Supreme Court of our new world order
has just asserted that the government *can* control speech between doctor and
patient—heretofore one of the most sacred of privacy privileges—when the
clinic receives federal funds and the topic of conversation is reproductive
choice?

These ironies of free-speech opportunism have been accompanied by a   10
breathtaking effort to rewrite our history. The multiculturalist reforms on
campus have been characterized as being at odds with the two moral touch-
stones of recent political memory: the World War II-era fight against Nazi
theory of Aryan supremacy and the American anti-slavery and civil rights
movements. Both of these struggles were in fact fought over—among other
things—the sort of contested social meanings that can be traced directly to
the present university discussions. The new interpretation of these two con-
tests, however, rewrites them as triumphs of the inevitable, forward-marching
progress of modern liberal individualism. Commentators from George Will to
Shelby Steele have consistently depicted Martin Luther King, Jr., for example,
as having pursued the higher moral ground of individual achievement rather
than the validation of African-American collective social identity—as though
these notions were inherently in opposition to one another. We are to imagine, for example, that the brave people who faced fire hoses and police dogs
and who sat-in at lunch counters in the 1950s and 1960s were after nothing
more than, say, the market freedom of an individual black American to eat a
grilled cheese sandwich in the company of raving bigots. Conservative opponents of multiculturalism would have us forget about the other part of that
struggle: the fight to expand the social space of all blacks and to re-articulate
the political semantics of the collective identity of the descendants of slaves.

***

Another striking paradox is the way that much of this backlash proceeds   11
in the name of democratic values, while mounting a sustained assault precisely on the democratic process of academic self-governance. The academic
Right devotes itself to attacks on changes in curricula and conduct codes that
have been adopted only after lengthy deliberation and votes by the faculty
senates (such as in the Stanford Western civilization reforms or the Berkeley

ethnic studies requirement), administrative committees, or student bodies. More curiously still, these assaults are typically said to be conducted in defense of something like "a free marketplace of ideas." Yet the recent multiculturalist changes might accurately be viewed as shifts in an intellectual marketplace where several positions have been rising in value, while another, older position, adamantly refusing to innovate, has been steadily losing its market share. There is a certain irony, therefore, in the spectacle of William Bennett and company engaged in a kind of status brokerage, trading on their appointed positions of authority for advantage they cannot gain via democratic votes in faculty senates or in the governing bodies of professional organizations.

Such distortions of the debate have worked to obscure what could be a genuine opportunity. The market idea, considered not simply as the nineteenth-century social-Darwinist mechanism whereby big fish eat little fish for the greater good, might serve as a multidimensional matrix for the representation of certain types of social information. If, for example, we could ever get to the point where we can honestly speak of having achieved a level playing-field in the marketplace of ideas (for this is precisely what is at stake in the present debates), then we might begin to understand the market as one means of representing multicentered networks of social interaction. Just as the American monetary system went off the gold standard in 1934, it is now time to get off the traditional *rational man* standard (the straight, white, male, Christian, English-speaking, middle-class individualist) as the universal measure of humanity. It is time to initiate a *perestroika* of personhood—to make a world in which all of us, in our multiple, overlapping, individual and collective identities can come to terms.

12

Questions

1. According to the authors, why does the conservative right oppose speech codes?
2. How is power associated with a particular curriculum?
3. Do you believe that restriction on speech in the interest of political correctness will lead to repression of other civil liberties?
4. How would Fish respond to this article?

The Wrong Way to Reduce Campus Tensions

THE NATIONAL ASSOCIATION OF SCHOLARS

The members of the National Association of Scholars attack preferential hiring of minorities to the possible exclusion, in their view, of sometimes better-qualified candidates who may not be minorities. They declare that higher education must enable the student to deal with contrary or unpleasant ideas and that shielding them from such ideas is detrimental in the long run. This reading is from Beyond PC *(1992).*

The academic community is alarmed by reports of intergroup tension at many colleges, including those long committed to equal opportunity. Unfortunately, educators have failed to reassess some recent policies and practices that, far from promoting tolerance and fairness, are undermining them. Worse yet, many have seized upon incidents of conflict to call for the extension of these policies and practices. They include: 1

- A willingness to admit students widely disparate in their level of preparation in order to make the campus demographically representative
- Preferential hiring for faculty and staff positions determined by race, ethnicity, and gender
- Racially or ethnically exclusive financial aid and academic counseling programs, as well as special administrators, ombudsmen, and resource centers assigned to serve as the putative representatives of selected student groups
- Punitive codes restricting "insensitive" speech
- Mandatory "sensitivity training" for incoming freshmen and sometimes for all students, faculty, and staff
- Requirements that students take tendentious courses dealing with groups regarded as victimized
- A failure to enforce campus rules when violated by those promoting these policies or other "politically correct" causes.

The National Association of Scholars believes that these policies and practices   2
involve either the application of a double standard or the repudiation of appropriate

400

intellectual criteria. Consequently, they undercut the academy's special sense of common purpose and prompt, divisive calculations of group interest. Specifically, we believe what follows.

The admission of seriously underprepared students creates unrealistic ex- 3 pectations and frequently leads to frustration and resentment. Moreover, policies that target specific minority groups unfairly stigmatize all students in such groups, reinforcing negative stereotypes.

Two-track hiring threatens to produce a two-tiered faculty instead of a 4 genuinely integrated one. While such hiring may well create "role models," they will be the wrong kind, encouraging the belief that it is the assertion of group power instead of the pursuit of individual achievement that reaps the most abundant rewards.

Disadvantaged students deserve ample assistance, yet disadvantage need 5 not coincide with race or ethnicity. Those excluded are often frustrated by seeing individuals who may be no worse off than themselves receiving special treatment solely because of ancestry. Furthermore, bureaucracies created to serve or champion particular groups tend to have vested interests in empha- sizing differences, fostering complaints, and maintaining the separation of those groups.

Safeguarding intellectual freedom is of critical importance to the acad- 6 emy. Thus, it is deeply disturbing to see the concept of "discriminatory ha- rassment" stretched to cover the expression of unapproved thoughts about selected groups or criticism of policies assumed to benefit them. Higher edu- cation should prepare students to grapple with contrary or unpleasant ideas, not shield them from their content. What is more, if a highly permissive atti- tude toward the excoriation of the "privileged" accompanies the censorship of critical views about other groups, a backlash is predictable.

Tolerance is a core value of academic life, as is civility. College authorities 7 should ensure that these values prevail. But tolerance involves a willingness, not to suppress, but to allow divergent opinions. Thus, "sensitivity training" programs designed to cultivate "correct thought" about complicated norma- tive, social, and political issues do not teach tolerance but impose orthodoxy. And when these programs favor manipulative psychological techniques over honest discussion, they also undermine the intellectual purposes of higher education and anger those subjected to them.

If entire programs of study or required courses relentlessly pursue issues 8 of "race, gender, and class" in preference to all other approaches to assessing the human condition, one can expect the increasing division of the campus along similar lines.

The discriminatory enforcement of campus regulations can only sap the 9 legitimacy of academic authority and create a pervasive sense of mistrust. In- deed, should students feel that repeated violations not only go unpunished, but are actually appeased, the reckless may be tempted to take matters into their own hands. The final stage of discredit will be reached when students and faculty see in such appeasement attempts by administrators to justify their own programs of campus "reform."

The policies just described are generally well-intentioned. Nonetheless, if the   10
goal were deliberately to aggravate campus tensions, the same policies might well
be adopted. On the premise that the fair treatment of individuals can do as much to
correct the current situation as the doctrine of collective guilt has done to create it,
the National Association of Scholars urges the following:

- Admitting inadequately prepared students only when realistic provision can be made for remediation
- Maintaining nondiscriminatory hiring policies
- Eliminating all forms of institutional segregation and preferential treatment determined by race and ethnicity, together with administrative positions that foster ethnic dissension
- Protecting the expression of diverse opinion
- Avoiding programs that attempt to impose "politically correct" thinking
- Adding or retaining ethnic or gender studies courses only when they have genuine scholarly content and are not vehicles for political harangue or recruitment
- Enforcing campus rules, even with respect to those who feel they are violating them in a good cause.

The National Association of Scholars believes that the surest way to achieve ed-   11
ucational opportunity for all and maintain a genuine sense of academic community
is to evaluate each individual on the basis of personal achievement and promise. It
is only as individuals united in the pursuit of knowledge that we can realize the
ideal of a common intellectual life.

Questions

1. How do policies intended to promote tolerance instead heighten racial tensions?
2. Would Fish agree with the stance of the National Association of Scholars?

Literacy and Cultural Literacy

E. D. HIRSCH, JR.

E. D. Hirsch, Jr., was educated at Cornell and Yale universities. He has taught at Williams College, Yale, and since 1966 at the University of Virginia, where he is now Kenan Professor of English. He has been a Guggenheim Fellow and an advisor to the National Council on Education Research.

His position in this piece is that to be truly successful and democratic a society must ensure that its members are culturally literate. Such literacy extends beyond reading and writing into a proficiency with a wide base of knowledge about themselves and the world they live in. People who do not have cultural literacy in the present society are, according to Hirsch, "disenfranchised." Traditional bases of knowledge and a traditional curriculum do not mean conservative indoctrination. Hirsch's plea is for universal literacy to liberate all strata of society and enable this country, by knowing its own culture intimately and then generalizing knowledge to other nations, to deal comfortably with the world culture. This reading is from Cultural Literacy *(1987).*

The Decline of Literate Knowledge

This book explains why we need to make some very specific educational 1 changes in order to achieve a higher level of national literacy. It does not anatomize the literacy crisis or devote many pages to Scholastic Aptitude Test scores. It does not document at length what has already been established, that Americans do not read as well as they should. It takes no position about methods of initial reading instruction beyond insisting that content must receive as much emphasis as "skill." It does not discuss teacher training or educational funding or school governance. In fact, one of its major purposes is to break away entirely from what Jeanne S. Chall has called "the great debate" about methods of reading instruction. It focuses on what I conceive to be the great hidden problem in American education, and I hope that it reveals this problem so compellingly that anyone who is concerned about American education will be persuaded by the book's argument and act upon it.

The standard of literacy required by modern society has been rising 2 throughout the developed world, but American literacy rates have not risen to meet this standard. What seemed an acceptable level in the 1950s is no longer acceptable in the late 1980s, when only highly literate societies can prosper economically. Much of Japan's industrial efficiency has been credited to its almost universally high level of literacy. But in the United States, only two thirds of our citizens are literate, and even among those the average level is too low and should be raised. The remaining third of our citizens need to be brought as close to true literacy as possible. Ultimately our aim should be to attain universal literacy at a very high level, to achieve not only greater economic prosperity but also greater social justice and more effective democracy. We Americans have long accepted literacy as a paramount aim of schooling, but only recently have some of us who have done research in the field begun to realize that literacy is far more than a skill and that it requires large amounts of specific information. That new insight is central to this book.

Professor Chall is one of several reading specialists who have observed   3
that "world knowledge" is essential to the development of reading and writing skills.[1] What she calls world knowledge I call cultural literacy, namely, the network of information that all competent readers possess. It is the background information, stored in their minds, that enables them to take up a newspaper and read it with an adequate level of comprehension, getting the point, grasping the implications, relating what they read to the unstated context which alone gives meaning to what they read. In describing the contents of this neglected domain of background information, I try to direct attention to a new opening that can help our schools make the significant improvement in education that has so far eluded us. The achievement of high universal literacy is the key to all other fundamental improvements in American education.

Why is literacy so important in the modern world? Some of the reasons,   4
like the need to fill out forms or get a good job, are so obvious that they needn't be discussed. But the chief reason is broader. The complex undertakings of modern life depend on the cooperation of many people with different specialties in different places. Where communications fail, so do the undertakings. (That is the moral of the story of the Tower of Babel.) The function of national literacy is to foster effective nationwide communications. Our chief instrument of communication over time and space is the standard national language, which is sustained by national literacy. Mature literacy alone enables the tower to be built, the business to be well managed, and the airplane to fly without crashing. All nationwide communications, whether by telephone, radio, TV, or writing are fundamentally dependent upon literacy, for the essence of literacy is not simply reading and writing but also the effective use of the standard literate language. In Spain and most of Latin America the literate language is standard written Spanish. In Japan it is standard written Japanese. In our country it is standard written English.

Linguists have used the term "standard written English" to describe both   5
our written and spoken language, because they want to remind us that standard spoken English is based upon forms that have been fixed in dictionaries and grammars and are adhered to in books, magazines, and newspapers. Although standard written English has no intrinsic superiority to other lan-

guages and dialects, its stable written forms have now standardized the oral forms of the language spoken by educated Americans.[2] The chief function of literacy is to make us masters of this standard instrument of knowledge and communication, thereby enabling us to give and receive complex information orally and in writing over time and space. Advancing technology, with its constant need for fast and complex communications, has made literacy ever more essential to commerce and domestic life. The literate language is more, not less, central in our society now than it was in the days before television and the silicon chip.

The recently rediscovered insight that literacy is more than a skill is based   6
upon knowledge that all of us unconsciously have about language. We know instinctively that to understand what somebody is saying, we must understand more than the surface meanings of words; we have to understand the context as well. The need for background information applies all the more to reading and writing. To grasp the words on a page we have to know a lot of information that isn't set down on the page.

Consider the implications of the following experiment described in an ar-   7
ticle in *Scientific American*.[3] A researcher goes to Harvard Square in Cambridge, Massachusetts, with a tape recorder hidden in his coat pocket. Putting a copy of the *Boston Globe* under his arm, he pretends to be a native. He says to passers-by, "How do you get to Central Square?" The passers-by, thinking they are addressing a fellow Bostonian, don't even break their stride when they give their replies, which consist of a few words like "First stop on the subway."

The next day the researcher goes to the same spot, but this time he pre-   8
sents himself as a tourist, obviously unfamiliar with the city. "I'm from out of town," he says. "Can you tell me how to get to Central Square?" This time the tapes show that people's answers are much longer and more rudimentary. A typical one goes, "Yes, well you go down on the subway. You can see the entrance over there, and when you get downstairs you buy a token, put it in the slot, and you go over to the side that says Quincy. You take the train headed for Quincy, but you get off very soon, just the first stop is Central Square, and be sure you get off there. You'll know it because there's a big sign on the wall. It says Central Square." And so on.

Passers-by were intuitively aware that communication between strangers   9
requires an estimate of how much relevant information can be taken for granted in the other person. If they can take a lot for granted, their communications can be short and efficient, subtle and complex. But if strangers share very little knowledge, their communications must be long and relatively rudimentary.

In order to put in perspective the importance of background knowledge   10
in language, I want to connect the lack of it with our recent lack of success in teaching mature literacy to all students. The most broadly based evidence about our teaching of literacy comes from the National Assessment of Educational Progress (NAEP). This nationwide measurement, mandated by Congress, shows that between 1970 and 1980 seventeen-year-olds declined in

their ability to understand written materials, and the decline was especially striking in the top group, those able to read at an "advanced" level.[4] Although these scores have now begun to rise, they remain alarmingly low. Still more precise quantitative data have come from the scores of the verbal Scholastic Aptitude Test (SAT). According to John B. Carroll, a distinguished psychometrician, the verbal SAT is essentially a test of "advanced vocabulary knowledge," which makes it a fairly sensitive instrument for measuring levels of literacy.[5] It is well known that verbal SAT scores have declined dramatically in the past fifteen years, and though recent reports have shown them rising again, it is from a very low base. Moreover, performance on the verbal SAT has been slipping steadily *at the top*. Ever fewer numbers of our best and brightest students are making high scores on the test.

Before the College Board disclosed the full statistics in 1984, antialarmists   11
could argue that the fall in average verbal scores could be explained by the rise in the number of disadvantaged students taking the SATs. That argument can no longer be made. It's now clear that not only our disadvantaged but also our best educated and most talented young people are showing diminished verbal skills. To be precise, out of a constant pool of about a million test takers each year, 56 percent more students scored above 600 in 1972 than did so in 1984. More startling yet, the percentage drop was even greater for those scoring above 650—73 percent.[6]

In the mid-1980s American business leaders have become alarmed by the   12
lack of communication skills in the young people they employ. Recently, top executives of some large U.S. companies, including CBS and Exxon, met to discuss the fact that their younger middle-level executives could no longer communicate their ideas effectively in speech or writing. This group of companies has made a grant to the American Academy of Arts and Sciences to analyze the causes of this growing problem. They want to know why, despite breathtaking advances in the technology of communication, the effectiveness of business communication has been slipping, to the detriment of our competitiveness in the world. The figures from NAEP surveys and the scores on the verbal SAT are solid evidence that literacy has been declining in this country just when our need for effective literacy has been sharply rising.

I now want to juxtapose some evidence for another kind of educational   13
decline, one that is related to the drop in literacy. During the period 1970–1985, the amount of shared knowledge that we have been able to take for granted in communicating with our fellow citizens has also been declining. More and more of our young people don't know things we used to assume they knew.

A side effect of the diminution in shared information has been a notice-   14
able increase in the number of articles in such publications as *Newsweek* and the *Wall Street Journal* about the surprising ignorance of the young. My son John, who recently taught Latin in high school and eighth grade, often told me of experiences which indicate that these articles are not exaggerated. In one of his classes he mentioned to his students that Latin, the language they were studying, is a dead language that is no longer spoken. After his pupils

had struggled for several weeks with Latin grammar and vocabulary, this news was hard for some of them to accept. One girl raised her hand to challenge my son's claim. "What do they speak in Latin America?" she demanded.

At least she had heard of Latin America. Another day my son asked his 15 Latin class if they knew the name of an epic poem by Homer. One pupil shot up his hand and eagerly said, "The Alamo!" Was it just a slip for *The Iliad?* No, he didn't know what the Alamo was, either. To judge from other stories about information gaps in the young, many American schoolchildren are less well informed than this pupil. The following, by Benjamin J. Stein, is an excerpt from one of the most evocative recent accounts of youthful ignorance.

> I spend a lot of time with teen agers. Besides employing three of them part-time, I frequently conduct focus groups at Los Angeles area high schools to learn about teen agers' attitudes towards movies or television shows or nuclear arms or politicians. . . .
>
> I have not yet found one single student in Los Angeles, in either college or high school, who could tell me the years when World War II was fought. Nor have I found one who could tell me the years when World War I was fought. Nor have I found one who knew when the American Civil War was fought. . . .
>
> A few have known how many U.S. senators California has, but none has known how many Nevada or Oregon has. ("Really? Even though they're so small?") . . . Only two could tell me where Chicago is, even in the vaguest terms. (My particular favorite geography lesson was the junior at the University of California at Los Angeles who thought that Toronto must be in Italy. My second-favorite geography lesson is the junior at USC, a pre-law student, who thought that Washington, D.C. was in Washington State.) . . .
>
> Only two could even approximately identify Thomas Jefferson. Only one could place the date of the Declaration of Independence. None could name even one of the first ten amendments to the Constitution or connect them with the Bill of Rights. . . .
>
> On and on it went. On and on it goes. I have mixed up episodes of ignorance of facts with ignorance of concepts because it seems to me that there is a connection. . . . The kids I saw (and there may be lots of others who are different) are not mentally prepared to continue the society because they basically do not understand the society well enough to value it.[7]

My son assures me that his pupils are not ignorant. They know a great 16 deal. Like every other human group they share a tremendous amount of knowledge among themselves, much of it learned in school. The trouble is that, from the standpoint of their literacy and their ability to communicate with others in our culture, what they know is ephemeral and narrowly confined to their own generation. Many young people strikingly lack the information that writers of American books and newspapers have traditionally taken for granted among their readers from all generations. For reasons explained in this book, our children's lack of intergenerational information is a serious problem for the nation. The decline of literacy and the decline of shared knowledge are closely related, interdependent facts.

The evidence for the decline of shared knowledge is not just anecdotal. In 1978 NAEP issued a report which analyzed a large quantity of data showing that our children's knowledge of American civics had dropped significantly between 1969 and 1976.[8] The performance of thirteen-year-olds had dropped an alarming 11 percentage points. That the drop has continued since 1976 was confirmed by preliminary results from a NAEP study conducted in late 1985. It was undertaken both because of concern about declining knowledge and because of the growing evidence of a causal connection between the drop in shared information and in literacy. The Foundations of Literacy project is measuring some of the specific information about history and literature that American seventeen-year-olds possess.   17

Although the full report will not be published until 1987, the preliminary field tests are disturbing.[9] If these samplings hold up, and there is no reason to think they will not, then the results we will be reading in 1987 will show that two thirds of our seventeen-year-olds do not know that the Civil War occurred between 1850 and 1900. Three quarters do not know what *reconstruction* means. Half do not know the meaning of *Brown decision* and cannot identify either Stalin or Churchill. Three quarters are unfamiliar with the names of standard American and British authors. Moreover, our seventeen-year-olds have little sense of geography or the relative chronology of major events. Reports of youthful ignorance can no longer be considered merely impressionistic.[10]   18

My encounter in the seventies with this widening knowledge gap first caused me to recognize the connection between specific background knowledge and mature literacy. The research I was doing on the reading and writing abilities of college students made me realize two things.[11] First, we cannot assume that young people today know things that were known in the past by almost every literate person in the culture. For instance, in one experiment conducted in Richmond, Virginia, our seventeen- and eighteen-year-old subjects did not know who Grant and Lee were. Second, our results caused me to realize that we cannot treat reading and writing as empty skills, independent of specific knowledge. The reading skill of a person may vary greatly from task to task. The level of literacy exhibited in each task depends on the relevant background information that the person possesses.   19

* * *

The lack of wide-ranging background information among young men and women now in their twenties and thirties is an important cause of the illiteracy that large corporations are finding in their middle-level executives. In former days, when business people wrote and spoke to one another, they could be confident that they and their colleagues had studied many similar things in school. They could talk to one another with an efficiency similar to that of native Bostonians who speak to each other in the streets of Cambridge. But today's high school graduates do not reliably share much common information, even when they graduate from the same school. If young people meet as strangers, their communications resemble the uncertain, rudimentary explanations recorded in the second part of the Cambridge experiment.   20

My father used to write business letters that alluded to Shakespeare. These   21
allusions were effective for conveying complex messages to his associates, because, in his day, business people could make such allusions with every expectation of being understood. For instance, in my father's commodity
business, the timing of sales and purchases was all-important, and he would
sometimes write or say to his colleagues, "There is a tide," without further
elaboration. Those four words carried not only a lot of complex information,
but also the persuasive force of a proverb. In addition to the basic practical
meaning, "Act now!" what came across was a lot of implicit reasons why immediate action was important.

For some of my younger readers who may not recognize the allusion, the   22
passage from *Julius Caesar* is:

> There is a tide in the affairs of men
> Which taken at the flood leads on to fortune;
> Omitted, all the voyage of their life
> Is bound in shallows and in miseries.
> On such a full sea are we now afloat,
> And we must take the current when it serves,
> Or lose our ventures.

To say "There is a tide" is better than saying "Buy (or sell) now and you'll
cover expenses for the whole year, but if you fail to act right away, you may
regret it the rest of your life." That would be twenty-seven words instead of
four, and while the bare message of the longer statement would be conveyed,
the persuasive force wouldn't. Think of the demands of such a business communication. To persuade somebody that your recommendation is wise and
well-founded, you have to give lots of reasons and cite known examples and
authorities. My father accomplished that and more in four words, which
made quoting Shakespeare as effective as any efficiency consultant could
wish. The moral of this tale is not that reading Shakespeare will help one rise
in the business world. My point is a broader one. The fact that middle-level
executives no longer share literate background knowledge is a chief cause of
their inability to communicate effectively.

The Nature and Use of Cultural Literacy

The documented decline in shared knowledge carries implications that go far   23
beyond the shortcomings of executives and extend to larger questions of educational policy and social justice in our country. Mina Shaughnessy was a
great English teacher who devoted her professional life to helping disadvantaged students become literate. At the 1980 conference dedicated to her
memory, one of the speakers who followed me to the podium was the Harvard historian and sociologist Orlando Patterson. To my delight he departed
from his prepared talk to mention mine. He seconded my argument that
shared information is a necessary background to true literacy. Then he ex-

tended and deepened the ideas I had presented. Here is what Professor Patterson said, as recorded in the *Proceedings* of the conference.

> Industrialized civilization [imposes] a growing cultural and structural complexity which requires persons to have a broad grasp of what Professor Hirsch has called cultural literacy: a deep understanding of mainstream culture, which no longer has much to do with white Anglo-Saxon Protestants, but with the imperatives of industrial civilization. It is the need for cultural literacy, a profound conception of the whole civilization, which is often neglected in talk about literacy.

Patterson continued by drawing a connection between background information and the ability to hold positions of responsibility and power. He was particularly concerned with the importance for blacks and other minorities of possessing this information, which is essential for improving their social and economic status.

> The people who run society at the macro-level must be literate in this culture. For this reason, it is dangerous to overemphasize the problems of basic literacy or the relevancy of literacy to specific tasks, and more constructive to emphasize that blacks will be condemned in perpetuity to oversimplified, low-level tasks and will never gain their rightful place in controlling the levers of power unless they also acquire literacy in this wider cultural sense.

Although Patterson focused his remarks on the importance of cultural literacy for minorities, his observations hold for every culturally illiterate person in our nation. Indeed, as he observed, cultural literacy is not the property of any group or class.

> To assume that this wider culture is static is an error; in fact it is not. It's not a WASP culture; it doesn't belong to any group. It is essentially and constantly changing, and it is open. What is needed is recognition that the accurate metaphor or model for this wider literacy is not domination, but dialectic; each group participates and contributes, transforms and is transformed, as much as any other group. . . . The English language no longer belongs to any single group or nation. The same goes for any other area of the wider culture.[12]

As Professor Patterson suggested, being taught to decode elementary reading materials and specific, job-related texts cannot constitute true literacy. Such basic training does not make a person literate with respect to newspapers or other writings addressed to a general public. Moreover, a directly practical drawback of such narrow training is that it does not prepare anyone for technological change. Narrow vocational training in one state of a technology will not enable a person to read manuals that explain new developments in the same technology. In modern life we need general knowledge that enables us to deal with new ideas, events, and challenges. In today's world, general cultural literacy is more useful than what Professor Patterson terms

24

"literacy to a specific task," because general literate information is the basis for many changing tasks.

Cultural literacy is even more important in the social sphere. The aim of universal literacy has never been a socially neutral mission in our country. Our traditional social goals were unforgettably renewed for us by Martin Luther King, Jr., in his "I Have a Dream" speech. King envisioned a country where the children of former slaves sit down at the table of equality with the children of former slave owners, where men and women deal with each other as equals and judge each other on their characters and achievements rather than their origins. Like Thomas Jefferson, he had a dream of a society founded not on race or class but on personal merit.

In the present day, that dream depends on mature literacy. No modern society can hope to become a just society without a high level of universal literacy. Putting aside for the moment the practical arguments about the economic uses of literacy, we can contemplate the even more basic principle that underlies our national system of education in the first place—that people in a democracy can be entrusted to decide all important matters for themselves because they can deliberate and communicate with one another. Universal literacy is inseparable from democracy and is the canvas for Martin Luther King's picture as well as for Thomas Jefferson's.

Both of these leaders understood that just having the right to vote is meaningless if a citizen is disenfranchised by illiteracy or semiliteracy. Illiterate and semiliterate Americans are condemned not only to poverty, but also to the powerlessness of incomprehension. Knowing that they do not understand the issues, and feeling prey to manipulative oversimplifications, they do not trust the system of which they are supposed to be the masters. They do not feel themselves to be active participants in our republic, and they often do not turn out to vote. The civic importance of cultural literacy lies in the fact that true enfranchisement depends upon knowledge, knowledge upon literacy, and literacy upon cultural literacy.

To be truly literate, citizens must be able to grasp the meaning of any piece of writing addressed to the general reader. All citizens should be able, for instance, to read newspapers of substance, about which Jefferson made the following famous remark:

> Were it left to me to decide whether we should have a government without newspapers, or newspapers without a government, I should not hesitate a moment to prefer the latter. But I should mean that every man should receive those papers and be capable of reading them.[13]

Jefferson's last comment is often omitted when the passage is quoted, but it's the crucial one.

Books and newspapers assume a "common reader," that is, a person who knows the things known by other literate persons in the culture. Obviously, such assumptions are never identical from writer to writer, but they show a remarkable consistency. Those who write for a mass public are always making judgments about what their readers can be assumed to know, and the judgments are closely similar. Any reader who doesn't possess the knowledge assumed in a piece he or she reads will in fact be illiterate with respect to that particular piece of writing.

Here, for instance, is a rather typical excerpt from the *Washington Post* of   30
December 29, 1983.

> A federal appeals panel today upheld an order barring foreclosure on a Missouri farm, saying that U.S. Agriculture Secretary John R. Block has reneged on his responsibilities to some debt ridden farmers. The appeals panel directed the USDA to create a system of processing loan deferments and of publicizing them as it said Congress had intended. The panel said that it is the responsibility of the agriculture secretary to carry out this intent "not as a private banker, but as a public broker."

Imagine that item being read by people who are well trained in phonics,   31
word recognition, and other decoding skills but are culturally illiterate. They might know words like *foreclosure,* but they would not understand what the piece means. Who gave the order that the federal panel upheld? What is a federal appeals panel? Where is Missouri, and what about Missouri is relevant to the issue? Why are many farmers debt ridden? What is the USDA? What is a public broker? Even if culturally illiterate readers bothered to look up individual words, they would have little idea of the reality being referred to. The explicit words are just surface pointers to textual meaning in reading and writing. The comprehending reader must bring to the text appropriate background information that includes knowledge not only about the topic but also the shared attitudes and conventions that color a piece of writing.

Our children can learn this information only by being taught it. Shared   32
literate information is deliberately sustained by national systems of education in many countries because they recognize the importance of giving their children a common basis for communication. Some decades ago a charming book called *1066 and All That* appeared in Britain.[14] It dealt with facts of British history that all educated Britons had been taught as children but remembered only dimly as adults. The book caricatured those recollections, purposely getting the "facts" just wrong enough to make them ridiculous on their face. Readers instantly recognized that the book was mistaken in its theory about what Ethelred-the-Unready was unready for, but, on the other hand, they couldn't say precisely what he *was* unready for. The book was hilarious to literate Britons as a satire of their own vague and confused memories. But even if their schoolchild knowledge had become vague with the passage of time, it was still functional, because the information essential to literacy is rarely detailed or precise.

This haziness is a key characteristic of literacy and cultural literacy. To understand the *Washington Post* extract literate readers have to know only   33
vaguely, in the backs of their minds, that the American legal system permits a court decision to be reversed by a higher court. They would need to know

only that a judge is empowered to tell the executive branch what it can or cannot do to farmers and other citizens. (The secretary of agriculture was barred from foreclosing a Missouri farm.) Readers would need to know only vaguely what and where Missouri is, and how the department and the secretary of agriculture fit into the scheme of things. None of this knowledge would have to be precise. Readers wouldn't have to know whether an appeals panel is the final judicial level before the U.S. Supreme Court. Any practiced writer who feels it is important for a reader to know such details always provides them.

Much in verbal communication is necessarily vague, whether we are conversing or reading. What counts is our ability to grasp the general shape of what we are reading and to tie it to what we already know. If we need details, we rely on the writer or speaker to develop them. Or if we intend to ponder matters in detail for ourselves, we do so later, at our leisure. For instance, it is probably true that many people do not know what a beanball is in baseball. So in an article on the subject the author conveniently sets forth as much as the culturally literate reader must know.   34

> Described variously as the knockdown pitch, the beanball, the duster and the purpose pitch—the Pentagon would call it the peacekeeper—this delightful stratagem has graced the scene for most of the 109 years the major leagues have existed. It starts fights. It creates lingering grudges. It sends people to the hospital. . . . "You put my guy in the dirt, I put your guy in the dirt."[15]

To understand this text, we don't have to know much about the particular topic in advance, but we do require quite a lot of vague knowledge about baseball to give us a sense of the whole meaning, whether our knowledge happens to be vague or precise.

The superficiality of the knowledge we need for reading and writing may be unwelcome news to those who deplore superficial learning and praise critical thinking over mere information. But one of the sharpest critical thinkers of our day, Dr. Hilary Putnam, a Harvard philosopher, has provided us with a profound insight into the importance of vague knowledge in verbal communication.[16]   35

> Suppose you are like me and cannot tell an elm from a beech tree. . . . [I can nonetheless use the word "elm" because] *there is a division of linguistic labor. . . .* It is not at all necessary or efficient that everyone who wears a gold ring (or a gold cufflink, etc.) be able to tell with any reliability whether or not something is really gold. . . . Everyone to whom the word "gold" is important for any reason has to *acquire* the word "gold"; but he does not have to acquire the *method of recognizing* if something is or is not gold.

Putnam does acknowledge a limit on the degrees of ignorance and vagueness that are acceptable in discourse. "Significant communication," he observes, "requires that people know something of what they are talking about." Nonetheless, what is required for communication is often so vague   36 and superficial that we can properly understand and use the word *elm* without being able to distinguish an elm tree from a beech tree. What we need to know in order to use and understand a word is an initial stereotype that has a few vague traits.

> Speakers are *required* to know something about (stereotypic) tigers in order to count as having acquired the word "tiger"; something about elm trees (or anyway about the stereotype thereof) to count as having acquired the word "elm," etc. . . . The nature of the required minimum level of competence depends heavily upon both the culture and the topic, however. In our culture speakers are not . . . required to know the fine details (such as leaf shape) of what an elm tree looks like. English speakers are *required by their linguistic community* to be able to tell tigers from leopards; they are not required to be able to tell beech trees from elm trees.

When Putnam says that Americans can be depended on to distinguish   37
tigers and leopards but not elms and beeches, he assumes that his readers will agree with him because they are culturally literate. He takes for granted that one literate person knows approximately the same things as another and is aware of the probable limits of the other person's knowledge. That second level of awareness—knowing what others probably know—is crucial for effective communication. In order to speak effectively to people we must have a reliable sense of what they do and do not know. For instance, if Putnam is right in his example, we should not have to tell a stranger that a leopard has spots or a tiger stripes, but we would have to explain that an elm has rough bark and a beech smooth bark if we wanted that particular piece of information conveyed. To know what educated people know about tigers but don't know about elm trees is the sort of cultural knowledge, limited in extent but possessed by all literate people, that must be brought into the open and taught to our children.

Besides being limited in extent, cultural literacy has another trait that is   38
important for educational policy—its national character. It's true that literate English is an international language, but only so long as the topics it deals with are international. The background knowledge of people from other English-speaking nations is often inadequate for complex and subtle communications within our nation. The knowledge required for national literacy differs from country to country, even when their national language is the same. It is no doubt true that one layer of cultural literacy is the same for all English-speaking nations. Australians, South Africans, Britons, and Americans share a lot of knowledge by virtue of their common language. But much of the knowledge required for literacy in, say, Australia is specific to that country, just as much of ours is specific to the United States.

For instance, a literate Australian can typically understand American   39
newspaper articles on international events or the weather but not one on a federal appeals panel. The same holds true for Americans who read Australian newspapers. Many of us have heard "Waltzing Matilda," a song known to

every Australian, but few Americans understand or need to understand what the words mean.

> Once a jolly swagman camped by a billy-bong,
> Under the shade of a kulibar tree,
> And he sang as he sat and waited for his billy-boil,
> "You'll come a-waltzing, Matilda, with me."

Waltzing Matilda doesn't mean dancing with a girl; it means walking with a kind of knapsack. A *swagman* is a hobo, a *billy-bong* is a brook or pond, a *kulibar* is a eucalyptus, and *billy-boil* is coffee.

The national character of the knowledge needed in reading and writing was   40
strikingly revealed in an experiment conducted by Richard C. Anderson and others at the Center for the Study of Reading at the University of Illinois. They assembled two paired groups of readers, all highly similar in sexual balance, educational background, age, and social class.[17] The only difference between the groups was that one was in India, the other in the United States. Both were given the same two letters to read. The texts were similar in overall length, word-frequency distribution, sentence length and complexity, and number of explicit propositions. Both letters were on the same topic, a wedding, but one described an Indian wedding, the other an American wedding. The reading performances of the two groups—their speed and accuracy of comprehension—split along national lines. The Indians performed well in reading about the Indian wedding but poorly in reading about the American one, and the Americans did the opposite. This experiment not only reconfirmed the dependence of reading skill on cultural literacy, it also demonstrated its national character.

Although nationalism may be regrettable in some of its worldwide politi-   41
cal effects, a mastery of national culture is essential to mastery of the standard language in every modern nation. This point is important for educational policy, because educators often stress the virtues of multicultural education. Such study is indeed valuable in itself; it inculcates tolerance and provides a perspective on our own traditions and values. But however laudable it is, it should not be the primary focus of national education. It should not be allowed to supplant or interfere with our schools' responsibility to ensure our children's mastery of American literate culture. The acculturative responsibility of the schools is primary and fundamental. To teach the ways of one's own community has always been and still remains the essence of the education of our children, who enter neither a narrow tribal culture nor a transcendent world culture but a national literate culture. For profound historical reasons, this is the way of the modern world.[18] It will not change soon, and it will certainly not be changed by educational policy alone.

The Decline of Teaching Cultural Literacy

Why have our schools failed to fulfill their fundamental acculturative respon-   42
sibility? In view of the immense importance of cultural literacy for speaking,

listening, reading, and writing, why has the need for a definite, shared body of information been so rarely mentioned in discussions of education? In the educational writings of the past decade, I find almost nothing on this topic, which is not arcane. People who are introduced to the subject quickly understand why oral or written communication requires a lot of shared background knowledge. It's not the difficulty or novelty of the idea that has caused it to receive so little attention.

Let me hazard a guess about one reason for our neglect of the subject. We have ignored cultural literacy in thinking about education—certainly I as a researcher also ignored it until recently—precisely because it was something we have been able to take for granted. We ignore the air we breathe until it is thin or foul. Cultural literacy is the oxygen of social intercourse. Only when we run into cultural illiteracy are we shocked into recognizing the importance of the information that we had unconsciously assumed. 43

To be sure, a minimal level of information is possessed by any normal person who lives in the United States and speaks elementary English. Almost everybody knows what is meant by *dollar* and that cars must travel on the right-hand side of the road. But this elementary level of information is not sufficient for a modern democracy. It isn't sufficient to read newspapers (a sin against Jeffersonian democracy), and it isn't sufficient to achieve economic fairness and high productivity. Cultural literacy lies *above* the everyday levels of knowledge that everyone possesses and *below* the expert level known only to specialists. It is that middle ground of cultural knowledge possessed by the "common reader." It includes information that we have traditionally expected our children to receive in school, but which they no longer do. 44

During recent decades Americans have hesitated to make a decision about the specific knowledge that children need to learn in school. Our elementary schools are not only dominated by the content-neutral ideas of Rousseau and Dewey, they are also governed by approximately sixteen thousand independent school districts. We have viewed this dispersion of educational authority as an insurmountable obstacle to altering the fragmentation of the school curriculum even when we have questioned that fragmentation. We have permitted school policies that have shrunk the body of information that Americans share, and these policies have caused our national literacy to decline. 45

At the same time we have searched with some eagerness for causes such as television that lie outside the schools. But we should direct our attention undeviatingly toward what the schools teach rather than toward family structure, social class, or TV programming. No doubt, reforms outside the schools are important, but they are harder to accomplish. Moreover, we have accumulated a great deal of evidence that faulty policy in the schools is the chief cause of deficient literacy. Researchers who have studied the factors influencing educational outcomes have found that the school curriculum is the most important controllable influence on what our children know and don't know about our literate culture.[19] 46

It will not do to blame television for the state of our literacy. Television watching does reduce reading and often encroaches on homework. Much of 47 it is admittedly the intellectual equivalent of junk food. But in some respects, such as its use of standard written English, television watching is acculturative.[20] Moreover, as Herbert Walberg points out, the schools themselves must be held partly responsible for excessive television watching, because they have not firmly insisted that students complete significant amounts of homework, an obvious way to increase time spent on reading and writing.[21] Nor should our schools be excused by an appeal to the effects of the decline of the family or the vicious circle of poverty, important as these factors are. Schools have, or should have, children for six or seven hours a day, five days a week, nine months a year, for thirteen years or more. To assert that they are powerless to make a significant impact on what their students learn would be to make a claim about American education that few parents, teachers, or students would find it easy to accept.

Just how fragmented the American public school curriculum has become 48 is described in *The Shopping Mall High School,* a report on five years of first-hand study inside public and private secondary schools. The authors report that our high schools offer courses of so many kinds that "the word 'curriculum' does not do justice to this astonishing variety." The offerings include not only academic courses of great diversity, but also courses in sports and hobbies and a "services curriculum" addressing emotional or social problems. All these courses are deemed "educationally valid" and carry course credit. Moreover, among academic offerings are numerous versions of each subject, corresponding to different levels of student interest and ability. Needless to say, the material covered in these "content area" courses is highly varied.[22]

Cafeteria-style education, combined with the unwillingness of our 49 schools to place demands on students, has resulted in a steady diminishment of commonly shared information between generations and between young people themselves. Those who graduate from the same school have often studied different subjects, and those who graduate from different schools have often studied different material even when their courses have carried the same titles. The inevitable consequence of the shopping mall high school is a lack of shared knowledge across and within schools. It would be hard to invent a more effective recipe for cultural fragmentation.

The formalistic educational theory behind the shopping mall school (the 50 theory that any suitable content will inculcate reading, writing, and thinking skills) has had certain political advantages for school administrators. It has allowed them to stay scrupulously neutral with regard to content.[23] Educational formalism enables them to regard the indiscriminate variety of school offerings as a positive virtue, on the grounds that such variety can accommodate the different interests and abilities of different students. Educational formalism has also conveniently allowed school administrators to meet objections to the traditional literate materials that used to be taught in the schools. Objectors have said that traditional materials are class-bound, white, Anglo-Saxon, and Protestant, not to mention racist, sexist, and excessively Western. Our schools have tried to offer enough diversity to meet these objections from liberals and enough Shakespeare to satisfy conservatives. Caught between ideological parties, the schools have been attracted irresistibly to a quantitative and formal approach to curriculum making rather than one based on sound judgments about what should be taught.

Some have objected that teaching the traditional literate culture means   51
teaching conservative material. Orlando Patterson answered that objection when he pointed out that mainstream culture is not the province of any single social group and is constantly changing by assimilating new elements and expelling old ones.[24] Although mainstream culture is tied to the written word and may therefore seem more formal and elitist than other elements of culture, that is an illusion. Literate culture is the most democratic culture in our land: it excludes nobody; it cuts across generations and social groups and classes; it is not usually one's first culture, but it should be everyone's second, existing as it does beyond the narrow spheres of family, neighborhood, and region.

As the universal second culture, literate culture has become the common   52
currency for social and economic exchange in our democracy, and the only available ticket to full citizenship. Getting one's membership card is not tied to class or race. Membership is automatic if one learns the background information and the linguistic conventions that are needed to read, write, and speak effectively. Although everyone is literate in some local, regional, or ethnic culture, the connection between mainstream culture and the national written language justifies calling mainstream culture *the* basic culture of the nation.

The claim that universal cultural literacy would have the effect of pre-   53
serving the political and social status quo is paradoxical because in fact the traditional forms of literate culture are precisely the most effective instruments for political and social change. All political discourse at the national level must use the stable forms of the national language and its associated culture. Take the example of *The Black Panther,* a radical and revolutionary newspaper if ever this country had one. Yet the *Panther* was highly conservative in its language and cultural assumptions, as it had to be in order to communicate effectively. What could be more radical in sentiment but more conservative in language and assumed knowledge than the following passages from that paper?

> The present period reveals the criminal growth of bourgeois democracy since the betrayal of those who died that this nation might live "free and indivisible." It exposes through the trial of the Chicago Seven, and its law and order edicts, its desperate turn toward the establishment of a police state. (January 17, 1970)

> In this land of "milk and honey," the "almighty dollar" rules supreme and is being upheld by the faithful troops who move without question in the name of "law and order." Only in this garden of hypocrisy and inequality can a murderer not be considered a murderer—only here can innocent people be charged with a crime and be taken to court with the confessed criminal testifying against them. Incredible? (March 28, 1970)

In the United States, the world's most technologically advanced country, one million youths from 12 to 17 years of age are illiterate—unable to read as well as the average fourth grader, says a new government report. Why so much illiteracy in a land of so much knowledge? The answer is because there is racism. Blacks and other Nonwhites receive the worst education. (May 18, 1974)

The last item of the Black Panther Party platform, issued March 29, 1972, begins

10. WE WANT LAND, BREAD, HOUSING, EDUCATION, CLOTHING, JUSTICE, PEACE AND PEOPLE'S CONTROL OF MODERN TECHNOLOGY.

When in the course of human events it becomes necessary for one people to dissolve the political bands which have connected them with another, and to assume among the powers of the earth the separate and equal station to which the laws of nature and nature's God entitle them, a decent respect to the opinions of mankind requires that they should declare the causes which impel them to the separation.

And so on for the first five hundred of Jefferson's words without the least hint, or need of one, that this is a verbatim repetition of an earlier revolutionary declaration. The writers for *The Black Panther* had clearly received a rigorous traditional education in American history, in the Declaration of Independence, the Pledge of Allegiance to the Flag, the Gettysburg Address, and the Bible, to mention only some of the direct quotations and allusions in these passages. They also received rigorous traditional instruction in reading, writing, and spelling. I have not found a single misspelled word in the many pages of radical sentiment I have examined in that newspaper. Radicalism in politics, but conservatism in literate knowledge and spelling: to be a conservative in the *means* of communication is the road to effectiveness in modern life, in whatever direction one wishes to be effective.

To withhold traditional culture from the school curriculum, and therefore   54
from students, in the name of progressive ideas is in fact an unprogressive action that helps preserve the political and economic status quo. Middle-class children acquire mainstream literate culture by daily encounters with other literate persons. But less privileged children are denied consistent interchanges with literate persons and fail to receive this information in school. The most straightforward antidote to their deprivation is to make the essential information more readily available inside the schools.

* * *

Providing our children with traditional information by no means indoc-   55
trinates them in a conservative point of view. Conservatives who wish to preserve traditional values will find that these are not necessarily inculcated by a traditional education, which can in fact be subversive of the status quo. As a child of eleven, I turned against the conservative views of my family and the Southern community in which I grew up, precisely because I had been given a traditional education and was therefore literate enough to read Gunnar Myrdal's *An American Dilemma,* an epoch-making book in my life.

Although teaching children national mainstream culture doesn't mean   56
forcing them to accept its values uncritically, it does enable them to understand those values in order to predict the typical attitudes of other Americans. The writers for *The Black Panther* clearly understood this when they
quoted the Declaration of Independence. George Washington, for instance, is
a name in our received culture that we associate with the truthfulness of the
hero of the story of the cherry tree. Americans should be taught that value
association, whether or not they believe the story. Far from accepting the
cherry-tree tale or its implications, Oscar Wilde in "The Decay of Lying" used
it ironically, in a way that is probably funnier to Americans than to the
British audience he was addressing.

> [Truth telling is] vulgarizing mankind. The crude commercialism of America,
> its materializing spirit, its indifference to the poetical side of things, and its
> lack of imagination and of high unattainable ideals, are entirely due to that
> country having adopted for its national hero a man who, according to his
> own confession, was incapable of telling a lie, and it is not too much to say
> that the story of George Washington and the cherry tree has done more
> harm, and in a shorter space of time, than any other moral tale in the whole
> of literature. . . . And the amusing part of the whole thing is that the story of
> the cherry tree is an absolute myth.[25]

For us no less than for Wilde, the values affirmed in traditional literate culture can serve a whole spectrum of value attitudes. Unquestionably, decisions
about techniques of conveying traditions to our children are among the most
sensitive and important decisions of a pluralistic nation. But the complex
problem of how to teach values in American schools mustn't distract attention from our fundamental duty to teach shared content.

The failure of our schools to create a literate society is sometimes excused   57
on the grounds that the schools have been asked to do too much. They are
asked, for example, to pay due regard to the demands of both local and national acculturation. They are asked to teach not only American history but
also state and city history, driving, cardiopulmonary resuscitation, consumerism, carpentry, cooking, and other special subjects. They are given the
task of teaching information that is sometimes too rudimentary and sometimes too specialized. If the schools did not undertake this instruction, much
of the information so provided would no doubt go unlearned. In some of our
national moods we would like the schools to teach everything, but they cannot. There is a pressing need for clarity about our educational priorities.

As an example of the priorities we need to set, consider the teaching of   58
local history in the Commonwealth of Virginia. Suppose Virginians had to
choose between learning about its native son Jeb Stuart and Abraham Lincoln. The example is arbitrary, but since choices have to be made in education, we might consider the two names emblematic of the kind of priority
decision that has to be made. Educational policy always involves choices between degrees of worthiness.

The concept of cultural literacy helps us to make such decisions because it places a higher value on national than on local information. We want to make our children competent to communicate with Americans throughout the land. Therefore, if Virginians did have to decide between Stuart and Lincoln they ought to favor the man from Illinois over the one from Virginia. All literate Americans know traditional information about Abraham Lincoln but relatively few know about Jeb Stuart. To become literate it's therefore more important to know about Lincoln than about Stuart. The priority has nothing to do with inherent merit, only with the accidents of culture. Stuart certainly had more merit than Benedict Arnold did, but Arnold also should be given educational priority over Stuart. Why? Because Benedict Arnold is as much a part of our national language as is, say, Judas. 59

To describe Benedict Arnold and Abraham Lincoln as belonging to the national language discloses another way of conceiving cultural literacy—as a vocabulary that we are able to use throughout the land because we share associations with others in our society. A universally shared national vocabulary is analogous to a universal currency like the dollar. Of course the vocabulary consists of more than just words. *Benedict Arnold* is part of national cultural literacy; *eggs Benedict* isn't. 60

NOTES

1. For rising standards of literacy, see R. L. Thorndike, *Reading Comprehension Education in Fifteen Countries: An Empirical Study* (New York: Wiley, 1973). On the connection between high literacy and Japan's economic performance, see Thomas P. Rohlen, "Japanese Education: If They Can Do It, Should We?" *American Scholar* 55, I (Winter 1985–86): 29–44. For American literacy rates, see Jeanne Chall, "Afterword," in R. C. Anderson et al., *Becoming a Nation of Readers: The Report of the Commission on Reading* (Washington, D. C.: National Institute of Education, 1985), 123–24. On "world knowledge" in literacy, see Jeanne S. Chall, *Stages of Reading Development* (New York: McGraw-Hill, 1983), 8.

2. The two classical discussions of the stabilizing effects of mass literacy on oral speech are Henry Bradley, *The Making of English,* revised edition by Simeon Potter (London: Macmillan, 1968), and Otto Jespersen, *Mankind, Nation, and Individual from a Linguistic Point of View,* Midland edition (Bloomington: Indiana University Press, 1964). Wider bibliographical references to this subject may be found in the first two chapters of my *Philosophy of Composition* (Chicago: University of Chicago Press, 1977).

3. The experiment is described in R. M. Krauss and S. Glucksberg, "Social and Nonsocial Speech," *Scientific American* 236 (February 1977): 100–105.

4. National Assessment of Educational Progress, *Three National Assessments of Reading: Changes in Performance, 1970–1980* (Report 11-R-01) (Denver: Education Commission of the States, 1981). The percentage of students scoring at the "advanced" level (4.9 percent) has climbed back to the very low levels of 1970. See *The Reading Report Card: Progress Toward Excellence in Our Schools, Trends in Reading Over Four*

National Assessments, 1971–1984 (Princeton, N.J.: Educational Testing Service No. 15-R-01, 1986).

5. John B. Carroll, "Psychometric Approaches to the Study of Language Abilities," in C. J. Fillmore, D. Kempler, and S.-Y. Wang, eds., *Individual Differences in Language Abilities and Language Behavior* (New York: Academic Press, 1979), 29.

6. The College Board, *College-Bound Seniors: Eleven Years of National Data from the College Board's Admission Testing Program, 1973–83* (New York, 1984). The College Board has sent me further details from an unpublished report that shows the breakdown of scores over 600 between 1972 and 1984. The percentage of students who scored over 600 was 7.3 percent in 1984 and 11.4 percent in 1972. The percentage scoring over 650 was 3.0 percent in 1984 and 5.29 percent in 1972.

7. Benjamin J. Stein, "The Cheerful Ignorance of the Young in L.A.," *Washington Post,* October 3, 1983. Reprinted with the kind permission of the author.

8. *Changes in Political Knowledge and Attitudes, 1969–76: Selected Results from the Second National Assessments of Citizenship and Social Studies* (Denver: National Assessment of Educational Progress, 1978).

9. The Foundations of Literacy Project under a grant from the National Endowment for the Humanities, has commissioned NAEP, now conducted by the Educational Testing Service of Princeton, to probe the literary and historical knowledge of American seventeen-year-olds.

10. I am breaking no confidences as a member of the NAEP panel in revealing these pretest figures. They were made public on October 8, 1985, in a press release by NEH Chairman John Agresto, which stated in part: "Preliminary findings indicate that two-thirds of the seventeen-year-old students tested could not place the Civil War in the correct half century; a third did not know that the Declaration of Independence was signed between 1750 and 1800; half could not locate the half century in which the First World War occurred; a third did not know that Columbus sailed for the New World 'before 1750'; three-fourths could not identify Walt Whitman or Thoreau or E. E. Cummings or Carl Sandburg. And one-half of our high school seniors did not recognize the names of Winston Churchill or Joseph Stalin."

11. See Chapter 2, pages 42–47.

12. Orlando Patterson, "Language, Ethnicity, and Change," in S. G. D'Eloia, ed., *Toward a Literate Democracy: Proceedings of the First Shaughnessy Memorial Conference, April 3, 1980,* special number of *The Journal of Basic Writing* III (1980): 72–73.

13. Letter to Colonel Edward Carrington, January 16, 1787, taken from *The Life and Selected Writings of Thomas Jefferson,* ed. A. Koch and W. Peden (New York: Random House, 1944), 411–12.

14. W. C. Sellar and R. J. Yeatman, *1066 and All That: A Memorable History of England, Comprising All the Parts You Can Remember, Including 103 Good Things, 5 Bad Kings, and 2 Genuine Dates* (London: Methuen, 1947).

15. Melvin Durslag, "To Ban the Beanball," *TV Guide,* June 8–14, 1985, 9.

16. H. Putnam, "The Meaning of Meaning," in *Philosophical Papers, Volume 2: Mind, Language and Reality* (Cambridge: Cambridge University Press, 1975), 227–48.

17. See M. S. Steffensen, C. Joag-Des, and R. C. Anderson, "A Cross-Cultural Perspective on Reading Comprehension," *Reading Research Quarterly 15,* I (1979): 10–29.

18. This is fully discussed in Chapter 3.

19. See H. J. Walberg and T. Shanahan, "High School Effects on Individual Students," *Educational Researcher* 12 (August-September 1983): 4–9.

20. "Up to about ten hours a week, there is actually a slight positive relationship between the amount of time children spend watching TV and their school achievement, including reading achievement. Beyond this point, the relationship turns negative and, as the number of hours per week climbs, achievement declines sharply." R. C. Anderson et al., *Becoming a Nation of Readers,* 27.

21. Walberg and Shanahan, "High School Effects on Individual Students," 4–9.

22. Arthur G. Powell, Eleanor Farrar, and David K. Cohen, *The Shopping Mall High School: Winners and Losers in the Educational Marketplace* (Boston: Houghton Mifflin, 1985), 1–8.

23. The neutrality and avoidance of the schools are described in detail in *The Shopping Mall High School.*

24. Patterson, "Language, Ethnicity, and Change," 72–73.

25. Oscar Wilde, "The Decay of Lying" (1889).

Questions

1. How does Hirsch define cultural literacy? Why does he feel cultural literacy is important?

2. Hirsch deplores what he calls "shopping mall high schools." Was your high school based on the shopping mall or cafeteria model? What is the rationale behind this model? Do you agree with Hirsch's evaluation of this model?

3. How does Hirsch respond to the assertion that imposing traditional culture on children is, in reality, forcing them to accept the status quo? Do you find his defense adequate? Would Hirsch be an advocate for a multicultural canon? Why or why not?

4. Contrast Hirsch's position with that of Gitlin in the following article.

On the Virtues of a Loose Canon

TODD GITLIN

Todd Gitlin is a professor of sociology and director of the Mass Communications Program at the University of California, Berkeley.

Here, Gitlin attacks the excesses of both right- and left-wing critics in the political correctness debate. He charges that too often individuals align themselves with an interest group as an end in itself, and that intellectual curiosity and openness in some groups become stifled because of attachment to group identity. He points out that the literary canon has always changed, that cultural literacy in our society is weak, and that our society is in trouble if we do not learn to respect differences. This selection is from the News Perspective Quarterly *(1991).*

I understand the "political correctness" controversy as the surface of a deeper fault line—a trauma in American cultural identity. 1

America's current identity crisis was precipitated by several events. First, the collapse of the Cold War denied the United States an opponent in the tug-of-war between capitalism and communism. When the enemy let go of the rope, the American "team"—constituted to hold the line against tyranny—was dropped on its collective ass. We are now on the prowl for a new enemy, something or someone to mobilize against: Noriega, drugs, Satan, Saddam Hussein, or the newest bogey: "political correctness"—a breed of left-wing academic intolerance and exclusion that ends up shackling not only free speech but free-flowing intellectual inquiry—a perversion of a sensible multicultural program of tolerance and inclusion. 2

Though political correctness is rightly condemned for its flights of excess, opponents often fail to separate multiculturalism from the PC version of tribalism. Indeed, some of the Right's intolerance is aimed not at the message but at the messengers: immigrants of color—mostly Asian and Hispanic—whose numbers have greatly increased on campuses since the sixties. These groups, along with African Americans and women, now want access—not just to the corridors of the academy but to its curriculum. 3

Let's face it: some of the controversy over the canon and the new multiculturalism has to do with the fact that the complexion of the United States—on its campuses and in the country as a whole—is getting darker. In 1960, 94 percent of college students were white. Today almost 20 percent are nonwhite or Hispanic and about 55 percent are women. 4

424

It is the confluence of these events—the end of the Cold War and the 5
transformation of the "typical American"—that appears to have stirred up a
particularly vocal reaction at this time to the multicultural movement within
the academy. Just note the degree of alarm, the alacrity with which the media
have jumped on this issue. *Newsweek,* the *Atlantic,* the *New Republic,* and *New
York* jumped up with cover stories on race, multiculturalism, and the politically correct movement on college campuses. The *New York Times* has given
extensive coverage to the PC trend. And George Bush, knowing a no-risk issue when he sees it, gave the commencement address to the University of
Michigan at Ann Arbor on "the new intolerance" of political correctness
sweeping college campuses, what he called "the boring politics of division
and derision"—an ironic comment coming from the man who elevated race-
baiting, through his Willie Horton commercials, to an art form.

In important ways, hysteria rules the response to multiculturalism. Aca- 6
demic conservatives who defend a canon, tight or loose, sometimes sound as
if American universities were fully and finally canonized until the barbarians
showed up to smash up the pantheon and install Alice Walker and Toni Mor-
rison in place of the old white men. These conservatives act as if we were
floating along in unadulterated canon until sixties radicals came along and
muddied the waters. Moreover, the hysterics give the misleading impression
that Plato and St. Augustine have been banned.

The tight canonists don't take account, either, of the fact that the canon 7
has always been in flux, constantly shifting under our feet. Literary historian
Leo Marx made the point that when he was in school it was a fight to get
good, gay Walt Whitman into the canon, and to get John Greenleaf Whittier,
Henry Wadsworth Longfellow, and James Russell Lowell out.

Still, without doubt there *has* been a dilution of essential modes of critical 8
reasoning, the capacity to write, and a general knowledge of the contours of
world history and thought. And this is to be deplored and resisted.

Indeed, there is a side of the academic conservatives argument I agree 9
with. There are a shocking number of students not only in run-of-the-mill
segments of higher education but in elite institutions who are amazingly uneducated in history, literature, and the fundamentals of logic, who don't
know the difference between an argument and an assertion. There *is* a know-
nothing mood in some quarters that refuses to understand that the ideas and
practices of many a dead white male have been decisive in Western—and
therefore world—history.

But the stupidification of our students cannot be blamed simply on shifts 10
in the canon. Cultural illiteracy has crept into our educational process for a
variety of reasons. In fact, America's higher illiteracy—to call it by a name
Thorstein Veblen might have appreciated—is largely a function of the so-far
irresistible force of popular culture as the shaper of popular discourse. By popular discourse, I mean not only the way we speak on the street but the way we
speak as presidents and presidential candidates. This is a culture in which
"read my lips" or "make my day" constitutes powerful and persuasive speech.

We live in a sound-bite culture, one that has taken anti-elitism as its sa-   11
cred principle. In the United States, to master a vocabulary that is superior to
the mediocre is to be guilty of disdain, of scorning democracy. Though conservatives will not be happy to hear about it, this leveling principle has the
full force of market capitalism working for it, a force that insists that the only
standard of value is a consumer sovereignty—what people will buy. Since
what people will buy are slogans and feel-good pronouncements, it is not surprising that schools and universities have degraded themselves in a frantic
pursuit of the lowest common denominator.

This said, we must also condemn the bitter intolerance emanating from   12
much of the academic left—steadily more bitter with each passing Republican year as students who feel politically helpless go looking for targets of convenience. The Right exaggerates the academic left's power to enforce its
prejudices, but is rightly appalled by a widespread self-righteous illiberalism.
Academic freedom—the irreducible prerequisite of a democratic society—
goes by the board when students at Berkeley and Michigan disrupt classes
(whether of a prejudiced anthropologist or a liberal sociologist, respectively).
With the long-overdue withering of Marxism, the academic left has degenerated into a loose aggregation of margins—often cannibalistic, romancing the
varieties of otherness, speaking in tongues.

In this new interest-group pluralism, the shopping center of identity poli-   13
tics makes a fetish of the virtues of the minority, which, in the end, is not
only intellectually stulifynig but also politically suicidal. It creates a kind of
parochialism in which one is justified in having every interest in difference
and no interest in commonality. One's identification with an interest group
comes to be the first and final word that opens and terminates one's intellectual curiosity. As soon as I declare I am a Jew, a black, a Hispanic, a woman, a
gay, I have no more need to define my point of view.

It is curious and somewhat disturbing that this has become a position on   14
the Left since, as Isaiah Berlin has eloquently pointed out in his essays on nationalism, adherents of these views walk head-on into the traditional nationalist trap—a trap that led participants of the German *Sturm und Drang*
movement against French cultural imperialism, in the end, to fascism, brutal
irrationalism, and the oppression of minorities.

But there is an interesting difference between the German *Sturm und*   15
Drang and our own "Storm and Stress" reaction to monochromatic presenta-
tions of history and literature. The Romantics of that period were opposing a
French-imposed imperialism. What imperialism is being imposed in the
United States? Is it the hegemony of Enlightenment ideals of reason and
equality, the values of universalism?

If America's multiculturalism means respect for actual difference, we   16
should uphold and encourage this reality against the white-bread, golden-
arch version of Disneyland America.

On the other hand, if multiculturalism means there is nothing but differ-   17
ence, then we must do everything we can to disavow it. We cannot condone
the creation by the Left of separate cultural reservations on which to frolic.

There *are* unities—to recognize, to appreciate, deplore, or whatever, but at least to acknowledge. There is America's strange admixture of individualism and conformity. There is the fact of American military, political, cultural, and—still—economic power on a world scale. There are shared myths that cut across tribal lines. We may deplore the ways in which America recognizes itself. Indeed, the Persian Gulf War, the Academy Awards, or the Super Bowl are not high notes in the symphony of civilization, though that is when our culture seems to collectively acknowledge itself. Nonetheless, the United States is also a history, an organization of power and an overarching culture. The world is interdependent and America is not simply a sum of marginalities.

Authentic liberals have good reason to worry that the elevation of "differ-   18 ence" to a first principle is undermining everyone's capacity to see, or change, the world as a whole. And those who believe that the idea of the Left is an idea of universal interdependence and solidarity—of liberty, equality, fraternity-and-sorority—have reason to mourn the sectarian parochialism of the academic left. To mourn and to organize, so that the Right does not, by default, monopolize the legacy of the Enlightenment.

We badly need a careful accounting of the intellectual, social, and cul-   19 tural nature and roots of the new illiteracies and conformities—as well as the academy's high-level efforts to integrate hitherto submerged materials and populations.

It is not a contradiction to say that America has a real culture and also to   20 say that this culture is conflicted, fragile, constantly in need of shoring up. The apparent contradiction is only its complexity. In fact, the identity we promote by way of giving lip service to certain ideals about life, liberty, and the pursuit of happiness is riddled with contradiction, or at least with tension. Ours is not a relaxed or natural ideology, nor was the French Revolution's program of liberty, equality, fraternity. The point is that we can't maximize all values simultaneously.

That is why part of the multicultural program is very important. What is   21 required in a general multicultural program, which is *not* a program for group narcissism, is an understanding of one's own vantage point but also the vantage point of others. If we don't infuse multiculturalism with a respect for the other, all we have is American-style tribalism—a perfect recipe for a home-grown Yugoslavia.

Questions

1. How does Gitlin account for the rise of political correctness? How does his account differ from those of other writers in this chapter?

2. According to Gitlin what are the causes of our increasing cultural illiteracy? What is his solution?

3. Compare Gitlin's view of the dangers of political correctness with those of other authors in this chapter.

Writing Assignments

The following writing assignments are concerned with the topic of political correctness. Before developing an argument on any of these assignments, be sure that you understand the controversy by completing the following exercises:

- Write responses to exploration questions.
- Read several articles in this chapter or elsewhere to discover at least two perspectives on the topic.
- Create a list of opposing viewpoints and consider the potential consequences of each.
- Examine the underlying assumptions behind each viewpoint.

To help you understand the issues and develop ideas, you can use the following form:

The conflict in this issue is between _____ and

_____.

I am more inclined to agree with _____.

because _____.

However, it is possible that some of my readers may believe that

_____.

Exploration Questions

1. Does your college have a speech code? What kinds of expressions are censored? Do you think that speech codes are beneficial?
2. Do you think off-color jokes are harmful or beneficial? Can you give examples from your experience to support your position?
3. How would you describe the racial climate at your school? Is there much interaction between races? Why or why not?
4. What kinds of programs can encourage racial interaction and eradicate prejudice?
5. When you studied history, did you learn about the roles played by minorities and women? Did your study of history have an effect on your ethnic or racial identity? Did it have an effect on your view of others?

ASSIGNMENT 1

The political correctness movement has been particularly important on college campuses, and many involved in the movement have suggested that particular laws and policies should be instituted on campuses to foster sensitivity and eradicate prejudice and stereotypical thinking. Such laws could take the form of a prescribed set of speech and behavior codes that some educators believe ought to be encouraged through special courses and policies. Those in favor of such laws believe that justice to racial minorities and women will occur only through specific legislation. Opponents, however, maintain that sensitivity cannot be instituted by law and that such restrictions will impinge significantly on the rights of free speech and possibly create a backlash.

Based on your reading of several articles in this chapter, write an argumentative essay in response to the following question: To what extent should colleges and universities mandate political correctness through the passage of particular rules or laws?

ASSIGNMENT 2

One component of the political correctness debate focuses on the extent to which the body of literature studied in school and deemed the literary canon reflects and fosters ethnic and gender bias. Consequently, there has been a recent reevaluation of which works should be included in the high school and college curriculum, particularly in history and literature classes and regarding the works of women and minorities. Others believe, however, that the entire notion of the literary canon is irrelevant because the political correctness debate is really about the distribution of power.

Based on the readings in this chapter, write an argumentative essay in which you address the following question: What is the role of the college curriculum in fostering ethnic and racial equality in a multicultural society?

8 ■ Diversity in Men and Women

Gender is a category that will not go away.
DEBORAH TANNEN, *YOU JUST DON'T UNDERSTAND*

In the survey reprinted here, "Political Agendas: Is There a Gender Gap?" the popular media psychologist, Dr. Joyce Brothers, claims that men and women are likely to differ in their political opinions, and she illustrates her point by summarizing typical responses to a series of questions (see page 438). The questions and the responses she maintains are representative do indeed suggest that men and women frequently differ in their views on various social issues and, by implication, in other important ways as well. By reflecting on some of these differences you can begin to think about the subject of this chapter—issues concerned with men and women in a diverse society. Read through Dr. Brothers's questions, and think about how you would respond and the extent to which you were able to predict Dr. Brothers's results. Would you have expected that women are more likely to vote than men? Did you know that women are more likely to advocate government involvement with issues of child care and homelessness or that they tend to be more tolerant of issues relating to homelessness, homosexuality, and AIDS? Would you have predicted that men are more likely than women to be in favor of the death penalty?

Although men and women differ from one another in significant ways, whether those differences are physically or culturally based has been a subject of debate throughout the ages. The stereotype, of course, is that women "naturally" tend to be the "weaker" sex, less dominant, less prone to violence, and more nurturing and expressive, whereas men "naturally" are the "stronger" sex, dominant, sometimes aggressive, less nurturing, and more inclined to action than to expressing their feelings. However, the women's and men's movements, as well as an increased awareness of gender role variation in other cultures, has posed a challenge to this stereotype, raising questions about the origin of gender behavior and the best way to address gender differences in a diverse society.

DRABBLE reprinted by permission of UFS, Inc.

Nature or Nurture?

In examining the origin of gender role in a diverse society, it is important to consider the question of whether gender behavior is biologically or culturally determined. During the 1970s, feminists strongly believed that differences in behaviors and consequent career and identity choices were due simply to an environment that offered more attractive opportunities to men. This position suggested that women chose the nurturing, domestic roles simply because men didn't want them but that in an enlightened society, where women had more choices, all forms of work, the more and the less desirable, would be shared. In her essay from *Time,* "Sizing Up the Sexes," Christine Gorman challenges that perspective, claiming that biological differences may play more of a role in determining gender behavior than has been currently fashionable to believe. The essay does make the qualification, however, that the concept of what is innate is difficult to determine because it is possible that learning can affect brain chemistry.

The Women's Movement

The extent to which gender role behavior is biologically determined was an issue of particular significance during the early days of the women's movement of the 1960s, a movement which is often associated with the publication in 1963 of Betty Friedan's *The Feminine Mystique.* Exposing some of women's dissatisfactions with traditional women's roles, particularly those of housewife and mother, the book led to the establishment of the National Organization of Women (NOW), which has devoted itself to raising women's consciousness about feminist issues and to supporting legislative measures

SALLY FORTH By Greg Howard and Craig MacIntosh

DID YOU CHECK IF THE DOORS ARE DEADBOLTED?

I DID IT LAST NIGHT. IT'S YOUR TURN.

BUT WHAT IF THERE'S A BAD GUY CROUCHED BY THE DOOR?

OH, ALL RIGHT. I'LL GO.

FEMINISM TAKES AN INTERESTING TWIST WHEN THERE'S A BAD GUY CROUCHED BY THE DOOR.

LET ME KNOW WHEN THERE'S A BAD WOMAN CROUCHED DOWN THERE, AND I'LL TAKE MY TURN.

Copyright © 1992. Reprinted with special permission of King Features Syndicate.

such as the Equal Rights Amendment and laws to institutionalize equal opportunity.

The women's movement and the accompanying development of feminist issues has been accompanied by an increased participation of women in the workplace. Yet in many instances, despite their so-called liberation, women find themselves juggling work commitments with primary responsibility for home and child care, dual demands that are less likely to be assumed by men. In fact, some have said that the 1980s and 1990s have seen a retrenchment of women from the feminist positions they held in the 1960s and 1970s, with women once again choosing to embrace motherhood and domesticity rather than juggle the multiplicity of tasks that a career combined with motherhood requires. Susan Faludi, however, in her controversial *Backlash: The Undeclared War Against Women,* argues that the idea that women prefer to return to more traditional roles is a mere fabrication of the media, designed to keep women down. Faludi cites the media's tendency to blame the feminist movement for imaginary psychological and social ills that plague modern women, viewing it as a thinly disguised effort to undermine the struggle for equality. It is not equality that makes women miserable, Faludi maintains, but "the rising pressure to halt, and even to reverse, women's quest for equality."

Judy Syfers' essay, "I Want a Wife," published in the first issue of *Ms.* in 1971 and frequently anthologized since, makes the case that being a wife in the traditional sense is as exhausting as having a career and far less personally rewarding. In this essay, Syfers gives an exhausting catalogue of a wife's duties and concludes with an exasperated "My God, who *wouldn't* want a wife?" The excerpt from Betty Friedan's *The Second Stage* explores some of the effects of the feminist movement on contemporary women and raises the issue of whether some of the apparent gains of the movement may in fact be illusory. Friedan argues that it is now necessary to move beyond the original goals of the women's movement to a "second stage"—a stage in which women can get beyond the battle of the sexes and begin to openly discuss the importance of family and of women's need to give and receive love, a stage that may involve the cooperation of men.

An issue that has a significant effect on the ability of women to combine a career and motherhood is the extent to which men participate in house-

Copyright © 1992. Reprinted with special permission of King Features Syndicate.

work and child care. Most studies suggest that although there have been some changes in the amount of time spent on household tasks by men and women, women still spend considerably more time in housework, taking responsibility for meal preparation and cleanup as well as for housecleaning, whereas men spend more time in outdoor tasks. Moreover, "having it all"—that is, working and taking care of a child, is difficult for both men and women because society does not provide a support system and because domestic or "women's" work continues to be undervalued, whether performed by men or women.

The Men's Movement

With the increase of women in the workplace and a greater awareness of the extent to which gender role expectations are culturally rather than biologically determined, some men are coming to realize that they, as well as women, have been limited in their possibilities. Men now believe that they would like to expand their life choices and break away from societal stereotypes of what it means to be a man. Consequently, a number of male liberationist groups now exist, such as The National Organization for Changing Men, founded in 1982, whose aim is to expand men's consciousness and provide support.

One result of the men's movement has been to evaluate the meaning of traditional masculinity in a diverse society where stereotypical roles are undergoing rapid change. One view of traditional masculinity maintains that its more extreme characteristics, such as abusive violence, irresponsible sexuality, gun fetishes, etc.—represent attempts to prove manhood in a society in which gender differences have been steadily declining. Thus, it is possible that the late twentieth century will be characterized by a gradual change in gender role expectations—greater diversity among both men and women and a less rigid association of manhood with competitive work and womanhood with perfect mothering, in other words, a more balanced view.

"*I'm just so impressed with what you're saying
about the victimization of men.*"

Drawing by Koren © 1992 The New Yorker Magazine, Inc.

Some men, however, believe that the feminine position on masculinity
has gone too far. Warren Farrell argues in his article, "We Should Embrace Traditional Masculinity," that traditional masculinity is often misinterpreted by
women, who have attacked gender behavior unfairly. He asserts that male socialization actually leaves men both physically and emotionally vulnerable,
and points out that male socialization offers a great deal that is valuable, in
particular, generosity as expressed through labor, the value of fairness, and a
veneration of action, leadership, and responsibility. Robert Bly in "The Pillow
and the Key," an excerpt from his best selling *Iron John,* maintains that modern men have become mummified, de-energized by feminist concepts of masculinity until they no longer know who they are. Bly laments that there is
not enough "father" in American society, and urges men to rediscover that
masculinity, that is, to get in touch with their fierce and wild side to reclaim
lost energy and glory in their manhood. To tap the "Wild Man," or the male
spirit, Bly maintains that men need mentors, older men who can sever the
attachment to the mother.

In a response to Bly, however, Jane Caputi and Gordene O. MacKenzie in
their essay, "Pumping Iron John," assert that Bly's concept of masculinity represents simply a return to stereotypical gender roles that will perpetuate sexism and exacerbate sexual inequality. The authors argue that Bly's conception
of masculinity endorses patriarchy and a "hatred of the feminine." What is
needed, they maintain, is a "gender transcendence movement." In another

response entitled "Robert Bly: Turning 'Yogurt Eaters' into 'Wild Men,' Susan Faludi describes how Bly moved from the peace movement in the 1960s, in which he encouraged men to foster their pacifistic femininity, to become a leader of the masculine movement. Faludi says that Bly is not concerned with inculcating equality or harmony between the sexes; instead, she feels that he is concerned with power and "how to wrest it from women and how to mobilize it for men."

Male Friendships

One issue emerging from the men's movement concerns the extent to which men are capable of close male friendships and the role that culture plays in influencing such friendships. Stereotypically, American males are depicted as unemotional and aloof toward other men, capable of only limited intimacy; however, in some cultures, this stereotype does not pertain. In "The Relationship Between Male-Male Friendship and Male-Female Marriage," Walter Williams discusses the stereotype of male friendship in his comparison of the concept of friendship and marriage in Native American and Asian cultures. Williams claims that the way in which traditional American men relate to one another is not innate but, in fact, culturally determined. In many societies, Williams claims, men fulfill their friendship needs by having close relationships with other men, just as women do, whereas American men, fearing the homosexual label, seek to fulfill these needs in their wives. Williams claims that the real culprit in preventing strong male friendships is our idealization of romantic love—we expect our spouses to be our "sexual playmate, economic partner, kinship system, best friend, and everything else"—but this ideal often leads to disappointment.

Several articles examine stereotypical views of minority men and women in a diverse society. Maxine Baca Zinn, in "Chicano Men and Masculinity," challenges the assumption that dominance in male Chicanos is entirely cultural; rather, she maintains, it can be traced to social inequality which men compensate for by assuming "macho" roles. Zinn argues that machismo is not simply a cultural heritage stemming from powerlessness and subordination. Rather, machismo results from socioeconomic status—the family is often the only sphere in which the Chicano male is able to assert his authority and dominance.

One issue affecting both black men and black women is whether the cultivation of a strong African and African-American identity would facilitate social and economic progress within black culture. Richard Majors, co-founder and chairman of the National Council of African-American Men, suggests that African culture is already of significance in the concept of "cool" within the black community. In "Cool Pose: The Proud Signature of Black Survival," Majors discusses the origins of this concept, traces it to factors within African culture, and maintains that black males adopt a "Cool Pose" because they have been denied access to "the dominant culture's acceptable avenues" of self-expression. Majors argues that this posture of control, toughness, and detachment denies the expression of fear and affection, and may explain such problems as black-on-black crime.

The issue of whether gender behavior is naturally or culturally determined is unlikely to be resolved in the near future. However, examining the roles that men and women play in different cultures is likely to spark reflection on the topic and at least minimize stereotypical gender role expectations.

Political Agendas: Is There a Gender Gap?

DR. JOYCE BROTHERS

Dr. Joyce Brothers is a renowned psychologist whose column is syndicated nationally. Educated at Cornell and Columbia universities, she has had several television shows since the late 1950s. She has written a number of books including What Every Woman Should Know About a Man, *and in 1956, she was a winner of the $64,000 question in the television program of the same name.*

Here, Dr. Brothers presents an informal survey designed to test your responses concerning political issues. Her conclusions are that women seem to have broader sympathies on many subjects and tend to be more tolerant and less dogmatic than men. This selection is from the Los Angeles Times *(1992).*

Some predict that this is the year of the woman in politics. Do women have   1
different priorities and attitudes about government, and if so, how do they
differ? Here's a chance to compare your views with those of some experts:

1. It's Election Day. It's raining, everything's gone wrong in your personal   2
   and business day and you figure your vote won't make a difference anyway, so you decide not to vote. You are more likely to be:
   MALE ( )   FEMALE ( )

2. Government should stay out of child care and leave it up to the families,   3
   with all funding coming from private sources. If you believe this and vote
   against government support for child care, you're more likely to be:
   MALE ( )   FEMALE ( )

3. Voters who place homelessness and poverty near the top of their list of   4
   priorities for government assistance are more apt to be:
   MALE ( )   FEMALE ( )

4. A proposed national family medical leave plan would allow homosexuals   5
   who live together to be considered as couples. If you would vote against
   this inclusion, you're more likely to be:
   MALE ( )   FEMALE ( )

5. There's a new conflict in a Third World country where American prestige   6
   may be on the line. Some feel that in order to save face, protect economic

438

interests and improve America's image as a world force, we should send in troops. If you support military intervention, you're more likely to be:
MALE ( )   FEMALE ( )

6. The man running for mayor whose political and economic views you support has recently been accused of being a homosexual. If you stop campaigning for him and switch your vote, chances are you're a:
MALE ( )   FEMALE ( )

7. You've just been named to a prominent position in the mayor's office. If you view the position primarily as a steppingstone to higher office, more money, control and power, you're more likely to be:
MALE ( )   FEMALE ( )

8. When you think of law-and-order issues, sexual harassment, rape and family violence are relatively low on your list. Chances are you're:
MALE ( )   FEMALE ( )

9. As a representative of your district, you're involved in a heated debate with colleagues. Compromise and negotiation are vital. If you find your gender gives you some advantages, chances are you're:
MALE ( )   FEMALE ( )

10. You support the death penalty. You're more likely to be:
MALE ( )   FEMALE ( )

Answers

Before you check your answers, remember that we're dealing in generalities. There are plenty of men and women who cross over on all these issues.

1. MALE. Women are more likely to get to the polls and vote than men. In 1988, 5,924,630 more women than men voted for President.

2. MALE. While large numbers of today's men are concerned with getting more help from the government with child care, more women than men favor support for working parents and child care.

3. FEMALE. According to a poll conducted by Life magazine, 50% more women than men believe poverty and homelessness should be an "extremely important" government priority.

4. MALE. Studies show that women are more tolerant of differences in sexual preferences. Life magazine's poll showed 80% of women would favor such a proposal, compared with 62% of the men questioned.

5. MALE. Women are generally much less concerned with "saving face" or maintaining image. They are more likely to want to continue negotiation and less likely to use force under any circumstances.

6. MALE. Female voters tend to be more tolerant of all issues relating to homosexuals and more compassionate and vigilant about the needs of those afflicted with AIDS.

7. MALE. Women who enter the political race are generally less concerned   19
with money, power and prestige and more concerned with specific issues.
Women in politics are less likely to view the office as a steppingstone.

8. MALE. Because females are much more likely to be victims of such crimes,   20
tougher laws regarding the offenses are usually high on their list.

9. FEMALE. In such a situation women often have a distinct advantage.   21
Most men find it easier to back down from a strong stand when talking to
a woman than when dealing with a male competitor.

10. MALE. Males are more likely than females to support the death penalty,   22
whereas women are more apt to choose life imprisonment.

If you answered eight of 10 of these questions correctly, you're better in-   23
formed than most on this issue.

Questions

1. What types of assumptions about gender differences guided your answers? Were
you surprised by any of the answers? Why or why not?

2. Why do you think women are more likely to vote than men?

3. Why do you think women are more concerned with poverty and homelessness?

4. Why are women less likely to view a promotion as a stepping stone than men?

Sizing Up the Sexes

CHRISTINE GORMAN

Journalist Christine Gorman summarizes findings by scientists who have discovered that varying hormone levels and neurological differences have some effect on gender differences such as women's intuition and men's capacity for visual-spatial tasks. However, in the final analysis, "it may be impossible to say where nature ends and nurture begins because the two are so intimately linked." This selection is from Time *(1992).*

What are little boys made of?
What are little boys made of?
Frogs and snails
And puppy dogs' tails,
That's what little boys are made of.

What are little girls made of?
What are little girls made of?
Sugar and spice
And all that's nice,
That's what little girls are made of.
                                          ANONYMOUS

Many scientists rely on elaborately complex and costly equipment to probe   1
the mysteries confronting humankind. Not Melissa Hines. The UCLA behavioral scientist is hoping to solve one of life's oldest riddles with a toybox full
of police cars, Lincoln Logs and Barbie dolls. For the past two years, Hines
and her colleagues have tried to determine the origins of gender differences
by capturing on videotape the squeals of delight, furrows of concentration
and myriad decisions that children from 2½ to 8 make while playing. Although both sexes play with all the toys available in Hines' laboratory, her
work confirms what most parents (and more than a few aunts, uncles and
nursery-school teachers) already know. As a group, the boys favor sports cars,
fire trucks and Lincoln Logs, while the girls are drawn more often to dolls and
kitchen toys.

But one batch of girls defies expectations and consistently prefers the boy   2
toys. These youngsters have a rare genetic abnormality that caused them to
produce elevated levels of testosterone, among other hormones, during their
embryonic development. On average, they play with the same toys as the
boys in the same ways and just as often. Could it be that the high levels of

testosterone present in their bodies before birth have left a permanent imprint on their brains, affecting their later behavior? Or did their parents, knowing of their disorder, somehow subtly influence their choices? If the first explanation is true and biology determines the choice, Hines wonders, "Why would you evolve to want to play with a truck?"

Not so long ago, any career-minded researcher would have hesitated to ask 3 such questions. During the feminist revolution of the 1970s, talk of inborn differences in the behavior of men and women was distinctly unfashionable, even taboo. Men dominated fields like architecture and engineering, it was argued, because of social, not hormonal, pressures. Women did the vast majority of society's child rearing because few other options were available to them. Once sexism was abolished, so the argument ran, the world would become a perfectly equitable, androgynous place, aside from a few anatomical details.

But biology has a funny way of confounding expectations. Rather than 4 disappear, the evidence for innate sexual differences only began to mount. In medicine, researchers documented that heart disease strikes men at a younger age than it does women and that women have a more moderate physiological response to stress. Researchers found subtle neurological differences between the sexes both in the brain's structure and in its functioning. In addition, another generation of parents discovered that, despite their best efforts to give baseballs to their daughters and sewing kits to their sons, girls still flocked to dollhouses while boys clambered into tree forts. Perhaps nature is more important than nurture after all.

Even professional skeptics have been converted. "When I was younger, I 5 believed that 100% of sex differences were due to the environment," says Jerre Levy, professor of psychology at the University of Chicago. Her own toddler toppled that utopian notion. "My daughter was 15 months old, and I had just dressed her in her teeny little nightie. Some guests arrived, and she came into the room, knowing full well that she looked adorable. She came in with this saucy little walk, cocking her head, blinking her eyes, especially at the men. You never saw such flirtation in your life." After 20 years spent studying the brain, Levy is convinced: "I'm sure there are biologically based differences in our behavior."

Now that it is O.K. to admit the possibility, the search for sexual differ- 6 ences has expanded into nearly every branch of the life sciences. Anthropologists have debunked Margaret Mead's work on the extreme variability of gender roles in New Guinea. Psychologists are untangling the complex interplay between hormones and aggression. But the most provocative, if as yet inconclusive, discoveries of all stem from the pioneering exploration of a tiny 3-lb. universe: the human brain. In fact, some researchers predict that the confirmation of innate differences in behavior could lead to an unprecedented understanding of the mind.

Some of the findings seem merely curious. For example, more men than 7 women are lefthanded, reflecting the dominance of the brain's right hemisphere. By contrast, more women listen equally with both ears while men favor the right one.

Other revelations are bound to provoke more controversy. Psychology 8
tests, for instance, consistently support the notion that men and women perceive the world in subtly different ways. Males excel at rotating three-dimen-
sional objects in their head. Females prove better at reading emotions of
people in photographs. A growing number of scientists believe the discrepancies reflect functional differences in the brains of men and women. If true,
then some misunderstandings between the sexes may have more to do with
crossed wiring than cross-purposes.

Most of the gender differences that have been uncovered so far are, statis- 9
tically speaking, quite small. "Even the largest differences in cognitive function are not as large as the difference in male and female height," Hines
notes. "You still see a lot of overlap." Otherwise, women could never read
maps and men would always be lefthanded. That kind of flexibility within
the sexes reveals just how complex a puzzle gender actually is, requiring
pieces from biology, sociology and culture.

Ironically, researchers are not entirely sure how or even why humans pro- 10
duce two sexes in the first place. (Why not just one—or even three—as in
some species?) What is clear is that the two sexes originate with two distinct
chromosomes. Women bear a double dose of the large X chromosome, while
men usually possess a single X and a short, stumpy Y chromosome. In 1990
British scientists reported they had identified a single gene on the Y chromosome that determines maleness. Like some kind of biomolecular Paul Revere,
this master gene rouses a host of its compatriots to the complex task of turning a fetus into a boy. Without such a signal, all human embryos would develop into girls. "I have all the genes for being male except this one, and my
husband has all the genes for being female," marvels evolutionary psychologist Leda Cosmides, of the University of California at Santa Barbara. "The
only difference is which genes got turned on."

Yet even this snippet of DNA is not enough to ensure a masculine result. 11
An elevated level of the hormone testosterone is also required during the
pregnancy. Where does it come from? The fetus' own undescended testes. In
those rare cases in which the tiny body does not respond to the hormone, a
genetically male fetus develops sex organs that look like a clitoris and vagina
rather than a penis. Such people look and act female. The majority marry and
adopt children.

The influence of the sex hormones extends into the nervous system. Both 12
males and females produce androgens, such as testosterone, and estrogens—
although in different amounts. (Men and women who make no testosterone
generally lack a libido.) Researchers suspect that an excess of testosterone before birth enables the right hemisphere to dominate the brain, resulting in
lefthandedness. Since testosterone levels are higher in boys than in girls, that
would explain why more boys are southpaws.

Subtle sex-linked preferences have been detected as early as 52 hours after 13
birth. In studies of 72 newborns, University of Chicago psychologist Martha
McClintock and her students found that a toe-fanning reflex was stronger in
the left foot for 60% of the males, while all the females favored their right.

However, apart from such reflexes in the hands, legs and feet, the team could find no other differences in the babies' responses.

One obvious place to look for gender differences is in the hypothalamus, a lusty little organ perched over the brain stem that, when sufficiently provoked, consumes a person with rage, thirst, hunger or desire. In animals, a region at the front of the organ controls sexual function and is somewhat larger in males than in females. But its size need not remain constant. Studies of tropical fish by Stanford University neurobiologist Russell Fernald reveal that certain cells in this tiny region of the brain swell markedly in an individual male whenever he comes to dominate a school. Unfortunately for the piscine pasha, the cells will also shrink if he loses control of his harem to another male.

Many researchers suspect that, in humans too, sexual preferences are controlled by the hypothalamus. Based on a study of 41 autopsied brains, Simon LeVay of the Salk Institute for Biological Studies announced last summer that he had found a region in the hypothalamus that was on average twice as large in heterosexual men as in either women or homosexual men. LeVay's findings support the idea that varying hormone levels before birth may immutably stamp the developing brain in one erotic direction or another.

These prenatal fluctuations may also steer boys toward more rambunctious behavior than girls. June Reinisch, director of the Kinsey Institute for Research in Sex, Gender and Reproduction at Indiana University, in a pioneering study of eight pairs of brothers and 17 pairs of sisters ages 6 to 18 uncovered a complex interplay between hormones and aggression. As a group, the young males gave more belligerent answers than did the females on a multiple-choice test in which they had to imagine their response to stressful situations. But siblings who had been exposed in utero to synthetic antimiscarriage hormones that mimic testosterone were the most combative of all. The affected boys proved significantly more aggressive than their unaffected brothers, and the drug-exposed girls were much more contentious than their unexposed sisters. Reinisch could not determine, however, whether this childhood aggression would translate into greater ambition or competitiveness in the adult world.

While most of the gender differences uncovered so far seem to fall under the purview of the hypothalamus, researchers have begun noting discrepancies in other parts of the brain as well. For the past nine years, neuroscientists have debated whether the corpus callosum, a thick bundle of nerves that allows the right half of the brain to communicate with the left, is larger in women than in men. If it is, and if size corresponds to function, then the greater crosstalk between the hemispheres might explain enigmatic phenomena like female intuition, which is supposed to accord women greater ability to read emotional clues.

These conjectures about the corpus callosum have been hard to prove because the structure's girth varies dramatically with both age and health. Studies of autopsied material are of little use because brain tissue undergoes such dramatic changes in the hours after death. Neuroanatomist Laura Allen and neuroendocrinologist Roger Gorski of UCLA decided to try to circumvent some of these problems by obtaining brain scans from live, apparently healthy people. In their investigation of 146 subjects, published in April, they confirmed that parts of the corpus callosum were up to 23% wider in women than in men. They also measured thicker connections between the two hemispheres in other parts of women's brains.

19   Encouraged by the discovery of such structural differences, many researchers have begun looking for dichotomies of function as well. At the Bowman Gray Medical School in Winston-Salem, N.C., Cecile Naylor has determined that men and women enlist widely varying parts of their brain when asked to spell words. By monitoring increases in blood flow, the neuropsychologist found that women use both sides of their head when spelling while men use primarily their left side. Because the area activated on the right side is used in understanding emotions, the women apparently tap a wider range of experience for their task. Intriguingly, the effect occurred only with spelling and not during a memory test.

20   Researchers speculate that the greater communication between the two sides of the brain could impair a woman's performance of certain highly specialized visual-spatial tasks. For example, the ability to tell directions on a map without physically having to rotate it appears stronger in those individuals whose brains restrict the process to the right hemisphere. Any crosstalk between the two sides apparently distracts the brain from its job. Sure enough, several studies have shown that this mental-rotation skill is indeed more tightly focused in men's brains than in women's.

21   But how did it get to be that way? So far, none of the gender scientists have figured out whether nature or nurture is more important. "Nothing is ever equal, even in the beginning," observes Janice Juraska, a biopsychologist at the University of Illinois at Urbana-Champaign. She points out, for instance, that mother rats lick their male offspring more frequently than they do their daughters. However, Juraska has demonstrated that it is possible to reverse some inequities by manipulating environmental factors. Female rats have fewer nerve connections than males into the hippocampus, a brain region associated with spatial relations and memory. But when Juraska "enriched" the cages of the females with stimulating toys, the females developed more of these neuronal connections. "Hormones do affect things—it's crazy to deny that," says the researcher. "But there's no telling which way sex differences might go if we completely changed the environment." For humans, educational enrichment could perhaps enhance a woman's ability to work in three dimensions and a man's ability to interpret emotions. Says Juraska: "There's nothing about human brains that is so stuck that a different way of doing things couldn't change it enormously."

22   Nowhere is this complex interaction between nature and nurture more apparent than in the unique human abilities of speaking, reading and writing. No one is born knowing French, for example; it must be learned, changing the brain forever. Even so, language skills are linked to specific cerebral centers. In a remarkable series of experiments, neurosurgeon George

Ojemann of the University of Washington has produced scores of detailed maps of people's individual language centers.

First, Ojemann tested his patients' verbal intelligence using a written exam. Then, during neurosurgery—which was performed under a local anesthetic—he asked them to name aloud a series of objects found in a steady stream of black-and-white photos. Periodically, he touched different parts of the brain with an electrode that temporarily blocked the activity of that region. (This does not hurt because the brain has no sense of pain.) By noting when his patients made mistakes, the surgeon was able to determine which sites were essential to naming.

Several complex sexual differences emerged. Men with lower verbal IQs were more likely to have their language skills located toward the back of the brain. In a number of women, regardless of IQ, the naming ability was restricted to the frontal lobe. This disparity could help explain why strokes that affect the rear of the brain seem to be more devastating to men than to women.

Intriguingly, the sexual differences are far less significant in people with higher verbal IQs. Their language skills developed in a more intermediate part of the brain. And yet, no two patterns were ever identical. "That to me is the most important finding," Ojemann says. "Instead of these sites being laid down more or less the same in everyone, they're laid down in subtly different places." Language is scattered randomly across these cerebral centers, he hypothesizes, because the skills evolved so recently.

What no one knows for sure is just how hardwired the brain is. How far and at what stage can the brain's extraordinary flexibility be pushed? Several studies suggest that the junior high years are key. Girls show the same aptitudes for math as boys until about the seventh grade, when more and more girls develop math phobia. Coincidentally, that is the age at which boys start to shine and catch up to girls in reading.

By one account, the gap between men and women for at least some mental skills has actually started to shrink. By looking at 25 years' worth of data from academic tests, Janet Hyde, professor of psychology and women's studies at the University of Wisconsin at Madison, discovered that overall gender differences for verbal and mathematical skills dramatically decreased after 1974. One possible explanation, Hyde notes, is that "Americans have changed their socialization and educational patterns over the past few decades. They are treating males and females with greater similarity."

Even so, women still have not caught up with men on the mental-rotation test. Fascinated by the persistence of that gap, psychologists Irwin Silverman and Marion Eals of York University in Ontario wondered if there were any spatial tasks at which women outperformed men. Looking at it from the point of view of human evolution, Silverman and Eals reasoned that while men may have developed strong spatial skills in response to evolutionary pressures to be successful hunters, women would have needed other types of visual skills to excel as gatherers and foragers of food.

The psychologists therefore designed a test focused on the ability to discern and later recall the location of objects in a complex, random pattern. In series of tests, student volunteers were given a minute to study a drawing that contained such unrelated objects as an elephant, a guitar and a cat. Then Silverman and Eals presented their subjects with a second drawing containing additional objects and told them to cross out those items that had been added and circle any that had moved. Sure enough, the women consistently surpassed the men in giving correct answers.

What made the psychologists really sit up and take notice, however, was the fact that the women scored much better on the mental-rotation test while they were menstruating. Specifically, they improved their scores by 50% to 100% whenever their estrogen levels were at their lowest. It is not clear why this should be. However, Silverman and Eals are trying to find out if women exhibit a similar hormonal effect for any other visual tasks. 30

Oddly enough, men may possess a similar hormonal response, according to new research reported in November by Doreen Kimura, a psychologist at the University of Western Ontario. In her study of 138 adults, Kimura found that males perform better on mental-rotation tests in the spring, when their testosterone levels are low, rather than in the fall, when they are higher. Men are also subject to a daily cycle, with testosterone levels lowest around 4 p.m. and peaking around 4 a.m. Thus, says June Reinisch of the Kinsey Institute: "When people say women can't be trusted because they cycle every month, my response is that men cycle every day, so they should only be allowed to negotiate peace treaties in the evening." 31

Far from strengthening stereotypes about who women and men truly are or how they should behave, research into innate sexual differences only underscores humanity's awesome adaptability. "Gender is really a complex business," says Reinisch. "There's no question that hormones have an effect. But what does that have to do with the fact that I like to wear pink ribbons and you like to wear baseball gloves? Probably something, but we don't know what." 32

Even the concept of what an innate difference represents is changing. The physical and chemical differences between the brains of the two sexes may be malleable and subject to change by experience: certainly an event or act of learning can directly affect the brain's biochemistry and physiology. And so, in the final analysis, it may be impossible to say where nature ends and nurture begins because the two are so intimately linked. 33

Questions

1. Why is it so difficult to determine whether "nature" or "nurture" is responsible for gender differences?

2. What is the possible neurological reason for the fact that more men than women can read a map upside-down?

3. Compare some of the gender assumptions you listed from Dr. Joyce Brothers's quiz with some of the findings in this essay. Are there any biological explanations for the different political behavior of men and women?

Introduction: Blame It on Feminism

SUSAN FALUDI

Susan Faludi is a Pulitzer Prize-winning journalist for the Wall Street Journal. *She has served as a staff writer for* Ms., *and has contributed to numerous magazines. She is the author of* Backlash: The Undeclared War
Against Women *(1991).*

   *In this excerpt, Faludi argues that the media's tendency to blame the
feminist movement for imaginary psychological and social ills that plague
modern women is only a thinly disguised effort to undermine the struggle for
equality. It is not equality that makes women miserable but "the rising pressure to halt, and even to reverse, women's quest for equality." This excerpt is
from* Backlash.

To be a woman in America at the close of the 20th century—what good for- 1
tune. That's what we keep hearing, anyway. The barricades have fallen, politicians assure us. Women have "made it," Madison Avenue cheers. Women's
fight for equality has "largely been won," *Time* magazine announces. Enroll
at any university, join any law firm, apply for credit at any bank. Women
have so many opportunities now, corporate leaders say, that we don't really
need equal opportunity policies. Women are so equal now, lawmakers say,
that we no longer need an Equal Rights Amendment. Women have "so
much," former President Ronald Reagan says, that the White House no
longer needs to appoint them to higher office. Even American Express ads are
saluting a woman's freedom to charge it. At last, women have received their
full citizenship papers.

   And yet. . . 2

   Behind this celebration of the American woman's victory, behind the 3
news, cheerfully and endlessly repeated, that the struggle for women's rights
is won, another message flashes. You may be free and equal now, it says to
women, but you have never been more miserable.

   This bulletin of despair is posted everywhere—at the newsstand, on the 4
TV set, at the movies, in advertisements and doctors' offices and academic
journals. Professional women are suffering "burnout" and succumbing to an
"infertility epidemic." Single women are grieving from a "man shortage." The
New York Times reports: Childless women are "depressed and confused" and
their ranks are swelling. *Newsweek* says: Unwed women are "hysterical" and

448

crumbling under a "profound crisis of confidence." The health advice manuals inform: High-powered career women are stricken with unprecedented outbreaks of "stress-induced disorders," hair loss, bad nerves, alcoholism, and even heart attacks. The psychology books advise: Independent women's loneliness represents "a major mental health problem today." Even founding feminist Betty Friedan has been spreading the word: she warns that women now suffer from a new identity crisis and "new 'problems that have no name.'"

How can American women be in so much trouble at the same time that 5 they are supposed to be so blessed? If the status of women has never been higher, why is their emotional state so low? If women got what they asked for, what could possibly be the matter now?

The prevailing wisdom of the past decade has supported one, and only 6 one, answer to this riddle: it must be all that equality that's causing all that pain. Women are unhappy precisely *because* they are free. Women are enslaved by their own liberation. They have grabbed at the gold ring of independence, only to miss the one ring that really matters. They have gained control of their fertility, only to destroy it. They have pursued their own professional dreams—and lost out on the greatest female adventure. The women's movement, as we are told time and again, has proved women's own worst enemy.

"In dispensing its spoils, women's liberation has given my generation 7 high incomes, our own cigarette, the option of single parenthood, rape crisis centers, personal lines of credit, free love, and female gynecologists," Mona Charen, a young law student, writes in the *National Review,* in an article titled "The Feminist Mistake." "In return it has effectively robbed us of one thing upon which the happiness of most women rests—men." The *National Review* is a conservative publication, but such charges against the women's movement are not confined to its pages. "Our generation was the human sacrifice" to the women's movement, *Los Angeles Times* feature writer Elizabeth Mehren contends in a *Time* cover story. Baby-boom women like her, she says, have been duped by feminism: "We believed the rhetoric." In *Newsweek,* writer Kay Ebeling dubs feminism "the Great Experiment That Failed" and asserts "women in my generation, its perpetrators, are the casualties." Even the beauty magazines are saying it: *Harper's Bazaar* accuses the women's movement of having "lost us [women] ground instead of gaining it."

In the last decade, publications from the *New York Times* to *Vanity Fair* to 8 the *Nation* have issued a steady stream of indictments against the women's movement, with such headlines as WHEN FEMINISM FAILED or THE AWFUL TRUTH ABOUT WOMEN'S LIB. They hold the campaign for women's equality responsible for nearly every woe besetting women, from mental depression to meager savings accounts, from teenage suicides to eating disorders to bad complexions. The "Today" show says women's liberation is to blame for bag ladies. A guest columnist in the *Baltimore Sun* even proposes that feminists produced the rise in slasher movies. By making the "violence" of abortion more acceptable, the author reasons, women's rights activists made it all right to show graphic murders on screen.

At the same time, other outlets of popular culture have been forging the   9
same connection: in Hollywood films, of which *Fatal Attraction* is only the
most famous, emancipated women with condominiums of their own slink
wild-eyed between bare walls, paying for their liberty with an empty bed, a
barren womb. "My biological clock is ticking so loud it keeps me awake at
night," Sally Field cries in the film *Surrender,* as, in an all too common transformation in the cinema of the '80s, an actress who once played scrappy
working heroines is now showcased groveling for a groom. In prime-time
television shows, from "thirtysomething" to "Family Man," single, professional, and feminist women are humiliated, turned into harpies, or hit by
nervous breakdowns; the wise ones recant their independent ways by the
closing sequence. In popular novels, from Gail Parent's *A Sign of the Eighties* to
Stephen King's *Misery,* unwed women shrink to sniveling spinsters or inflate
to fire-breathing she-devils; renouncing all aspirations but marriage, they beg
for wedding bands from strangers or swing sledgehammers at reluctant bach-
elors. We "blew it by waiting," a typically remorseful careerist sobs in Freda
Bright's *Singular Women;* she and her sister professionals are "condemned to
be childless forever." Even Erica Jong's high-flying independent heroine literally crashes by the end of the decade, as the author supplants *Fear of Flying's*
saucy Isadora Wing, a symbol of female sexual emancipation in the '70s, with
an embittered careerist-turned-recovering-"co-dependent" in *Any Woman's
Blues*—a book that is intended, as the narrator bluntly states, "to demonstrate
what a deadend the so-called sexual revolution had become, and how desperate so-called free women were in the last few years of our decadent epoch."

Popular psychology manuals peddle the same diagnosis for contemporary   10
female distress. "Feminism, having promised her a stronger sense of her own
identity, has given her little more than an identity *crisis,*" the best-selling advice manual *Being a Woman* asserts. The authors of the era's self-help classic
Smart Women/Foolish Choices proclaim that women's distress was "an unfortunate consequence of feminism," because "it created a myth among women
that the apex of self-realization could be achieved only through autonomy,
independence, and career."

In the Reagan and Bush years, government officials have needed no   11
prompting to endorse this thesis. Reagan spokeswoman Faith Whittlesey declared feminism a "straitjacket" for women, in the White House's only policy
speech on the status of the American female population—entitled "Radical
Feminism in Retreat." Law enforcement officers and judges, too, have
pointed a damning finger at feminism, claiming that they can chart a path
from rising female independence to rising female pathology. As a California
sheriff explained it to the press, "Women are enjoying a lot more freedom
now, and as a result, they are committing more crimes." The U.S. Attorney
General's Commission on Pornography even proposed that women's professional advancement might be responsible for rising rape rates. With more
women in college and at work now, the commission members reasoned in
their report, women just have more opportunities to be raped.

Some academics have signed on to the consensus, too—and they are the   12
"experts" who have enjoyed the highest profiles on the media circuit. On
network news and talk shows, they have advised millions of women that
feminism has condemned them to "a lesser life." Legal scholars have railed
against "the equality trap." Sociologists have claimed that "feminist-inspired"
legislative reforms have stripped women of special "protections." Economists
have argued that well-paid working women have created "a less stable American family." And demographers, with greatest fanfare, have legitimated the
prevailing wisdom with so-called neutral data on sex ratios and fertility
trends; they say they actually have the numbers to prove that equality
doesn't mix with marriage and motherhood.

Finally, some "liberated" women themselves have joined the lamenta-   13
tions. In confessional accounts, works that invariably receive a hearty greeting from the publishing industry, "recovering Superwomen" tell all. In *The
Cost of Loving: Women and the New Fear of Intimacy,* Megan Marshall, a Har-
vard-pedigreed writer, asserts that the feminist "Myth of Independence" has
turned her generation into unloved and unhappy fast-trackers, "dehumanized" by careers and "uncertain of their gender identity." Other diaries of mad
Superwomen charge that "the hard-core feminist viewpoint," as one of them
puts it, has relegated educated executive achievers to solitary nights of frozen
dinners and closet drinking. The triumph of equality, they report, has merely
given women hives, stomach cramps, eye-twitching disorders, even comas.

But what "equality" are all these authorities talking about?   14

If American women are so equal, why do they represent two-thirds of all   15
poor adults? Why are nearly 75 percent of full-time working women making
less than $20,000 a year, nearly double the male rate? Why are they still far
more likely than men to live in poor housing and receive no health insurance, and twice as likely to draw no pension? Why does the average working
woman's salary still lag as far behind the average man's as it did twenty years
ago? Why does the average female college graduate today earn less than a
man with no more than a high school diploma (just as she did in the '50s)—
and why does the average female high school graduate today earn less than a
male high school dropout? Why do American women, in fact, face one of the
worst gender-based pay gaps in the developed world?

If women have "made it," then why are nearly 80 percent of working   16
women still stuck in traditional "female" jobs—as secretaries, administrative
"support" workers and salesclerks? And, conversely, why are they less than 8
percent of all federal and state judges, less than 6 percent of all law partners,
and less than one half of 1 percent of top corporate managers? Why are there
only three female state governors, two female U.S. senators, and two Fortune
500 chief executives? Why are only nineteen of the four thousand corporate
officers and directors women—and why do more than half the boards of Fortune companies still lack even one female member?

If women "have it all," then why don't they have the most basic require-   17
ments to achieve equality in the work force? Unlike virtually all other indus-

trialized nations, the U.S. government still has no family-leave and child care programs—and more than 99 percent of American private employers don't offer child care either. Though business leaders say they are aware of and deplore sex discrimination, corporate America has yet to make an honest effort toward eradicating it. In a 1990 national poll of chief executives at Fortune 1000 companies, more than 80 percent acknowledged that discrimination impedes female employees' progress—yet, less than 1 percent of these same companies regarded *remedying* sex discrimination as a goal that their personnel departments should pursue. In fact, when the companies' human resource officers were asked to rate their department's priorities, women's advancement ranked last.

If women are so "free," why are their reproductive freedoms in greater   18
jeopardy today than a decade earlier? Why do women who want to postpone childbearing now have fewer options than ten years ago? The availability of different forms of contraception has declined, research for new birth control has virtually halted, new laws restricting abortion—or even *information* about abortion—for young and poor women have been passed, and the U.S. Supreme Court has shown little ardor in defending the right it granted in 1973.

Nor is women's struggle for equal education over; as a 1989 study found,   19
three-fourths of all high schools still violate the federal law banning sex discrimination in education. In colleges, undergraduate women receive only 70 percent of the aid undergraduate men get in grants and work-study jobs—and women's sports programs receive a pittance compared with men's. A review of state equal-education laws in the late '80s found that only thirteen states had adopted the minimum provisions required by the federal Title IX law—and only seven states had anti-discrimination regulations that covered all education levels.

Nor do women enjoy equality in their own homes, where they still shoul-   20
der 70 percent of the household duties—and the only major change in the last fifteen years is that now middle-class men *think* they do more around the house. (In fact, a national poll finds the ranks of women saying their husbands share equally in child care shrunk to 31 percent in 1987 from 40 percent three years earlier.) Furthermore, in thirty states, it is still generally legal for husbands to rape their wives; and only ten states have laws mandating arrest for domestic violence—even though battering was the leading cause of injury of women in the late '80s. Women who have no other option but to flee find that isn't much of an alternative either. Federal funding for battered women's shelters has been withheld and one third of the 1 million battered women who seek emergency shelter each year can find none. Blows from men contributed far more to the rising numbers of "bag ladies" than the ill effects of feminism. In the '80s, almost half of all homeless women (the fastest growing segment of the homeless) were refugees of domestic violence.

The word may be that women have been "liberated," but women them-   21
selves seem to feel otherwise. Repeatedly in national surveys, majorities of women say they are still far from equality. Nearly 70 percent of women polled

by the *New York Times* in 1989 said the movement for women's rights had only just begun. Most women in the 1990 Virginia Slims opinion poll agreed with the statement that conditions for their sex in American society had improved "a little, not a lot." In poll after poll in the decade, overwhelming majorities of women said they needed equal pay and equal job opportunities, they needed an Equal Rights Amendment, they needed the right to an abortion without government interference, they needed a federal law guaranteeing maternity leave, they needed decent child care services. They have none of these. So how exactly have we "won" the war for women's rights?

Seen against this background, the much ballyhooed claim that feminism   22
is responsible for making women miserable becomes absurd—and irrelevant. As we shall see in the chapters to follow, the afflictions ascribed to feminism are all myths. From "the man shortage" to "the infertility epidemic" to "female burnout" to "toxic day care," these so-called female crises have had their origins not in the actual conditions of women's lives but rather in a closed system that starts and ends in the media, popular culture, and advertising—an endless feedback loop that perpetuates and exaggerates its own false images of womanhood.

Women themselves don't single out the women's movement as the   23
source of their misery. To the contrary, in national surveys 75 to 95 percent of women credit the feminist campaign with *improving* their lives, and a similar proportion say that the women's movement should keep pushing for change. Less than 8 percent think the women's movement might have actually made their lot worse.

* * *

What actually is troubling the American female population, then? If the   24
many ponderers of the Woman Question really wanted to know, they might have asked their subjects. In public opinion surveys, women consistently rank their own *inequality,* at work and at home, among their most urgent concerns. Over and over, women complain to pollsters about a lack of economic, not marital, opportunities; they protest that working men, not working women, fail to spend time in the nursery and the kitchen. The Roper Organization's survey analysts find that men's opposition to equality is "a major cause of resentment and stress" and "a major irritant for most women today." It is justice for their gender, not wedding rings and bassinets, that women believe to be in desperately short supply. When the *New York Times* polled women in 1989 about "the most important problem facing women today," job discrimination was the overwhelming winner; none of the crises the media and popular culture had so assiduously promoted even made the charts. In the 1990 Virginia Slims poll, women were most upset by their lack of money, followed by the refusal of their men to shoulder child care and domestic duties. By contrast, when the women were asked where the quest for a husband or the desire to hold a "less pressured" job or to stay at home ranked on their list of concerns, they placed them at the bottom.

As the last decade ran its course, women's unhappiness with inequality   25
only mounted. In national polls, the ranks of women protesting discrimina-

tory treatment in business, political, and personal life climbed sharply. The proportion of women complaining of unequal employment opportunities jumped more than ten points from the '70s, and the number of women complaining of unequal barriers to job advancement climbed even higher. By the end of the decade, 80 percent to 95 percent of women said they suffered from job discrimination and unequal pay. Sex discrimination charges filed with the Equal Employment Opportunity Commission rose nearly 25 percent in the Reagan years, and charges of general harassment directed at working women more than doubled. In the decade, complaints of sexual harassment nearly doubled. At home, a much increased proportion of women complained to pollsters of male mistreatment, unequal relationships, and male efforts to, in the words of the Virginia Slims poll, "keep women down." The share of women in the Roper surveys who agreed that men were "basically kind, gentle, and thoughtful" fell from almost 70 percent in 1970 to 50 percent by 1990. And outside their homes, women felt more threatened, too: in the 1990 Virginia Slims poll, 72 percent of women said they felt "more afraid and uneasy on the streets today" than they did a few years ago. Lest this be attributed only to a general rise in criminal activity, by contrast only 49 percent of men felt this way.

While the women's movement has certainly made women more cognizant of their own inequality, the rising chorus of female protest shouldn't be written off as feminist-induced "oversensitivity." The monitors that serve to track slippage in women's status have been working overtime since the early '80s. Government and private surveys are showing that women's already vast representation in the lowliest occupations is rising, their tiny presence in higher-paying trade and craft jobs stalled or backsliding, their minuscule representation in upper management posts stagnant or falling, and their pay dropping in the very occupations where they have made the most "progress." The status of women lowest on the income ladder has plunged most perilously; government budget cuts in the first four years of the Reagan administration alone pushed nearly 2 million female-headed families and nearly 5 million women below the poverty line. And the prime target of government rollbacks has been one sex only: one-third of the Reagan budget cuts, for example, came out of programs that predominantly serve women—even more extraordinary when one considers that all these programs combined represent only 10 percent of the federal budget.

The alarms aren't just going off in the work force. In national politics, the already small numbers of women in both elective posts and political appointments fell during the '80s. In private life, the average amount that a divorced man paid in child support fell by about 25 percent from the late '70s to the mid-'80s (to a mere $140 a month). Domestic-violence shelters recorded a more than 100 percent increase in the numbers of women taking refuge in their quarters between 1983 and 1987. And government records chronicled a spectacular rise in sexual violence against women. Reported rapes more than doubled from the early '70s—at nearly twice the rate of all other violent crimes and four times the overall crime rate in the United States. While the homicide rate declined, sex-related murders rose 160 percent between 1976 and 1984. And these murders weren't simply the random, impersonal by-product of a violent society; at least one-third of the women were killed by their husbands or boyfriends, and the majority of that group were murdered just after declaring their independence in the most intimate manner—by filing for divorce and leaving home.

By the end of the decade, women were starting to tell pollsters that they 28 feared their sex's social status was once again beginning to slip. They believed they were facing an "erosion of respect," as the 1990 Virginia Slims poll summed up the sentiment. After years in which an increasing percentage of women had said their status had improved from a decade earlier, the proportion suddenly shrunk by 5 percent in the last half of the '80s, the Roper Organization reported. And it fell most sharply among women in their thirties—the age group most targeted by the media and advertisers—dropping about ten percentage points between 1985 and 1990.

Some women began to piece the picture together. In the 1989 *New York* 29 *Times* poll, more than half of black women and one-fourth of white women put it into words. They told pollsters they believed men were now trying to retract the gains women had made in the last twenty years. "I wanted more autonomy," was how one woman, a thirty-seven-year-old nurse, put it. And her estranged husband "wanted to take it away."

The truth is that the last decade has seen a powerful counterassault on 30 women's rights, a backlash, an attempt to retract the handful of small and hard-won victories that the feminist movement did manage to win for women. This counterassault is largely insidious: in a kind of pop-culture version of the Big Lie, it stands the truth boldly on its head and proclaims that the very steps that have elevated women's position have actually led to their downfall.

The backlash is at once sophisticated and banal, deceptively "progressive" 31 and proudly backward. It deploys both the "new" findings of "scientific research" and the dime-store moralism of yesteryear; it turns into media sound bites both the glib pronouncements of pop-psych trend-watchers and the frenzied rhetoric of New Right preachers. The backlash has succeeded in framing virtually the whole issue of women's rights in its own language. Just as Reaganism shifted political discourse far to the right and demonized liberalism, so the backlash convinced the public that women's "liberation" was the true contemporary American scourge—the source of an endless laundry list of personal, social, and economic problems.

But what has made women unhappy in the last decade is not their 32 "equality"—which they don't yet have—but the rising pressure to halt, and even reverse, women's quest for that equality. The "man shortage" and the "infertility epidemic" are not the price of liberation; in fact, they do not even exist. But these chimeras are the chisels of a society-wide backlash. They are part of a relentless whittling-down process—much of it amounting to outright propaganda—that has served to stir women's private anxieties and break their political wills. Identifying feminism as women's enemy only furthers the ends of a backlash against women's equality, simultaneously deflecting attention from the backlash's central role and recruiting women to attack their own cause.

Some social observers may well ask whether the current pressures on women actually constitute a backlash—or just a continuation of American society's long-standing resistance to women's rights. Certainly hostility to female independence has always been with us. But if fear and loathing of feminism is a sort of perpetual viral condition in our culture, it is not always in an acute stage; its symptoms subside and resurface periodically. And it is these episodes of resurgence, such as the one we face now, that can accurately be termed "backlashes" to women's advancement. If we trace these occurrences in American history (as we will do in a later chapter), we find such flare-ups are hardly random; they have always been triggered by the perception—accurate or not—that women are making great strides. These outbreaks are backlashes because they have always arisen in reaction to women's "progress," caused not simply by a bedrock of misogyny but by the specific efforts of contemporary women to improve their status, efforts that have been interpreted time and again by men—especially men grappling with real threats to their economic and social well-being on other fronts—as spelling their own masculine doom.   33

The most recent round of backlash first surfaced in the late '70s on the fringes, among the evangelical right. By the early '80s, the fundamentalist ideology had shouldered its way into the White House. By the mid-'80s, as resistance to women's rights acquired political and social acceptability, it passed into the popular culture. And in every case, the timing coincided with signs that women were believed to be on the verge of breakthrough.   34

Just when women's quest for equal rights seemed closest to achieving its objectives, the backlash struck it down. Just when a "gender gap" at the voting booth surfaced in 1980, and women in politics began to talk of capitalizing on it, the Republican party elevated Ronald Reagan and both political parties began to shunt women's rights off their platforms. Just when support for feminism and the Equal Rights Amendment reached a record high in 1981, the amendment was defeated the following year. Just when women were starting to mobilize against battering and sexual assaults, the federal government stalled funding for battered-women's programs, defeated bills to fund shelters, and shut down its Office of Domestic Violence—only two years after opening it in 1979. Just when record numbers of younger women were supporting feminist goals in the mid-'80s (more of them, in fact, than older women) and a majority of all women were calling themselves feminists, the media declared the advent of a younger "postfeminist generation" that supposedly reviled the women's movement. Just when women racked up their largest percentage ever supporting the right to abortion, the U.S. Supreme Court moved toward reconsidering it.   35

In other words, the antifeminist backlash has been set off not by women's achievement of full equality but by the increased possibility that they might win it. It is a preemptive strike that stops women long before they reach the   36 finish line. "A backlash may be an indication that women really have had an effect," feminist psychologist Dr. Jean Baker Miller has written, "but backlashes occur when advances have been small, before changes are sufficient to help many people. . . . It is almost as if the leaders of backlashes use the fear of change as a threat before major change has occurred." In the last decade, some women did make substantial advances before the backlash hit, but millions of others were left behind, stranded. Some women now enjoy the right to legal abortion—but not the 44 million women, from the indigent to the military work force, who depend on the federal government for their medical care. Some women can now walk into high-paying professional careers—but not the more than 19 million still in the typing pools or behind the department store sales counters. (Contrary to popular myth about the "have-it-all" baby-boom women, the largest percentage of women in this generation remain typists and clerks.)

As the backlash has gathered force, it has cut off the few from the many— 37 and the few women who have advanced seek to prove, as a social survival tactic, that they aren't so interested in advancement after all. Some of them parade their defection from the women's movement, while their working-class peers founder and cling to the splintered remains of the feminist cause. While a very few affluent and celebrity women who are showcased in news articles boast about having "found my niche as Mrs. Andy Mill" and going home to "bake bread," the many working-class women appeal for their economic rights—flocking to unions in record numbers, striking on their own for pay equity and establishing their own fledgling groups for working women's rights. In 1986, while 41 percent of upper-income women were claiming in the Gallup poll that they were not feminists, only 26 percent of low-income women were making the same claim.

***

Women's advances and retreats are generally described in military terms: 38 battles won, battles lost, points and territory gained and surrendered. The metaphor of combat is not without its merits in this context and, clearly, the same sort of martial accounting and vocabulary is already surfacing here. But by imagining the conflict as two battalions neatly arrayed on either side of the line, we miss the entangled nature, the locked embrace, of a "war" between women and the male culture they inhabit. We miss the reactive nature of a backlash, which, by definition, can exist only in response to another force.

In times when feminism is at a low ebb, women assume the reactive 39 role—privately and most often covertly struggling to assert themselves against the dominant cultural tide. But when feminism itself becomes the tide, the opposition doesn't simply go along with the reversal: it digs in its heels, brandishes its fists, builds walls and dams. And its resistance creates countercurrents and treacherous undertows.

The force and furor of the backlash churn beneath the surface, largely in- 40 visible to the public eye. On occasion in the last decade, they have burst into view. We have seen New Right politicians condemn women's independence, antiabortion protesters firebomb women's clinics, fundamentalist preachers damn feminists as "whores" and "witches." Other signs of the backlash's wrath, by their sheer brutality, can push their way into public consciousness for a time—the sharp increase in rape, for example, or the rise in pornography that depicts extreme violence against women.

More subtle indicators in popular culture may receive momentary, and   41
often bemused, media notice, then quickly slip from social awareness: A report, for instance, that the image of women on prime-time TV shows has suddenly degenerated. A survey of mystery fiction finding the numbers of female characters tortured and mutilated mysteriously multiplying. The puzzling news that, as one commentator put it, "So many hit songs have the B-word [bitch] to refer to women that some rap music seems to be veering toward rape music." The ascendancy of virulently misogynist comics like Andrew Dice Clay—who called women "pigs" and "sluts" and strutted in films in which women were beaten, tortured, and blown up—or radio hosts like Rush Limbaugh, whose broadsides against "femi-Nazi" feminists made his syndicated program the most popular radio talk show in the nation. Or word that in 1987, the American Women in Radio & Television couldn't award its annual prize for ads that feature women positively: it could find no ad that qualified.

These phenomena are all related, but that doesn't mean they are some-   42
how coordinated. The backlash is not a conspiracy, with a council dispatching agents from some central control room, nor are the people who serve its ends often aware of their role; some even consider themselves feminists. For the most part, its workings are encoded and internalized, diffuse and chameleonic. Not all of the manifestations of the backlash are of equal weight or significance either; some are mere ephemera, generated by a culture machine that is always scrounging for a "fresh" angle. Taken as a whole, however, these codes and cajolings, these whispers and threats and myths, move overwhelmingly in one direction: they try to push women back into their "acceptable" roles—whether as Daddy's girl or fluttery romantic, active nester or passive love object.

Although the backlash is not an organized movement, that doesn't make   43
it any less destructive. In fact, the lack of orchestration, the absence of a single string-puller, only makes it harder to see—and perhaps more effective. A backlash against women's rights succeeds to the degree that it appears *not* to be political, that it appears not to be a struggle at all. It is most powerful when it goes private, when it lodges inside a woman's mind and turns her vision inward, until she imagines the pressure is all in her head, until she begins to enforce the backlash, too—on herself.

In the last decade, the backlash has moved through the culture's secret   44
chambers, traveling through passageways of flattery and fear. Along the way, it has adopted disguises: a mask of mild derision or the painted face of deep "concern." Its lips profess pity for any woman who won't fit the mold, while it tries to clamp the mold around her ears. It pursues a divide-and-conquer strategy: single versus married women, working women versus homemakers,

middle- versus working-class. It manipulates a system of rewards and punishments, elevating women who follow its rules, isolating those who don't. The backlash remarkets old myths about women as new facts and ignores all appeals to reason. Cornered, it denies its own existence, points an accusatory finger at feminism, and burrows deeper underground.

Backlash happens to be the title of a 1947 Hollywood movie in which a 45 man frames his wife for a murder he's committed. The backlash against women's rights works in much the same way: its rhetoric charges feminists with all the crimes it perpetrates. The backlash line blames the women's movement for the "feminization of poverty"—while the backlash's own instigators in Washington pushed through the budget cuts that helped impoverish millions of women, fought pay equity proposals, and undermined equal opportunity laws. The backlash line claims the women's movement cares nothing for children's rights—while its own representatives in the capital and state legislatures have blocked one bill after another to improve child care, slashed billions of dollars in federal aid for children, and relaxed state licensing standards for day care centers. The backlash line accuses the women's movement of creating a generation of unhappy single and childless women— but its purveyors in the media are the ones guilty of making single and childless women feel like circus freaks.

To blame feminism for women's "lesser life" is to miss entirely the point 46 of feminism, which is to win women a wider range of experience. Feminism remains a pretty simple concept, despite repeated—and enormously effective—efforts to dress it up in greasepaint and turn its proponents into gargoyles. As Rebecca West wrote sardonically in 1913, "I myself have never been able to find out precisely what feminism is: I only know that people call me a feminist whenever I express sentiments that differentiate me from a doormat."

The meaning of the word "feminist" has not really changed since it first 47 appeared in a book review in the *Athenaeum* of April 27, 1895, describing a woman who "has in her the capacity of fighting her way back to independence." It is the basic proposition that, as Nora put it in Ibsen's *A Doll's House* a century ago, "Before everything else I'm a human being." It is the simply worded sign hoisted by a little girl in the 1970 Women's Strike for Equality: I AM NOT A BARBIE DOLL. Feminism asks the world to recognize at long last that women aren't decorative ornaments, worthy vessels, members of a "special-interest group." They are half (in fact, now more than half) of the national population, and just as deserving of rights and opportunities, just as capable of participating in the world's events, as the other half. Feminism's agenda is basic: It asks that women not be forced to "choose" between public justice and private happiness. It asks that women be free to define themselves— instead of having their identity defined for them, time and again, by their culture and their men.

The fact that these are still such incendiary notions should tell us that 48 American women have a way to go before they enter the promised land of equality.

Questions

1. Describe in your own words what Faludi means by the media's "backlash." Can you think of recent examples of this backlash in the newspaper or in news magazines?

2. What does Faludi mean when she says that the media's representation of women as miserable constitutes "propaganda"? What does she mean when she says that the rhetoric of those against women's rights "charges feminists with all the crimes it perpetuates"?

3. Examine a current women's magazine (*Vogue, Glamour, Mademoiselle*). How do its advertisements, articles, and features define what it means to be a woman? Can you find evidence of "backlash"? How influential do you think these magazines are on the reader's ideas of feminism?

4. How do you think Faludi would react to Gorman's essay? What similarities and differences can you note?

I Want a Wife

JUDY SYFERS

Judy Syfers has an undergraduate degree in painting from the University of Iowa and has been an active voice in the women's movement for years.

In this essay, Syfers gives an exhausting catalogue of a wife's "duties" and concludes with an exasperated "My God, who wouldn't want a wife?" This essay was originally printed in the first issue of Ms. *in 1971.*

I belong to that classification of people known as wives. I am A Wife. And, not altogether incidentally, I am a mother.

Not too long ago a male friend of mine appeared on the scene fresh from a recent divorce. He had one child, who is, of course, with his ex-wife. He is looking for another wife. As I thought about him while I was ironing one evening, it suddenly occurred to me that I, too, would like to have a wife. Why do I want a wife?

I would like to go back to school so that I can become economically independent, support myself, and, if need be, support those dependent upon me. I want a wife who will work and send me to school. And while I am going to school I want a wife to take care of my children. I want a wife to keep track of the children's doctor and dentist appointments. And to keep track of mine, too. I want a wife to make sure my children eat properly and are kept clean. I want a wife who will wash the children's clothes and keep them mended. I want a wife who is a good nurturant attendant to my children, who arranges for their schooling, makes sure that they have an adequate social life with their peers, takes them to the park, the zoo, etc. I want a wife who takes care of the children when they are sick, a wife who arranges to be around when the children need special care, because, of course, I cannot miss classes at school. My wife must arrange to lose time at work and not lose the job. It may mean a small cut in my wife's income from time to time, but I guess I can tolerate that. Needless to say, my wife will arrange and pay for the care of the children while my wife is working.

I want a wife who will take care of *my* physical needs. I want a wife who will keep my house clean. A wife who will pick up after my children, a wife who will pick up after me. I want a wife who will keep my clothes clean, ironed, mended, replaced when need be, and who will see to it that my personal things are kept in their proper place so that I can find what I need the minute I need it. I want a wife who cooks the meals, a wife who is a *good* cook. I want a wife who will plan the menus, do the necessary grocery shopping, prepare the meals, serve them pleasantly, and then do the cleaning up while I do my studying. I want a wife who will care for me when I am sick

461

and sympathize with my pain and loss of time from school. I want a wife to go along when our family takes a vacation so that someone can continue to care for me and my children when I need a rest and change of scene.

I want a wife who will not bother me with rambling complaints about a   5
wife's duties. But I want a wife who will listen to me when I feel the need to explain a rather difficult point I have come across in my course of studies. And I want a wife who will type my papers for me when I have written them.

I want a wife who will take care of the details of my social life. When my   6
wife and I are invited out by my friends, I want a wife who will take care of the babysitting arrangements. When I meet people at school that I like and want to entertain, I want a wife who will have the house clean, will prepare a special meal, serve it to me and my friends, and not interrupt when I talk about things that interest me and my friends. I want a wife who will have arranged that the children are fed and ready for bed before my guests arrive so that the children do not bother us. I want a wife who takes care of the needs of my guests so that they feel comfortable, who makes sure that they have an ashtray, that they are passed the hors d'oeuvres, that they are offered a second helping of the food, that their wine glasses are replenished when necessary, that their coffee is served to them as they like it. And I want a wife who knows that sometimes I need a night out by myself.

I want a wife who is sensitive to my sexual needs, a wife who makes love   7
passionately and eagerly when I feel like it, a wife who makes sure that I am satisfied. And, of course, I want a wife who will not demand sexual attention when I am not in the mood for it. I want a wife who assumes the complete responsibility for birth control, because I do not want more children. I want a wife who will remain sexually faithful to me so that I do not have to clutter up my intellectual life with jealousies. And I want a wife who understands that *my* sexual needs may entail more than strict adherence to monogamy. I must, after all, be able to relate to people as fully as possible.

If, by chance, I find another person more suitable as a wife than the wife I   8
already have, I want the liberty to replace my present wife with another one. Naturally, I will expect a fresh, new life; my wife will take the children and be solely responsible for them so that I am left free.

When I am through with school and have a job, I want my wife to quit   9
working and remain at home so that my wife can more fully and completely take care of a wife's duties.

My God, who *wouldn't* want a wife?   10

Questions

1. What is the tone of Syfers's essay? Do you think she fairly documents a wife's "duties"?

2. Syfers's article was published over twenty years ago. Do you find it dated? Why or why not?

3. Do you agree with her definition of a wife? What do you expect from a spouse?

4. Can Syfers's article be considered sexist? Why or why not?

How to Get the Women's Movement Moving Again

BETTY FRIEDAN

Betty Friedan (b. 1921) is the author of The Feminine Mystique *(1963) that sparked the feminist movement in America. She is also the founder of the National Organization for Women (NOW), and served as its first president (1966–1970). She has lectured extensively on feminism and has served as a visiting lecturer at many universities including Yale and the University of Southern California.*

In the following excerpt, Friedan explores some of the effects of the feminist movement on contemporary women and wonders if some of the apparent gains of the movement may in fact be "illusory." She argues that a "second stage" is needed in the feminist movement—a stage in which women can get beyond the battle of the sexes and begin to openly discuss "the importance of family, of women's need to give and get love." This excerpt is from The Second Stage *(1986).*

This is addressed to any woman who has ever said "we" about the women's movement, including those who say: "I'm not a feminist, but. . ." And it's addressed to quite a few men.   1

It's a personal message, not at all objective, and it's in response to those who think our modern women's movement is over—either because it is defeated and a failure, or because it has triumphed, its work done, its mission accomplished. After all, any daughter can now dream of being an astronaut, after Sally Ride, or running for President, after Geraldine Ferraro.   2

I do not think that the job of the modern women's movement is done. And I do not believe the movement has failed. For one thing, those of us who started the modern women's movement, or came into it after marriage and children or from jobs as "invisible women" in the office, still carry the glow of "it changed my whole life," an aliveness, the satisfaction of finding our own voice and power, and the skills we didn't have a chance to develop before.   3

I do believe, though, that the movement is in trouble. I was too passionately involved in its conception, its birth, its growing pains, its youthful flowering, to acquiesce quietly to its going gently so soon into the night. But, like a lot of other mothers, I have been denying the symptoms of what I now feel forced to confront as a profound paralysis of the women's movement in America.   4

I see as symptoms of this paralysis the impotence in the face of funda-   5
mentalist backlash; the wasting of energy in internal power struggles when
no real issues are at stake; the nostalgic harking back to old rhetoric, old
ideas, old modes of action instead of confronting new threats and new problems with new thinking: the failure to mobilize the young generation who
take for granted the rights we won and who do not defend those rights as
they are being taken away in front of our eyes, and the preoccupation with
pornography and other sexual diversions that do not affect most women's
lives. I sense an unwillingness to deal with the complex realities of female
survival in male-modeled careers, with the new illusions of having it all in
marriage and equality in divorce, and with the basic causes of the grim feminization of poverty. The potential of women's political power is slipping away
between the poles of self-serving feminist illusion and male and female opportunism. The promise of that empowerment of women that enabled so
many of us to change their own lives is being betrayed by our failure to mobilize the next generation to move beyond us.

Evidence of the movement's paralysis has been impinging on my own life   6
in many ways:

■ Over the last few years, I've noticed how the machinery for enforcing   7
the laws against sex discrimination in employment and education has been
gradually dismantled by the Reagan Administration, and how the laws' scope
has been narrowed by the courts, with little public outcry. Professional lobbyists for women's organizations objected, of course, but there have been no
mass protests from the women in the jobs and professions that those laws
opened to them. In the early days of the National Organization for Women,
nearly 20 years ago, we demanded and won an executive order banning government contracts to companies or institutions guilty of sex discrimination;
it was the first major weapon women could use to demand jobs. Some officials in the Administration are proposing the order's elimination. The Reagan
Administration is also urging the courts to undo recent movement victories
regarding equal pay for work of comparable value.

■ The crusade against women's right to choice in the matter of childbirth   8
and abortion, preached from the pulpits of fundamentalist churches and by
the Catholic hierarchy, first achieved a ban on Federal aid to poor women
seeking abortion, then the elimination of United States Government aid to
third-world family-planning programs that counsel abortion. The Attorney
General announced in the summer of 1985 that he would seek to reverse the
historical Supreme Court decision, Roe v. Wade, which in 1973 decreed that
the right of a woman to decide according to her own conscience when and
whether and how many times to bear a child was as basic a right as any the
Constitution originally spelled out for men.

At a recent meeting to mobilize women in mass communications to help   9
save that right, I was amazed to hear a one-time radical feminist suggest that
abortion should not be defended in terms of a woman's right. "Women's
rights are not chic in America anymore," she argued.

■ The main interest of many feminist groups in various states in recent   10
years seems to be outlawing pornography. Laws prohibiting pornography as a
form of sex discrimination and violation of civil rights have been proposed in
Minnesota, Indiana, California and New York. A former NOW leader who
practices law in upstate New York was startled, when she dropped in on a
feminist fund-raiser, to be asked to support a nationwide ban on sexually explicit materials. When she warned, "A law like that would be far more dangerous to women than the most obscene pornography," she was greeted with
incomprehension and hostility.

■ At a black-tie banquet at the Plaza Hotel in New York in September   11
1985, I proudly watched a sparkling parade of champion women athletes as
they entertained the corporate donors who sponsor their games and scholar-
ships through the 11-year-old Women's Sports Foundation. The women
champions in basketball, judo, gymnastics, tennis, skiing, swimming, boxing,
running and sports-car and dogsled racing paraded down the runway in se-
quined miniskirts and satin jumpsuits, clasping their hands over their heads
in the victory gesture. They gave credit to parents and teachers, but not one
mentioned the recent Supreme Court decision regarding Grove City College
in Pennsylvania. That decision threatens to remove school athletic programs
from the protection of the law banning sex discrimination in Federally assisted education—which is what provided crucial athletic training to these
new female champions in the first place.

■ At another reception, one of the many new networks of women corpo-   12
rate executives, a woman in her late thirties, holding a job a woman had
never been given before in a large insurance company, told me: "If my slot
became open today, they wouldn't give it to a woman. Not because I haven't
done a good job—I keep getting raises. But they've stopped talking about getting more women on the board—or in the company. The word has gone out
from the White House: They don't have to worry anymore about women and
blacks. Its over.". . .

■ At one company, executives who faced class-action suits a decade ago   13
now boast that their best new employees are the women. They were shocked
when one of their star superwomen, on a rung very near the top, became
pregnant with her second child and announced she was quitting. The boss
even offered her an extended maternity leave, which is not required by law or
union contract, but she quit anyway. "You may never have another chance
like this," her colleagues, male and female, protested. "I'll never have these
years with my children again," she answered. Most of them did not understand. They figured that whatever guilt or pressure she suffered trying to juggle baby and demanding job was her peculiar "personal problem." That sort
of thing is not discussed as a woman's movement problem, requiring a political solution, in her professional network.

■ Another longtime feminist mother, with three "yuppie" daughters—   14
banker, lawyer, talent agent—says, regretfully, "They're not feminists . . . they
take all that for granted." She goes on to tell me that "Janey's problem is her
love life and her job, and Ann's is her kids and her job, and Phyllis thinks

maybe she should go back and get an MBA. With all that and exercise class, they don't have time for the meetings we used to go to. Why do they have to be feminists when they never had to suffer like we did?". . .

* * *

. . . Aware of these symptoms, and yet denying my own sense that the   15
American women's movement was over, not ready to admit defeat but wanting to move on to other things myself, I went to Kenya in the summer of 1985 out of a sheer sense of historic duty to see the thing through to its end. Most card-carrying American feminists were not even bothering with the meeting in Nairobi. NOW had scheduled its own convention in New Orleans at the same time as the United Nations World Conference of Women.

Ten years earlier, when the modern women's movement was spreading   16
from America to the world, I had joined women wanting to organize in their countries in appealing to the UN to call a world assembly of women. At the first two world women's meetings, in Mexico in 1975 and Copenhagen in 1980, I had seen the beginnings of international networking among women broken up by organized disrupters led by armed gunmen shouting slogans against "imperialism" and "Zionism." I had been appalled at the way the official male delegates from Arab countries and other third-world and Communist nations that control the UN showed contempt for women's rights, using those conferences mainly to launch a new doctrine of religious and ethnic hate, equating Zionism and racism. And I had been repelled by the way the delegates from Western countries, mostly male officials or their wives and female flunkies, let them thereby rob those conferences of the moral and political weight they might have given to the advance of women worldwide. This year, the United States delegation had instructions from President Reagan to walk out if the question of Zionism was included in the conclusions reached at Nairobi.

To my amazement, the women's movement emerged in Nairobi with suf-   17
ficient strength worldwide to impose its own agenda of women's concerns over the male political agenda that had divided it before. Despite, or because of, the backlash and other problems they face at home, nearly 17,000 women from 159 nations assembled, some 14,000 having paid their own way or been sent by volunteer, church or women's groups to the unofficial forum that is part of every such UN conference. Some traveled by plane three and four days, or by bus from African villages.

Whole new worlds of women's skills, strength, expertise and a new confi-   18
dence in themselves and each other became visible in 1800 workshops at the unofficial world forum on the Nairobi University campus. Women in saris and African Kangas, blue jeans and summer dresses, overflowed into the corridors, discussing "New Dimensions of Women's Spirituality," "Women as the Driving Force in Development," "The Economic Value of Women's Unpaid Work," "Getting Benefits for Part-time Workers," "Female Sexuality in Different Religious Traditions." The new women lawyers and jurists from Asia, Africa and Latin America used international law, backed up by the media skills of black and white veterans of American civil rights and women's movements, to force the Kenyan government to let us double up and stay in the

hotel rooms from which they were going to evict us because of the unexpected numbers of official delegates and journalists. The scholars from centers of women's studies that now exist in 32 nations got beyond "defining
everything in terms of our subordination to men" to new feminist thinking,
based on women's own experience, "embracing rather than denying biological differences between the sexes," as a brilliant woman scholar from Trinidad
put it. New women theologians compared notes in the way their scriptures
(Bible, Talmud, Koran) have been distorted by the fundamentalists trying to
use every religion's authority to put women down. Across the lines of capitalism, communism, socialism and different levels of development, we found
common roots of economic discrimination against women in the unpaid and
undervalued housework and child care which women everywhere are still expected to do on top of paid work, for which women everywhere are still paid
less than work of comparable value done by men.

There was a bypassing, or bridging, of the old, abstract ideological con-   19
flicts that had seemed to divide women before—a moving beyond the old
rhetoric of career versus family, equality versus development, feminism versus socialism, religion versus feminism, or feminism as an imperialist capitalist arrogance irrelevant to poor third-world women. What took the place of
all this was a discussion of concrete strategies for women to acquire more
control of their lives. Third-world revolutionaries, Arab and Israeli women, as
well as Japanese, Greeks and Latins, gathered under a baobab tree where,
every day at noon, like some African tribal elder, I led a discussion on "Future
Directions of Feminism.". . .

. . . I and other Americans—as many black as white among the 2,000 of   20
us at Nairobi—went home strengthened, resolved not to accept backward-
nation status for American women. For though we had gone to Nairobi sub-
dued by our own setbacks and sophisticated enough not to offer Western
feminism as the answer to the problems of women of the third world, it was
truly humiliating to discover that we are no longer the cutting edge of modern feminism or world progress toward equality. Even Kenya has an equal
rights clause in its Constitution!

***

How can we let the women's movement die out here in America when   21
what we began is taking hold now all over the world? I would like to suggest
10 things that might be done to break the blocks that seem to have stymied
the women's movement in America:

1. Begin a new round of consciousness-raising for the new generation.   22
These women, each thinking she is alone with her personal guilt and pressures,
trying to "have it all," having second thoughts about her professional career,
desperately trying to have a baby before it is too late, with or without husband,
and maybe secretly blaming the movement for getting her into this mess, are
almost as isolated, and as powerless in their isolation, as those suburban housewives afflicted by "the problem that had no name" whom I interviewed for
"The Feminine Mystique" over 20 years ago. Those women put a name to their
problem; they got together with other women in the feminist groups and began to work for political solutions and began to change their lives.

That has to happen again to free a new generation of women from its   23
new double burden of guilt and isolation. The guilts of less-than-perfect
motherhood and less-than-perfect professional career performance are real
because it's not possible to "have it all" when jobs are still structured for men
whose wives take care of the details of life, and homes are still structured for
women whose only responsibility is running their families. I warned five
years ago that if the women's movement didn't move into a second stage and
take on the problems of restructuring work and home, a new generation
would be vulnerable to backlash. But the movement has not moved into that
needed second stage, so the women struggling with these new problems view
them as purely personal, not political, and no longer look to the movement
for solutions. . . .

2. Mobilize the new professional networks and the old established vol-   24
unteer organizations to save women's rights. We can't fight fundamentalist
backlash with backward-looking feminist fundamentalism. Second-stage feminism is itself pluralistic, and has to use new pluralist strengths and strategies.
The women who have been 30 and 40 percent of the graduating class from
law school or business school and 47 percent of the journalism school classes,
the ones who've taken women's studies, the women who grew up playing Little League baseball and cheered on those new champion women athletes, the
new professional networks of women in every field, every woman who has
been looking to those networks only to get ahead in her own field, must now
use her professional skills to save the laws and execute orders against sex
discrimination in education and employment. They must restore the enforcement machinery and the class-action suits that opened up all these
opportunities to her in the first place.

The last time the ladies with briefcases went to Washington from the   25
"new girl" networks like Women's Forum was to get the deadline for ERA extended, nearly a decade ago. The dismantling of the laws of sex discrimination shows how much we need that Constitutional underpinning. But new
symbolic marches for ERA are not what we need now but urgent, immediate
concrete strategies to save the laws themselves. And this can't be left to the
few professional lobbyists on feminist organization payrolls. . . .

. . . America's first movement for women's rights died out after winning   26
the vote, four generations ago, because women didn't tackle the hard political tasks of restructuring home and work so that women who married and
had children could also earn and have their own voice in the decision-making mainstream of society. Instead, those women retreated behind a cultural
curtain of female "purity," focusing their energies on issues like prohibition,
much like the pornographic obsession of some feminists today.

3. Get off the pornography kick and face the real obscenity of poverty.   27
No matter how repulsive we may find pornography, laws banning books or
movies for sexually explicit content could be far more dangerous to women.
The pornography issue is dividing the women's movement and giving the
impression on college campuses that to be a feminist is to be against sex.
More important, it is diverting energies that need to be spent in saving the
basic rights now being destroyed and in facing the new problems of eco-

nomic and emotional survival, for young women and old. And feminists joining forces with the Far Right to outlaw pornography are strengthening the Right's campaign to weaken constitutional protections of all our freedoms and rights, including women's basic right to control her own body. . . .

. . . 4. Confront the illusion of equality in divorce. Economists and feminists have been talking a lot lately about "the feminization of poverty" in theoretical terms, but the American women's movement has not developed concrete strategies that get at its root cause. It's not just a question of women earning less than men—though as long as women do not get equal pay for work of comparable value, or earn Social Security or pensions for taking care of children and home, they are both economically dependent on marriage and motherhood and pay a big economic price for it. And this is as true for divorced aging yuppies as for welfare mothers. Not many women or men want to face the fact that the overwhelming majority of the truly poor in this country, regardless of race, religion or husband's economic status, are women alone, and children in families headed by women. 28

A startling new book by the sociologist Lenore J. Weitzman, "The Divorce Revolution: The Unexpected Social and Economic Consequences for Women and Children in America," reveals that in the 1970s, when 48 states adopted "no-fault" divorce laws treating men and women "equally" in divorce settlements—laws feminists originally supported—divorced women and their children suffered an immediate 73 percent drop in their standard of living, while their ex-husbands enjoyed a 42 percent rise in theirs. The legal profession, including women lawyers, sought and won passages in those laws that merely enjoined the judge to "equitable" distribution of property, requiring the wife to "prove" that her contribution was equal to her husband's. (Feminists like myself were almost alone then in demanding truly equal division.) 29

In dividing "marital property," Lenore Weitzman reports, judges have systematically overlooked the major assets of many marriages—the husband's career assets that the wife helped make possible, his professional education that she may have helped support, the career on which he was able to concentrate because she ran the home, and his salary, pension, health insurance and earning power that resulted. They have also ignored the wife's years of unpaid housework and child care (not totally insured by Social Security in the event of divorce) and her drastically diminished job prospects after divorce. And, for most, the "equal" division of property means the forced sale of the family home—which used to be awarded to the wife and children. Child support, which has often been inadequate, unpaid and uncollectible, usually ends when the child is 18, just as college expenses begin. Thus the vicious cycle whereby an ever-increasing majority of the truly poor in America are families headed by women. 30

When those "no fault" divorce "reform" laws were first passed, feminists in the first brave flush of "independence" repudiated women's need for alimony; a generation of "displaced housewives" paid a bitter price. 31

A new generation of feminist lawyers and judges has now drafted, and must get urgent grass-roots political support for, the kind of law needed, a law that treats marriage as a true economic partnership—and includes fairer stan- 32 dards of property division, maintenance and child support. It should be a law that does not penalize women who have chosen family over, or even together with, professional career.

5. Return the issue of abortion to the matter of women's own responsi- 33 ble choice. I think feminists have been so traumatized by the fundamentalist crusade against abortion and all the talk of fetuses and when life begins that they are in danger of forgetting the values that make abortion a feminist issue in the first place. Those pictures of revived fetuses raise new moral questions. And, in fact, hard new thinking is being done in the medical and religious communities about the use of technology to keep unwanted life alive at both extremes of the life cycle. New, hard thinking is required here of feminist theories and leaders generally, as well as the new women doctors and midwives. . . .

I think women who are young, and those not so young, today must be 34 able to choose when to have a child, given the necessities of their jobs. They will indeed join their mothers, who remember the humiliations and dangers of backstreet butcher abortions, in a march of millions to save the right of legal abortion. I certainly support a march for women's choice of birth control and legal abortion. NOW has called for one in the spring of 1986.

6. Affirm the differences between men and women. New feminist think- 35 ing is required if American women are to continue advancing in a man's world, as they must, to earn their way, and yet "not become like men." This fear is heard with more and more frequency today from young women, including many who have succeeded, and some who have failed or opted out of male-defined careers. More books, like Carol Gilligan's *In a Different Voice,* and consciousness-raising sessions are needed. First-stage feminism denied real differences between women and men except for the sexual organs themselves. Some feminists still do not understand that true equality is not possible unless those differences between men and women are affirmed and until values based on female sensitivities to life begin to be voiced in every discipline and profession, from architecture to economics, where, until recently, all concepts and standards were defined by men. This is not a matter of abstract theory alone but involves the restructuring of hours of work and patterns of professional training so that they take into account the fact that women are the people who give birth to children. It must lead to concrete changes in medical practice, church worship, the writing of history, standards of ethics, even the design of homes and appliances.

7. Breakthrough for older women. Though the great majority of Ameri- 36 cans living vitally now through their sixties, seventies and eighties are women (men still die prematurely, part of the price they seem to pay for machismo dominance), the women's movement has never put serious energy into the job that must be done to get women adequately covered by Social Security and pensions, especially those women now reaching sixty-five who spent many years as housewives and are ending up alone. The need for more independent and shared housing for older women now living alone in suburban houses they can't afford to sell, or lonely furnished rooms—and the need

for services and jobs or volunteer options that will enable them to keep on living independent, productive lives—has never been a part of the women's movement agenda. But that first generation of feminist mothers, women now in their sixties, is a powerful political resource for the movement as these women retire from late or early professional or volunteer careers. Women in their fifties and sixties are shown by the polls to be more firmly committed than their daughters to the feminist goals of equality. Let the women's movement lead the rest of society in breaking the spell of the youth cult and drawing on the still enormous energies and the wisdom that may come to some of us in age. Or will we have to start another movement to break through the age mystique, and affirm the personhood of women and men who live beyond that dread ceiling of sixty-five—my own next birthday!

8. Bring in the men. It's passé, surely, for feminists now to see men only   37
as the enemy, or to contemplate separatist models for emotional or economic survival. Feminist theorists like Barbara Ehrenreich cite dismal evidence of the "new men" opting out of family responsibilities altogether. But in my own life I seem to see more and more young men, and older ones—even former male chauvinist pigs—admitting their vulnerability and learning to express their tenderness, sharing the care of the kids, even though most of them may never share it equally with their wives.

And as men let down their masks of machismo, and admit their depen-   38
dence on the women in their lives, women may admit a new need to depend on men, without fear of sinking back into the old abject subservience. After all, even women who insist they are not, and never will be, feminists have learned to defend themselves against real male brutality. Look at Charlotte Donahue Fedders, the wife of that Security and Exchange commissioner, who testified in divorce court about his repeated abuse—his repeated beatings caused black eyes and a broken eardrum. At one time, a woman in her situation would have kept that shame a secret. The Reagan Administration had to ask him to resign, because wife-beating is no longer politically acceptable, even in conservative America in 1985.

I don't think women can, or should try to, take the responsibility for lib-   39
erating men from the remnants of machismo. But there has to be a new way of asking what do men really want, to echo Freud, a new kind of dialogue that breaks through or gets behind both our masks. Women cannot restructure jobs or homes just by talking to themselves. As a movement, we have to figure out a new kind of second stage consciousness-raising and a new kind of political organization that bring men in as organic partners.

9. Continue to fight for real political power. Feminists do not now, and   40
in fact never really did support a woman just because she is a woman. In the '82 elections, NOW actually opposed Millicent Fenwick's Senate race in New Jersey and Margaret Heckler in Massachusetts because, though they had supported ERA, they went along with Reagan's nuclear missile buildup and cuts in social programs and legal protections for women. The "gender gap" that emerged in American politics, when women, for the first time voting independently of men, defeated governors, senators and congressmen who

seemed to threaten their values of peace and social concerns, did not operate as strongly in '84 against Reagan as it did in '80, despite the presence of Ferraro on the ticket. Did the onslaught of the bishops and the attempt to tarnish her for collusion in her husband's brutally exposed business dealings rule her out as an embodiment of women's hopes? Did she fail to raise that "different voice" for women in that disastrous campaign? Or did the male backlash against Democratic values prevail also, or sufficiently, among women to offset what had seemed to be her stunning significance.

There is no substitute for having women in political offices that matter. 41 Women are discovering that they have to fight, as men do, in primaries where victory is not certain, and not just wait for an "open seat.". . .

. . . 10. Move beyond single-issue thinking. Even today, I do not think 42 women's rights are the most urgent business for American women. The important thing is somehow getting together with men who also put the values of life first to break through the paralysis that fundamentalist backlash has imposed on all our movements. It is not only feminism that is becoming a dirty word in America, but also liberalism, humanism, pluralism, environmentalism and civil liberties. The very freedom of political dissent that enabled the women's movement to start here has been made to seem unsafe for today's young men as well as young women. I think the yuppies are afraid to be political.

Women may have to think beyond "women's issues" to join their ener- 43 gies with men to redeem our democratic tradition and turn our nation's power to the interests of life instead of the nuclear arms race that is paralyzing it. I've never, for instance, seen the need for a separate women's peace movement. I'm not really sure that women, by nature, are more peace-loving than men. They were simply not brought up to express aggression the way men do (they took it out covertly, on themselves and on their men and children, psychologists would say). But the human race may not survive much longer unless women move beyond the nurture of their own babies and careers to political decisions of war and peace, and unless men who share the nurture of their children take responsibility for ending the arms race before it destroys all life. . . .

Questions

1. According to Friedan, what was the first stage of feminism fighting for? Why do women need to proceed to a second stage? What is this second stage?

2. Friedan seems to feel that the first stage of feminism—the fight for equality—has been accomplished. Would Faludi agree with her stand?

3. Can you think of ways in which the feminist movement has affected your life? What are the positive effects? The negative effects?

4. What role should men play in the second stage? Do you think men will be willing to participate?

5. Compare the issues that Friedan addresses with those discussed in the Faludi selection. Where are the major differences and similarities?

We Should Embrace Traditional Masculinity

WARREN FARRELL

Warren Farrell is the only male to be elected three times to the board of directors of the National Organization for Women (NOW). He completed his Ph.D. at New York University in 1974 and has taught at Rutgers University and Brooklyn College. He has also been a special assistant to the president of New York University. His books include The Liberated Man: Beyond Masculinity *and* Why Men Are the Way They Are.

Farrell argues that traditional masculinity is often misinterpreted by women and that they have attacked gender behavior somewhat unfairly. He asserts that male socialization actually leaves men both physically and emotionally "vulnerable." This selection is from To Be a Man *(1991).*

Every virtue, taken to the extreme, becomes a vice. For the past twenty years   1
I have critiqued traditional masculinity because masculinity has been taken to the extreme. And taken to the extreme it creates anxiety, homicide, rape, war, and suicide; not taken to the extreme it has many virtues not to be tossed out with the bathwater.

Praise of men is an endangered species. But the good about men is not.   2
And when something good is being endangered it needs special attention. And so, for a rare moment in recent history, here is special attention to what's good about male socialization. . . .

* * *

Giving/Generosity. Why do we think of women as giving of themselves and   3
men as giving gifts? Because women's socialization teaches direct giving—as listening nurturers, cooks of men's meals, and doing more of his wash than he does of hers. He may give by working in a coal mine and contracting black lung so his child can attend college as he never could, but his giving is done at the mine—where we don't see it. The result of his giving is a check. With women's giving we appreciate more than the result, we appreciate the process: we see her cook the meal, serve it, and usually clean it up. We don't see him wading through water in a dark and damp mine shaft, or driving a truck at 2 A.M. on his fourth cup of coffee, behind schedule in traffic and with no time to nap. We see him at home withdrawing from the coffee.

He may spend much of his life earning money to finance a home his wife   4
fell in love with, but we don't think of him as giving when he's away from

473

home nearly as much as we think of her as giving when she cleans up his dishes.

Sometimes a man's giving is reflexive and role-based, such as when he re-   5
flexively picks up a tab at a restaurant. We forget this is also giving: fifty dollars for dinner and drinks may represent a day's work in after-tax income. Theater tickets, gas, and babysitters are another day's work. We don't think of his picking up these tabs as being as giving as when a woman spends two days preparing a special meal for him. Both forms of giving are role-based; hers are just more direct. . . .

Fairness. The best thing emerging from sports, games, work rules, win-   6
ning, and losing is fairness. Not necessarily honesty—fairness. In Little League, when I trapped a ball in my glove just after a bounce, the umpire credited me with catching a fly. I volunteered to the umpire that I hadn't. The umpire, embarrassed, changed the decision. The angry coach bawled me out. The other coach bawled out my coach for bawling me out. They disagreed on honesty. But neither would have disagreed with the fairness of a neutral umpire making the decision.

Male socialization teaches the value of a careful system of rules, within   7
which anyone can work to gain advantage, and some of which can be gotten around (with possible consequences). Once mastered, the rules give everyone a much more equal chance than they would have had without the rules. To men, mastering these rules feels like survival—survival of themselves and their family. A lifetime of practicing these rules gives many men a sixth sense for fairness. Groups of men and women who have disregarded these rules as "too male" or "too establishment," as did the Students for a Democratic Society in the sixties and seventies, soon evolve into backstabbing elites which self-destruct.

Male Action

Nurturing. Carl wasn't great at expressing feeling. And he didn't under-   8
stand fully that sometimes Cindy just needed a listening ear. His way of supporting her was to volunteer to help Cindy with the problem that was making her upset. For Carl, taking Cindy seriously meant taking Cindy's problem seriously, and taking Cindy's problem seriously meant trying to find a solution. To him this was an act of love. Anything less, like just standing around when she was hurting, was an act of cruelty. "If Cindy's bleeding," he'd say, "find a solution. . . . Don't just stand there with that sickening supportive smile on your face while the woman I love is bleeding to death!" *Solutions are male nurturance.* . . .

Leadership. Accusations that "men have the power" have appeared more   9
frequently in the past decade and a half than appreciation for the billions of hours sacrificed by men to give themselves the leadership training to get that power. Or the benefits of the leadership itself. For example, few articles

explain how male socialization has trained millions of leaders to lead thousands of businesses that are now providing millions of women with opportunities for leadership that might not exist were it not for male leadership.

Outrageousness. While women are socialized to get male attention by being "good girls" or not offending male egos, men are being socialized to get female attention by standing out. One way a man can stand out is to be outrageous. The best part of outrageousness is the barriers it breaks to allow all of us more freedom to experiment with discovering more of ourselves. The Beatle's hair, considered outrageous at the time, permitted a generation to experiment with their hair; Elvis the Pelvis allowed a generation to experiment with their sexual selves; the Wright Brothers were told it was scientifically impossible to fly—and suicidal to try; and Salvador Dali, Picasso, and Copernicus looked at the world in ways considered outrageous in their time; in retrospect, we can see that they freed us to live in a way we could not have dreamed of before.   10

Male Psychology

To Keep Emotions Under Control. Although in relationships this tight lid leads to a "male volcano" after months of repressed emotions, the flip side is our dependence on this male trait in crisis situations. Dirk recalls a head-on collision. "Five cars crashed. There was glass and blood everywhere. Four of us guys ran from car to car, following the screams and preparing tourniquets. We stopped two cars to recruit passengers to redirect traffic, called the police, and removed a woman and her son from a car that burst into flames a minute later."   11

The newspapers reported the accident. But no headlines read, "Men Control Their Emotions in Order to Save Lives of Women and Children." They ran a picture—not of four men standing next to the women and children they saved, but of the five cars that collided.   12

Ego Strength. When women reevaluate what goes wrong in a relationship the unspoken assumption is that this takes ego strength. When men compete fiercely to be number one, we see it as a reflection of their fragile egos (which it can be) and call it strategizing, *rather than recognizing the ego strength required to conduct a self-reevaluation immediately after a loss.* A man needs to ask, "What did *I* do wrong?" And then, when he finds the answer, rather than credit himself with his introspection, he must focus immediately on correcting it before the next game...   13

To Express Anger. "One minute we were shouting and calling each other names. A minute later we were concentrating on the next play." The male tendency to take sports seriously combined with the willingness to express feelings intensely leads many adult men to say, "I lose my temper for a minute, then it's done with." The positive side of male anger is the quick,   14 intense release of emotions, with the subsequent calm that follows the storm. If the intensity is understood, and not exacerbated, grudges are rarely held. The intensity, like all powerful energy, can be harnessed—and channeled into powerful lovemaking . . .

Male Strength

To Save Her Life at the Risk of His Own. I described in the introduction [of   15
my book] how my younger brother Wayne died in an avalanche as he ventured ahead to check out a dangerous area alone rather than have his woman friend share the risk or do it herself. No news account of his death discussed this as an example of men's willingness to forfeit their lives for the women they love. We read of accounts of women lifting automobiles to save the life of a child, but not to save the life of a husband. Frequently, a woman who hears about this difference gets defensive even though she says she wants to appreciate men more.

There is nothing to be defensive about. It is not a statement that men are   16
better. Members of each sex do what they are socialized to do both to give themselves the feeling of being part of a whole and to deviate a bit to feel like an individual. This makes both sexes equal—with different programming. A man's dying for a woman he loves doesn't make him better at all, but part of his socialization leaves him vulnerable. My brother was quite vulnerable.

To Give Up on His Life for His Beliefs. Some men give up their lives at war   17
because they believe in their country; others do it because if they cannot be a hero they'd rather not live; others do it to support families. Others risk their lives in war so that if they live, they will earn enough money and status to "earn" a wife. Men with different class or ethnic backgrounds do the same in the CIA, FBI, State Department, and Mafia: their beliefs or their willingness to support their families are as important as their entire existence.

For these men, these are not empty words. While the worst part of this is   18
an extraordinary statement of male insecurity and compensation for power-lessness, the best part is the extraordinary conviction men have for their beliefs and their families. It is a statement (within their value system) of the importance of values, responsibility, and quality of life: theirs and their family's. . . .

Male Responsibilities

Self-sufficiency. We don't call men "career men," because the word *career* is   19
built into the word *man*. Self-sufficiency is built into masculinity. . . .

Male socialization is an overdose in self-sufficiency. There are no fairy   20
tales of a princess on a white horse finding a male Sleeping Beauty and sweeping him off to a castle; no fairy tales glorifying a man who is not self-suffi-cient. When the going gets tough, he doesn't talk it through, he gets going.

How do these fairy tales translate into reality? Liberation has been de-   21
fined as giving women the "right to choose": to choose the option of being at
home or being at work. *Men do not learn they have the right to choose to be at
home. That would imply someone else would have to take care of him at home.* A
man doesn't learn to expect that. He learns, instead, "The world doesn't owe
you a living." Self-sufficiency implies *earning* rights. The right to choose, he
learns, comes from choosing, for example, to take a job that pays a lot so he
has more choices when he is away from the job. As a result of a man's training to take care of himself, millions of women have been freer to look at their
own values—and to criticize men—than they would be if they had to support
them. . . .

Risk Taking. The male socialization to take risks on the playing field pre-   22
pares a man to take risks investing in stocks, businesses, and conglomerates.
To invest in his career with years of training, and then extra training. A plastic surgeon may have risked from age five to thirty-five as a student or part-
time student, underpaid and overworked, in order, during the second half of
his life, to be able to earn a half million dollars a year. . . .

On numerous levels, male socialization teaches men to risk a lot and be   23
willing to fail a lot—and all for the hope of being rewarded a lot. (Conversely,
if he doesn't risk, he doesn't expect the rewards.) If he survives, he will then
be able to provide a security for his wife and children that he never had for
himself. . . .

To Develop Identity. The pressure on men to be more than self-sufficient,   24
which forced them to take risks and self-start, to sort out their values quickly,
to learn how and when to challenge authority, and to invent, resulted, at
best, in the development of *identity.* Identity arises out of seeing both how we
fit in and how we don't fit in—but especially how we don't fit in. The foundation of society is here before we arrive and after we pass. Identity is discovering our uniqueness in that continuity. As we take risks, and challenge what
exists, the friction between ourselves and society makes all the boundaries
clearer. Which is how we develop identity, and why the best parts of male socialization are helpful in developing identity. Of course, most men sell a good
portion of their identity out to institutions just as most women sell out to a
man. But the part of a man true to the values he has sorted out still challenges, still takes risks, still benefits from the development of identity. . . .

Responsibility. Male socialization is a recipe book of taking responsibility.   25
From the responsibility of getting a job at age fourteen so he can pay for his
first date's food and tickets, to performing adequately within view of the girl
he wants to ask out to increase his chances of acceptance, to actually asking
his first date out, to arranging for his parents to drive, then, in later years, to
borrowing the car, then driving himself, then taking initiatives—all of these
are responsibility. . . .

My study of male-female language-pattern differences reflects the male   26
training to take responsibility. Men are much less likely to use phrases like
"This happened to me," and much more likely to use phrases like "I did this."

What Males Can Do

Sense of Efficacy. In the process of learning to take risks, men get especially   27
strong training in learning what is and what is not effective—a sense of efficacy. In the process of trying a wide variety of jobs, we learn what we are effective at. We are socialized with a different attitude toward lost
investments—as experiences that fine-tune us to the questions we must ask
to prevent the next loss. We see the loss as an investment in investing. Tin-
kering for hours under a hood teaches him by trial and error how to be effective with a car (I said teaches him—it hasn't taught me!).

Once again, this is reflected in male-female language differences. Men are   28
much less likely to say, "Maybe we can get Bill to do that," and much more
likely to say, "Maybe if I try. . . ."

Doing Rather Than Complaining. To become effective, men learn to make   29
the unarticulated distinction between two types of complaining: "I'm helpless" versus "This is the complaint, now here's the solution." Men are not tolerant enough of other men complaining, "I'm helpless." But the best part of
this intolerance is the pressure it exerts on a man to get rid of the problem
that created the complaint.

Pushing the Limits of One's Talents. Doing may be better than complaining,   30
but doing is not enough. A man's pressure to earn as much as he can with his
talents means a constant pushing of the limits of each and every talent to discover which one can support him best. When people hear "pushing the limits of one's talents" they think of talents as raw capability; they feel that job
advancement involves an expansion of talents and an application of talents
toward an appropriate job and frequent promotions. Successful people learn
that pushing the limits of one's talents also means balancing the politics of
everyone else's egos while making themselves shine; balancing facade with
personal integrity; and selling themselves repeatedly without appearing as if
they're selling. The struggle to master the complex politics of advancement is
the real pushing of the limits of one's talents.

The recent focus on discrimination has made us feel that the formula for   31
success is qualifications plus lack of discrimination. That one-two approach
has limited our appreciation of the extraordinary subtlety and range of talents required for advancement.

Male Flexibility

Sense of Humor. Whether it's Woody Allen's ability to laugh at the   32
schlemiel in himself or George Carlin's ability to laugh at masculinity itself,

one of the best things that emerges from men's training to see life as a game is the ability to laugh both at our own roles in the game and at the game itself. Even the most traditional and serious of male systems are mocked, such as Bill Murray in *Stripes* mocking the military. It is difficult to find movies similarly mocking the traditional female role—for example, a movie mocking motherhood. . . .

Change Without Blame. Although men have made fewer changes than women, what changes they have made—as in fathering—have occurred without movements that blamed women. Fifteen years ago, few men were sensitive to orgasms or clitorises. Few had heard of the ERA. Few fathers-to-be joined their wives in the delivery room, in the preparation for the birth of their child. But soon, men had changed in all these ways. 33

The changes that occurred happened without attacking women with equal-but-opposite rhetoric, such as "Women hold a monopoly of power over the child," or "Women have a fragile mothering ego perpetuated by a quiet matriarchy that sends men into the field to die while women conspire to sleep in warm beds at home." Nor did men respond to blame by labeling it psychological abuse. 34

When we hear the phrase "the battle between the sexes," there is an unspoken assumption that both sexes have been blaming equally. The battle, though, could easily be called "the female attack on men," not "the male attack on women." There is a distinction between responding to blame and initiating it. Men have changed less, but they have also blamed less. 35

Questions

1. According to Farrell what is good about male socialization?
2. Does Farrell convince you that feminist attacks on traditional masculinity are unfair? Why or why not?
3. How would Faludi react to Farrell's position? Whose position do you favor?

The Pillow and the Key

ROBERT BLY

Robert Bly won the National Book Award for Poetry in 1967 for his collection entitled The Light Around the Body. *Educated at Harvard and the University of Iowa, he was a peace activist in the 1960s, held "Great Mother" conferences in the 1970s, ran workshops for men in the 1980s, and his most recent book* Iron John: A Book About Men *(1990) was a bestseller. He has held a Fulbright scholarship, has been a Guggenheim Fellow, and has written numerous books of poetry.*

In this reading, Bly explains the myth of "Iron John" as "the fundamental historical split in the psyche between primitive man and the civilized man." He argues that the feminization of men is inadequate—in order to tap the "Wild Man," or the male spirit, men need mentors, older men who can sever the attachment to the mother. This reading is from Iron John.

We talk a great deal about "the American man," as if there were some con- 1
stant quality that remained stable over decades, or even within a single
decade.

The men who live today have veered far away from the Saturnian, old- 2
man-minded farmer, proud of his introversion, who arrived in New England
in 1630, willing to sit through three services in an unheated church. In the
South, an expansive, motherbound cavalier developed, and neither of these
two "American men" resembled the greedy railroad entrepreneur that later
developed in the Northeast, nor the reckless I-will-do-without culture settlers
of the West.

Even in our own era the agreed-on model has changed dramatically. Dur- 3
ing the fifties, for example, an American character appeared with some consistency that became a model of manhood adopted by many men: the Fifties
male.

He got to work early, labored responsibly, supported his wife and chil- 4
dren, and admired discipline. Reagan is a sort of mummified version of this
dogged type. This sort of man didn't see women's souls well, but he appreciated their bodies; and his view of culture and America's part in it was boyish
and optimistic. Many of his qualities were strong and positive, but underneath the charm and bluff there was, and there remains, much isolation, deprivation, and passivity. Unless he has an enemy, he isn't sure that he is alive.

The Fifties man was supposed to like football, be aggressive, stick up for 5
the United States, never cry, and always provide. But receptive space or intimate space was missing in this image of a man. The personality lacked some

480

sense of flow. The psyche lacked compassion in a way that encouraged the unbalanced pursuit of the Vietnam war, just as, later, the lack of what we might call "garden" space inside Reagan's head led to his callousness and brutality toward the powerless in El Salvador, toward old people here, the unemployed, schoolchildren, and poor people in general.

The Fifties male had a clear vision of what a man was, and what male responsibilities were, but the isolation and one-sidedness of his vision were dangerous. 6

During the sixties, another sort of man appeared. The waste and violence of the Vietnam war made men question whether they knew what an adult male really was. If manhood meant Vietnam, did they want any part of it? Meanwhile, the feminist movement encouraged men to actually look at women, forcing them to become conscious of concerns and sufferings that the Fifties male labored to avoid. As men began to examine women's history and women's sensibility, some men began to notice what was called their *feminine* side and pay attention to it. This process continues to this day, and I would say that most contemporary men are involved in it in some way. 7

There's something wonderful about this development—I mean the practice of men welcoming their own "feminine" consciousness and nurturing it—this is important—and yet I have the sense that there is something wrong. The male in the past twenty years has become more thoughtful, more gentle. But by this process he has not become more free. He's a nice boy who pleases not only his mother but also the young woman he is living with. 8

In the seventies I began to see all over the country a phenomenon that we might call the "soft male." Sometimes even today when I look out at an audience, perhaps half the young males are what I'd call soft. They're lovely, valuable people—I like them—they're not interested in harming the earth or starting wars. There's a gentle attitude toward life in their whole being and style of living. 9

But many of these men are not happy. You quickly notice the lack of energy in them. They are life-preserving but not exactly life-giving. Ironically, you often see these men with strong women who positively radiate energy. 10

Here we have a finely tuned young man, ecologically superior to his father, sympathetic to the whole harmony of the universe, yet he himself has little vitality to offer. 11

The strong or life-giving women who graduated from the sixties, so to speak, or who have inherited an older spirit, played an important part in producing this life-preserving, but not life-giving, man. 12

I remember a bumper sticker during the sixties that read "WOMEN SAY YES TO MEN WHO SAY NO." We recognize that it took a lot of courage to resist the draft, go to jail, or move to Canada, just as it took courage to accept the draft and go to Vietnam. But the women of twenty years ago were definitely saying that they preferred the softer receptive male. 13

So the development of men was affected a little in this preference. Non-receptive maleness was equated with violence, and receptive maleness was rewarded. 14

Some energetic women, at that time and now in the nineties, chose and   15
still choose soft men to be their lovers and, in a way, perhaps, to be their sons.
The new distribution of "yang" energy among couples didn't happen by accident. Young men for various reasons wanted their harder women, and women
began to desire softer men. It seemed like a nice arrangement for a while, but
we've lived with it long enough now to see that it isn't working out.

I first learned about the anguish of "soft" men when they told their sto-   16
ries in early men's gatherings. In 1980, the Lama Community in New Mexico
asked me to teach a conference for men only, their first, in which about forty
men participated. Each day we concentrated on one Greek god and one old
story, and then late in the afternoons we gathered to talk. When the younger
men spoke it was not uncommon for them to be weeping within five minutes. The amount of grief and anguish in these younger men was astounding
to me.

Part of their grief rose out of remoteness from their fathers, which they   17
felt keenly, but partly, too, grief flowed from trouble in their marriages or relationships. They had learned to be receptive, but receptivity wasn't enough
to carry their marriages through troubled times. In every relationship something *fierce* is needed once in a while: both the man and the woman need to
have it. But at the point when it was needed, often the young man came up
short. He was nurturing, but something else was required—for his relationship, and for his life.

The "soft" male was able to say, "I can feel your pain, and I consider your   18
life as important as mine, and I will take care of you and comfort you." But he
could not say what he wanted, and stick by it. *Resolve* of that kind was a different matter.

In *The Odyssey*, Hermes instructs Odysseus that when he approaches   19
Circe, who stands for a certain kind of matriarchal energy, he is to lift or show
his sword. In these early sessions it was difficult for many of the younger men
to distinguish between showing the sword and hurting someone. One man, a
kind of incarnation of certain spiritual attitudes of the sixties, a man who had
actually lived in a tree for a year outside Santa Cruz, found himself unable to
extend his arm when it held a sword. He had learned so well not to hurt anyone that he couldn't lift the steel, even to catch the light of the sun on it. But
showing a sword doesn't necessarily mean fighting. It can also suggest a joyful decisiveness.

The journey many American men have taken into softness, or receptivity,   20
or "development of the feminine side," has been an immensely valuable journey, but more travel lies ahead. No stage is the final stop.

Finding Iron John

One of the fairy tales that speak of a third possibility for men, a third mode, is   21
a story called "Iron John" or "Iron Hans." Though it was first set down by the
Grimm brothers around 1820, this story could be ten or twenty thousand
years old.

As the story starts, we find out that something strange has been happen- 22
ing in a remote area of the forest near the king's castle. When hunters go into
this area, they disappear and never come back. Twenty others go after the
first group and do not come back. In time, people begin to get the feeling that
there's something weird in that part of the forest, and they "don't go there
anymore."

One day an unknown hunter shows up at the castle and says, "What can 23
I do? Anything dangerous to do around here?"

The King says: "Well, I could mention the forest, but there's a problem. 24
The people who go out there don't come back. The return rate is not good."

"That's just the sort of thing I like," the young man says. So he goes into 25
the forest and, interestingly, he goes there *alone,* taking only his dog. The
young man and his dog wander about in the forest and they go past a pond.
Suddenly a hand reaches up from the water, grabs the dog, and pulls it down.

The young man doesn't respond by becoming hysterical. He merely says, 26
"This must be the place."

Fond as he is of his dog and reluctant as he is to abandon him, the hunter 27
goes back to the castle, rounds up three more men with buckets, and then
comes back to the pond to bucket out the water. Anyone who's ever tried it
will quickly note that such bucketing is very slow work.

In time, what they find, lying on the bottom of the pond, is a large man 28
covered with hair from head to foot. The hair is reddish—it looks a little like
rusty iron. They take the man back to the castle, and imprison him. The King
puts him in an iron cage in the courtyard, calls him "Iron John," and gives
the key into the keeping of the Queen.

* * *

Let's stop the story here for a second. 29

When a contemporary man looks down into his psyche, he may, if condi- 30
tions are right, find under the water of his soul, lying in an area no one has
visited for a long time, an ancient hairy man.

The mythological systems associate hair with the instinctive and the sex- 31
ual and the primitive. What I'm suggesting, then, is that every modern male
has, lying at the bottom of his psyche, a large, primitive being covered with
hair down to his feet. Making contact with this Wild Man is the step the
Eighties male or the Nineties male has yet to take. That bucketing-out process
has yet to begin in our contemporary culture.

As the story suggests very delicately, there's more than a little fear around 32
this hairy man, as there is around all change. When a man begins to develop
the receptive side of himself and gets over his initial skittishness, he usually
finds the experience to be wonderful. He gets to write poetry and go out and
sit by the ocean, he doesn't have to be on top all the time in sex anymore, he
becomes empathetic—it's a new, humming, surprising world.

But going down through water to touch the Wild Man at the bottom of 33
the pond is quite a different matter. The being who stands up is frightening,
and seems even more so now, when the corporations do so much work to
produce the sanitized, hairless, shallow man. When a man welcomes his re-

sponsiveness, or what we sometimes call his internal woman, he often feels warmer, more companionable, more alive. But when he approaches what I'll call the "deep male," he feels risk. Welcoming the Hairy Man *is* scary and risky, and it requires a different sort of courage. Contact with Iron John requires a willingness to descend into the male psyche and accept what's dark down there, including the *nourishing* dark.

For generations now, the industrial community has warned young busi-   34
nessmen to keep away from Iron John, and the Christian church is not too fond of him either.

Freud, Jung, and Wilhelm Reich are three investigators who had the   35
courage to go down into the pond and to accept what they found there. The job of contemporary men is to follow them down.

Some men have already done this work, and the Hairy Man has been   36
brought up from the pond in their psyches, and lives in the courtyard. "In the courtyard" suggests that the individual or the culture has brought him into a sunlit place where all can see him. That is itself some advance over keeping the Hairy Man in a cellar, where many elements in every culture want him to be. But, of course, in either place, he's still in a cage.

The Loss of the Golden Ball

Now back to the story.   37

One day the King's eight-year-old son is playing in the courtyard with the   38
golden ball he loves, and it rolls into the Wild Man's cage. If the young boy wants the ball back, he's going to have to approach the Hairy Man and ask him for it. But this is going to be a problem.

The golden ball reminds us of that unity of personality we had as chil-   39
dren—a kind of radiance, or wholeness, before we split into male and female, rich and poor, bad and good. The ball is golden, as the sun is, and round. Like the sun, it gives off a radiant energy from the inside.

We notice that the boy is eight. All of us, whether boys or girls, lose some-   40
thing around the age of eight. If we still have the golden ball in kindergarten, we lose it in grade school. Whatever is still left we lose in high school. In "The Frog Prince," the princess's ball fell into a well. Whether we are male or female, once the golden ball is gone, we spend the rest of our lives trying to get it back.

The first stage in retrieving the ball, I think, is to accept—firmly, defi-   41
nitely—that the ball has been lost. Freud said: "What a distressing contrast there is between the radiant intelligence of the child and the feeble mentality of the average adult."

So where is the golden ball? Speaking metaphorically, we could say that   42
the sixties culture told men they would find their golden ball in sensitivity, receptivity, cooperation, and nonaggressiveness. But many men gave up all aggressiveness and still did not find the golden ball.

The Iron John story says that a man can't expect to find the golden ball   43
in the feminine realm, because that's not where the ball is. A bridegroom

secretly asks his wife to give him back the golden ball. I think she'd give it to him if she could, because most women in my experience do not try to block men's growth. But she can't give it to him, because she doesn't have it. What's more, she's lost her own golden ball and can't find that either.

Oversimplifying, we could say that the Fifties male always wants a   44
woman to return his golden ball. The Sixties and Seventies man, with equal lack of success, asks his interior feminine to return it.

The Iron John story proposes that the golden ball lies within the mag-   45
netic field of the Wild Man, which is a very hard concept for us to grasp. We have to accept the possibility that the true radiant energy in the male does not hide in, reside in, or wait for us in the feminine realm, nor in the ma-cho/John Wayne realm, but in the magnetic field of the deep masculine. It is protected by the *instinctive* one who's underwater and who has been there we don't know how long.

In "The Frog Prince" it's the frog, the un-nice one, the one that everyone   46
says "Ick!" to, who brings the golden ball back. And in the Grimm brothers version the frog himself turns into the prince only when a hand throws him against the wall.

Most men want some nice person to bring the ball back, but the story   47
hints that we won't find the golden ball in the force field of an Asian guru or even the force field of gentle Jesus. Our story is not anti-Christian but pre-Christian by a thousand years or so, and its message is still true—getting the golden ball back is incompatible with certain kinds of conventional tameness and niceness.

The kind of wildness, or un-niceness, implied by the Wild Man image is   48
not the same as macho energy, which men already know enough about. Wild Man energy, by contrast, leads to forceful action undertaken, not with cru-elty, but with resolve.

The Wild Man is not opposed to civilization; but he's not completely con-   49
tained by it either. The ethical superstructure of popular Christianity does not support the Wild Man, though there is some suggestion that Christ himself did. At the beginning of his ministry, a hairy John, after all, baptized him.

When it comes time for a young male to talk with the Wild Man he will   50
find the conversation quite distinct from a talk with a minister, a rabbi, or a guru. Conversing with the Wild Man is not talking about bliss or mind or spirit or "higher consciousness," but about something wet, dark, and low—what James Hillman would call "soul."

The first step amounts to approaching the cage and asking for the golden   51
ball back. Some men are ready to take that step, while others haven't yet bucketed the water out of the pond—they haven't left the collective male identity and gone out into the unknown area alone, or gone with only their dog.

The story says that after the dog "goes down" one has to start to work   52
with buckets. No giant is going to come along and suck out all the water for you: that magic stuff is not going to help. And a weekend at Esalen won't do it. Acid or cocaine won't do it. The man has to do it bucket by bucket. This

resembles the slow discipline of art: it's the work that Rembrandt did, that Picasso and Yeats and Rilke and Bach did. Bucket work implies much more discipline than most men realize.

The Wild Man, as the writer Keith Thompson mentioned to me, is not simply going to hand over the golden ball either. What kind of story would it be if the Wild Man said: "Well, okay, here's your ball"?   53

Jung remarked that all successful requests to the psyche involve deals. The psyche likes to make deals. If part of you, for example, is immensely lazy and doesn't want to do any work, a flat-out New Year's resolution won't do any good. The whole thing will go better if you say to the lazy part: "You let me work for an hour, then I'll let you be a slob for an hour—deal?" So in "Iron John," a deal is made: the Wild Man agrees to give the golden ball back if the boy opens the cage.   54

The boy, apparently frightened, runs off. He doesn't even answer. Isn't that what happens? We have been told so often by parents, ministers, grade-school teachers, and high-school principals that we should have nothing to do with the Wild Man that when he says "I'll return the ball if you let me out of the cage," we don't even reply.   55

Maybe ten years pass now. On "the second day" the man could be twenty-five. He goes back to the Wild Man and says, "Could I have my ball back?" The Wild Man says, "Yes, if you let me out of the cage."   56

Actually, just returning to the Wild Man a second time is a marvelous thing; some men never come back at all. The twenty-five-year-old man hears the sentence all right, but by now he has two Toyotas and a mortgage, maybe a wife and a child. How can he let the Wild Man out of the cage? A man usually walks away the second time also without saying a word.   57

Now ten more years pass. Let's say the man is now thirty-five . . . have you ever seen the look of dismay on the face of a thirty-five-year-old man? Feeling overworked, alienated, empty, he asks the Wild Man with full heart this time: "Could I have my golden ball back?"   58

"Yes," the Wild Man says, "If you let me out of my cage."   59

Now something marvelous happens in the story. The boy speaks to the Wild Man, and continues the conversation. He says, "Even if I wanted to let you out, I couldn't, because I don't know where the key is."   60

That's so good. By the time we are thirty-five we don't know where the key is. It isn't exactly that we have forgotten—we never knew where it was in the first place.   61

The story says that when the King locked up the Wild Man, "he gave the key into the keeping of the Queen," but we were only about seven then, and in any case our father never told us what he had done with it. So where is the key?   62

I've heard audiences try to answer that one: 63
"It's around the boy's neck."   64
No.   65
"It's hidden in Iron John's cage."   66
No.   67

"It's inside the golden ball."	68
No.	69
"It's inside the castle . . . on a hook inside the Treasure Room."	70
No.	71
"It's in the Tower. It's on a hook high up on the wall!"	72
No.	73

The Wild Man replies, "The key is under your mother's pillow." 74

The key is not inside the ball, nor in the golden chest, nor in the safe . . . 75 the key is under our mother's pillow—just where Freud said it would be.

Getting the key back from under the mother's pillow is a troublesome 76 task. Freud, taking advice from a Greek play, says that a man should not skip over the mutual attraction between himself and his mother if he wants a long life. The mother's pillow, after all, lies in the bed near where she makes love to your father. Moreover, there's another implication attached to the pillow.

Michael Meade, the myth teller, once remarked to me that the pillow is 77 also the place where the mother stores all her expectations for you. She dreams: "My son the doctor." "My son the Jungian analyst." "My son the Wall Street genius." But very few mothers dream: "My son the Wild Man."

On the son's side, he isn't sure he wants to take the key. Simply transfer- 78 ring the key from the mother's to a guru's pillow won't help. Forgetting that the mother possesses it is a bad mistake. A mother's job is, after all, to civilize the boy, and so it is natural for her to keep the key. All families behave alike: on this planet, "The King gives the key into the keeping of the Queen."

Attacking the mother, confronting her, shouting at her, which some 79 Freudians are prone to urge on us, probably does not accomplish much—she may just smile and talk to you with her elbow on the pillow. Oedipus' conversations with Jocasta never did much good, nor did Hamlet's shouting.

A friend mentioned that it's wise to steal the key some day when your 80 mother and father are gone. "My father and mother are away today" implies a day when the head is free of parental inhibitions. That's the day to steal the key. Gioia Timpanelli, the writer and storyteller, remarked that, mythologically, the theft of the key belongs to the world of Hermes.

And the key has to be *stolen*. I recall talking to an audience of men and 81 women once about this problem of stealing the key. A young man, obviously well trained in New Age modes of operation, said, "Robert, I'm disturbed by this idea of stealing the key. Stealing isn't right. Couldn't a group of us just go to the mother and say, 'Mom, could I have the key back?'?"

His model was probably consensus, the way the staff at the health food 82 store settles things. I felt the souls of all the women in the room rise up in the air to kill him. Men like that are as dangerous to women as they are to men.

No mother worth her salt would give the key anyway. If a son can't steal 83 it, he doesn't deserve it.

"I want to let the Wild Man out!"	84
"Come over and give Mommy a kiss."	85

Mothers are intuitively aware of what would happen if he got the key: 86 they would lose their boys. The possessiveness that mothers typically exercise on sons—not to mention the possessiveness that fathers typically exercise on daughters—can never be underestimated.

The means of getting the key back varies with each man, but suffice it to say that democratic or nonlinear approaches will not carry the day.   87

One rather stiff young man danced one night for about six hours, vigorously, and in the morning remarked, "I got some of the key back last night."   88

Another man regained the key when he acted like a wholehearted Trickster for the first time in his life, remaining fully conscious of the tricksterism. Another man stole the key when he confronted his family and refused to carry any longer the shame for the whole family.   89

We could spend days talking of how to steal the key in a practical way. The story itself leaves everything open, and simply says, "One day he stole the key, brought it to the Wild Man's cage, and opened the lock. As he did so, he pinched one of his fingers." (That detail will become important in the next part of the story.) The Wild Man is then free at last, and it's clear that he will go back to his own forest, far from "the castle."   90

What Does the Boy Do?

At this point a number of things could happen. If the Wild Man returns to his forest while the boy remains in the castle, the fundamental historical split in the psyche between primitive man and the civilized man would reestablish itself in the boy. The boy, on his side, could mourn the loss of the Wild Man forever. Or he could replace the key under the pillow before his parents got home, then say he knows nothing about the Wild Man's escape. After that subterfuge, he could become a corporate executive, a fundamentalist minister, a tenured professor, someone his parents could be proud of, who "has never seen the Wild Man."   91

We've all replaced the key many times and lied about it. Then the solitary hunter inside us has to enter into the woods once more with his body dog accompanying him, and then the dog gets pulled down again. We lose a lot of "dogs" that way.   92

We could also imagine a different scenario. The boy convinces, or imagines he could convince, the Wild Man to stay in the courtyard. If that happened, he and the Wild Man could carry on civilized conversations with each other in the tea garden, and this conversation would go on for years. But the story suggests that Iron John and the boy cannot be united—that is, cannot experience their initial union—in the castle courtyard. It's probably too close to the mother's pillow and the father's book of rules.   93

We recall that the boy in our story, when he spoke to the Wild Man, told him he didn't know where the key was. That's brave. Some men never address a sentence to the Wild Man.   94

When the boy opened the cage, the Wild Man started back to his forest. The boy in our story, or the thirty-five-year-old man in our mind—however you want to look at it—now does something marvelous. He speaks to the Wild Man once more and says, "Wait a minute! If my parents come home   95 and find you gone, they will beat me." That sentence makes the heart sink, particularly if we know something about child-rearing practices that have prevailed for a long time in northern Europe.

As Alice Miller reminds us in her book *For Your Own Good,* child psycholo- 96
gists in nineteenth-century Germany warned parents especially about *exuber-ance.* Exuberance in a child is bad, and at the first sign of it, parents should be severe. Exuberance implies that the wild boy or girl is no longer locked up. Puritan parents in New England often punished children severely if they acted in a restless way during the long church services.

"If they come home and find you gone, they will beat me." 97

The Wild Man says, in effect, "That's good thinking. You'd better come 98
with me."

So the Wild Man lifts the boy up on his shoulders and together they go 99
off into the woods. That's decisive. We should all be so lucky.

As the boy leaves for the forest, he has to overcome, at least for the mo- 100
ment, his fear of wildness, irrationality, hairiness, intuition, emotion, the body, and nature. Iron John is not as primitive as the boy imagines, but the boy—or the mind—doesn't know that yet.

Still, the clean break with the mother and father, which the old initiators 101
call for, now has taken place. Iron John says to the boy, "You'll never see your mother and father again. But I have treasures, more than you'll ever need." So that is that.

Going Off on the Wild Man's Shoulders

The moment the boy leaves with Iron John is the moment in ancient Greek 102
life when the priest of Dionysus accepted a young man as a student, or the moment in Eskimo life today when the shaman, sometimes entirely covered with the fur of wild animals, and wearing wolverine claws and snake verte-brae around his neck, and a bear-head cap, appears in the village and takes a boy away for spirit instruction.

In our culture there is no such moment. The boys in our culture have a 103
continuing need for initiation into male spirit, but old men in general don't offer it. The priest sometimes tries, but he is too much a part of the corporate village these days.

Among the Hopis and other native Americans of the Southwest, the old 104
men take the boy away at the age of twelve and bring him *down* into the all-male area of the kiva. He stays *down* there for six weeks, and does not see his mother again for a year and a half.

The fault of the nuclear family today isn't so much that it's crazy and full 105
of double binds (that's true in communes and corporate offices too—in fact, in any group). The fault is that the old men outside the nuclear family no longer offer an effective way for the son to break his link with his parents without doing harm to himself.

The ancient societies believed that a boy becomes a man only through rit- 106
ual and effort—only through the "active intervention of the older men."

It's becoming clear to us that manhood doesn't happen by itself; it   107
doesn't happen just because we eat Wheaties. The active intervention of the
older men means that older men welcome the younger man into the ancient,
mythologized, instinctive male world.

One of the best stories I've heard about this kind of welcoming is one that   108
takes place each year among the Kikuyu in Africa. When a boy is old enough
for initiation, he is taken away from his mother and brought to a special
place the men have set up some distance from the village. He fasts for three
days. The third night he finds himself sitting in a circle around the fire with
the older men. He is hungry, thirsty, alert, and terrified. One of the older men
takes up a knife, opens a vein in his own arm, and lets a little of his blood
flow into a gourd or bowl. Each older man in the circle opens his arm with
the same knife, as the bowl goes around, and lets some blood flow in. When
the bowl arrives at the young man, he is invited to take nourishment from it.

In this ritual the boy learns a number of things. He learns that nourish-   109
ment does not come only from his mother, but also from men. And he learns
that the knife can be used for many purposes besides wounding others. Can
he have any doubt now that he is welcome among the other males?

Once that welcoming has been done, the older men teach him the   110
myths, stories, and songs that embody distinctively male values: I mean not
competitive values only, but spiritual values. Once these "moistening" myths
are learned, the myths themselves lead the young male far beyond his personal father and into the moistness of the swampy fathers who stretch back
century after century.

In the absence of old men's labor consciously done, what happens? Initi-   111
ation of Western men has continued for some time in an altered form even
after fanatics destroyed the Greek initiatory schools. During the nineteenth
century, grandfathers and uncles lived in the house, and older men mingled a
great deal. Through hunting parties, in work that men did together in farms
and cottages, and through local sports, older men spent much time with
younger men and brought knowledge of male spirit and soul to them.

Wordsworth, in the beginning of "The Excursion," describes the old man   112
who sat day after day under a tree and befriended Wordsworth when he was
a boy:

> He loved me; from a swarm of rosy boys
> Singled me out, as he in sport would say,
> For my grave looks, too thoughtful for my years.
> As I grew up, it was my best delight
> To be his chosen comrade. Many a time
> On holidays, we wandered through the woods . . .

Much of that chance or incidental mingling has ended. Men's clubs and   113
societies have steadily disappeared. Grandfathers live in Phoenix or the old
people's home, and many boys experience only the companionship of other
boys their age who, from the point of view of the old initiators, know nothing at all.

During the sixties, some young men drew strength from women who in turn had received some of their strength from the women's movement. One could say that many young men in the sixties tried to accept initiation from women. But only men can initiate men, as only women can initiate women. Women can change the embryo to a boy, but only men can change the boy to a man. Initiators say that boys need a second birth, this time a birth from men. 114

Keith Thompson, in one of his essays, described himself at twenty as a typical young man "initiated" by women. His parents divorced when Keith was about twelve, and he lived with his mother while his father moved into an apartment nearby. 115

Throughout high school Keith was closer to women than to other men, and that situation continued into college years, when his main friends were feminists whom he described as marvelous, knowledgeable, and generous, and from whom he learned an enormous amount. He then took a job in Ohio state politics, working with women and alert to the concerns of women. 116

About that time he had a dream. He and a clan of she-wolves were running in the forest. Wolves suggested to him primarily independence and vigor. The clan of wolves moved fast through the forest, in formation, and eventually they all arrived at a riverbank. Each she-wolf looked into the water and saw her own face there. But when Keith looked in the water, he saw no face at all. 117

Dreams are subtle and complicated, and it is reckless to draw any rapid conclusion. The last image, however, suggests a disturbing idea. When women, even women with the best intentions, bring up a boy alone, he may in some way have no male face, or he may have no face at all. 118

The old men initiators, by contrast, conveyed to boys some assurance that is invisible and nonverbal; it helped the boys to see their genuine face or being. 119

So what can be done? Thousands and thousands of women, being single parents, are raising boys with no adult man in the house. The difficulties inherent in that situation came up one day in Evanston when I was giving a talk on initiation of men to a group made up mostly of women. 120

Women who were raising sons alone were extremely alert to the dangers of no male model. One woman declared that she realized about the time her son got to high-school age that he needed more hardness than she could naturally give. But, she said, if she made herself harder to meet that need, she would lose touch with her own femininity. I mentioned the classic solution in many traditional cultures, which is to send the boy to his father when he is twelve. Several women said flatly, "No, men aren't nurturing; they wouldn't take care of him." Many men, however—and I am one of them—have found inside an ability to nurture that didn't appear until it was called for. 121

Even when a father is living in the house there still may be a strong covert bond between mother and son to evict the father, which amounts to a conspiracy, and conspiracies are difficult to break. One woman with two sons had enjoyed going each year to a convention in San Francisco with her hus- 122 band, the boys being left at home. But one spring, having just returned from a women's retreat, she felt like being private and said to her husband: "Why don't you take the boys this year?" So the father did.

The boys, around ten and twelve, had never, as it turned out, experienced their father's company without the mother's presence. After that experience, they asked for more time with their dad.

When the convention time rolled around the following spring, the mother once more decided on privacy, and the boys once more went off with their father. The moment they arrived back home, the mother happened to be standing in the kitchen with her back to the door, and the older of the two boys walked over and put his arms around her from the back. Without even intending it, her body reacted explosively, and the boy flew across the room and bounced off the wall. When he picked himself up, she said, their relationship had changed. Something irrevocable had happened. She was glad about the change, and the boy seemed surprised and a little relieved that he apparently wasn't needed by her in the old way.

This story suggests that the work of separation can be done even if the old man initiators do not create the break. The mother can make the break herself. We see that it requires a great deal of intensity, and we notice that it was the woman's body somehow, not her mind, that accomplished the labor.

Another woman told a story in which the mother-son conspiracy was broken from the boy's side. She was the single parent of a son and two daughters, and the girls were doing well but the boy was not. At fourteen, the boy went to live with his father, but he stayed only a month or so and then came back. When he returned, the mother realized that three women in the house amounted to an overbalance of feminine energy for the son, but what could she do? A week or two went by. One night she said to her son, "John, it's time to come to dinner." She touched him on the arm and *he* exploded and *she* flew against the wall—the same sort of explosion as in the earlier story. We notice no intent of abuse either time, and no evidence that the event was repeated. In each case the psyche or body knew what the mind didn't. When the mother picked herself off the floor, she said, "It's time for you to go back to your father," and the boy said, "You're right."

The traditional initiation break clearly is preferable, and sidesteps the violence. But all over the country now one sees hulking sons acting ugly in the kitchen and talking rudely to their mothers, and I think it's an attempt to make themselves unattractive. If the old men haven't done their work to interrupt the mother-son unity, what else can the boys do to extricate themselves but to talk ugly? It's quite unconscious and there's no elegance in it at all.

A clean break from the mother is crucial, but it's simply not happening. This doesn't mean that the women are doing something wrong: I think the problem is more that the older men are not really doing their job.

The traditional way of raising sons, which lasted for thousands and thousands of years, amounted to fathers and sons living in close—murderously close—proximity, while the father taught the son a trade: perhaps farming or carpentry or blacksmithing or tailoring. As I've suggested elsewhere, the love unit most damaged by the Industrial Revolution has been the father-son bond.

There's no sense in idealizing preindustrial culture, yet we know that to- 130 day many fathers now work thirty or fifty miles from the house, and by the time they return at night the children are often in bed, and they themselves are too tired to do active fathering.

The Industrial Revolution, in its need for office and factory workers, 131 pulled fathers away from their sons and, moreover, placed the sons in compulsory schools where the teachers are mostly women. D. H. Lawrence described what this was like in his essay "Men Must Work and Women as Well." His generation in the coal-mining areas of Britain felt the full force of that change, and the new attitude centered on one idea: that physical labor is bad.

Lawrence recalls that his father, who had never heard this theory, worked 132 daily in the mines, enjoyed the camaraderie with the other men, came home in good spirits, and took his bath in the kitchen. But around that time the new schoolteachers arrived from London to teach Lawrence and his classmates that physical labor is low and unworthy and that men and women should strive to move upward to a more "spiritual" level—higher work, mental work. The children of his generation deduced that their fathers had been doing something wrong all along, that men's physical work is wrong and that those sensitive mothers who prefer white curtains and an elevated life are right and always have been.

During Lawrence's teenage years, which he described in *Sons and Lovers,* 133 he clearly believed the new teachers. He wanted the "higher" life, and took his mother's side. It wasn't until two years before he died, already ill with tuberculosis in Italy, that Lawrence began to notice the vitality of the Italian workingmen, and to feel a deep longing for his own father. He realized then that his mother's ascensionism had been wrong for him, and had encouraged him to separate from his father and from his body in an unfruitful way.

A single clear idea, well fed, moves like a contagious disease: "Physical 134 work is wrong." Many people besides Lawrence took up that idea, and in the next generation that split between fathers and sons deepened. A man takes up desk work in an office, becomes a father himself, but has no work to share with his son and cannot explain to the son what he's doing. Lawrence's father was able to take his son down into the mines, just as my own father, who was a farmer, could take me out on the tractor, and show me around. I knew what he was doing all day and in all seasons of the year.

When the office work and the "information revolution" begin to domi- 135 nate, the father-son bond disintegrates. If the father inhabits the house only for an hour or two in the evenings, then women's values, marvelous as they are, will be the only values in the house. One could say that the father now loses his son five minutes after birth.

When we walk into a contemporary house, it is often the mother who 136 comes forward confidently. The father is somewhere else in the back, being inarticulate. This is a poem of mine called "Finding the Father":

My friend, this body offers to carry us for nothing—as the ocean carries logs.   137
So on some days the body wails with its great energy; it smashes up the boulders, lifting small crabs, that flow around the sides.

Someone knocks on the door. We do not have time to dress. He wants us   138
to go with him through the blowing and rainy streets, to the dark house.

We will go there, the body says, and there find the father whom we have   139
never met, who wandered out in a snowstorm the night we were born, and
who then lost his memory, and has lived since longing for his child, whom
he saw only once . . . while he worked as a shoemaker, as a cattle herder in
Australia, as a restaurant cook who painted at night.

When you light the lamp you will see him. He sits there behind the door   140
. . . the eyebrows so heavy, the forehead so light . . . lonely in his whole body,
waiting for you.

The Remote Father

The German psychologist Alexander Mitscherlich writes about this father-son   141
crisis in his book called *Society Without the Father.* The gist of his idea is that if
the son does not actually see what his father does during the day and
through all the seasons of the year, a hole will appear in the son's psyche, and
the hole will fill with demons who tell him that his father's work is evil and
that the father is evil.

The son's fear that the absent father is evil contributed to student   142
takeovers in the sixties. Rebellious students at Columbia University took over
the president's office looking for evidence of CIA involvement with the university. The students' fear that their own fathers were evil was transferred to
all male figures in authority. A university, like a father, looks upright and decent on the outside, but underneath, somewhere, you have the feeling that it
and he are doing something demonic. That feeling becomes intolerable because the son's inner intuitions become incongruous with outer appearances.
The unconscious intuitions come in, not because the father is wicked, but
because the father is remote.

Young people go to the trouble of invading the president's office to bridge   143
this incongruity. The country being what it is, occasionally they do find letters from the CIA, but this doesn't satisfy the deeper longing—the need of the
son's body to be closer to the father's body. "Where is my father . . . why
doesn't he love me? What is going on?"

The movie called *The Marathon Man* concentrates on the young American   144
male's suspicion of older men. The main character, played by Dustin Hoffman, loses his father, a leftist driven to suicide in the McCarthy era. The plot
puts the young man in dangerous contact with a former concentration camp
doctor, whom Hoffman must confront and defeat before he can have any
peace with his own dead father.

When the demons are so suspicious, how can the son later make any   145
good connection with adult male energy, especially the energy of an adult
man in a position of authority or leadership? As a musician he will smash
handcrafted guitars made by old men, or as a teacher suspicious of older

writers he will "deconstruct" them. As a citizen he will take part in therapy rather than politics. He will feel purer when not in authority. He will go to northern California and raise marijuana, or ride three-wheelers in Maine.

There's a general assumption now that every man in a position of power   146
is or will soon be corrupt and oppressive. Yet the Greeks understood and praised a positive male energy that has accepted authority. They called it Zeus energy, which encompasses intelligence, robust health, compassionate decisiveness, good will, generous leadership. Zeus energy is male authority accepted for the sake of the community.

The native Americans believe in that healthful male power. Among the   147
Senecas, the chief—a man, but chosen by the women—accepts power for the sake of the community. He himself owns virtually nothing. All the great cultures except ours preserve and have lived with images of this positive male energy.

Zeus energy has been steadily disintegrating decade after decade in the   148
United States. Popular culture has been determined to destroy respect for it, beginning with the "Maggie and Jiggs" and "Blondie and Dagwood" comics of the 1920s and 1930s, in which the man is always weak and foolish. From there the image of the weak adult man went into animated cartoons.

The father in contemporary TV ads never knows what cold medicine to   149
take. And in situation comedies, "The Cosby Show" notwithstanding, men are devious, bumbling, or easy to outwit. It is the women who outwit them, and teach them a lesson, or hold the whole town together all by themselves. This is not exactly "what people want." Many young Hollywood writers, rather than confront their fathers in Kansas, take revenge on the remote father by making all adult men look like fools.

They attack the respect for masculine integrity that every father, under-   150
neath, wants to pass on to his grandchildren and great-grandchildren. By contrast, in traditional cultures, the older men and the older women often are the first to speak in public gatherings; younger men may say nothing but still aim to maintain contact with the older men. Now we have twenty-seven-year-olds engaged in hostile takeovers who will buy out a publishing house and dismantle in six months what an older man has created over a period of thirty years.

I offered my help in undermining Zeus energy during my twenties and   151
thirties. I attacked every older man in the literary community who was within arrow range, and enjoyed seeing the arrows pass through his body, arrows impelled by the tense energy bottled in my psyche. I saw many parts of my father's daytime life, his work habits, and his generous attitude toward working men; but he was inaccessible in some other way, and the hole in me filled with demons, as Mitscherlich predicted. Older men whom I hardly knew received the anger.

When a son acts on that fear of demonism it makes him flat, stale, iso-   152
lated, and dry. He doesn't know how to recover his wet and muddy portion. A few years ago, I began to feel my diminishment, not so much on my "feminine" side as on my masculine side. I found myself missing contact with men—or should I say my father?

I began to think of him not as someone who had deprived me of love or   153
attention or companionship, but as someone who himself had been deprived, by his father and his mother and by the culture. This rethinking is
still going on.

Every time I see my father I have new and complicated feelings about   154
how much of the deprivation I felt with him came willingly and how much
came against his will—how much he was aware of and unaware of.

Jung said something disturbing about this complication. He said that   155
when the son is introduced primarily by the mother to feeling, he will learn
the female attitude toward masculinity and take a female view of his own father and of his own masculinity. He will see his father through his mother's
eyes. Since the father and the mother are in competition for the affection of
the son, you're not going to get a straight picture of your father out of your
mother, nor will one get a straight picture of the mother out of the father.

Some mothers send out messages that civilization and culture and feeling   156
and relationships are things which the mother and the daughter, or the
mother and the sensitive son, share in common, whereas the father stands
for and embodies what is stiff, maybe brutal, what is unfeeling, obsessed, ra-
tionalistic: money-mad, uncompassionate. "Your father can't help it." So the
son often grows up with a wounded image of his father—not brought about
necessarily by the father's actions, or words, but based on the mother's observation of these words or actions.

I know that in my own case I made my first connection with feeling   157
through my mother. She provided me my first sense of discrimination of feeling. "Are you feeling sad?" But the connection entailed picking up a negative
view of my father, who didn't talk very much about feelings.

It takes a while for a son to overcome these early negative views of the fa-   158
ther. The psyche holds on tenaciously to these early perceptions. Idealization
of the mother or obsession with her, liking her or hating her, may last until
the son is thirty, or thirty-five, forty. Somewhere around forty or forty-five a
movement toward the father takes place naturally—a desire to see him more
clearly and to draw closer to him. This happens unexplainably, almost as if
on a biological timetable.

A friend told me how that movement took place in his life. At about   159
thirty-five, he began to wonder who his father really was. He hadn't seen his
father in about ten years. He flew out to Seattle, where his father was living,
knocked on the door, and when his father opened the door, said, "I want you
to understand one thing. I don't accept my mother's view of you any longer."

"What happened?" I asked.   160

"My father broke into tears, and said, 'Now I can die.'" Fathers wait. What   161
else can they do?

I am not saying that all fathers are good; mothers can be right about the   162
father's negative side, but the woman also can be judgmental about masculine traits that are merely different or unexpected.

If the son learns feeling primarily from the mother, then he will probably   163
see his own masculinity from the feminine point of view as well. He may be
fascinated with it, but he will be afraid of it. He may pity it and want to

reform it, or he may be suspicious of it and want to kill it. He may admire it, but he will never feel at home with it.

Eventually a man needs to throw off all indoctrination and begin to dis- 164 cover for himself what the father is and what masculinity is. For that task, ancient stories are a good help, because they are free of modern psychological prejudices, because they have endured the scrutiny of generations of women and men, and because they give both the light and dark sides of manhood, the admirable and the dangerous. Their model is not a perfect man, nor an overly spiritual man.

In the Greek myths, Apollo is visualized as a golden man standing on an 165 enormous accumulation of the dark, alert, dangerous energy called Dionysus. The Wild Man in our story includes some of both kinds of energy, both Apollo and Dionysus.

The Bhutanese make masks of a bird-headed man with dog's teeth. That 166 suggests a good double energy. We all know the temple guardians set before Oriental temple doors. A guardian is a man with bulging brows and fierce will, foot raised as if to dance, who lifts a club made of a flower. The Hindus offer as an image of masculinity Shiva, who is both an ascetic and a good lover, a madman and a husband. He has a fanged form called Bhairava, and in that aspect he is far from the niceness suggested by the conventional Jesus.

There's a hint of this Bhairava energy when Christ goes wild in the tem- 167 ple and starts whipping the moneychangers. The Celtic tradition offers as a male image Cuchulain—when he gets hot, his shin muscles switch around to the front and smoke comes out of the top of his head.

These powerful energies inside men are lying, like Iron John, in ponds we 168 haven't walked past yet. It is good that the divine is associated with the Virgin Mary and a blissful Jesus, but we can sense how different it would be for young men if we lived in a culture where the divine also was associated with mad dancers, fierce fanged men, and a being entirely underwater, covered with hair.

All of us, men and women both, feel some fear as we approach these im- 169 ages. We have been trying for several decades, rightly, to understand the drawbacks of the destructive, macho personality type, and in that regard I think it is helpful to keep in mind the distinctions between the Wild Man and the savage man.

When a man gets in touch with the Wild Man, a true strength may be 170 added. He's able to shout and say what he wants in a way that the Sixties-Seventies man is not able to. The approach to, or embodying of, receptive space that the Sixties-Seventies man has achieved is infinitely valuable, and not to be given up. But as I wrote in a poem called "A Meditation on Philosophy":

When you shout at them, they don't reply.
They turn their face toward the crib wall, and die.

The ability of a male to shout and to be fierce does not imply domina- 171 tion, treating people as if they were objects, demanding land or empire, holding on to the Cold War—the whole model of machismo.

Women in the 1970s needed to develop what is known in the Indian tra-   172
dition as Kali energy—the ability really to say what they want, to dance with
skulls around their neck, to cut relationships when they need to.

Men need to make a parallel connection with the harsh Dionysus energy   173
that the Hindus call Kala. Our story says that the first step is to find the Wild
Man lying at the bottom of the pond. Some men are able to descend to that
place through accumulated grief. However, connecting with this Kala energy
will have the effect also of meeting that same energy in women. If men don't
do that, they won't survive.

Men are suffering right now—young men especially. Now that so many   174
men have gotten in touch with their grief, their longing for father and mentor connections, we are more ready to start seeing the Wild Man and to look
again at initiation. But I feel very hopeful.

At this point, many things can happen.   175

Questions

1. What does Bly mean when he says that the new man of the 90s is "life-preserv-
    ing" but not "life-giving"?

2. What do you think the "Wild Man" represents? What does Bly mean when he
    says "once the golden ball is gone, we spend the rest of our lives trying to get it
    back"?

3. What kinds of images of men do the media promote? Do you agree with Bly that
    most of the images represent the father figure as "weak and foolish"?

Pumping Iron John

JANE CAPUTI AND GORDENE O. MACKENZIE

Jane Caputi and Gordene O. MacKenzie teach American Studies at the University of New Mexico, Albuquerque. Caputi is the author of The Age of Sex Crime.

Caputi and MacKenzie argue that Bly's conception of masculinity endorses patriarchy and a "hatred of the feminine." They argue that his insistence on the rigidity of gender leads to inequality and enmity; what is needed is a "gender transcendence movement." This selection is from Women Respond to the Men's Movement *(1992).*

> *[Gender] difference exists in every cell of the body.*
> ROBERT BLY, *IRON JOHN*[1]

The January 20, 1992, issue of *Time* magazine tries to tell us just what kind of a year it is going to be for women and men. The headline reads: "Why Are Men and Women Different?" Right away we notice that another question is not being asked: *Are* men and women different? The title itself presumes and enforces sexual difference. A subtitle continues: "It isn't just upbringing. New studies show they are born that way." A dark-haired boy and a blond girl (dressed not too subtly in red, white, and blue) stand together. The backdrop is a brick wall. She is looking at him, with an expression of grinning indulgence, one hand placed shyly against his elbow. He uses one of his hands to raise the cuff of his shirt so that he can flex his biceps, which he lovingly gazes upon. She is looking at him; she is touching him. He is oblivious to her; he is touching himself. They both gaze at his small swollen muscle. She is pumping him up with her attention, touch, and gaze. He is pumping himself. They are both pumping iron john. The message couldn't be clearer. The women's movement and contemporary women are up against a (brick) wall. The so-called "Wild Men" of the contemporary "men's movement," who incessantly drum out the message of innate gender difference and, implicitly, inequality between women and men, must be chanting "Ho!"

Robert Bly's *Iron John,* the bible of the men's movement, topped the bestseller lists for much of 1991. In this work, Bly laments the lot of "soft" and "faceless" men who remain under the maiming influence of the mother and/or dominant female lovers. He proclaims that we live in a world bereft of male initiation and that this is a society in which there is "not enough father," leaving men "wounded" and beset with grief. Although we'll expand

499

upon these points later, we must take a moment here to seriously question Bly's credibility as a cultural observer. Doesn't the man go to the movies or watch television—ritual activities in themselves, where stories of boys turning into men and paeans to father power are omnipresent. Many of the most popular films of all time concern some aspect of male initiation, e.g., *Star Wars, Home Alone, Top Gun,* and just about anything by Steven Spielberg, e.g., *Jaws, E.T.* and *Hook.* Television, of course, is a medium notorious for its father fixation, from "Father Knows Best" to "The Cosby Show." With some notable exceptions ("Roseanne"), all too frequently mothers play second banana ("Home Improvement"), or have been disappeared by the story line altogether ("Davis Rules," "Full House"), even though, in reality, there are many more single female parents than male. As a recent headline in the *New York Times* (May 26, 1991) summed up current TV demographics: "Poof! The Mommies Vanish in Sitcomland."

Such trends are highly significant, for the mass media serve as our cul-   3
ture's primary dispensary of myth and ritual. Here, stories are told that transmit and reinforce mainstream values, that tell us how the world works, instruct us as to what is normal or deviant, right or wrong, that form both the individual and the collective psyche. Robert Bly himself is fully aware of the power of story to affect consciousness. In *Iron John,* he dives deeply into the patriarchal archives, surfacing with a Grimm Brothers' tale ("Iron John"), which he offers as an alchemical parable for modern men. In his view, Iron John, a.k.a. the "Wild Man," is the source of "true masculinity" repressed and denied in modern culture, the figure with whom Bly believes all men must connect in order to transmute from boys to men.

In the fable, Iron John is a wild, extremely hairy man who lives in a state   4
of enchantment in a forbidding forest, beneath a deep lake. The king has him brought back to the castle, where he is kept locked up in an iron cage. The king's son accidentally rolls his golden ball into the cage. To get it back, he agrees to steal the key to the cage from under his mother's pillow, and free Iron John. Dreading punishment, the prince runs away with Iron John, eventually undergoing various ordeals of initiation until, aided by his hairy mentor, he proves his manhood by besting an enemy in battle and marrying a princess, at which point Iron John is freed from his enchantment.

During the past two decades, the contemporary women's movement has   5
questioned and rejected rigid sex and gender stereotypes, creating new myths and definitions of female power, and naming ourselves to be "Wild," that is, undomesticated and outside of the bounds of patriarchy (most vividly, in Mary Daly's *Gyn/Ecology,* 1978).[2] The feminist movement also challenged men to invent new definitions of "masculinity" and to make a qualitative break from a world ordered by a "masculinity" understood to be aggressive, violent, and unemotional. At first some women might be hopeful that the men's movement would concern itself with these sorts of radical changes, but, despite some double-talk to the contrary, the song these wild men are singing is "Return to Gender" (that is, rigid bipolar gender roles). Just as David Duke and his followers responded to the pressures of antiracist move-

ments with the founding of the National Association for the Advancement of White People, much of the activity going on under the rubric of the "men's movement" (composed largely of white middle-class men) is a form of masculinist nationalism, that is, a reconstellation of patriarchal rules and roles and an attempt to consolidate cockocratic[3] power in response to challenges from the women's movement. The "men's movement," as epitomized by Bly's writings, while portending/pretending to be a movement for liberation is actually a manifestation of an authoritarian backlash and joins the political and religious right in reinforcing separatism, hierarchy, contempt for the "other," and invidious distinctions between women and men.

Zeus Juice[4]

In his pursuit of "true masculinity," Bly urges a return not only to hairy fairy tales, but to ancient manly deities, notably the Greek god Zeus. Zeus, as Robert Graves extensively demonstrates, was an incessant rapist, molesting both mortal women and ancient goddesses. Moreover, his reign ushered in an era of blight for women. As Graves notes: ". . . the hitherto intellectually dominant Greek woman degenerated into an unpaid worker and breeder of children wherever Zeus and Apollo were the ruling gods."[5] Bly expediently ignores these factors and instead rhapsodizes over Zeus as the embodiment of: "positive male energy . . . Zeus energy, which encompasses intelligence, robust health, compassionate decisiveness, good will, generous leadership. Zeus energy is male authority accepted for the good of the community."[6] Antipatriarchal women and men would do well to defy Bly, the iron-age guru, exhorting us to give over our power to rapist divinities and self-styled father figures "for our own good." [6]

Bly neatly reverses the real meaning of Zeus' "masculinity" and such doublethinking inversion structures much of the movement. If we understand Zeus not as a rapist, but as a benevolent authority, we can more readily accept elite men as victims, not victimizers. In much of men's movement ideology, men identify themselves as victims: of absent fathers, of a contaminating and encompassing "femininity," and of angry feminists and insubordinate wives and girlfriends. [7]

Some estimates suggest that over a quarter of a million men have participated in "men only" workshops, conferences, and weekend fraternal "adventures." Here, frequently in wilderness settings, they engage in drum beating, screaming, chanting, sweat lodging, dancing, crying, hugging, and playing Big Daddy to one another in a dying world (and no doubt terrorizing whatever indigenous animal life still exists). According to the tenets of the men's movement, it is of paramount importance that younger men overcome their distrust of older men and bond together in son-father dyads to heal their wounds. In Bly's view, men have been deprived of initiation into manhood due to the structuring of industrial society that removed fathers from the home. This absent father syndrome, allegedly, is the source of men's deepest grief. To address this pain and to become truly "masculine," Bly contends [8] that men need a surrogate father figure or "male mother" (not unlike Bly himself).

We would not deny that men, even socially elite men, feel grief and have been victimized. All were at one time boys and, as Kate Millet points out, the rules of patriarchal domination are twofold: Men shall dominate women, and elder men shall dominate younger men.[7] In patriarchy, any group perceived as "weaker" or "other" is stereotyped as "feminine," including women, people of color, and even male children. As such, boyhood in patriarchy is frequently an ignominious state. Boys can be humiliated by their fathers with impunity; they, like girls, are sexually exploited by adults, most frequently by adult males; and they are sent off to war (by governmental father figures) to be maimed and killed. By urging men to heal the wound with their fathers, Bly is urging a truce between elite men, asking younger men to identify with their prior oppressors and unite with the fathers in opposition to women and "others," effectively consolidating patriarchal power.   9

Bly writes: "As I've participated in men's gatherings since the early 1980s, I've heard one statement over and over from American males, which has been phrased in a hundred different ways: 'There is not enough father.'"[8] This alleged father lack plagues not only individual men, but our entire culture, which, Bly contends, is desperately hungering for "the King." If so, this is extremely alarming, for a yearning for paternal authority figures smacks not of therapeutic healing, but of fascism. As Gertrude Stein, writing in 1937, warned: "There is too much fathering going on just now and there is no doubt about it fathers are depressing. Everybody nowadays is a father, there is father Mussolini and father Hitler and father Roosevelt and father Stalin . . . and there are ever so many more ready to be one."[9] Again, it seems incredible that Bly can gaze upon a world dominated by father figures—father Bush, father Schwartzkopf, father Turner, father Yeltsin, Jehovah, Allah, God the father, and John Paul Too—and see an *absent* father. Of course, Bly (and other men's movement leaders) would contend that many military and political leaders are not *true* fathers, but "shadow" fathers or "Poisoned Kings." This is tantamount to denying the culpability of the Church for the Inquisition by arguing that those who implemented it were not *true* Christians. Bly's argument is riddled further with doublethink, because the archetypes of and routes to "masculinity" that he explicitly prescribes can lead only to this type of "poisoned" (more accurately *poisoning*) father.   10

For example, we must question Bly's use of a fairy tale as a source of positive gender roles. Feminists for decades have been pointing out the all too grim meaning of many of these stories for women. As Andrea Dworkin observed, in these tales women are either passive lumps of beauty, hence "good," *or* active and powerful, hence malevolent (and often ugly) witches.[10] In "Iron John," the boy becomes a man by slaying the enemy in battle and marrying a princess, neatly fulfilling patriarchal roles and expectations. The princess, of course, is obsessed with the prince (the original pretty woman who loves too much) and, like a piece of property, is passed from father to husband. There is no challenge to male dominance or traditional gender roles   11

here. Bly overtly denies a desire to reconstitute the patriarchy, yet his glorifi-
cation of rapist divinities and sexist fairy tales belies that statement. Congruent with this is his recurrent use of *soft* as the primary descriptive of failed
"masculinity." All power resides with the fraternity of the *hard* on Captain
Bly's Ship of Snools.[11] When ironclad men shout "Ho," savvy women sigh
"ho, ho, hum." Haven't we heard all this before?

Bly's endorsement of sexual inequality also is revealed in his constant   12
admonishment that "even the best intentioned women cannot give [the
questing man] what is needed." What is required, it seems, is a kind of psychic semen: "When a father and a son spend long hours together . . . we
could say that a substance almost like food passes from the older body to the
younger. . . . A physical exchange takes place. . . . The younger body learns at
what frequency the masculine body vibrates."[12] This sounds frighteningly
like psychic and/or physical incest and evinces both pedophilia and a characteristic patriarchal phenomenon: homophobic homoeroticism. This dynamic
easily is recognizable in the patterns of traditional fraternal organizations
such as organized sports, college fraternities, the military, and the Catholic
clergy. Such brotherhoods vehemently taboo liberating, erotic expression between men, but at the same time profoundly encourage contempt for the
female and worship of the male, and engage in all sorts of homophobic/
homosexual ritual (e.g., the spanking games of college fraternities, the sexual
byplay of football language and gesture, and the sadomasochistic and erotically charged hierarchies of the military and the church). These all-male institutions are the true model for the separatist men's movement and long have
functioned as a breeding ground of patriarchal attitudes and values (allowing
older men to pass their prejudices on to younger men), and the chief setting
for rites of "masculine" initiation (which frequently entail sexual abuse of
women and/or younger men). So resistant are these groups to integration of
the sexes that one member of the Yale Skull and Bones Society recently
threatened that there would be a rash of "date rape" in the "medium-term
future" if women insisted upon joining that organization.[13] Such rapism is
the true face of the "Zeus energy" that Bly so blithely extols.

It is important to distinguish between the separatism (sometimes tempo-   13
rary) of oppressed groups and the entrenched separatism of many elite patriarchal groups. Simply put, when women and other oppressed groups
structure their organizations and lifestyles according to separatist principles,
it is usually a survival technique, employed because the power elites invariably treat us as inferiors, victimizing us (even to the point of killing us),
thwarting our efforts for political change, and, in general, rendering life ugly,
snoolish, and boring. When men structure their organizations and life-styles
according to separatist principles, it is due to traditional elitist and exclusionary tactics, serving to consolidate male power and to institutionalize fear and
loathing of the "Other." As Julia Sugarbaker (Dixie Carter) acidly observed on
a 1991 episode of "Designing Women" that lampooned the separatism of the
men's movement, such wild men deem women to be the "impure ones" who
would "pollute the men's sacred circle."

Separating from the Mother, Or, "I Used to Love Her, But I Had to Kill Her"[14]

Along with that questionable juicy bonding with the father, Bly demands   14
that the son commit psychic matricide. In his words, it is crucial that boys
make "a clean break" from the original focus of their love, the mother. It's kill
or be killed, as Bly spells it out, for "when women, even women with the best
intentions, bring up a boy alone, he may in some way have no male face, or
he may have no face at all."[15] Here, Bly clearly aligns himself with the legions
of mother haters and mother blamers who have swelled the ranks of "masculine" authority for centuries.

A popular 1991 T-shirt reads: "Shut Up Bitch," and *Iron John* essentially   15
transmits that same command. Bly's call for the radical rupture from the
mother signals a greater renunciation and silencing of everything female and
"feminine" in order to keep up "masculinity." A November 22, 1991, Oprah
Winfrey show dedicated to the men's movement groveled to that movement's prejudices by restricting its audience to males. (Have women ever
been so indulged?) Self-avowed men's movement leaders and a "Santa
Fe–style" long-haired drumming white man preened on the stage. Engaging
in group drumming, they sought to "release the beast" within and encouraged men in the audience to express antipathy and anger to women. One audience member was met with rousing cheers when he stated: "When my TV
talks too much, I can mute it. [Unfortunately] I can't do that to my girlfriend." Such are the fantasies of late twentieth-century techno-wild men.

Bly's demand that the boy separate from the mother is by no means   16
unique. This dictum pervades psychoanalytic, social learning, and sociobio-
logical theories, and we see it propagated everywhere in popular culture
(from *Psycho* to *Home Alone*). Currently, fearful parents can take an insufficiently "masculine" boy to gender clinics run by "male mothers" such as
Richard Green, author of *The Sissy Boy Syndrome*. These clinics force the
young boy into conforming to "masculine" norms, inciting him to kill off
anything remotely "feminine" or motherlike in himself, often through
bizarre behavior modification techniques. "Feminine" behavior, such as playing with dolls, is punished, while "masculine" behavior, such as pulling all
the hair off a female doll, is rewarded. One "sissy boy" actually was deemed
cured after he beat his mother and sisters with a stick.[16]

Other "male mothers," gender theorists such as Robert Stoller and John   17
Money, have promoted transsexual surgery as a solution to extreme "femininity" in boys. Such a mutilating procedure is accepted and legitimated because it supports the ingrained patriarchal belief that one's genitals and
gender identity must line up according to the ironclad rule of "masculine"/male, "feminine"/female. Individuals who do not fulfill cultural stereotypes of sex and gender then become not only targets of violence, but
stigmatized as mentally ill. Ironically, all of these father figures protest too
much. Each, in his own way, goes to extraordinary lengths to guide (bully)
males into "true manhood." As this very state of affairs indicates, "masculinity"
is *not* something males are just "born into." Rather, many males have to go

through behavior modification, shock treatment, and "born-again" cult type experiences in order to achieve it. Remarkably, some extremely tenacious types succeed in resisting "masculinity" (e.g., the drag queens of Jennie Livingston's 1991 documentary *Paris Is Burning*) and surgical "solutions," but they then remain cultural outcasts. Implicit in the labors of male mothers Bly and Green is a hatred of the "feminine" and an urge to force it into its ordained place—females. Such ideology creates a climate of fear and loathing and legitimates emotional and physical violence against women and the "feminine," even when the "feminine" is embodied by males.

From Iron to Irony

The many dictionary definitions of *iron* include "inflexible," "unrelenting," [18] and "harsh" as well as "weaponry" and "something . . . used to bind, confine or restrain . . . captivity." Bly intends "Iron John" to be a transformative metaphor and a model of benevolent, affirming "masculinity." Nevertheless, it actually functions as a perfect metaphor for the inflexible prison of gender difference that patriarchy requires. Clearly, anatomical sexual difference exists, but having a vulva or a penis does not compel "gender," that is, sex-linked traits and behaviors. Despite *Time* magazine's magical invocation of "new studies," the question of whether or not there are innate gender differences is fundamentally a matter of ideology, not "science."

Bly mandates gender difference and eternal opposition between men and [19] women. Indeed, he celebrates that rigid opposition, recoiling in horror from any flexibility or fluidity. In grand ironmonger style, he heaps scorn upon fluidity as a "copper" or conductive mode of being that reduces men to crippled ghouls: "The more the man agrees to be copper, the more he becomes neither alive nor dead, but a third thing, an amorphous, demasculinized, half-alive psychic conductor."[17] Yet, what is so abhorrent in the notion of "the third thing," let alone a fourth or a fifth? As Virginia Woolf once noted, "the two sexes [genders] are quite inadequate, considering the vastness and variety of the world."[18] The tradition of the Native American *Berdache*—transgendered individuals, generally males who live as women—is one example of a "copper" mode of being, indicating the possibility of movement between what Bly would have us believe are two fixed spheres. So, too, are the traditions of Drag Kings and Queens (persons curiously unremarked upon in Bly's discussion of archetypal royalty). Devoted to pumping Iron John, that is, emphasizing and rejoicing in the rigidity of two, polar genders, Bly leads us only further into narrowness, inequality, and enmity.

In *Borderlands/La Frontera*, Gloria Anzaldúa underscores the dire need to [20] break down the dualistic paradigm, the foundation of opposition "between the white race and the colored, between males and females." The real alchemical work for both women and men is not to render ourselves into inflexible iron, but to become, in Anzaldúa's words, *"mestizaje"*—a "third element," divergent, plural, holistic—mocking and rendering irrelevant the bipolar paradigm.[19]

Such mockery and reversal of expectation suggests that one way out of   21
the bonds of gender would be to develop a grounding, not in iron, but in
irony. *Irony* is "a state of affairs . . . that is the reverse of what was . . . a result
opposite to and as if in mockery of the appropriate result." Perhaps, as that
superb ironist Valerie Solanas once suggested, males are really "feminine" and
females are really "masculine."[20] Perhaps even more to the reverse of expectation, and Wildly contrary to iron man myth, is that these two categories of
gender are themselves historical social constructs that shackle the full range
of human expression. "Masculine"/"feminine" are immutable facts only in
the world/cage forged by those who would cast all men in the mold of Iron
John. Women and men sick of being kept in irons might respond to the
men's movement by mocking its revival of hoary archetypes, profoundly un-
suitable for a world in which enmity and opposition overwhelm us. In a spirit
of Irony, we might create a gender transcendence movement.

Bly bitterly complains about a *lack* of father and the need to summon   22
Iron John as a savior for lost "masculinity." Yet, in truth, our world is plagued
by a gross surfeit of father power and we suffer under the sign of Iron John.
Like the Yoruban God Ogun, whom he resembles, "the wild man in the
woods . . . the Father of Technology . . . the policeman, the military, the one
who feeds on war,"[21] Iron John is an archetype of antagonistic masculinity.
Contrary to Bly, Iron John needs not to be summoned *out* of the forest, but
guided back into it. He needs to be tucked in for a very long snooze at the
bottom of a very deep lake.

NOTES

1. Robert Bly, *Iron John: A Book About Men* (Reading, MA: Addison-Wesley, 1990), p.
    234.
2. Mary Day, *Gyn/Ecology: The Metaethics of Radical Feminism* (Boston: Beacon Press,
    1978).
3. *Cockocratic* is derived from *Cockocracy,* which means "the state of supranational,
    supernatural erections; the place/time where the air is filled with the crowing of
    cocks, the joking of jocks, the droning of clones, the sniveling of snookers and
    snudges, the noisy parades and processions of prickers: pecker order." See Mary
    Daly with Jane Caputi, *Webster's First New Intergalactic Wickedary of the English
    Language* (Boston: Beacon Press, 1987), p. 191.
4. "Zeus Juice" was suggested by our very funny friend, Dorothy Johnson.
5. Robert Graves, *The Greek Myths* (2 vols.) (New York: Penguin Books, 1955), Vol. 1,
    p. 117.
6. Bly, p. 22.
7. Kate Millett, *Sexual Politics* (Garden City, NY: Doubleday, 1970), p. 25.
8. Bly, p. 92.
9. Gertrude Stein, *Everybody's Autobiography* (New York: Vintage, 1937, 1973), p. 133.
10. Andrea Dworkin, *Woman Hating* (New York: E. P. Dutton and Co., 1975), pp.
    31–49.

11. *Snool* is a word pirated from ordinary dictionaries by Mary Daly in *Pure Lust: Elemental Feminist Philosophy* (Boston: Beacon Press, 1984), which she redefines to "Name agents of the atrocities of the sadostate" (p. 21). Daly with Caputi further defines *snool* in the *Wickedary* as "normal inhabitant of sadosociety, characterized by sadism and masochism combined; stereotypic hero and/or saint of the sadostate" (p. 227).

12. Bly, p. 93.

13. See Phyllis Theroux, "Man and Animal at Yale," *New York Times*, Sept. 25, 1991, Sec. A, p. 23. See also "Correction," *New York Times*, Sept. 26, 1991, Sec. A., p. 23.

14. Guns n' Roses, "Used to Love Her," *Live Like a Suicide*, Geffen Records, 1988.

15. Bly, p. 17.

16. Richard Green, *The "Sissy Boy Syndrome" and the Development of Homosexuality* (New Haven: Yale University Press, 1987). See also Richard Green and John Money, eds., *Transsexualism and Sex Reassignment* (Baltimore: The Johns Hopkins University Press, 1969) and Richard Green, *Sexual Identity Conflict in Children and Adults* (New York: Basic Books, 1974).

17. Bly, p. 171.

18. Virginia Woolf, *A Room of One's Own* (New York: Harcourt, Brace and World, 1929, 1957), p. 91.

19. Gloria Anzaldúa, *Borderlands La Frontera: The New Mestiza* (San Francisco: Spinsters/Aunt Lute Book Company, 1987), pp. 79–80.

20. Valerie Solanas, *The Scum Manifesto* (New York: Olympia Press, 1967, 1968), p. 6.

21. Luisah Teish, *Jambalaya: The Natural Woman's Book of Personal Charms and Practical Rituals* (San Francisco: Harper & Row, 1985), pp. 125–26.

Questions

1. Why do the authors condemn Bly's view of what it means to be masculine? Do you agree with some of the problems they find in Bly's argument?

2. Do you agree with the authors that men essentially have to undergo "behavior modification" to learn how to be masculine? Is this assertion true to your own experience? If so, how?

3. How do you think Bly would respond to this attack on his explanation for male dissatisfaction?

Robert Bly: Turning "Yogurt Eaters" into "Wild Men"

SUSAN FALUDI

Susan Faludi is a Pulitzer Prize-winning journalist for the Wall Street Journal. *She has served as a staff writer for* Ms, *and has contributed to numerous
magazines. She is the author of* Backlash: The Undeclared War Against
Women *(1991). Her articles on feminist issues have been published widely.*

*Here, Faludi describes how Bly moved from the peace movement in the
1960s in which he encouraged men to foster their pacifistic "femininity" to
become a leader of the "masculine" movement. Faludi says that Bly is not
concerned with inculcating equality or harmony between the sexes; instead,
he is concerned with power and "how to wrest it from women and how to
mobilize it for men." This selection is from* Backlash.

> *It is a massive*
> *masculine shadow,*
> *fifty males sitting together*
> *in ball or crowded room,*
> *lifting something indistinct*
> *up into the resonating night.*
> ROBERT BLY, "FIFTY MALES SITTING TOGETHER"

"All of you men who are going to the men's weekend tomorrow, remember to   1
bring a large stone." Shepherd Bliss, a stern-faced man with rounded shoulders, is standing in front of the crowded back room at the Black Oak book-
store in Berkeley. So many have showed up for the evening's event that scores
must be turned away; they linger out front, listening via wall speakers. Inside,
more than a hundred people are elbowing each other for a closer view of the
dais, where poet Robert Bly will soon appear, "coming out of hibernation," as
Bliss puts it, to read his latest works.

Bliss, whose recent transformation includes changing his first name from   2
Walter to Shepherd and his profession from army officer to psychologist, is
one of Bly's chief spokesmen in the New Age masculinist community. But at
the moment, he is being a bit closemouthed about the stones. They will be
using them to build a "monument to Hermes," but that's all he'll say. He
doesn't want to get too specific because there are ladies in the room tonight.

Suddenly, the men on stage begin to beat on conga drums. The hibernat-   3 ing bear himself, roused from his great sleep in the "far north"—Moose Lake, Minnesota, to be exact—lumbers down the aisle. Just turned sixty, Bly, with his tangled white mane and rounded belly, looks a little like Father Christmas. His heritage, as he will tell listeners several times that evening, is Norse, and something in his pose—perhaps the way he plants his feet as if manning a storm-swept deck—suggests that he intends his audience take him for a Viking.

We no longer have images of "real men," Bly says, as the men continue the drum beat. Stereotypical sissies have replaced macho men. "Woody Allen is just as bad—a negative John Wayne," he says, raising his voice to a nasal squeak in imitation. "Men used to make models for what a man is from the *Iliad* and the *Odyssey* and places like that." On the all-male weekend, he promises, he will bring back these role models for male edification: "One of the things we do is go back to the very old stories, five thousand years ago, where the view of a man, what a man is, is more healthy."   4

Two decades earlier, Bly was a Berkeley hero for another reason: a '60s peace activist, the poet gained fame for his literary stand against the Vietnam War. When he won the National Book Award in 1967 for his poetry collection "The Light Around the Body," he gave the money to a draft-resistance group and blasted American literary smugness at the awards ceremony: "Since we are murdering a culture in Vietnam at least as fine as our own, have we the right to congratulate ourselves on our cultural magnificence?"   5

Back then, Bly lauded women who encouraged draft-age young men to resist the war and flee to Canada. To bring peace into the world, Bly argued, men and women both should embrace their feminine principle; the life-preserving nature, he maintained, resided in both sexes but was unhealthily repressed in men. In the "Great Mother" conferences he conducted in the '70s, gatherings open to both sexes, Bly tried to foster that "feminine" peace-loving spirit.   6

But as the peace movement sputtered and the years passed, Bly was no longer commanding crowds—nor receiving national awards he could reject. By the early '80s, he was even, he confessed, starting to feel less than manly. "I began to feel diminished," Bly writes, "by my lack of embodiment of the fruitful male—or the moist male." It wasn't his loss of early prominence, however, that he identified as the problem. It was his "missing contact with men" and his overexposure to strong and angry women, including his own mother, who were speaking out about the mistreatment they had endured from men in their lives. (In his family's case, as Bly recalls, his mother was re-acting to his father, a remote and chilly alcoholic.) He feared that he and men like him had allied themselves *too* closely with such women, and conse-quently taken "a female view" of their fathers and their own masculinity. He decided he'd made a mistake with his earlier recommendation: "If someone says to me now, 'There is something missing on your feminine side,' I say, 'No, what is missing is the masculine,'" Bly told *Whole Earth* magazine in 1988. He worried that he was only "superficially" manly. Men had awakened their feminine principle only to be consumed by it. They had gone "soft."   7

To remedy this latest imbalance, Bly began running all-male workshops   8
to reintroduce men to "the deep masculine." Soon he was leading wilderness weekend retreats where men dressed in tribal masks and wild-animal
costumes, beat drums and rediscovered "the beast within." While Warren
Farrell and even neoconservative men like George Gilder at least sought to
be heard by women, Bly believed strict separatism was the soft male's only
salvation.

By the mid-'80s, Bly was drawing crowds again; hundreds of men were   9
paying $55 for a single lecture, $300 for a two-day retreat. By the end of the
decade, Bly was back in the media throne, too, meriting a ninety-minute TV
special with Bill Moyers, feature treatment in the *New York Times Magazine,*
and tributes from traditional men's magazines and New Age periodicals. He
was lionized in both *Gentlemen's Quarterly* and *Yoga Journal.* Mainstream
newspapers hailed him as the "Father Figure to the New, New Man." By 1990,
his self-published pamphlets on the masculinity crisis had been compiled
and reissued in hard cover by a leading publisher—and the book, *Iron John,*
quickly scaled the *New York Times* best-seller list.

Bly's success inspired scores of imitators; by the late '80s, the men's move-   10
ment had turned into a cottage industry complete with lecture series ("Moist
Earthy Masculinity, for Men Only"), books (*Phallos: Sacred Image of the Masculine*), newsletters ("New Warrior News"), tapes ("The Naive Male"), radio
shows ("Man-to-Man with Jerry Johnson"), and even board games ("A Game
of Insights for Men Only"). This new men's movement wasn't just another
California curiosity. "Brotherhood lodges" sprang up in Tulsa, Oklahoma;
Washington, D.C., supported six men's organizations offering "wild man" rituals; "The Talking Stick: A Newsletter About Men" issued from Frederick,
Maryland; the Austin, Texas, "Wild Man Gatherings" got booked months in
advance; and the Men's Center in Minneapolis drew enough men to keep up
a daily schedule of "playshops." In New York City and Oakland, California,
the Sterling Institute of Relationships' $400 "Men, Sex and Power" weekends
taught "wimps" to become "real men," dressing up like gorillas, beating their
chests, and staging fistfights. These seminars alone enrolled more than ten
thousand men in the 1980s. Bly's weekend retreats logged fifty thousand men
in the last half of the '80s alone. Nor were attendants marginalized drifters.
On Bly's retreat roster were lawyers, judges, doctors, accountants, and corporate executives; at one wilderness experience, the group included several vice
presidents of Fortune 500 companies and two television-station owners.

The New Age masculinists claimed to bear no ill-will toward the women's   11
movement. The two movements were running on "parallel tracks," as Bly's
disciples liked to emphasize. When a woman asked Bly at the Black Oak poetry reading for his view of feminism, the poet assured her, "I support
tremendously the work of that movement." The only reason he doesn't invite
women to most of the events, he explained, is because men "can be more
honest when women aren't around." But Bly's writings and speeches suggest
other reasons, too, for the poet's ban on women.

"I remember a bumper sticker [advocating draft-dodging] during the '60s   12
that read WOMEN SAY YES TO MEN WHO SAY NO," he writes in "The Pillow & the
Key," his 1987 manifesto of New Age masculinism. ". . . The women were definitely saying that they preferred the softer receptive male, and they would
reward him for being soft: 'We will sleep with you if you are not too aggressive and macho.'" That, Bly suggests, was the first of many female jabs that
would deflate the male psyche. "The development of men was disturbed a little there," he writes, "interfered with."

The arrival of the women's movement in the early '70s increased the in-   13
terference. "What Men Really Want," a written "dialogue" between Bly and
fellow New Age masculinist Keith Thompson, outlines the problem:

BLY: I see the phenomenon of what I would call the "soft male" all over the country
     today. Sometimes when I look out at my audiences, perhaps half the young males
     are what I'd call soft. . . . Many of these men are unhappy. There's not much en-
     ergy in them. They are life-preserving but not exactly life-giving. And why is it
     you often see these men with strong women who positively radiate energy?
THOMPSON: Perhaps it's because back in the sixties, when we looked to the women's
     movement for leads as how we should be, the message we got was that the new
     strong women *wanted* soft men.
BLY: I agree. That's how it felt.

In short, the Great Mother's authority has become too great. "Men's soci-   14
eties are disappearing, partly under pressure from women with hurt feelings,"
he writes. Too many women are "raising boys with no man in the house."
The single mother's son has become "a nice boy who now not only pleases
his mother but also the young woman he is living with."

To restore the nice boy's male identity, Bly proposes, he must quit taking   15
cues from mother and "go down into the psyche and accept what's dark
down there." As a key guide to the journey, Bly offers "The Story of Iron
John," borrowed from a Grimm's Brothers' fairy tale. In the story, a hairy
"wild man" is locked up in an iron cage near the royal castle; the key to the
cage is under the queen's pillow. One day the young prince loses his prized
"golden ball" when it rolls into an abandoned pond, and he can only retrieve
it by stealing the key from mother and freeing the wild man. The young man,
in the words of Bly's sidekick Keith Thompson, "has to take back the power
he has given to his mother and get away from the force field of her bed. He
must direct his energies away from pleasing Mommy."

At Bly's all-male "mythopoetic" weekends, the not-so-young princes re-   16
claim their golden balls, with a few adjustments for modern times. At one
such weekend—located at a Bible camp in Mound, Minnesota—the "wild
men" build their lairs with plastic lounge chairs. Journalist Jon Tevlin, who
attended the event, recalls a typical wild-man encounter that weekend, led by
the omnipresent Shepherd Bliss.

As he [Bliss] spoke of recovering the "wild man within" that first night, Shep-   17
herd slowly dropped to his knees. "Some of you may want to temporarily

leave the world of the two-leggeds, and join me in the world of the four-leggeds," he said. One by one, we slid from our orange Naugahyde chairs onto an orange shag carpet ripped straight out of the 1960s. "You may find yourself behaving like these four-leggeds; you may be scratching the earth, getting in contact with the dirt and the world around you."

As he spoke, people began pawing at the ground. . . . "You may find your-   18
self behaving like the most masculine of all animals—the ram," Shepherd said in a coaxing voice. . . . "You may find unfamiliar noises emerging from your throats!". . . There were gurgles and bleats, a few wolf calls. . . . Out of the corner of my eye, I saw Shepherd coming toward me, head down, tufts of white hair ringing a bald spot. . . . Meanwhile, I felt a slight presence at my rear, and turned to see a man beginning to sniff my buttocks.

"Woof!" he said.   19

The question of how to improve relations with women, in or out of bed,   20
gets remarkably short shrift on these weekends. "In two full days women were hardly mentioned," Trip Gabriel writes of a "Wild-Man Gathering" in Texas. Writers Steve Chapple and David Talbot, who attended Bly's "Love, Sex and Intimate Relationships" weekend in California, report that none of these three billed topics were on the agenda:

Men young and old are beating drums and wailing about the fathers they never knew. They are laying bare their deepest shame and, more than a little bit, heaping scorn on the dominating women in their lives. Surprisingly, though, sex is not at all a hot topic at these gatherings. The New Man seems infinitely more fascinated with himself than with the ladies.

When one of the men is asked to draw his "ideal mate," Chapple and Talbot note, he draws himself in bed alone, "whacking off," as he puts it.

But maybe the lack of relationship-talk shouldn't have been so surprising.   21
The true subject of Bly's weekends, after all, is not love and sex, but power—how to wrest it from women and how to mobilize it for men. Indeed, the Bly retreat that Chapple and Talbot attended opened with a display of "power objects," which each man was instructed to bring from home. On this weekend, the trophies included a .380-caliber automatic pistol. Bly may be an advocate of world peace, but as the general of the men's movement, he is overseeing a battle on the domestic front—and he withholds his dovish sentiments from the family-circle conflict. At a 1987 seminar, attended by one thousand men, a man in the audience told Bly, "Robert, when we tell women our desires, they tell us we're wrong." Bly instructed, "So, then you bust them in the mouth." After someone pointed out that this statement seemed to advocate violence against women, Bly amended it, "Yes. I meant, hit those women verbally!"

* * *

"What's the matter? Too much yogurt?" Bly is shouting. He is midway   22
through a two-day lecture at the Jung Center in San Francisco—one of the rare events to which he will admit women. He is back in his sea captain's pose, hands on hips, scowling at this audience of more than four hundred.

"There's too much passivity and naïveté in American men today," he says, as he begins to pace the stage. "There's a disease going around, and women have been spreading it. Starting in the '60s, the women have really invaded men's areas and treated them like boys."

A woman in the audience asks if he's saying that the women's movement 23 is to blame. "The men's movement is not a response to the women's movement," he says. A few moments later, though, he is back to warning men in the audience to beware of "the force-field of women." When another woman in the crowd points out the contradiction, he gets mad. He picks up the microphone and marches over to the troublemaker, a frail elderly woman clutching a flowered tote bag. He sticks his face in hers and yells into the microphone, "It's women like you who are turning men into yogurt-eaters." Embarrassed, the woman tries to appease the fuming poet; in a quavery voice, she asks if he has "any suggestions" about how she can improve her relationship with her emotionally distant husband. "Why don't you stop making demands and leave him alone," Bly shouts. "Just leave him alone."

On the second day of the Jung Center weekend, Bly announces that he 24 will tell a fairy tale. He explains that he often relies on old myths because they are more "advanced" than rational or psychological analysis. "No one's being blamed," he says. "In mythological thinking, rather than saying, 'I'm mad at you,' you are saying, 'There's a witch in the room who is doing this to us.' The witch is a third party in the relationship." Yet the invoking of a third-party "witch" turns out to be a dodge—a way to represent the feminist monster in a form men can revile without apology. As Bly puts it, "You can't make generalizations about men and women anymore" without offending someone. "So it must be mythologically stated."

Today's story is another Grimm's Brothers tale, "The Raven," in which a 25 hero, enfeebled by a witch and a variety of overbearing women, must rediscover his manhood by battling giants before he can claim the princess. When the story is over, Bly asks his listeners to identify which part of the story most fits their personal situation. When hardly any of the men choose the part in which the hero storms the glass mountain, Bly is disgusted. "You are all in the 'feminine waiting' part," he grumbles. "I want to see action. I want to see anger. You've got to get out there and kill the giants." Bly entreats the men to "growl," and throws up his hands at the tepid response. "C'mon, c'mon. Show your teeth. Show some anger."

A young man raises his hand. "But Robert, Gandhi didn't resort to vio- 26 lence to achieve his ends." Bly stomps his foot. "You're all so naïve. You're full of all kinds of weak ideas that soupy philosophers, including Gandhi, have encouraged."

It's time for a lunch break. As the audience streams out, the woman with 27 the flower tote bag approaches Bly and hands him a note. He jams it into his shirt pocket, then stalks off without speaking—to a back room, where two gray-haired women from the Jung Center are setting out his meal.

For months, Bly has refused requests for an interview—his media inter- 28 views are largely with men—but today he accedes to a brief conversation over lunch. Between man-size bites of a sandwich, the poet says he bars women from most of his events because men need a sanctuary from a female-dominated world. "There's no place for the warrior in this country. The feminists have taken over from the Catholic priests." And this is only the start of the female incursion. "I just see it getting worse and worse. Men will become more and more insecure, farther from their own manhood. Men will become more like women, women will try to be more like men. It's not a good prospect."

What evidence does he have that all this is happening, or that feminism   29
is actually turning men "soft"? The venerable poet flies into a sudden rage. "I don't need evidence. I have brains, that's how I know. I use my brains." He refuses to answer any more questions and swivels his chair until he's facing the side wall. An uncomfortable silence falls over the room; the two women from the Jung Center try to coax him back to good spirits with murmured compliments about his "brilliance" and offers of more apple juice. He says nothing for a while, then, apparently remembering the other woman who made him mad earlier, he dips inside his shirt pocket and fishes out the note. He shakes his head, snorts, then starts to read it out loud: "I was very hurt and angry at the way you simply dismissed my comments and made fun of me." What hurt most of all, she wrote, was the way he attacked her when she said she wanted more emotional support from her husband. She needs that support, she wrote, because she is battling ovarian cancer. Bly says sarcastically, "Oh, so I can't understand ovarian cancer unless I've gone through it?" He stuffs the note back in his pocket and polishes off his sandwich.

Questions

1. Describe your reaction to the representation of Bly in this article.
2. How would you describe Faludi's tone? How does she explain Bly's involvement in the men's movement?
3. What is your reaction to the proceedings at one of Bly's camps? What is the purpose of the role-playing?

The Relationship Between Male-Male Friendship and Male-Female Marriage

WALTER L. WILLIAMS

Walter L. Williams is an associate professor of anthropology at the University of Southern California. He took his Ph.D. at the University of North Carolina and has taught at the University of California, Los Angeles, and the University of Cincinnati. His most recent book is Javanese Lives: Women and Men in Modern Indonesian Society, *a study that emerged from his Fulbright scholarship trip to Indonesia in 1987–1988.*

In this selection, Williams argues that Americans suffer from alienation and a lack of emotional support because our culture prohibits intimate friendships with members of the same sex. The real culprit is our idealization of romantic love—we expect our spouses to be our "sexual playmate, economic partner, kinship system, best friend, and everything else"—but this ideal often "only leads to grief." This reading is from Men's Friendships *(1992).*

Very often popular critics complain about problems of alienation resulting from men's inability to develop intimate friendships. Humans, like other social animals, need and want intimacy, yet many men feel an inability to express that part of their being freely. This lack of close friendships is decried by many (see, for example, Brod, 1987; Franklin, 1984; Kilgore, 1984; Kimmel & Messner, 1989; Miller, 1983; Pleck & Pleck, 1980). Yet suggestions for change are inevitably greeted with a chorus of disbelievers who dismiss such relationships among men as being utopian, unrealistic, or even "unnatural." Given our observation of the way most American men act, we tend to think that this is the only way men *can* behave and still be "men." We might acknowledge, and even admire, the intense friendships that often exist among gay men, but this intensity itself seems to suggest that such friendships are not part of the standard masculine pattern. If men wish to retain their sense of being masculine, if they wish to be successful, if they wish to keep from being "emasculated," then close friendship seems to be the inevitable casualty. 1

Such a viewpoint is understandable, given our ignorance of other realistic alternatives. If the only point of reference is from within contemporary American culture, this viewpoint is easy to accept because so few "successful" white heterosexual men seem to challenge it. When examining men's friend- 2

515

ships from the perspective of other cultures, however, it is the American style that seems strange.

Not enough research has been done on this subject to draw valid general-   3
izations, but what investigation has been done on male friendships shows a quite different pattern from one culture to another. And within any particular culture, there is variation based on class, ethnic background, sexuality, and other differences. Masculinity, no less than other aspects of personality, is a socially constructed achieved status (Gilmore, 1990). The lack of intimacy and demonstrated affection among American men is quite unlike the situation in many other cultures. Many Americans may be aware, from newspaper photographs, that the acceptable style of formal greeting for men in France, Russia, and other European cultures is to embrace and kiss each other. Some of us may even be aware that Arab leaders often are seen walking arm in arm, or holding hands as they talk. Yet most of us are so ignorant of men's daily behavior in much of the non-Western world that we do not realize the peculiarity of men's interactions in the United States. In short, contemporary American mainstream masculinity is rather unique in its suppression of displays of affection, and of close and intimate friendships, between adult men.

Most of human history has occurred in small-scale societies where people   4
know one another much more closely than in modern cities. For about 99% of our history as a species, humans existed in small hunter-gatherer bands. In more recent epochs, pastoral herdsmen or settled agricultural villages emerged. Only within the last century, and only in certain areas of the world, have urban populations surpassed rural ones. Perhaps it is time for us to examine the ways of life of these various social patterns and to see what lessons we might learn about how better to conduct our own social relations. This chapter focuses on male friendship patterns in other cultures, using select examples as a means of demonstrating not only that intimate relationships among men are realistic and possible but also that these kinds of relationships have indeed existed in many other times and places.

Friendship Across Cultures

To understand the differences between friendship in other cultures and   5
friendship in contemporary America, it is necessary to look at some diverse examples; however, very little ethnographic data exist. While marriage patterns have been analyzed exhaustively by ethnographers, hardly any anthropological attention has been devoted to friendship—even though friendship is universal behavior. Friendships are often unstructured and spontaneous, thus fitting poorly with anthropologists' theories about the structures of society (Leyton, 1974). Gilmore (1990) has recently written the first cross-cultural study of manhood as an institutionalized social category; but despite the importance of his work, there is still a lack of cross-cultural focus on men's friendships.

The most extensive anthropological study of friendship remains *Friends*   6
and Lovers, by Robert Brain (1976). Based largely on his fieldwork in Africa,

Brain's book provides numerous examples where friendships are encouraged by being ceremonialized and formalized in society. In southern Ghana, for example, same-sex best friends go through a marriage ceremony similar to that performed for husbands and wives. This same-sex marriage, for members of the noble class as well as commoners, includes the payment of "brideprice" to the parents of the younger friend. Among the Bangwa of Cameroon, where Brain did most of his research, social pressure is directed to every child to encourage him to pair up with a best friend, much in the same way that other societies pressure everyone to find a spouse. Cautionary myths are told about the misfortunes falling to a self-centered person who neglects to make a friend. A major theme of popular songs is the celebration of friendships, in contrast to Western pop music, which emphasizes heterosexual romance and sex. In fact, Bangway same-sex friendships are even more durable than male-female marriages. These friendships typically last from adolescence through old age, while marriages commonly split up when children reach adulthood.

Once a year, in the major Bangwa ceremony at the king's palace, men exchange gifts and formally proclaim their friendships as continuing for another year. When a man dies, his funeral ceremony is paid for by his best friend rather than his family. The friend's public mourning is treated even more seriously than the lament of the deceased's widow and children. Throughout the life course, friendship is publicly recognized and ceremonialized among the Bangwa in multiple ways that are not even verbalized among most American men (Brain, 1976).   7

The institution of "godparenthood," so often commented upon by anthropologists as a form of "fictive kinship" to give a child the advantage of an extra set of parents, is also often a means of formally recognizing friendships. Godparenthood institutionalizes the relationship between the parents of the child and their best friend. In some areas of Latin America, two men will perform a rite of baptism that makes them "godbrothers" (Brain, 1976). Such ceremonies formalize and give social and religious respect to friendship in a way that modern American society does not. Even though the mythic basis for such a ceremony in Judeo-Christian cultures exists in the Biblical story of Jonathan and David, there is a noticeable lack of ritual in Protestant Christian churches that celebrates close friendships. The Catholic Church even warns its priests and seminary students against forming "particular friendships," thus depriving its unmarried clergy of *any* form of intimate relationship. On the sports field, probably the place most encouraging of same-sex camaraderie in modern America, the emphasis is on team loyalty, competition, and success—rather than on particular friendships.   8

North American Indian Friendships

How do other cultures manage to encourage these intense friendships among men? In order to understand the important role of such friendships, I turn to my own research with North American Indians. As with many other cultures, same-sex friendships among aboriginal North Americans were emotionally   9 intense because marriages were not the center of a person's emotional life. Marriage was primarily an economic arrangement between women and men to produce offspring and gather food. This arrangement had its basis in a division of labor by gender. Although wide ranges of activities were open for both women and men, in most pre-Columbian American societies there existed a basic division between masculine tasks and feminine tasks. While some individual males or females had the option of doing the tasks usually associated with the other sex, by taking on a highly respected *berdache* gender role that mixed the masculine and feminine aspects together, most people limited their skills to either masculine or feminine ones (Williams, 1986).

By dividing the necessary tasks of each family into "men's work" and   10
"women's work," people only had to learn half of the necessary skills, and gained the expertise of their spouse in tasks that were different from their own skills. Because many Native American societies did not have social taboos against homosexual behavior, same-sex marriages were also recognized, just as long as one of the spouses took on a berdache role and agreed to do the labor of the other sex. The emphasis of the culture was to encourage marriage and parenthood (either by procreation or adoption), not to try to dictate what kind of sexual behavior a person should engage in. As a result, homosexually inclined individuals were not alienated, and family ties were quite strong. By marrying, a person could gain the assistance and support of the spouse's kin group, and thus could double the number of relatives to whom one could turn for support in time of need.

For American Indian societies, as with most societies in all of human his-   11
tory, marriage has primarily been an economic arrangement. Marriage partners in many of these situations might or might not be sexually attracted to each other, but they did expect to be able to depend on each other and their kinsmen for economic support. They had little expectation that they would be each other's best friend. Other than when they were engaging in sex, husbands and wives kept a certain respectful emotional distance from each other. They would bring their resources home to provide food for their spouse and children; they would eat at home and sleep there (at least some of the time). But American Indian men, like those in many other cultures, would not spend much of their leisure time at home. In some native societies husbands and wives did not even sleep together. Among groups as disparate as the Cherokees in the Southeast and the Yupik Eskimos of Alaska, males above age 10 regularly slept in the village "men's house," a sort of community center for males that doubled as the men's sleeping quarters, while the women and small children slept in their own individual houses.

Friendships in such sex-segregated societies followed the same pattern.   12
For friendship, men's primary psychological needs would be met by their long-term friends from childhood. And those friendships were, of course, with persons of the same gender. Men usually had deep feelings of love for their mothers, aunts, grandmothers, and sisters, based on their intimacy in early childhood, but the only adult male who would experience continued close friendships with women was the androgynous berdache, who moved back and forth between the separated gender worlds of men and women. Be-

cause of their in-between gender status, berdaches (or their masculined fe-male counterpart) often served as a go-between to negotiate agreements or settle disputes between men and women. In some groups, like the Cheyenne Indians of the Plains, men were so shy around women that they would often ask berdaches to negotiate proposals of marriage.

In such a situation, where each sex felt such shyness in dealing with the other, they each turned to same-sex friends for primary intimacy needs. Early Western explorers often commented upon the especially warm friendships that existed between an Indian man and his "blood brother." A nineteenth-century United States Army officer, for example, reported about "brothers by adoption" that he observed from his years on the frontier. Speaking of Indian male pairs, he pointed out the contrast with more reserved friendships among white men. He said that Arapaho males "really seem to 'fall in love' with men; and I have known this affectionate interest to live for years." The union of two men was often publicly recognized in a Friendship Dance that they would do together (Trumbull, 1894, pp. 71–72, 165–166). 13

One of these friendships among Lakotas was described by Francis Park-man, who met the two men during his journey on the Oregon Trail in 1846. They were, he wrote: 14

> [I]nseparable; they ate, slept, and hunted together, and shared with one an-other almost all that they possessed. If there be anything that deserves to be called romantic in the Indian character, it is to be sought for in friendships such as this, which are common among many of the prairie tribes. (Parkman, 1969, pp. 280–283)

This is not to suggest that these special friendships should be equated with homosexuality. The emphasis for the Indian men was a close emotional bond, which might well be nonsexual in many or maybe most of these friendships. If two close friends engaged in sexual activity, that would be con-sidered their own private business, which would not be publicly mentioned. Even if they were known to be sexual with each other, they would not be la-beled as a distinct category like "homosexual." As long as they continued to follow a masculine lifestyle, they would not be socially defined as a berdache. And they certainly would not be stigmatized for their erotic acts. The socially recognized part of their relationship was their deep friendship; native com-munities honored that. What this meant is that Native American men were allowed to develop intense friendships, and even to be able to express their love for their blood brother friend, without worry that they would be stigma-tized. Except for the berdache, any concept like "homosexual" was foreign to the thinking and social world of American Indians. 15

Friendship and Marriage: Andalusia and Java

The pattern of friendship that traditionally existed among Native Americans, where a man gets his intimate needs met more by his male friends than by his wife, is quite common in various areas of the world. When Brandes (1987) did his field research in rural areas of Andalusia, Spain, he found that both 16 men and women feel more comfortable revealing their deeper thoughts to a same-sex friend than to their spouse. Brandes was told by his male informants that the home is basically women's space; for men it is "only for eating and sleeping." Men in Andalusia spend most of their leisure time with their male friends at the local tavern. When their teenaged sons become old enough to be brought into the men's friendship sphere, then the men take over the raising of the adolescent males; otherwise men are not much involved in the rearing of younger children. Except for harvest season, when adults are busy working long hours, a man is expected to spend several hours each day with his best friend. He goes home only in the evening for a late dinner just before bedtime. Since any association between an unrelated woman and man would arouse suspicion of adultery, men and women avoid close social interaction with the other sex.

It should be noted that these intense male-male friendships in Andalusia   17
are not seen as a threat to the family in any way. Marriage is strong, but is kept within its bounds of economic co-dependence, food consumption, sex, and sleeping. Marriage relationships between husbands and wives are close, but are not expected to answer one's personal intimacy needs, which are met by one's same-sex friends. As a result of this system, people have two types of close bonds: the structured mixed-sex marriage-kinship system, and the unstructured same-sex friendships networks. These two bonds strengthen and complement each other, providing supportive allegiances and psychological outlets from the pressures of life. Rather than threaten each other, each of these two bonds has its restricted area and does not try to impose on the other. The two together work better than either marriage or friendship would by itself (Brandes, 1987).

My thinking on the complementary relationship between close friend-   18
ships and marriage partnerships has also been influenced by my fieldwork on the island of Java, which is the most populous island in the archipelago of Indonesia. In 1987 and 1988 I lived in the classical court city of Yogyakarta, where Javanese culture remains strong. Javanese people show a strong sense of reserve in terms of public interaction between women and men, even when they are married. A scandal would ensue if a husband and wife kissed in public, and except for younger urbanites, who have been influenced by American movies and television shows to adopt more Westernized lifestyles, it is rare even to see a Javanese man and woman holding hands in public. This reserve is part of a larger pattern of the limits placed on male-female intimacy. One reason that such reserve exists has to do with arranged marriages. Traditionally, there was no such thing as dating between proper young women and men in Java. Marriages were arranged by parents, with the bride and groom often meeting each other for the first time at their wedding ceremony. Before marriage, people spend most of their time with same-sex friends rather than in heterosexual dating.

Many Americans are shocked to hear of such a custom as arranged mar-   19
riages, yet our shock is no greater than the shock felt by Javanese who observe American patterns of relationships. I have had several fascinating

conversations with Indonesians on this topic. While they admire the material wealth of the United States, Indonesians often wonder "why Americans seem so intent on making themselves miserable." After watching American movies together, I noticed how often they expressed puzzlement about the way Americans experience so much stress by falling in and out of love. "Why," they asked me, "do Americans experience such fragile personal relationships?" One Indonesian spoke for many when he told me that he had the impression that "Americans don't seem to have a hold on anything. They don't seem committed—to their relationships, their friends, or to anything else." It is obvious to them that Western romanticism and traditional forms of family life are not working for many Americans.

In the United States, various groups have called for a "return to the traditional family" as a cure for society's ills. Yet, the nuclear family seems to be less and less able to deal with the realities of the stresses facing people in modern America. Progressive voices have not really articulated a vision for the future, beyond merely accepting the fact that divorce and singlehood are becoming more and more common. The question is, are there other alternatives to the patriarchal nuclear family that will help to prevent an increasing sense of alienation in the lifestyle of the twenty-first century? The extended family is long gone from the American scene, and the nuclear family seems likewise destined. One-to-one relationships continue to be made and broken in fairly similar patterns among both heterosexual couples and homosexual couples. Can people live comfortably with the uncertainty of not knowing how long their partnership will last? These are questions that terrify many, and people are pulled between their desires for the adventure of love and the security of a long-term relationship. Magazines are filled with articles telling worried spouses "how to keep your husband/wife in love with you." 20

No one seems to be asking the question that maybe it is precisely the romantic ideal of "being in love" that is itself the problem with contemporary marriages. It is in this regard that we might be able to learn something from Indonesian patterns. It became quite evident to me, during my time in Java, that Indonesian husbands and wives do not seem to feel the necessity of "being in love" all the time. In their view, such romantic ideals only lead to grief, because they promote so much longing that families are broken apart. 21

In Indonesia, under the influence of Westernization, younger people are beginning to choose their marriage partner by "falling in love," but the older generation questions the ideal of romantic love as the primary basis for one's emotional life. I interviewed elderly husbands and wives whose marriages had been arranged by their parents, asking them how they could have adjusted to life together without getting to know each other and falling in love beforehand. They told me it was precisely *because* of their nonromantic approach that their marriage worked. They pointed out that even if two young people know each other intimately for several years, and think that they are completely right for each other, they are so inexperienced in human relationships that they cannot possibly know anything definite about the other person. Plus, individuals change so much over the life course that it does not 22 matter much what kind of person the other one was at that moment. The important advantage of an arranged marriage, in the Javanese view, is that the two young people are *not* "in love," and therefore they are not disillusioned later when they fall out of love. (For interviews with elderly Javanese, where they detail their thoughts about arranged marriages and friendship patterns, see Williams, 1991).

Such nonemotional marriages work because they are complemented by people's emotional needs being met by same-sex friendships. The strong balance between marriage and friendship is most strikingly presented in the context of wedding ceremonies that I observed in Java. The most obvious difference from an American wedding was that all the men sat on one side of the room while the women sat together on the other side of the room. The seating pattern was consciously designed to reflect the separateness of women and men. Weddings are a big event in the villages, reflecting the importance of the family in Javanese culture. 23

In contrast to an American wedding, which focuses on the love between the bride and groom, a Javanese wedding ceremony emphasizes the economic and social obligations of the new couple to each other, to their future children, to their parents and other relatives, and to the community as a whole. The couple sits down together on the wedding seat, the bride on the women's side, and the groom on the men's, indicating that they retain their closeness to their same-sex friends, even while becoming husband and wife. 24

Throughout the ceremony, the major emphasis is the economic obligation of the bride and groom. Nowhere does "love," or any expression of emotion between the two partners, put in an appearance. After thinking about the meaning of this ceremony, and talking with Javanese people about the role of marriage, love, and friendship in their lives, I think that perhaps this deliberate deemphasis on love in a marriage is—ironically, to us—one of the reasons for its stability. Instead of an ideal of romantic love, Indonesians seem to have more realistic expectations for a marriage, keeping it more or less restricted to its economic and procreative functions. (For further elaboration of the Javanese wedding ceremony, see Williams, 1991). 25

In the Javanese view, marriage should not be too intimate. To them, a person's intimacies are best kept where they were already located before two people got married: with their same-sex friends. A man continues to have his relatives and male age-mates as his most intimate friends, and a woman does likewise with her female friends and relatives. They do not expect that their spouse will be either some knight in shining armor or a princess in perpetual beauty, and so they are not disappointed later. As in Andalusia, friendship is not antipathetic to the marriage bond, but they are complementary to each other. One's sexual partner is not expected to also be one's best friend. Given the economic importance of marriage in Javanese village life, the exaltation of friendship among one's same-sex friends serves as a balancing point. 26

As their separated seating at the Javanese wedding ceremony makes clear, women are not expected to separate themselves from other women and give all their emotional support to their husbands. Both they and their husbands are getting many of their emotional needs met by their same-sex friends. If 27 husbands and wives do not sit together at a ceremony as symbolic as a wedding, why should it be expected for them to be together otherwise? In their workday, men and women are likewise often separated. Women spend much of their time at the market, selling their family's food produce to other women. Markets for food sales are primarily women's spaces, with men seldom involved. At their domestic work, women are either in the kitchen or at the riverbank, washing their clothes in company with other women. Men are off plowing with the oxen, or working in all-male labor gangs in the fields or the irrigation canals.

During the evening hours in a typical Javanese village, after the day's work is completed, husbands and wives will each go their separate ways. Women will visit and chat with other women, while the men will gather among themselves. They may be involved with an arts organization or a dance group, and each of these groups is either all-male or all-female. Men may play musical instruments, or women may join a singing group, but there is little overlap between the sexes in many of their leisure activities.   28

The Future of Friendship

Strong extended family kinship networks have often not been able to survive the extensive geographical mobility characteristic of modern America. Relatives are separated as the capitalist job market has forced many people to migrate to other locations. Under these pressures, "the family" has been reduced from its original extended form (the most common type of family among humans) to a mere nuclear remnant of parents and children. In modern America, a person's "significant other" has now become practically the sole person with whom he or she can be intimate. For many couples, this is too much to ask of their relationships, as the significant other is expected simultaneously to be sexual playmate, economic partner, kinship system, best friend, and everything else. Because of the dictatorship of the romantic ideal, many Americans expect their spouse to meet all their emotional needs. That is doubly difficult to do while both partners are also holding down full-time employment outside the home.   29

As more American marriages become households where both spouses have jobs outside the home, there is less energy left for being emotionally supportive of one's partner. Even these rump nuclear family marriages are, therefore, in increasing numbers of cases, falling apart. The flip side of the American ideal of individual freedom and progress is thus often a legacy of individual alienation and loneliness.   30

In contrast, by not expecting the marriage relationship to fulfill all of a person's needs, many other cultures allow people more emotional closeness to same-sex friends. To take one example, in some cultures, families are not often broken up over the issue of homosexuality. In such a situation, in fact, there is not as much emotional need for homosexually inclined individuals to construct a separate homosexual identity. There will, of course, still be a certain percentage of people who erotically prefer a same-sex partner, but that inclination may be fulfilled within the friendship bond. There is no social   31 pressure for persons to leave their marriage just because they desire same-sex erotic contacts. Sexual desires may have little to do with family bonding, because the marriage is not assumed to be sexually exclusive.

Same-sex friendships need not, of course, include a sexual component, but as far as the society is concerned, the important factor is the friendship rather than the sexual behavior. The person might be sexually involved with a same-sex friend while also being heterosexually married. Both forms of bonding occur, and a person does not have to choose one over the other. This flexibility resolves to the advantage of society and the individual. There is a looseness and an adaptiveness that allow for close intimate interaction with both sexes within the dual bonds of marriage and friendship.   32

In cultures that do not stigmatize same-sex eroticism, and do not divide up people into "homosexuals" and "heterosexuals," there is remarkable freedom from worry among males that others will perceive them to be members of a distinct "homosexual" category. This freedom from worry demonstrates that much of the inhibition that contemporary American men feel about their friendships is due to the fear that others might categorize them as homosexual. This can most clearly be seen by contrasting the behavior of late twentieth-century Indian men with their non-homophobic ancestors. As contemporary Indian people have absorbed more and more mainstream white American values, through Christian missionaries, government schools, off-reservation residence, and television, they have become more homophobic. On reservations today, friendships are not as intense as among past generations. American Indian men's alienation from each other is a "miner's canary" to warn us of the even more extreme alienation going on among mainstream Americans. Friendships among heterosexual men are one of the main casualties of homophobia.   33

Given all these pressures, which restrict men's expressions of their feelings and increase their stress levels, it will be valuable to get some concrete ideas as to how we can get beyond some of these dilemmas facing American men. A cross-cultural analysis is one possible source of knowledge regarding how men can conceptualize their intimacy needs.   34

First, it is necessary to move beyond the view that every person is either exclusively heterosexual or exclusively homosexual. Two facts emerge from the anthropological literature: (a) There is a diversity in individual sexual inclinations, with some persons clearly preferring the other sex and some clearly preferring the same sex, but many (probably a majority) having a mixture of erotic feelings for both sexes; and (b) for most people, healthy human operation requires the spreading around of intimacy to a wider circle of people. This is the most common pattern, in the extended family networks and the close friendships, of probably the majority of cultures, yet this is precisely what twentieth-century American culture has failed to do. Since our geographical mobility precludes the reestablishment of extended family kinship systems for most Americans, it behooves us to reexamine the cross-cultural data on friendships and to try to start building alternative forms of relationships on this basis.   35

Perhaps it is time for us to begin a more fundamental public discourse   36
questioning the primacy of the male-female romantic ideal (i.e., "the traditional family") as sufficient for meeting human intimacy needs by itself. Many
Americans know that something is wrong with their lives, but the only solution they hear is popular music's refrain that they should fall in love, and the
allied heterosexist "pro-family" rhetoric. Perhaps a new rhetoric of friendship
needs to be emphasized. It is not an exaggeration to say that there has been a
denigration of friendship in the United States. The pro-heterosexual, pro-mar-
riage discourse has almost obliterated intense same-sex friendships. This is not
to suggest that people should abandon their sexual partners, but that they
should expect less of such a partner than his or her total emotional support.

In the 1970s, radical feminist separatists' and gay men's friendship net-   37
works emerged as never before. New possibilities seemed to be emerging. By
the 1980s, however, as a drive for social respectability set in, fueled by the
AIDS crisis, gay men and lesbians tended to settle into same-sex couplehoods
that mirror the American heterosexual marriage rather than the more widespread intimacy patterns of many other cultures.

As we prepare for a new century, a revitalization of the psychological and   38
social importance of friendship should become a high priority. Ironically, the
AIDS crisis has brought out the importance of friendship "buddy" networks, as
well as domestic partners, as caregivers within the gay and lesbian community.
In the non-gay community as well, more attention must be given to ceremoni-
alizing and ritualizing friendship relationships in the same way that romantic
relationships and marriages have been. More serious respect can be given, from
one's partner as well as by society at large, for the importance of friends. Since
sexual attractions are often subject to change over the years, maybe more people will be living the slogan that "lovers come and go, but friends remain."

Certainly, these suggestions do not imply that all people will evolve new   39
kinds of relationships, but it does imply the need for equal social respect being given for a variety of friendship types. It suggests that, rather than regret-
ting the passing of a traditional form of marriage that has already disappeared
for many people, Americans will be better served by paying more attention to
our needs for close intimate friendships. The problem is not the breakdown
of marriage as much as it is the need to develop wider distributions of individuals to whom we can express our intimacy. In this society, women are doing this much more successfully than are men. Before American men dismiss
the possibility of anything different, they might educate themselves to the
necessity of getting over barriers to intimacy with friends, whether this is due
to homophobia or to a competitive ethos at the workplace. We already have,
in the examples from other cultures, many functioning models that have well
served the emotional needs of men for centuries. These models bear further
investigation. Those who have highly developed friendships can recognize
the power of these relationships to carry us forward into the future. For at
least some of us, maybe this is a better place to focus our intimacies, rather
than placing all our hopes on some romantic love that might later turn sour
and then become so disruptive in our lives.

If our society is to survive, when traditional family patterns are evolving   40
and geographical mobility strains the limits of intergenerational connections,
it is up to innovative individuals to search out new forms for intimate relationships beyond sexual partnerships. We need to analyze and nurture our
long-term close friendship networks as the best possible base on which to
build an emotionally satisfying future.

REFERENCES

Brain, R. (1976). *Friends and lovers.* New York: Basic Books.

Brandes, S. (1987). Sex roles and anthropological research in rural Andalusia. *Women's Studies, 13,* 357–372.

Brod, H. (Ed.). (1987). *The making of masculinities: The new men's studies.* Boston: Allen & Unwin.

Franklin, C. (1984). *The changing definition of masculinity.* New York: Plenum.

Gilmore, D. (1990). *Manhood in the making: Cultural concepts of masculinity.* New Haven, CT: Yale University Press.

Kilgore, J. (1984). *The intimate man: Intimacy and masculinity in the 80s.* Nashville, TN: Abingdon.

Kimmel, M., & Messner, M. (Eds.). (1989). *Men's lives.* New York: Macmillan.

Leyton, E. (Ed.). (1974). *The compact: Selected dimensions of friendship* (Newfoundland Social and Economic Papers No. 3). Toronto: University of Toronto Press and Memorial University of Newfoundland.

Miller, S. (1983). *Men and friendship.* Boston: Houghton Mifflin.

Parkman, F. (1969). *The Oregon Trail.* Madison: University of Wisconsin Press.

Pleck, E. H., & Pleck, J. H. (1980). *The American man.* Englewood Cliffs, NJ: Prentice-Hall.

Trumbull, H. C. (1894). *Friendship the master passion.* Philadelphia: Wattles.

Williams, W. L. (1986). *The spirit and the flesh: Sexual diversity in American Indian culture.* Boston: Beacon.

Williams, W. L. (1991). *Javanese lives: Women and men in modern Indonesian society.* New Brunswick, NJ: Rutgers University Press.

Questions

1. In your experience is Williams's view of American male friendship accurate? In what way?

2. Williams argues that our idealization of romantic love precludes our ability to form strong friendships, and leads only to grief. Can you think of ways in which our culture (for example, the media) idealizes romantic love? Can you think of instances in which same-sex friendship is idealized?

3. Would the Java model of social relationships work in the U.S.? Why or why not?

4. How would Williams respond to Bly?

Chicano Men and Masculinity

MAXINE BACA ZINN

Maxine Baca Zinn teaches sociology at Michigan State University. She has written widely in the areas of family relations, Chicano studies, and gender studies.

Here, Zinn argues that machismo is not simply a cultural heritage stemming from powerlessness and subordination. Rather, machismo results from socioeconomic status—the family is often the only sphere in which the Chicano male is able to assert his authority and dominance. This reading is from Men's Lives *(1989).*

Only recently have social scientists begun to systematically study the male role. Although men and their behavior had been assiduously studied (Pleck and Brannon, 1978), masculinity as a specific topic had been ignored. The scholar's disregard of male gender in the general population stands in contrast to the preoccupation with masculinity that has long been exhibited in the literature on minority groups. The social science literature on Blacks and Chicanos specifically reveals a long-standing interest in masculinity. A common assumption is that gender roles among Blacks are less dichotomous than among Whites, and more dichotomous among Chicanos. Furthermore, these differences are assumed to be a function of the distinctive historical and cultural heritage of these groups. Gender segregation and stratification, long considered to be a definitive characteristic of Chicanos, is illustrated in Miller's descriptive summary of the literature:

> Sex roles are rigidly dichotomized with the male conforming to the dominant-aggressive archetype, and the female being the polar opposite—subordinate and passive. The father is the unquestioned patriarch—the family provider, protector and judge. His word is law and demands strict obedience. Presumably, he is perpetually obsessed with the need to prove his manhood, oftentimes through excessive drinking, fighting, and/or extramarital conquests (1979:217).

The social science image of the Chicano male is rooted in three interrelated propositions: (1) That a distinctive cultural heritage has created a rigid cult of masculinity, (2) That the masculinity cult generates distinctive familial and socialization patterns, and (3) That these distinctive patterns ill-equip Chicanos (both males and females) to adapt successfully to the demands of modern society.

527

The machismo concept constitutes a primary explanatory variable for both family structure and overall subordination. Mirandé critically outlines the reasoning in this interpretation: 3

> The macho male demands complete deference, respect and obedience not only from the wife but from the children as well. In fact, social scientists maintain that this rigid male-dominated family structure has negative consequences for the personality development of Mexican American children. It fails to engender achievement, independence, self-reliance or self worth—values which are highly esteemed in American society. . . . The authoritarian Mexican American family constellation then produces dependence and subordination and reinforces a present time orientation which impedes achievement (1977:749).

In spite of the widely held interpretation associated with male dominance among Chicanos, there is a growing body of literature which refutes past images created by social scientists. My purpose is to examine empirical challenges to machismo, to explore theoretical developments in the general literature on gender, and to apply both of these to alternative directions for studying and understanding Chicano men and masculinity. My central theme is that while ethnic status may be associated with differences in masculinity, those differences can be explained by structural variables rather than by references to common cultural heritage.   4

Theoretical Challenges to Cultural Interpretations: The Unversality of Male Dominance

The generalization that culture is a major determinant of gender is widely accepted in the social sciences. In the common portrayal of Chicanos, exaggerated male behavior is assumed to stem from inadequate masculine identity.   5

> The social science literature views machismo as a compensation for feelings of inadequacy and worthlessness. This interpretation is rooted in the application of psychoanalytic concepts to explain both Mexican and Chicano gender roles. The widely accepted interpretation is that machismo is the male attempt to compensate for feelings of internalized inferiority by exaggerated masculinity. "At the same time that machismo is an expression of power, its origin is ironically linked to powerlessness and subordination." The common origins of inferiority and machismo are said to lie in the historical conquest of Mexico by Spain involving the exploitation of Indian women by Spanish men thus producing the hybrid Mexican people having an inferiority complex based on the mentality of a conquered people (Baca Zinn, 1980:20).

The assumption that male dominance among Chicanos is rooted in their history and embedded in their culture needs to be critically assessed against recent discussions concerning the universality of male dominance. Many anthropologists consider all known societies to be male dominant to a degree (Stockard and Johnson 1980:4). It has been argued that in all known societies   6 male activities are more highly valued than female activities, and that this can be explained in terms of the division of labor between domestic and public spheres of society (Rosaldo, 1973). Women's child-bearing abilities limit their participation in public sphere activities and allow men the freedom to participate in and control the public sphere. Thus in the power relations between the sexes, men have been found to be dominant over women and to control economic resources (Spence 1978:4).

While differing explanations of the cause of male dominance have been advanced, recent literature places emphasis on networks of social relations between men and women and the status structures within which their interactions occur. This emphasis is crucial because it alerts us to the importance of structural variables in understanding sex stratification. Furthermore, it casts doubt on interpretations which treat culture (the systems of shared beliefs and orientations unique to groups) as the cause of male dominance. If male dominance is universal, then it cannot be reduced to the culture of a particular category of people. 7

Challenges to Machismo

Early challenges to machismo emerged in the protest literature of the 1960s and 1970s and have continued unabated. Challenges are theoretical, empirical, and impressionistic. Montiel, in the first critique of machismo, set the stage for later refutations by charging that psychoanalytic constructs resulted in indiscriminate use of machismo, and that this made findings and interpretations highly suspect (1970). Baca Zinn (1975:25) argued that viewing machismo as a compensation for inferiority (whether its ultimate cause is seen as external or internal to the oppressed), in effect blames Chicanos for their own subordination. Sosa Riddell proposed that the machismo myth is exploited by an oppressive society which encourages a defensive stance on the part of Chicano men (1974). Delgado (1974:6) in similar fashion, wrote that stereotyping acts which have nothing to do with machismo and labeling them as such was a form of societal control. 8

Recent social science literature on Chicanos has witnessed an ongoing series of empirical challenges to the notion that machismo is the norm in marital relationships (Grebler, Moore and Guzman, 1970; Hawkes and Taylor, 1975; Ybarra, 1977; Cromwell and Cromwell, 1978: Cromwell and Ruiz, 1979; Baca Zinn, 1980a). The evidence presented in this research suggests that in the realm of marital decision making, egalitarianism is far more prevalent than macho dominance. 9

Cromwell and Ruiz find that the macho characterization prevalent in the social science literature is "very compatible with the social deficit model of Hispanic life and culture" (1979:355). Their re-analysis of four major studies on marital decision making (Cromwell, Corrales and Torsellio, 1973; Delchereo, 1969; Hawkes and Taylor, 1975 and Cromwell and Cromwell, 1978) concludes that "the studies suggest that while wives make the fewest unilateral decisions and husbands make more, joint decisions are by far the most common in these samples . . ." (1979:370). 10

Other studies also confirm the existence of joint decision making in Chi-   11
cano families and furthermore they provide insights as to factors associated
with joint decision making, most importantly that of wives' employment. For
example, Ybarra's survey of 100 married Chicano couples in Fresno, California found a range of conjugal role patterns with the majority of married Chicano couples sharing decision making. Baca Zinn (1980a) examined the
effects of wives' employment outside of the home and level of education
through interviews and participation in an urban New Mexico setting. The
study revealed differences in marital roles and marital power between families with employed wives and nonemployed wives. "In all families where
women were not employed, tasks and decision making were typically sex segregated. However, in families with employed wives, tasks and decision making were shared" (1980a:51).

Studies of the father role in Chicano families also called into question the   12
authoritative unfeeling masculinized male figure (Mejia, 1976; Luzod and
Arce, 1979). These studies are broadly supportive of the marital role research
which points to a more democratic egalitarian approach to family roles. Luzod and Arce conclude:

> It is not our contention to say that no sex role differences occur within Chi-
> cano families, but rather demonstrate the level of importance which both the
> father and mother give to respective duties as parents as well as the common
> hopes and desires they appear to share equally for their progeny than was
> commonly thought. It therefore appears erroneous to focus only on maternal
> influences in the Chicano family since Chicano fathers are seen as being im-
> portant to the children and moreover may provide significant positive influ-
> ences on the development of their children (1979:19).

Recent empirical refutations of super-masculinity in Chicano families   13
have provided the basis of discussions of the Chicano male role (Valdez,
1980; Mirandé, 1979, 1981). While these works bring together in clear fashion impressionistic and empirical refutations of machismo, they should be
considered critical reviews rather than conceptual refutations. In an important essay entitled, "Machismo: Rucas, Chingasos, y Chingaderas" (1981), Mirandé critically assesses the stereotypic components of machismo, yet he
asserts that it also has authentic components having to do with the resistance
of oppression. While this is a significant advance, it requires conceptual focus
and analysis.

Uunanswered Questions, Unresolved Issues and Unrecognized Problems

The works discussed above provide a refutation of the simplistic, one-dimen-   14
sional model of Chicano masculinity. As such they constitute important contributions to the literature. My own argument does not contradict the general
conclusion that machismo is a stereotype, but attempts to expand it by posing some theoretical considerations.

In their eagerness to dispute machismo and the negative characteristics   15
associated with the trait, critics have tended to neglect the phenomenon of
male dominance at societal, institutional, and interpersonal levels. While the
cultural stereotype of machismo has been in need of critical analysis, male
dominance does exist among Chicanos. Assertions such as the following require careful examination:

> There is sufficient evidence to seriously question the traditional male domi-
> nant view (Mirandé, 1979:47).

Although male dominance may not typify marital decision making in Chicano families, it should not be assumed that it is nonexistent either in families or in other realms of interaction and organization.

Research by Ybarra (1977) and Baca Zinn (1980) found both egalitarian   16
and male dominant patterns of interaction in Chicano families. They found
these patterns to be associated with distinct social conditions of families,
most notably wives' employment. The finding that male dominance can be
present in some families but not in others, depending on specific social characteristics of family members, is common in family research.

The important point is that we need to know far more than we do about   17
which social conditions affecting Chicanos are associated with egalitarianism
and male dominance at both micro and macro levels of organization. Placing
the question within this framework should provide significant insights by en-
larging the inquiry beyond that of the culture stereotype of machismo. It is
necessary to guard against measuring and evaluating empirical reality against
this stereotype. The dangers of using a negative ideal as a normative guide are
raised by Eichler (1980). In a provocative work, she raises the possibility that
the literature challenging gender stereotypes, while explicitly attempting to
overcome past limitations of the gender roles research may operate to reinforce the stereotype. Thus, it could be argued that energy expended in refuting machismo may devote too much attention to the concept, and overlook
whole areas of inquiry. We have tended to assume that ethnic groups vary in
the demands imposed on men and women. "Ethnic differences in sex roles
have been discussed by large numbers of social scientists" (Romer and Cherry,
1980:246). However, these discussions have treated differences as cultural or
subcultural in nature. Davidson and Gordon are critical of subcultural explanations of differences in gender roles because they "fail to investigate the
larger political and economic situations that affect groups and individuals.
They also fail to explain how definition of the roles of women and men, as
well as those associated with ethnicity, vary over time and from place to
place" (1979:124).

1. What specific social conditions are associated with variation in general
    roles among Chicanos?
2. If there are ethnic differences in gender roles, to what extent are these a
    function of shared beliefs and orientations (culture) and to what extent

are they a function of men's and women's place in the network of social relationships (structure)?

3. To what extent are gender roles among Chicanos more segregated and male dominated than among other social groups?

4. How does ethnicity contribute to the subjective meaning of masculinity (and femininity)?

Structural Interpretations of Gender Roles

There is a good deal of theoretical support for the contention that masculine   18
roles and masculine identity may be shaped by a wide range of variables having less to do with culture than with common structural position. Chafetz calls into question the cultural stereotype of machismo by proposing that it is a socioeconomic characteristic:

> . . . more than most other Americans, the various Spanish speaking groups in this country (Mexican American, Puerto Rican, Cuban), . . . stress dominance, aggressiveness, physical prowess and other stereotypical masculine traits. Indeed the masculine sex role for this group is generally described by reference to the highly stereotyped notion of machismo. In fact, a strong emphasis on masculine aggressiveness and dominance may be characteristic of most groups in the lower ranges of the socioeconomic ladder (1979:54).

Without discounting the possibility that cultural differences in male roles   19
exist, it makes good conceptual sense to explain these differences in terms of sociostructural factors. Davidson and Gordon suggest that the following social conditions affect the development of gender roles in ethnic groups: (1) the position of the group in the stratification system, (2) the existence of an ethnic community, (3) the degree of self identification with the minority group (1978:120). Romer and Cherry more specifically propose that ethnic or subcultural sex role definitions can be viewed as functions of the specific and multiple role demands made on a given subgroup such as skilled or unskilled workers, consumers, etc., and the cultural prism through which these role expectations are viewed (1980:246). Both of these discussions underscore the importance of the societal placement of ethnics in the shaping of gender roles. This line of reasoning should not be confused with "culture of poverty" models which posit distinctive subcultural traits among the lower class. However, it can be argued that class position affects both normative and behavioral dimensions of masculinity.

The assumption that Chicanos are more strongly sex typed in terms of   20
masculine identity is called into question by a recent study. Senour and Warren conducted research to question whether ethnic identity is related to masculine and feminine sex role orientation among Blacks, Anglos and Chicanos. While significant sex differences were found in all categories, Senour and Warren concluded that Mexican American males did not emerge as super masculine in comparison to Black and Anglo males (1976:2).

There is some support for this interpretation. In roles dealing with masculinity among Black males, Parker and Kleiner (1977) and Staples (1978) find that role performance must be seen in light of the structurally generated inequality in employment, housing, and general social conditions. Staples writes: 21

> . . . men often define their masculinity in terms of the ability to impregnate women and to reproduce prolifically children who are extensions of themselves, especially sons. For many lower income black males there is an inseparable link between their self image as men and their ability to have sexual relations with women and the subsequent birth of children from those sexual acts. At the root of this virility cult is the lack of role fulfillment available to men of the underclass. The class factor is most evident here, if we note that middle class black males sire fewer children than any other group in this society (1978:178).

What is most enlightening about Staples' discussion of masculinity is that it treats male behavior and male identity not as a subcultural phenomenon, but as a consequence of social structural factors associated with race and class.

A thoughtful discussion of inequality, race, and gender is provided by Lewis (1977). Her analysis enlarges upon Rosaldo's model of the domestic public split as the source of female subordination and male dominance discussed earlier. It has pertinent structural considerations. Lewis acknowledges the notion of a structural opposition between the domestic and public spheres which offers useful insights in understanding differential participation and evaluation of men and women. Nevertheless, she argues that its applicability to racial minority men and women may be questionable since historically Black men (like Black women) have been excluded from participation in public sphere institutions. Lewis asserts: 22

> What the black experience suggests is that differential participation in the public sphere is a symptom rather than a cause of structural inequality. While inequality is manifested in the exclusion of a group from public life, it is actually generated in the groups' unequal access to power and resources in a hierarchically arranged social order. Relationships of dominance and subordination, therefore, emerge from a basic structural opposition between groups which is reflected in exclusion of the subordinate group from public life (1977:342).

Lewis then argues that among racially oppressed groups, it is important to distinguish between the public life of the dominant and the dominated societies. Using this framework we recognize a range of male participation from token admittance to the public life of the dominant group to its attempts to destroy the public life within a dominated society. She points to the fact that Mexican American men have played strong public roles in their own dominated society, and as Mexican Americans have become more assimilated to the dominating society, sex roles have become less hierarchical. The signifi- 23 cant feature of this argument has to do with the way in which attention is brought to shifts in power relationships between the dominant society and racial minorities, and how these shifts effect changes in relationships between the sexes. Lewis' analysis makes it abundantly clear that minority males' exclusion from the public sphere requires further attention.

Chicano Masculinity as a Response to Stratification and Exclusion

There are no works, either theoretical or empirical, specifically devoted to the impact of structural exclusion on male roles and male identity. However, there are suggestions that the emphasis on masculinity might stem from the fact that alternative roles and identity sources are systematically blocked from men in certain social categories. Lillian Rubin, for example, described the martial role egalitarianism of middle class professional husbands as opposed to the more traditional authoritarian role of working class husbands in the following manner: 24

> . . . the professional male is more secure, has more status and prestige than the working class man, factors which enable him to assume a less overtly authoritarian role within the family. There are, after all, other places, other situations where his authority and power are tested and accorded legitimacy. At the same time, the demands of his work role for a satellite wife require that he risk the consequences of a more egalitarian family ideology. In contrast, for the working class men, there are few such rewards in the world outside the home. The family is usually the only place where he can exercise power, demand obedience to his authority. Since his work role makes no demands for wifely participation, he is under fewer and less immediate external pressures to accept the egalitarian ideology (Rubin, 1976:99).

Of course, Rubin is contrasting behaviors of men in different social classes, but the same line of thinking is paralleled in Ramos' speculation that for some Chicanos what has been called "machismo" may be a "way of feeling capable in a world that makes it difficult for Chicanos to demonstrate their capabilities" (Ramos, 1979:61).

We must understand that while maleness is highly valued in our society, it interacts with other categorical distinctions in both manifestation and meaning. As Stoll (1974:124) presents this idea, our society is structured to reward some categories in preference to others (e.g., men over women) but the system is not perfectly rational. First the rewards are scarce, second, other categories such as race, ethnicity and other statuses are included in the formula. Furthermore, the interaction of different categories with masculinity contributes to multiple societal meanings of masculinity, so that "one can never be sure this aspect of one's self will not be called into dispute. One is left having to account for oneself, thus to be on the defensive" (Stoll, 1974:124). It is in light of the societal importance attributed to masculinity that we must assess Stoll's contention that "gender identity is a more profound personal con- 25 cern for the male in our society than it is for women, because women can take it for granted that they are female" (Stoll, 1974:105). This speculation may have implications for Chicanos as well. Perhaps it will be found that ethnic differences in the salience of gender are not only one of degree but that their relative significance has different meanings. In other words, gender may not be a problematic identifier for women if they can take it for granted, though it may be primary because many still participate in society through their gender roles. On the other hand, men in certain social categories have had more roles and sources of identity open to them. However, this has not been the case for Chicanos or other men of color. Perhaps manhood takes on greater importance for those who do not have access to socially valued roles. Being male is one sure way to acquire status when other roles are systematically denied by the workings of society. This suggests that an emphasis on masculinity is not due to a collective internalized inferiority, rooted in a subcultural orientation. To be "hombre" may be a reflection of both ethnic and gender components and may take on greater significance when other roles and sources of masculine identity are structurally blocked. Chicanos have been excluded from participation in the dominant society's political–economic system. Therefore, they have been denied resources and the accompanying authority accorded men in other social categories. My point that gender may take on a unique and greater significance for men of color is not to justify traditional masculinity, but to point to the need for understanding societal conditions that might contribute to the meaning of gender among different social categories. It may be worthwhile to consider some expressions of masculinity as attempts to gain some measure of control in a society that categorically denies or grants people control over significant realms of their lives.

Turner makes this point about the male posturing of Black men: "Boastful, or meek, these performances are attempts by black men to actualize control in some situation" (Turner, 1977:128). Much the same point is made in discussions of Chicanos. The possibility has been raised that certain aggressive behaviors on the part of Chicano men was "a calculated response to hostility, exclusion, and racial domination," and a "conscious rejection of the dominant society's definition of Mexicans as passive, lazy, and indifferent" (Baca Zinn, 1975:23). Mirandé (1981:35) also treats machismo as an adaptive characteristic, associated with visible and manifest resistance of Chicano men to racial oppression. To view Chicano male behavior in this light is not to disregard possible maladaptive consequences of overcompensatory masculinity, but rather to recast masculinity in terms of responses to structural conditions. [26]

Differences in normative and behavioral dimensions of masculinity would be well worth exploring. Though numerous recent studies have challenged macho male dominance in the realm of family decision making, there is also evidence that patriarchal *ideology* can be manifested even in Chicano families where decision making is not male dominant. Baca Zinn's findings of *both* male dominant and egalitarian families revealed also that the ideology of patriarchy was expressed in all families studied: [27]

Patriarchal ideology was expressed in statements referring to the father as the "head" of the family, as the "boss," as the one "in charge." Informants continually expressed their beliefs that it "should be so." Findings confirmed that while male dominance was a cultural ideal, employed wives openly challenged that dominance on a behavioral level (1979:15).

It is possible that such an ideology is somehow associated with family solidarity. This insight is derived from Michel's analysis of family values (cited in Goode, 1963:57). Drawing on cross cultural studies, she reports:

. . . the concept of the strength or solidarity of the family is viewed as being identical with the father . . . the unity of the family is identified with the prerogatives of the father.

If this is the case, it is reasonable to suggest that the father's authority is strongly upheld because family solidarity is important in a society that excludes and subordinates Chicanos. The tenacity of patriarchy may be more than a holdover from past tradition. It may also represent a contemporary cultural adaptation to the minority condition of structural discrimination.

Conclusion

The assumption that male dominance among Chicanos is exclusively a cultural phenomenon is contradicted by much evidence. While many of the concerns raised in this paper are speculative in nature, they are nevertheless informed by current conceptualization in relevant bodies of literature. They raise the important point that we need further understanding of larger societal conditions in which masculinity is embedded and expressed. This forces us to recognize the disturbing relationship between the stratification axes of race, class and sex. To the extent that systems of social inequality limit men's access to societally valued resources, they also contribute to sexual stratification. Men in some social categories will continue to draw upon and accentuate their masculinity as a socially valued resource. This in turn poses serious threats to sexual equality. We are compelled to move the study of masculinity beyond narrow confines of subcultural roles, and to make the necessary theoretical and empirical connections between the contingencies of sex and gender and the social order.

REFERENCES

Baca Zinn, Maxine.
    1975 "Political Familism: Toward Sex Role Equality in Chicano Families," *International Journal of Chicano Studies Research.* 6:13–26.
    1980a "Employment and Education of Mexican American Women: The Interplay of Modernity and Ethnicity in Eight Families." *Harvard Educational Review* 50:47–62.
    1980b "Gender and Ethnic Identity Among Chicanos." *Frontiers:* V(2)18–24.

Chafetz, Janet Saltzman.
  1974 *Masculine/Feminine or Human.* E. E. Ithica, Ill.: Peacock Publishers, Inc.

Cromwell, Vicky L. and Ronald E. Cromwell.
  1978 "Perceived Dominance in Decision-Making and Conflict Resolution Among Anglo, Black and Chicano Couples." *Journal of Marriage and the Family.* 40(Nov):749–759.

Cromwell, Ronald E. and Rene E. Ruiz.
  1979 "The Myth of Macho Dominance in Decision Making Within Mexican and Chicano Families." *Hispanic Journal of Behavioral Sciences.* 1:355–373.

Davidson, Laurie and Laura Kramer Gordon
  1979 "The Sociology of Gender." Rand McNally College Publishing Co.

Delgado, Abelardo.
  1974 "Machismo." *La Luz.* (Dec.):6.

Eichler, Margrit.
  1980 *The Double Standard: A Feminist Critique of Feminist Social Science.* St. Martin's Press.

Grebler, Leo, Joan W. Moore and Ralph C. Guzman.
  1970 *The Mexican American People: The Nation's Second Largest Minority.* The Free Press.

Hawkes, Glenn R. and Minna Taylor.
  1975 "Power Structure in Mexican and Mexican-American Farm Labor Families." *Journal of Marriage and the Family.* 37:807–811.

Hyde, Janet Shibley and B. G. Rosenberg.
  1976 Half the Human Experience. *The Psychology of Women.* D. C. Heath and Company.

Lewis, Diane K.
  1977 "A Response to Inequality: Black Women, Racism, and Sexism." *SIGNS: Journal of Women in Culture and Society.* 3:339–361.

Luzod, Jimmy A. and Carlos H. Arce.
  1979 "An Exploration of the Father Role in the Chicano Family." Paper presented at the National Symposium on the Mexican American Child. Santa Barbara, California.

Mejia, Daniel P.
  1976 Cross-Ethnic Father Role: Perceptions of Middle Class Anglo American Parents, Doctoral Dissertation, University of California, Irvine.

Miller, Michael V.
  1975 "Variations in Mexican-American Family Life: A Review Synthesis." Paper presented at Rural Sociological Society, San Francisco, California.

Mirandé, Alfredo.
  1977 "The Chicano Family: A Reanalysis of Conflicting Views." *Journal of Marriage and the Family.* 39:747–756.
  1979 "A Reinterpretation of Male Dominance in the Chicano Family." *Family Coordinator.* 28(4), 473–497.
  1981 "Machismo: Rucas, Chingasos, y Chingaderas." *De Colores,* Forthcoming.

Montiel, Miguel.
  1970 "The Social Science Myth of the Mexican American Family." *El Grito.* 3:56–63.

Parker, Seymour and Robert J. Kleiner.
  1977 "Social and Psychological Dimensions of the Family Role Performance of the Negro Male." Pp. 102–117 in Doris Y. Wilkinson and Ronald L. Taylor (editors), *The Black Male in America.* Nelson Hall.

Pleck, Joseph H. and Robert Brannon.
  1978 "Male Roles and the Male Experience: Introduction." *Journal of Social Issues.* 34:1–4.

Ramos, Reyes.
  1979 "The Mexican American: Am I Who They Say I Am?" Pp. 49–66 in Arnulfo D. Trejo (editor), *The Chicanos as We See Ourselves.* The University of Arizona Press.

Riddell, Adaljiza Sosa.
  1974 "Chicanas and El Movimiento" *Aztlan.* 5(1 and 2):155–165.

Romer, Nancy and Debra Cherry.
  1980 "Ethnic and Social Class Differences in Children's Sex-Role Concepts." *Sex Roles.* 6:245–263.

Rosaldo, Michelle and Louise Lamphere.
  1974 *Woman, Culture, and Society.* Stanford: Stanford University Press.

Rubin, Lillian.
  1976 *Worlds of Pain.* Basic Books.

Senour, Maria Neito and Lynda Warren.
  1976 "Sex and Ethnic Differences in Masculinity, Femininity and Anthropology." Paper presented at the meeting of the Western Psychological Association, Los Angeles, California.

Spence, Janet T. and Robert L. Helmreich.
  1978 *Masculinity and Femininity: The Psychological Dimensinos, Correlates and Antecedents.* University of Austin Press.

Staples, Robert.
  1978 "Masculinity and Race: The Dual Dilemma of Black Men." *Journal of Social Issues.* 34:169–183.

Stockard, Jean and Miriam M. Johnson.
  1980 *Sex Roles.* Englewood Cliffs, New Jersey: Prentice-Hall.

Stoll, Clarice Stasz.
  1974 *Male and Female: Socialization, Social Roles, and Social Structure.* William C. Brown Publishers.

Taylor, Ronald L.
  1977 "Socialization to the Black Male Role." Pp. 1–6 in Doris Y. Wilkinson and Ronald L. Taylor (editors), *The Black Male in America.* Nelson Hall.

Turner, William H.
  1977 "Myths and Stereotypes: The African Man in America." Pp. 122–144 in Doris Y. Wilkinson and Ronald L. Taylor (editors), *The Black Male in America.* Nelson Hall.

Valdez, Ramiro.
  1980 "The Mexican American Male: A Brief Review of the Literature." *Newsletter of the Mental Health Research Project,* I.D.R.A. San Antonio: 4–5.

Ybarra-Soriano, Lea.
  1977 *Conjugal Role Relationships in the Chicano Family.* Ph.D. diss. University of California at Berkeley.

Questions

1. What is the traditional explanation for machismo? How is Zinn's explanation different?
2. Why is machismo less prevalent among the middle class?
3. According to Zinn, is it more difficult to be male or to be female in Chicano society? Why?

Cool Pose: The Proud Signature of Black Survival

RICHARD MAJORS

Richard Majors is the author of Cool Pose: The Dilemmas of Black Manhood in America *(1992). He is an assistant professor of psychology at the University of Wisconsin, Eau Claire, and co-founder and chairman of the National Council for African-American Men.*

    Majors argues that black males adopt a "Cool Pose" because they have been denied access to "the dominant culture's acceptable avenues" of self-expression. However, this posture of control, toughness, and detachment denies the expression of fear and affection, and may explain such problems as black-on-black crime. This reading is from Men's Lives *(1989).*

Just when it seemed that we black males were beginning to recover from past injustices inflicted by a dominant white society, we find once again that we are being revisited in a similar vein. President Reagan's de-emphasis of civil rights, affirmative action legislation and social services programs; the rise of black neoconservatives and certain black feminist groups; harshly critical media events on television (e.g., the CBS documentary "The Vanishing Family—Crisis in Black America") and in films (e.g., *The Color Purple*); and the omnipresent problems of unemployment and inadequate health care, housing, and education—all have helped to shape a negative political and social climate toward black men. For many black men this period represents a *New Black Nadir*, or lowest point, and time of deepest depression. [1]

Black people in general, and the black man in particular, look out on a world that does not positively reflect their image. Black men learned long ago that the classic American virtues of thrift, perseverance and hard work would not give us the tangible rewards that accrue to most members of the dominant society. We learned early that we would not be Captains of Industry or builders of engineering wonders. Instead, we channeled our creative energies into construction of a symbolic universe. Therefore we adopted unique poses and postures to offset the externally imposed "zero" image. Because black men were denied access to the dominant culture's acceptable avenues of expression, we created a form of self-expression—the "Cool Pose."[1-3] [2]

Cool Pose is a term that represents a variety of attitudes and actions that serve the black man as mechanisms for survival, defense and social competence. These attitudes and actions are performed using characterizations and roles as facades and shields. [3]

540

Cool Culture

Historically, coolness was central to the culture of many ancient African civi- 4
lizations. The Yorubas of Western Nigeria (900 B.C. to 200 A.D.) are cited as
an example of an African civilization where cool was integrated into the social fabric of the community.[4] Uses of cool ranged from the way a young man
carried himself before his peers to the way he impressed his elders during the
initiation ritual. Coolness helped to build character and pride for individuals
in such groups and is regarded as a precolonial cultural adaptation. With the
advent of the modern African slave trade, cool became detached from its indigenous cultural setting and emerged equally as a survival mechanism.

Where the European saw America as the promised land, the African saw it 5
as the land of oppression. Today, reminders of Black America's oppressive past
continue in the form of chronic underemployment, inadequate housing, inferior schools, and poor health care. Because of these conditions many black
men have become frustrated, angry, confused and impatient.

To help ease the pain associated with these conditions, black men have 6
taken to alcoholism, drug abuse, homicide, and suicide. In learning to mistrust the words and actions of dominant white people, black males have
learned to make great use of "poses" and "postures" which connote control,
toughness, and detachment. All these forms arise from the mistrust that the
black males feel towards the dominant society.

For these black males, particular poses and postures show the white man 7
that "although you may have tried to hurt me time and time again, I can take
it (and if I am hurting or weak, I'll never let you know). They are saying loud
and clear to the white establishment, "I am strong, full of pride, and a survivor." Accordingly, any failures in the real world become the black man's
secret.

The Expressive Life Style

On the other hand, those poses and postures that have an expressive quality 8
or nature have become known in the literature as the "expressive life style."[5]
The expressive life style is a way in which the black male can act cool by actively displaying particular performances that emphasize creative expression.
Thus, while black people historically have been forced into conciliatory and
often demeaning positions in American culture, there is nothing conciliatory
about the expressive life style.

This dynamic vitality will not be denied even in limited stereotypical 9
roles—as demonstrated by Hattie McDaniel, the maid in *Gone With the Wind*
or Bill "Bojangle" Robinson as the affable servant in the Shirley Temple
movies. This abiding need for creative self-expression knows no bounds, and
asserts itself whether on the basketball court or in dancing. We can see it in
black athletes—with their stylish dunking of the basketball, their spontaneous dancing in the end zone, and their different styles of handshakes (e.g.,
"high fives")—and in black entertainers with their various choreographed

"cool" dance steps. These are just a few examples of black individuals in their professions who epitomize this creative expression. The expressive life style is a dynamic—not a static—art form, and new aesthetic forms are always evolving (e.g., "rap-talking" and breakdancing). The expressive life style, then, is the passion that invigorates the demeaning life of blacks in White America. It is a dynamic vitality that transforms the mundane into the sublime and makes the routine spectacular.

A Cultural Signature

Cool Pose, manifested by the expressive life style, is also an aggressive assertion of masculinity. It emphatically says, "White man, this is my turf. You can't match me here." Though he may be impotent in the political and corporate world, the black man demonstrates his potency in athletic competition, entertainment and the pulpit with a verve that borders on the spectacular. Through the virtuosity of a performance, he tips the socially imbalanced scales in his favor. "See me, touch me, hear me, but, white man, you can't copy me." This is the subliminal message which black males signify in their oftentimes flamboyant performance. Cool Pose, then, becomes the cultural signature for such black males.   10

Being cool is a unique response to adverse social, political and economic conditions. Cool provides control, inner strength, stability and confidence. Being cool, illustrated in its various poses and postures, becomes a very powerful and necessary tool in the black man's constant fight for his soul. The poses and postures of cool guard, preserve and protect his pride, dignity and respect to such an extent that the black male is willing to risk a great deal for it. One black man said it well: "The white man may control everything about me—that is, except my pride and dignity. That he can't have. That is mine and mine alone."   11

The Cost

Cool Pose, however, is not without its price. Many black males fail to discriminate the appropriate uses of Cool Pose and act cool much of the time, without regard to time or space.[6] Needless to say, this can cause severe problems. In many situations a black man won't allow himself to express or show any form of weakness or fear or other feelings and emotions. He assumes a facade of strength, held at all costs, rather than "blow his fronts" and thus his cool. Perhaps black men have become so conditioned to keeping up their guard against oppression from the dominant white society that this particular attitude and behavior represent for them their best safeguard against further mental or physical abuse. However, this same behavior makes it very difficult for these males to let their guard down and show affection, even for people that they actually care about or for people that may really care about them (e.g., girlfriends, wives, mothers, fathers, "good" friends, etc.).   12

When the art of being cool is used to put cool behaviors ahead of emotions or needs, the result of such repression of feelings can be frustration.   13

Such frustrations sometimes cause aggression which often is taken out on those individuals closest to such men—other black people. It is sadly ironic, then, that the same elements of cool that allow for survival in the larger society may hurt black people by contributing to one of the more complex problems facing black people today—black-on-black crime.

Further, while Cool Pose enables black males to maintain stability in the face of white power, it may through inappropriate use render many of them unable to move with the mainstream or evolve in healthy ways. When misused, cool can suppress the motivation to learn, accept or become exposed to stimuli, cultural norms, aesthetics, mannerisms, values, etiquette, information or networks that could help them overcome problems caused by white racism. Finally, in a society which has as its credo, "A man's home is his castle," it is ironic that the masses of black men have no castle to protect. Their minds have become their psychological castle, defended by impenetrable cool. Thus, Cool Pose is the bittersweet symbol of a socially disesteemed group that shouts, "We are" in face of a hostile and indifferent world that everywhere screams, "You ain't." 14

Cool and the Black Psyche

To be fully grasped, Cool Pose must be recognized as having gained ideological consensus in the black community. It is not only a quantitatively measured "social reality" but a series of equally "real" rituals of socialization. It is a comprehensive, officially endorsed cultural myth that became entrenched in the black psyche with the beginning of the slave experience. This phenomenon has cut across all socioeconomic groups in the black community, as black men fight to preserve their dignity, pride, respect and masculinity with the attitudes and behaviors of Cool Pose. Cool Pose represents a fundamental structuring of the psyche of the black male and is manifested in some way or another in the daily activities and recreational habits of most black males. There are few other social or psychological constructs that have shaped, directed or controlled the black male to the extent that the various forms of coolness have. It is surprising, then, that for a concept that has the potential to explain problems in black male and black female relationships, black-on-black crime, and black-on-black pregnancies, there is such limited research on this subject. 15

In the final analysis, Cool Pose may represent the most important yet least researched area with the potential to enhance our understanding and study of black behavior today. 16

NOTES

1. Majors, R. G., Nikelly, A. G., "Serving the Black Minority: A New Direction for Psychotherapy." *J. for Non-white Concerns*, 11:142–151 (1983).
2. Majors, R. G., "The Effects of 'Cool Pose': What Being Cool Means." *Griot*, pp. 4–5 (Spring, 1985).

3. Nikelly, A. G. & Majors, R. G. "Techniques for Counseling Black Students," *Techniques: J. Remedial Educ. & Counseling*, 2:48–54 (1986).

4. Bascom, W., *The Yoruba of Southwestern Nigeria*. (New York: Holt, Rinehart & Winston, 1969).

5. Rainwater, L., *Behind Ghetto Walls*. (Chicago: Aldine, 1970).

6. Majors, R. G., "Cool Pose: A New Hypothesis in Understanding Anti-Social Behavior in Lower SES Black Males," unpublished manuscript.

Questions

1. Describe what Majors means by "Cool Pose." Has this form of expression been stereotyped by the media?

2. What is your definition of "cool"? Does it correspond to the definition given by Majors?

3. Does Majors's concept of a "Cool Pose" contribute to cultural misunderstanding?

Writing Assignments

The following writing assignments are concerned with the topic of diversity among men and women. Before developing an argument on any of these assignments, be sure that you understand the controversy. Complete the following activities:

■   Write responses to exploration questions.

■   Read several articles in this chapter or elsewhere to discover at least two perspectives on the topic.

■   Create a list of opposing viewpoints and consider the potential consequences of each one.

■   Examine the underlying assumptions behind each viewpoint.

To help you understand the issues and develop ideas, you can use the following form:

The conflict in this issue is between _____ and

_____ .

I am more inclined to agree with _____

because _____ .

However, it is possible that some of my readers may believe that

_____ .

Exploration Questions

1. As a child, were you treated differently than siblings of the opposite sex? Did you have different responsibilities and choices? Discuss the extent to which your family may have instilled specific sex role behaviors.

2. Although schools are now at least somewhat conscious of their role in perpetuating sex stereotyping, they still may contribute to them. Discuss the extent to which your school reinforced sex role behaviors. Can you recall specific ways in which "traditional masculinity" was reinforced?

3. What advantages are there to being a woman? What advantages are there to being a man?

4. How are men portrayed in the media in terms of their participation in family life? How do the media portray women within the family structure?

5. If you were a member of a club dedicated to helping men fulfill their potential, what would you focus on?

6. Why do you think household labor time is associated with level of education? Why do men with more education do a higher share of household labor?

7. It is said that our idealization of romantic love precludes our ability to form strong friendships between the sexes. Can you think of ways in which our culture (for example, the media) idealizes romantic love? Can you think of instances in which same-sex friendship is idealized?

8. If you woke up tomorrow and discovered that you had changed sex, how would your life be different?

ASSIGNMENT 1

The reevaluation of women's role in society and increased activity on behalf of equality for women was bound to have an effect on men. Many men are now reexamining their own prescribed roles and discovering that they had been just as limited by such prescriptions as were women. They too believe that they would like to maximize their life choices and they see the women's movement as providing a liberating impetus for men. Some men, of course, resist, believing that the women's movement has impinged upon their own traditionally defined power base. Still others point out that the women's movement has unfairly relegated men to the position of the enemy; they point out that there is a prevailingly anti-male attitude among women, which is just as pervasive as the anti-female prejudice attributed to men.

Read several articles in this chapter concerned with men's rights, and write an argumentative essay in response to the following question: Is there a need for a men's movement? Be sure to narrow your topic so that you address specific issues.

ASSIGNMENT 2

Although most people now acknowledge that women should be treated equally with men, it is also recognized that a number of women's issues still exist. Betty Friedan, in her book, *The Second Stage*, examines several of these issues, among them, discrimination against older women, the difficulty of obtaining adequate child care, and the uncertainties facing women who "want it all"—career, marriage, and children.

Read several articles in this book concerned with current women's issues (Chapters 8, 9, 10, and 11 have articles you can use). Locate a controversial issue, and examine various viewpoints on it. Then write a five to six page argumentative essay addressing the following question: Which are the most important issues facing women today?

In writing your essay, you should begin by exploring your own perspective on the topic (how you were socialized, your own plans for the future) and then incorporating the perspective of others. Support your position by referring to current controversies in the newspaper.

Using Data

ASSIGNMENTS

1. According to the table, are black or white women more likely to be without a spouse? Do any of the articles in this chapter explain this tendency (for instance, the essays by Leslie and Korman, and Billingsley)?

2. Why do you think the percentage of single mothers steadily increased? Are white and black female family householders now more likely to be alone because of divorce or the death of a spouse or because they never married?

3. According to the table, are women now having more or less children than they did in 1970?

Female Family Householders with No
Spouse Present—Characteristics, by Race: 1970 to 1989

Characteristic	White					Black				
	1970	1980	1985	1988	1989	1970	1980	1985	1988	1989
Female family householder	4,185	6,052	6,941	7,235	7,342	1,349	2,495	2,964	3,074	3,223
Percent of all families (%)	9.1	11.6	12.8	12.9	13.0	28.3	40.3	43.7	42.8	43.5
Median age (yr)	50.4	43.7	42.7	42.2	42.5	41.3	37.4	38.0	38.1	37.2
Marital status (%)										
Single (never married)	9.2	10.6	11.9	15.1	15.7	16.2	27.3	33.4	35.9	38.5
Married, spouse absent	18.5	16.9	16.0	15.7	14.7	39.7	28.6	21.1	23.2	22.2
Separated	11.4	13.9	13.8	12.6	12.2	33.8	26.8	19.3	20.3	19.3
Other	7.2	3.0	2.1	3.0	2.5	5.9	1.8	1.7	2.9	2.9
Widowed	47.0	32.7	28.3	27.0	26.7	29.9	22.2	21.2	18.8	17.3
Divorced	25.3	39.8	43.8	42.2	43.0	14.2	21.9	24.5	22.1	22.0
Presence of children under 18 (%)										
No own children	52.0	41.2	43.5	43.8	43.6	33.5	28.1	34.5	34.3	32.7
With own children	48.0	58.8	56.5	56.2	56.4	66.6	71.9	65.5	65.7	67.3
1 child	18.8	28.1	28.9	28.5	28.9	19.1	26.3	27.5	28.1	29.8
2 children	15.0	19.9	18.6	18.9	18.7	14.4	23.2	21.6	20.2	19.7
3 children	7.8	7.4	6.4	6.4	6.4	12.5	11.1	10.1	10.5	10.8
4 or more children	6.4	3.4	2.6	2.4	2.4	20.6	11.3	6.3	6.9	7.0
Children per family (number)	1.00	1.03	0.96	0.94	0.95	1.83	1.51	1.29	1.23	1.24

Based on U.S. Bureau of the Census estimates.

9 ■ Diversity and the Family

Happy families are all alike, but each
unhappy family is unhappy in its own way.
TOLSTOY, *ANNA KARENINA*

Whenever this statement from Tolstoy is quoted, people usually nod, implying their belief that the statement has validity. However, if one carefully examines the ideas in the statement, it becomes clear that several facets of it are
not true today and probably were not true in Tolstoy's day. Certainly, in a diverse society all happy families cannot be alike because models of what constitutes an ideal family differ from culture to culture. And if all happy families
are not alike, one cannot then presume similarity among unhappy families
either.

Perhaps the element in Tolstoy's statement that comes closest to the truth
is implied—that family happiness significantly affects individual happiness
and that problems with the family are not uncommon. It is true that the portrayals of families in literature—from the biblical tale of Cain and Abel, to figures from Greek drama such as Oedipus and Medea, to Shakespearean
characters such as Hamlet and King Lear, to the novels of James Baldwin and
Gabriel Marquez—indicate the relationship between family happiness and individual happiness in a variety of cultures. They also suggest that confusion,
emotional turbulence, and conflict are also parts of family life.

Despite their problems and despite periodic statements that the family is
in decline, the idea of family remains an important social construct in most
cultures, often providing economic as well as emotional support. The topic of
family is, therefore, relevant to the overall subject of diversity. The readings
in this chapter examine the role of the family in American society, discuss the
question of what is deemed best for children, and explore how the concept of
the family differs according to culture.

Is the Family Desirable?

In most cultures, when the word "family" is mentioned, it frequently connotes something positive and respectable. People are usually proud of having

a big family or a successful family, and if a member of a family has achieved something of note, whether that achievement is intellectual, social, or monetary, family members are often inclined to boast, feeling that they are entitled to share that success. Conversely, if a family member does something shameful, family members partake equally of the shame, and sometimes do whatever they can to disassociate themselves from the family. Family values, family gatherings, and family viewing all suggest that the family is something important, a significant component of the culture, and something worth preserving and supporting.

Some people believe, however, that the family, particularly in its so-called ideal form in Western culture, is not necessarily a desirable model either for peaceful and productive human interaction or for raising children. These people believe that other models might facilitate greater equality and harmony for society as a whole as well as provide greater support for individual endeavor. One work that views the family in a negative light is Marge Piercy's futuristic novel, *Woman on the Edge of Time*, which postulates a society in which relationships are not based on familial blood ties. Piercy's novel castigates the traditional concept of family, condemning the idea that parents should love only their own biological children, which she perceives as limiting, or the idea that the family should be the vehicle for communicating cultural values, thereby perpetuating racism and ethnocentricity. Piercy's novel also repudiates the idea that children should maintain close ties with their family because family obligations are likely to conflict with professional and personal possibilities. Moreover, Piercy's novel makes the case that the traditional model of the family has contributed to societal inequities and has been especially exploitive of women.

The Family in the United States

Whatever Piercy's objections to the family might be, Americans, for the most part, like to think of themselves as a family-oriented society—Christmas at home around a fire, fourth of July barbecues, family picnics—a part of the mythology of picture-postcard American family life, particularly as presented in the media. Reacting against this stereotype, social historian Stephanie Coontz, in her book, *The Way We Never Were: American Families and the Nostalgia Trap,* argues that the myth of the traditional family is demoralizing and ultimately dysfunctional, placing "impossible burdens and guilt on both parents and children." Coontz, in a reprinted interview by Peggy Taylor, examines the concept of idealized families as portrayed in television and by politicians, pointing out that the stereotypical family in which the father worked and the mother's sole responsibility was to nurture children at home existed in only a very few instances, even in the family-oriented 1950s. Coontz's book presents many common beliefs about the family as simple myths, such as the idea that the biological mother is the best person to care for a child and the belief that the traditional family model of mother, father, and two kids provides the best environment for raising children.

In another perspective on the family in America, Richard Rodriguez states in "Family Values," that Americans, in some ways, are actually anti-family: their promotion of individualism and the high regard they have for the pioneer spirit implies a breaking away from traditional patterns and forging a new life away from home. Rodriguez questions whether Americans have ever truly valued the family and argues that despite the recent emphasis on family values, the tendency in America has been to break away from the family.

The extent to which the concept of family is an integral part of American culture is further explored by Arlene Skolnick in an excerpt from her book, *Embattled Paradise: The American Family in an Age of Uncertainty*, entitled "The State of the American Family." Skolnick argues that despite rumors to the contrary, the family has not declined; rather, it has changed because of economic and demographic factors. She warns that to blame our social ills on the lack of family values places an unfair burden on individual responsibility when the explanation for problems such as poverty, drug abuse, and declining academic achievement is largely due to the widening gap in our economic structure. Skolnick characterizes American culture as a tension between communitarian and individualistic impulses—an ambivalent yearning for autonomy on the one hand and attachment to family and community on the other. Citing the often divergent opinions of family scholars, she stresses that it is difficult to define a traditional family, even within so-called mainstream American families, and discusses the modifications on the traditional nuclear family that have occurred since the 1960s as a result of the two-worker family becoming the cultural norm.

Certainly, economic concerns have always played a significant role in determining family structure, and especially today, it has become increasingly difficult for one person to support a family. Katha Pollitt, in "Why I Hate 'Family Values' (Let Me Count the Ways)," contends that the apparent decline of family values lies "not in moral collapse but in our failure to acknowledge and adjust to changing social relations." She maintains that the dissolution of the family insofar as there is an increase in the number of poor, single mothers is not a problem of individual values but is a "problem of money."

Sar A. Levitan and Richard S. Belous also discuss the relationship of the family to economic factors, tracing the relationship between the modern concept of the family and the rise of industrialization. They point out in "The Family in the Welfare State" that before the industrial revolution the family was the primary source of economic necessities and education. Subsequently, the social surplus created by industry led to the creation of public education, health care, and other institutions, resulting in what is referred to as "the welfare state." The article then discusses some of the advantages and disadvantages of the nuclear family as opposed to the extended family and community networks of the past, and speculates about whether governmental programs ought to provide additional support for families.

FAMILY VALUES AND "MURPHY BROWN"

The role of the family within American culture was brought to public attention in the spring of 1992 in the television program "Murphy Brown." Here, the fictional character, Murphy Brown, a highly educated and professionally successful newscaster, chose to bear a child as a single parent after despairing over ever finding the ideal man and hearing the biological clock ticking away. Murphy Brown's decision, ultimately leading to the birth of the child, elicited public condemnation from Vice President Dan Quayle, who castigated the program as a threat to family values, a pronouncement that generated a storm of controversy over the decline of family values and about what constitutes an acceptable family in a diverse society. People with more conservative values believed that the Murphy Brown decision epitomized the erosion of traditional mores begun in the 1960s, which has led to a fragmented society in which single motherhood is associated with poverty and a variety of social problems. However, Katha Pollitt points out (whether or not reality can be significantly influenced by a television show), the fortysomething, educated, professional Murphy Brown bears little resemblance to the millions of middle- and lower-class single mothers who find themselves in desperate financial straits as a result of poor employment prospects and fathers who fail to contribute support. Pollitt also believes that people preach about family values as a substitute for taking concrete action, such as providing practical information about sexuality and birth control to teenagers to prevent unwanted pregnancies. Other commentators have pointed out that the child of an intelligent, loving, affluent, educated, mature single mother such as Murphy Brown is certainly more likely to be provided with emotional and financial support than the average child coming into the world.

CHILDREN, CHILD REARING, AND CHILD CARE

Implicit in the Murphy Brown controversy is the idea that a two-parent household—the traditional model in which the man is primary breadwinner and the woman provides primary child care—provides the best environment for children, a theory that has never been established definitively and is difficult, if not impossible, to prove. As Ludmilla Jordanova points out in "Children in History: Concepts of Nature and Society," studying children and evaluating what is best for them is extremely complex because the way in which anyone approaches such a study is influenced heavily by cultural preconceptions concerning nature and nurture. For example, the widely accepted contemporary notion that child development occurs in stages came into existence only during the last few centuries, and it was only in the nineteenth century that the concept of adolescence originated. The question arises as to whether the concepts of childhood and adolescence are discoveries, that is, recognition of a preexisting state, or inventions, that is, creations of the human mind. Jordanova also points out that aside from historical considerations, each society treats childhood and children differently, and that considerable variation exists even among different parts of a single society concerning the relationship of children to sexuality and labor.

One of the major issues associated with women's desire for professional equality with men is that of child care. Extended families are no longer available to take on that role and some men still do not perceive this as one of their major responsibilities. Bell Hooks addresses the issue of child care in her essay "Revolutionary Parenting." She argues that although women are socialized to believe that they have the natural capacity and the duty to raise children, this consciousness needs to be revolutionized because the healthiest conditions for the child result when the father and other parental figures provide models. Hooks believes that motherhood had been devalued by early feminists but is currently being romanticized by white bourgeois women. She rejects both extremes in favor of a practical approach in which child rearing would be shared equally by both sexes. She also advocates the establishment of community-based, public child-care centers as a means of overcoming the isolation of parents and children.

The Family in Different Cultures

Several articles in this chapter discuss how the family is viewed in black families, Mexican-American families, and gay families. The selection from Andrew Billingsley's recently published book, *Climbing Jacob's Ladder: The Enduring Legacy of African-American Families*, however argues against the idea that it is the deterioration of the black family that causes black social problems. Billingsley asserts that the black family structure is strong because of community support; what is needed, he maintains, is for social institutions to be changed so that "they function as well for blacks as they do for whites."

Stuart A. Queen and Robert W. Habenstein in "The Mexican-American Family" describe some of the characteristics of Mexican-American families living in border towns and isolated villages in the Southwest; they discuss differences in gender roles and the effect of industrialization on traditional family structure. They point out that although the majority of Mexican-American families remain monogamic and patriarchal, socioeconomic factors are changing the strong nuclear structure of these families and that the "depressed occupational status" of the Mexican male and the influence of American culture has begun to weaken the family as a functioning unity. The article concludes with a comparison of Mexican-American families to black families.

The last two articles in the chapter examine the issue of whether gay family life can support the notion of family values. The article "Gays Under Fire" discusses several controversial issues associated with the gay movement, such as whether gay couples should be allowed to adopt children and whether gay marriages should be recognized legally. The article by Eric Marcus cites his own relationship in support of the idea that gay couples do live happy, family-centered lives.

Emotionally charged issues such as family values and determining what conditions are best for raising children generate conflict even in relatively homogeneous societies. And, in a culturally diverse society in which differing lifestyles and value systems collide on a daily basis, awareness and understanding of these differences is critical for survival.

The Way We Never Were

INTERVIEW BY PEGGY TAYLOR

Editor of the New Age Journal, *Peggy Taylor interviewed social historian Stephanie Coontz, author of* The Way We Never Were: American Families and the Nostalgia Trap *(1992).*

   This interview focuses on Coontz's position that the myth of the traditional family is demoralizing and ultimately dysfunctional, placing "impossible burdens and guilt on both parents and children."

The Family. To the sound-bite-hungry politician, it's a once-proud institution   1
whose lamentable "breakdown" and loss of "values" is the root cause of everything from drug abuse and unemployment to Murphy Brown's pregnancy. To many in the recovery movement, it's a cruel crucible grinding out generations of dysfunctional adult children. To many others, it's something just vaguely unsatisfying: a patchwork of relationships, struggles, joys, and somehow unfulfilled expectations—never quite living up to what we imagine it's supposed to be.

   From almost every perspective, it seems, The Family is in the doghouse.   2
And one main reason, argues social historian Stephanie Coontz, is because we view our families through a cloud of myths and misunderstandings. From clichés such as "A man's home is his castle" to political rhetoric about the lost "traditional" families of years past to scenes of domestic perfection exhibited by the TV Cleavers, Bradys, and Huxtables, we have been indoctrinated with images of a family life that has never existed and that—despite the longings of some politicians—could not be lived by real people today. Not only do these idealized images block us from making sound public policy, Coontz contends, but they damage us on a personal level—by fostering guilt.

   "Even as children, my students and colleagues tell me, they felt guilty be-   3
cause their families did not act like those on television," she writes in her new book, *The Way We Never Were: American Families and the Nostalgia Trap* (Basic Books, 1992). "Perhaps the second most common reaction is anger—a sense of betrayal or rage when you and your family cannot live as the myths suggest you should be able to."

   Coontz has spent much of her career questioning conventional thinking   4
on social issues. As a student at the University of California, Berkeley, and at the University of Washington, she achieved some renown as an antiwar activist, eventually serving as a national coordinator of the National Peace Action Coalition. The single mother of an eleven-year-old boy, she has been a professor at Washington's Evergreen State College—known for its progressive approach to education—for the past sixteen years, specializing in family

553

history, social history, and women's history. With the publication of *The Way We Never Were,* her first book aimed at a general readership, Coontz is fast emerging as a progressive voice in a "family values" debate that has up till now been dominated by the right wing.

We recently spent a leisurely afternoon together in Seattle.   5

NEW AGE JOURNAL: *You talk a lot about the myths that shape our ideas about fam-*   6
ily. What do you mean?

STEPHANIE COONTZ: We have a whole range of images of how the family is sup-   7
posed to be—partly drawn from television series, partly drawn from grandparents' stories, partly drawn from books like *Little House on the Prairie.* And
then there are political myths that chase around in our heads about how the
family is supposed to "go it alone" and how a man's home is his castle, how
there didn't used to be outside interference with the family.

These political myths collide or sometimes coalesce with our personal   8
myths—that our parents, or somebody's parents, used to be perfect; that
there was a time when there were women who stayed home and baked cook-
ies and gave their children nothing but unconditional love. And fathers came
home from their jobs and, even though they had to work, weren't too tired to
teach the boys how to fix the car. And they gave their children good advice
about what to do in school and how to build character. So then we ask ourselves, why aren't we able to do that? Or why didn't this happen to us?

These myths are very dysfunctional, because they focus us on what sup-   9
posedly happened in the past, on what has disappeared. There's a tendency,
then—one greatly exacerbated by recent electoral campaigns—to say that all
the problems we have now in America, from poverty to social alienation to
crime to drug use, are a result of the collapse of the family. I would argue that
that's just not the case.

Well, let's talk about some of these myths, take some of them apart a little bit.   10

A good way to start is with this idea of the "traditional family" that politi-   11
cians keep referring to. And you have to ask, Which traditional family do you
have in mind? I always try to ask anybody who says this to me, "Name a year,
a section of the population, a region of the country, where you think the family worked." Well, you can tell a lot about the politics of the people you're
talking with by what year they pick and what family. The religious conservatives will generally pick colonial New England, the Puritan era. The more soft
conservative ones, and even some liberals, and a few feminists who want to
celebrate female nurturing, will pick the Victorian Age, with its gender division of labor, the separate spheres, the protection of childhood. Politicians often pick the pioneer family as an example of the independent, self-reliant
spirit, which if it still existed would mean they wouldn't have to fund any social programs. And harassed working parents often look back to the '50s as a
time when it was so much easier to raise kids. Even those of us who don't
want to return to an earlier era are constantly measuring ourselves against
one or another of those myths—with demoralizing consequences.

So let's look at one family model in detail, say the Victorian family.   12

The model of the Victorian family is the one that most of us imbibed   13
when we read the Louisa May Alcott stories, such as *Little Women.* I still find
them attractive. I've even tried to get my son to read them in spite of the fact
that I know what really went on in that era. The Louisa May Alcott stories are
about a family that had this wonderful division of labor in it, that was not
oppressive, but where males and females each had their own jobs to do. The
men were not as patriarchal as in colonial days, but they represented the family to the outside world. They were the breadwinners. The mothers stayed
home and took care of the children and the children themselves had a greatly
lengthened childhood. They were not exposed too early to knowledge of evil
and complexity and ambiguity, or sex, death, and violence as most of us feel
our kids are today.

Some people modify this model a little bit and say that women ought to   14
have the right to work too, even though they didn't then, and they ought to
have the right to vote. But fundamentally, they say, there really is no substitute for this kind of nurturing family and some division of labor, and this
protection of childhood.

But there are a number of problems with this model. First of all, people   15
forget that it prevailed in only a tiny minority of the population. And the
condition for its prevalence in that tiny minority, then as now, was the ability
to exploit a lower class of immigrants and poor who did the arduous housework, made the clothes cheap enough so that they could be bought ready-
made, and freed up the Victorian housewife from her former chores in the
home. You find this even today—a lot of the families who think they have
solved this problem are the ones who hire new immigrants to clean their
house and be their nannies. And it's really not much of a solution, because of
what happens to the kids of those women who are cleaning those houses. So,
then as now, the lengthening of childhood for that privileged middle class
meant a foreshortening of childhood for many, many more children all
around the world.

Another problem is that the Victorian division of labor created tremen-   16
dous misunderstandings between men and women—misunderstandings that
we are still trying to get over today. At the time, it created a marriage crisis.
Because women felt they were so different from men and had so little in common with men, their most intense relationships, sensual as well as emotional,
were with other women. Relationships between men and women were very
stilted. Even today, when we're less repressed sexually, you see the same sort
of problems being worked through. Men and women, to the extent that they
are defined as opposites, have to give up half of themselves in order to attract
their other half. The communication problems caused by this are still haunt-
ing us.

What about the '50s? What's wrong with the Father Knows Best *family?*   17

The '50s were a very contradictory period. First of all, that time was not   18
really as family oriented as those television shows liked to pretend. But even
when it was, there were tremendous problems. It's true that there was a high
rate of family formation, there was a falling rate of divorce, although it's

important to note that America has had the highest divorce rate in the world ever since 1889—this is not an invention of the '60s. It's part of the American romanticization of love. But the '50s did see a fall in the divorce rate, a fall in the age of marriage, a rise in fertility. Something that's not usually mentioned by proponents of the '50s, however, is that it also saw a tremendous widening, for the first time in a hundred years, in the educational gap between men and women.

So the first thing to understand about the '50s family is that it was a   19
fluke, it was a seven-year aberration, in contradiction to a hundred years of other trends—and those seven years were hardly idyllic. A third of American children lived in poverty, even though there were far fewer single-parent homes; that's much higher than today's 20 percent. So not everybody was schmoozing in front of the Hot Point.

But the other thing that is so interesting about the '50s is that it was the   20
source of a lot of the things that modern cultural conservatives who say we should go back to the '50s bewail. This was the period when the youth market was first invented and shows like *The Howdy Doody Show* began to pander to kids. This was the period when television and family life became saturated with commercialism. Look at those shows. They are walking advertisements for freezers, refrigerators, stoves, cars, household consumer items.

People are generally surprised to learn that there were many more births to   21
teen-agers in the '50s than there are today. Teens didn't "just say no." They just said "yes," but then they could afford to get married because the government subsidized early marriage and parents did as well. It was also a time of an expanding economy, so that young men could support a family. More than 60 percent of men aged twenty to twenty-four could support a family above the poverty level back then, as opposed to only 42 percent who can do so today.

And if you want to talk about big government, think about the way the   22
government in the '50s pried into people's political associations, sexual lives, even reading habits. This was not an idyllic time for women either. They were repressed and oppressed, and when a woman got raped or battered people assumed *she* had done something wrong. I mean, wife beating was considered natural; the wife was considered to have provoked it. And girls who complained about incest were told by therapists that they were engaging in unconscious oedipal fantasies. So in all these ways it wasn't idyllic.

But wasn't there this idea that mothers were supposed to be happy at home with   23
their kids in the suburbs?

Yes, and it turns out that many of them were miserable. Tranquilizers, for   24
example, were a typical '50s invention—invented specifically with women in mind. The ads for tranquilizers in medical journals always pictured a distraught housewife in the doctor's office. The ads said: This is who needs it, this is who needs it.

Mother's little helpers.   25

Really! It's also important to remember that one of the reasons the '50s   26
family model was viable at all was because there was unprecedented government financing.

How so?   27

It was primarily through things like the GI Bill, which gave significant   28
stipends for veterans to go to school. The government also made it much easier for middle-class and lower-middle-class people to buy homes, by under-
writing loans so banks could afford to ask for very low down payments. They
also embarked on a massive road-building campaign, which turned out to be
an extraordinary, unprecedented subsidization of private home building, because the roads essentially acted as conduits to open up new suburban areas
of the country.

Meanwhile, while all of this was being financed by the public purse, not a   29
dime was going to mass transit in the city, with the result, of course, that it
became more and more difficult to construct a viable urban life.

All of the government policies were directed toward getting people to re-   30
treat into private homes in suburbia. Not only do I think this was an unsatisfactory kind of family life, as we know now from the tales of people who were
abused in '50s families and couldn't get out of it until the '70s, when there
was a women's movement to support them, but I think it's also very ironic
that conservatives want us to go back to this when they're not willing to
engage in the social spending that would allow for it. The '50s family style
received far more resources from the government than modern welfare
provides, only we didn't call it welfare. If you're in the middle class it's called
entitlement: if you're poor, it's called welfare.

So what about the pioneer, the mythical pioneer family?   31

That's another favorite myth, and I have a personal connection to it, be-   32
cause my grandfather was a logger and I was raised on it. But we were all
raised on it, with the *Little House on the Prairie* books and the TV shows.

The myth is that you have the lone pioneer—either the man who went   33
out West on his own and then called for his family, or who met the local
schoolteacher and married her—or the family as a whole, like in *Little House
on the Prairie,* who went out into the wilderness, carved themselves out their
little utopia, and held off the Indians and the bears single-handedly. Just
building their little empire and raising their kids and going it alone—too
proud to ask for handouts.

The truth is astonishing, actually. The '50s family and the pioneer family   34
are in a neck-and-neck race for the honor of who received the most subsidization from the federal government. And the poor much-maligned welfare families of today are just left in the dust. First of all, the pioneer family didn't get
out there alone. After all, the West was already an inhabited society, and it required a massive army effort supported by the federal government to destroy
the Indian societies and to take half of Mexico. That wasn't done by a few individual volunteers.

The first industries and transportation out West were also supported by   35
the federal government. The railways and the big logging companies were the
result of federal giveaways. The railroad companies were given free sections of
heavily wooded land ten miles on either side of the railroad. They didn't
know what to do with the land, so they'd sell it off to friends and those

people would log it and eventually make millions of dollars. So fortunes like the Weyerhausers' were originally based on federal giveaways to the railroad companies. It wasn't bootstrap enterprise.

The same is true for the little family that would move out West. Sure, a   36
few families did move and go it alone. Most often, however, they moved into already existing communities, and they could not have survived without the help of their neighbors. The evidence is absolutely clear that despite the ideology of individualism in the West, people were extremely cooperative, relying tremendously on the sharing of animals, of tools, and of resources and labor. But even such cooperation still required the backdrop of federal investment—right up until the twentieth century, when the further opening up of the West to farming was accompanied by the electrification campaign and the irrigation campaign, all of which were subsidized by the federal government. The West is still, mile for mile and person for person, more heavily subsidized by the federal government than the East. So this flies in the face of all of our myths.

And you say in your book that the Little House on the Prairie *books are a*   37
myth in themselves.

That's right. The story is that Laura Ingalls Wilder's daughter Rose Wilder   38
Lane was a freelance journalist in the 1930s who was so rabidly anti–New Deal that she decided to quit writing in order to avoid paying taxes to the government. She went back home and tried to make it living with her mother on the prairie. She edited her mother's books and turned them into mass-market items. The historians who've studied Rose's past, Linda Kerber for instance, can show that she edited those books with a very particular kind of ideological stance—to get rid of the instances of cooperation and to create the myth of the isolated family that stood on its own two feet and either made it or failed to make it all on its own merits.

So not only is this myth historically untrue, there's actual evidence that   39
the myth itself was consciously created in part by one of the early opponents of welfare.

So how does this myth affect us in our families today?   40

Well, it plays itself out in a number of ways. First of all, the idea that fam-   41
ilies can and should make it alone stands in the way of our realistically assessing what kind of support families need and how they can go about getting it. It lets us forget the fact that the family is a very small social institution that goes through ups and downs economically. Never in history has the family been able to go it alone. There has never been a natural family economy in which families have been able to take care of all of their needs—taken care of elders and fully provided for children. Families have always needed help from outside the family unit. Sometimes that help has been inadequate, but there's always been that help. This myth of self-sufficiency, then, prevents us from giving that help when it's needed. And when we do give help, or when we're forced into giving help, we do it begrudgingly and we do it in a moralizing way—as evidenced by our current welfare system. We say, "You are a bad family, you're not being right, because you need that."

And then you see things happen, like farmers in the Midwest committing suicide   42
several years ago when business turned bad and they started losing their farms to the
bank. It wasn't their fault that they were losing—they couldn't control the weather or
the prices—but they took it very personally, as if they were somehow morally bad.

That's a good example of the bad effects of this myth on the personal   43
level. Interestingly, this myth is more widespread in America than anywhere
else in the world. I once read a comparative study, done by psychologists, of
Europe and America in the Great Depression. They found that Europeans
were far more likely to understand their unemployment as a consequence of
some breakdown in the economic system or political system than were Americans, who were far more likely to experience it as a failure of gender roles—as
a male weakness. And the result, of course, is that we turn inward. The men
commit suicide, as in the case of the farming crisis, or they feel depressed.
The women blame them and nag them, saying: "What kind of a man are you
that you can't support your family?" So, on a personal level, this myth is extremely destructive, because it leads people to overemphasize their responsibility for things and then to experience ill fortune as a personal failure, or as
personal betrayal.

The self-sufficiency myth has a psychological component as well. It tells   44
us that the family should be everything to each other psychologically, that
you should be able to get everything you need from your family. And I think
that has a lot to do with the tensions that we find in families. Most societies
in history have not been so unrealistic. They know that sometimes a mom
and a child don't get along together, and that in fact it is so common that
you've got to allow for it. Among the Cheyenne, for example, a girl is expected to have strained, even hostile, relations with her mother and to go to
her aunt for comfort and guidance. You've got to have institutions that allow
for this very frequent misfit between a mother's personality or a father's personality and a child, to find another outlet, instead of the way we do it,
which is to say, By God, you make it work, and if you don't make it work it's
going to destroy your life, because we give you no other options.

There seems to be a belief in our culture now that if there's a child who's in dis-   45
tress, something's wrong with the mother.

That's right. In every way, we load too much on the family. If we see a   46
child in distress, we blame the parents, and as you say, particularly the
mother—mothers get bashed all the time on this, and parents blame themselves as well. So we overload the family emotionally, we overload it economically. We say, if you had a good father and mother, you should be able to be
self-sufficient. And then the logical corollary of that is this nonsense we're
hearing about how the majority of poverty in America is caused by single-parent families. After Quayle's talk and the L.A. riots, I heard a nationally known
economist come on the radio and say that if we could just convince Americans not to have children until they are married and have jobs, then we
would solve all of America's poverty problems. And I thought, Tell that to the
74,000 GM workers who were married and had jobs and just got laid off.
Family structure has nothing to do with the poverty they're facing.

The majority of increase in poverty in the '80s and '90s has been among   47
two-parent families. The poverty rate of young married couples with children
more than doubled between 1973 and 1990. Yes, it's true that poverty tends to
be tougher and longer lasting in single-parent families—partly because of discriminatory wages paid to women—but we have to remember that a lot of
one-parent families (though not all, of course) are one-parent families *because*
of economic trouble. A 1991 census study found that in more than half the
cases where a family falls into poverty (and is coded by the economists as having fallen into poverty because the father left), the family was already in economic stress *before* the father left, usually because the father had just lost his
job. And then, because the father buys into, often, the male breadwinner routine, he is so distressed by the poverty that it actually breaks up the family life.

So I just find this outrageous. The myth of the self-sufficient family puts   48
impossible burdens and guilt on both parents and children. And on a social
level, it lets the politicians off the hook so they can say, "It's not a problem
with our economy, it's not a problem of us tripling the national debt in ten
years, it's a problem of you people not keeping your families together."

One of the arguments being made is that the traditional family, with the stay-   49
at-home mom, is the best place to raise healthy children. And there have been stud-
ies done on maternal/infant bonding and the importance of the relationship to the
mother, and so on.

This is one of those things that has a kernel of truth in it that has been   50
terribly distorted. It is certainly true that babies need continuous, loving, predictable adult guidance around them for the first eighteen months of life, but
it doesn't always have to be the natural parent. There are many societies in
which there are large extended families where the child gets passed around
from one to another and doesn't find any trauma involved in that at all.

There are plenty of studies done that suggest that a variety of caregivers, if   51
they're consistent, and a variety of exposure to many adults, is extremely
healthy for children. And that, in fact, a better predictor of long-term adjustment is how well a child is able to bond with a secondary caregiver, not just
with the mother. If the child has been locked into an overly intense relationship with the mother, it turns out not to be good for their development.

Other cultures have a far more fluid notion of family. In Hawaii, for ex-   52
ample, they have an adoption system called *hanai.* Children are so important
and so valued in traditional Hawaiian culture that if you don't have a child
it's considered kind of a tragedy, and people are eager to give you theirs. I
found that some of my best students had been raised by hanai moms.

They simply give up their children?   53

Yes. Of course they don't lose contact, and the hanai relationship usually   54
links extended kin and neighbors even more tightly, despite the physical separation—at least as traditionally practiced. And so in most traditional Hawaiian communities, there is still a very strong sense of these blurred family
boundaries where you "hanai" a child to someone else, or you may ask for a
child. And if you were my sister and didn't have a child, I might say, oh, take
one of mine and raise it as the hanai mom.

I think we have this idea that there's nothing more tragic than to take the child 55
away from its parents or to take the child away from its siblings.

That's because we have, if you think about it, a tragically limited sense of 56
love and obligation in our society, and the only way we can imagine giving
love is within the private nuclear family unit. If you think about it, only the
lower animals behave that way. Not the higher animals. There's never a one-
parent family among whales, for example—not because father and mother
are always both there, but because there's always another adult sharing the
parenting, what they call the nurse. Chimpanzees, our closest relatives,
ravens, most intelligent of the birds, all have this sharing beyond the family.
It's only ants and bees and slime molds that operate on the instinct of genetic
relatedness. So, who do we want to be like?

Well, if you put it that way . . . definitely the slime molds. [Laughs.] But I was 57
struck by what you said in your book, that if we place all the importance of parent-
ing on the parents alone, you're only one divorce, one death, away from total chaos.

Yes, this notion that love is something that just has to flow along biologi- 58
cal lines, that blood is thicker than water, is really frightening. And it's tragic
to see people who think that they are teaching their family a moral outlook
on life by simply emphasizing what you owe to your brother or your sister or
your father—what a truncated sense of social responsibility and morality
these kids are growing up with. It's the idea that hey, if I give a toy to my
child, I've made the children of the world happy. And what a deformed idea
of social reciprocity that is. So I would think that it's important to take a more
blurred notion of family.

What I hear from so many people is, If I can't do anything else in the world, if 59
at least I can raise one healthy child then I've done something.

Right. People really mean this, and it comes, I think, from very good in- 60
tentions. But you can't raise a healthy child by focusing all your energies on
raising a healthy child, because what are you teaching that child? You're
teaching that child that he or she is the center of the universe and that it is
sufficient morality to just pick one person to be responsible to.

You would do a lot better for that child by taking him with you a couple 61
of days a week to a soup kitchen and saying, "I'm sorry, you're going to have
to eat this food tonight instead of your favorite dish I make at home. It's not
the best food money can buy. It's what other people have to eat and you can
help cook it and serve it." We need to teach people to be able to exist in communities even if you're not siblings or lovers, and you can't raise a healthy
child if the only message that child is getting from you, is, Ah, I'm getting
this because I'm part of this person's bloodline.

I think this emphasis on just raising your own kid well comes from the 62
social realities of our times. There's just a sense of defeat in so many areas of
life—politics, the economy, the environment. And the result is that instead of
having the social confidence to look outward and make connections with
others, people begin to say, Well, let's retreat, let's carve ourselves out a little
oasis from which we can watch the rest of our social world turn into a desert.
And we want to protect our children from the pain of what's going on in the

world. But I don't think that's healthy. I think it's far healthier to talk to them about what's going on—to say, Our economy is falling apart, the United States is now fifty-first in the world in terms of what it's doing for infrastructure, we waste a third of the nation's fresh water every day in leaky pipes, we're destroying our environment. This is a problem. It's not a problem that our love as parent and child—important and intense as this may be—is going to solve. We're going to have to go beyond our family, link up with other people, and work for social change. That outward focus is what not only solidifies the child's ability to participate in the community, it actually is the best recipe for a healthy family.

Whenever you say the word family, *the picture that still comes to mind for me is mother, father, two kids. And you're a single mother. What do you advocate for a single parent? I mean, for a lot of the single parents I know, the issue of isolation is so major in their lives.*   63

Yes. Single-parent families do face special problems in America. A lot of the problems they face, however, are precisely because we have clung too much to tradition rather than changing to adjust to modern realities. Our society is still organized around the belief that families don't need any outside help because they're all headed by couples. So you have someone who can stay home to wait for something to be delivered, or somebody who's going to be free during the day to go and do a school conference, or whatever. This assumption that there will be two parents there makes it impossible for a one-parent family to measure up, and then we blame the one-parent family for not living up to it. It's a wonderful double bind.   64

And, of course, another large part of the problem is our false stereotypes and perceptions about single-parent families. A number of studies have been done where they show a videotape of a child to teachers—who should know better—and in one instance they'll give the case history of this child as being from a two-parent family, and another instance as being from a one-parent family. Consistently the teachers rate the child more negatively on a whole scale of behaviors when they think he comes from a one-parent family. It becomes a self-fulfilling prophecy.   65

I encounter this myself from time to time. My son tests in the ninety-seventh percentile of everything and is inordinately proud—too proud—of the fact that he never got his name on the board [for bad behavior] once in his entire elementary school history. At the end of one year, when I went in to say good-bye to his teacher, she said to me, "I just want you to know that your child is the most together boy"—and I started to smile, and there was this pause that gave me time to get my smile very broad—"of a one-parent family that I have ever met." And my smile just kind of froze. I would like to know why that modifier was there. He was the top student in the class. He was the most well-behaved in the class. He was very popular. Why was that modifier there, you know? And imagine the poor kids whose single parents are not professors and aren't friends with the principal the way I was, and don't have all the things going for them that allowed her to see my child as the most together child—of a single-parent family—she'd ever met.   66

There were earlier studies done where all they had to do was tell a teacher that 67
certain children in the class were problems and others were good students and, in-
evitably, the teacher would behave unconsciously in such a way that the "problem"
kids would do much worse than the others.

Right. And now all you have to do is say this is a single-parent child. 68

So many problems are caused by assumptions like this. Let me tell you a 69
personal anecdote: When I was in my Lamaze class, I was the only single
mother in it, and when I had my baby, a lot of people from the class called.
And they would come over and bring me food. My students frequently came
over and spent the night to help me out, because I'd had a C section. Every
time one of my fellow Lamaze people had a baby, I'd call, and maybe two
weeks later I'd bring them dinner. And every time, the woman practically
wept and said, Oh, it's just so nice to not have to make dinner. And I thought,
Well, where is your husband? Well, the husband was working, so it was hard
for him to make dinner. And all of their friends assumed that because they
were a couple, they wouldn't need any help. Here was an instance where I was
actually better off because I was single, and so people assumed I would need
some help. If you have social networks that recognize you need help, whether
you're a two-parent or a one-parent family you're going to be a lot better off.

Most societies in human history have felt that parenting is far too large a 70
job to even be entrusted to two people—no less one—and so they have lots of
wider networks.

You make quite a case in your book about day care not being harmful to kids, 71
and yet there's that feeling—well, you know, you have a baby and six weeks later
you shuffle him or her off to day care—that it may not be in the kid's best interest.
Do you know what I mean?

Absolutely. Even though you can mobilize a lot of statistics to show that 72
day care doesn't necessarily hurt and in some cases can be very beneficial, we
all know anecdotally of cases where kids simply aren't getting enough time or
attention from their parents or from anybody else. That's absolutely true.
I don't think, though, that the problem is day care. I know plenty of instances in history when children were not with their families for huge periods
of the day—much longer than today—when children still were getting a lot
of time and attention from adults, including but not necessarily limited to
their parents.

So I don't see the problem as one of day care. I do see a problem with our 73
general priorities of how we spend time in our society. This is not a kid-
friendly culture; it's not a society in which we sit around and, as I learned to
do in Hawaii over the last six months, "talk story," and involve the kids in
talking story. We have a tremendous gap between adult recreation and children's recreation, unless of course it's television, which is no recreation at all
and no interaction at all. And then we have this tremendous lack of distinction between what adults and children watch, and I'm as horrified as any
right-winger by the sorts of things that are on television. I'm embarrassed to
sit around with my son and see the kinds of distortions that he gets about
what sex is all about on television. I think it's terrible.

A large part of the problem is not with parents working but with what   74
people do *after* they work. When I was little, my mom worked for some of
those years, but when my parents socialized they took me with them. We all
went to the same place to socialize, and all the kids were put together in the
same bed and went to sleep in the same bed and it was a wonderful environment. It wasn't one-on-one parental time, and that's probably good. It wasn't
vested with so much energy—Oh, I've been away all day, now I've got to relate to this child. If you have a life that is child oriented—and I don't mean
child centered, but is oriented toward building a community of kids and
adults that the kids can interact with—I think that's the key to a healthy development.

So speaking to people who are really trying to make changes but are stuck in   75
these myths: Where can we go from here?

There are two levels that we have to work on. The first one is to get past   76
our American discomfort with history and really look at the truth behind the
myths, so that we can erase all of those old tapes about what a family should
be. When we do that, we will eventually end up letting ourselves off the hook
a little. That doesn't mean that we will not keep the good aspects of the consciousness raising that's gone on in the last twenty years. We should remember what we've learned, that the family is a social system that's very critical in
people's lives, and we should do our best to make it function in a more loving
and fair way. But we should be very cautious of falling into the trap of thinking that that's anything more than a baseline, a precondition for making
things better—both in our own families and for other families.

So the next step is to understand that the family does not exist, cannot   77
exist, isolated from other social institutions. There is no way I can build a
utopia in my family and allow the rest of the world to go to hell, because the
rest of the world is going to affect my family relations. So I need to worry
about more than my own family, but at home I can let myself off the hook a
little. I'll do my best, and if sometimes I don't do great as a parent, I'm going
to say, No sweat, that's OK. What I really need to do is connect my family to
larger social networks, movements, ideas, and institutions that can supplement me when I do well and compensate for me when I do badly as a parent.
Because you can't be everything to everyone.

Can you give me an example of how you'd do that?   78

Well, it can take place on many different levels. It can take place in com-   79
munities that are able to build neighborhood associations and social support
systems. But I think even more than that, given the severity of the crisis of
obligation in twentieth-century America, we have to take part in forging the
social networks that are not now here, or that have been destroyed over the
last thirty years, and in building a more participatory economy and policy.

Some of these problems do have to be solved at the larger level. That   80
sounds overwhelming to people, but what I would say is that (a) we have evidence that small starts can have big impact, we have concrete evidence of
small ways that you can get involved that will have larger implications; and
(b) even if you don't accomplish everything you shoot for, the process of

shooting for it is going to create much healthier families than staying home and trying to pretend that you can close out the rest of the world. The process of taking your child to be involved in a political action, in an environmental cleanup, in a demonstration, in a rally, in a lobbying effort, will teach your child so much more about social responsibility and love and obligation than just sitting at home and reading to him, important though that may be. I think it's worth it. I think your reach should exceed your grasp. That's the healthiest thing for a family.

Questions

1. What is the myth of the ideal family? Why does Coontz feel that this myth is ultimately dysfunctional? Do you agree with Coontz's views?

2. What types of families are represented on television? Why are the representations of these families unrealistic? Why do these idealized representations cause guilt in the viewer?

3. Contemporary politicians have blamed poverty, crime, and drug abuse on the collapse of the traditional family. Why would Coontz disagree with this assessment?

4. Summarize Coontz's main points.

Family Values

RICHARD RODRIGUEZ

Of Mexican-American heritage, Richard Rodriguez was born in San Francisco in 1944. He graduated from Stanford University in 1967, received a master's degree from Columbia University in 1969, and continued his graduate study at the University of California, Berkeley. Rodriguez is now a full-time writer and is particularly known for Hunger of Memory *(1982) and* Days of Obligation: An Argument with My Mexican Father *(1992).*

In this article, Rodriguez questions whether Americans have ever truly valued the family. He argues that despite the recent emphasis on family values the tendency in America has been to break away from the family. This reading is from the Los Angeles Times *(1992).*

I am sitting alone in my car, in front of my parents' house—a middle-aged 1 man with a boy's secret to tell. What words will I use to tell them? I hate the word *gay,* find its little affirming sparkle more pathetic than assertive. I am happier with the less polite *queer.* But to my parents I would say *homosexual,* avoiding the Mexican slang *joto* (I had always heard it said in our house with hints of condescension), though *joto* is less mocking than the sissy-boy *maricon.*

The buzz on everyone's lips now: Family values. The other night on TV, 2 the vice president of the United States, his arm around his wife, smiled into the camera and described homosexuality as "mostly a choice." But how would he know? Homosexuality never felt like a choice to me.

A few minutes ago Rush Limbaugh, the radio guy with a voice that re- 3 minds me, for some reason, of a butcher's arms, was banging his console and booming a near-reasonable polemic about family values. Limbaugh was not very clear about which values exactly he considers to be family values. A divorced man who lives alone in New York?

My parents live on a gray, treeless street in San Francisco not far from the 4 ocean. Probably more than half of the neighborhood is immigrant. India lives next door to Greece, who lives next door to Russia. I wonder what the Chinese lady next door to my parents makes of the politicians' phrase *family values.*

What immigrants know, what my parents certainly know, is that when 5 you come to this country, you risk losing your children. The assurance of family—continuity, inevitability—is precisely what America encourages its children to overturn. *Become your own man.* We who are native to this country

566

know this too, of course, though we are likely to deny it. Only a society so guilty about its betrayal of family would tolerate the pieties of politicians regarding family values.

On the same summer day that Republicans were swarming in Houston 6 (buzzing about family values), a friend of mine who escaped family values awhile back and who now wears earrings resembling intrauterine devices, was complaining to me over coffee about the Chinese. The Chinese will never take over San Francisco, my friend said, because the Chinese do not want to take over San Francisco. The Chinese do not even *see* San Francisco! All they care about is their damn families. All they care about is double-parking smack in front of the restaurant on Clement Street and pulling granny out of the car—and damn anyone who happens to be in the car behind them or the next or the next.

Politicians would be horrified by such an American opinion, of course. But 7 then, what do politicians, Republicans or Democrats, really know of our family life? Or what are they willing to admit? Even in that area where they could reasonably be expected to have something to say—regarding the relationship of family life to our economic system—the politicians say nothing. Republicans celebrate American economic freedom, but Republicans don't seem to connect that economic freedom to the social breakdown they find appalling. Democrats, on the other hand, if more tolerant of the drift from familial tradition, are suspicious of the very capitalism that creates social freedom.

How you become free in America: Consider the immigrant. He gets a job. 8 Soon he is earning more money than his father ever made (his father's authority is thereby subtly undermined). The immigrant begins living a life his father never knew. The immigrant moves from one job to another, changes houses. His economic choices determine his home address—not the other way around. The immigrant is on his way to becoming his own man.

When I was broke a few years ago and trying to finish a book, I lived with 9 my parents. What a thing to do! A major theme of America is leaving home. We trust the child who forsakes family connections to make it on his own. We call that the making of a man.

Let's talk about this man stuff for a minute. America's ethos is anti-domestic. We may be intrigued by blood that runs through wealth—the Kennedys or the Rockefellers—but they seem European to us. Which is to say, they are movies. They are Corleones. Our real pledge of allegiance: We say in America that nothing about your family—your class, your race, your pedigree—should be as important as what you yourself achieve. We end up in 1992 introducing ourselves by first names.

What authority can Papa have in a country that formed its identity in an 11 act of Oedipal rebellion against a mad British king? Papa is a joke in America, a stock sitcom figure—Archie Bunker or Homer Simpson. But my Mexican father went to work every morning, and he stood in a white smock, making false teeth, oblivious of the shelves of grinning false teeth mocking his devotion.

The nuns in grammar school—my wonderful Irish nuns—used to push 12 Mark Twain on me. I distrusted Huck Finn, he seemed like a gringo kid I would steer clear of in the schoolyard. (He was too confident.) I realize now, of course, that Huck is the closest we have to a national hero. We trust the story of a boy who has no home and is restless for the river. (Huck's Pap is drunk.) Americans are more forgiving of Huck's wildness than of the sweetness of the Chinese boy who walks to school with his mama or grandma. (There is no worse thing in America than to be a mama's boy, nothing better than to be a real boy—all boy—like Huck, who eludes Aunt Sally, and is eager for the world of men.)

There's a bent old woman coming up the street. She glances nervously   13
as she passes my car. What would you tell us, old lady, of family values in America?

America is an immigrant country, we say. Motherhood—parenthood—is   14
less our point than adoption. If I had to assign gender to America, I would note the consensus of the rest of the world. When America is burned in effigy, a male is burned. Americans themselves speak of Uncle Sam.

Like the Goddess of Liberty, Uncle Sam has no children of his own. He   15
steals children to make men of them, mocks all reticence, all modesty, all memory. Uncle Sam is a hectoring Yankee, a skinflint uncle, gaunt, uncouth, unloved. He is the American Savonarola—hater of moonshine, destroyer of stills, burner of cocaine. Sam has no patience with mamas' boys.

You betray Uncle Sam by favoring private over public life, by seeking to   16
exempt yourself, by cheating on your income taxes, by avoiding jury duty, by trying to keep your boy on the farm.

Mothers are traditionally the guardians of the family—against America—   17
though even Mom may side with America against queers and deserters, at least when the Old Man is around. Premature gray hair. Arthritis in her shoulders. Bowlegged with time, red hands. In their fiercely flowered housedresses, mothers are always smarter than fathers in America. But in reality they are betrayed by their children who leave. In a thousand ways. They end up alone.

We kind of like the daughter who was a tomboy. Remember her? It was al-   18
ways easier to be a tomboy in America than a sissy. Americans admired Annie Oakley more than they admired Liberace (who, nevertheless, always remembered his mother). But today we do not admire Annie Oakley when we see Mom becoming Annie Oakley.

The American household now needs two incomes, everyone says. Mean-   19
ing: Mom is *forced* to leave home out of economic necessity. But lots of us know lots of moms who are sick and tired of being mom, or only mom. It's like the nuns getting fed up, teaching kids for all those years and having those kids grow up telling stories of how awful Catholic school was! Not every woman in America wants her life's work to be forgiveness. Today there are moms who don't want their husbands' names. And the most disturbing possibility: What happens when Mom doesn't want to be Mom at all? Refuses pregnancy?

Mom is only becoming an American like the rest of us. Certainly, people   20
all over the world are going to describe the influence of feminism on women (all over the world) as their "Americanization." And rightly so.

Nothing of this, of course, will the politician's wife tell you. The politi- 21
cian's wife is careful to follow her husband's sentimental reassurances that
nothing has changed about America except perhaps for the sinister influence
of deviants. Like myself.

I contain within myself an anomaly at least as interesting as the Republi- 22
can Party's version of family values. I am a homosexual Catholic, a communi-
cant in a tradition that rejects even as it upholds me.

I do not count myself among those Christians who proclaim themselves 23
protectors of family values. They regard me as no less an enemy of the family
than the "radical feminists." But the joke about families that all homosexuals
know is that we are the ones who stick around and make families possible.
Call on us. I can think of 20 or 30 examples. A gay son or daughter is the only
one who is "free" (married brothers and sisters are too busy). And, indeed, because we have admitted the inadmissible about ourselves (that we are
queer)—we are adepts at imagination—we can even imagine those who refuse
to imagine us. We can imagine Mom's loneliness, for example. If Mom needs
to be taken to church or to the doctor or ferried between Christmas dinners,
depend on the gay son or lesbian daughter.

I won't deny that the so-called gay liberation movement, along with fem- 24
inism, undermined the heterosexual household, if that's what politicians
mean when they say family values. Against churchly reminders that sex was
for procreation, the gay bar as much as the birth-control pill taught Americans not to fear sexual pleasure. In the past two decades—and, not coincidentally, parallel to the feminist movement—the gay liberation movement
moved a generation of Americans toward the idea of a childless adulthood. If
the women's movement was ultimately more concerned about getting out of
the house and into the workplace, the gay movement was in its way more
subversive to Puritan America because it stressed the importance of play.

Several months ago, the society editor of the morning paper in San Fran- 25
cisco suggested (on a list of "must haves") that every society dame must have
at least one gay male friend. A ballet companion. A lunch date. The remark
was glib and incorrect enough to beg complaints from homosexual readers,
but there was a truth about it as well. Homosexual men have provided
women with an alternate model of masculinity. And the truth: The Old Man,
God bless him, is a bore. Thus are we seen as preserving marriages? Even Republican marriages?

For myself, homosexuality is a deep brotherhood but does not involve 26
domestic life. Which is why, my married sisters will tell you, I can afford the
time to be a writer. And why are so many homosexuals such wonderful
teachers and priests and favorite aunts, if not because we are freed from the
house? On the other hand, I know lots of homosexual couples (male and female) who model their lives on the traditional heterosexual version of domesticity and marriage. Republican politicians mock the notion of a
homosexual marriage, but ironically such marriages honor the heterosexual
marriage by imitating it.

"The only loving couples I know," a friend of mine recently remarked,   27
"are all gay couples."

This woman was not saying that she does not love her children or that   28
she is planning a divorce. But she was saying something about the sadness of
American domestic life: the fact that there is so little joy in family intimacy.
Which is perhaps why gossip (public intrusion into the private) has become a
national industry. All day long, in forlorn houses, the television lights up a
freakish parade of husbands and mothers-in-law and children upon the stage
of Sally or Oprah or Phil. They tell on each other. The audience ooohhhs.
Then a psychiatrist-shaman appears at the end to dispense prescriptions—the
importance of family members granting one another more "space."

The question I desperately need to ask you is whether we Americans have   29
ever truly valued the family. We are famous, or our immigrant ancestors were
famous, for the willingness to leave home. And it is ironic that a crusade under the banner of family values has been taken up by those who would otherwise pass themselves off as patriots. For they seem not to understand
America, nor do I think they love the freedoms America grants. Do they understand why, in a country that prizes individuality and is suspicious of authority, children are disinclined to submit to their parents? You cannot
celebrate American values in the public realm without expecting them to
touch our private lives. As Barbara Bush remarked recently, family values are
also neighborhood values. It may be harmless enough for Barbara Bush to recall a sweeter America—Midland, Texas, in the 1950s. But the question left
begging is why we chose to leave Midland, Texas. Americans like to say that
we can't go home again. The truth is that we don't want to go home again,
don't want to be known, recognized. Don't want to respond in the same old
ways. (And you know you will if you go back there.)

Little 10-year-old girls know that there are reasons for getting away from   30
the family. They learn to keep their secrets—under lock and key—addressed
to Dear Diary. Growing up queer, you learn to keep secrets as well. In no place
are those secrets more firmly held than within the family house. You learn to
live in closets. I know a Chinese man who arrived in America about 10 years
ago. He got a job and made some money. And during that time he came to
confront his homosexuality. And then his family arrived. I do not yet know
the end of this story.

The genius of America is that it permits children to leave home, it permits   31
us to become different from our parents. But the sadness, the loneliness of
America, is clear too.

Listen to the way Americans talk about immigrants. If, on the one hand,   32
there is impatience when today's immigrants do not seem to give up their
family, there is also a fascination with this reluctance. In Los Angeles, Hispanics are considered people of family. Hispanic women are hired to be at the
center of the American family—to baby-sit and diaper, to cook and to clean
and to ease the dying. Hispanic attachment to family is seen by many Americans, I think, as the reason why Hispanics don't get ahead. But if Asians privately annoy us for being so family oriented, they are also stereotypically

celebrated as the new "whiz kids" in school. Don't Asians go to college, after all, to honor their parents?

More important still is the technological and economic ascendancy of Asia, particularly Japan, on the American imagination. Americans are starting to wonder whether perhaps the family values of Asia put the United States at a disadvantage. The old platitude had it that ours is a vibrant, robust society for being a society of individuals. Now we look to Asia and see team effort paying off.

In this time of national homesickness, of nostalgia, for how we imagine America used to be, there are obvious dangers. We are going to start blaming each other for the loss. Since we are inclined, as Americans, to think of ourselves individually, we are disinclined to think of ourselves as creating one another or influencing one another.

But it is not the politician or any political debate about family values that has brought me here on a gray morning to my parents' house. It is some payment I owe to my youth and to my parents' youth. I imagine us sitting in the living room, amid my mother's sentimental doilies and the family photographs, trying to take the measure of the people we have turned out to be in America.

A San Francisco poet, when he was in the hospital and dying, called a priest to his bedside. The old poet wanted to make his peace with Mother Church. He wanted baptism. The priest asked why. "Because the Catholic Church has to accept me," said the poet. "Because I am a sinner."

Isn't willy-nilly inclusiveness the point, the only possible point to be derived from the concept of family? Curiously, both President Bush and Vice President Quayle got in trouble with their constituents recently for expressing a real family value. Both men said that they would try to dissuade a daughter or granddaughter from having an abortion. But, finally, they said they would support her decision, continue to love her, never abandon her.

There are families that do not accept. There are children who are forced to leave home because of abortions or homosexuality. There are family secrets that Papa never hears. Which is to say there are families that never learn the point of families.

But there she is at the window. My mother has seen me and she waves me in. Her face asks: Why am I sitting outside? (Have they, after all, known my secret for years and kept it, out of embarrassment, not knowing what to say?) Families accept, often by silence. My father opens the door to welcome me in.

Questions

1. Both Coontz and Rodriguez refer to traditional family values. How would you define traditional family values?

2. Compare Coontz's and Rodriguez's perceptions of the American family. How are they the same? How are they different?

3. How does Rodriguez's perception of the American family compare to your own? How much independence from family were you encouraged to develop?

The State of the American Family

ARLENE SKOLNICK

Arlene Skolnick (b. 1933) is a research psychiatrist at the Institute of Human Development at the University of California, Berkeley. She is the author of The Intimate Environment: Exploring Marriage and Family *(1987).*

In this selection, she argues that the family has not declined but has changed because of economic and demographic factors. She points out that to blame our social ills on the lack of family values places an unfair burden on individual responsibility, when the explanations for such problems as poverty, drug abuse, and declining academic achievement are largely due to the widening gap in our economic structure. Skolnick is a member of the Berkeley Women's Research group that helped launch some of the ideas in the book Embattled Paradise: The American Family in an Age of Uncertainty *(1991), from which this selection was taken.*

The American family does not exist. Rather, we are creating many American families, of diverse styles and shapes. . . . We have fathers working while mothers keep house; fathers and mothers both working away from home; single parents; second marriages bringing together people from unrelated backgrounds; childless couples; unmarried couples, with and without children; gay and lesbian parents. We are living through a period of historic change in American family life.

"THE 21ST CENTURY FAMILY"
NEWSWEEK (1990)

The feminist revolution of this century has provided the most powerful challenge to traditional patterns of marriage. Yet paradoxically, it may also have strengthened the institution by giving greater freedom to both partners, and by allowing men to accept some of the traditionally female values.

HELGE RUBENSTEIN
THE OXFORD BOOK OF MARRIAGE

572

The debate about whether the family in America is falling apart, here to stay,   1
or better than ever has continued unabated since the 1970s, like an endless
cocktail party conversation. There is of course no way of resolving the issue.
"Most of us," observes Joseph Featherstone, "debate these matters from our
general instinct of where history is tending, from our own lives and those of
our friends. . . . One of the difficult things about the family as a topic is that
everyone in the discussion feels obliged to defend a particular set of choices."

While the argument shows no signs of reaching a resolution, some of the   2
debaters have wandered away. Others have switched sides. Most of the radical
voices who celebrated the death of the family have disappeared. Those who
denounced the family as an oppressive institution and lamented its persistence have also passed from the scene, although continuing critical attacks
have granted them a kind of immortality. Meanwhile, the ranks of the optimists who think the family is alive and well have thinned considerably. Recently, one family researcher did publish a book entitled *The Myth of Family
Decline,* but generally there is less talk of family decline and decay in the media and more of it among social scientists.

There is no doubt that the family transformations of recent times have   3
left a great deal of disruption in their wake. But those who lament "the decline of the family" lump together an array of serious problems, as well as
changes that are not necessarily problems at all: divorce, the sexual revolution, working mothers, the rising age of marriage, teenage pregnancy, abortion, childhood poverty, child abuse, domestic violence, the economic effects
of no-fault divorce for women and children, the failure of many divorced fathers to pay child support and maintain contact with their children, an increase in the percentage of people living alone, young people "postponing"
adulthood and refusing to leave home, latchkey children, the "dysfunctional
family," drug use in the ghettos and suburbs, problems of minority families.

Wrapping these issues in one big package labeled "decline of the family"   4
muddles rather than clarifies our understanding of family change. Some of
these problems arise out of the old plague of poverty, which has grown worse
over the past decade; others are by-products of an American economy afflicted by recession, inflation, and industrial decline and dislocation.

Still other difficulties are a result of the mismatch between the new reali-   5
ties of family life and social arrangements based on earlier family patterns.
For example, the problem of "latchkey children" could be remedied if we had
the will to do so—through afterschool programs, or a lengthening of the
school day, or flexible work schedules for parents. And at least some of the
painful consequences of divorce are products of the legal policies and practices governing the dissolution of marriage. No-fault divorce is a classic case
of unintended consequences: what looked like reform of an unfair, degrading
way of dealing with marital breakdown turned into an economic disaster for
older homemakers and mothers with young children. Yet here, too, the worst
features of the system can be remedied—for example, by postponing the sale
of the family home until children are grown.

Moralistic cries about declining families and eroding values hinder public   6
discussion about the kinds of modifications that can be made in other social
institutions to alleviate current strains in family life. Framing the issue in
terms of "the declining family" also leads to an overemphasis on personal and
moral failings as the source of family and social problems, and draws attention away from the social sources of family change that have been discussed
throughout this book: the economic and demographic factors that have
drawn women into the workplace, the life-course revolutions that have reshaped families as well as the processes of growing up and growing old, and so
on. The popularity of recent critiques of individualism reflects a strong American tradition of blaming serious social problems on individual moral character rather than on institutions and economic structures. For example, there
was a tendency in the early 1930s—given voice by F. Scott Fitzgerald—to
blame the Great Depression on the hedonism and immorality of the jazz age.

Without an economic catastrophe or government takeover by religious   7
extremists, as in *The Handmaid's Tale,* women are not going to return to full-
time domesticity, and unhappy couples will seek to remedy their unhappiness through divorce. Most people no longer feel there is a conflict between
the family and the feminist search for equality. We need less hand wringing
and more social ingenuity to help the families we do have work better. As E. J.
Dionne has recently suggested, the American public is ready for a new "center" that makes peace between the liberal values of the 1960s and the work
and family values of the 1980s.

INDIVIDUALISM VERSUS ATTACHMENT

It is not clear why social scientists have become so much more pessimistic   8
than they used to be. The deepening gloom does not correspond to marked
shifts in demographic trends. In the 1980s, for example, such vital indicators
of family life as divorce rates and birthrates, which had changed sharply in
the 1970s, leveled off. Toward the end of the 1980s, new births reached baby-
boom levels, confounding the expectations of demographers. As a 1990 review of trends in family life put it, "Predictions of childlessness and
large-scale abandonment of family life for this generation, a generation supposedly obsessed with individual fulfillment and achievement, will not be
realized."

Some family scholars may have been reacting against their overly opti-   9
mistic assessments of family change in the 1970s. Responding to alarm about
the impending "death of the family," many researchers, pointing to demographic and survey evidence of persisting commitments to family life, argued
that the family was "here to stay." Emphasizing the benefits of recent
trends—more freedom from the constraints of sex roles, greater opportunities
for women, closer and more satisfying marriages—they tended to downplay
the costs and hardships that come with changes. As if to compensate for that
optimism, in the 1980s they stressed the negative.

But family scholars in recent years also seem to have been influenced by   10
the pessimistic views of American character and culture that began to dominate intellectual discourse in the mid-1970s. The landmark work in this genre
during the 1980s was the widely acclaimed, widely discussed, best-selling
book *Habits of the Heart,* by Robert Bellah and his colleagues. Six years after
The Culture of Narcissism, this new work continued the critique of individualism that had become prominent in the 1970s.

A work of interpretive social science based on interviews with mostly   11
middle-class people in California and elsewhere, *Habits of the Heart* presents a
far gentler and more complex picture of Americans than had Lasch's blighted
portrait. Indeed, Bellah and his co-authors reported that "if there are vast
numbers of a selfish, narcissistic me-generation in America, we did not find
them." The complaint is more subtle; instead of applying a psychiatric diag-
nostic label to an entire population, the book takes issue with American individualism in its contemporary version. While observing that "individualism
lies at the very core of American culture" and that it is closely linked to "[o]ur
highest and noblest aspirations, not only for ourselves, but for those we care
about, for our society and the world," Bellah and his colleagues criticize both
"utilitarian individualism"—the pursuit of self-interest and success—and "expressive individualism"—the pursuit of happiness, the belief in each person's
"unique core of feeling and intuition." The book argues that the two kinds of
individualism have perniciously combined to form the therapeutic ethos,
which forms the model for many relationships. Yet the authors portray Americans not as asocial loners, devoid of family ties and community spirit, but
merely as lacking a moral language to justify the commitments they do have.

Speaking to widely shared anxieties about social and cultural change, the   12
book has played a surprisingly large role in the newly pessimistic discourse
about the family on the part of social scientists. It is not uncommon to find
works presenting hard statistical data on family trends that cite *Habits of the
Heart* as evidence for a corrosive new individualism that can explain the trends.

Yet, as a number of critics have pointed out, the book's analyses are varia-   13
tions on older themes in the critique of modernity, such as the decline of
community, the isolation of the self, the loss of religious certitude. Its criticism of "lifestyle enclaves"—communities of people who are socially or economically similar, as opposed to the "genuine" communities of the
past—resembles the attack on suburbia in the 1950s. Like those earlier critiques, it contrasts a romantic vision of the past with a jaundiced vision of
the present. Above all, *Habits of the Heart* represents the latest addition in an
ongoing pessimistic discourse on the self, that, along with its optimistic
counterpart, has been a persistent but largely unnoticed feature of American
cultural life.

The fact that these recent attacks on individualism strike such responsive   14
chords in the American public suggests that moral and communitarian values
are alive and well. American culture has always been marked by an ambivalent yearning for autonomy on the one hand and attachment to family and
community on the other. It is not simply that Americans are individualistic

or communitarian, but that the tension between these impulses is a central theme in American culture. Yet most writings on American character ignore this duality and the psychological and social tensions it creates. And aiming criticism at personal and moral failings not only is in keeping with American religiosity—we are the most religious of Western countries, in both belief and churchgoing—but promises that we can solve our problems through changes of heart rather than through the difficult and divisive route of political and social change. But the problems of family life are located less in the realm of personal defects and declining values and more in the difficulties of making and maintaining families in a time of sweeping social change, in a society that is neglectful of families and their needs.

The most recent extended argument for the decline of the family from a   15
family scholar has been put forth by David Popenoe. Popenoe is precise about what he means by "family decline." Since the 1960s, he argues, four major trends have signaled a "flight" from the traditional nuclear family as both ideal and reality: declining birthrates, the sexual revolution, the movement of mothers into the workplace, and the divorce revolution. Citing *Habits of the Heart,* Popenoe suggests that the trends toward expressive individualism and the therapeutic attitude have contributed to family decline. He is also precise about what he means by "traditional nuclear family": it is "focused on the procreation of children" and consists of "a legal, lifelong, sexually exclusive, heterosexual, monogamous marriage, based on affection and companionship, in which there is a sharp division of labor (separate spheres) *with the female as full-time housewife and the male as primary provider and ultimate authority*" (italics added).

Popenoe's argument illustrates that the debate over the declining family   16
is often not so much about the decline of family life as about preference for a particular pattern of family and gender arrangements. He is certainly correct in claiming that what he defines as the traditional nuclear family is no longer dominant. Yet his definition is an essentially nineteenth-century portrait of family and gender roles, today favored by conservatives and the New Right but no longer shared by a majority of Americans. Clearly, the two-worker nuclear family is becoming the new cultural norm, and, while most people describe themselves as strongly pro-family, they favor a more symmetrical version of marriage.

Traditionalists like Popenoe place too much emphasis on family structure   17
and not enough on the emotional quality of family life. Structural characteristics like divorce or maternal employment, as another researcher observes, "are weak predictors of the consequences most of us really care about: personal and family well-being, economic mobility, educational attainment, children's health."

THE OZZIE AND HARRIET DEBATE

While Popenoe mourns the decline of the traditional nuclear family as he de-   18
fines it, another family researcher has recently complained that it is more

common than generally assumed and ought to be given more recognition. David Blankenhorn argues that reports of the deaths of Ozzie and Harriet have been greatly exaggerated. This debate is a prime example of the family as a "great intellectual Rorschach blot."

Since the 1970s we have been hearing that the kind of family that domi- 19 nated the family imagery of the 1950s now constitutes only about 10 percent of American households. Conservatives, liberals, and radicals all use that figure to document the decline of the family—but it is both true and extremely misleading. For example, as we have seen, because of lengthening life spans and smaller families, the share of adult life devoted to raising children has become much smaller. Such statistics have been used to overemphasize the changes in American families, as Blankenhorn observes. In 1987, he points out, the "workadaddy-housewife family" constituted more like 33.3 percent of families with preschool children and 35 percent of all families with children under eighteen.

The 10 percent figure comes from estimating the proportion of depen- 20 dent children/breadwinner/housewife families out of all 89.5 million households in America in 1987. These households include families not yet or no longer living with children under eighteen, such as honeymooners and empty-nesters, as well as nonfamily households: people who live alone, students who room together, and the like. In the 1950s, the heyday of the Ozzie and Harriet family, this method of calculation would have shown only one-third of households to be made up of traditional families.

Blankenhorn's concern is that the 10 percent figure tells "traditional" 21 families that they are "old fashioned, outmoded, irrelevant." Although he correctly points out that statistics have often been misused to generate a sense of crisis or to score ideological points, Blankenhorn is also guilty of massaging the data to make his points. For example, he criticizes those who count as "working mothers" women who are employed part-time, claiming they categorize working mothers this way in order to "diminish the importance of stay at home mothers." His solution is to combine part-time employees with mothers who do not work at all, arguing that "well over half" of mothers of preschoolers are employed either part-time or not at all. To make the numbers of at-home and part-time-worker mothers add up to more than half, Blankenhorn adds the 7 percent of Ozzieless families—those with preschoolers headed by a single mother not in the work force.

If combining mothers who work full-time and part-time obscures the dif- 22 ferences between two different life-styles, combining part-time employment with full-time mothering obscures still more. Part-time workers have many of the same needs and face many of the same pressures and tensions as full-time workers, but to a lesser degree: finding good child care, dealing with a sick child, being pulled between the demands of work and the needs of the family. For social policy purposes, it makes good sense to consider part-time employees as working parents.

Further, what looks like an Ozzie and Harriet family in the 1980s and 23 1990s may not truly reflect the 1950s model in either ideal or reality. In the 1950s women were assumed to be housewives and mothers almost by definition, and most women did define themselves as such. Today's stay-at-home mother may still think of herself as a high-powered professional. Many career women choose to stay home while their children are small. By and large today's women consider paid work as one of their roles in life, even if they are not working at the moment.

We need to take a life-course perspective. If we define "the family" as existing only during that short time of life spent as a married couple with children under eighteen, we are ignoring the lives of the vast majority of Americans. Although virtually all people live in family households early in life and the vast majority live in family households as adults, many of us will experience significant periods of living apart. The prevailing family types are variants of the nuclear family that have been around for a long time, if not in great number. The current Ozzie and Harriet debate reveals that the meaning of statistics on family life is not straightforward. In a highly charged atmosphere, statistics can easily become ideological weapons. At best, it is often difficult to make sense of the trends.

THE STATE OF THE CHILDREN

Anxiety about the state of the family often focuses most intensely on the young. Children are not only profoundly vulnerable to any trouble in the family; they also embody the future for both their parents and the society. Thus people worry about their own children as well as other people's children. Today the vast majority of people—nearly three out of four in one survey, both parents and nonparents—believe that the quality of life for America's children has declined since their own childhood.

Yet this worry, like worries about the declining family in general, is often built on a muddled mixture of issues. With the huge increase in working mothers, divorce, and single-parent families, today's children certainly grow up in very different circumstances than did children only a few decades ago. Most have working mothers, fewer brothers and sisters, and a good chance of spending time in group care. By the time they reach adulthood, at least half of American children, according to current estimates, will spend some time living in a single-parent family. How children are faring under these circumstances is an issue with profound implications for the future of our society.

Yet many of problems afflicting children that came to public attention in the 1970s and 1980s—physical and sexual abuse, for example—had long histories. Further, a good deal of our current anxiety focuses on issues that are not directly part of family life: the state of children's health, the failings of our educational system, sex and violence in the media, drugs, unsafe schools and streets.

Alarming stories about the state of children and young people have become a media staple in recent years. We hear of "epidemics" of teen pregnancy, suicide, and drug use, and of the increasing poverty of children, the dire effects of divorce, the plight of latchkey children. We also hear of child abuse, incest, and sexual molestation. Pictures of missing children appear on milk cartons all over the country. Many of the changes in children's lives should indeed cause us concern, but many claims about threats to children are wildly exaggerated.

To put today's anxieties into perspective, it is useful to recall that the sup- 29 posed golden age of family life, the 1950s, was beset by a number of crises concerning children and youth. Shocking reports of juvenile delinquency, gang fights, all-night drinking parties, and sex clubs in teenage suburbia appeared in the mass media. In the professional literature, sociologists and psychologists analyzed the problems of alienated youth and the decline of parental authority. Congress held hearings on the corrupting influence of comic books on the nation's children. In 1955, a book entitled *1,000,000 Delinquents* correctly predicted the number of adolescents who would be brought to court the following year. "Teenagers on the Rampage" was the title of a *Time* magazine report on violence in the nation's high schools. Meanwhile, a widely proclaimed educational crisis for schoolchildren of all ages alarmed Americans. A 1955 best-seller, Rudolph Flesch's *Why Johnny Can't Read,* described America as a nation of illiterates.

To point to the hysteria of an earlier time is not to minimize the difficul- 30 ties facing today's children and young people. But cries of alarm and doom need to be subjected to serious scrutiny. Making sense of the changes in children's lives in recent years is more complicated than most people assume. Several family researchers have recently published comprehensive assessments of the state of children and young people in America. In general, these reports show that, while the well-being of children has worsened in some ways, not all of the news concerning America's children is bad—in fact, some of it is good.

These studies generally agree that it is not useful to take one indicator— 31 say, teenage suicide or SAT scores—as a general measure of child welfare. As Nicholas Zill and Carolyn Rogers point out, children's well-being is a "multi-faceted phenomenon." Analyzing trends in indicators of children's economic, physical, and psychological well-being since the 1960s, Zill and Rogers challenge the widespread assumptions that the overall condition of children is deteriorating.

Taken together, these studies present a mixed picture of children's 32 prospects. On the plus side, the average American child's physical health has improved dramatically since the 1960s. Although our infant mortality rates are higher than those of most other industrial societies, both our infant and child mortality rates have dropped considerably. Declining family size has increased most children's share of the family's material resources, even though overall family income has declined since the 1970s. The educational level of most parents has risen since the 1950s, a gain that has been most striking among black women.

On the other side of the ledger, troubling social behavior on the part of 33 young people—delinquency, drug use, early sexual activity—has increased over the past several decades. But many of these trends leveled off or declined in the 1980s. Teenage suicide is frequently cited as an indicator of the emotional well-being of American youth in general, and its recent rise blamed on changing family patterns. (Teenage suicide rates more than doubled between 1960 and the mid-1980s.) But suicide rates are notoriously slippery; changes in reported rates could reflect fluctuating practices in reporting deaths as suicides, or the greater availability of lethal weapons. The number of suicide attempts is much larger than the number of completed suicides, but statistics on attempts are not as reliable.

Suicide may therefore not be a valid indicator of the overall psychological well-being of a population. As Zill and Rogers observe, some groups in the population have relatively low rates of suicide and, at the same time, relatively high rates of depression. Despite the rise in suicide rates, the vast majority of children do not seem to be depressed, unhappy, or alienated, and survey measures of children's life satisfaction and emotional well-being have not changed in recent years.   34

Now, as in the past, many of the difficulties facing children arise out of economic factors. During the 1980s overall poverty rates increased, and children became the poorest segment of the population; since 1988, one out of five children has lived below the poverty line. Several factors have led to the large increase in child poverty in recent years. One is the general decline in wages, especially for younger men in their peak child-rearing years. The enormous growth of poverty among working people *not* living in inner-city underclass communities is one of the untold stories of the 1980s. A second source of child poverty is the rise of single-parent families due to divorce and out-of-wedlock births. The impact on children of both of these trends has been worsened by shortsighted government policies—cutbacks or inadequate investments in housing, health care, child care, and other social supports.   35

Other stresses arise out of the time pressures parents experience and other dilemmas of balancing work and family. Although there is little that government or business can do directly to reverse trends in family structure, policy choices such as child care, parental leave, opportunities for both parents to work part-time while children are young, and measures to fight poverty and joblessness can alleviate some of the current strains on families.   36

Surprisingly, the evidence linking family changes such as divorce and maternal employment to declines in children's well-being is weaker than most people think. In 1986, a widely discussed article by Peter Uhlenberg and David Eggebeen argued that the condition of American teenagers had steadily worsened in recent decades. This decline, they said, was linked to recent changes in family structure.   37

Later, more detailed studies of trends in various measures of child and adolescent well-being do not, however, support a familial explanation of negative trends such as drug use, crime, or declining academic achievement. For example, many negative indicators leveled off in the late 1970s and 1980s, at a time when the family-disintegration hypotheses would have predicted increases. Further, as the sociologists Frank Furstenberg and Gretchen Condran point out, the worrisome behavioral trends among youth in the 1960s and   38

1970s were also found among people in their twenties and thirties. Since these young adults had grown up during the years of postwar family stability, their problem behavior cannot be attributed to changing family patterns.

Much public concern and recent research has focused on the effects of   39
maternal employment on young children. But despite the widespread belief to the contrary, the research literature shows that children whose mothers work are no more likely to suffer from developmental problems or behavioral difficulties than are children of stay-at-home mothers. Maternal employment alone reveals little about the well-being of a child. A working mother's attitudes, the amount of emotional and practical support she receives, and the quality of available child care play a tremendous role in her morale and the functioning of the family. The most depressed mothers are those who want to work and can't, and those who would like to be full-time homemakers but must work. A recent review of the research literature on working mothers in two-parent families concludes:

> Where this pattern itself produces difficulties, they often seem to stem mainly from the slow pace with which society has adapted to this new family form. . . . It is the disequilibrium of social change that creates problems; the typical American family is a dual-wage family, but neither social policy nor social attitudes are in synchrony with this fact.

The evidence on divorce is more mixed. Few would deny that it is often a   40
stressful experience for children or that children are best off with two parents in a good marriage. Even most children whose parents have a bad marriage would probably prefer to have them stay together. Yet we know surprisingly little about the long-term effects of divorce on children. Is it uniformly devastating to all children who go through it? Does it create deep psychological wounds that never heal?

A relatively small number of largely middle-class white children has   41
served as the basis for much current research about the impact of divorce on children. In 1989, Judith Wallerstein and Sandra Blakeslee published *Second Chances,* a book describing the lives of a sample of 131 children of divorce whom Wallerstein had been studying for the previous fifteen years. The detailed psychological portraits of these now-grown children were poignant, and the conclusions of the book disturbing.

Wallerstein and Blakeslee state that almost half of the young men and   42
women in the study were worried, underachieving, self-deprecating, and angry. This bad news about divorce was widely publicized; reports on the book in the media elicited many comments from adults who retained painful, vividly detailed memories of their parents' divorce. Yet other divorce researchers, while respectful of the book's clinical insights, suggest that it exaggerates the extent of the long-term harmful effects of divorce.

There can be little doubt, though, that the time around the breakup of a   43
marriage is a crisis for all concerned. The experiences associated with divorce and remarriage often increase a child's risk of developing problems of various

kinds—psychological, social, and academic. But clearly not all children whose parents divorce develop such problems. Researchers in recent years have begun to focus on differences in children's responses to divorce and the conditions that influence whether they do well or poorly. One factor is the child's own temperament. Some children are more vulnerable than others to adversity and change; "difficult" children are especially likely to become targets of a stressed parent's anger.

The major factor influencing a child's long- and short-term well-being   44
after divorce is the relationship with the parents, especially with the custodial parent, usually the mother. A child who can maintain a warm, supportive relationship with one or both parents, or with a grandparent or other adult, has a much better chance of dealing successfully with the stresses of divorce.

Most researchers now regard divorce not as one event but as part of a long   45
process in which the divorce itself may not be the critical variable. It is not always easy to separate the effects of divorce from the effects of the circumstances that accompany it: conflict between the parents before and after separating; economic loss as a result of the divorce; disruptions in the child's life due to losing the family home, changing schools, and so forth.

There is increasing evidence that parental conflict, whether in the form of   46
shouting or hitting or cold hostility, which may exist in both intact and divorcing families, is a key factor in children's psychological well-being. Yet studies of the effects of divorce rarely compare divorced families to intact families with high levels of conflict. A 1986 study found some children, long before their parents separated, already showing the kinds of behavioral problems that have been viewed as effects of divorce.

In 1968, the psychologists Jeanne and Jack Block began a study of three-   47
year-olds and assessed them periodically for years afterward. When the children were fourteen, the researchers looked back at their data and discovered that those children, especially boys, whose parents would later divorce were rated long before the marriage ended as more aggressive and impulsive and more likely to be in conflict with their parents. Of course, we don't know whether parental conflict led to difficulties for these children, or whether difficult children were creating problems for their parents' marriage. But it is clear that these children's problems did not result from the divorce itself. Recently, a large-scale before-and-after study of the effects of divorce found similar results as had the Blocks in their small sample; a British study of 17,000 families found that many of the problems children exhibited after divorce had existed earlier.

The economic disruptions of divorce often compound the emotional   48
problems. Large numbers of children lose not only their father's presence in the home but his financial support. Their standard of living declines dramatically, and they must adjust to a new home, a new school, new household routines. Policy changes in the economic arrangements following divorce could greatly reduce the stress and disruption children experience.

If we care about children, we need to focus less on the form of the fami-   49
lies they live in and more on ways of supporting their well-being in all kinds

of families. We need to accept the fact that while the family is here to stay, so are divorce, working mothers, and single-parent families. As the anthropologist Paul Bohannon suggests, we need cultural models of the successful divorce and the successful postdivorce family—one that does the least harm to children and leaves them with good relationships with both parents.

The impact of divorce on children's lives seems to be more harsh in America than in other countries. The United States has been less careful than others to ensure that children are provided for after their parents' marriage ends. As the economist Sylvia Hewlett points out, there are two models of divorce reform in Western Europe. In France, for example, no-fault divorce requires that the father continue to support the wife and children in their current lifestyle. In Sweden, child support is publicly provided, and tailored to the needs of one-parent families. In the United States, however, we have failed to provide either public or private supports for children in the wake of divorce.

American society is prepared to deplore the plight of children and to exhort parents to fix it. It is less willing to make the kinds of investments in children's well-being that other advanced nations do. Our empty calls for parental sacrifice, "lovingly packed lunchboxes," and a return to the traditional family will do little to improve the quality of children's lives.

"A HIGH RISK AND HIGH STRESS SOCIETY"

In the early 1980s three American corporations asked a group of British scholars to make reliable projections about the social, economic, political, and cultural trends that would shape America in the next ten years. The portrait of the emerging American society they produced was not flattering. America, they argued, was becoming "a high risk and high stress society."

The future these researchers foresaw offered less economic opportunity, greater risks of downward mobility, fewer public efforts to respond to social needs, and a widening gap between haves and have-nots. Under these circumstances, people would experience greater stress and anxiety than at any other time in America's postwar history. Americans, they predicted, would also be torn between the competing goals of success at work and family happiness.

Increasingly, people would turn to marriage and the family to make life worthwhile, looking for intimacy, personal fulfillment, and a haven from the high-stress world. Yet, tensions and instability would remain high in the very place to which people would turn for security. Strains arising out of changing family relationships would be intensified by increasing poverty and falling standards of living.

In the 1970s and 1980s two kinds of economic changes had profound effects on families—the structural shifts that came with the move to a postindustrial society, and a downturn in the economy that ushered in a prolonged period of low growth; one economist labeled it a "quiet depression." The cyclical change exacerbated the dislocations resulting from the decline of manufacturing and the loss of blue-collar jobs. In the 1980s, government policies and social program cuts made them even worse. Obviously, economic change cannot explain all of the structural changes in family life, but it has played a much larger role than is generally acknowledged. Meanwhile, the celebration of "traditional family values" masked the decimation of the American family dream.

Haves and Have-nots

By the late 1980s, the economic inequality produced during the Reagan years had become increasingly evident. As Kevin Phillips pointed out, "shifts of 3 to 5% of national income from the grass roots to the top 1% of the population have hurt the bottom half of Americans by effects ranging from small-town decay to urban crime, weakened families, and lost economic opportunity for the unskilled." While it is possible to quibble with these percentages, the most dramatic effects were plain to see: homelessness and the growth of an underclass in the nation's ghettos. Economic change also turned once-thriving industrial regions into Rust Belts, while farm states like Iowa witnessed a replay of the Great Depression, with boarded-up small towns and farm families packing up their belongings and heading west. In 1988 the *Wall Street Journal* observed that the United States "is in the midst of a coast to coast, border to border collapse of much of its rural economy," involving about a quarter of the nation's population.

For most of the 1980s, these harsh changes were disguised by the paradox of a growing economy. Supporters of Reaganomics could point to twenty million new jobs (mostly low-paying, low-benefit positions in sales and service), a host of other favorable economic indicators, and the many visible signs of an uneven prosperity, such as rising sales of luxury goods like Mercedes-Benzes and BMW's. While large numbers of middle-class Americans were slipping down the economic scale, or barely clinging to middle-class living standards, large segments of the upper middle class were prospering, especially two-earner professional families.

"We knew that something was wrong," observed the economist Frank Levy in 1987, "but we lacked the language to describe it." Conservatives dominated national debates on the both the family and the economy. Blaming the growth of "the welfare state" during the 1960s and 1970s for the nation's economic problems and for undermining poor families, they attributed the widening gap between rich and poor to the increase of single-parent families. For their part, many left-leaning social critics continued to fight the cultural battles of the 1970s, ignoring the growth of economic inequality and railing against consumerism and narcissism, especially as personified by the yuppie.

Conservatives blamed increasing poverty rates on changes in family structure. Yet the widening gap between rich and poor could not be attributed solely to the increase in single-parent families—unmarried women and their children. Moreover, recent research supports the view that among the persistently poor, family breakups and teenage childbearing are largely a response to, rather than a cause of, persistent poverty. Further, while married-couple families tended to fare much better in the 1980s than did other kinds of households, the growth of inequality also showed up strikingly among intact families and among working Americans. Of the twenty million people who fell below the Census Bureau's poverty line in 1987, nearly 60 percent were from families with at least one member working full-time or part-time. Throughout most of the postwar era, poverty was almost synonymous with being unemployed. The 1980s saw the rise of the working poor; by mid-decade the salary offered by nearly one-third of full-time jobs could not keep a family of four above the poverty line.

The Myth of the Yuppie

The 1980s were particularly hard on young people, women, minorities, blue-collar workers, the unskilled, and those without a college education. Young adults across the range of social classes devised a number of strategies to cope with declining real earnings. According to one study, "they postponed marriage, both spouses entered the labor market, they had fewer children, and they went into debt." The same four strategies were undertaken by the much-maligned yuppie. 60

Yuppies formed one piece of the confused media imagery of the baby-boom generation, the leading edge of whom was thirtysomething as the 1980s began. The yuppie stereotype took on a life of its own. A variant of the myth of narcissism and the earlier myth of suburbia, the yuppie presented a more acceptable target of resentment than the truly rich millionaires who were the real beneficiaries of Reaganomics. Yet the yuppie was a misleading symbol of the baby-boom generation and the national economy. There were no more young families with incomes over $35,000 than there had been in the early 1970s (in constant dollars). Moreover, back then, more families attained this level of income with only one earner. 61

The generation that followed the baby boomers fared still worse in the 1980s. According to a 1988 study by the William T. Grant Foundation, the economic changes of the 1980s fell hardest on children, youths in their teens and twenties, and young families. Media images of "a generation on the skids," the report argues—unstable and irresponsible, unwilling to grow up and make commitments to family and work, beset by drugs, crime, and out-of-wedlock pregnancy—are harmful and misleading. The majority of young people are staying in school, working in one or more jobs, saying no to drugs, and avoiding premature marriage and childbearing. To the extent that problems do exist, they cannot be blamed on "moral decay": *The primary problem lies with the economy, and the paths for youth who enter it, rather than with the youth themselves. Education can certainly help, but it is no cure-all for massive changes in the labor market"* (italics in original). 62

A Growing Underclass

The most malignant effects of the declining fortunes of the young have fallen on those who are both poor and members of minorities. In the 1970s and 63

1980s there was a decline in marriage rates among black women and a dramatic rise in black female-headed households. Many African-American observers agreed that there was indeed a crisis in the black family. In contrast to what many feared, however, changes in black families were not "leading indicators" of future changes in white family life; rather, the family patterns of the two groups were moving farther apart than they had ever been in this century.

While not all differences between black and white families could be explained by spreading poverty, many of the more disturbing changes associated with the rise of a ghetto underclass were linked to the economic changes of recent years. A number of scholars, most notably William Julius Wilson, have argued that the social pathologies that have emerged in inner-city black neighborhoods over the last twenty years are a response to powerful economic forces. Manufacturing declined or moved to the suburbs, eliminating many well-paying, unskilled jobs. High unemployment led to more persistent and concentrated poverty and a set of mutually reinforcing problems—increased welfare dependence, high rates of family disruption, high crime rates, drug use, and so on. 64

Further, the growth of a population of unemployed and unemployable young men reduced the pool of potential marriage partners, leading to a decline in marriage rates and an increase in the number of unmarried mothers. Growing numbers of young women, suspecting that they will never find a husband able to help support a family, see no advantage to marriage or waiting to have a child. 65

One ethnographic study of a poor black community in the late 1980s describes teenage childbearing as an alternative life-course strategy adopted in response to economic and social constraints. Faced with limited prospects of an economically viable marriage, young women invest in a vertical kin system, relying on female relatives for emotional and practical support. As one fourteen-year-old mother explained: "Ever since I can remember I always expected to have a baby when I was 15 or 16 but I never believed I would ever have a chance to get a husband. One of the things my grandmother always said, 'Pay your dues to your kin because they will take care of you.'" 66

Although various aspects of Wilson's analysis have been challenged, his overall argument that unemployment, underemployment, and poverty have profound effects on family life are indisputable. Glen Elder's studies of children and families in the Great Depression, and Katherine Newman's recent study of job loss and subsequent downward mobility in the 1980s, provide vivid portraits of what happens when families get caught in the undertow of economic decline. 67

During the 1980s conservative arguments dominated debates about poverty and the underclass: people were poor because of flaws in their attitudes, values, and behavior; because a "culture of poverty" was passed along from generation to generation, untouched by external circumstance; and because government social policies created perverse incentives. Conservative critics such as George Gilder and Charles Murray made "welfare" the key to 68 the many troubles that beset America in the 1970s and 1980s—economic stagnation, high taxes, crime in the streets, moral decline. These arguments fit the mood and intuitions of the public during the Reagan years. Poverty in America was typified by Reagan's image of the Cadillac-driving "welfare queen" and the strutting black stud who appeared on a Bill Moyers television documentary on the crisis of the black family and boasted of how many babies he had made.

In the early 1990s, poverty and its attendant ills are still being defined as 69 moral and personal, but the rhetoric has begun to shift. There is a little less talk of declining cultural values, a little more about reordering national priorities. The appearance of homeless people all over America in the mid-1980s has transformed American cities; homelessness—especially homeless families, women, and children—signify a kind of poverty that few can defend. Slowly, a consensus has begun to grow among liberals and conservatives, especially on the part of American business, that destitution and rampant social pathology, whatever their sources, are not good for the country and will in the long run be costly to taxpayers.

DEFYING THE "LOGIC OF INDUSTRIALISM"

America is not the only country to have experienced a historic change in 70 family life in recent years. As I discussed earlier, other societies have seen similar changes in sex roles, divorce rates, and family structure—but their public policy responses have been very different. By the end of the 1980s there was increasing awareness in the media that America lagged far behind other industrial nations in family and social policy. Stories appeared about French prenatal care and preschools, the Canadian health care system, German apprenticeship training, and the like.

The gap between rhetoric about family values and American willingness 71 to address the needs of families may have stretched in recent years, but it is not new. Since the nineteenth century, Americans have looked to the family as the source of individual and social salvation. Europeans, by contrast, have looked at the family as a fragile institution in need of support from the wider society.

Most European countries conceive of family policy as something required 72 by the "logic of industrialism"—the need of families no longer living on the land, dependent on wages and salaries, for help in dealing with unemployment, major illness, the dependencies of old age. Hence the unquestioned role of governments in virtually all industrial countries in supplying a considerable array of family supports—health care, child allowances, housing allowances, support for working parents with children that includes child care, parental leave, short work days for parents—as well as an extensive array of services at the other end of the life cycle, for the aged.

In a study of family policy in eighteen "rich democracies," the sociologist 73 Harold Wilensky found some striking differences in the politics of the family as well as in family policies. Americans debate endlessly about emotionally charged moral issues like abortion, sex education, and gay rights, while in Europe, family policy is part of general economic policy. Support for children and families in America has been generally based on the assumption that families are inadequate if they are not self-sufficient. Other countries provide a range of supports for children and families across income groups, not just for the poor, with no stigma attached to them.

Several factors, according to Wilensky, seem to account for innovative   74 and expansive social policies in other countries. Among these are the extent of industrial development, high levels of women in the labor force, and strong Left and Catholic parties, both of which share a strong interest in supporting families, despite differences in ideas about women's place. A large aging population is also a factor. Older people are strong supporters of family policy, including support for child care, in the United States as well as other countries. There is little evidence for the generational war that some commentators have described. Framing policy issues in terms of young against old is a deceptive and politically opportunistic way of avoiding more fundamental issues of economic inequality in America.

Paradoxically, Americans have a stronger sense of both familistic values   75 and family crisis than do other advanced countries. We have higher marriage rates, a more home-centered way of life, and greater public devotion to family values, yet also greater rates of instability—divorce, single-parent families, and teenage pregnancies—than other countries.

Eventually, despite our unique cultural and political traditions, it seems   76 likely that the logic of industrialism will prevail, and America will converge with other countries in providing support for families. The proportion of old people rising and will leap to new heights when the baby-boom generation ages. The proportion of women at work is also likely to remain high or even increase. Today's policy debates over child care, parental leave, health insurance, and care for the elderly are a preview of the future.

The current "stalled revolution" (in Arlie Hochschild's phrase) in family   77 life is not likely to last indefinitely. In the 1980s a concern for family values was harnessed to a conservative drive to dismantle the already fragmented and relatively ungenerous systems of public provision that had grown out of the New Deal and the Great Society. In the 1990s, family values might be harnessed to revitalize a new thrust for public and private sector policies in support of children and families.

RECONSTRUCTING THE DREAM

After almost three decades of social upheaval and cultural civil war, there are   78 signs that the family debate in America has entered a new stage. By the early 1990s, the polarized political climate that had prevailed for more than a decade seemed to be fading and the contours of a new consensus began to emerge. Most Americans, according to survey data and in-depth studies of attitudes, have already made peace between the liberal values of the 1960s—self-fulfillment, equal opportunity for women—and the traditional work and family values of the 1980s. The most dramatic evidence of such a shift was the formation in 1991 of an unusual alliance of a group of well-known liberals and New Right conservatives; disregarding the issues that continue to divide them, such as abortion, they joined forces to press for specific family support issues on which they could agree.

Further, despite continuing talk of family decline, the outlines of a new 79 American family are beginning to be seen. It is more diverse, more fragile, more fluid than in the past. The image of a vast, homogenized middle class that was mythologized in the 1950s applies even less to today's realities than it did then. Yet contrary to some critics, the middle class, and middle-class aspirations for family life, have not disappeared. Although there is much more tolerance for variation, lifelong heterosexual marriage, with children, remains the preferred cultural norm.

The New American Dream mixes the new cultural freedoms with many of 80 the old wishes—marital and family happiness, economic security, home ownership, education of children. But the new dream is more demanding than the old, and even the basics—a secure job, a home, health care, education—are becoming more difficult to achieve. The new life course has more twists and turns than it did in the past; it offers greater opportunities for autonomy, but greater risks of loneliness. Further, even the middle class faces more travails than in the past: divorce, time pressures, and the dilemmas of raising children in a world that has grown more dangerous, competitive, and uncertain.

The meaning of other aspects of family change can also be debated endlessly, but the argument obscures a complex reality: the glass is both half full 81 and half empty. It is possible to be optimistic about the future of the family and still be concerned about the number of children who live in poverty, the disruptions of divorce, the difficulties of balancing work and family.

On one issue, however—the centrality of family in the lives of most 82 Americans—the optimists are surely correct and the pessimists wrong. For better or worse, family life, and an idealized image of what the family should be, remain at the source of our greatest joys, our deepest worries, our most painful hurts.

It is possible to build a convincing case for either the optimistic or the 83 pessimistic view of recent changes. Pessimists point to high divorce rates as evidence that the family is falling apart and that people are no longer capable of deep and lasting commitments. Optimists argue that getting divorced is not the same thing as rejecting marriage. Besides, they point out, three-quarters of divorced people remarry, and higher rates of divorce only indicate that marriage has become so important that people are no longer willing to put up with the kinds of unsatisfying, conflicted, or "empty-shell" marriages earlier generations tolerated.

When people are polled about the most important elements in a good 84 life, they place family values—"a happy marriage," love, and emotional support—at the top of the list. Through all the years of dramatic changes in the leading family indicators, surveys have shown that about 90 to 95 percent of young men and women—the alleged Me generation—have planned to marry. National surveys also show that, once married, the vast majority of people report being "very satisfied" or "very happy" with their marriages. But the pollster Lou Harris recently reported that while 87 percent of men say they would remarry their wives, only 76 percent of women say they would remarry their husbands. And contrary to notions of a male "flight from commitment," a greater proportion of men than women marry and remarry.*

Not only have young people continued to value marriage but they expect   85
to have children. Between 1971 and 1979, despite the supposed Me Decade, less than 1 percent of young women considered having no children as the "ideal family situation." Similarly, surveys of both sexes during the 1980s revealed that young adults felt a near-universal urge to have children. In one study of parents and children, 88 percent of the parents said they would choose to have children again, and 71 percent described their families as "close and intimate." Needless to say, what people say to polltakers may not reflect the realities of their family lives; we may not wish to bare our souls or air the family's dirty linen when the survey researcher comes to call. Still, the upbeat answers reveal what people see as the prevailing cultural values.

Further, numerous surveys show that despite talk about the disappear-   86
ance of the extended family, family ties beyond the nuclear family persist. Regardless of mobility, most Americans had ready access to members of their family, nearly 90 percent having at least one household of relatives living nearby. Sixty percent of these people saw nearby relatives at least once a week. Those with no relatives nearby, or who saw nearby relatives less often than once a month, comprised about 30 percent of the population. It seems likely that most of these people were in touch with their families by mail and phone, visited on holidays, and mobilized to help one another during emergencies. Clearly, the image of contemporary Americans as isolated, rootless loners is far from reality.

How, then, to account for the widespread belief in the isolated nuclear   87
family and the lack of kin ties in contemporary society? Part of the answer may be that the highly educated (especially professional) middle class is more geographically mobile than other segments of the population, and less involved with kin on a daily basis. For the less educated, the working class, and lower middle class, as well as some ethnic groups, social life largely revolves around relatives. Since social critics tend to be members of the upper middle

---

*The "male flight from commitment" is the subject of Barbara Ehrenreich's book *The Hearts of Men*. She argues that a "playboy" ethic led men to reject the breadwinner role in favor of a fun-filled bachelor life. The notion that men today are reluctant to marry and take on family responsibilities fits with the experience of large numbers of women. And certainly, many men have fled responsibilities for their children after divorce. Yet, as Lillian Rubin points out, "something is wrong with the picture as drawn." It leaves out the vast majority of men who do make a commitment to marriage, kids, mortgages, and the like. Most men can't afford the affluent bachelor life, and those who can are less likely to remain single than those at the bottom of the income scale.

class, in their discourse on the excesses of individualism they are likely to be projecting their own life-styles onto the population as a whole.

Whatever the reasons, it is clear that a certain cynical stance toward marriage and family, once considered sophisticated and modern, now seems old-fashioned. As a sign of the times, big weddings are back in style. Even feminists are more likely to choose a traditional wedding with all the trappings: a long white gown, a reception for a hundred relatives and friends, a honeymoon. This shift in the emotional and intellectual mood has permeated popular culture. 88

In the 1950s it became almost a convention for Broadway and Hollywood to portray marriages as unhappy, especially if the spouses were middle-class or middle-aged. *Who's Afraid of Virginia Woolf?*—both the play and the film—is a prime example of the genre. Joseph Heller's best-selling 1974 novel *Something Happened* was one of a number of novels that offered a similar message at the time. A depressing family saga, the book presented in a more naked way a message common to many literary works of the period. Its "hero," Slocum, is totally disaffected from both his corporate job and his suburban family. In both places, but especially the home, the prevailing emotions are boredom, indifference, isolation, and unhappiness, punctuated by anxiety and hatred. 89

By the end of the 1970s, such a view of middle-class life had begun to seem stale. After the upheavals of the 1960s and early 1970s, the problem seemed to shift from too much social order to too little, from a stifling, seemingly all-powerful system to a sense of chaos and social disintegration. People across the political spectrum groped for symbols of stability and yearned for attachment, roots, tradition. 90

During the 1980s, these longings fastened on the family. Once again, family and children came to be reinvested with deep-seated values, in an almost religious revitalization easily exploited by politicians and advertisers. The family had arisen like a phoenix from the challenges of ideological assault and demographic upheaval to reclaim its status as a sacred symbol, affecting even those who had been at the forefront of cultural and political revolt. "The new consensus," observed one feminist critic, "is that the family is our last refuge, our only defense against universal predatory selfishness, loneliness, and rootlessness; the idea that there could be a desirable alternative to the family is no longer taken seriously." 91

The new familistic mood even penetrated into the avant-garde. Woody Allen's films trace the transition from the celebration of liberated sex (*Play It Again, Sam* in 1972) to the search for "relationships" (*Annie Hall* in 1977) to the celebration of family bonds, family rituals, and children (in the recent *Hannah and Her Sisters, Radio Days,* and even the dark comedy *Crimes and Misdemeanors*). The work of the avante-garde playwright Sam Shepard has followed a similar odyssey. Shepard himself went from being an East Village bohemian to becoming the embodiment of the all-American hero in his film portrayal of the test pilot Chuck Yeager (*The Right Stuff*). His stormy dramas of the 1960s and 1970s portrayed fractured, alienated families like those of 92

O'Neill, Williams, and Albee; his later plays portray versions of the same vaguely autobiographical characters reuniting and reconciling. A recent play, observes one critic, "finds its mystery not in lies of the mind [the play's title], but in loves of the heart."

Yet if the past has any lesson to teach, it is that inflated expectations for family life are a recipe for personal disenchantment and social neglect. The emphasis on the home as the source of both personal happiness and social order has been responsible for the recurring sense of crisis concerning children and the family that has afflicted American culture since the 1820s. For almost two centuries, social critics have been both singing the praises of the family and decrying its failures. 93

The vision of the family as an earthly paradise was a nineteenth-century invention. But the most vivid portrayals of the family have been profoundly ambivalent. In what could be called the "high tragic" tradition—including Greek drama and Shakespeare, as well as the Bible, fairy tales, and the novel—the family is portrayed as a powerfully emotional setting, seething with dark Freudian passions. To Freud, such figures as Cain and Abel, Oedipus and Medea, Hamlet and Lear, and the witches and ogres of fairy tales present disguised versions of the emotions of ordinary family life. 94

As Freud and others have recognized, ambivalence and conflict are woven into the fabric of family life; they arise from the intimacy and commitment that provide its distinct benefits. Nor is it simply the isolated nuclear family that is prone to accumulate tension and conflict. A large body of anthropological evidence suggests that extended kin groups not only confer security and belonging but give rise to intense conflicts that cannot be openly dealt with, but may emerge in explosive form. 95

Rather than yearning for an elusive perfected family, we would be wiser to consider new social arrangements that fit the kinds of families we now have and the kinds of lives we now lead. We need both political will and social creativity in order to devise ways, for example, of living with divorce and of coming to grips with the implications of living in history's first mass-longevity society. Our traditions have not prepared us for the long and fluid lives we live today. The current celebration of marriage and family does not take into account that most of us will spend parts of our lives living apart from family. We need to think of how to supply substitutes for the comforts and companionship of home. 96

We also need to think of how to encourage a broader sociability. Middle-class Americans have substituted a vision of the ideal home for a vision of the ideal city. As a result, our lives are divided between home and work, leaving us yearning for a broader sense of community. Yet what we may be missing is not the idealized small town of our imagined past, but that "third realm" of sociability and social cohesion beyond the home and the workplace—public spaces and informal meeting places—that our European counterparts take for granted as part of the good life. 97

There are no quick, easy, or cheap fixes for the problems of family life today. And there is good reason to believe that we may never solve some of the 98 dilemmas of family—our paradoxical needs for autonomy and attachment, for privacy and community, the ambivalence built into deep emotional bonds, the tensions stirred by intense intimacy, conflicts between genders and generations. But there is much that could be done to alleviate some of the major, outer sources of stress and strains; sooner or later, policy makers will translate rhetoric and genuine public concern about children and families into ways of addressing the new realities of family life.

Without minimizing our current troubles or our attempts to resolve them, we need to remember that many of the most vexing issues that confront us derive from the very benefits of modernization, benefits too easily forgotten in our yearnings for a lost past. There was no problem of elder care when most people died before they grew old; the problems of adolescence were unknown when work began in childhood; education was a privilege for the well-to-do; and a person's place in society was determined at birth. And when most people were illiterate and living on the margins of survival, only aristocrats could worry about sexual satisfaction and self-fulfillment.   99

However great the difficulties of the present appear, there is no point in giving in to the lure of nostalgia. There is no golden age of family life to long for, no past pattern that, if only we had the moral will to return to, would guarantee us happiness and security. Family life is always bound up with the economic, demographic, and cultural predicaments of specific times and places. We are no longer a nation of pioneers, Puritans, farmers, or postwar suburbanites. We must shatter the myths that blind us and find ways to cope with our present, the place where social change and family history have brought us.   100

Questions

1. Why does Skolnick object to the decline in family values as an explanation for some of our social problems? Do you agree with her argument?

2. How have recent economic factors influenced American families?

3. According to Skolnick, a central theme in American culture is "an ambivalent yearning for autonomy on the one hand and attachment to family and community on the other." Have you experienced a similar tension?

4. How do American and European attitudes toward the role of government in family affairs differ? Why does Skolnick feel that the American belief in self-sufficiency is destructive?

5. Would Coontz agree with Skolnick's argument? Why or why not?

Why I Hate "Family Values"
(Let Me Count the Ways)

KATHA POLLITT

Katha Pollitt is the author of Antarctic Traveller *(1982).*

Here, Pollitt contends that the apparent decline of family values lies "not in moral collapse but in our failure to acknowledge and adjust to changing social relations." The dissolution of the family insofar as there is an increase in the number of poor, single mothers is not a problem of individual values, but is a "problem of money." This selection is from the Nation *(1992).*

Unlike many of the commentators who have made Murphy Brown the most famous unmarried mother since Ingrid Bergman ran off with Roberto Rossellini, I actually watched the notorious childbirth episode. After reading my sleep-resistant 4-year-old her entire collection of Berenstain Bears books, television was all I was fit for. And that is how I know that I belong to the cultural elite: Not only can I spell "potato" correctly, and many other vegetables as well, I thought the show was a veritable riot of family values. First of all, Murph is smart, warm, playful, decent and rich: She'll be a great mom. Second, the dad is her ex-husband: The kid is as close to legitimate as the scriptwriters could manage, given that Murph is divorced. Third, her ex spurned *her*, not, as Dan Quayle implies, the other way around. Fourth, she rejected abortion. On TV, women have abortions only in docudramas, usually after being raped, drugged with birth-defect-inducing chemicals or put into a coma. Finally, what does Murph sing to the newborn? "You make me feel like a natural woman"! Even on the most feminist sitcom in TV history (if you take points off *Kate and Allie* for never so much as mentioning the word "gay"), anatomy is destiny.

That a show as fluffy and genial as *Murphy Brown* has touched off a national debate about "family values" speaks volumes—and not just about the apparent inability of Dan Quayle to distinguish real life from a sitcom. (And since when are TV writers part of the cultural elite, anyway? I thought they were the crowd-pleasing lowbrows, and *intellectuals* were the cultural elite.) The *Murphy Brown* debate, it turns out, isn't really about Murphy Brown; it's about inner-city women, who will be encouraged to produce fatherless babies by Murph's example—the trickle-down theory of values. (Do welfare moms watch *Murphy Brown?* I thought it was supposed to be soap operas, as in "they just sit around all day watching the soaps." Marriage is a major obsession on the soaps—but never mind.) Everybody, it seems, understood this substitu-

1

2

594

tion immediately. After all, why get upset about Baby Boy Brown? Is there any doubt that he will be safe, loved, well schooled, taken for checkups, taught to respect the rights and feelings of others and treated to *The Berenstain Bears Visit the Dentist* as often as his little heart desires? Unlike millions of kids who live with both parents, he will never be physically or sexually abused, watch his father beat his mother (domestic assault is the leading cause of injury to women) or cower beneath the blankets while his parents scream at each other. And chances are excellent that he won't sexually assault a retarded girl with a miniature baseball bat, like those high school athletes in posh Glen Ridge, New Jersey; or shoot his lover's spouse, like Amy Fisher; or find himself on trial for rape, like William Kennedy Smith—children of intact and prosperous families every one of them. He'll probably go to Harvard and major in semiotics. Maybe that's the problem. Just think, if Murph were married, like Dan Quayle's mom, he could go to DePauw University and major in golf.

That there is something called "the family"—Papa Bear, Mama Bear, Brother Bear and Sister Bear—that is the best setting for raising children, and that it is in trouble because of a decline in "values," are bromides accepted by commentators of all political stripes. The right blames a left-wing cultural conspiracy: obscene rock lyrics, sex ed, abortion, prayerless schools, working mothers, promiscuity, homosexuality, decline of respect for authority and hard work, welfare and, of course, feminism. (On the *Chicago Tribune* Op-Ed page, Allan Carlson, president of the ultraconservative Rockford Institute, found a previously overlooked villain: federal housing subsidies. With all that square footage lying around, singles and unhappy spouses could afford to live on their own.) The left blames the ideology of postindustrial capitalism: consumerism, individualism, selfishness, alienation, lack of social supports for parents and children, atrophied communities, welfare and feminism. The center agonizes over teen sex, welfare moms, crime and divorce, unsure what the causes are beyond some sort of moral failure—probably related to feminism. Interesting how that word keeps coming up.   3

I used to wonder what family values are. As a matter of fact, I still do. If abortion, according to the right, undermines family values, then single motherhood (as the producers of *Murphy Brown* were quick to point out) must be in accord with them, no? No. Over on the left, if gender equality, love and sexual expressivity are desirable features of contemporary marriage, then isn't marriage bound to be unstable, given how hard those things are to achieve and maintain? Not really.   4

Just say no, says the right. Try counseling, says the left. Don't be so lazy, says the center. Indeed, in its guilt-mongering cover story "Legacy of Divorce: How the Fear of Failure Haunts the Children of Broken Marriages," *Newsweek* was unable to come up with any explanation for the high American divorce rate except that people just didn't try hard enough to stay married.   5

When left, right and center agree, watch out. They probably don't know what they're talking about. And so it is with "the family" and "family values." In the first place, these terms lump together distinct social phenomena   6 that in reality have virtually nothing to do with one another. The handful of fortysomething professionals like Murphy Brown who elect to have a child without a male partner have little in common with the millions of middle- and working-class divorced mothers who find themselves in desperate financial straits because their husbands fail to pay court-awarded child support. And neither category has much in common with inner-city girls like those a teacher friend of mine told me about the other day: a 13-year-old and a 12-year-old, impregnated by boyfriends twice their age and determined to bear and keep the babies—to spite abusive parents, to confirm their parents' low opinion of them, to have someone to love who loves them in return.

Beyond that, appeals to "the family" and its "values" frame the discussion   7
as one about morals instead of consequences. In real life, for example, teen sex—the subject of endless sermons—has little relation with teen childbearing. That sounds counterfactual, but it's true. Western European teens have sex about as early and as often as American ones, but are much less likely to have babies. Partly it's because there are far fewer European girls whose lives are as marked by hopelessness and brutality as those of my friend's students. And partly it's because European youth have much better access to sexual information, birth control and abortion. Or consider divorce. In real life, parents divorce for all kinds of reasons, not because they lack moral fiber and are heedless of their children's needs. Indeed, many divorce because they *do* consider their kids, and the poisonous effects of growing up in a household marked by violence, craziness, open verbal warfare or simple lovelessness.

* * *

Perhaps this is the place to say that I come to the family-values debate   8
with a personal bias. I am recently separated myself. I think my husband and I would fall under *Newsweek*'s "didn't try harder" rubric, although we thought about splitting up for years, discussed it for almost a whole additional year and consulted no fewer than four therapists, including a marital counselor who advised us that marriage was one of modern mankind's only means of self-transcendence (religion and psycho-analysis were the others, which should have warned me) and admonished us that we risked a future of shallow relationships if we shirked our spiritual mission, not to mention the damage we would "certainly" inflict on our daughter. I thought he was a jackass—shallow relationships? *moi?* But he got to me. Because our marriage wasn't some flaming disaster—with broken dishes and hitting and strange hotel charges showing up on the MasterCard bill. It was just unhappy, in ways that weren't going to change. Still, I think both of us would have been willing to trudge on to spare our child suffering. That's what couples do in women's magazines; that's what the Clintons say they did. But we saw it wouldn't work: As our daughter got older, she would see right through us, the way kids do. And, worse, no matter how hard I tried to put on a happy face, I would wordlessly communicate to her—whose favorite fairy tale is "Cinderella," and whose favorite game is Wedding, complete with bath-towel bridal veil—my resentment and depression and cynicism about relations between the sexes.

The family-values types would doubtless say that my husband and I made   9
a selfish choice, which society should have impeded or even prevented.
There's a growing sentiment in policy land to make divorce more difficult. In
When the Bough Breaks, Sylvia Ann Hewlett argues that couples should be
forced into therapy (funny how ready people are to believe that counseling,
which even when voluntary takes years to modify garden-variety neuroses,
can work wonders in months with resistant patients who hate each other).
Christopher Lasch briefly supported a constitutional amendment forbidding
divorce to couples with minor children, as if lack of a separation agreement
would keep people living together (he's backed off that position, he told me
recently). The Communitarians, who flood *The Nation*'s mailboxes with self-
promoting worryfests, furrow their brows wondering "How can the family be
saved without forcing women to stay at home or otherwise violating their
rights?" (Good luck.) But I am still waiting for someone to explain why it
would be better for my daughter to grow up in a joyless household than for
her to live as she does now, with two reasonably cheerful parents living
around the corner from each other, both committed to her support and coop-
erating, as they say on *Sesame Street,* in her care. We may not love each other,
but we both love her. Maybe that's as much as parents can do for their children, and all that should be asked of them.

But, of course, civilized cooperation is exactly what many divorced par-   10
ents find they cannot manage. The statistics on deadbeat and vanishing dads
are shocking—less than half pay child support promptly and in full, and
around half seldom or never see their kids within a few years of marital
breakup. Surely, some of this male abdication can be explained by the very
thinness of the traditional paternal role worshiped by the preachers of "values"; it's little more than breadwinning, discipline and fishing trips. How
many diapers, after all, has Dan Quayle changed? A large percentage of American fathers have never changed a single one. Maybe the reason so many fathers fade away after divorce is that they were never really there to begin
with.

* * *

It is true that people's ideas about marriage are not what they were in the   11
1950s—although those who look back at the fifties nostalgically forget both
that many of those marriages were miserable and that the fifties were an atypical decade in more than a century of social change. Married women have
been moving steadily into the work force since 1890; beginning even earlier,
families have been getting smaller; divorce has been rising; sexual activity has
been initiated even earlier and marriage delayed; companionate marriage has
been increasingly accepted as desirable by all social classes and both sexes. It
may be that these trends have reached a tipping point, at which they come to
define a new norm. Few men expect to marry virgins, and children are hardly
"stigmatized" by divorce, as they might have been a mere fifteen or twenty
years ago. But if people want different things from family life—if women, as
Arlie Hochschild pointed out in *The Second Shift,* cite as a major reason for
separation the failure of their husbands to share domestic labor; if both sexes

are less willing to resign themselves to a marriage devoid of sexual pleasure, intimacy or shared goals; if single women decide they want to be mothers; if teenagers want to sleep together—why shouldn't society adapt? Society is, after all, just us. Nor are these developments unique to the United States. All over the industrialized world, divorce rates are high, single women are having babies by choice, homosexuals are coming out of the closet and infidelity, always much more common than anyone wanted to recognize, is on the rise. Indeed, in some ways America is behind the rest of the West: We still go to church, unlike the British, the French and, now that Franco is out of the way, the Spanish. More religious than Spain! Imagine.

I'm not saying that these changes are without cost—in poverty, loneli-   12
ness, insecurity and stress. The reasons for this suffering, however, lie not in moral collapse but in our failure to acknowledge and adjust to changing social relations.

We still act as if mothers stayed home with children, wives didn't need to   13
work and men earned a "family wage." We'd rather preach about teenage "promiscuity" than teach young people—especially young women—how to negotiate sexual issues responsibly. If my friend's students had been prepared for puberty by schools and discussion groups and health centers, the way Dutch young people are, they might not have ended up pregnant, victims of what is, after all, statutory rape. And if women earned a dollar for every dollar earned by men, divorce and single parenthood would not mean poverty. Nobody worries about single fathers raising children, after all; indeed, paternal custody is the latest legal fad.

What is the point of trying to put the new wine of modern personal rela-   14
tions in the old bottles of the sexual double standard and indissoluble marriage? For that is what most of the current discourse on "family issues" amounts to. No matter how fallacious, the culture greets moralistic approaches to these subjects with instant agreement. Judith Wallerstein's travesty of social science, *Second Chances,* asserts that children are emotionally traumatized by divorce, and the fact that she had no control group is simply ignored by an ecstatic press. As it happens, a recent study in *Science* did use a control group. By following 17,000 children for four years, and comparing those whose parents split with those whose parents stayed in troubled marriages, the researchers found that the "divorce effect" disappeared entirely for boys and was very small for girls. Not surprisingly, this study attracted absolutely no attention.

Similarly, we are quick to blame poor unmarried mothers for all manner   15
of social problems—crime, unemployment, drops in reading scores, teen suicide. The solution? Cut off all welfare for additional children. Force teen mothers to live with their parents. Push women to marry in order to attach them to a male income. (So much for love—talk about marriage as legalized prostitution!)

New Jersey's new welfare reform law gives economic coercion a particu-   16
larly bizarre twist. Welfare moms who marry can keep part of their dole, but

only if the man is *not* the father of their children. The logic is that, married or not, Dad has a financial obligation to his kids, but Mr. Just Got Into Town does not. If the law's inventors are right that welfare policy can micromanage marital and reproductive choice, they have just guaranteed that no poor woman will marry her children's father. This is strengthening the family?

Charles Murray, of the American Enterprise Institute, thinks New Jersey   17
does not go far enough. Get rid of welfare entirely, he argued in *The New York Times:* Mothers should marry or starve, and if they are foolish enough to pre-fer the latter, their kids should be put up for adoption or into orphanages. Mickey Kaus, who favors compulsory low-wage employment for the poor, likes orphanages too.

None of those punitive approaches will work. There is no evidence that   18
increased poverty decreases family size, and welfare moms aren't likely to meet many men with family-size incomes, or they'd probably be married al-ready, though maybe not for long. The men who impregnated those seventh graders, for example, are much more likely to turn them out as prostitutes than to lead them to the altar. For one thing, those men may well be married themselves.

The fact is, the harm connected with the dissolution of "the family" is   19
not a problem of values—at least not individual values—it's a problem of money. When the poor are abandoned to their fates, when there are no jobs, people don't get to display "work ethic," don't feel good about themselves and don't marry or stay married. The girls don't have anything to postpone motherhood for; the boys have no economic prospects that would make them reasonable marriage partners. This was as true in the slums of eigh-teenth-century London as it is today in the urban slums of Latin America and Africa, as well as the United States. Or take divorce: The real harm of divorce is that it makes lots of women, and their children, poor. One reason, which has got a fair amount of attention recently, is the scandalously low level of child support, plus the tendency of courts to award a disproportionate share of the marital assets to the man. The other reason is that women earn much less than men, thanks to gender discrimination and the failure of the work-place to adapt to the needs of working mothers. Instead of moaning about "family values" we should be thinking about how to provide the poor with decent jobs and social services, and about how to insure economic justice for working women. And let marriage take care of itself.

Family values and the cult of the nuclear family is, at bottom, just an-   20
other way to bash women, especially poor women. If only they would get married and stay married, society's ills would vanish. Inner-city crime would disappear because fathers would communicate manly values to their sons, which would cause jobs to spring up like mushrooms after rain. Welfare would fade away. Children would do well in school. (Irene Impellizeri, anti-condom vice president of the New York City Board of Education, recently gave a speech attributing inner-city children's poor grades and high dropout rates to the failure of their families to provide "moral models," the way immi-

grant parents did in the good old days—a dangerous argument for her, in particular, to make; doesn't she know that Italian-American kids have dropout and failure rates only slightly lower than black and Latino teens?)

When pundits preach morality, I often find myself thinking of Samuel   21
Johnson, literature's greatest enemy of cant and fatuity. What would the eighteenth-century moralist make of our current obsession with marriage? "Sir," he replied to Boswell, who held that marriage was a natural state, "it is so far from being natural for a man and woman to live in the state of marriage that we find all the motives which they have for remaining in that connection, and the restraints which civilized society imposes to prevent separation, are hardly sufficient to keep them together." Dr. Johnson knew what he was talking about: He and his wife lived apart. And what would he think of our confusion of moral preachments with practical solutions to social problems? Remember his response to Mrs. Thrale's long and flowery speech on the cost of children's clothes. "Nay, madam," he said, "when you are declaiming, declaim; and when you are calculating, calculate."

Which is it going to be? Declamation, which feeds no children, employs   22
no jobless and reduces gender relations to an economic bargain? Or calculation, which accepts the fact that the Berenstain Bears, like Murphy Brown, are fiction. The people seem to be voting with their feet on "the family." It's time for our "values" to catch up.

Questions

1. Why did Dan Quayle attack Murphy Brown? Why does Pollitt think his denunciation is misguided? Do you agree with Pollitt's view? Why or why not?

2. Both liberals and conservatives agree that family values have declined. How do their explanations differ?

3. Pollitt agrees that the typical family has changed. How has it changed? Why does Pollitt say that the apparent decline of the family is not a problem of values but of money?

4. How does Pollitt's perception of the family compare with that of Coontz?

The Family in the Welfare State

SAR A. LEVITAN AND RICHARD S. BELOUS

Sar A. Levitan is a professor of economics and the director for the Center of Social Policy Studies at George Washington University. He is the author of more than thirty books on labor policy and minorities, including Working for the Sovereign *(1983) and* Working But Poor: America's Contradiction *(1987). Richard S. Belous is the author of* More Than Subsistence: Minimum Wages for the Working Poor *(1979) and* Creating a Strong Post-Cold War Economy *(1990).*

In this selection, Levitan and Belous argue that social welfare policies are based on assumptions about family structure and therefore influence family life. Both contend that the major welfare question is whether policies should encourage a return to the family as it existed earlier in the century or whether policies should adapt to changing family structures. This reading is from What's Happening to the American Family? *(1981).*

> *Blanche Dubois: I have always depended on the kindness of strangers.*
> TENNESSEE WILLIAMS,
> *A STREETCAR NAMED DESIRE*

PROBLEMS AND POLICIES

In the past the family may not always have been the best haven from a heart- 1
less world, as Blanche Dubois discovered, but it was the main mechanism of support in times of trouble. However, economic and social changes in many cases have shifted responsibilities for individuals in need from the family to the state. Numerous families in the welfare state now depend on the impersonal kindness of strangers to help them cope and retain viable households.

Adjustments to dramatic economic and social changes never have been 2
easy. During the initial wave of industrialization workers may have obtained a higher standard of living, but at the cost of altered living and household arrangements. Older supporting mechanisms could not function in this new environment.

Josiah Wedgwood, one of England's pioneering industrial entrepreneurs, 3
reportedly told disgruntled employees to ask their parents for a realistic description of living conditions prior to the industrial revolution and then

601

compare those accounts with their present state. The comparisons could only be highly favorable toward life under the then new and emerging mode of production, Wedgwood fervently believed. It is not as clear whether Wedgwood's workers saw the situation in the same light.

While industrialization created the conditions for rapid economic growth   4 and rising living standards, it also brought new problems. The establishment of national markets and large urban factories made employment and wages highly dependent upon the vagaries of new economic forces; the unpredictable and invisible hand could decimate as well as uplift. Also, the factory system tended to depersonalize the relationship between employer and workers. Industrialization often reduced the skill level and social status of labor. A growing number of workers were required to uproot themselves and leave the land for jobs in the expanding factories located in urban centers.

Nuclear Families

The economic and social transformations fostered a rapid rise in the gross na-   5 tional product, but at a considerable toll. A growing urban poor population and the destruction of established household patterns were byproducts of these changes. There is a growing debate among historians as to how extensive the extended family was in American society, and it appears to have been much more common in Europe than in the New World, because many of the immigrants in America were younger adults who left their parents and most other kin in their native countries.

However, when the United States was an agricultural society dotted with   6 villages and small towns, it was not uncommon to find three generations all living under the same roof. But since relatively few people lived beyond the biblical threescore and ten, and most died at a much younger age—as late as 1920 life expectancy at birth was 54 years—demographic factors suggest that sustained three-generation families could not have been widespread. In this environment, trades and skills were passed down from parent to child, and the extended family also shouldered the responsibility for the care of its elderly members and other relatives who could not fend for themselves. The rural family was often almost self-sufficient. Even when trading with the rest of the community, a family enterprise involved almost all its members. The family filled the primary roles as provider of economic necessities and education. In addition to its varied functions, the family in effect was a social security system.

As the industrial revolution progressed, the family was overshadowed by   7 other institutions in performing some of its earlier functions. Economic production moved from household to factory. New and expanding manufacturing industries required a mobile labor force, and people moved where the jobs were. Beyond employment, the social surplus generated by the highly productive industrial sector provided the resources to create public education, health care and other institutions. Providing basic education to all youngsters was one of the first major family activities in which the government became involved. Before the New Deal in America—or Bismarck in Germany and Lloyd George in England—the options were work, starve, or turn to one's family for support. Now with a vast web of income transfer and in-kind programs, an individual has many more options.

Many roles undertaken by the modern welfare state were at one time the major responsibility of the family. In fact, the founding fathers in framing the Constitution did not assign to the federal government any jurisdiction over family affairs. The various states were given the powers to pass "family laws" covering sex, marriage, responsibility for rearing children, and divorce, and it was assumed that government regulation of these essentially personal affairs would be kept to a minimum. 8

While the extended family, even when it existed, was often not the wellspring of bucolic bliss depicted by some fertile romantic minds, it had several qualities that the more urban nuclear family could not match. Compared with the extended family, the nuclear family had a much higher potential of being unstable. With more adults in the household, the extended family could absorb added responsibilities created by the death, illness, unemployment, separation, or divorce of one member, whereas a similar tragedy could crush the smaller nuclear unit. Thus, the nuclear family in the industrialized world had lost many of the traditional supports of the past. These families were playing a game of chance. If the breadwinner could hang on to a stable job with good pay, the household would be a winner compared with extended families or rural life. However, if the breadwinner died or had some mishap, then the members of the nuclear family could experience a more wrenching form of destitution than they would have endured within extended family units. 9

High mobility may have increased the possibilities for better jobs, but it has often reduced family and community ties and increased the sense of alienation and loneliness. As an indication of the rapid residential mobility within the population, the average American moves 14 times in his or her lifetime, and roughly one of five Americans moves each year. 10

As mobility reduced the roles played by the family, the void was seldom filled by other private institutions, so the government established programs to shoulder some of the responsibilities once performed by the family. Most of these programs were designed to cure a specific social pathology—such as destitution among the elderly population—and no real thought was given as to how a specific program would link up or interrelate with other policies affecting families. For better or for worse the welfare state has become an integral part of our economy and society. This institutional change has had a dramatic impact on American family life. 11

Toward a Comprehensive Policy?

Although the champions of a comprehensive family policy—whatever that may mean—continue to be heard, the government has tended to step into family situations only when families have failed or are being failed. Cam- 12 paigning for the presidency in 1976, Jimmy Carter expressed a deep concern about the "loss of stability and the loss of values" within American society. The root cause of this problem was "the steady erosion and weakening of our families," he asserted. The solution, Carter insisted, was to design a strong "pro-family" policy that would encourage families to remain together. Such a policy would include a system of income transfers that would raise families out of destitution, encourage work, and provide the in-kind goods and services required to stabilize family life. Our lack of a formal comprehensive family policy was the "same thing as an antifamily policy," he asserted. In the name of a strong "pro-family" policy, Ronald Reagan campaigned during the 1980 election on a platform that opposed the Equal Rights Amendment and abortion and favored prayer in public schools. His position in each case would lead to stronger and more stable families, Reagan insisted.

Presidents Carter and Reagan touched on what appears to be a very sensitive theme; issues concerning the future of the American family have become controversial political items. But needless to say, neither spelled out what would constitute the complete elements of a comprehensive pro-family policy. While some advocates call for the creation of new programs to improve family life, some critics argue that the welfare state has contributed to the erosion of the work ethic and caused some of the difficulties experienced by American families. Welfare, the opponents charge, has led not only to family breakups, encouraging husbands to desert their wives and fathers to leave their children, but it has also made bearing children out of wedlock profitable. The criticisms take a variety of twists and turns, each faulting the welfare state and its presumed deleterious impact on the family. One analyst has asserted that the welfare state has created a new class of "helping professionals" who have taken over too many parenthood and family life responsibilities. The assumption has been that social engineering directed by this new class has been expanded into more and more activities once left to individuals and their families, on the assumption that these helping professionals can do a better job than the one "wretchedly performed by most parents." But, instead of improving conditions, these social engineers have left families less able to cope in the world and even more dependent on the services provided by this new class. Just as the rural family became dependent upon a highly complex food distribution system, today's family must seek a growing list of supporting services outside the home. Despite good intentions, according to this formulation, the welfare state has weakened the family and forced it to turn to public resources.

America does not appear to be alone in this trend, nor has it even been the leader. In France, helping professionals started to exert an enormous influence on family life before a similar trend was established in the United States.

In a presumably conservative era, a growing number of critics have questioned the efficacy and desirability of many government efforts. However, it appears that governmental activities affecting households were more a response to, than a cause of, changing living conditions. The breakdown of the extended family preceded the establishment of the social security system in the 1930s. Payments to the elderly may have given more senior citizens the chance to maintain households independent of their children, but this freedom of choice can have many social benefits for individuals and society. It is far easier to damn the growth of the welfare state than to fashion realistic social, political, and economic alternatives. Faced with having their mother-in-law move in with them, many critics apparently would prefer the separate living arrangements made possible by the social security system. Given the current distribution of the total economic pie, one may wonder whether American family life would be measurably improved if the assistance provided by the welfare state were eliminated or vastly reduced. In most cases, government action was required because numerous families did not have the resources to cope with dire problems affecting their households. Far from leading to a weakening of family bonds, the welfare state enabled many families to remain together.

It would be more persuasive to argue that all too often the programs designed by the welfare state ignore the fact that most people live in families. For example, analysis of labor force measurements count individuals as employed, unemployed, or not in the labor force, too frequently ignoring the economic status of their families. The official statistics count the unemployed worker who is the sole support of a household the same as the one who lives in a household with a total income that exceeds the national median. Economic hardship can only be understood when one considers not only the work experience of the individual but the total family income. Many government social programs set their goals, collect data, and provide benefits on the basis of individual needs and do not consider the larger picture of household living conditions. 16

Surveys of American attitudes show highly conflicting views about the relationship of the welfare state and family policy. One national sample found that four of five individuals thought that the federal government is spending too much money. However, when questioned about specific social and family related areas as health, education, and housing, the vast majority said that the federal government should allocate more funds in each case. Given this American love-hate relationship with government, it is understandable why calls to reduce government involvement in people's lives have directly coincided with a mounting effort to expand social programs. 17

It is easy to call for a coordinated pro-family policy on the campaign trail or during congressional oversight hearings. However, it is much more difficult to propose an acceptable package of programs that would win a consensus. As Martin Rein has noted, "government cannot affirm its objectives, because it cannot articulate the normative direction toward which it is moving." Given our highly pluralistic society, there is little likelihood that a consensus will develop on a single comprehensive policy for the family. 18

Policymakers may agree on the desirability of "stabilizing" the family, but they may differ sharply on the type of family that the government should stabilize. Some would tilt government policies in favor of households in which a 19 husband is the sole breadwinner supporting a full-time housewife and several children. When the ethos was to move into suburbia and live the "good life," it appeared sound social policy to pass legislation favoring home ownership and a highway system that made suburban family life possible. Tax laws, social security, and other government benefits and obligations were structured in such a way that they encouraged household formations agreeing with this once-predominant social norm.

However, social norms have become highly diverse, and prospective   20 changes in the structure of American families may increase this diversity. Husband-wife couples, who made up about 75 percent of all households in 1960, comprised less than 65 percent of all total by the end of the 1970s and may represent only 55 percent of all American households by 1990. Even within husband-wife families there have been major changes, and more can be expected. By 1990 only about half of all married couples may have children under 15 years of age in the house, comprising one of every four households, instead of the three of seven ratio that prevailed in 1960, and one of three in 1978.

With these changes in mind, should policies encourage a return to the   21 family as it existed in the 1950s, or should they support and encourage currently diverse preferences? The appropriate answers are not at all clear. Some traditionalists view adjustment of our institutions—including education, social security, tax laws, health care system—to accommodate the new forces as fueling the fire that is destroying once widely held norms that they believe should be supported and sustained. Others believe that it is neither wise nor even possible to reverse the current trends in living arrangements, arguing that family policy should be neutral and even-handed to all types of household arrangements, thus avoiding the need to specify what type of family life the government is trying to stabilize. Still others want a family policy that is neither neutral nor protective of traditions; they advocate policies that would speed up the changes; or even would make it easier to split up a husband-wife family.

If strict neutrality sounds like a worthwhile goal in relation to household   22 types, then the specifics must be considered. Should families that have children be expected to pay the same taxes as childless households that have the same income? Or should home-owning families receive favorable tax treatment vis-à-vis renting families? Strict neutrality may appeal in principle, but it would gore some favorite oxen.

The 1980 White House Conference on Families has demonstrated the dif-   23 ficulties of reaching a consensus on specific areas of a family policy. Considering that family issues and values are deeply personal matters, and given the wide diversity of social norms, it is difficult to hammer out even general goals and objectives.

Even if the ends could be agreed upon, questions would arise concerning   24 the means of attaining these objectives. For example, how would fertility or divorce rates respond to specified shifts in the tax code? For that matter, can any legislative enactments change the basic trends that have affected American family life? Government actions *do,* of course, have a profound impact on many aspects of daily living within households, but there are limits as to what can be realistically accomplished within constitutional constraints. And the experience with the proposed Equal Rights Amendment shows the obstacles to achieving some consensus by way of constitutional change.

What about Other Countries?

An examination of several foreign countries' experiences with family policies demonstrates real differences in the pathologies that were highlighted for remedial treatment, compared with current conditions in the United States. The Scandinavian countries are often cited as models of a family policy. However, close examination of the direction taken in these countries indicates that it would be difficult and probably undesirable to duplicate similar programs in the United States.

While they may be currently called family policies in the Scandinavian nations, these programs were almost always labeled as population policies by their original advocates. In Sweden, Gunnar and Alva Myrdal were among the first and most persuasive advocates of policies to increase the annual crop of babies. During the 1930s, Swedish economists and sociologists experienced dramatic changes in their views regarding demographic growth. Prior to the Great Depression, social scientists in Sweden shared the belief that their country would be facing problems associated with overpopulation. Toward the end of the 1800s, the renowned Swedish economist Knut Wicksell launched a major campaign that made Malthusian population theory a topic of household conversation. Wicksell was concerned that if their population continued to grow unchecked, Scandinavian countries would not be able to feed their citizenry and that their per capita income would plummet as population increases would vastly outstrip the realistic prospects for economic growth.

Initially Wicksell's views received a cold reception, and he was threatened with the loss of his academic post for pressing his unpopular population theories. However, in time his views were accepted, and they became the dominant viewpoint. It could be argued that his Malthusian preachments were so persuasive as to halt population growth. But, without denying the might of the pen, it seems that world economic depression and other factors associated with industrialization may have had a greater impact on population trends than the scholarly debates. The Swedish fertility rate declined and—coupled with migration—threatened a population decline.

Whatever the causes of the declining birth rate, by the 1930s the problem was the opposite from what Wicksell had posed. Nor were the changed conditions only the concern of technical experts and policymakers. Alva Myrdal observed that the situation raised deep emotional and ideological conflicts. Many feared that the decline was destined to take the form of an "incessant and self-perpetuating liquidation of the people." The population issue was viewed as a concern affecting all of society. The outcome could not be left to chance or some invisible hand, and active government policies were viewed as a necessity even by conservative political circles within these countries. Fears about depopulation "acted as a godfather" to Scandanavian family policies.

Beyond national pride, the threat of depopulation posed other serious   29
problems to the Scandanavian nations. The revolution in demographic thought coincided with the rising influence of Keynesian macroeconomic ideas. Declines in population could be a major force halting economic development and causing long-term economic stagnation. A population reversal would reduce demand for goods and services, and it would harshly dampen capital investment in new technology. It would also have the effect in the long run of producing dire labor shortages, and it could make a country more highly dependent upon other nations. Moved by these concerns, most of the Scandinavian nations established high ranking government commissions to explore policies that might lead to population growth.

The policies, whose initial impetus was a concern over population   30
growth, resulted in expansion of the welfare state. The rationale behind reducing the financial costs of having and rearing children was that if the price of progeny were lowered, potential parents would have more children, just as they would presumably buy more of any other commodity if its price were marked down. A 1937 law provided free maternity, obstetrical services, and child-health care. Government backed low-cost loans for home furnishings and other items were also made to newly married couples. In 1948 these efforts were expanded to include universal family allowances to support all children up to the age of 16, apparently with little consideration that the meager allowances could hardly encourage greater fertility among the affluent. Later, the system was amended to include a rent allowance for households with children, and a supplemental formula was devised to provide a larger allowance to destitute families.

All of the developed industrial countries, except the United States, have   31
family allowance systems providing some modest payments regardless of family income. Because the allowances are most often universal, the actual cash value has often remained small—typically between 5 to 10 percent of a country's median wage for one child and slightly higher for more youngsters.

Population policy advocates, such as the Myrdals, were interested not   32
only in quantity but also in the quality of the next generation. Family planning support was provided to avert the birth of more unwanted children. Once the children were born the next step was to improve the environment in which children were raised. The goal of the emerging welfare state was to assure that all goods and services deemed essential for parents and children would become either free or subsidized.

Family policy in Sweden in the 1970s branched out to consider other   33
problems such as sexual equality in households. As in the United States, the Swedish tax code was based on the assumption of a household consisting of one male worker, a full-time housewife, and one or more children, but this model became less representative as women entered the labor force. To end what was, in effect, a marriage tax penalty, the Swedish tax code was revised in the 1970s to allow individual taxation for husband-wife families.

To assist or encourage women to enter the labor force, Sweden also ex-   34
panded its child care services, but the demand still exceeds the supply. In
1974, a "child leave" system was also instituted that entitled gainfully employed parents to divide 9 months of child care leave during which they receive 90 percent of their regular income. Thus, during the 1970s Swedish
social welfare efforts were revised to better reflect the gradual replacement of
the one-earner family by the two-breadwinner household.

Should the United States emulate this model of a family policy? To be   35
sure, many of its features could be included in American social welfare programs. For example, as far as the U.S. Internal Revenue Service is concerned,
two cannot always live as cheaply as one; multi–pay check families often pay
higher income taxes than they would if they were not married and had the
same total income. However, the United States is far more heterogeneous
than other industrialized nations. It is also appears to lack any specific central unifying principle, such as the former depopulation fears of other nations, which could unite American concerns in this area. Considering U.S.
concerns about the limits to growth and environmental factors, it does not
appear that pronatalist policies could provide the key spark to motivate an
integrated American family policy. The emotional hassles generated by the
1980 White House family conferences are ample evidence of the concerns
and obstacles that lie in the path of any attempt to formulate a consensus on
a family policy.

West Germany does provide an example of how other concerns can result   36
in the formation of family policies. After World War II, it appeared to policy-
makers that the only German institution that remained firm despite the dev-
astation was the family. As it appeared to be in relatively good shape, it was
decided that the family should be used as a healthy building block in the
foundation of efforts to revitalize the country. While Americans express
many anxieties regarding modern family life, no one family issue or group of
issues has captivated our attention the way fertility rates (or postwar fears in
Germany) provided a springboard for other nations.

Instead of designing an explicitly coordinated family policy, the American   37
welfare state has settled for a series of disparate programs that affect families.
Avoiding a grand design, these programs are expanding gradually and incre-
mentally, and they are adapting to the changing needs. Underlying the diverse proposals, but modest programmatic efforts, is the recognition that, for
better or worse, American families will remain in a period of transition, and
the resulting society will continue to have highly pluralistic living arrangements. This view, however, is not universally accepted, and voices are raised
championing family policies suitable for a puritanical or Victorian society.

What can be accomplished is an easing of the period of transition by ac-   38
tive social policies that seek to provide a basic living standard and essential
services for all types of families. Such a policy would ensure that children are
not raised in deprivation; it would keep them dry, warm, and fed no matter
what type of household they live in. A realistic approach to these problems
would be first to examine the already existing social efforts in these areas, and
then to determine what changes are desirable and probable.

PROGRAMS AFFECTING FAMILIES

The United States may lack a coordinated family policy, but the government   39
has instituted myriad programs that affect households. The Family Impact
Seminar of the George Washington University has found 270 different federal
programs, administered by 17 different departments and agencies, that have
a direct impact on American families. Any family that pays taxes, receives
benefits or contributes to the government's massive income transfer system,
or is involved with the public schools or courts, or seeks employment, training, or other social services is touched in some way by the far-reaching welfare state. Indeed, it seems almost impossible to establish policies that do not
affect families. Like Molière's hero who spoke prose all his life but was not
aware of the fact, American policymakers keep on designing new programs
without recognizing their family implications.

The programs' basic assumptions about family life, however, often have   40
been hidden and not fully stated. Assumptions that may have made sense
during the 1930s may no longer reflect the shifting conditions and social
mores that prevail today. Sometimes policymakers have ignored the ramifica-
tions of specific programs. Few politicians are on record as favoring policies
that discourage marriage, but, as noted earlier, some programs may have such
an impact.

Programs aimed at solving a specific problem unrelated to families may   41
nevertheless have a tangential impact upon them. Reducing youth unemployment and retraining workers displaced by technological changes have
been the goals of several government efforts. That the alleviation of these
problems also could have a beneficial impact on American family life cannot
be denied because workers with stable and sufficient earnings may be in a
better position to lead stable family lives. However, family-related objectives
often have not been explicitly considered in these programs, as their design
or evaluation have tended to view the target population only as individuals
and not as members of household units.

Basic Needs

In the welfare state, the concept of what constitutes basic needs is continually   42
expanding to include food, income, health care, shelter, education, social services, and even assistance for heating homes. The Social Security Act of 1935
has been the cornerstone in this effort. In fashioning this legislation, the Roosevelt administration and Congress concluded that shifting economic and social realities had created conditions requiring federal intervention, because
the then-existing arrangements of mutual aid—including family, private, and
local assistance—could not meet the complex needs of an advanced industrialized society. The diminished nuclear family could not cope on its own with
major bouts of massive unemployment or other disasters causing the loss of
income. In the early stages of drafting the proposal, some New Dealers advocated a social security system that included provision for family subsidy,

health care, and maternity benefits. However, the final package was much less ambitious and limited to what were then considered basic necessities.

It remained for later generations to expand the definition of basic needs. 43 Helping all families to obtain minimal adequate living conditions requires a sustained long-term effort. The problems faced by many households in need are due not so much to cyclical slumps in economic conditions as to deep-rooted structural problems within society. Efforts to provide the basics for all households and to raise families out of poverty have met with some success. Poverty has been significantly reduced, even though liberals and conservatives may argue a good deal over the specifics.

Despite conceptual and technical problems of measurement, the federal 44 government has devised a poverty index that has gained wide acceptance. The index reflects the different consumption requirements of families based on size and composition, sex and age of the family head, and farm and non-farm residence. The 1981 poverty thresholds follow:

Number of family members	Nonfarm
1	$3,800
2	4,900
3	5,800
4	7,400
5	8,800
6	9,900

The number of families in destitution declined significantly during the 45 1960s and 1970s. While more than one of every five families were poor at the start of the 1960s, this level had fallen to one of ten two decades later. But these gains were not evenly distributed by size or type of family. The chances of being in poverty are highly related to family structure. More than one-third of female-headed families remain poor, as do more than one-seventh of families with children under 18 (figure 1).

The population of families in poverty also demonstrates other important 46 differences in personal characteristics when compared with all American families. About one of four heads of poverty households completed fewer than eight years of elementary school education, compared with only about one of ten for all household heads. Place of residence also affects the incidence of destitution within families. Rural families face a much higher chance of living in destitution than do urban households. Husband-wife families experience a lower poverty rate than other family types. However, of the 5 million families classified in 1979 as living in poverty, 46 percent were husband-wife families, 51 percent were headed by females, and the remainder were male-headed families with no wife present.

The principal economic support of almost 30 percent of all American 47 families no longer comes from the earnings of a male head. This, of course, is due to several reasons. In about 14 percent of families, there is no male head to provide any support. Also, with an increased percentage of wives in the work force, their earnings plus earnings of other family members may exceed that of the traditional provider.

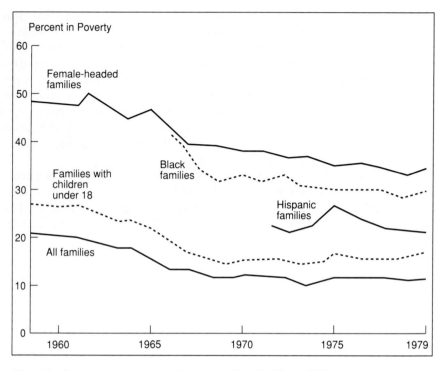

Figure 1. Despite improvement, about one of ten families still lives in poverty. (U.S. Department of Commerce, Bureau of the Census.)

Having an employed head may reduce the probability that a family will   48
be in destitution, yet many heads are among the ranks of the working poor. A
job for these working poor heads—even full-time employment—is no sure escape from poverty. About half of the heads of poverty households work during the year, and nearly 1 million of them work full time, full year.

Alternative definitions and concepts have a major impact on poverty esti-   49
mates. The Congressional Budget Office (CBO) has estimated that in the absence of government transfer payments about 25 percent of all American
families would have been in poverty during 1976. However, government cash
transfers are included in the official poverty index, and this inclusion reduced
the proportion of destitute American families to about 10 percent. If in-kind
programs were included, such as subsidized housing and food stamps, then
the percentage in poverty would be reduced even further.

Government programs may not have eliminated poverty within all fami-   50
lies, but they have vastly reduced the chances for almost all types of households. Destitution has been most highly reduced among households with
heads 65 and over. Close to 1 million poor families are headed by an elderly
adult. Without government transfer payments the number of poverty families with an elderly head would have been 60 percent greater, and the number
of destitute families headed by females would have been almost 25 percent

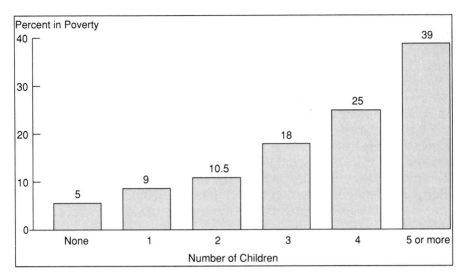

Figure 2. Larger families faced a greater risk of economic hardship. (U.S. Department of Commerce, Bureau of the Census.)

greater. While the free market has continually reduced the proportion of families living below the official poverty threshold, many more households would have been counted among the poor in the absence of governmental intervention.

The welfare state has done, however, very little to aid two-parent families with children. Low-income families are frequently driven into poverty by the addition of family members (figure 2). Indeed, family size and poverty are closely related, with 57 percent of poor children coming from families with five or more members. A higher incidence of poverty among larger families is to be expected in a society where need is ignored as a factor in wage determination and where the necessity of child care often hinders the wife or female family head from earning needed income. As noted earlier, the United States is the only major industrial nation that makes no provision for family allowances. 51

In general, government policies to help the poor include four types of programs: (1) cash support; (2) direct provisions of necessities such as food, shelter, and medical care; (3) preventive and compensatory efforts for children and youth; and (4) attempts to restructure existing institutions to help families adapt to those institutions. 52

Various categories of families have different needs. Family heads and young people with their life's work ahead of them must have not only mere daily subsistence but also encouragement and support for acquiring the skills sought by employers. For the aged and their families, medical care and nursing homes are of primary concern. Children also need health care and the basic education to assure them opportunities in the future. 53

Also, certain services, such as child care, are being demanded by families   54
with incomes higher than the median. Government social welfare efforts and
the system used to finance these efforts have a pervasive impact on family decisions. Government policies may affect the choice of a place of residence or
the decision to purchase or rent shelter, and may have an impact on the determination to marry. The financial prospects of ending a marriage can be altered by government transfer payments and in-kind aid programs. Whether
one enters the labor market could well depend on the governmental child
care policies in many cases. This is not to say that people act like cold computers and just calculate economic costs and benefits before they make decisions regarding love, marriage, and family life. Any analysis that ignores the
irrational and emotional aspects bound up in these decisions is likely to be
off the mark. However, households cannot totally ignore the impact of government policies.

Realistic Goals

It is difficult to fashion social welfare efforts and the system to finance these   55
programs without having an impact upon family life, even though the assumptions made about the effects of the programs may not be spelled out. A
major problem underlying recent policies is that governmental interventions
fail to pay adequate heed to changing family structure and attitudes about its
roles. The basic assumptions concerning the typical American family that
prevailed during the 1930s, when many of the current programs were initiated, no longer fit American family life. Furthermore, given the rapid changes
that American families are experiencing, grand designs for a new comprehensive family policy are likely to be based on misleading assumptions or values
that lack a predominant consensus. Marginal changes in current intervention
policies addressed to emerging problems are likely to be more productive.

Both Democratic and Republican administrations in recent years have   56
shown a distinct propensity to oversell their proposals. The Johnson administration promised that the Great Society programs would "open the doors of
learning . . . rewarding leisure . . . and opportunity . . . to everyone." The revenue sharing system launched in the early 1970s was far less than the "second American revolution" touted by the Nixon administration. After years of
debate, numerous presidential proposals for a unified welfare system have
failed to become law. A grand design of family policy is likely to meet a similar fate. While it may be far less dramatic, incremental reform of the already
existing system provides the most realistic approach to helping families during this rough period of transition.

Questions

1. Within your own community, do families take on responsibilities for some of the
    obligations noted by Levitan and Belous? If so, how is it possible for this to hap-
    pen? Are there any trade-offs? If not, would it be desirable if it were possible?

2. Why has the welfare state taken on a greater role in aiding families in the last century?
3. Do you feel that welfare policies should encourage a return to the traditional family or should they "pay heed to changing family structure and attitudes about its roles"? What do the authors conclude?

Children in History: Concepts of Nature and Society

LUDMILLA JORDANOVA

Ludmilla Jordanova has been a lecturer in history at the University of Essex since 1980, and is the author of Lamarck *(1980).*

In this selection, Jordanova discusses the difficulty of defining childhood, and argues that historical definitions are inadequate, especially the analogy of the child with nature. Because the definition of childhood is a cultural construct, she feels that it is important to recognize the extent to which these constructs mold the experience of children. This reading is from Children, Parents, and Politics *(1989).*

Introduction

Children have recently become news. Child abuse, incest, and murder frequently occupy the headlines. Television and radio programmes are regularly devoted to these subjects. This media attention contains a drama and a voyeurism of which we should be properly sceptical. Furthermore, it may serve to confirm a sense of complacency among 'normal' parents—they are not the abusers in question. Present-day reactions to the ill-treatment of children are certainly complex enough without the additional problem of history. By this I mean that implicit historical claims are often contained in media presentations and in received opinion. Currently there is an immediate sense of crisis about the treatment of children, despite a recognition that any visible increases in child abuse may be in the reporting rather than in the occurrence itself. Readers, viewers, and listeners easily feel a sense of urgency, mixed with fear at the magnitude of contemporary ills, when they learn of damaged children. Many treatments of the subject advance a covert historical thesis which is highly morally charged. Our perceptions of contemporary issues are clearly moulded by such an unspoken historical consciousness, within which the past is often idealised and the present depicted as a decline. Of course, our implicit historical sense can go in the opposite direction morally speaking, as it does in relation to child labour. When the work of the young is considered, the past becomes barbaric and exploitative, the present enlightened by the discovery of the importance of play, which thereby becomes the antithesis of work. Because we so often construct and deploy historical myths to organise contemporary tensions, it is important to assess what kind of historical knowledge is possible about children.

616

We might put this same point in another way. It is common to find the dichotomy traditional/modern used in connection with current social ills, including those where children are at issue.[1] For many people, the abuse of children symbolises the negative aspects of modern life. We can easily see how widespread the identification between children and social well-being is from the prevalent use by politicians of phrases like 'our children's future', which raise questions about the present and the future in deliberately emotive terms. As a result, there is little commitment to thinking logically about children's social position, partly for the understandable reason that we are all deeply implicated, emotionally, in child welfare. Yet, until we face up to this problem, discussions of children will continue to be muddled in ways that are seldom apparent.

I want to suggest that children pose special intellectual challenges to us. This is partly because the state of being a child is temporary and hard to define. Indeed, the process of becoming an adult involves a number of fundamental shifts which, certainly from an adult perspective and probably also from a child's, are so dramatic that a gradualist language modelled on small-scale, incremental growth seems hopelessly inadequate. There are two issues, to which we shall return, which focus the problem with particular force—work and sex.

Historical writing participates in the construction of our ideas of childhood. The history of childhood has been used as a way of speaking about other social transformations, precisely because it can so easily be taken to symbolise them. Discussions about children and childhood, past or present, are suffused with moral assumptions. Furthermore, we often use such discourses as a way of speaking about other concerns. I also wish to suggest that using a language which refers to children in terms of nature, as I believe we have done for almost three centuries, is profoundly problematic. A general commitment to speaking of children in a language permeated by natural imagery (tender, pure, innocent, plantlike) and to thinking about them as asocial or presocial has certain consequences of which we should be fully aware. The term 'nature' itself is highly complex, giving rise to meanings which are not consistent with one another; indeed, this may be one reason why it plays such a central role in our social thinking. This role is particularly crucial in relation to the child. The languages of nature used about children are a major vehicle for our moral concerns.

The moral notions we use when speaking about children can usefully be explored historically. This enables us to put them in a larger perspective by exploring both continuity and change. One possible spin-off of a historical approach is that it can prevent us from taking any particular set of attitudes or behaviours as 'natural' or 'normal'. By examining the historical variety of the position of children and of ideas about childhood, and by tracing back some of the steps by which we arrived at our present situation, we can achieve a more dispassionate analysis. Studying children historically is not, however, without its difficulties. What, for example, is the proper object of inquiry? Such a question is less simple-minded than it sounds, since 'child' is not a simple descriptive category. Is age the major criterion or does this shift with class, gender, and historical period? How can a person be a child in some respects (e.g. living at home, being under parental authority) and not in others (e.g. being economically and sexually active)? We might propose that the historian study those deemed children at a specific time and place—a solution which allows for changes in concepts of the child, but not for the problem of simultaneously conflicting attributions. Furthermore, is the study of children different from the study of childhood? To this we must answer yes, since the first implies a study of groups of persons, the second that of a state of being. In the latter case, how can the historian examine such an abstraction? The only way is through those domains which consider children in general: the law, medicine, social policy, and so on. A full history of childhood has to engage with the complexity of the history of ideas.

    Yet there is something inherently unsatisfactory about studying the history of childhood without any reference to specific historical personages. It offends deeply held beliefs about authenticity and historical method. Historians persist in searching for the voice of children themselves, in their diaries and autobiographies and in literature written expressly for them.[2] Such a search is based on an illusion about both the nature of childhood and of history. Children, I submit, are constructed in particular social settings; there can be no authentic voice of childhood speaking to us from the past because the adult world dominates that of the child. Thus, while we can study particular children, provided suitable materials exist, and examine general ideas about childhood, we cannot capture children's past experiences or responses in a pure form.   6

    The desire for historical authenticity has also emerged forcefully in relation to women and the working class. The child, the woman, and the worker have all been treated as 'other', that is, as outside mainstream culture and separate from dominant social groups, and hence as not requiring the historical treatment reserved for the adult male members of elites, who become the 'norm'. In reacting against this, radical historians have sought the authentic voice of those who not only could not speak for themselves before, but were often assumed to have no tongues. There are now lively debates about the extent to which it is possible to bring women and the working class back through a study of their distinctive behaviours, ideas, and writings. In a similar vein some historians of childhood claim to be giving to the young their own, autonomous history.[3] There are, however, different kinds of otherness involved in these three instances. For example, the otherness of women is based on the depth of gender difference which, however you define it, can readily be seen as constitutive of social relations in general. For the most part we understand men and women, male and female, to be separated by a profound gulf. The peculiarity of the otherness we assign to children is paradoxical in that we have all experienced childhood—hence to make the child other to our adult selves we must split off a part of our past, a piece of ourselves. This accounts for the profound ambivalence which informs our attitudes to children and which is relived when we become parents ourselves. It may be   7 that women and workers have simply spoken with the voices of the dominant discourse, although many historians would deny this. Children, however, have inevitably done so, since there can be no alternative for them. Their passage into being is inexorably a coming into language, a language which is, for the child, a given. There are no special sources available to historians or to others which avoid this trap. The quest for an authentic other is not fulfilled by children—nor, indeed, by any other group. Like children, both women and 'the people' have often been analogised with nature. We remain convinced that for children the comparison is valid, and this makes us imprisoned by it. This long-standing analogy is reinforced by our lively biological sense of the processes of procreation, a fresh consciousness of children—at least when babies—as wonders of nature.

The relationship between children, childhood, and nature has existed at a number of different levels. It is as complex as our ideas about nature itself: the state of childhood may be seen as pure, innocent, or original in the sense of primary; children may be analogised with animals or plants, thereby indicating that they are natural objects available for scientific and medical investigation; children could be valued as aesthetic objects for their beauty and physical perfection—but they could equally well be feared for their instinctual, animal-like natures. Two fundamental points, therefore, arise out of the association between children and nature: First, the polyvalency of nature led to a variety of concepts of childhood, and second, these diverse meanings of childhood were deeply imbued with moral values.

Children could be used by scholars as a tool for revealing historically shifting meanings of nature. In fact, historians generally use them for different purposes, themselves products of the sentimentalising of children which the association with nature has brought. It is therefore necessary to discuss first how historians have approached these matters before considering some historical material which sheds more direct light on the matter. Throughout we should remember the power of language to shape our ideas. Historians, like everyone else, have worked from commonly held assumptions about children, without attending to the constraints—moral, cultural, and linguistic—on their own frameworks.

HISTORIANS AND CHILDREN

Historians have 'discovered' children and childhood only relatively recently. It was Philippe Ariès who started the trend with his book *Centuries of Childhood*.[4] Although much criticised, it is nonetheless treated by non-historians as a definitive account which establishes certain 'truths' about the subject that are now common knowledge. The volume is a marvellously rich piece of historical writing, drawing on an impressive range of sources, some little used by historians—paintings, architecture, costume, literature, and so on. Ariès advances the thesis that in medieval society children were seen merely as small adults and treated casually. They participated in adult society because no special provisions were made for them. This situation changed, he suggests, over a long period of time, roughly the sixteenth to eighteenth centuries, with other major social transformations. The end result was a society which associated children firmly with the domestic sphere and hence with women and with education. Children came to be treated as a particular class of persons, to whom special conditions apply and for whom special provision must therefore be made. A subsidiary thesis concerns parental attitudes towards children. In times of high mortality, children were less valued as individuals, parents were more 'cruel', mourned their children less, and were generally indifferent to them. These attitudes also underwent a radical transformation, so that by the nineteenth century recognisably 'modern' emotions existed. *Centuries of Childhood* has, however, significant limitations. Ariès relies heavily on French materials, with the result that it may be illegitimate to generalise from his account. Furthermore, he simply assumes that there have been dramatic changes in the understanding and so also in the experience of childhood. He also takes it for granted that these changes are integral to larger social and cultural transformations.

There can be no doubt that there are serious shortcomings in Ariès's   11
work, but the fundamental question remains how and why his work gripped people's imaginations so forcibly. Certainly it had novelty value; possibly he told them things they wanted to hear about children. Ariès made early modern society an 'other' with respect to children. It could be distanced, put aside, rendered safe by an account which perpetually allows readers to say 'not like us'. The flipside of this is a reinforcement of the readers' own values and attitudes, and a yardstick with which to judge how far society has come. In fact, Ariès implies a somewhat negative interpretation of modern views when he stresses the isolation and lack of sociability of the modern family in general and of women and children in particular. He often romanticised the past to celebrate traditional values. Nonetheless, Ariès may be criticised for treating the present as a norm. Whereas early modern society had no notion of childhood, we now have an elaborate one. Their absence is defined by our presence. This particular aspect of Ariès's argument has prompted much critical comment, largely in relation to the logic of historical argument.[5]

Here I want to stress another aspect of the debate. Arguments among his-   12
torians of childhood have implicit value systems built into them, and judgement is passed on people long dead. This is most obvious when we look at areas that involve 'cruelty' and violence, for there is abundant historical evidence of gross physical chastisement, economic exploitation, and parental neglect. For us, cruelty to children is such an emotive topic that we lapse all too easily into confusion. Faced with evidence of infanticide, abandonment, murder, and child labour, we are at a loss as to how to construct historical arguments adequate to their explanation.[6] There is a genuine problem of imagination here. Unless scholars are willing to think deeply about violence towards children, which inevitably involves facing their own feelings, they have few options available. They can either deny the validity of the evidence or the interpretative procedures applied to it—for example, by appealing to

the 'untypical' nature of infanticide—or they can seek other explanations— such as citing the ubiquity of poverty as a cause of harsh treatment of children. Those who espouse the first position often refer to the constancy of human nature in their support. It is, they imply, 'natural' for parents to love and cherish their children, and denying that this was always the case degrades the members of past societies. They have to produce counter-evidence to show that cruelty and violence were not typical.[7] Those who take up the second position generally use a form of economic determinism as their framework. Under the guiding notion of the 'family economy', they point out that shedding children could have been the only way that a family as a whole could survive.[8] Infanticide and abandonment, they argue, were forms of behaviour manifested by those pushed to extremes by hardship and degradation. Similarly, children who were sent to work, often very young, must be understood in the context of a society which took child labour for granted. This began to change only at the end of the eighteenth century, in philanthropic circles, while legislation designed to put a stop to child labour altogether did not come in Britain until the late nineteenth century and was then by no means wholly successful.

Indeed, it is hard to deny that both of these positions have some validity,   13 although they contain refusals to imagine unfamiliar attitudes and forms of behaviour. A few historians have taken a third approach that solves some of these problems. They take the phenomena (infanticide, abandonment, murder, labour, and so on), accept their existence, and then seek to interpret them in terms of the value system of the time. They refuse the moralism implicit in so much historical writing on children. At the same time, they challenge traditional historiography by assuming that uncovering the 'meaning' that has been given to events and experiences in the past is an important and valid historical procedure.[9] It follows directly from this that those who concern themselves with material conditions must consider belief systems as an integral part of historical research. This approach also involves defending the study of 'atypical' behaviour on the grounds that it offers special insights into larger social patterns. In recent years we have come to associate the belief that the normal and the abnormal are closely linked, each existing only in relation to the other, with the work of Michel Foucault.[10] In fact, the idea that the study of deviance—defined relatively, not absolutely—reveals the norm, has existed for some time among sociologists who argue that our understanding of general social patterns may be dramatically sharpened by studying abnormal behaviour. This third approach is open to the complex position of children in past societies, and it requires the historian to be equally alive to a symbolic level.

It was implicit in Ariès's book that stages of life are historically con-   14 structed. The idea of there being definable 'ages of man' is an old one; these ages were commonly depicted in Renaissance art. But their function was not to display socially distinct categories, but to act as *memento mori*, reminding people of their own mortality as part of the larger theme of *vanitas*.[11] Historians frequently claim that 'childhood' came to be recognized as a separate developmental category first and then, in the nineteenth century, 'adolescence' came into existence. The language we use to speak about such historical processes is crucial. Were these in fact 'inventions'—that is, creations of the human mind—or were they 'discoveries'—that is, recognitions of a state existing outside the realm of ideas? If childhood and adolescence are inventions, then they may be understood in the same terms as other cultural products. If they are discoveries, 'the child' and 'the adolescent' become natural, timeless categories, waiting in the wings of history for just recognition. Discussing the problems inherent in historical language highlights the general difficulties already noted in defining children.

These difficulties are immediately apparent if we ask the simple questions 'What is a child?' and 'What is an adolescent?' There are no clear-cut boundaries here—a child in one culture could be a parent or prostitute at the same age elsewhere. There can be no neat way of defining children simply in terms of their age. Turning to general characteristics shared by all children provides no straightforward solutions either. What do new-borns and nine-year-olds have in common? Our answer to such a question would probably include the following characteristics: dependence upon parents, economic and sexual inactivity, living in the parental home, an absence of legal and political rights. Most of these criteria do not apply to past societies. Furthermore, different parts of a single society treat children and childhood differently. This makes historical generalisation fraught with difficulties, all the more so when present-day assumptions are foisted on the past.

Many past societies had little formal apparatus for dealing with children, hence their position was governed by contingencies. Early modern England, it seems, operated without any clear legal defintion of 'child'. Children could be called as witnesses, if, in the opinion of the judge, they seemed able to give testimony. With no legal controls on age of work, a child might be self-sufficient economically at quite a young age. Children of that era who were apprenticed, were, at least in theory, subject to the physical discipline of their masters or mistresses, who sometimes beat them to death.[12]

In a society at any one time, no general definition of childhood exists, although there have been occasions when powerful sectors, such as the law, have provided relatively coherent and systematic accounts of what a child is, particularly in relation to rights. However, far from lapsing into defeatism on account of the difficulty of providing general definitions, we should recognise that it opens up some interesting possibilities. Classes, groups, and individuals are constantly negotiating and renegotiating in many different contexts what children are, using perpetual social and conceptual policing which is hard to reconstruct historically.

There is a controversial school of the history of childhood which has not been mentioned so far: psychohistory. Historians using Freudian techniques and theories inevitably place special emphasis on childhood, since psychoanalytic theory accords a privileged place to the child. For many psychohistorians this involves studying individual or collective biographies, using evidence of early experience as a major source. Although this method can help us to understand the childhood of particular individuals, it does not necessarily illuminate the historical aspects of the nature of childhood itself. This is partly because it employs a genetic model, based on biology, to explain a logic of personal development. Stressing the 'evolutionary' processes that parent–child relationships have undergone has resulted in a flat, one-dimensional history. Although it is possible to apply psychoanalytic insights to the history of childhood in a wide variety of ways, one in particular, associated with Lloyd de Mause and the journal he founded, has dominated the field. De Mause argued that societies undergo developmental processes in relation to children just as individuals do and that these can be understood psychoanalytically. Whereas in the past parents were repressive and sadistic, in more recent times they have been increasingly willing to accept the individuality of children. Parents, it seems, are growing up. The maturity of the mid-twentieth century, called the helping mode, was arrived at via five earlier modes which characterised successive historical periods: the infanticidal, abandonment, ambivalent, intrusive, and socialization modes.[13] It is frequently alleged that psychohistory reduces historical phenomena to the psychology of past individuals. It is perfectly possible, however, to apply these same ideas to groups and cognitive structures to uncover both the deep investments we have in seeing children in particular ways and the complex determinants of their lives.

Writing the history of childhood leads us to ask questions about the adequacy of our intellectual tools, calling our entire worldview into question. We must decide, for example, whether children are constructed differently by different societies, whether human nature is trans-historical, and to what extent the material circumstances of a culture guide its theories and practices in relation to children. Curious though it may seem, historians are reluctant not only to raise such matters but even to blend different approaches, as if too much else hangs on their choices. The only way to avoid the trap of a biologism according to which all parents naturally love their children or of an economic determinism in which children are either liabilities or assets to be used in family survival strategies is to examine the place of children in a given society as a whole, without exempting them from the larger multi-faceted changes all societies have undergone. 19

Sources and Interpretation

Historians have a wealth of material through which they can understand the child as a social and cultural product. Indeed, it is hard to think of an area of life which does not, in some way or other, bear on the nature of childhood. But some sources are more revealing than others, partly because they pertain to children and childhood quite directly. The role of educational theory and practice is the most obvious example, although historians of education have had relatively little to say about the construction of childhood, perhaps because they have conventionally given priority to the development of formal educational institutions. Of course, educational sources are limited in that 20 schooling has paid scant attention to tiny children—hence they reveal little about children in their first years of life—and in that many are biased towards the education of boys, since in the past that of girls was often of a less formal kind. Nonetheless, we can learn much from the teaching methods used, the books provided, and the organisation of the school. Interpreting these materials can be tricky, however. If we use a present-day definition of 'good' teaching, as some historians of education do, early books for children (an eighteenth-century phenomenon) are easily dismissed as inappropriate and tedious—a value judgement with little historical merit.[14]

Those who study childhood give particular weight to autobiographies 21 and diaries. This is part of a larger trend towards the use of such sources, discernible in many fields of social history, produced by the drive for authenticity mentioned above. This material requires scrupulous interpretation. We cannot take at face value accounts of intimate relationships provided by the participants, especially when it comes to relationships as complex and ambivalent as those between parents and children. But however these texts are used, they remain products of individual lives and may reveal little about the general state of childhood. There is an issue here of different, although related, levels of generality. It is mistaken to assume that if we aggregate numerous individual accounts we arrive at insights of a more general or abstract nature. Rather, we should seek appropriate sources which are themselves of that kind.

In this respect, medicine, like the law, is a promising area. The nature and 22 extent of medical interest in children has been far from constant. The development of specific children's facilities (i.e. hospitals and dispensaries) was a feature of the late eighteenth and nineteenth centuries, while an organised field of medical knowledge—paediatrics—did not emerge until the later nineteenth century. There is an extensive medical literature on child-rearing which goes back at least to the seventeenth century, although it grew vastly in the eighteenth century. This literature is of particular interest because it sought to give a coherent account of children in naturalistic terms. A medical framework dictated that an internally consistent, observationally based account be produced. Significantly, this account had to be accessible to the middle-class readership to whom such works were addressed. If children raise contradictory issues for adults, then a domain dedicated to the elimination of conceptual wrinkles will prove especially revealing. Neither medical nor legal writings, however, have offered simple solutions to the conceptual complexity of the category 'child'.

Widely varied sources indicate that the general drive towards naturalism 23 during the eighteenth century included the child—indeed, the child became a paradigm of the natural.[15] Being the heirs of this same intellectual tradition, we find it hard to step outside it and see it for what it really is—a cultural construct. To designate something as natural is not only to give it a form of otherness, but also certain kinds of priority, and to treat it as both primitive and ideal. Two things follow from the recourse to nature. First, epistemologically speaking, 'nature' is a privileged domain, in a sharp, because relatively novel, way in the late seventeenth and eighteenth centuries. Nature, because it was deemed the unique source of valid knowledge, endowed observational accounts of childhood with particular authority. Simultaneously, the medical writer's status as the possessor of natural knowledge and the child's status as natural object were affirmed. Medical practitioners, ever attentive to ways of creating and reinforcing their status, relied heavily on the validity of their knowledge in making larger claims. Second, languages of nature are highly metaphorical. We must recognise that the associations, resonances, and meanings which language, the primary analytical tool, gives rise to can never be fully determined by authors.[16]

The question of growth, especially important within a naturalistic per- 24
spective, exemplifies the difficulties people experienced in the past of finding the appropriate language. It is self-evident that children grow and at some point become adults. But how does this take place? What other processes are similar? Can we account for emotional and intellectual growth in the same terms as physical growth? How do we know when these processes are complete? What parts of growing up are 'natural', what parts not so? Are we to characterise unnatural developments in terms of pathology, of environmental mishaps, or of parental inadequacy? Although we can, and generally have, answered these questions in biological/naturalistic terms, our responses embody social and cultural shifts. Many eighteenth-century medical writings about children insisted upon the naturalness of their development. For example, teething was redefined as a normal event, its status as disease rejected. Swaddling came to be widely condemned on the grounds that the healthy infant body does not require such human manipulation. This constituted an attack on the attitudes and customs of specific social groups. The cult of breast-feeding in this period, often associated with Rousseau, is another case where social issues—here concern about mothering and criticism of wet-nursing—were expressed in a language of nature.[17]

It was not that people suddenly changed their child-rearing habits, but 25
that a group of middle-class professionals and intellectuals strove to rethink the nature of childhood as a part of their approach to 'nature'. This project was not confined to medicine, but also involved such areas as social and political theory and the law. Writings in these areas help us reconstruct the imaginative field childhood inhabited during that specific period. They also indicate points of tension and difficulty in relation to childhood. Rousseau's writings, for example, reveal that the role of the mother and, more generally, the nature of womanhood caused him particular problems.[18] Numerous contemporary writings tell the same story. In effect, a guarantee about the quality of mothering was sought which would certify the legitimacy of children and ensure their survival. It is certainly not coincidental that the art and literature of the period displays a considerable sentimentalisation of both mothers and young children.[19] If we took this at face value we might see no more than romanticism. Looked at with an awareness of the uses to which childhood and nature were being put, it appears rather different. It signals considerable social tension about parental roles, about who should control a child's up-

bringing—in fact about gender divisions in general. We could extend this analysis to include relationships between servants and children, about which there was also widespread concern.[20] When writers advise parents to police the contact between children and those who care for them, they both evoke the idea of children as natural—they are plants, for example, easily distorted or destroyed by poor gardening—and express conflicts between classes, mediated in this case through control over children.

These examples, although brief, should establish three points. First, it is impossible to separate children from their social and cultural setting; all domains contain implications for them, just as they can be used in a wide variety of arguments as emblems or symbols. Second, although our ideas about children and childhood are a product of history, it is also possible—and certainly easier—to gain a measure of distance from historical materials than from our own culture. This distance from the past, like that of anthropologists from the societies they study, is intellectually productive. It enables us to understand value systems different from our own, which should no longer be seen as the norm or as a peak of progress. Complacency is a formidable enemy. We tend to oscillate between self-congratulation for our enlightened views of children and self-abnegation for our ill treatment of them. Third, no single type of source material provides an authoritative historical picture, while the value of all sources depends on their interpretation. 26

Two specific issues illustrate the rewards and difficulties of historical approaches: sexuality and work. Present-day attitudes towards the latter are certainly characterised by self-congratulation: We believe that in Western societies we have abolished the iniquity of economically active children. A historical perspective on the fundamental change from having most children in the work force to placing all children in full-time education may be illuminating. By contrast, we have a distinctly self-punishing attitude to the sexuality of children, which goes right to the heart of current concerns. We agonise about teenage pregnancy, contraception for the young, AIDS, and incest. Sex in relation to children is popularly perceived as a crisis issue. Here too a historical perspective may be valuable. 27

Sexuality

We have constructed a mythical past for children. One element of this mythology is the idea that sexuality was repressed, often quite brutally, in the Victorian period, but that twentieth-century attitudes are altogether more enlightened. This fits neatly with a view commonly expressed by historians—that the early modern period knew little sexual inhibition, hence there was no taboo associated with childhood sexuality. Michel Foucault argued, however, that what appeared as Victorian repression was rather a compulsion to create discourses about sexuality.[21] What people apparently feared and deplored, such as children masturbating, they spoke and wrote about endlessly. For Foucault, it is essential to put the new discourses on sexuality in the context of power relations in the society as a whole; the sexuality of children is 28 no exception to this. Since the publication of Volume One of Foucault's *History of Sexuality* (French edition, 1976, English edition, 1978), there has been a veritable explosion of writings on that subject. Many of these were written from a particular vantage point—by active members of the gay communities, for example. Scholars have also studied the male construction of female sexuality. Yet very little attention has been paid to children. This may be partly because no academic groups expressly serve their interests, and there are doubtless additional reasons. What sources are available for such an enquiry, for instance? Furthermore, in a setting where personal relations are regulated more by custom than by law, as was the case in Europe before the late nineteenth century, we might expect little comment on such matters. Whether the omission is to be blamed on the sources or on those who study them, the fact remains that historians have approached sexuality and the young through a limited range of topics: bridal pregnancy and illegitimacy, courtship customs, masturbation, and prostitution. Only in the case of masturbation were children truly involved.[22] In each case, however, the society in question had to erect some conventions, if not laws, to help its members think about whether a particular action was acceptable or not. The fact that customary controls played an important role does not mean that moral boundaries were shaky or ill-patrolled. The task of analysing the extent to which past societies understood sexual behavior in age-related terms is just beginning. It does seem clear that criteria for judging the sexual activities of the young shifted, and that, from roughly the mid-eighteenth century on, many commentators found custom, with its strong associations with both ritual and material life, inadequate; they sought norms more rooted in 'nature'.

Although we live in a post-Freudian age, in which it is widely accepted [29] that children possess latent sexuality, we nonetheless think of children as beings who are not actively sexual. Furthermore, we now regulate these matters by law as well as by convention. The state of childhood is one which, although preparatory for adulthood, is supposed to be free from the burden of sexual relationships. Those who attack or use children for sexual purposes violate such a deeply felt code that they are often treated as if they have forfeited their human status. Here, the conviction that it is 'unnatural' for children to have sexual relationships is scarcely amenable to purely rational analysis. The difficulty of deciding when children may be sexually active cannot be resolved in any simple way; the age of consent is a mere token in this respect. It does not prevent sexual relations by the under-aged, while by contrast many people may not experience sex until very much later. Growing up is a gradual process, hard to assess with any accuracy and varying markedly from individual to individual. We persist with a commitment to thinking in terms of the exact age of children because it appears objective, because such information is readily available, and because it is customary to do so.

The present situation, relatively speaking, is of recent origin. We may [30] contrast it with that of eighteenth-century England, when there was little regulation of youth by any kind of institutional authority, no compulsory registration of births, little formal control on age of marriage, and only a rudimentary educational system. Contemporaries seemed uninterested in the exact age of children—for example, coroners investigating child death rarely gave a precise age, mentioning only that it was an infant, a child, or giving just an approximate age. Age was, however, becoming an issue in relation to prostitution and illicit sexual activity. The dissolute husband in Hogarth's barbed satire `Marriage à la Mode' (1742–4) consorted with a childlike girl whom he infected with VD.[23] In condemning prostitution, the zealous philanthropist Jonas Hanway was particularly worried about the use of young girls in their early teens, despite the fact that he was less interested in immorality *per se* than in the disruption of family life occasioned by prostitution. Institutions were founded to save girls from lives of sin.[24] It is of course true that these anxieties were far more acute in relation to girls than to boys. Nonetheless, the condemnation of masturbation in the eighteenth century, which was directed principally at boys, also suggests both that sexuality and children were somehow to be separated, and that the regulation of sexual behaviour was problematic.

There were, of course, sound economic reasons why societies regulated, 31 by whatever means, the sexual activities of the young. This may well have operated at an unconscious level. Adolescent marriage—because the girl became pregnant, for example—brought higher levels of fertility and, consequently, harsher economic burdens. Illegitimate children posed dramatic problems for their mothers, sometimes solved only by infanticide, or, less drastically, by abandonment. What past societies sought to control was not so much sexuality itself as the formation of new households and lives. Yet by the late eighteenth century a new factor had come into the equation—the association of children with nature expressed in art and literature as well as in medicine and social thinking generally. This naturalism produced a logical trap. Ideas about nature were part of larger patterns of thinking within which nature was often paired with another term, its antithesis—commonly society or culture. Eighteenth-century concepts of nature were also all-embracing, covering the whole material world, the entirety of observable reality. Separating nature from society allowed the naturalness of children—pure, innocent, asexual— to be contrasted with the uncleanness of the corrupt adult world. But an inclusive approach validated sexuality as part of nature, hence how could it be depraved?[25] These views co-existed uneasily. It is indeed hard to reconcile the belief that children are natural and asexual with the view that sexuality is integral to nature.

An excellent example is one of the most popular novels ever written, *Paul* 32 *et Virginie* (1787) by Bernardin de Saint-Pierre.[26] It was an enormously powerful statement about nature. Set on Mauritius, it concerns two children who grow up together, are so close they think of themselves as brother and sister, fall in love, and yet do not marry. The reasons they do not, even at the level of the plot, are quite complex. If we ask why the writer refused to imagine such an eventuality, then we can consider the possibility that although for him romantic love was part of nature, at the same time it posed threats to a particular vision of nature. Thus, Virginie's love for Paul—and his for her—is presented in glowing terms, while her puberty is accompanied by turbulent weather mirroring her own confusion. At the point of her new sexual awareness, things begin to go wrong. She remains a virgin until she drowns in a shipwreck, frozen, as it were, at a moment of intense emotion and sexual purity.

I have used this example because, although it is hardly 'representative', it conveys exceptionally vividly the association between children and nature in the late eighteenth century and the difficulties sexuality posed to that association. Legal devices to deal with the problem, like an age of consent, are only one type of solution. They are inadequate because incapable of addressing the symbolic transformation that takes place when children become sexually active. Children themselves may not experience these changes as symbolic, but they are perceived as such at the level of group responses and mental structures. Possibly modern reactions to the sexuality of children are bound up with our conviction that sex is related to individual liberty; the rights of each person to pleasure. When children become sexually active they assert their autonomy. This autonomy is connected in our minds with the adult world and the marketplace that constitutes its environment, while sexual activity is nonetheless seen as natural. Once again, the child in its passage to adulthood is caught in the conceptual labyrinth formed from our notions of 'nature'. Similar issues arise when we consider the economic activities of children, although these are more straightforward since they have fewer troubling implications for adults. 33

Child Labour

Work is an exceptionally difficult concept. It has a number of different uses, and context is often the only clue to meaning. When we state that children no longer 'work' we mean that they no longer endure long hours of labour daily, under the control of an employer, for which they may or may not have received wages. Yet children are not now free to do as they please, and, although they do not receive payment for attending school, it certainly counts as 'work' in one sense. Nonetheless, few children are expected to be economically self-sufficient or to bear responsibility for others in this respect. Here, indeed, is a marked contrast with the past. It is easy to say that until the late nineteenth and early twentieth centuries the mass of the population took child labour for granted; it is much harder to assess with any accuracy the actual distribution of different kinds of work. A child could be economically active in four main ways. First, children could undertake work which was paid either in cash or in kind; or they could be apprenticed, which required a fee without providing wages, but put them in the care of masters who undertook to feed and clothe children who were indirectly bringing some economic benefit to themselves and their families. Second, children leaving home affected the family budget quite directly, either positively by no longer requiring sustenance, or negatively by withdrawing their labour. Third, children 34 made a significant contribution when they took care of younger children to enable their parents, especially the mother, to work. Finally, they might work with the parents and so help to raise their productivity.

This was the situation until the late eighteenth and early nineteenth cen-   35
turies: it was seldom condemned; indeed, contemporary commentators often stressed the simple, uncomplicated expectation that children 'do their bit'. Violence by masters against their apprentices was certainly not condoned, although it could be difficult to deal with such brutality through legal channels, but neither was it much debated in public until the 1770s. Thereafter, the debates slowly began, mostly centred on chimney sweeps. Why that particular occupation, when children undertook hundreds of different jobs? Because it was visible, it affected young children (roughly five upwards), and it had tremendous symbolic potential (black, dirt, sin, slavery, and so on). On what grounds was it deplored? Children were tender, impressionable, vulnerable, pure, deserving of parental protection, and hence all too easily corrupted by the market-place. Two main justifications existed for this characterisation of children: a Christian one, which portrayed children as in a 'sacred state of life'; and an ideological one, according to which they were somehow 'naturally' incompatible with the world of commodities.[27]

The historical moment when child labour was no longer taken for   36
granted, even if only by a limited number of people, is particularly relevant to the leading theme of this paper: the application of concepts of nature and society to children and childhood. Although up to that point societies had regulated child labour by a variety of mechanisms, some more formal than others, these social conventions came, gradually, to seem inadequate. This sense of inadequacy was composed of many different elements. In the early days of movements critical of existing child labour practices, two features stand out. One is that legislative control of some kind was sought; the other, that children were presented as *naturally* ill-suited to heavy labour, although exactly why and how this conception arose is not yet understood. We may note that few commentators recommended the total *abolition* of child labour; they wanted it regulated and humanised.[28] Nonetheless, the logic of the ar-. guments about the inherent vulnerability of children led to notions of and institutions for their protection. 'Better' mothering and full-time education were the centerpieces of the new view of childhood.

Conclusion

It is neither possible nor desirable to produce a summary history of children   37
or of childhood. The very project of writing the history of these subjects is fraught with difficulties caused by the nature of the sources, by the problems intrinsic to the writing of history, and by our present-day attitudes towards and deep investments in childhood. Writing the history of children and childhood thus presents some serious challenges. One way of understanding the problems historians face is by unravelling the implications of associating children with nature. Deriving from the naturalism of the eighteenth cen-

tury, this association gave rise to contradictory formulations of the essential characteristics of childhood. One of the main points of tension was how the transition from child—in the domain of nature—to adult—in the social and cultural domain—could be conceptualised. I have focused on two themes to illustrate these issues: sexuality and work. Because past societies thought about these matters in a way so different from our own, historical materials offer us the chance to see how children fit into an unfamiliar context, and hence to infer what facets of a society most forcefully determine the nature of childhood within them. They also enable us to put the contemporary situation in perspective, appreciate its antecedents, and avoid treating it as the norm.

Yet I have sounded a note of caution on source materials, none of which [38] unproblematically reveals historical 'truths' about children. Particular care needs to be exercised in the treatment of sources. In this essay I have suggested that analysing the language used in relation to the child is a valuable exercise. The history of institutions and legislation can also be revealing, as can direct records of the lives of children. But especially if we want to move from a social history of children to a more general history of childhood, we need a related methodological shift from material which is largely descriptive to that which is more abstract. This should provide greater insight into the structures of thinking about children at specific times. If it is the case that societies invent concepts of childhood, both consciously and unconsciously, then it is important to recognise the extent to which these mould the experience of children.

NOTES

1. R. Williams, *Keywords: A Vocabulary of Culture and Society,* 2nd ed. (London: Fontana, 1983), discusses these and many of the other concepts mentioned in this essay.

2. For example, L. Pollock, *Forgotten Children: Parent–Child Relations from 1500–1900* (Cambridge: Cambridge University Press, 1983); J. Burnett, *Useful Toil: Autobiographies of Working People from the 1820's to the 1920's* (London: Allen Lane, 1974); J. Walvin, *A Child's World: A Social History of English Childhood 1800–1914* (Harmondsworth: Penguin, 1982); P. Demers and G. Moyles, eds., *From Instruction to Delight. An Anthology of Children's Literature to 1850* (Toronto: Oxford University Press, 1982) (see esp. pp. 302–6 for a bibliography of work in this field).

3. The general interest in authenticity is exemplified by some of the contributions to *History Workshop Journal;* for the concern with giving children their own history see J. R. Gillis, *Youth and History: Tradition and Change in European Age Relations 1770–present* (New York: Academic Press, 1981; revised ed.).

4. P. Ariès, *Centuries of Childhood* (Harmondsworth: Penguin, 1973). The first French edition, under the title *L'Enfant et la vie familiale sous L'ancien régime,* was in 1960, the first English one in 1962.

5. Critiques of Ariès include A. Wilson's 'The Infancy of the History of Childhood: An Appraisal of Philippe Ariès', *History and Theory 19,* 1980, 132–53, and R.

Vann's, 'The Youth of *Centuries of Childhood*', *History and Theory 21*, 1982, 279–97. Pollock, *Forgotten Children*, Chapter 1, is also critical of Ariès.

6. W. L. Langer, 'Infanticide: A Historical Survey', *History of Childhood Quarterly 1*, 1974, 353–65, and 2, 1974, 129–34; A. Forrest, *The French Revolution and the Poor* (Oxford: Basil Blackwell, 1981), Chapter 7; I. Pinchbeck and M. Hewitt, *Children in English Society*, 2 volumes (London: Routledge & Kegan Paul, 1969 and 1973); M. D. George, *London Life in the Eighteenth Century* (Harmondsworth: Penguin, 1966, first published 1925), especially Chapter 5.

7. Pollock, *Forgotten Children;* S. Wilson, 'The myth of motherhood a myth', *Social History 9*, 1984, 181–98.

8. O. Hufton, 'Women and the Family Economy in Eighteenth-Century France', *French Historical Studies 9*, 1975, 1–22; O. Hufton, *The Poor in Eighteenth-Century France* (Oxford: Oxford University Press, 1974); K. Snell, *Annals of the Labouring Poor* (Cambridge: Cambridge University Press, 1985). M. Anderson, *Approaches to the History of the Western Family* (London: Macmillan, 1980), discusses a number of the approaches mentioned in this essay.

9. D. Sabean, *Power in the Blood: Popular Culture and Village Discourse in Early Modern Germany* (Cambridge: Cambridge University Press, 1984); H. Medick and D. Sabean, eds., *Interest and Emotion. Essays on the study of family and kinship* (Cambridge: Cambridge University Press, 1984), especially Chapter 3, by Regina Schulte on infanticide.

10. M. Foucault, *The History of Sexuality, Volume 1: An Introduction* (London: Allen Lane, 1979); M. Foucault, ed., *I, Pierre Rivière* (Harmondsworth: Penguin, 1978); P. Rabinow, ed., *The Foucault Reader* (Harmondsworth: Penguin, 1986).

11. James Hall, *Dictionary of Subjects and Symbols in Art* (London: John Murray, 1979, revised ed.).

12. George, *London Life*, Chapter 5; J. Rule, *The Experience of Labour in Eighteenth-Century Industry* (London: Croom Helm 1981), Chapter 4; Pinchbeck and Hewitt, *Children in English Society*, Chapter 9 (Volume 1) and Chapter 14 (Volume 2).

13. L. de Mause ed., *The History of Childhood* (London: Souvenir, 1976); see also *The Psychohistory Review and Journal of Psychohistory*, formerly *History of Childhood Quarterly*. The application of psychoanalysis to the history of childhood is also discussed in D. Hunt, *Parents and Children in History: the Psychology of Family Life in Early Modern France* (New York: Basic Books, 1980), Chapter 1 (N.B. Chapter 2 discusses Ariès); M. Poster, *Critical Theory of the Family* (London: Pluto, 1978), especially Chapters 1 and 7; and L. J. Jordanova, 'Fantasy and History in the Study of Childhood', *Free Associations. Psychoanalysis, Groups, Politics, Culture 2*, 1985, 110–22. For an impressive defence of the value of psychoanalysis to history in general see P. Gay, *Freud for Historians* (Oxford: Oxford University Press, 1985).

14. Some standard works on the history of education are: B. Simon, *Studies in the History of Education* (London: Lawrence and Wishart, 1960); G. Sutherland, *Elementary Education in the Nineteenth Century* (London: Historical Association, 1970); W. Armytage, *Four Hundred Years of English Education* (Cambridge: Cambridge University Press, 1965). P. McCann, ed., *Popular Education and Socialization in the Nineteenth Century* (London: Methuen, 1977), is a valuable collection of recent research.

15. D. G. Charlton, *New Images of the Natural in France* (Cambridge: Cambridge University Press, 1984), especially Chapters 7 and 8; L. Jordanova, ed., *Languages of Nature. Critical Essays on Science and Literature* (London: Free Association Books, 1986), especially the chapters by Pilkington and Jordanova; J. H. Plumb, 'The New World of Children in 18th Century England', *Past and Present 67*, 1975, 64–95.

16. Jordanova, *Languages of Nature.*

17. J.-J. Rousseau, *Emile* (London: Dent, 1974, first published 1762); J. Bloch, 'Rousseau's reputation as an authority on childcare and physical education in France before the Revolution', *Paedagogica Historica 14*, 1974, 5–33.

18. J. B. Elshtain, *Public Man, Private Woman: Women in Social and Political Thought* (Oxford: Basil Blackwell, 1982), pp. 147–70; J. B. Elshtain, *Meditations on Modern Political Thought. Masculine/Feminine Themes from Luther to Arendt* (New York: Praeger, 1986), Chapter 4; J. Schwartz, *The Sexual Politics of Jean-Jacques Rousseau* (Chicago: University of Chicago Press, 1984); S. M. Okin, *Women in Western Political Thought* (London: Virago, 1980), part 3.

19. Charlton, *New Images of the Natural*, especially Chapter 8; C. Duncan, 'Happy Mothers and Other Ideas in 18th Century Art', *Art Bulletin 60*, 1973, 570–83.

20. C. Fairchilds, *Domestic Enemies. Servants and their Masters in Old Regime France* (Baltimore: Johns Hopkins University Press, 1984), Chapters 6 and 7; L. J. Jordanova, 'The Popularisation of Medicine: Tissot on Onanism', *Textual Practice 1*, 1987. Tissot was a major eighteenth-century exponent of the view that relations between children and servants should be closely scrutinised.

21. Foucault, *The History of Sexuality*, pp. 17–49; this section is also in Rabinow, *The Foucault Reader*, pp. 301–29.

22. R. H. MacDonald, 'The Frightful Consequences of Onanism: Notes on the History of a Delusion', *Journal of the History of Ideas 28*, 1967, 423–31; E. H. Hare, 'Masturbatory Insanity: The History of an Idea', *Journal of Mental Science 108*, 1962, 1–25; R. P. Neumann, 'Masturbation, Madness and the Modern Concepts of Childhood and Adolescence', *Journal of Social History 8*, 1975, 1–27. Sexuality and the young is also discussed in E. Shorter, *The Making of the Modern Family*, (London: Collins, 1976), Chapters 3 and 4, and John Gillis, *Youth and History.*

23. See Plate 3 of William Hogarth's 'Marriage à la Mode,' conveniently reproduced in *Marriage à la Mode by William Hogarth. With a Commentary on the Pictures and a Note on the Painter by Michael Levy* (London: National Gallery, 1970).

24. [J. Hanway], *Thoughts on the Plan for a Magdalen House for Repentant Prostitutes* (London: Waugh, 1758); J. S. Taylor, *Jonas Hanway. Founder of the Marine Society. Charity and Policy in Eighteenth-Century Britain* (London: Scolar, 1985).

25. On eighteenth-century sexuality see J.-G. Boucé ed., *Sexuality in 18th Century Britain* (Manchester: Manchester University Press, 1982) and *Représentations de la Vie Sexuelle*, a special issue of *Dix-Huitième Siècle*, 12, 1980.

26. J. H. Bernardin de Saint-Pierre, *Paul et Virginie*, first published 1787; *Paul and Virginia* (London: Peter Owen, 1982), ed. and trans. J. Donovan; P. Robinson, 'Virginie's Fatal Modesty: Some Thoughts on Bernardin de Saint-Pierre and Rousseau', *British Journal for Eighteenth-Century Studies 5*, 1982, 35–48.

27. J. Hanway, *A Sentimental History of Chimney-Sweepers* (London: Dodsley, 1785);

Taylor, *Jonas Hanway*; H. Cunningham, 'Child Labour in the Industrial Revolution', *The Historian*, Spring 1987; L. J. Jordanova, 'Conceptualising Childhood in the Eighteenth Century: The Problem of Child Labour', *British Journal for Eighteenth-Century Studies*, 10, 1987, 189–99.

28. Hanway is a good example of this position. For the more general historical issues surrounding changing work patterns see N. Smelser, *Social Change in the Industrial Revolution* (London: Routledge, 1959).

Questions

1. Why does Jordanova feel that it is important to define childhood? How would you define childhood?

2. Why does Jordanova object to the comparison between children and nature? How did this concept originate?

3. It has been said that the concept of childhood has been lost as children become more and more sophisticated. Do you agree with this idea?

4. In the culture with which you are most familiar, characterize the way in which children are perceived in terms of "naturalness," development, and responsibilities.

Revolutionary Parenting

BELL HOOKS

Bell Hooks writes about feminist issues affecting African-American women.
Among her publications are Talking Back *(1989) and* From Margin to Center *(1984).*

In this selection, Hooks argues that women are socialized to believe that they have the natural capacity and the duty to raise children. This consciousness needs to be revolutionized, because it is healthiest for the child when the father as well as other parental figures provide models. This reading is from From Margin to Center.

During the early stages of contemporary women's liberation movement, feminist analyses of motherhood reflected the race and class biases of participants. Some white middle class, college-educated women argued that motherhood was a serious obstacle to women's liberation, a trap confining women to the home, keeping them tied to cleaning, cooking, and child care. Others simply identified motherhood and childrearing as the locus of women's oppression. Had black women voiced their views on motherhood, it would not have been named a serious obstacle to our freedom as women. Racism, availability of jobs, lack of skills or education and a number of other issues would have been at the top of the list—but not motherhood. Black women would not have said motherhood prevented us from entering the world of paid work because we have always worked. From slavery to the present day black women in the U.S. have worked outside the home, in the fields, in the factories, in the laundries, in the homes of others. That work gave meager financial compensation and often interfered with or prevented effective parenting. Historically, black women have identified work in the context of family as humanizing labor, work that affirms their identity as women, as human beings showing love and care, the very gestures of humanity white supremacist ideology claimed black people were incapable of expressing. In contrast to labor done in a caring environment inside the home, labor outside the home was most often seen as stressful, degrading, and dehumanizing. 1

These views on motherhood and work outside the home contrasted sharply with those expressed by white women's liberationists. Many black women were saying "we want to have more time to share with family, we want to leave the world of alienated work." Many white women's liberationists were saying "we are tired of the isolation of the home, tired of relating only to children and husband, tired of being emotionally and 2 economically dependent; we want to be liberated to enter the world of work." (These voices were not those of working class white women who were, like black women workers, tired of alienated labor.) The women's liberationists who wanted to enter the work force did not see this world as a world of alienated work. They do now. In the last twenty years of feminist movement many middle class white women have entered the wage earning work force and have found that working within a social context where sexism is still the norm, where there is unnecessary competition promoting envy, distrust, antagonism, and malice between individuals, makes work stressful, frustrating, and often totally unsatisfying. Concurrently, many women who like and enjoy the wage work they do feel that it takes too much of their time, leaving little space for other satisfying pursuits. While work may help women gain a degree of financial independence or even financial self-sufficiency, for most women it has not adequately fulfilled human needs. As a consequence women's search for fulfilling labor done in an environment of care has led to reemphasizing the importance of family and the positive aspects of motherhood. Additionally, the fact that many active feminists are in their mid to late 30s, facing the biological clock, has focussed collective attention on motherhood. This renewed attention has led many women active in the feminist movement who were interested in childrearing to choose to bear children.

Although early feminists demanded respect and acknowledgment for housework and child care, they did not attribute enough significance and value to female parenting, to motherhood. It is a gesture that should have been made at the onset of feminist movement. Early feminist attacks on motherhood alienated masses of women from the movement, especially poor and/or non-white women, who find parenting one of the few interpersonal relationships where they are affirmed and appreciated. Unfortunately, recent positive feminist focus on motherhood draws heavily on sexist stereotypes. Motherhood is as romanticized by some feminist activists as it was by the nineteenth century men and women who extolled the virtues of the "cult of domesticity." The one significant difference in their approach is that motherhood is no longer viewed as taking place primarily within the framework of heterosexual marriage or even heterosexual relationships. More than ever before, women who are not attached to males, who may be heterosexual or lesbian, are choosing to bear children. In spite of the difficulties of single parenting (especially economic) in this society, the focus is on "joys of motherhood," the special intimacy, closeness, and bonding purported to characterize the mother/child relationship. Books like Phyllis Chesler's *With Child: A Diary of Motherhood* rhapsodizes over the pleasures and joys of childbirth and child care. Publication of more scholarly and serious works like Jessie Bernard's *The Future of Motherhood*, Elisabeth Badiner's *Mother Love*, Nancy Friday's *My Mother/My Self*, and Nancy Chodorow's *The Reproduction of Mothering* reflect growing concern with motherhood.

This resurgence of interest in motherhood has positive and negative implications for feminist movement. On the positive side there is a continual need for study and research of female parenting which this interest promotes and encourages. In the foreword to *Of Woman Born,* Adrienne Rich states that she felt it was important to write a book on motherhood because it is "a crucial, still relatively unexplored area for feminist theory." It is also positive that women who choose to bear children need no longer fear that this choice excludes them from recognition by feminist movement, although it may still exclude them from active participation. On the negative side, romanticizing motherhood, employing the same terminology that is used by sexists to suggest that women are inherently life-affirming nurturers, feminist activists reinforce central tenets of male supremacist ideology. They imply that motherhood is a woman's truest vocation; that women who do not mother, whose lives may be focused more exclusively on a career, creative work, or political work are missing out, are doomed to live emotionally unfulfilled lives. While they do not openly attack or denigrate women who do not bear children, they (like the society as a whole) suggest that it is *more* important than women's other labor and more rewarding. They could simply state that it *is* important and rewarding. Significantly, this perspective is often voiced by many of the white bourgeois women with successful careers who are now choosing to bear children. They seem to be saying to masses of women that careers or work can never be as important, as satisfying, as bearing children.

This is an especially dangerous line of thinking, coming at a time when 5 teenage women who have not realized a number of goals, are bearing children in large numbers rather than postponing parenting; when masses of women are being told by the government that they are destroying family life by not assuming sexist-defined roles. Through mass media and other communication systems, women are currently inundated with material encouraging them to bear children. Newspapers carry headline stories with titles like "motherhood is making a comeback"; women's magazines are flooded with articles on the new motherhood; fashion magazines have special features on designer clothing for the pregnant woman; television talk shows do special features on career women who are now choosing to raise children. Coming at a time when women with children are more likely to live in poverty, when the number of homeless, parentless children increases by the thousands daily, when women continue to assume sole responsibility for parenting, such propaganda undermines and threatens feminist movement.

To some extent, the romanticization of motherhood by bourgeois white 6 women is an attempt to repair the damage done by past feminist critiques and give women who mother the respect they deserve. It should be noted that even the most outrageous of these criticisms did not compare with sexism as a source of exploitation and humiliation for mothers. Female parenting is significant and valuable work which must be recognized as such by everyone in society, including feminist activists. It should receive deserved recognition, praise, and celebration within a feminist context where there is renewed effort to re-think the nature of motherhood, to make motherhood neither a compulsory experience for women nor an exploitative or oppressive one, to make female parenting good effective parenting whether it is done exclusively by women or in conjunction with men.

In a recent article, "Bringing Up Baby," Mary Ellen Schoonmaker stressed   7
the often made point that men do not share equally in parenting:

> Since the early days of ambivalence toward motherhood, the overall goal of
> the women's movement has been a quest for equality—to take the oppression
> out of mothering, to join "mothering" to "parenting," and for those who
> choose to have children to share parenting with men and with society in gen-
> eral. Looking back over the past twenty years, it seems as if these goals have
> been among the hardest for the women's movement to reach.
>
> If men did equally share in parenting, it would mean trading places with
> women part of the time. Many men have found it easier to share power with
> women on the job than they have in the home. Even though millions of
> mothers with infants and toddlers now work outside the home, many
> women still do the bulk of the housework . . .

Men will not share equally in parenting until they are taught, ideally from
childhood on, that fatherhood has the same meaning and significance as
motherhood. As long as women or society as a whole see the mother/child relationship as unique and special because the female carries the child in her
body and gives birth, or makes this biological experience synonymous with
women having a closer, more significant bond to children than the male parent, responsibility for child care and child rearing will continue to be primarily women's work. Even the childless woman is considered more suited to
raise children than the male parent because she is seen as an inherently caring nurturer. The biological experience of pregnancy and childbirth, whether
painful or joyful, should not be equated with the idea that women's parenting is necessarily superior to men's.

Dictionary definitions of the word "father" relate its meaning to accept-   8
ing responsibility, with no mention of words like tenderness and affection,
yet these words are used to define what the word mother means. By placing
sole responsibility for nurturing onto women, that is to say for satisfying the
emotional and material needs of children, society reinforces the notion that
to mother is more important than to father. Structured into the definitions
and the very usage of the terms father and mother is the sense that these two
words refer to two distinctly different experiences. Women and men must define the work of fathering and mothering in the same way if males and females are to accept equal responsibility in parenting. Even feminist theorists
who have emphasized the need for men to share equally in childrearing are
reluctant to cease attaching special value to mothering. This illustrates feminists' willingness to glorify the physiological experience of motherhood as
well as unwillingness to concede motherhood as an arena of social life in
which women can exert power and control.

Women and society as a whole often consider the father who does equal   9
parenting unique and special rather than as representative of what should
be the norm. Such a man may even be seen as assuming a "maternal" role.
Describing men who parent in her work *Mother Love,* Elisabeth Badinter
comments:

Under the pressure exerted by women, the new father mothers equally and in the traditional mother's image. He creeps in, like another mother, between the mother and the child, who experiences almost indiscriminately as intimate a contact with the father as with the mother. We have only to notice the increasingly numerous photographs in magazines showing fathers pressing newborns against their bare chests. Their faces reflect a completely motherly tenderness that shocks no one. After centuries of the father's authority or absence, it seems that a new concept has come into existence—father love, the exact equivalent of mother love. While it is obvious that women who parent would necessarily be the models men would strive to emulate (since women have been doing effective parenting for many more years), these men are becoming parents, effective fathers. They are not becoming mothers.

Another example of this tendency occurs at the end of Sara Ruddick's es-   10
say "Maternal Thinking." She envisions a time in which men will share equally in childrearing and writes:

> On that day there will be no more "fathers," no more people of either sex who have power over their children's lives and moral authority in their children's worlds, though they do the work of attentive love. There will be mothers of both sexes who live out a transformed maternal thought in communities that share parental—care practically, emotionally, economically, and socially. Such communities will have learned from their mothers how to value children's lives.

In this paragraph, as in the entire essay, Ruddick romanticizes the idea of the "maternal" and places emphasis on men becoming maternal, a vision which seems shortsighted. Because the word "maternal" is associated with the behavior of women, men will not identify with it even though they may be behaving in ways that have traditionally been seen as "feminine." Wishful thinking will not alter the concept of the maternal in our society. Rather than changing it, the word paternal should share the same meaning. Telling a boy acting out the role of caring parent with his dolls that he is being maternal will not change the idea that women are better suited to parenting; it will reinforce it. Saying to a boy that he is behaving like a good father (in the way that girls are told that they are good mothers when they show attention and care to dolls) would teach him a vision of effective parenting, of fatherhood, that is the same as motherhood.

Seeing men who do effective parenting as "maternal" reinforces the   11
stereotypical sexist notion that women are inherently better suited to parent, that men who parent in the same way as women are imitating the real thing rather than acting as a parent should act. There should be a concept of effective parenting that makes no distinction between maternal and paternal care. The model of effective parenting that includes the kind of attentive love Ruddick describes has been applied only to women and has prevented fathers from learning how to parent. They are allowed to conceive of the father's role solely in terms of exercising authority and providing for material needs. They

are taught to think of it as a role secondary to the mother's. Until males are taught how to parent using the same model of effective parenting that has been taught to women, they will not participate equally in child care. They will even feel that they should not participate because they have been taught to think they are inadequate or ineffective childrearers.

Men are socialized to avoid assuming responsibility for childrearing and   12
that avoidance is supported by women who believe that motherhood is a sphere of power they would lose if men participated equally in parenting. Many of these women do not wish to share parenting equally with men. In feminist circles it is often forgotten that masses of women in the United States still believe that men cannot parent effectively and should not even attempt to parent. Until these women understand that men should and can do primary parenting, they will not expect the men in their lives to share equally in childrearing. Even when they do, it is unlikely that men will respond with enthusiasm. People need to know the negative impact that male non-participation in childrearing has on family relationships and child development.

Feminist efforts to point out to men what they lose when they do not   13
participate in parenting tend to be directed at the bourgeois classes. Little is done to discuss non-sexist parenting or male parenting with poor and working class women and men. In fact, the kind of maternal care Ruddick evokes in her essay, with its tremendous emphasis on attention given children by parents, especially mothers, is a form of parental care that is difficult for many working class parents to offer when they return home from work tired and exhausted. It is increasingly difficult for women and men in families struggling to survive economically to give special attention to parenting. Their struggle contrasts sharply with the family structure of the bourgeoisie. These white women and men are likely to be better informed about the positive effects of male participation in parenting, who have more time to parent, and who are not perpetually anxious about their material well being. It is also difficult for women who parent alone to juggle the demands of work and childrearing.

Feminist theorists point to the problems that arise when parenting is   14
done exclusively by an individual or solely by women: female parenting gives children few role models of male parenting; perpetuates the idea that parenting is a woman's vocation; and reinforces male domination and fear of women. Society, however, is not concerned. This information has little impact at a time when men, more than ever before, avoid responsibility for childrearing and when women are parenting less because they work more but are parenting more often alone. These facts raise two issues that must be of central concern for future feminist movement: the right of children to effective child care by parents and other childrearers; the restructuring of society so that women do not exclusively provide that care.

Eliminating sexism is the solution to the problem of men participating   15
unequally or not at all in child care. Therefore more women and men must recognize the need to support and participate in feminist movement. Masses

of women continue to believe that they should be primarily responsible for child care—this point cannot be over emphasized. Feminist efforts to help women unlearn this socialization could lead to greater demands on their part for men to participate equally in parenting. Making and distributing brochures in women's health centers and in other public places that would emphasize the importance of males and females sharing equally in parenting is one way to make more people aware of this need. Seminars on parenting that emphasize non-sexist parenting and joint parenting by women and men in local communities is another way more people could learn about the subject. Before women become pregnant, they need to understand the significance of men sharing equally in parenting. Some women in relationships with men who may be considering bearing children do not do so because male partners make it known that they will not assume responsibility for parenting. These women feel their decision not to bear children with men who refuse to share parenting is a political statement reinforcing the importance of equal participation in parenting and the need to end male dominance of women. We need to hear more from these women about the choices they have made. There are also women who bear children in relationships with men who know beforehand that the man will not participate equally in parenting. It is important for future studies of female parenting to understand their choices.

Women need to know that it is important to discuss child care with men 16 before children are conceived or born. There are women and men who have made either legal contracts or simply written agreements that spell out each individual's responsibility. Some women have found that men verbally support the idea of shared parenting before a child is conceived or born and then do not follow through. Written agreements can help clarify the situation by requiring each individual to discuss what they feel about parental care, who should be responsible, etc. Most women and men do not discuss the nature of childrearing before children are born because it is simply assumed that women will be caretakers.

Despite the importance of men sharing equally in parenting, large num- 17 bers of women have no relationship to the man with whom they have conceived a child. In some cases, this is a reflection of the man's lack of concern about parenting or the woman's choice. Some women do not feel it is important for their children to experience caring, nurturing parenting from males. In black communities, it is not unusual for a single female parent to rely on male relatives and friends to help with childrearing. As more heterosexual and lesbian women choose to bear children with no firm ties to male parents, there will exist a greater need for community-based child care that would bring children into contact with male childrearers so they will not grow to maturity thinking women are the only group who do or should do childrearing. The childrearer does not have to be a parent. Childrearers in our culture are teachers, librarians, etc. and even though these are occupations which have been dominated by women, this is changing. In these contexts, a child could experience male childrearing. Some female parents who raise their children without the mutual care of fathers feel their own positions are undermined when they meet occasionally with male parents who may provide a good time but be totally unengaged in day-to-day parenting. They sometimes have to cope with children valuing the male parent more because he is male (and sexist ideology teaches them that his attentions are more valuable than female care). These women need to know that teaching their children non-sexist values could help them appreciate female parenting and could eradicate favoritism based solely on sexist standards.

Because women are doing most of the parenting, the need for tax-funded   18
public child care centers with equal numbers of non-sexist male and female workers continues to be a pressing feminist issue. Such centers would relieve individual women of the sole responsibility for childrearing as well as help promote awareness of the necessity for male participation in child raising. Yet this is an issue that has yet to be pushed by masses of people. Future feminist organizing (especially in the interests of building mass-based feminist movement) could use this issue as a platform. Feminist activists have always seen public child care as one solution to the problem of women being the primary childrearers. Commenting on the need for child care centers in her article "Bringing Up Baby," Mary Ellen Schoonmaker writes;

> As for child care outside the home, the seemingly simple concept envisioned by the women's movement of accessible, reliable, quality day care has proven largely elusive. While private, often overpriced sources of day care have risen to meet middle class needs, the inadequacy of public day care remains an outrage. The Children's Defense Fund, a child advocacy and lobbying group in Washington, D.C., reports that perhaps six to seven million children, including preschoolers, may be left at home alone while their parents work because they can't afford day care . . .

Most child care centers, catering either to the needs of the working classes or the bourgeoisie, are not non-sexist. Yet until children begin to learn at a very early age that it is not important to make role distinctions based on sex, they will continue to grow to maturity thinking that women should be the primary childrearers.

Many people oppose the idea of tax-funded public child care because   19
they see it as an attempt by women to avoid parenting. They need to know that the extent to which the isolated parenting that women do in this society is not the best way to raise children or treat women who mother. Elizabeth Janeway makes this point in her most recent book *Cross Sections*, emphasizing that the idea of an individual having sole responsibility for childrearing is the most unusual pattern of parenting in the world, one that has proved to be unsuccessful because it isolates children and parents from society:

> . . . How extreme that family isolation can be today is indicated by these instances listed in a study undertaken for the Massachusetts Advisory Council on Education . . . This group found:

1. Isolation of wage earners from spouses and children, caused by the wage earners' absorption into the world of work.

2. The complementary isolation of young children from the occupational world of parents and other adults.

3. The general isolation of young children from persons of different ages, both adults and other children.

4. The residential isolation of families from persons of different social, ethnic, religious, and racial backgrounds.

5. The isolation of family members from kin and neighbors.

Such isolation means that the role of the family as the agent for socializing children is inadequately fulfilled at present whether or not mothers are at work outside the home. Children are now growing up without the benefit of a variety of adult role models of both sexes and in ignorance of the world of paid work. Returning women to a life centered in home and family would not solve the fundamental loss of connection between family and community. The effort by the women's movement to see that centers for child care are provided by society is not an attempt to hand over to others the duties of motherhood but to enlist community aid to supplement the proper obligations of parents, as was often the practice in the past.

Ideally, small, community-based, public child care centers would be the best way to overcome this isolation. When parents must drive long distances to take children to day care, dependency on parents is increased and not lessened. Community-based public child care centers would give small children great control over their lives.

Child care is a responsibility that can be shared with other childrearers, [20] with people who do not live with children. This form of parenting is revolutionary in this society because it takes place in opposition to the idea that parents, especially mothers, should be the only childrearers. Many people raised in black communities experienced this type of community-based child care. Black women who had to leave the home and work to help provide for families could not afford to send children to day care centers and such centers did not always exist. They relied on people in their communities to help. Even in families where the mother stayed home, she could also rely on people in the community to help. She did not need to go with her children every time they walked to the playground to watch them because they would be watched by a number of people living near the playground. People who did not have children often took responsibility for sharing in childrearing. In my own family, there were seven children and when we were growing up it was not possible for our parents to watch us all the time or even give that extra special individual attention children sometimes desire. Those needs were often met by neighbors and people in the community.

This kind of shared responsibility for child care can happen in small com- [21] munity settings where people know and trust one another. It cannot happen in those settings if parents regard children as their "property," their "possession." Many parents do not want their children to develop caring relationships with others, not even relatives. If there were community-based day care centers, there would be a much greater likelihood that children would develop ongoing friendships and caring relationships with adult people rather than their parents. These types of relationships are not formed in day care centers where one teacher takes care of a large number of students, where one never sees teachers in any context other than school. Any individual who has been raised in an environment of communal child care knows that this happens only if parents can accept other adults assuming parental type care for their children. While it creates a situation where children must respect a number of caretakers, it also gives children resources to rely on if their emotional, intellectual, and material needs are not met solely by parents. Often in black communities where shared childrearing happens, elderly women and men participate. Today many children have no contact with the elderly. Another hazard of single parenting or even nuclear family parenting that is avoided when there is community-based childraising is the tendency of parents to over-invest emotion in their children. This is a problem for many people who choose to have children after years of thinking they would not. They may make children into "love objects" and have no interest in teaching them to relate to a wide variety of people. This is as much a problem for feminist women and men who are raising children as it is for other parents.

Initially, women's liberationists felt that the need for population control 22 coupled with awareness of this society's consumption of much of the world's resources, were political reasons not to bear children. These reasons have not changed even though they are now ignored or dismissed. Yet if there were less emphasis on having one's "own" children and more emphasis on having children who are already living and in need of child care, there would be large groups of responsible women and men to share in the process of childrearing. Lucia Valeska supported this position in an essay published in a 1975 issue of *Quest*. "If All Else Fails, I'm Still a Mother":

> To have our own biological children today is personally and politically irresponsible. If you have health, strength, energy, and financial assets to give to children, then do so. Who, then will have children? If the childfree raise existing children, more people than ever will "have" children. The line between biological and nonbiological mothers will begin to disappear. Are we in danger of depleting the population? Are you kidding?
>
> Right now in your community there are hundreds of thousands of children and mothers who desperately need individual and community support . . .

Some people who choose not to bear children make an effort to participate in childrearing. Yet, like many parents, most people without children assume they should be uninterested in child care until they have their "own" children. People without children who try to participate in childrearing must confront the suspicions and resistance of people who do not understand their interest, who assume that all people without children do not like them. People are especially wary of individuals who wish to help in childrearing if they do not ask for pay for their services. At a time in my life when my companion and I were working hard to participate in childrearing we had children stay with us in our home for short periods of time to give the parent, usually a single mother, a break and to have children in our lives. If we explained the principle behind our actions, people were usually surprised and supportive but wary. I think they were wary because our actions were unusual. The difficulties we faced have led us to accept a life in which we have less interaction with children than we would like, the case for most people who do not have children. This isolation from children has motivated many feminists to bear children.

Before there can be shared responsibility for childrearing that relieves   23
women of the sole responsibility for primary child care, women and men must revolutionize their consciousness. They must be willing to accept that parenting in isolation (irrespective of the sex of the parent) is not the most effective way to raise children or be happy as parents. Since women do most of the parenting in this society and it does not appear that this situation will alter in the coming years, there has to be renewed feminist organizing around the issue of child care. The point is not to stigmatize single parents, but to emphasize the need for collective parenting. Women all over the United States must rally together to demand that tax money spent on the arms race and other militaristic goals be spent on improving the quality of parenting and child care in this society. Feminist theorists who emphasize the hazards of single parenting, who outline the need for men to share equally in parenting, often live in families where the male parent is present. This leads them to ignore the fact that this type of parenting is not an option for many women (even though it may be the best social framework in which to raise children). That social framework could be made available in community-based public day care centers with men and women sharing equal responsibility for child care. More than ever before, there is a great need for women and men to organize around the issue of child care to ensure that all children will be raised in the best possible social frameworks; to ensure that women will not be the sole, or primary, childrearers.

Questions

1. Which parent was most present in your home when you were being raised? Why does Hooks feel it is important that fathers share responsibility in raising children?

2. How has the feminist attitude toward motherhood changed? Why has it changed? How are the attitudes of black women toward motherhood different from those of white women?

3. Why does Hooks object to describing male parenting as "maternal"? Do you agree with her position?

4. According to Hooks, why is it important that women are not the sole, or primary, childrearers?

Climbing Jacob's Ladder: The Enduring Legacy of African-American Families

ANDREW BILLINGSLEY

Andrew Billingsley has written extensively on the African-American experience. He is a professor and chair of the department of family studies at the University of Maryland and a consultant to the National Urban League. Also, he received the Du Bois, Johnson and Frazier Award in 1992, and in 1991, he was the recipient of the Distinguished Scholar Award. He is the author of Climbing Jacob's Ladder: The Enduring Legacy of African-American Families *(1992).*

In this selection, Billingsley argues against Daniel P. Moynihan's assertion that it is the deterioration of the black family that causes black social problems. He asserts that the black family structure is strong because of community support; social institutions need to be changed so that they function as well for blacks as they do for whites. This selection is from Climbing Jacob's Ladder.

The supreme test of how well families function is how well they care for their members, particularly their dependent members, and most especially their children. The same test may be applied to the community and the larger society that surrounds them. 1

Children are the centerpiece of African-American family life. As we will see, they depend on adult family members in various and changing family structures. The ability of their families to care for them depends in turn on the resources of their surrounding community and social policies emanating from the larger society. But by the early 1990s not only African-American families but significant sectors of their communities and the larger society had become acutely concerned. 2

THE AFRICAN-AMERICAN FAMILY CRISIS

"Today, compared to 1980," declared Marian Wright Edelman of the Children's Defense Fund in 1990, "black children are *more* likely to be born into poverty, lack early prenatal care, have a single mother, have an unemployed 3

646

parent, be unemployed themselves as teenagers, and not go to college after high school graduation." Moreover, the following national trends affect black children in startling proportions:

- Today, the United States ranks eighteenth in the world behind Spain and Singapore in overall infant mortality. American black infant mortality rates place the United States twenty-eighth in the world, behind the overall rates of Cuba and Bulgaria.

- A black baby born in Indianapolis, Detroit, or in the shadow of the White House and Capitol was more likely to die in the first year of life in 1986 than a baby born in Jamaica, Trinidad and Tobago, Chile, Panama, Romania, or the Soviet Union. Black infant mortality rates in 1986 were equivalent to white infant mortality rates in 1970.

- If recent trends continue, in the year 2000 more than a third of all black births will be to a mother who did not receive early prenatal care.

- One in five of all American children has a single parent and one child in five is poor. By the year 2000, one in four will have a single parent and one in four will be poor.

What is happening to black children? One of the best barometers is suggested by changes in their living arrangements over the past few decades. As late as 1960 some 67 percent of black children under eighteen lived with both parents (Table 1). By 1988 this proportion had declined to 38.6 percent. Meanwhile the proportion living with their mothers only rose from nearly 20 percent in 1960 to over 51 percent by 1988. Over the same period the proportion of black children living with their fathers only rose from 2 percent to 3 percent. Meanwhile those living with other relatives declined from nearly 10 percent to just over 6 percent, while those living with nonrelatives declined slightly from 1.5 percent to 1 percent. With all these changes, however, it is notable that as late as 1988 some 99 percent of all black children lived with adults who were related to them. Such is the elasticity of the black family. Yet when other barometers are checked, one fact stands out: children are not the only ones in jeopardy.

Internal strife has made homicide the leading cause of death for young black men, just ahead of preventable accidents and just behind suicide. Domestic strife causes unprecedented numbers of African-American mothers and fathers to war against their own children, against each other, and against their parents. Child abuse, sibling abuse, spouse abuse, elder abuse, and fratricide—while by no means unique to black people—are relatively new in such numbers.

More young black males go to jail than to college, and it costs five times as much per year to keep them there. By the end of the 1980s a definitive report from Jewelle Taylor Gibbs of the University of California at Berkeley on the status of young black males concluded that they are "an endangered species." A brilliant series of analyses led her to conclude, "In American soci-

Table 1. Living Arrangements of Children 1960–1988

	Distribution	
Living Arrangement	Number	%
Total children under 18		
1960	8,650,000	100.0
1970	9,422,000	100.0
1980	9,375,000	100.0
1988	9,699,000	100.0
Living with two parents		
1960	5,795,000	67.0
1970	5,508,000	58.5
1980	3,956,000	42.2
1988	3,739,000	38.6
Living with mother only		
1960	1,723,000	19.9
1970	2,783,000	29.5
1980	4,117,000	43.9
1988	4,959,000	51.1
Living with father only		
1960	173,000	2.0
1970	213,000	2.3
1980	180,000	1.9
1988	288,000	3.0
Living with other relatives		
1960	827,000	9.6
1970	820,000	8.7
1980	999,000	10.7
1988	620,000	6.4
Living with nonrelatives only		
1960	132,000	1.5
1970	97,000	1.0
1980	123,000	1.3
1988	94,000	1.0

Source: U.S. Bureau of the Census, *Current Population Reports, Population Characteristics, Marital Status and Living Arrangements,* March 1988.

ety today, no single group is more vulnerable, more victimized, and more violated than young black males in the age range 15 to 24. In a scholarly essay on the plight of black men, the poet Haki Madhubuti remarked with unmistakable feeling, "The major piece of education I absorbed after twelve years of public education was that I was a problem, inferior, ineducable, and a victim. And as a victim I began to see the world through the eyes of a victim."

By the end of the 1980s, stimulated in part by the findings of the 1980 census, many family specialists, black leaders, professionals, public officials, and people in the media began to discuss the African-American family crisis. The idea of such a "crisis" was buttressed by research findings. Essentially it consisted of a cluster of conditions with devastating consequences reflected in Figure 1. They include family problems such as divorce, stress, marital conflict, domestic violence, and teen pregnancy; and dependent children behav-

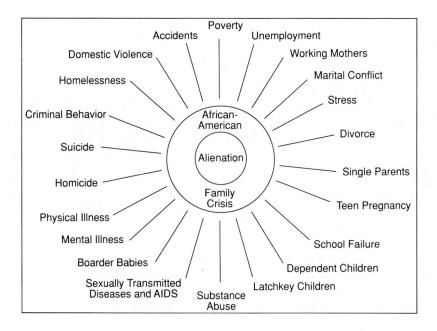

Figure 1. The African-American family crisis. (Andrew Billingsley.)

ioral problems such as school failure. Other conditions include substance abuse, sexually transmitted diseases and AIDS, physical and mental illness, criminal behavior, homicide, suicide, homelessness, and accidents.

Several characteristics stand out. First, almost all the conditions are more common and crippling among African-American families than among families in the nation as a whole.   8

Second, none of these conditions is exclusive or indigenous to African-American families. All of them afflict other American families as well. Numerically, most of the victims of these conditions are white. The proportion of sufferers, however, is higher among the black population.   9

Third, all of these conditions seem to have become more widespread, and more severe, in the decades since the 1960s. To some extent, this is because of greater social awareness of them. But mostly, the conditions themselves have worsened.   10

Fourth, each is either caused directly or aggravated substantially by social conditions. The United States leads many of the other industrial societies in the incidence of the problems, but trails many other industrialized nations in institutionalizing prevention and treatment. These conditions do not arise, exist, or operate in isolation. They often work together. Poverty, unemployment, and stress are highly interrelated. Reinforcing each other, they impact on divorce, single parenthood, teen pregnancy, and school failure. Substance abuse, illness, and domestic violence interact to produce dependent children, boarder babies, and marital conflict. Antisocial behavior such as crime in   11 general and homicide in particular, as well as suicide and accidents, intertwine with other problems. Homelessness is the evidence of a whole cluster of problems. With so many elements overlapping, the crisis can seem overwhelming. A growing sense of alienation or estrangement leads to a hopelessness which often borders on despair.

One final point comes through nonetheless. Not one of these problems 12 affects all or even a majority of African-American families. For example, the most widespread problem, unemployment, affects about a third.

As Patricia Raybon observed succinctly in a letter published in *Newsweek* 13 in 1989:

> Day after day, week after week, this message—that black America is dysfunctional and unwhole—gets transmitted across the American landscape. Sadly, as a result, America never learns the truth about what is actually a wonderful, vibrant, creative community of people.
>
> Most black Americans are not poor. Most black teenagers are not crack addicts. Most black mothers are not on welfare. Indeed, in sheer numbers, more white Americans are poor and on welfare than are blacks. Yet one never would deduce that by watching television or reading American newspapers and magazines.
>
> Why does the American media insist on playing this myopic, inaccurate picture game?
>
> . . . I want America to know us—all of us—for who we really are. To see us in all of our complexity, our subtleness, our artfulness, our enterprise, our specialness, our liveliness, our American-ness. That is the real portrait of black Americans—that we are strong people, surviving people, capable people. That may be the best kept secret in America. If so, it's time to let the truth be known.

THE AFRICAN-AMERICAN COMMUNITY

One of the most powerful truths about families is that they cannot be strong 14 unless they are surrounded by a strong community. Can black families look to their communities for assistance in meeting their responsibilities, particularly to their children? What is the capability and the responsibility of the black community? These are questions on which knowledgeable analysts differ markedly. The African-American community, as a context for helping families protect their children and youth, has itself undergone enormous changes during recent decades. Some analysts hold that as an organized entity, with guiding norms, values, and institutions, this community has virtually ceased to exist. Others point to the many dysfunctional aspects of community life. And while all these characterizations are based on fact, they in no sense constitute the whole truth.

The fact is that the African-American community exists, and is both 15 weak and strong. Even as it is undergoing constant change, major generative elements endure. The community is capable of providing resources and assistance. Any community composed of 30 million people, most of whom live in families, most of whom are no longer poor, with combined annual income exceeding $300 billion, more than 400,000 black-owned business firms, some 75,000 black-owned churches, a hundred black colleges, and numerous other organizations, with a common history, common identity, and successful struggles against the adversities of life, cannot reasonably be defined as impotent.

A community cannot be accurately defined by its limitations alone. A wholistic definition includes its strengths as well. Nor are these the worst of times for African-American families. Slavery, Jim Crow, and abject poverty were all much worse. Neither is it necessary to wait for another Harriet Tubman, Frederick Douglass, Marcus Garvey, Ida B. Wells, Earl Warren, Rosa Parks, Martin Luther King, Jr., Malcolm X, Lyndon B. Johnson, or Thurgood Marshall to usher in reforms. Scholars, leaders, organizations, and citizens generally—both black and white—who grasp the generative features of the African-American experience can harness this resource. With it, they can build communities that can sustain families that will be better able to protect, guide, and care for their children and youth.

What specifically do we mean by "African-American community"? According to James Blackwell:

> The black community can be perceived as a social system. Within the community value consensus and congruence exists; a significant segment of its constituents share norms, sentiments, and expectations. . . . Even though diversity exists within the community, its members are held together by adherence to commonly shared values and goals.

Thus, the black community is not just isolated individuals and families as presented by most sociological studies.

We take issue, however, with another of Blackwell's views, that the African-American community is held together by "white oppression and racism." There is strong evidence to support our view that the African-American people have reasons of their own to cling together, quite apart from external oppression. For example, the black church does not exist simply because the white church is oppressive. Black religion is a qualitatively different experience altogether and exists parallel with but not subservient to white religion. The black fraternal organizations might have been necessary because of exclusion from white organizations, but their persistence and growth are driven by forces internal to the black experience as much as by external hostility.

People of African descent in America constitute a community in four respects. First, geographically, most black families live in neighborhoods where most of their neighbors are also black. In conducting a national survey of black Americans in 1989, we found that 80 percent of a national sample of black adults live in neighborhoods that are predominantly black. This occurs sometimes out of economic necessity, and sometimes because of racist exclusionary practices which prevent people from exercising freedom of choice.

Whatever the reasons, there are African-American communities in every part of the nation which exist as enclaves.

A second sense of community among African-Americans that is less 21 widely known or accepted in the larger society is a shared set of values, which helps to define them.

The traditional values of the community, many of them intact today, 22 have been articulated by a number of scholars. One group of black scholars headed by John Hope Franklin, Eleanor Holmes Norton, and twenty-eight others summarized these values in a statement published by the Joint Center for Political and Economic Studies in 1987. In an era when many public officials and even scholars were asserting an absence of values among the African-American people, these scholars wrote:

> Blacks have always embraced the central values of the society, augmented those values in response to the unique experiences of slavery and subordination, incorporated them into a strong religious tradition, and espoused them fervently and persistently. These values—among them, the primacy of family, the importance of education, and the necessity for individual enterprise and hard work—have been fundamental to black survival. These community values have been matched by a strong set of civic values, ironic in the face of racial discrimination—espousal of the rights and responsibilities of freedom, commitment to country, and adherence to the democratic creed.

Thirdly, most black people, wherever they live, continue to identify with their heritage to some considerable degree. Many persons who move out of black neighborhoods or who never lived in one have relatives and friends who have stayed; others return to go to churches, barber shops, and beauty parlors. Even individuals who seldom visit these neighborhoods have a potentially powerful connection with black causes and issues.

For example, witness their response on Sunday, February 18, 1990, as Nel- 23 son Mandela was released from twenty-seven years of imprisonment for fighting against the apartheid system in South Africa. Roger Wilkins captured the spirit of the occasion in an op-ed article in *The New York Times* a few days later:

> When the son of an African noble house goes defiantly to prison to continue his struggle for freedom, part of us goes with him. And when we get reports of his growth, stubborn dignity, calm, commanding presence and wisdom, we swell again and think of our ancient heritage and bonds of blood.
> There was a surge of pride when the world for the first time gave a black man his regal due during his lifetime. So when the day finally came, we clapped, cheered and cried at the sight of a king—our cousin, the king—walking in the sunshine.

Finally, it is appropriate to speak of an African-American community in 24 terms of a set of institutions and organizations which grow out of the African-American heritage, identify with it, and serve primarily African-

American people and families. The repeated assertion that the black community is not organized misses the mark. Organization is widespread. There is an organization, agency, or institution for every conceivable function in the black community today. They are, however, sometimes small and uncoordinated, and uncooperative with others. And they sometimes spring up and dissolve too soon to complete their missions. But they anchor the community and can be galvanized into collective action when circumstances or leadership commands.

Four sets of organizations have been preeminent throughout the history   25
of the community. These are the church, the school, the business enterprise, and the voluntary organization. All these have undergone enormous change since the end of World War II. Even so, a majority of African-American adults belong.

Fully 70 percent of black adults belong to just one, namely the black   26
church, which is easily the strongest and most representative. The black church embodies all the four senses of community. Ordinarily located in neighborhoods where a majority of the families are of African-American descent, it embraces traditional African-American values. It identifies with both the struggles and achievements of African-American people, and it is institutionalized with an enduring organizational structure and mission.

It is appropriate, then, to speak of the African-American community in ei-   27
ther, all, or any combination of the above respects. The African-American community, at bottom, is the organized or collective expression of the African-American people in the United States.

Robert Bellah, in *Habits of the Heart,* has given voice to the concept that a   28
real community is "one that does not forget its past. In order not to forget that past, a community is involved in retelling its story, its constitutive narrative, and in so doing, it offers examples of the men and women who have embodied and exemplified the meaning of the community. These stories of collective history and exemplary individuals are an important part of the tradition that is so central to a community of memory." He could be speaking directly of the African-American community as he observes: "At times, neighborhoods, localities, and regions have been communities in America, but that has been hard to sustain in our restless and mobile society. Families can be communities, remembering their past, telling the children the stories of parents' and grandparents' lives, and sustaining hope for the future—though without the context of a larger community that sense of family is hard to maintain."

This definition raises several questions. For instance, does the African-   29
American community include persons of West Indian ancestry? In our conception it does as long as they live in the United States, since they are obviously of African descent. And while there are individuals from time to time of West Indian or Caribbean ancestry living in the United States who do not wish to identify with the African-American community, that is an individual matter and we are speaking of collectivities.

What about individual African-American natives of the United States   30
who choose not to identify with the African-American community? Certain
blacks wish to distance themselves from their heritage. More than one such
individual has been heard to say that he or she is an American who just happens to be black. We have found that this is an acute minority view. In a national study of black households, adults were asked how they prefer to be
identified. A small minority of 8 percent want to be called just "American."
Nearly three times as many, or some 20 percent, prefer just "black." In keeping with the double consciousness Du Bois wrote about, an overwhelming 70
percent preferred the identity of black *and* American.

Nothing in this definition has referred to skin color, texture of hair, or   31
rhythm in the stride. While these may indicate African heritage, they are not
the same thing. The real thing is the sense of peoplehood with a common anchor in African history and the American experience.

THE LARGER SOCIETY

Every American family insures the well-being of its children with the help of   32
policies, programs, and resources generated within the larger society. Full employment, certain Constitutional guarantees, education, and health care, for
example, require resources far beyond the ones that can be generated within
any limited community. Therefore, the African-American community has a
major responsibility to use its resources to focus the attention of the wider society on the needs of its families and children. Through organized, persistent
efforts, the community has to enlighten, persuade, cooperate, pressure, and
lead in order to make sure that the appropriate national resources flow its
way and are channeled effectively.

Any minority community which allows the larger society's majority com-   33
munity to define its character, determine its needs, and design policies and programs to meet those needs is likely to suffer perpetual disadvantage. At the
same time, any community which proposes to ignore the collaboration of
forces in that larger society and go it alone is likely to suffer the same fate. Joint
action is complex, taxing, and difficult, but clearly indispensable to progress.

The public sector, the private for-profit sector, the voluntary nonsectarian   34
sector, and the religious sector all control resources to which African-American people continue to make enormous contributions. It is not a question of
blacks being supplicants, or begging alms of others. Blacks do more than their
fair share of the hard work, pay more than their fair share of taxes, contribute
more than their fair share of personnel to the military, spend most of their income to keep the consumer economy going, contribute great amounts to
charity and to voluntary service, to culture and leisure activities, and provide
many of the customers and clients for private and nonprivate enterprises.
They are entitled to the resources they need to maintain their independence,
stability, and their viability. Blacks, in other words, are an intricate and con-

tributing part of this amorphous national society. But what is the nature of this society? How does it go about influencing African-American families for good and for ill?

We have identified twelve key systems through which society influences 35 African-American families. These are the economic system, the political system, the health system, the housing system, the educational system, the welfare system, the criminal justice system, and the military system, as well as the transportation, recreation, communications, and religious systems. They may be conveniently considered in four major sectors: government, private business, voluntary nonsectarian, and religious. They often collaborate and interact.

The government sector includes politics and government at all levels. The 36 private business sector includes the profit-making enterprises. Many of the twelve societal systems are subsystems of these two sectors, sometimes independently and sometimes jointly. For example, the military system is part of the government sector, as is the criminal justice system. Other systems such as health, welfare and education, and transportation are derivatives of both the government and private business sectors. The government sector plays a preeminent role because it, more than any other sector, has historically stood as an obstacle to the freedom, independence, and opportunity available to African-American families. And conversely, government leadership has enabled the greatest measure of progress over the past century.

The private business sector consists of ideas, practices, and institutions, 37 which control the production and distribution of goods and services. When it works optimally it provides jobs, income, and wealth, distributed on an equitable basis. Profits earned are used to perpetuate the business and to distribute rewards to those eligible. The private business sector provides most of the jobs for African-American people that make it possible for families to meet their basic obligations. It is dependent on vigorous family functioning in both its instrumental domain, providing food, clothing, shelter, and other basic necessities; and in its more expressive domain, providing love and care for all its members.

The voluntary sector is the largest sector of all. As President George Bush's 38 theme of "the thousand points of light" suggests, it has enormous power, status, and place in American society. It consists of those ideas, practices, and institutions which operate for the general welfare of the people without pursuing a profit and without pursuing a sectarian purpose. This is the fastest growing sector of American society, and it virtually exploded with the onset of the postindustrial era. The United Way, the American Red Cross, family agencies, foundations, and a plethora of professional associations are typical of the voluntary sector.

Finally, there is the religious sector. This is composed of a wide range of 39 ideas, values, institutions, and practices oriented to particular religious and spiritual traditions. Most have at bottom a set of moral values, which are humanitarian and family oriented. They have been, are, and can be even more helpful in the struggle of African-American families for viability.

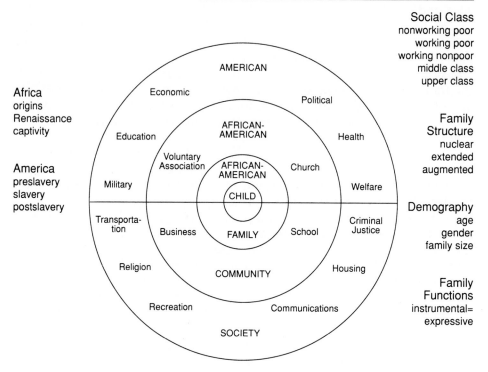

HISTORY   CONTEMPORARY SOCIETY   CONTEMPORARY
                                                                   FAMILY PATTERNS

AMERICAN

Economic   Political

Africa
origins
Renaissance
captivity
Education   AFRICAN-   Health
                         AMERICAN
                Voluntary
                Association   AFRICAN-   Church
America   AMERICAN
preslavery   Military   Welfare
slavery   CHILD
postslavery

Transporta-   Criminal
tion   Business   FAMILY   School   Justice

Religion   COMMUNITY   Housing

Recreation   Communications

SOCIETY

Social Class
nonworking poor
working poor
working nonpoor
middle class
upper class

Family
Structure
nuclear
extended
augmented

Demography
age
gender
family size

Family
Functions
instrumental=
expressive

Figure 2. A whole perspective. (Andrew Billingsley.)

Systems of Contemporary Society

Figure 2 sketches out the broad implications of this analysis. It suggests that knowing the truth about black families today requires a profound appreciation of certain large-scale influences. First, a careful observer recognizes that the family which surrounds and sustains the child is in turn surrounded and sustained by the black community and by the wider American society. Whatever considerable influence history has had, it is moderated through these forces of contemporary society. A dozen segments of the wider society are identified. Each has an impact. In addition, there are certain segments or institutions within the African-American community which are particularly powerful in their effects on family life. Finally, as a consequence of how society and the community operate, certain distinct patterns of family life emerge. These are reflected in social class, family structure, age structure, and gender distinctions.

40

SOCIETY'S ADVANTAGE

Working through its various sectors, society both assists and blocks families   41
in their efforts to meet their basic responsibilities even though families are
not passive entities and also influence society. In the late 1960s, prominent
sociologist Nathan Glazer made a comment that remains particularly pertinent to this point. "It is clear that society makes families and families make
society," Glazer wrote in his introduction to a new edition of E. Franklin Frazier's pace-setting *The Negro Family in the United States,* originally published in
1939, "but what is not clear is the relative influence of the two."

This was a Solomonic response to a raging theoretical controversy. Glazer   42
had collaborated with Senator Daniel P. Moynihan in a 1963 study on ethnic
and racial groups in New York City, *Beyond the Melting Pot.* In 1965, Moynihan published a study that became infamous. It was called *The Negro Family:
The Case for National Action.* In it he seemed to say that families make society.
He claimed that certain weaknesses he identified within African-American
families caused the difficulties black people experienced in the larger society
in education, employment, and politics. "The white family," he argued, "has
achieved a high degree of stability and is maintaining that stability." Moreover, he argued that because of that strong family structure, white people do
better in society. Black people do not do as well because of a weak family
structure. "At the heart of the deterioration of the fabric of negro society, is
the deterioration of the negro family. It is the fundamental source of weakness at the present time."

Moynihan's thesis seemed to reinforce the policy perspective that there   43
was less need for changing the structure of society, less need for civil rights
legislation and affirmative action, and more need for changing the internal
structure of African-American families by putting a man in charge of every
house.

We argued, along with others, that Moynihan had it all backward. We ar-   44
gued that society makes families and that it was the difficulties experienced
by African-Americans in the wider society (their economic, political, and educational deprivation) which caused the patterns of instability within families
that Moynihan identified. Consequently, we argued that by changing the
structure of social institutions so that they would function as well for blacks
as they do for whites, and as well for female-headed families as they do for
male-headed families, and as well for poor families as they do for more privileged families, both family stability and more effective family functioning
would follow.

After reflecting on two decades of research in the social sciences since   45
then, we would now state our position somewhat differently. Recent studies
of African-American families seem to bear out Nathan Glazer. However, to
avoid the either-or mode of thought, we propose that families make society
and society makes families. We add to that observation, however, the view
that while the influence between families and society flows in both directions, society has the advantage. This is, in part, because society is older,

larger, stronger, more continuous and, thus, more powerful and has more re-sources at its command. Though contemporary analysts of African-American families still have some difficulty with the idea of the supremacy of society over families, this proposition is really not new. Aristotle expressed it this way: "The state is by nature clearly prior to the family and to the individual, since the whole is of necessity prior to the part." It is an idea which can help us all understand better both the structure and the functioning of contempo-rary African-American families as these intimate associations struggle to help their members adapt to the pressures and opportunities inherent in their communities and their larger society. The so-called black family crisis is not of their own making; nor is it the worst crisis they ever faced and survived.

We will show that within the range of family structures, within the range   46 of community institutions and initiatives, and within the larger society, there are enormous pressures making it difficult for families to be strong. Just as im-portant, however, we will identify a set of strengths and resources in family, community, and society, with the potential for generating policies, programs, and practices which can help families meet their responsibilities.

In the next section we ask what we can learn from the history of the   47 African-American people that will help us understand better the value they place on family life. What struggles have they faced in trying to protect and enhance their families? What successful efforts can they look back to for guidance and inspiration? Reflecting on their past, we uncover ideas that could help more families meet the future effectively. We also gain more in-sight into the way that society's influence works.

Questions

1. According to Billingsley, black families have strong community support. Why then are black families perceived to be in a crisis? According to the author, what is the cause of this crisis? How does his explanation differ from the views of other sociologists?

2. What role does the various types of communal support play in your own life? How do these communal supports strengthen family structure?

3. How would Hooks perceive Billingsley's portrayal of black families? Would they agree?

The Mexican American Family

STUART A. QUEEN AND ROBERT W. HABENSTEIN

Stuart A. Queen (b. 1890) is the author of The American City *(1953). Robert W. Habenstein (b. 1914) began his career in sociology late after serving in the armed forces and completing a Ph.D. that dealt with funeral directing. He has been a professor at the University of Missouri and is the author of eight books, including a number of studies on the family.*

In this excerpt, Queen and Habenstein point out that although the majority of Mexican-American families remain monogamic and patriarchal, socioeconomic factors are changing the strong nuclear structure of these families. The "depressed occupational status" of the Mexican male as well as the influence of American culture has begun to weaken the family as a functioning unit. This selection is from The Family in Various Cultures *(1974).*

FAMILY STRUCTURE

Familism and Family Solidarity

Within this constellation of cultural values an overriding assumption is that the family remains the single most important social unity. The theme of family honor and unity diffuses throughout Mexican American society, irrespective of social class variation or geographical location. The upper class rancher and the lowly crop picker both think of themselves first as family members and second as individuals.[1] It is a familism that extends beyond husband, wife, and children to relatives on both sides. In center city enclaves the ideal of familism persists even when the dominance of the male role becomes weakened. It is the main focus of obligations and also a source of emotional and economic support, as well as recognition for accomplishment.[2] William Madsen, a student of Mexican Americans in South Texas, writes:

> The family is a sanctuary in a hostile world full of envy and greed. The Mexican-American child who has been humiliated by Anglos at school knows that he will receive love and understanding from his mother. The wife who has been abused by her husband can seek help and guidance from her parents. Any Latin boy with a brother knows he need never stay alone in a fight. As long as one member of the family has a house and food, none of his close relatives will lack shelter or meals.[3]

659

But, obligations to the family provide the other side of the coin. Individualism and individual needs must accommodate to the collective needs of the family—as these needs come to be defined by the patriarchal father. "The strength with which a person is bound to his family," observes anthropologist Arthur J. Rubel, "so overshadows all other bonds in importance that it contributes to the atomistic nature of the neighborhood."[4]

One reason that Mexican American family organization can encompass a full set of primary roles with ramified age and sex differentiation is its size. Mexican families by ordinary American standards are quite large. "They are so large," remarks Joan Moore, "as to make Mexican participation in the ordinary material rewards of American life much more marginal than that of most other populations identified by the census."[5] High fertility and the presence of many young families assure continued growth of the number of Mexican Americans, at least through the remainder of the century. 2

Family and Kinship

The Mexican American family in the first instance exists as a sharply definable nuclear unit of husband, wife, and children. The specificity of roles is reinforced by the denotative kinship terminology used among family members, contrasted with the generally classificatory system operating in the more inclusive kinship system.[6] The family is highly monogamic and, as indicated above, strongly patriarchal. While the enveloping extended kinship system is bilateral and mother's and father's kin of generally equal importance, special recognition is given to mother's sisters. Both sets of grandparents are revered but not the siblings of grandparents. First cousins are especially important collateral kin and, as Rubel indicates, "are said to be somewhat like one's sisters and brothers."[7] 3

Ritual Kinship: Compadrazgo

An important integrative social usage that has prevailed through several centuries is a form of ritual kinship involving the special linkage of two persons or groups as *compadres*. While the *compadrazgo* may take a number of forms, notably coparenthood, by providing fictive kinship linkages, its effect is to generate social and interpersonal cohesion and thus to reduce the potential extrafamilial conflict that might arise in a highly family-centered society. Coparenthood, which is considered the most important, links two families through the baptismal ritual. The godparents, *compadres,* will have been chosen with care from outside the kinship circle and the male, the most important *compadre,* will hopefully be a man of goodness, status, and respect in the community. The bond having been established ritually, the interaction henceforth will be carried on between the younger person and his coparent in the context of prescribed formality and mutual respect. They are expected to visit each other and cultivate a close relationship. And, in any kind of trouble, *compadres* have the right to call on each other for help and advice.[8] 4

The Marriage Institution

The traditional norms of Mexican American culture prescribe endogamy, for- 5
mal courtship, chaperonage, permission from both sets of parents to marry,
and a great circumspection in courtship behavior. The services of a go-between, *portador,* may be secured by the parents. Madsen elaborates:

> A proper *portador* is a respected member of the community who may be an
> older woman of good family or a man of good reputation. The *portador* makes
> the proposal to the girl's parents and they take the matter for consideration
> for a period of at least two weeks in order to discuss it with their daughter. A
> polite refusal delivered to the *portador* carries no offense to the boy's family.
> The *portador* who brings back an acceptance is rewarded with a handsome
> gift.[9]

Rubel tells of an earlier custom of exchanging potential spouses, the girl
spending several months on trial at the home of the boy's parents and vice
versa (*intercambio*). After the proposal had been accepted the boy would send
food or money to the girl's parents for several months, and after thus demonstrating ability to provide would marry and live at the home of the girl until
he could establish a separate household.[10]

Parental involvement in courtship and marriage continues, but not with- 6
out resistance of the younger generation. Elopements have increased, but the
common pattern is for a period of engagement followed by an elaborate
wedding.

> The approaching wedding of a daughter is publicly announced at a dance
> sponsored by *her* parents, and there at the dance the parents of the girl are in-
> troduced to the gathering by the master of ceremonies. Their obligations to-
> ward her met, *they* are honored as well as she. The financial outlay for such
> an announcement is considerable, but after all, it is a life's work to prepare a
> daughter to become a worthy wife and mother.[11]

The lavishness of the wedding, as Madsen notes, varies with social class. 7

> Lower class marriages are customarily celebrated with an outdoor barbecue
> and beer party. Wedding celebrations among the elite sometimes fill the ball-
> rooms of the largest hotels where champagne and imported French delicacies
> are served in addition to a towering wedding cake. Regardless of these differ-
> ences, the symbolism is the same. By uniting their children in marriage, the
> two families have become *compadres* to each other. It is a relationship that en-
> dures as long as the marriage.[12]

Residence of the newlyweds tends to be matrilocal. The bride's mother is not
anxious to lose a daughter from the intimate circle of familiars upon whom
she is forced to depend for friendship, confidences, and assurance.[13] The
groom, who has been restive under the authority and control of the *jefe de la
casa,* is assured whatever freedom that can come from geographical separa-

tion, and at the same time he will have fewer qualms about a wife continuing her associations with mother and intimates than reconstructing a set of social and personal relationships in a strange setting. Mothers-in-law fare no better in the Mexican than in the Anglo-Saxon tradition, and the wife would prefer to avoid her spouse's mother. Finally, the marriage behind and the residence established, the groom settles down as the authoritarian head of household, a role for which he has served a lengthy, often trying apprenticeship.

Role Behavior and Life Cycle

Again, the role prescriptions described in this section emanate from, and em-   8
phasize the norms and values of, traditional Mexican culture. As such they should be seen to have operated either as acknowledged cultural ideals or to have persisted in common everyday experiences and so taken for granted as to have been seldom thought about consciously. Their closest approximation to reality would be found along the border areas, particularly in South Texas.

Childhood

The Mexican American infant is wanted, cherished, pampered, and thor-   9
oughly "spoiled."

> The small child is regarded as an *angelito* as yet uncontaminated by human sin and error. He receives adoring affection from mother and father alike. The father may drop his dignity to cradle a child, care for his needs, or even crawl on hands and knees to play with him. Such behavior is confined to the home.[14]

But awareness of gender comes early. The son-father relationship soon becomes asymmetrical and remains so throughout the life of both. The father very early in the child's life exemplifies the patriarchal parental role and the socialization process is long and difficult, as the son must constantly try to measure up to the demands and expectations of his father. A certain amount of distance and formality develops once the son is judged to have reached the ability to reason and to accept responsibility. The father must hold his own in male society, not only for himself, as a *macho*, but as the representative of his family unit. The lessons of male childhood are as demanding as they are endless. The mother, acting as a buffer between father and son, tends to indulge the latter, only to contribute to the tension when her favoritism is suspected or becomes apparent to the father.

Father-daughter relations throughout the latter's childhood are less dis-   10
tant and severe. "This is partly because the daughter is not expected to emulate him in any way," says Peñalosa, "nor is she at all a threat to his male status."[15] Mother-daughter relationships during early childhood are very close, with the mother dominating in much the same way as the father does the son. The daughter receives the most attention from the mother, even

more than the son. "Because of the close relationship prevailing between mother and daughter on both emotional and household chore level," continues Peñalosa, " . . . the daughter ordinarily manages full identification with the mother."[16]

By the time childhood gives way to the teens both son and daughter have experienced no difficulty finding appropriate role models. The differentiation process has been reinforced in innumerable ways. Boys are expected to emulate fathers, to learn masculine ways, and to gain independence from maternal solicitude and pampering. Since a succession of children is the expectable occurrence, the boy will find himself dislodged from the favored position by the next born, and his narcissistic needs threatened.[17] The dynamics of coming of age for the male center around the psychogenic, emotional needs generated in infancy and reinforced by maternal solicitude, with these in turn coming into conflict with the clear cultural demands for manliness, independence, and maturity.   11

The adolescent male is encouraged and given the freedom to move about and gain experience in an expanding social world, the world which he must someday master as representative of his own family. Ordinarily he will join in with informal youth groups, *palomillas,* which afford him an opportunity to test his manliness against his peers. Thus he begins to develop a reputation centered on skill, knowledge, experience, and ability, from which his social status and prestige in the community is eventually derived.[18]   12

The adolescent female must learn a culturally defined role of an opposite yet complementary character to that of male *machismo.* Her social world is constricted and is home and mother-centered—but there is much more to it than learning housewifery. The female occupies a virtually sanctified position in Mexican and Mexican American society. Revered as a symbol of purity, she must grow up virginal, compassionate, submissive, aware that in the meaning of things she exists to complement but never to compete with the manly male. She finds herself less likely to be in conflict with her mother than the son with his father as she enters, in effect, a sisterhood made up of all the females of the extended kin group. Within it ambivalence, mistrust, and suppressed hostility toward the dominant male (whatever the psychogenic roots) are learned and/or reinforced. Biologically impelled toward males, yet long instructed that in the weakness of her sex she is incapable of resisting male exploitation, her refuge lies in early marriage and entrance as quickly as possible into the fully expressive, if sexually suppressed, role of motherhood.   13

Adult Roles

Perhaps enough has already been said about the traditional male role in Mexican American culture. A deeper look into the symbolic underpinning of the role, however, may be instructive. Octavio Paz, one of Mexico's greatest writers, has analyzed the *macho* or masculine role as incorporating superiority, aggressiveness, insensitivity, and invulnerability, all subsumable under one   14 word, *power,* " . . . force without the discipline of any notion of order: arbitrary power, the will without reins and without a set course."[19] Beneath the more public or cognitive meanings of honor, strength, and masculinity lie subjective, symbolic associations leading back to and rooted subconsciously in earlier histories of two rather frightful peoples, the warring, sacrificing Aztecs, and their medieval Spanish conquerors.[20] Spelled out in day-to-day role activities, however, *machismo* calls for an aloof authoritarian head of family, directing its activities, arbitrating disputes, policing behavior, and, as already indicated, representing the family to community and society.

The adult female finds security in motherhood, a sainted role, to be dif-   15
ferentiated from the spousal role. The latter is clearly the more difficult for its focus is on husband-wife interaction in all its concrete reality. Twin ambivalencies present themselves: the husband, having long been socialized in the tradition of the sexual conquest of "bad" girls and the ascetic veneration of the "good," finds it difficult to assimilate sexual intercourse with the wife as an act of mutuality involving gratification and fulfillment equally shared; the wife, aware from earliest socialization that as a weaker female she cannot trust herself in sexual matters, denies herself or makes no sexual advances toward the spouse. The husband, free to continue the social activities enjoyed before marriage, finds conquests of other females ego building, and, as he makes no effort to deny such activities to his friends, they become just another means of demonstrating *machismo.*

The effect, as indicated above, is to take the husband out of the home and   16
to consign the wife to an early and permanent role of motherhood. Each child becomes the object for expression of strong affective sentiments, themselves generated in the wife's childhood socialization. The wife and mother vies with all other family members in possessiveness toward the children, her rationalization being that only she can properly serve and minister to their needs. The latter include formal religious education and the providing of an appropriate religious atmosphere in the home. In a sense the home becomes an extension of the Catholic church with its mixture of indigenous folk beliefs, and the mother symbolically becomes the embodiment of the Virgin of Guadalupe.

Grandparenthood has always been a well established status and, as al-   17
ready noted, grandparents are revered by their own adult children and by grandchildren alike. But prestige is not coterminous with power, and the authority of the father takes precedence. Children may go to their grandparents with questions they might be afraid to bother the father about, but if there are decisions to be made the children will be referred to their father. Reporting child's-eye views of life in an urban *barrio* in Houston, Mary Ellen Goodman and Alma Beman report that grandmothers as well as mothers fill many domestic roles in the child's world, but again when small rules are disobeyed discipline falls to the mother.[21] Still, grandmothers will compete actively for the attention and affection of grandchildren, more so than the grandfather, understandable in relation to the intimacy world of children and females. "In contrast to the father and his relationship to the children," Murillo points

out, "the mother continues to be close and warm, serving and nurturing even when her children are grown, married, and have children of their own."[22]

SOCIAL INTEGRATION AND SOCIAL PROBLEMS

Function and Strain

Let us know briefly review the Mexican American family as a functioning unity. In rural and *barrio* society familism, as a normative prescription emphasizing family needs and family reputation over all other matters, provided the *context of meaning* for intrafamilial behavior and gave reality and importance to the roles all its family members would play. This meaning has long been grounded in tradition and undergirded by a symbol system incorporating elements of two medieval cultures, Spanish and indigenous native. Moreover, the social and interactive arena within which the drama of everyday family life would be played and individual family roles enacted was constricted, embracing in the first instance the nuclear family of husband, wife, and children, and in the second extending only moderately to include close collateral and lineal relatives. Beyond that, neighboring and community participation was or could easily become erratic, and unsystematized in the sense of an incomplete articulation of wider social roles. Community life would be beset by contingencies that are present when constituent family members, age and sex groups turn in on themselves, retreat to the sanctuary of their homes, and find difficulty in establishing social networks. [18]

Yet within this arena an exchange and balance of expected behaviors operated smoothly enough to guarantee family continuity for generation after generation. Only one role called for serious, sustained, critical involvement with social systems external to the family, that of husband, provider, and protector of the family name. Assuredly economic contingencies were ever present, and the hazards of a personal contest system whereby one's *macho* was always on the line would make the male role difficult but seldom impossible. The embracing system of cultural values detailed at the beginning of this chapter always provided a rationale for Mexican Americans to downgrade the demands of the Western Protestant ethic. The centrality of the work ethic for Anglo Americans has as its reciprocal a residual anxiety attached to one's being physically present in the home when there's work to be done elsewhere. It is clear that the strictures to find meaning in life through vocational activity are neither so meaningful for Mexican Americans nor so all-embracing as they have been for Anglo Americans. The home is the social and personal center of gravity for the people of the *barrio* and the *hacienda* alike. And, it must also be remembered, each home is a religious sanctuary serving as a physical and spiritual extension of the church, centering around the wife as Holy Mother and objects of religious significance that are found everywhere in Mexican American homes. [19]

Finally, a number of social arrangements or mechanisms have served to link families to each other and to assure at least a modicum of social integra- [20]

tion at the extrafamilial level. These we recall as the woman's kin and sociability groups, the husband's drinking companions, the *palomillas,* i.e., peer groups for youth, the *compadre* relationships generated through the *compadrazgo* system, and the pervasive religious community, sensuously and symbolically glorifying the miracle of the Holy Family in fiestas, other religious observances, and through the services of the Catholic ministry.

Disjunction and Change

Our last task will be to look at the internal weaknesses of the traditional Mexican American family in the context of social change.[23] Conflicts within any family are of course inevitable, but their genesis and importance will vary significantly. Husband-wife discord in Mexican and Mexican American families has never been uncommon. The asymmetrical nature of the husband's role, with his prerogative to express himself personally, socially, and sexually in the community at large, while the wife must stay at home, mind the family, and serve the husband in all his needs, gives rise to a sense of injustice on the part of the female—particularly in a world society where modernity increasingly prescribes equality of the sexes. The enshrinement of womanhood clashes with the particularity and individuality of each wife as a person with human needs. Given the increasing vocational opportunities for women,[24] as well as the demands of external institutions, agencies, schools, secondary associations, City Hall, etc., the wife finds herself with an expanded secular role to play. `21`

The higher the family income the more likely there will be a departure from traditional ethnic norms.[25] The *macho* role of the husband includes his function as provider, but in a world of rising expectations and standards of living, the longstanding depressed occupational status of the male[26] frustrates the breadwinner's role and often leads him into heavy drinking, rows with friends and neighbors, and abusive behavior at home. The tendency to withdraw rather than to challenge authority and status reported by most students of Mexican-American culture suggests that the *macho* role is not correlatively supported by ego strength. In any event, mistreated wives still have as one recourse a further retreat into the inner sanctum of religion or the emotionally supportive group of female intimates. However, it is not unknown for the wife to fight back, to scorn the husband for his weakness and improvidence. Divorce, anathema to the Catholic church, provided no way out, but desertion always has. Husbands who migrate to look for work may not return; others simply flee the family. Technology and the urban tropism have moved persons and families everywhere, but geographical mobility does not insure better job opportunities. When the occupational base of the provider is undermined or jeopardized it is a sociological truism that family form and solidarity are likewise threatened. *Machismo* might coexist with uncertain employment in the small village and the *barrio,* but the city apartment or flat does not provide the same climate of refuge as did the village *casa. Mañana* has only a hollow echo. Desertion rates are increasing, and when divorce statistics are combined with separation statistics the result is as dismaying as it is `22` indicative of the deterioration of family unity.[27] The Mexican American family in this regard fares no better than the American black. Significantly, both groups at the low income level have a large proportion of female household heads.

Education, in the context of small parochial schools taught by members of a religious teaching order,[28] seldom if ever operated to separate children from their parents. Family solidarity and the virtues of family life would as a matter of course be emphasized in parochial education. The predominance of formal public school education has meant that greater opportunities and resources could be made available to children of Mexican Americans and provide the means for breaking out of the culture of poverty cycle. But consensus seems to favor the proposition that the American public school system has been particularly deficient in its impact on Spanish and Mexican-Spanish vernacular-speaking children and their families. For one, the confusing and ego damaging experiences in school lead to early dropping out, despite the general high value that Mexican peoples in the abstract have placed on intelligence and learning. The child's personal problem of thinking in one language and being asked to learn by thinking in another is compounded by the experience of bringing the foreign language into the home, of using it or some variety of it with brothers and sisters in front of noncomprehending parents. Also, as Murillo and others have indicated, the child often finds himself caught up in the clash between authoritarian values embedded in the family structure and the democratic ideals learned at school.[29] Again, children may be kept home from or even taken out of school by parents who put matters involving the family as a whole over the needs of any member. Migratory workers' children are virtually guaranteed discontinuous and abortive schooling.

The desires of the young to escape the domination of the old gets expressed in both conflict and avoidance. As much as possible the father will be avoided by the older offspring. The mother, where and if possible, will be dominated by both sons and daughters—particularly the former, who vie for the favorable treatment that was once their birthright. Brothers of varying ages avoid each other except in the presence of an external threat from a nonfamily source. The young wish to date and marry freely. Chaperonage, the *portado,* even parental consent for marriage may be relegated to the category of "old-fashioned." Elopements are common and intermarriages are on the increase. The division of labor breaks down as older children stay on in school and/or are diverted from household chores by homework and school activities. The increase in the number of working mothers makes for further complications.

All familial roles and the contexts of family interaction, it seems, are undergoing change. Some internal tensions arising in the wake of a changing society have already been discussed. However, a few of the macrolevel changes noted earlier remain to be elaborated. One of these is the revolution taking place in agricultural technology. Mechanization and the application of rational, corporation-style modes of organization in the planting, growing, harvesting, and marketing of agricultural products have meant a continuing reduction of stoop labor. For Mexican Americans who have always been heavily employed in this kind of work, mechanization poses a threat to their livelihood more significant than that presented by the *braceros* and the wet-backs who competed when labor was more scarce. Not only does the market for farm labor lessen but a concomitant development, that of increasing marginality and economic hazard of small scale farming, has made it difficult for Mexican Americans to succeed as farmer-entrepreneurs. Lack of capital and credit, the crushing forces of corporate competition, labor militancy, jurisdictional disputes and strikes, all in one combination or another loom up as obstacles to the maintenance of the family farm and the farm family.

The "pull" of urban centers—Los Angeles, San Antonio, Chicago, Kansas City—then, must be seen partly as a consequence of the "push" occasioned by the lack of promise for any kind of economically based good life in village and country. Inner cities have always been the point of urban entry for migrants, and when the migration is large scale the reproduction of familiar institutions is expectable. However, the urban *barrio* remains to be more thoroughly studied, not merely for the replication of traditional social structures but for adaptations and changes that represent responses to new environmental problems.[30] 26

Certainly one of the important "inputs" into the urban mix is the demographic fact that Mexican Americans have the highest birth rate of all the larger minority groups, and that in view of a decreasing death rate, the proportion and concentration of urban Mexican Americans in American society can only increase. The matter of physical concentration is crucial but must be seen against some evidence of dispersion and assimilation into the American mainstream. It can be shown that opportunities to do better in the labor force are increasing, and the elaboration of a social class as against an earlier caste system is advanced as a corollary development. Thus the future of the Mexican American is held by some to lie in the realm of blending into Anglo American society, with a tincture effect occurring as Mexican culture is absorbed into the American mainstream. That such assimilation, even if it were desirable, is in the realm of possibility is doubted by the thousands of politicized Mexican Americans who have redefined their problem as victimization through suppression and exploitation. The conception of *la Raza* and the redesignation of Mexican Americans as "Chicanos"—a political stratagem—represent the frustration responses of Americans of Spanish-Mexican ancestry whose hopes for an equal sharing of the affluence of the world's richest nation still remain remote in their minds. Thus the counter-assimilation moves and the power sought by militant leaders are based on the proposition that the bulk of Mexican American urban migrants will remain concentrated in the center of the nation's cities. 27

CONCLUSION

The Mexican American family differs historically from the black American family because of its early and continued unity. For Negroes slavery, emancipation but with exclusion as a separate and inferior race, and a wide variety 28 of forms of social and economic discrimination could scarcely produce other than a fragile monogamy with the male provider facing an uphill struggle for status, authority, and ego strength, both inside the family and out. Despite conquest and subjugation Mexicans—and later Mexican Americans—have always enjoyed nuclear family unity: husband, wife, and child, with other primary collateral and affinal relatives usually close at hand. If neither group could experience economic verisimilitude in the past, it has been the Mexican and Mexican American family that could relegate such matters to a secondary order of value and still keep its unity of organization. Both groups remain part of a great underclass of American society. Should it be their collective fate to pile up in the disintegrating and blighted urban centers the prospect for family change will increase just to the extent that adaptations and accommodations, or breakdowns, are generated in face of family, community-, and minority-wide crises. For the Mexican American family there will undoubtedly be a number of structural changes, the most significant of which will be the equalization of spousal roles.

NOTES

1. William Madsen, *The Mexican-Americans of South Texas* (1964), p. 44.

2. *Ibid.;* Murillo, *op cit.,* pp. 103–105. Joan Moore feels, however, that familism seems to be declining in the big cities of the southwest. See her *Mexican Americans* (1970), pp. 116–118.

3. Madsen, *op. cit.,* p. 44.

4. Arthur J. Rubel, "Across the Tracks" (1966), in *Mexican Americans in the United States: A Reader,* John Burma, ed. (1970), Chap. 3, p. 211.

5. Moore, *op. cit.,* p. 57.

6. Rubel, *op. cit.,* p. 211.

7. *Ibid.* This paragraph paraphrases Rubel's description of Mexican American family structure.

8. Madsen, *op. cit.,* p. 47.

9. *Ibid.,* p. 56. By permission of Holt, Rinehart and Winston.

10. Rubel, *op. cit.,* p. 216.

11. *Ibid.,* p. 217. By permission of University of Texas Press.

12. Madsen, *op. cit.,* p. 57. By permission of Holt, Rinehart and Winston.

13. Rubel, *op. cit.,* pp. 217–218.

14. Madsen, *op. cit.,* p. 51. By permission of Holt, Rinehart and Winston.

15. Fernando Peñalosa, "Mexican Family Roles," *Journal of Marriage and the Family,* 30 (Nov., 1968), p. 686.

16. *Ibid.,* p. 687.

17. *Ibid.,* p. 686.

18. Murillo, *op. cit.,* p. 105.

19. Octavio Paz, "The Sons of La Malinche," in *Introduction to Chicano Studies,* Livie Isauro Duran and H. Russell Bernard, eds. (1973), p. 24. "The Sons of La Malinche" was originally a chapter in *The Labyrinth of Solitude* (1961).

20. Aztecs slaughtered hundreds of thousands of victims in propitiatory rituals; the Conquistadors killed the necessary thousands it took to subjugate the Indian civilizations and, through spreading disease to and by starvation, torture, executions, and working enslaved natives to death, assisted in the decimation of *millions* more.

21. Mary Ellen Goodman and Alma Beman, "Child's-Eye Views of Life in an Urban Barrio," in *Chicanos: Social and Psychological Perspectives, op. cit.,* p. 112.

22. Murillo, *op. cit.,* p. 104.

23. Cf. Chap. 15, "The Family, Variations in Time and Space" in Leo Grebler, Joan W. Moore, and Ralph Guzman, *The Mexican-American People* (1970), pp. 350–377.

24. *Ibid.,* p. 206. Mexican American female participation in the labor force remains low, much lower, for example, than for Negro females. In the southwest areas, California, particularly Los Angeles, their participation is highest.

25. *Ibid.,* p. 582.

26. Labor force participation for Mexican American males is lower than for Anglos and is concentrated in the middle and lower ranges of the occupational hierarchy. Unemployment rates, by the same token, are higher. The absorption of rural migrants into urban labor markets becomes an increasingly critical problem.

27. *Op. cit.,* pp. 130–131. In their Mexican American Study Project at Los Angeles Grebler, Moore, and Guzman found that "When separations and divorces are combined, Anglo women show the lowest incidence, Spanish-surname females rank next, and non-whites by far the highest."

28. Parochial schools never figured very prominently in Mexican society and were banned by the Constitution of 1912. In the United States a continuing effort has been made by the Catholic church, particularly since World War II, to build and bring Mexican Americans to parochial schools. Possibly a fifth of all Mexican American youth attend such schools.

29. Murillo, *op. cit.,* p. 105.

30. One excellent sociological study has been carried out by Anthony G. Dworkin, part of which is readably summarized in his "No Siesta Mañana: The Mexican American in Los Angeles," in *Our Children's Burden,* Raymond W. Mack, ed. (1968), pp. 387–439.

Questions

1. Describe some of the factors that have historically reinforced Mexican family unity. What are some of the socioeconomic factors that are threatening that unity?

2. What is the woman's place in Mexican culture? How does she derive her power? How is she disempowered?

3. What similar factors have led to the disintegration of both Mexican-American and African-American families?

4. Why are Mexican-American families better able to withstand these socioeconomic factors than African-American families?

Gays Under Fire

NEWSWEEK

*This article documents the increasing incidents of "gay-bashing" and dis-
crimination against homosexuals. It claims that in the face of this conservative backlash, gays are pursuing a legislative agenda that will deliver basic
civil liberties. This reading is from* Newsweek *(1992).*

Peter O'Donnell, a city councilor in Portland, Maine, had seen enough. In the   1
early morning hours last Feb. 2, Benjamin Kowalsky, a 33-year-old commu-
nity-development worker suffering from AIDS, was chased down and attacked by three rock-throwing youths who yelled, "Hey faggot, we're going to
get you." Ten days later another gay man was severely beaten by a gang of 10
men. This time police collared some of the assailants, but the victim declined
to press charges for fear of losing his job. After eight other attacks, O'Donnell
introduced an ordinance barring anti-gay discrimination in housing, employment and credit. The city council passed it by a 7-1 vote on May 12.

The reaction was swift and angry. Within three weeks a group called Con-   2
cerned Portland Citizens gathered 2,000 signatures—enough to put the issue
to a November referendum. Organizers claim the ordinance will send the city
of 61,500 down a slippery slope of gay promiscuity, AIDS and pedophilia. The
Christian Civic League of Maine, another group fighting the law, called it
"the most critically significant moral issue facing Maine people, probably in
the history of our state." O'Donnell is astonished. "It blows me away that
people who profess to Christian values and family values take up shields and
spears to defend discrimination."

Portland's lavender scare is no isolated case. Gay America's struggle for ac-   3
ceptance has reached a new and uncertain phase. A series of modest gains
over the last several years—in civil rights, national political clout, funding for
AIDS research and visibility in popular culture—has provoked a powerful
backlash. A well-coordinated counteroffensive by the religious right is underway in city halls, school boards and state legislatures to stymie—and even roll
back—what its leaders regard as an intolerable gay advance out of the closet
and into the social mainstream. In November, Oregon voters will be asked to
classify homosexuality as "abnormal, wrong, unnatural and perverse," and
bar the state from passing any law protecting citizens on the basis of sexual
orientation. A similar measure is on the fall ballot in Colorado. This month
California Gov. Pete Wilson, under pressure from the fundamentalist wing of
the state Republican Party, is expected to veto an anti-gay-discrimination bill

671

Table 1. Newsweek Poll

Should homosexuals have equal rights in job opportunities?
78%   Yes   17%   No

Is homosexuality an acceptable alternative lifestyle?
41%   Yes   53%   No

Are gay rights a threat to the American family and its values?
45%   Yes   51%   No

Which apply to you?
43%   Have a friend or acquaintance who is gay
20%   Work with someone you know who is gay
 9%   Have a gay person in your family

Should homosexuals be hired in each of the following occupations (percent saying yes):
83%   Salesperson
64%   A member of the president's cabinet
59%   Armed forces
59%   Doctors
54%   High-school teachers
51%   Elementary-school teachers
48%   Clergy

Newsweek Poll, Aug. 27, 1992

for the second time in a year. For many gays, a symbolic low point came during the Republican National Convention in Houston last month, where repeated attacks on "the homosexual lifestyle" evoked images of moral decay and unraveling family life. Conservative Doberman Pat Buchanan told delegates that gay rights have no place "in a nation we still call God's country."

The blatant rhetoric only turned off most Americans, and Republican   4
campaign strategists quickly backed President George Bush and his surrogates away from overt gay-bashing. But the public remains deeply ambivalent about gay and lesbian aspirations—torn between a basic impulse to be tolerant and a visceral discomfort with gay culture. A *Newsweek* Poll found that an overwhelming 78 percent of the public believes gay men and women should enjoy the same access to job opportunities as heterosexuals. By better than a two-thirds majority, those surveyed approve of health insurance and inheritance rights for gay spouses. But on issues closer to the emotional core of family life, the public sentiment cools. Only 32 percent believe gays should be able to adopt children; just 35 percent approve of legally sanctioned gay marriages. Fifty-three percent still don't consider homosexuality "acceptable" behavior. Asked whether gay rights was a threat to the American family and its values, 45 percent said yes.

For many gays and lesbians, the threats are more than rhetorical: anti-gay   5
harassment and violence increased 31 percent last year in five major U.S. cities (New York, San Francisco, Chicago, Boston and Minneapolis-St. Paul), according to the National Gay and Lesbian Task Force Policy Institute. Gay advocates acknowledge that an increased sense of social approval has made

Table 2. Newsweek Poll

How do you feel about each of the following homosexual rights?

	Approve	Disapprove
Health Insurance for gay spouses	67%	27%
Inheritance rights for gay spouses	70%	25%
Social security for gay spouses	58%	35%
Legally sanctioned gay marriages	35%	58%
Adoption rights for gay spouses	32%	61%

In general, how important is the issue of gay rights to your presidential vote?
40%   Very, or somewhat important
57%   Not too, or not at all important

Do you think the candidates have:

	Clinton	Bush
Gone too far in supporting gay rights	16%	5%
A position that is about right	44%	41%
Gone too far in opposing gay rights	3%	27%

For this *Newsweek* Poll, The Gallup Organization interviewed 547 registered voters by phone Aug. 27, 1992. Margin of error +/- 5 percentage points. "Don't know" and other responses not shown. The *Newseek* Poll © 1992 by *Newsweek*, Inc.

victims more likely to report incidents. But they also say that the escalating numbers don't describe the qualitative change in the violence. Drive-by slurs and egg-tossings have given way with more frequency to nail-studded baseball bats and switchblades. "You've got people who get picked up outside of a bar and tied up with duct tape and are beaten. They are sliced with razors," says Peg Yeates, leader of San Francisco's Street Patrol, a Guardian Angels-style organization. The new attacks take a range of forms, from fundamentalist gay-bashing to ridicule in the workplace.

Rage on the Right

It's possible to trace the right wing's anti-gay campaign to a bullwhip. It was   6
photographed hanging from the late Robert Mapplethorpe's derrière and featured in his 1989 retrospective partially funded by the National Endowment for the Arts (NEA). The bullwhip came at an opportune moment for the religious right. The Berlin wall and the contras had fallen; Reagan was a memory. Gay-bashing was always a staple for right-wing fund raisers. But taxpayer-subsidized dirty art—homosexual art, no less—kindled a new and lucrative source of outrage. Morris Chapman, president-elect of the 15 million-member Southern Baptist Convention, predicts that "in the 1990s homosexuality will be what the abortion issue has been in the 1980s."

For fundamentalists, the anti-gay animus is rooted in Biblical injunctions   7
against same-sex unions. Corinthians promises that homosexuals (along with fornicators, idolaters, adulterers and thieves) shall never inherit the kingdom of God. Other conservatives are opposed to creating a class of people legally protected on the basis of sexual behavior they regard as abhorrent. "We surely

love their souls," Jerry Falwell wrote in a 1991 letter to followers, describing his "national battle plan" to fight gay rights. "But we must awaken to their wicked agenda for America!"

Other familiar faces on the right are mobilizing as well. Pat Robertson's   8
Christian Coalition—with 2.2 million names in its computer files—will convene a meeting of a thousand activists in Virginia Beach, Va., this fall to discuss "the homosexual-rights agenda and how to defeat it," according to executive director Ralph Reed. The Rev. Lou Sheldon, a former Robertson protégé whose Anaheim-based Traditional Values Coalition has affiliates in 15 states and a web of interrelated fund-raising arms, pushed for the 1989 repeal of gay-rights ordinances in Irvine and Concord, Calif. Last month he helped force California educators to withdraw proposed sex-education and health-curriculum guidelines that described "families headed by parents of the same sex" as "part of contemporary society." He's also coordinating an attempt to block congressional approval of a law that would allow unmarried District of Columbia employees (gay and straight) to register as partners and enroll in city-sponsored health-care plans. "We're just protecting the heterosexual ethic," he says.

Backlash at the Ballot Box

The most bitter battleground is Oregon, where a movement heavily financed   9
by Christian fundamentalists is attempting to all but codify gays and lesbians out of existence. A petition drive by the Oregon Citizens Alliance (OCA) has produced Ballot Measure 9, which would void portions of the state's hate-crimes law and invalidate the phrase "sexual orientation" in any statute where it now appears. It also requires educators to set curriculum standards equating homosexuality with pedophilia, sadism and masochism as behaviors "to be discouraged and avoided." Despite new scientific evidence that homosexuality may have genetic origins, OCA members talk openly of "curing" gays.

Gays and lesbians, fearing they'll be effectively stripped of their citizen-   10
ship, are fighting desperately. "If we lose, we lose everything," says Donna Red Wing of Portland's Lesbian Community Project. "Our children could be taken from us, our lives could be wiped out at the ballot box." Despite big-name opposition, from Rep. Les AuCoin to the Roman Catholic Church to Gov. Barbara Roberts, state political experts give the measure an even chance of passage.

The campaign has spawned a mean season in a state with a national im-   11
age for tolerance and progressive politics. Opponents of the measure have documented an escalating volume of violence, burglaries and verbal intimidation. In the rural southern Oregon town of Wolf Creek, Dean Decent says violence against him and eight other gay men in the area has grown more brazen. "Now that the homophobes have blown up the car and shot at the trailer, when they drive by and yell it doesn't seem so bad," says Decent, a

32-year-old professional quilt maker. Unlikely alliances have formed. In an emotional meeting recently, gay activists and migrant farm workers in the Willamette Valley shared stories about racism and homophobia, pledging to support one another's struggles. Fear has bolted some closet doors but opened others. The Rev. Gary Wilson, of Portland's Metropolitan Community Church, says gay parishioners are "sitting down writing letters to everybody they know that they've never come out to saying, 'I am a gay person, I am a lesbian person; if you support Measure 9, you're destroying my life.'"

A new strain of gay-bashing has entered local races in other states. Six 12 months ago Dick Mallory was a pro-choice Texas Republican courting gay votes in his campaign to unseat state Rep. Glen Maxey, the only openly gay member of the state legislature. Mallory recently ran radio ads in the Austin area asking voters if they want to be represented by "an avowed homosexual." Mallory says he's found Christ. Maxey argues that he's found a Republican consultant. Perhaps the most virulent gay-baiting campaign is in Kansas. Supporters of Baptist minister Fred Phelps, who lost the August Democratic senatorial primary to state legislator Gloria O'Dell, continue to picket the Topeka streets with signs reading BULL DIKE (*sic*) O'DELL and NO SPECIAL LAWS FOR FAGS. O'Dell, 46, says she's heterosexual.

Closet in the Office

Some private employers have tried to minimize homophobia in the work- 13 place, offering bias workshops and opportunities for gay employees to meet. A smaller handful have established spousal benefit programs for same-sex couples. But office culture still can be a bleak frontier. Gay workers tread warily, coming out to a trusted few, usually remaining closeted to higher-ups. Steven Greenberg and Mikael Hollinger, two day administrative assistants at San Francisco's Nestlé Beverage Co., would take lunch-hour walks down the city's Embarcadero to speak freely. Soon their strolls had mutated into a vicious office rumor—that they were having sex together in a company restroom.

Last March they were fired. Nestlé denies any anti-gay bias and says they 14 were terminated for poor performance, although Greenberg says he had been given a raise three weeks earlier. The two joined five other gay men last month in filing job-discrimination lawsuits against several San Francisco area employers, including Ricoh Corp. and Transworld Systems, alleging that they were harassed, ridiculed and dismissed because they were gay.

Even in companies that take gay-bashing seriously, the atmosphere 15 among coworkers can be oppressive. When Nancy Logan worked as an auditor for a major Cleveland bank three years ago, a colleague would shake in a repulsed manner as she passed her desk. "Any time I walked into the ladies' room and she was there, she would walk out," says Logan. She complained to management, which transferred the other employee. But Logan says she was told that the only reason the company supported her was that she was "low key," in other words, not out. She quit shortly afterward and remains closeted in her new job.

The Next Battle

Even in the chill of resurgent gay-hating, there's a sense of victory at hand for many American gays and lesbians. The struggle against AIDS has matured into a broad political and social movement. Last July's Democratic National Convention symbolized the sea change: 13 pro-gay speakers addressed a Madison Square Garden audience that included 108 openly gay delegates, alternates and party officials. Twenty-one states and 130 municipalities now offer gays and lesbians some form of legal protection against discrimination. An estimated 10,000 children are being raised by lesbians who conceived them through artificial insemination. Hollywood, which has lagged far behind television in realistic portrayals of gays, is changing its act. At least six major gay or AIDS-themed films are in development, including Gus Van Sant's "The Mayor of Castro Street," about martyred San Francisco supervisor Harvey Milk.   16

For some activists, the signs of greater acceptance make the new vehemence even more shocking. "It's reminded us of our precarious position in society, and just how deep homophobia runs," says Cathy Siemens, a Portland, Ore., real-estate agent. "Should we withdraw and protect ourselves or continue to march out of the closet?" Nearly all say no—that the backlash is affirmation of their new power and a last hurrah for the kind of blatant gay-bashing on display at the convention in Houston. "It's the bellows of dying elephants," says Peter Gomes, minister of Harvard University's Memorial Church.   17

If there's a consensus among gay political strategists, it's that the best defense is a good offense. In some cases, that means renewed "outings" of closeted public officials who have promoted anti-gay policies. The Advocate, a gay magazine, recently exposed a congressman with an anti-gay voting record. Others say that press attention to Republican hypocrisy in its condemnation of gays will also help. Last week's Washington Post Style section profiled Dee Mosbacher, the lesbian daughter of former Bush-Quayle campaign chairman Robert Mosbacher.   18

Others are pursuing a legislative agenda that will deliver basic civil liberties. "The right to have a job without losing it and the right to walk down the street without getting beaten up" would be a good start, says Gregory King of the Human Rights Campaign Fund, a gay political-action committee. Topping the list is passage of the Civil Rights Amendments Act of 1991, a federal law that would offer sexual orientation the same protections as race, creed, color, national origin and disability. Another priority is increased funding for AIDS research. New victories will certainly bring new scapegoating. "As we become more visible we become targets," says Houston lesbian activist Annise Parker. In time, though, Parker hopes that the Buchanans and the   19

Robertsons will seem evermore shrill and marginal. In time, she believes, "the basic decency of the American people will take over."

Questions

1. Why is it that much of the anti-gay backlash has been initiated by the Christian right? What is the rationale behind their accusations that gays threaten family values?

2. According to the author, what initiated the recent outrage against gays?

3. Do you agree that gays should be protected under the Civil Rights Amendment?

4. Do you think that children should be educated to be aware of different lifestyles, including those of gays?

5. What are your feelings about the results of the *Newsweek* polls?

They're Not Telling the Truth

ERIC MARCUS

Eric Marcus is the author of Making History: The Struggle for Gay and Lesbian Equal Rights, 1945–1990: An Oral History *(1992).*

In this article, Marcus argues that the Republican rhetoric that mandates that gays are not "normal" and are a threat to family values is misguided and encourages anti-gay crusaders. He points out that since homosexuality is not a choice, the threat that homosexual couples will force their sexual orientation on adopted children is absurd.

It started in the middle of the night over Labor Day weekend three years ago. Barry and I were fast asleep when our new downstairs neighbor and his friends, all federal Drug Enforcement Administration officers, began pounding on the ceiling below our bedroom. In their drunken stupor they yelled, "We're coming to get the faggots! We've got an AK-47 in the car! Bang, bang, you're dead!" Listening to what the religious right and the Republican Party have been saying about us lately, I imagine our old neighbor has felt vindicated. After all, he and his buddies were simply trying to scare a couple of "anti-family" homosexuals, people the president told them are not normal, who the vice president said made the wrong choice, who Pat Robertson believes are not fit to be parents and for whom Pat Buchanan said AIDS was "nature's retribution."

Hearing these and other statements about who I am, I've felt the same anger, disgust and confusion I felt in the days after Barry and I were threatened in our own home. "Why are they attacking us?" "Did we do anything to deserve this?" Very quickly, I realized that we hadn't done anything wrong. It was our neighbor who was wrong. And the anti-gay crusaders are also wrong. They're not telling the truth about who I am.

The life Barry and I live is not the Ozzie and Harriet ideal, but we're not the only Americans who don't live that near-mythical model—including Ozzie and Harriet. Nonetheless, most people would find our family life very familiar and anything but anti-family. Just last month we attended Barry's twin brother's wedding, where Barry and his brother James were best men. In January, when my mother had a heart attack, I flew home to look after her. We've had both families over for holidays, gone to my niece's and nephew's birthdays, attended funerals together and helped our friends through hard times.

678

President Bush said I'm not normal. I don't know what he means. Bush's   4
left-handedness isn't normal either, if "normal" means "in the majority." But
like being left-handed, being gay doesn't diminish my humanity, my normal
wish to love, be loved, contribute and prosper. When I heard Dan Quayle say
on "Good Morning America" and "Prime Time Live" that I had made the
"wrong choice," I wanted to ask him what choice he was referring to. When I
realized I was gay I also realized I *did* have a choice, but not between homosexuality and heterosexuality. I could choose to live in the closet, maybe even
marry a woman and pretend to be who I'm not, or I could be honest about
who I am and live my life openly—no easy thing to do. I didn't choose to be
gay, but I did choose to tell the truth. That's what my parents taught me.

During the presidential campaign I've heard many people say that gay   5
and lesbian people are unfit parents and that we shouldn't be allowed to
adopt. There's no question that some gay people make rotten parents. Same
with some heterosexual parents. Those who condemn us won't come right
out and say it, but they'd like you to believe we'll "make our kids gay" or that
we'll molest them. But that's not what our siblings and heterosexual friends
with kids think. They know you can't make somebody gay who isn't gay by
nature. They also know that if their kids are going to be molested that overwhelmingly the most likely person to do the molesting is a heterosexual
male. And if their kids happen to be gay, they know that we're fine role models. Two heterosexual couples have asked us if we would be the guardians of
their children should something happen to them. And Barry is godfather to a
little boy named Lucas, who just celebrated his first birthday.

City lifestyle: In a television interview last month, President Bush said that   6
he would still love his grandchild if he found out he was gay, but he wouldn't
want him to promote his gay lifestyle. Would somebody please tell me what a
gay lifestyle is? One may choose a country-club lifestyle, a Western lifestyle, a
city lifestyle, but there is no such thing as a gay lifestyle—just as there is no
such thing as a heterosexual lifestyle. Homosexual lifestyles, like heterosexual
lifestyles, run the gamut. They defy classification. And the only way I can
"promote" my sexual orientation is to show other gay and lesbian people by
my example that you can be homosexual, live outside the closet and lead a
full, happy, family-centered life.

I'm convinced the president doesn't really believe what he and some of   7
his supporters are saying about me. If he did, he wouldn't tolerate the many
gay men and women he and those in his administration have appointed to
responsible jobs in the White House, the Department of Defense, the National Endowment for the Arts and virtually every other government agency.
But the anti-gay campaign has nothing to do with telling the truth. Instead,
it's about trying to scare Americans into thinking that if they vote for Bill
Clinton, the awful homosexuals—me included!—will destroy America's family values.

Barry and I were lucky with our bigoted downstairs neighbor. Our land-   8
lords, a lovely heterosexual couple, evicted him without hesitation. While we

now feel safe in our own home, as long as the anti-gay campaigners continue to spread their message of ignorance and hate, our nation will remain a hostile, dangerous and sometimes deadly place for us, our friends and millions of America's gay and lesbian citizens.

Questions

1. Describe your reaction to Marcus's article.
2. Why are many people adverse to the idea of allowing homosexual couples to adopt children?
3. Why do many conservatives feel that homosexuality is a threat to family values?
4. What points of agreement do you note between Marcus's article and the *Newsweek* piece? Are there points of disagreement?

Writing Assignments

The following writing assignments are concerned with the topic of diversity in the concept of the family. Before developing an argument on any of these assignments, be sure that you understand the controversy by completing the following exercises:

- Write responses to exploration questions.
- Read several articles in this chapter or elsewhere to discover at least two perspectives on the topic.
- Create a list of opposing viewpoints and consider the potential consequences of each.
- Examine the underlying assumptions behind each viewpoint.

To help you understand the issues and develop ideas, you can use the following form:

The conflict in this issue is between _____ and

_____.

I am more inclined to agree with _____

because _____.

However, it is possible that some of my readers may believe that

_____.

Exploration Questions

1. Was family life important in your upbringing? Do you believe that the traditional family is the best arrangement for raising children?

2. Do you plan to have children? If so, what type of role do you envision yourself playing? What sort of child care do you expect to have?

3. What view of the family is depicted on television? Do you think it is realistic?

4. Do you think that business should play a role in helping employees care for their children? What sort of role should they play?

5. How would you define "family values"?

6. Do you believe that women are naturally more nurturing than men? Why or why not?

7. Are you more inclined toward restrictive or permissive parenting? Explain what is meant by permissive and restrictive.

8. Do you think that the subject of alternate lifestyles should be discussed with children? Why or why not?

ASSIGNMENT 1

In Marge Piercy's futuristic novel, *Woman on the Edge of Time,* the concept of the family as we know it is no longer in existence. Piercy's society, like that depicted in Aldous Huxley's *Brave New World,* views the family as primitive and destructive, fostering unhealthy, blood-based emotional allegiances, perpetuating prejudice, and frequently causing psychological damage to children. Based on your readings in this chapter and on your own concept of the role of the family, write an argumentative essay in response to the following question: What is the role of the family in an increasingly changing, diverse society?

ASSIGNMENT 2

The recent controversy over family values has raised the issue of what type of home environment is best for raising children. Although in the past it has been assumed that the traditional family (consisting of a mother, father, and children) provides the most secure and nurturing home life for children, the increasing acceptance of alternative lifestyles, including that of gay couples, suggests that other models might be equally suitable or perhaps more desirable. Based on your own concept of what is important in raising children and on your reading of several selections in this chapter, write an argumentative essay in which you address the following question: Should gay couples be allowed to adopt children? Why or why not?

ASSIGNMENT 3

One of the ways in which one society distinguishes itself from another is the way in which it views its children. The familiar saying that "children should be seen and not heard" is one such view, and it suggests that a well-behaved child should be undemanding and proper and should not intrude on the world of adults. Think about your own concept of what children are or should be, note how children are depicted in the media, and reflect on the discussion of nature versus nurture in the readings in this chapter. Then, write an argumentative essay addressing the following question: What is the prevailing view of children in American culture? Does this view reinforce American values?

Using Data

1. After studying the table below, what can you conclude about how the American household has changed since 1960? In what ways has it changed?

2. Does this table support Levitan's and Belous's study about how the American family has changed? Could the table be used to support Taylor's and Pollitt's assertion that the ideal nuclear family is an illusion?

3. Has the incidence of female householders increased or decreased?

4. How could this table be used in the debate over family values?

Households, Families, Subfamilies, Married Couples, and Unrelated Individuals: 1960–1990

Type of Unit	1960	1970	1975	1980	1985	1987	1988	1989	1990	Percent Change 1970-1980	Percent Change 1980-1990
Households..........................	52,799	63,401	71,120	80,776	86,789	89,479	91,066	92,830	93,347	27.4	15.6
Average size	3.33	3.14	2.94	2.76	2.69	2.66	2.64	2.62	2.63	—	—
Family households	44,905	51,456	55,563	59,550	62,706	64,491	65,133	65,837	66,090	15.7	11.0
Married couple	39,254	44,728	46,951	49,112	50,350	51,537	51,809	52,100	52,317	9.8	6.5
Male householder[1]	1,228	1,228	1,485	1,733	2,228	2,510	2,715	2,847	2,884	41.1	66.4
Female householder[1]	4,442	5,500	7,127	8,705	10,129	10,445	10,608	10,890	10,890	58.3	25.1
Nonfamily households	7,895	11,945	15,557	21,226	24,082	24,988	25,933	26,994	27,257	77.7	28.4
Male householder	2,716	4,063	5,912	8,807	10,114	10,652	11,310	11,874	11,606	116.8	31.8
Female householder	5,179	7,882	9,645	12,419	13,968	14,336	14,624	15,120	15,651	57.6	26.0
One person......................	6,896	10,851	13,939	18,296	20,602	21,128	21,889	22,708	22,999	68.6	25.7
Families	45,111	51,586	55,712	59,550	62,706	64,491	65,133	65,837	66,090	15.4	11.0
Average size	3.67	3.58	3.42	3.29	3.23	3.19	3.17	3.16	3.17	—	—
Married couple	39,329	44,755	46,971	49,112	50,350	51,537	51,809	52,100	52,317	9.7	6.5
Male householder[1]	1,275	1,239	1,499	1,733	2,228	2,510	2,715	2,847	2,884	39.9	66.4
Female householder[1]	4,507	5,591	7,242	8,705	10,129	10,445	10,608	10,890	10,890	55.7	25.1
Unrelated subfamilies.........	207	130	149	360	526	566	537	473	534	176.9	48.3
Married couple....................	75	27	20	20	46	37	38	49	68	—	—
Male reference persons[1].......	47	11	14	36	85	77	46	26	45	—	—
Female reference persons[1] ...	85	91	115	304	395	452	452	398	421	234.1	38.5
Related subfamilies.............	1,514	1,150	1,349	1,150	2,228	2,286	2,397	2,278	2,403	-	109.0
Married couple....................	871	617	576	582	719	712	765	775	871	-5.7	49.7
Father-child[1]	115	48	69	54	116	123	152	103	153	—	—
Mother-child[1]	528	484	705	512	1,392	1,451	1,480	1,400	1,378	5.8	169.1
Married Couples..................	40,200	45,373	47,547	49,714	51,114	52,286	52,613	52,924	53,256	9.6	7.1
With own household	39,254	44,728	46,951	49,112	50,350	51,537	51,809	52,100	52,317	9.8	6.5
Without own household	946	645	596	602	764	749	803	824	939	-6.7	56.0
Percent without.................	2.4	1.4	1.3	1.2	1.5	1.4	1.5	1.6	1.8	—	—
Unrelated individuals..........	11,092	14,988	19,100	26,426	30,518	31,914	33,124	34,499	35,384	76.3	33.9
Nonfamily householders	7,895	11,945	15,557	21,226	24,082	24,988	25,933	26,994	27,257	77.7	28.4
Secondary individuals..........	3,198	3,043	3,543	5,200	6,436	6,926	7,191	7,505	8,127	70.9	56.3
Male	1,746	1,631	2,087	3,006	3,743	3,947	4,081	4,241	4,711	84.3	56.7
Female.............................	1,451	1,412	1,456	2,194	2,693	2,978	3,110	3,264	3,416	55.4	55.7

[1] No spouse present.

Based on U.S. Census Bureau estimates.

10 ■ Diversity and the Workplace

No dream comes true until you wake up and go to work!

A man has happiness in the palms of his hands if he can fill his days with real work.

The plain fact is that human beings are happy only when they are striving for something worthwhile.

The above sayings attest to the value that American culture has always placed on work, not only as a means of putting bread on the table but as the enterprise contributing most significantly to human happiness and to the formation of identity. "What do you do?" we frequently ask new acquaintances. We ask that question not only to know how someone might fill his or her days or what particular skills that person might have but also more fundamental questions such as "What kind of a person are you?" and "Where do you fit into the social hierarchy?" or "How powerful or important a person are you?" In American society, work not only defines human identity but also helps determine the degree of control one has over one's circumstances. Frequently, it is a mark of status.

The readings in this chapter focus on several issues concerned with controversies that arise over equitable access to and value for work, addressing questions such as the following: Who should be hired? Should preferences be given to one group over another? What can be done to ensure that people are treated fairly in the workplace? What does "fair" treatment mean? Several articles discuss the concept of equal opportunity and the attempt over the past thirty years to mandate equality in the workplace through affirmative action policies. Other readings examine differing concepts of work and the effect those differences can have on the workplace environment. Finally, a number of articles examine how women and minorities are treated in the workplace, evaluate the extent to which workplace equality has actually been attained, and explore the changes that are likely to occur as society becomes increasingly diverse.

The Workplace and Equal Opportunity

Ideologically, the United States has always professed a strong belief in the concept of equality for all of its citizens. One of the earliest and best known articulations of this belief is stated in the Declaration of Independence:

> We hold these truths to be self-evident, that All Men are Created Equal, that they are endowed by their Creator with certain unalienable Rights, that among these are Life, Liberty, and the pursuit of Happiness.

Many of us had to memorize this statement and others like it in school, and as children, we accepted the statement without reflecting very seriously on its meaning. However, if one thinks about this statement, it becomes clear that not all men (or women) are truly created equal because some people are smarter than others, some are stronger, some are more talented, etc. Despite the nobility of the statement and the attractiveness of the ideal it represents, it was written at a time when in some states, more than one-half of the members of the white population were temporarily enslaved as indentured servants, legally required to work for a period of years to pay for their passage to America. Moreover, the statement did not apply to black men or to women of any race. The idea that all people are created equal, then, was not a reality in the early days of American colonialism, nor has it been realized since.

In general, the statement has come to be interpreted as referring not to the actual condition of equality but to the potential for equality inherent in all human beings—what is usually referred to as equality of opportunity. The Fourteenth Amendment provides a more recent legal foundation for this concept, leading ultimately to the first affirmative action programs that emerged from the passage of the Civil Rights Act of 1964 and later altered and expanded through other legislation, presidential orders, and Supreme Court decisions.

The Fourteenth Amendment

The Fourteenth Amendment was a post–Civil War amendment added to the Constitution in 1868 to expand the Thirteenth Amendment as the basis for federal civil rights authority. It was also intended to ensure Southern compliance with newly established political rights for blacks. The amendment declares that "all persons born or naturalized in the United States and subject to the jurisdiction thereof, are citizens of the United States and the State wherein they reside" and that "no state shall deprive any person of life, liberty, or property without due process of law." This clause, known as the "due process clause," ultimately allowed the court to apply most Bill of Rights guarantees to the states and also enabled the Supreme Court to engage in a substantive review of state policies, particularly those regulating private property rights. The amendment also contains the statement that no state shall deny to any person within its jurisdiction the equal protection of laws, a provision that was intended to prohibit unjustified classifications that might discriminate unreasonably. However, early attempts to do so were unsuccessful because the Supreme Court held that congressional power might be used only in a remedial fashion in cases where the state was itself an active participant in discrimination. Despite this limitation, the Fourteenth Amendment provided the basis for most of the affirmative action policies originating in the 1960s.

Affirmative Action and Diversity

Why was affirmative action necessary, when discrimination in employment, education, voting, and housing was already illegal before 1964? As the word "action" in the name implies, the concept of affirmative action was instituted to motivate employers to actively compensate for discrimination that may have occurred in the past, even if the discrimination was not intentional. Employers could no longer say, "I did the best I could to institute equality." With affirmative action programs, they had to take concrete steps (affirmative action) to make it happen. In the 1971 case of *Griggs v. Duke Power Company*, the Supreme Court ruled that the act was intended to *rectify* inequities in employment practices and not simply to motivate employers to hire minorities. The Supreme Court claimed that "practices, procedures, . . . neutral on their face, and even neutral in terms of intent, cannot be maintained if they operate to 'freeze' the status quo of prior discriminatory employment practices."

The Supreme Court also required that employers administer job-related tests to prospective employees and to abolish other tests that might be discriminatory—those with a hidden agenda of eliminating a disproportionately high percentage of women and minorities, for example. Employers now had to demonstrate that such tests were a "business necessity," a term that was more clearly defined in later Supreme Court decisions to signify the safe and efficient operation of a business. Under the new ruling, an employer would have to prove that the business could not be operated safely unless all employees possessed sufficient knowledge of the material covered on the test.

Affirmative action policies also highlighted several other discriminatory employment practices such as advertising job openings in an informal, "word-of-mouth" fashion, recruiting personnel at educational institutions attended predominantly or exclusively by whites or males, excluding women from jobs based on their marital status, requiring women to quit their jobs upon becoming pregnant, and specifying job qualifications (either educational or physical) which do not pertain to the nature of the job. In particular, affirmative action policies raised the possible requirement that any employer who contracts or subcontracts with the federal government must attempt to increase the proportions of women and minorities on their payroll. The courts maintained that whenever the proportions of such employees are lower than those in the available, qualified labor market, an act of discrimination could be presumed. If such a case arose, the employer would have to demonstrate that the disproportions in hiring did not result from discrimination. Such requirements, as set forth by the Equal Opportunity Employment Act of 1972 and by executive orders, applied to federal contractors or subcontractors with contracts of more than $50,000 and fifty or more employees, to all state governments unconditionally, and to all local governments with fifteen or more employees. Similar guidelines were also established by many state and local governments.

These rules on government contracts applied to a more significant percentage of the work force than the alternative case-by-case enforcement of federal civil rights laws. The case-by-case approach had required an employer to be found guilty of discrimination before any remedial action could be taken, whereas the contract-enforcement system required accused employers to provide evidence that they had made a bona fide attempt to overcome past patterns of underemploying women and minorities.

The Impact of Affirmative Action

Over the past thirty years, many facets of life have been affected by affirmative action policies. In some instances, attempts to enforce policies of equal opportunity have led to the establishment of quotas or proposed goals for the increased targeting or preferential hiring of minorities and women. However, policies involving quotas have been criticized as having created a new form of discrimination against white males. The issue of reverse discrimination was tried by the Supreme Court in 1978 in the case of *Regents of the University of California v. Bakke,* in which the Supreme Court ruled five to four against the use of quotas. This decision consequently left a great deal of uncertainty as to which types of affirmative action were to be considered desirable or permissible. A ground-breaking case in this area was *Steelworkers v. Weber* (1979), in which the Supreme Court upheld the use of affirmative action-related quotas by private employers and unions.

Although affirmative action policies were instituted over thirty years ago, the issue of how effective they have been in providing true equality of opportunity in a diverse society is still being debated, as are the ethical dilemmas arising when any one group is privileged above another. Some blacks, like Shelby Steele, a professor at San Jose University, believe that affirmative action actually works against their race because it fosters feelings of unworthiness. Other blacks feel that although some progress has been made, discrimination still exists, although sometimes it is exercised by more subtle means.

Perspectives Included in the Readings

The articles concerned with affirmative action and issues arising from attempts to institute equality of opportunity in the workplace address a variety of perspectives. Nathan Glazer in "The Affirmative Action Stalemate" traces the history of affirmative action laws, which, he believes, resulted in considerable progress for racial minorities and women. However, he points out that at the present time, the controversy about affirmative action appears to be in a stalemate in that neither side seems able to advance and that both are waiting for some major case to decide whether affirmative action represents a transgression of the equal protection laws guaranteed by the Fourteenth Amendment and the stated commitment to color blind policies of the Civil Rights Act of 1964 or whether affirmative action policies, even those that include the use of quotas, constitute a legitimate approach to compensating for past discrimination. Glazer maintains that the concept of affirmative action is now very much entrenched in American business and that despite concerns over quotas, most people wish such policies to be maintained because the condition of minorities, African-Americans in particular, still needs considerable improvement.

The *Business Week* article, "Race in the Workplace: Is Affirmative Action Working?" points out that although affirmative action policies may benefit some groups, there are always trade-offs in that compensation for past discrimination against some people can result in new discrimination against others. It also suggests that despite some gains for blacks and other minorities, old-boy networks tend to favor white males, inhibiting minority advancement. In a 1991 Harris Executive poll, sixty-five percent of corporate executives insist that business will extend hiring and promotion to women and minorities without the need of affirmative action policies simply because of the changing labor supply and the benefits of a diverse work force. Affirmative action, however, remains a sensitive issue for both whites and blacks. Reacting against accusations that affirmative action policies can adversely affect the self-esteem of those who benefit from them, Stephen L. Carter in "Racial Preferences? So What?" begins his article with the statement, "I got into law school because I am black." However, he makes the point that it is not *how* someone gets into a school or gets a particular job but what that person does with the opportunity that matters.

Several articles address different concepts of how work is regarded by subgroups within American society. Bob Baker's article, "Buzzword with Bite: Work Ethic," examines the impact that the term "work ethic" has on minorities and discusses the results of a study contrasting black and Hispanic employment situations. Baker explores some of the social and economic factors that have contributed to the absence of the work ethic in members of the urban ghettos. He asserts that although employers insist that pride and dedication are crucial to success, some social scientists argue that the growth of minimum-wage jobs and cuts in health benefits and pensions have diminished employee loyalty and commitment to work. John Paul Fieg's article, "Attitudes Toward Work," contrasts traditional work values of Americans with those of Thais, and points out that the so-called puritan work ethic is changing so that many workers of all backgrounds are now more concerned with security, job satisfaction, shorter work weeks, and less pressure. This article is useful in highlighting the values usually associated with the work ethic.

There is no question that the workplace environment is undergoing considerable change and reevaluation as the work force becomes more diverse. It is equally true that when stereotypical views of other races and cultures are maintained, they can interfere significantly with daily workplace harmony. Acknowledging the existence of prejudice in the workplace, Studs Terkel, in "An Interview with C.P. Ellis," recounts a situation in which a worker has been able to overcome deeply entrenched prejudice and stereotypical thinking. In this interview, an ex-president of the Ku Klux Klan explains that he joined the organization because he "had to hate somebody." However, after working on an interracial committee to solve racial problems in the school system, he was "born again," and has come to the realization that poor blacks and whites have a common enemy—upper-class whites.

Diversity in the workplace also has a significant impact on the home environment and when women enter the work force, they frequently have to assume primary responsibility for domestic chores as well, a dual responsibility that sometimes places a strain on marriage. Phyllis Moen, in "Women's Two Roles: A Contemporary Dilemma," discusses several models of maintaining a home while being actively engaged in employment, and examines the effect of working women on marriages and the family dynamic. Moen shows that although about one-half of all married mothers with children are in the labor force, traditional ideologies mandating that a woman's primary sphere is the home have not changed. She posits that working mothers still do most of the housework and that some men (especially older men) experience some degree of depression and low self-esteem when their wives work.

The days when the man worked all day to provide support and the woman stayed at home caring for the children are unlikely to return. Although presumably the ambition and work-centeredness of the 1980s is going to be replaced by a yearning for self-fulfillment and leisure in the 1990s, it is quite likely that people will continue to find fulfillment and identity through their work. And because the workplace will be populated by people from many different backgrounds, understanding diverse attitudes toward work and being able to work in harmony with many different types of people will become increasingly important.

The Affirmative Action Stalemate

NATHAN GLAZER

Nathan Glazer publishes frequently on social issues, particularly those pertaining to affirmative action and immigration. Among his many publications are Clamor at the Gates: The New American Immigration *(1985) and* Limits of Social Policy *(1988).*

In this article, Glazer argues that affirmative action has been sustained by the actual condition of blacks that "imposes itself on the American conscience." However, he also points out that when affirmative action is interpreted as the imposition of numerical quotas, the result is racial hostility. This article is from Public Interest *(1988).*

Ten years ago the Supreme Court handed down its first decision on affirmative action. It dealt with the case of an applicant who had been denied admission to a medical school, while minority applicants with lesser academic qualifications had been admitted to fill a quota the medical school had set. The Supreme Court ruled, five to four, that quotas were illegal and that the applicant should be admitted. A different five-man majority (only Justice Powell was included in both majorities) also ruled that it was legitimate to take race into account in making admissions decisions. The Court seemed to have come down on both sides of the issue.

While the case was raised over admission to an educational institution, the Court's schizophrenia shaped the many decisions over employment that have come down year after year. Those affected by affirmative action—employers and employees, enforcement agencies and lawyers, applicants to selective programs and good jobs, jobholders threatened with termination—have waited for that final, clear decision that tells us just how to separate the constitutional and the legal in preference for minorities from the unconstitutional and illegal. But the Court has shown a remarkable skillfulness in chopping up the issue into finer and finer pieces—still without drawing that clear line that settles the controversy over affirmative action. Nor, in an eight-justice court, can we expect a conclusion to this Perils-of-Pauline routine in the present session.

This situation conforms neatly with the conditions usually associated with trench warfare: neither side seems able to advance, though attacks are mounted by both, and neither is weak enough to surrender. Even more remarkable, this stasis has characterized the issue for a dozen years despite a series of kaleidoscopic political changes that many expected to lead either to

691

a rapid reduction in the scope of affirmative action or to its unchallenged institutionalization as the way in which Americans make decisions on employment, promotion, and admission to selective institutions of higher education. Thus we have moved from a Nixon presidency, which might have been expected to oppose affirmative action, but under which its procedures were formalized and extended; to a Ford administration, which tried to take some action to limit affirmative action, but retreated in the face of effective opposition from civil rights organizations; to a Carter administration, which was comfortable with it and in some ways extended it (as in appointments to the federal judiciary); to a Reagan administration, which is hostile to it—and which, as of this writing, seven years after it came into office, and after two electoral victories, presides over affirmative action requirements that are just about identical to those first formulated in the late 1960s and early 1970s.

Court Battles

The battles of politics—in presidential elections, in Congress, in the regulatory and administrative agencies—have left the overall structure of affirmative action unchanged through more than four presidential terms, and three transitions of power. Nor, surprisingly, have matters changed much in the federal courts, despite extended and endless battles. Almost every year since the mid-1970s, we have, it seems, awaited with hope or anxiety the determination of some major case by the Supreme Court that would tell us whether affirmative action transgressed the "equal protection of the laws" guaranteed by the Fourteenth Amendment and the apparent commitment to colorblindness of the Civil Rights Act of 1964, or whether, on the contrary, it was a legitimate approach to overcoming the heritage of discrimination and segregation by improving the condition of American blacks. But from the first major affirmative action decision to the most recent decisions of 1986, the Supreme Court has been split, with five-to-four or six-to-three decisions encompassing a range of conflicting positions in both majority and minority. We will, it seems, be living with the issues raised by affirmative action for a long time.

Policies we may legitimately call "affirmative action" have been undertaken in three crucial areas: jobs and employment, desegregation of public schools, and housing. In each American blacks have suffered from severe deprivation, rooted in racist prejudice, expressed in formal or informal discrimination and segregation. This is the basic underlying ground for affirmative action: it is because the heritage of prejudice and discrimination still weighs heavily on black Americans that the question of affirmative action cannot be expected to find easy resolution.

The term "affirmative action" appears in two places in American law. We find it in the Civil Rights Act of 1964, Title VII, dealing with discrimination in employment: "If the court finds that the respondent has intentionally engaged in or is intentionally engaging in an unlawful employment practice . . . , the court may . . . order such affirmative action as may be appropriate, which may include, but is not limited to, reinstatement or hiring of employees, with or without back pay . . ., or any other equitable relief as the court deems appropriate." This applies to all employers of over fifteen persons. And it appears again in Executive Order 11246, applying to federal contractors, and imposing "affirmative action" on employment and promotion as a condition for receiving federal contracts. There is no similar requirement, either in the Civil Rights Act or in its 1972 revision or elsewhere, for "affirmative action" in admission to institutions of higher learning.* Yet the term has been widely applied to the practices of colleges, universities, and professional schools attempting to voluntarily increase minority enrollment. The first major case decided by the Supreme Court dealing with affirmative action arose in the context of higher education, but was widely interpreted as having some application to employment practices. This was the case of Allen Bakke, who sued the University of California because he was denied admission to the Medical School of the University of California at Davis, despite having higher grades than successful minority applicants, and received relief in the complex five-to-four decision in 1978, which simultaneously legitimated practices that could have denied him that admission.

Affirmative action in employment originally meant going beyond non- 7 discrimination: an employer who discriminated could not only be ordered to desist from his discriminatory practices, but could be required to compensate those against whom he had discriminated, as the references to back pay and reinstatement in the Civil Rights Act make clear. The federal contractor providing goods and services to the federal government was not only bound by the Civil Rights Act, like all other employers, but also, regardless of whether he had ever discriminated, had to go beyond its requirements, by engaging in "affirmative action" to make his employment and promotion opportunities available and accessible to minority applicants.

Controversy and the Written Law

Affirmative action in employment became controversial only when it went be- 8 yond the written language of the Civil Rights Act and the Executive Order, and began to require employers to hire or promote specific numbers of minority applicants or employees. Federal courts and the Equal Employment Opportunity Commission effected this radical extension of the law by interpreting Title VII of the Civil Rights Act of 1964 and 1972, and by the Office of Federal Contract Compliance Programs' enforcement of the Executive Order. "Quotas" or "goals and timetables" became the buzzwords of choice in disputes over the appropriate degree of "affirmative action." Back pay to those who proved discrimination, or requirements for advertising, recruiting, or training by federal contractors, which seem to be what the Civil Rights Act and the

---

*The one exception to this rule are the universities covered by the *Adams* v. *Richardson* litigation: public institutions (primarily in the south), formerly restricted to whites or blacks, that are now required to fulfill affirmative action goals in the recruitment of students.

Executive Order call for, are not what we have in mind when we speak about the controversy over affirmative action, though they have a better claim to be called affirmative action than court-ordered quotas or agency-required goals and timetables. But under expanded federal regulations and judicial decisions, affirmative action has become a matter of setting statistical goals or quotas by race for employment or promotion. The expectation of color blindness that was paramount in the mid-1960s has been replaced by policies mandating numerical requirements. That is what we mean today by affirmative action.

The critic of quotas or goals and timetables is regularly attacked for opposing affirmative action, even though he may well support the clear intention of the "affirmative action" of Title VII as understood in 1964, as well as the "affirmative action" mandated by the Executive Order of 1965. But there is no point arguing with changes in the meaning of words: whatever the term meant in the 1960s, since the 1970s affirmative action has come to mean quotas and goals and timetables.   9

In the same way, whatever desegregation of schools meant when the Supreme Court declared the unconstitutionality of segregation in 1954, or when Congress defined it in the Civil Rights Act of 1964, desegregation today has come to mean busing. The supporter of busing is thus said to support "desegregation," the opponent of busing is attacked for defending "segregation," even though the latter term originally meant state-ordered or city-ordered segregation of the races. But it has come to mean black concentration in schools, regardless of cause, even if that cause is residential concentration or parental choice.   10

In the early 1970s, the setting of statistical goals was becoming the favored means of advancing minority representation in employment and desegregating the schools; even the geographical redistribution of minority populations was being proposed. The 1954 decision of the Supreme Court declaring segregation in public schools unconstitutional, endorsed by Congress in the Civil Rights Act of 1964, had been reshaped, through court interpretations, into racial numerical requirements in schools, so that each had to attain such and such a proportion of minority and majority. The facts of residential distribution made it inevitable that such a requirement could be implemented only by transporting students to schools out of their neighborhoods: "busing" thus became the issue in public education that paralleled "affirmative action" in employment. And we also saw efforts in the early 1970s to redistribute the black population through government action, so that it would not be so highly concentrated in the central cities. Concentration led inevitably to black-majority schools, and many believed, to reduced opportunities for employment. Here, too, the ambition was some numerical goal spelling the end of residential segregation and discrimination, but the policies with which the federal government tried to implement these aims were weak and without effect. The struggle to redistribute the black population through the construction of subsidized housing in white suburbs continues; the impact of such policies has been quite moderate, however, so (unlike affirmative action and busing) they have not become crucial national issues.   11

An Old Pattern: Immigration and Advancement

The mere fact that a kind of stasis prevails, in which affirmative action is nei-   12
ther eliminated nor expanded, is surprising. In 1975, when I published *Affir-mative Discrimination*, expansion seemed to be in the cards. If fixed numbers
of blacks and other minorities had to be employed or promoted, why would
such a requirement not be extended to other groups, since so many could
claim to have met prejudice and discrimination? As these measures were im-plemented, what hope was there, since they gave advantage to some groups,
that they would ever be abandoned? If busing was implemented in some
cities under the lax standards set by the Supreme Court for finding state-sanc-tioned segregation, why would it not spread to all major cities? Once insti-tuted, how could the assignment of students by race ever end? If these
policies became a permanent part of America's polity and society, how could
we ever attain the ideal of a color-blind society based on individual rights, at
which American liberals had long aimed?

Undergirding these concerns was a conception of American society and   13
the role of race and ethnicity in it. We had seen many groups become part of
the United States through immigration, and we had seen each in turn over-coming some degree of discrimination to become integrated into American
society. This process did not seem to need the active involvement of gov-ernment, determining the proper degree of participation of each group in
employment and education. It had not happened that way in the past, and
there was no reason to think it had to happen that way in the future. What
was needed was that barriers to economic activity and education not be im-posed, and that they be lifted where they existed. These barriers had been
overwhelming for blacks, the one major group in American society (aside
from American Indians) that does not owe its origins to free immigration.
They had been lifted through the success of the civil rights struggle, and one
could expect the economic and educational advancement of blacks that had
been evident in the 1960s to continue. If progress could be expected to con-tinue, why were quotas and goals, busing, and numerical targets for enroll-ment necessary?

I did not expect—nor should anyone have expected—that each group   14
would reflect some national average in occupation and education, because
the effects of history, past experiences, and yes, discrimination and segrega-tion would continue to be felt. But the laws against discrimination were pow-erful and powerfully enforced. Blacks had made great progress in the 1960s
without affirmative action. They were becoming prominent in public em-ployment—in which they had more than "their share" of jobs (though not of
the best jobs). In other areas, blacks had less than "their share." But how dif-ferent was this from Irish domination of police forces in the past, or Jewish
concentration in small business? If this was the way things had worked in the
past, I believed they would work that way in the future; the introduction of
affirmative action and busing threatened only to increase racial and ethnic
conflict, without achieving much for the advancement of blacks. Further, as

with many government policies, affirmative action was poorly adapted even to its central objectives, because along with blacks it had targeted American Indians, Asians, and Hispanics; the latter two were mixtures of very different groups, some of which could make no claims to special governmental solicitude and "fair shares" in view of their economic and educational progress.

One fear and one hope were not realized in the dozen years since the publication of *Affirmative Discrimination*. The fear was that affirmative action would spread beyond the initial groups targeted for government concern to include others; that the opportunity of individual Americans would come to depend on their racial and ethnic group; that ethnic and social conflict would escalate as rigid boundaries determined opportunity. This has not happened. The unrealized hope was that the progress of blacks would continue, making it evident that such measures were unnecessary.   15

Affirmative action has not spread markedly beyond the initial groups defined as its beneficiaries. In some areas (that of set-asides for minorities for government contracts) there has been some moderate expansion—for example, Asian Indians are now classified as minority contractors and may get the benefits of minority set-asides—but on the whole the original line dividing the benefited from all others has held. Within the initial boundaries, affirmative action, particularly as it affects blacks and women, has been institutionalized and has become an accepted part of the American economic scene. It will be very hard to uproot. There is now a serious question whether one should try.   16

Stalemate

The stability we see is not only one of exhaustion and equally-matched political forces; it is also one of institutionalization—the acceptance of affirmative action as a legitimate norm by employers, even grudgingly by employees. When the Reagan administration began, after some years of quiescence that disappointed those who thought it would move against affirmative action, to finally bestir itself on this issue, it found, to its surprise, that business wanted no change in affirmative action requirements. Cities and counties did not want to be released from the consent decrees requiring goals or quotas in employment and promotion. "Businessmen like to hire by the numbers," announced a September 16, 1985 article in *Fortune*. It points out, accurately, that "so far, in spite of the Administration's rumblings, nothing much has happened that affects the way companies run their affirmative action programs. The Labor Department's Office of Federal Contract Compliance Programs, which enforces equal opportunity in companies that do business with the federal government, has gone right on enforcing the rules." (A proposal by the Department of Justice in August 1985 to modify affirmative action requirements for federal contractors ran into opposition within the Administration itself, as the Department of Justice was challenged by the Labor Department. After two years, matters now stand where they have always stood: the rules remain unaltered.) The *New York Times* reported a similar finding on March 3, 1986: big business had no argument with affirmative   17 action requirements, even though small businesses found the rules and the paperwork they required frustrating, excessive, and unrealistic.

Affirmative action had become a norm of employer behavior. As the economic columnist Robert J. Samuelson wrote in the *Washington Post* of July 11, 1984:

> These pressures [the aggressive use of anti-discrimination laws, including affirmative action] have changed the ways labor markets work. Many firms have overhauled personnel policies. Recruitment has been broadened. Tests unrelated to qualifications have been abandoned. Promotions are less informal. When positions become open, they are posted publicly so anyone (not just the boss's favorite) can apply. Formal evaluations have been strengthened so that, when a manager selects one candidate over another (say, a white man over a woman), there are objective criteria.
>
> Equally important, women and blacks increasingly are plugged into the informal information and lobbying networks that remain critical in hiring and promotion decisions.

Even more revealing than commentary and analysis is the sort of pragmatic advice that is handed out to business. Consider for example the warnings given in the "Small Business" column of the *Wall Street Journal* on February 4, 1985:

> What's wrong with asking a woman job applicant these questions: Who takes care of your children when you're at work? What if they get sick? How does your husband feel about your taking business trips? What would he say if a male employee went too?
>
> They may seem like reasonable questions. But in fact they could be construed as biased against women and could embroil the employer in charges of discriminating against female job applicants in violation of federal or state laws because male applicants aren't asked such questions.
>
> Employment laws contain many traps for the unwary. More are being created in court decisions. . . .
>
> Don't ask if someone has ever been arrested. (Because blacks are arrested more than whites, a federal court has held, such a question can be discriminatory against blacks.) However, asking about criminal convictions is usually safe. And not hiring a convicted felon can be justified as a business necessity for such reasons as not being able to bond the person.
>
> Restrictive job requirements can get a company in trouble, too. It may be discriminatory to have an educational barrier to a position (only high school grads need apply) if it can't be justified as necessary to doing the job.

Entrenchment and Legitimation

Affirmative action has been institutionalized not only in business but also in government, which does not want to upset the applecart either. Thus, when the Justice Department requested that fifty-one cities, counties, and states operating under court orders and consent decrees requiring quotas or goals

18

19

20

consider revising them, the governments involved were not eager to be released from these requirements. They may have fought them initially (ironically, almost all were the result of Justice Department suits under previous administrations), but once the quotas had been set, the state and local governments were willing to live with them.

Affirmative action is so well entrenched that the very government agencies   21
of an administration that opposes quotas and goals report to the Equal Employment Opportunity Commission on their progress toward meeting affirmative action numerical goals! Only three agencies have resisted this requirement: the Department of Justice, the National Endowment for the Humanities, and the Federal Trade Commission. But a hundred others have not.

The institutionalization of affirmative action suggests that even with   22
changes in its composition the Supreme Court will pause before considering the uprooting of processes so well established, involving thousands of employees, affecting the expectations of millions. And the Court is the only potential threat to continuing affirmative action. If the administration of Ronald Reagan has done so little in seven years through administrative action, it is hardly likely it will do more in its remaining time. The "stroke of the pen" that could have radically modified or eliminated the requirement to set hiring and promotion goals by race and sex for tens of thousands of government contractors has not been delivered. To those who find affirmative action an abomination, this is a tragedy. To those who feared its demise, it is a relief. In Congress, a point of view that may well reflect the opinions of a minority always holds sway. The protection of affirmative action is in the hands of the Congressmen who care, reflecting the views of civil rights organizations; most others stay away from the issue. "Civil Rights Lobby Plays Defense But Wins," ran a *Washington Post* headline on June 7, 1986. The *Post's* summary is correct: the civil rights lobby had blocked the nomination of William Bradford Reynolds, a critic of quotas and goals who was in charge of civil rights for the Justice Department, as Associate Attorney General; by leaking a Justice Department plan to change affirmative action requirements it had started an uproar that led the Administration to retreat into silence; it had blocked an Administration nomination to the general counsel of the EEOC; it had blocked a number of lesser judicial appointments. And it has since defeated Robert Bork's nomination to the Supreme Court.

This strength must give one pause; it seems to make nonsense of polls   23
showing that three-quarters of Americans oppose quotas. The success of the civil rights lobby suggests that the actual structure of decision making cannot be deduced from public opinion polls, party platforms, or Congressional opinion. Many players are involved; of these, the Court remains the strongest. But I believe the underlying force that keeps the system of numerical quotas and goals intact is the actual condition of blacks. It is the unrealized hope for black improvement, a hope that could have with reason been entertained in the early 1970s, that sustains affirmative action in employment and promotion, minority preference in admission to institutions of higher education, and busing in a number of major cities.

It is thus the condition of the black population of the United States, not 24 the state of their rights, or the practices that affect them, that lends the strongest support to affirmative action. Other racial and minority groups are covered by affirmative action, but it is not *their* fate or *their* power or *their* claim on the American conscience that motivates this massive machinery. Japanese and Chinese moved ahead despite discrimination. Newer Asian immigrants—Filipinos, Koreans, Vietnamese, Asian Indians—can for the most part expect to do well. The Hispanic Americans are a mixed collection indeed, from the upwardly mobile Cubans to the depressed Puerto Ricans, but they would hardly have had the power to institute affirmative action or to sustain it. (Women are a separate story; their numbers ensure their protection by affirmative action.) It is the blacks who quite rightly affect the conscience of America: they were enslaved and rigidly kept down after emancipation by massive public and private discrimination and prejudice. If they had made rapid progress despite their grim history, we would undoubtedly never have felt the pressures to institute race-conscious policies in employment and discrimination. In some respects, they have made great progress. But the mass of misery characterizing their poor stands as the great argument for affirmative action.

We have seen a substantial reduction of the gap in earnings between 25 blacks and whites, but we have seen other key measures of black well-being decline; the most important are the great increase in black female-headed families and children born out of wedlock, and the decline in the percentage of black males in the labor force. Many factors have been at work, and some measures of long-term well-being have been matched by other measures of decline. Would matters have been worse in the absence of affirmative action? That case can be made. Would they have been better in its absence? Even that case can be made. Thus Thomas Sowell and others argue that the employer who knows he must be careful in dealing with blacks in regard to promotions, pay, and terminations (because of the threat of charges of discrimination) will more cautiously select his black employees, so that the opportunities of less-skilled blacks will decline. However this argument is decided, it seems clear that the problems that now concern black leaders—teen-age pregnancies, family breakup, drugs, female-headed families, declining participation in the work force—will hardly be solved by affirmative action.

Affirmative Action and the Black Condition

If it is the condition of blacks, imposing itself on the American conscience, 26 that sustains affirmative action, the obvious question is what affirmative action does for that condition.

Although we know much more about this now than we did a dozen years 27 ago, there is still room for argument as to the effect of affirmative action on the black condition. All firms with over fifteen employees are covered by the antidiscrimination provisions of Title VII; all firms with more than one hundred employees must provide EEO-1 forms to the Equal Employment Opportunity Commission listing the numbers of each group they employ at each occupational level. Federal contractors with more than $50,000 in contracts and fifty employees must maintain affirmative action plans and report to the EEOC on how their employees break down by ethnic and racial group and occupation. It should be easy to compare firms covered by affirmative action with those not so covered. That has been done. The results are generally positive but surprisingly varied. Certainly black employment has increased in or shifted to the firms that report to EEOC and are covered by affirmative action. James P. Smith and Finis Welch, authors of *Closing the Gap: Forty Years of Economic Progress for Blacks,* report:

> Black men were 10 percent less likely to work in covered firms in 1966. By 1980, however, they were 20 percent more likely to work in EEOC reporting firms. To put these changes in another way, less than half (48 percent) of black male workers were employed in EEOC covered firms in 1966; the figure rose to 60 percent by 1980.
>
> The largest employment changes occurred between 1966 and 1970 (the first four years of reporting). Between those years, there was a 20 percent increase in the number of blacks working in covered firms. The trend continued at a diminished pace until 1974, and then apparently stabilized.

The rapid increase of the period 1966–1970 came *after* the adoption of   28
the Civil Rights Act banning discrimination, but *before* the regulations for affirmative action were firmed up and began to be widely enforced. Nevertheless, affirmative action *per se* has had its effect: within the covered sector, black jobs shifted toward firms with contracts with the federal government. Between 1970 and 1980, black employment in non-federal contractor firms that report to the EEOC grew by 5 percent. Among federal contractors, total black employment expanded by more than 15 percent.

> As large as those increases in total employment seem, they pale next to changes within the managerial and professional jobs. Black managers and professionals were half as likely as white managers and professionals to work in covered firms in 1966. By 1980, black managers and professionals were equally likely to be found in covered firms.

Jonathan Leonard's analyses also show a great increase in black employment among federal contractors.

But to concentrate only on the firms covered by affirmative action is to   29
miss something. Smith and Welch add:

> Affirmative action resulted in a radical reshuffling of black jobs in the labor force. It shifted black male employment towards EEOC covered firms and industries, and particularly into firms with federal contracts. Reshuffling is the right term, because the mirror image is that black employment in the non-covered sector plummeted.

Despite the increases in the number of blacks employed by EEOC-covered   30
firms and federal contractors, Smith and Welch, looking at the overall gap between black and white earnings for the entire period between 1940 and 1980,
find that affirmative action must have had only a slight effect. Blacks improved their position both before affirmative action and after it. Improved
education, the migration of blacks from south to north, the narrowing of the
difference in earnings between north and south, and the collapse of discrimination in earnings against blacks in the south after the Civil Rights Act of
1966 seem to have played the greatest role in reducing the gap between black
and white earnings in recent decades. "The slowly evolving historical forces
we have emphasized in this report—education and migration—were the primary determinant of the long-term black economic improvement." At best,
write Smith and Welch, "affirmative action has marginally altered black wage
gains during this long-term period."

Whatever the truth as to the impact of affirmative action (in terms of   31
generating improvements for blacks in some areas, while causing decline in
others), it seems clear that uprooting affirmative action would be very difficult. The Reagan administration is as determined an opponent as we are ever
likely to see. But after about fifteen years of affirmative action, we have created expectations among blacks and practices in business and government
that sustain it. Whatever black doubts about affirmative action there may be
(and they do exist), moving against it would appear to black leaders, and to
other blacks, as an attack on their interests and their well-being. A dozen
years ago affirmative action was newly established, and the recollection of
the intention of color blindness was strongly fixed in the minds of liberals
and blacks. Today affirmative action looks back on a long history, and the
memory of what was intended in 1964 recedes further and further into the
distance.

How Much Affirmative Action?

I believe opposition to affirmative action is often founded on a liberal vision   32
as devoted to equality as that of its proponents. But principle often must give
way to practicality and prudence: rather than an all-out assault, which it
seems must fail, the issue now is to define, as some Supreme Court decisions
do, where, when, for whom, and what kind of affirmative action is legitimate. Thus we should consider (though one is aware of the enormous political difficulties involved) eliminating Asians and Hispanics from the
affirmative action categories. They would of course retain the protection all
Americans have against discrimination on grounds of race, ethnicity, or national background. If such a limitation were possible—it could easily be done
administratively—it would begin to send the message that we view affirmative action as a temporary expedient, to be increasingly dispensed with, in
various areas, for various groups, over time. We should make clear, even if it is
politically impossible to change the affirmative action regulations affecting
blacks, that these are to be reviewed at regular intervals to determine their

necessity or efficacy. Ideally, we should aim at a society in which individuals are treated without regard to race and ethnicity for purposes of employment, promotion, or admission into selective institutions: this is the kind of society, it is clear, that the majority of blacks would like to live in.

No other issue of statistical goal-setting for minority improvement remains as controversial as that of affirmative action in employment. Busing is maintained in many communities, but it is hard to believe that a new, major busing program can be instituted in any large city. Whites have always opposed it, and blacks by now are disillusioned with its promise, even when it is instituted under the best of circumstances. One has the impression the civil rights leadership continues to demand busing without any conviction that it will get more, or that if it does it will do much for the education of blacks. Just as the theme of self-help becomes the dominant one in discussions of the social problems of blacks, so it becomes increasingly important in discussions of education. It is almost inevitable that this should be so, as the educational systems of our largest cities come increasingly under black leadership. 33

The Housing Issue

The campaign for residential integration has been even less successful than that for busing. The *Gautreaux* litigation in Chicago was originally designed to get subsidized housing built in white areas there. It failed in that; and it has had very little success in its later emanation, as an effort to get blacks into subsidized suburban housing. The *Mt. Laurel* litigation in New Jersey also aimed at residential integration by overcoming restraints on subsidized housing in white suburbs. Subsidized housing would make it possible for low-income people to move into higher-income towns, and would also increase the number of blacks in those towns. It has had almost as tortuous a course as the *Gautreaux* litigation, with as modest results. Residential integration does proceed, but on the basis of the economic progress of blacks, not on the basis of the governmentally-required insertion of subsidized housing for low-income and black families into middle-class areas that resist it. 34

The issue of housing for blacks—like the issue of education—has always been complicated, because two objectives, not necessarily consistent or in harmony, are aimed at: in education, better *and* integrated education; in housing, better *and* integrated housing. In education, the attempt to produce a higher measure of integration in the schools through busing leads to "white flight," increased disorder, disruptions of education, and, in the short run at least, no major improvement. (Admittedly, one may ask whether improvement would be greater if the integration objective was abandoned; but one could answer, why not? Many school systems, after all, are led by blacks, administered by blacks, and strongly committed to improving the education of blacks.) In housing, we have a similar conflict. The policy of creating or maintaining a measure of integration is generally implemented by restricting the number of units in a development made available to blacks, in order to reduce white fears of a black majority that would lead them to move out, thus 35 creating a segregated community. Ironically, this issue has recently pitted the Administration's chief opponent of any policy discriminating on the basis of race against a chief critic of goals and quotas in employment, who was appointed by the Administration to the United States Commission on Civil Rights. Assistant Attorney General William Bradford Reynolds has argued in federal court against an arrangement limiting the number of apartments available to blacks in Starrett City in Brooklyn, New York (a plan that was instituted to maintain Starrett City as an integrated development). Morris Abram, a lawyer who first achieved prominence fighting for civil rights in the South, defends Starrett City.

My own position is pragmatic: where integration can be maintained, as it   36 has been in Starrett City, such policies should be allowed to continue. One would be distressed to see a policy of color blindness adhered to so absolutely that examples of residential integration, valuable—and few—as they are, and dependent on color-conscious policies, could not be maintained. But such a policy differs from a quota or goal in employment in a number of key respects: it does not undermine the rights or expectations of the previous tenants—indeed, it maintains them, for they expected and were provided with an integrated community when they moved in; it does not lower the standards for admission, by including, for example, families that would be disruptive or would be unable to pay the rent. Racial quotas in housing thus do not threaten the living environment; indeed, they protect against its deterioration. In employment, on the other hand, goals and quotas are inseparable from attacks on testing and standards.

Lessons

The most important lesson from the study of public policies designed to im-   37 prove the condition of blacks is that people will resist what government does to improve it directly more than they will any individual's effort to improve his own position. The black in a job finds no problem with his colleagues; but a problem may arise when that job is gained through quotas and goals in a particularly egregious manner. The black family sending its children to a white majority school will find no problem, if it is a neighborhood school, a private school, or a Catholic school; it may have a problem when the assignment to a school is made by government against prevalent expectations of how children are assigned to or select schools. The black family in a white majority neighborhood rarely runs into trouble; but a policy designed to spread low-income black families into middle-income areas, black or white, through subsidized housing, does mean trouble. No American can be satisfied with the overall condition of black Americans, despite progress in recent decades; but government actions that aim at statistical goals for minorities are not likely to do better in improving that condition than the work and efforts of blacks in an open and, it is to be hoped, more prosperous society. That government should prevent and punish discrimination is universally accepted by Americans. When government tries to determine how many members of a particular ethnic group should get certain jobs or promotions, attend particular schools, or live in designated areas, however, it runs into widespread opposition.

Questions

1. How do you think the Supreme Court should have decided in the case that Glazer presents in the first paragraph? Defend your position.
2. Summarize the two sides to the affirmative action issue.
3. Explain Glazer's assertion that "opposition to affirmative action is often founded on a liberal vision as devoted to equality as that of its proponents."

Race in the Workplace: Is Affirmative Action Working?

BUSINESS WEEK

In this article, the authors discuss the backlash against affirmative action that can occur when the government interprets what should be a legal defense against discrimination. Although affirmative action has its problems, the authors conclude that it must nevertheless be retained as a symbol of America's commitment to civil rights. This article is from Business Week *(1991).*

- **1941**   President Roosevelt encourages minority employment by ordering defense contractors to cease discriminatory practices in hiring; first such Presidential effort

- **1953**   President Eisenhower creates a committee to receive complaints about discrimination, covering all federal contractors, including subcontractors. Still no sanctions for noncompliance

- **1961**   As the fight against segregation in the South intensifies, President Kennedy introduces the term "affirmative-action" and puts teeth in minority hiring rules for government contractors. Creates commission to investigate contractors' practices, impose sanctions, collect employment statistics

- **1963**   Two hundred thousand blacks and whites rally in Washington for equal rights

- **1965**   A year after Congress passes the Civil Rights Act, President Johnson issues an order requiring companies that do business with the government to put affirmative-action plans in writing

- **1969**   President Nixon mandates hiring quotas for construction companies in Philadelphia

- **1978**   The Supreme Court strikes down University of California affirmative-action plan

- **1985**   Attorney General Meese challenges affirmative action in Supreme Court cases

- **1989**   The Supreme Court shocks civil rights groups with a string of decisions that make it difficult to win discrimination suits in court, triggering a national debate on hiring quotas

- **1990**   President Bush vetoes a civil rights bill that would have overturned five high court rulings

"Every black person in every corporation has to ask: 'If I were white, where would I be now?'"
A BLACK MANAGER AT MASSACHUSETTS MUTUAL LIFE INSURANCE CO. IN SPRINGFIELD

"Minorities get too fair a shake. And pretty soon we won't be able to afford the luxury."
A WHITE STOCKBROKER AT DEAN WITTER REYNOLDS INC. IN NEW YORK

Call it affirmative action. Or minority outreach. Or perhaps you prefer "managing diversity," the newest, politically well-scrubbed name for policies aimed at bringing minorities into the business mainstream through preferential hiring and promotion. But however you describe such hiring based on race, U.S. society must come to grips with a sobering fact: Some 25 years into a national drive—and 50 years since the government first embraced the idea—to give blacks and other minorities a foothold in white, male-dominated Corporate America, the ideal of racial equality remains elusive, and the means of attaining it increasingly controversial.

Affirmative action encompasses both race and gender. Indeed, women have been among its greatest beneficiaries. But the discussion of race stirs the fiercest emotions. And as Washington's nasty partisan battle over the civil rights bills shows, affirmative action itself remains shrouded in ignorance, mistrust, and political cynicism. "The term conjures up the vilest of connotations," says Virginia Governor L. Douglas Wilder. "It has become like a four-letter word."

It wasn't always that way, of course. In 1964, the Civil Rights Act banned discrimination in employment and ordered that all hiring be color-blind. Affirmative action, established by a series of Presidential directives going back to Lyndon B. Johnson's in 1965, was to make up for past injustices, overcome continuing discrimination, and ultimately to provide equal job opportunities for blacks and whites. Unhappily, those aims sometimes contain a painful contradiction: Compensating for past discrimination against some people can create fresh discrimination against others. When companies make extraordinary efforts to hire or promote minority workers, they may penalize white workers.

Old-Boy Network. Small wonder that some companies have had trouble accepting the spirit of affirmative action. Not that business has entirely shirked its duty. Since the 1970s, most major companies and many smaller ones have adopted formal written policies to recruit minorities. Result: Affirmative action has produced major gains for black job-seekers. The percentage of blacks in the work force has risen by 50% in the past 25 years—a solid advance even taking into account a larger black population. The biggest gains were in the South and by black women. Many jobs came in government itself, where as many as 850,000 blacks found jobs in the social-welfare bureaucracy from 1960 to 1976. Huge numbers of blacks have moved into the middle class.

In 1989, about 5% of all managers in the U.S. were black. That's a fivefold increase since 1966 and a 30% increase since 1978. Still, there's a long road ahead. Nearly 97% of senior executives in the biggest U.S. companies are white. And while blacks make up 12.7% of the private-sector work force, only 5% of all professionals are black.

Part of the problem for black managers is the so-called old-boy network. Jason Wright, a black vice-president at RJR Nabisco Inc., says: "The reality of life in America is that if you're white, most of the people you know are white. If someone says to you, 'Do you know anyone for this job?,' the people you recommend will probably be white."

Furthermore, overall progress seems to be slowing. After dramatic income gains in the 1960s and 1970s, blacks have been losing economic ground for the past decade. And the good-paying manufacturing jobs that once were a doorway to economic security for working-class blacks are harder to come by in an increasingly service-based economy.

The idea that affirmative action isn't moving fast enough or far enough is reinforced by the widespread view in the black community that, ever since Ronald Reagan took office, Republicans have been using the White House bully pulpit to equate preferential hiring with racial quotas. Blacks feel, with some justification, that this is part of a deliberate political strategy to stampede blue-collar Democrats toward the GOP. "Prior to 1980, companies were learning to live with the new order," says John E. Jacob, president of the National Urban League. "After Reagan began to challenge affirmative action, companies began to question it." Result: a decade of backsliding and "a grade of C+ for Corporate America," Jacob says.

While blacks fret that the drive for racial equality is slowing, many whites think it has gone far enough. In happier economic times, companies could give hiring preferences to blacks without necessarily taking away white workers' jobs. That's much harder now. Corporate restructurings have slashed the ranks of middle managers, and new technologies have wiped out millions of low-skill jobs. Now, as the economic pie shrinks, whites increasingly begin to fear that affirmative action puts their careers in jeopardy.

Doubts and Questions. Even those whites who still support affirmative action in principle think it can lead to too-rapid advancement of unprepared minorities. One white employee at United Technologies Corp.'s Hamilton Standard Div. in Windsor Locks, Conn., says he works for a black foreman who isn't up to the job—and is hurting his unit's morale. "I don't know if he's there because management thinks he's qualified, or because he's black," he says.

Whites aren't the only ones questioning race-based preferences these days. Some black intellectuals, such as Shelby Steele, who teaches at San Jose State University, say affirmative action works against their race. By singling blacks out for special treatment, Steele argues, it stigmatizes them as unworthy and creates a sense of victimization. Such feelings, he says, can stifle attempts to throw off the bonds of dependency and poverty that have plagued many blacks.

Other blacks are equally dissatisfied with preferential hiring, but for different reasons. They acknowledge that affirmative action has expanded opportunity but believe that many companies lose interest in black advancement once a hiring goal has been met. Some black middle managers feel they are being shunted into human resources or public relations—jobs that often spell "dead end" in the corporation.   12

It's not that way at every company, of course. Some corporations' commitment to equal opportunity goes far beyond lip service and a government mandate—not for altruistic reasons, but for pragmatic ones. Minorities, who now make up 28% of the U.S. population, have become a major force in the domestic economy, and businesses want to reach these growing markets.   13

"Corporate America isn't stupid," says Henry L. Warren, vice-president for planning and control at Arkansas Power & Light Co. "Companies are able to see that the customers they'll provide service to are changing." To serve these nonwhite customers, companies need a multiracial work force. Furthermore, for a company to ignore the rising numbers of minority workers—non-whites now account for 22% of the labor market—is to let a valuable talent pool go untapped. Affirmative action "is not just the right thing to do," asserts American Telephone & Telegraph Chairman Robert E. Allen. "It's a business necessity."   14

But not all managers have come around to this enlightened view. Many companies hire just enough minority workers to satisfy the government and protect themselves against discrimination suits. "I've had people tell me, 'We need a woman for this,' or 'I need a black,'" during job interviews, says an investor-relations manager for a New York-based mining company. "Quotas will be set and met in certain staff jobs." (Many workers and executives interviewed for this story spoke on condition of anonymity.)   15

Black workers contend that once hired, they often meet with indifference or outright hostility. A black woman middle manager who has been with a large New York insurance company for 10 years complains that minority managers have a tough time advancing because plum jobs are often filled before they are ever posted. "It's Corporate America, and we didn't create it. It's their game and their rules."   16

Assembly Line. The current debate over proposed civil rights legislation produces only more anger and confusion. Democrats claim they merely want to restore the intent of civil rights laws by making it easier for minorities to win discrimination lawsuits. Republicans are using the Democrats like a trampoline for pushing that most dreaded of all measures, a "quota bill."   17

In fact, the passage of the Democratic bill—or a GOP alternative—would make very little difference in how blacks are treated by corporations. That's because affirmative action is now so deeply ingrained in American corporate culture that changes at the margin of the law won't have much impact. The machinery hums along, nearly automatically, at the largest U.S. corporations.   18

They have turned affirmative action into a smoothly running assembly line, with phalanxes of lawyers and affirmative-action managers. "Whether we have new civil rights legislation or not is irrelevant to us," insists AT&T's Allen, who earlier this year tried unsuccessfully to broker a civil rights bill acceptable to both large corporations and minority activists.

Not every corporation functions on automatic pilot. Some highly visible companies, such as IBM, American Express, and Xerox, have embraced aggressive hiring and promotion programs for women and minorities. Although these models of equal opportunity cut across diverse fields, the key ingredient often seems to be a sustained top-down push from a chief executive. "Without commitment from a CEO," says Randall Kinder, a black senior vice-president at Equitable Financial Cos., "it just doesn't work." 19

Price Waterhouse is one firm where the message comes straight from the top. In 1989, as the accounting giant was reeling from adverse publicity from an embarrassing sex-discrimination case, new CEO Shaun F. O'Malley set up an advisory committee on women and minorities. He invited prominent black accountants to serve on the panel. Then, "to make sure everyone knew how important it was, I made myself chairman." Adds O'Malley: "About 6% of our work force is black now. We want more. But more of the best." 20

In 1973, AT&T settled a landmark government discrimination suit by agreeing to hire and promote more minorities. The court order expired in 1979, but, with CEO Allen pushing hard, the company continues its aggressive recruiting of blacks. Today, minorities make up nearly 21% of AT&T's work force. And 17% of the company's managers are minorities, up from 12% in 1984. 21

AT&T also encourages its minority workers' participation in race-based support groups. These forums, which often have branches at every work site around the country, offer black managers a chance to share ideas, solve problems, and develop the networks white men have long relied on. AT&T's Black Managers' Group is one of 12 such affinity groups. All branches of the BMG, which was set up in the early '70s, meet twice a year for two-day conferences. Such race-based advocacy networks are increasingly common among progressive companies. 22

To get past the emotional charge carried by affirmative action, some employers have embraced a new catchphrase: managing diversity. Sometimes, this is to settle lawsuits. Northwest Airlines Inc. agreed to spend $1.2 million on cultural-diversity training for all managers and to provide cash incentives for managers who meet minority hiring goals. Pillsbury Co. settled a class action, in part by agreeing to spend $1.76 million to set up a "cultural diversity and training fund." The program will, among other things, promote "ethnic cuisine and specialty events in the Pillsbury cafeteria." 23

Some of these earnest efforts can be easily lampooned. But many companies are serious about making their workplaces more congenial to minorities. Du Pont Chairman Edgar S. Woolard Jr. encourages workers to confront their biases in five-day workshops. The company also sponsored an all-expenses-paid conference for black managers to discuss how African-American culture 24 can improve the company's bottom line. Managers who feel their heritage is valued are more productive, says one long-time Du Ponter.

Hard Times

Yet plenty of corporations still duck the issue of hiring preferences. One large   25
publisher based in the Midwest scrapped its voluntary affirmative-action plan when it failed to meet its own goals. What went wrong? A company official says it was lack of interest at the top. "There was no buy-in to the program," she says. "It's still a good-old-boy network."

Even the best of corporate intentions can be undone by economic hard   26
times. Take Equitable, the New York-based financial-services company. The firm spent years building its image among black managers as a "good" company. Now, after changing top management, Equitable is in the midst of a painful restructuring. Its black middle managers believe that affirmative action has been a casualty and worry that black advancement will suffer.

"We have maintained some semblance of affirmative action," says Dar-   27
wen Davis, a black senior vice-president and 25-year Equitable veteran. But, he says, because of the company's "financial and internal problems, these are all back-burner issues." For example, the Black Officers' Council Davis used to head no longer meets. Equitable denies that it has reduced its commitment to affirmative action.

For other businesses, distaste for hiring blacks still exists. The owner of a   28
small western Pennsylvania plastics company says he hired a black woman three years ago "to do the right thing." But after he passed her over for pro-motion, she sued, claiming race discrimination. The case is still in court, but the owner says he won't hire other blacks: "I don't need all the aggravation."

Racial stereotypes persist as well. The owner of a small foundry near Pitts-   29
burgh says he has had blacks on the payroll for years and has been fully satis-fied with their work. But he says he will not actively recruit them. "It's not like it was in the old days," he says, "when you gave a black man a job and he appreciated it and didn't try to stir things up."

No CEO, surrounded by lawyers and affirmative-action advisers, would ad-   30
mit to such views. But some big companies have established practices that can end up being just as discriminatory. It's called hiring by the numbers.

Affirmative action is not supposed to be synonymous with quotas. But   31
virtually all companies doing business with the federal government must set annual plans, sometimes in the shape of numerical goals or timetables, for in-creasing employment of women and minorities. Companies often agree to meet specific hiring goals when they settle discrimination suits. In effect, quotas are prohibited and required at the same time—which can make com-pliance a nightmare.

Since the system encourages companies to focus on numbers of blacks on   32
the payroll, rather than on individuals, companies face no penalty if their policies establish a revolving door, where a fixed percentage of black employ-ees come and go, simply filling the same slots. Presto: instant compliance.

"It can be difficult to get managers to move past the numbers," says   33
William F. Holmes, vice-president at Employment Advisory Services Inc., a
Washington consulting firm. "Everything they do is numbers. They have a
production quota. Why not just have a human-resources quota?"

There is also some evidence that the current system may be setting a ceil-   34
ing on minority hiring and promotion. Says Donald L. Huizenga, president of
Larson Foundries in Grafton, Ohio: "We don't have to go out and hire minorities because our percentage [of minority workers] is higher than the community of Grafton. If it weren't, we would be going out and recruiting." In
nearly lily-white Grafton, 14% of Larson's work force is black or Hispanic.

Those blacks who make it into management ranks can find life lonely—   35
and frustrating. Of 92 top management jobs at Hughes Aircraft Co., for example, only two are filled by blacks—the vice-presidents for communications
and workplace diversity. "Rarely do I see a black man or woman with profit-
and-loss responsibility," says Norman Hatter Jr., a black human-resources director for Du Pont's engineering staff. "That's where we really need to be."

Intellectuals such as Steele see an even deeper problem. In a collection of   36
provocative essays on black-white relations, Steele writes: "One of the most
troubling effects of racial preferences for blacks is a kind of demoralization,
an enlargement of self-doubt." Even when blacks get a promotion, says University of Pennsylvania sociologist Elijah Anderson, they "run the risk of being seen as tokens. And that's a very difficult thing to handle."

The kind of hiring by the numbers that bothers Steele is just what angers   37
many whites. Their anger doesn't seem to be based on personal experience,
since, according to one recent poll, fewer than 1 in 10 whites say they have
been victims of reverse discrimination. Still, when companies hire or promote blacks who are considered unqualified by their colleagues, it creates bitterness. "I question the factoring of affirmative action into hiring," says
David J. Pandolfi, a white AT&T technician in Springfield, Mass. "It handicaps
a company's future growth if an employer has to hire an unqualified individual in order to appease a politician."

Of course, "there are a lot of dumb white people who get breaks, and no-   38
body seems too upset about that," notes William T. Coleman Jr., who as
Transportation Secretary was the highest-ranking black in the Ford Administration. Still, Pandolfi expresses the feelings of millions of workers. It is understandable given affirmative action's legacy of racial tension, tokenism, and
purely mechanistic compliance.

No question, the cost is high. But is affirmative action worth it? Yes. It's   39
an important symbol of America's commitment to civil rights. More than
that, it's an effective club. A deep vein of prejudice still runs through U.S. society, despite all the upbeat talk about the increasingly diversified work force.
Government-mandated hiring preferences prod companies into integrating
their work force, and in the past 25 years of affirmative action, blacks and
other minorities have benefited socially and economically. Individual businesses and the economy have profited, not lost. Until America comes up with
a better idea, it's wise to stick with a policy that, despite its flaws, is both a
moral imperative and an economic necessity.

Questions

1. What is the difference between preferential hiring and racial quotas?

2. Do you agree with the assertion that singling out blacks for preferential treatment stigmatizes them as unworthy and creates a sense of victimization?

3. Why does the phrase "affirmative action" carry an emotional charge? Why is "managing diversity" perhaps a better catchphrase?

Racial Preferences? So What?

STEPHEN L. CARTER

Stephen L. Carter (b. 1954) is a lawyer and law professor at Yale University and author of Reflections of an Affirmative Action Baby *(1991).*

Here, Carter, who is black, discusses some of the psychological effects that occur when affirmative action is practiced in education, such as the sensitivity and shame its beneficiaries often experience. However, Carter argues that what is important is not that a minority benefits from racial preference, but how the individual performs given the initial advantage. This reading is from Reflections of an Affirmative Action Baby.

I

I got into law school because I am black.   1

As many black professionals think they must, I have long suppressed this   2
truth, insisting instead that I got where I am the same way everybody else
did. Today I am a professor at the Yale Law School. I like to think that I am a
good one, but I am hardly the most objective judge. What I am fairly sure of,
and can now say without trepidation, is that were my skin not the color that
it is, I would not have had the chance to try.

For many, perhaps most, black professionals of my generation, the matter   3
of who got where and how is left in a studied and, I think, purposeful ambiguity. Some of us, as they say, would have made it into an elite college or professional school anyway. (But, in my generation, many fewer than we like to
pretend, even though one might question the much-publicized claim by
Derek Bok, the president of Harvard University, that in the absence of preferences, only 1 percent of Harvard's entering class would be black.) Most of us,
perhaps nearly all of us, have learned to bury the matter far back in our
minds. We are who we are and where we are, we have records of accomplishment or failure, and there is no rational reason that anybody—employer,
client, whoever—should care any longer whether racial preference played any
role in our admission to a top professional school.

When people in positions to help or hurt our careers *do* seem to care, we   4
tend to react with fury. Those of us who have graduated professional school
over the past fifteen to twenty years, and are not white, travel career paths
that are frequently bumpy with suspicions that we did not earn the right to
be where we are. We bristle when others raise what might be called the qualification question—"Did you get into school or get hired because of a special
program?"—and that prickly sensitivity is the best evidence, if any is needed,

713

of one of the principal costs of racial preferences. Scratch a black professional with the qualification question, and you're likely to get a caustic response, such as this one from a senior executive at a major airline: "Some whites think I've made it because I'm black. Some blacks think I've made it only because I'm an Uncle Tom. The fact is, I've made it because I'm good."

Given the way that so many Americans seem to treat receipt of the benefits of affirmative action as a badge of shame, answers of this sort are both predictable and sensible. In the professional world, moreover, they are very often true: relatively few corporations are in a position to hand out charity. The peculiar aspect of the routine denial, however, is that so many of those who will bristle at the suggestion that they themselves have gained from racial preferences will try simultaneously to insist that racial preferences be preserved and to force the world to pretend that no one benefits from them. That awkward balancing of fact and fiction explains the frequent but generally groundless cry that it is racist to suggest that some individual's professional accomplishments would be fewer but for affirmative action; and therein hangs a tale.

For students at the leading law schools, autumn brings the recruiting season, the idyllic weeks when law firms from around the country compete to lavish upon them lunches and dinners and other attentions, all with the professed goal of obtaining the students' services—perhaps for the summer, perhaps for a longer term. The autumn of 1989 was different, however, because the nation's largest firm, Baker & McKenzie, was banned from interviewing students at the University of Chicago Law School, and on probation—that is, enjoined to be on its best behavior—at some others.

The immediate source of Baker & McKenzie's problems was a racially charged interview that a partner in the firm had conducted the previous fall with a black third-year student at the school. The interviewer evidently suggested that other lawyers might call her "nigger" or "black bitch" and wanted to know how she felt about that. Perhaps out of surprise that she played golf, he observed that "there aren't too many golf courses in the ghetto." He also suggested that the school was admitting "foreigners" and excluding "qualified" Americans.

The law school reacted swiftly, and the firm was banned from interviewing on campus. Other schools contemplated taking action against the firm, and some of them did. Because I am black myself, and teach in a law school, I suppose the easiest thing for me to have done would have been to clamor in solidarity for punishment. Yet I found myself strangely reluctant to applaud the school's action. Instead, I was disturbed rather than excited by this vision of law schools circling the wagons, as it were, to defend their beleaguered minority students against racially insensitive remarks. It is emphatically not my intention to defend the interviewer, most of whose reported questions and comments were inexplicable and inexcusable. I am troubled, however, by my suspicion that there would still have been outrage—not as much, but some—had the interviewer asked only what I called at the beginning of the chapter the qualification question.

I suspect this because in my own student days, something over a decade 9 ago, an interviewer from a prominent law firm addressed this very question to a Yale student who was not white, and the student voices—including my own—howled in protest. "Racism!" we insisted. "Ban them!" But with the passing years, I have come to wonder whether our anger might have been misplaced.

To be sure, the Yale interviewer's question was boorish. And because the 10 interviewer had a grade record and résumé right in front of him, it was probably irrelevant as well. (It is useful here to dispose of one common but rather silly anti–affirmative action bromide: the old question, "Do you really want to be treated by a doctor who got into medical school because of skin color?" The answer is, or ought to be, that the patient doesn't particularly care how the doctor got *into* school; what matters is how the doctor got *out*. The right question, the sensible question, is not "What medical school performance did your grades and test scores predict?" but "What was your medical school performance?") But irrelevance and boorishness cannot explain our rage at the qualification question, because lots of interviewers ask questions that meet the tests of boorishness and irrelevance.

The controversy is not limited to outsiders who come onto campus to re- 11 cruit. In the spring of 1991, for example, students at Georgetown Law School demanded punishment for a classmate who argued in the school newspaper that affirmative action is unfair because students of color are often admitted to law school on the basis of grades and test scores that would cause white applicants to be rejected. Several universities have considered proposals that would deem it "racial harassment" for a (white?) student to question the qualifications of nonwhite classmates. But we can't change either the truths or the myths about racial preferences by punishing those who speak them.

This clamor for protection from the qualification question is powerful ev- 12 idence of the terrible psychological pressure that racial preferences often put on their beneficiaries. Indeed, it sometimes seems as though the programs are not supposed to have any beneficiaries—or, at least, that no one is permitted to suggest that they have any.

And that's ridiculous. If one supports racial preferences in professional 13 school admissions, for example, one must be prepared to treat them like any other preference in admission and believe that they make a difference, that some students would not be admitted if the preferences did not exist. This is not a racist observation. It is not normative in any sense. It is simply a fact. A good deal of emotional underbrush might be cleared away were the fact simply conceded, and made the beginning, not the end, of any discussion of preferences. For once it is conceded that the programs have beneficiaries, it follows that some of us who are professionals and are not white must be among them. Supporters of preferences must stop pretending otherwise. Rather, some large segment of us must be willing to meet the qualification question head-on, to say, "Yes, I got into law school because of racial preferences. So what?"—and, having said it, must be ready with a list of what we have made of the opportunities the preferences provided.

Now, this is a costly concession, because it carries with it all the baggage   14
of the bitter rhetorical battle over the relationship between preferences and
merit. But bristling at the question suggests a deep-seated fear that the dichotomy might be real. Indeed, if admitting that racial preferences make a
difference leaves a funny aftertaste in the mouths of proponents, they might
be more comfortable fighting against preferences rather than for them.

So let us bring some honesty as well as rigor to the debate, and begin at   15
the beginning. I have already made clear my starting point: I got into a top
law school because I am black. Not only am I unashamed of this fact, but I
can prove its truth.

As a senior at Stanford back in the mid-1970s, I applied to about half a   16
dozen law schools. Yale, where I would ultimately enroll, came through fairly
early with an acceptance. So did all but one of the others. The last school, Harvard, dawdled and dawdled. Finally, toward the end of the admission season, I
received a letter of rejection. Then, within days, two different Harvard officials
and a professor contacted me by telephone to apologize. They were quite frank
in their explanation for the "error." I was told by one official that the school
had initially rejected me because "we assumed from your record that you were
white." (The words have always stuck in my mind, a tantalizing reminder of
what is expected of me.) Suddenly coy, he went on to say that the school had
obtained "additional information that should have been counted in your favor"—that is, Harvard had discovered the color of my skin. And if I had already made a deposit to confirm my decision to go elsewhere, well, that, I was
told, would "not be allowed" to stand in my way should I enroll at Harvard.

Naturally, I was insulted by this miracle. Stephen Carter, the white male,   17
was not good enough for the Harvard Law School; Stephen Carter, the black
male, not only was good enough but rated agonized telephone calls urging
him to attend. And Stephen Carter, color unknown, must have been white:
How else could he have achieved what he did in college? Except that my college achievements were obviously not sufficiently spectacular to merit acceptance had I been white. In other words, my academic record was too good for
a black Stanford University undergraduate, but not good enough for a white
Harvard law student. Because I turned out to be black, however, Harvard was
quite happy to scrape me from what it apparently considered somewhere
nearer the bottom of the barrel.

My objective is not to single out Harvard for special criticism; on the con-   18
trary, although my ego insists otherwise, I make no claim that a white student with my academic record would have been admitted to any of the
leading law schools. The insult I felt came from the pain of being reminded
so forcefully that in the judgment of those with the power to dispose, I was
good enough for a top law school only because I happened to be black.

Naturally, I should not have been insulted at all; that is what racial prefer-   19
ences are for—racial preference. But I was insulted and went off to Yale instead, even though I had then and have now absolutely no reason to imagine
that Yale's judgment was based on different criteria than Harvard's. Hardly
anyone granted admission at Yale is denied admission at Harvard, which

admits a far larger class; but several hundreds of students who are admitted at Harvard are denied admission at Yale. Because Yale is far more selective, the chances are good that I was admitted at Yale for essentially the same reason I was admitted at Harvard—the color of my skin made up for what were evidently considered other deficiencies in my academic record. I may embrace this truth as a matter of simple justice or rail against it as one of life's great evils, but being a member of the affirmative action generation means that the one thing I cannot do is deny it. I will say it again: I got into law school because I am black. So what?

II

One answer to the "So what?" question is that someone more deserving than I—someone white—may have been turned away. I hardly know what to make of this argument, for I doubt that the mythical white student on the cusp, the one who almost made it to Yale but for my rude intervention, would have done better than I did in law school.* Nor am I some peculiar case: the Yale Law School of my youth trained any number of affirmative action babies who went on to fine academic performances and are now in the midst of stellar careers in the law.

Even in the abstract, what I call the "fairness story" has never struck me as one of the more convincing arguments against preferential policies. The costs of affirmative action differ from the costs of taxation only in degree, not in kind. People are routinely taxed for services they do not receive that are deemed by their government necessary to right social wrongs they did not commit. The taxpayer-financed "bailout" of the weak or collapsed savings-and-loan institutions is one example. Another is the provision of tax dollars for emergency disaster assistance after a hurricane devastates a coastal community. The people who bear the costs of these programs are not the people who caused the damage, but they still have to pay.

Like many, perhaps most, of America's domestic policies, affirmative action programs are essentially redistributive in nature. They transfer resources from their allocation in the market to other recipients, favored for social policy reasons. Much of the attack on affirmative action is fueled by the same instinct—the same American dream—that stands as a bulwark against any substantial redistribution of wealth. In America, most people like to think, it

20

21

22

†*It has always struck me as quite bizarre that so many otherwise thoughtful people on both sides of the affirmative action controversy seem to think so much turns on the question of how the beneficiaries perform. I would not dismiss the inquiry as irrelevant, but I am reluctant to say that it is the whole ball game. It may be the case, as many critics have argued, that the affirmative action beneficiary who fails at Harvard College might have performed quite well at a less competitive school and gone on to an excellent and productive career that will almost surely be lost because of the shattering experience of academic failure; but one must weigh this cost (and personal choice) against the tale of the student who would not have attended Harvard without affirmative action and who succeeds brilliantly there. It may be that those who do less well in school because of preferences outnumber those who do better, but such statistics are only the edge of the canvas, a tiny part of a much larger and more complex picture, and that is why I think the energy devoted to the qualification question is largely wasted.

is possible for anyone to make it, and those who do not have been victims principally of their own sloth or lack of talent or perhaps plain bad luck—but not of anybody else's sinister plottings. Seymour Martin Lipset, among others, has argued plausibly that a stable democracy is possible only when an economically secure middle class exists to battle against radical economic reforms that the wealthier classes would otherwise resist by using means outside the system. In America, that middle class plainly exists, and racial preferences are among the radical reforms it is willing to resist.

Sometimes the fervent opposition of the great majority of white Americans to affirmative action is put down to racism, or at least racial resentment, and I do not want to argue that neither motivation is *ever* present. But affirmative action programs are different from other social transfers, and the way they differ is in the basis on which the favored and disfavored groups are identified. The basis is race, and sometimes sex—and that makes all the difference.   23

I say that race is different not because I favor the ideal of a color-blind society; indeed, for reasons I discuss [elsewhere], I fear that the rhetoric of color blindness conflates values that are best kept separate. Race is different for obvious historical reasons: the world in general, and this nation in particular, should know well the risks of encouraging powerful institutions to categorize by such immutable characteristics as race. Besides, even were race as a category less controversial, there is still the further fairness argument, that the sins for which the programs purportedly offer compensation are not sins of the current generation.   24

Many proponents of preferential policies, however, insist that the current generation of white males deserves to bear the costs of affirmative action. "White males," we are told, "have had exclusive access to certain information, education, experience, and contacts through which they have gained unfair advantage." In the words of a leading scholar, "[W]e have to say to whites, 'Listen, you have benefited in countless ways from racism, from its notions of beauty [and] its exclusion of minorities in jobs and schools.'" The argument has a second step, too: "For most of this country's history," wrote one commentator, "the nation's top universities practiced the most effective form of affirmative action ever; the quota was for 100 percent white males." The analogy is fair—indeed, it is so fair that it wins the endorsement of opponents as well as supporters of affirmative action—but what does it imply? For proponents of preferences, the answer is clear: if white males have been for centuries the beneficiaries of a vast and all-encompassing program of affirmative action, today's more limited programs can be defended as simply trying to undo the most pernicious effects of that one. That is how, in the contemporary rhetoric of affirmative action, white males turn out to deserve the disfavored treatment that the programs accord.*   25

---

*Even accepting this dubious rhetorical construct, it is easy to see that racial preferences call for sacrifices not from white males as a group but from the subgroups of white males most likely to be excluded by a preference benefitting someone else—that is, the most disadvantaged white males, those who, by hypothesis, have gained the least from racism.

But there is risk in this rhetoric. To make race the determining factor not 26
simply of the favored group but of the disfavored one encourages an analytical structure that seeks and assigns reasons in the present world for disfavor-
ing one group. The simplest structure—and the one that has come, with
mysterious force, to dominate the terms of intellectual and campus debate—
is what Thomas Sowell has called "social irredentism," an insistence that all
members of the disfavored dominant group bear the mantle of oppressor. Affirmative action, then, becomes almost a punishment for the sin of being
born the wrong color and the wrong sex.

All of this carries a neat historical irony. The personalization of affirma- 27
tive action, the specification of white males as the villains, has diluted the
message of the black left of the 1960s and early 1970s, which often (but by no
means always) joined forces with the white left to insist that the problems
were systemic, not individual. In those halcyon days of campus radicalism,
the race struggle was widely described as hand-in-glove with the class struggle. Racial justice was said to be impossible under capitalism, and the principal debate among radical students was over what form of socialism was best
for black people—a separate society or an integrated one, central planning or
local communities?

As for affirmative action, well, sophisticated nationalists understood that 28
it was part of the problem. By funneling the best and brightest young black
men and women into the white-dominated system of higher education, the
critics argued, the programs would simply skim the cream from our community, co-opting into the (white) mainstream those who should have been our
leaders. An attack on efforts to substitute enhanced educational opportunities
for racial justice was a principal focus of Robert Allen's provocative 1969 book
Black Awakening in Capitalist America. "The black student," Allen warned, "is
crucial to corporate America's neocolonial plans." The best and brightest
among black youth, he argued, instead of criticizing capitalism from the outside, would be trained to serve it from the inside. Nationalist reviewers
agreed. For example, Anne Kelley wrote in *The Black Scholar* that "the emphasis on higher education for black students" was part of a "neo-colonialist
scheme" that was "designed to stabilize the masses."

But the language of protest is quite different now, and the success of affir- 29
mative action is one of the reasons; to paraphrase John le Carré, it is hard to
criticize the system when it has brought you inside at its own expense. Affirmative action programs in education are designed to move people of color
into productive roles in capitalist society, and the best sign that they are
working is the way the argument has shifted. White males have replaced "the
society" or "the system" or "the establishment" in the rhetoric of racial justice, perhaps because the rhetoric of justice is no longer under the control of
genuine radicals. The modern proponents of preferences rarely plan to spend
their lives in community organizing as they await the revolutionary moment,
and there is no particular reason that they should. They are liberal reformers,
not radical revolutionaries; with the collapse of communism as a force in the
world, nobody seems to think any longer that the solution is to burn every-

thing down and start over. On campuses nowadays, especially in the professional schools, the students of color seem about as likely as their white classmates to be capitalists to their very fingertips; they have no desire to kill the golden goose that the (white male) establishment has created. Or, to switch metaphors, today's affirmative action advocates want mainly to share in the pie, not to see it divided up in some scientific socialist redistribution.

III

Which helps explain, I think, why the "So what?" that I advocate is not easy   30
to utter. Students of color are in the professional schools for the same reason white students are there: to get a good education and a good job. Because so many people seem to assume that the beneficiaries of affirmative action programs are necessarily bound for failure, or at least for inferiority, there is an understandable tendency for people of color to resist being thought of as beneficiaries. After all, who wants to be bound for failure? (Especially when so many beneficiaries of racial preferences really *don't* succeed as they would like.) Better not to think about it; better to make sure nobody else thinks about it either. Rather than saying, "So what?" better to say, "How dare you?"

I understand perfectly this temptation to try to make the world shut up,   31
to pursue the fantasy that doubts that are not expressed do not exist. When I listen to the labored but heart-felt arguments on why potential employers (and, for that matter, other students) should not be permitted to question the admission qualifications of students of color, I am reminded uneasily of another incident from my own student days, a shining moment when we, too, thought that if we could only stifle debate on the question, we could make it go away.

The incident I have in mind occurred during the fall of 1978, my third   32
year in law school, a few months after the Supreme Court's decision in *Regents of the University of California v. Bakke,* which placed what seemed to many of us unnecessarily severe restrictions on the operation of racially conscious admission programs. The air was thick with swirling critiques of racial preferences, most of them couched in the language of merit versus qualification. Everywhere we turned, someone seemed to be pointing at us and saying, "You don't belong here." We looked around and saw an academic world that seemed to be doing its best to get rid of us.

So we struck back. We called the critics racist. We tried to paint the question of our qualifications as a racist one. And one evening, when the Yale Political Union, a student organization, had scheduled a debate on the matter (the title, as I recall, was "The Future of Affirmative Action"), we demonstrated. All of us.

Our unanimity was astonishing. Then as now, the black students at the   34
law school were divided, politically, socially, and in dozens of other ways. But on this issue, we were suddenly united. We picketed the Political Union meeting, roaring our slogan *("We are not debatable! We are not debatable!")* in tones of righteous outrage. We made so much noise that at last they threw wide the doors and invited us in. In exchange for our promise to end the demonstra-

tion so that the debate could be conducted, we were offered, and we accepted, the chance to have one of our number address the assembly. That task, for some reason, fell to me.

I remember my rising excitement as I stood before the audience of immaculately attired undergraduates, many of them still in their teens. There was something sweet and naive and appealing about the Political Union members as they sat nervously but politely in their tidy rows, secure (or, perhaps, momentarily insecure) in their faith that a commitment to openness and debate would lead to moral truth. But I set my face against the smile that was twitching there, and tried to work up in its stead a glower sufficient to convey the image of the retributive fury of the radical black left. (Having missed those days in college, I thought perhaps to rekindle them briefly.) And while some of the kids seemed annoyed at the intrusion, others looked frightened, even intimidated, which I suppose was our goal. I spoke briefly, pointing out that it was easy for white people to call for color-blind admissions when they understood perfectly well that none of the costs would fall on them. I carefully avoided the word *racism,* but I let the implication hang in the air anyway, lest I be misunderstood.

And then we marched out again, triumphantly, clapping and chanting rhythmically as though in solemn reminder that should the Political Union folks get up to any more nonsense, we might return and drown them out again. (A few of the undergraduates and one of the speakers joined us in our clapping.) We were, for a shining moment, in our glory; the reporters were there, tapes rolling, cameras clicking; in our minds, we had turned back the calendar by a decade and the campuses were in flames (or at least awash with megaphones and boycotts and banners and an administration ready to compromise); the school would meet us with a promise of justice or we would tear it down!

Then all at once it was over. We dispersed, returning to our dormitory rooms and apartments, our law review and moot court activities, our long nights in the library to prepare for class and our freshly cleaned suits for job interviews, our political differences and our social cliques. We returned to the humdrum interests of law school life, and suddenly we were just like everybody else again. Absolutely nothing had changed. *Bakke* was still the law of the land. There was no magic, the campus was not in flames, and there had never been a shining moment. There was only the uneasy tension of our dual existence. The peculiar uncertainty provoked by affirmative action was still with us, and our outrage at being reminded of its reality was undiminished. And as for the eager young minds of the Political Union, I suppose they held their debate and I suppose somebody won.

IV

The demonstration at the Political Union seems very long ago now, not only in time but in place: Could that really have been Yale? Could that really have been *us?* (I look around at the chanting faces in my memory and pick out their subsequent histories: this one a partner in an elite law firm, that one an investment banker, this one a leading public interest lawyer, that one another partner, this one in the State Department, that one a professor at a leading law school, this one a prosecuting attorney, that one in the legal department of a Fortune 100 corporation, and so on.) We are not the people we were then, but the fact that the debate was held over our boisterous objections seems not to have diverted our careers. We are a successful generation of lawyers, walking advertisements, it might seem, for the bright side of affirmative action. Our doubts, seen from this end of the tunnel, seem vague and insubstantial.

At the time, however, the doubts, and the anger, were painfully real. I do   39
not want to suggest that the doubts have persisted into our careers or those of other black professionals—I am as irritated as anybody else by the frequent suggestion that there lurks inside each black professional a confused and un-certain ego, desperately seeking reassurance—but it is certainly true that as long as racial preferences exist, the one thing that cannot be proved is which people of color in my generation would have achieved what they have in their absence.

At this point in the argument many of us are told, as though in reassur-   40
ance, "Oh, don't worry, you're not here because of affirmative action—you're here on merit." But it is not easy to take this as quite the compliment it is pre-sumably meant to be. In the first place, it continues the opposition of merit to preference that has brought about the pain and anger to begin with. More important, and perhaps more devastating, it places the judgment on how good we are just where we do not want it to be: in the minds and mouths of white colleagues, whose arrogant "assurances" serve as eloquent reminders of how fragile a trophy is our hard-won professional status.

Very well, perhaps we were wrong in our youthful enthusiasm to try to   41
stifle debate, but that is not the point of the story. The point, rather, is that our outrage was misdirected. Even at the time of my glowering diatribe, I real-ized that not all of what I said was fair. Looking back, I have come to under-stand even better how much of my message—our message—was driven by our pain over *Bakke* and the nation's changing mood. "Don't you under-stand?" we were crying. "We have fought hard to get here, and we will not be pushed back!"

Our anguish was not less real for being misdirected. Whether one wants   42
to blame racial preferences or white racism or the pressures of professional school or some combination of them all, our pain was too great for us to con-sider for an instant the possibility that victory in the battle to "get here" did not logically entail affirmative action. We were not prepared to discuss or even to imagine life without preferences, a world in which we would be chal-lenged to meet and beat whatever standards for admission and advancement were placed before us. We wanted no discussion at all, only capitulation. All we saw was that the Supreme Court had given us the back of its hand in *Bakke* (we even wore little buttons: FIGHT RACISM, OVERTURN BAKKE) and the forces of reaction were closing in.

Now that I am a law professor, one of my more delicate tasks is convinc-   43
ing my students, whatever their color, to consider the possibility that perhaps

the forces of reaction are *not* closing in. Perhaps what seems to them (and to many other people) a backlash against affirmative action is instead (or in addition) a signal that the programs, at least in their current expansive form, have run their course. Or perhaps, if the programs are to be preserved, they should move closer to their roots: the provision of opportunities for people of color who might not otherwise have the advanced training that will allow them to prove what they can do.

My students tend to disagree, sometimes vehemently. The bad guys are   44
out there, they tell me, and they are winning. And one of the reasons they are winning, as I understand it, is that they get to set the rules. A couple of years ago, for example, a student complained to me that people of color are forced to disguise their true voices and write like white males in order to survive the writing competition for membership on the *Yale Law Journal.* One critic has argued that university faculties employ a "hierarchical majoritarian" standard for judging academic work—a standard that is not sensitive to the special perspective people of color can bring to scholarship. And all over the corporate world, I am led to believe, the standards of what counts as merit are designed, perhaps intentionally, to keep us out.

Nowadays, racial preferences are said to be our tool for forcing those bad   45
guys—the white males who run the place, the purveyors, so I am told, of so much misery and the inheritors of so much unearned privilege—to acknowledge that theirs is only one way of looking at the world. Anyone who can't see the force of this argument is evidently a part of the problem. White people who ask whether the quest for diversity contemplates a lowering of standards of excellence are still charged with racism, just as in the old days. (The forces of reaction *are* closing in.) People of color who venture similar thoughts are labeled turncoats and worse, just as they always have been. (Don't they *know* that academic standards are a white male invention aimed at maintaining a eurocentric hegemony?) And through it all, the devotion to numbers that has long characterized the affirmative action debate continues.

Certainly the proportions of black people in the various professions are   46
nothing to shout about. In my own field of law teaching, for example, a study prepared for the Society of American Law Teachers shows that only 3.7 percent of faculty members are black at law schools that are, as the report puts it in an unfortunate bit of jargon, "majority-run." In other professions, too, although the numbers have generally improved in recent years, the percentages of black folk remain small. On medical school faculties, for example, 1.9 percent of the professors are black. On university faculties generally, just 4 percent of the faculty members are black. For lawyers and judges, the figure is 2.3 percent. For physicians, 3.3 percent. Financial managers, 4.3 percent. (And, as long as we're at it, for authors, 0.4 percent, about 1 out of 250.)

But while we might agree on the desirability of raising these numbers, the   47
question of strategy continues to divide us. To try to argue that purported racism in professional standards is not a plausible explanation for most of the data is to risk being dismissed for one's naïveté. And as to my oft-stated preference for returning to the roots of affirmative action: well, the roots, as it

turns out, had the matter all wrong. My generation, with its obsessive concern with proving itself in the white man's world, pressed an argument that was beside the point. Had we but understood the ways in which our experiences differ from those of the dominant majority, it seems, we would have insisted on an affirmative action that rewrites the standards for excellence, rather than one that trains us to meet them.

Questions

1. Why do you think recipients of affirmative action treat its benefits as a badge of shame? Do you feel ashamed when you receive preferential treatment? Why?

2. Why is Carter unashamed of the fact that he was accepted at Yale because he was black?

3. Do you agree with Carter's analogy between affirmative action and taxation?

4. How does Carter's view of affirmative action compare to Glazer's view?

Buzzword with Bite: Work Ethic

BOB BAKER

Bob Baker is a reporter for the Los Angeles Times, *and he specializes in labor relations.*

In this article, Baker explores some of the social and economic factors that have contributed to the absence of the work ethic in members of the urban ghettos. He points out that although employers insist that pride and dedication are crucial to success, some social scientists argue that the growth of minimum-wage jobs and cuts in health benefits and pensions have diminished employee loyalty and commitment to work. This selection is from the Los Angeles Times *(1992).*

Don't use my name, the businessman says. He knows he's playing with 1
loaded words and he's afraid they'll backfire.

He's a middle-aged black man who runs a downtown Los Angeles indus- 2
trial company with three dozen workers, and he can count his black employees on one hand. That's because he hires immigrants. They accept the minimum wage work and—here come the loaded words—"they have a higher work ethic."

Olivia Fernandez treads gingerly, too. Fernandez is a lecturer for the Na- 3
tional Assn. of Working Women. She visits job training classes at housing projects and pumps students full of tips about how to keep jobs once they get them: How to be prompt, assertive, cut wasted time, follow directions, set goals, take responsibility.

She is, in short, teaching the work ethic. 4

Except that Fernandez never uses those words. 5

"It's a turn-off," she says. 6

Work ethic, a phrase spoken with simple pride for generations, has become 7
another American buzzword. Like the popular Republican Party campaign slogan, "family values," it is freighted with so many social overtones, historical tensions and stereotypes that honest debate has become practically impossible.

And yet in the wake of the Los Angeles riots, that debate is inevitable. 8

Encouraging a purposefulness about work is a crucial, if abstract, part of 9
Los Angeles' recovery from the riots.

One of the prime goals of Rebuild L.A. is to create 60,000 jobs in "ne- 10
glected" communities, in addition to restoring the jobs lost in the violence.

725

In many of those neighborhoods, more than half the residents are unem-   11
ployed, due in part to the disappearance of industrial jobs during the past
two decades. Many of the jobless have grown discouraged and stopped looking for work. Some have grown dependent on a welfare system that reduces
or cuts off benefits to recipients who earn outside income. Others have entered a parallel work ethic—the drug culture—in which drug dealing and rob-
bing are commonly described as "getting paid."

In reaching out to the hard-core unemployed, traditional training must   12
be expanded to teach concepts of conscientiousness, dedication and personal
planning, job training specialists say.

"It's not only teaching them how to use a computer, it's teaching them   13
how to act in the work environment. That's a totally different culture," said
Yolanda Martinez-Weiss, a Long Beach adult school teacher who hires Olivia
Fernandez as a supplemental lecturer.

For people who have never worked, or been unemployed for years, the   14
transition to a daily job carries hidden difficulties.

"You get relaxed. You say, 'Oh, well, I can sleep to 10, I can get up when I   15
want,'" said Betty Bryant, 39, the mother of a 6-year-old son. Bryant is studying to be a pharmacy technician at a job training school, after spending the
past eight years on welfare.

However, addressing these kinds of personal adjustments inevitably raises   16
hackles because of the way *work ethic* has been bandied about.

* * *

Among minorities, there is widespread suspicion that employers who fret   17
about the loss of the work ethic are using the phrase as a sanitized way of
grousing about having to deal with people of color. Even in sports, syntax is
suspect. Traditionally, sportswriters and broadcasters have been more likely to
praise the "work ethic" of white stars, such as retired Boston Celtic Larry Bird,
while applauding black standouts for their "natural ability."

The debate transcends race.   18

U.S. business leaders, under stiff pressure from foreign competition to in-   19
crease productivity, have complained for years that the American work force
is growing more poorly educated, less able to adjust to rapid technological
change and less devoted to company goals. Many employers believe, in the
words of one industrial psychologist, that too many of these workers remain
stuck in a "psychology of entitlement" that took hold in the less competitive
1950s and '60s as the economy expanded and wages soared.

A 1987 study by a team of researchers from eight nations, who surveyed   20
nearly 15,000 workers, found that only 30% of Americans said they considered work "one of the most important things in my life," third after the
Japanese (44%) and the Yugoslavians (31%).

Some workplace analysts contend that American employers have inadver-   21
tently sabotaged the work ethic in their obsession to keep labor costs competitive. Fundamental changes in the overall economy, such as relentless
corporate "downsizing," the growth of low-paying service sector and part-
time jobs and cuts in health benefits and pensions, have diminished employee loyalty and commitment to work, they suggest.

"The real killers of the work ethic are [minimum-wage] jobs that pay less   22
than what one can live on," said Elliot Liebow, a retired anthropologist who
authored the landmark 1967 book "Tally's Corner," which chronicled the
lives of a small group of urban "streetcorner men" in Washington, focusing
on the attitudes that led poor, unemployed people to sometimes turn down
jobs.

"If you can't support yourself on the goddamned job, how can you value   23
it?" Liebow said. "And yet we think the work ethic is something *in* people,
something immutable, as though it were independent of the nature of work."

Social scientists believe that a number of forces shape a person's attitude   24
toward work. As a result, attitudes sometimes differ sharply between different
economic classes and cultures.

A detailed study of 2,490 poverty-level parents living in Chicago's inner-   25
city neighborhoods by University of Chicago sociologist William Julius Wilson and a team of colleagues, released last year, found Mexican immigrants
were more successful in seeking and keeping jobs than African-Americans because of significantly stronger home and neighborhood "networks."

Immigrants were far more likely to have family members and acquain-   26
tances who provided information about jobs and social support to assist
working parents, the study said.

The study attempted to answer one of the most popular and sensitive so-   27
cial questions in America: Why have sharp ethnic differences in "labor force
participation"—the proportion of a population working or actively looking
for work—developed since the 1960s, when the participation rate in all
groups was around 80%?

In South Los Angeles, for example, the 1990 Census found that 70% of   28
the area's 113,000 Latino men 16 or older were employed, with 9% unemployed and 18% not looking for work. By contrast, of 100,000 black men,
only 45% were working, 12% were unemployed and a staggering 42% were
not looking for work.

The Chicago study found that Mexican immigrants were better able to   29
find jobs because they could plug into a tight subculture established by a
chain of prior immigrants, some of whom came from the same villages. It
also found that the larger families of Mexican immigrants created indirect advantages in looking for work.

Ghetto blacks, meanwhile, lived in more racially segregated neighbor-   30
hoods with a much higher concentration of poor people than Mexican immigrants.

Black men were less likely than Mexican immigrants to have a close   31
friend who was employed, and twice as likely to say that most of their friends
had lost jobs due to companies moving or closing. Among working male parents, Mexican immigrants were far more likely than blacks to have found
their job through a friend.

***

The Chicago study is part of an uneasy debate among social researchers   32
about the degree to which personal responsibility versus "situational" dynamics should be blamed for problems such as joblessness.

Increasingly, however, attention is being paid to more complicated the-   33
ories.

For example, to explain high black male joblessness, sociologist Wilson   34
folds together several trends that occurred in the past two decades: the decline of manufacturing jobs, which disproportionately affected minorities;
the fact that the service industries that replaced those jobs paid significantly
less, required higher levels of education and were often located in the harder-
to-reach suburbs, and the flight of the black middle class from the inner
cities, leaving behind an isolated class of poor people without role models.

Libby Tracy, a black teen-ager who grew up in the Jordan Downs project   35
in Watts, was recently reminded how isolated his neighborhood had become
from the working world after he obtained a summer job as a counselor in a
private dropout prevention program.

"I told my homeboys I was working, and the first thing they said is: 'Are   36
they taking applications?' I bet 80 people asked me that. Ain't nobody down
here working," said Tracy, who was a street gang member until he was shot in
the leg last year. He now attends college.

Few of the people he knows read newspaper want ads because most of the   37
jobs advertised there require experience, Tracy said.

However, he said few of those people would consider taking a job at the   38
minimum wage of $4.25 an hour.

"People want something better than average," he said. "If they get $6, $7   39
an hour, they can live on that."

Immigrants are far more likely to pool their earnings from minimum-   40
wage jobs and live together in more clustered surroundings.

***

"That's how we pay the rent. We live 10 people to an apartment," said   41
Juan Gutierrez, an immigrant from Honduras who spends his days waiting
for infrequent construction work at one of several dozen Los Angeles street
corners where immigrant day laborers gather.

The black downtown business owner who hires primarily immigrants   42
said he relies heavily on his immigrant workers for leads.

"The day after you put the word out," he said, clapping his hands for em-   43
phasis, "someone is here: a brother, a nephew, a niece."

The University of Chicago study found Mexican immigrants had fewer   44
difficulties with child care because of the presence of a second adult in the
house. (Eighty-four percent of Mexican immigrant mothers lived with at least
one other adult, compared to only 29% of black mothers.) The extra adult
also made it easier for one adult to take advantage of government surplus
food giveaways or soup kitchens while the second worked, allowing minimal
incomes to be stretched further.

"In the [housing] projects, it's harder for both parents to work because   45
you have kids at home," said Tracy. "You can't leave them alone or the [so-
cial] welfare people get on you. And to begin with, you don't have many
[poor black] families with two parents."

As a result, black parents live closer to the edge than Mexican immi-   46
grants, the Chicago study said, making them "more susceptible to stressful,

income-related disruptions" and making it "harder to be a reliable employee."

Poor blacks were more likely than poor Mexican immigrants to suffer a   47
telephone or electrical disconnection due to inability to pay, more likely to
have been evicted and less likely to have a car that ran or a savings account.

The Chicago study shows that high joblessness among poor blacks "has   48
become a well-institutionalized social fact that cannot easily be swept away
with 'workfare' [requiring able-bodied welfare recipients to work] or other
programs designed to enforce a proper work ethic," university researcher
Martha Van Haitsma said. "Even the most zealous worker requires certain social supports if he is to maintain a strong attachment to the work force."

Van Haitsma emphasized that black and Mexican immigrant parents   49
looked at work from dramatically different worlds.

Immigrants were likely to be highly motivated—having possessed the   50
ambition to come here—while ghetto blacks were likely to be people who had
not been successful enough to move to better neighborhoods. Immigrants
had no welfare experience and were willing to work in minimum-wage jobs—
which paid more than they earned in Mexico—while blacks said they could
not survive on those wages.

More than 70% of black parents surveyed in the study thought that peo-   51
ple have a right to public assistance without working. Only one-third of the
Mexican immigrants thought that.

The Chicago study also surveyed 185 Chicago-area companies and found   52
that employers viewed inner-city workers—particularly black men—as unstable, uncooperative, dishonest and uneducated.

The employers, whose names were not used in the study, spoke frankly   53
and often about ethic differences.

"They're not as wired to the clock in keeping time and being on time as   54
someone else who was raised in a family where the father went to work everyday," said the owner of a construction firm about minority workers. "It's just
cultural difference."

Albert H. Yee, professor of educational psychology at Florida Interna-   55
tional University, said Americans suffer from the belief that a person's work
ethic is inherited.

"We perceive a lot of behavior in genes," Yee said. "People think, 'Why   56
are you good in math and I'm not? Your genes are better.'"

The American work ethic secularized the Protestant Reformation's view of   57
work, which held that God had called everyone to some productive vocation.
By the mid-19th Century, popular American morality held that in a hard,
stern world full of material demands, it was everyone's social duty to produce.
Even the lowest form of work was not merely virtuous but necessary to ward
off evil and idleness.

That romanticized notion of work was—and remains—at odds with Euro-   58
pean culture. After all, European folk legends describe "milk and honey Edens
free from work," writes Daniel T. Rogers, a Princeton University historian
who has studied the evolution of the American work ethic. To Europeans, "to
work was to do something wearisome and painful, scrabbling in the stubborn

soil. It was the mark of men entrapped by necessity and thus men who were not wholly free."

***

As work in America became industrialized and assembly line jobs replaced jobs that had offered independent expression, the idea that all work offered dignity became harder to maintain.   59

Allen Steinberg, a history professor at the University of Iowa, contends that American workers never bought into the notion of work as a socially redeeming activity.   60

"That idea was forced upon workers by the middle and upper classes," Steinberg said. "Workers have always been told that industrious activity would allow you to become a self-sufficient property-owning person, whether it meant owning a farm or a workshop in the 19th Century, or becoming a well-educated professional now.   61

"But that goal is not achievable by working hard at [low] wage labor and manual work. By that, all you do is get to keep your job; you don't gain independence. That's the contradiction."   62

Adds Juliet Schor, an associate professor of economics at Harvard University and author of "The Overworked American," which notes that the average working American puts in 163 more hours a year than 20 years ago: "The work ethic was transformed into an ethic of work-and-spend. The whole idea of the job became a paycheck."   63

The depersonalizing computerization of many jobs since the 1970s, combined with a tendency of many Americans to work longer hours at stagnant wages, has strengthened the contrast between work as salvation and work as alienating drudgery.   64

"Jobs for many Americans are insignificant," said Donna Schaper, pastor of a church in Riverhead, N.Y., and author of a forthcoming book, "Shelter for the Spiritually Homeless." "The anxiety about keeping jobs that don't feed our spirits is a cruel hoax. . . . That hoax is the work ethic in America today."   65

Questions

1. Why is the phrase "work ethic" freighted with so many social overtones, historical tensions, and stereotypes?

2. Why is it considered offensive when Larry Bird is praised for his "work ethic" whereas a black athlete is applauded for his "natural ability"?

3. Baker cites a statistic that shows that only thirty percent of Americans considered work "one of the most important things in my life." Why is this statistic considered a problem? Should work be the most important aspect in one's life? Why or why not?

4. According to Lieber, the work ethic is dependent upon the nature of our work: "If you can't support yourself on the goddamned job, how can you value it?" If you have ever held a minimum-wage or low-paying job, did you find it difficult to feel dedicated to your job?

Attitudes Toward Work

JOHN PAUL FIEG

John Paul Fieg (b. 1941) lived in Thailand as a Peace Corps volunteer. After returning to the United States and obtaining a law degree at George Washington University and working at the Washington International Center and the East West Center in Hawaii, he returned to Thailand where he was an English specialist at Sukhothai Thammathirat University for four years. He is currently teaching at the Pacific International Language School in Hawaii and is the author of A Common Core: Thais and Americans *(1989).*

In this selection, Fieg compares American and Thai attitudes toward work, change, ambition, and success and shows that although Thai immigrants are adapting to the American view that work and ambition are "morally good" and that individual determination is the key to success, Thais are still more inclined to attribute success or failure to forces outside the individual. This reading is from A Common Core.

Work and Play

The idea that work per se is morally good and that there is a direct relation- 1
ship between hard work and success—the cornerstone of what came to be known as the Puritan, the Protestant, or simply, the work ethic—has left an indelible imprint on the American psyche. Since the ethic endures today, long after the passing of the Puritan colonists, and has in its grip Catholic and Jewish Americans as well as Protestants, it will be referred to here as simply the work ethic. By whatever name, the ethic taught (and experience seemed to bear out) that hard work had its rewards in the U.S. The American worker gained a reputation for immense productivity based on discipline, determination, and long hours of unremitting toil.

Though there is talk now of a changing work ethic in the sense that many 2
workers appear more concerned with security, job satisfaction, shorter work weeks, and a generally looser rein while on the job, the fact remains that most Americans still look with disfavor on the idle person, the loafer, the one who wastes time on anything but a steady job. Time for work has traditionally been viewed as separate from time for recreation or fun. Work is what one does to earn a living. It is supposed to be satisfying in itself. Physical

731

labor is a positive value in the American lexicon and work provides the framework in which one pursues achievements. It is not necessarily supposed to be fun, that is, pursued as play, nor is it to be confused with leisure, which is something that provides relief from the pressures and constrictions of work. Life to the American, then, is essentially compartmentalized. There is a time for hard, hopefully satisfying, but not necessarily enjoyable, work followed by time for relaxation. Americans even speak of a person's social life as if it were a separate life from the life lived on the job.

Thais do not look at work or life in this way. The lofty place that work occupies in the mental priority list of most Americans would be substituted by most Thais with *sanùke* (fun, enjoyment, having a good time). Just as Americans tend to view work per se as a good thing, so Thais generally regard sanùke per se as a good thing. This seems almost heretical to the average American, raised in a culture where play is viewed as an escape from reality and having fun is seen as a normal, necessary, but temporary retreat from adult responsibility. 3

From the Thai standpoint, however, if something is not sanùke, it is scarcely worth doing. Unlike the compartmentalized approach of Americans, Thais have more of an expectation that all of their activities will be suffused with sanùke. Work, study, and even religious services must have at least an element of sanùke if they are to absorb a Thai's interest; in fact, one of the reasons why there have been so few Thai converts to Christianity has undoubtedly been the failure of the missionaries to make their religion appear more sanùke. 4

Thais particularly enjoy sanùke activities which are novel and diverting. In the past there was a tendency to plunge energetically into new activities, tasks or projects which were fun, but then to lose interest when the novelty wore off, leaving the project unfinished. This is less true today when both city dwellers and farmers work long and hard at tasks which further the economic development of their country. Nevertheless, Thais still like to punctuate their work or introduce into it, more frequently than Americans, activities that are designed purely for the enjoyment they provide, transforming the task from work to fun. 5

One representative of an American foundation which supports Thai projects noted that often he calls on Thai organizations and government offices to explain the work of his foundation. He is frequently asked by Thais why he does this kind of work. "I go into a serious discussion about objectives, etc.," says the American, "but then I tell them I do this kind of work because I like it, because it's sanùke, and they understand right away." 6

Western-trained Thai technocrats might demur to the above characterization of what might be termed the "traditional" (predominantly rural) Thai approach to work and fun. Schooled in the rigors of modern business practices, they may have internalized Western values to such an extent that they can rightly say that their approach more closely parallels the American model than it does the traditional Thai pattern. 7

Change

Change may well be the only constant in American society. Lacking deep-rooted traditions, Americans feel comfortable with change, thrive on change, and almost feel that it is a civic, if not moral, duty to bring change about more or less continuously. This attitude of necessity implies a certain dissatisfaction with things as they are, for if one were content with the status quo, there would obviously be no need to change it. Like the work ethic, this notion of change stems in part from the Puritan view that evil which exists in the world must be rooted out.

Americans have thus long felt a sense of mission not only to renew and perfect their own society but also to serve as a model for all mankind. Originally this took the more passive form of the Puritan "City on a Hill" (American society), whose exemplary light was to shine out for all to see. Over the course of the nation's history, the sense of mission took on a more active character as Americans, not content simply to light up their own hill, felt compelled to transport the light overseas so that none could miss it. Though no doubt based on good intentions, this attempt to impose their perspectives on others led to charges that the United States was attempting to impose its way of life on the rest of the world.

Though secular in nature, such enterprises as foreign aid, the Peace Corps, and numerous other American institutions of diplomacy and foreign relations are deeply rooted in the idea that the United States has a special mission in the world. The impact of this more generalized, secular missionary zeal, whose message is simply "the American way," has been far greater than that of the original religious doctrine from which it sprang.

Embodied in the whole notion is the idea that human beings must improve their lot by instigating change; this in turn conforms to the American view of nature described earlier, in which humans are the masters of their environment and can alter it to suit their needs. Americans speak highly of "change agents" working to bring about meaningful change, clearly indicating that it is up to the individual to take an active role in modifying the status quo. Consequently, Americans tend to look despairingly and somewhat patronizingly on more traditional societies (often referring to them as "hidebound"), which seem either unwilling or unable to change.

Like Americans, Thais do believe in change, but they have never felt the same compulsion as Americans to bring it about. Their concept of change and a person's role in it differ in a fundamental way from the American view. For in the Buddhist sense, change is the most certain thing of all; it is what existence is all about—constant cycles of *ùbàt* (birth, beginning, springing up) and *wíbàt* (death, ending, passing away). Since change is so all-pervasive, it would be presumptuous, foolish, and certainly futile for humans to interject themselves in an active way into this process.

The point is that everything is going to change by itself—government, companies, mundane problems are going to come and go. Instead of worrying about how and when these changes are going to occur, it's better to simply keep one's emotions under control, restrain one's concern over life's vicissitudes, and try to develop the wisdom to see how transitory all things really are. Eschewing the American's active approach to change, Thais would agree fervently with Milton: "They also serve who only stand and wait."

This point of view is not congenial to the American mentality, for Americans tend not to look at things in this long-range manner. Based on their experiences, Americans believe that by bringing about change, they can help improve the human condition, at least in a material sense, and that they can do it now. Because they have conquered many formerly deadly diseases, have improved sanitary conditions and medical treatment, and have pioneered the development of numerous beneficial consumer goods, Americans can argue forcefully that more people are living longer and more comfortably than in the past. This is good; let's keep trying to improve things even more. 14

Thais might counter that no matter how much you change things, no matter how many diseases are wiped out, no matter how pure the water and how clean the air, fundamental facts of existence will remain. Mankind will still suffer, grow old, and die. From the American perspective, this Thai view seems defeatist or at best fatalistic. From the Thai perspective, the American position looks rash and futile. 15

Who is right? In a sense, both are. It is just that the American view, shaped by the belief that a person has only one go-around on this earth, tends to be more short-range. The Thai idea, influenced by the cyclical Buddhist concept of existence, is much longer-range. 16

This is not to say that human-initiated change never occurs in Thailand, for in fact throughout its history Thailand has been generally receptive to change. Within the broad, long-range conceptual framework outlined above, there have generally been ruling elites or Western-influenced professionals, who—like Americans—strove to better certain aspects of the status quo. Here it might be said that Thai pragmatism as well as a penchant for present comfort took precedence over the abstract Buddhist doctrine. Thais have thus tended to borrow elements from other societies, modifying them if necessary to fit smoothly into the Thai cultural mosaic. 17

In recent years there has been considerable change in Thailand. New, modern skyscrapers in Bangkok, like those of the Bangkok Bank, the Thai Farmer's Bank and others, symbolize these changes and indicate that Thailand is adapting to the styles and practices of contemporary international business. One observer comments, "Politically, Thailand has advanced more in the past ten years than any other country in the region. The development of the institution of representative government and the mechanics and channels for the preservation of basic individual freedoms (such as the media and ad hoc protest groups) have all been significant." The Royal Thai government's five-year national development plan charts the course of change and growth in Thailand. 18

But while significant changes are taking place in Thailand today, Americans and Thais may have different approaches to change in the workplace. One major reason is that change often brings out underlying conflict, which 19

Thais much prefer to avoid. Thais, responding on the basis of deeply in-grained, culturally based attitudes, are much more likely to prefer retaining the status quo than to go through the painful, soul-searching process of iden-tifying problems and placing blame for things that require change. Another major reason for preserving the status quo is the wish to avoid inconvenienc-ing another person with the change and, perhaps, inciting anger and possible retribution.

"People are more important than anything," said one Thai personnel offi-   20
cer whose American company has recently had to lay employees off in re-sponse to difficult economic times. "Very seldom would a Thai organization lay a lot of people off. Thais feel that they can't trust American organizations because they don't offer complete job security." On the other hand, Thais consider working for an American company to be good experience. "I like it," said a Thai. "It means there are always new opportunities to achieve new things."

One American businessman in Thailand notes that Thais are willing to   21
accept change in an organization but, like their American counterparts, they like to have the reasons for it spelled out. They also appreciate a chance to give feedback on the proposed change. However, an American boss who says, "Tell me what you think; my door is always open," won't get much response. Some alternative method for seeking reaction must be found, such as nomi-nating one member of the staff to collect comments or requesting that the staff comment through a group memo where no one person is responsible for any opinion expressed.

Thais themselves are not likely to initiate change in a work situation.   22
They are taught by their culture and their educational training, which em-phasize rote learning and deference to seniors, not to challenge the system that is in place. But there are ways to get them to participate in organizational development, or the change process. As an experiment, one American execu-tive organized a brainstorming day for all staff and was amazed at the num-ber of sound, creative ideas that came out of it. He had always thought that his Thai staff members, being quiet and reserved, did not think much about the company's operations. He was delighted to find that when encouraged to speak up in a nonthreatening setting, they were full of ideas.

Ambition

Americans have tended to view ambition in a generally positive light; it is   23
something a person should have in order to be successful in life. Underlying this concept of ambition is the assumption that personal achievement is largely a matter of individual determination. One will be rewarded if only one works hard enough. "Where there's a will, there's a way." Americans cite numerous instances of poor children, sometimes unable to speak English, who have risen to great heights as business tycoons, political leaders, scien-tists, entertainers, or athletes largely because of their own hard work and de-termination. This notion that one can literally go from "rags to riches,"

popularized in the Horatio Alger stories, has inspired many an American to put in prodigious amounts of time and effort in an attempt to improve his or her lot in life.

Since achievement obviously requires an all-out effort, Americans place a great emphasis on being active, keeping busy, and above all "doing" something. It is the person who performs visible deeds rather than the contemplative intellectual who is accorded high prestige in American society. Inventors are more praised than poets; doctors of medicine outrank doctors of philosophy. This "doing" orientation in American life is reflected in numerous colloquial expressions: "How're you *doing*?" "What do you *do* for a living?" "What do you want to *do* when you grow up?" One should be active, energetic, and steadfast in pursuit of a distant goal. 24

The traditional Thai view of ambition has been considerably lower key. Central to the Thai attitude is the idea of *karma,* which might be thought of as the sum total of merit and demerit that a person has inherited from a previous life and the store of rewards and punishments which accordingly must be enjoyed or endured in this life. 25

There is clearly an element of predestination here, for as one has sown in one's past life, so will one reap in this life. Thai parents consequently tend not to encourage their children to be ambitious or pressure them to achieve. If they are destined to arrive at some position—say, to become prime minister—it will simply happen. This does not mean that a person should be totally passive and fatalistic since appropriate action is called for to ensure a satisfactory position in one's next life. But given the many lifetimes one has in which to work out one's religious destiny, achievement in this life does not loom as large in the total picture of existence as it does for an American who views this life as a single journey. 26

Since Buddhism teaches that a craving for power and prestige will only bring suffering or unhappiness, one who manifests a strong ambition to attain these goals has traditionally been looked at with disapproval by Thai society, for that person is perceived as being solely interested in worldly goods. This does not mean, however, that Thais don't take advantage of opportunities that present themselves; they would attribute it to a good karma and make the most of it. 27

Apart from Buddhist undergirding, which has tended to diminish overt manifestations of ambition, the Thai temperament itself, inclined to sanùke more than to striving, has played its part in restraining obsession with achievement. Thus, relatively easy work with adequate pay has generally been preferable to hard work with higher pay. And the best combination of all, from the standpoint of many Thais, would be an easy job and good pay. For hand in hand with a preference for sanùke goes a corresponding desire to be *sabaaj* (comfortable, untroubled). 28

Many Thais are therefore surprised and not a little amused when Americans either can't get a job because they are overqualified or else take a job for which they are overqualified and then complain that the work isn't challenging enough. Such a solution would seem ideal to many a Thai, since in work- 29

ing at less than full capacity—perhaps one step below their actual ability—
Thais would feel more at ease or sabaaj than in a more demanding job where
they felt pressured to perform up to their supposed full potential. (Interestingly, if Americans followed this pattern, they would never have to worry
about the "Peter Principle," for no one would ever reach his or her own level
of incompetence!)

The usual caveat must be added that the above description does not fully   30
apply to Westernized Bangkokians, who tend to share with Americans a preference for a demanding, prestigious position. As one young, enterprising Thai
professional pointed out, the Thai expression, "Don't set your ambitions beyond your station," was coined no doubt by some high-ranking noble who
clearly had a vested interest in seeing that those below him in the hierarchy
adhered to it. But this young professional and other Western-trained Thais
want to use the skills they have acquired abroad and appear willing to sacrifice some "sabaaj-ness" to tackle demanding jobs which will allow them to
live up to their potential. It will be interesting to see what new pattern may
emerge as sanùke and sabaaj link up with the work ethic and Theravada Buddhism tries to accommodate Horatio Alger.

Inherent in American concepts of individualism and ambition is a con-   31
stant struggling or striving to improve one's position or, as we said earlier, to
carve out one's niche or station in life. Since achievement is viewed as largely
a matter of individual effort and since status is determined chiefly by how
successful one is in this individualistic pursuit, the motivating factor of competition is a strong stimulant to goad the American ever upward. For it is
through competition that the best rise to the top, and achievement where
competition is lacking—whether it be in the political, economic, or athletic
realm—is looked on with mingled distrust and disdain by most Americans.

Thus, Americans are generally hostile to one-party or individual rule of   32
any kind. They have set up elaborate antitrust laws to ensure competition in
business and pay the ultimate tribute to an athlete by calling that person a
good competitor. While this competitive cast to American society is viewed as
ruthless by some outsiders, most Americans accept and even thrive in such an
atmosphere; even those bested in the competition give at least grudging respect to those who ultimately win out and are stimulated to try that much
harder the next time.

Although, as we have commented before, Thais share certain individual-   33
istic tendencies with Americans, the hierarchical nature of their social order—
based as it is on deference to rank—combined with the generally restrained
approach to ambition and achievement have served to preclude competition
as a significant motivating force. In addition Buddhism supposedly teaches
that craving for wealth and power will only bring unhappiness. What then
motivates a Thai to engage in hard work, particularly in the private sector,
where, as noted earlier, the titles and prestige associated with government
service have been unavailable?

Here we quite simply run into a discrepancy between what one would   34
expect a Thai to do based on a literal reading of Buddhist scripture (i.e.,

renounce worldly goods) and what is actually happening in contemporary Thai (especially urban) society, where it is difficult to detect any significant deficiency in materialistic drive. This should not be particularly surprising, for a clear parallel could be drawn to American society. If someone who had never been to the United States looked on the Bible as predictive of American behavior, he would no doubt have some trouble if, on coming to the United States, he tried to reconcile the obvious materialism he saw all around him with the Sermon on the Mount.

A Thai may be a Buddhist, but he is also a pragmatist, a realist, and a   35
seeker of present enjoyment rather than other-worldly bliss. While the over-all influence of Buddhist thought on Thai society can hardly be overemphasized, it is clear that some of the traditional practices of the religion do not mesh well with a modern, urban, materialistic way of life.

But what would induce a Thai to work for an American company as op-   36
posed to a Thai company or the Thai government, where the prestige assumedly would be greater? Given the materialistic strain in Thai society, it should not come as a complete surprise that the chief motivating factor is money, for Thais can earn considerably more working for an American company than they could for either a Thai company or the Thai government. But there are several other important reasons as well. First, they view working with an American company as the best way to learn the latest techniques and procedures in the field. Second, they consider the American management system to be streamlined, efficient, and effective, which has its attractions despite the cross-cultural adjustment that may be called for in working within it. Third, there is usually a good program of overseas training. Fourth, they appreciate the fact that promotion will be forthcoming, if earned, and will not depend on flattering the boss. Additional positive features of working for an American company include modern office facilities (furniture, machines, telephones, etc.), good employee benefits, and the chance to practice English.

It sounds good so far, but there are two serious drawbacks, chief of which is a lack of security. Despite the advantages listed above, there is always the   37
nagging fear that they may be laid off or even fired if market conditions or their performance so warrants. In this respect, American efficiency, which they generally appreciate, appears rather heartless, and they fear the harsh suddenness with which the axe might fall. The other drawback is a belief that some American companies reserve top-level jobs for American expatriate staff—hardly conducive to good employee morale and motivation.

Taking Risks and Failure

Risk-taking on the part of Americans is based on well-established precedent: 38
their forebears gave up everything they had in Europe (which admittedly in many cases wasn't much), gambled their lives on a dangerous ocean voyage, and then often risked everything again by moving from settled communities to face the uncertainties of life on the frontier. "Nothing ventured, nothing gained" became the watchword, and whether it was panning for gold in Cali-

fornia, plunging heavily into the stock market, or venturing a final dollar to set up one's own business, the American historically has been willing and even eager to risk it all on one turn of the wheel.

Though the abandon of decades past has to a certain extent given way to an ever increasing concern for financial security—for the steady return rather than the dramatic windfall—simple statistics on mobility and new business start-ups indicate that vast numbers of Americans are still ready to set off for greener pastures at the drop of a well-placed suggestion. 39

The vastness of the land and the opulence of its resources have reinforced the American's belief that the limits to achievement are found only within the individual. If one tries hard enough, one will ultimately succeed. Failure will generally not be attributed to a lack of resources, the government, fate or other external causes. It will most often be attributed to lack of effort, skill, persistence or whatever on the part of the individual. Success and failure, defined as they are in such intensely personal terms, can lead to considerable ego inflation for those who make it and a corresponding deflation for those who don't. 40

Thais tend not to view life in such all-or-nothing terms. Traditionally more concerned with comfort and security than all-out individual achievement, Thais have not generally been bold risk-takers. Since government positions offered both comfort and security as well as the coveted titles, Thais have been content to blend smoothly into the benign bureaucracy rather than strain and struggle to get ahead in the competitive business environment. 41

Apart from its failure to provide titled positions, business has generally not been in tune with the Thai temperament. One outspoken Thai quickly catalogued five reasons why this is so: (1) Thais don't like to take the risks which business requires; (2) Thais are relatively easily satisfied and see no reason to struggle to get more; (3) business involves being under pressure, which is not particularly appealing; and (4) Thais don't like to cheat others (apparently an unfortunate *sine qua non* for doing business in the eyes of many Thais). 42

Having said this, we should point out that many, many Thais have had successful careers in business—from banking, to real estate, cattle ranching, poultry farming and orchid raising—on a high-powered international scale. Hundreds of Thais study business in the United States, and Thailand's ethnic Chinese citizens contribute a great deal of business expertise to the country. As Thailand develops, so does the size and sophistication of Thailand's businesses. 43

The Thai word for a person who is a failure (*khon lóm lĕw*) conveys considerably less stigma than does the corresponding English word. There is more of a tendency, both on the part of the society and the individual, to attribute that unhappy state to outside forces, such as fate, demerit from a past life, or simple lack of inherited capacity, for which one is in no way at fault. Though from the individual's standpoint there might be an element of human rationalization involved as well, the fact remains that a Thai would probably not go through the same painful introspection as would an American similarly situated. 44

There are signs, however, that traditional Thai attitudes toward govern-   45
ment service and business are changing, perhaps significantly, and that the
former is no longer viewed in the wholly positive light it once was. Ambitious, materialistic, and willing to take risks, a growing number of well-educated urban Thais are challenging some long-held cultural values concerning
work, comfort and prestige. Call it Western, modern, or simply pragmatic,
this drive to achieve will no doubt further the development of Bangkok along
the lines of the industrialized West. It may also further widen the gap between residents of the island-like capital and their more traditional up-coun-
try kinsmen.

Questions

1. Why would the Thai concept of *sanùke* seem heretical to the average American?
    Why do we draw a line between work and fun?

2. Do you feel guilty or lazy if you are not working or productive in some way? Ex-
    plain how this is a cultural attitude. If your primary culture is not American, de-
    scribe how your attitude toward work may be different.

3. Compare the American and Thai attitudes toward change and ambition. With
    which do you agree?

4. Fieg gives two examples of adages that typify American attitudes ("Nothing ven-
    tured, nothing gained"; "Where there's a will, there's a way"). Think of some
    other common maxims. How do they reflect the American mentality?

An Interview with C. P. Ellis

STUDS TERKEL

Studs Terkel (b. 1912) has written several collections of oral histories, among them Working *(1974),* The Good War *(1974), and* American Dreams: Lost and Found *(1980).*

In this interview, an ex-president of the Ku Klux Klan explains to Terkel that he joined the organization because he "had to hate somebody." However, after working on an interracial committee to solve racial problems in the school system, he is "born again," and has now come to believe that poor blacks and whites have a common enemy—upper-class whites. This selection is from American Dreams.

We're in his office in Durham, North Carolina. He is the business manager of the 1 *International Union of Operating Engineers. On the wall is a plaque: "Certificate of Service, in recognition to C.P. Ellis, for your faithful service to the city in having served as a member of the Durham Human Relations Council. February 1977."*

At one time, he had been president (exalted cyclops) of the Durham chapter of 2 *the Ku Klux Klan.*

He is fifty-three years old. 3

My father worked in a textile mill in Durham. He died at forty-eight years 4 old. It was probably from cotton dust. Back then, we never heard of brown lung. I was about seventeen years old and had a mother and sister depending on somebody to make a livin'. It was just barely enough insurance to cover his burial. I had to quit school and go to work. I was about eighth grade when I quit.

My father worked hard but never had enough money to buy decent 5 clothes. When I went to school, I never seemed to have adequate clothes to wear. I always left school late afternoon with a sense of inferiority. The other kids had nice clothes, and I just had what Daddy could buy. I still got some of those inferiority feelin's now that I have to overcome once in a while.

I loved my father. He would go with me to ball games. We'd go fishin' to- 6 gether. I was really ashamed of the way he'd dress. He would take this money and give it to me instead of putting it on himself. I always had the feeling about somebody looking at him and makin' fun of him and makin' fun of me. I think it had to do somethin' with my life.

My father and I were very close, but we didn't talk about too many inti-   7
mate things. He did have a drinking problem. During the week, he would work every day, but weekend he was ready to get plastered. I can understand when a guy looks at his paycheck and looks at his bills, and he's worked hard all the week, and his bills are larger than his paycheck. He'd done the best he could the entire week, and there seemed to be no hope. It's an illness thing. Finally you just say: "The heck with it. I'll just get drunk and forget it."

My father was out of work during the depression, and I remember going   8
with him to the finance company uptown, and he was turned down. That's something that's always stuck.

My father never seemed to be happy. It was a constant struggle with him   9
just like it was for me. It's very seldom I'd see him laugh. He was just tryin' to figure out what he could do from one day to the next.

After several years pumping gas at a service station, I got married. We had   10
to have children. Four. One child was born blind and retarded, which was a real additional expense to us. He's never spoken a word. He doesn't know me when I go to see him. But I see him, I hug his neck. I talk to him, tell him I love him. I don't know whether he knows me or not, but I know he's well taken care of. All my life, I had work, never a day without work, worked all the overtime I could get and still could not survive financially. I began to say there's somethin' wrong with this country. I worked my butt off and just never seemed to break even.

I had some real great ideas about this great nation. (Laughs.) They say to   11
abide by the law, go to church, do right and live for the Lord, and every-thing'll work out. But it didn't work out. It just kept gettin' worse and worse.

I was workin' a bread route. The highest I made one week was seventy-five dollars. The rent on our house was about twelve dollars a week. I will   12
never forget: outside of this house was a 265-gallon oil drum, and I never did get enough money to fill up that oil drum. What I would do every night, I would run up to the store and buy five gallons of oil and climb up the ladder and pour it in that 265-gallon drum. I could hear that five gallons when it hits the bottom of that oil drum, splatters, and it sounds like it's nothin' in there. But it would keep the house warm for the night. Next day you'd have to do the same thing.

I left the bread route with fifty dollars in my pocket. I went to the bank   13
and I borrowed four thousand dollars to buy the service station. I worked seven day a week, open and close, and finally had a heart attack. Just about two months before the last payments of that loan. My wife had done the best she could to keep it runnin'. Tryin' to come out of that hole, I just couldn't do it.

I really began to get bitter. I didn't know who to blame. I tried to find   14
somebody. I began to blame it on black people. I had to hate somebody.

Hatin' America is hard to do because you can't see it to hate it. You gotta have somethin' to look at to hate. (Laughs.) The natural person for me to hate would be black people, because my father before me was a member of the Klan. As far as he was concerned, it was the savior of the white people. It was the only organization in the world that would take care of the white people. So I began to admire the Klan.

I got active in the Klan while I was at the service station. Every Monday 15 night, a group of men would come by and buy a Coca-Cola, go back to the car, take a few drinks, and come back and stand around talkin'. I couldn't help but wonder: Why are these dudes comin' out every Monday? They said they were with the Klan and have meetings close-by. Would I be interested? Boy, that was an opportunity I really looked forward to! To be part of somethin'. I joined the Klan, went from member to chaplain, from chaplain to vice-president, from vice-president to president. The title is exalted cyclops.

The first night I went with the fellas, they knocked on the door and gave 16 the signal. They sent some robed Klansmen to talk to me and give me some instructions. I was led into a large meeting room, and this was the time of my life! It was thrilling. Here's a guy who's worked all his life and struggled all his life to be something, and here's the moment to be something. I will never forget it. Four robed Klansmen led me into the hall. The lights were dim, and the only thing you could see was an illuminated cross. I knelt before the cross. I had to make certain vows and promises. We promised to uphold the purity of the white race, fight communism, and protect white womanhood.

After I had taken my oath, there was loud applause goin' throughout the 17 buildin', musta been at least four hundred people. For this one little ol' person. It was a thrilling moment for C.P. Ellis.

It disturbs me when people who do not really know what it's all about are 18 so very critical of individual Klansmen. The majority of 'em are low-income whites, people who really don't have a part in something. They have been shut out as well as the blacks. Some are not very well educated either. Just like myself. We had a lot of support from doctors and lawyers and police officers.

Maybe they've had bitter experiences in this life and they had to hate 19 somebody. So the natural person to hate would be the black person. He's beginnin' to come up, he's beginnin' to learn to read and start votin' and run for political office. Here are white people who are supposed to be superior to them, and we're shut out.

I can understand why people join extreme right-wing or left-wing groups. 20 They're in the same boat I was. Shut out. Deep down inside, we want to be part of this great society. Nobody listens, so we join these groups.

At one time, I was state organizer of the National Rights party. I organized 21 a youth group for the Klan. I felt we were getting old and our generation's gonna die. So I contacted certain kids in schools. They were havin' racial problems. On the first night, we had a hundred high school students. When they came in the door, we had "Dixie" playin'. These kids were just thrilled to death. I begin to hold weekly meetin's with 'em, teachin' the principles of the

Klan. At that time, I believed Martin Luther King had Communist connections. I began to teach that Andy Young was affiliated with the Communist party.

I had a call one night from one of our kids. He was about twelve. He said: "I just been robbed downtown by two niggers." I'd had a couple of drinks and that really teed me off. I go downtown and couldn't find the kid. I got worried. I saw two young black people. I had the .32 revolver with me. I said: "Nigger, you seen a little young white boy up here? I just got a call from him and was told that some niggers robbed him of fifteen cents." I pulled my pistol out and put it right at his head. I said: "I've always wanted to kill a nigger and I think I'll make you the first one." I nearly scared the kid to death, and he struck off. 22

This was the time when the civil rights movement was really beginnin' to peak. The blacks were beginnin' to demonstrate and picket downtown stores. I never will forget some black lady I hated with a purple passion. Ann Atwater. Every time I'd go downtown, she'd be leadin' a boycott. How I hated—pardon the expression, I don't use it much now—how I just hated that black nigger. (Laughs.) Big, fat, heavy woman. She'd pull about eight demonstrations, and first thing you know they had two, three blacks at the checkout counter. Her and I have had some pretty close confrontations. 23

I felt very big, yeah. (Laughs.) We're more or less a secret organization. We didn't want anybody to know who we were, and I began to do some thinkin'. What am I hidin' for? I've never been convicted of anything in my life. I don't have any court record. What am I, C.P. Ellis, as a citizen and a member of the United Klansmen of America? Why can't I go to the city council meeting and say: "This is the way we feel about the matter? We don't want you to purchase mobile units to set in our schoolyards. We don't want niggers in our schools." 24

We began to come out in the open. We would go to the meetings, and the blacks would be there and we'd be there. It was a confrontation every time. I didn't hold back anything. We began to make some inroads with the city councilmen and county commissioners. They began to call us friend. Call us at night on the telephone: "C.P., glad you came to that meeting last night." They didn't want integration either, but they did it secretively, in order to get elected. They couldn't stand up openly and say it, but they were glad somebody was sayin' it. We visited some of the city leaders in their home and talk to 'em privately. It wasn't long before councilmen would call me up: "The blacks are comin' up tonight and makin' outrageous demands. How about some of you people showin' up and have a little balance?" I'd get on the telephone: "The niggers is comin' to the council meeting tonight. Persons in the city's called me and asked us to be there." 25

We'd load up our cars and we'd fill up half the council chambers, and the blacks the other half. During these times, I carried weapons to the meetings, outside my belt. We'd go there armed. We would wind up just hollerin' and fussin' at each other. What happened? As a result of our fightin' one another, 26 the city council still had their way. They didn't want to give up control to the blacks nor the Klan. They were usin' us.

I began to realize this later down the road. One day I was walkin' down- 27
town and a certain city council member saw me comin'. I expected him to shake my hand because he was talkin' to me at night on the telephone. I had been in his home and visited with him. He crossed the street. Oh shit, I began to think, somethin's wrong here. Most of 'em are merchants or maybe an attorney, an insurance agent, people like that. As long as they kept low-income whites and low-income blacks fightin', they're gonna maintain control.

I began to get that feeling after I was ignored in public. I thought: Bull- 28
shit, you're not gonna use me any more. That's when I began to do some real serious thinkin'.

The same things is happening in this country today. People are being 29
used by those in control, those who have all the wealth. I'm not espousing communism. We got the greatest system of government in the world. But those who have it simply don't want those who don't have it to have any part of it. Black and white. When it comes to money, the green, the other colors make no difference. (Laughs.)

I spent a lot of sleepless nights. I still didn't like blacks. I didn't want to 30
associate with 'em. Blacks, Jews, or Catholics. My father said: "Don't have anything to do with 'em." I didn't until I met a black person and talked with him, eyeball to eyeball, and met a Jewish person and talked to him, eyeball to eyeball. I found out they're people just like me. They cried, they cussed, they prayed, they had desires. Just like myself. Thank God, I got to the point where I can look past labels. But at that time, my mind was closed.

I remember one Monday night Klan meeting. I said something was wrong. 31
Our city fathers were using us. And I didn't like to be used. The reactions of the others was not too pleasant: "Let's just keep fightin' them niggers."

I'd go home at night and I'd have to wrestle with myself. I'd look at a 32
black person walkin' down the street, and the guy'd have ragged shoes or his clothes would be worn. That began to do somethin' to me inside. I went through this for about six months. I felt I just had to get out of the Klan. But I wouldn't get out.

Then something happened. The state AFL-CIO received a grant from the 33
Department of HEW, a $78,000 grant: how to solve racial problems in the school system. I got a telephone call from the president of the state AFL-CIO. "We'd like to get some people together from all walks of life." I said: "All walks of life? Who you talkin' about?" He said: "Blacks, whites, liberals, conservatives, Klansmen, NAACP people."

I said: "No way am I comin' with all those niggers. I'm not gonna be asso- 34
ciated with those type of people." A White Citizens Council guy said: "Let's go up there and see what's goin' on. It's tax money bein' spent." I walk in the door, and there was a large number of blacks and white liberals. I knew most of 'em by face 'cause I seen 'em demonstratin' around town. Ann Atwater was there. (Laughs.) I just forced myself to go in and sit down.

The meeting was moderated by a great big black guy who was bushy- 35
headed. (Laughs.) That turned me off. He acted very nice. He said: "I want
you all to feel free to say anything you want to say." Some of the blacks stand
up and say it's white racism. I took all I could take. I asked for the floor and I
cut loose. I said: "No, sir, it's black racism. If we didn't have niggers in the
schools, we wouldn't have the problems we got today."

I will never forget. Howard Clements, a black guy, stood up. He said: "I'm 36
certainly glad C.P. Ellis come because he's the most honest man here
tonight." I said: "What's that nigger tryin' to do?" (Laughs.) At the end of
that meeting, some blacks tried to come up shake my hand, but I wouldn't do
it. I walked off.

Second night, same group was there. I felt a little more easy because I got 37
some things off my chest. The third night, after they elected all the committees, they want to elect a chairman. Howard Clements stood up and said: "I
suggest we elect two co-chairpersons." Joe Beckton, executive director of the
Human Relations Commission, just as black as he can be, he nominated me.
There was a reaction from some blacks. Nooo. And, of all things, they nominated Ann Atwater, that big old fat black gal that I had just hated with a purple
passion, as co-chairman. I thought to myself: Hey, ain't no way I can work with
that gal. Finally, I agreed to accept it, 'cause at this point, I was tired of fightin',
either for survival or against black people or against Jews or against Catholics.

A Klansman and a militant black woman, co-chairmen of the school com- 38
mittee. It was impossible. How could I work with her? But after about two or
three days, it was in our hands. We had to make it a success. This give me another sense of belongin', a sense of pride. This helped this inferiority feelin' I
had. A man who has stood up publicly and said he despised black people, all of
a sudden he was willin' to work with 'em. Here's a chance for a low-income
white man to be somethin'. In spite of all my hatred for blacks and Jews and
liberals, I accepted the job. Her and I began to reluctantly work together.
(Laughs.) She had as many problems workin' with me as I had workin' with her.

One night, I called her: "Ann, you and I should have a lot of differences 39
and we got 'em now. But there's somethin' laid out here before us, and if it's
gonna be a success, you and I are gonna have to make it one. Can we lay aside
some of these feelin's?" She said: "I'm willing if you are." I said: "Let's do it."

My old friends would call me at night: "C.P., what the hell is wrong with 40
you? You're sellin' out the white race." This begin to make me have guilt
feelin's. Am I doin' right? Am I doin' wrong? Here I am all of a sudden makin'
an about-face and tryin' to deal with my feelin's, my heart. My mind was beginnin' to open up. I was beginnin' to see what was right and what was
wrong. I don't want the kids to fight forever.

We were gonna go ten nights. By this time, I had went to work at Duke 41
University, in maintenance. Makin' very little money. Terry Sanford give me
this ten days off with pay. He was president of Duke at the time. He knew I was
a Klansman and realized the importance of blacks and whites getting along.

I said: "If we're gonna make this thing a success, I've got to get to my kind 42
of people." The low-income whites. We walked the streets of Durham, and we

knocked on doors and invited people. Ann was goin' into the black community. They just wasn't respondin' to us when we made these house calls. Some of 'em were cussin' us out. "You'r sellin' us out, Ellis, get out of my door. I don't want to talk to you." Ann was gettin' the same response from blacks: "What are you doin' messin' with that Klansman?"

One day, Ann and I went back to the school and we sat down. We began 43 to talk and just reflect. Ann said: "My daughter came home cryin' every day. She said her teacher was makin' fun of me in front of the other kids." I said: "Boy, the same thing happened to my kid. White liberal teacher was makin' fun of Tim Ellis's father, the Klansman. In front of other peoples. He came home cryin'." At this point—(he pauses, swallows hard, stifles a sob)—I begin to see, here we are, two people from the far ends of the fence, havin' identical problems, except hers bein' black and me bein' white. From that moment on, I tell ya, that gal and I worked together good. I begin to love the girl, really. (He weeps.)

The amazing thing about it, her and I, up to that point, had cussed each 44 other, bawled each other. We didn't know we had things in common.

We worked at it, with the people who came to these meetings. They 45 talked about racism, sex education, about teachers not bein' qualified. After seven, eight nights of real intense discussion, these people, who'd never talked to each other before, all of a sudden came up with resolutions. It was really somethin', you had to be there to get the tone and feelin' of it.

At that point, I didn't like integration, but the law says you do this and 46 I've got to do what the law says, okay? We said: "Let's take these resolutions to the school board." The most disheartening thing I've ever faced was the school system refused to implement any one of these resolutions. These were recommendations from the people who pay taxes and pay their salaries. (Laughs.)

I thought they were good answers. Some of 'em I didn't agree with, but I 47 been in this thing from the beginning, and whatever comes of it, I'm gonna support it. Okay, since the school board refused, I decided I'd just run for the school board.

I spent eighty-five dollars on the campaign. The guy runnin' against me 48 spent several thousand. I really had nobody on my side. The Klan turned against me. The low-income whites turned against me. The liberals didn't particularly like me. The blacks were suspicious of me. The blacks wanted to support me, but they couldn't muster up enough to support a Klansman on the school board. (Laughs.) But I made up my mind that what I was doin' was right, and I was gonna do it regardless what anybody said.

It bothered me when people would call and worry my wife. She's always 49 supported me in anything I wanted to do. She was changing, and my boys were too. I got some of my youth corps kids involved. They still followed me.

I was invited to the Democratic women's social hour as a candidate. 50 Didn't have but one suit to my name. Had it six, seven, eight years. I had it cleaned, put on the best shirt I had and a tie. Here were all this high-class wealthy candidates shakin' hands. I walked up to the mayor and stuck out my hand. He give me that handshake with that rag type of hand. He said: "C.P., I'm glad to see you." But I could tell by his handshake he was lyin' to me. This was botherin' me. I know I'm a low-income person. I know I'm not wealthy. I know they were sayin': "What's this little ol' dude runnin' for school board?" Yet they had to smile and make like they're glad to see me. I begin to spot some black people in that room. I automatically went to 'em and that was a firm handshake. They said: "I'm glad to see you, C.P." I knew they meant it—you can tell about a handshake.

Every place I appeared, I said I will listen to the voice of the people. I will 51 not make a major decision until I first contacted all the organizations in the city. I got 4,640 votes. The guy beat me by two thousand. Not bad for eighty-five bucks and no constituency.

The whole world was openin' up, and I was learnin' new truths that I had 52 never learned before. I was beginnin' to look at a black person, shake hands with him, and see him as a human bein'. I hadn't got rid of all this stuff. I've still got a little bit of it. But somethin' was happenin' to me.

It was almost like bein' born again. It was a new life. I didn't have these 53 sleepless nights I used to have when I was active in the Klan and slippin' around at night. I could sleep at night and feel good about it. I'd rather live now than at any other time in history. It's a challenge.

Back at Duke, doin' maintenance, I'd pick up my tools, fix the commode, 54 unstop the drains. But this got in my blood. Things weren't right in this country, and what we done in Durham needs to be told. I was so miserable at Duke, I could hardly stand it. I'd go to work every morning just hatin' to go.

My whole life had changed. I got an eighth-grade education, and I 55 wanted to complete high school. Went to high school in the afternoons on a program called PEP—Past Employment Progress. I was about the only white in class, and the oldest. I begin to read about biology. I'd take my books home at night, 'cause I was determined to get through. Sure enough, I graduated. I got the diploma at home.

I come to work one mornin' and some guy says: "We need a union." At 56 this time I wasn't pro-union. My daddy was anti-labor too. We're not gettin' paid much, we're havin' to work seven days in a row. We're all starvin' to death. The next day, I meet the international representative of the Operating Engineers. He give me authorization cards. "Get these cards out and we'll have an election." There was eighty-eight for the union and seventeen no's. I was elected chief steward for the union.

Shortly after, a union man come down from Charlotte and says we need a 57 full-time rep. We've got only two hundred people at the two plants here. It's just barely enough money comin' in to pay your salary. You'll have to get out and organize more people. I didn't know nothin' about organizin' unions, but I knew how to organize people, stir people up. (Laughs.) That's how I got to be business agent for the union.

When I began to organize, I began to see far deeper. I began to see people 58 again bein' used. Blacks against whites. I say this without any hesitancy: management is vicious. There's two things they want to keep: all the money and all the say-so. They don't want these poor workin' folks to have none of that. I begin to see management fightin' me with everything they had. Hire antiunion law firms, badmouth unions. The people were makin' a dollar ninety-five an hour, barely able to get through weekends. I worked as a business rep for five years and was seein' all this.

Last year, I ran for business manager of the union. He's elected by the workers. The guy that ran against me was black, and our membership is seventy-five percent black. I thought: Claiborne, there's no way you can beat that black guy. People know your background. Even though you've made tremendous strides, those black people are not gonna vote for you. You know how much I beat him? Four to one. (Laughs.)   59

The company used my past against me. They put out letters with a picture of a robe and a cap: Would you vote for a Klansman? They wouldn't deal with the issues. I immediately called for a mass meeting. I met with the ladies at an electric component plant. I said: "Okay, this is Claiborne Ellis. This is where I come from. I want you to know right now, you black ladies here, I was at one time a member of the Klan. I want you to know, because they'll tell you about it."   60

I invited some of my old black friends. I said: "Brother Joe, Brother Howard, be honest now and tell these people how you feel about me." They done it. (Laughs.) Howard Clements kidded me a little bit. He said: "I don't know what I'm doin' here, supportin' an ex-Klansman." (Laughs.) He said: "I know what C.P. Ellis come from. I knew him when he was. I knew him as he grew, and growed with him. I'm tellin' you now: follow, follow this Klansman." (He pauses, swallows hard.) "Any questions?" "No," the black ladies said. "Let's get on with the meeting, we need Ellis." (He laughs and weeps.) Boy, black people sayin' that about me. I won 134 to 41. Four to one.   61

It makes you feel good to go into a plant and butt heads with professional union busters. You see black people and white people join hands to defeat the fascist issues they use against people. They're tryin' the same things with the Klan. It's still happenin' today. Can you imagine a guy who's got an adult high school diploma runnin' into professional college graduates who are union busters? I gotta compete with 'em. I work seven days a week, nights and on Saturday and Sunday. The salary's not that great, and if I didn't care, I'd quit. But I care and I can't quit. I got a taste of it. (Laughs.)   62

I tell people there's a tremendous possibility in this country to stop wars, the battles, the struggles, the fights between people. People say: "That's an impossible dream. You sound like Martin Luther King." An ex-Klansman who sounds like Martin Luther King. (Laughs.) I don't think it's an impossible dream. It's happened in my life. It's happened in other people's lives in America.   63

I don't know what's ahead of me. I have no desire to be a big union official. I want to be right out here in the field with the workers. I want to walk through their factory and shake hands with that man whose hands are dirty. I'm gonna do all that one little ol' man can do. I'm fifty-two years old, and I ain't got many years left, but I want to make the best of 'em.   64

When the news came over the radio that Martin Luther King was assassinated, I got on the telephone and begin to call other Klansmen. We just had a real party at the service station. Really rejoicin' cause that son of a bitch was dead. Our troubles are over with. They say the older you get, the harder it is for you to change. That's not necessarily true. Since I changed, I've set down and listened to tapes of Martin Luther King. I listen to it and tears come to my eyes 'cause I know what he's sayin' now. I know what's happenin'. 65

POSTSCRIPT: *The phone rings. A conversation.*

"*This was a black guy who's director of Operation Breakthrough in Durham. I had called his office. I'm interested in employin' some young black person who's interested in learnin' the labor movement. I want somebody who's never had an opportunity, just like myself. Just so he can read and write, that's all.*" 66

Questions

1. What reasons does C. P. Ellis give for joining the Ku Klux Klan? Can you understand his reasoning? Do we all need someone to hate? Why?
2. How does C. P. change once he starts to work with blacks?
3. In what way is C. P. "born again"? Have you had a similar experience?

Women's Two Roles: A Contemporary Dilemma

PHYLLIS MOEN

Phyllis Moen teaches sociology at Cornell University and is a former program director of sociology for the National Science Foundation. She has published many articles concerned with women's roles both within and beyond the family, and she is the author of Women's Two Roles: A Contemporary Dilemma *(1992) from which this selection is an excerpt.*

Here, Moen shows that although about one-half of all married mothers with children are in the labor force, traditional ideologies mandating that a woman's primary sphere is the home have not changed. She posits that working mothers still do most of the housework and that some men (especially older men) experience some degree of depression and low self-esteem when their wives work.

> *Of all the rationales offered for women's presence in the home, the myth of motherhood seems the most persuasive and the least questionable in its premises and conclusions, for even if the housewife role and the wife role are capable of change, the maternal role is not.*
>
> OAKLEY 1974:186

Family life in the United States has changed markedly throughout this century, but most dramatically so since the baby boom years of the 1950s. Young people increasingly postpone marriage; a small but growing number forgo it altogether. Similarly, more couples now delay childbearing and give birth to fewer children. They are also more likely to divorce, which, in conjunction with an acceleration in the proportion of births outside marriage, has led to a substantial growth in the number of single-parent families. Residential mobility has been a long-term trend, with families both moving to the suburbs and relocating to communities promising greater economic growth and employment opportunities. And there has been a progressive trend toward gender equality, as evidenced by the narrowing of the gap between men and women in educational achievement. Within this constellation of change, the expanding number of employed mothers of young children has had a particularly broad and strong impact on family life. 1

THE CHANGING SHAPE OF MARRIAGE

Women increasingly want to have it both ways: a happy home life and a suc-   2
cessful career. But for most employed mothers, having it both ways means
having two jobs: one at home and one at work, with little help on the home
front. The relationships between men and women in society are being redefined, but the relationships between husbands and wives are slow to change.
This points to the transitional nature of this revolution in gender roles, with
men and women holding ambiguous and often conflicting expectations for
themselves and for their spouses. For example, the belief that the husband
should be the principal occupational achiever remained deeply rooted into
the 1970s, as expressed by the college men interviewed in an in-depth study
conducted by sociologist Mirra Komarovsky (1976). These men paid lip service to the principle of equality, asserting that mothers of preschoolers
should be able to take full-time jobs, "provided, of course, that the home was
running smoothly, the children did not suffer and the wife did not interfere
with her husband's career." In fact, the most common attitude among these
college men can be described as that of a "modified traditionalist," advocating the sequential pattern of women's employment, i.e., leaving their jobs for
child rearing and then returning to work when their children are school age.
Komarovksy's findings are consistent with those of large-scale surveys of nationally representative samples of men. As documented in Chapter 2, even in
the mid-1980s, most men believed there could be no substitute for a mother's
care during the preschool years. A major portion (62.7%) of men interviewed
in 1985, regardless of educational level, agreed that a preschool child is likely
to suffer if his or her mother works.[1]

Ambivalent—even contradictory—values, ideologies, and personal prefer-   3
ences appear to be deeply entrenched: "It is only fair to let a woman do her
own thing, if she wants a career. Personally, though, I would want my wife at
home" (Komarovsky 1976, p. 34). These internal conflicts reflect in some
ways what some observers see as an inherent clash between the goals of
women's equality and of family well-being. Historian Carl Degler sees these as
being "at odds" with one another (1980), and George Gilder describes
women's growing equality as "catastrophic" to the emotional health of men
in our society (1986). Is the employment of wives truly a "catastrophe" for
husbands? Or, to the contrary, might men actually benefit from it? These
questions cannot be answered without first addressing another issue: continuity and change in the division of family work—housework and child
care—between husbands and wives.

The Division of Labor

Women may have come a long way in terms of employment and gender-role   4
attitudes, but the fact remains that, whether or not employed, they continue
to perform by far the greatest share of family work. This has been a consistent
finding throughout nearly thirty years of research.[2]

Some scholars explain the persistence of this traditional division of labor   5
in terms of "resource theory"—husbands and fathers simply do not have the
time to devote to domestic activity, given their heavy involvement in occupations (Blood and Wolfe 1960). Others see it as a "system of exchange"—men
provide the family with income and social status, and their wives in turn assume the burden of domestic chores (Scanzoni 1970, 1978). This second perspective is closely in tune with the "new home economics" approach of
economist Gary Becker, who suggests that the traditional division of labor
makes sense as a means of maximizing household "utility" (Becker 1981; Berk
and Berk 1983).

But if wives are also working, if they also are bringing home a paycheck,   6
what then? Both these interpretations imply a trend toward more equitable
sharing of domestic work as wives and mothers themselves face the time constraints of employment and gain status and income from their work.

In contrast, the feminist perspective says that women's heavy domestic   7
load is a consequence of patriarchy, the domination of women by men in all
sectors of society. According to this view, gender roles within the household
are deeply embedded within the larger system of social relations; employment may increase women's economic resources and even improve their self-
esteem, but it will not lighten their burden at home (Hartmann 1981;
Sokoloff 1980, 1988; Walby 1986).

Time-use data collected in the 1960s and early 1970s revealed that a hus-   8
band's contribution to domestic work was unrelated to whether his wife was
employed. However, by the late 1970s, men with employed wives did spend
more time each week in housework and child care than did husbands who
were sole breadwinners.[3] This trend over the 1970s decade may represent a
significant shift in men's and women's roles, especially since the family work
of husbands with wives who are *not* employed has also increased over the
years. But it is important to note that husbands typically "help" their wives
rather than assume a major responsibility for particular household tasks
(Geerken and Gove 1983; Pleck 1985, 1986).

Consider, for example, the greater involvement of fathers in child care   9
when their wives are employed. Typically their participation is limited to
playing with the children or to caring for them when their wives are not present. Still, the fact that fathers of young children are spending more time in
child care does suggest at least the beginnings of a convergence in the domestic responsibilities of men and women.[4]

This convergence can also be seen in the changes occurring in the amount   10
of time devoted to housework, as women spend less time in household work
(as a result of their smaller families and increased employment) and men
spend slightly more. In 1965 married women did more than five times as
much housework as did married men, but by 1985 they did only twice as
much. The trends from 1965 to 1985 in the average hours per week spent in
housework by parents of preschoolers show mothers cutting their time in
housework by almost one third and fathers more than doubling their housework hours. Beyond doubt this is a remarkable change.

The principal factors that seem to influence the division of household   11
work between spouses are as follows:

- Husband's income—the higher his income, the less likely he is to share in domestic work.
- Wife's earnings—the more she earns, the more her husband is involved with housework.
- Presence of children—having young children increases the likelihood of a husband's domestic involvement.
- Wife's education—the greater the wife's education, the greater the husband's involvement, at least in some tasks.
- Husband's education—the higher the husband's level of education, the greater his share of the housework.
- Husband's work hours—the more hours the husband spends on the job, the less his involvement in housework and child care.[5]

These effects of husbands' and wives' education and the presence of   12
preschoolers may be changing over time, with younger cohorts of husbands
more influenced by these factors than older cohorts. The influence of another
variable, race, may also be changing. Studies in the early 1970s found that
black husbands did more work around the home than white husbands. However, race has not been a significant predictor of housework in later studies.[6]

The last half of the 1970s may have been a real turning point in the dis-   13
tribution of housework between husbands and wives. Where change particularly appears to have occurred is among fathers of young children. These
fathers in the late 1970s and 1980s appeared to be more involved in the family's domestic work than ever before, *regardless* of whether their wives were
employed.[7]

But there is more to housework and child care than meets the eye. Men   14
may be putting in time around the house, but women remain burdened with
the principal *responsibility* for family life. As Robert and Rhona Rapoport
noted in their study of professional couples in Great Britain in the 1960s:

> It is the wife who must remember about things that have to be done in the
> home, even though they may have negotiated an agreement to share respon-
> sibilities. The husband simply forgets once he has left the house, wiping his
> mind clean of domestic concerns because he has been programmed by soci-
> ety to shift his attention to external concerns. (1976:368)

In fact, economist Heidi Hartmann (1981) suggests that the care and feeding
of *husbands* may require more household work than they themselves contribute.[8]

Social psychologists Joseph Pleck and Michael Lamb and their colleagues   15
specify four factors that should influence the involvement of fathers in the
care of their young children: motivation, skills, social supports, and the ab-

sence of institutional barriers.[9] "Institutional barriers" include the ways in which jobs are structured, leaving little time available for child care. These barriers are central to the feminist perspective, which underscores the fact that women's domestic work frees men to devote full time to their jobs, emotionally as well as physically. This view suggests that the division of household work cannot become truly equitable until basic changes are made in the workplace, erasing the myth of the unencumbered (male) worker.

Division of Power

Some social scientists explain men's power in conventional marriages in exchange terms: Husbands provide the income and status and, thereby, "earn" an entitlement to be the principal decision makers. According to this perspective, wives' employment, which increases their resources and options, should produce a greater equity in household decision making. Studies over the years have, in fact, affirmed the relationship between wives' earning power and their power in the marriage. Working-class wives in particular seem to gain the most from employment, possibly since their earnings are so critical to the family economy.[10] 16

Feminist scholars locate the source of the power inequity between husbands and wives in the larger system of patriarchy and its ideology of male dominance. The exploitation of women at home and at work, they argue, augers to the benefit of men. Accordingly, it is not apt to disappear easily, regardless of the recent trends in women's employment. Indeed, from a feminist perspective, women's roles, resources, and relationships both at home and in the workplace serve to perpetuate gender inequalities (Reskin 1988; Sokoloff 1980, 1988). 17

The research evidence suggests that, although employment appears to increase a wife's power in family decision making, equality of power between husbands and wives has yet to be realized. Given the ways in which women typically accommodate their jobs to their family obligations, along with persistent occupational segregation and gender discrimination, the fact is that wives seldom approach their husbands in earnings capacity. In most cases the financial resources they bring to the marriage merely supplement the income earned by their husbands. The lives of husbands and wives remain seriously constrained by gender expectations. Thus, the division of power between husbands and wives, like the division of household work, remains markedly skewed, but in the opposite direction. 18

Implications for the Marital Relationship

> Each marriage bears the footprints of economic and cultural trends which originate far outside marriage. (Hochschild 1989:11)

Social scientists address the effects of a wife's employment on the quality of marriage from several viewpoints. One postulates a positive outcome: 19

Dual-earner couples should have more in common since they share the wage-earning (and may come to share the homemaking) role. This view builds on a long sociological tradition associating role sharing with the warmth of relationships between spouses.[11]

But others predict negative outcomes. These scholars feel that the tradi-   20 tional division of labor between spouses may well be the most effective way of managing the multiple demands of family life. Accordingly, a "working" wife may mean competition between husband and wife, or, at the very least, the working wife and mother may disrupt her husband's and children's lives by failing to do all that needs to be done at home.[12]

Are husbands and wives less satisfied with their marriages when both   21 spouses work? To answer that question we have to consider the evolution of women's roles over time. Married women's employment might have been problematic for marriage during the 1950s when it was considered somewhat deviant, but the social climate has changed. Early research on that topic did, in fact, find less marital satisfaction among dual-employed couples than among those in which the wife was a full-time homemaker. But, by the late 1960s and early 1970s, this difference had disappeared (Axelson 1963; Feld 1963; Nye 1974b).

A major survey of couples conducted in the late 1960s by Susan Orden   22 and Norman Bradburn (1969) illuminated the issue by looking at both marital satisfactions and tensions—recognizing that they are not the same thing—and by separating out employed women who *wanted* to work from those who preferred to be homemakers (contrast committed and captive women). They found that employed women who did not want to be in the labor force, those captive to the work role, had both much tension and little satisfaction in their marriages. Moreover, these researchers discovered an important life-cycle difference. When preschoolers were in the home, both husbands and wives evaluated their marriages more positively when the wives were not in the labor force. Employed wives who were committed to the work role and whose children were school age were the most positive in describing their marriages, as were their husbands. For parents of high schoolers, however, the wife's employment made little difference in marital satisfaction.

More recent investigations highlight the importance of gender-role atti-   23 tudes—especially those of the husband—in moderating the links between the wife's employment and both spouses' marital satisfaction. When husbands are more egalitarian in their attitudes and values, they report a higher quality marriage, regardless of whether their wives are employed. Similarly, employed wives report higher levels of marital satisfaction when their husbands are more supportive and share in the care of children (Philliber and Hiller 1983; Kessler and McRae 1982).

There is evidence also that the *nature* as well as the mere fact of the wife's   24 employment must be taken into account. Two studies conducted in the early 1960s found that part-time women workers had higher levels of marital satisfaction than full-time workers. And recent studies suggest that the conditions of work for both parents must be considered, with stress on the job associated with marital conflict and strain.[13]

What may be critical too is a wife's status and earnings *relative to those of*   25 *her husband.* Men whose wives are more successful than they are may be particularly dissatisfied with their marriages. But the evidence on this issue is still ambiguous.[14]

Historical trends concerning the effects of a wife's employment on her (or   26 her husband's) marital satisfaction are by no means clear from the evidence on hand. Some surveys report no difference in levels of marital satisfaction as a function of the wife's employment; others find husbands of employed wives less satisfied with their marriages than single-earner husbands.[15]

But what do we mean by "marital satisfaction"? Studies use various mea-   27 sures of marital adjustment, ranging from reported happiness, conflict, and satisfaction to joint recreational activities and the absence of negative comments about the spouse. Different findings may be a result of different measures used. There is also the problem of "selection bias": The unhappiest couples are not studied because they have probably already been divorced! In fact, wives who work are more likely than full-time homemakers to divorce their husbands. Marriages bonded only by financial dependency are less likely to continue once wives attain some degree of economic independence through employment (Booth, Johnson, and Whyte 1984; Cherlin 1981).

This suggests that the trend in women's employment may have a positive   28 impact on the quality of marriages, since fewer women will either enter into or remain in marriages simply for financial reasons. When both spouses work, the marriage benefits in terms of more income but suffers in terms of the availability and flexibility of time. And couple decisions—whether to move, when to have a child—become more complicated when two jobs are involved. Most likely a wife's employment follows various pathways in affecting her marriage: altering how she sees herself, the time she has for and the demands placed upon the marital relationship, her (and their) resources, and how her husband sees himself. Whether the wife's employment is good (or bad) for the husband and, by connotation, for the marriage depends, as we shall see below, on how the husband feels about his wife's being employed.

Implications for Husbands' Well-Being

Some studies indicate that wives' employment may have deleterious effects   29 on the mental health of their husbands. Trend data are admittedly sparse; the earliest study, based on only thirty married couples in 1965, reported higher levels of depression among husbands with employed wives (Rosenfield 1980). In addition, data from a 1976 survey of a large, nationally representative sample, analyzed by sociologists Ronald Kessler and James McRae (1982), reveal an association between wives' employment and depression and low self-esteem among husbands. These relationships persist even after taking into account the husbands' ages and incomes as well as the number and ages of children. Kessler and McRae tested for the possibility of role overload by including in their analysis whether or not the husbands of employed wives frequently do housework or are involved in child care. However, these family chores were found not to be related to the psychological distress of husbands—with one small exception. Fathers with working wives who did *not* assist in child care were *more* likely to report ill health and psychological anxiety than those participating in caretaking.[16]

Another analysis of these data, which tested the effects of wives' incomes (both absolute level and as a proportion of total family income) on husbands' well-being, found that husbands' improved mental health goes hand in hand with increases in their wives' incomes. This suggests that it is something other than the loss of status and power as the sole breadwinner that produces mental distress in the husbands of employed wives. [30]

Kessler and McRae also discovered that the negative effects of a wife's employment are greatest in mid-life; young husbands and husbands approaching retirement are less likely to show mental distress in conjunction with their wives' employment. They suggest that this finding may reflect both age and cohort effects. Older men may have accommodated to the situation (age effect); younger men may be more liberal regarding women's roles (cohort effect). Thus, at least part of the negative impact of a wife's employment on her husband's well-being should diminish with the passage of time, as younger cohorts replace older ones, because younger couples are more accepting of this new life-style. [31]

Missing in the Kessler and McRae study is any measure of the husband's attitudes toward sex roles in general and toward his own wife's employment in particular. This gap is filled in another nationwide survey of couples conducted in 1978. In this study Catherine Ross, John Mirowsky, and Joan Huber (1983) found that the deleterious effects of a wife's employment are greatly increased if the husband does not *want* his wife to be employed. Conversely, men who supported their wives' employment reported the lowest depression levels. As in the earlier study conducted by Kessler and McRae, this research found that neither the wife's earnings nor the husband's involvement in housework had any effect on the husband's depression. A husband's preference for his wife to be employed was negatively correlated with age; that is, younger men were more apt than older ones to approve of their wives' employment. This again suggests that future cohorts of husbands may find having a working wife less problematic than has been true in the past. [32]

Other studies suggest that characteristics of the wife's job may affect the husband's well-being. For example, having a wife who works part-time has been shown to have a salutary effect on her husband's psychological health.[17] [33]

Historical trend data on the well-being of husbands can be considered on two levels. First, husbands of employed wives generally have been psychologically worse off than husbands with wives who were homemakers. Second, this effect may be disappearing as new cohorts of younger husbands accept and even endorse the employment of their wives. [34]

TRADING TIME FOR MONEY

> The institutions of the society make no allowances for alternative conceptions of time. They impose rigid and standard time schedules on all. (Harriman 1982:4)

Time has become the new scarcity in American families. As a fixed commodity, the time allocated to employment is necessarily unavailable for other activities, including family affairs. When mothers of young children combine domestic work with paid work, their families gain in income and the women themselves may gain in self-esteem. What is *lost* is time—for the couples, for the families, and for the women themselves. Time constraints in working families are experienced disproportionately by women, and these constraints are especially problematic for single-parent mothers.

Time pressures necessarily limit the number of joint activities working parents can undertake—with their children and with each other. The competition for time between work and family is seldom resolved; rather, obligations to both are juggled in a time-budgeting process that is often unsatisfactory for both parents and their children.

The early years of childbearing are especially demanding. Infants and preschoolers not only take more time, but they also impose demands that cannot fit into a rigid, predetermined schedule.[18] Sociologist John Robinson, examining time use in a 1973 national survey, found that, "other factors being equal, a child under four years of age received 50 percent more of a mother's contact time and three times as much of her primary activity time than a comparable child beyond the preschool age of four" (1977:80).

Working mothers with jobs have more to do than those who do not work outside the home, but they spend less time on housework.[19] Moreover women generally, whether employed or not, are spending less and less time on housework, as time-use studies show. In fact, from 1965 to 1985, the amount of time spent on household tasks decreased more sharply for *nonemployed* women (ten-hour per week drop) than for employed women (three-hour per week drop).

Still, women with paid jobs put in fewer hours on domestic chores than do full-time homemakers. Housework is somewhat elastic—expanding to fill open hours and contracting when time is scarce. This explains why employed women spent on average 41 percent less time in housework than did nonemployed women in 1965. It also explains why women in the 1960s spent as much time doing housework as did women in the 1920s to 1950s, despite the advances in household technology.

But today women are having fewer children and hold less exacting housekeeping standards—hence the reduction in time spent on domestic chores. There have been societal adjustments as well: the burgeoning number of restaurants and fast-food chains, microwave dinners, and take-out meals available in grocery stores and delis, for example, along with the proliferation of vendored services such as housecleaning and child care. But raising children is not nearly so flexible as housework. Parents, especially mothers, "invest" in their children; they assume that the more quality time they spend with their children, the better their development will be. Thus, it should come as no surprise that employed single-parent mothers spend *less* time in household chores than do those who are not employed, but the *same* amount of time in child care.

Economists Russell Hill and Frank Stafford (1974, 1980) report that college-educated women give up sleep in order to care for their children and that the amount of time these women spend with their children does not diminish with their employment. But Barbara Willer (1986), drawing on data from the 1977 Quality of Employment Survey, found that employed mothers of preschoolers with higher income levels spent less time with their children than did those with lower incomes. This finding suggests that women may, in fact, make trade-offs between income and family time. Nevertheless, with the hours spent on the job, in housework, and in child care, employed mothers of young children put in, on average, an eighty–hour week in the 1970s; fathers in such families spent only sixty-five hours overall. Trends in time use by men and women may well be converging, but they are converging at a very modest pace.[20]   41

Family Payoffs

The paychecks of single-parent women are crucial to supporting their families. Working wives also make a significant contribution to the economic security and well-being of their families. In 1986 wives' earnings represented about one-fourth of total family income, and wives working full-time and year-round contributed nearly 40 percent, roughly the same proportion (39%) as in 1977 (Hayghe 1978; U.S. Bureau of the Census 1986).   42

But the extent to which the earnings potential of women can be realized is determined by a host of cultural and institutional factors, including employment opportunities, prevailing wage rates, and the "costs" of employment. For many mothers of preschoolers, the expense and the complexity of arranging for child care makes full-time employment impossible. Single-parent mothers in particular tend to hold unstable or low-paying jobs, often in tandem with low, erratic, or even no child support payments from their children's fathers (Garfinkel and McLanahan 1986; Weitzman 1985).   43

The escalating costs of raising a family, in conjunction with the rise in the incidence of single-parent families, make the employment of mothers of young children increasingly consequential. Even when it is not essential to put bread on the table, the employment of wives and mothers provides a financial cushion for the family economy, as well as the wherewithal to achieve a better quality of life. In fact, one-fourth of the mothers in two-earner families surveyed in 1986 said they were working to enable the family to enjoy a higher standard of living. Not surprisingly, blue-collar workers and those with lower levels of household income were more likely to describe their reason for working as "economic necessity."[21]   44

An additional benefit of maternal employment to families is the mother's　45
higher morale. Both professional and blue-collar women workers report
greater happiness and satisfaction than full-time homemakers in studies conducted throughout the 1970s and 1980s. As one woman reported, "I'm nicer
to my family when I get out of the house. I'm more independent, satisfied,
and happier at home."[22] This sense of satisfaction, however, has been found
to be contingent on women's preference for employment. The committed
benefit the most; the captives benefit not at all. Moreover, the actual conditions of employment also affect a woman's sense of well-being. And, as we
have seen in Chapter 3, women can be satisfied with working yet still endure
role strains and overloads.

Family Costs

About one-third of the workers interviewed in a 1977 national survey re-　46
ported experiencing "work-family interference," typically related to time constraints (Moen and Dempster-McClain 1987). Nine years later, in a 1986
survey, little had changed; 30 percent of the employed parents reported that
their work put stress on their family lives. More wives than husbands reported not having enough time to spend with children and spouses because
of work, and both husbands and wives in two-earner families experienced
more time pressures than did husbands in traditional one-earner situations or
single-parent women (Opinion Research Corporation 1987).

　　Analysis of data from the 1977 survey underscored the relationship be-　47
tween work/family strains and preferred work/time involvement. Mothers
(and fathers) who reported such strains were five times more likely to prefer
spending less time working. The 1986 survey found that those parents experiencing work/family strains were the least likely to describe their families as
open in communicating with each other, close knit, basically happy, mutually helpful, or supportive. Again, the full-time women workers under strain
in meshing their work and family responsibilities may well be the captive and
conflicted workers—on the job but wishing they were working less or not at
all at this stage of their lives when their children are young. Part of their
strain can be attributed to the glacial pace of institutional change. Mothers
increasingly work outside the home, but they have little opportunity to reduce their hours temporarily as necessary or to take an extended leave of absence. Neither are there enough quality, affordable, and accessible child-care
arrangements available to working families.

　　Work/family strain is not the special province of women. A 1989 *New York*　48
Times survey of mothers and fathers with children under age 18 found that
83 percent of the mothers and 72 percent of the fathers felt torn between the
demands of their jobs and wanting to spend more time with their families at
least sometimes. About one-third of both men and women respondents felt
that children and family life suffered most when a woman tries to combine a
job, marriage, and children (Cowan 1989).

Marriage. The amount of time working couples spend in employment is   49
typically "negotiated" between spouses as a trade-off between family time
and financial needs. These decisions are made against a backdrop of deeply
embedded cultural expectations. One such expectation is that fathers should
work at least a forty–hour week. But mothers also are commonly locked into
jobs where standard hours are prescribed, regardless of family needs. Both the
number of hours worked and their scheduling necessarily determine the
amount of time husbands and wives spend together and with their children.
Shift work, for example, permits some parents to share in the care of their
children. On the other hand, work in the evening and at night may exacerbate scheduling difficulties for husbands and wives.[23]

In the end, having both spouses work—regardless of their work sched-   50
ules—typically means that couples spend less time together eating meals,
watching television, socializing, engaging in sports, and entertaining. This
limitation on "togetherness" frequently has deleterious effects on the quality
of the marriage (Kingston and Nock 1987; Booth, Johnson, and Whyte 1984).

Children. Despite women's best intentions, the inevitable outcome of ma-   51
ternal employment is some reduction in the amount of time children spend
with their mothers. There are three dimensions to the "time with children"
issue.

The first is simply the *number of hours* in a day or week children spend   52
with their mothers. Some might argue that children of employed mothers do
not lose on this count because (1) working mothers, especially those with
young children, may work less than a standard forty–hour week when it is
financially feasible; (2) mothers may forgo other activities in their lives
(such as sleep and personal care) to compensate for their hours on the job;
and (3) children may be kept up later at night or awakened earlier in the
morning in order to spend as much time as possible with their mothers.

Second, children may lose hours spent with their mothers, but what is   53
lost in *quantity* may be well surpassed by the *quality* of the time mothers devote to their children. And third, children may also benefit from spending
additional time with their fathers.

The evidence bearing on these three possibilities is ambiguous, partly be-   54
cause different investigators employ quite different methods, ranging from
merely asking parents for rough time estimates to having them keep detailed
time-use diaries. Moreover, "time with children" can mean one-on-one togetherness or simply occupying the same room at the same time. And "children" in one study may be defined as those under age 6, while in another
study it includes all those under age 20. But after collating the findings from
a variety of studies with a range of coding methods, definitions, and samples,
the following trends seem to emerge:

1. Employed mothers do in fact spend less time in all types of activities   55
with their children than do full-time homemakers. The greatest difference
(after taking into account socioeconomic status, income, race, and parents'

ages) is, not surprisingly, in the time spent with preschoolers during the work week. Working mothers of young children spend fewer minutes per day with their children in play, education, child care, "fun" activities, homemaking, and meals. This is also true of working mothers of school-age children, although the contrast with full-time homemakers in this case is not as striking.

2. Differences between working and stay-at-home mothers in the amount 56
of time they spend with their children depend on the activity considered. For example, time spent talking with preschool children or in watching television with them does *not* vary by the mother's employment status. The largest difference, again not surprisingly, is in being with children while doing household chores. The two groups of mothers differ by only about a half-hour in time spent actually caring for children during the work week. Thus, it might appear that the quality time between mothers and preschoolers is not sacrificed when mothers are in the labor force, but "quality" is in the eye of the beholder and is very difficult to gauge in any objective fashion.

3. Fathers in dual-earner families tend to spend *less* time per workday 57
with their children than do fathers who are traditional, single-earners. Clearly, fathers do not compensate in any major way for their wives' absence from the home. In fact, the only activity in which the husbands of employed wives seem consistently to engage in more with their children than do single-earner husbands is television watching on Sundays! However, fathers of *preschoolers* tend to spend more time with their children while their wives are away at work. This is especially true when wives work in the evening or at night or when the fathers themselves are on night or evening shifts (Presser 1986, 1989; Hoffman 1989).

NOTES

1. Data are taken from the General Social Survey (Mason and Lu 1988).

2. There is a range of studies and reviews on this topic (Berk and Berk 1979; Berk 1985; Blood and Wolfe 1960; Geerken and Gove 1983; Farkas 1976; Robinson 1977; Pleck 1983, 1985; Walker and Woods 1976; Huber and Spitze 1983; Coverman 1985; Hill and Stafford 1974, 1980; Juster 1985; Coverman and Sheley 1986; Hochschild 1989; Menaghan and Parcel 1990).

3. Although some early community studies reported that husbands of employed wives were more likely to share *somewhat* in household tasks (Hoffman 1963b; Blood and Wolfe 1960) than men married to full-time homemakers, nationally representative time-use studies showed no difference by wife's employment status. However, studies did report that changes had occurred by the late 1970s (Coverman 1985; Huber and Spitze 1983; Nickols and Metzen 1982; Weingarten 1978; Pleck 1985).

4. For overviews of this shift, see Gecas (1976), Ericksen, Yancey, and Ericksen (1979), Berk and Berk (1979), Nock and Kingston (1988), Pleck (1985), Coverman and Sheley (1986), Robinson (1985), and Juster (1985).

5. For the effects of husband's income and wife's earnings, see Ericksen, Yancey, and Ericksen (1979), and Ross, Mirowsky, and Huber (1983). For the effects of the pres-

ence of children, see Berk and Berk (1979), Berk (1985), Juster (1985), Coverman (1985), and Coverman and Sheley (1986). For education effects, see Ericksen, Yancey, and Ericksen (1979), Walker and Woods (1976), Duncan and Duncan (1978), and Ross, Mirowsky, and Huber (1983). For the effect of the husband's work hours, see Crouter et al. (1987), Pleck (1983, 1985), Robinson (1977), and Walker and Woods (1976).

6. Shifts by cohort are reported in Farkas (1976) and Pleck (1985). Changes by race are seen by contrasting the studies conducted by Farkas (1976) and Ericksen, Yancey, and Ericksen (1979) with those conducted by Ross, Mirowsky, and Huber (1983) and Coverman and Sheley (1986). The overall trends in men's involvement in housework and child care by no means illustrate a steady linear increase over the years. Comparisons of surveys conducted in Detroit in 1955 and 1971 reveal no systematic movement over that period toward equality in the distribution of household tasks (Duncan and Duncan 1978). A time-use study of 750 urban households conducted in the 1970s found only a minimal increase in the husbands' involvement accompanying wives' employment (Berk and Berk 1979; see also general overviews by Miller and Garrison 1982; Pleck 1985).

   Part of the difficulty in gauging long-term trends in the sexual division of labor is the fact that social scientists use quite different measures of it, ranging from single-item questions to complicated time diaries. Adding to the complexity of interpretation, husbands and wives at all stages of the life course are typically grouped together in a single analysis.

7. See, for example, Daniels and Weingarten (1982), Coverman and Sheley (1986), Juster (1985), and Pleck (1985).

8. Prior to 1910 the traditional middle-class arrangement was for a servant to do the housework. Even during World War II wives typically joined the labor force only when their husbands were drafted. Even women without children felt a responsibility to take care of their husbands (Long 1958:125).

9. Pleck (1986); Pleck, Lamb, and Levine (1985); Lamb and Sagi (1983). For the feminist theoretical perspective, see also Hartmann (1976), Sokoloff (1980, 1988), and Walby (1986).

10. For an exchange perspective, see Bernard (1981) and Scanzoni (1970, 1978). Several early studies (Blood 1963; Hoffman 1963b; Bahr 1974; Gillespie 1971) and reviews (Moore and Hofferth 1979; Rallings and Nye 1979) are available.

11. See Bott (1957), Blood (1963), Dizard (1968), Aldous (1983), and Simpson and England (1981).

12. This perspective also has a long tradition of acceptance in the sociological literature (Parsons 1942; Parsons and Bales 1966), and it is embraced by economist Gary Becker (1981) as well.

13. There is both early (Axelson 1963; Nye 1963) and more recent evidence (Staines and Pleck 1983; Pleck 1985; Hochschild 1989).

14. See the discussions by Parsons (1942) and by Oppenheimer (1977). A study by Philliber and Hiller (1983), for example, reports that, when the wife's job is more prestigious than her husband's, either she is likely to move to a lower status job or the marriage is apt to end in divorce. Other investigators do not confirm this finding (Oppenheimer 1977; Huber and Spitze 1980).

15. Some studies report no differences (Campbell, Converse, and Rodgers 1976; Wright 1978; Locksley 1980; Glenn and Weaver 1978); others have found that

husbands of employed wives were less satisfied with their marriages than single-earner husbands (Geerken and Gove 1983; Crouter et al. 1987).

16. Three other studies, also with small or select samples, have produced inconsistent results regarding the psychological well-being of husbands of employed wives (Burke and Weir 1976; Booth 1977, 1979; Roberts and O'Keefe 1981). Campbell (1984) notes that, during World War II, women in unhappy marriages, on the verge of divorce, prepared for this contingency by getting a job. Hence, any correlation between the wife's employment and the husband's dissatisfaction is not surprising. For the salutary consequences of fathers' child care, see also Baruch and Barnett (1986a).

17. See Moen (1989) and Wethington (1992).

18. The age of children is more important than their number in establishing the amount of time spent in child care—at least for mothers (Berk 1985; Pleck 1985; Coverman and Sheley 1986).

19. Studies conducted over the 1970s document this fact (Vanek 1974, 1980; Walker and Woods 1976; Robinson 1977; Geerken and Gove 1983).

20. See Sanik and Mauldin (1986) for women giving up sleep and Hochschild (1989) for examples of women's double day. Similarly, working wives during World War II also cut back on their hours of sleep to cope with their multiple demands (Campbell 1984).

21. See Opinion Research Corporation (1987). However, "economic necessity" is a social decision. If the employment of wives and mothers is not socially sanctioned, as was the case in the United States prior to World War II, then expected standards of living will adjust accordingly. And, as more women are employed, the definition of what is an adequate or comfortable standard of living changes (Hernandez 1989). The wife's employment is also a protection against the ravages of unemployment (Moen, Kain, and Elder 1983).

22. See Opinion Research Corporation (1987:39). Some studies look at morale (Birnbaum 1975; Ferree 1976, 1987; Veroff, Douvan, and Kulka 1981; Kessler and McRae 1982); others look at preference for employment (Gove and Zeiss 1987; Whitham and Moen 1992).

23. See Nock and Kingston (1988), Hood and Golden (1979), Presser (1986, 1988, 1989), Presser and Cain (1983), and Staines and Pleck (1984).

Questions

1. Why has the deeply entrenched ideology of the two spheres impeded governmental intervention into family life?

2. Moen argues that because men benefit from traditional domestic and workplace arrangements, they are reluctant to see them altered. How do they benefit from the traditional arrangements?

3. Why do some men view the employment of wives as a catastrophe?

4. When you were a child did your mother work? Why did she work? If so, did your father do more of the housework?

5. What is the difference between captive and committed working mothers?

Writing Assignments

The following writing assignments are concerned with the topic of diversity in the workplace. Before developing an argument on any of these assignments, be sure that you understand the controversy by completing the following exercises:

- Write responses to exploration questions.
- Read several articles in this chapter or elsewhere to discover at least two perspectives on the topic.
- Create a list of opposing viewpoints and consider the potential consequences of each.
- Examine the underlying assumptions behind each viewpoint.

To help you understand the issues and develop ideas, you can use the following form:

The conflict in this issue is between _____ and

_____.

I am more inclined to agree with _____.

because _____.

However, it is possible that some of my readers may believe that

_____.

Exploration Questions

1. Have you ever held a job? Describe it. What sort of job was it? How did you get this job? Did you believe that you had the possibility to advance in this job?
2. Do you believe that people in the United States have equal opportunities to become successful? Why or why not?
3. Do you think it is the task of government to ensure that everyone has equal opportunity, or do you believe that government interference in this matter is ultimately doomed to be unfair to someone? Explore your attitude toward the role of government in mandating equal opportunity.
4. Have you ever received preferential treatment in a work-related situation? If so, how did you feel about it?
5. Why is there still a discrepancy between the wages of men and women? Why is there still a discrepancy between the wages of blacks and whites?
6. If you are a man, do you expect your wife to work after you have children? Do you expect to share in the housework and child care? If you are a woman, do you expect to work after you have children? Do you expect your husband to share in the housework and child care?

7. Are the students on your campus members of minority racial or ethnic groups? What is the prevailing attitude on campus toward these groups?

8. Characterize the work ethic of your family and community.

ASSIGNMENT 1

Affirmative action policies have been in place for over twenty years, and many believe that the spirit that motivated their passage has now been so well incorporated into American business that such policies are no longer necessary. Others believe that the goal of providing equal opportunity for all people in the United States has not been met and that we still have a long way to go to achieve workplace equality. Read several selections in this chapter and then write an argumentative essay answering the following question: Is affirmative action still necessary?

ASSIGNMENT 2

On occasion, the concept of equal opportunity comes into conflict with the freedom associated with free enterprise. In an argumentative essay, define how the concept of equal opportunity might conflict with the idea of free enterprise and discuss your position on which concept should win out when such a conflict exists. Use specific instances to illustrate your position.

ASSIGNMENT 3

Write an argumentative essay examining the extent to which work is linked to identity in American society. Do you think that the value placed on particular types of work and the acclaim given to those who perform such work are reasonable or fair?

Using Data

1. What conclusions can you draw from the following graph? How could this graph be used in the debate over the effectiveness of affirmative action programs (as they apply to both racial minorities and women)?

2. Can this graph be used to support or refute any of the assertions by the authors in this chapter?

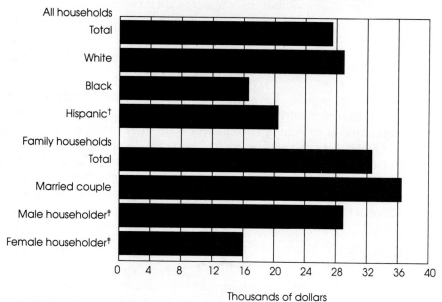

Median Household Income: 1989

All households
Total

White

Black

Hispanic†

Family households
Total

Married couple

Male householder†

Female householder†

0   4   8   12   16   20   24   28   32   36   40

Thousands of dollars

†Hispanic persons may be of any race.
†Spouse not present.
Data are based on U.S. Bureau of the Census estimates.

11 ■ Diversity and the Media

Of course I know it's true. I saw it on television.

It has become a cliché of our culture that everything is getting worse, that the world is falling apart, and that once upon a time, the quality of life was, in many respects, better. People shake their heads, agree that society is in a general state of disintegration and cite as examples the increase of crime, violence, divorce, pornography, and illegitimacy, and denounce the decline of literacy, educational values, morality, and the work ethic. Moreover, whenever anyone looks for the primary cause of this pervasive degeneration, television (as well as other forms of media) is frequently cited as the culprit—presumably responsible for illiteracy and excess consumerism. Television and movies are said to incite children to violence or at least encourage a greater tolerance for violence, thus contributing to an increase in crime.

In addition, the media are blamed for an overall decline in morality and values, and in the context of the issues addressed in the previous chapters, have also been accused of fostering racial, ethnic, and sexual inequality by depicting men and women and minority groups in terms of stereotypes. During the past several years, social analysts are claiming that the media are having an even more insidious and pervasive impact than has been generally acknowledged—they point out that the media influence not only how we perceive reality but, in fact, that the media actually create that reality through the power of the image. At their most invasive, media images have become a substitute for actual experience.

The readings in this chapter focus on controversies concerned with the role that the media (television in particular) has played in a diverse society. Several readings discuss how the use of rapid images and sound bites both influence our perception of reality and, to some extent, become the only reality people know. Other selections focus on the impact of television on viewer perception, using the Rodney King beating and the subsequent riots in Los Angeles as examples. Finally, other readings discuss how the media have portrayed men, women, and minorities, and evaluate the extent to which such portrayals contribute to the perpetuation of stereotypes.

769

The Media and Reality

Because television is a visual medium, its primary mode of presentation is the image—viewers see a series of images when they watch television news, and it is these images, rather than any accompanying commentary, that viewers tend to remember. So compelling are television and video images that often they linger in viewers' minds, influencing what they believe is true and giving them the impression that they are actually present at the scene. This influence is forceful even when viewers are aware that they may be seeing only part of what actually occurred or a skewed version of it. When viewers are unaware of how they may be influenced by visual stimuli, they may be easily deceived by what they see. A sequence of events can be depicted non-sequentially, or a crucial event can be left out. Sometimes distortion can occur when particular scenes are given emphasis, such as what some say occurred during the Los Angeles riots when the repeated showing of the same fires gave the impression that the entire city was ablaze.

Aside from influencing our view of reality, television also has the power to disseminate culture and its accompanying values, not only throughout the United States but throughout the world. Whereas a particular fashion or custom popularized in a big city once took months or even years to come to the attention of people in a small town, now it can be communicated with the click of a switch, resulting in an amazing homogeneity that some people believe is not necessarily desirable. Adolescents in small towns as well as large cities in the United States can watch the popular television show "Beverly Hills 90210." On the basis of the program, they may then share a perception of what is "in" and what is "out," and consequently, may imitate the style or behavior of the characters even though their own environment may be quite different from the Beverly Hills scene. Through easy access to cable and video, adolescents in other countries may also tune in, thus joining an adolescent culture and an adolescent value system that transcends national boundaries.

John Lippman, in "Tuning in the Global Village," points out that television has spread pop culture throughout the world, a phenomenon that is not necessarily considered beneficial. Lippman examines the possibility that television does not only relay pictures of a particular reality but that it actually determines the nature of that reality, resulting in a fragmented "sound-bite" perception of the world. Although the empowered elite of developing countries have tried to limit "borderless television," they have found it nearly impossible to impede the spread of Western culture with all of its attendant disadvantages, particularly its emphasis on consumerism.

Michael Ventura, in "Report from El Dorado," makes the point that media now control our lives to such an extent that "in its most common form, media substitute a fantasy of experience or (in the case of news) an abbreviation of experience" for actual reality. Thus, Ventura claims, in today's society, we do not live our experiences, we simply absorb them. Given this phenomenon, the problem of trying to define and share a culture becomes extremely problematic because today's culture does not exist anywhere—it consists simply of a number of images.

If our concept of reality is shaped by the media, we might question the view of reality the media chooses to project, particularly in its portrayal of minority ethnic and racial groups. One concern is that television perpetuates racism with its stereotypical presentation of minorities. In "Advertising: The Media's Not-So-Silent Partner," Clint C. Wilson II and Félix Gutiérrez trace racist imagery in the history of advertising. From Aunt Jemima to the Frito Bandito, these images indicate an insensitivity on the part of corporate America, which, until recently, focused its campaigns toward the majority audience. With increased awareness of the importance of blacks and Latinos as consumers, however, advertisers have become more sensitive to these groups, although this is still not the case for Asians.

News Coverage

The 1992 riots in Los Angeles after the Rodney King verdict called attention to the role of television news in both reflecting and shaping reality. As Joe Saltzman, formerly with CBS television and now a professor of journalism at the University of Southern California, has noted, "All videotape is inaccurate . . . Lighting, camera angle, and video speed all affect the way viewers perceive actions on videotape and all contribute to the potential for distortion" (*Los Angeles Times,* February 14, 1993). Because of its capacity to distort, television has been blamed for perpetuating racism by depicting minorities only in terms of a narrow stereotype and giving the impression that the stereotype reflects the norm. For example, during the Los Angeles riots, the television broadcasted images of looters running uncontrolled through smoky ruins, feeding the prejudice that contributed to the riots in the first place. Moreover, the media coverage of the King verdict and the ensuing riots provided a sense of immediacy, intimacy, and drama that kept the civic temperature at a steady boil. Television's search for the dramatic gave the impression that the entire city of Los Angeles was about to explode when, in fact, only a small section of the city was affected.

If television presents a distorted picture of reality, the question arises as to what, if anything, can or should be done about it because freedom of expression is of particular importance in American culture. Burton M. Leiser, in "The Case For Censorship," traces the reasoning of those who advocate censorship since the time of Plato, and argues that only a libertarian approach to freedom of speech in which freedom of opinion is absolute can guarantee democratic principles. Despite his belief in freedom of opinion, Leiser does not condone speech that is intended to be used as "weapons of destruction and harm to others."

The Depiction of Minorities

Several articles discuss the way in which particular groups are represented by the media. In "Stereotypes and American Indians," Joann Sebastian Morris points out how television propagates the stereotypes of Native Americans as "simple, lazy, wasteful, and humorless; they are depicted as lacking intelligence and English-speaking skills, and adhering to primitive religions." This portrayal of Native Americans in film ignores tribal diversity and creates a distorted view of reality.

The media have also played a role in influencing how the general public views gay society and the problem of AIDS. Gara LaMarche and William B. Rubenstein, in "The Love That Dare Not Speak," point out that although AIDS has led in some instances to a more open forum for discussing homosexuality, it has simultaneously provided additional opportunities for censorship. They contend that homosexual discourse upsets "an 'asexual' public discourse" and threatens "uninformed, but deeply held, assumptions about what is moral." Censorship, they maintain, should be at the forefront of the gay and lesbian agenda.

The Media and Women

It has become a truism that the media also helps shapes our conception of masculinity and femininity. In "When Men Put on Appearances," Diane Barthel examines how visual and verbal symbols are used to construct images of masculinity and to associate these images with specific products. Barthel feels that our consumer decisions are socially constructed rather than biologically based and supports her position with examples of ads for clothing, sports fashion, cars, watches, and cologne. Barthel argues that advertisers plant an image in the minds of men of what it means to be masculine: "visual and verbal symbols are used to construct images of masculinity and to associate these images with specific products."

The impact of the media on the women's movement is addressed by Susan Faludi in "The Media and the Backlash," an excerpt from her recent book, *Backlash: The Undeclared War Against American Women.* Faludi asserts that the media have contributed to an anti-feminist feeling in America by emphasizing the difficulties some women have experienced in attempting to balance career goals with commitments to marriage and children. According to Faludi, it was the media that popularized phrases such as the "biological clock," the "Mommy track," and other phrases suggesting that liberation does not bring happiness and that a return to more traditional feminine roles may be the solution to the problem. Faludi maintains that the media depict single women as lonely and unfulfilled, thus promoting the message that marriage is the answer to modern women's alleged unhappiness.

It is unlikely that the influence of the media will decline as technology becomes more advanced and as various forms of media become affordable to a larger population. Therefore, it is important that we understand the potential of the media to influence what we believe about the world. In addition to their impact on our concept of reality, our understanding of political and social issues, and our perception of minorities and men and women, the media influence our conception of other facets of society explored in this book, such as how we view people who do not speak English as a first language, and our concept of family and work. In a rapidly changing, increasingly diverse society, in which divisiveness and hostility pose a threat to survival, it is especially important to understand the power of the media in order to separate appearance from reality, and perhaps to harness that power in the interest of peace, understanding, mutual respect, and cooperation.

Tuning in the Global Village

JOHN LIPPMAN

John Lippman is a staff writer for the Los Angeles Times.

In this article, Lippman documents how the global television economy is growing at a blistering rate, spreading American pop culture worldwide. He argues that although the empowered elite of developing countries have tried to limit borderless television, they have found it nearly impossible to impede the spread of Western culture. This selection is from the Los Angeles Times *(1992).*

1. Historians looking at the 20th Century from the next millennium will likely pinpoint 1945 as the most pivotal year since the voyage of Columbus.

2. Two nuclear bombs exploded over Japanese cities, providing a glimpse of the apocalypse. And an obscure British radar officer named Arthur C. Clarke found that it's possible to relay pictures around the world almost instantly by bouncing radio signals off a few satellites orbiting high above the Equator.

3. Both developments changed the course of humankind.

4. Asked once what had caused the stunning collapse of communism in Eastern Europe, Polish leader Lech Walesa pointed to a nearby TV set. "It all came from there."

5. If it has helped topple totalitarian governments and promote global democracy, television has also—for better or for worse—led a modern Crusade, spreading pop culture over the Earth as medieval knights once spread Christendom.

6. In fact, nearly 30 years after Canadian philosopher Marshall McLuhan coined the phrase "global village" to describe how the electronics revolution was shrinking the world and shortening the time between thought and action, the Media Millennium is at hand.

7. More than half of Americans alive today may not remember a time without TV in their home. They're surprised if someone *doesn't* have 25 or 30 channels to choose from. But for much of the globe, television is still relatively new—and changing fast.

8. It only arrived last summer in Vanuatu, a scattered archipelago with 165,000 people in the southwest Pacific formerly known as the New Hebrides. Crowds mobbed appliance stores to watch the new state-owned network's first broadcast—the opening of the 1992 Olympic Games in Barcelona.

9. But thanks to Arthur Clarke, places like Vanuatu are fast going the way of the rooftop antenna. Today, there is hardly any spot on Earth untrammeled

by a satellite "footprint"—the area, sometimes spanning whole continents, within reach of signals from its parabolic antennas.

The rapid inroads of satellite-based "borderless television" are changing   10
the way the world works, the way it plays, even the way it goes to war and makes peace. Even countries that have long limited what their citizens can watch on nationalized TV are slowly being forced to relax their vice-like grip.

Madonna writhes on MTV videos from Bahrain to Bangladesh. A deputy   11
police chief in Moscow is distracted during an interview by Super Channel, a British cross between MTV and "Entertainment Tonight," which blares incessantly in many Russian homes and offices. Dozens of pan-European satellite channels, beaming everything from highbrow French talk shows to Dutch pornography, trespass national borders without visas. "Los Simpsons" becomes a top-rated TV show in Colombia and Argentina.

A New Economy

Spurred by technological advance and the worldwide trend toward privatiza-   12
tion, a global TV economy is growing at a blistering rate. Consider:

- More than 1 billion TV sets now populate the globe—a 50% jump over   13
the last five years. The number is expected to continue growing by 5% annually—and by more than double that in Asia, where half the world's population lives.

- Worldwide spending for television programming is now about $65 bil-   14
lion, and the tab is growing by 10% per year, according to Neal Weinstock, media project director for the New York research firm Frost & Sullivan Inc. TV programs are a major U.S. export now worth about $2.3 billion annually.

- The number of satellite-delivered TV services around the world is more   15
than 300 and climbing rapidly, says Mark Long, publisher of the World Satellite Almanac. More than half of those services emanate from the United States—everything from the Arts & Entertainment Network to Total Christian Television. Truly global "super channels" such as MTV reach hundreds of millions of households, while CNN is seen in 137 countries.

- Scores of new communications satellites are planned for launch in just   16
the next five years, which will mean a huge jump in the number of spaceborne TV channels.

The cultural, political and economic effects of this global television revo-   17
lution are enormous.

TV sets are more common in Japanese homes than flush toilets. Virtually   18
every Mexican household has a TV, but only half have phones. Thai consumers will buy a TV set before an electric fan or even a refrigerator.

Parents in China complain that teen-agers are humming jingles from   19
Nabisco and Coca-Cola commercials. Russians in the ecological sinkhole of Tyumen, in Siberia, rank the fate of Marianna, the beleaguered heroine of a Mexican TV-produced soap opera titled "The Rich Also Cry," as their third

biggest worry in life—after acquiring weapons for self-defense and raising their kids. Turkish schoolchildren adopt an argot dubbed "Turkilize" picked up from German-, French- and English-language satellite channels beamed in from Western Europe.

Kuwait City rooftops are a sea of parabolic antennas. Vans roam Bogota streets with miniature satellite dishes on the roof and a megaphone blaring promises of hookups for $150. In New Delhi, "dish wallahs" nail satellite receivers to crowded apartment buildings. Nearly 20% of all Polish households have installed a dish over the last three years. Ivory Coast distributors have so flooded the dish market that they can no longer even give them away.

The Iraqi army carted away 50,000 satellite dishes when retreating from Kuwait—inspiring some CNN staffers to joke that what the Iraqis really wanted was uncensored television, not oil. Philippine troops surprised a guerrilla camp in the mountains because the revolutionaries were engrossed watching MTV from a homemade satellite hookup. Fiji schools reported record absenteeism and "TV hangovers" after live satellite television was introduced for the first time because students stayed up until 3 a.m., mesmerized by American sitcoms.

Shaping History

Whether in the situation room at the White House or in living rooms at home, it is clear to viewers that television is no longer simply a limp witness to history.

Television is how most people now experience history, as happened when viewers watched live satellite pictures of Scud missiles whistling down on Israel during the Gulf War. Conversely, history is now shaped by television—a reality eloquently symbolized by East German youths when they hoisted MTV flags over the Berlin Wall as it was torn down.

Oxford political scientist Timothy Garton Ash dubs television "the third superpower" whose influence will only grow as satellites and cable revolutionize its content.

A complex set of problems and issues arise from that power.

Ash warns that borderless TV threatens to make even more painfully obvious the economic gulf between rich nations and poor ones. Diplomats in Libya contend that television is undermining the regime of Moammar Kadafi by tempting the country's relatively poor and otherwise largely sheltered population with the consumer product delights seen in Italian commercials.

Even more alarming to some is the prospect of a world full of couch potatoes. The French now spend more time watching TV than working. Spanish schoolchildren watch more than their American counterparts.

Some worry that all that TV watching will make the rest of the world lose its appetite for reading—as has already happened to two generations of Americans.

With satellites beaming down literally hundreds of TV channels over whole continents and oceans, countries lose control over the information crossing their borders—an unstoppable migration of ideas, images and culture that raises basic questions about the meaning of national sovereignty in the modern world.

"The nation-state is less and less able to control what goes in and out of   30
it," said Everrete E. Dennis, a media scholar and executive director of the Freedom Forum Media Studies Center. "It really makes customs and other nuances from the past kind of irrelevant."

What is happening around the world is the outcome of nearly two   31
decades of global deregulation, spreading capitalism and advances in technology that are making electronic communications perhaps the world's preeminent growth industry.

"Technology has made it possible to add a number of channels in a vari-   32
ety of ways," said Eli Noam, an expert in global television at Columbia University's Graduate School of Business in New York. "And the old state-run broadcasting systems are running out of steam."

While international radio dates to the 1930s, borderless TV did not ma-   33
ture until the 1980s.

Billions in Advertising

The surge in communications satellites hurled into orbit—literally hundreds   34
since 1965, with more than 70 additional "birds" planned through 1996—
stems from the mushrooming demand for telecommunications pathways to transmit telephone, data and TV signals around the world.

The global market for communications satellites is projected to reach $6.1   35
billion in 1996. Satellite time is now so readily available it costs a paltry $750 to $1,000 an hour for a link between North America and Europe.

Many of the new channels are being financed by advertising generated   36
from an increasingly industrialized world looking for new outlets for its consumer and manufactured goods.

In Europe, TV advertising is expected to more than double to $36 billion   37
by the turn of the century. The Pacific Rim's nascent TV ad market—just emerging from years of heavy-handed government regulation—has already reached $14 billion. With worldwide satellite networks, the Holy Grail of marketing—global advertising—is finally a reality.

Europe, with a potential market of 320 million viewers, today has twice as   38
many hours of programming to fill as it did a couple of years ago. The number of channels has exploded—to 120 from 39 in the past decade—and could reach 250 within three years. More than 95% of the homes in Belgium now get at least 25 cable TV channels—the highest penetration anywhere in the world. Satellite channels attract half of the TV audience in some Western European countries.

Ever higher-powered satellites not only carry more programs but also al-   39
low for smaller and cheaper receiving dishes, making it virtually impossible for governments to regulate their spread. When the Colombian government

ordered that the country's estimated 300,000 owners register their satellite dishes, only 50 complied.

"In another five years, there will be direct broadcast satellite all over the Arab world," said Abdallah Schleifer, professor of television journalism at American University in Cairo. "And whether [people] want it or not, everyone is going to have access."   40

Historically, the empowered elite have always sought to suppress the wider distribution of ideas, wealth, rights and, most of all, knowledge.   41

This is as true today as it was 536 years ago, when the German printer Gutenberg invented movable type to print the Bible. For two centuries afterward, government tightly controlled what people could read through the widespread exercise of "prior restraint."   42

Then, in 1695, the English Parliament abolished pre-publication censorship—an act as significant for freedom of the press as the 1791 ratification of the First Amendment to the Constitution of the United States.   43

Some governments still go to mind-boggling lengths to make the news fit their political purposes.   44

When Korean Air Lines Flight 007 was shot down by the Russians in 1983, killing 269 people, the top story on the South Korean evening news was about President Chun Doo Hwan instructing village leaders to start a road cleanup campaign.   45

The Chinese government doctored videotape of the 1989 Tian An Men Square massacre, reversing the order of events to make it appear the killings were a justified reaction to mob violence.   46

Just as censorship of the printed word could not continue with the emergence of democracy in 17th-Century Britain and 18th-Century America, so today suppression of the electronic media is thwarted by technology and rapidly growing economies around the world.   47

The growing middle class in newly industrialized Thailand is typically growing impatient with old-style government censorship.   48

Currency traders complained that Bangkok banks racked up huge losses during the Gulf War because they didn't have instant access to news of market-moving developments. A little over a year later, when officials tried to censor news reports of violent attacks against anti-government demonstrators in Bangkok, Thais scrambled to buy gray-market satellite dishes so they could see unfettered foreign news broadcasts.   49

Ever since the Gulf War, customers dine at one of Kuwait City's most popular seafront restaurants in front of a battery of giant-screen television sets tuned variously to CNN, BBC-TV, Kuwait's own two government channels and a state-run station in nearby Bahrain. Over dinner, they debate the contents.   50

If you can't lick 'em, some governments apparently feel, you may as well join 'em. There are presently more than 40 established or planned government-run satellite TV channels. Many have the same propagandistic purpose as their terrestrial predecessors, but some are reacting to the new marketplace.   51

Egypt's Space Channel, for example, originally launched to entertain   52
homesick Egyptian troops in the Saudi desert during the Gulf War, is seen as a
response to Middle Eastern Broadcasting's Pan-Arabic news channel, owned
by Saudis with royal connections.

Like ambitious states that want to join the nuclear club, a country today   53
barely ranks as a world-class power unless it lofts a satellite bearing its own
acronym: Asiasat, Aussat, Turksat, Thaicom, Arabsat, Insat, Indonesia's Palapa
and Spain's Hispasat, to name but a few.

"It's frequently a question of political sovereignty, not just economic ra-   54
tionality," said Meherro Jussawalla, a research economist with the East-West
Center in Honolulu. "Each country wants to control its own satellite system
for domestic purposes."

Cultural Control

Even more than on politics, however, the greatest influence of satellite televi-   55
sion is on culture. Whereas it used to take decades or centuries for one culture
to seep into another, television today can spread lasting images in a matter of
seconds.

"Foolish programs coming in foreign languages to our cable television   56
stations are as much a danger to us as some attacks on our frontier," threatening Israel's culture, heritage and language, Foreign Minister Shimon Peres said
not long ago.

Ironically, Peres shares this concern with Islamic fundamentalists in Alge-   57
ria who now call satellite receiving dishes—*les antennes paraboliques* in
French—*les antennes diaboliques.*

While devout Muslims march through the streets of Algiers, satellite TV   58
programs from France's TV5 and Italy's RAI 1 show naked women astride
naked men and an Italian strip game show called "Tutti Frutti."

Furious British politicians are seemingly powerless to block a porno-   59
graphic satellite channel beamed from Holland called "Red Hot Dutch."
Spanish intellectuals worry that Mexico's booming export of *telenovelas* (soap
operas) masks its cultural imperialist ambitions. American Christmas shows
in Ethiopia caused a rush among Ethiopians to find Christmas trees.

Occasionally, the attempts to block these images are comical.   60

On Egyptian TV, which abides by strict Islamic code, kisses on reruns of   61
"Dallas" and "Falcon Crest" are edited out after the first split-second smooch.
Even that's too racy for neighboring Saudi Arabia, which protests that viewers
in Jeddah can receive the Egyptian TV signals and people in the south can
watch Yemen's televised Parliament.

When Pakistan—a country where even state-run TV's female newscasters   62
are veiled—allowed CNN into the country, Islamic religious leaders quickly
objected that the most popular show on the network was "Style," featuring
stunning women modeling the latest fleshy fashions. At first, authorities tried
to superimpose black bars on the screen to block out the women's skin. But

the models moved so fast that several knees and elbows sneaked through. Finally, the authorities blacked out the entire picture, permitting only the audio track of the latest creations from Paris and Milan.

Satellite dishes "bring in all kinds of evil and corruption," said Saudi Arabia's chief Islamic scholar, Sheik Abdul Azziz ibn Baz, who ruled that the dishes violate tenets of Islam.

The roots of such fears can run deep, as they do between Japan and South Korea, where Koreans remember Japan's colonization and attempts to wipe out its language and culture.

When Japan started satellite broadcasting, Korea—fearing another cultural invasion—protested and demanded that Japan adjust its "footprint" to exclude the country.

Neither quotas nor religious edicts are likely to slow the onslaught of borderless television. Rather than homogenizing the world, it is likely that the revolution will instead lead to a greater diversity in programming, especially as developing states become more sophisticated in the use of the medium.

The global village won't be called "Dallas."

Questions

1. According to Lippman, what are some of the drawbacks of borderless television?

2. What are some of the advantages and disadvantages of the ease in which cultures are spread by global television?

3. Pick a particular culture with which you have had little direct contact. To what extent has your view of this culture been influenced by how it is portrayed on television?

Report from El Dorado

MICHAEL VENTURA

Michael Ventura (b. 1945) is a columnist for the L. A. Weekly. *He is the au-thor of* Mollyhawk Poems *(1977),* Shadow Dancing in the U.S.A. *(1985), and* Night Time Losing Time *(1989).*

In this essay, he asserts that media images have replaced American cul-ture and history. He goes on to argue that television acts as a panacea whose fundamental message is "It's all right." This selection is from Shadow Dancing in the U.S.A. *(1988).*

To go from a job you don't like to watching a screen on which others live   1
more intensely than you . . . is American life, by and large.

This is our political ground. This is our artistic ground. This is what we've   2
done with our immense resources. We have to stop calling it "entertainment"
or "news" or "sports" and start calling it what it is: our most immediate environment.

This is a very, very different America from the America that built the in-   3
dustrial capacity to win the Second World War and to surge forward on the
multiple momentums of that victory for thirty years. That was an America
that worked at mostly menial tasks during the day (now we work at mostly
clerical tasks) and had to look at each other at night.

I'm not suggesting a nostalgia for that time. It was repressive and bigoted   4
to an extent that is largely forgotten today, to cite only two of its uglier aspects. But in that environment America meant *America:* the people and the
land. The land was far bigger than what we'd done with the land.

This is no longer true. Now the environment of America is media. Not the   5
land itself, but the image of the land. The focus is not on the people so much
as it is on the interplay between people and screens. What we've done with
the land is far more important now than the land—we're not even dealing
with the land anymore, we're dealing with our manipulation and pollution
of it.

And what we've done with the very concept of "image" is taking on far   6
more importance for many of us than the actual sights and sounds of our
lives.

For instance: Ronald Reagan stands on a cliff in Normandy to commemo-   7
rate the day U.S. Army Rangers scaled those cliffs in the World War II invasion. Today's Rangers reenact the event while some of the original Rangers, in
their sixties now, look on. Except that it is the wrong cliff. The cliff that was

actually scaled is a bit further down the beach, but it's not as photogenic as this cliff, so this cliff has been chosen for everybody to emote over. Some of the old Rangers tell reporters that the historical cliff is over yonder, but the old Rangers are swept up (as well they might be) in the ceremonies, and nobody objects enough. This dislocation, this choice, this stance that the real cliff is not important, today's photograph is more important, is a media event. It insults the real event, and overpowers it. Multiplied thousands of times over thousands of outlets of every form and size, ensconced in textbooks as well as screenplays, in sales presentations as well as legislative packages, in religious revivals as well as performance-art pieces, this is the process that has displaced what used to be called "culture."

* * *

"I'm not even sure it's a culture anymore. It's like this careening hunger   8
splattering out in all directions."

Jeff Nightbyrd was trying to define "culture" in the wee hours at the Four   9
Queens in Las Vegas. It was a conversation that had been going on since we'd become friends working on the *Austin Sun* in 1974, trying to get our bearings now that the sixties were *really* over. He'd spent that triple-time decade as an SDS organizer and editor of *Rat,* and I'd hit Austin after a few years of road-roving, commune-hopping, and intensive (often depressive) self-exploration—getting by, as the song said, with a little help from my friends, as a lot of us did then. This particular weekend Nightbyrd had come to Vegas from Austin for a computer convention, and I had taken off from my duties at the *L.A. Weekly* for some lessons in craps (at which Jeff is quite good) and to further our rap. The slot machines clattered around us in unison, almost comfortingly, the way the sound of a large shaky air-conditioner can be comforting in a cheap hotel room when you're trying to remember to forget. We were, after all, trying to fathom an old love: America.

There are worse places to indulge in this obsession than Las Vegas. It is   10
the most American, the most audacious, of cities. Consuming unthinkable amounts of energy in the midst of an unlivable desert (Death Valley is not far away), its decor is based on various cheap-to-luxurious versions of a 1930s Busby Berkeley musical. Indeed, no studio backlot could ever be more of a set, teeming with extras, people who come from all over America, and all over the world, to see the topless, tasteless shows, the Johnny Carson guests on parade doing their utterly predictable routines, the dealers and crap-table croupiers who combine total boredom with ruthless efficiency and milk us dry—yet at least these tourists are risking something they genuinely value: money. It's a quiz show turned into a way of life, where you can get a good Italian dinner at dawn. Even the half-lit hour of the wolf doesn't faze Las Vegas. How could it, when the town has survived the flash of atom bombs tested just over the horizon?

The history books will tell you that, ironically enough, the town was   11
founded by Mormons in 1855. Even their purity of vision couldn't bear the intensity of this desert, and they abandoned the place after just two years. But they had left a human imprint, and a decade later the U.S. Army built a

fort here. The settlement hung on, and the railroad came through in 1905. During the Second World War the Mafia started to build the city as we know it now. Religious zealots, the Army, and the Mafia—quite a triad of founding fathers.

Yet one could go back even further, some 400 years, when the first Euro- 12 peans discovered the deserts of the American West—Spaniards who, as they slowly began to believe that there might be no end to these expansive wilds, became more and more certain that somewhere, somewhere to the north, lay El Dorado—a city of gold. Immeasurable wealth would be theirs, they believed, and eternal youth. What would they have thought if they had suddenly come upon modern Las Vegas, lying as it does in the midst of this bleached nowhere, glowing at night with a brilliance that would have frightened them? We have built our desert city to their measure—for they were gaudy and greedy, devout and vicious, jovial and frenzied, like this town. They had just wasted the entire Aztec civilization because their fantasies were so strong they couldn't see the ancient cultural marvels before their eyes. The Aztecs, awed and terrified, believed they were being murdered by gods; and in the midst of such strangeness, the Spaniards took on godlike powers even in their own eyes. As many Europeans would in America, they took liberties here they would never have taken within sight of their home cathedrals. Their hungers dominated them, and in their own eyes the New World seemed as inexhaustible as their appetites. So when Nightbyrd described our present culture as "a careening hunger splattering out in all directions," he was also, if unintentionally, speaking about our past. Fittingly, we were sitting in the midst of a city that had been fantasized by those seekers of El Dorado 400 years ago. In that sense, America had Las Vegas a century before it had Plymouth Rock. And our sensibility has been caught between the fantasies of the conquistadors and the obsessions of the Puritans ever since.

Yes, a fitting place to try to think about American culture. 13

"There are memories of culture," Nightbyrd was saying, "but the things 14 that have given people strength have dissolved. And because they're dissolved, people are into distractions. And distractions aren't culture."

Are there even memories? The media have taken over our memories. That 15 day Nightbyrd had been driving through the small towns that dot this desert, towns for which Vegas is only a dull glow to the southwest. In a bar in one of those towns, "like that little bar in *The Right Stuff*," he'd seen pictures of cowboys on the wall. "Except that they weren't cowboys. They were movie stars. Guys who grew up in Glendale [John Wayne] and Santa Monica [Robert Redford]." Surely this desert had its own heroes once, in the old gold-mining towns where a few people still hang on, towns like Goldfield and Tonopah. Remembering those actual heroes would be "culture." Needing pictures of movie stars for want of the real thing is only a nostalgia for culture.

Nostalgia is not memory. Memory is specific. One has a relationship to a 16 memory, and it may be a difficult relationship, because a memory always makes a demand upon the present. But nostalgia is vague, a sentimental wash that obscures memory and acts as a narcotic to dull the importance of the present.

Media as we know it now thrives on nostalgia and is hostile to memory.   1
In a television bio-pic, Helen Keller is impersonated by Mare Winningham.
But the face of Helen Keller was marked by her enormous powers of concentration, while the face of Mare Winningham is merely cameo-pretty. A memory has been stolen. It takes a beauty in you to see the beauty in Helen
Keller's face, while to cast the face of a Mare Winningham in the role is to
suggest, powerfully, that one can come back from the depths unscathed. No
small delusion is being sold here. Yet this is a minor instance in a worldwide,
twenty-four-hour-a-day onslaught.

An onslaught that gathers momentum every twenty-four hours. Remem-   18
ber that what drew us to Las Vegas was a computer fair. One of these new
computers does interesting things with photographs. You can put a photograph into the computer digitally. This means the photograph is in there
without a negative or print, each element of the image stored separately. In
the computer, you can change any element of the photograph you wish, replacing it or combining it with elements from other photographs. In other
words, you can take composites of different photographs and put them into a
new photograph of your own composition. Combine this with computer
drawing, and you can touch up shadows that don't match. When it comes
out of the computer the finished product bears no evidence of tampering
with any negative. The possibilities for history books and news stories are infinite. Whole new histories can now be written. Events which never happened can be fully documented.

The neo-Nazis who are trying to convince people that the Holocaust   19
never happened will be able to show the readers of their newsletter an
Auschwitz of well-fed, happy people being watched over by kindly S.S. men
while tending gardens. And they will be able to make the accusation that
photographs of the *real* Auschwitz were created in a computer by manipulative Jews. The Soviet Union can rewrite Czechoslovakia and Afghanistan, the
United States can rewrite Vietnam, and atomic weapons proponents can
prove that the average resident of Hiroshima was unharmed by the blast. On
a less sinister, but equally disruptive, level, the writers of business prospec-
tuses and real-estate brochures can have a field day.

Needless to say, when any photograph can be processed this way then all   20
photographs become suspect. It not only becomes easier to lie, it becomes far
harder to tell the truth.

But why should this seem shocking when under the names of "entertain-   21
ment" and "advertising" we've been filming history, and every facet of daily
life, in just this way for nearly a century now? It shouldn't surprise us that the
ethics of our entertainment have taken over, and that we are viewing reality
itself as a form of entertainment. And, as entertainment, reality can be rewritten, transformed, played with, in any fashion.

These considerations place us squarely at the center of our world—and we   22
have no choice, it's the only world there is anymore. *Electronic media has done
for everyday reality what Einstein did for physics:* everything is shifting. Even the
shifts are shifting. And a fact is not so crucial anymore, not so crucial as the

process that turns a fact into an image. For we live now with images as much as facts, and the images seem to impart more life than facts *precisely because they are so capable of transmutation, of transcendence, able to transcend their sources and their uses.* And all the while the images goad us on, so that we become partly images ourselves, imitating the properties of images as we surround ourselves with images.

This is most blatant in our idea of "a vacation"—an idea only about 100 years old. To "vacation" is to enter an image. Las Vegas is only the most shrill embodiment of this phenomenon. People come here not so much to gamble (individual losses are comparatively light), nor for the glittery entertainment, but to step into an image, a daydream, a filmlike world where "everything" is promised. No matter that the Vegas definition of "everything" is severely limited, what thrills tourists is the sense of being surrounded in "real life" by the same images that they see on TV. But the same is true of the Grand Canyon, or Yellowstone National Park, or Yosemite, or Death Valley, or virtually any of our "natural" attractions. What with all their roads, telephones, bars, cable-TV motels, the visitors are carefully protected from having to *experience* the place. They view its image, they camp out in its image, ski down or climb up its image, take deep breaths of its image, let its image give them a tan. Or, when they tour the cities, they ride the quaint trolley cars of the city's image, they visit the Latin Quarter of its image, they walk across the Brooklyn Bridge of its image—our recreation is a *re*-creation of America into one big Disneyland.

And this is only one way we have stripped the very face of America of any content, any reality, concentrating only on its power as image. We also elect images, groom ourselves as images, make an image of our home, our car, and now, with aerobics, of our very bodies. For in the aerobics craze the flesh becomes a garment, susceptible to fashion. So it becomes less *our* flesh, though the exercise may make it more serviceable. It becomes "my" body, like "my" car, "my" house. What, within us, is saying "my"? What is transforming body into image? We shy away from asking. In this sense it can be said that after the age of about twenty-five we no longer *have* bodies anymore—we have possessions that are either more or less young, which we are constantly trying to transform and through which we try to breathe.

It's not that all this transformation of realities into un- or non- or supra-realities is "bad," but that it's unconscious, compulsive, reductive. We rarely make things more than they were; we simplify them into less. Though surely the process *could*—at least theoretically—go both ways. Or so India's meditators and Zen's monks say. But that would be to *increase* meaning, and we seem bent on the elimination of meaning. We're Reagan's Rangers, climbing a cliff that *is* a real cliff, except it's not the cliff we say it is, so that the meaning of both cliffs—not to mention of our act of climbing—is reduced.

As I look out onto a glowing city that is more than 400 years old but was built only during the last forty years, as I watch it shine in blinking neon in a desert that has seen the flash of atom bombs, it becomes more and more plain to me that America is at war with meaning. America is form opposed to content. Not just form *instead* of content. Form opposed. Often violently. There are few things resented so much among us as the suggestion that what we do *means*. It *means* something to watch so much TV. It *means* something to be obsessed with sports. It *means* something to vacation by indulging in images. It means something, and therefore it has consequences. Other cultures have argued over their meanings. We tend to deny that there is any such thing, insisting instead that what you see is what you get and that's *it*. All we're doing is having a *good time,* all we're doing is making a buck, all we're doing is enjoying the spectacle, we insist. So that when we export American culture what we are really exporting is an attitude toward content. Media is the American war on content with all the stops out, with meaning in utter rout, frightened nuances dropping their weapons as they run.

* * *

"Media is the history that forgives," my friend Dave Johnson told me on   27
a drive through that same desert a few months later. We love to take a weekend every now and again and just *drive.* Maybe it started with reading *On the Road* when we were kids, or watching a great old TV show called *Route 66* about two guys who drove from town to town working at odd jobs and having adventures with intense women who, when asked who they were, might say (as one did), "Suppose I said I was the Queen of Spain?" Or maybe it was all those rock 'n' roll songs about "the road"—the road, where we can blast our tape-decks as loud as we want, and watch the world go by without having to touch it, a trip through the greatest hologram there is, feeling like neither boys nor men but both and something more, embodiments of some ageless, restless principle of movement rooted deep in our prehistory. All of which is to say that we're just as stuck with the compulsion to enter the image as anybody, and that we love the luxuries of fossil fuel just as much as any other red-blooded, thickheaded Americans.

Those drives are our favorite time to talk, and, again, America is our old-   28
est flame. We never tire of speaking of her, nor of our other old girlfriends. For miles and miles of desert I thought of what Dave had said.

"Media is the history that forgives." A lovely way to put it, and quite un-   29
Western. We Westerners tend to think in sets of opposites: good/bad, right/wrong, me/you, past/present. These sets are often either antagonistic (East/West, commie/capitalist, Christian/heathen) or they set up a duality that instantly calls out to be bridged (man/woman). But Dave's comment sidesteps the dualities and suggests something more complex: a lyrical impulse is alive somewhere in all this media obfuscation. It is the impulse to redeem the past—in his word, to *forgive* history—by presenting it as we would have most liked it to be.

It is one thing to accuse the media of lying. They are, and they know it,   30
and they know we know, and we know they know that we know, and nothing changes. It is another to recognize the rampant lying shallowness of our media as a massive united longing for . . . innocence? For a sheltered child-like state in which we need not know about our world or our past. We are so desperate for this that we are willing to accept ignorance as a substitute for

innocence. For there can be no doubt anymore that this society *knowingly* accepts its ignorance as innocence—we have seen so much in the last twenty years that now we know what we *don't* see. Whenever a TV show or a movie or a news broadcast leaves out crucial realities for the sake of sentimentality, we pretty much understand the nature of what's been left out and why.

But American media *forgives* the emptiness and injustice of our daily life by presenting our daily life as innocent. Society, in turn, forgives American media for lying because if we accept the lie as truth then we needn't *do* anything, we needn't change.   31

I like Dave's line of thought because it suggests a motive—literally, a motive force—for these rivers of glop that stream from the screens and loudspeakers of our era. Because, contrary to popular belief, profit is *not* the motive. That seems a rash statement to make in the vicinity of Las Vegas, but the profit motive merely begs the question: *why* is it profitable? Profit, in media, is simply a way of measuring attention. Why does what we call "media" attract so much attention?   32

The answer is that it is otherwise too crippling for individuals to bear the strain of accepting the unbalanced, unrewarding, uninspiring existence that is advertised as "normal daily life" for most people who have to earn a living every day.   33

Do those words seem too strong? Consider: to go to a job you don't value in itself but for its paycheck, while your kids go to a school that is less and less able to educate them; a large percentage of your pay is taken by the government for defenses that don't defend, welfare that doesn't aid, and the upkeep of a government that is impermeable to the influence of a single individual; while you are caught in a value system that judges you by what you own, in a society where it is taken for granted now that children can't communicate with their parents, that old people have to be shut away in homes, and that no neighborhood is *really* safe; while the highest medical costs in the world don't prevent us from having one of the worst health records in the West (for instance, New York has a far higher infant mortality rate than Hong Kong), and the air, water, and supermarket food are filled with God-knows-what; and to have, at the end of a busy yet uneventful life, little to show for enduring all this but a comfortable home if you've "done well" enough; yet to *know* all along that you're living in the freest, most powerful country in the world, though you haven't had time to exercise much freedom and don't personally have any power—this is to be living a life of slow attrition and maddening contradictions.   34

Add to this a social style that values cheerfulness more than any other attribute, and then it is not so strange or shocking that the average American family watches six to eight hours of network television a day. It is a cheap and sanctioned way to partake of this world without having actually to live in it.   35

Certainly they don't watch so much TV because they're bored—there's far too much tension in their lives to call them bored, and, in fact, many of the products advertised on their favorite programs feature drugs to calm them down. Nor is it because they're stupid—a people managing the most techni-   36 cally intricate daily life in history can hardly be written off as stupid; nor because they can't entertain themselves—they are not so different from the hundreds of generations of their forebears who entertained themselves very well as a matter of course. No, they are glued to the TV because one of the most fundamental messages of television is: "It's all right."

Every sitcom and drama says: "It's all right." Those people on the tube go   37
through the same—if highly stylized—frustrations, and are exposed to the same dangers as we are, yet they reappear magically every week (every day on the soap operas) ready for more, always hopeful, always cheery, never questioning the fundamental premise that this is the way a great culture behaves and that all the harassments are the temporary inconveniences of a beneficent society. It's going to get even *better,* but even now *it's all right.* The commercials, the Hollywood movies, the universal demand in every television drama or comedy that no character's hope can ever be exhausted, combine in a deafening chorus of: *It's all right.*

As a screenwriter I have been in many a film production meeting, and   38
not once have I heard any producer or studio executive say, "We have to lie to the public." What I have heard, over and over, is, "They have to leave the theater feeling good." This, of course, easily (though not always) translates into lying—into simplifying emotions and events so that "it's all right." You may measure how deeply our people know "it" is *not* all right, not at all, by how much money they are willing to pay to be ceaselessly told that it is. The more they feel it's not, the more they need to be told it is—hence Mr. Reagan's popularity.

Works that don't say "It's all right" don't get much media attention or   39
make much money.

The culture itself is in the infantile position of needing to be assured,   40
every day, all day, that this way of life is good for you. Even the most disturbing news is dispensed in the most reassuring package. As world news has gotten more and more disturbing, the trend in broadcast journalism has been to get more and more flimflam, to take it less seriously, to keep up the front of "It's really quite all right." This creates an enormous tension between the medium and its messages, because everybody knows that what's on the news is *not* all right. That is why such big money is paid to a newscaster with a calm, authoritative air who, by his presence alone, seems to resolve the contradictions of his medium. Walter Cronkite was the most popular newscaster in broadcast history because his very presence implied: "As long as I'm on the air, you can be sure that, no matter what I'm telling you, *it's still all right.*"

Which is to say that the media has found it profitable to do the mother-   41
ing of the mass psyche. But it's a weak mother. It cannot nurture. All it can do is say it's all right, tuck us in, and hope for the best.

Today most serious, creative people exhaust themselves in a sideline com-   42
mentary on this state of affairs, a commentary that usually gets sucked up into the media and spewed back out in a format that says "It's all right. What this guy's saying is quite all right, what this woman's singing is all right, all right." This is what "gaining recognition" virtually always means now in

America: your work gets turned inside out so that its meaning becomes "It's all right."

Of course, most of what exists *to make media of,* to make images of, is   43
more and more disorder. Media keeps saying, "It's all right" while being fixated upon the violent, the chaotic, and the terrifying. So the production of media becomes more and more schizoid, with two messages simultaneously being broadcast: "It's all right. We're dying. It's all right. We're all dying." The other crucial message—"We're dying"—runs right alongside *It's all right.*

Murder is the crux of much media "drama." But it's murder presented   44
harmlessly, with trivial causes cited. Rare is the attempt, in all our thousands of murder dramas, to delve below the surface. We take for granted now, almost as an immutable principle of dramatic unity, that significant numbers of us want to kill significant numbers of the rest of us. And what are all the murders in our media but a way of saying "We are being killed, we are killing, we are dying"? Only a people dying and in the midst of death would need to see so much of it in such sanitized form *in order to make death harmless.* This is the way we choose to share our death.

Delete the word "entertainment" and say instead, North Americans de   45
vote an enormous amount of time to the ritual of sharing death. If this were recognized as a ritual, and if the deaths were shared with a respect for the realities and the mysteries of death, this might be a very useful thing to do. But there is no respect for death in our death-dependent media, there is only the compulsion to display death. As for the consumers, they consume these deaths like sugar pills. Their ritual goes on far beneath any level on which they'd be prepared to admit the word "ritual." So we engage in a ritual we pretend isn't happening, hovering around deaths that we say aren't real.

It is no coincidence that this practice has thrived while the Pentagon uses   46
the money of these death watchers to create weapons for death on a scale that is beyond the powers of human imagination—the very same human imagination that is stunting itself by watching ersatz deaths, as though intentionally crippling its capacity to envision the encroaching dangers. It is possible that the Pentagon's process could not go on without the dulling effects of this "entertainment."

When we're not watching our screens, we're listening to music. And, of   47
course, North Americans listen to love songs at every possible opportunity, through every possible orifice of media. People under the strain of such dislocating unrealities need to hear "I love you, I love you," as often as they can. "I love you" or "I used to love you" or "I ought to love you" or "I need to love you" or "I want to love you." It is the fashion of pop-music critics to discount the words for the style, forgetting that most of the world's cultures have had songs about *everything,* songs about work, about the sky, about death, about the gods, about getting up in the morning, about animals, about children, about eating, about dreams—about everything, along with love. These were songs that everybody knew and sang. For a short time in the late sixties we moved toward such songs again, but that was a brief digression; since the First World War the music that most North Americans listen to has been a

music of love lyrics that rarely go beyond adolescent yearnings. Either the song is steeped in the yearnings themselves, or it is saturated with a longing for the days when one could, shamelessly, feel like an adolescent. The beat has changed radically from decade to decade, but with brief exceptions that beat has carried the same pathetic load. (The beat, thankfully, has given us other gifts.)

It can't be over-emphasized that these are entertainments of a people   48
whose basic imperative is the need not to think about their environment. The depth of their need may be measured by the hysterical popularity of this entertainment; it is also the measure of how little good it does them.

* * *

Media is not experience. In its most common form, media substitutes a   49
fantasy of experience or (in the case of news) an abbreviation of experience for the living fact. But in our culture the absorption of media has become a substitute for experience. We absorb media, we don't live it—there is a vast psychological difference, and it is a difference that is rarely brought up.

For example, in the 1940s, when one's environment was still one's *envi-*   50
ronment, an experience to be lived instead of a media-saturation to be absorbed, teenagers like Elvis Presley and Jerry Lee Lewis didn't learn their music primarily from the radio. Beginning when they were small boys they sneaked over to the black juke joints of Louisiana and Mississippi and Tennessee, where they weren't supposed to go, and they listened and learned. When Lewis and Presley began recording, even though they were barely twenty they had tremendous authority because they had experience—a raw experience of crossing foreign boundaries, of streets and sounds and peoples, of the night-to-night learning of ways that could not be taught at home.

This is very different from young musicians now who learn from a prod-   51
uct, not a living ground. Their music doesn't get to them till it's been sifted through elaborate corporate networks of production and distribution. It doesn't smack of the raw world that exists before "product" can even be thought of.

The young know this, of course. They sense the difference intensely, and   52
often react to it violently. So white kids from suburban media culture invented slam dancing (jumping up and down and slamming into each other) while black kids from the South Bronx, who have to deal with realities far more urgent than media, were elaborating the astounding graces of break dancing.

Slam dancing was a dead end. Break dancing, coming from a living   53
ground, goes out through media but becomes ultimately transformed into another living ground—the kids in the elementary school down the street in Santa Monica break dance. Which is to say, a grace has been added to their lives. A possibility of grace. With the vitality that comes from having originated from a living ground. The media here is taking its proper role as a channel, not as a world in itself. It's possible that these kids are being affected more in their bodies and their daily lives by the South Bronx subculture than by high-gloss films like *Gremlins* or *Indiana Jones and the Temple of Doom.* Even through all this static, life can speak to life.

Of course, break dancing inevitably gets hyped, and hence devalued, by   54
the entertainment industry, the way Elvis Presley ended up singing "Viva Las
Vegas" as that town's most glamorous headliner. He went from being the nu-
minous son of a living ground to being the charismatic product of a media
empire—the paradigm of media's power to transform the transformers. The
town veritably glows in the dark with the strength of media's mystique.

We do not yet know what life *is* in a media environment. We have not yet   55
evolved a contemporary culture that can supply the definition—or rather,
supply the constellation of concepts in which that definition would live and
grow. These seem such simple statements, but they are at the crux of the
American dilemma now. An important aspect of this dilemma is that we've
barely begun a body of thought and art which is focused on what is really
alive in the ground of a media-saturated daily life. For culture always proceeds
from two poles: one is the people of the land and the street; the other is the
thinker. You see this most starkly in revolutions: the ground swell on the one
hand, the thinker (the Jefferson, for instance) on the other. Or religiously, the
ground swell of belief that is articulated by a Michelangelo or a Dante. The
two poles can exist without each other but they cannot be effective without
each other.

Unless a body of thought connects with a living ground, there is no pos-   56
sibility that this era will discover itself within its cacophony and create, one
day, a post-A.D. culture. It is ours to attempt the thought and seek the
ground—for all of us exist between those poles. We are not only dying. We
are living. And we are struggling to share our lives, which is all, finally, that
"culture" means.

Questions

1. How are TV images able to transform history? What are the advantages and dangers of the power of the image to represent reality?

2. What types of images enter your mind when you think of a vacation? Do you
   agree with Ventura's assertion that to "vacation" is to enter an image?

3. What does Ventura mean when he says that the image has replaced culture?

4. According to Ventura, why do people watch so much television? Do you agree
   with his explanation?

5. Would Ventura agree with Lippman?

Advertising: The Media's Not-So-Silent Partner

CLINT C. WILSON II AND FÉLIX GUTIÉRREZ

Clint C. Wilson II is an associate professor of journalism at the University of Southern California. He has published widely on ethnic minorities and mass media, including Minorities and the Media *(1985) a:.d* Black Journalists in Paradox *(1991). He has also worked as a professional journalist for several Los Angeles newspapers and is a founder of the Black Journalists Association of Southern California. Félix Gutiérrez (b. 1943) received his Ph.D. from Stanford University. He was a professor of journalism at the University of Southern California and has received numerous Education in Journalism Awards. He has published widely on Latinos and the media, notably* Minorities and the Media: Diversity and the End of Mass Communication *(with Clint C. Wilson II, 1985). He is currently vice-president of the Gannett Foundation.*

Wilson and Gutiérrez argue that traditionally advertisers have promoted images of minorities that reflect the prejudices of the white majority. They believe that although advertisers are now more racially sensitive, their ads are still harmful to minorities insofar as they "promote consumption of their products as a shortcut to the good life, a quick fix for low-income consumers." This selection is from Minorities and the Media.

In the late 1960s a lovable cartoon character appeared on television screens and in magazines across the United States. Named the Frito Bandito, the cartoon figure of a mustachioed Mexican bandit with six-gun, broad sombrero, and a sinister smile went around houses sneaking Fritos corn chips from unsuspecting mothers. "Bullet"-riddled "wanted" posters produced as part of an advertising campaign for the snack food advised housewives to buy two bags of the corn chips, because "he loves cronchy Fritos corn chips so much he'll stop at nothing to get yours. What's more he's cunning, clever—and sneaky."[1] Television commercials featured youngsters sneaking corn chips from the family supply, then biting into the crunchy chips as "Mexican"-style mustaches appeared on their faces.

The Frito Bandito was a lovable, and successful, salesman for the Frito-Lay Corporation, maker of the corn chips. He was described by the director of advertising for the company as a "simple character, which is intended to make you laugh; in turn, we hope that this laughter will leave our trademark implanted in your memory."[2] But many Latinos, particularly Chicano activist and civic groups, did not react to the Frito Bandito with laughter. They pointed out that the cartoon character was nothing more than a humorous version of the stereotype Mexican bandit, one who perpetuated and reinforced the stereotype of Mexicans as mustachioed thieves. Protests were organized against Frito-Lay and boycotts threatened against television stations airing the commercials. After some local television stations were persuaded in 1970 that the cartoon character was racially offensive and agreed not to air the advertisement, Frito-Lay announced it would cancel what had been a highly successful advertising campaign.

A little more than ten years later, Frito-Lay launched yet another advertising campaign playing on the Anglo perceptions of Latinos and Latin America. But this time the approach was very different. The product was Tostitos, another corn chip produced by the company, but one that was touted as being authentically Mexican. Rather than featuring a gun-toting mustachioed bandit under a broad sombrero, the campaign was centered on a tall, distinguished Latino, reminiscent of the "Latin lovers" who populated earlier generations of Hollywood movies. He spoke with a Spanish accent, but this time it was a lilting, cultured accent that resounded with careful pronunciations of consonants and vowels that highlighted the correct pronunciation of the company's product. 3

In each commercial the stately spokesman told viewers about his fond memories of his growing up as a young boy in his Latin American homeland. Among his fondest memories were coming home from school and play to finding warm corn chips that had just been prepared. He told viewers how good they tasted and how much he missed them. But, he continued, now corn chips with that same authentic taste and shape were now available in the United States to everyone, not just those fortunate enough to come from Latin America. He praised the Tostito corn chips available in plastic bags at local stores and attested to their authenticity. 4

This time there were no protests against the commercials from Latino organizations, no threats of boycotts against the product, and no angry letters to the regulatory agencies overseeing broadcasting or advertising. This time Frito-Lay had struck the right chord with Latinos and non-Latinos. The company played on the accepted imagery of Latinos and Latin America, but instead of reinforcing the image of the sneaky Mexican bandit, the company played on the romantic image of the distinguished, cultured Latino, perhaps more a product of Spain than of Mexico. The campaign, which also ran in media directed to Latinos in the United States, represented a change in the thinking at Frito-Lay, from seeing Latinos as the object of humorous stereotypes to portraying them as people with a romantic past that could be brought into your home through the purchase of Tostitos. It was a transition that illustrated an evolution in advertising, an industry that has been identified as essential to the American character in the United States. 5

Advertising and Media in the Land of Plenty

In 1950 historian David M. Potter was invited by the Wahlgreen Foundation   6
to prepare six lectures on the American character and the impact of economic
abundance on shaping the character of the people living in the United States.
In these lectures, which were later published in a revised form in a book titled
People of Plenty, Potter identified advertising as the "institution of abundance," that unique part of the society "that was brought into being by abundance, without previous existence in any form, and, moreover, an institution
which is peculiarly identified with American abundance."[3] He also noted that
media scholars up to that time had not recognized the central role that advertising has placed in shaping and developing media in the United States.

As Potter and subsequent scholars have noted, the development of advertis-   7
ing as a revenue source for print and, later, broadcast media required media
managers to develop news and entertainment content that would attract the
largest possible number of people. This gave birth to the term "mass media,"
which describes the ability of the media to attract the large audience to which
advertisers wanted to transmit their commercial messages. The circulation and
rating figures are the bread and butter of the media, since they translate into increased advertising insertions and higher advertising rates. The media attract the
mass audience by developing content with a broad appeal that often is directed
at the lowest common denominator of culture in the audience. The advertising,
like the editorial and entertainment material it supports in newspapers, magazines, radio, and television, is also geared to appeal to a mass audience that
might produce buyers. This mass appeal by both advertisers and the media they
support is targeted to the audience in the majority, not to racial or other minorities who might happen to pick up a newspaper or listen to a radio program.

Far from being an appendage to the media industry, Potter described ad-   8
vertising as a force that dictates the editorial and entertainment content of
the media, which depend on advertising dollars for their revenues. Mass media charge artificially low subscription fees to boost their circulation, which
force the media to depend on advertisers even more for their revenues. This,
in turn, is accompanied by editorial or programming philosophies that place
a priority on attracting the largest possible audience. Media content, wrote
Potter, is nothing more than the bait to attract the audience and hold its
attention between the commercial messages:

> What this means, in functional terms, it seems to me, is that the newspaper
> feature, the magazine article, the radio program, do not attain the dignity of
> being ends in themselves. They are rather means to an end: that end, of
> course, is to catch the reader's attention so that he will then read the adver-
> tisement or hear the commercial, and to hold his interest until these essential
> messages have been delivered. The program or the article becomes a kind of
> advertisement in itself—becomes the "pitch," in the telling language of the
> circus barker. Its function is to induce people to accept the commercial, just
> as the commercial's function is to induce them to accept the product."[4]

According to Potter, the development of content as bait for the mass au-   9
dience means that the mass media include material that will attract the most
people and, at the same time, delete material with the potential of offending
or leaving out any potential members of the audience. This places some rigid
constraints on media editorial and entertainment content.

> First, a message must not deal with subjects of special or out-of-the-way inter-
> est, since such subjects by definition have no appeal for the majority of the
> audience. Second, it must not deal with any subject at a high level of matu-
> rity, since many people are immature, chronologically or otherwise, and a
> mature level is one which, by definition, leaves such people out. Third, it
> must not deal with matters which are controversial or even unpleasant or dis-
> tressing, since such matters may, by definition, antagonize or offend some
> members of the audience.[5]

Advertising and Minorities

Given the social and legal restrictions on the participation of racial minorities   10
in the society of the United States during much of this country's history, it is
not hard to see how the desire to cater to the perceived views of the mass audience desired by advertisers has resulted in entertainment and news content
that largely ignores minorities, treats them stereotpyically when they were
recognized, and largely avoids grappling with such issues as segregation, discriminatory immigration laws, land rights, and other controversies that affected certain minority groups more than they do the White majority. While
the portrayal of racial minorities is amply analyzed in other chapters of this
book, it is important to recognize that those portrayals have been, to a large
extent, supported by a system of advertising that requires the media to cater
to the perceived attitudes and prejudices of the White majority and that also
reinforces such images in its own commercial messages. For years, advertisers
in the United States have reflected the place of racial minorities in the social
fabric of the nation by either ignoring them or, when they have been included in advertisements for the mass audience, by processing and presenting
them so as to make them palatable salespersons for the products being advertised. These portrayals have largely mirrored the stereotyped images of minorities in the entertainment media, which, in turn, were designed to reflect
the perceived values and norms of the White majority society. In this way,
minority portrayals in advertising have paralleled and reinforced the images
of minorities in other media.

The history of advertising in the United States is replete with minority   11
images that, like the Frito Bandito, respond to and reinforce the preconceived
image that many White Americans apparently have of Blacks, Latinos,
Asians, and Native Americans. Over the years advertisers have employed
Latin spitfires such as Chiquita Banana, Black mammies such as Aunt
Jemima, and noble savages such as the Santa Fe Railroad's Super Chief to
pitch their products to a predominantly White mass audience of consumers.

In 1984 the Balch Institute for Ethnic Studies in Philadelphia sponsored an exhibit of more than 300 examples of racial and ethnic images used by corporations in magazines, posters, trade cards, and story boards. In an interview with the advertising trade magazine *Advertising Age,* institute director Mark Stolarik quoted the catalog for the exhibit, which capsulized the evolution of minority images and how they have changed.

> Some of these advertisements were based on stereotypes of various ethnic groups. In the early years, they were usually crude and condescending images that appealed to largely Anglo-American audiences who found it difficult to reconcile their own visions of beauty, order and behavior with that of non-Anglo-Americans. Later, these images were softened because of complaints from the ethnic groups involved and the growing sophistication of the advertising industry.[6]

The advertising examples in the exhibit include positive White ethnic   12
stereotypes, such as the wholesome and pure image of Quakers in an early Quaker Oats advertisement and the cleanliness of the Dutch in a turn-of-the-century advertisement for Colgate soaps. But they also featured a late-nineteenth-century advertisement showing an Irish matron threatening to hit her husband over the head with a rolling pin because he didn't smoke the right brand of tobacco. Like Quaker Oats, some products even incorporated a racial stereotype image on the package or product line being advertised, such as Red Man Chewing Tobacco.

"Lawsee! Folks sho' whoops with joy over AUNT JEMIMA PANCAKES,"   13
shouted a bandanna-wearing Black mammy in a magazine advertisement for Aunt Jemima pancake mix, which featured a plump Aunt Jemima on the box. Over the years Aunt Jemima has lost some weight, but the stereotyped face of the Black servant continues to be featured on the box. Earlier advertisements for Cream of Wheat featured Rastus, the Black servant on the box, in a series of magazine cartoons with a group of cute but ill-dressed Black children. Some of the advertisements played on the stereotypes ridiculing Blacks. In one, a Black schoolteacher, standing behind a makeshift lectern made out of a boldly lettered Cream of Wheat box, asks the class, "How do you spell Cream of Wheat?" Others appeared to promote racial integration, such as a magazine advertisement captioned "Putting It Down in Black and White," which showed Rastus serving bowls of the breakfast cereal to Black and White youngsters sitting at the same table.

Racial imagery was also integrated into the naming of trains by the Santa   14
Fe railroad, which called one of its passenger lines the Super Chief and featured highly detailed portraits of the noble Indian in promoting its service through the southwestern United States. In another series of advertisements, the railroad used cartoons of Native American children to show the service and sights passengers could expect when they traveled the Santa Fe line. General Motors advertised its Pontiac automobile with the slogan "Pontiac Heap Fine Car."

These and other portrayals catered to the mass audience mentality by ei-   15
ther neutralizing or making humor of the negative perceptions that many
Whites may have had of racial minorities. The advertising images, rather
than showing minorities as they really were, portrayed minorities as filtered
through Anglo eyes. This presented an out-of-focus image of racial minorities, but one that was palatable, and even persuasive, to the White majority
to which it was directed. In the mid-1960s Black civil rights groups targeted
the advertising industry for special attention, protesting both the lack of integrated advertisements and the stereotyped images that the advertisers continued to use. The effort, accompanied by support from federal officials, resulted
in the overnight inclusion of Blacks as models in television advertising in
1967 and a downplaying of the images that many Blacks found objection-
able. "Black America is becoming visible in America's biggest national advertising medium," reported the *New York Times* in 1968. "Not in a big way yet,
but it is a beginning and men in high places give assurances that there will be
a lot more visibility."[7]

But the advertising industry did not generalize the concerns of Blacks, or   16
the concessions made in response to them, to other groups. At the same time
that some Black concerns were being addressed with integrated advertising,
other groups were being ignored or singled out for continued stereotyped
treatment in such commercials as those featuring the Frito Bandito.

Among the Latino advertising stereotypes cited in a 1969 article by sociol-   17
ogist Tomás Martínez[8] were commercials for Granny Goose chips featuring
fat gun-toting Mexicans; an advertisement for Arrid underarm deodorant
showing a dusty Mexican bandito spraying his underarms after a hard ride as
the announcer intoned, "If it works for him it will work for you"; and a magazine advertisement featuring a stereotypical Mexican sleeping under his
sombrero as he leans against a Philco television set. Especially offensive to
Martínez was a Liggett & Meyers commercial for L&M cigarettes that featured
Paco, a lazy Latino who never "feenishes" anything, not even the revolution
he is supposed to be fighting. In response to a letter complaining about the
commercial, the director of public relations for the tobacco firm defended the
commercial's use of Latino stereotypes:

> "Paco" is a warm, sympathetic and lovable character with whom most of us
> can identify because he has a little of all of us in him, that is, our tendency to
> procrastinate at times. He seeks to escape the violence of war and to enjoy the
> pleasure of the moment, in this case, the good flavor of an L&M cigarette.[9]

Although the company spokesman claimed that the character had been   18
tested without negative reactions from Latinos (a similar claim was made by
Frito-Lay regarding the Frito Bandito), Martínez roundly criticized the advertising images and contrasted them to what he saw as the gains Blacks were
then making in the advertising field:

> Today, no major advertiser would attempt to display a black man or woman
> over the media in a prejudiced, stereotyped fashion. Complaints would be

forthcoming from black associations and perhaps the FCC. Yet, these same advertisers, who dare not show "step'n fetch it" characters, uninhibitedly depict a Mexican counterpart, with additional traits of stinking and stealing. Perhaps the white hatred for blacks, which cannot find adequate expression in today's ads, is being transferred upon their brown brothers.[10]

In 1970 a Brown Position Paper prepared by Latino media activists Armando Rendon and Domingo Nick Reyes charged that the media had transferred the negative stereotypes it once reserved for Blacks to Latinos, who had become "the media's new nigger."[11] The protests of Latinos soon made the nation's advertisers more conscious of the portrayals that Latinos found offensive. But, as in the case of the Blacks, the advertising industry failed to apply the lessons learned from one group to other racial minorities.   19

Although national advertisers withdrew much of the advertising that negatively stereotyped Blacks and Latinos, sometimes replacing them with images of affluent, successful images that were as far removed from reality as the portrayals of the past, the advances made by those groups were not shared with Native Americans and Asians. Native Americans, no longer depicted as either noble savage or cute cartoon characters, have all but disappeared from broadcast commercials and print media advertising. On the other hand, Asians, particularly Japanese, have been dealt more than their share of commercials depicting them in stereotypes that cater to the fears and stereotypes of White America. As was the case with Blacks and Latinos, it has taken organized protests from Asian-American groups to get the message across to the corporations and their advertising agencies.   20

In the mid-1970s a Southern California supermarket chain agreed to remove a television campaign in which a young Asian karate-chopped his way down the stores aisles cutting prices for customers. Nationally, several firms whose industries have been hard-hit by Japanese imports fought back through commercials, if not in the quality or prices of their products. One automobile company featured an Asian family carefully looking over a new car and commenting on its attributes in heavily accented English. Only after they bought it did they learn it was from the United States, not Japan. Another automobile company that markets cars manufactured in Japan under an English-language name showed a parking lot attendant opening the doors of the car, only to find the car speaking to him in Japanese. For several years Sylvania television ran a commercial boasting that its television picture had been selected repeatedly over competing brands as an off-screen voice with a Japanese accent repeatedly asked, "What about Sony?" When the announcer responded that the Sylvania picture had also been selected over Sony's, the off-screen voice faded away, shouting what sounded like a string of Japanese expletives. A 1982 *Newsweek* article observed that "attacking Japan has become something of a fashion in corporate ads" because of resentment over Japanese trade policies and sales of Japanese products in the United States, but quoted Motorola's advertising manager as saying, "We've been as careful as we can be" not to be racially offensive.[12]   21

But many of the television and print advertisements including Asians fea-   22
tured images that are racially insensitive, if not offensive. A commercial for a
laundry product showed a Chinese family that used an "ancient Chinese
laundry secret" to get their customers' clothes clean. Naturally, the Chinese
secret turned out to be the packaged product paying for the advertisement.
Companies pitching everything from pantyhose to airlines featured Asian
women coiffed and costumed as seductive China dolls to promote their products, some of them draped in a Chinese setting and others attentively caring
for the needs of the Anglo men in the advertisement. One airline boasted that
those who flew with it would be under the care of the "Singapore girl."

Asian women appearing in commercials are often featured as China dolls,   23
with the small, darkened eyes, straight hair with bangs, and a narrow slit
skirt. Another common portrayal features the exotic, tropical Pacific Islands
look, complete with flowers in the hair, a sarong or grass skirt, and shell orna-
mentation. Asian women hoping to become models have sometimes found
that they must conform to these stereotypes or lose assignments. One Asian
American model was told to cut her hair with bangs when she auditioned for
a beer advertisement. When she refused, the beer company decided to hire
another model with shorter hair cut in bangs.[13]

The lack of a sizable Asian community or market in the United States is   24
sometimes cited as the reason that Asians are still stereotyped in advertising
and, except for children's advertising, are rarely presented in integrated settings. However the growth rate and income of Asians living in the United
States would seem to indicate Asians have the potential for overcoming the
stereotyping and lack of visibility that Blacks and Latinos have already challenged. By the mid-1980s there are a few signs that advertising is beginning
to integrate Asian Americans into crossover advertisements that, like the Tostitos campaign, are designed to have a broad appeal. In one commercial, television actor Robert Ito was featured telling how he loves to call his relatives in
Japan because the calls make them think that he is rich, as well as successful,
in the United States. Of course, he adds, it is only because the long-distance
rates of the AT&T are so low that he is able to call Japan so often.

In the 1970s, mass-audience advertising in the United States became   25
more racially integrated than in any time in the nation's history. Blacks, and
to a much lesser extent Latinos and Asians, could be seen in television commercials spread across the broadcast week and in major magazines. In fact,
the advertisements on network television often appeared to be more fully integrated than the television programs they supported. Like television, gen-
eral-circulation magazines also experienced an increase in the use of Blacks,
although studies of both media showed that most of the percentage increase
had come by the early 1970s. By that time the percentage of prime-time television commercials featuring Blacks had apparently leveled off at about 10
percent. Blacks were featured in only between 2 and 3 percent of magazine
advertisements as late as 1978. That percentage, however small, was a sharp
increase from the .06 percent of news magazine advertisements reported in
1960.[14]

The gains were also socially significant, since they demonstrated that   26
Blacks could be integrated into advertisements without triggering a backlash
among potential customers in the White majority. Both sales figures and research conducted since the late 1960s have shown that the integration of
Black models into television and print advertising does not adversely affect
sales or the image of the product. Instead, a study by the American Newspaper Publishers Association showed, the most important influences on sales
are the merchandise and the advertisement itself. In fact, while triggering no
adverse affect among the majority of Whites, integrated advertisements were
found to be useful in swaying Black consumers, who respond favorably to
positive Black role models in print advertisements.[15] Studies conducted in the
early 1970s also showed that White consumers did not respond negatively to
advertising featuring Black models, although their response was more often
neutral than positive.[16] However, one 1972 study examining White backlash
did show that an advertisement prominently featuring darker-skinned Blacks
was less acceptable to Whites than those featuring lighter-skinned Blacks as
background models.[17] Perhaps such findings help explain why research conducted later in the 1970s revealed that, for the most part, Blacks appearing in
magazine and television advertisements were often featured as part of an integrated group.[18]

Although research findings have showed that integrated advertisements   27
do not adversely affect sales, the percentage of Blacks and other minorities in
general-audience advertising has not increased significantly since the numerical gains made through the mid-1970s. Those minorities who do appear in
advertisements are often depicted in upscale or integrated settings, an image
that the Balch Institute's Stolarik criticized as taking advertising "too far in
the other direction and created stereotypes of 'successful' ethnic group members that are as unrealistic as those of the past."[19] Equally unwise, from a
business standpoint, was the low numbers of Blacks appearing in advertisements. At the conclusion of a 1983 study, marketing professor Lawrence
Solely wrote:

> Advertisers and their ad agencies must evaluate the direct economic conse-
> quences of alternative strategies on the firm. If it is believed that the presence
> of Black models in advertisements decreases the effectiveness of advertising
> messages, only token numbers of Black models will be used. Previous studies
> have found that advertisements portraying Black models do not elicit nega-
> tive affective or conative responses from consumers. Given the consistency of
> the research findings, more Blacks should be portrayed in advertisements. If
> Blacks continue to be underrepresented in advertising portrayals, it can be
> said that this is an indication of prejudice on the part of the advertising in-
> dustry, not consumers.[20]

Analysis

The relationship between racial minorities and advertising has undergone   28
dramatic changes since the early 1960s. Blacks have been the most visible in

the changes that have occurred in both mainstream and segmented advertising, although Spanish-speaking Latinos also have become more important as a market segment. In spite of experiencing the greatest percentage growth of any racial group in the years between 1970 and 1980, Asian Americans still had not been recognized as a major consumer force by advertisers in the mid-1980s. But, given the projected growth figures for Asians in the United States, it appears inevitable that the group will be increasingly important as a market segment in the future, particularly if Asian Americans continue to demonstrate income and education levels above national norms and if they respond to racially sensitive advertising in media directed to Asian Americans. Native Americans, divided between the cities and rural areas, have become largely invisible in mainstream advertising. The noble Super Chief has gone the way of the passenger train he once advertised, as have the caricatures that once stereotyped Native Americans in advertising. The small percentage of the population in urban areas that Native Americans make up and their geographic dispersion in rural areas make them less attractive for mainstream advertisers looking at potential market segments. As far as advertising is concerned, it appears that Native Americans will continue to be treated as the most invisible minority.

National advertisers in mass-audience media appear to be reluctant to 29
learn from the experiences with one group in dealing with others. Thus Blacks, Latinos, Asians, and Native Americans have all had to wage individual battles against stereotyping and racially offensive advertisements. Blacks, the most visible racial minority in network television and general-interest magazine advertising, still constitute only a very small percentage of the characters in those media. Asians and Latinos are still infrequently used in mainstream advertisements. Gains have been noted in the use of Black celebrities, such as Bill Cosby, the Jacksons, and Reggie Jackson, in advertising with a "crossover" appeal to both Blacks and non-Blacks. Given the use of different languages and the smaller sizes of the groups, it would appear that integration of Latinos and Asians into mainstream advertising will most likely follow the "crossover" model, such as the Tostitos commercial or the Robert Ito long-distance telephone spot. Such advertisements afford the advertiser the advantage of reaching the majority of potential consumers, including English-speaking Latinos and Asians.

Minority-formatted publications and broadcasters depend on advertising 30
to support their media. They have benefited from the increased emphasis on market segmentation by promoting the consumption patterns of the audiences they reach and their own effectiveness in delivering persuasive commercial messages to their readers, listeners, and viewers. But advertising is also a two-edged sword; advertisers expect to take more money out of a market segment than they invest in advertising to that segment. Black and Spanish-language media will benefit from the advertising dollars of national corporations only as long as they are the most cost-effective way for advertisers to persuade Blacks and Latinos to use their products. This places the minority media in an exploitative relationship with their audience, who,

because of language, educational, and economic differences sometimes, are exposed to a narrower range of media than Whites. Advertisers support the media that deliver the audience with the best consumer profile at the lowest cost, not necessarily the media that best meet the information and entertainment needs of their audience.

The slick, upscale lifestyle used by national advertisers is more a goal than   31
a reality for most Blacks and Latinos. It is achieved through education, hard work, and equal opportunity. Yet advertisers promote consumption of their products as a shortcut to the good life, a quick fix for low-income consumers. The message to their low-income audience is clear: You may not be able to live in the best neighborhoods, wear the best clothes, or have the best job, but you can drink the same liquor, smoke the same cigarettes, and drive the same car as those who do. At the same time, advertising appeals playing on the cultural or historical heritage of Blacks and Latinos make the products appear to be "at home" with minority consumers. Recognizing the importance of national holidays and the forgotten minority history, they have joined with Blacks and Latinos in commemorating dates, events, and persons. But they also piggyback their commercial messages on the recognition of events, leaders, or heroes. Persons or events that in their time represented protest against slavery, oppression, or discrimination are now used to sell products.

Advertising, like mining, is an extractive industry. It enters the ghetto   32
and barrio with a smiling face to convince all within its reach that they should purchase the products advertised and purchase them often. It has no goal other than to stimulate consumption of the product; the subsidization of the media is merely a by-product. But owners of minority-formatted media, having gained through the increased advertising investments of major corporations, now have greater opportunities to use those increased dollars to improve news and entertainment content and thus better meet their social responsibility to their audience. Unlike advertisers, who may support socially responsible activities for the purpose of promoting their own images, minority publishers and broadcasters have a long, though sometimes spotty, record of advocating the rights of the people they serve. Their growing dependence on major corporations and national advertising agencies should do nothing to blunt that edge as long as the audiences they serve continue to confront a system of inequality that keeps them below national norms in education, housing, income, health, and other social indicators.

NOTES

1. "Using ethnic images—An advertising retrospective," *Advertising Age,* June 14, 1984, p. 9.
2. Tomás Martínez, "How advertisers promote racism," *Civil Rights Digest,* Fall 1969, pp. 8–9.
3. David M. Potter, *People of Plenty* (University of Chicago Press, 1954), p. 166.
4. Ibid., pp. 181–182.

5. Ibid., pp. 184–185.
6. "Using ethnic images."
7. Cited in Philip H. Dougherty, "Frequency of blacks in TV ads," *New York Times,* May 27, 1982, p. D19.
8. Martínez, "How advertisers promote racism," p. 10.
9. Ibid., p. 11.
10. Ibid., pp. 9–10.
11. Domingo Nick Reyes and Armando Rendón, *Chicanos and the Mass Media* (National Mexican American Anti-Defamation Committee, 1971).
12. Joseph Treen, "Madison Ave. vs. Japan, Inc.," April 12, 1982, p. 69.
13. Ada Kan, "Asian models in the media," unpublished term paper, Journalism 466: Minority and the Media, University of Southern California, December 14, 1983, p. 5.
14. Studies on the increase of Blacks in magazine and television commercials cited in James D. Culley and Rex Bennett, "Selling Blacks, selling women," *Journal of Communication,* Autumn 1976, Vol. 26, No. 4, Autumn 1976, pp. 160–174; Lawrence Solely, "The effect of Black models on magazine ad readership," *Journalism Quarterly,* Vol. 60, No. 4, Winter 1983, p. 686; and Leonard N. Reid and Bruce G. Vanden Bergh, "Blacks in introductory ads," *Journalism Quarterly,* Vol. 57, No. 3, Autumn 1980, pp. 485–486.
15. Cited in D. Parke Gibson, *$70 billion in the black* (Macmillan, 1979), pp. 83–84.
16. Laboratory studies on White reactions to Blacks in advertising cited in Solely, "The effect of black models," pp. 585–587.
17. Carl E. Block, "White backlash to Negro ads: Fact or fantasy?" *Journalism Quarterly,* Vol. 49, No. 2, Summer 1972, pp. 258–262.
18. Culley and Bennett, "Selling Blacks, selling women."
19. "Using ethnic images," p. 9.
20. Solely, "The effect of black models," p. 690.

Questions

1. Can you think of any advertisements that you have recently seen that use racial stereotypes to sell their products? Why would advertisers feel that these types of ads are effective?

2. Do you think advertisers should have some type of ethical standard? Why or why not?

3. Do you think that promoting products associated with the good life to minorities that are unable to afford them is unethical?

The Case for Censorship

BURTON M. LEISER

Burton M. Leiser is the author of Custom, Law and Morality: Conflict and Continuity in Social Behavior *(1969),* Liberty, Justice, and Morals: Contemporary Value Conflicts *(1973), and* Values in Conflict: Life, Liberty and the Rule of Law *(1981). He is a professor of philosophy at Drake University, and has published articles on a wide variety of topics including philosophy, biblical criticism, archaeology, and religion.*

In this excerpt, Leiser argues that only a libertarian approach to freedom of speech in which freedom of opinion is absolute can guarantee democratic principles. However, despite his belief in freedom of opinion, he does not condone speech that is intended to be used as "weapons of destruction and harm to others." This article is from Liberty, Justice, and Morals.

The Case for Censorship

The reasoning of those who advocate censorship has changed little since Plato first attempted to rationalize it in his *Republic* and again in his later writings. In the *Republic* Plato declared: "If our commonwealth is to be well-ordered, we must fight to the last against any member of it being suffered to speak of the divine, which is good, being responsible for evil. Neither young nor old must listen to such tales, in prose or verse. Such doctrine would be impious, self-contradictory, and disastrous to our commonwealth."[1]

After setting up a system of dogmatic education, he urged his followers to "take the greatest care not to overlook the least infraction of the rule against any innovation upon the established system of education." He even went so far as to advocate legislation against the introduction of new fashions in music, for in his opinion changes in the conventions of music endanger the whole fabric of society. "It is here," in art, music, poetry, and literature, according to Plato, "that lawlessness easily creeps in unobserved . . . in the guise of a pastime, which seems so harmless." But it is not harmless, for "little by little, this lawless spirit gains a lodgement and spreads imperceptibly to manners and pursuits; and from thence with gathering force invades men's dealings with one another, and next goes on to attack the laws and the constitution with wanton recklessness, until it ends by overthrowing the whole structure of public and private life."[2] If innovation is to be curbed, the best place to begin is in the mind, by crushing the inquiring spirit. For the person who asks probing questions, who raises doubts about the system or its values, poses a threat to a rigidly controlled totalitarian regime. Therefore, Plato concluded, "one of the best laws will be the law forbidding any young men to enquire which laws are right or wrong; but with one mouth and one voice they must all agree that the laws are all good, for they came from God; and anyone who says the contrary is not to be listened to."[3]

By this time in his life, Plato was a long way from the views he had espoused early in his career, shortly after the execution of Socrates on charges of corrupting the youth; that is, of "agitating" among the young people of Athens for a rethinking of Athenian values and the Athenian way of life. But he did offer a rationale for censorship that has been appealed to time and time again in subsequent centuries. The argument proceeds under the assumption that the present regime is ordained by God, or at least that it possesses God's sanction and blessing. A further assumption is that only those with special insights or special training are qualified to ordain or even to advocate change in the delicate and highly complex operations of the society. Those who lack such special insights or training, being unqualified, should be discouraged from inquiring too deeply into the structure of the state or its policies and should be forbidden to publish any thoughts they may have on reforms; for such thoughts are subversive, because they are not in accord with the official policies of the state, or the Church, as the case may be. False doctrines—that is, those doctrines that are inconsistent with those that are taught by the state—must be suppressed. For if people are seduced into believing them, they will begin to lose confidence in the state as the final arbiter and purveyor of right and truth. If ordinary citizens may decide for themselves what to believe, they may also attempt to decide for themselves what conduct is right and what conduct is wrong; and this could lead to anarchy, to rebellion, and, as Plato said, to the destruction of the whole structure of public and private life.

Thomas Hobbes put the case for censorship in much the same terms: 4

It is annexed to the sovereignty to be judge of what opinions and doctrines are averse and what conducing to peace, and consequently on what occasions, how far, and what men are to be trusted withal in speaking to multitudes of people, and who shall examine the doctrines of all books before they be published. For the actions of men proceed from their opinions, and in the well-governing of opinions consists the well-governing of men's actions, in order to their peace and concord. And though in matter of doctrine nothing ought to be regarded but the truth, yet this is not repugnant to regulating the same by peace. For doctrine repugnant to peace can no more be true than peace and concord can be against the law of nature.[4]

Censorship rests upon the assumption that the sovereign or some person 5 or committee appointed by him possesses the truth and is the final judge of right and good, and that the ruler is charged with the responsibility of seeing that false or harmful doctrines are not spread abroad. During long periods of history certain propositions have been considered, by virtually all authorities,

to be self-evidently true. Anyone who expressed doubts about those propositions was branded a heretic or a madman. Yet those same propositions are
now known—or believed, at any rate—to be false. Giordano Bruno was
burned at the stake for insisting that the earth was not in the center of the
universe, but that it revolved around the sun.

The Persecution of Galileo

When Galileo announced that he had discovered four satellites revolving   6
around Jupiter, he concluded that this was a decisive argument in favor of the
Copernican (heliocentric) hypothesis. Until this discovery, opponents of
the Copernican theory had argued that the earth could not revolve around
the sun, for if it were moving along an orbit around the sun, the moon would
be left behind. Now he could show that there was a planet moving through
an orbit carrying four moons along with it. The objections offered to his book
The Starry Messenger (*Siderius Nuncius*), in which he announced his discoveries
and his conclusions, boiled down to the following: (1) His theory contradicted common sense and everyday experience, for everyone could see the
sun rising in the east and setting in the west. (2) The theory of earth moving
through space was contrary to the laws of physics. (3) If the earth moved, astronomers on earth should be able to detect parallax in their observations of
the stars, but no such observations had ever been recorded. (4) The Copernican theory contradicted Scripture, for Joshua would scarcely have commanded the sun to stand still if it did not move,[5] the Psalmist declared
explicitly that God had established the earth on its foundation, not to be
moved forever,[6] and Ecclesiastes stated that the sun rises and sets and hastens
to the place where it will rise again.[7] Galileo responded by observing that the
Bible was not intended to be a source of scientific information and that its authors used ordinary language and figures of speech in order not to confuse
their readers. Nevertheless, he conceded that any scientific propositions that
were not rigorously demonstrated and that were contrary to Scripture should
be considered to be false.

In 1616 eleven theologians were assigned the task of judging Galileo's   7
work. After five days of deliberation, they announced their verdict: The heliocentric theory, they said, "is philosophically foolish and absurd, and formally
heretical, inasmuch as it expressly contradicts the doctrines of holy scripture
in many places both according to their literal meaning and according to the
common exposition and interpretation of the holy fathers and learned theologians." Copernicus's works were put on the Index until they could be
purged of any suggestion that the theory presented in them was anything
more than a very tentative hypothesis, and all books (including those of
Galileo) that attempted to reconcile the Copernican theory with the Bible
were condemned.

Nevertheless, in 1632 Galileo managed to publish another important   8
work, *A Dialogue Concerning the Two Chief World-Systems*, with a license
from the Holy Office and a dedication to Pope Urban VIII. The Jesuits, after

examining the book, concluded that it treated the Copernican system not as a hypothesis but as an established fact, and they denounced it as being more dangerous than all the heresies of Luther and Calvin. The Inquisition forbade all further sales of the book and ordered the confiscation of all outstanding copies. Galileo, sixty-eight years old and very ill, was summoned to the Inquisition to answer the charges of heresy. In its hearings, which dragged on for several months, the Inquisition produced a document that had allegedly been discovered in the files of the 1616 case. In it, Bellarmine, the chief hearing officer, was reported to have ordered Galileo in absolute terms not to hold, teach, or defend the Copernican hypothesis in any way. Galileo, according to the document, expressed his consent to that order. In the new hearings, Galileo denied that any such injunction had been issued, and he denied further that he had ever agreed to comply with such a decree. He insisted throughout his trial that he had no memory of such an injunction. The Inquisition decided that Galileo had obtained the license to publish his book fraudulently, that it had been "extorted" under false pretenses, because he was under orders not to publish his opinions on the Copernican theory. On the strength of the Bellarmine document they were able to prosecute Galileo for "vehement suspicion of heresy," and were successful, at last, in forcing the sick and aged philosopher to recite a formula in which he "abjured, cursed, and detested" his past errors and heresies, swore that he would never again say or assert anything that would give anyone cause to suspect him of harboring heretical thoughts, and promised to denounce any heretic or anyone suspected of heresy to the Holy Office. He was sentenced to life imprisonment and spent the remainder of his life under house arrest in Florence.

There is a general consensus (not universally accepted) among historians, based upon evidence uncovered when the file on Galileo's trial was published in 1877, that the Bellarmine document was a forgery, planted in the 1616 file to give the Holy Office the ammunition it needed to convict Galileo. Without it they had no case, because Galileo's book had the *imprimatur*. It was necessary to prove that the *imprimatur* had been obtained fraudulently in order to nullify it.   9

In the course of time, refined instruments enabled astronomers to observe the parallax that was not perceptible with the instruments of Galileo's time, and the laws of physics were revised to account for the phenomena that had been newly discovered. Common sense was shown to be fallible, as were Aristotelian and Biblical doctrines that had been accepted throughout the scholarly world for many centuries.[8]   10

* * *

The persecution of men like Bruno and Galileo illustrates how the disregard of civil liberties and official refusal to allow opinions contrary to established dogmas to be expressed openly and freely can retard the progress of science and the expansion of human knowledge. Countless other men in every field have been subjected to similar persecutions by state churches and totalitarian regimes. They have been deprived of the opportunity to pursue their researches and to publish their findings, and, what is more important,   11 the rest of the world has been deprived of the opportunity to hear what they have had to say and to pass judgment upon their opinions.

The Libertarian Response

More than 100 years ago John Stuart Mill published his essay *On Liberty,* part of which was devoted to establishing the proposition that there should be no restraints on the voicing of opinions, no matter how radical or heretical they might seem to be, no matter how wrong they might be in the light of the "truths" allegedly "known" and "held sacred" by the community.

Mill argued, first of all, that "we can never be sure that the opinion we are endeavouring to stifle is a false opinion." And he argued that even if we were sure that it was false, "stifling it would be an evil still."[9]

No one is infallible, he said. Even the most superficial study of history reveals the grave errors that men have made in the past—men who were invested with great power and authority and were thought by their contemporaries to be very wise—in the conduct of their personal affairs and in their conduct of the affairs of the communities or organizations over which they held sway.

Mill's advocacy of complete freedom from censorship was based upon the principle that the state has no right to legislate on any matter that restricts the citizens' freedoms except in those areas where such restriction is necessary to protect the persons or property of others. Legislation restricting the individual's freedom in order to protect him from harming himself was, in Mill's opinion, insupportable. If censorship was intended to protect people against hurting themselves, it was unjustifiable on the grounds of this basic principle. And if it was intended to protect other persons against harm that might arise because of the spread of false or vicious doctrines or beliefs, then Mill replied that the evil and the harm arising from censorship itself far outweighed any harm that might come from the spread of supposedly evil or false opinions. The harm that resulted from the persecution of Giordano Bruno and Galileo is a case in point. It is impossible to estimate how far the advance of science was set back by the intolerant attitude taken by the Church to the Copernican hypothesis and those who advocated it. As it happened, the Copernican theory eventually won out, in spite of all the effort that went into extirpating it. On the basis of these examples, and others that might be adduced, some people maintain that truth cannot be permanently lost by persecution; rather, they say, if it survives persecution and intolerance, it is established ever the more firmly. Truth, according to this view, may be subjected to trial by ordeal. But such a trial is no more rational when applied to doctrines than it is when applied to persons. Mill noted that persecution is a strange reward to bestow upon those who have endeavored to enlighten mankind. More importantly, there is no guarantee that the truth will survive the persecution and martyrdom of its defenders. Because the losers seldom write the history books, it is impossible to estimate how many people have endured needless suffering because of the suppression of discoveries and theories that might have contributed to human happiness, if they had been given a free forum.

We may flatter ourselves into believing that we no longer persecute heretics or burn those who express unpopular opinions. But we would do well to look at the question more closely. There are among us those who maintain that our society exhibits grave weaknesses, that it is sick unto death, that it ought to be replaced by a new and better social order. These dissidents sometimes express their opinions in a manner that is quite offensive to many of their fellow citizens, who are incensed at any suggestion that their country is not the greatest country in the world or that certain laws and social norms are oppressive and evil. The latter may conclude that those who express such opinions are part of an international conspiracy to take over the world and impose a totalitarian form of government over free people everywhere. When the expression of such unpopular views is accompanied by a life style that is deemed to be undesirable or improper (for example, by living in communes, wearing beards or long hair, wearing garments that are not in keeping with the fashions of the day, engaging in interracial dating or marriage), the members of the community express their intolerance and disapproval by refusing employment to the dissidents, by harassing them legally and in other ways, and in the last resort, by running them out of town.

Mill argued that such official and unofficial intolerance of persons and groups whose views differ from those of the majority is itself a kind of tyranny that ought not to be tolerated, for it tends to stifle discussion, and no one can be so certain that his views are correct that he should prevent those with other opinions, on even the most vital issues, from having their say. Not the greatest evil attendant upon such intolerance is the harm done to those who are not heretics, for their mental development is cramped and their characters are robbed of that healthy skepticism and robust spirit of inquiry that is never welcome where spiritual oppression reigns. They are intimidated by fear of being exposed to public scorn and ridicule if any of their views should turn out to be unacceptable, and their intellects are thus deprived of the stimulation that disagreement and a rich diversity of opinions engenders.

This brings us to another possibility—that the opinions being suppressed are in fact false. Even then, in Mill's opinion, they should be permitted free expression, for they encourage everyone who encounters them to search once again for the roots of his beliefs, for the grounds upon which they are based. Nothing is so destructive to meaningful belief, even in religion, than lack of genuine discussion and blind adherence to orthodox or received opinions. In the course of time unexamined beliefs become empty and meaningless slogans, platitudes and clichés that have no more impact upon those who utter them than do the babblings of a parrot.

More often than not, however, the full truth is found neither in the received opinion nor in that of the dissenters, but in some combination of the two. Only by permitting free expression of both opinions, then, and by encouraging reasoned argument to proceed between opposing factions can the real truth be found.

All of this leads to the conclusion that there should be no restraints on   20
freedom of information, that the community as a whole, and its individual
members, benefit from free and open communication and free expression of
all opinions.

Those who live in a free society choose to govern themselves, even   21
though self-government entails certain dangers against which the subjects of
totalitarian regimes are protected. One of these dangers, if it can be called
that, is the danger of slipping into error. Those who live in a free society
choose not to be protected against error; they must therefore assume the responsibility of searching for the truth. As another great libertarian, Alexander
Meiklejohn, put it:

> We have adopted it [i.e., the search for truth] as our "way of life," our method
> of doing the work of governing for which, as citizens, we are responsible.
> Shall we, then, as practitioners of freedom, listen to ideas which, being op-
> posed to our own, might destroy confidence in our form of government?
> Shall we give a bearing to those who hate and despise freedom, to those who,
> if they had the power, would destroy our institutions? Certainly, yes! Our
> action must be guided, not by their principles, but by ours. We listen, not
> because they desire to speak, but because we need to hear. If there are
> arguments against our theory of government, our policies in war or in peace,
> we the citizens, the rulers, must hear and consider them for ourselves. That is
> the way of public safety. It is the program of self-government.[10]

A self-governing nation is one that is prepared to take the risks that Plato   22
and Hobbes and the other defenders of totalitarianism would concentrate in
the hands of a few. It has not yet been shown how the few—whether they be
called philosopher–kings, sovereigns, or commissars—are to be chosen in
such a way as to avoid error on their own part and assure those who live under their dominion that their best interests will be served if they are kept in
ignorance about matters that the few decide may be harmful to them, and if
they permit the few to make decisions for them.

The Limits of Liberty

Even the most liberal philosophers have recognized that there must be limits   23
to speech and to the use of the press and that some of those limits may be imposed and enforced by law. In the last chapter, we observed that freedom of
speech does not mean that everyone is free to speak on any topic whenever
and wherever he pleases. The discussion there centered upon only one respect in which freedom of expression must be restricted and regulated. There
are others, even in the most liberal society.

Any society must have rules governing its members' behavior, including   24
their oral behavior. No deliberative body, whether it is a court, a legislature, a
professional society, a faculty meeting, or a committee meeting, can grant un-
limited rights of free expression to anyone—even its own members—without
finding itself reduced to chaos and utter frustration of its efforts to achieve its

professed aims. Rules of order have been established because without them, it would be impossible to carry any meeting to a reasonable, effective conclusion. The chairman of a meeting must have some means of controlling the members so that those who wish to be heard may have an opportunity to speak, and so that those who wish to listen to the proceedings may be able to hear what the speakers are saying. During such a meeting, those who have not been recognized by the chair do not have the right to speak, no matter how important they may conceive their statements to be, no matter how urgent they may believe it is that the group hear what they have to say. If they feel that they have the right to disrupt the orderly procedures of the meeting in order to have their way, they must acknowledge the right of those who are conducting the meeting to expel them or to prevent them from gaining access to the hall in order to avoid such disruption. For unless one can demonstrate that the meeting is illegal or so dangerous to the well-being of society that it cannot be permitted to go on, one is on very dangerous ground by claiming to have a right to disrupt it. This stand is particularly dangerous, because undoubtedly there will be others who will harbor similar sentiments about the meetings of one's own groups and organizations. It is very difficult to maintain that I have the right to disrupt your meetings and to deny that you have the right to disrupt mine. It is not easy to demonstrate that I have the right to do my thing without interference from you while at the same time insisting that you do not have the right to do your thing without interference from me.

Of course, there are people who behave in accordance with an ethic similar to this. When Hitler was getting organized, he had groups of bullies stationed at meetings of democratic parties and societies who heckled, shouted, and rioted in an effort (successful, in the end) to destroy them. At his own meetings, though, these same bullies were posted with strict orders to bash in the heads of any who were so bold as to attempt to interfere with the orderly progress of the agenda. Stalinists, Maoists, and fascists of all stripes have had the same double standard wherever they have attempted to assume power. Not by the orderly process of parliamentary debate, not by an attempt to arrive at the truth through the free expression and exchange of ideas and opinions, but by theatrical role playing, by provocative harassment, by violence and by playing on emotions, they have attempted to destroy the workings of democratic deliberative bodies and to impose their own iron-disciplined machines upon those who were unable or unwilling to fend off their attacks. 25

It is sometimes forgotten that the purpose of a meeting, any meeting, is not unregulated talk, but the conduct of some kind of business. A meeting of any deliberative body is not for the purpose of hearing everyone who wishes to speak say whatever comes to mind, but to hear everything that is worth being said on the subject under discussion so that an informed decision may be reached. Freedom of speech does not mean that speech is totally immune to regulation, but that *no expression of opinion ought to be suppressed because the opinion itself is considered to be false, heretical, harmful, or subversive.* Even the expression of opinions that are generally acknowledged to be true, saintly, 26 beneficial, and patriotic is out of order when the speaker does not have the floor or when his opinions are irrelevant to the goals of the meeting. Opinions as such ought not to be regulated, and there should be public forums for the expression of all opinions, but there are places and occasions when the expression of any opinion, or the expression of opinions on certain subjects, is out of place and may be declared out of order.

Some forms of verbal expression are not expressions of opinion at all and therefore do not come under the protection of the First Amendment or of the liberal theory of freedom of speech and press. Suppose, for example, that someone has concluded that the president of the Chase Manhattan Bank, being a symbol of capitalism and of the military–industrial complex, should be assassinated. Suppose he delivers himself of this opinion before a mob of angry demonstrators in front of the home of that bank official. And suppose that his words tend to inflame the passions of the mob to such a degree that they storm the house and cause serious injury to its occupants. Certainly such speech ought not to be protected. 27

Suppose that a group of pranksters decides to play a "joke" on the audience assembled in an old theater whose exits are narrow and not easily accessible from the center aisles. During a tense moment in the performance, the pranksters shout "Fire!" and create a panic in the crowd. That single word, uttered in the proper circumstances, can be as damaging as a match lit in an explosive atmosphere. The pain and suffering that might be caused to members of the audience as they rush toward the exits cannot be excused or justified on the ground that free speech is at stake. No legal protection has ever been granted to anyone to use words as weapons to harm others. Just as matches and knives may be used freely and legitimately for certain purposes but not for others, so also may words be used for some purposes but not for others. The use of words as a means of communicating information and opinion is relatively (but not absolutely) unrestricted in free societies; but their use as weapons of destruction and harm to others has always been limited. 28

Some statements are so damaging to individual citizens that their utterance or publication may subject those who are responsible for them to civil or criminal actions under the laws of defamation of character, slander, or libel. A well-known basketball coach was once accused by a leading national magazine of having accepted bribes to throw important games. Such an accusation, unsubstantiated but widely read, could have destroyed his professional career, and certainly must have caused him and his family months of anguish. A rumor that a certain physician was mentally unbalanced and that he had started to molest his female patients began to circulate in the small town in which he lived. His practice dried up overnight, though there was not a scintilla of truth to the rumor. A high school teacher was accused by a local newspaper of being a communist, though she had never had the slightest interest in politics. In none of these cases could the protection of the right of free speech or freedom of the press be invoked, for they are invasions of the privacy of the individual concerned. The public interest is not served by such statements, and the law provides the opportunity for persons damaged 29 by such false charges to seek compensation through damage suits in the courts. For certain kinds of slander and libel there are criminal penalties as well.

In the common-law countries truth is a defense against a charge of libel or slander. That is, if a person accused of libel can prove that he has published the truth, then no damages can be assessed against him. But in some states truth is not always a defense, for it is believed that some matters should not be afforded the protection of the law when they are widely published, even if they are true. Unless some matter of public welfare is at stake, for example, no one has the right to publish the fact that a particular individual is an alcoholic, that he suffers from severe depressions, or that he has frequent arguments with his wife. Though such reports may be true, no public interest is served by publishing them, and public reports of such facts may cause grievous harm, acute embarrassment, or great anguish to the parties involved. Therefore, on such private matters, laws of slander and libel can be brought to bear to protect persons against their public exposure.

Where private rights, including the right to privacy, come into conflict with the right to speak and to publish freely, the latter may have to give way to the former, particularly when no public interest is served by publication of such material. The courts have held, for example, that exposés of the private lives of public figures are relatively immune to the libel laws, because such exposés may be relevant to public decisions on matters of public policy. Defamatory statements directed against the private conduct of a public official or of a private citizen are not protected by the Constitution of the United States, for purely private defamation has little to do with the political ends of a self-governing society. But where public officials or public matters are concerned, the balance is shifted in favor of freedom of expression rather than against it.[11] Newspapers cannot be required, either, to adhere to a standard that provides that *only* the truth shall be a defense against libel action, particularly where criticism of public officials is at issue; for if critics of public officials and their actions had to guarantee the truth of all their statements under threat of criminal or civil liability, there would be a stifling effect upon them, amounting to a kind of self-censorship. Some libel laws require, therefore, that the person pressing the complaint must demonstrate not only that the report was false, but also that it was made maliciously, with actual knowledge of its falsity, and with reckless disregard of whether it was false or not.[12]

Another area in which the law places restrictions upon the publication of statements, even though they may be true, is in the divulging of the contents of private communications without the permission of the sender or receiver. If a telephone lineman overhears a conversation while repairing a cable, he does not have the right to divulge the contents of that conversation to any other person, and in many states he may be held criminally liable if he does. On the other hand, however, if a telephone employee discovers that the company's lines are being used for unlawful purposes, he may be *required* to furnish such information to the appropriate law enforcement officers or agencies and may be punished if he fails to do so. Thus, there are times when one must remain silent, and there are other times when silence is forbidden. One is not always justified in divulging the truth, nor is one always justified in respecting other persons' privacy.

If truth is not always protected, it is evident that falsehoods should not 33 be. The utterance of some falsehoods is prohibited by criminal law, because they cause so much mischief and are potentially so destructive and so costly that they cannot be justified on the usual grounds reserved for free speech.

A person who initiates or circulates a false report or warning of a fire, ex- 34 plosion, crime, or other emergency under circumstances in which it is likely that public alarm or inconvenience will result cannot plead that he was justified in doing so because of his rights to speak freely. The public inconvenience caused by such false reports is so great that the freedom to make them is not protected by the law, and does not deserve to be protected. On the contrary, legislators are perfectly justified in imposing penalties upon persons who deliberately engage in such public mischief.

Similarly, some kinds of statements may be prohibited, whether they are 35 true or false. The rights of freedom of expression do not extend to the protection of persons who reveal secrets with which they have been entrusted. Ideas, like material goods, can be stolen or misappropriated. A man working for a chemical company or a pharmaceutical firm might learn the formulas of valuable compounds that had recently been discovered or the methods for producing certain compounds inexpensively. Freedom of speech does not extend to permission for him to reveal these secrets to competing companies which might then use them to take business away from the company for which he had been working. Similarly, attorneys, accountants, and physicians do not have the right to reveal facts about their clients that they have learned in confidential conversations with them, or through their examination of documents relating to their clients' personal lives or businesses. Freedom of the press does not grant a professor the right to publish his students' grades or the contents of letters of recommendation that might have been written to the university at the time of their admission to the institution. To allow such breaches of confidence would undermine the trust that persons put in one another in a number of sensitive areas. For certain kinds of assistance to be given to people, complete trust must prevail. In recognition of this, governments have foregone their customary right to compel people to testify about one another when the relation between them is of such a nature that breach of confidence would not be in the public interest. Thus, lawyers, doctors, ministers, and others are generally immune from the state's power to require that people reveal what they know about one another when called upon to do so in court or in other legitimate governmental inquiries. However, public interest sometimes requires that the right to silence and respect for the confidentiality of the doctor–patient relationship be superseded. Physicians may be *required to volunteer* information, even though no official of the state has requested it; and they may be held criminally liable if they fail to make certain reports. If a given patient is discovered to have the plague, for example, it would clearly be in the public interest for the doctor to be compelled to report the fact to the appropriate officials so that the patient might be quarantined, others inoculated, and other steps taken to prevent the spread of the disease. Similarly, if a physician discovers that a child is being beaten, severely maltreated, or neglected in such a way as to endanger its life or its physical or psychological well-being, he may be required by law to report these facts to the proper agencies, so that they may take appropriate action to protect the child against further abuse. The public interest is better served in such cases as these by breaking the trust ordinarily existing between doctor and patient.

There are other areas where the line is not so easily drawn and where   36
there is considerable room for disagreement. One is illustrated by a case that made the headlines in 1971. A physician in England was asked by the minor daughter of a friend of his for a prescription for contraceptives. He reported the request to her father, under the assumption that his duty to look after the welfare of his patient (the young lady) would be best served by informing her father of her sexual activities. Not all of his colleagues in the medical profession agreed, for they considered it to be a gross violation of the doctor–patient relationship and a breach of professional ethics. Other medical men, however, concluded that it was quite appropriate for him to involve the girl's parents, because they were, after all, her legal guardians and had a responsibility to look after her conduct and her well-being. Whatever one may think of this physician's motives, one must ask what the consequences would be if young people had no assurance that their communications with their doctors would be held in the strictest confidence, particularly where such sensitive problems as contraception, pregnancy, venereal disease, and drug abuse are concerned. There is reason to believe that there would soon cease to be any doctor–patient relationship in such cases, for the young people concerned would stop seeking medical advice from competent physicians. Where there is fear of breach of confidence, many young people have taken their chances on home remedies or black market medicine rather than risk exposure.

These are only some examples of types of speech and publication that are   37
not permitted, even in the most liberal society. The advertiser cannot claim the right to publish what he will about his product, whether it is true or false, under the First Amendment guarantee of freedom of the press, for that guarantee does not apply to commercial advertisements. It applies to expressions of opinion, to the expression of ideas, and to artistic expressions, but publications offering things for sale do not come under the same protection. They *are* protected, though, under the due process clause of the Fifth Amendment, which says that no one "may be deprived of life, liberty, or property without due process of law." The vendor may circulate his advertisements freely, unless he is enjoined against doing so by due process of law. But it is quite clear that his liberty to publish statements about his products is *not* the same as that referred to in the First Amendment's absolute prohibition against restraints upon freedom of the press.

The liberty to speak is not absolute. Nor is the liberty to publish what one   38
pleases completely unrestricted. There are subjects, such as those about which one has been given confidential or secret information, about which one may not be at liberty to speak. And there are facts, such as those whose publication

may harm persons who have a right to be protected against such injury, that one ought not to publish, even if they have been verified. There are occasions when one has no right to speak at all, and others when, if one speaks, one must confine oneself to a particular topic. In his own living room, a person may wander from topic to topic at will and hold forth at length on his favorite subject if he so chooses. But he may be restrained from doing this at a meeting or at a rally or in a courtroom where such musings are not on the agenda. A salesman may not (or should not) make false claims for his merchandise, and if he does, there should be sanctions that can be applied against him.

Yet the libertarian claims that freedom of speech and freedom of the press are, or should be, absolute. If it is proper to restrict the freedom of the salesman, to restrain him against disseminating false information whose worst effect may be to deprive his customer of a few dollars, how can it be improper to forbid political, moral, and religious hucksters from spreading false doctrines that may weaken our morals and destroy our society? The libertarian replies by pointing out that the salesman is peddling merchandise, whereas the others are dealing with ideas. There are standard tests for determining whether the claims the salesman makes for his merchandise are true—tests that everyone, including the salesman himself, will acknowledge to be valid. But there are no standard tests for determining whether the clergyman's claims are true; no scales to weigh the capitalist's views against those of the communist; no test to provide an infallible, or even a highly probable, judgment as to whether one economic theory is to be preferred over another.

And finally, the libertarian replies by observing, as Alexander Meiklejohn did, that the free man is prepared to take the risks of living in a society that offers the liberty to speak, to publish, and to think false or incorrect or even harmful thoughts; for the risks of living in a society where those liberties do not exist are so much greater.

NOTES

1. Plato, *Republic,* tr. by F. M. Cornford (New York: Oxford University Press, 1945), p. 72 (378d).

2. Ibid., p. 115 (424a ff.).

3. Plato, *Laws,* tr. by B. Jowett, 634d.

4. Thomas Hobbes, *Leviathan,* Chapter 18. In Library of Liberal Arts Edition (Indianapolis: Bobbs-Merrill, 1958), p. 147.

5. Joshua 10:12–13.

6. Psalms 103:5.

7. Ecclesiastes 1:5.

8. For an excellent review of the principal facts about this controversy, see the article on Galileo by Giorgia D. de Santillana in the 1967 edition of *Encyclopedia Britannica.* For more details, see Will and Ariel Durant, *The Age of Reason Begins* (Vol. 7 of

The Story of Civilization) (New York: Simon and Schuster, 1961), Chapter 22. Galileo's own writings are available in a number of translations. See also H. Butterfield, *The Origins of Modern Science* (London: G. Bell, 1957), Lane Cooper, *Aristotle, Galileo, and the Tower of Pisa* (Ithaca, N.Y.: Cornell University Press, 1935), Hermann Kesten, *Copernicus and His World* (New York: Roy, 1945), and D. W. Singer, *Giordano Bruno, His Life and Thought* (New York: Schuman, 1950).

9. John Stuart Mill, *On Liberty*, Chapter 2.

10. Alexander Meiklejohn, *Political Freedom: The Constitutional Powers of the People* (New York: Oxford University Press, 1965), p. 57.

11. See Justice Goldberg's concurring opinions in *New York Times Company* v. *Sullivan* (376 U.S. 255).

12. See Justice Brennan's opinion, for the Court, in the *New York Times* case cited in note 11.

Questions

1. What is the rationale behind Plato's advocacy of censorship? Do you agree with his position as outlined by Leiser? What are the dangers in his position?

2. Why did John Stuart Mill insist on absolute freedom of speech? Why did he consider any form of censorship dangerous?

3. According to Leiser what kinds of speech should not be protected?

Stereotypes and American Indians

JOANN SEBASTIAN MORRIS

Joann Sebastian Morris works with the American Indian Educational Commission in Los Angeles.

    In this essay, Morris argues that American Indians have traditionally been depicted as lazy, vicious, and unintelligent. Also, the portrayal of American Indians in film ignores tribal diversity and creates a distorted view of reality. This selection is from Television and the Socialization of the Minority Child *(1982).*

It is interesting to note that many people still consider research into the effects of television viewing to be relatively new. The general public is itself basically unaware of the actions of numerous researchers and community action groups concerned with this issue. As early as 1960, American Indian groups began protesting the television portrayal of tribal peoples. In that year the Oklahoma Legislature, after receiving considerable pressure from its large American Indian population, denounced the portrayal of American Indians in a resolution which read in part, 1

> There is no excuse for TV producers to ignore the harm that may be done the children of America by repetitious distortion of historical facts pertaining to the way of life of any race or creed, including the American Indian. Many television programs show Indians as bloodthirsty marauders and murderers (U.S. Commission on Civil Rights, 1977).

To the extent that children's behavior and values are affected by television, relations between Indian and non-Indian youngsters are affected by television's narrow and usually stereotyped portrayal of American Indians. The most common Indian characters viewed on the television screen are depicted as simple, lazy, wasteful, and humorless; they are shown as lacking intelligence and English-speaking skills and as believing in heathenistic nonsense for a religion. This portrayal was begun in the cheaply made western films and later carried over into television westerns. 2

    The stereotype's visual image is generally that of a Plains Indian. There are hundreds of tribes still in existence, each with its own housing style, language, religion, and other distinguishing cultural aspects. Yet the differences are obscured by the monotonous image ascribed to American Indians by tele- 3

818

vision producers, directors, and writers. American Indians are all visualized as wearing beaded and fringed leather garb, hunting buffalo, living in tipis, and moving constantly. Those tribal groups who wore woven cotton garments, those who ate fish or acorns as their staple, those who resided in open-air or subterranean houses, along with those who moved only once a year or were sedentary are all obscured in the name of simplifying someone's concept of an American Indian for a television audience. Tribal diversity is especially lacking when American Indian characters are used in historical scenes in which they play minor roles. The unimportance of their individual and collective identity is underscored. They become faceless, nameless, and tribeless.

American Indian women are either ignored altogether or included solely 4 as background characters. They are relegated to lesser roles in which they generally depict quiet, passive, dull, and hard-working women. The respect and independence experienced by many American Indian women from numerous tribes is never delineated for television audiences. One does not see portrayals of Navajo or Mohawk women who live in matrilineal societies and wield considerable power in the governmental affairs and economics of the tribe.

Other negative and erroneous stereotypes continue to surface in televi- 5 sion programming. In television programs depicting the time immediately after the taming of the West, American Indian characters are rarely seen. When included, their role is still not a positive or popular one. They are frequently represented as half-breeds, perhaps in an attempt to depict the merging of two cultures. That many American Indian people who survived the transition period underwent massive cultural shock is never addressed. When the culture conflict is acknowledged, it is generally represented by a character who is pathetic, alcoholic, and occasionally begging.

Even when contemporary American Indians are shown on television, the 6 majority of programs including them continue to be of a documentary style. They may discuss life on a particular reservation, but most do not relay information about American Indians residing in urban areas, even though one-half of the American Indian population currently resides in nonreservation settings. On those rare occasions when American Indians are depicted in a contemporary setting, they are too often stereotyped as militant activists. Although this is one reality for some American Indians, the portrayal is still a negative one, particularly in the eyes of non-Indian viewers.

Rarely have Indian portrayals been positive or contemporary with their 7 time. Whether the time period illustrated is historical or depicts the period of contact and cultural confusion or whether it stresses contemporary life, the role of the American Indian is generally not a positive one. Few social scientists have attempted to explain this overall negative image of the American Indian. Some American Indians argue that in order to justify the unfair treatment afforded most American Indian groups, even those considered "friendly," early American leaders had to convince the uninformed majority to believe that all Indians were untrustworthy, uncivilized, and unworthy of fair treatment. In such a climate was born the first anti-Indian public relations campaign.

Negative references to American Indians was the easiest way to influence   8
public attitudes. Another tactic was to simply ignore American Indians as
members of American society to keep them out of the national conscience of
sympathetic Americans. Either way, the result remained the same: An unfair
and inaccurate image of American Indians was created.

During interviews with a variety of television industry personnel con-   9
ducted by Thomas Baldwin and Colby Lewis, it was discovered that among
the networks' guidelines regarding the portrayal of minorities there exist
many specific "do's" and "don'ts" regarding American Indians. Baldwin and
Lewis learned that in westerns, certain types of violence are not to be inflicted
on Indians. One such guideline states that "Your Indians have to decide to
give up before a fight (U.S. Commission on Civil Rights, 1977)." Not only are
American Indians shown as savages, but as inept savages at that, helpless victims of the white man's superiority.

The limitations imposed on television producers are acknowledged, but   10
not condoned, by informed American Indian community members. We recognize that most television producers feel that they do not have sufficient
time to develop complex situations or characters. We further understand their
need to move the action rapidly and to simplify characters for easy viewer
identification. Yet, by oversimplifying situations and stereotyping characters,
television creates a distorted view of reality. This is dangerous since it has been
found that children, particularly the very young, believe that television presents them with a valid picture of the real world (Paul, 1971).

For American Indians, who are generally portrayed negatively and only in   11
an historical context, this spells disaster. It is little wonder that so many ele-
mentary-school-age children believe that American Indians are bad and,
thankfully, do not exist any longer. It is hard for them to make the transition
from the forest creature they have always heard about to the American Indian
guest lecturer standing before them in the classroom wearing everyday
clothes and speaking Standard English. This contradiction between the television image and the real world should not exist today.

Questions

1. What view of American Indians were you raised with? Do you think it has influ-
    enced you in any way?

2. Morris says that "few social scientists have attempted to explain the overall nega-
    tive image of the American Indian." Why do you think that Native Americans
    have traditionally been portrayed so negatively? Are there any recent exceptions?

The Love That Dare Not Speak

GARA LAMARCHE AND
WILLIAM B. RUBENSTEIN

Gara LaMarche is the program director of PEN American Center's Freedom-to-Write Committee. William B. Rubenstein is director of the ACLU's Lesbian and Gay Rights Project.

LaMarche and Rubenstein document the rise of anti-gay censorship. They contend that homosexual discourse upsets "an 'asexual' public discourse" and threatens "uninformed, but deeply held, assumptions about what is moral." This reading is from the Nation *(1990).*

"Congress shall make no law . . . abridging the freedom of speech . . . except 1
when the speech is by or about lesbians and gay men." The First Amendment hasn't yet been amended that way, but it's not at all obvious if one considers a flurry of recent censorship incidents, all involving homophobia:

■ Congress, spurred by Senator Jesse Helms, bars the National Endow- 2
ment for the Arts from funding "homoerotic" art, thereby equating art involving gay themes with obscenity. Now, all N.E.A. grant recipients must sign an oath declaring, among other things, that their art is free of homoeroticism. Meanwhile, the N.E.A.'s governing body, the National Council on the Arts, overrides the unanimous recommendations of its peer review panel and cancels grants to four performance artists, three of whom are openly gay.

■ Congress amends a District of Columbia law prohibiting discrimination 3
on the basis of sexual orientation. The amendment allows religiously affiliated educational institutions to discriminate against lesbians, gay men and gay rights advocates.

■ Offended by safe-sex education materials produced with private funds 4
by Gay Men's Health Crisis, Congress—again incited by Helms—effectively cuts off government funds for AIDS education targeted at the gay community by prohibiting the Centers for Disease Control from funding educational programs that might "promote or encourage directly, homosexual activity."

■ Facing criticism from conservative members of Congress, the Secretary 5
of Health and Human Services disavows a government report on youth suicide that found a remarkable prevalence of suicide among, and called for an end to discrimination against, gay youth.

This censorious mentality is hardly limited to acts of the federal govern- 6
ment. For instance, while most people are aware that there has been a sharp

rise in book-banning incidents in public schools and libraries during recent years, they may not realize that many books are blacklisted solely because they treat homosexuality sympathetically:

- In Saginaw, Michigan, *Young, Gay and Proud* is attacked as obscene by the American Family Association.   7
- *Just Hold On* is removed from school libraries in Vancouver, Washington.   8
- *The Lord is My Shepherd and He Knows I'm Gay,* by the Rev. Troy Perry, and *View from Another Closet,* by Janet Bodes, are attacked as "pornographic" in Michigan.
- Conservatives try to ban *Understanding Gay Relatives and Friends* in Indiana on the theory that it attempts to "get people to accept the homosexual lifestyle, like there is nothing wrong with it."   9
- A Pennsylvania high school library removes Jerzy Kozinski's *Being There* because "the main character has a homosexual experience."   10
- In Arlington Heights, Texas, a school principal prohibits the school paper from publishing the results of a student survey on attitudes toward homosexuality.   12

This is far from an exhaustive list. From Utah (where education officials   13
attempted to ban references to gay victims from a visiting international Holocaust exhibit) to Memphis (where an ordinance prohibits minors from attending live performances that deal with homosexuality in any way), speech is being censored because it deals with homosexuality.

If these incidents are reminiscent of the McCarthy era, that may be be-   14
cause there's been nothing like them since those terrible days of repression. Indeed, some of this censorship might be attributed to the similarities between today's America and that of the 1950s. McCarthyism arose following the conclusion of World War II as the country, having defeated an external enemy, searched for internal enemies. The targets of the 1950s witch hunts were both Communists and other leftists, labeled "subversives," and homosexuals, labeled "sexual perverts." Today, as the cold war mentality collapses, enemies are again being found at home, but this time lesbians and gay men are leading the list.

Some of this censorship might also be considered a backlash to the in-   15
creased awareness of lesbian and gay issues brought about by the AIDS epidemic. Several incidents of censorship can be tied directly to AIDS:

- The Texas legislature grudgingly backed AIDS education only after at-   16
taching a requirement that courses warn students that homosexuality is an unacceptable life style and a state crime.
- Shenandoah, Iowa, school officials canceled a drama class's production   17
of *Warren—A True Story,* a play about a person with AIDS, because it was not sufficiently critical of homosexuality.
- And someone in Springfield, Missouri, took a more violent approach,   18
firebombing the home of Brad Evans, a Southwest Missouri State University student who spoke out in support of the production on campus of Larry Kramer's play *The Normal Heart.*

Because AIDS has led, in some instances, to a more open discourse about   19
homosexuality, it has simultaneously provided new opportunities for censorship. However, neither the current repressive climate nor the spread of AIDS can explain what motivates antigay censorship in the first place. After all, antigay crusaders such as Anita Bryant flourished during the more liberated, pre-AIDS era of the 1970s.

A third important factor contributing to the current censorship arises   20
from the particular manner in which our society regulates sexual orientation. Aiming to keep lesbians and gay men "in the closet," society's oppression of homosexuals is based on censorship—of speech as much as, if not more than, conduct. Society rarely polices homosexual conduct directly, although the Supreme Court gave it the green light to do so in *Bowers v. Hardwick,* upholding Georgia's sodomy law. Instead, society polices the *expression* of sexual identity, turning "coming out" into a political declaration. As more lesbians and gay men make this declaration, society fights back by muzzling expression—increasingly, with violence.

Finally, speech by and about gay themes is inordinately censored because   21
it is situated at the confluence of a number of other repressive forces within our society: the muting of discourse about sexuality of any kind; the cold rejection of "difference," whether based on race, gender, ethnicity, disability, sexual orientation or any other factor; and the packaging of sexual orientation as an issue of "morality." Such speech challenges these powerful oppressions, upsetting an "asexual" public discourse and threatening uninformed, but deeply held, assumptions about what is moral. It is therefore censored, just as other threats to these forces—from a woman's right to reproductive freedom to 2 Live Crew—are controlled.

Opposition to all censorship has been, and must remain, a central tenet   22
of the lesbian and gay rights movement. Given the nature of the struggle for gay rights, lesbians and gay men have a special stake in the First Amendment. Straight supporters of free speech must ask themselves what they would be doing if, within the span of one year, Congress passed four laws restricting speech by and about African-Americans or women; if antiracism courses were forced to give equal time to the Ku Klux Klan; if there was a wave of book bannings involving works by Latino authors about their ethnic experience. Then they need to speak out—loud and often.

Questions

1. How do the authors account for the recent public backlash against gay themes? Why do you think people feel threatened by homosexual discourse?

2. Recently, there has been considerable controversy over whether gays and lesbians ought to be allowed in the military. How would the authors explain the extreme reactions on both sides?

When Men Put on Appearances

DIANE BARTHEL

Diane Barthel (b. 1949) is an assistant professor at State University of New York, Stony Brook. She is the author of Putting on Appearances: Gender and Advertising *(1988).*

   In this essay, Barthel argues that masculinity is a social construction that is manipulated by advertisers. Advertisers plant an image in the minds of men of what it means to be masculine: "visual and verbal symbols are used to construct images of masculinity and to associate these images with specific products." This reading is from Men, Masculinity, and the Media *(1992).*

Advertising invites us into a privileged, exciting world of appearances. Adver- 1
tising conveys information, but that is just the beginning. Some critics, in fact, believe it embeds its limited information in a whirlpool of disinformation. The more claims are made for a product, the more this seems to be the case. Simple bits of hardware, for example, are advertised with brand name, small illustration, and price. But other products aim at a more abstract form of construction, namely self-construction. This chapter examines how visual and verbal symbols are used to construct images of masculinity and to associate these images with specific products.

   Advertising is big business. A large corporation like Philip Morris or Gen- 2
eral Motors will spend $200 million to $300 million on magazine advertising alone. The top 15 companies who advertised in magazines in 1989 spent a total of $1.7 billion on magazine advertising—in addition to the $3.9 billion they spent on television advertising. What they are buying is the chance of catching our attention, or of slipping the product into our minds while we are in a state of relative inattention and relaxation. One recent study showed that the typical reader spends an average of 25 to 35 minutes daily looking at magazines, during which time he or she would be exposed to 65 to 70 advertisements. About 35 of these will be seriously scanned. In addition, the average television viewer sees 95 to 100 commercials daily, seriously watching about 60 of them. Yet polls suggest that people respond more favorably to magazine advertising than to television advertisements (Christenson & Redmond, 1990). Is this response a form of art appreciation or social enculturation? Is it the medium or the message that turns people on? And what do both medium and message have to do with masculinity?

As Georg Simmel recognized (1978), we use goods not simply to do a 3
job—to clothe us, shelter us, get us from point A to point B. We also use
goods as extensions of ourselves. They extend our power. They communicate
our sense of ourselves to others. And they give that sense back to us again.
Sometimes, however, instead of extending our power, they become the locus
of power. By finding our identities in and through products, we actually hand
over our identities. Marx (1976) saw how people empower goods, treating
them like magical fetishes to be worshipped. When such *commodity fetishism*
occurs, we no longer have power over goods. Rather, they have power over
us. They rule our lives and determine our actions.

We use consumer goods to define and reinforce definitions of what is 4
masculine and what is feminine. The idea that these definitions are not *natural* but rather are *socially constructed* is given weight and credibility when we
look at how such definitions have changed over time.

In earlier centuries, fashionable gentlemen wore ruffles of lace, colorful 5
tights, and pantaloons. Eighteenth-century gentlemen favored colorful silks and
considered it only proper to appear in public heavily powdered and bewigged.
By the nineteenth century, the Industrial Revolution imposed stricter standards
of serious masculine behavior and appearance. The Doctrine of Separate Spheres
encouraged a strict divide between the man's world and the woman's world,
and this divide was symbolically communicated by appearance. As other gentlemen increasingly retreated into a dark and somber standard, from black top hat
and coat down to conservative suit and shoes, the "dandy" was singled out for
derision, due to what was seen as his extravagant attention to the details of
dress. For most status-conscious middle-class men, competitive dressing focused
on the cut and the fabric and the quality of the tailoring.

In the twentieth century, young men rebelled against this standard either 6
by wearing sports clothes as street clothes or playing with innovations such
as the zoot suit. But the standard of serious dress for serious men remained,
susceptible only to relatively minor changes, compared with earlier transformations. Recent history has seen a movement from the 1950s "man in the
gray flannel suit" to the 1960s psychedelic breakout, complete with beads,
bellbottoms, and Indian motifs. Men in the 1970s continued to explore their
feelings, enjoying some new freedoms and communicating their sentiments
through their appearance. But corporate conformity never totally disappeared. In the 1980s, it was back with a vengeance, updated to serve the
times. The new male role model was the young man on the make: neither a
stoic, inner-directed achiever (Riesman, 1950) nor a dull, outer-directed organization man (Whyte, 1957). The new achiever was out to win, out for power
and the perks that go with it. He knew that, in the end, "whoever has the
most toys wins." Merchandisers, advertisers, and retailers loved him. This
new achiever was a challenge, at times difficult, but he could be sold. As we
enter the nineties he is still out there, a little chastened by economic reverses
but still raring to go, struggling and shopping his way the top. He is one of
capitalism's most successful products: a consumer and a gentleman. Let us
examine what he is sold, and of what stuff he is made.

The Corporate Game

"Clothes make the man" is an adage with some truth to it. Dressing for success took the point to the extreme as the acquisition of the "power look" came to precede the acquisition of power itself. Yet this new achiever, this yuppie hell-bent-for-corporate-glory, was he not merely a hard-living, free-spending version of the earliest corporate conformist?   7

For all their glamour, it certainly seemed so from the advertisements in men's magazines such as *GQ, M,* and *Esquire,* and more general interest magazines, ranging from *Fortune* and *Forbes* to *Sports Illustrated.* In page after page the solitary male figure appears handsomely turned out in a three-piece suit and top coat. He is the existential executive. He either stares out confidently at the camera or seems lost in his own deep, important thoughts. Sometimes he is on his way to a power lunch. Sometimes he stands scrutinizing the business pages; sometimes he makes a call on a cordless phone. The backdrop to his activities is a panoramic view through a skyscraper window of other corporate towers. This is a common advertising technique, which tells us that the man modeling the suit is a high-powered executive able to buy and sell those who are below him, both literally and figuratively (Marchand, 1985). If there is furniture, it is either expensively modern, sleek and avant-garde, or more often polished old-worldly, solid oak or mahogany complemented by leather sofa and armchairs.   8

The executive pictured may be above the riffraff, but even at these exalted heights he is not above the competition. A hotel advertisement depicts a late-night work session in an upper-story office. Discussion comes to a full stop when a male executive turns in amazement to address a commanding-looking female executive, who is holding a credit card and a phone: "You're checking into your hotel over the phone? Who do *you* know?" She answers confidently: "Hyatt."   9

It is the very real threat of women invading such centers of power that makes the social construction, and perpetual *re-construction,* of masculinity so important. Men must show that they have the right stuff, that they have what it takes. In the 1950s, C. Wright Mills described what it took to become part of the power elite: 10

> The fit survive, and fitness means, not formal competence . . . but conformity with the criteria of those who have already succeeded. To be compatible with the top men is to act like them, to look like them, to think like them: to be of and for them—or at least to display oneself to them in such a way as to create that impression. This is, in fact, what is meant by "creating"—a well-chosen word—"a good impression." This is what is meant—and nothing else—by being a "sound man," as sound as a dollar. (1956)

To create a good impression in today's highly competitive world, a man must know how to recognize, as Bally of Switzerland puts it, "the difference between dressed, and well dressed." Casual T-shirts and jeans are fine for college students and economic dropouts. But the man looking to climb the cor-   11 porate ladder has to learn both how to read the messages given off by other men's appearances (polished and confidant or cheap and sleazy) *and* how to send the right messages himself. As a shoe advertisement says, "Powerful men leave strong impressions"—and not just on thick carpets. A man's clothes speak for him before he opens his mouth. It is up to him to make sure they say the right things. It is a tough world out there. This message is reinforced by the lawyer role model in a clothing advertisement, who says, "Sometimes the right suit is the best defense." In this case, the right suit is a double-breasted charcoal wool with a discreet pin-stripe, set off by a patterned red silk tie (just a touch assertive) and a muted silk handkerchief (not to overdo the effect). Even the right wallet can be seen as a "high interest investment." Plastic or bright colors just won't do.

America has no traditional aristocracy. Its self-made men have to create   12
their own place in time, assert their own importance. One way they do this is by linking themselves to status symbols that legitimate their recent upward mobility. For American millionaires, this once meant castles in Wales or property in the South of France. To the upwardly mobile men of today, advertisements promise that, even if they do not own a castle in Wales, they can look as if they do. Barbour jackets and Burberry raincoats have become easily recognized status symbols. Suits and jackets are advertised as having "the perfection of tradition," transcending "time and trend."

These and similar advertisements for status clothes emphasize fine crafts-   13
manship, natural fibers, and traditional styling. Key words are value, quality, and sophistication. "Distinguished by an air of traditional refinement, today's classic sportscoat suggests a most suitable alternative." The square-jawed model with the tortoiseshell glasses sits in the soft light of an expensive lamp, as though he were relaxing in his private library. This impression is reinforced by the thick volume he holds in his hand. The "gentleman in his library" is a common advertising image of the gentleman at home. This is man the thinker, surrounded by his treasures: his leather-bound volumes, his old photographs, his private collection of Renaissance bronzes, his Parker Duofold Roller ball pen. It is this sort of image that is promoted by Ralph Lauren, the boy from Brooklyn who encourages others to act out their fantasies through his brands marketed with such prestigious names as Chaps and Polo University Club.

Such advertisements are appealing in part because they show the gentle-   14
man at leisure: relaxed, cosseted, choosing how to dispose of his time. But men on the make have a far different relationship to time. Life in the fast lane does not allow time for quiet contemplation. Advertisements promise commodities that will help men beat time, winning their way to the finish line. A brand of personal organizers puts it simply: "Either you run your life or it runs you." A deodorant imagines a high-pressure situation likely to affect the business traveler: "You're at gate 3. Your plane leaves from gate 33 in two minutes. Only one deodorant will turn on extra protection for the last hundred yard dash." A shoe brand reminds corporate climbers that the clock never stops ticking. "Tuesday 10 AM . . . Clock in. Another day at the firm

begins as time flies in the fast track . . ." The confident young man shown looks as though he can handle time, insofar as he has put his foot on the base of the standing clock, the sole prop pictured to drive the point home.

With all this pressure, why bother striving for success unless, of course, 15 one gets a kick out of wearing three-piece suits? This question has been around a long time. Once men were motivated to achieve by advertisements that linked the individual's desire for more goods with the nation's prosperity and growth. As in Mandeville's eighteenth-century "Fable of the Bees," individual vices (such as envy and greed) added up to public virtues when they expanded markets and promoted production. Now, however, the capitalist realism (Schudson, 1984) of advertising images is so well accommodated in the public mind that advertising seldom needs to appeal to patriotism. Private self-interest is good and goal enough, and it does not even need to pretend to be enlightened self-interest at that. Like popular inspirational speakers, advertisements reinforce self-indulgence and self-promotion with buzz phrases like "Enjoy" and "You're worth it."

Advertisements provide a whole panoply of seductive goods and glitter- 16 ing prizes not only for fast-track finishers but also as encouragement along the way. The consumer goals are meant to justify the means: spending one's time and energies chasing after the gold ring. Consumerism becomes an end in itself—more definitive, more physical, more real than any abstract (love, patriotism, fulfillment) can ever be. As the advertisement for Wild Turkey puts it, "It's okay to pay the price for success. Just make sure you're reimbursed."

Back to Nature

All work makes a dull boy; there has to be time for play. That is why week- 17 ends were invented. Time off allows for psychic and physical batteries to be re-charged. It allows man to come to terms with nature and with himself. But this is not an unmediated encounter. Rather, judging by advertisements, a whole set of consumer goods are necessary to accomplish the transition from work style to weekend style. And a consumer and a gentleman does everything with style. As the successful executive in the sports jacket says, "I take my weekends very seriously."

Man at leisure needs the right pair of shoes. Rugged shoes. Hardworking 18 shoes. Shoes that are worn by men who do a real man's job: that is, who don't sit in an office shuffling paper and making phone calls. Advertisements wax poetic about rugged shoes that are "as comfortable on the forest floor as on the shoe store carpet," that allow man to "go toe to toe with Mother Nature and keep dry every step of the way," shoes that "cover a lot of territory." Unlike dress shoes, perpetually polished to perfection to make the right impression, even if it is the wrong impression, these are honest shoes for honest guys:

> You knew exactly what you wanted . . .
> an honest pair of waterproof handsewns.

They had to be great looking, comfortable and keep
your feet dry. No splashy colors, nothing rubber,
you trashed the gummys years ago . . .

In other words, real men are not dumb kids. They know quality and they   19
will settle for nothing less, nothing flashy, nothing ineffectual. Such advertisements are accompanied by images of trees, rocks, and cool moss, of sun-
beams breaking through clouds to shine on a solitary walker. Man in nature.
Protected by Gore-Tex.

Honest shoes demand honest clothes. Thoreau warned that one should be   20
careful of any activity that demanded the buying of new clothes. New clothes
always suggest some measure of dishonesty, some impression-management
going on. The most honest clothes are old clothes, clothes that have grown
on you and literally "become you." But not everyone has old clothes. Some
people have to buy new clothes that are deliberately made to look old. Since
"everyone agrees that a denim shirt ought to look as though years of wearing
and washing went into that perfect, faded shade of blue," Banana Republic
promises that all its shirts are "washed and finished to a weathered shade of
indigo." These shirts are pre-laundered, if not pre-lived in: They save their
owners years of life experience. Other brands promise more layers of life experience than most people can crowd or even care to crowd into their holidays
and weekends. Ralph Lauren's advertisements are heavily symbolic of the
good life lived elsewhere, which can become yours here and now: the country
retreat, the faithful dog, the fishin' 'n' huntin' gear, the piles of *National Geographic,* and stacks of cozy wool blankets. Such images are for men who never
have to mow the lawn on weekends—or who wish they never had to.

When the gentleman-consumer goes back to nature, he confronts his   21
own nature. From underneath the modern-day corporate conformist there
emerges the Great American Individualist. But even an individualist needs
the right goods to express his autonomy. He needs Oshkosh sportswear, "Because life becomes clearer when you don't watch it through a window." He
drinks Suntory Japanese beer, "for those who drink to the beat of a different
drummer," And he wears Timberland boots, like the outdoorsman in the advertisement, sitting pensive in front of a waterfront shack with his trusty
hound. He is "an individualist who has two good reasons to abandon the
comforts of civilization. One, his passion for the outdoors. Two, his trust in
Timberland gear."

Advertisers call this "mass-marketing individuality." Each consumer fan-   22
cies himself an individual wearing and using the same goods as millions of
other men. The original and still-present image of the rugged individualist is
the Marlboro Man, riding through the Big Country, doing a man's job in a
man's way. Men who do jobs that women can do must find other ways of being masculine. One way is to distill the essence of masculinity. If they can't
join in the activity, they can at least have the attitude. For Jean Baudrillard,
this attitude is one of *exigence:* the masculine attitude of demanding the best
and achieving perfection.

Power and Perfection

> All of masculine advertising insists on rule, on choice, in terms of rigor and inflexible minutiae. He does not neglect a detail . . . It is not a question of just letting things go, or of taking pleasure in something, but rather of distinguishing himself. To know how to choose, and not to fail at it, is here the equivalent of the military and puritanical virtues: intransigence, decision, *virtus*. (Baudrillard, 1970)

The male mode of exigence is found in advertisements ranging from cigarettes: "Buck the System," to group insurance: "Accept no substitutes." It is most in evidence in car advertisements, where the keywords are masculine: power, precision, performance.   23

Sometimes the car is a woman. It responds to the touch and the will of the male driver more directly and pliantly than any real woman with a mind of her own. The car's sexy, streamlined body attracts him: "Pure shape, pure power, pure Z. It turns you on." As the juxtaposition of shape and power suggests, the car is not simply the Other. It is also an extension of the owner. As he turns it on, he turns himself on. Its power is his power. Through it, he overpowers other men and seduces women. "How well does it perform? How well can you drive?"   24

The car, like the driver, has to have the right attitude, a masculine attitude. The slick monochromatic skin, like a Bond Street suit, makes a good first impression. But the car, like the driver, must have what it takes underneath. It must be able to go the distance faster and better than the competition. Both car and driver "pass the entrance exam" that others fail: "Going from zero to traffic speed in the length of an on-ramp can be a real test of nerve for the average sedan owner." But then Toyota's V-6 engine "is not at all average." Other advertisements refer to competition in the world of business. "To move ahead fast in this world, you've got to have connections." Ferrari says, simply, "We are the competition."   25

In this competition between products, owners are almost superfluous. The cars fight it out among themselves. The advertisements suggest the power of the automobile to bestow its qualities on the owner. Pontiac's sport couple has "the motivation to match its looks" and "a level of refinement" to complement its "formidable performance potential." It is a car to live up to. BMW gets back to basics in its stark black-and-white "anti-advertising" advertisement, which reads, simply: "Deeds, not words." That is the serious attitude, a manly attitude, an attitude of *exigence* appropriate to a car "engineered like no other car in the world."   26

As Todd Gitlin points out, most of the drivers in these advertisements are young white males, loners empowered by the car that makes their escape possible, that allows them to transcend everyday reality into some higher realm of experience and existence. Gitlin stresses the advertisements' "emphasis on surface, the blankness of the protagonist: his striving toward self-sufficiency to the point of displacement from the recognizable world." Even the Chrysler advertisements that co-opt Bruce Springsteen's "Born in the USA" for their   27

"Born in America" campaign lose the original political message, "ripping off Springsteen's angry anthem, smoothing it into a Chamber of Commerce ditty as shots of just plain productive-looking folks, black and white . . . whiz by in a montage-made community." As Gitlin comments, "None of Springsteen's losers need apply—or rather, if only they would roll up their sleeves and see what good company they're in, they wouldn't feel like losers any longer" (1986).

This is a world of patriarchal order in which the individual male can and   28
must challenge the father. He achieves identity by breaking loose of the family structure and breaking free of the pack. At a certain point, though, he grows up. He comes to value his father. Maybe he becomes a father himself. The father-son relationship is translated into advertising's glowing stereotypes and put in the service of a new role model: the New Man.

The New Man

Men's liberation has emphasized the need for men to invest themselves emo-   29
tionally in relationships. This need was frustrated by the straitjacket of traditional expectations regarding the strong, silent male. The old stereotype meant that men grew up never really knowing their fathers, never hearing them say they loved their sons. The old stereotype meant that men had a hard time expressing deep emotion, whether with friends or with lovers. The emergence of the New Man was meant to change all that.

It has changed appearances in some advertisements. Dad has broken his   30
silence. In women's magazines, it is mother who gives advice. In men's magazines, by contrast, mother is almost always absent, out-of-sight, outgrown. When she is present, it is as someone the young man must *still* distance himself from, as in the Nike advertisement depicting a lone runner on the Golden Gate Bridge at sunset, with the accompanying copy: "Mothers, there's a mad man running in the streets. And he's snarling at dogs. And he still has four more miles to go." Nike says, "Just do it." Do it regardless of what mother and all mother-substitutes say or think.

While the young man must still maintain distance between himself and   31
his mother, he proves his New Man status by breaking down the distance between himself and his father. There's a newly discovered warmth to the relationship. "You used to hate it when he told you what to do. Now sometimes you wish he would." How to celebrate the *rapprochement*? "What are you saving the Chivas for?"

Alcohol used to be an honorific product used predominantly by males. As   32
Veblen (1919) recognized, it was a status good used to strengthen bonds and confirm the privileges of masculine identity. Ladies were meant to stay off the stuff. It is still used to impress and strengthen male ties. "How to choose a Scotch to impress your dad:"

> Maturity. Sophistication. Taste. All characteristics much admired in fathers, and, coincidentally, in fine Scotch . . .

There are also family traditions in style and manner. In a Brooks Brothers   33
advertisement, a white-haired figure in a tuxedo, identified as "grandfather,"
smiles beneficently down on "grandson" in his spiffy navy blazer: "Who says
charm isn't hereditary?"

Madison Avenue did not oppose the New Woman, but instead welcomed   34
her. She was a new type, and she needed new products. So too with the New
Man. The New Father wants to spend "quality time" with his children. He
soon appeared in their company in advertisements for products ranging from
watches to underpants. In one advertisement, a young executive carries his
baby on his back in a pouch, and smiles broadly at the camera: "Success is
knowing which appointments to keep." This suggests one can be both a high-
powered executive *and* a responsible, caring, sharing father. But will he really
bring the baby into the board meeting? A man and a boy appear on horse-
back to sell Levi's shoes; another pair snuggles in loving embrace, if uncertain
relationship, selling Calvin Klein's Eternity.

Besides being free to love his children, the New Man is also free to express   35
himself emotionally. Clothing offers one of the most immediate forms of self-
expression. He can be like the man in the Ermenegildo Zegna soft suit, "relaxed, carefree, easy as he wants to be." He can wear Fathom cologne, even if
few others can fathom his emotional depths. "For men of motion whose feelings run deep." The idea of men in motion is visually, if tritely, communicated by a male runner in swim trunks. The deep emotions are similarly
communicated by a man and a woman silhouetted against a sunset, and by
another inset of a solitary male. The depth of feeling is also communicated by
a large pair of eyes that stares out uncomprehendingly over the whole blue-
toned double-page spread.

The New Man may be artistic, and still be a Real Man, as long as he has   36
inner strength, and as long as that inner strength sells. The model with the
trendy eyeglasses is posed in front of his own (ghastly) oil painting. "Even
when he's by himself, he's never alone. Creativity is his constant companion.
Public or private he makes statements, and the world echoes." Artists can be
envied when they pull off the trick of both doing what they want *and* getting
rich at it. Artists, presumably, have no bosses breathing down their necks. A
real-life artist poses in front of his sizable painting. "My dream was to be a
fine artist. So the fact that I can paint every day and I have an audience out
there . . . For me, that's it. I have reached the point of Delirium" (brand
name).

The New Man is a gift to advertisers. He continues a trend that, according   37
to Barbara Ehrenreich (1983), started in the fifties. The old masculine definition of the serious, uptight male stoically shouldering family responsibilities
was challenged by a new philosophy. The *Playboy* philosophy said that boys
just want to have fun, and *should* have fun. The hippies of the sixties had
their own philosophy: "Make love, not war." "If it feels good, do it." Men of
the nineties continue to feel they have the right to self-expression and self-
indulgence, to love and be loved, or, at least, to fool around a bit. Advertisements suggest ways to facilitate the process.

Wives and Lovers

Wives are seldom seen in advertisements for men's status goods. When seen, 38
they are usually selling "comfortable," products such as sweat clothes, rather
than the more glamorous products, such as fine liquors or automobiles. Pregnant wives are particularly useful for selling insurance and airbags: products
meant to appeal to a man's sense of responsibility. An insurance company advertisement shows a pair of expectant parents, the husband placing a protective arm around his pregnant wife. He has made "A promise to dig the seat
belts out from under the seats . . . A promise to reserve comment on the latest
additions to your wardrobe . . . A promise that a safe world will mean more
than night lights and teddy bears." The advertisement goes on to warn about
broken promises, thus calling up not just masculine responsibility but masculine guilt. Has the reader purchased enough insurance? Has he had airbags in-
stalled in *his* automobile?

By contrast, the beautiful young women in provocative clothes who 39
drape themselves over the male models in clothing advertisements look like
anything but wives. They are lovers devoted to the men in their trendy out-
fits and their flash automobiles. The real prizes are the gorgeous Guess girls
falling over the guys in the Guess men clothes. Where do they find them?

Advertising has encouraged a "feminization" of culture, as it puts all po- 40
tential consumers in the classic role of the female: manipulable, submissive,
seeing themselves as objects. The feminization of culture is evident in men's
advertisements, where many of the promises made to women are now being
made to men. If women's advertisements cry, "Buy this product and he will
notice you," men's advertisements similarly promise that female attention
will follow immediately upon purchase, or shortly thereafter. "They can't stay
away from Mr. J." Much as in the advertisements directed at women, the advertisements for men's products promise that these products will do the talking for you: "For the look that says come closer." "All the French you'll ever
need to know."

Along with this process, men have been encouraged to use a whole range 41
of beauty care products that have been primarily associated with women. Precisely because these products are so similar to women's products, advertisers
rely heavily on language and visual symbolism to convey the impression that
these are men's products. The need to legitimate such products is captured in
a men's magazine cover that asked, in large letters: "Are you man enough for
mousse?"

Men's fragrances need masculine-sounding names: Brut, Boss, English 42
Leather, or Hero ("Everyone needs a hero"). They must convince the suspicious male that he can be both "romantico" and "virile." One strategy is to
focus the camera on muscular male bodies in perfect physical condition: the
male body as symbolic of sex and power. Personal products marketed for men
must also have masculine scents: musky, woodsy, seashore, or citrus. In fact,
they can smell of virtually anything except flowers. It is not simply because
flowers are colorful and delicate that they are equated with femininity. It is

also because their one purpose in life, botanically speaking, is to attract fertilization. Given the possible confusion, men are told to head for the woods, wearing Aspen: "As compelling as the land that inspired it. As natural as the man who wears it."

Packaging for men's products avoids pastels and emphasizes instead rich   43
golds, browns, and blacks. Names are changed to protect the ego, if not the innocent: Cosmetics become "skin supplies" and "grooming gear." Hair permanents are sold to promote the "Manly Look," and it required a sportscaster's personal assurance that it really is okay before men would use hair spray: "Years ago, if someone had said to me, 'Hey Al, do you use hair spray?' I would have said, 'No way, baby!'"

"That was before I tried Consort Pump." Having tried the hair spray, the   44
sportscaster vouches for the fact that his hair looked neither stiff nor phony, nor, presumably, feminine. It really is "Grooming Gear for Real Guys."

The New Man lowers his resistance to formerly feminine products, but in   45
service of a traditional masculine goal. The payoff is still good sex, and lots of it. Not surprisingly, sex is most consistently and insistently used to sell alcohol. Sometimes the magic formula for getting good sex is quite explicit: "Always pamper her with Martell cognac. And always, always, be a tiger in bed." Sometimes it is more subtle and implicit. A man and a woman on a waterfront deck look out over the sunset. The brandy is close at hand. The copy reads, "There are some occasions when Courvoisier does mix with water." Similarly, the Hennessy cognac advertisement shows an attractive woman smiling beguilingly at the reader and holding up her brandy snifter. "You're a wanted man." Clearly, the brandy has something to do with her positive attitude.

Masculine Nostalgia

There are other games in town, and other memories to be made and trea-   46
sured. Sports serves as a metaphor for the male: a special arena free of life's contradictions and contaminations, where a man can test himself and be tested. Sports terms and icons are used to sell a remarkable range of goods, from jackets to tires, from shoes to savings bonds. Once again, we find the qualities of the product transferred to the consumer. TAG-Heuer watches possess endurance and precision, qualities found among "those who thrive on pressure." Dial soap provides "extra inning relief." Sports stars, such as Orel Hershiser and Jim Palmer, transfer their magic to the product, allowing the consumer to share vicariously in their achievements.

The world of sports is colorful and challenging. It is, above all, a man's   47
world. By comparison, the real world seems dull and banal. While there is a certain amount of macho posturing in the presence of high technology, in the computer rooms and at desktop terminals, it is not the same thing as being physically tested by a physically demanding job.

Not surprisingly, a number of advertisements take the consumer back to   48
his past. For it is only there that a secure sense of manhood can be recaptured, in however mythic a form. The highly successful movie, *Field of*

Dreams, resurrected long-dead baseball players, who looked like the strong, simple, mostly silent heroes of yesteryear. It is an image directly simulated in an American Express advertisement featuring Tom Seaver, clad in rolled-up white pants and a white singlet, standing as if contemplating a pitch, baseball behind his back, against the eerie light of evening. His trusty dog is at his side.

There are many different boyhood dreams, not all having to do with baseball or dogs, although there are lots of dogs in advertisements directed at men: Men also dream of cars. Beautiful cars.   49

Cars to kill for. One brand of men's clothes is advertised as being "as classic as a '55 Thunderbird," with most of the two-page spread taken up by the Thunderbird. The clothes only turn the reader on by association. Corvette relies upon its classic dream-car status to condescend to criticize the "rag-tag collection of pseudo 'sports cars' that, over the years, have challenged Corvette's supremacy." Mazda evokes the streetscapes of small-town America, when the bright red convertible in the showroom was every boy's dream. "We stood in the glow of a streetlight, our faces pressed against the glass, hypnotized by visions of Route 66, road racing, and rock and roll."   50

Other dreams have to do with the romance of flight: The Ralph Lauren model in his sportsman's sweater stands confidently on the pontoon of his seaplane in the rugged lake country, the "bombardier watch" advertises "rugged precision for land, sea, or air." Sometimes a man has to travel far for adventure, leaving behind the girl foolish enough to prefer "rum you could see through." He prefers rum you can't see through, and other mysterious satisfactions of the tropics: "the club with no name, the curious but delicious daiquiri, and the waiter with the bamboo cane."   51

These are dreams of escape. Back home, in everyday adulthood, the man finds himself weighed down by the pressures of competition, achievement, and conformity. These pressures, ironically, are reinforced by the mass of advertising he encounters—even when he doesn't think he's paying attention to it. Is there really any way he can succeed on his own terms? Is there really any way he can be his own man, rather than, in fact, just another walking advertisement for the capitalist system and its attendant dreams of individual success at whatever cost?   52

The New Role Models

There are still plenty of sports stars selling hair cream and dirt bikes. Lately, however, a new role model has been added: the ordinary person who has done, or is doing, extraordinary things. As in advertisements for the Gap, the models are interesting people with interesting faces, if not household names. In a glossy, four-page spread, Timex presents three such heroes, one woman and two men: 53

> The most remarkable people in this world don't appear on movie screens or in sports arenas or on television tubes. They drive cabs and work in offices

and operate machinery. They're just ordinary people like us who happened to have experienced something extraordinary. And survived.

The woman in her early fifties skied to the magnetic North Pole, surviving polar bear confrontations, blizzards, and near starvation. The older man survived being sucked into an offshore water-intake pipe for a nuclear power plant, traveling 1,650 feet at 50 miles per hour. He was finally spat out into a canal at the power station. The younger man walked around the world alone. The 21,000-mile trek took him 4 years, and included a wild boar attack and being arrested as a spy (four times). The fact that some of these adventures were undertaken voluntarily, whereas others just happened, suggests to us that any of us can be extraordinary. The ordinary—our everyday selves, the inexpensive Timex watch—can be transformed into the extraordinary.   54

A second example. A clothing company proposes "Heroes for Today":   55

> The old heroes were often but a chimera. Men like Coop and the Duke, who saved the day before heading off into a technicolored sunset. Paladins of our imagination. But, today's heroes are those men and women who are guided by principles based on real and lasting values. Those who help to mend the torn fabric of the earth. And those who still seek the adventurous life. Before they head off, they don't call wardrobe. They call us. Eddie Bauer.

This is the new anti-advertising. But it is still advertising. It tells us that we are too knowing and wise to be taken in by the old advertising and its old-fashioned heroes, who were, after all, a bit obvious. So it offers us new heroes to whom we can relate in a way we no longer can to John Wayne or Gary Cooper. All that shooting was bad for the environment.   56

CONCLUSION

It has been argued, persuasively, that at some level the media reflect society. It is also argued that the media actively shape society, though it is very difficult to prove direct relationships of causes and effects (cf. Tuchman, Daniels, & Benet, 1978). Much of the power of advertising is indirect. Sometimes it directly influences us to rush out and buy a product. Advertisers wish it could and would do this more often. What it often does do is to plant an image in our minds—an image of the good life, of how the product can help facilitate its achievement, and an appealing, if flattering, picture of the people we would like to be.   57

Such new role models suggest new options, a new choice of heroes. It is their connection with their sponsors that remains problematic. These people are not distinctive or admirable because they wear Timex watches or Eddie Bauer sports clothes. As Simmel (1978) recognized, true distinction does not come from money but from character and applications, from people creating worthy selves in and through society. Material goods are necessary, but they   58 are not sufficient. As Weber (1905) said of materialism in general, it should be worn lightly, like a cloak. But material goods have become more like a security blanket in an uncertain world. Social status and financial success are used to compensate for either devaluation or loss of other goals and possible achievements.

Righting the balance depends not on the actions of advertisers, but of consumers. We must unravel the cultural meanings in the messages to see how their images of masculinity exist to promote not individual identity but corporate profits. The meaning of masculinity is neither predetermined nor hidden from view: It is out there *in* society, because it is *of* society. It can be altered, shaped, and molded. Ultimately, it is ours, to do with as we will. This chapter represents one step in this process of reclamation.

59

Questions

1. What does Barthel mean when she says that definitions of masculinity are not natural but are socially constructed?
2. What types of images of masculinity do advertisers use to sell their products?
3. Consider the clothes you are wearing right now. To what extent has your choice of styles or name brands been influenced by advertising? Do you find any of the images discussed by Barthel appealing? Why?
4. Choose two or three advertisements and discuss how the advertisers use images of masculinity to sell their products. Comment on why the ad is effective.

The Media and the Backlash

SUSAN FALUDI

Susan Faludi is a Pulitzer Prize–winning journalist for the Wall Street Journal. *She previously served as a staff writer for* Ms., *has contributed to numerous magazines, and is the author of the bestselling* Backlash: The Undeclared War Against American Women *(1991).*

In this excerpt, Faludi documents the media's backlash against women and the feminist movement. She believes that trend stories that claim that professional women are abandoning the work force or are more happy at home are more wishful than factual. This selection is from Backlash *(1991).*

The press first introduced the backlash to a national audience—and made it 1 palatable. Journalism replaced the "pro-family" diatribes of fundamentalist preachers with sympathetic and even progressive-sounding rhetoric. It cosmeticized the scowling face of antifeminism while blackening the feminist eye. In the process, it popularized the backlash beyond the New Right's wildest dreams.

The press didn't set out with this, or any other, intention; like any large 2 institution, its movements aren't premeditated or programmatic, just grossly susceptible to the prevailing political currents. Even so, the press, carried by tides it rarely fathomed, acted as a force that swept the general public, powerfully shaping the way people would think and talk about the feminist legacy and the ailments it supposedly inflicted on women. It coined the terms that everyone used: "the man shortage," "the biological clock," "the mommy track" and "postfeminism." Most important, the press was the first to set forth and solve for a mainstream audience the paradox in women's lives, the paradox that would become so central to the backlash: women have achieved so much yet feel so dissatisfied; it must be feminism's achievements, not society's resistance to these partial achievements, that is causing women all this pain. In the '70s, the press had held up its own glossy picture of a successful woman and said, "See, she's happy. That must be because she's liberated." Now, under the reverse logic of the backlash, the press airbrushed a frown into its picture of the successful woman and announced, "See, she's miserable. That must be because women are too liberated."

"What has happened to American women?" ABC asked with much con- 3 sternation in its 1986 special report. The show's host Peter Jennings promptly answered, "The gains for women sometimes come at a formidable cost to them." *Newsweek* raised the same question in its 1986 story on the "new problem with no name." And it offered the same diagnosis: "The emotional fallout of feminism" was damaging women; an "emphasis on equality" had robbed them of their romantic and maternal rights and forced them to make "sacrifices." The magazine advised: "'When the gods wish to punish us, they answer our prayers,' Oscar Wilde wrote. So it would seem to many of the women who looked forward to 'having it all.'" (This happens to be the same verdict *Newsweek* reached when it last investigated female discontent—at the height of the feminine-mystique backlash. "American women's unhappiness is merely the most recently won of women's rights," the magazine reported then.)

The press might have looked for the source of women's unhappiness in   4
other places. It could have investigated and exposed the buried roots of the backlash in the New Right and a misogynistic White House, in a chilly business community and intransigent social and religious institutions. But the press chose to peddle the backlash rather than probe it.

The media's role as backlash collaborator and publicist is a familiar one in   5
American history. The first article sneering at a "Superwoman" appeared not in the 1980s press but in an American newspaper headline at the turn of the century. Feminists, according to the late Victorian press, were "a herd of hysterical and irrational she-revolutionaries," "fussy, interfering, faddists, fanatics," "shrieking cockatoos," and "unpardonably ridiculous." Feminists had laid waste to the American female population; any sign of female distress was surely another "fatal symptom" of the feminist disease, the periodicals reported. "Why Are We Women Not Happy?" the male-edited *Ladies' Home Journal* asked in 1901—and answered that the women's rights movement was debilitating its beneficiaries.

As American studies scholar Cynthia Kinnard observed in her bibliogra-   6
phy of American antifeminist literature, journalistic broadsides against women's rights "grew in intensity during the late 19th century and reached regular peaks with each new suffrage campaign." The arguments were always the same: equal education would make women spinsters, equal employment would make women sterile, equal rights would make women bad mothers. With each new historical cycle, the threats were simply updated and sanitized, and new "experts" enlisted. The Victorian periodical press turned to clergymen to support its brief against feminism; in the '80s, the press relied on therapists.

The 1986 *Newsweek* backlash article, "Feminism's Identity Crisis," quoted   7
many experts on women's condition—sociologists, political scientists, psychologists—but none of the many women supposedly suffering from this crisis. The closest the magazine came was two drawings of a mythical feminist victim: a dour executive with cropped hair is pictured first at her desk, grimly pondering an empty family-picture frame, and then at home, clutching a clock and studying the hands—poised at five minutes to midnight.

The absence of real women in a news account that is allegedly about real   8
women is a hallmark of '80s backlash journalism. The press delivered the backlash to the public through a series of "trend stories," articles that claimed to divine sweeping shifts in female social behavior while providing little in

the way of evidence to support their generalizations. The trend story, which may go down as late-20th-century journalism's prime contribution to its craft, professes to offer "news" of changing mores, yet prescribes more than it observes. Claiming to mirror public sentiment, its reflections of the human landscapes are strangely depopulated. Pretending to take the public's pulse, it monitors only its own heartbeat—and its advertisers'.

Trend journalism attains authority not through actual reporting but through the power of repetition. Said enough times, anything can be made to seem true. A trend declared in one publication sets off a chain reaction, as the rest of the media scramble to get the story, too. The lightning speed at which these messages spread has less to do with the accuracy of the trend than with journalists' propensity to repeat one another. And repetition became especially hard to avoid in the '80s, as the "independent" press fell into a very few corporate hands.

Fear was also driving the media's need to dictate trends and determine social attitudes in the '80s, as print and broadcast audiences, especially female audiences, turned to other news sources and advertising plunged—eventually falling to its lowest level in twenty years. Anxiety-ridden media managements became preoccupied with conducting market research studies and "managing" the fleeing reader, now renamed "the customer" by such news corporations as Knight-Ridder. And their preoccupations eventually turned up in the way the media covered the news. "News organizations are moving on to the same ground as political institutions that mold public opinion and seek to direct it," Bill Kovach, former editor of the *Atlanta Journal-Constitution* and the Nieman Foundation's curator, observed. "Such a powerful tool for shaping public opinion in the hands of journalists accustomed to handling fact is like a scalpel in a child's hands: it is capable of great damage."

Journalists first applied this scalpel to American women. While '80s trend stories occasionally considered the changing habits of men, these articles tended to involve men's latest hobbies and whimsies—fly fishing, beepers, and the return of the white shirt. The '80s female trends, by contrast, were the failure to find husbands, get pregnant, or properly bond with their children. NBC, for instance, devoted an entire evening news special to the pseudo-trend of "bad girls," yet ignored the real trend of bad boys: the crime rate among boys was climbing twice as fast as for girls. (In New York City, right in the network's backyard, rape arrests of young boys had jumped 200 percent in two years.) Female trends with a more flattering veneer surfaced in women's magazines and newspaper "Style" pages in the decade, each bearing, beneath new-and-improved packaging, the return-to-gender trademark: "the New Abstinence," "the New Femininity," "the New High Monogamy," "the New Morality," "the New Madonnas," "the Return of the Good Girl." While anxiety over AIDS has surely helped fuel promotion of these "new" trends, that's not the whole story. While in the '80s AIDS remained largely a male affliction, these media directives were aimed almost exclusively at women. In each case, women were reminded to reembrace "traditional" sex roles—or suffer the consequences. For women, the trend story was no news report; it was a moral reproach.

The trends for women always came in instructional pairs—the trend that   12
women were advised to flee and the trend that they were pushed to join. For
this reason, the paired trends tended to contradict each other. As one woman
writer observed wryly in an *Advertising Age* column, "The media are having a
swell time telling us, on the one hand, that marriage is 'in' and, on the other
hand, that women's chances of marrying are slim. So maybe marriage is 'in'
because it's so hard to do, like coal-walking was 'in' a year ago." Three contradictory trend pairs, concerning work, marriage, and motherhood, formed the
backlash media's triptych: Superwoman "burnout" versus New Traditionalist
"cocooning"; "the spinster boom" versus "the return of marriage"; and "the
infertility epidemic" versus "the baby boomlet."

Finally, in female trend stories fact and forecast traded places. These arti-   13
cles weren't chronicling a retreat among women that was already taking
place; they were compelling one to happen. The "marriage panic," as we have
seen, didn't show up in the polls until after the press's promotion of the Har-
vard-Yale study. In the mid-'80s, the press deluged readers with stories about
how mothers were afraid to leave their children in "dangerous" day care centers. In 1988, this "trend" surfaced in the national polls: suddenly, almost 40
percent of mothers reported feeling fearful about leaving their children in day
care; their confidence in day care fell to 64 percent, from 76 percent just a
year earlier—the first time the figure had fallen below 70 percent since the
survey began asking that question four years earlier. Again, in 1986 the press
declared a "new celibacy" trend—and by 1987 the polls showed that the proportion of single women who believed that premarital sex was acceptable had
suddenly dropped six percentage points in a year; for the first time in four
years, fewer than half of all women said they felt premarital sex was okay.

Finally, throughout the '80s the media insisted that women were fleeing   14
the work force to devote themselves to "better" motherhood. But it wasn't
until 1990 that this alleged development made a dent—a very small one—in
the labor charts, as the percentage of women in the work force between
twenty and forty-four dropped a tiny 0.5 percent, the first dip since the early
'60s. Mostly, the media's advocacy of such a female exodus created more guilt
than flight: in 1990, a poll of working women by Yankelovich Clancy Shul-
man found almost 30 percent of them believed that "wanting to put more energy into being a good homemaker and mother" was cause to consider
quitting work altogether—an 11 percent increase from just a year earlier and
the highest proportion in two decades.

The trend story is not always labeled as such, but certain characteristics   15
give it away: an absence of factual evidence or hard numbers; a tendency to
cite only three or four women, typically anonymously, to establish the trend;
the use of vague qualifiers like "there is a sense that" or "more and more"; a
reliance on the predictive future tense ("Increasingly, mothers will stay home
to spend more time with their families"); and the invocation of "authorities"
such as consumer researchers and psychologists, who often support their assertions by citing other media trend stories.

Fortune's 1986 cover photo featured Janie Witham, former IBM systems   16
engineer, seated in her kitchen with her two-year-old daughter on her lap.

Witham is "happier at home," *Fortune*'s cover announced. She has time now to "bake bread." She is one of "many women, including some of the best educated and most highly motivated," wrote the article's author, *Fortune* senior writer Alex Taylor III, who are making "a similar choice" to quit work. "These women were supposed to lead the charge into the corridors of corporate power," he wrote. "If the MBAs cannot find gratification there [in the work force], can *any* [his italics] women?"

The *Fortune* story originated from some cocktail chatter at a *Fortune* editor's class reunion. While mingling with Harvard Business School classmates, Taylor's editor heard a couple of alumnae say they were staying home with their newborns. Suspecting a trend, he assigned the story to Taylor. "He had this anecdotal evidence but no statistics," Taylor recalls. So the reporter went hunting for numbers.   17

Taylor called Mary Anne Devanna, research coordinator at Columbia Business School's Center for Research in Career Development. She had been monitoring MBA women's progress for years—and she saw no such trend. "I told him, 'I don't believe your anecdotes are right,'" she recalls. "'We have no evidence that women are dropping out in larger numbers.' And he said, 'Well, what would convince you?'" She suggested he ask *Fortune* to commission a study of its own. "Well, *Fortune* apparently said a study would cost $36,000 so they didn't want to do one," she says, "but they ended up running the story anyway."   18

Instead of a study, Taylor took a look at alumni records for the Class of '76 from seventeen top business schools. But these numbers did not support the trend either: in 1976, the same proportion of women as men went to work for large corporations or professional firms, and ten years later virtually the same proportion of women and men were still working for these employers.   19

Nonetheless, the story that Taylor wrote stated, "After ten years, significantly more women than men dropped off the management track." As evidence, Taylor cited this figure: "Fully 30 percent of the 1,039 women from the class of '76 reported they are either self-employed or unemployed, or they listed no occupation." That would seem newsworthy but for one inconvenient fact: 21 percent of the *men* from the same class also were self-employed or unemployed. So the "trend" boiled down to a 9 percentage-point difference. Given that working women still bear primary responsibility for child care and still face job discrimination, the real news was that the gap was so *small*.   20

"The evidence is rather narrow," Taylor concedes later. "The drop-out rates of men and women are roughly the same." Why then did he claim that women were fleeing the work force in "disquieting" numbers? Taylor did not actually talk to any of the women in the story. "A [female] researcher did all the interviews," Taylor says. "I just went out and talked to the deep thinkers, like the corporate heads and social scientists." One woman whom Taylor presumably did talk to, but whose example he did not include, is his own wife. She is a director of corporate communications and, although the Taylors have two children, three years old and six months old at the time of the interview,   21 she's still working. "She didn't quit, it's true," Taylor says. "But I'm struck by the strength of her maternal ties."

The *Fortune* article passed lightly over political forces discouraging busi-   22
nesswomen in the '80s and concluded that women flee the work force because they simply would "rather" stay home. Taylor says he personally
subscribes to this view: "I think motherhood, not discrimination, is the overwhelming reason women are dropping out." Yet, even the ex-IBM manager
featured on the cover didn't quit because she wanted to stay home. She left
because IBM refused to give her the flexible schedule she needed to care for
her infant. "I wish things had worked out," Witham told the magazine's interviewer. "I would like to go back."

Three months later, *Fortune* was back with more of the same. "A woman   23
who wants marriage and children," the magazine warned, "realizes that her
Salomon Brothers job probably represents a choice to forgo both." But *Fortune* editors still couldn't find any numbers to support their retreat-of-the-
businesswoman trend. In fact, in 1987, when they finally did conduct a
survey on business managers who seek to scale back career for family life,
they found an even smaller 6 percent gender gap, and 4 percent *more* men
than women said they had refused a job or transfer because it would mean
less family time. The national pollsters were no help either: they couldn't
find a gap at all; while 30 percent of working women said they might quit if
they could afford it, 30 percent of the men said that too. And contrary to the
press about "the best and brightest" burning out, the women who were well
educated and well paid were the least likely to say they yearned to go home.
In fact, a 1989 survey of 1,200 Stanford business-school graduates found that
among couples who both hold MBAs and work, the husbands "display more
anxiety."

Finally *Fortune* just turned its back on these recalcitrant career women   24
and devoted its cover instead to the triumph of the "trophy wife," the young
and doting second helpmate who "make[s] the fifty- and sixty-year-old CEOs
feel they can compete"—unlike that selfish first wife who failed to make her
husband "the focus of her life" and "in the process loses touch with him and
his concerns." *Fortune* wasn't the only publication to resort to this strategy.
Esquire, a periodical much given to screeds against the modern woman, devoted its entire June 1990 issue to a dewy tribute to "the American Wife," the
traditional kind only. In one memorable full-page photo, a model homemaker was featured on her knees, happily scrubbing a toilet bowl.

Questions

1. What does Faludi mean by backlash journalism? Why does she call such stories morality plays? Why do you think this type of journalism has become so popular?

2. Some of the trends described by the media include cocooning, neotraditionalism, and mommy-tracking. What do these phrases mean? Since there is little statistical

evidence for these trends, why does the media continue to promote these types of stories?

3. To what extent do you believe that people's perceptions of women's roles are influenced by the media?

4. Do you think that Faludi would be in favor of censorship to counterbalance what she perceives as a backlash against women?

Writing Assignments

The following writing assignments are concerned with the topic of the role of the media in a diverse society. Before developing an argument on any of these assignments, be sure that you understand the controversy by completing the following exercises:

- Write responses to exploration questions.

- Read several articles in this chapter or elsewhere to discover at least two perspectives on the topic.

- Create a list of opposing viewpoints and consider the potential consequences of each.

- Examine the underlying assumptions behind each viewpoint.

To help you understand the issues and develop ideas, you can use the following form:

The conflict in this issue is between _____ and

_____.

I am more inclined to agree with _____

_____.

because _____.

However, it is possible that some of my readers may believe that

_____.

Exploration Questions

1. What are your favorite television programs? Can you think of programs in which ethnic and racial minorities appear?

2. Do you watch news on television? What is your opinion of television news?

3. Do you believe that you are influenced by television? Why or why not?

4. Do you think that television should be censored to make sure it does not present a prejudiced view of ethnic and racial minorities?

5. What are the benefits of television?
6. How does television depict women? Men?
7. What view of racial and ethnic minorities does television promote?
8. Does the media reinforce American culture? Why or why not?

ASSIGNMENT 1

Read several selections in this chapter discussing the role of the media in the portrayal of ethnic and racial minorities, and familiarize yourself with a few television programs in which these minorities appear. Write an argumentative essay addressing the following question: How does the media portray ethnic and racial minorities?

In examining this topic, you should include a discussion of the extent to which you think that the media influences our perception of reality. Also, be sure to narrow your topic sufficiently to explore this issue in depth. Do not merely list examples.

ASSIGNMENT 2

Every year it seems as if Americans are spending more time watching television, and there are those who claim that television has become an increasingly significant influence on American culture. Others, however, maintain that television does not really influence the culture—it merely reflects it. Read several articles in this chapter concerned with the role of the media in a diverse society, and then write an argumentative essay responding to the following question: Does television create or reflect American culture?

ASSIGNMENT 3

One of the most powerful criticisms leveled at television news is that it contributes to societal violence by subjecting viewers to a nightly dose of sensationalism and crime, thereby desensitizing viewers to acts of violence. As a solution, it has been proposed that television be censored to reduce or even eliminate violence through the creation of a censorship board that would monitor what was shown. Others believe, however, that to censor anything on television is a slippery slope leading to total censorship and a Big Brother mentality. Based on your personal feelings about television and your reading of several articles in this chapter, write an argumentative essay in response to the following question: Should further restrictions be placed on television in the interest of reducing violence?

Using Data

1. What types of people (according to sex, race, age group, and education) watch the most television? How would you account for some of these statistics (for instance, the fact that women appear to log more hours in front of the set than men)?

2. Is the average hours of television watched surprising to you (lower or higher than you expected)? How do your own viewing habits compare with your respective age group and sex in the table?

3. Of the top-rated television shows listed, do any promote racial stereotypes as several of the authors in this section have contended?

4. Do any of the top-rated shows support Faludi's thesis that the media tends to project images of women that suggest a return to traditional gender roles is more conducive to happiness?

Average Television Viewing Time, 1992

		Mon.-Fri. 10am- 4:30pm	Mon.-Fri. 4:30pm- 7:30pm	Mon.-Sun. 8-11pm	Sat. 7am-1pm	Mon.-Fri. 11:30pm- 1am
Total Persons		4:50	4:21	9:23	:50	1:13
Total Women (yr)	18+	5:20	3:50	10:40	:43	1:28
	18-24	5:59	3:44	7:42	:41	1:19
	25-54	5:14	3:59	10:03	:40	1:25
	55+	8:47	7:11	13:07	:46	1:37
Total Men (yr)	18+	4:02	2:58	9:45	:44	1:22
	18-24	3:35	2:49	6:40	:35	1:25
	25-54	3:11	3:20	9:23	:45	1:25
	55+	6:20	6:53	12:19	:46	1:27
Female Teens		3:11	3:59	7:17	:52	:37
Male Teens		3:54	3:30	7:52	:54	:35
Children (yr)	2-5	6:07	4:22	5:42	1:31	:22
	6-11	2:14	3:53	6:32	1:20	:21

Note: Data are hours and minutes per week.
Source: Nielsen Media Research, Feb. 1992

Favorite Syndicated Programs, 1992

Program	TV House- holds	Women	Men	Teens	Children	Program	TV House- holds	Women	Men	Teens	Children
Wheel of Fortune	17.5	14.8	10.3	4.7	4.9	Inside Edition	8.0	5.9	4.4	1.9	1.0
Jeopardy	14.5	11.9	8.3	3.6	3.0	Donahue	7.2	5.6	2.7	1.0	0.6
Oprah Winfrey	12.9	11.0	4.0	4.7	1.7	Golden Girls	7.2	5.6	3.3	3.9	2.5
Star Trek- Next Gen.	11.8	7.2	9.6	6.7	5.5	Cheers	7.1	4.7	5.0	3.3	1.8
						Full House	7.1	5.9	2.2	10.8	14.0
Wheel of Fort. (Wknd)	10.4	8.7	6.1	2.2	2.6	Hard Copy	6.8	4.9	3.9	1.7	0.9
Entertainment Tonight	9.8	7.4	5.5	2.8	1.8	Married With Children	6.8	4.1	4.6	6.8	4.4
Jeopardy (Wknd)	9.1	7.5	5.5	1.8	1.9	Sally Jessy Raphael	6.8	5.6	2.0	1.2	0.7
Current Affair	8.8	6.2	5.4	2.8	1.9						

Note: Data are percentages.
Source: Nielsen Media Research, Feb. 1992.

America's Favorite Prime-Time Television Programs, 1991

Program	TV Households	Women	Men	Teens	Children	Program	TV Households	Women	Men	Teens	Children
60 Minutes	23.4	18.2	17.3			American Detective			9.5		
Roseanne	20.6	15.2	11.0	17.1	14.4	Amer. Funniest Videos			8.9		10.9
CBS Sunday Movie	18.9	17.5	10.0			FBI The Untold Stories			8.9		
Home Improvement	18.3	12.6	9.2	17.7	18.2	ABC Sunday Movie			9.0		
Coach	17.6	14.0	9.9	14.1	9.0	ABC Monday Movie			9.0		
Murder, She Wrote	17.5	15.6	9.4			Beverly Hills 90210				20.5	9.0
Cheers	17.2	12.6	10.6			Blossom				16.9	11.9
Designing Women	17.1	14.0	9.5			Doogie Howser, MD				12.8	10.2
Major Dad	17.0	14.1	9.5			Drexells Class				12.6	9.8
NBC Sunday Movie	17.0	13.8	10.3	10.3		Family Matters				11.0	15.3
Unsolved Mysteries	17.0	13.5	10.7			Herman's Head				10.8	
Full House	16.0	11.2		16.8	19.5	In Living Color				14.6	
Murphy Brown	16.4	13.2	8.9			Married With Children				12.9	
Evening Shade	16.1	13.6	9.6			Roc				11.5	
48 Hours	15.6	11.5	10.6			Simpsons				16.0	16.2
Northern Exposure	14.8	11.7	9.0			Step By Step				10.5	15.0
Wings	14.7					Wonder Years				13.4	12.6
Fresh Prince	14.7			19.0	13.0	Amer. Funniest People					10.0
Cosby Show	14.6			10.5	9.1	Baby Talk					13.5
A Diff. World	14.5	11.2		12.0	9.6	Dinosaurs					14.9
CBS Tues. Movie		11.2				Billy					9.5
Golden Girls		11.2				Who's the Boss					9.0
In Heat of Night		11.5									
Matlock		11.5									

Note: Prime time = Mon.-Sat. 8pm-11pm & Sun. 7pm-11pm, New York time. Data are percentages.
Source: Nielsen Media Research

III

■ Appendix

Appendix

■ Acknowledging Your Sources*

Avoiding Plagiarism

The term "plagiarism" is derived from the Latin word "plagiarius" or kidnaper. Thus, to plagiarize means to steal, to take what is not yours. In current usage, to plagiarize is to take the ideas of another writer and pass them off as your own. It is the unacknowledged borrowing of sources. This section is designed to help you determine the difference between common knowledge and sources that must be documented. It will also show you how to properly document the authorities you cite. Proper documentation is important because it allows your readers to easily locate your references.

Although today plagiarism is considered a serious academic offense (often resulting in a failing grade, or worse), in earlier times the unacknowledged borrowing of sources was not a problem. In fact, in the Middle Ages, to mimic or echo another author's ideas, style, or actual words was considered the highest compliment. Originality was not valued, nor was an author considered the owner of his work. Shakespeare never published his own plays and those who did felt free to amend them as they wished—at one point *King Lear* was even given a happy ending! It was not until the eighteenth century that an author's writing was seen as a personal expression and a personal possession.

When you include information from published works within your own text, remember that an author's words and ideas are considered a form of permanent property owned by the writer. If you use another writer's ideas and acknowledge your source, you are borrowing. If you do not document your source, you are stealing. And the theft of ideas is considered one of the deadly sins of the academic world. Below is a practical discussion of how to incorporate material from outside sources into the body of your text and how to properly document those sources. The two most commonly used types of documentation styles are the MLA (Modern Language Association) and the APA (American Psychological Association). The MLA style would be best for

* This section was written by Kathleen Forni, instructor at the University of Southern California.

the assignments in this book; however, the method of documentation varies according to discipline, so check with your instructor on which method to use.

Some useful manuals that can be found in your library include:

MLA Handbook For Writers of Research Papers. 3rd ed. (New York: MLA, 1988).
This explains the MLA system that is preferred in most disciplines in the humanities, including philosophy, religion, and history.

Publication Manual of the American Psychological Association. 3rd ed. (Washington, D.C.: APA, 1983).
This outlines the APA system that is preferred in most disciplines in the social sciences, including sociology, political science, and economics.

The Chicago Manual of Style. 13th ed. (Chicago: University of Chicago Press, 1982).
This method uses a system of footnotes inserted into the text. It is often required for research papers in history and for some humanities publications.

What kind of information must you document? Some kinds of information are considered common knowledge. This is information that most people know, and therefore does not require a reference. For instance, the statement that the Los Angeles riots occurred in the spring of 1992 is common knowledge, but any commentary on that incident, for instance, the number of arrests, or the extent of the damage, would require a reference. Similarly, the fact that Malcolm X was a civil rights leader who was assassinated is common knowledge; however, if you referred to a social historian who claimed that Malcolm X did not condone racial violence, as is commonly assumed, then it is important that you acknowledge that point of view through a citation. Sometimes it is difficult to determine whether something is common knowledge because for someone it may be new information. In general, though, well-known facts are considered common knowledge; opinions and observations on these facts must be documented.

Distinguishing Between Primary and Secondary Sources

When you are citing your sources you need to be aware that there is a difference between primary and secondary sources. A primary source provides primary knowledge of your topic. It is the original work or document upon which your paper is based. Primary sources would include such items as the Declaration of Independence, a novel, or a poem. If you are writing about a particular person, a statement made by that person would constitute a primary source.

A secondary source is any type of commentary on the primary source. For instance, an article that analyzes the Declaration of Independence is a secondary source. A critical commentary on a work of literature is a secondary source. A statement made about the person who is the subject of your paper is a secondary source. For instance, if you are writing a paper on President Clinton's views on the economy, his own statements about proposed tax increases are primary sources but newspaper articles commenting on his statements would be secondary sources.

It is important to differentiate between primary and secondary sources so that you do not confuse your reader. For instance, the following sentence was written by an observer and is, therefore, a secondary source:

> It seems that the President wants his staff to reflect the diversity of the American population.

However, the next sentence was spoken by the President in a press conference and is, therefore, a primary source:

> At a press conference in Washington Clinton promised, "My staff will reflect the cultural diversity of the American people."

How Many Sources to Use?

It is a common assumption that the more sources you use the stronger your position. It is important to remember, though, that the function of sources is not only to support your own position, but also to accurately represent the opposing side of your argument. Moreover, if you use too many sources, your paper reads like a long list of quotations and your personal voice or position gets lost. Do not try to let your sources write your paper for you.

In deciding to use a source consider how it advances your argument. Are you using the source as an example? Are you using it as an authority to support your own views? Are you using it to adequately represent the opposition? These questions will help you decide on how many sources to use. As for specific numbers, I would suggest at least four but no more than ten. It is also helpful to ask your instructor for advice. Remember, the key is to use enough sources to support your position, but not so many that your voice is lost.

The MLA System

PARENTHETICAL REFERENCE

When you write a research paper you include information from secondary sources either in the form of direct quotes, summary, or paraphrase. According to the new MLA system, that information must be acknowledged by parenthetical reference within the body of your paper and through a "Works Cited" page at the end. The parenthetical reference is meant to provide enough information so that your reader can locate the full reference in the Works Cited.

A parenthetical reference consists of the author's name (or an abbreviated title if the author's name is missing) and a page number. Here is an example:

> Lippman says that television "has helped topple totalitarian governments, and promote global democracy" (774).

Note that since Lippman's name appears in the sentence it does not need to be repeated within the parentheses with the page number. Your readers have enough information here to locate Lippman in the Works Cited section if they desired to peruse Lippman's article. Note also the placement of the quotation marks, the parentheses, and the period. The period goes at the very end, after the parentheses, not inside the quote (this is a common mistake). Follow these conventions correctly or it will annoy and confuse your reader.

If you do not include the name of your source in the course of your sentence then it is necessary to include the name and page number in the parentheses:

> It is commonly acknowledged that television "has helped topple totalitarian governments, and promote global democracy" (Lippman 774).

Note that there is no comma between the name of the author and the page number.

Sometimes you may have two sources by the same author. In this case, to allow your reader to locate the source within the Works Cited section you would have to include the title of the work with the author's name in the parentheses. For example:

> It is commonly acknowledged that television "has helped topple totalitarian governments, and promote global democracy" (Lippman, "Tuning in the Global Village" 774).

If the work you are referring to is a book, the title is underlined to indicate italics. If it is an essay or an article, the title is put in quotation marks.

LONG QUOTATIONS

For quotations that are more than four typed lines (not in the source, but in your paper) writers use block quotations, in which the quote is indented ten spaces and double-spaced. The parenthetical reference occurs two spaces after the punctuation at the end of the block. Notice also that quotation marks are omitted. Here is an example:

> In "Fenimore Cooper's Literary Offenses" Mark Twain criticizes Cooper for his lack of realism:
>
> > Another stage property he pulled out of his box pretty frequently was his broken twig. He prized his broken twig above all the rest of his effects, and worked it the hardest. It is a restful chapter in any book of his when somebody doesn't step on a dry twig and alarm all the reds and

whites for two hundred yards around. Every time a Cooper person is in peril, and absolute silence is worth four dollars a minute, he is sure to step on a dry twig. There may be a hundred handier things to step on, but Cooper requires him to turn out and find a dry twig; and if he can't do it, go and borrow one. (Twain 524)

THE WORKS CITED PAGE: BOOKS

References on the Works Cited page consist of the author, title, and the publication information (city, publisher, and publication date). The items are arranged in alphabetical order by the last name of the author. If no author is listed, use the first significant word of the title. Each citation begins at the left margin and additional lines in each citation should be indented five spaces. Double-space between each line and between each citation. The title "Works Cited" should be placed one inch down from the top of the page. Then double-space between the title and the first citation.

James D. Lester suggests the following scheme for including information in a Works Cited page (note that 1, 3, and 8 are required):

1. Author
2. Chapter or part of a book
3. Title of the book
4. Editor, translator, or compiler
5. Edition
6. Number of volumes
7. Name of the series
8. Place, publisher, and date
9. Volume Number of this book
10. Page Numbers

Here are some examples you can use as models:

A BOOK WITH ONE AUTHOR

Rose, Kathleen. Socialization and the Inner City. Los Angeles: Embassy

   Press, 1991.

TWO OR MORE BOOKS BY THE SAME AUTHOR

Rose, Kathleen. Socialization and the Inner City. Los Angeles: Embassy

   Press, 1991.

Dropping Out: Alternatives to Academic Careers. New York:

   Leisure Press, 1992.

A BOOK BY TWO AUTHORS

Johnson, William and Marily Reid. Emancipating Your Children.

   Berkeley: Dome Press, 1987.

A BOOK WITH THREE AUTHORS

Agassi, Arnold, Jerome Connors and Malcolm McEnroe. <u>Tennis Etiquette</u>. London: Hillman, 1989.

A BOOK WITH FOUR OR MORE AUTHORS

Dessing, Harmond et al. <u>The Fear of Intimacy</u>. Los Angeles: Coward Press, 1987.

A BOOK WITH A TRANSLATOR OR EDITOR

Ulysses, Stephen. <u>The Agony of the Artist</u>. Trans. Buck Mulligan. Dublin: Whiner Press, 1985.

A CHAPTER THAT IS PART OF AN ANTHOLOGY OR COLLECTION

Stearns, Eliot. "Can Notes Elucidate Meaning?" <u>Understanding Poetry</u>, Ed. Edward Pound. 3rd ed. London: Cryptic Books, 1982.

AN INTRODUCTION, PREFACE, FOREWORD, OR AFTERWORD

Simpson, Bart. Introduction. <u>Life Is Unfair</u>. By Homer Simpson. Los Angeles: Larson Books, 1991. i–ix.

THE WORKS CITED PAGE: PERIODICALS

James D. Lester suggests the following sequence for listing references to periodicals on the Works Cited page.

1. Author   2. Title of the article   3. Name of periodical   4. Volume, issue and page number

Enter the author's last name at the margin, followed by a comma, then the author's first name, followed by a period.

The title of the article should be enclosed in quotation marks followed by a period placed inside the closing quotation marks.

The name of the periodical is then underlined with no following punctuation.

References to volume, dates, issue and page number depend on the type of periodical you are citing.

In general, magazines begin with page one in each issue, whereas journals tend to have continuous pagination for an entire year. This distinction be-

tween separate and continuous pagination determines the sort of information you should include. A volume number, year, and page numbers are sufficient for journal entries since they are paginated continuously. However, for
magazines, omit the volume number and provide a month or even a specific
day in the case of weekly publications. Here are some examples:

MAGAZINE (MONTHLY)

Hoss, Dirk. "How Old is Too Young?" <u>Maturity</u> May 1990: 21–23.

MAGAZINE (WEEKLY)

Joseph, James. "Hands-On Experience." <u>Volunteer</u> 6 Sept. 1982:

      19–23.

There is no mark of punctuation between the name of the magazine and the
date. If the magazine does not indicate the name of the author, begin with
the title of the article as shown below:

"Economy in Chaos." <u>Time</u> 11 Mar. 1991: 60–61.

Note also that arabic, not roman, numerals are used.

JOURNAL

For journal entries, you should include the volume number, the year within
parentheses, followed by a colon and inclusive page numbers. Here is an example:

Tripper, John W. "Dogs That Chew Too Much." <u>The Canine Courier</u> 20

      (1989): 262–269.

If the journal begins each issue with number one, add an issue number
following the volume number. Separate the volume number from the issue
number with a period. Here is an example:

Phorney, Bill. "Extracting Canine Incisors: Pros and Cons." <u>Journal of</u>

      <u>American Dentistry</u> 9.6 (1988): 9–12.

NEWSPAPER

For newspaper entries, provide the author's name, the title of the article, the
name of the newspaper as it appears on the front page (*New York Times* not
The New York Times) and the complete date (day, month, year). Page numbers
are listed according to how they actually appear on the page. If the article
does not continue on the next page, that is, if it is not printed consecutively,
write only the first page number and add a plus sign (+). Thus, if the article
begins on page four and continues on page twenty-one, you should write 4+.

Here is an example of a newspaper citation:

Reid, Anne. "Dining Out Will Save Your Marriage." <u>San Francisco</u>

<u>Chronicle</u> 22 Jan. 1989: 23.

OTHER TYPES OF SOURCES

Some sources are neither books nor periodicals. Here are some other possibilities.

An Interview

If the interview is published, treat it as a work in a collection:

Bly, Robert. Interview. <u>Interviews with Robert Bly</u>. By John Schaffer.

Chicago: Westwood Press, 1988.

If you are citing a personal interview, identify it by date:

Burton, Theresa. Personal interview. 6 Nov. 1989.

A Broadcast Interview

Clinton, Hillary. Interview. Morning Edition. National Public Radio.

KCRW, Los Angeles. 7 Jan. 1993.

Material from a Computer Service

"Civil Disobedience." <u>Grolier's Online Encyclopedia</u>. 1988.

The APA System

PARENTHETICAL REFERENCE

In the APA system, you should refer to outside sources within the body of your text and include enough information so that the reader will be able to locate the source in the References page at the end of your paper. In the APA system the year of publication is included in parentheses immediately after mention of the author's name. If you do not mention the author by name in the sentence in which you are referring to his or her work, then you should include the author's name (or a short title if the author's name is missing) and the year of publication, separated by a comma enclosed in parentheses at the end of the sentence. If you quote from your source, you must also add the page number in your parentheses, with "p." preceding the page number. For example:

Harding (1993) insists that "proposed budget cuts in our universities threaten the quality of undergraduate education" (p. 6).

In the APA system as in the MLA system you do not need to include Harding's name in the parentheses because it already appears in the text. Thus, the reader is already aware of the author's name and would be able to find the rest of the information about the source in the References section. Note also the placement of the quotation marks, the parentheses, and the period.

In the example below, Harding's name is not mentioned in the course of the sentence. Therefore, it is necessary to include her name as well as the page number within the parentheses:

Administrators overlook the fact that "proposed budget cuts in our universities threaten the quality of undergraduate education" (Harding, 1993, p. 6).

A WORK WITH TWO OR MORE AUTHORS

If a work has two authors, refer to both within the text. For example:

In a recent study of single mothers (Kelly & Rose, 1991), it was discovered that . . .

or

Kelly and Rose (1991) discovered that . . .

Note that the ampersand (&) is used only in parentheses.

If a work has several authors (fewer than six) they should be mentioned in the first reference:

Kelly, Rose, Mangan, Burgess and Dyer (1991) argue that . . .

However, in subsequent references, you can use "et al." ("and the rest"):

Kelly et al. (1991) argue that . . .

THE REFERENCES PAGE

Similar to the Works Cited page in the MLA system, there are also three main components in the References page—the author, title, and publication information (city, publisher, and publication date). Again, the sources are arranged in alphabetical order by the last name of the author. If no author is listed, use the first significant word of the title. Each citation begins at the left margin and additional lines in each citation are indented three spaces. Double-space between each line and double-space between each citation. Two spaces follow a period, one space follows a comma, semicolon, or colon. The title "References" is placed one and one-half inches from the top of the page. Double-space between the title and the first citation.

Below are some of the major differences between APA and MLA style:

1. Initials, instead of full first names, are used for authors.
2. Titles of books and articles do not use capital letters, except for the first word.
3. Titles of articles do not use quotation marks.
4. There is a greater emphasis on the year of publication.

Here are some examples you can use as models:

REFERENCES PAGE: BOOKS

A BOOK WITH ONE AUTHOR

Rose, K. (1991). <u>Socialization and the inner city</u>. Los Angeles: Embassy Press.

Notice that the author's first name is indicated by an initial and that only the first word of the title is capitalized.

TWO OR MORE BOOKS BY THE SAME AUTHOR

Rose, K. (1991). <u>Socialization and the inner city</u>. Los Angeles: Embassy Press.

Rose, K. (1992). <u>Dropping out: Alternative to academic careers</u>. New York: Leisure Press.

Notice that two or more books by the same author are listed in chronological order.

A BOOK WITH TWO AUTHORS

Reverse all authors' names and separate them with commas. Use an ampersand (&) before the last author.

Johnson, W, & Reid, M. (1987). <u>Emancipating your children</u>. <u>Berkeley</u>: Dome Press.

A BOOK WITH A TRANSLATOR OR EDITOR

Ulysses, S. (1985). <u>The agony of the artist</u>. (Buck Mulligan, Trans.)

      Dublin: Whiner Press.

A CHAPTER THAT IS PART OF AN ANTHOLOGY OR COLLECTION

Stearns, E. (1982). Can notes elucidate meaning? In Edward Pound

      (Ed.) <u>Understanding Poetry</u> (pp. 56–71). London: Cryptic

      Books.

REFERENCES PAGE: PERIODICALS

ARTICLE IN A JOURNAL WITH CONTINUOUS PAGINATION

Hoss, D. (1990). How old is too young? <u>Maturity, 12</u>, 21–23.

    The number following the title of the journal is the volume number. Notice that the title is underlined. Also note that commas separate the journal title, volume number, and page numbers.

ARTICLE IN A JOURNAL PAGINATED SEPARATELY IN EACH ISSUE

Joseph, J. (1982). Hands-on experience. <u>Volunteer 6</u> (12), 19–23.

In the case above you follow the volume number "6" with the issue number (12) which is placed in parentheses.
If the journal does not indicate the name of the author, begin with the title of the article as shown below:

Economy in chaos. (1991, Mar. 11). <u>Time</u>, pp. 60–61.

GENERAL INTEREST MAGAZINES
General interest magazines which are usually published monthly or weekly often cite the date of publication rather than the volume number. For example:

Tripper, J. (1989, April). Dogs that chew too much. <u>The Canine</u>

      <u>Courier</u>, pp. 262–269.

NEWSPAPERS
If you are citing a newspaper article, provide the author's name, the title of the article, the name of the newspaper as it appears on the front page (*San Francisco Chronicle*, not *The San Francisco Chronicle*) and the complete date

(day, month, year). Page numbers are listed according to how they actually appear on the page. For example:

Reid, A. (1989, Jan. 22). Dining out will save your marriage. San

   Francisco Chronicle, p. 23.

OTHER TYPES OF SOURCES

Interviews

In the APA system personal interviews are not included in the reference list but are cited in the body of the paper. Here is an example of how to incorporate a personal interview into your text:

John Gaunt (personal communication, June 21, 1990) indicated

   that . . .

Published interviews are cited as works in a book or periodical:

Keidis, A. (1987, July). Censorship in the nineties. (Interview).

   Rolling Stone, pp. 4–7.

Material from a Computer Service

Civil Disobedience. (1988) Grolier's Online Encyclopedia, New York,

   New York.

General Instructions

If the examples above do not provide enough information, consult a style manual. Finally, it is important to remember the following:

1. Acknowledge all secondary source material. Do not risk plagiarizing either deliberately or inadvertantly.
2. Ask your instructor which style of documentation to use or look at journals in your discipline to see which style is preferred.
3. Do not guess the correct form when documenting sources—keep a set of citation conventions handy. Make sure that spacing and punctuation is accurate. Since documentation is detailed, it can be time consuming. Leave plenty of time to do it correctly.

■ Acknowledgments

CHAPTER 2

"Multiculturalism: Building Bridges or Burning Them" by Sharon Bernstein. Copyright, 1992, Los Angeles Times. Reprinted by permission.
James Lynch, "The Multicultural Education: The Context and the Case," *Batsford Academic*, pp. 9–23, copyright © 1983.
Stuart Wolpert, "Study Details How Race Affects Neighborhood Choices," reprinted from UCLA TODAY. Copyright © 1992. Reprinted with permission.

CHAPTER 3

Alfee Enciso, "Living Under 'A Veil of Denial,'" reprinted from *Los Angeles Times*. Copyright © 1992. Reprinted with permission of the author.

CHAPTER 4

Marcia Eldredge, "Educating Tomorrow's Worker: Are We Ignoring Today's Girls?" This article was originally published in *National Business Woman* magazine. Copyright © 1992. Reprinted with permission.
Joel Kotkin, "Perilous Illusions About Los Angeles," reprinted from *Los Angeles Times*. Copyright © 1992 by Joel Kotkin. Reprinted by permission of Melanie Jackson Agency.

CHAPTER 5

Diane Ravitch, "Multiculturalism: E Pluribus Plures." Reprinted from *The American Scholar*, Volume 59, No. 3, Summer 1992. Copyright © 1992 by the author.
Itabari Njeri, "Beyond the Melting Pot." Copyright, 1991, *Los Angeles Times*. Reprinted by permission.
Arthur M. Schlesinger, Jr., "The Decomposition of America," reprinted from *The Disuniting of America*. This book was first published by Whittle Books as part of The Larer Agenda Series. Copyright © 1992. Reprinted by arrangements with Whittle Communications, L. P.

CHAPTER 6

Richard E. Porter. Copyright © 1991 by Wadsworth Publishing Co. Shirley N. Weber is the Associate Professor of Africana Studies, at San Diego State University. Reprinted by permission of the author.

Wayne Lionel Aponte, "Talkin' White," reprinted from *Essence Magazine.* Copyright © 1989. Reprinted with permission.

CHAPTER 7

John M. Ellis, "The Origins of PC," reprinted from *The Chronicle of Higher Education.* Copyright © 1992. Reprinted by permission of John M. Ellis (Professor of German Literature, University of California, Santa Cruz).

Ruth Perry, "A Short History of the Term 'Politically Correct,'" reprinted from *Women's Review of Books.* Copyright © 1992. Reprinted with permission of the author.

Dinesh D'Souza, "The Visigoths in Tweed" reprinted from *Forbes Magazine.* Copyright © 1991 by The Sagalyn Agency. Reprinted with permission.

Nat Hentoff, "'Speech Codes' and Free Speech," reprinted from *Dissent Magazine.* Copyright © 1991. First appeared in the fall issue of 1991. Reprinted with permission.

Stanley Fish, "There's No Such Thing as Free Speech and It's a Good Thing, Too," reprinted from a shorter version that appeared in the *Boston Review.* Copyright © 1992. Reprinted with permission of the author.

Charles R. Lawrence, III, "The Debate over Placing Limits on Racist Speech Must Not Ignore the Damage It Does to Its Victims," reprinted from *The Chronicle of Higher Education.* Copyright © 1989. Reprinted with permission of the author Charles R. Lawrence, III, Professor of Law, Stanford University.

Richard Perry, "Freedom of Hate Speech," reprinted from *Tikkun,* Volume 6, No. 4. Copyright © and reprinted by permission of *Tikkun,* a bi-monthly Jewish critique of politics, culture, and society.

The National Association of Scholars, "The Wrong Way to Reduce Campus Tensions," from *Beyond PC,* ed. by Patricia Aufderheide. Copyright © 1992. Reprinted by permission.

"Literacy and Cultural Literacy," reprinted from *Cultural Literacy* by E. D. Hirsch, Jr. Copyright © 1987 by Houghton Mifflin Company. Reprinted by permission of Houghton Mifflin Company. All rights reserved.

Todd Gitlin, "On the Virtues of a Loose Canon," reprinted from *Racism Will Always Be with Us.* Copyright © Summer 1991. Reprinted with permission of the New Perspectives Quarterly.

CHAPTER 8

Dr. Joyce Brothers, "Political Agendas: Is There a Gender Gap?" Reprinted from Los Angeles Times. Copyright © 1992. Reprinted with permission.

Christine Gorman, "Sizing Up the Sexes." Copyright 1992 Time Inc. Reprinted by permission.

From *Backlash* by Susan Faludi. Copyright © 1991 by Susan Faludi. Reprinted by permission of Crown Publishers, Inc.

Judy Syfers, "I Want a Wife," reprinted from *Ms. Magazine.* Copyright © 1971. Reprinted with permission.

CHAPTER 9

CHAPTER 10

CHAPTER 11

■ Index

Index of Authors and Titles